American Speech, the journal of the American Dialect Society, has for fifty years included a regular collection of neologisms called "Among the New Words." Complete documentation is given for all citations, which are fuller than those given in most dictionaries. British as well as American sources have been consulted. John Algeo, with the assistance of Adele Algeo, has prepared a complete index and glossary to all the words cited in this column from 1941 to 1991. The original articles themselves are reproduced in this book, photographically reduced but still large enough to be easily readable. For the first time this valuable resource is accessible in a single alphabetical format.

It is a fascinating record. A survey of "Among the New Words" reveals much about the origin and early use of these expressions and the social climate in which they prospered. This book will appeal to all those interested in language and the introduction of new words, whether from a social, cultural, or linguistic point of view. Language scholars will find it essential as a record of language change over half a century. Cultural historians will find its coverage comparable to a documentary report of the chief public preoccupations in each decade.

In addition to the index and glossary, Professor Algeo has written an introduction which is virtually a primer on new-word formation. Citing copiously from the collection that follows, Algeo describes the patterns of new words and discusses some of the motives for devising new words.

FIFTY YEARS AMONG THE NEW WORDS

FIFTY YEARS

AMONG THE NEW WORDS

A Dictionary of Neologisms, 1941–1991

Edited by JOHN ALGEO

University of Georgia

With the assistance of Adele S. Algeo

This book is a publication in the Centennial Series of the American Dialect Society in celebration of the beginning of its second century of research into language variation.

CAMBRIDGE UNIVERSITY PRESS

Published by the Press Syndicate of the University of Cambridge
The Pitt Building, Trumpington Street, Cambridge CB2 1RP
40 West 20th Street, New York, NY 10011–4211, USA
10 Stamford Road, Oakleigh, Victoria 3166, Australia

First published 1991
First paperback edition 1993

Printed in the United States of America

Library of Congress Cataloging-in-Publication Data

Fifty years among the new words ; a dictionary of neologisms.
1941–1991 / edited by John Algeo, with the assistance of Adele S. Algeo.

p.   cm.

Includes index.

ISBN 0–521–41377–X
1. English language–New words–Dictionaries.   I. Algeo, John.
II. Algeo, Adele S.
PE1630.F5   1991
423'.1–dc20   91–26694
                                                            CIP
A catalog record for this book is available from the British Library.

ISBN 0-521-41377-X hardback
ISBN 0-521-44971-5 paperback

CONTENTS

ACKNOWLEDGMENTS

The Publisher wishes to acknowledge with gratitude the loan of nine rare issues of *American Speech* from Professor Allen Walker Read for reproduction in this book. We also wish to acknowledge the generosity of John and Adele Algeo for providing us with copies of many of the issues of *American Speech* reproduced here from their own collection.

INTRODUCTION

A community is known by the language it keeps, and its words chronicle the times. Every aspect of the life of a people is reflected in the words they use to talk about themselves and the world around them. As their world changes – through invention, discovery, revolution, evolution, or personal transformation – so does their language. Like the growth rings of a tree, our vocabulary bears witness to our past.

When we talk about writing books today, our use of the words *write* and *book* fossilize a culture much different from ours. For *write* comes from a root word that meant 'to scratch', and *book* from one that also gives us *beech* (tree), thus suggesting that early records were scratched on beech wood. While our linguistic ancestors still dwelled on the European continent, they discovered the paved road (*via strata*) of the Romans, and borrowed the second half of the Latin term to become our *street*. Having translated themselves to the British Isles, they played host to the Danes, who paid for the hospitality with words like *they* and *sky,* and to the Normans, who brought with them *chair* and *table.* As English speakers went on meeting new situations and developing new manners and morals, the vocabulary of English went on changing too.

Today the English word stock is a multileveled record of the history of English speakers. And, as we have not yet reached the end of history, neither have we reached the end of our vocabulary. This volume is a record, partial and imperfect to be sure, of some changes in English words during the fifty years 1941–1991. The changes were recorded, in the first instance, in a semiregular column called "Among the New Words" published in the journal *American Speech.* That journal had been founded in 1925 at the instigation of the Sage of Baltimore, H. L. Mencken, whose avocation was studying the language of America. Its first editors were a troika of distinguished scholars, Louise Pound, Kemp Malone, and Arthur Kennedy. In 1971, the journal acquired sponsorship by the scholarly organization dearest to Mencken's heart – the American Dialect Society; its current editor is Ronald R. Butters of Duke University.

In 1941 Dwight L. Bolinger, who had been writing a column on new words ("The Living Language") for a magazine published in Los Angeles, transferred his work to *American Speech* and renamed it "Among the New Words." Bolinger continued to edit the feature until 1944, when it came under the guidance of I. Willis Russell, who looked after it for forty-two years, until his death in 1985. During the first fifty years of the feature's publication in *American Speech,* it appeared in 113 installments, with 222 persons acknowledged as contributors of citations or other assistance.

Still appearing in practically every issue of *American Speech,* "Among the New Words" is the longest-running documentary record of new English words. Although dictionaries of new words have become increasingly popular in recent years, in one sense, English lexicography began with new-words books. The first monolingual English dictionaries recorded "hard words" exclusively, and so were mainly glossaries of unusual new words in the language intended to help ambitious yuppies of the seventeenth century keep up with the knowledge explosion of their day. In that sense, "Among the New Words" is in a very old tradition.

The motive behind "Among the New Words" is, however, quite different from that of the early "hard words" dictionaries. They were do-it-yourself books intended to help "unskilled," that is, unschooled, persons educate themselves in the buzzwords of their age. The aim of "Among the New Words" is more detached. When *American Speech* began publication, it had a motto blazoned on its cover: "They haif said. Quhat say they? Lat thame say."

That cryptic motto (traceable to an inscription over a door at Marischal College in Aberdeen, but with antecedents going back to magical amulets of the late

Classical period) has several interpretations. But most probably it was intended as a statement of editorial policy: The aim of *American Speech* was to observe and record the language of the populace, without concern for correcting it – to be descriptive, not prescriptive, in its approach to its subject, to glory in the vernacular.

So too, the aim of "Among the New Words" has always been to catch change in our vocabulary on the wing, to record it, to marvel at it, and when possible to explain it. The feature has been a dispassionate, albeit sometimes amused, observer of the lexical and social flux of our society, especially as change in our words interacts with and reflects change in our folkways and mores. A fitting motto for "Among the New Words" might be this: "Et Verba Nova et Origines Exquirere" (To seek out new words and their origins).

It would be incorrect to say that the mission of the column is to boldly go where none have gone before, because the quest for neologisms is an old one. However, "Among the New Words" is distinguished by how it has gone about its mission, especially by the evidence it presents. A characteristic feature of its entries is their extensive documentation. New words are shown as they are used in real language through many, often long, quotations for which full source information is given.

The body of this volume reprints the 113 installments that originally appeared between 1941 and 1991. These installments include many of the significant words added to the English vocabulary during those decades. However, they also omit some significant words and include a good many insignificant ones. The principles on which words were chosen for "Among the New Words" explain both the omissions and the inclusions.

COLLECTING NEW WORDS

1. What is a new word?

For "Among the New Words," a NEW WORD is a form or the use of a form not recorded in general dictionaries. The form may be one that is usually spelled as a single word (*guesstimate*) or a compound (*sandwich generation*) or even an idiomatic phrase (*out of the loop, go double platinum*).

The form of the word itself may be novel, a shape that has not before been seen or heard in English (*flextime, phillumenist, ecotage*), or the newness may lie in a novel use of an existing form. In the latter case, the novelty may be in what the word refers to (*turf* as 'a location, subject, or responsibility claimed as one's own'), the word's grammar (*looney tunes* developing from the name of an animated cartoon to an adjective 'erratic, absurd'), or even its relationship to those who use it (British *toyboy* entering American use via supermarket tabloids).

The early installments of "Among the New Words"

tried to include words that were new in an absolute sense – words that had come into use within a few years before their documentation in the column. It is often difficult, however, to be sure of when a word was actually first formed, and some words have a long underground existence before they are reported. So the column eventually adopted an operational definition of *new:* A word is "new" if it (or a particular use of it) does not appear in general dictionaries at the time it is included in the column.

The list of dictionaries taken as touchstones for "newness" changes as fresh ones are published and old ones are revised. At the time of this writing, the following works are being consulted as the column's dictionaries of record:

Random House Webster's College Dictionary, 1991.
Oxford English Dictionary, 2d ed., 1989.
World Book Dictionary (Thorndike-Barnhart), 1989.
Webster's New World Dictionary, 3d College ed., 1988.
Random House Dictionary, 2d ed. Unabridged, 1987.
Webster's Ninth New Collegiate Dictionary, 1983.
Webster's Third New International Dictionary, 1961.

Except for the two major dictionaries of record (the *OED* and *Webster's Third*), the list is limited to significant American dictionaries published during the preceding ten years.

British dictionaries (other than the *OED*) are consulted only for words suspected to be of British origin, and the inclusion of a word in a British dictionary does not exclude it from "Among the New Words" if it appears to have extended its use from British to American English. On the other hand, occasional installments of "Among the New Words" or particular entries in an installment document British new words, regardless of their use in American English. The additional British dictionaries of record for "Among the New Words" are currently the following:

Concise Oxford Dictionary, 8th ed., 1990.
Chambers English Dictionary, 1988.
Collins Concise Dictionary, 2d ed., 1988.
Collins Dictionary, 2d ed., 1986.
Longman Dictionary, 1984.
Reader's Digest Great Illustrated Dictionary, 1984.

Dictionaries specializing in new words are also routinely consulted, and a word entered in one of them is not usually included in "Among the New Words" unless the editors have citational evidence providing additional information about the word. The new-word glossaries currently consulted are these:

Third Barnhart Dictionary of New English, 1990.
Longman Register of New Words, vol. 1, 1989; vol. 2, 1990.
New New Words Dictionary, 1988.
Longman Guardian New Words, 1986.
12,000 Words, 1986.

In addition to such books, the other major periodical record of neologisms regularly consulted is *The Barnhart Dictionary Companion*, 1982–.

A form or use that is not adequately accounted for

in such dictionaries is a "new word" and thus a candidate for inclusion in the column, and normally only words not entered in them are included. Consequently, if a recently coined word appears in a new dictionary, it will never appear in "Among the New Words." The column is therefore a record of such new words as have not yet made their way into dictionaries at the time the column is being prepared.

On the other hand, "Among the New Words" does not scruple to include words that would not usually appear in any general dictionary: nonce words and stunt words. A NONCE WORD is one coined for a particular use and unlikely to become a permanent part of the vocabulary. A STUNT is a nonce word intended as a joke or a clever display of the coiner's virtuosity. Such words are not included in "Among the New Words" if they have nothing else to recommend them; the column does not seek to record the merely novel and cute. When, however, stunt and other nonce words illustrate a pattern of word formation or are especially indicative of the life of the time or otherwise exemplify something important about language, they may find their way into "Among the New Words."

The proliferation of Watergate words is a case in point. Many of the *Water-* and *-gate* forms were ephemeral, of no intrinsic interest. But they showed how rapidly a new suffix can come into widespread use, they were highly topical in American society, and many exemplified a spirit of play that has as much claim to being a central function of language as any of the more sober purposes usually set forth as humanity's reason for talking.

2. How are new words found?

The identification of potential new-word candidates and the gathering of documentary evidence – that is, citations with source information – is the major task in preparing "Among the New Words." The column can be written only because, from its beginning, words and citations have been contributed by members of the band of volunteer workers listed in the Index to Contributors.

New contributors join the band every year. They watch for words that strike them as new uses in whatever material they customarily read or listen to. Because printed evidence is easy to gather, most of the new words are attested from newspapers, magazines, and books. However, speech and other forms of writing are equally valid sources of evidence. The dominance of printed citations is a matter of convenience, not intended to privilege the published word over the spoken or handwritten. Oral and manuscript citations are used when they are available.

Some contributors do preliminary checking in one of the dictionaries of record listed above, but verifying "newness" is the responsibility of the editors. Contributors need primarily an awareness of what is likely to be novel and an inclination to gather citations as they come upon them in their ordinary reading and listening.

If the material to be cited is disposable, such as a newspaper or popular magazine, contributors underline the word in red or highlight it, tear out the page, and send it to the editors. The page must contain the name of the publication, the date, and the page number. If that information is not printed on the page, it has to be written on the tear sheet by the contributor.

If the material is not disposable, the preferred method of collecting is to copy the page xerographically (with source information – author, title, place, publisher, date, and page number – added by hand as necessary), and then to treat the copies in the same way as tear sheets. If it is not convenient to copy pages, handwritten or typed quotations with source information are sent on either sheets of paper or four-by-six slips.

An oral citation, which may be handwritten or typed, should consist whenever possible of a full sentence containing the new word. Source information includes the date the sentence was heard and its circumstances (if a broadcast, the radio or TV station call letters and city; if in a conversation or public speech, a brief description of the occasion). Some identification of the speaker is often useful: the name of a public figure or a brief characterization of a private person – sex, approximate age, etc.

All citations are added to the New Words files of the American Dialect Society, which are the basis for "Among the New Words." Those files are in any of three forms, depending on how the citations were gathered: slips, tear sheets or clippings, and computer records.

All active contributors are members of the American Dialect Society's New Words Committee by virtue of their contributions. They receive an irregular newsletter reporting on the state of the committee's work and listing new words for which citations are especially sought. In each installment those who supplied citations for that installment are listed, and once a year active contributors are acknowledged.

THE MAKING OF NEW WORDS

There are six basic etymological sources for new words: CREATING, BORROWING, COMBINING, SHORTENING, BLENDING, and SHIFTING. Each of those six, however, has a number of important subtypes, so the total number of distinct sources is large. All six of the basic types and a number of subtypes have been represented during the fifty years of "Among the New Words." There is also a seventh category of words whose source is unknown. Etymologists strive, ever unsuccessfully, to reduce the membership of that category to zero.

1. Creating

Some new words are made from nothing or, at least, not from existing words. This source is the least productive of the six; most new words derive in one way or another from old words. The purest kind of creating would be to make a word completely from scratch, creation ex nihilo. Theoretically, it should be possible to make up words in that fashion; but in fact there are no such words of which we can be sure. To make something out of nothing does not seem to be a human talent.

Another kind of creating is to make a word whose sound resembles some sound in nature: the *moo* of a cow or the *pow* of a blow to the chin. Such words are called IMITATIVE, ECHOIC, or ONOMATOPOETIC. Instances in this book are *bebop, bleep, blimp, burp, gack, gobbledygook* or *gobbledegook*, and *re-bop*. *Gobbledygook*, which is said to imitate the sound of a turkey, is based partly on the existing echoic *gobble* but extends that word with a new echo.

2. Borrowing

A more productive source of new words is to borrow them from other languages. A great proportion of the total English vocabulary is composed of words made from ultimately foreign elements. However, many such words were actually formed in English, so the extremely high percentage of borrowing sometimes reported for English is exaggerated. Yet many loanwords did enter English in the past, and we continue to borrow words from other languages as they fill a need in English.

Simple loanwords Simple LOANWORDS are ADOPTED directly into English, sometimes with minor modifications of pronunciation needed to make them conform to English sound patterns, and sometimes with spelling changes of a similar kind, but with no major change of form. Ever since 1066 French has been the main source of LOANS into English, and it is the most prolific contributor in this volume, being the source of the following:

brouhaha, chichi, discotheque, lettrisme, lettrist, magicienne, maquis, marché légal, marché noir, marché parallèle, messagerie, Minitel, Minitelist, nacelle, (la) nouvelle cuisine, nouvelle cuisinier, plastique, plastiqueur, repechage.

French, however, also borrows from English, and sometimes the borrowing doubles back upon itself, so that we have items that combine French and English: *les shorts, Watergaffe.*

German was the source of a fair number of loanwords at the time of World War II, most military in nature:

blitzkrieg, buna, Festung Europa, flak, sometimes respelled in a more English-looking fashion as *flack, Herrenvolk, Luftwaffe, panzer, schnorchel* with variants *schnorkel, schnorkle,* and eventually *snorkel, sitzkrieg,* and *Wuwa.*

Spanish has provided a few loanwords, especially of American Spanish origin, relating to politics, music, and drugs: *Fidelismo, Fidelista, mambo, (el-)primo, rubia (de la costa).* Portuguese is likewise of the American variety, heavy on music: *bossa nova, lambada, lambaderia.* Russian loans are political in their overtones: *perestroika, sputnik, Tass.*

Other languages provide a smattering of loans: Afrikaans *apartheid*, Arabic *intifada(h)*, Modern Hebrew *Israeli*, Kikuyu *Mau Mau*, Norwegian *rumptaske*, Panjabi *bhangra*, Swedish *jul otta*.

Adapted loanwords Some loans involve remodeling of meaningful parts of their form (morphological change), rather than only adjustments of pronunciation or spelling (phonological or orthographic change). They are ADAPTED from their foreign word pattern to a more native one. A foreign ending may be omitted, as in *dol* from Latin *dolor;* in the case of *Lettrism* and *Fidelism,* the French *-isme* and Spanish *-ismo* were replaced by the corresponding English *-ism.* In *spelunker, cybernetics, ataractic, ataraxic,* and *emporiatrics,* the grammatical endings of Latin *spelunca* and of Greek *kybernetes, ataraktos, ataraxia,* and *emporos* were omitted and the suffixes *-er, -ics, -ic,* and *-iatrics* added, with other spelling changes to naturalize the orthography. *Rhochrematics* compounds two Greek roots, *rho-* and *chremat-*, and adds the suffix *-ics.*

Ever since the Renaissance, English has raided the classical languages for impressive-sounding root words. So extensive has such learned borrowing been that a large number of Greek and Latin roots are now a part of English, used like any other elements to make compounds and affixed derivatives. However, we still sometimes go back to the classical sources to borrow roots when we need a fancy term, especially in medicine or technology.

Loan translations Instead of borrowing the form of a foreign word, English sometimes borrows its meaning, rendering the foreign sense by appropriate words already in the language. Such borrowings, called CALQUES or LOAN TRANSLATIONS, may exist alongside the corresponding simple loans they translate. Instances are the French *animator, basket, fourth force,* and *new cuisine* (beside *nouvelle cuisine*); German *Fortress Europe* (beside *Festung Europa*) and *guestworker* (for which the simple loan *Gastarbeiter* also exists, although it is generally used only for guestworkers in Germany); Russian *apparatus* (for which there is also the simple loan *apparat,* usual only in the context of communism), and *fellow traveler;* Spanish *blonde from the coast* (beside *rubia de la costa*); and Chinese *barefoot doctor.*

3. Combining

A far more productive source of new words – indeed, by most counts, the most productive of all – is to combine existing words or word parts (technically known as MORPHEMES) into a new form. Such combinations are said to be of two types: COMPOUNDS and DERIVATIVES. The difference is that a compound combines two or more full words or bases, whereas a derivative combines a base with one or more affixes.

A BASE is the part of a word to which prefixes and suffixes may be added. It may be an independent word, such as *comb* in *uncombed*, or it may be a morpheme that does not occur alone as a separate word, such as the *kemp* of *unkempt*. An AFFIX is a PREFIX if it comes before a base (like *un-*), and a SUFFIX, if after a base (like *-ed* or *-t*). A combination of bases or of a base and affix to which another affix may be added is called a STEM; so in *short-timer*, the combination of bases, *short-time*, is the word's stem, and in *activity*, the combination of base and suffix, *active*, is likewise a stem.

The theoretical distinction between base and affix is, however, neater than the reality. Affixes are sometimes used as independent words, as *ism* and *ology* are. On the other hand, independent words may be used in an affix-like way and eventually become affixes. An example is the word *like*, which is a kind of suffix in *affix-like*. Its Old English source word, *lic*, is also the origin of the suffix *-ly*. So *like*, *-like*, and *-ly* are historically all developments of the same word, though today they are a base-word, a quasi-affix, and an ordinary affix.

A different kind of example is *anthrop(o)-*, which combines with a word in *anthropogenesis* and with a suffix in *anthropoid* but is not used alone. A form like *anthrop(o)-* or *-like* is called a COMBINING FORM and can be regarded as either a base or an affix. The distinction between the compounding of bases and derivation by affixes is a useful one, but there are combinations that can be looked at in either way.

Prefixes Traditional prefixes are well represented among new words. The following occur in this volume: *anti-*, *be-*, *bi-*, *bin-*, *contro-*, *counter-*, *crypto-*, *de-*, *electro-*, *ergo-*, *exo-*, *extra-*, *hydro-*, *hyper-*, *hypo-*, *infra-*, *inter-*, *kilo-*, *maxi-*, *mega-*, *mini-*, *mono-*, *multi-*, *neo-*, *non-*, *off-*, *out-*, *over-*, *paleo-*, *pluto-*, *post-*, *pre-*, *proto-*, *quadri-* (with variants *quadra-* and *quadro-*), *quasi-*, *re-*, *retro-*, *semi-*, *sub-*, *super-*, *thermo-*, *tri-*, *turbo-*, *ultra-*, *un-*, *under-*, *up-*, *urbi-*, and *xeri-* or *xero-*.

New prefixes or new senses of old prefixes often develop to augment the list of traditional ones. For example, *aer(o)-* is a form meaning 'air' that combines with other word parts, as in *aerate* and *aerobic*. However, because of its association with *aeronautics* and the British *aeroplane*, it has acquired the sense 'aviation' as in *aeropause* and *aeropolitics*. Similarly, *agriculture* was a loanword from Middle French, ultimately from Latin *agricultura*, in which *agri-* was a combining form of the Latin word for 'field', *ager*. Today, however, that form has taken on the sense of the whole word *agriculture* and become a prefix, as in *agribusiness*. *Bio-* continues its earlier sense of 'life' but is sometime used more specifically to mean 'biological', as in *biorobot*, which is not a living machine, but one used in biological experiments.

Docu- has the sense 'in a documentary style' in forms like *docu-pulp*, *docu-reenactment*, and *documusical*. *Eco-* has taken on the sense 'ecology, ecological' in a very large number of words (*eco-awareness*, *ecodefender*, *ecopolicy*, etc.) and is a vogue affix today. Another currently much used form is *Eur(o)-*, which has both the general sense 'European' and the more specific one 'pertaining to the EC (European Community)'. *Execu-* in *execu-crime* means 'executive, white-collar'. *Heli-* used in the sense 'helicopter' balances the short form *copter* in showing how English speakers have divided the full form despite its etymology, which is *helico-pter* 'spiral-wing'.

Micro- has its usual sense of 'small', but in addition has developed a new use as in *microcook* 'cook in a microwave oven'. Similarly, *para-* acquired a new meaning in *paradoctor* 'a medical person making parachute calls', *parastreaker* 'a naked parachutist', and *paratrooper* 'member of a parachute troop', along with a score of other such words. *Petrochemical*, *petrodiplomat*, *petrodollar*, and *petropolitics* are concerned with petroleum rather than with rocks. *Psychodrama*, *psychohistory*, and *psycholinguistics* are not about the soul but are respectively playacting used as psychotherapy, history from a psychoanalytical standpoint, and study of the psychological aspects of language.

Radio-poison is poisoning from radioactive fallout. *Strato-suit*, *stratocruiser*, and *stratopen* refer not to clouds or layers, but to things used in the stratosphere. A *telecourse* is not just distant, but is taught by television; a *teleprompter* is a nearby device showing television performers what to say; and a *telethon* is a televised show to raise money.

Suffixes Suffixes are more numerous than prefixes, and they are more frequent. Traditional suffixes, or combinations of suffixes, that have been used to form recent new words are *-able*, *-ac*, *-aceous*, *-age*, *-aire*, *-(al)ly*, *-(i)ana*, *-ate*, *-ation*, *-cide*, *-dom*, *-ectomy*, *-ed*, *-ee*, *-eer*, *-eering*, the extremely productive *-er* (which has several uses), *-(e)ry*, *-ese*, *-esque*, *-ette* (whose recent use is more pejorative than it once was), *-eur*, *-euse*, *-ey*, *-fication*, *-fy*, *-grapher*, *-graphy*, *-ian*, *-iatrics*, *-ic*, *-ical*, *-ics*, noun-forming *-ie* or *-y*, *-in*, *-ing*, *-ion*, *-ish*, the very popular *-ism* with a pseudo-Spanish variant *-ismo*, *-ist*, *-ite*, *-ity*, *-ium*, *-ive*, *-ization*, *-ize*, *-latry*, *-less*, *-let*, *-logist*, *-logy*, *-ly*, *-ment*, *-metrician*, *-ness*, *-oid*, *-or*, *-osis*, *-phile*, *-phobe*, *-ster*, *-stress*, *-tomy*, *-wise*, and adjective forming *-y*.

Some suffixes are positioned oddly, especially when converting phrases like "lust after" or "speed up" into words. In *lustable-after* (beside *lust-afterable*) the suffix

-able is interposed rather than put at the end of the word. In *speeder-upper* and a number of similar forms, *-er* is reduplicated.

The placename element *-(s)ville* is used also to form words with a metaphorical allusion to place. *Hooverville* was a 1930s instance, and a more recent one that never found its way into "Among the New Words" is *dullsville*. Although *photogenic* originally meant 'produced by light', by the 1920s it had come to mean 'good as a subject for photography' and in that sense was the source of a new meaning for the suffix *-genic* in *mediagenic, phonogenic, radiogenic,* and *telegenic*. Although the suffix *-nik* is older in English, it received a double-barreled boost in the late 1950s from *sputnik* and *beatnik;* later examples are *discothequenik, folknik, gatenik,* and *neatnik*.

Derivatives sometimes have linking vowels or consonants added to the stem of a word before an affix for ease of pronunciation or by association with related words. So the complex suffix *-arianism* of *communitarianism* carries over the *t* from that word and from others like *Rotarianism* to the new form *cosmotarianism*. Similarly, the *-ateer* of *pulpateer* reflects the vowel and *t* of *pamphleteer* or *profiteer*. The same linking sounds (*at*) occur in *ismatism* as an echo of such medical terms as *rheumatism* and *astigmatism*.

Some new suffixes are formed, just as some prefixes are, by a process of blending. Thus, *breath* and *analyzer* were blended in a tradename "Breathalyzer," and the ending *-(a)lyzer* was extended as a suffix to *eye(a)lyzer*. The old words *secretariat* and *proletariat* are the source of the suffix *-ariat* in *infantariat* and *salariat*. Similarly, blends of *inflation* have produced a voguish new suffixal form *-flation* in *gradeflation, oilflation, taxflation;* it also occurs as the stem in *un-flation,* an alternative to the much older *deflation*. Another suffix created by fracturing a word is *-holic* from *alcoholic;* the prototypical form seems to have been *workaholic* in the late 1960s.

The ending of *broadcast* has become a new suffix *-cast,* used in forms like *narrowcast, telecast,* and *newscast*. Other derivatives from it are the *-caster* of *sportscaster* and the *-casting* of *beercasting* (beer-advertising on TV). The second part of *Watergate* became a suffix for a political scandal complicated by efforts at a cover-up, but was used jokingly in many stunt words from *Abdulgate* to *Winegate*. There is no reason why the last syllable of *Watergate* should have become a suffix, except that it was short, snappy, and suggested an opening for satire.

A shortage of various commodities during World War II resulted in illegal dealers in them; consequently the older term *bootlegger* (originally 'one who carries contraband in his boot legs') became the source of a new suffix, *-legger* in *foodlegger, tirelegger, gas legger,* and the like. The early clipping of *automobile* to *auto* left the second half of the word for use as a suffixal form; the prototype, *bookmobile,* is from the

1920s, but a later example is *bloodmobile*. Although *sandwich* has no connection with *sand* (anymore than *hamburger* does with *ham*), its first syllable has been replaced by various words indicating fillings: *duckwich, Spamwich, turkeywich*.

Argonaut begat *astronaut* as early as 1880; later suffixal uses of *-naut* for explorers of the watery or stellar deeps are *aquanaut, bathynaut, cosmonaut,* and *hydronaut*. Other terms for spaceship passengers have first parts describing the traveler: *plastinaut* (a plastic dummy) and *chimp(o)naut*. Only a vague sense of spaciness seems to connect the foregoing to the blend *Reaganaut* 'a supporter of Ronald Reagan'. *Economic(s)* has been clipped to a suffixal *-(o)nomic(s),* as in *Fordonomics* and *Reaganomic;* the suffix is especially favored when it can be blended with a word ending in *n*: *McGovernomics, Nixonomics, electionomics*.

Panorama yielded the suffix *-rama* (ultimately from Greek *horama* 'a view') as early as the first half of the nineteenth century. General Motors used the form in its etymological sense as part of the name of their exhibition at the 1939 New York World's Fair, *Futurama;* since that time the suffix has become diverse and vaguer in meaning. The suffix *-(a)thon* is the kind of innovation linguistic pecksniffery loves to hate. Of this suffix, the *Oxford English Dictionary,* 2d ed., looking down a very long and censorious nose, remarks: "barbarously extracted f. MAR)ATHON, used occas. in the U.S. (*talkathon, walkathon*), rarely in Britain, to form words denoting something carried on for an abnormal length of time." The events so named are often fund-raisers for charity.

The suffix *-iad,* abstracted from *Olympiad,* is used for a different sort of quadrennial event in *presidentiad*. The abstraction of *-on* from *aileron* to add to *deceler(ate)* in *deceleron* 'an aircraft brake' added another sense to the several scientific and technological uses of the *-on* suffix. On the other hand, the abstraction of *-onics* from *electronics* in order to make *bionics* produced a new suffix. The playful, joking suffix *-aroo, -eroo,* or *-roo,* probably abstracted from *buckaroo,* occurs in words like *switcheroo*.

The rare suffix *-ere* in *gomere* 'female gomer' (a gomer being an undesirable emergency-room patient) perhaps reflects such French gender distinctions as *couturier/couturière* and *cuisinier/cuisinière,* although the analogy is imperfect. The *-erie* of *shooterie* likewise seems to be modeled on French as a variant of the more usual *-ery*. The *-ers* of *bleepers* is perhaps the British slang suffix of *champers*.

New suffixes are still occasionally borrowed from the classical languages, such as *-tron* from Greek to form names for devices or facilities of scientific study. It has doubtless been reinforced by its similarity to the ending of the word *electron*. Endings suggestive of the inflections of classical languages are sometimes added to words for effect, without adding any very precise meaning. The Greek-looking *-os* in the trademark *Domestos* is an example, as is the Latin-looking *-us* in *goofus*.

Near the borderline between suffixation and compounding is the formative *happy*, which does not look much like a suffix because it is usually spelled with either a hyphen (*headline-happy*) or a space (*flak happy*). However, its meanings are different from those of the independent word *happy*. Suffixal *happy* has two senses: 'confused and disoriented from' (*battle-happy*) and 'impulsive or obsessive about' (*trigger-happy, power-happy*). Both senses are negative, whereas the independent word *happy* is normally positive in its meanings. The prototype of the use was probably *slaphappy*, from the 1930s, which already had the seed of both senses, specifically 'punch-drunk' and 'irresponsibly zany'. The suffix radiated in its uses during World War II.

Another borderline suffix is the prepositional *-in*, with three senses: 'a public protest' (prototype *sit-in*, also *pray-in*), 'a place to which one comes' (prototype *drive-in*, also *fly-in*), 'a large group entertainment' (prototype *love-in*, also *streak-in*). Similar are *-off* and *-out*. Although *play-off* is from the nineteenth century, *bake-off* is a mid-twentieth-century form. *Punch-out*, with an intensifying sense of *-out*, suggests the older *knock-out*. *Brown-out* and *dim-out* are obviously patterned after the older *black-out*. *Fallout* and *cookout* involve yet other senses of the suffix, directional and locational.

Compounds Compounds, the result of joining two or more bases, are the most numerous type of combination.

About 90 percent of new compounds are nouns. Adjectives and verbs account for less than 10 percent, and other parts of speech are even rarer. Several factors account for the preponderance of nouns. There are more new things to name than there are new events or qualities. We rarely come upon a new action or characteristic, but often invent or discover new objects. Also English prefers to put semantic information into nouns and use a few dummy verbs like *have*, *take*, and *do* with them; we "dine" less often than we "have dinner," "rest" less often than "take a rest," "research" less often than "do research." Moreover, it is easy in English to use a noun to modify another noun, so we have less need for distinctive adjectives. On the whole, the English vocabulary favors nouns.

Compounds generally consist of two (occasionally more) words combined as a lexical unit. They are usually written with a space between them (*architectural barrier*), less often solid (*blacktop*) or with a hyphen (*user-friendly*). There is, however, a good deal of variation: *toyboy* or *toy-boy*, *spaceship* or *space ship*, *product mix* or *product-mix*, *tinseltown*, *tinsel-town*, or *tinsel town*.

(a) Suffix-like compounds. Compounds are sometimes formed according to a pattern of using a particular word in first or last position, very much like an affix. During World War II, United States military forces were based at various locations around the world, so forms like *Aleutian-based, Italy-based, Marianas-based, Saipan-based* were frequent. Common nouns were also used as the first elements of *-based* compounds: *carrier-based, homebased, shore-based*. Although less prolific now than it was in the 1940s, the pattern still produces new forms: *reality-based*.

Other forms with similar popular suffix-like use are *-bashing* (especially in British use: *fag-bashing, granny-bashing, Paki-bashing, square-bashing, yuppy-bashing*), the enduring *-burger* (*nutburger, SPAMburger*), *-buster*, which enjoyed a fad in the 1940s (*atom-buster, belly buster, blockbuster, crime buster, gangbuster, ghost buster* 'an exposer of fraudulent mediums' rather than the later 'exorcist', *knuckle buster, racket buster, trust-buster, union-buster*, and many others), *circuit* (*Borscht circuit, chicken-patty circuit, subway circuit*), *curtain* (*bamboo curtain, iron curtain, paper curtain*), *-hop* (*bed-hop, city-hop, job-hop, museum-hop, table-hop*), *-intensive* (*earnings-intensive, fuel-intensive, time-intensive*), *look* (*bare look, layered look*), *-mania* (*condomania, Olliemania*), *privilege* (*executive privilege, journalistic privilege, judicial privilege*), *-speak* (*businessspeak, computerspeak, Haigspeak, Valley Girl-speak*), and many others.

(b) Prefix-like compounds. Certain other words are favored as the first element of compounds and so are prefix-like. *Bamboo* was used with the sense 'native' with reference to the Philippines in *bamboo English, bamboo government, bamboo telegraph*; later *bamboo English* was used also for English influenced by Japanese and Korean. *Big* has similar prefixal use in *big banking, big labor, big money*, and *big oil*. *Golden* in *golden handshake, golden parachute, golden shackle*, and many other combinations refers to a financial settlement benefiting the employee or the employer. Other such initial elements are *living, motor, power, shock, sky*, and many more.

(c) Classical compounds. In its early history, English borrowed a great many compounds from Latin and Greek (although most Greek words were filtered through Latin, and even today new loans from Greek are generally represented in English as though they had passed through Roman mouths and hands). Because we adopted a large number of classical compounds, we also adopted the classical pattern for forming them. In English, if we want to compound two words, we generally just stick them together: *self + rule = self-rule*. In Greek, it was generally necessary to have a vowel between two compounded bases: *aut + o + nomia = autonomia*, which we borrowed as *autonomy*.

When we form new compounds in English, using morphemes from the classical languages, we often combine them more or less according to the classical pattern. So *o*'s pop up in many new words like *chemosphere* and *magnetosphere*, which otherwise might just as well have been "chemical sphere" and "magnetic sphere." "New Latin" and "New Greek" compounds include *Legionella pneumophila* (the bacillus of Legionnaire's disease), *Homo habilis*, and *zinjanthropus*, although the Romans and Hellenes would hardly have known what to make of them.

(d) Letter compounds. Some compounds consist of a noun and one or more letters of the alphabet. The letters often stand for words, as the *A* in *A-bomb* is for "atom," and thus the word is a compound of an acronym (see below) and another word. Military use favors such letter compounds, but they are also used in other circumstances as cryptic short forms (*Q fever*, for "query" because of questions about the nature of the illness) or euphemisms (*F-word* and many humorous imitations of that pattern).

In other cases, however, the letter has a different origin. It may represent a point in a series, as *Baker Day* (with *baker* as the signaler's name for the letter *B*) is the second day in a military operation. Occasionally, the letter merely reduplicates the first letter of a following noun: *H-hour*. Sometimes it is a pun: *U-Drive* for "you drive." Although there have been no examples in "Among the New Words," the letter is sometimes iconic, as in *S curve* and *V neck*. In a few cases, the meaning of the letter is unknown, as in *g-string*.

(e) Alphanumeric compounds. Some compounds are made of combinations of letters and numerals (*V-1* 'a German bomb'), sometimes of numerals alone (*1080* 'a rat poison'), sometimes of letters and numerals joined with an ordinary word (*vitamin B$_{12}$*). The parts may be individually significant, as in *1947N* the name of a comet, the fourteenth (hence *N*) discovered in 1947. Or they may be from an arbitrary system of classification, like *4F* as the designation for those rejected for military service during World War II. Often the motivation for the parts of the compound fades from awareness, as in *20-20* 'perceptive, accurate' from the ability to see normally with both eyes at a distance of twenty feet.

(f) Sound patterns in compounds. Sound repetition plays a part in a few compounds. At the greatest extreme of repetition, some compounds reduplicate a word: *bleep bleep*, *lurgy lurgy*, *ping-ping-pong-pong* (which puts one instance of the reduplicated word inside the other), *quad-quad*, *short shorts*, *zero-zero*.

Rime plays a part in others: *brain drain*, *creepie-peepie*, *fuddie-duddie*, *Hacky Sack*, *Ike-liker*, *jet set*, *no-show*, *peepie-creepie*, *shock frock*, *shock jock*, *surround sound*, *tot lot*, *toyboy*, *wait state*.

Alliteration is probably at least a supporting motive behind such compounds as *baby bust*, *belly bundle*, *bumble bomb*, *buzz bomb*, *chump change*, *death dust*, *double-digit* (which is more popular than the synonymous but unalliterative *double-figure*), *down and dirty*, *gas guzzler*, *glower and grin*, *hidden hunger*, *hollow hunger*, *lend-lease*, *metermaid*, *roid rage*, *sky scout*, *sweepswinger*.

The assonance of the vowels contributes to the effect of *brass hat*, *date rape*, *eager beaver*, *fanny pack*, *hit list*, *hot rod*, *jampacked*, *punch-drunk*, *whirlybird*.

Some compounds combine sound effects; alliteration and assonance in *fanny flask*, *sword and sorcery*, *winkie-wiggling*; alliteration and consonance (the repetition of consonant sounds after the vowel) in *Tinseltown*, *war-weary*.

(g) Respelled compounds. Unconventional spelling has long been a device of trade names to make a distinctive commercial label out of an ordinary word or phrase ("Holsum," "Bestovall"). In that tradition is the British *Filofax* (from "file of facts") for a loose-leaf notebook with filler pages of many kinds.

(h) Compound phrases. Some items are new "words" in the sense that they have a single idiomatic meaning, yet look and behave as though they were phrases. Verbal idioms like *turn over* (the ball in a football game) and *rev it up* (of an engine) are such phrases of one kind. Others are prepositional phrases used adjectivally or adverbially, such as *on the beam* and *behind the curve*. Others are complex noun phrases, such as *discrimination in reverse* or *back-to-the-basics*.

4. Shortening

A new word can be made by omitting some part of an old word.

Clipping The simplest form of shortening is by CLIPPING an expression at the boundary between its main parts (its primary morpheme boundary). Thus, *DNA fingerprinting* loses its first element by FORE CLIPPING to become *fingerprinting*, and *billboard antenna* loses its second element by HIND CLIPPING to become *billboard*. Such clipped forms usually look like merely a new use of the short form, but they are derived from an original longer expression, usually a compound, but sometimes an affixed word, as in the hind clipping of the suffix *-ie* from *yuppie* to make *yup*.

Other examples of fore clipping: *(Big) Bang*, *(architectural) barrier*, *(Smokey) Bear*, *(Hotel) de Gink*, *(user-) friendly*, *(gas) guzzler*, *(escalation) index*, *(couch) potato*, *(landing) strip*, *(ear) wire*.

Other examples of hind clipping: *Anderson (shelter)*, *baka (bomb)*, *department (store)*, *disco(theque)*, *doodle(bug)*, *double-digit (figure)*, *four-channel (sound/equipment)*, *giveaway (show)*, *heavy (bomber)*, *jet(-propelled plane)*, *Legionnaire's (disease)*, *mach (number)*, *main (course)*, *Mexican (marijuana)*, *Michoacan (marijuana)*, *micro(wave)*, *Molotov (cocktail)*, *nickel (bag)*, *nouvelle (cuisine)*, *nylon (hose)*, *palazzo (pants)*, *Panama (red)*, *percentage (of the winnings/profits)*, *platinum (record album)*, *probable (casualty)*, *robot (bomb)*, *security (blanket)*, *sniffer (and snorter)*, *soap (opera)*, *Streakers (Party)*, *string (bikini)*, *take-home (pay)*, *weekend (party)*.

A combination of both fore and hind clipping produces *(lysergic) acid (diethylamide)*.

(a) Internal clipping. Many shortened forms omit, not a whole main element of the original form, but only part of one of the main elements. Thus, *parachutist* was formed from *parachute* + *-ist*, which are its main elements. In *chutist*, only part of the first element was clipped. The clipping was still at a morpheme boundary, since *parachute* consists of *para* + *chute*, but it was not at the primary boundary within the word.

Other instances of such internal clipping: *biopic* from *bio(graphical) pic(ture)*, *Cabbage (Patch) Kid*, *Cominform* from *Com(munist) Inform(ation Bureau)*, *computeracy* from *computer (liter)acy*, *computerate* from *computer (liter)ate*, *demoth(ball)*, *(gold-)fish bowl*, *Legionnaire('s disease)*, *maître d'(hôtel)*, *microwave (oven)-proof*, *peak(-load) pricing*, *photo op(portunity)*, *physia* with respelling from *physio(therapist)*, *(car) pooler*, *(car) pooling*, *quad(riphony)*, *rehab(ilitation)*, *sencit* from *sen(ior) cit(izen)*, *Syncom* from *syn(chronous) com(munications satellite)*, *tiptank* from *(wing)tip tank*, *twi(light)-night*, *2–4-Di(chlorophenoxyacetic acid)*, *stepping* from *step (danc)ing*.

(b) Innovative clipping. In yet other cases, forms are clipped not at a morpheme boundary at all, but instead at a point that does not correspond to any part of the original word structure. New morphemes are created by such clipping. For example, *condominium* has the structure *con* + *domin-ium*; its clipping to *condo* was at no morphological boundary and so made a new word element.

Other instances of such innovative clipping: *amtrac* or *amphtrack* from *am(ph(ibious) trac(tor)*, *Amvets* from *Am(erican) Vet(eran)s*, *avgas* from *av(iation) gas(oline)*, *bascart* from *bas(ket) cart*, *blacketeer* from *black (mark)eteer*, *(be)bop*, *bra(ssière)*, *capcom* from *cap(sule) com(municator)*, *Cominch* from *Com(mander) in Ch(ief)*, *comsymp* from *com(munist) symp(athizer)*, *conelrad* from *con(trol of) el(ectromagnetic) rad(iation)*, *conillum* from *con(trol of) illum(ination)*, *(heli)copter*, *corti(co)s(ter)one*, *cyborg* from *cyb(ernetic) org(anism)*, *fax* respelled from *facs(imile transmission)*, *hazchem* from *haz(ardous) chem(icals)*, *Juco* from *ju(nior) co(llege)*, *mimstud* from *mi(ddle-aged) m(ale) st(ick-in-the-m)ud*, *mod(ern)*, *Nip(ponese)*, *nuke* respelled from *nuc(lear ship/weapon)*, *nonsked* or *non-sched(uled airline)*, *op(tical) art*, *prefab(ricated)*, *prop(eller)-stop*, *quas(i-stell)ar (object)*, *sitcom* from *sit(uation) com(edy)*, *tr(ans)axle*, *twee(t)* as a lisping pronunciation of *sweet*, *Valgirl* from *(San Fernando) Val(ley) girl*.

Alphabetism ALPHABETISMS or INITIALISMS are abbreviations using the initial letters of the words of an expression, pronounced by the alphabetical names of the letters. One of the most successful is *TV*. Sometimes the letter names are spelled out, as in *Jaycee* or *Elsie* (for *LC*, landing craft, with a pun on the female name). Occasionally alphabetical names other than the conventional ones are used, as in *ack-ack*, with a

British signal corps name for the letters *AA*, although the echoic value of *ack-ack* in suggesting the sound of antiaircraft fire also doubtless played a part.

Other alphabetisms: *AA, A-B-C, ABL, ACS, AMG, AT, BW, CAT, CATV, CFA, CPK, CRP, DDT, DE, dh, DI, DNB, DP, DPH, E, EAM, ETO, EVA, FFI, FM, FVT, GCA, GEM, IBM, ICBM, IMP, LCI, LCM, LCR, LCT, LCVP, LFC, LP, LST, MLF, MTB, MVA, OCD, ODT, OGO, OPA, OWI, PET, POW, PTFP, PV, PW, RDX, ROK, RV, sro, SST, TBS, TD, TOFC, TSO, TV, UNO, USO, VIP, WLB.*

Acronymy The term ACRONYM is used in several ways, but here it is a form made of the initial letters of the words of an expression, like an alphabetism, but pronounced according to the normal rules of English orthography. An example is *scuba* 'self-contained underwater breathing apparatus'. Some forms are either alphabetisms or acronyms; for example *ROK* is pronounced with letter names "are-oh-kay" when it stands for 'Republic of Korea' but as an orthographic word sounding like "rock" when it is used for a soldier of the ROK army.

Many acronyms are homonyms with another word and thus pun on it. Frequently the acronym is invented for the sake of the pun. Thus the *ZIP* of *ZIP Code* is said to stand for 'Zone Improvement Plan', but there can be little doubt that the word was chosen to suggest that the numerical postal codes would speed up mail delivery.

Yuppie, an acronym for 'young urban professional' plus the suffix *-ie*, has radiated a large number of similar terms, often involving puns. They include *bluppy, dink, droppies* with a pun on "drop (out)," *dumpie, dumpy* with puns on "dump," *flyer, guppie, guppy* (variously, 'grown-up pauper', 'gay urban professional', 'greedy upwardly mobile professional' or 'green yuppie'), *nuppie, sampy, serf, skippie, yap, yappie, yuca, yumpo*.

Instead of an initial letter only, sometimes several letters or a whole syllable is used. Thus in *CREEP* 'Committee for the Re-Election of the President', the syllable "Re" enters the acronym. And in *Fin-Creep* 'Financial Committee to Re-Elect the President', so do the first three letters of the first word. If a word is made up chiefly from syllables or groups of letters, it would usually be called a clipping. Acronyms are clippings in which most of the parts are reduced to single letters. A form like *loran* 'long-range navigation' is often called an acronym, but it is close to a form like *sitcom* 'situation comedy', which is usually called a clipping.

Some forms mix the alphabetic and acronymic principles, pronouncing the word partly with letter names and partly in the normal spelling-pronunciation way. The alphabetic part of such forms usually spells out the letter names. An example is *veep* 'vice president', in which "vee" is an alphabetical spelling and "p" is acronymous. Another is *umtee* 'Universal Military Trainee', in which "tee" may represent either the letter name or be a mid clipping of *T(rain)ee*.

Other acronyms: *ANZUS, BEV, Cincus, DOVAP, DRAM, E-COM, ELAS, ENIAC, Fido, flip, Fosdic, FOSDIC, gleep, jato, LEM, LOCA, lox, MOL, Mouse, nab, NERVA, OPEC, Ovra, PABA, PAC, piat, radar, REM, Sage, SHAEF, snafu, SPARS, STOL, sug, thobber, UNIVAC, UNRRA, WAAF, WAAS, WAC, WASP, WAVES, WOWS, zert*.

Phonetic elision   The omission of a sound is not always a deliberate decision to shorten a word (a morphological remodeling); it is sometimes a result of phonetic processes (APHESIS, APOCOPE, SYNCOPE). Normally, such processes make alternate pronunciations of an old word rather than a new word. But occasionally the elided form may be treated as a new word. *Stonewash* 'bleached in streaks' (of denim cloth) is an apocopated form of *stonewashed*, omitting the final [t] sound. *Fax* is a commercial respelling of a pronunciation of *facts* with elided [t], as also partly is *Ceefax*, a BBC teletext service punning on "see facts."

Back formation   BACK FORMATION is the process of shortening a word by omitting what is, or is thought to be, an affix or other constituent morpheme. The noun *zipper*, originally a trademark for a kind of slide fastener, was the origin of the verb *zip* 'to open or close with a zipper', formed by omitting the *-er* ending, as though it were the agent suffix on a verb.

The process of back formation often involves METANALYSIS – a reinterpretation of how a form is structured. So, *shotgun marriage* was a compound of those two nouns; from it, however a verb was formed by omitting the final *-age* as though that suffix had been added to an original *shotgun-marry*. The word was thus reanalyzed from *shotgun + marriage* to *shotgun marry + -age*.

Occasionally a backformation omits a prefix, like *ruly English* from *unruly*, or substitutes whole words, like the verb *jump-shoot* in basketball from the noun *jump-shot*. But most back formations omit suffixes and thus are a process of "de-suffixation." The following examples are listed by the omitted suffix:

-ed: brown off, chicken-fry, custom-make, fair-trade, field test, flight test, gift-wrap, jet-propel, polyunsaturate

-er or *-or:* baby sit, bargain-hunt, book-keep, chain-smoke, city-edit, cliff-hang, copyread, fellow-travel, guest-conduct, housepaint, pinchhit, script-write, sharecrop, tenant-farm

-ing: air condition, bellyland, brainstorm, brainwash, breast feed, breath-test, Christmas-shop, compulsory-test, contour-plow, crash land, double-park, fact-find, featherbed, grass-feed, hedgehop, lip-read, night-drive, patternbomb, pistol-whip, plea-bargain, price fix, pubcrawl, quisle, radar-track, soft-land, stock-take, touch dance, window-shop

-ion: air-evacuate, automate, mass-produce, noun-incorporate, trial subscribe

5. Blending

The process of simultaneously combining and shortening is BLENDING. A blend is a word made by joining two or more forms but omitting at least part of one. This simple process has a number of variations, some quite complex.

Blending with clipped first element   The word that begins the blend may have had its ending shortened:

adenovirus < aden(oid) + o + virus
aeroneer < aeron(aut) + -eer
Alcometer < alco(hol) + meter
bar-b-burger < bar-b-(cue) + burger
Binac < bin(ary) + -ac
build-down < build(-up) + down
femspeak < fem(inine) + speak
hit lady < hit (man) + lady
hit woman < hit (man) + woman
hot lederhosen < hot (pants) + lederhosen
near collision < near (miss) + collision
Okie < Ok(lahoman) + -ie
ploughperson's < plough(man)'s + person
synchrocyclotron < synchro(nize) + cyclotron
transaxle < trans(mission) + axle
vidspud < vid(eo) + spud
Waterbungler < Water(gate) + bungler

The blending of the words may be encouraged by an overlapping of sounds, usually at the point where the words join:

gazunder < gazu(mp) + *u*nder
lumberjill < lumber*j*(ack) + *j*ill
niacin < ni(cotinic) aci(d) + -in
robomb < ro*b*(ot) + *b*omb
smist < s*m*(oke) + *m*ist
smurk < s*m*(oke) + *m*urk
triathlete < tri*athl*(on) + *athl*ete
videot < *vide*(o) + *vide*ot
Watergimmick < Water*g*(ate) + *g*immick
Watergoof < Water*g*(ate) + *g*oof
yup-scale < y*up*(pie) + *up*-scale

Or the overlapping sound may be at the beginning or end of the word:

droodle < d*r*(aw) + *d*oodle
filipin < filip*in*(o) + -*in*

A number of puns based on *Watergate*, some fairly complex in the words they combine, belong to this general type:

Waterbugger < *Water*(gate) + *waterbug* + *bugg*[ing] + -*er* + bugger
Waterbuggery < *Water*(gate) + *waterbug* + *bugg*[ing] + buggery
Waterbugging < *Water*(gate) + *waterbug* + *bugging*
Waterfallout < *Water*(gate) + *waterfall* + *fall-out*

In the following example, the clipping comes in the middle of the first expression, so the other word is inserted into it:

safe computer practice < *safe* (sex) *practice + computer*

Although the computer term *bit* is usually said to be a clipping in origin, it clearly puns on the familiar noun meaning 'a small piece' and so is a blend:

bit < *b*(inary dig)*it + bit*

Similarly, the advice to Britons on how to cope with bombs falling during the wartime blitz is an obvious punning blend:

Bob 'Ope < *bob* (and) *hope + Bob Hope*

Blending with clipped second element As a mirror image of the usual pattern above (clipping the end of the first element), the beginning of the last element of the blend may be clipped:

airbrasive < air + (a)brasive
Asialationist < Asia + (iso)lationist
Bean-o-tash < bean + (succ)otash
beefcake < beef + (cheese)cake
bookvertising < book + (ad)vertising
car hop < car + (bell)hop
carlegging < car + (boot)legging
cartnapper < cart + (kid)napper
cartnapping < cart + (kid)napping
cheeseburger < cheese + (ham)burger
daddy track < daddy + (mommy) track
fanzine < fan + (maga)zine
Fleur-o-lier < fleur + o + (chande)lier
gasahol < gas + (alc)ohol
grass trap < grass + (speed) trap
gray market < gray + (black) market
gray marketeer < gray + (black) marketeer
grayout < gray + (black)out
hot war < hot + (cold) war
Little Bang < little + (Big) Bang
low-rise < low + (high)-rise
lukewarm pants < lukewarm + (hot) pants
middlebrow < middle + (high/low)-brow
monokini < mono- + (bi)kini
moonquake < moon + (earth)quake
Popsicle < pop + (i)cicle
potatophernalia < potato + (para)phernalia
Pretoriastroika < Pretoria + (pere)stroika
quadriminium < quadri- + (condo)minium
radiobotage < radio + (sa)botage
radioboteur < radio + (sa)boteur
RV-cationer < RV + (va)cationer
slumlord < slum + (land)lord
space opera < space + (soap) opera
spud-ucopia < spud + (corn)ucopia
squadrol < squad + (pat)rol
tank-dozer < tank + (bull)dozer
turkeyfurter < turkey + (frank)furter
uraniumaire < uranium + (million)aire
xericscaping < xeric + (land)scaping
yuppieback < yuppie + (paper)back

The following blend of this kind is possibly reinforced by a pun on the name of a literary character:

Tinman < *tin* + (Iron)*man* + *Tinman* [of Oz]

And the following certainly puns on both halves of the word:

margie-wanna < *margie* + *wanna* [= want a] + *m*(a)*rijuana*

Such blends may also be reinforced by overlapping sounds, usually the final sounds of the first element and the beginning sounds of what is left of the clipped second element:

aerobat < ae*ro* + (ac)*ro*bat
autotel < aut*o* + (h)*o*tel
beefalo < bee*f* + (buf)*f*alo
bidvertiser < bi*d* + (a)*d*vertiser
boatel < b*o*at + (h)*o*tel
confrontainment < confron*t* + (enter)*t*ainment
dramedy < dra*ma* + (co)*me*dy
ear-condition < ear + (ai)*r*-condition
ecotage < eco- + (sab)*o*tage
ecoteur < eco- + (sab)*o*teur
electionomics < electi*on* + (ec)*on*omics
fanference < fa*n* + (co)*n*ference
go-show < g*o* + (n)*o*-show
hairsatz < hai*r* + (e)*r*satz
handie-talkie < handy + (walk)*ie*-talkie
inner space < inn*er* + (out)*er* space
jetomic < je*t* + (a)*t*omic
jigaboo < ji*g* + (bu)*g*aboo
McGovernomics < McGover*n* + (eco)*n*omics
Nixonomics < Nix*on* + (ec)*on*omics
pencilatelist < pen*cil* + (ph)*il*atelist
Reaganaut < Reaga*n* + (argo)*n*aut
Reaganomic < Reaga*n* + (eco)*n*omic
Reaganomics < Reaga*n* + (eco)*n*omics
rockumentary < ro*ck* + (do)*c*umentary
Tenderoni < tend*er* + (mac)*ar*oni
trainasium < trai*n* + (gym)*n*asium

More elaborate sound effects sometimes link the two elements of a blend. In the following, the *poc* of *apocolypse* has been METATHESIZED (or reversed in order) to overlap the *co* of *eco-*:

ecopolypse < *eco-* + (a)*pocolypse*

Cockney riming slang belongs to the general category of blending:

porky pie < porky p*ie* + (l)*ie*

A similar expression is that for a book about the author's parent:

slap-and-yell < slap *and y*ell + (kiss) *and* (t)*ell*

The informal term for a helicopter seems to blend the latter half of the formal term with a metaphor derived from the whirling blades:

chopper < ch*opper* + (helic)*op*(t)*er*

Overlapping of the initial sounds of the blended words can reinforce the clipping:

cowfeteria < *cow* + *c*(a)feteria
Dixiecrat < *Dixie* + *D*(emo)crat
Dixiecratic < *Dixie* + *D*(emo)cratic
turkeymallies < *turkey* + *t*(a)males

The last part of the final element is clipped in

snort < *snor*t + *schnor*(chel).

Double clipping and insertion is illustrated by

bleepity-bleep < *bleep* + *bl*(ank)ety-*bl*(ank).

Blending with both elements clipped   Both elements entering into a blend may be clipped; the most usual pattern is to clip the end of the first element and the beginning of the second one:

appestat < appe(tite) + (thermo)stat
avionics < avi(ation) + (electr)onics
buppie < b(lack) + (y)uppie
Clari-phane < clari(ty) + (cello)phane
cockapopso < cockapo(o) + (Lhasa a)pso
Eisencrat < Eisen(hower) + (Demo)crat
globflation < glob(al) + (in)flation
guppie < g(reen) + (y)uppie
Hurri-Buster < Hurri(cane) + (tank)-buster
infotainment < info(rmation) + (enter)tainment
magdraulic < mag(netic) + (hy)draulic
medflation < med(ical) + (in)flation
Panagate < Pana(ma) + (Water)gate
Perma-lastic < perma(nent) + (e)lastic
plench < pl(iers) + (wr)ench
quadminium < quad(ri-) + (condo)minium
republocrat < republ(ican) + (dem)ocrat
rockoon < rock(et) + (ball)oon
simulcast < simul(taneous) + (broad)cast
sluppy < Sl(oane) + (y)uppy
smaze < sm(oke) + (h)aze
soaperatic < soap (opera) + (op)eratic
spammer < sp(ace) + (h)ammer
squack < squ(aw) + (sh)ack
suppie < s(outhern) + (y)uppie
synchrotron < synchro(nize) + (cyclo)tron
tenigue < ten(sion) + (fat)igue

The letters or sounds where the clipped elements come together may be identical and thus overlapping:

Aluminaut < alumi*n*(um) + (argo)*n*aut
autel < au*t*(o) + (ho)*t*el
cafetorium < cafe*t*(eria) + (audi)*t*orium
Eisenhopper < Eisen*h*(ower) + (grass)*h*opper
infomercial < info[r]*m*(ation) + (c)o*mm*ercial
motel < m*ot*(or) + (h)*ot*el
orature < ora(l) + (lite)*r*ature
patriotute < patrio*t*(ic) + (prosti)*t*ute
republicrat < republi*c*(an) + (demo)*c*rat
vocumentary < voc(al) + (d)o*c*umentary

A more complex example is the following:

Britcom < Br*it*(ish) com(edy) + (s)*itcom*

The following term from climatology blends two expressions and puns on a third:

icehouse < *ice* (age) + (green)*house* + *icehouse*

The last parts of two or more elements may be clipped:

Alcan < Al(aska) + Can(ada)
bacitracin < baci(llus subtilis) + Trac(y) + -in
Benelux < Be(lgium) + Ne(therlands) + Lux(embourg)
cockapoo < cocke(r spaniel) + poo(dle)
plexipave < plexi(glass?) + pave(ment)
telecon < tele(type) + con(versation)

Although *Argy* is basically a clipped diminutive of *Argentine* used in British English, during the Falklands War it seems to have been interpreted as a pun on the first part of another British expression meaning 'a wrangle':

Argy < *Arg*(entine) + *-y* + *argy*(-bargy)

A few blends clip the vowel of the first word, the initial consonant of the second, and reinforce the blend with overlapping final sounds:

Chunnel < Ch(a)*nnel* + (t)u*nnel*
huppie < h(i)*ppy* + (y)u*ppie*
skort < sk(i)*rt* + (sh)*ort*

A complex example is the following, a joke verb formed from the name of a British Labour Party spokesman, involving comic back formation and a pseudo-acronym:

meach < [Michael] *Meach*(er) + *m*(ake) *e*(xtravagant) *a*(dditional) *c*(ommitments) *h*(ourly)

Blending by overlapping sounds only   Some blends incorporate the whole of two sources, coalescing their overlapping words:

atomic bomber < atomic *bomb* + *bomb*er
insecurity blanket < in*security* + *security* blanket
milk wagon run < *milk* wagon + *milk* run
microwave oven-proof < microwave *oven* + *oven*-proof
milk-rounded up < milk-*round* + *round*ed up
red-hot pants < red-*hot* + *hot* pants

In other cases, the overlapping elements are sounds rather than whole words:

between-ager < be*tween* + *teen*-ager
futurama < futu*re* + -rama
globaloney < glob*al* + *bal*oney
guesstimate < gu*ess* + *est*imate
infanticipate < inf*ant* + *ant*icipate
Japanazi < Jap*an* + *Naz*i
omnibuster < omni*bus* + *bus*ter
quackupuncture < qu*ack* + *ac*upuncture

Some puns are of this type:

bangalore (torpedo) < *Bangalore* + [possibly] *bang* + *galore*
bellehop < *belle* + *belle*hop
jiggle-o < *jiggle* + *-o-* + *gigolo*
pot likker < *pot* + *likker* + *pot liquor*
seabee < *CB* + *sea* + *bee*
tutu < *too too* + *tutu*

Some blends are of homophonic spellings (the first example being probably a misspelling):

straiten-outer < *straight*en out + *-er* + *strait*
playwrite < *play* + *write* + *playwright*

6. Shifting

In addition to combining, shortening, and blending, English also shifts forms into new uses. The SHIFT may be in grammar, meaning, circumstances of use, or even form.

Shift of form A simple way to shift a form is to reverse the order of words, such as *boy toy* (from *toy boy*), or the order of letters, such as *yarg*, the name of a cheese said to be a reverse spelling of the name of the family that makes it, *Gray*.

Another is to change the sounds in a word, as the vowel of *goomer* was shifted from *gomer* (perhaps under the influence of words like *goon* and *goof*) or the initial consonant of *Vatergatski* was changed to make it Russian-looking. In *jeepers*, the whole final syllable was changed to euphemize the exclamatory use of *Jesus*.

Shift of circumstances *Stomp* began as a dialect pronunciation of *stamp* but is now an alternative word in standard use. When it became part of general English, it shifted its circumstances.

Shift of grammar English very freely shifts a word from one grammatical use to another, especially noun to adjective or verb, and verb to noun. Not all languages have this freedom to change a word's part of speech without using affixes or otherwise modifying its form. But British English easily makes a verb, *to bath*, out of a noun, even though we already have a related verb, *to bathe*, and American does the same with *to guest* for the phrase "to be a guest on a program." Such grammatical shifts often annoy people who are easily annoyed by language change: *to contact* as a verb and *hopefully* as a sentence adverb have been favorite subjects of outrage. The process of making and using such shifts is, however, of honorable antiquity and current vitality.

Adjectives are shifted from adverbs (*back-to-work*), interjections (*yah-boo*), prefixes (*mega-*), verbs (*built-in*, *jiggle*, *see-through*, *stand-up*, *turnaway*, *write-in*), proper nouns (*Buck Rogers*, *Colombo*, *looney tunes*), and especially common nouns (*acid*, *altered-state*, *back burner*, *ball park*, *bananas*, *blue collar*, *bobby-sock*, *bottom line*, *broad spectrum*, *budget*, *cafeteria*, *caretaker*, *chiclet*, *clutch*, *command*, *conglomerate*, *costume*, *crash*, *cutting edge*, *dime store*, *flash*, *front burner*, *fruitcake*, *girlie*, *girly*, *hotshot*, *key*, *latchkey*, *lend-lease*, *monkey-wrench*, *OPEC*, *page three*, *plastic*, *pushbutton*, *quad*, *raunch*, *reality*, *real time*, *red feather*, *shoe-leather*, *smarm*, *smokestack*, *strawhat*, *Teflon*, *test-tube*).

Nouns are shifted from adjectives (*audible*, *durable*, *effective*, *fast-food*, *flak happy*, *lovely*, *middlebrow*, *plastic*, *quadrasonic*, *quadriphonic*, *separate*, *spectacular*), clauses (*whodunit*), interjections (*bebop*, *bleep*), proper nouns (*archie*, *Barney*, *corrigan*, *Dunkirk*, *Edgar*, *Gertrude*, *gomer*, *joad*, *looney tunes*, *Mae West*, *Marilyn Monroe*, *melvin*, *Miranda*, *murphy*, *Oscar*, *Pearl Harbor*, *quisling*, *smokey ((the) bear)*, a number and preposition (*twofer*), a prefix (*Anglo*), and especially verbs (*backup*, *blackout*, *blowby*, *blowout*, *call-up*, *cease-fire*, *checkoff*, *countdown*, *cutback*, *flashback*, *fly-past*, *handoff*, *hang-up*, *hold-up*, *know-how*, *meltdown*, *overkill*, *quadricast*, *recap*, *retread*, *rollback*, *run-around*, *run-through*, *rundown*, *scrub*, *send-in*, *shoo-in*, *sit-in*, *sitdown*, *sound off*, *spinoff*, *spiral*, *splashdown*, *stay-put*, *streak*, *takeover*, *ustabie*, *wannabe*, *wind-up*).

Verbs are shifted from adjectives (*fast-forward*, *gavel-to-gavel*, *out*, *short*), interjections (*bonk*), and especially nouns (*air-cover*, *air drop*, *atombomb*, [*energy*] *audit*, *bleep*, *blitz*, *blueprint*, *booby trap*, *bookend*, *bore-sight*, *bucket drive*, *burn*, *burp*, *bypass*, *cap*, *car hop*, *car pool*, *cartop*, *case*, *channel*, *clipper*, *clock*, *cornrow*, *crash-dive*, *cutback*, *deck*, *dense pack*, *depth-charge*, *dim-out*, *flash-photograph*, *flour-paste*, *formula-diet*, *glide bomb*, *ground transport*, *gun*, *hand-fight*, *hand-sign*, *high-pressure*, *highball*, *index*, *jeep*, *jump-pass*, *kickturn*, *lend-lease*, *liposuction*, *lug*, *mastermind*, *microfilm*, *microwave*, *Miranda*, *necklace*, *needle*, *outhouse*, *pancake*, *ping-pong*, *pinpoint*, *plane-crash*, *premiere*, *pressure*, *prong*, *quarter-back*, *redshirt*, *rev*, *road test*, *RV*, *script*, *shovel-pass*, *side-line*, *sit-in*, *skyrocket*, *spearhead*, *speed-zone*, *spiral*, *spot check*, *stick-handle*, *test-pilot*, *wedgie*, *weekend*, *whistle stop*, *wolf-pack*, *wolf-whistle*, *yup*). Transitive verbs are made from intransitive ones (*burp*, *shop*).

Interjections are made out of proper nouns (*Geronimo*).

Shift of meaning Shifting the meaning of a word, that is, the way the word is applied to things, is extremely common. It is often hard to decide, however, when the use of a word for one thing rather than another is a new meaning and when it is just an incidental variation. After all, no two things are identical; everything and every experience is unique. So in one sense, every use of a word is a new reference. When we talk about shift of meaning, however, we mean a major change in the kind of thing to which a word is applied.

Words naturally shift their meanings over time, as they are used in new circumstances. For example, English borrowed *ablation* from Latin in the sixteenth century in its etymological sense of 'removal, a carrying away' (from *ab-* 'off, away' and *latum* 'carried'). By the seventeenth century, it was being used in medicine in the more specific sense of 'remission of a disease'; and by the eighteenth century, it had acquired another medical sense, 'surgical removal'. In the nineteenth century, it developed a geological sense 'the melting of glacial ice or the wearing away of a rock by water'. In the mid twentieth century, it acquired a sense recorded in "Among the New Words": 'the melting of the outer surface (of a space capsule) by atmospheric friction'. These (and some other) uses are listed as separate senses in the *Oxford English Dictionary*, but they are clearly specializations of the original, etymological sense.

Specialization of meaning is a common type of semantic shift. Other examples are the British use of *frame* for 'a portable stand to assist the handicapped in walking, a walker', *jiggle* 'move in a sexually suggestive way', *streak* 'run naked in public'. Other common types of semantic shift are generalization of meaning (*blue print* 'any detailed plan', *full-dress* 'complete in all details', *tabloid* '(of television) characterized by investigative stories, celebrity interviews, and a lurid treatment of taboo subjects)'; metaphor (*fast lane* 'the reckless pursuit of excitement', *spin* 'the interpretation of an event for public presentation', *virus* 'a surreptitiously introduced and self-replicating computer program'); and metonymy (*bamboo* 'native', *hacky sack* 'a game played with a Hacky Sack beanbag', *scuttlebutt* 'a rumor').

7. Source unknown

Some words have origins that are unknown in whole or in part: *Beeloo, dweeb, Exton, hassle, jitteroptera, Promin, shmoo, snazzy, snoozamorooed, Volscan, wuss(y)*. *Webster's Third* guesses that *hassle* is a blend of *haggle* and *tussle;* and *Webster's New World* guesses that *snazzy* blends *snappy* and *jazzy*. *Shmoo,* a benevolent creature from Al Capp's comic strip "Li'l Abner," suggests the Yiddish *schm-* words, especially *schmooze* and *schmuck,* but also *moo* and other possibilities. The uncertainty about the origin of such words makes them puzzles to tease the etymologist.

8. Summary

The neologisms recorded in "Among the New Words" during the fifty years between 1941 and 1991 are divided among the major etymological types as reported in Table 1 (with percentages rounded off to whole numbers).

Every collection of new words is biased by the interests, purposes, and resources of the collector. So it is instructive to compare the etymological sources from "Among the New Words" with those of words in two other collections, analyzed according to the same principles. That comparison is made in Table 2.

The three counts agree that English makes overwhelmingly most of its words by combining existing elements into new forms. They also agree that the next most productive process, although a distant second, is shifting existing words to new uses and that the third process is shortening words. Blending and borrowing are minor processes, and creating new words out of new material is an insignificant source for the vocabulary.

Although the English vocabulary continues to grow at a prodigious rate, most new words are constructed from its existing resources. The types of word making that introduce new word elements (morphemes) are those that are least productive: creating, borrowing, blending, and shortening. Indeed, the more likely to produce new morphemes a process is, the less frequently it is used. The English vocabulary seems to follow what Otto Jespersen called the Principle of Efficiency, a kind of linguistic Occam's razor: to make much with little.

THE MOTIVES FOR NEW WORDS

The need for new words is both pragmatic and esthetic. Pragmatically, when there are new things to talk about, we need new words to name them. Or sometimes we want to talk about old things in a new way. Changes in society, whether material or intellectual, call for new words; and the more intense the social change, the more need we have to name new things or rename old ones. Thus invention, discovery, exploration, war, commerce, and revolution all breed neology.

But language is not limited to the practical values of conceptualization, communication, management, and cooperation. Language is also a field for play and poetry. Lady Macbeth's "No, this my hand will

Table 1. *New words, 1941–1991 (% by types)*

Combining	68
(Compounds 40)	
(Suffixes 20)	
(Prefixes 8)	
Shifting	17
(Semantic 11)	
(Grammatical 6)	
Shortening	8
Blending	5
Borrowing	2
Creating (below .5)	
Unknown (below .5)	
Total	100%

Table 2. *New words from three sources (% by types)*

	ANW	BDNE	LRNW
Combining	68.3	63.9	54.3
(Compound forms	40.3	29.8	36.3)
(Affixed forms	28.0	34.1	18.0)
Shifting	17.4	14.2	19.4
Shortening	7.6	9.7	10.0
Blending	4.6	4.8	9.8
Borrowing	1.6	6.9	4.3
Unknown	.3	.5	2.2
Creating	.2		

ANW = "Among the New Words," 1941–1991
BDNE = *Barnhart Dictionary of New English since 1963*
LRNW = *Longman Register of New Words,* Vol. 1

rather / The multitudinous seas incarnadine" is the *Oxford English Dictionary's* first recorded use of the verb *incarnadine* and its first use of *multitudinous* applied to the ocean. Shakespeare did not necessarily originate either use, but they must both have been new in his time. Why did he not instead have that most ambitious lady say simply that her hand would redden the massy seas? There is something sublime and overwhelming about the words he used. There is a ponderous playfulness in them. We use some new words because we take delight in them.

The new words recorded in this volume tell us something about the world and our reactions to it during the fifty-year period during which they were gathered. They reflect changes in material and intellectual culture. And they show us something of the way human beings cope with problems and laugh at the absurdities of life.

When the column began in 1941, the world was already embroiled in the greatest war of the twentieth century. So it is not surprising that the first word in the index is *AA* 'anti-aircraft', recorded in the issue of *American Speech* for December 1941. Words from various wars and military actions are scattered throughout the volume: *airlift, balloon bomb, cease-fire, intifada, overkill* (as though there were a possibility of "under-kill"). War terms are sometimes pacified: *flak* began as German AA fire, but became just criticism, and the threatening *schnorchel* became the friendly *snorkel.* Moreover, after the war in Europe, *fraternizing* was no longer something *G.I. Joe* did with his buddies.

The changes that have swept society here and abroad during the last half of the century are mirrored in such words as *affirmative action, apartheid, asphalt jungle, desegregation, freedom ride, Jim Crowism, reverse integration, sit-in, tokenism.* The *common market* did not exist and had no name when "Among the New Words" began; by 1992 it was scheduled to revolutionize the *Euromarket.* Heads of government have been connected by a *hot line* on which they discuss issues that are really *key.* And *perestroika* now seems somewhat unstructured behind the former *iron curtain.*

The law and policing have evolved. Once *fingerprinting* was done with fingers, before we knew about DNA, and the *lie detector* was *on the cutting edge. Gangbusters* came on like . . . well, gangbusters. The *hit list,* which started in the register of organized crime, moved to that of disorganized politics. Miranda's brave new world now requires that a *Miranda* be read to every suspect to avoid the specter of a *police state.* People began to worry about leaving a *paper trail. Do-it-yourself* terrorists rejoiced in the *plastic bomb.*

Within the memory of a generation still living, technological changes have revolutionized daily life. It is hard now to realize that there was a time when we were not able to *air condition* our houses or cars,

when rockets did not *blast off,* and there was no *cable TV* on which *couch potatoes* could watch *documentaries* or their favorite *soap operas* during the *family hour* instead of the *jiggle factor.* In those dimly remembered times, the *condo* was not yet a place where one went home to *microwave* a *prepackaged* dinner by *pushbutton,* after shopping at the *discount house. Latchkey kids* had not yet flown away to leave their parents as *empty nesters.*

In transportation, the *parking meter* competed with the *parking deck. Superhighways* were punctuated with *toll plazas.* A near miss in air traffic became a *near collision* whether above a *hub-and-spoke* airport or a *stolport.* For people who had a *hang-up* about *hotpants,* there was the option of *pedal pushers,* not necessarily worn only when riding a *bike path.*

Art frequently leads life. The cinematic *flashback* became a synonym for sudden memory, and now we can *fast-forward* through life as well as on a VCR. Once the *little magazines* were avant-garde, and *pop art* vied with *op art. Rock 'n rollers* came to seem like sweet innocents when the *lambada* came in. *Step-dancing* replaced *streaking* as an innocent pastime. The Disney company developed *theme parks,* with something for everybody – even the *thirtysomething* crowd. Those who love a mystery found that the *flying saucer* was their cup of tea. Others settled for a *whodunit.* Sports changed with the *designated hitter,* not to mention *roid rage.*

The sport of politics was enlivened by *dirty tricks,* a new name for an old game bungled by the *Waterbuggers.* The *exit poll* allowed elections to be decided before Californians got to vote, even when there was no *front-runner* on a *whistlestop* tour of the country. *Influence peddling* did not originate in this period, but the term did, though it helped if the peddler was *in the loop.* Elections got decided by *photo ops* and *sound bites,* and anointed a *Teflon* president.

Although it is hard to believe that human nature has changed much in fifty years, the terms by which we insult one another have. The *jerk* of the 1940s became the *dweeb* of the 1980s. *Yuppies* were a new breed. *Gomer* seems to have come from the television character Gomer Pyle, but has entered the folklore of doctors and hospitals.

The universe is a bigger and stranger place than it used to be, now full of *quasars* and *radio stars. Cosmonauts* have gone for *spacewalks. Safe computer practice* is needed to avoid the deadly *electronic virus.* Hackers hunt for the *trapdoor* that bypasses normal controls. And others long for a *user-friendly* system whose price is *in the ball park.*

Technology and social progress have their downside, however. *DDT* began as a boon and ended as a timebomb in the environment. But *eco-awareness* led to *ecoaction* to preserve *endangered species. Fallout* was just a disagreement before it became something more radioactive. On the other hand, a *meltdown* was imminent disaster before it became just an uncontrolled process. The threat of *nuclear winter* breathes its frosty breath through the *ozone hole*.

The availability of the courts led to *defensive medicine,* by which doctors over-treat patients in order to defend themselves against the danger of malpractice suits. *Legionnaire's disease* was a challenge to the *wonder drugs. Double-digit* interest rates were once called usury. The *mommy track* is a kind of deadend. *Shrink-wrap* protects not just the product, but the producer as well – if you break it on a computer program, you have agreed to the terms of purchase.

Culinary innovation has been matched by lexical. In the era before *fast-food* had a name and the *empty calory* had been discovered, the *cheeseburger* was unchallenged by *polyunsaturates.* People sometimes cooked out of doors then, but they had not learned to call the meal a *cookout.* At restaurants, the *maitre d'* led the way to *nouvelle cuisine.*

Some changes are of attitude rather than of substance. Americans have never been as comfortable with the notion of "class" as Britons are, so they were happy to exchange "working class" for *blue-collar worker.* They also naturalized the exotic brassière as a thoroughly domestic *bra* and filled them with *falsies.*

They left the *g-string* to Gypsy Rose Lee, but made the *string-bikini* available to all. During this period, religious fundamentalists learned to call dogma *creation science,* and sharp bookkeepers traded "doctoring the books" for *creative accounting.* The *New Age* has turned out to be old stuff.

Before the *teleprompter* ended the need to jot notes on a shirt cuff, people talked *off the cuff.* Textbooks were once not *dumbed-down* in keeping with the ideals of *educationism* or its *gobbledygook.* Salesmen developed the *hard sell* and the *soft sell,* operating out of an *industrial park. Parkinson's Law* (that work expands to fill the time available for its completion) is perhaps the most insightful explanation ever offered for human dithering. It also doubtless explains why mail is slower with *ZIP codes.*

The last word in the index is *zippered* 'equipped with a slide fastener'. That is somehow an appropriate way to end – not on a Great Truth or a Fearful Warning, but with a small convenience. When some of us were wee lads and lasses, life was all buttons or hooks and eyes. The zipper may not be one of the great achievements of the Western world, but it does make life easier. So maybe our changing culture and vocabulary show that there is yet hope in the little things. . . . Zippered. It is not a bad ending.

REFERENCES

Barnhart Dictionary Companion. Vols. 1–. Ed. Clarence L. Barnhart and David K. Barnhart. Cold Spring, NY: Lexik House, 1982–.

Barnhart Dictionary of New English since 1963. By Clarence L. Barnhart, Sol Steinmetz, and Robert K. Barnhart. Bronxville, NY: Barnhart, 1973.

Chambers English Dictionary. Ed. Sidney I. Landau, W. S. Ramson, Catherine Schwarz, George Davidson, Anne Seaton, Virginia Tebbit. Cambridge: Chambers–Cambridge, 1988.

Collins Concise Dictionary, 2d ed. Ed. Patrick Hanks. London: Collins, 1988.

Collins Dictionary, 2d ed. Ed. Patrick Hanks. London: Collins, 1986.

Concise Oxford Dictionary, 8th ed. Ed. R. E. Allen. Oxford: Clarendon, 1990.

Longman Dictionary. Harlow, Essex: Longman, 1984.

Longman Guardian New Words. Ed. Simon Mort. Harlow, Essex: Longman, 1986.

Longman Register of New Words, vol. 1. By John Ayto. Harlow, Essex: Longman, 1989.

Longman Register of New Words, vol. 2. By John Ayto. Harlow, Essex: Longman, 1990.

New New Words Dictionary. By Harold LeMay, Sid Lerner, and Marian Taylor. New York: Ballantine, 1988.

Oxford English Dictionary, 2d ed. Oxford: Clarendon, 1989.

Random House Dictionary, 2d ed. Unabridged. Ed. Stuart Berg Flexner. New York: Random House, 1987.

Random House Webster's College Dictionary. Ed. Robert B. Costello. New York: Random House, 1991.

Reader's Digest Great Illustrated Dictionary. 2 vols. Ed. Robert Ilson. London: Reader's Digest, 1984.

Third Barnhart Dictionary of New English. By Robert K. Barnhart, Sol Steinmetz, with Clarence L. Barnhart. Bronx, NY: H. W. Wilson, 1990.

12,000 Words. Ed. Frederick C. Mish. Springfield, MA: Merriam–Webster, 1986.

Webster's New World Dictionary, 3d College ed. Ed. Victoria Neufeldt and David B. Guralnik. New York: Webster's New World, 1988.

Webster's Ninth New Collegiate Dictionary. Ed. Frederick C. Mish. Springfield, MA: Merriam–Webster, 1983.

Webster's Third New International Dictionary. Ed. Philip Babcock Gove. Springfield, MA: Merriam, 1961.

World Book Dictionary (Thorndike–Barnhart), 2 vols. Ed. Clarence L. Barnhart and Robert K. Barnhart. Chicago: World Book, 1989.

INDEX OF NEW WORDS WITH GLOSSES
FIFTY YEARS AMONG THE NEW WORDS
A DICTIONARY OF NEOLOGISMS, 1941–1991

This index to "Among the New Words" in *American Speech* between 1941 and 1991 includes (1) headwords, (2) variant forms following headwords in lemmas, (3) secondary or run-in forms within an entry, (4) forms mentioned in the introduction (forematter) of an installment although without an entry in that installment, and (5) a few additional forms used in illustrative citations but not otherwise treated. Thus the index includes all forms entered or mentioned in "Among the New Words" and a few merely exemplified. The last are, strictly speaking, not subjects of "Among the New Words" but are indexed here as of potential interest.

A single entry of this index includes variant and related forms that are close in alphabetical order. Other variants have separate entries at their appropriate places in the alphabetical sequence. Different senses, even when they correspond to distinct parts of speech or etymologies, are in the same entry if their forms have the same spellings.

Most of the glosses in the index are based on those in "Among the New Words," with only slight revision. The original glosses were derived from the citational evidence available at the time the entries were written. Therefore, an index gloss suggests the meaning of its form, but should not be taken as a full definition. Some forms are mentioned casually in the forematter of an installment without a definition, and some entries have no definition and only citations that do not clearly indicate the meaning of the form. In such cases no definition is given in the index unless the meaning of the form is obvious from other evidence.

Index entries are referred to the issue in which they appear by volume and issue number and by date as well. References are placed after the forms and senses to which they apply. The notation "forematter" in a reference indicates that the form is mentioned in the introduction to an installment but has no entry in that installment.

Other conventions:

Small capital letters in a gloss indicate that the form so printed has an entry in the index.

also: The following form or forms used in a gloss are synonymous with the indexed form and have entries in the index. (That is, *also* and small capitals are both cross-references, small capitals in the primary definition of a form, and *also* preceding synonyms. Cross-referencing is extensive but does not exhaust the possibilities; in particular, forms that are close to one another alphabetically are not usually cross-referenced because the user can easily see them.)

British: The form so labeled is believed to be British rather than American, or the evidence for the form is British, even though the form is in general English use rather than limited to the British Isles.

cf.: The following form is related.

cited s.v.: The indexed form is cited in a note to the following form in "Among the New Words."

from: The following form is an etymon of the indexed form and helps to explain its meaning.

illus. s.v.: The indexed form occurs in a citation for the following form, but does not itself have an entry.

see: The indexed form is an orthographic or morphological variant of the following form and is treated in "Among the New Words" under the latter.

s.v.: The indexed form is treated in "Among the New Words" as a run-in entry under the following form.

AA an antiaircraft gun; antiaircraft, *also* ack-ack, archie, flack, flak [16.4 Dec. 1941; 21.3 Oct. 1946 forematter]

A-B-C (of warfare and weapons) atomic-bacteri(ologic)al-chemical [30.4 Dec. 1955]

Abdulgate [56.4 Winter 1981 *s.v.* -gate]

ABL Automated Biological Laboratory, a module equipped to search for life on Mars and to send reports back to earth by radio [44.1 Feb. 1969]

ablate (in astrophysics) to remove by melting or vaporizing; **ablating; ablation; ablative** (of material coating a space capsule's nose to protect the inner parts) with a high heat-vaporization point [35.4 Dec. 1960]

Able-Day, Able Day (from *able,* the signaller's word for *A + day*) Atom bomb day, 30 June 1946, when the Bikini atomic bomb was tested [23.1 Feb. 1948]

A-bomb an atomic bomb [21.2 Apr. 1946]

Acapulco red; Acapulco gold types of marijuana [57.4 Winter 1982]

acid lysergic acid diethylamide, LSD [44.1 Feb. 1969]; (of clothing made from denim cloth) bleached, with light-colored streaks, *also* frosted, iced, stonewash; **acid jeans; acid overalls; acid-washed; acid-washing process** [65.1 Spring 1990 *s.v.* acid]

ack-ack *see* AA [16.4 Dec. 1941]

acquaintance rape forced sexual intercourse with a person known to the victim [64.4 Winter 1989]

acronym a word formed from the initial letters of other words [23.3–4 Oct.-Dec. 1948]

ACS anti-reticular-cytotoxic serum, a serum to stimulate the reticular cells of the connective-tissue system [23.1 Feb. 1948]

action girl a woman who looks for the action by drifting from one party to another in search of rich or famous men [63.3 Fall 1988]

action point (in the World Football League) the point after touchdown, to be attempted by running or passing the football across the goal line [51.3–4 Fall-Winter 1976]

activate to call (a military unit) into active service [20.2 Apr. 1945]

active (of a satellite) provided with instrumentation [36.3 Oct. 1961]

actorishness *British* the quality of being like an actor [63.2 Summer 1988]

ADA-er, A.D.A.-er *prob.* a member of Americans for Democratic Action [33.4 Dec. 1958]

A-Day, A day Alabama day at the University of Alabama; attack day (a Pacific theater version of the European D day) [21.3 Oct. 1946 forematter]; ABLE-DAY [23.1 Feb. 1948]

adenovirus, adeno-virus a virus causing respiratory disease, first discovered in the adenoids [34.1 Feb. 1959]

adflation an increase in the cost of advertising space or time [58.4 Winter 1983 *s.v.* -flation]

aerial walkway a walkway suspended across an enclosed court within a building such as a hotel [57.2 Summer 1982]

aerobat a stunt flier [44.1 Feb. 1969]

aerobee a rocket [24.1 Feb. 1949]

aerocab a helicopter taxi between an airport and a downtown area [30.4 Dec. 1955]

aeroneer an enthusiast of model airplanes [18.1 Feb. 1943 forematter]

aeropause the region above the present ceiling of inhabited aircraft flights, i.e., 79,000 ft. [28.1 Feb. 1953]

aeropolitics political and economic development as influencing, and as influenced by, the development and application of aviation [24.4 Dec. 1949]

aerosol bomb a spray can of insect repellant [21.3 Oct. 1946]

affirmative action positive action taken toward any goal, opposed to passive failure to take action that would produce the opposite effect; specif. positive steps taken to eliminate discrimination against members of minority groups, esp. in employment, as opposed to a mere lack of overt discrimination against minorities [49.3–4 Fall-Winter 1974]

afterboomer a BABY BUSTER [64.1 Spring 1989]

afterburner, after-burner a ramjet engine coupled to the rear of a conventional turbojet engine for added power [25.3 Oct. 1950]; a device attached to an exhaust pipe to complete the oxidation of gasoline and so prevent pollution [35.1 Feb. 1960]

aftergate [56.4 Winter 1981 *s.v.* -gate]

against-ism expressing one's principles as opposition to that with which one disagrees, having predominantly negative attitudes; *cf.* for-ism [32.4 Dec. 1957]

agribusiness an enterprise that produces, processes, and distributes farm products; a business related to agriculture, such as the manufacture of farm equipment or agricultural experimentation [35.4 Dec. 1960]

ahead of the curve in the forefront, on the cutting edge, anticipating developments [65.3 Fall 1990 *s.v.* curve]

airboat, air boat a small boat equipped with an airplane motor and rudder, used in shallow water [25.1 Feb. 1950]

air-borne [19.3 Oct. 1944 forematter]

airbrasive a fine, almost pinpoint, stream of compressed air into which a suitable finely divided abrasive agent has been introduced for use in dentistry [21.4 Dec. 1946]

air bridge, air-bridge, airbridge an established air route, orig. across water; specif. the Berlin airlift of 1948–49 [25.3 Oct. 1950]; *British* a movable walkway connecting an airplane to the terminal [62.3 Fall 1987]

air condition *v.* [31.3 Oct. 1956]

air-cover *v.* [31.3 Oct. 1956]

air drop *v.* [31.3 Oct. 1956]

air-evacuate *v.* [31.3 Oct. 1956]

airgraph *British* V-mail [18.1 Feb. 1943 forematter; 19.3 Oct. 1944]

air letter an airmail letter [23.2 Apr. 1948]

airlift, air lift air service for the transportation of personnel or cargo, sometimes supplemental to other forms of transport such as rail and water [23.3–4 Oct.-Dec. 1948]; to transport by an airlift [31.3 Oct. 1956]

air-mailer a person who tosses garbage out of windows [33.4 Dec. 1958]

airmark *v.* [31.3 Oct. 1956]

air motorway *British* the controlled air space used by airliners [62.3 Fall 1987]

airpark, air park a small landing field for private planes, attractively landscaped to make it acceptable to neighboring communities [19.4 Dec. 1944]

air-sea rescue a method of rescuing fliers forced down on the water [21.2 Apr. 1946; 22.2 Apr. 1947]

airstrip, air strip a hurriedly prepared strip of land for temporary use by landing aircraft, usu. fighter planes [20.2 Apr. 1945]

airtrooper a soldier who arrives after the paratroops and helps to hold or exploit what has been gained [33.4 Dec. 1958]

aisle-hop [48.1–2 Spring-Summer 1973 *s.v.* hop]

aisle-sitter a drama critic [29.1 Feb. 1954]

Alcan the Alaska Highway [19.1 Feb. 1944]

alcohol arcade *British* a drinking place [62.3 Fall 1987]

Alcometer *British* an instrument for measuring degree of intoxication by analyzing the breath, a drunkometer [62.3 Fall 1987]

alert an air-raid alarm [16.2 Apr. 1941]

Aleutian-based [20.2 Apr. 1945 forematter]

all-outer an advocate of an all-out policy, as of aid to Britain or of national defense [17.2 Apr. 1942]

all-ticket *British* (of a sporting or musical event) accessible only by an admission ticket secured in advance [62.3 Fall 1987]

altered-state pertaining to a change in consciousness due to drug use, disease, near-death experience, war experiences, imaginary experiences, etc. [60.3 Fall 1985]

Altergate an incident involving the alteration of Congressional transcripts [59.2 Summer 1984 *s.v.* -gate]

alternate state of consciousness a state of consciousness differing from the normal in perceptions or impressions [60.3 Fall 1985]

Aluminaut a submarine for research in the ocean depths [40.3 Oct. 1965 *s.v.* -naut]

America Firster a member of the America First Committee [17.3 Oct. 1942]

American look [45.3–4 Fall-Winter 1970 *s.v.* look]

AMG *perh.* American Military Government [21.3 Oct. 1946 forematter]

aminopterin a chemical used to treat leukemia [24.1 Feb. 1949]

amtrac; amphtrack an amphibious tractor [20.2 Apr. 1945]

Amvets an organization of American Veterans of World War II [21.4 Dec. 1946]

anchor a military position used as a base for operations [17.3 Oct. 1942 forematter; 17.4 Dec. 1942]

ancient astronaut an extraterrestrial traveler who, according to E. von Däniken and others, visited Earth in prehistoric times and brought genetic, intellectual, and technological advances to the ancestors of modern humanity [59.4 Winter 1984]

Anderson (shelter) a small British air-raid shelter [18.2 Apr. 1943; 22.2 Apr. 1947]

Anglo (esp. in New Mexico) an American of English-speaking descent [18.4 Dec. 1943]

animator one who organizes or leads an activity, a facilitator [64.2 Summer 1989]

answer to score after an opponent has scored [56.4 Winter 1981]

anthologer one who puts together an anthology [33.4 Dec. 1958]

anti-anti-communist one who opposes those who attack communism or communists [30.2 May 1955]

anticipate to expect [17.3 Oct. 1942 forematter]

anti-fluoridationist one who disapproves of the fluoridation of water [30.2 May 1955]

anti-gas guzzler in opposition to automobiles with low gas-milage [54.1 Spring 1979]

anti-G-suit *see* G-suit [21.2 Apr. 1946]

anti-marijuana opposing the use of marijuana [57.4 Winter 1982]

anti-Nounspeak opposing the extensive use of attributive nouns [59.2 Summer 1984]

antipersonnel mine a mine operating on a hair-trigger trip mechanism, exploding with a shrapnel effect [18.4 Dec. 1943]

anti-pot antimarijuana [57.4 Winter 1982]

antiproton, anti-proton an elementary particle of matter, the negatively charged counterpart of a proton [31.4 Dec. 1956]

anti-Reagan; anti-Ronald Reagan in opposition to U.S. President Ronald Reagan [57.3 Fall 1982]

anti-supply-sider an opponent of supply-side economics [56.4 Winter 1981]

anti-Titoist one opposed to Marshal Tito of Yugoslavia or his policies [25.2 May 1950]

anti-woggism disdain of foreigners, esp. Middle-Easterners [32.4 Dec. 1957]

ANZUS Australia, New Zealand, and the United States [28.4 Dec. 1953]

A-OK, A-O.K.; A-okay excellent, fine [38.3 Oct. 1963]

A-105 a germicide [22.2 Apr. 1947 forematter]

apartheid the policy of the South African government espousing racial segregation (white, black, Asian, and colored or half- caste) and rule by a white minority over a black majority [28.1 Feb. 1953]

apparatus a political organization, esp. under Russian or Soviet influence [26.1 Feb. 1951]

appease to bribe (an aggressor or potential aggressor); **appeasement; appeaser** [16.2 Apr. 1941]

appestat appetite thermostat, an appetite-regulating function of the brain [29.3 Oct. 1954]

appointments diary *British* a book with a day-by-day calendar in which appointments may be written, an engagement book, date book, calendar [62.4 Winter 1987]

aquanaut an underwater explorer; a skin diver [44.1 Feb. 1969]

aquascope a diving chamber with wide plastic windows for undersea photography [29.3 Oct. 1954]

A-question the question whether someone has committed adultery [63.4 Winter 1988 *s.v.* question]

archie *see* AA [16.4 Dec. 1941]

architectural barrier any feature of a building or other construction that prevents or hinders access or use by handicapped persons [50.1–2 Spring-Summer 1975]

area bombing bombing that attempts to hit every part of a predetermined section of land, esp. cities with the greatest possible destruction of civilian life and property, *also* carpet bombing, saturation bombing [20.4 Dec. 1945; 26.2 May 1951]

area rule (in aerodynamics) the principle that, given a theoretically ideal design for an airplane fuselage with minimum air resistance, the increased drag caused by the addition of wings can be partly offset by reducing the area of the fuselage at any point along the root of the wing by an amount equal to the area of the wing at that point, or by adding in front of or behind the wing an area equal to that of the wing [31.4 Dec. 1956]

arena staging; arena theatre a seating arrangement in which the audience sits on all sides of the acting area, *also* theater in the round; **arena** (of theater layout) *as in* ~ style, ~ establishment [26.4 Dec. 1951]

Argy *British* Argentinean [62.3 Fall 1987]

-ariat *suffix* (from *proletariat, secretariat*) [18.1 Feb. 1943 forematter]

-aroo *suffix* (with festive associations) [16.4 Dec. 1941 forematter; 17.4 Dec. 1942 forematter]

art-gallery-hop [48.1–2 Spring-Summer 1973 *s.v.* hop]

Asia-firster, Asia firster one who considers Asia more important than Europe for American policy [33.4 Dec. 1958]

Asialationist a person advocating concentration on Asian rather than European affairs [33.2 May 1958]

asphalt jungle a large city [34.1 Feb. 1959]

asylee one who seeks political asylum in the United States but does not have official recognition as a refugee under the Refugee Act of 1980 [57.1 Spring 1982]

AT [21.3 Oct. 1946 forematter]

ataractic a tranquilizer drug; **ataraxic** (of drugs) tranquilizing [34.1 Feb. 1959]

A-10 a germicide [22.2 Apr. 1947 forematter]

Atlantic Community a political grouping of the United States, the United Kingdom, France, South America, Australia, Belgium, Canada, Central America, Cuba, the Scandinavian countries, the Dominican Republic, Ireland, Haiti, Iceland, Liberia, Luxembourg, Mexico, the Netherlands, New Zealand, the Philippines, Portugal, South Africa, Spain, Italy, Greece, and Switzerland [24.4 Dec. 1949]

atombomb, atom bomb an ATOMIC BOMB; **atom-bomb,** to drop an atom bomb on [21.2 Apr. 1946]; **atom bombing** an attack by dropping an atomic bomb [21.4 Dec. 1946]

atom-buster [23.3–4 Oct.-Dec. 1948 *s.v.* buster]

atomic age the period after 6 August 1945, when the first atomic bomb was dropped [21.3 Oct. 1946]

atomic bomb a bomb utilizing the atom's nuclear binding energy, which is released by chain bombardment of the nucleus by neutrons; a destructive or explosive issue, remark, etc. [21.2 Apr. 1946; 22.2 Apr. 1947; 25.3 Oct. 1950 forematter]

atomic bomber [21.2 Apr. 1946]

atomic bombing *see* atom bombing [21.4 Dec. 1946]

atomic clock a clock in which the nitrogen atom of a molecule of ammonia is utilized to obtain virtually perfect accuracy [25.1 Feb. 1950]

atomic cocktail an alcoholic drink, presumably strong in effect; a radioactive liquid medicine [29.1 Feb. 1954]

atomic curtain [25.3 Oct. 1950 forematter]

atomic garden a garden of radioactive plants [33.2 May 1958]

atomic rocket a rocket engine powered by a nuclear reactor [40.2 May 1965]

atomic veteran; atomic vet a veteran exposed to radiation from atomic weapons or testing [65.1 Spring 1990]

atom-smasher any machine such as the cyclotron and betatron that furnishes projectiles used to bombard the nuclei of atoms [23.3–4 Oct.-Dec. 1948]

audible a football technique in which the quarterback comes to the line of scrimmage and then changes the play originally called in the huddle in order to combat the defensive alignment [44.2 May 1969]

auding listening with retentive understanding [35.4 Dec. 1960]

audioconferencing *British* teleconferencing in which more than two people are connected by telephone for an electronic meeting [63.1 Spring 1988]

audit a survey of a building and its equipment to ascertain their condition and to recommend needs; to make an energy audit of (a building) [57.2 Summer 1982]

Australia-based [20.2 Apr. 1945 forematter]

autel (from *auto* + *hotel*) a motel [24.2 Apr. 1949 forematter]

auto camp [24.2 Apr. 1949 forematter]

autocide death by automobile [39.3 Oct. 1964 *s.v.* -cide]

auto court a motel [24.2 Apr. 1949]

auto-happy having a deep interest in and desire for automobiles [22.3 Oct. 1947 *s.v.* happy]

auto inn [24.2 Apr. 1949 forematter]

automania an excessive concern with having and operating automobiles; **automaniac** one given to automania, esp. an enthusiast of antique cars [39.2 May 1964]

automate to introduce automation; to make automated [33.2 May 1958]

automated characterized by automation [31.1 Feb. 1956]

automation the use of automatically operating machinery in place of labor [25.3 Oct. 1950]

automobiliana things having to do with automobiles as hobbies or objects of collection [30.4 Dec. 1955]

automotel; autotel [24.2 Apr. 1949 forematter]

auto sales *British* a location for automatic vending machines [62.3 Fall 1987]

avgas aviation gasoline [27.3 Oct. 1952]

avionics the application of electronics to aviation [25.3 Oct. 1950]

axis a politico-military alliance between two or more powers; specif. the Rome-Berlin alliance, and later the Rome-Berlin-Tokyo alliance; something detrimental to the anti-Axis powers [17.4 Dec. 1942]

B *prefixal form* bar, *as in* B-drink, B joint, B-girl [30.2 May 1955]

baby-bound awaiting the birth of a baby, pregnant [17.4 Dec. 1942 forematter]

baby bust a period of sharp decrease in the birthrate; **baby buster** one born during a baby bust, specif. in the U.S. 1965–74, *also* afterboomer, flyer [64.1 Spring 1989]

baby flat-top an escort carrier converted from a cargo ship [19.3 Oct. 1944]

babyroo [16.4 Dec. 1941 forematter]

baby sit, baby-sit to mind children while their parents or guardians are out [24.1 Feb. 1949; 31.3 Oct. 1956]

baby-tend *v.* [31.3 Oct. 1956]

bachelorette [17.4 Dec. 1942 forematter]

bacitracin an antibiotic [23.3–4 Oct.-Dec. 1948]

back burner low priority, *as in* on the/a ~ 'of low priority', put on the/a ~ 'assign low priority to'; **back-burner** *attrib.* having low priority [54.2 Summer 1979]

backer-upper a position in football: linebacker, backer-up [33.4 Dec. 1958]

backlighting *British* an internal lighting source for LCD displays on laptop computers [63.1 Spring 1988]

backpack a portable life-support system for U.S. astronauts outside their spacecraft; the jet-powered unit used by U.S. astronauts to maneuver outside the Shuttle without a tether, *also* jet(-powered) ~ [59.4 Winter 1984]

backstage under cover, not claiming attention, covert, concealed [17.2 Apr. 1942 forematter; 17.3 Oct. 1942]

back to back, back-to-back one after another, consecutive [30.4 Dec. 1955]

back to the basics, back-to-the-basics; back to basics, back-to-basics (pertaining to) education with emphasis on proficiency in verbal and mathematical skills, fundamental knowledge of a traditional kind, and assessment of competency [56.3 Fall 1981 *also* forematter]

back-to-work (of a plan or movement) involving a return to industrial employment, esp. in the face of union opposition [17.2 Apr. 1942]

backup, back-up a substitute or alternate, used in case of failure of the primary equipment or procedure [35.4 Dec. 1960]

backward type [23.2 Apr. 1948 forematter]

bacteriological warfare [23.2 Apr. 1948 forematter]

bad type [23.2 Apr. 1948 forematter]

bafflegab ambiguous or incomprehensible speech, esp. of bureaucrats or military officers [28.3 Oct. 1953]

baiter *suffixal form* one who heckles; **baiting** *suffixal form* heckling [17.2 Apr. 1942]

baka (bomb) a piloted rocket plane that carries its pilot to certain death by diving into a target [22.3 Oct. 1947]

bake-off a recipe and baking competition [29.4 Dec. 1954]

Baker Day (from *baker*, the signaler's word for *B + day*) the day when the second (hence B) atomic bomb was exploded during Operation Crossroads, 25 July 1946 [23.1 Feb. 1948]

balding becoming bald [22.3 Oct. 1947]

balladeering performing ballads [18.1 Feb. 1943 forematter]

ballistic furious, raging, angry, *also* nuclear [65.2 Summer 1990]

balloon bomb an incendiary bomb launched by Japan against the West Coast [44.1 Feb. 1969]

balloon buster, balloon-buster [23.3–4 Oct.-Dec. 1948 *s.v.* buster]

balloon-type [24.3 Oct. 1949 *s.v.* type]

balloteer [18.1 Feb. 1943 forematter]

ball park a missile recovery area near Hawaii [44.1 Feb. 1969]; one's own territory, area of competence or concern; the general area, approximate range; **ball-park** *attrib.* within a reasonable or acceptable range, *esp. in* ~ figure [51.1–2 Spring-Summer 1976]

Baltic Wall defensive installations on the Baltic seacoast of East Germany, Poland, and the USSR [26.4 Dec. 1951]

bamboo native, pertaining to natives; **bamboo Americans** sailors who take native Pacific islanders as mistresses and go native; **bamboo English** broken English spoken in the Philippine Islands; **bamboo telegraph** unknown but efficient means of communication among Philippine natives; **bamboo wireless** unknown but efficient means of communication among Philippine natives [21.4 Dec. 1946]; **bamboo curtain** [25.3 Oct. 1950 forematter]; **bamboo ferry** a civilian ferry carrying natives from Manila to Cavite; **bamboo fleet** a fleet assigned to Philippine waters; **bamboo government** the Philippine civil government; **bamboo juice** a strong variety of whiskey; **bamboo railroad** a native-run railroad operating in rural districts of the Philippines [21.4 Dec. 1946 forematter]

banana; **banana cake** a crazy person, nut, zany or eccentric person; **banana** *attrib.* insane, crazy, nutty; **go bananafish** *nonce* go bananas [51.3–4 Fall-Winter 1976]

bananas eccentric, excited, crazy, nutty, *esp. in* go ~, drive (somebody) ~, *also* whamfartbananas; **Bananasville** craziness, nuttiness; **bananologist** *stunt* one who practices the art of being bananas; **bananology** *stunt* the science of being bananas [51.3–4 Fall-Winter 1976]

Band-busters name of an orchestra [23.3–4 Oct.-Dec. 1948 *s.v.* buster]

Bang *British, see* Big Bang [62.3 Fall 1987]

bangalore (torpedo) a length of pipe filled with explosive, used in series to clear a path through mine fields and barbed wire [19.3 Oct. 1944]

banjo buster, banjo-buster one who plays the banjo [23.3–4 Oct.- Dec. 1948 *s.v.* buster]

bar-b-burger; **barbecue burger** [18.2 Apr. 1943 forematter]

barefoot doctor a paramedical worker in rural China [51.3–4 Fall-Winter 1976]

bare look [45.3–4 Fall-Winter 1970 *s.v.* look]

bar-fly an habitué of drinking places [17.2 Apr. 1942; 17.3 Oct. 1942 forematter]

bargain-hunt *v.* [31.3 Oct. 1956]

bargaining chip something, such as an arms program or diplomatic maneuver, that can be used to gain an advantage or effect a concession [49.1–2 Spring-Summer 1974]

barge buster [23.3–4 Oct.-Dec. 1948 *s.v.* buster]

bar happy, bar-happy (army use) eager for promotion [19.1 Feb. 1944 forematter; 22.3 Oct. 1947 *s.v.* happy]

barhop [47.3–4 Fall-Winter 1972 *s.v.* hop]

bariatrics the study of obesity [44.2 May 1969]

bark-happy (of dogs) inclined to bark [22.3 Oct. 1947 *s.v.* happy]

Barney an award for cartoonists of merit, a silver cigarette box with sketches of Barney Google and Snuffy Smith on it [23.1 Feb. 1948 forematter]

barrier an ARCHITECTURAL BARRIER; **barrier-free** without an architectural barrier [50.1–2 Spring-Summer 1975]

barrier cream a cream that protects the hands from dyestuffs, chemicals, oils, acids, and other harmful substances [30.2 May 1955]

bascart basket cart, a supermarket shopping cart [30.4 Dec. 1955]

baseball diplomacy a Soviet-bloc term for Nixon's trip to Communist China [46.3–4 Fall-Winter 1971]

based *suffixal form* established with a base at, on, or in [19.3 Oct. 1944 forematter; 20.2 Apr. 1945 forematter]; *cf.* reality-based

bashing *suffixal form, British* [62.4 Winter 1987 forematter]

basket a group of negotiating proposals for consideration without linkage to other issues; the part of an agreement corresponding to a negotiating basket [65.2 Summer 1990]

basketeer [18.1 Feb. 1943 forematter]

bat bomb a bomb that is guided to its target by radio waves sent out by a mechanism in its nose [23.3–4 Oct.-Dec. 1948]

Batgate an incident involving the overruling of umpires in baseball [59.2 Summer 1984 *s.v.* -gate]

bathinette a portable bathtub for infants [16.4 Dec. 1941]

bath sheet *British* a large bath towel [62.3 Fall 1987]

bathynaut a deep-sea investigator in a diving vehicle [40.3 Oct. 1965 *s.v.* -naut]

bathyscaphe a submarine vehicle that descends into the sea suspended from a steel and aluminum container filled with lightweight gasoline [23.2 Apr. 1948]

batoneer [18.1 Feb. 1943 forematter]

battle-happy [22.3 Oct. 1947 *s.v.* happy]

battleship buster a bomb that can smash through armor [23.3–4 Oct.-Dec. 1948 *s.v.* buster]

battle-test *v.* [31.4 Dec. 1956]

battlewagon a battleship [17.4 Dec. 1942; 22.2 Apr. 1947; 23.1 Feb. 1948]

bazooka (from a type of horn invented by Bob Burns) an antitank rocket gun [20.2 Apr. 1945]

B day Bond day, beginning of a campaign to sell war bonds [21.3 Oct. 1946 forematter]

Beach Buster a naval tracked amphibious vehicle also known as the LVT–3 [23.3–4 Oct.-Dec. 1948 *s.v.* buster]

beach-head a military invasion point established on a beach in territory being invaded; a fortified position on a beach [17.2 Apr. 1942]

beak buster, beak-buster a boxer [23.3–4 Oct.-Dec. 1948 *s.v.* buster]

beam a constant unidirectional radio signal transmitted from a flying field for the guidance of pilots; **off the beam** wrong, insane; **on the beam** on the right track, right, sane [18.1 Feb. 1943]

beam pad, beam-pad a liner in an aircraft helmet that protects the head from blows by distributing the load like a beam and absorbing the force like a pad [31.4 Dec. 1956]

beam-rider guidance a system for guiding missiles along a radar beam tracking the target; (fig.) control of human behavior, as by a wife of a husband [30.4 Dec. 1955]

Bean-o-tash (from *succotash*) [18.4 Dec. 1943 forematter]

bear, Bear (in CB slang) a state trooper; any law enforcement officer; **bear report** information broadcast by users of citizen band radios concerning the location of police officers [51.3–4 Fall-Winter 1976]

bebop, be-bop a form of discordant jazz in which notes are played rapidly with accents more on the upbeat than the downbeat, *also* bop, rebop [24.1 Feb. 1949]

be-Cabbaged having the Cabbage Patch Kid trademark or decorated with images of the Cabbage Patch Kids [59.4 Winter 1984]

bed-hop to have many sexual partners [54.1 Spring 1979 *s.v.* hop]

bed-make *v.* [31.4 Dec. 1956]

bed show *British* a pornographic entertainment [62.3 Fall 1987]

beefalo a hybrid of beef cattle and buffalo [51.1–2 Spring-Summer 1976]

beefcake, beef cake exposure of the male chest [29.4 Dec. 1954]

beef up to strengthen, reinforce; **beefed up, beefed-up** reinforced, strengthened, augmented; **beefing up** reinforcing [27.1 Feb. 1952 *s.v.* beef]

beefer a football player [16.2 Apr. 1941 forematter]

Beeloo a robot bomb [19.4 Dec. 1944 forematter]

beercasting advertising beer on TV [31.1 Feb. 1956]

beetle-borne [20.2 Apr. 1945 forematter]

behind the curve lagging behind current needs or trends [65.3 Fall 1990 *s.v.* curve]

bellehop a female bellhop [17.4 Dec. 1942 forematter]

belly bundle a parachute pack worn on the stomach [31.1 Feb. 1956 *illus. s.v.* parapack]

belly buster landing on one's stomach; a joke; a comedian [23.3–4 Oct.-Dec. 1948 *s.v.* buster]

bellyland, belly-land to land in a plane without using its landing gear [24.1 Feb. 1949; 31.3 Oct. 1956]

belt a moving assembly line [17.2 Apr. 1942 forematter; 17.3 Oct. 1942]

belt bag a pouchlike container strapped around the waist, *also* fanny pack [65.1 Spring 1990]

belt out to sing with great energy and a strongly accented rhythm [30.2 May 1955]

Benelux the economic union of Belgium, the Netherlands, and Luxembourg [23.2 Apr. 1948]

benthoscope a deep-sea diving chamber that moves on wheels [25.3 Oct. 1950]

berkelium an atomic element in the 97th place on the periodic table [26.4 Dec. 1951]

best-sellerdom the status of a book with high sales [26.1 Feb. 1951]

best-sellerism the promotion of books as best-sellers [32.4 Dec. 1957]

between-ager an adolescent aged 11–14 [33.4 Dec. 1958]

BEV billion electron volts, a measurement of the energy of subatomic particles [29.3 Oct. 1954]

bevatron a type of cyclotron or atom smasher, capable of hurling protons and neutrons at ten billion electric volt capacity [24.3 Oct. 1949; 25.3 Oct. 1950 *illus. s.v.* cosmotron]

bhangra *British* a style of music combining traditional Indian modes and a disco beat [63.1 Spring 1988]

bicycle path; bicycle trail; bicycle way a path for cyclists, *also* bike path, cycling trail; **bicycle boulevard; bicycle lane** a path for cyclists running parallel to a road or walkway [46.1–2 Spring-Summer 1971]

bidvertiser (from *advertiser*) [18.4 Dec. 1943 forematter]

big *prefixal form* formed or conducted on large scale; **big art; big banking; big broadcasting; big education; big labor; big military; big money; big oil; big steel** [49.1–2 Spring-Summer 1974]

Big Bang *British* the immediate consequences of the October 1986 deregulation of the London Stock Exchange; any sudden forceful beginning; **Big Banger** one involved with the Big Bang on the London Stock Exchange [62.3 Fall 1987]

big lie a lie boldly and confidently told as the truth, used as a propaganda technique esp. in totalitarian states [27.3 Oct. 1952]

big-shotism [32.4 Dec. 1957]

bikebuster [23.3–4 Oct.-Dec. 1948 *s.v.* buster]

bike lane; bike path; bike route; bike trail; bikeway a BICYCLE PATH; BICYCLE LANE [46.1–2 Spring-Summer 1971]

bikini a skimpy two-piece bathing suit [25.2 May 1950]

billboard (antenna) a large rectangular antenna of billboard proportions, mounted on tall uprights [39.2 May 1964]

Billygate [56.4 Winter 1981 *s.v.* -gate]

Binac *trademark* a type of computer [25.2 May 1950]

binaural (of broadcasting and recording) transmitted on two channels so that different elements of sound reach each ear of the hearer; **binaurality** a three-dimensional effect from binaural sound transmission [29.1 Feb. 1954]

bio- *prefix* biology, biological [60.4 Winter 1985]

bioacoustics, bio-acoustics the science concerned with the impact of sound impulses on living beings [39.2 May 1964]

bioastronautics the study of the needs for human life during travel in outer space [35.1 Feb. 1960]

bio business the development, manufacture, and distribution of advanced biological products [60.4 Winter 1985 *s.v.* bio-]

biochip a proposed device composed of small proteins, capable of carrying out many of the electronic functions now performed by silicon chips [60.4 Winter 1985 *s.v.* bio-]

biocide the destruction of the tissues of the body by the unphysiologic habits of civilization; the destruction of living species by indirect chemical or nuclear poisons [39.2 May 1964]

biodegradable (of a detergent) made from chemicals that are quickly broken down by the bacteria in soil and water, *also* soft [40.3 Oct. 1965]

bioelement one of the lighter elements, esp. those of which living matter is composed [60.4 Winter 1985 *s.v.* bio-]

biofuture the biological future; the potential course of one's state of health [60.4 Winter 1985 *s.v.* bio-]

biomining the use of natural or genetically modified bacteria to extract metals from ores or pollutants from contaminated materials [60.4 Winter 1985 *s.v.* bio-]

bionics the study of living creatures to improve human-made mechanisms [38.3 Oct. 1963]

biopic biographical picture, a movie based on the life of a famous person [31.4 Dec. 1956]

bioproduction the manufacture of industrial chemicals by using bacteria or similar organisms developed specifically for a task [60.4 Winter 1985 *s.v.* bio-]

bio-reactor a tank for industrial-scale bioproduction [60.4 Winter 1985 *s.v.* bio-]

bio-robot an automated device designed to carry out laboratory procedures in molecular biology [60.4 Winter 1985 *s.v.* bio-]

biosatellite a satellite carrying an animal or plant to study the effect of space conditions on living beings [39.3 Oct. 1964]

biotron a facility or building for the study of living organisms in a variety of environments [40.3 Oct. 1965]

Bircher one who belongs to the John Birch Society; **Birchism** the extreme right-wing beliefs and practices of the John Birch Society [37.2 May 1962]; **Birchite** pertaining to or associated with the John Birch Society [37.2 May 1962 *illus. s.v.* comsymp]

bird a guided missile [27.3 Oct. 1952]

birdieback pertaining to combined transportation of freight by land and air [32.2 May 1957 *illus. s.v.* fishyback]

birth by blood, as opposed to adoptive, *esp. in* ~ mother, father, parent [58.4 Winter 1983]

bit binary digit, a mathematical unit of information [29.3 Oct. 1954]

bitchy (of a woman) sexy [17.2 Apr. 1942 forematter; 17.4 Dec. 1942]

bite (of a propeller) [18.2 Apr. 1943 forematter]; a SOUND BITE [64.3 Fall 1989]

bizone a geographical area split into two zones by political, social, or economic boundaries; **bizonal** pertaining to a bizone [25.1 Feb. 1950]

black cab *British* a licensed, metered taxicab of a standard design, usu. black (but increasingly of other colors), available at taxi ranks or cruising [62.3 Fall 1987]

blacketeer a black-market operator [18.1 Feb. 1943 forematter]; **black marketeer; black marketer** [20.3 Oct. 1945]

black-marketeering [18.1 Feb. 1943 forematter]

Black Monday a day, 19 October 1987, marked by the greatest American stock market crash since the Great Depression [63.3 Fall 1988]

black nationalist a believer in the supremacy of the Negro [39.3 Oct. 1964]

blackout a lapse of consciousness [17.2 Apr. 1942]

black spot *British* a focus of deprivation or danger; a difficult place, event, or situation [62.3 Fall 1987]

black taxi *British, see* black cab [62.3 Fall 1987]

blacktop a macadam or similar black road-surface (used generally of the cheaper grades) [16.2 Apr. 1941]

blandspeak a type of science fiction writing with a dull vocabulary and "brain-crunching" syntax [59.2 Summer 1984 *s.v.* speak]

blast away to be launched, to take off [34.1 Feb. 1959]

blast-down a landing of a space ship [34.1 Feb. 1959]

blast off *v., see* blast away; **blastoff, blast-off** (of a rocket) a launch, take-off [34.1 Feb. 1959]

bleep a toot, squeak or other meaningless sound; specif. a short high-pitched sound produced by various electronic devices, or such a sound superimposed on the soundtrack of a televised program in order to eliminate certain words regarded as objectionable; (of broadcast and printed material) to censor; *also* **bleep bleep; bleepers; bleeping; bleepity-bleep** a substitute for a word regarded as vulgar, controversial, or otherwise censorable [51.3–4 Fall-Winter 1976]

blenderize to process in an electric blender [57.1 Spring 1982]

blimp (onomatopoeic, or from *b*[*alloon*] + *limp,* or [*Model*] *B-limp*) a nonrigid airship [18.2 Apr. 1943 forematter; 19.3 Oct. 1944 forematter]

blimpcasting transmitting messages in large letters on the side of a blimp [25.2 May 1950]

blitz to attack in the manner of the blitzkrieg [16.2 Apr. 1941]

blitz buggy, blitz-buggy a small, maneuverable military vehicle [17.2 Apr. 1942 forematter; 17.3 Oct. 1942]

blitzkrieg [23.2 Apr. 1948 forematter]

blockbuster, block-buster, block buster an aerial bomb large enough to demolish a block of houses; an exceptionally large, powerful, or effective person or thing [19.3 Oct. 1944; 23.3–4 Oct.-Dec. 1948 *s.v.* buster]; an intoxicating drink [23.3–4 Oct.- Dec. 1948 *s.v.* buster]

blockhouse a reinforced structure from which missile launches are controlled and observed [34.1 Feb. 1959]

blocktime the mandatory hours of work in a flexible work-time system [54.1 Spring 1979]

blonde from the coast a kind of Columbian marijuana, *also* rubia de la costa [57.4 Winter 1982]

blood-bath a massacre [17.2 Apr. 1942]

blood chip; blood chit a notice offering Chinese peasants a reward for helping downed fliers to elude capture [31.1 Feb. 1956]

bloodmobile a mobile unit for receiving donations of blood [29.1 Feb. 1954]

Bloody Monday *British* Black Monday [63.3 Fall 1988]

blowby, blow-by unburned gasoline vapors forced by leaky piston rings into a car's crankcase, thence emitted as fumes [36.3 Oct. 1961]

blow dead to cause (a football) to be dead (i.e., out of play) by the blowing of the referee's whistle [48.1–2 Spring-Summer 1973]

blow job a military jet plane [26.3 Oct. 1951]

blowout, blow-out the lateral destructive effect of a hydrogen bomb, *esp. in* limit of ~ [30.2 May 1955]

blowtorch, blow torch *see* blow job [26.3 Oct. 1951]

Blue Circuit [24.4 Dec. 1949 forematter]

blue collar, blue-collar pertaining to an industrial or manual employee who works for hourly wages, *esp. in* ~ worker [35.4 Dec. 1960]

blueprint any detailed plan [17.2 Apr. 1942; 22.2 Apr. 1947; 24.3 Oct. 1949]; to devise (a plan) [17.2 Apr. 1942]

bluppy *British* black urban professional [62.3 Fall 1987]

boatel a hotel accessible by boat, *also* botel [35.1 Feb. 1960]

boat people those who sail on yachts, the yachting set; people who live on junks, *also* water people; refugees who flee their countries on a boat [55.2 Summer 1980]

bobby socks; bobbysox, bobby-sox anklets, esp. when worn by teenage girls; **bobby-sock** pertaining to bobby socks or those who wear them; **bobbysock brigade; bobby socks brigade, bobby-socks brigade; bobby sox brigade, bobby-sox brigade** girls of school age found loitering around drug stores, taverns, military installations, movies, and railroad and bus terminals; **bobby socker, bobby-socker; bobby-sockser; bobby soxer, bobby-soxer** a girl 12–17 years old [20.3 Oct. 1945]

Bob 'Ope (from *bob down and 'ope* + *Bob Hope*) a ROBOT BOMB [19.4 Dec. 1944 forematter]

body-dancing dancing in which the partners maintain physical contact, *also* touch dancing [50.1–2 Spring-Summer 1975]

body jewelry [48.1–2 Spring-Summer 1973]

body-plane to bodysurf, ride a wave on one's chest without a surfboard [31.4 Dec. 1956]

bog-buster [23.3–4 Oct.-Dec. 1948 *s.v.* buster]

bogey; bogie an unidentified airplane that may be friendly or unfriendly [21.2 Apr. 1946; 33.2 May 1958 *illus. s.v.* skunk]

boil, on the *British* under active consideration [62.3 Fall 1987]

bomb an explosive shell dropped from an aircraft [17.3 Oct. 1942 forematter]; *cf.* A-bomb, H-bomb, V-bomb

bombardier one who bombs, esp. from aircraft [17.3 Oct. 1942; 22.2 Apr. 1947]

Bombay mix *British* a cocktail food made of nuts and other crunchy ingredients flavored with Indian spices [62.3 Fall 1987]

bomb bay, bomb-bay that portion of the fuselage where the bombs are lodged [20.4 Dec. 1945]

bomb carpet [26.3 Oct. 1951 *illus. s.v.* carpet bombing]

bombcasting [18.2 Apr. 1943 forematter]

bombee the victim of a bombing attack [16.4 Dec. 1941 forematter]

bomber's moon a moon giving light for bombing operations [20.4 Dec. 1945]

bomb happy shocked and demoralized from heavy bombing [19.1 Feb. 1944 forematter]

bomb run; bombing run a bombing plane's course from a predetermined point on the ground (called "initial point" or I.P.) to the point where its bombs are released [20.4 Dec. 1945]

bonanza baby one born between 1911 and 1916 and therefore entitled to higher Social Security benefits than those born later, *also* windfall baby [64.4 Winter 1989]

bonk *British* to copulate [62.3 Fall 1987]

bonus-sign *v.* [31.3 Oct. 1956]

boob-baiting [17.2 Apr. 1942 *s.v.* baiter]

boob tuber a couch potato [63.3 Fall 1988]

booby trap *n.* [20.3 Oct. 1945 forematter]; **booby-trap** *v.* [31.3 Oct. 1956]

bookburner, book burner one who wishes to suppress the dissemination of ideas; **book burning, book-burning** the suppression of the dissemination of ideas, esp. through the print media [29.3 Oct. 1954]

bookend to enclose, bracket, precede and follow; to close off, separate; to end, conclude in a way appropriate to the beginning [64.1 Spring 1989]

booking hall *British* an office where reservations are made [63.1 Spring 1988 *s.v.* hall]

book-keep *v.* [31.4 Dec. 1956]

book-match *v.* [31.3 Oct. 1956]

bookvertising (from *advertising*) [18.4 Dec. 1943 forematter]

boom *British* the arm of a barrier used to regulate vehicles at a customs station [62.3 Fall 1987]

boot a naval recruit [19.1 Feb. 1944]

booth-hop [47.3–4 Fall-Winter 1972 *s.v.* hop]

bootleg (of automobile sales) offered for sale by a used-car dealer but acquired from an overstocked new-car dealer; **bootlegging** the practice of selling new cars at cut-rate prices through used-car dealers who do not hold factory franchises [30.4 Dec. 1955]

boot money *British* money paid by a manufacturer to the members of a sports, esp. rugby, team to use the company's product, specif. athletic shoes [62.3 Fall 1987]

boozebuster [23.3–4 Oct.-Dec. 1948 *s.v.* buster]

bop BEBOP, REBOP music [24.2 Apr. 1949]; **bopper** one who listens to bebop or rebop [24.2 Apr. 1949]

bore-sight to have under direct aim or fire [31.3 Oct. 1956]

borne *suffixal form* [19.3 Oct. 1944 forematter; 20.2 Apr. 1945 forematter]

Borscht circuit the resort hotels of the Catskill Mountains, where borscht is supposed to be a favorite dish; a type of show business associated with those hotels [24.4 Dec. 1949 forematter]

bossa nova a dance music of Brazil that combines the rhythm of the samba with jazz music; **bossa novist** one who plays bossa nova music [40.2 May 1965]

botel *see* boatel [35.1 Feb. 1960]

bottleneck buster [23.3–4 Oct.-Dec. 1948 *s.v.* buster]

bottlenecker one guilty of obstructing national defense [16.2 Apr. 1941 forematter]

bottom (profit) line the last line of a financial report; specif. the line that summarizes the net profit (or loss) or the earnings per share of a corporation or other organization, or the line of an income tax return on which the taxpayer signs; hence, a definitive argument, statement, or answer, summary, punch line, clincher, *esp.* **on the bottom line** *and* **when you get down to the bottom line**; the lower limit; the lowest rank or quality; **bottom-line** *attrib.* fundamental, ultimate; **bottom-line syndrome** a disposition to judge everything in terms of profit and loss [48.3–4 Fall-Winter 1973]

boulder-hop [48.1–2 Spring-Summer 1973 *s.v.* hop]

bounce-pass to pass (a basket ball) by bouncing [31.3 Oct. 1956]

boutique beer; boutique brew a MICROBREW [65.4 Winter 1990]

boutique-hop [47.3–4 Fall-Winter 1972 *s.v.* hop]

bowl a hookah, water pipe used by some marijuana smokers [57.4 Winter 1982]

boy toy, boy-toy a young woman as an object of sexual interest; a handsome young man, TOY BOY; a man as an object of sexual interest [65.4 Winter 1990]

bra a brassière; an article of clothing resembling a brassière, as a detached section of a bathing suit [16.2 Apr. 1941]; a cover for the front end of a car, *also* car bra, nose bra *or* mask [65.4 Winter 1990]

bracket creep the movement of wage earners into higher income tax brackets as a result of wage increases intended to offset inflation [56.4 Winter 1981]

bracketeer a member of certain social brackets of income [17.4 Dec. 1942 forematter; 18.1 Feb. 1943 forematter]

brain buster [23.3-4 Oct.-Dec. 1948 *s.v.* buster]

brain drain the departure of educated and talented people, frequently scientists or academics, who go from one city or country to another (originally from the U.K. to the U.S.) for better pay and working conditions [40.2 May 1965]

brainstorm, brain storm pertaining to brainstorming; to engage in brainstorming; **brainstormer** one who engages in brainstorming; **brainstorming, brain storming** thinking up ideas prolifically with no evaluation or discussion until the production has finished [33.2 May 1958]

brain trust a group acting in an advisory capacity; **brain truster** a member of a brain trust [22.2 Apr. 1947]; **brains trust** *British* [22.2 Apr. 1947 forematter]

brainwash *v.* [31.3 Oct. 1956]; **brainwashing, brain washing** a systematic eradication of old loyalties and beliefs by psychological techniques [27.1 Feb. 1952]

branching a characteristic of a form of automated instruction, by which detailed instruction in some part of a subject is put on a branch of the program that a more knowledgeable student can omit [38.3 Oct. 1963]

Brannanism [32.4 Dec. 1957]

brass curtain [25.3 Oct. 1950 forematter]

brass hat a military official [16.2 Apr. 1941]

breast feed *v.* [31.3 Oct. 1956]

breath pack *British* an implement for giving breath tests to persons suspected of being drunk drivers [62.3 Fall 1987]

breath-test *British* to administer a breath test to (drivers suspected of excessive consumption of alcohol) [62.3 Fall 1987]

brewpub a small brewery combined with a restaurant; **brewpublike** [65.4 Winter 1990]

bridge buster [23.3–4 Oct.-Dec. 1948 *s.v.* buster]

bridge-head a military salient in hostile territory [17.2 Apr. 1942]

bridge streaking streaking across a bridge [48.1–2 Spring-Summer 1973]

Briefingate the stealing of Jimmy Carter's briefing book for a TV debate by Ronald Reagan's campaign workers [59.2 Summer 1984 *s.v.* -gate]

Britain-based; British-based [19.3 Oct. 1944 forematter; 20.2 Apr. 1945 forematter]

Britcom a British television comedy [64.1 Spring 1989]

British-type [23.2 Apr. 1948 *s.v.* type]

broad spectrum, broad-spectrum (of drugs and antibiotics) effective against a wide range of infections [35.1 Feb. 1960]

broncobuster, bronco-buster; broncho-buster [23.3–4 Oct.-Dec. 1948 part II]

bronze buster a sculptor [23.3–4 Oct.-Dec. 1948 *s.v.* buster]

brouhaha a to-do, fuss [32.2 May 1957]

brown *British* being of a racial category perceived as having a skin color between white and black, specif. Asian, Indian [62.3 Fall 1987]

brownie buster, brownie-buster a freight car burglar [23.3–4 Oct.-Dec. 1948 *s.v.* buster]

brown off *British* to depress, sadden, annoy, irritate [62.3 Fall 1987; 62.4 Winter 1987 forematter]

brownout a semidarkening of a city, as distinguished from a blackout [20.2 Apr. 1945]

brush-buster a cowboy in brush country; a machine that cuts through brush [23.3–4 Oct.-Dec. 1948 *s.v.* buster]

brushfire war, brush-fire war, brush fire war a small controllable localized war [33.2 May 1958]

brutalitarianism the use of brutality as an instrument of government [30.2 May 1955]

B$_{12}$ *see* vitamin B12 [24.4 Dec. 1949]

bubble a stock market boom followed by a sudden crash [63.3 Fall 1988]

bubble chamber a detector for high-speed subatomic particles that records the track of an ionizing particle in a liquid [32.2 May 1957]

bubble-gummer an adolescent, esp. one who chews bubble gum and blows bubbles [33.4 Dec. 1958]

bucket drive to collect money for charity by public solicitation with bucket-like containers [65.1 Spring 1990]

Buck Rogers fantastically ingenious [28.3 Oct. 1953]

budget conducing to economical spending of household funds [17.2 Apr. 1942]

budget motel a motel economically built on a simple scale, featuring only the necessities demanded by travelers, and offering rooms at low rates [48.1–2 Spring-Summer 1973]

bug a hidden microphone; **bugging** the installation of concealed microphones [31.4 Dec. 1956]; **bug** a small two-person lunar excursion vehicle [39.2 May 1964]

build-down; builddowning a proposed reduction of nuclear weapons by eliminating more than one missile or warhead for each new one deployed [60.1 Spring 1985]

built-in automatic, concomitant, inevitably resulting, inherent [30.2 May 1955]

bull-buster a crook who habitually resists arrest [23.3–4 Oct.- Dec. 1948 s.v. buster]

bumble bomb a ROBOT BOMB [19.4 Dec. 1944 forematter]

bump to displace (another worker with less priority on the job, because of lack of seniority or veteran status) [22.3 Oct. 1947]

buna a synthetic rubber developed in Germany, made by polymerization of butadiene [18.2 Apr. 1943]

bunker atmosphere a mood of last-ditch defensiveness in response to imminent loss of political power; **bunker mentality** a last-ditch defensive reaction, as to growing criticism or imminent loss of political power [64.1 Spring 1989]

buppie black yuppie [64.2 Summer 1989]

burger *suffixal and free form* [18.2 Apr. 1943 forematter]

Burma bridge part of a rope course through trees, used as a training exercise [39.2 May 1964]

Burma Road the road from Burma to China, used as a military supply route; a supply route of similar nature or importance [17.4 Dec. 1942]

burn anger, a showing of anger; to show anger [16.4 Dec. 1941]

burp a belch; to belch; to cause (a baby) to belch [16.2 Apr. 1941]

bury-in the integration of a cemetery [36.4 Dec. 1961 s.v. in]

bus-back pertaining to a cargo-carrying service of hitching 1½-ton semitrailers to regularly scheduled intercity passenger busses [37.2 May 1962]

bush-buster a hillbilly [23.3–4 Oct.-Dec. 1948 s.v. buster]

bushing high-pressure selling in which a potential car buyer is pressured into spending more for a car than an advertised price [33.2 May 1958]

bush pilot a commercial pilot who flies over relatively uninhabited country, like Alaska [23.1 Feb. 1948]

businessspeak a type of insider language used by business people [59.2 Summer 1984 s.v. speak]

buster *suffixal form* (from *trustbuster, gangbuster*) [18.1 Feb. 1943 forematter; 23.3–4 Oct.-Dec. 1948 part II]; *cf.* blockbuster, factory buster, gangbuster, union-buster; a BABY BUSTER [64.1 Spring 1989]

bustle buster [23.3–4 Oct.-Dec. 1948 s.v. buster]

butterfly bomb a bomb with wings that open up upon its release to slow its speed of descent [21.2 Apr. 1946]

buttery *British* a small kitchen or coffee-making counter in the residence hall of a school or college [62.3 Fall 1987]

button buster, button-buster a joke; a comedian [23.3–4 Oct.-Dec. 1948 s.v. buster]

buzz (in aviation) to fly close to the ground, esp. in a spirit of frolic or showing-off; **buzzer** one who buzzes; **buzzing** the act of flying an airplane dangerously close to the ground [20.2 Apr. 1945]

buzz bomb, buzz-bomb a robot bomb [19.4 Dec. 1944]

BW biological warfare [24.4 Dec. 1949]

by-liner a newspaper columnist [33.4 Dec. 1958]

bypass to pass up, disregard; specif. to outflank [18.4 Dec. 1943]

Cabbage (Patch) Kid; Cabbage Patch doll; Cabbage Patcher *trademark* a soft-bodied doll sold with adoption papers, *also* CPK; **Cabbage Patch (doll)** any item that sells spectacularly, such as the Cabbage Patch Kid doll, a popular fad that passes quickly [59.4 Winter 1984]

cab happy [22.3 Oct. 1947 s.v. happy]

cabineteer a presidential cabinet member [18.1 Feb. 1943 forematter; 23.3–4 Oct.-Dec. 1948]

cablespeak [59.4 Winter 1984 s.v. speak]

cable TV a subscription service transmitting TV signals from a master antenna to individual sets, *also* CATV, wire TV [47.3–4 Fall-Winter 1972]

cactus happy (in army use) bemused from living in cactus patches [19.1 Feb. 1944 forematter]

cafe coronary death by choking on food, mistaken for a heart attack [54.1 Spring 1979]

cafeteria; cafeteria-style; cafeteria-type (affording) choice from a list of options (as of fringe-benefit plans, contraceptives, etc.) [65.3 Fall 1990]

cafetorium a room usable as both a cafeteria and an auditorium [30.2 May 1955]

californium an atomic element in the 98th place on the periodic table [26.4 Dec. 1951]

call *prefixal form* prostitution, esp. by the use of a telephone to make engagements [17.3 Oct. 1942]; **call boy** a male prostitute [58.1 Spring 1983]; **call girl; call woman** prostitute; **call house** house of prostitution [17.2 Apr. 1942 forematter]

call-up a summons to active military service [26.4 Dec. 1951]

calorie-intensive [60.1 Spring 1985 s.v. intensive]

camelback uncured rubber with wings tapered from the shoulders, applied to a worn tire to make new tread [18.4 Dec. 1943]

camp *suffixal form*, as in auto ~, tourist ~, motor~ [24.2 Apr. 1949 forematter]

campus theater circuit [24.4 Dec. 1949 forematter]

cannibalize to dismantle an unserviceable vehicle to provide spare parts for other vehicles [20.3 Oct. 1945]; **cannibal** *British* produced by cannibalizing automobiles [62.3 Fall 1987]

canyon-hop [48.1–2 Spring-Summer 1973 *s.v.* hop]

cap *British* to put a limit on, restrict [62.3 Fall 1987]

capcom, Cap Com; capsule communicator, Capsule Communicator a person stationed at the command communicator console in the control center who is the only person designated to talk directly with the astronauts orbiting overhead [40.2 May 1965]

capsulize to express succinctly [29.3 Oct. 1954]

captive audience an audience so situated that it must listen involuntarily [26.3 Oct. 1951 *s.v.* captive]

car bra a cover for the front end of a car, *also* bra, nose bra *or* mask [65.4 Winter 1990]

car cannibal *British* one who cannibalizes cars [62.3 Fall 1987]

card (*in* play the – card) a particular gambit or tactic used to gain an advantage or attain a goal in political maneuvering, *esp. in* play the China ~, Russia ~, *also* Canadian ~, Cuba ~, draft ~, Mexican ~, Olympics-boycott ~, Soviet ~ [58.4 Winter 1983]

card-covered *British* (of a book) bound in stiff paper covers [62.3 Fall 1987]

care assistant *British* a social welfare worker who looks after severely handicapped people by visiting them frequently and taking care of their needs [63.1 Spring 1988]

careerism placing one's personal professional ambitions above all other values [35.4 Dec. 1960]

caregiver an unpaid companion or nurse for the elderly, chronically ill, or handicapped, usu. a family member; **caregiving** providing companionship or nursing for the elderly, chronically ill, or handicapped without pay; **care recipient** an elderly, chronically ill, or handicapped person who receives caregiving [64.2 Summer 1989]

caretaker interim or stopgap [24.1 Feb. 1949]

car hop a waiter or waitress who serves customers in parked automobiles [16.2 Apr. 1941]; **carhop** *v.* [31.3 Oct. 1956]

carlegging car bootlegging, selling a new car by an overstocked dealer for resale in another area by a used-car dealer at below the usual price for new cars [30.4 Dec. 1955]

carpark, car-park, car park *mainly British* an automobile parking area [31.1 Feb. 1956; 34.1 Feb. 1959]

carpet bombing; carpet raid AREA BOMBING to prepare for the advance of ground troops; [26.3 Oct. 1951; 27.1 Feb. 1952]; **carpet of bombs** [26.3 Oct. 1951 *illus. s.v.* carpet bombing]

car pool an arrangement for sharing transportation in private automobiles, *also* pooling [18.4 Dec. 1943]; **carpool** to travel in a car pool; **carpooler** member of a car pool, *also* pooler; **car-pool it** to travel in a car pool, *also* pool it [51.3–4 Fall-Winter 1976]

carrier-based; carrier-borne [19.3 Oct. 1944 forematter; 20.2 Apr. 1945 forematter]

Cartergate the infiltration of Jimmy Carter's campaign by Ronald Reagan's campaign staff to give him an edge in the TV debates [53.3 Fall 1978 *s.v.* -gate; 59.2 Summer 1984 *s.v.* -gate]

cartnapper; cartnaper one who steals a grocery cart; **cartnapping** the act of stealing a grocery cart [39.3 Oct. 1964]

cartop *v.i.* to load and transport a boat on top of an automobile; (of a boat) to be loaded and transported on the top of a car; *v.t.* to load and transport (a small boat or other bulky object) on top of an automobile; to use a cartop boat on (a body of water); **cartoppable** (of a boat) of such size and weight that it can be loaded and transported on top of a car; **car-topper** one who cartops [47.3–4 Fall-Winter 1972]

case to study or plan (a crime, esp. the setting of a crime) so as to preclude accidents [16.4 Dec. 1941]

cash dispensing machine *British* an automatic bank teller, often outside a bank, from which money can be withdrawn by inserting a card and keying in an identification number; **cashpoint** *British* a cash dispensing machine; a cash-register counter [62.4 Winter 1987]

-cast *suffix* (from *broadcast*) [18.2 Apr. 1943 forematter]

castle-hop [47.3–4 Fall-Winter 1972 *s.v.* hop]

Castroism the communistic and revolutionary ideas and practices of Fidel Castro, *also* Fidelismo [36.3 Oct. 1961]

CAT clear air turbulence, invisible WIND SHEER [54.1 Spring 1979]

catbird seat an advantageous position or situation, *esp. in* sitting in the ~ [29.4 Dec. 1954]

categorical of a federal grant-in-aid designed for a specific project [58.2 Summer 1983]

catfish circuit [24.4 Dec. 1949 forematter]

Catholic-baiter [17.2 Apr. 1942 *s.v.* baiter]

Cattlegate [53.3 Fall 1978 *s.v.* -gate]

CATV Community Antenna Television, *also* cable TV [47.3–4 Fall-Winter 1972]

catwalk an aerial walkway [57.2 Summer 1982]

Caudleism [32.4 Dec. 1957]

cavalry mounted soldiery [18.1 Feb. 1943 forematter]

CCFer supporter of the Cooperative Commonwealth Federation [33.4 Dec. 1958]

C day Clarion [radio] day; Car day, when new cars were to be available again after WWII [21.3 Oct. 1946 forematter]

cease-fire a cessation of military action, truce [26.2 May 1951]

ceiling an upper limit [16.4 Dec. 1941]; **hit the ceiling** [18.1 Feb. 1943 forematter]

cell a nucleus within a larger organization, intriguing for a special interest [16.4 Dec. 1941]

cellular using many low-powered transmitters, each forming a cell bounded by its transmitting range, within a large call area, thus making possible an increased number of simultaneous calls from mobile radio-telephones [58.1 Spring 1983]

cemetery-hop [47.3–4 Fall-Winter 1972 *s.v.* hop]

cent (of words or things, after a large numeral) important or pretentious, *as in* 75¢ word [17.3 Oct. 1942 *s.v.* dollar]

centaurette a female centaur in the film *Fantasia* [17.4 Dec. 1942 forematter]

central staging a seating arrangement in which the audience sits on all sides of the acting area, *also* theater in the round [26.4 Dec. 1951]

certified mail recorded mail for which the recipient must sign [31.1 Feb. 1956]

CFA College Football Association [57.2 Summer 1982]

chain-in a demonstration for integration in which the demonstrators chain themselves, e.g., to seats in the gallery of a state legislature [38.3 Oct. 1963 *s.v.* in]

chain reaction a series of causally linked events [23.1 Feb. 1948]

chain-smoke *v.* [31.3 Oct. 1956]

chain-whip *v.* [31.3 Oct. 1956]

chairborne [20.2 Apr. 1945 forematter]

change-up (in baseball) an unexpected, slow pitch designed to throw off a batter's timing [25.1 Feb. 1950]

channel a channeler or medium; to serve as a medium through whom other intelligences communicate, *as in* ~ spirits, ~ed voices; **channeling** communicating with spirits through a medium [63.3 Fall 1988]

channeler one who attempts to swim the English Channel [33.4 Dec. 1958]; one who communicates with spirits, a medium [63.3 Fall 1988]

channel-hop [47.3−4 Fall-Winter 1972 *s.v.* hop]

chase aircraft; chase airplane; chase plane a fast plane that helps to test a new aircraft by following it closely and radioing observations and advice to the test pilot [40.2 May 1965]

chateau-hop [48.1−2 Spring-Summer 1973 *s.v.* hop]

chat line a computerized telephone service for engaging in conversation, often of a sexual or pornographic nature, with another subscriber to the service or with someone employed by the service for this purpose [64.1 Spring 1989]

checkbook baseball the practice of paying unusually large amounts of money for and to a few players on a baseball team in an effort to produce a winning or championship team; **checkbook journalism** the payment of large sums of money to public figures for televised interviews [51.3−4 Fall-Winter 1976]

checkoff an arrangement whereby a livestock producer contributes for each animal marketed a fee for a promotional program; an arrangement whereby taxpayers indicate whether they wish a dollar of their income tax to be used for public financing of political campaigns [48.1−2 Spring-Summer 1973]

cheeseburger [18.2 Apr. 1943 forematter]

cheesecake a display, esp. photographic, of beautiful women with bare flesh exposed [18.4 Dec. 1943]

chemosphere the region 26 to 70 miles above the earth, rich in photochemical activity [26.3 Oct. 1951]

chestwise of the chest [63.2 Summer 1988 *s.v.* -wise]

chichi, chi-chi smart, pretentious, affected; stylishness, flair [25.2 May 1950]

chicken à la king and mashed potatoes circuit speaking engagements at the Kiwanis, Rotary, and Elks clubs [24.4 Dec. 1949 forematter]

chicken-fry to cook (esp. steak) by breading and frying [31.4 Dec. 1956]

chicken-patty circuit speaking tours sponsored by women's clubs in the smaller cities and towns of the United States [24.4 Dec. 1949 forematter]

chiclet, Chiclet (of a computer keyboard) having keys smaller and closer together than those on a typewriter and lacking full movement; **Chiclet Syndrome** [60.1 Spring 1985]

childspeak precocious or naively amusing language attributed to children in material intended for adults [63.2 Summer 1988 *s.v.* speak]

chimponaut; chimpnaut a chimpanzee sent into space in place of a human astronaut [40.3 Oct. 1965]

Chinacard, play to use relations with China as a factor in foreign relations between the U.S. and the USSR [58.4 Winter 1983 forematter]

China syndrome an accident in which the failure of cooling systems causes the core of a nuclear reactor to overheat to the melting point of the fuel and the reactor vessel, a meltdown [56.2 Summer 1981]

chin buster, chin-buster a boxer [23.3−4 Oct.-Dec. 1948 *s.v.* buster]

chloromycetin a drug of the penicillin-streptomycin family [23.3- 4 Oct.-Dec. 1948]

chocolate circuit [24.4 Dec. 1949 forematter]

chopper a helicopter [29.3 Oct. 1954]

Christmas-shop *v.* [31.3 Oct. 1956]

chump change a small amount of money [65.1 Spring 1990]

Chunnel a tunnel running under the English Channel [39.3 Oct. 1964]

churning buying and selling large blocks of stock with little or no change of price [30.4 Dec. 1955]

chutist a parachutist [17.3 Oct. 1942 forematter; 17.4 Dec. 1942]

-cide *suffix* death by [39.3 Oct. 1964]

cigar look [45.3−4 Fall-Winter 1970 *s.v.* look]

Cincus a Naval command [21.2 Apr. 1946 forematter]

CIOer one who is a member of the CIO [33.4 Dec. 1958]

circle staging; circle theatre a seating arrangement in which the audience sits on all sides of the acting area, *also* theater in the round [26.4 Dec. 1951]

circuit *suffixal form* [24.4 Dec. 1949 forematter]

circuit breaker a measure to prevent tax-burden overloads on low- and middle-income households by the state's assuming a part of property taxes when they exceed a specified percentage of income [60.3 Fall 1985]

circuitry a system of electronic circuits, circuits collectively [33.2 May 1958]

Citronella Circuit summer theaters [24.4 Dec. 1949 forematter]

city-buster an aerial bomber; an atomic bomb [23.3−4 Oct.-Dec. 1948 *s.v.* buster]

city-edit *v.* [31.3 Oct. 1956]

city-hop to travel frequently between cities [47.3−4 Fall-Winter 1972 *s.v.* hop; 48.1−2 Spring-Summer 1973 *s.v.* hop; 54.1 Spring 1979 *s.v.* hop]

city shorts HOT PANTS [46.1−2 Spring-Summer 1971 forematter]

civilianization the adding of civilians to the services [31.1 Feb. 1956]

civil righter; civil-rightist one who protests the abuse of civil rights [44.1 Feb. 1969 *also* forematter]

clamgate [59.2 Summer 1984 *s.v.* -gate]

clapometer *British* a machine that registers the volume of an audience's response, applause meter [62.3 Fall 1987]

Clari-phane (from *cellophane*) [18.4 Dec. 1943 forematter]

classic car a beautiful, well engineered car built between 1925 and 1942 [31.1 Feb. 1956]

clay buster, clay-buster a trapshooter [23.3–4 Oct.-Dec. 1948 *s.v.* buster]

clean (of hydrogen bombs) with low radioactive side effects [32.2 May 1957]

cleaner-upper a product used to clean [33.4 Dec. 1958]

cliff-hang *v.* [31.4 Dec. 1956]

cliometrician a historian who relies upon statistics and computerized data; **cliometrics** the study of history using statistics and computerized data [51.1–2 Spring-Summer 1976]

clipper, Clipper to ship by clipper plane; to go by clipper plane [17.2 Apr. 1942 forematter; 17.3 Oct. 1942]

clock *British* to turn back the odometer of a used car to increase its sales value [62.3 Fall 1987]

close coupled *British* (of a toilet fixture) having the water tank joined with the toilet bowl as a single piece [62.3 Fall 1987]

close dancing TOUCH DANCING [50.1–2 Spring-Summer 1975]

cloud buster, cloud-buster a flying fortress; (in baseball) a fly ball [23.3–4 Oct.-Dec. 1948 *s.v.* buster]

clubmobiler [33.4 Dec. 1958]

clutch *attrib.* (in sports) in a critical situation [26.2 May 1951; 26.4 Dec. 1951]

coach *euphemism* (of travel) third class [17.2 Apr. 1942 forematter]

coal dust curtain [25.3 Oct. 1950 forematter]

coalgate [56.4 Winter 1981 *s.v.* -gate]

cockapoo a hybrid of a cocker spaniel and a poodle [54.1 Spring 1979]

cockapopso a hybrid of a cockapoo and a Lhasa apso [54.1 Spring 1979]

cocktail circuit [24.4 Dec. 1949 forematter]

cocooning staying at home and indulging in sedentary pursuits such as eating and watching television [63.3 Fall 1988]

code play *British* a drama with a covert meaning [63.1 Spring 1988]

coffee hog [18.2 Apr. 1943 forematter]

coke, Coke a drink of Coca-Cola [18.1 Feb. 1943 forematter; 19.1 Feb. 1944]

coke bottle an airplane shape [31.4 Dec. 1956 *illus. s.v.* wasp waist]

cold-call *British* to attempt to sell a product, esp. stock shares, over the telephone to an unprepared and unwilling potential customer; **cold-caller** *British* one who cold-calls [62.3 Fall 1987]

cold (nuclear) fusion nuclear fusion at ordinary temperature and without elaborate machinery, *also* fusion in a bottle *or* jar, tabletop fusion [65.2 Summer 1990]

cold rubber a synthetic rubber made at near-freezing temperatures [25.1 Feb. 1950]

cold war a prolonged contest for national advantage, conducted by diplomatic, economic, and psychological rather than military means [23.2 Apr. 1948]; any determined opposition [26.1 Feb. 1951]

collar bone *British* a thin strip of material, such as bone, used to stiffen a shirt collar, a collar stay [62.3 Fall 1987]

Colombo pertaining to an alliance of India, Pakistan, Ceylon, Burma, and Indonesia, which initially met at Colombo, *esp. in* ~ powers, ~ prime ministers [30.4 Dec. 1955]

colonize to infiltrate, as by Communists; **colonizer** infiltrator, spy [30.4 Dec. 1955]

colorcast *v.* [31.3 Oct. 1956]

combat-load *v.* [31.3 Oct. 1956]

come out (of athletes) to turn professional before eligibility to play on a college team is exhausted, esp. at the end of the junior year [65.4 Winter 1990]

cometoid a phase in a comet's decline, a chunk of ice too small to be observed as a comet but still unmelted as it enters the Earth's atmosphere [35.1 Feb. 1960]

comic *British, derogatory* a tabloid newspaper [62.3 Fall 1987]

Cominch a Naval command [21.2 Apr. 1946 forematter]

Cominform Communist Information (i.e., propaganda) Bureau [24.1 Feb. 1949]

comitology *stunt* the scientific study of committees [46.3–4 Fall-Winter 1971]

command controlled by radio signals from the ground, a ship, or an airplane, *esp. in* ~ missile; **command guidance** *often attrib.* (of missiles) control by such signals [30.4 Dec. 1955]

commando [17.4 Dec. 1942 forematter]

common market, Common Market an alliance with no customs barriers between the member states and the same tariff against outside goods, originally between France, West Germany, Italy, Belgium, the Netherlands, and Luxembourg [35.4 Dec. 1960]

communitarianism communal living as by Shakers or the Oneida community [32.4 Dec. 1957]

community college a two-year, nonresidential college serving local needs [25.2 May 1950 *s.v.* community]

company buster, company-buster an employee of a mining company who works above ground [23.3–4 Oct.-Dec. 1948 *s.v.* buster]

company townism [32.4 Dec. 1957]

compartment-hop [48.1–2 Spring-Summer 1973 *s.v.* hop]

compatibility the ability of TV color signals to be picked up by a black-and-white set; **compatible** (of a TV color system) able to be picked up by black-and-white sets [26.3 Oct. 1951]

completer one who owns a copy of every book in a series or of a particular kind [29.3 Oct. 1954]

complex a cluster of related buildings or other structures, *specif.* industrial ~, rail bridge ~, highway ~, ~ of apartments [40.2 May 1965]

compulsory-test *British* to test (someone) compulsorily [62.3 Fall 1987]

computeracy *British* computer literacy, knowledge about computers; **computerate** *British* computer literate [62.3 Fall 1987]

computer conferencing *British* a meeting conducted by storing and distributing messages to the participants by means of a computer system [63.1 Spring 1988 *illus. s.v.* teleconferencing]

computerspeak the jargon of computer users [59.2 Summer 1984 *s.v.* speak]

computer virus a program maliciously inserted into a computer to alter or destroy other computer programs, *also* electronic virus, silent virus, software virus [64.3 Fall 1989 *s.v.* virus]

comsymp, com-symp (Birch Society use) a communist sympathizer [37.2 May 1962]

concerteer a concert-goer [18.1 Feb. 1943 forematter]

conciliationism [32.4 Dec. 1957]

concrete, in immovable, unalterable [58.1 Spring 1983]

concussion grenade a cardboard, hand-grenade-sized container of explosive, intended to shock or stun rather than to kill [29.1 Feb. 1954]

condo a condominium; **condomania** a vogue for condominiums [47.3–4 Fall-Winter 1972]

conelrad control of electromagnetic radiation, a plan for broadcasting warnings of enemy attack to the public without broadcasting beams usable to locate targets [29.1 Feb. 1954]

confrontainment a TV program on which participants engage in verbal confrontation, a form of TABLOID TV [65.1 Spring 1990]

congaroo a conga dancer [17.4 Dec. 1942 forematter]

congeneric a business conglomerate [44.2 May 1969]

conglomerate a corporate enterprise that achieves product or service diversity through the acquisition of existing independent companies, usu. in situations where earnings and security price relationships and expectations indicate profitable outcomes for the parties involved; pertaining to a group of companies that operate in separate markets and are held together by ties of financial and administrative authority; **conglomeration** any act of increasing the number of a firm's external markets; a conglomerate or the action of forming one; **conglomerator** a conglomerate entrepreneur, one who forms or manages a conglomerate [44.2 May 1969]

conillum (from *con*[*trol of*] *illum*[*ination*]) a plan restricting outdoor advertising signs and floodlights [30.2 May 1955]

conk buster, conk-buster cheap liquor; an intellectual Negro [23.3–4 Oct.-Dec. 1948 *s.v.* buster]

conscriptee one conscripted for military service [16.4 Dec. 1941 forematter]

consensus All-American a football player chosen as a member of several All-American teams [60.1 Spring 1985]

consumerism [32.4 Dec. 1957]

contact (of flying) (within) sight of the ground [22.3 Oct. 1947]

contact lens a lens fitted to the eyeball [17.2 Apr. 1942 forematter; 17.3 Oct. 1942]

continent-hop [48.1–2 Spring-Summer 1973 *s.v.* hop]

contour couch a couch in a space vehicle designed to fit the form of an astronaut's body [37.2 May 1962]

contour-plow *v.* [31.3 Oct. 1956]

contourscape (from *landscape, seascape*) [18.4 Dec. 1943 forematter]

contract beer a MICROBREW sold outside the area where it is made [65.4 Winter 1990]

contract buster, contract-buster a professional horse breaker [23.3–4 Oct.-Dec. 1948 *s.v.* buster]

contronym a word with two senses that seem to contradict each other [39.2 May 1964]

conventional type [23.2 Apr. 1948 *s.v.* type]

conventioneer one who attends a convention [17.2 Apr. 1942; 18.1 Feb. 1943 forematter; 23.3–4 Oct.-Dec. 1948]

cook *in* What's ~ing? [18.1 Feb. 1943 forematter]; to make (something) radioactive by putting it in an atomic pile [27.3 Oct. 1952]

cookout, cook-out a cooking of a meal outdoors [28.4 Dec. 1953]

cook with gas; cook with electricity; cook with radar (used in the progressive) make progress, be successful, [21.4 Dec. 1946]

coolie *British* an uncritical fan of popular music [62.3 Fall 1987]

cool pants HOT PANTS [46.1–2 Spring-Summer 1971 forematter]

Cooperette a female employee of CCA (*perh.* Cooperative Consumer Association); **Co-operette,** a member of the women's auxiliary of the Co-operative Club [17.4 Dec. 1942 forematter]

coop happy out of one's mind from being shut up [22.3 Oct. 1947 *s.v.* happy]

coordinate *euphemism* censor, regiment [17.2 Apr. 1942 forematter]

cop buster, cop-buster [23.3–4 Oct.-Dec. 1948 *s.v.* buster]

copette a policewoman [18.2 Apr. 1943 forematter]

copter a helicopter [24.1 Feb. 1949]

copycode a technique for preventing the copying of compact-disk recordings [65.1 Spring 1990]

copyread *v.* [31.3 Oct. 1956]

corn row a tight hair braid close to the scalp; **cornrow** to divide the hair into geometric sections and braid the sections flat to the scalp [46.3–4 Fall-Winter 1971]

corny old-fashioned, sentimental, stale, yokelish, esp. as applied to music [18.1 Feb. 1943 forematter; 19.1 Feb. 1944]

corrigan something done backwards; one who acts in a way contrary to expectations [16.2 Apr. 1941]

cortisone a synthesized hormone of the outer cortex of the adrenal gland [26.1 Feb. 1951]

cosmonaut a Russian astronaut; **cosmonautical** pertaining to cosmonauts [37.2 May 1962]

cosmotarianism [32.4 Dec. 1957]

cosmotron a type of atom smasher [25.3 Oct. 1950]

cost out *British* to estimate or determine the cost of [62.3 Fall 1987]

costume *euphemism* (of jewelry) artificial, imitation [17.2 Apr. 1942 forematter]

cottage colony a group of resort cabins or cottages clustered with stores or entertainment facilities [34.1 Feb. 1959]

cottage court [24.2 Apr. 1949 forematter]

couch potato; couch rat one who spends time reclining and watching television, *also* potato, sofa spud, spud, telespud, videot, vidspud; **couch potatoing** lounging as a couch potato; **couch tomato** a female couch potato [63.3 Fall 1988]

countdown, count down, count-down an audible counting off of a certain length of time; the minutes before a missile is to be fired [29.3 Oct. 1954]; a period immediately preceding a critical decision or turning point; a roll call of states at a political convention [35.4 Dec. 1960]

counter-escalation an escalation of hostilities in a given location as the counterpart of an escalation elsewhere [40.3 Oct. 1965]

counter-productive producing results contrary to what was hoped or expected [45.3–4 Fall-Winter 1970]

country-hop [47.3–4 Fall-Winter 1972 *s.v.* hop; 48.1–2 Spring- Summer 1973 *s.v.* hop]

coup-type [23.2 Apr. 1948 *s.v.* type]

courtesy patrol *euphemism* mounted police [17.2 Apr. 1942 forematter]

court-ordered pertaining to an action carried out in compliance with a court ruling [55.2 Summer 1980]

courtworthy [16.2 Apr. 1941 forematter]

coventrize; coventryize to bombard (an open city) into ruins, as Coventry was on 14–15 Nov. 1940 [16.2 Apr. 1941]

cowbarn circuit summer theaters [24.4 Dec. 1949 forematter]

cowboy economics individualistic, exploitative economic practices; **cowboy economy** exploitation of the environment without concern for the effects produced on it [54.1 Spring 1979]

cowfeteria a feeding arrangement for cows from which they may eat as they choose [35.1 Feb. 1960]

CPK a CABBAGE PATCH KID [59.4 Winter 1984]

crackpottism; crackpotism eccentric and extreme ideas [31.1 Feb. 1956]

crack-upee [16.4 Dec. 1941 forematter]

crash protective in a crash or used to rescue those involved in a crash, *as in* ~ cushion, ~ pad; ~ boat, ~ truck, ~ wagon [25.2 May 1950]; done, carried out in the shortest time possible, *as in* ~ dive (of a submarine), ~ job, ~ program [29.3 Oct. 1954]; (of a TV program) using violent action for entertainment [65.1 Spring 1990]

crashdive *v.* [18.2 Apr. 1943 forematter]

crash land, crash-land to land a plane with a portion or all of the essential landing equipment ineffective [20.4 Dec. 1945; 31.3 Oct. 1956]; **crash landing** [20.4 Dec. 1945]

crash show; crash television; crash TV [65.1 Spring 1990 *s.v.* crash]

crawler-transporter a transport vehicle used to maneuver large pieces of aerospace equipment; **crawlerway** a wide and deep-bedded track for crawler-transporters [44.1 Feb. 1969]

creation science the belief that scientific evidence supports a literal interpretation of the biblical account of creation; **creation scientist** one who accepts creation science [58.1 Spring 1983]

creative inventive or imaginative, esp. for the purpose of conveying a false impression or perpetrating a fraud; **creative accountant** an accountant who finds ways to justify fanciful figures on a client's statement of earnings; **creative accounting** the practice of making financial statements appear favorable by the way in which accounts or transactions are recorded; **creative bookkeeping** creative accounting; **creativity** the ability to do creative accounting [56.2 Summer 1981]

creative finance; creative financing financial inducements used to sell houses when interest rates are high, such as adjustable interest rates, assumption of existing low-interest mortgages, and barter or exchange [57.2 Summer 1982]

creative pause the lull in fighting after the Nazi conquest of Crete (coined by German propagandists); any temporary cessation of fighting [17.2 Apr. 1942 forematter; 17.4 Dec. 1942]

credit worthy [16.2 Apr. 1941 forematter]

CREEP Committee for the Re-Election of the President, Richard Nixon's 1972 campaign organization [47.3–4 Fall-Winter 1972]

creeper lane, creeper-lane a lane on a steeply rising road in which trucks can move slowly in low gear [30.4 Dec. 1955]

creepie-peepie a hand-held television camera, *also* peepie-creepie, walkie-lookie [28.3 Oct. 1953]

crewman member of an airplane crew [21.2 Apr. 1946]

crime buster [23.3–4 Oct.-Dec. 1948 *s.v.* buster]

cronyism the appointment of close friends to government posts [31.1 Feb. 1956]

cross-check to check from many points of view [29.1 Feb. 1954]

crowding out reducing the availability of credit to nonfederal borrowers as a result of heavy borrowing by the U.S. Treasury [57.2 Summer 1982]

Crown privilege the absolute right of the British government to object to producing a document in court on the ground that it would be against the public interest to do so [55.2 Summer 1980]

CRP *see* CREEP [47.3–4 Fall-Winter 1972]

cruise control a device that maintains an automobile's cruising speed at the velocity set by the driver [59.1 Spring 1984]

cryobiologist a specialist in cryobiology; **cryobiology** the study of the effects of extreme cold on living systems; **cryosurgery** the use of freezing as a surgical tool [38.3 Oct. 1963]

crypto-communist someone with a hidden or secret communist affiliation; **cryptofascist, crypto-fascist** someone with a hidden or secret fascist affiliation [24.1 Feb. 1949]

cuff, off the informal; informally, extemporaneously [17.2 Apr. 1942 forematter; 17.3 Oct. 1942]

cuff, on the on credit [17.2 Apr. 1942 forematter; 17.3 Oct. 1942 forematter]

cuffo concert [18.1 Feb. 1943 *illus. s.v.* concerteer, forematter]

curtain *suffixal form* a barrier or obstruction [25.3 Oct. 1950 forematter]; *cf.* paper curtain

curtains finis, esp. death by violence [17.2 Apr. 1942; 17.3 Oct. 1942 forematter]

curvaceous (of the human figure) showing curves [16.2 Apr. 1941]

curve forefront, cutting edge, *esp. in* ahead of the ~, *also* behind the ~ [65.3 Fall 1990]

customizer one who changes the appearance of a car to make it reflect personal taste and preference [38.3 Oct. 1963]

custom-make *v.* [31.3 Oct. 1956]

cutback, cut-back a sharp cut in the production of raw materials or manufactured goods, as for the armed services, due to a sudden or unforeseen lessening of demand; a reduction [19.3 Oct. 1944; 20.3 Oct. 1945]; **cut back** to reduce [20.3 Oct. 1945]

cutting edge the vanguard, frontier, forefront, *esp. in* on the ~; advanced, innovative, pioneering, prominent; *also* front edge [60.1 Spring 1985]

cybernated automated, computerized *esp. in* ~ society, ~ world; **cybernation** automation, computerization [41.2 May 1966]

cybernetics the scientific field of control and communication theory encompassing both mechanical and animal subjects [24.4 Dec. 1949]

cyborg (from *cyb[ernetic] org[anism]*) a human being with some organs altered or replaced by mechanical devices to permit more efficient life in an environment different from the normal one [38.3 Oct. 1963]

cycling trail a BICYCLE TRAIL [46.1–2 Spring-Summer 1971]

daddy track work arrangements that allow men time away from company business for parental responsibilities; *cf.* mommy track [65.2 Summer 1990]

Dallasgate [53.3 Fall 1978 *s.v.* -gate]

dam buster, dam-buster [23.3–4 Oct.-Dec. 1948 *s.v.* buster]

dampish *British* (of Conservative politicians) inclined not to be firm in supporting right-wing Conservative policies [63.1 Spring 1988]

dandelioneer a state employee delegated to dig dandelions [18.1 Feb. 1943 forematter]

date rape sexual intercourse forced by a person with whom the victim has a social engagement [64.4 Winter 1989]

daughter track responsibility placed upon women to care for aging relatives, *also* granny track [65.3 Fall 1990]

Davis Cupper one who has competed in the Davis Cup [33.4 Dec. 1958]

day *suffixal form* [21.3 Oct. 1946 forematter]; *cf.* D Day, V day, VE-Day, V-J Day

DCer one who works the Double Crostic puzzle [33.4 Dec. 1958]

D Day, D day, D-Day, D-day a cryptic designation for the date of a military action, such as an attack on a local front or the start of an invasion, specif. 11 May 1944; *in* D-day

minus one 'the day before D-day', D-day plus one 'the day after D-day' [19.4 Dec. 1944; 21.3 Oct. 1946 forematter]

DDT an insecticide, dichloro-diphenyl-trichloro-ethane [20.2 Apr. 1945]

DE [21.3 Oct. 1946 forematter]

deadender, dead ender one who is at a dead end in life, a derelict [33.4 Dec. 1958]

death ray bomb a neutron bomb [37.2 May 1962 *illus. s.v.* neutron bomb]

death sand; death dust invisible radioactive particles that kill silently [26.3 Oct. 1951]

death squad a group that murders their enemies or political opponents [60.3 Fall 1985]

debarker a device that removes the bark from lumber [33.4 Dec. 1958]

debategate the stealing of Jimmy Carter's briefing book for a TV debate by Ronald Reagan's campaign workers [59.2 Summer 1984 *s.v.* -gate]

debrief; debriefing, de-briefing the process of questioning and instructing after an operation [28.3 Oct. 1953]

deceleron an aircraft brake [28.3 Oct. 1953]

decimal inch an inch divided into ten parts [54.1 Spring 1979]

deck *usu. in passive* to tackle someone in football [46.3–4 Fall-Winter 1971]

deck-hop [47.3–4 Fall-Winter 1972 *s.v.* hop]

declassify to remove security restrictions on access to documents or information [26.2 May 1951]

decolonization the nationalization of foreign-owned enterprises [18.2 Apr. 1943 forematter; 19.1 Feb. 1944]

deconglomeration the act of breaking up a conglomerate into its smaller companies [44.2 May 1969]

deconstructivist architecture building design using sloping walls, tilted columns, diagonal lines, warped façades, and a generally distorted appearance [65.1 Spring 1990]

decontamination removal of destructive gas and chemicals launched in an air attack [17.2 Apr. 1942]

deep (in sports) possessing (a specified amount of) reserve strength in available substitutes [23.3–4 Oct.-Dec. 1948]

deep-fat-fry *v.* [31.3 Oct. 1956; 31.4 Dec. 1956]

deepfreezer, deep freezer a food locker maintaining a temperature well below freezing [25.2 May 1950]

defense-happy enthusiastic about defensive tactics in sports [22.3 Oct. 1947 *s.v.* happy]

defensive medicine practices by physicians that serve more to protect the physician in case of a malpractice suit than to manage or treat the patient's ailment, such as the ordering of clinically unnecessary tests and X-rays [51.3–4 Fall-Winter 1976]

de-fuzzer a device that removes the fuzz from a peach [33.4 Dec. 1958]

degauss to neutralize or offset a magnetic field; **degaussing** [18.2 Apr. 1943]

De Gink *see* Hotel de Gink [22.2 Apr. 1947]

deglamorize to deprive of glamor or charm; **deglamorization** [18.2 Apr. 1943]

dehumidification a rustproofing technique for ships [22.2 Apr. 1947]

demand-side pertaining to the economic theory put forth by John Maynard Keynes that to cure a lagging economy, one creates demand through government spending or tax cuts, and to cure inflation, one depresses demand by cutting spending or raising taxes [56.4 Winter 1981]

demothball; demoth to ready (stored ships or planes) for action [26.4 Dec. 1951]

denazify, de-Nazify to eradicate Nazi doctrines and adherents; **denazification, de-Nazification** [21.4 Dec. 1946]

dense pack a method of deploying ICBMs, specif. the MX missile, in silos close to one another; to deploy (missiles) in densely distributed silos [58.4 Winter 1983]

department *British* a department store [63.1 Spring 1988]

deportee one who is deported [16.4 Dec. 1941 forematter]

depth (in sports) the amount of reserve strength a team has in substitutes [23.3–4 Oct.-Dec. 1948]

depth-charge *v.* [31.4 Dec. 1956]

depth interview a long discursive interview without a questionnaire [26.2 May 1951]

depurge to restore to good standing a person once purged for antidemocratic or hostile actions; **depurgee** one so restored [27.3 Oct. 1952]

derived four-channel [48.1–2 Spring-Summer 1973 *s.v.* four-channel *n.*]

desegregate to bring about a condition in which all ethnic groups, esp. African Americans, can avail themselves of the same facilities, such as motion picture theaters and public schools; **desegregation, de-segregation** [30.2 May 1955]

designate (with allusion to *designated hitter*) delegate, assign [46.3–4 Fall-Winter 1971 forematter]

designated base runner a designated runner [46.3–4 Fall-Winter 1971]

designated driver a person selected to abstain from intoxicants at a party or bar and to drive an automobile for other persons afterwards [64.4 Winter 1989]

designated hitter In the American League, a tenth player who may, if the manager chooses, be named in the line-up to bat for the pitcher, but anywhere in the batting order [46.1–2 Spring-Summer 1971]

designated homer; designated HR a home run hit by a designated hitter [46.3–4 Fall-Winter 1971]

designated pinch hitter, designated pinch-hitter *see* designated hitter, *also* DPH; any substitute, replacement, or stand-in [46.1–2 Spring-Summer 1971; 46.3–4 Fall-Winter 1971]

designated runner an additional baseball player who may eventually be added to the lineup to run for the catcher [46.3–4 Fall-Winter 1971]

designated Saturday *British* a Saturday reserved for particular soccer matches [63.1 Spring 1988]

designee a designated hitter [46.3–4 Fall-Winter 1971]

desk copy *euphemism* free copy [17.2 Apr. 1942 forematter]

detainee *euphemism* prisoner [17.2 Apr. 1942 forematter]

deviationism (in Communism) divergence from an orthodox line of thought; **deviationist** (in Communism) one who diverges from an orthodox line of thought [26.2 May 1951]

De Votoism [32.4 Dec. 1957]

dewbathe *v.* [31.3 Oct. 1956]

dh, DH *see* designated hitter [46.1–2 Spring-Summer 1971]

DI, D.I. DISCOMFORT INDEX, a measure of the human discomfort resulting from the combination of temperature and humidity [36.4 Dec. 1961]

diamondgate [56.4 Winter 1981 *s.v.* -gate]

dianetics L. Ron Hubbard's name for his so-called science of the mind [26.3 Oct. 1951]

diary *British* a record of future engagements [62.4 Winter 1987 *cited s.v.* appointments diary]

dime bag a packet containing 10 dollars worth of an illicit drug [57.4 Winter 1982]

dime store a store dealing in low-priced commodities; cheap or paltry [22.2 Apr. 1947]

dim-out a lowering of lights as a protective measure in wartime; to dim lights protectively [17.3 Oct. 1942]

dim-viewer one who takes a dim view or criticizes [33.4 Dec. 1958]

dink; dinkie double income no kids, one of a couple with separate incomes and no children and consequently money for a high standard of living [64.2 Summer 1989]

dinosaur a heavy element that came into being at the birth of the universe but decayed out of existence within a few weeks, *usu. in* ~ element [40.2 May 1965]

dirty (of hydrogen bombs) with high radioactive side effects; **dirtiness** the amount of radioactivity generated by a bomb [32.2 May 1957]

dirty trick a malicious act, usu. covert, esp. one directed toward a political opponent, *also* soggy-trick; **dirty-trickery** the practice of performing dirty tricks; **dirty-trickster** one who performs dirty tricks [49.3–4 Fall-Winter 1974]; **dirty campaign trick** a dirty trick in a political campaign; **dirty work** disreputable activity, esp. in politics [49.3–4 Fall-Winter 1974 forematter]

disc-er [33.4 Dec. 1958]

disc-intensive (of computers) [60.1 Spring 1985 *s.v.* intensive]

disclosing serving to reveal, by means of vegetable dye preparations, the plaque or food particles adhering to inadequately cleaned tooth surfaces, *as in* ~ agent, ~ solution, ~ tablet, ~ wafer; **disclosure tablet** a disclosing tablet, one that releases a vegetable dye preparation to reveal plaque or food particles adhering to inadequately cleaned tooth surfaces [50.1–2 Spring-Summer 1975]

disco discotheque [40.2 May 1965]

discographer [33.4 Dec. 1958]

discomfort index, Discomfort Index *see* DI, a measure of the human discomfort resulting from the combination of temperature and humidity [36.4 Dec. 1961]

discotheque, discothèque a usu. small, intimate night club for dancing, esp. currently fashionable dances, esp. to recorded music; (of clothing) appropriate for wear to a discotheque; **discothequenik** one who frequents a discotheque [40.2 May 1965]

discount house a store where prices are below those listed on the product or generally charged [29.4 Dec. 1954]

discrete four-channel [48.1–2 Spring-Summer 1973 *s.v.* four- channel *n.*]

discrimination in reverse discrimination in favor of members of a group formerly discriminated against [57.1 Spring 1982]

discussion-type [23.2 Apr. 1948 *s.v.* type]

diskery a company that manufactures phonograph records [36.3 Oct. 1961]

displaced person a refugee; one of those the Germans forcibly removed from their native lands to work as slave laborers, *also* DP [21.2 Apr. 1946]

disposable income income available for use after taxes [26.4 Dec. 1951]

ditch to bring a disabled aircraft down on the water; **ditching** [20.2 Apr. 1945]

dit-happy (army use) very fast in operating a telegraph key [19.1 Feb. 1944 forematter]

diversionism [32.4 Dec. 1957]

Dixiecrat a Democrat who opposed the civil rights program of the Truman Administration and the civil rights plank of the 1948 platform of the Democratic Party; one of those who convened at Birmingham, Alabama, to nominate their own candidates on a platform of states' rights [23.3–4 Oct.-Dec. 1948]; **Dixiecratic** pertaining to the Southern Democrats who left the Democratic Party [27.3 Oct. 1952]; **Dixiecratism** the principles and practice of Southern conservative Democrats [26.2 May 1951]

Dixiegop a coalition of Republicans and conservative Southern Democrats [25.3 Oct. 1950]

DJ-day D day in Japan [21.3 Oct. 1946 forematter]

DNA fingerprinting identification, esp. for legal purposes, by analyzing the structure of the DNA in an individual's cells, *also* genetic fingerprinting; **DNA print** the distinctive structure of the DNA in an individual's cells, used as a means of identification, *also* genetic fingerprint [64.4 Winter 1989]

DNB [21.3 Oct. 1946 forematter]

Dr. Spin a SPIN DOCTOR [63.3 Fall 1988]

docu- *prefix* documentary; **docu-autobio-musico-"Journey"** a documentary-autobiographical-musical film, *Journey through the Past*; **docudramatize** to treat (a subject) in the style of a docudrama; **docuhistory** a work that combines historical fact with the imagination of the author; **docu-musical** a program with songs and dramatic re-creations; **docu-pulp** sensational, unintelligent writing about history in a documentary style; **docu-re-creation** a program that attempts to re-create historical reality in the minds of TV audiences; **docu-reenactment** a program that uses little footage of actual events, but offers instead a re-creation of historical events; **docu-schlock** a light magazine-style program that combines entertainment with information, *also* infotainment, reality programming; **docu-soap opera** a docudrama in the manner of a soap opera [60.4 Winter 1985]

document something proved or supported by documentary evidence, as a film or novel; documentary [17.4 Dec. 1942 forematter; 18.2 Apr. 1943]

documentary a film dealing with factual matter and utilizing real-life film footage, a documentary film [17.2 Apr. 1942; 22.2 Apr. 1947]

dogcaster one who conducts a radio program about dogs [18.2 Apr. 1943 forematter]

do-gooder one who officiously does good acts [24.1 Feb. 1949]

do-it-yourself the practice of doing oneself such things as working with wood and finishing; **do-it-yourselfer** one who practices do-it-yourself activities; **do-it-yourselfing** the activity of do-it-yourself; **do-it-yourselfism** the practice of do-it-yourself [30.4 Dec. 1955]

dol a unit of pain [25.3 Oct. 1950]

dollar (of words or things, after a numeral) important or pretentious, *as in* two-~ word, $4 word, five-~ word, five-~ term, five-~ question, ten-~ word, $15 word, $64 question, $64 problem [17.3 Oct. 1942; 20.3 Oct. 1945]

dollar diplomacy [46.3–4 Fall-Winter 1971 forematter]

dollar gap a trade imbalance resulting from an excess of imports from a dollar area, such as the U.S., over exports to that area [25.3 Oct. 1950]

dolorimeter an instrument for measuring pain [25.3 Oct. 1950]

Domestos *trademark, British* a bleach or disinfectant used to clean toilets and sinks [62.4 Winter 1987]

domino theory (of drugs) the belief that use leads to addiction to progressively more harmful drugs, *also* stepping-stone hypothesis [57.4 Winter 1982]

doodle; doodlebug a ROBOT BOMB [19.4 Dec. 1944 forematter]

doodler a trifler, dawdler; one who idly draws nonsense figures, as when speaking over a telephone [18.1 Feb. 1943]

doorbuster [23.3–4 Oct.-Dec. 1948 *s.v.* buster]

doorkey children, door-key children; door-key kids children of working parents who come to school with door keys hung around their necks and return after school to empty houses [29.4 Dec. 1954]; *cf.* latchkey

doorstep *British* a sandwich made with thick slices of bread [63.1 Spring 1988]

double-blind pertaining to an experiment in which neither the experimentee nor the experiment-administrator knows the terms of the experiment, as a drug test in which neither patient nor doctor knows whether the former is getting a drug or a placebo [38.3 Oct. 1963]

double-digit; double-figure between 10 and 99, esp. percent; *usu. pl.* double-digit figures, *also* two-digit [49.1–2 Spring-Summer 1974]

double-park to park on a street outside the curb area provided for parking, parallel to another car parked by the curb; **doubleparking, double-parking** parking a car parallel to another car parked by a curb [24.4 Dec. 1949]

doublethink the power of holding two contradictory beliefs in one's mind simultaneously and accepting both of them [28.4 Dec. 1953]

double zero ZERO-ZERO [64.1 Spring 1989]

dough-happy [22.3 Oct. 1947 *s.v.* happy]

DOVAP Doppler velocity and position, a system for tracking rockets [26.1 Feb. 1951]

down and dirty fiercely and unsportingly competitive, no holds barred, intensely applied; crude, coarse, scandalous, or sexually suggestive; **down if not dirty** funky but not lurid [65.3 Fall 1990]

downgrading placing in a lower grade or rank; reducing in size or quality [22.3 Oct. 1947]

down range station, down-range station one of a series of posts from which the flight of missiles is monitored [29.3 Oct. 1954]

down-size (of a car) to reduce the length and weight [55.2 Summer 1980]

downtown-and-dirty *stunt* streetwise and fiercely competitive [65.3 Fall 1990 *s.v.* down and dirty]

DP, D.P. *see* displaced person [21.2 Apr. 1946]

DPH designated pinch hitter, *see* designated hitter [46.1–2 Spring-Summer 1971]

draft-ager one who is of an age for the draft [33.4 Dec. 1958]

drag one's feet; drag one's elbows to stall, hold back, delay, slow up; **dragging of heels** dragging one's feet [28.3 Oct. 1953 *s.v.* drag]

DRAM *British* a dynamic random access memory chip [63.1 Spring 1988]

dramedy; dramady a TV program combining comedy and drama [64.3 Fall 1989]

draw in *British* to stop a vehicle by the side of the road, to pull over [63.1 Spring 1988]

Dread Weed, The marijuana [57.4 Winter 1982]

dream up to improvise, originate in an imaginative way, conceive mentally, imagine [18.1 Feb. 1943; 22.3 Oct. 1947]

dress out to put on athletic garb; to put athletic garb on (someone) [25.1 Feb. 1950]

drink driving *British* driving a vehicle under the influence of alcohol, drunk driving [63.1 Spring 1988]

drip a dull, tedious person [17.3 Oct. 1942 forematter]

drive-in integrated patronage of a segregated motel or roadside ice-cream stand [36.4 Dec. 1961 *s.v.* in]

drone a small, remote-controlled military plane launched from a MOTHER SHIP [22.3 Oct. 1947]

droodle a witty drawing, more contrived than a doodle, designed to mystify the viewer until it is explained; **droodling** [36.3 Oct. 1961]

droop a person disliked because of languidness [17.2 Apr. 1942 forematter; 17.3 Oct. 1942]

drop earring an earring that dangles down from the lobe [45.3–4 Fall-Winter 1970]

drop out to refuse to participate in the usual activities of society; **dropoutism** the practice of dropping out of society [47.3–4 Fall-Winter 1972]

droppies *British* disillusioned, relatively ordinary professionals, preferring independent employment situations [62.4 Winter 1987 forematter]

drugfastness, drug-fastness the ability of bacteria, specifically those causing illness, to alter themselves and render drugs or antibiotics useless in their eradication [28.1 Feb. 1953]

drunkometer, drunk-o-meter a device utilizing potassium permanganate and sulfuric acid to measure alcohol consumption [24.1 Feb. 1949]

dry drunk an emotional state of depression, impatience, intolerance, irritability, nervousness, and confusion experienced by alcoholics remaining sober over an extended period [31.4 Dec. 1956]

dry run something done for practice only, as a dress rehearsal [19.3 Oct. 1944]

duck an amphibious truck [19.4 Dec. 1944]

duck, break one's *British* to do a thing for the first time [63.1 Spring 1988]

duckwich (from *sandwich*) [18.4 Dec. 1943 forematter]

dudette a female patron of a dude ranch [17.4 Dec. 1942 forematter]

dumb down to revise so as to appeal to those of little education or intelligence; specif. to write (a textbook) on a lower intellectual or educational level than that formerly expected of the group for whom it is intended or to reduce the requirements of (a job) for less well educated workers; to teach (a student) with material intended for those at a lower grade level; to cause (someone) to be or appear less intelligent; **dumb-down,** reduced in requirements for the basic skills of literacy and numeracy, *as in* ~ job [63.4 Winter 1988]

Dumbo an air-sea rescue plane [21.2 Apr. 1946]

dumb up to dumb down [63.4 Winter 1988]

dumpie downwardly mobile middle-aged professional [64.2 Summer 1989]; **dumpy** *British* downwardly *or* doubtfully mobile professional, one who expects little success and who does not strive for it [62.4 Winter 1987]

Dunkirk a defeat similar to that suffered by the British at Dunkirk, Belgium, June 1940 [17.3 Oct. 1942]; a defeat (in general) [17.2 Apr. 1942 forematter]

durable something durable [29.1 Feb. 1954]

dust-bowler an inhabitant of the Dust Bowl [16.2 Apr. 1941 forematter]

dustup, dust-up a quarrel, row [29.1 Feb. 1954]

dweeb (teenage slang) an unattractive, unsophisticated person, a nerd, wimp; **dweebish** [65.3 Fall 1990]

D-word detente [63.4 Winter 1988 *s.v.* word]

Dynamite Meteor a robot bomb [19.4 Dec. 1944 forematter]

E [21.3 Oct. 1946 forematter]

eager beaver an excessively industrious worker [23.3–4 Oct.-Dec. 1948]

EAM, E.A.M. Ethnikon Apeleutherotikon Metopon, the National Liberation Front, a left-wing Greek resistance group [21.2 Apr. 1946]

ear-condition *v.* [31.4 Dec. 1956]

ear jewel an earring or other ear ornament; **ear jewelry** ear jewels [45.3–4 Fall-Winter 1970]

earnings-intensive pertaining to an activity that requires much money [60.1 Spring 1985 *s.v.* intensive]

ear-pinner-backer one who pins back ears, or criticizes vigorously [33.4 Dec. 1958]

earthquake bomb a six-ton bomb that penetrates into the earth so deeply that, when its delayed-action fuse explodes, the result is comparable to an earthquake [20.2 Apr. 1945]

earwire, ear wire a wire or post that goes through a pierced ear hole and holds an ornament; a wire that attaches an ornament to the ear; an earring, *also* wire [46.1–2 Spring-Summer 1971]

ear-worthy [16.2 Apr. 1941 forematter]

Eastlandism [32.4 Dec. 1957]

E-boat [21.3 Oct. 1946 forematter]

eco- *prefix* ecology, ecological [47.3–4 Fall-Winter 1972; 63.4 Winter 1988 forematter]; **ecoaction; eco-award; eco-awareness; Eco-Bag; Eco-Commando; eco-consciousness; ecoconversion; eco-design; eco-detergent; eco-drunk; eco-enthusiast; Eco-Farm; ecofreak** one concerned about ecology; **Ecogame; Eco-Gemini; eco-house; eco-journalism; Eco-land; ecology freak** *see* ecofreak; **ecomanagement; ecomodel; Eco-Now; econut; eco-palace; eco-philosophy; Eco-plastics; ecopolicy; ecopolypse; eco-prophet; eco-pundit; eco-skit; ecosteel; ecotactics; ecotage; ecoteur; eco-unit; eco-version** [47.3–4 Fall-Winter 1972 *s.v.* eco]; **eco-anarchism** an anarchistic theory of ecology; **ecocommunity** a human community living in balance with the environment; **ecodefender** one engaged in ecodefense, *also* monkeywrencher; **ecodefense** the sabotage of companies and institutions exploiting or threatening the environment, *also* ecotage, monkeywrenching; **ecodisaster** the disappearance of many species in an environment; **ecofact** a natural object, such as seeds or bones, found with artifacts, revealing how ancient peoples responded to their surroundings; **ecomenu** a selection of simple, healthful foods that make minimal demands on the environment; **econote** a short article on ecology; **ecoraider** an ecodefender [63.4 Winter 1988]

E-COM *trademark* Electronic Computer Originated Mail [59.1 Spring 1984]

E-day Education day; Eisenhower day [21.3 Oct. 1946 forematter]

Edgar an award for writers of detective stories, a porcelain bust of Edgar Allan Poe [23.1 Feb. 1948 forematter]

editorial-ism [32.4 Dec. 1957]

Edsel (from an automobile named after Edsel Ford) a product that does not meet the needs of the time, a failure despite great effort on the part of the producer [60.3 Fall 1985]

educationism the enforcement by schools of education of inflated course requirements and irrelevant standards that discourage talented persons from becoming teachers [32.4 Dec. 1957]

-ee *suffix* one passively related to the referent of the stem [16.4 Dec. 1941 forematter]

-eer *suffix* (from *engineer,* etc.) one energetically or excessively engaged in; to engage energetically or excessively in [18.1 Feb. 1943 forematter]

effective an agency (object, organization, etc.) that successfully effects a desired result [16.4 Dec. 1941]

egg, to lay an (esp. of commercial entertainment) to fail [16.2 Apr. 1941]

egghead, egg-head, egg head *derogatory* an intellectual [28.4 Dec. 1953]; **eggheadism** [32.4 Dec. 1957]

eightfold way the SU-3 THEORY, a rule explaining the grouping of nuclear particles into families, or multiplets, of eight or ten members with the same mass, hypercharge, and isotopic spin [40.2 May 1965]

Eisencrat a Democrat who supported Eisenhower [29.4 Dec. 1954]

Eisenhopper a mechanical grasshopper used by Dwight Eisenhower as a joke to relieve tension at staff meetings [29.3 Oct. 1954]

Eisenhowerism the political ideas associated with Dwight D. Eisenhower [32.4 Dec. 1957]

ELAS, E.L.A.S. Ellinikos Laikos Apeleutherotikos Stratos, the military arm of EAM [21.2 Apr. 1946]; **ELASer** [33.4 Dec. 1958]

elder care pertaining to caregiving, *in* ~ program [64.2 Summer 1989]

election-happy [22.3 Oct. 1947 *s.v.* happy]

electionomics economic policies or actions considered primarily from the standpoint of their possible effect on the election of candidates advocating them [46.1–2 Spring-Summer 1971]

electrojet, electro-jet an electric current that is generated by tidal movements of the atmosphere and flows in the ionosphere [34.1 Feb. 1959]

electroluminescence light from an electric current passing through a powdered phosphor bound in plastic and sprayed on the surface of a glass plate; **electroluminescent** producing electroluminescence [34.1 Feb. 1959]

Electromaster Range [18.2 Apr. 1943 forematter]

electronic operating by electricity, specif. through computer or television [63.4 Winter 1988]; (of surveillance) using electronic instruments [47.3–4 Fall-Winter 1972]

electronic battlefield a combat area supplied with electronic detectors and other devices [63.4 Winter 1988 *s.v.* electronic]

electronic brain a computer [25.2 May 1950]

electronic desk a workstation combining the functions of a telephone, telephone dialer, calculator, typewriter, personal computer, appointments calendar, and address book [63.4 Winter 1988 *s.v.* electronic]

electronic dialer a miniature computer that remembers telephone numbers and can dial them at the touch of a button [63.4 Winter 1988 *s.v.* electronic]

electronic evangelist a preacher on television, televangelist; **electronic evangelistic peer** an electronic evangelist considered relatively to other television evangelists [63.4 Winter 1988 *s.v.* electronic]

electronic-fuel-injected equipped with an electronically controlled fuel injection system [56.3 Fall 1981]

electronic kiosk a form of telecommunications for newspapers and radio stations [63.4 Winter 1988 *s.v.* electronic]

electronic letter box communication by computers [63.4 Winter 1988 *s.v.* electronic]

electronic meeting *British* a meeting of several persons by means of TELECONFERENCING [63.1 Spring 1988]

electronic press the television news media [63.4 Winter 1988 *s.v.* electronic]

electronic security arch a metal detector [63.4 Winter 1988 *s.v.* electronic]

electronic squealer a type of body scanning metal-detector [63.4 Winter 1988 *s.v.* electronic]

electronic time bomb a COMPUTER VIRUS [63.4 Winter 1988 *s.v.* electronic]

electronic vandalism the propagation of a COMPUTER VIRUS [63.4 Winter 1988 *s.v.* electronic]

electronic virus a COMPUTER VIRUS [64.3 Fall 1989 *s.v.* virus]

electronic wallet a smart card used for financial transactions [63.4 Winter 1988 *s.v.* electronic]

electronic yoga biofeedback [63.4 Winter 1988 *s.v.* electronic]

electronuclear, electro-nuclear using nuclear power to produce electricity [32.2 May 1957]

elephant buster one who breaks elephants [23.3–4 Oct.-Dec. 1948 *s.v.* buster]

eleventh commandment *often humorous* any rule observed, or to be observed, as strictly as if it were an addition to the Ten Commandments [60.3 Fall 1985]

el-primo see primo [57.4 Winter 1982]

Elsie LC, landing craft [21.2 Apr. 1946 *illus. s.v.* LCVP]

emporiatrics travel medicine, medical care for travelers [64.2 Summer 1989]

empty calorie a calorie in foods that possess little or no nutritional value, *also* naked calorie [41.2 May 1966; 54.1 Spring 1979]; **empty-caloried** possessing calories but little or no nutritional value [54.1 Spring 1979 *s.v.* empty calorie]

empty nest a demographic group composed of parents whose children no longer live in the parental home; **empty-nest depression** empty-nest syndrome, the feelings of sadness parents often experience when their children leave home; **empty nester** one who no longer has a child living at home; **empty-nest syndrome** changes in the mental and emotional state of parents whose children have grown up and moved away from home, a form of depression [46.3–4 Fall-Winter 1971]

endangered species a group of animate or inanimate objects threatened with extinction or destruction [58.1 Spring 1983]

energy crisis a shortage of fossil fuels and power-generating facilities, with a resulting conflict of energy and environmental objectives [47.3–4 Fall-Winter 1972]

energy guzzler a household appliance that uses much electricity or gas [54.1 Spring 1979]

energy-intensive [60.1 Spring 1985 *s.v.* intensive]

ENIAC electronic numerical integrator and computer [24.2 Apr. 1949]

enrouter one who is en route somewhere [33.4 Dec. 1958]

enterprise zone a location, usu. urban, with unemployment above the national average and concentrations of low and poverty-level incomes, allowed to attract businesses by offering such incentives as lower payroll and capital gains taxes and favorable depreciation schedules, *also* urban enterprise zone [58.2 Summer 1983]

equitist one who believes in equal rights and fairness under the law for all people, regardless of race, sex, nationality, or religion [64.2 Summer 1989]

-er *suffix* someone or something associated with [16.2 Apr. 1941 forematter; 33.4 Dec. 1958 forematter; 34.2 May 1959 forematter]

ergosphere [48.3–4 Fall-Winter 1973 *illus. s.v.* gravitational radiation]

escalate to increase the intensity of hostilities, leading to greater violence; **escalation** [40.3 Oct. 1965]

escalation index an automatic adjustment of income, interest, taxes, etc. to the inflation rate [50.1–2 Spring-Summer 1975]

escape speed; escape velocity (of rockets) a speed that overcomes the pull of gravity [29.4 Dec. 1954]

escort carrier a small aircraft carrier used in convoys [21.2 Apr. 1946]

escort-type [23.2 Apr. 1948 *s.v.* type]

essentialism an educational doctrine stressing time-proven techniques and disciplines, esp. as opposed to the practices of progressivism; **essentialist** an adherent of essentialism in education [19.1 Feb. 1944]

ETO European Theater of Operations [23.1 Feb. 1948]

-ette *suffix* a woman worker [17.4 Dec. 1942 forematter; 18.2 Apr. 1943 forematter]

Eurafrican embracing Europe and Africa [35.4 Dec. 1960 *illus. s.v.* common market]

Euratom a proposed West European pool of atomic research: European Atomic Agency [35.4 Dec. 1960]

Euro- *prefix* European, esp. Western European; pertaining to the European money market or the European Economic Community or Common Market [59.1 Spring 1984; 62.4 Winter 1987 forematter]

Euro-banker *British* a European banker [62.4 Winter 1987]

Eurobanking [59.1 Spring 1984 *s.v.* Euro-]

Euro-bomb *British* an atomic bomb controlled by European governments [62.4 Winter 1987]

Eurocommunism, Euro-Communism, Euro-communism a revision in doctrine and strategy by the principal Communist parties of Western Europe, by which they claim independence from Russia and adherence to democratic principles; **Eurocommunist, Euro-Communist** an adherent or advocate of Eurocommunism [54.2 Summer 1979]

Eurocompany [59.1 Spring 1984 *s.v.* Euro-]

Euroconvertible, Euro-convertible *British* [62.4 Winter 1987]

Eurodebt [59.1 Spring 1984 *s.v.* Euro-]

Eurodefence *British* policies for the defense of Europe by European governments [62.4 Winter 1987]

Eurodeposit [59.1 Spring 1984 *s.v.* Euro-]

Euro D-mark [59.1 Spring 1984 *s.v.* Euro-]

Eurodollar, Euro dollar a dollar deposit in a U.S. bank by foreigners outside the U.S. [39.2 May 1964]

Euro event *British* an artistic performance involving elements from several European countries [62.4 Winter 1987]

Eurofinancing [59.1 Spring 1984 *s.v.* Euro-]

Euroflation inflation in Europe [58.4 Winter 1983 *s.v.* -flation; 59.1 Spring 1984 *s.v.* Euro-]

Euro-loan [59.1 Spring 1984 *s.v.* Euro-]

Euromark [59.1 Spring 1984 *s.v.* Euro-]

Euromarket, Euro-market; Euromart the European Economic Community, or Common Market [35.4 Dec. 1960; 59.1 Spring 1984 *s.v.* Euro-]

Euromast a television tower in Rotterdam [59.1 Spring 1984 *s.v.* Euro-]

Euro-Mediterranean [59.1 Spring 1984 *s.v.* Euro-]

Euromissile a missile deployed in Europe [59.1 Spring 1984 *s.v.* Euro-]

Euronote a financial note sold in Europe but issued in non-European currency [59.1 Spring 1984 *s.v.* Euro-]

Euro-nymphet [59.1 Spring 1984 *s.v.* Euro-]

European type [24.3 Oct. 1949 *s.v.* type]

Europe firster one who considers Europe more important than Asia for American policy [33.4 Dec. 1958 *illus. s.v.* Asia-firster]

Eurosteel the European steel industry [59.1 Spring 1984 *s.v.* Euro-]

Euro-sterling convertible market *British* [62.4 Winter 1987 *illus. s.v.* Euro-banker]

Euro strategic of or dealing with European strategy [59.1 Spring 1984 *s.v.* Euro-]

Eurosubsidy a government subsidy given to a European firm, esp. one exporting its products to the U.S. and underselling American manufacturers [59.1 Spring 1984 *s.v.* Euro-]

Euro-summit *British* a meeting of the heads of government of European nations [62.4 Winter 1987]

Euro(Swiss) franc [59.1 Spring 1984 *s.v.* Euro-]

Euroterrorism [59.1 Spring 1984 *s.v.* Euro-]; **Euro terrorist** *British* a European terrorist, esp. one attacking NATO [62.4 Winter 1987]

Eurotransplant a computerized file of Europeans who need kidney transplants [59.1 Spring 1984 *s.v.* Euro-]

Eurotunnel *British* the Anglo-French company building a rail tunnel under the English channel [62.4 Winter 1987]

Eurounion a labor union composed of workers in the countries of Europe, specifically in the Common Market [59.1 Spring 1984 *s.v.* Euro-]

Euroville a city in which the permanent headquarters of the European Economic Community were to be located [59.1 Spring 1984 *s.v.* Euro-]

Eurovision the European Television Network, with transmitters in various European nations [30.2 May 1955]

Euroyen Japanese yen held by Europeans [59.1 Spring 1984 *s.v.* Euro-]

EVA extravehicular activity in space [41.2 May 1966]

evacuee one who is evacuated [16.4 Dec. 1941 forematter]

excavationist *British* an archeological excavator [63.1 Spring 1988]

excursion class *British* (of airplanes) second class [63.1 Spring 1988]

execu-crime white-collar crime; specif. crime committed by executives in the operation of their offices [64.2 Summer 1989]

executive privilege a privilege associated with being an executive; the claimed right of the executive branch of the government to withhold information from the legislative or judicial branches, based upon the separation of powers [48.3-4 Fall-Winter 1973 *also s.v.* privilege; 55.2 Summer 1980]

exhibition *British* (of buildings) a model, serving as a typical or prime example of its type; intended for demonstration or show rather than use [63.1 Spring 1988]

exit poll a poll of the preferences of voters taken as they leave the voting place; **exit polling** [56.4 Winter 1981]

exosociety, exo-society an intelligent social order beyond the solar system [39.2 May 1964]

exotic fuel a fuel containing chemicals of very high rating, e.g., a combination of hydrogen with boron or lithium [35.4 Dec. 1960]

expansion (of a professional football team) existing as a result of the expansion of a league [44.2 May 1969]

expendable (military use) that may be expended or sacrificed, as in order to preserve more valuable equipment or to delay an enemy [18.2 Apr. 1943]

explosive decompression the sudden, violent release of pressure, as from a ruptured, pressurized vehicle at high altitude or in outer space, like a burst balloon [29.4 Dec. 1954]

export-intensive [60.1 Spring 1985 *s.v.* intensive]

exposure extensive viewing of a public person by audiences, esp. on TV [33.2 May 1958]

ex-reporter's privilege [48.3-4 Fall-Winter 1973 *s.v.* privilege]

Exton a Du Pont plastic [18.1 Feb. 1943 forematter; 19.1 Feb. 1944]

extravehicular pertaining to use in space exploration outside a space vehicle [41.2 May 1966]

eyealyzer; eyelyzer an instrument for detecting the amount of alcohol one has consumed by measuring the alcohol in the vapors emitted from the eyes [64.4 Winter 1989]

eyewitnesser eyewitness report [33.4 Dec. 1958]

faceless regarded not as an individual, but as a member of a group or an impersonal means to an end; of secret identity, anonymous [30.4 Dec. 1955]

face square *British* a wash cloth [63.1 Spring 1988]

facility *British* a service; specif. food service [63.1 Spring 1988]

fact-find *v.* [31.4 Dec. 1956]; **fact finder, fact-finder** a researcher, investigator [23.3-4 Oct.-Dec. 1948]

factory buster, factory-buster a six-ton missile [21.2 Apr. 1946; 23.3-4 Oct.-Dec. 1948 *s.v.* buster]

factory-ship *v.* [31.4 Dec. 1956]

fag-bashing *British* beating up homosexuals [62.4 Winter 1987 forematter]

fair one an arranged open fight between representatives of two gangs to settle differences between the groups, contrasted with *rumble* [39.2 May 1964]

fair-trade *usu. as participle* fair-traded, to require the sale of a product at a listed price; **fair trading** [29.4 Dec. 1954]

fallout, fall-out the descent of radioactive particles to earth from an atomic explosion [29.1 Feb. 1954 *s.v.* fall out]

falsie *usu. pl.* a breast-shaped filler for a brassiere cup [25.1 Feb. 1950]

family an operating unit of the Cosa Nostra in a particular geographic area [39.2 May 1964]

family (TV) hour; family time; family viewing hour; family viewing time the two-hour period of prime television time during which programs may not be aired if they are unsuitable for children or if they might offend some viewers, *also* FVT [51.3–4 Fall-Winter 1976]

family viewing (of TV programs) suitable for children, not offensive to viewers generally, *see* family hour [51.3–4 Fall-Winter 1976]

fanciable *British* sexually attractive [63.1 Spring 1988]

fancyism a voguish expression like "historical perspective" [59.2 Summer 1984 *illus. s.v.* Newspeakism]

fanference a conference of fantasy fiction fans [27.3 Oct. 1952 *illus. s.v.* fanzine]

fan-jet (engine) a jet engine in which a ducted fan or ducted propeller is used to take in air to augment the gases of combustion in the jet stream [39.3 Oct. 1964]

fanny flask a flask carried in a belt around the waist [65.1 Spring 1990]

fanny pack a pouchlike container strapped around the waist, *also* belt bag, rumptaske [65.1 Spring 1990]

fanzine a magazine for fans of fantasy fiction [27.3 Oct. 1952]

fast food mass-produced, standardized food sold in restaurants specializing in quick but minimal service; **fast-food** pertaining to fast food [46.1–2 Spring-Summer 1971]

fast-forward *British* to move rapidly forward on a video-recorder tape; to move rapidly forward in time [62.4 Winter 1987]

fast lane the life style of those who desire immediate gratification and lack restraint and commitment [59.4 Winter 1984]

father (of a chapel) *British* the chairman of a printers' or journalists' local union [63.1 Spring 1988]

fattypuff *British* one inclined to put on weight, a pleasingly plump, socially agreeable person [62.4 Winter 1987]

fax facsimile transmission; specif. facsimile newspaper [24.3 Oct. 1949]; *British* facts (a commercial spelling, as in *Ceefax*, a BBC information broadcasting system, and FILOFAX) [62.4 Winter 1987; 63.2 Summer 1988]

F day Flight day [21.3 Oct. 1946 forematter]

featherbed (in railroading) pertaining to or protecting featherbedding, *as in* ~ practices, ~ rules [19.4 Dec. 1944; 35.1 Feb. 1960]; **featherbedding** limiting of work or output to spread jobs and prevent unemployment [19.4 Dec. 1944]

feederliner [33.4 Dec. 1958]

fellow-travel *v.* [31.4 Dec. 1956]

fellow traveler one who does not accept all of another's aims, but has enough in common to accompany in a comradely fashion part of the way [16.2 Apr. 1941]

fellow traveler circuit [24.4 Dec. 1949 forematter]

fellow-traveling an act or acts characteristic of fellow travelers [16.4 Dec. 1941]

feminine hygiene *euphemism* contraception [17.2 Apr. 1942 forematter]

femspeak language characteristics of the women's liberation movement [63.2 Summer 1988 *s.v.* speak]

fence buster, fence-buster one who hits a home run in baseball [23.3–4 Oct.-Dec. 1948 *s.v.* buster]

Festung Europa FORTRESS EUROPE [19.3 Oct. 1944]

FFI, F.F.I. the French Forces of the Interior [21.2 Apr. 1946]

Fidelismo; Fidelism the revolutionary doctrines and practices of Fidel Castro, *also* Castroism; **Fidelista** a follower of Fidel Castro, an adherent to his program [36.3 Oct. 1961]

Fido Fog Investigation Dispersal Operation, a system of gasoline-filled pipes around an airfield that dissipate fog by heating the air with vaporized gasoline burning from hundreds of jets [21.2 Apr. 1946]

field test, field-test *v.* [31.3 Oct. 1956; 31.4 Dec. 1956]

fifth basket environmental problems, drugs, international terrorism and missile proliferation as topics for Soviet-American negotiation [65.2 Summer 1990]

fifty-oner (modeled on *forty-niner*) a miner in 1951 [33.4 Dec. 1958]

52-20 club, 52-20 Club veterans' unemployment compensation for 52 weeks at $20 a week [24.1 Feb. 1949]

fighterbomber, fighter-bomber, fighter bomber a regulation pursuit airplane fitted with an under-fuselage mounting for carrying a 500-pound delayed-action bomb [20.4 Dec. 1945]

fighter strip an airstrip [20.2 Apr. 1945]

fight-happy punch drunk [22.3 Oct. 1947 *s.v.* happy]

filipin an antibiotic, antifungal agent discovered in soil from the Philippines [32.2 May 1957]

fill in supply with information, *esp.* ~ on [31.4 Dec. 1956]; **fill-in** a brief sketch of background information, *esp. in* give a ~ [27.1 Feb. 1952]

Filofax *trademark, British* a PERSONAL ORGANISER [62.4 Winter 1987]

Fin-Creep Financial Committee to Re-Elect the President, Richard Nixon, in the 1972 campaign [47.3–4 Fall-Winter 1972]

finding a presidential authorization for covert actions, usu. undertaken by the CIA [63.3 Fall 1988]

finger-catch *v.* [31.3 Oct. 1956]

fingerprinting DNA fingerprinting [64.4 Winter 1989]

fire bomb, fire-bomb an incendiary bomb [21.4 Dec. 1946]

fireman a relief pitcher in baseball [26.2 May 1951]

firepower, fire-power the relative force and intensity of an army's explosive weapons; the ballistic force or destructive capability of a weapon [17.3 Oct. 1942 forematter; 17.4 Dec. 1942; 22.2 Apr. 1947]

firestorm, fire storm an intense, widespread fire whose heat creates strong air currents, resulting esp. from massive bombing [29.4 Dec. 1954]; a public outcry, excited controversy [49.1–2 Spring-Summer 1974]

firette a woman firefighter [17.4 Dec. 1942 forematter]

first termer one serving a first term in public office [16.2 Apr. 1941 forematter]

fishbite a WEDGY [65.3 Fall 1990 forematter]

fish bowl *see* goldfish bowl [28.3 Oct. 1953]

fish-in a protest action against fishing restrictions [39.3 Oct. 1964 *s.v.* in]

fishing expedition (in law) random questioning of a witness without definite purpose in the hope of eliciting useful information [48.1–2 Spring-Summer 1973; 49.3–4 Fall-Winter 1974]

fishyback, fishy-back pertaining to coordinated land-water transportation of freight by truck-trailers carried on ships; **fishybacking** transporting freight by truck-trailers carried on ships [32.2 May 1957]

fission-fusion-fission pertaining to a U-bomb or explosive device in which a plutonium or U–235 (fission) bomb triggers a hydrogen (fusion) explosion, from which fast neutrons fission a mantle of uranium (U–238) wrapped around the entire device [34.1 Feb. 1959]

5-incher a gun with a bore of 5 inches [33.4 Dec. 1958]

five percenter, five-percenter, five-per-center, 5 percenter one who helps a business get government contracts in return for a percentage fee [25.1 Feb. 1950 *s.v.* five]; **five percentism, 5 percentism** the practice of charging fees for helping to obtain government contracts [25.1 Feb. 1950]

fixit shop, fix-it shop a repair shop [28.3 Oct. 1953]

flack *see* flak [17.3 Oct. 1942]

flag advertising *British* advertising by a group, such as solicitors, under a single identification or logo [63.1 Spring 1988]

flag plot *v.* [31.3 Oct. 1956]

flag station; flag stop a small town or minor stop on a railroad line [28.1 Feb. 1953 forematter]

flak antiaircraft fire, *also* ack-ack [17.2 Apr. 1942 forematter; 17.3 Oct. 1942; 21.3 Oct. 1946 forematter]

flak happy suffering combat fatigue; affected by sodium pentothal [22.3 Oct. 1947 *s.v.* happy]; **Flak Happy** name of a Flying Fortress [19.1 Feb. 1944 forematter]

flash sudden and violent [16.4 Dec. 1941]; *British* (extension of military use) a piece of cloth sewn to a garment as an ornament, advertising, or identification [63.1 Spring 1988]

flashback an interruption in the sequence to introduce an event prior to those being presented [18.1 Feb. 1943]

flash-photograph *v.* [31.3 Oct. 1956]

flat-footed, catch to catch (one) in such a way that a prompt defense or other suitable reaction is impossible [18.1 Feb. 1943]

-flation *suffix* inflation [58.4 Winter 1983]

flattener-outer [33.4 Dec. 1958]

flat-top an aircraft carrier [19.3 Oct. 1944]

fleet-based [19.3 Oct. 1944 forematter; 20.2 Apr. 1945 forematter]

Fleur-o-lier (from *chandelier*) [18.4 Dec. 1943 forematter]

flexible (work) time; flexitime; flextime a work schedule that allows an employee to choose working hours within certain guidelines [54.1 Spring 1979]

flight deliver *v.* [31.3 Oct. 1956]

flight engineer an officer responsible for the engines of an airplane [23.1 Feb. 1948 *s.v.* flight]

flight test *v.* [31.3 Oct. 1956]; **flight testing** taking an aircraft through trial runs [22.3 Oct. 1947]

flip, Flip floating instrument platform, a vessel used for oceanic research that flips into a bow-up position for making observations [41.2 May 1966]

flipping a renewal of a loan with additional interest, charging interest on interest; **flipper** one who renews a small loan with added interest, a loan shark [47.3–4 Fall-Winter 1972]

flitter bomb a ROBOT BOMB [19.4 Dec. 1944 forematter]

float (of currency) to fluctuate in value on the international exchange according to demand; **floating** [45.3–4 Fall-Winter 1970]

Floodgate a purported scandal involving Congressman Daniel Flood [59.2 Summer 1984 *s.v.* -gate]

floor a lower limit [16.4 Dec. 1941]

flour-paste *v.* [31.3 Oct. 1956]

fly-bomb a robot bomb [19.4 Dec. 1944 forematter]

flyboy an airforce pilot [26.1 Feb. 1951]

fly-by-wire a method of controlling a space rocket in which the pilot uses a manual stick to operate normally automatic fuel jets [38.3 Oct. 1963]

flyer fun-loving youth en route (to success), *also* baby buster [64.1 Spring 1989]

fly-in an outdoor movie theater that customers can fly to and watch from their planes, an aeronautical drive-in movie [29.4 Dec. 1954; 30.2 May 1955]

flying bomb *see* buzz bomb [19.4 Dec. 1944]

flying boxcar, flying box-car, flying box car a cargo plane; a bomber [20.4 Dec. 1945]

flying disc; flying disk a disk-shaped unidentified flying object [24.1 Feb. 1949]

flying jeep the Aeronica L–3 Defender, the Piper L–4B–4, or the Taylorcraft L–2A airplane [21.2 Apr. 1946]

flying laboratory an experimental airplane equipped with various testing instruments [24.3 Oct. 1949]

flying saucer *see* flying disc [24.1 Feb. 1949]; **flyingsaucerism** belief in the reality of flying saucers [32.4 Dec. 1957]

flying stovepipe a RAMJET aircraft [23.3–4 Oct.-Dec. 1948]

fly-past a review of aircraft [28.3 Oct. 1953]

FM frequency modulation [21.3 Oct. 1946 forematter]

folknik a folk singer or fan of folksongs and folk singers [41.2 May 1966]

folliette a female performer in the follies [17.4 Dec. 1942 forematter]

Folsomism [32.4 Dec. 1957]

foodgate [56.4 Winter 1981 *s.v.* -gate]

food hall *British* a grocery store or department [63.1 Spring 1988 *s.v.* hall]

foodlegger a wartime food racketeer [18.1 Feb. 1943 forematter]

food stylist one who prepares food to be photographed for advertisements, cook books, etc. [60.3 Fall 1985]

footbag a beanbag used in playing the game of HACKY SACK [64.2 Summer 1989]

footballing *British* resulting from or pertaining to football, i.e., soccer [63.1 Spring 1988]

footborne [20.2 Apr. 1945 forematter]

footlight-happy stagestruck [19.1 Feb. 1944 forematter]

footnotarianism scholarly documentation, esp. in footnotes [32.4 Dec. 1957]

Fordonomics U.S. President Gerald R. Ford's economic policies [49.3–4 Fall-Winter 1974]

forever wild (esp. of forest lands) legally protected against commercial development; **forever wilder** one who favors the preservation of forest lands in the wild state [60.4 Winter 1985]

for-ism expressing one's principles as support for that with which one agrees, having predominantly affirmative attitudes; *cf.* against-ism [32.4 Dec. 1957]

formula-diet *v.* [31.3 Oct. 1956]

fortbuster a small fuse [23.3–4 Oct.-Dec. 1948 *s.v.* buster]

Fortress Europe Europe within its outer defenses, described by Nazis as a fortress, *also* Festung Europa [19.3 Oct. 1944]

fortysomething pertaining to persons in their forties [65.2 Summer 1990]

Fosdic, FOSDIC Film Optical Sensing Device for Input to Computers, an electrical scanner that converts census data sheets to magnetic-tape records [35.4 Dec. 1960]

foundation-hop to move from one granting agency to another [54.1 Spring 1979 *s.v.* hop]

four-channel any of several methods for recording and playing back sound signals through four loudspeakers so that the listener hears, or has the illusion of hearing, separate elements of the original signal with lateral separation (as in conventional stereo) and also front-to-rear separation; the sound produced by any of these techniques; equipment for the playback of four-channel sound; *attrib.* designed for the recording, broadcasting, or reproduction of sound by dividing the original signal into four such distinct segments; *also* quadriphonic [48.1–2 Spring-Summer 1973]

4F [21.4 Dec. 1946 forematter]

four-letter word an obscene word; specif. one consisting of four letters [24.2 Apr. 1949 forematter; 25.2 May 1950]

4 percenter one who engages in influence peddling with the Government for a fee of four percent [29.3 Oct. 1954]

four-placer an airplane seating four persons [33.4 Dec. 1958]

fourth force (in French politics) an alliance of radicals and independent rightists, or of centrists and rightists [28.3 Oct. 1953]

fourth leader *British* the third and final humorous editorial in the Saturday *Times* newspaper [63.1 Spring 1988]

fourth termer one in a fourth term [33.4 Dec. 1958]

four-two-one syndrome a Chinese family pattern of single children over three generations with its consequent social problems [65.1 Spring 1990]

fox hole a hole in the ground where troops may hide, for protection or ambush [17.4 Dec. 1942 forematter; 18.2 Apr. 1943]

foxhole circuit, fox-hole circuit a theater circuit at the fighting fronts played by American troupes [21.3 Oct. 1946; 24.4 Dec. 1949 forematter]

frame *British* a portable stand used by an incapacitated or handicapped person as an aid in walking, a walker [63.1 Spring 1988]

frame of reference context, viewpoint, a set of ideas by which matters are interpreted [26.4 Dec. 1951]

fraternization the amicable intercultural association between people living in a different country and the indigenous people of that country; specif. military persons stationed overseas engaging in sexual liaisons with foreign nationals; **fraternize** to have close relations, usu. sexual (with a female enemy national); **fraternizing** [22.2 Apr. 1947]

fraud squad a unit investigating cases of suspected fraud, as in Medicaid claims [54.3 Fall 1979]

freedom concerning an organized protest of racial segregation or one who takes part in such a protest; **freedom ride** a protest against bus terminal segregation; **freedom rider** one who engages in freedom rides; **freedom stay-out; freedom walker** one who takes part in a walk protesting racial segregation [40.2 May 1965]

free enterprise the right of all people to work or trade where they like, save and invest according to their own judgment, run their businesses as they wish, and take the consequences of gain or loss, *also* private enterprise [22.2 Apr. 1947; 24.3 Oct. 1949]; **free-enterpriser** one who supports free enterprise [33.4 Dec. 1958]

free spinner a consultant or academic unassociated with a political campaign who analyzes events with relative objectivity; **free spinning** the unbiased analysis of political events [63.3 Fall 1988]

freeway an express highway [24.1 Feb. 1949]

free wheel pertaining to vehicles not confined by tracks [24.4 Dec. 1949]

free wheeling see free wheel; free, easy, open, unrestrained [24.4 Dec. 1949]

freeze (esp. of the standardization of industrial design so as to make mass production possible) to arrest, at a given stage, the expenditure of (money) or the development or evolution of (a product), *as in* ~ funds, ~ models [17.4 Dec. 1942 forematter; 19.1 Feb. 1944]

freeze-dried preserved by the extraction of moisture as vapor while the preserved substance is frozen; **freeze-drying** preservation by rapid freezing followed by dehydration by microwave energy [36.4 Dec. 1961]

French (of earrings) (with) a clip attachment, *in* ~ back [45.3–4 Fall-Winter 1970]

French-type [23.2 Apr. 1948 *s.v.* type]

friendly user-friendly, easy to operate, even without scientific or technical expertise [60.1 Spring 1985]

fringe parking vehicular parking on the outskirts of a city's business district [25.1 Feb. 1950]

frogman, frog man a diver wearing a wetsuit and fins and carrying oxygen for sustained underwater activity [26.2 May 1951]

front a political or other similar alliance arraying diverse forces; an outwardly respectable agent serving as a façade for a disreputable activity; an individual or group serving as the real or nominal head or representative of an enterprise or movement to lend it prestige, concealment, etc.; to act as a political front for [17.2 Apr. 1942 forematter; 17.3 Oct. 1942]; leading in a race, *see* front-running [26.3 Oct. 1951]

front burner high priority, *as in* put on the ~ 'give high priority to'; *attrib.* having high priority [54.2 Summer 1979]

front edge the CUTTING EDGE [60.1 Spring 1985]

front four the guards and tackles on the defensive unit of a football team [48.1–2 Spring-Summer 1973]

front organization an organization, esp. political, that lends its offices to some insidious purpose, giving the latter an air of respectability [16.2 Apr. 1941]

front runner, front-runner a candidate who is expected to win an election [28.3 Oct. 1953]

front-running (in sports) being in the lead throughout a race; leading, in first position [26.3 Oct. 1951; 28.3 Oct. 1953]; (of a broker or brokerage house) executing one's own trades before those of one's customers [63.3 Fall 1988]

frosted jeans jeans with white, frost-like streaks, *also* acid jeans [65.1 Spring 1990]

frozen food food frozen quickly to retain flavor and nourishment [23.2 Apr. 1948]

fruitcake crazy, nuts, bananas [51.3–4 Fall-Winter 1976]

fuddie-duddie; fuddy-duddy a fussy, ineffective person [16.2 Apr. 1941]

fuel cell a battery in which chemicals interact to produce an electric charge and by-products [36.4 Dec. 1961]

fuel-injected (of an engine) having the fuel supplied to the combustion chambers by a fuel injection system; (of an automobile) powered by such an engine [56.3 Fall 1981]

fuel-intensive [60.1 Spring 1985 *s.v.* intensive]

full-dress involving a display of activity for which full preparations are made; complete in all details, carried on by all possible means [17.3 Oct. 1942 forematter; 17.4 Dec. 1942; 29.1 Feb. 1954]

full surround-sound [48.1–2 Spring-Summer 1973 *s.v.* surround-sound]

fundraiser, fund-raiser, fund raiser an event held to raise money, esp. for a charitable or political organization; a product sold by members of an organization to raise money [51.3–4 Fall-Winter 1976; 55.2 Summer 1980]

furlough *usu. passive* to lay (employees) off work [35.4 Dec. 1960]

furnace a nuclear reactor [26.3 Oct. 1951]

fusion in a jar; fusion in a bottle COLD FUSION [65.2 Summer 1990]

futurama the General Motors exhibit at the World's Fair, 1939–40, portraying the future; any similar portrayal [17.3 Oct. 1942 forematter; 17.4 Dec. 1942]

Fuzzy Wuzzy Oscar an effigy of a Fiji Islander mounted on a fragment of Japanese airplane metal, presented to Humphrey Bogart and Greer Garson by General MacArthur's troops, *also* GI Oscar [23.1 Feb. 1948 forematter]

FVT FAMILY VIEWING TIME, *also* family (TV) hour [51.3–4 Fall-Winter 1976]

F-word fuck [63.4 Winter 1988 *s.v.* word]

gack a sweet gelatinous substance [65.1 Spring 1990]

gadget happy eager for gadgets [22.3 Oct. 1947 *s.v.* happy]

gageroos gags, jokes [16.4 Dec. 1941 forematter]

Gainesville green marijuana grown in Gainesville, Florida [57.4 Winter 1982]

galaxy-hop [47.3–4 Fall-Winter 1972 *s.v.* hop]

gallery-hop [47.3–4 Fall-Winter 1972 *s.v.* hop; 48.1–2 Spring-Summer 1973 *s.v.* hop]

gamecaster a sports reporter [18.2 Apr. 1943 forematter]

game-winner a hit in baseball or a kick in football that produces the winning score [57.2 Summer 1982]

gangbuster, gang-buster an officer engaged in breaking up organized crime [17.4 Dec. 1942 forematter; 18.2 Apr. 1943; 23.3–4 Oct.-Dec. 1948 *s.v.* buster]

gang-tackle *v.* [31.3 Oct. 1956]

garbage poll an estimation of an election trend by examining discarded sample ballots [56.4 Winter 1981 forematter]

garrison finish [17.4 Dec. 1942 forematter]

garrison state an isolationist country; a country whose resources are primarily diverted to military use; a police state [27.1 Feb. 1952]

gasahol a fuel consisting of 90 percent gasoline and 10 percent denatured alcohol [54.1 Spring 1979]

gas guzzler an automobile that has a high rate of gasoline consumption per mile; one who manufactures or drives such an automobile; **gas-guzzling** (of cars) consuming much gasoline [54.1 Spring 1979]

gas hog one who uses too much gasoline, esp. one who abuses gasoline-rationing privileges [17.3 Oct. 1942]

gas legger [18.1 Feb. 1943 forematter]

gasohol *see* gasahol [54.1 Spring 1979]

-gate *suffix* a scandal involving charges of corruption and usu. of coverup (added to a noun that in some way suggests the particular scandal), *also facetious* [53.3 Fall 1978; 54.4 Winter 1979 forematter; 56.4 Winter 1981; 59.2 Summer 1984]

gategate [56.4 Winter 1981 *s.v.* -gate]

gatenik a fancier of *-gate* words [56.4 Winter 1981]

Gaullism [32.4 Dec. 1957]

gavel-to-gavel from beginning to end, esp. of TV reportage of political conventions; to watch gavel-to-gavel TV coverage of a convention [57.1 Spring 1982]

gawker one who gawks [33.4 Dec. 1958]

gazunder *British* (of a potential property-buyer, usu. of residential property) to frustrate a property-seller by lowering the amount of money offered between the agreement to buy and the closing of the contract, thus requiring the seller either to accept less than expected or to look for another buyer; **gazundering; gazunderer** a property buyer who engages in gazundering [65.3 Fall 1990]

GCA Ground Controlled Approach, a radar system for guiding aircraft in blind landings [22.2 Apr. 1947]

Gee Whizzer a lightweight jet airplane [33.4 Dec. 1958]

GEM ground effect machine, a device that skims over the ground or water on streams of air at speeds up to 175 miles an hour [40.2 May 1965]

gender gap the difference between men and women in attitude toward an issue [58.2 Summer 1983]

gender struggle *British* a disagreement involving discrimination against a woman because of her sex [63.1 Spring 1988]

generational politics (of a candidate) appeal to voters on the basis of youth; **generational politician** a politician who relies on a youthful image to sway voters [63.3 Fall 1988]

genesis bean; genesis rock; genesis stone a specimen of lunar or meteoric material believed to retain characteristics of rock formed early in the development of the solar system [50.1–2 Spring-Summer 1975]

genetically engineered having a genetic code modified by technological means; **genetic engineer** one who modifies the genetic code in living organisms [57.2 Summer 1982]

genetic fingerprint the distinctive structure of the DNA in an individual's cells, used as a means of identification, *also* DNA print; **genetic fingerprinting** identification, esp. for legal purposes, by analyzing the structure of the DNA in an individual's cells, *also* DNA fingerprinting [64.4 Winter 1989]

genocide the extermination of racial and national groups [21.3 Oct. 1946]

Germany firster a German Social Democrat [33.4 Dec. 1958]

Geronimo the name of an Indian chief, used as a battle cry by U.S. paratroops during World War II [23.2 Apr. 1948]

Gertrude a small sterling silver kangaroo given to an author whose book has sold a million copies in a Pocket edition [23.1 Feb. 1948 forematter]

get-rich-quicker one who wishes to make a large amount of money easily and quickly through free enterprise [33.4 Dec. 1958]

G-410 a convenience designation of penta-chlor-phenol [22.2 Apr. 1947 forematter]

Ghana a nation formed from the former British crown colony of the Gold Coast and the protectorate of Togoland, named for an ancient African empire; **Ghanian** a citizen of Ghana [34.1 Feb. 1959]

ghillie look [45.3–4 Fall-Winter 1970 *s.v.* look]

ghost a faint second image on a TV screen [26.1 Feb. 1951]; an applicant who is accepted by a college but does not register [39.2 May 1964]

ghost buster, ghost-buster an exposer of spiritualistic mediums [23.3–4 Oct.-Dec. 1948 *s.v.* buster]

GI, G.I. an American soldier [21.2 Apr. 1946; 21.3 Oct. 1946 forematter]

gift-loan *v.* [31.3 Oct. 1956]

gift-price *v.* [31.3 Oct. 1956]

gift-wrap *v.* [31.3 Oct. 1956]

GI Joe, G.I. Joe *see* GI [21.2 Apr. 1946]

gin up to create, produce; to increase, encourage [64.1 Spring 1989]

GI Oscar Fuzzy Wuzzy Oscar [23.1 Feb. 1948 forematter]

girlie; girly (of publications and entertainment) featuring the display of scantily clad young women; a picture of a scantily clad young woman, a pin-up; a magazine that includes such pictures [30.4 Dec. 1955]; **girly** *British* pertaining to a group of women friends who meet frequently, *as in* ~ lunch [63.1 Spring 1988]

giveaway (show); giveaway program an audience-participation radio program in which the successful contestants receive prizes [24.4 Dec. 1949]

give-up the splitting of commissions between two or more brokerage houses on a single securities transaction [44.1 Feb. 1969]

glacier happy psychologically affected by living in Iceland [19.1 Feb. 1944 forematter]

glamorette [17.4 Dec. 1942 forematter]

glass ceiling unacknowledged prejudice based on race or sex that prevents corporate advancement in management [65.2 Summer 1990]

gleep graphite low energy experimental pile, an atomic pile in the U.K. [23.2 Apr. 1948]

glide bomb, glide-bomb to bomb, from an airplane, by descending at an angle of less than 65 degrees from the horizontal when releasing bombs; a bomb used in glide-bombing [20.4 Dec. 1945]

glide path the path of descent of an airplane described by a radio beam [26.2 May 1951]

glider-borne [19.3 Oct. 1944 forematter; 20.2 Apr. 1945 forematter]

gliding shift; gliding time; gliding work(ing) hours; gliding working time a flexible work time system in which workers change hours from day to day [54.1 Spring 1979]

global bomber a B–36 airplane that can carry an atomic bomb great distances [27.3 Oct. 1952]

globaler [33.4 Dec. 1958]

globaloney a foreign policy directed toward international welfare as distinct from narrowly national interests; any unrealistic foreign policy [65.2 Summer 1990]

Globemaster [21.2 Apr. 1946 forematter]

globflation global inflation [58.4 Winter 1983 *s.v.* -flation]

glower and grin the theatrical masks of tragedy and comedy [46.1–2 Spring-Summer 1971 *illus. s.v.* semi-porno]

glutenburger [18.2 Apr. 1943 forematter]

gobbledygook; gobbledegook talk or writing that is long, pompous, vague, involved, usu. with Latinized words; also talk or writing that is merely long, even though the words are fairly simple, with repetition of that which could have been said in a few words [20.3 Oct. 1945; 22.3 Oct. 1947]

Gobelism a linguistic expression associated with the comedian George Gobel, such as "Well, I'll be a dirty bird" or "Cri-mi-nentlies" [32.4 Dec. 1957]

go double platinum to sell two million copies of a record album [57.2 Summer 1982 *s.v.* platinum]

go-it-aloneism isolationism [32.4 Dec. 1957]

gold fish bowl, gold-fish bowl a place or circumstance open to public scrutiny [28.3 Oct. 1953]

golden *British* (in combination with a metaphorical noun) pertaining to a large financial benefit given to an employee on association with or severance from a business in order to protect the interests of either the employee or business [62.4 Winter 1987]

golden curtain [25.3 Oct. 1950 forematter]

golden goodbye *British* a retirement benefit [62.4 Winter 1987 *s.v.* golden]

golden handcuff incentives or perquisites offered to key employees to keep them from taking a position with a different employer [58.2 Summer 1983; *British* 62.4 Winter 1987 *s.v.* golden]

golden handshake; golden hello *British* a hiring bonus [62.4 Winter 1987 *s.v.* golden]

golden parachute a provision in an employment contract stipulating that in the event of a takeover by another company the employee, usu. an important executive, may resign without loss of salary and various perquisites until the completion of the contract period [58.2 Summer 1983; *British* 62.4 Winter 1987 *s.v.* golden]

golden shackle *British* a benefit designed to discourage resignations [62.4 Winter 1987 *s.v.* golden]

golden welcoming shake *British* a hiring bonus [62.4 Winter 1987 *s.v.* golden]

Goldingate [56.4 Winter 1981 *s.v.* -gate]

Goldwaterism the conservative policies of Barry Goldwater, Republican candidate for president in 1964 [40.2 May 1965; 40.3 Oct. 1965]; **Goldwaterite** an adherent of Goldwaterism [40.2 May 1965]

gomer a military trainee, regarded as stupid and clumsy; a member of the U.S. Marine Corps; a Communist Vietnamese soldier or airman; a stupid person; a hospital patient who is dirty, undesirable, senile, or unresponsive to treatment, esp. a poor or homeless older man who frequently seeks emergency-room treatment for minor or imaginary complaints; an older patient requiring long-term care; **gomere, gomerette** a female gomer; **gomeroid** resembling a gomer, gomerlike [64.2 Summer 1989]

gone platinum (of a recording artist) having made a record album that has sold a million copies [57.2 Summer 1982 *s.v.* platinum]

go-no go, go-no-go (of a rocket missile launch) so controlled at the end of the countdown as to permit an instantaneous change in decision on whether to launch or not; a specified point on a runway used as a decision point for aborting, beyond which take-off is inevitable [39.3 Oct. 1964]

good-bad type; good type [23.2 Apr. 1948 forematter]

goofus a stupid person [64.2 Summer 1989]

goomer *see* gomer [64.2 Summer 1989]

goon a ruffian, esp. a thug employed in labor disputes, *esp. in* ~ squad [18.2 Apr. 1943]

goose to feed (gasoline into an engine) in irregular spurts [18.1 Feb. 1943]

GOP-er a Republican [33.4 Dec. 1958]

go platinum to thrive, prosper, do very well; to sell in large numbers [57.2 Summer 1982 *s.v.* platinum]

go-show an airline passenger without a reservation who is sent to the airport in hope of securing the seat of a no-show [24.2 Apr. 1949]

goulash communism *British* communism as practiced in Eastern Europe, specif. Hungary [63.1 Spring 1988]

governmentese government-speak [59.4 Winter 1984 forematter]

government-speak jargon used by government officials, esp. those in the federal government [59.4 Winter 1984 *s.v.* speak]

grace-hoper one who hopes for grace; specif. an author who wants readers with understanding and appreciation [33.4 Dec. 1958]

gradeflation grade inflation [58.4 Winter 1983 *s.v.* -flation]

granny-bashing *British* the violent mistreatment of the elderly; *ironic* visiting old people as a form of community ser-

vice to help them with shopping and odd jobs or to entertain them [62.4 Winter 1987]

granny track the responsibility to care for aging parents, *also* daughter track [65.3 Fall 1990]

grass-feed *v.* [31.3 Oct. 1956]

grasshopper a high-winged cabin monoplane of the tandem type with low landing and take-off speeds enabling it to be operated from small fields [19.3 Oct. 1944]

grass rooter a politician in touch with the grass roots [33.4 Dec. 1958]

grass trap a stretch of highway where the police stop long-haired or bearded drivers who may be transporting marijuana [57.4 Winter 1982]

graveyard shift a shift in industry from about midnight to about 8 am [18.4 Dec. 1943]

gravitational radiation gravity conceived as a force emitted by bodies [48.3–4 Fall-Winter 1973]

gray intermediate, between extremes, indeterminate, *as in* ~ war, ~ area, ~ time [29.4 Dec. 1954]

gray market a market where goods can be bought legally but at exorbitant prices [23.2 Apr. 1948; 25.2 May 1950 forematter; 29.4 Dec. 1954 *s.v.* gray]; **gray marketeer, gray-marketeer** one who trades on the gray market [23.3–4 Oct.-Dec. 1948]

gray mobilization incomplete mobilization [27.3 Oct. 1952; 29.4 Dec. 1954 *s.v.* gray]

grayout, grey out (esp. of pilots) to become semiconscious [28.1 Feb. 1953; 29.4 Dec. 1954 *s.v.* gray]

great lie *see* big lie [27.3 Oct. 1952]

green curtain [25.3 Oct. 1950 forematter]

greeterette [17.4 Dec. 1942 forematter]

grey market *see* gray market [23.2 Apr. 1948]

grey marketeer *see* gray marketeer [23.3–4 Oct.-Dec. 1948]

gridcaster an announcer of football contests [18.2 Apr. 1943 forematter]

gridlock a complete stoppage, failure to make any progress [59.1 Spring 1984]

grief work the process by which a bereaved person deals with grief [58.2 Summer 1983]

ground to suspend the license of, to forbid (a person) to drive a car, *as in* ~ a jockey, ~ an automobile driver [30.4 Dec. 1955]

ground cushion the buoyancy a helicopter receives from the mass of air forced downward from its rotors [32.2 May 1957]

ground transport *v.* [31.3 Oct. 1956]

ground zero the point directly under a bomb's explosion in the air [27.3 Oct. 1952]

GR-S-10 a synthetic rubber [22.2 Apr. 1947 forematter]

g-string a breechcloth, esp. one used by a striptease dancer [16.2 Apr. 1941]

G-suit an anti gravity suit to prevent fliers from blacking out in steep dives [21.2 Apr. 1946]

guesstimate an estimate based on little information [28.3 Oct. 1953]

guest *euphemism* small in size [17.2 Apr. 1942 forematter]

guest-conduct to conduct an orchestra as a guest [26.1 Feb. 1951; 31.3 Oct. 1956]

guestimate *see* guesstimate [28.3 Oct. 1953]

guestworker, guest worker a Mexican laborer legally in the U.S. [59.1 Spring 1984]

guided missile a projectile guided by remote control [22.3 Oct. 1947]

Guilder a member of the American Newspaper Guild [16.2 Apr. 1941 forematter]

guinea pig any object of experimentation, esp. if conceived as victimized [16.4 Dec. 1941]

guitar look [45.3–4 Fall-Winter 1970 *s.v.* look]

gum bubbler [33.4 Dec. 1958]

gun to accelerate (an automobile) [17.2 Apr. 1942 forematter; 17.3 Oct. 1942 forematter]

gunboat diplomacy [46.3–4 Fall-Winter 1971 forematter]

gun buster [23.3–4 Oct.-Dec. 1948 *s.v.* buster]

guppie grown-up pauper [60.1 Spring 1985 forematter]; *British* Green yuppie, an ecological-minded yuppie [62.4 Winter 1987 *cited s.v.* guppy]

guppy a small, speedy snorkel submarine [24.1 Feb. 1949; 26.1 Feb. 1951]; *British* gay urban professional; greedy upwardly mobile professional [62.4 Winter 1987]

guzzler a GAS GUZZLER [54.1 Spring 1979]

Gymnasium Circuit [24.4 Dec. 1949 forematter]

hackie a cabbie [28.1 Feb. 1953]

Hacky Sack *trademark* a small beanbag used in a game whose object is to keep the bag in the air by the feet or other parts of the body except the hands and arms; the game played with such a beanbag [64.2 Summer 1989]

Haigspeak language characterized by pompous obscurity resulting from redundancy, the semantically strained use of words, and verbosity, associated with Alexander Haig, Secretary of State during Ronald Reagan's first two years as president [59.2 Summer 1984 *s.v.* speak; 63.2 Summer 1988 *s.v.* speak]

hair-doer hair-dresser [33.4 Dec. 1958]

hairsatz (from *ersatz*) [18.4 Dec. 1943 forematter]

hall *British* a place where services or commodities are sold, an office, shop, or department of a store [63.1 Spring 1988]

hall of famer a member of the baseball Hall of Fame [33.4 Dec. 1958]

Halseyism [32.4 Dec. 1957]

hammy characteristic of a ham actor [17.2 Apr. 1942]

hand-trim *v.* [31.4 Dec. 1956]

hand-fight *v.* [31.3 Oct. 1956]

handie-talkie a small, light WALKIE-TALKIE radio [18.4 Dec. 1943]

handoff, hand-off a handing of the ball from one player, usu. the quarterback, to another in American football; the ball so handed [26.2 May 1951]

hand-ride *v.* [31.3 Oct. 1956]

hand-sign *v.* [31.3 Oct. 1956]

hand-whip *v.* [31.3 Oct. 1956]

handy-talkie *see* handie-talkie [18.4 Dec. 1943]

hand zert a hand-operated space tool, such as a wrench whose handles must be squeezed to turn a bolt [40.3 Oct. 1965 *s.v.* zert]

hang-up a psychological or emotional problem; any problem or difficulty [48.1–2 Spring-Summer 1973]

happy *suffixal form* bored, fed-up, slightly goofy, jittery, confused because of or as manifested by; interested in, concerned about [19.1 Feb. 1944 forematter; 22.3 Oct. 1947]

happy-time weed marijuana [57.4 Winter 1982]

harbor happy [22.3 Oct. 1947 *s.v.* happy]

hard (of a detergent) not easily degraded by natural biological processes [40.3 Oct. 1965]

hard sell vigorous, high-pressure selling [30.4 Dec. 1955]

hardliner one who persists in a line of thinking, regardless of the consequences [40.2 May 1965]

hard news factual reports with figures and direct quotations that are more analytical and less exciting than "soft news" [29.4 Dec. 1954]

hardtop, hard top an indoor theater as opposed to a drive-in [32.2 May 1957]

harmonic convergence a gathering of people at sacred sites at a time supposedly predicted by the ancient Mayan calendar when the world was said to be in danger of destruction unless people came together in harmonious activities such as communal chanting, music, rituals, and meditation [63.3 Fall 1988]

Hashbury, (The) the Haight-Ashbury district of San Francisco, noted for drug use by its residents [57.4 Winter 1982]

hash pipe a pipe for smoking hashish [57.4 Winter 1982]

hassle; hassel an irritation, problem, struggle, argument [25.3 Oct. 1950]

hate-happy [19.1 Feb. 1944 forematter]

hazchem *British* (a warning sign) hazardous chemicals [63.1 Spring 1988]

H-bomb, H. bomb a hydrogen bomb [26.1 Feb. 1951]

H-day Howard College (in Birmingham) day [21.3 Oct. 1946 forematter]

headache band a headband worn as a fashionable accessory [35.1 Feb. 1960]

head booth a booth at an exhibition or fair where items of interest to drug users are shown [57.4 Winter 1982]

headline-happy [22.3 Oct. 1947 *s.v.* happy]

Hearingsgate charges that congressional transcripts were altered [59.2 Summer 1984 *s.v.* -gate]

heat-happy [22.3 Oct. 1947 *s.v.* happy]

heat hog [18.2 Apr. 1943 forematter]

heavy a heavy bomber [20.4 Dec. 1945]

hedgehop *v.* [31.3 Oct. 1956]

heel-dragging dragging one's feet [28.3 Oct. 1953 *s.v.* drag]

Heimlich maneuver; Heimlich hug a lifesaving technique of standing behind a choking victim, quickly grasping both arms around the victim's waist, one hand gripping the other wrist, and then pressing forcefully into the victim's diaphragm just below the ribs, thus compressing the lung and expelling the matter choking the victim; **Heimlich sign** a gesture made by grasping one's throat, recommended for use by a food-choked victim who is conscious but unable to speak [54.1 Spring 1979]

helibus a helicopter line for passengers [29.1 Feb. 1954]

helistop a helicopter taxi terminal [30.4 Dec. 1955 *illus. s.v.* aerocab]

hell bomb, Hell Bomb a hydrogen bomb [26.1 Feb. 1951]

Hell Dog; Hell Hound a robot bomb [19.4 Dec. 1944 forematter]

Herrenvolk the dominant class or race in a society [17.2 Apr. 1942]

H-Hour [19.4 Dec. 1944 *illus. s.v.* D-Day, *also* forematter]

hidden hunger consumption of a qualitatively inadequate diet over a prolonged period, leading to an unsatisfied feeling and consequent overeating [29.3 Oct. 1954]

highball to speed [17.4 Dec. 1942 forematter]

high-pressure to exert high pressure upon, esp. in order to make a sale; to obtain by high-pressure methods [16.4 Dec. 1941]

high rise, high-rise (of buildings) many-stories tall [39.3 Oct. 1964]

high-school-football-and-milk-shake-circuit [24.4 Dec. 1949 forematter]

high-speed hypnosis a trance-like state induced by monotonous, effortless driving at high speeds [29.4 Dec. 1954]

highway-buster a truck driver [23.3–4 Oct.-Dec. 1948 *s.v.* buster]

highway-hotel [24.2 Apr. 1949 forematter]

highway hypnosis a condition like hypnosis induced by driving for long periods of time [30.4 Dec. 1955]

highway inn [24.2 Apr. 1949 forematter]

hipism; hippism an expression used by or of hippies; the values and practices of hippies [48.1–2 Spring-Summer 1973]

hippy having prominent hips [16.2 Apr. 1941]

hit to indulge in, take to greedily [17.2 Apr. 1942 forematter; 17.3 Oct. 1942]; to complete a forward pass thrown to (a receiver) in football [24.1 Feb. 1949]

hit lady a woman who commits murder for hire [55.1 Spring 1980]

Hitler-happy [19.1 Feb. 1944 forematter]

Hitleristic pert. to or characteristic of Adolf Hitler [17.2 Apr. 1942 forematter; 17.3 Oct. 1942]

hit list a list of targets for assassins; a list of persons or programs against whom some action is to be taken [55.1 Spring 1980]

hit man one paid to attack others, physically or verbally; specif. a reviewer who writes highly critical notices; a hockey player who attacks the opposition's key players; **hit person; hit woman** [55.1 Spring 1980]

hobby-happy [22.3 Oct. 1947 *s.v.* happy]

hog *suffixal form* one who takes an unfair share [18.2 Apr. 1943 forematter]; *cf.* gas hog

hold-up *British* hose with elasticized tops worn without garters or garter belt, *also* stay-put [63.2 Summer 1988]

hollow hunger consumption of an inadequate quantity of food, as opposed to inadequate quality (or HIDDEN HUNGER) [29.3 Oct. 1954]

Hollywoodgate [53.3 Fall 1978 *s.v.* -gate; 59.2 Summer 1984 *s.v.* -gate]

Hollywood silk screen [25.3 Oct. 1950 forematter]

homebased [20.2 Apr. 1945 forematter]

home-shopping selling goods and services to phone-in viewers of cable TV; **home-shopper** one who purchases by telephone from television advertising [64.1 Spring 1989]

homogeneous reactor an atomic reactor in which a single solution serves as fuel, moderator, and cooling agent [29.3 Oct. 1954]

Homo habilis a creature evidenced by fossil remains found in East Africa by Louis Leakey, thought to be an ancestor of humanity about 2 million years ago [40.2 May 1965]

Homo transvaalensis Homo habilis [40.2 May 1965]

Honest John a field artillery rocket designed to carry a nuclear warhead [30.2 May 1955]

honey shot a TV view of a woman spectator, usu. young and pretty, at a public event [48.1–2 Spring-Summer 1973]

Hong Kong flu a variant of the influenza virus spread to the U.S. from the Orient [48.1–2 Spring-Summer 1973]

hoopster a person operating a hula hoop [39.2 May 1964]

hoot out of the ball park to make fun of (someone), laugh out of court [51.1–2 Spring-Summer 1976 *s.v.* ball park]

Hooverville a temporary, ramshackle town, inhabited usu. by migratory workers [17.3 Oct. 1942 forematter; 17.4 Dec. 1942]

hop *suffixal form* to move frequently from one (location or activity) to another [47.3–4 Fall-Winter 1972; 48.1–2 Spring-Summer 1973; 54.1 Spring 1979]; *cf.* table hop; **hopper** *suffixal form;* **hopping** *suffixal form* [47.3–4 Fall-Winter 1972 *s.v.* hop]; *cf.* island hopping

horizontal hotel [24.2 Apr. 1949 forematter]

horse cavalry mounted soldiery using horses rather than motorized conveyances [19.1 Feb. 1944]

horse-drawn-type [23.2 Apr. 1948 *s.v.* type]

horsefeathers [17.2 Apr. 1942 forematter; 17.3 Oct. 1942 forematter]

Hospital Circuit [24.4 Dec. 1949 forematter]

hot rapid, rapidly [18.2 Apr. 1943]; (of an airplane's landing speed) [27.3 Oct. 1952]; radioactive or radioactively contaminated [24.1 Feb. 1949]

Hotel de Gink, Hotel De Gink, Hotel d'Gink the nickname for visiting officers' quarters on a military base [22.2 Apr. 1947]

hot lederhosen HOT PANTS from a Bavarian designer [46.1–2 Spring-Summer 1971 forematter]

hot-line a communications line that is open at all times for use in emergencies [41.2 May 1966]

hotpants, hot pants, HotPants very short shorts for men or women, *also* city shorts, cool pants, les shorts, lukewarm pants, minipants, red-hot pants, short cuts, shortpants, short shorts, sports shorts [46.1–2 Spring-Summer 1971]

hot rod an automobile stripped for speed and increased in power, used by teenagers for racing and frustrating the police [24.3 Oct. 1949]

hotshot fast, snappy; (esp. in truck-freighting) offering through or nonstop service; excellent, important [18.2 Apr. 1943]

hot war a military conflict, as opposed to cold war [23.2 Apr. 1948]

housepaint v. [31.3 Oct. 1956]

H₂O gate [56.4 Winter 1981 s.v. -gate]

hub-and-spoke pertaining to a system of airplane routing in which many flights converge at a hub airport [64.1 Spring 1989]

hucksterism aggressive, ethically questionable commercialism [32.4 Dec. 1957]

hug of life a Heimlich maneuver [54.1 Spring 1979]

Hump the Himalayan mountain range between India and China as crossed by air traffic [21.2 Apr. 1946]

hump happy fatigued from flying the Hump [22.3 Oct. 1947 s.v. happy]

huppie British hippy yuppie [62.4 Winter 1987 forematter]

Hurri-Buster a Hurricane tank-buster [23.3–4 Oct.-Dec. 1948 s.v. buster]

hurricane buster an airplane [23.3–4 Oct.-Dec. 1948 s.v. buster]

hush puppy British a foot or shoe [62.4 Winter 1987]

huskiburger [18.2 Apr. 1943 forematter]

H-word Harvard [63.4 Winter 1988 s.v. word]

hydrogen bomb an atomic bomb using an isotope of hydrogen [26.1 Feb. 1951]

hydro-jet a means of propulsion by which water sucked into a cylinder is heated and expelled under pressure [27.3 Oct. 1952]

hydronaut an underwater explorer [40.3 Oct. 1965 s.v. -naut]

hypersonic moving at a speed greater than that of sound [25.2 May 1950]

hypo-happy [22.3 Oct. 1947 s.v. happy]

hypospray an air gun developed to inject drugs without breaking the skin [24.1 Feb. 1949]

IBM, I.B.M.; ICBM an intercontinental ballistic missile [32.2 May 1957]

iced jeans jeans with white streaks, also frosted jeans, acid jeans [65.1 Spring 1990]

icehouse, ice house a cooling of the earth's surface and lower atmosphere, triggering an ice age, esp. in ~ state [65.4 Winter 1990]

ice skiing [54.3 Fall 1979 forematter]

idea-intensive [60.1 Spring 1985 s.v. intensive]

idiot board a TELEPROMPTER; **idiot girl** a woman who holds up an idiot board or teleprompter [33.2 May 1958]

iffy contingent, doubtful [17.2 Apr. 1942]

Ike-liker one who supports Dwight D. Eisenhower [33.4 Dec. 1958]

image orthicon a highly sensitive television camera tube [23.2 Apr. 1948]

IMP interplanetary monitoring platform, an unmanned satellite for exploring regions beyond the earth's magnetic field and for helping to plan for protection of astronauts against radiation in space [41.2 May 1966]

imperial father British the head of all the combined Chapels (reportedly a title in the hierarchy of the printing unions) [63.1 Spring 1988]

in suffixal form a mass gathering for social protest or entertainment [36.4 Dec. 1961; 38.3 Oct. 1963; 39.3 Oct. 1964]

in-betweener an average or mediocre film [33.4 Dec. 1958]

incentive pay a pay increase based upon the amount of production; pay for piece work [21.4 Dec. 1946]

index an ESCALATION INDEX; to link (income, interest, taxes, etc.) to the consumer price index or an escalation index; **indexation** indexing; specif. attaching escalator clauses based on some relevant yardstick of inflation to various long-term contracts; **index bond** a bond whose level of repayment is tied to the price level; **indexed** tied to a cost-of-living index; **indexing** tying various money incomes to a cost-of-living index for the purpose of mitigating the costs of inflation on fixed money contracts, also monetary correction; **indexization, index-linking** indexing [50.1–2 Spring-Summer 1975]

India-based [19.3 Oct. 1944 forematter; 20.2 Apr. 1945 forematter]

individual working time a work plan in which each employee chooses a monthly work schedule from several fixed working schedules [54.1 Spring 1979]

industrial park; industrial district an area zoned for industry and supplied with the necessary facilities [35.1 Feb. 1960]

infantariat [18.1 Feb. 1943 forematter]

infanticipate (of childbirth) to be expectant [17.3 Oct. 1942 forematter; 17.4 Dec. 1942; 18.2 Apr. 1943 forematter]

infanticipation [18.2 Apr. 1943 forematter]

infighting, in-fighting contention among members of the same group [28.1 Feb. 1953]

inflight, in-flight during an airplane flight [28.4 Dec. 1953]

influence peddler one who sells the ability to influence decisions, esp. of government; **influence peddling** [27.3 Oct. 1952]

infomercial British an advertising magazine [63.1 Spring 1988]

informate to share information and authority widely, esp. in a business; to operate or communicate in a network pattern rather than hierarchically [65.1 Spring 1990]

information-intensive [60.1 Spring 1985 s.v. intensive]

infotainment [60.4 Winter 1985 illus. s.v. docu-schlock s.v. docu-]

infrastructure, infra-structure the underlying requirements and support for the functioning of a system or organization, such as communications and services; permanent installations for a military organization [28.4 Dec. 1953]

inner circler a member of the inner circle of government [16.2 Apr. 1941 forematter]

inner space the sea [35.4 Dec. 1960]; the unconscious levels of the psyche [40.3 Oct. 1965]

inning deliberately revealing the homosexuality esp. of a famous person, *also* outing [65.4 Winter 1990]

insect-borne [20.2 Apr. 1945 forematter]

insecurity blanket *stunt* [49.1–2 Spring-Summer 1974]

insistent type [23.2 Apr. 1948 forematter]

Institute *euphemism* (in an organization's name) a trust-like combination of businesses, *as in* American Meat ~ [17.2 Apr. 1942 forematter]

instructor-intensive [60.1 Spring 1985 *s.v.* intensive]

instrument cowl *British* the frame and rim around the instrument panel of an automobile serving to protect it and shield it from external light [63.1 Spring 1988]

intensive *suffixal form* requiring or containing a large quantity of [60.1 Spring 1985]

intensive care (of a section of a city) under special police patrol [47.3–4 Fall-Winter 1972]

interchange a place on the Pennsylvania Turnpike where vehicular traffic can enter or leave the pike [26.2 May 1951]

interior designed *British* (of a building's interior) with decorations and furnishings planned by an interior designer or decorator [63.1 Spring 1988]

interphone the telephone system in an aircraft [18.1 Feb. 1943]

intervention *British* a comment or question following a speech or academic paper [63.1 Spring 1988]

in the ball park in close proximity to what is expected or aimed at [51.1–2 Spring-Summer 1976 *s.v.* ball park]

in the loop part of the decision-making and information-disseminating pattern in a bureaucracy [63.3 Fall 1988 *s.v.* loop]

intifada, intifadah an uprising by Palestinians against Israeli occupation of the West Bank and the Gaza Strip [64.4 Winter 1989]; any popular political uprising [65.3 Fall 1990]

I/O-intensive involving much input and output on a computer [60.1 Spring 1985 *s.v.* intensive]

iron curtain [25.3 Oct. 1950 forematter]

Ironman, Iron Man Hawaii's very difficult and strenuous triathlon; a competitor who finishes the Ironman Triathlon [58.2 Summer 1983]

iron nonfraternization curtain [25.3 Oct. 1950 forematter]

iron triangle a threefold combination of legislative committees, administrative bureaus, and industries that influence federal appropriations to maintain funding for projects from which they all benefit [65.2 Summer 1990]

Iron Woman a female competitor who finishes the Ironman Triathlon [58.2 Summer 1983 *s.v.* Ironman]

island the superstructure on an aircraft carrier [21.2 Apr. 1946; 21.4 Dec. 1946]

island happy [22.3 Oct. 1947 *s.v.* happy]

island-hop [47.3–4 Fall-Winter 1972 *s.v.* hop; 48.1–2 Spring-Summer 1973 *s.v.* hop; **island hopping, island-hopping** moving from one island to another [21.3 Oct. 1946]

-ism *suffix* doctrine, practice, etc. associated with; a linguistic expression associated with [32.4 Dec. 1957 forematter]

ismatism [32.4 Dec. 1957]

isolation booth a glass-enclosed booth to which contestants on a quiz program may retire to consider the answer to a question [32.2 May 1957]

Israel the name of the Jewish national state formed in the twentieth century; **Israeli** pertaining to the nation state of Israel; citizen of Israel [24.1 Feb. 1949]

Italy-based [19.3 Oct. 1944 forematter; 20.2 Apr. 1945 forematter]

I-word impeachment [63.4 Winter 1988 *s.v.* word]

jam-buster [23.3–4 Oct.-Dec. 1948 *s.v.* buster]

jam doughnut *British* a doughnut with a jam filling, a jelly doughnut [63.1 Spring 1988]

jampacked, jam-packed filled full, tightly packed [22.3 Oct. 1947]

Janizariat; Janissariat the body of New Deal advisers and officials about President F. D. Roosevelt [17.2 Apr. 1942; 18.1 Feb. 1943 forematter]; **Janizary** a member of the Janizariat [17.2 Apr. 1942]

Japanazi pertaining to Japan and to Nazi Germany, esp. as military allies [18.1 Feb. 1943]

Jap-happy [22.3 Oct. 1947 *s.v.* happy]

jato, JATO jet-assisted take-off, for naval airplanes [21.2 Apr. 1946]

Jaycee [21.4 Dec. 1946 forematter]

jazzophile one who likes jazz music [35.1 Feb. 1960]

jeep to travel by jeep [20.3 Oct. 1945]

jeepers [17.2 Apr. 1942 forematter; 17.3 Oct. 1942 forematter]

jerk a stupid person, anyone viewed with dislike [17.4 Dec. 1942 forematter; 18.2 Apr. 1943]

jet jet-propelled plane [21.2 Apr. 1946]; **jet airplane** [20.2 Apr. 1945]

jet backpack a unit allowing an astronaut to maneuver outside a spacecraft, *also* backpack [59.4 Winter 1984 *illus. s.v.* backpack]

jet bridge a JETWAY [64.2 Summer 1989]

jet-lagged *British* affected or produced by jet lag [63.1 Spring 1988]

jetomic jet and atomic, *esp. in* ~ age [29.3 Oct. 1954]

jet plane *see* jet airplane [20.2 Apr. 1945]

jet-powered backpack a jet backpack [59.4 Winter 1984 *illus. s.v.* backpack]

jet-propel *v.* [31.4 Dec. 1956]

jet propulsion the act or method of propelling an airplane that runs without propellers and uses exhaust gases [20.2 Apr. 1945]

jet set, Jet Set, jet-set a group who travel internationally and are preoccupied with entertaining themselves; the younger generation in Russia who are attracted by foreign (esp. Western) culture; **jet-setter** one who belongs to the jet set [41.2 May 1966]

jet stream a narrow wind current located six to ten miles above the earth's surface and flowing from west to east [28.3 Oct. 1953]

jetway a movable passageway connecting an airport boarding lounge with an aircraft [64.2 Summer 1989]

jiffy the time required for an object moving at the speed of light to travel one centimeter [33.2 May 1958]

jigaboo a Negro [17.4 Dec. 1942 forematter]

jiggle (of a woman) to move in a sexually suggestive way, esp. to bounce the breasts; sexually suggestive dress or behavior; **jiggle factor** the use of sexual suggestiveness, esp. on TV to promote ratings; **jiggle-o** a sexually suggestive character or actress; **jiggly; jiggly syndrome** the popularity of sexually suggestive TV series [56.3 Fall 1981]

Jim Crowism discrimination against Negroes [17.2 Apr. 1942]

jitteringly *British* in a jittering or nervous manner [63.1 Spring 1988]

jitteroptera, Jitteroptera serious music based on American folk music [26.2 May 1951]

jivaroo [16.4 Dec. 1941 forematter]

jive-happy [22.3 Oct. 1947 *s.v.* happy]

joad *usu. in plural* a migratory worker [16.4 Dec. 1941]

job a large, powered, usu. locomotive machine, esp. an automobile or airplane [17.3 Oct. 1942 forematter; 17.4 Dec. 1942]

job-hop [47.3–4 Fall-Winter 1972 *s.v.* hop]

John Bircher a member of the extreme right-wing John Birch Society [37.2 May 1962]

join-in a demonstration for integration at white churches [38.3 Oct. 1963 *s.v.* in]

joint buster, joint-buster a burglar [23.3–4 Oct.-Dec. 1948 *s.v.* buster]

jolly-doggism [32.4 Dec. 1957]

journalistic privilege [48.3–4 Fall-Winter 1973 *s.v.* privilege]

Juco a junior college [17.2 Apr. 1942 forematter; 17.3 Oct. 1942]

judicial privilege [48.3–4 Fall-Winter 1973 *s.v.* privilege]

jugaroo a jail [17.4 Dec. 1942 forematter]

juicer a machine to extract fruit or vegetable juices [17.3 Oct. 1942 forematter; 17.4 Dec. 1942]

jul otta Christmas morning services in Swedish-American churches [16.2 Apr. 1941]

jumboize to enlarge (esp. a tanker ship by cutting off its bow and stern and welding them to a new larger midsection); **jumboized; jumboizing; jumboizer** one who makes things bigger [35.4 Dec. 1960]

jumpmaster a leader of parachute jumpers [18.2 Apr. 1943 forematter]

jump off, the [19.4 Dec. 1944 forematter]

jump-pass *v.;* **jump-shoot** *v.* [31.3 Oct. 1956]

jungle(s) a dangerous or lawless place; specif. a black district, a vice district, a hobo camp, a union members' meeting place, the rough in golf [24.2 Apr. 1949 forematter]

jungle-happy affected by a long stay in the jungle [22.3 Oct. 1947 *s.v.* happy]

junior miss a girl 13–16 years old [20.3 Oct. 1945]

junk TV show tabloid TV [65.1 Spring 1990]

Jupiter effect meteorological and seismic disturbances predicted to occur in 1982 when all nine planets were located on the same side of the sun, according to John Gribbin and Stephen Plagemann, authors of *The Jupiter Effect* [58.1 Spring 1983]

kamikazer a kamikaze pilot [33.4 Dec. 1958]

karate chop any action that adversely affects its object; a strong argument against [46.3–4 Fall-Winter 1971]

keister buster, keister-buster a safecracker [23.3–4 Oct.-Dec. 1948 *s.v.* buster]

Kenya bean *British* a kind of thin string bean [63.1 Spring 1988]

kettle buster a boilermaker [23.3–4 Oct.-Dec. 1948 *s.v.* buster]

key critical, of central importance [65.1 Spring 1990]

khaki-happy [22.3 Oct. 1947 *s.v.* happy]

Khrushchevism [32.4 Dec. 1957]

kickturn *v.* [31.3 Oct. 1956]

kidflation inflation affecting children and businesses whose customers are principally children or young people [58.4 Winter 1983 *s.v.* -flation]

kidney buster, kidney-buster a hard-riding truck, an army truck [23.3–4 Oct.-Dec. 1948 *s.v.* buster]

kilobuck (scientific slang) a thousand dollars; **kilogrand** (scientific slang) a million dollars, a megabuck [40.3 Oct. 1965 *illus. s.v.* megabuck]

kiloton a measure of explosive power equal to 1000 tons of TNT [28.3 Oct. 1953]

king cotton diplomacy [46.3–4 Fall-Winter 1971 forematter]

kiss-and-tell revealing confidential or private matters known through personal intimacy, *also* slap-and-yell, tattle-tale [64.1 Spring 1989]

kissamaroo [16.4 Dec. 1941 forematter]

kitcheneering [18.1 Feb. 1943 forematter]

Kivik Rocket a robot bomb [19.4 Dec. 1944 forematter]

kneel-in the attendance at white churches by blacks [36.4 Dec. 1961]

know-how special skill, acquired through practice, in carrying through a complicated process or operation [17.3 Oct. 1942 forematter; 17.4 Dec. 1942]

knowledgeable having or revealing knowledge and intelligence [35.4 Dec. 1960]

knowledge-intensive [60.1 Spring 1985 *s.v.* intensive]

knuck-buster; knuckle buster, knuckle-buster a crescent wrench [23.3–4 Oct.-Dec. 1948 *s.v.* buster]

Koreagate a scandal involving allegations that Leon Jaworski was working for himself instead of the Korean government in giving money to U.S. Congressmen [53.3 Fall 1978 *s.v.* -gate]

Kremlinology the study of Russian policy; **Kremlinologist** a specialist in Kremlinology [39.2 May 1964]

Laborgate [53.3 Fall 1978 *s.v.* -gate]

lackey (epithet used by communists) one subservient to capitalists or to capitalistic society [17.2 Apr. 1942 forematter; 17.4 Dec. 1942]

ladyfinger circuit the rounds of a newspaper society reporter [24.4 Dec. 1949 forematter]

lagged delayed [63.1 Spring 1988]

lambada an Afro-Brazilian dance involving close body contact, with positions and motions imitative of coitus; **lambaderia** a nightclub where the lambada is danced [65.4 Winter 1990]

lamburger [18.2 Apr. 1943 forematter]

Lancegate a scandal involving Bert Lance [53.3 Fall 1978 *s.v.* -gate]

land-based [19.3 Oct. 1944 forematter; 20.2 Apr. 1945 forematter]

landing mat a section of meshed steel 12 by 3 feet containing fasteners so that a number can be joined together to form a surface of any desired area, used as a landing surface for aircraft during the war and as reinforcement for concrete [23.1 Feb. 1948]

landing strip a cleared, drained, and graded strip used by planes in landing and taking off [20.2 Apr. 1945]

land-type [23.2 Apr. 1948 *s.v.* type]

laryngectomee one who has had the larynx removed as medical treatment [32.2 May 1957]

latchkey with little supervision after school hours because of a working mother, *as in* ~ child, ~ kid [40.2 May 1965]; *cf.* doorkey children

Latin Quarterette [17.4 Dec. 1942 forematter]

laughette [17.4 Dec. 1942 forematter]

law buster [23.3–4 Oct.-Dec. 1948 *s.v.* buster]

layered look [45.3–4 Fall-Winter 1970 *s.v.* look]

LCI landing craft for infantry, a vessel for disembarking troops on ramps extended on both sides of the bow [21.2 Apr. 1946]

LCM landing craft, mechanized *or* medium, a fifty-foot vessel carrying a tank or bulldozer [21.2 Apr. 1946]

LCR landing craft, rubber, a light, inflatable vessel for patrols of seven to ten persons [21.2 Apr. 1946]

LCT landing craft, tank, a hundred-foot vessel [21.2 Apr. 1946]

LCVP landing craft for vehicles and personnel, a 36-foot vessel [21.2 Apr. 1946]

L-day [21.3 Oct. 1946 forematter]

leader board (in golf) a board on which are listed the players with the best scores in a tournament; (in football) a listing of the teams with the best records [59.1 Spring 1984]

lead time the interval between the conception or design and the production of a product or finalization of a process [29.3 Oct. 1954]

leaflet drop *British* a delivery of leaflets to the mail slot of houses [63.1 Spring 1988]

lease-lend [17.3 Oct. 1942 forematter]; *see* lend-lease *adj.*, *v.t.* [17.4 Dec. 1942]

leaving present *British* a present given to one who is leaving, a goodby present [63.1 Spring 1988]

-legger *suffix* (from *bootlegger*) [18.1 Feb. 1943 forematter]

legging suit *British* a set of knit pants and matching blouse [63.1 Spring 1988]

Legionnaire's disease; Legion disease; Legionellosis; Legion fever; Legionnaire (disease); Legionnaires'; Legionnaire's fever; Legionnaire's illness a respiratory infection caused by the Legionella pneumophila, first identified among persons attending a convention of the American Legion in Philadelphia, 21–24 July 1976, *cf.* Pontiac fever; **Legionella pneumophila** a bacillus identified as the causative agent of Legionnaire's disease and of a similar but nonfatal illness, Pontiac fever; **Legion epidemic** the outbreak of a mysterious and sometimes fatal respiratory disease among those who had attended the state convention of the American Legion in Philadelphia, 21–24 July 1976 [56.2 Summer 1981]

legis-flation the rising cost of legislating [58.4 Winter 1983 *s.v.* -flation]

leg up, leg-up a boost [16.2 Apr. 1941]

LEM Lunar Excursion Module, a vehicle in which astronauts descend to and explore the surface of the moon [40.2 May 1965]

lend-lease the act of leasing or lending American military supplies to foreign powers; pertaining to the law authorizing such transactions; to supply (such military goods) [17.4 Dec. 1942; *v.t. also* 17.3 Oct. 1942 forematter]

les shorts HOT PANTS [46.1–2 Spring-Summer 1971 forematter]

letter bomb a small bomb sent in the mail to explode upon opening, *also* mail(-a-)bomb [46.3–4 Fall-Winter 1971]

lettergate [56.4 Winter 1981 *s.v.* -gate]

Lettrism; lettrisme the theory created by Isidore Isou of poetry as rhythmic architecture, using meaningless combinations of letters and invented letters [26.3 Oct. 1951]; **Lettrist** one who writes poetry in the mode of Lettrism [*illus. s.v.* Lettrism]

level playing field equal terms, par; **level the playing field** to create equality [64.1 Spring 1989]

Leyte-based [20.2 Apr. 1945 forematter]

LFC laminar flow control, an air-inhalation system for aircraft [39.3 Oct. 1964 *illus. s.v.* slit wing plane]

libel-sue *v.* [31.3 Oct. 1956]

libspeak the language of the women's liberation movement [59.2 Summer 1984 *s.v.* speak]

Libyagate [56.4 Winter 1981 *s.v.* -gate]

lie detector a polygraph, used as an aid in obtaining confessions from suspects [19.3 Oct. 1944]

lie-in [39.3 Oct. 1964 *s.v.* in]

lifeline a commercial, esp. British maritime, route [16.4 Dec. 1941]; the minimum amount of electricity or other utilities needed in a home, the basis for a proposed rate structure under which the lowest charge would apply to the minimum and higher charges to greater amounts [55.1 Spring 1980]

lifer a life-insurance agent [16.2 Apr. 1941 forematter]

Lilt *trademark, British* a grapefruit-and-pineapple-flavored carbonated beverage [62.4 Winter 1987]

limited series a series of TV programs [54.3 Fall 1979 forematter]

linear park a long narrow park along a riverbank or right-of-way [47.3–4 Fall-Winter 1972]

line buster a fullback [23.3–4 Oct.-Dec. 1948 *s.v.* buster]

line-check *v.* [31.4 Dec. 1956]

link worker *British* a social worker who specializes in assisting disadvantaged foreigners having a poor command of English to cope with the complexities of British bureaucracy and customs [63.1 Spring 1988]

Linus blanket a security blanket, with reference to the security blanket carried by the character Linus Van Pelt in Charles Schultz's comic strip "Peanuts" [49.1–2 Spring-Summer 1974]

lipofilling the transfer of fat from one part of the body to another by suction and injection [64.4 Winter 1989]

liposuction the removal of fat from the body by a process of suction; to remove fat from the body by suction [64.4 Winter 1989]

lip-read *v.* [31.3 Oct. 1956]

lipscape (from *landscape, seascape*) [18.4 Dec. 1943 forematter]

litterbug, litter-bug one who litters [27.1 Feb. 1952]

Little Bang *British* a preliminary March 1986 deregulation of the London Stock Exchange [62.3 Fall 1987]

little magazine; little review a magazine designed to print artistic work not commercially appealing to large-circulation periodicals or presses [23.2 Apr. 1948]

living re-creating for study and observation the activities involved in the usu. everyday life of the past; **living archeology** the replication of earlier lifestyles in a controlled fashion; **living (historical) farm; living-history farm** a farm operated with tools and techniques of an earlier period for purposes of historical demonstration; **living history** history made vivid by exhibits of documents or artifacts, reenactment of events, or demonstration of techniques and tools of the past; re-creation on a continuing or permanent basis of the life of the past; **living history park** a re-creation of a past community, e.g., a cotton plantation, for purposes of education and entertainment; **living museum** a residence that houses a collection of objects such as might be found in a museum; a building or other site where a bygone mode of living either is evoked by the reenactment of past events or by the display of artifacts or is re-created by persons living on the site as people lived in the past; **living ranch** a working ranch operated with the tools and methods of the past [55.1 Spring 1980]

LL 30 an anesthetic [22.2 Apr. 1947 forematter]

Load-Master Engine [18.2 Apr. 1943 forematter]

Lobogate a scandal involving athletics at the University of New Mexico, whose team nickname is Lobos (Spanish 'timber wolves') [59.2 Summer 1984 *s.v.* -gate]

lobstergate the eating of lobster at taxpayer's expense by the staff of the governor of Massachusetts [59.2 Summer 1984 *s.v.* -gate]

LOCA loss of coolant accident, an accident in which a nuclear reactor core suddenly loses its water and quickly becomes catastrophically overheated [56.2 Summer 1981]

longtime [17.3 Oct. 1942 forematter]

look *suffixal form* (in fashion) (of) a specified style [45.3–4 Fall-Winter 1970]

loon a radio-controlled missile [26.1 Feb. 1951]

looney tunes; loony tunes illogical, erratic, absurd or crazy in behavior; a person or persons acting in such a manner [64.4 Winter 1989]

loop the decision-making and information-disseminating pattern in a bureaucracy; *cf.* in the loop, out of the loop [63.3 Fall 1988]

loose cannon someone or something that has become uncontrollable [58.1 Spring 1983]

Loran long-range navigation, a system using radar impulses sent from ground stations to calculate the position of an airplane and the direction of a target [21.2 Apr. 1946]

lorry push *British* a stunt to raise money for charity by pushing a truck over a specified course [63.1 Spring 1988]

lovely a beautiful female movie star or other entertainer [22.2 Apr. 1947]

low-incomer a recipient of a low income [16.2 Apr. 1941 forematter]

low-rent cheap, low on the socioeconomic scale, crude, tasteless, tacky [64.4 Winter 1989]

low-rise (of buildings) two to five stories tall [39.3 Oct. 1964 *illus. s.v.* high-rise]

lox, L-O-X liquid oxygen [26.2 May 1951]

loyal opposition opposition toward a party in power, not verging upon disloyalty to fundamental national principles [17.2 Apr. 1942]

LP a long playing record disk [24.1 Feb. 1949]

LST landing ship, tank, a large, heavy vessel [21.2 Apr. 1946]

lucite, Lucite a plastic made by du Pont [17.2 Apr. 1942]

luftwaffe, Luftwaffe, *pl.* **Luftwaffen** the German air force [16.2 Apr. 1941]

lug an exaction, *esp. in* to put the ~ on 'to exact money for political purposes'; to make an exaction from [17.2 Apr. 1942 forematter; 17.3 Oct. 1942]

lukewarm pants HOT PANTS somewhat longer than usual [46.1–2 Spring-Summer 1971 forematter]

lumberjill a female lumberjack; a woman dressed in lumberjack-like plaid [33.2 May 1958]

lunatic fringe an extremist or unbalanced minority of an organization or movement [18.1 Feb. 1943 forematter; 19.1 Feb. 1944; 21.3 Oct. 1946]

lurch *British* to eye and chat up women, to attempt to attract, allure, seduce [63.1 Spring 1988]

lurgy lurgy psychologically affected by desert campaigning [19.1 Feb. 1944 *illus. s.v.* sand happy, forematter]

lustable; lustable-after; lust-afterable *British* worthy of lust [63.2 Summer 1988]

L-word liberal [63.4 Winter 1988 *s.v.* word]

lytic cocktail a combination of drugs that affects the nervous system's regulatory mechanisms, lowers body temperature, and produces a simulated hibernation [30.2 May 1955]

McCarthyism the overzealous search for communist sympathizers and agents named for its main proponent, Senator Joseph R. McCarthy; the use of innuendo, smear tactics, anonymous informants, and inquisitorial techniques [26.4 Dec. 1951]

McGeorge Bundyism [32.4 Dec. 1957]

McGovernomics George McGovern's policies for income redistribution, welfare reform and changes in the nation's tax structure [46.1–2 Spring-Summer 1971]

mach *see* mach number (followed by a number that is the ratio of speed of an airplane to the speed of sound, e.g., "mach 1" is the speed of sound, "mach .5" is half the speed of sound) [23.1 Feb. 1948]

machinespeak computer language [59.4 Winter 1984 *s.v.* speak]

mach number (named for Ernst Mach) the speed of an airplane as a ratio of the speed of sound in the same air [23.1 Feb. 1948]

Mae West a life preserver [19.3 Oct. 1944]

magdraulic (from *hydraulic*) [18.4 Dec. 1943 forematter]

magicienne *British* a female magician [63.2 Summer 1988]

magnetic bottle the magnetic field created by an electrical current that confines hot gas into a column (the PINCH EFFECT) and so prevents it from touching the walls of a material container [34.1 Feb. 1959 *illus. s.v.* pinch effect]

magnetosphere a radiation belt above the earth that traps electrical particles [38.3 Oct. 1963]

Magyar Martian theory a jocular proposal by Hungarian physicists at Los Alamos that Hungarians are Martians who have concealed their identity from earthly barbarians [59.4 Winter 1984 forematter]

mail bomb; mail-a-bomb a LETTER BOMB [46.3–4 Fall-Winter 1971]

mailshot *British* an information campaign by mail, bulk mailing [63.1 Spring 1988]

main *British* a main course [63.1 Spring 1988]

maitre d', maitre d'., maître d' a maître d'hôtel [35.1 Feb. 1960]

male-hop [47.3–4 Fall-Winter 1972 *s.v.* hop]

malling (esp. of teenagers) congregating in a shopping mall for entertainment by meeting peers, eating, and window-shopping; **mall-jam** to crowd together in a shopping area for social purposes; **mallie; mall rat** a young person who frequents shopping malls with friends as a pastime; **malling** an increase in the number of shopping malls (in a specified area) with loss of variety and quality in stores, *as in the* ~ *of America* [65.4 Winter 1990]

mambo a dance similar to the rumba [26.4 Dec. 1951]

Manhattan white a supposed variety of marijuana, NEW YORK CITY SILVER [57.4 Winter 1982]

mansion-hop [47.3–4 Fall-Winter 1972 *s.v.* hop]

man-tailored (of women's clothes) tailored after the manner of men's clothes [18.1 Feb. 1943 forematter; 19.1 Feb. 1944]

maquis French resistance fighters who have taken to the woods, mainly young men seeking escape from labor service in Germany or sought by the Germans [20.3 Oct. 1945]

marathon a group therapy session of prolonged duration [48.1–2 Spring-Summer 1973]

marché légal *French* legal market, white market [25.2 May 1950 forematter]

marché noir *French* black market [25.2 May 1950 forematter]

marché parallèle *French* illegal or black market [25.2 May 1950 forematter]

margie-wanna marijuana [57.4 Winter 1982]

Marianas-based [20.2 Apr. 1945 forematter]

marijuanaholic a chronic user of marijuana [57.4 Winter 1982]

Marilyn Monroe an airplane shape [31.4 Dec. 1956 *illus. s.v.* wasp waist]

market *suffixal form* (for types of trading activities) [25.2 May 1950 forematter]; *cf.* Common Market, Euro-sterling convertible market, Euromarket, white market

marry-in an interracial marriage [36.4 Dec. 1961 *s.v.* in]

Marshalls-based [20.2 Apr. 1945 forematter]

masculist *British* an advocate of men's rights or privileges [63.1 Spring 1988]

mass-produce to produce standardized items in large numbers [21.4 Dec. 1946]

master *suffixal form* (in trade names); (in common nouns) leader [18.2 Apr. 1943 forematter; 21.2 Apr. 1946 forematter]; *cf.* shackmaster, Skymaster, wedgiemaster

mastermind to engineer or direct as a master mind [17.2 Apr. 1942]

matrix four-channel [48.1–2 Spring-Summer 1973 *s.v.* four-channel *n.*]

Mau Mau, Mau-Mau a Kenya terrorist organization dedicated to driving Europeans out of Africa [31.4 Dec. 1956]

maxiseries a regular television series, esp. as opposed to a miniseries [54.3 Fall 1979]

M day, M-day Mobilization day; Moving day (in Canada); the day when meat was to be freely available at butcher shops after WWII [21.3 Oct. 1946 forematter]

meach *British* (stunt with allusion to Michael Meacher, a left-wing Labour spokesman) to make extravagant additional commitments hourly [63.2 Summer 1988]

measured (of a charge for telephone service) based on the amount of actual use instead of a flat monthly rate [58.2 Summer 1983]

meatlegger one who sells meat contrary to rationing restrictions [18.4 Dec. 1943]

medflation the rising cost of medical benefits [58.4 Winter 1983 *s.v.* -flation]

mediagate a scandal concerning the press's failure to serve blacks and other minorities [53.3 Fall 1978 *s.v.* -gate]; a sensational press treatment of a minor scandal, or a minor scandal given such treatment [59.2 Summer 1984 *s.v.* -gate]

mediagenic attractive to and on the mass media [51.1–2 Spring-Summer 1976]

Medicaid mill a medical clinic in which individuals on Medicaid are often recommended for unnecessary services, sometimes administered below standard, *cf.* mill patient [54.3 Fall 1979]

Mediterranean-based [20.2 Apr. 1945 forematter]

medium *euphemism* small in size [17.2 Apr. 1942 forematter]

medspeak medical jargon [59.2 Summer 1984 *s.v.* speak; 59.4 Winter 1984 *s.v.* speak]

Meet-the-People-burger (from the musical comedy *Meet the People*) [18.2 Apr. 1943 forematter]

me firstism placing one's own interests above those of others [32.4 Dec. 1957]

mega *British* big or important [63.1 Spring 1988]

megabuck (scientific slang) a million dollars [40.3 Oct. 1965]

megacorpse one million, as a unit measuring the number of deaths in a nuclear attack [39.3 Oct. 1964]

megadeath the death of a million persons [29.3 Oct. 1954]

megaton (of atomic weapons) the explosive power of one million tons of TNT [29.3 Oct. 1954]

melancholy type [23.2 Apr. 1948 forematter]

meltdown an uncontrollable and undesirable event [56.3 Fall 1981]; (of the stock market) a sudden catastrophic decline in financial value, *as in* market ~, financial ~, ~ Monday, i.e., BLACK MONDAY; *hyperbole* destruction from excessive use, *as in* "The telephone experiences ~ from teenage use"; a critically dangerous condition, *as in* educational ~ ; **melt down** (esp. of stock) to decline sizably and rapidly in value [63.3 Fall 1988]

melvin a WEDGY [65.3 Fall 1990 forematter]

me-neitherism [32.4 Dec. 1957]

menticide thought-control, brainwashing [27.1 Feb. 1952]

Merry-Go-Rounder an editor of the column "Washington Merry-Go-Round" [16.2 Apr. 1941 forematter]

messagerie a CHAT LINE [64.1 Spring 1989]

metermaid, meter maid a uniformed woman who patrols parking areas and enforces parking meter regulations by writing tickets for overparking [36.4 Dec. 1961]

methodolatry an excessive concern with method [28.3 Oct. 1953]

me-tooism (in politics) favoring the objectives of the opposition party [25.2 May 1950]

Metspeak imprecise, verbose, bureaucratic language used to blunt the statement of unpleasant facts, associated with the London Metropolitan Police [63.2 Summer 1988 *s.v.* speak]

Me TV TABLOID TV [65.1 Spring 1990]

Mexican marijuana from Mexico [57.4 Winter 1982]

MGer, M.G.er [33.4 Dec. 1958]

Michoacan marijuana from the state of Michoacán, Mexico [57.4 Winter 1982]

micro a microwave oven [55.2 Summer 1980]

microbial mining the extraction of metals by genetically engineered microbes [60.4 Winter 1985]

microbrew beer produced by a microbrewery, *cf.* contract beer, signature beer; **microbrewer** a brewer in a microbrewery; **microbrewery** a small brewery producing beer usu. for local consumption; **microbrewing** producing beer in a microbrewery [65.4 Winter 1990]

microcook to cook (something) in a microwave oven [55.2 Summer 1980]

microelectronics the miniaturization of electronic circuits through the development of chip technology [40.2 May 1965]

microfilm to photograph on microfilm [18.1 Feb. 1943 forematter; 19.1 Feb. 1944]

microgroove, micro-groove pertaining to a phonograph record with a much larger number of grooves than the conventional type [24.1 Feb. 1949]

micrometeor; micrometeorite a very small meteor, a tiny speeding particle of space dust [34.1 Feb. 1959]

micrometeoroid a very small meteoroid [40.2 May 1965]

micro-skirted wearing a very short skirt [46.3–4 Fall-Winter 1971]

microsleep, micro-sleep sleep of a few seconds duration with open eyes and bodily movement; momentary blackouts of consciousness [44.2 May 1969]

microwave a microwave oven; to cook or heat in a microwave oven; **microwave oven-proof; microwave-proof; microwave-safe** designed for or suitable for use in microwave cooking [55.2 Summer 1980]

middle-ager [33.4 Dec. 1958]

middlebrow, middle-brow pertaining or appealing to the tastes or habits of those who are neither highly cultivated nor uncultivated; a member of that middle group [26.1 Feb. 1951]

middle buster a double-moldboard plow [23.3–4 Oct.-Dec. 1948 *s.v.* buster]

midnighter one abroad at midnight [16.2 Apr. 1941 forematter]

mid-seasoner something, specif. a fashion, appearing in mid-season [33.4 Dec. 1958]

mileage percentage, profit, success, benefit [31.1 Feb. 1956]

milk round *British* (from a milk deliverer's route) the recruitment of college graduates by industry; **milk-rounded up** *British* (of college graduates) recruited for employment in industry [63.1 Spring 1988]

milk (wagon) run a routine sortie or bombing mission [20.3 Oct. 1945]

mill patient a patient who receives services from a MEDICAID MILL [54.3 Fall 1979]

mimstud *British, stunt* a middle-aged male stick-in-the-mud [63.1 Spring 1988]

mini-Watergate a small scale coverup or scandal [54.4 Winter 1979]

miniaturization the reduction in size of electronic components [28.3 Oct. 1953]

minicab *British* an unmarked, usu. nonmetered car of any of various designs, available chiefly by telephone [62.3 Fall 1987 *illus. s.v.* black cab]

miniconvention a small convention set up to consider strategy for the regular convention, usu. of a political party [49.3–4 Fall-Winter 1974]

mini-microwave oven; mini micro a small microwave oven [55.2 Summer 1980]

minipants HOT PANTS [46.1–2 Spring-Summer 1971 forematter]

miniseries a television series of limited duration [54.3 Fall 1979]

miniskirted wearing a miniskirt [46.3–4 Fall-Winter 1971]

mini-strike a short-lived, usu. localized labor strike [57.2 Summer 1982]

Minitel a French telecommunication system accessed by home computer terminals; a terminal in the French telecommunication system; **Minitelist** a user of the Minitel system [64.1 Spring 1989]

Miranda a warning read to those arrested; to read (suspects) their rights as required by the U.S. Supreme Court ruling in *Miranda vs Arizona* (1966); to bring into conformity with the requirements of the Miranda ruling [56.3 Fall 1981]

miss the boat (nonnautical use) [17.4 Dec. 1942 forematter]

Mixmaster [18.2 Apr. 1943 forematter]

MLF multilateral (nuclear) fleet *or* force [41.2 May 1966]

mob buster [23.3–4 Oct.-Dec. 1948 *s.v.* buster]

mod, Mod (from *modern*) a foppishly dressed, motor-scooter-riding member of a British teenage gang [41.2 May 1966]

modeler one interested in model airplanes [33.4 Dec. 1958]

Moist Master [18.2 Apr. 1943 forematter]

MOL manned orbiting *or* orbital laboratory [41.2 May 1966]

molecular electronics the use of certain properties of molecules in amplifying or controlling devices [37.2 May 1962]

mollybuster (telephone workers' jargon) a tamp for expanding anchors [23.3–4 Oct.-Dec. 1948 *s.v.* buster]

Molotov a Molotov cocktail [18.2 Apr. 1943 forematter]

Molotov breadbasket a type of bomb [18.4 Dec. 1943; 21.4 Dec. 1946]

Molotov cocktail a bottle filled with explosives and fitted with a fuse [18.2 Apr. 1943 forematter; 19.1 Feb. 1944]

momentarily momently, at any moment [19.4 Dec. 1944; 20.2 Apr. 1945 forematter; 21.3 Oct. 1946]

moment of truth a critical time for decision making [47.3–4 Fall-Winter 1972]

momism the inhibiting effect of matriarchy and maternal concern on masculine self-confidence [23.2 Apr. 1948]

mommy track; mom tracking work arrangements that permit flexible scheduling and fringe benefits for mothers, often perceived as blocking employment advancement, *cf.* daddy track [65.2 Summer 1990]

monad the S-shaped insignia of the Technocrats, signifying unity, balance, growth, and dynamic functioning for the security of the life processes, also dynamic equilibrium between production and distribution [18.2 Apr. 1943]

monetary correction INDEXING [50.1–2 Spring-Summer 1975]

monitoring screen; monitor screen a screen on which appears a telecast as it goes to the home viewer [26.3 Oct. 1951]

monkey-wrench pertaining to ECODEFENSE; **monkey-wrencher** an ECODEFENDER; **monkeywrenching** ECODEFENSE [63.4 Winter 1988]

monokini skimpy bathing trunks for men [40.3 Oct. 1965]

monolithic showing solidity or cohesion plus great size [18.2 Apr. 1943]

monophonic (of phonograph records) having only one sound track [36.3 Oct. 1961]

moon garden a garden in which vegetables are grown under reduced air pressure as an experiment in supplying food during space travel [36.3 Oct. 1961]

moonlighter a person who holds two or more jobs; **moonlighting** working a second job after the normal workday is done [33.2 May 1958]

moonquake a movement in the substance of the moon caused by artificial explosions or meteorite hits [36.3 Oct. 1961]

moonship, moon ship a spacecraft for travel to the moon [40.3 Oct. 1965]

moonshot, moon shot; moonshoot, moon shoot a launch of a rocket probe to the moon [37.2 May 1962]

moon suit a garment or container to protect humans on the surface of the moon [36.3 Oct. 1961]

mosquito boat a motor-torpedo boat [16.2 Apr. 1941]

motel [24.2 Apr. 1949 forematter]

mother plane; mother ship a plane that controls another plane (a DRONE) by means of electromagnetic waves; **mother tank** a tank that controls another tank [22.3 Oct. 1947 forematter]

motion sickness sickness or nausea caused by movement, as in a land, sea, or air vehicle [25.1 Feb. 1950]

motor camp; motor-camper; motor-camping [24.2 Apr. 1949 forematter]

motor court a collection of small houses clustered around a central service and administration building [24.2 Apr. 1949]

Motorgate a scandal concerning the submission of fraudulent warranty claims to General Motors [53.3 Fall 1978 *s.v.* -gate]; a scandal involving employees of an automobile manufacturer and dealership [59.2 Summer 1984 *s.v.* -gate]

motor-haul *v.* [31.4 Dec. 1956]

motor-hotel; motorist inn; motorist's inn; motor lodge [24.2 Apr. 1949 forematter]

mountain-hop [48.1–2 Spring-Summer 1973 *s.v.* hop]

Mounty-gate a scandal involving the Royal Canadian Mounted Police [59.2 Summer 1984 *s.v.* -gate]

Mouse Minimum Orbital Unmanned Satellite, Earth, a small orbiting automatic laboratory [30.2 May 1955]

mover and shaker a person of power and influence [60.3 Fall 1985]

MTB motor torpedo boat [21.3 Oct. 1946 forematter]

mudder (in sports) someone or something that performs well under muddy conditions [28.1 Feb. 1953]

Muldergate a scandal involving a South African cabinet member, Cornelius P. Mulder [59.2 Summer 1984 *s.v.* -gate]

mule-borne [19.3 Oct. 1944 forematter; 20.2 Apr. 1945 forematter]

multiseries one of several television series, with fewer segments than a regular series, that are scheduled to be televised in rotation in the same time slot; also such time-sharing shorter series collectively [54.3 Fall 1979]

murphy a WEDGY [65.3 Fall 1990 forematter]

museum-hop [47.3–4 Fall-Winter 1972 *s.v.* hop]

musicflation the rising cost of record albums [58.4 Winter 1983 *s.v.* -flation]

MVA Missouri Valley Authority [21.2 Apr. 1946]

nab (from *nut and bolt*) a wrench for use in space by weightless astronauts, permitting a twisting force without moving the body, a kind of ZERT [40.3 Oct. 1965]

nacelle (in aeronautics) [18.1 Feb. 1943 forematter]

naked calorie an EMPTY CALORIE [41.2 May 1966 forematter]

name famous, *esp. in* ~ band [18.1 Feb. 1943]

name calling the attempt to put people or things in a bad light by attaching to them a word with unpleasant connotations [22.3 Oct. 1947]

name dropper, name-dropper one who tries to impress by interlarding conversation with the names of prominent people [29.3 Oct. 1954]

narrow band *British* (of currency exchange rates with the dollar) a small range of fluctuation; **narrow banded** *British* (of currency exchange rates) held in a small range (of fluctuation with the dollar); **narrow banding** *British* keeping (currency exchange rates) in a small range of fluctuation (with the dollar) [63.1 Spring 1988]

narrowcast (play on *broadcast*) to gear broadcasting toward a demographic group that will pay for such programming; to transmit programs over subscription radio or cable television [53.3 Fall 1978]; **narrowcasting** subscription radio; cable television transmission [*illus. s.v.* narrowcast]

NASAgate [56.4 Winter 1981 *s.v.* -gate]

-naut *suffix* one who explores or investigates; that which is employed in exploration or investigation [40.3 Oct. 1965]

Naziphile one who favors National Socialism or National-Socialist Germany [18.1 Feb. 1943]

near collision a barely avoided collision of two airplanes (usu. called *near miss*) [64.1 Spring 1989]

near miss a fired shell that misses its intended target, but lands close enough to damage it [22.2 Apr. 1947]

neatnik one who is neat in personal habits [37.2 May 1962]

necklace to set fire to a gasoline-filled automobile tire around the neck of a victim [64.1 Spring 1989]

needle to goad, vex; to thread (one's way) [17.2 Apr. 1942]

needle stick an injury from accidental stabbing by a hypodermic needle, particularly one contaminated by prior use on an AIDS-infected person [65.3 Fall 1990]

negative amortization the rise in principal of a loan with a flexible interest rate, caused when the interest rises to the point that payments fail to cover the interest due [57.2 Summer 1982]

neo-Deweyism educational practice and theory based on the philosophy of John Dewey [32.4 Dec. 1957]

neo-Fascism, Neo-Fascism a revival of fascist theory and practice; **Neofascist, neo-Fascist, Neo-Fascist** pertaining to neo-Fascism, or the belief that it would have been better had National Socialist Germany or Fascist Italy been victorious in World War II [27.1 Feb. 1952]

neomycin an antibiotic derived from the same kind of organism that produces streptomycin [26.1 Feb. 1951]

neo-Tomism [32.4 Dec. 1957]

neptunium the 93rd element on the atomic chart [21.4 Dec. 1946]

NERVA, N.E.R.V.A. Nuclear Engine for Rocket Vehicle Application, a nuclear power source for a spaceship [40.3 Oct. 1965]

nerve gas a deadly gas sometimes used for military purposes, exposure to which causes death by paralysis of the central nervous system [26.2 May 1951]

netback pricing *British* calculating the price of a cargo of crude oil with reference to the value of products made from it [63.1 Spring 1988]

neural efficiency the efficiency of the brain in processing information as indicated by the speed with which it responds to flashes of light [51.3–4 Fall-Winter 1976]

neutron bomb a small thermonuclear warhead releasing neutrons that kill humans without damaging property [37.2 May 1962]

neutron star a star composed of closely packed neutrons, weighing from 10 to 100 billion tons per cubic inch, believed to be the remnant of an exploding star or supernova [40.3 Oct. 1965]

New Age a present or coming period in human history with emphasis on the spiritual, metaphysical, holistic, soothing music, astrology, affective responses, and harmonious relationships; **New Ager** one involved in New Age activities and attitudes [63.3 Fall 1988]

new cuisine a style of cooking, *also* nouvelle cuisine [58.1 Spring 1983]

New Dealism [16.4 Dec. 1941]

new look [45.3–4 Fall-Winter 1970 *s.v.* look]

new Nixonomics the radical change in economic policies made by Richard Nixon in 1971 [46.1–2 Spring-Summer 1971 *illus. s.v.* Nixonomics]

newscast [18.2 Apr. 1943 forematter]

news hole the amount of space (in print journalism) or air time (in broadcast journalism) available for news stories [51.3–4 Fall-Winter 1976]

news-men's privilege [48.3–4 Fall-Winter 1973 *s.v.* privilege]

Newspeakism the use of fashionable jargon, like *confrontation* and *chairperson* [59.2 Summer 1984]

newsworthy worthy of figuring in the news [16.2 Apr. 1941]

new type, new-type [23.2 Apr. 1948 *s.v.* type]

New York City silver (in urban folklore) a variety of marijuana, of high quality, growing in the sewers of New York, *also* Manhattan white, subway silver [57.4 Winter 1982]

New Yorkerism catchphrase originating in or popularized by *The New Yorker* magazine, such as "I say it's spinach, and I say the hell with it" [32.4 Dec. 1957]

New York white *see* New York City silver [57.4 Winter 1982]

niacin nicotinic acid, an antipellagra substance in enriched bread [17.3 Oct. 1942]

nice-nellieism the use of prudishly affected euphemisms [32.4 Dec. 1957]

nickel bag; nickel a packet containing 5 dollars worth of an illegal drug [57.4 Winter 1982]

night-drive *v.* [31.4 Dec. 1956]

NIH-204 a substance with some of the properties of Atabrine [22.2 Apr. 1947 forematter]

1947N a new comet so named because many astronomers saw it simultaneously, N because it was the 14th comet sighted in the year [23.2 Apr. 1948]

Nip Japanese [17.4 Dec. 1942 forematter; 18.2 Apr. 1943]

Nixonian pertaining to the ideas or actions of Richard M. Nixon [46.1–2 Spring-Summer 1971]

Nixonism [32.4 Dec. 1957]

Nixonomics the economic policies of Richard M. Nixon [46.1–2 Spring-Summer 1971]

NMRI-448 an insecticide; **NMRI 407; NMRI 201** repellents [22.2 Apr. 1947 forematter]

no-brainer a decision easily made; a stupid or incoherent person; a college course requiring little preparation or effort [64.2 Summer 1989]

noggie *British* a draftee, a conscript; **nogging** *British* the National Service, the draft [63.2 Summer 1988]

no-gooder [34.2 May 1959]

nominal equivalent in power (20,000 tons of TNT) to the atomic bomb dropped on Hiroshima, taken as the standard by which other bombs are rated [30.4 Dec. 1955]

nonfiction TV REALITY TV [65.1 Spring 1990]

nonindexed without linkage to an ESCALATION INDEX [50.1–2 Spring-Summer 1975]

non-pierced (of earrings) designed for unpierced ears [45.3–4 Fall-Winter 1970]

nonsked; non-sched an airline that flies on an unscheduled basis [25.1 Feb. 1950]

nonstreak a streaking event proposed for publicity without intention of its being held [48.1–2 Spring-Summer 1973]

nontechnology-intensive [60.1 Spring 1985 *s.v.* intensive]

nose at, have a *British* to poke one's nose into the business of, to watch, observe, spy on [63.2 Summer 1988]

nose bra; nose mask a cloth or plastic cover for the front end of a car, shielding the bumper and grill, with holes for the lights and front license plate, reputedly providing resistance to radar tracking, *also* bra, car bra, stealth auto *or* car bra [65.4 Winter 1990]

noshow, no-show, no show a person who reserves airline space, buys a ticket and then neglects to cancel the reservation after deciding not to travel [24.2 Apr. 1949]

notch a supposed reduction in Social Security benefits for those born 1917–21; the period of five years (1917–21) spanning the birth date of retirees who claim their Social Security benefits are inequitable; **notch baby; notchie** one born during 1917–21 who claims to be receiving a reduction in Social Security benefits; **notch year** a year within the period 1917–21, persons born during which claim to be receiving reduced Social Security benefits [64.4 Winter 1989]

noun-incorporate *v.* [31.3 Oct. 1956]

Nounspeak a style of writing or speech with many attributive nouns [59.2 Summer 1984 *s.v.* speak]

nouvelle cuisine, (la) a style of French cooking aiming at clear, fresh flavors and light textures instead of richness, *also* new cuisine; **nouvelle** prepared or served in the manner of the nouvelle cuisine; **nouvelle cuisinier** a chef or restaurateur who specializes in the nouvelle cuisine [58.1 Spring 1983]

nuclear furious, raging, angry, *also* ballistic [65.2 Summer 1990]

nuclear blackmail the attempt of one country to coerce another into responding to its demands by the threat of using nuclear weapons [41.2 May 1966]

nuclear reactor REACTOR [25.2 May 1950]

nuclear winter the cooling of the earth that some scientists believe would result if the explosion of nuclear weapons injected vast quantities of dust and smoke into the atmosphere, thus preventing sunlight from reaching the surface of the earth [60.3 Fall 1985]

nuke a weapon or ship powered by nuclear energy or firing nuclear devices [40.3 Oct. 1965]

nuppie nonworking urban professional [60.1 Spring 1985 forematter]

nutburger [18.2 Apr. 1943 forematter]

nut buster a mechanic [23.3–4 Oct.-Dec. 1948 *s.v.* buster]

N-word nigger [63.4 Winter 1988 *s.v.* word]

nylon nylon hose [16.2 Apr. 1941]

obliteration bombing blotting out by concentrated bombing [19.3 Oct. 1944; 20.4 Dec. 1945]

obstetographer [34.2 May 1959]

OCD Office of Civilian Defense [21.3 Oct. 1946 forematter]

O-day [21.3 Oct. 1946 forematter]

ODT Office of Defense Transportation [21.3 Oct. 1946 forematter]

off-load to unload from a transport vehicle [26.1 Feb. 1951]

off-street (of automobile parking or loading areas) not along the edge of a street [25.1 Feb. 1950]

off-the-ball *British* vindictive [63.2 Summer 1988]

OGO Orbiting Geophysical Observatory, a research satellite [39.3 Oct. 1964]

oil bomb an incendiary bomb filled with oil or gasoline [22.2 Apr. 1947]

oilflation inflation caused by the high cost of imported oil [58.4 Winter 1983 *s.v.* -flation]

oil patch an oil region; the petroleum industry [60.3 Fall 1985]

Okie an itinerant Oklahoman [16.4 Dec. 1941]

old-hat old-fashioned or trite [18.1 Feb. 1943]

Oligopithecus a prehistoric primate [39.3 Oct. 1964]

olive happy (army use) bemused from living outdoors [19.1 Feb. 1944 forematter]

Olliemania interest in Lt. Colonel Oliver North, esp. during the televised trial for his involvement in the Iran-Contra affair [63.3 Fall 1988]

-omics *see* -onomics [49.3–4 Fall-Winter 1974]

omnibuster one who steals a London bus [23.3–4 Oct.-Dec. 1948 *s.v.* buster]

one-stop (orig. of filling stations) supplying all the shopper's (esp. the motoring shopper's) needs, so as to remove the necessity of shopping at more than one place [18.1 Feb. 1943]

one-worldism cooperation among global powers, as through the UN [32.4 Dec. 1957]

-onomics *suffix* economics [49.3–4 Fall-Winter 1974]

OPA Office of Price Administration [21.3 Oct. 1946 forematter]

op art, Op Art, op-art optical art, intended to produce illusions, such as a sense of movement [40.3 Oct. 1965]

OPEC Organization of Petroleum Exporting Countries; belonging to that organization [49.1–2 Spring-Summer 1974]

open racially nonsegregated [39.3 Oct. 1964]

open city a city declared to be unfortified or undefended and hence under international law exempt from enemy bombardment [19.3 Oct. 1944; 22.2 Apr. 1947]

open occupancy racially unrestricted housing [35.1 Feb. 1960]

OPMer [34.2 May 1959]

opster one who practices op art [40.3 Oct. 1965]

orature oral literature [63.4 Winter 1988]

orphan drug a drug that is not tested or manufactured because there are so few patients who might benefit from it [58.4 Winter 1983]

Oscar a gold statuette awarded annually by the Academy of Motion Picture Arts and Sciences for achievement; a symbol of excellence [19.4 Dec. 1944; 23.1 Feb. 1948 forematter]

Oscarette the award Bob Hope gave the young Margaret O'Brien in 1945 [23.1 Feb. 1948 forematter]

out known and admittedly homosexual; to deliberately reveal the homosexuality of (esp. a public person); **outage; outing** a deliberate revelation of the homosexuality of a person, forcing out of the closet [65.4 Winter 1990]

outhouse *British* to house in a subsidiary rather than in a main location [63.1 Spring 1988]

out-Nounspeak to surpass in the use of Nounspeak [59.2 Summer 1984]

out-of-stater someone from outside the state [34.2 May 1959]

out of the ball park impossible or highly improbable [51.1–2 Spring-Summer 1976 *s.v.* ball park]

out of the loop not part of the decision-making and information-disseminating pattern in a bureaucracy [63.3 Fall 1988 *s.v.* loop]

out-of-towner one who visits or does not reside in a particular town [27.1 Feb. 1952]

outsource to purchase (parts) from an outside supplier, domestic or foreign [60.3 Fall 1985]

outyear, out year (in U.S. government) the year(s) beyond the current budget year [57.2 Summer 1982]

overexposure excessive availability of a public person for viewing by an audience, esp. on TV [33.2 May 1958 *illus. s.v.* exposure]

overflight a flight over an area, esp. for purposes of aerial photography or intelligence gathering [40.3 Oct. 1965 *illus. s.v.* spy in the sky]

over-jacket *British* a vest-like garment worn over a coat; specif. a luminous one to increase the wearer's visibility on a highway [63.1 Spring 1988]

overkill to wreak destruction far beyond an enemy's probable point of surrender; *also* **over-kill,** the power to wreak destruction far beyond an enemy's probable point of surrender [38.3 Oct. 1963]

overnight letter a letter guaranteed next-day delivery for a special fee [59.1 Spring 1984]

over the top [19.4 Dec. 1944 forematter]

Ovra [21.3 Oct. 1946 forematter]

OWI Office of War Information [21.3 Oct. 1946 forematter]

O-word Olympics [63.4 Winter 1988 *s.v.* word]

ozone hole a localized depletion in the ozone layer encircling the earth's atmosphere, specif. over Antarctica and the Arctic [64.2 Summer 1989]

ozoner a drive-in movie theater [28.3 Oct. 1953]

PABA [21.3 Oct. 1946 forematter]

PAC, P.A.C. the Political Action Committee of the Congress of Industrial Organizations [21.2 Apr. 1946]

Pacific-firster one who believes that the Pacific area is of greatest importance for U.S. policy [34.2 May 1959]

pack rape *New Zealand use* forced sexual intercourse with several persons, gang rape [64.4 Winter 1989]

paddy-hop [47.3–4 Fall-Winter 1972 *s.v.* hop]

page three *British* the third page of a tabloid newspaper, specif. *The Sun,* containing a large photograph of an unclothed young woman; appearing nude or seminude on the third page of a tabloid; beautiful, young, and like a pin-up [63.1 Spring 1988]

pajamagate [56.4 Winter 1981 *s.v.* -gate]

Paki-bashing *British* beating up Pakistanis [62.4 Winter 1987 forematter]

palazzo *usu. pl.;* **palazzo pants** long, wide-legged pants for women, usu. made of crepe, jersey, or other soft fabric; **palazzo sleeve** a very wide, flowing sleeve [47.3–4 Fall-Winter 1972]

paleomagnetism the study of the magnetization of ancient rocks [39.3 Oct. 1964]

Panagate [56.4 Winter 1981 *s.v.* -gate]

Panama-based [20.2 Apr. 1945 forematter]

Panama red; Panama marijuana of high quality from Panama [57.4 Winter 1982]

pancake to flatten, crush, *lit. and fig.* [17.4 Dec. 1942 forematter; 18.2 Apr. 1943]

panelist a member of a discussion or quiz panel, esp. on television [29.4 Dec. 1954]

panzer (of mechanized troops, esp. tanks) armored, *also fig. uses* [16.2 Apr. 1941]

paper curtain the use of money as protection; paperwork as an interference; censored news-reporting [25.3 Oct. 1950 forematter]; *British* censorship of news reports [63.2 Summer 1988]

paper trail evidence, esp. for a decision or of clandestine or improper action [63.3 Fall 1988]

para- *prefix* parachute [20.3 Oct. 1945 forematter]

parabomb [20.3 Oct. 1945 forematter]

parachute-streak to jump from an airplane with a parachute but otherwise naked [48.1–2 Spring-Summer 1973]

parade-happy [22.3 Oct. 1947 *s.v.* happy]

paradoctor a doctor who parachutes to deliver aid [20.3 Oct. 1945 forematter; 25.1 Feb. 1950]

paradrop, para-drop to drop by parachute [28.3 Oct. 1953]

parafemme French woman dropped by parachute [20.3 Oct. 1945 forematter]

parafrag bomb [20.3 Oct. 1945 forematter]

paramarine [20.3 Oct. 1945 forematter]

para-medic a medical corps person who parachutes from an aircraft to administer aid [27.3 Oct. 1952]

para-mine [20.3 Oct. 1945 forematter]

parapack; parapak a parachuted package; a parachute pack worn on the stomach [31.1 Feb. 1956]

parapacked supplies [20.3 Oct. 1945 forematter]

parapants [20.3 Oct. 1945 forematter]

parapooch; parapup a dog dropped in a parachute [20.3 Oct. 1945 forematter]

pararescueman an Air Force parachutist who rescues space capsules and their personnel from the ocean [38.3 Oct. 1963]

para-searcher a parachutist who helps stranded aviators [20.3 Oct. 1945 forematter]

parashooter; parashot [20.3 Oct. 1945 forematter]

para-ski (of parachute troops) equipped with skis; **para-skier** a member of a para-ski troop [18.1 Feb. 1943 forematter; 19.1 Feb. 1944; 20.3 Oct. 1945 forematter]

paraspotter [20.3 Oct. 1945 forematter]

paraspy [20.3 Oct. 1945 forematter]

parastreaker one who parachutes naked [48.1–2 Spring-Summer 1973]

paratroop *usu. pl.* a parachute troop; a paratrooper [18.1 Feb. 1943; 20.3 Oct. 1945 forematter]

paratrooper a member of a parachute troop [18.1 Feb. 1943]

Paratwill a shiny, rain-resistant fabric [20.3 Oct. 1945 forematter]

parenting the care or attention given to a child, by or as by a parent [58.1 Spring 1983]

parity a political concept holding that a farmer should receive prices for farm products equivalent in purchasing power to that of 1909–14 [18.4 Dec. 1943]

parking deck a multistoried structure for parking automobiles [47.3–4 Fall-Winter 1972]

parking meter a clocking device to charge for parking [23.1 Feb. 1948]

parking orbit a temporary staging orbit about the Earth from which a rocket departs for outer space [37.2 May 1962]

parking station a site for parking [34.1 Feb. 1959 *illus. s.v.* car park]

Parkinson's Law a principle stated by C. Northcote Parkinson that bureaucracies are inherently inefficient, phrased in various ways, such as "Work expands to fill the time available for its completion" and "Subordinates multiply at a fixed rate, regardless of the amount of work done"; **Parkinsonism** the trend of a bureau to expand; any of Parkinson's Laws [37.2 May 1962]

park-ride pertaining to a service that provides both remote parking for automobiles and transportation from the parking place to a destination [34.1 Feb. 1959]

parlay to make a small possession, endowment, etc. yield a large return [25.2 May 1950]

partner dancing TOUCH DANCING [50.1–2 Spring-Summer 1975]

party-hop [47.3–4 Fall-Winter 1972 *s.v.* hop]

party-liner one who adheres to the party line [16.2 Apr. 1941 forematter]

pass candy [18.2 Apr. 1943 forematter]

pass-fail, pass/fail pertaining to an academic class in which a student's work is evaluated in terms of passing or failing rather than by a letter grade [45.3–4 Fall-Winter 1970]

passive (of a satellite) without instrumentation [36.3 Oct. 1961]

patch-farm to farm (land) in patches [31.3 Oct. 1956]

patient zero a person who plays a key role in the spread of a disease; specif. the first person to introduce the Aids virus into America [64.2 Summer 1989]

patriotute a patriotic prostitute, a young woman who is sexually available to military men [21.3 Oct. 1946 *illus. s.v.* victory girl]

pattern-bomb *v.* [31.3 Oct. 1956]; **pattern bombing, pattern-bombing** bombing of an area by a formation of planes to increase the likelihood of hitting a target [20.4 Dec. 1945]

peace dividend an anticipated saving in military spending due to improved relations with Russia [65.4 Winter 1990]

peak-load pricing; peak pricing a rate structure under which the highest rates would be charged for electricity consumed at times of peak demand [55.1 Spring 1980]

Pearl Harbor the Japanese attack at Pearl Harbor, 7 Dec. 1941; a similar attack or danger [17.4 Dec. 1942]

pedal-in [39.3 Oct. 1964 *s.v.* in]

pedal pusher(s) women's knee-length trousers developed for bicycle-riding [21.4 Dec. 1946]

pedestal booth *British* a public telephone on a post, partially enclosed in a transparent wrap-around [63.2 Summer 1988]

peel off (of an airplane) to curve away from another aircraft [17.4 Dec. 1942 forematter; 18.2 Apr. 1943]

peepie-creepie a portable TV camera, *also* creepie-peepie, walkie-lookie [28.3 Oct. 1953]

Peglerism an expression in the manner of Westbrook Pegler [32.4 Dec. 1957]

pencilatelist (from *philatelist*) [18.4 Dec. 1943 forematter]

Pendergastism [32.4 Dec. 1957]

people *suffixal form* (used after the initial letter of a word under real or pretended taboo to make a jocular euphemism) [63.4 Winter 1988]

people-intensive [60.1 Spring 1985 *s.v.* intensive]

pepperroo a peppy story [17.4 Dec. 1942 forematter]

percentage a share of winnings or profits; a rake-off [18.1 Feb. 1943 forematter; 19.1 Feb. 1944]

perchery *British* (of eggs) from hens kept in a shed or barn [63.2 Summer 1988]

perestroika the Soviet policy of economic restructuring instituted by Mikhail Gorbachev [63.3 Fall 1988]; any radical change in economic policy [65.3 Fall 1990]

Perma-lastic (from *elastic*) [18.4 Dec. 1943 forematter]

personal organiser; personal planner *British* a notebook holding printed forms for organizing one's appointments, activities, and personal information; *specif.* Filofax or Time Manager [62.4 Winter 1987]

personhood personal identity and worth [54.1 Spring 1979]

personnel-intensive [60.1 Spring 1985 *s.v.* intensive]

personnel transfer capsule an underwater capsule in which aquanauts move to a decompression chamber on the deck of a ship [44.1 Feb. 1969]

PET *British* polyethylene terephthalate, a material used for bottles of carbonated drinks [63.2 Summer 1988]

pet rock a rock packaged with a "training manual" and sold as a novelty gift item; a fad that brings considerable profit to its promoter [56.3 Fall 1981]

petro- *prefix* petroleum; **petrobillions; petrodiplomat** a diplomat representing a country that traffics heavily in oil and petroleum products; **petrodollar** surplus dollars (or dollar claims or assets) that the oil-exporting countries accumulate in the oil-importing countries; **petrodollar-rich; petropolitics** [49.1–2 Spring-Summer 1974]

petrochemical, petro-chemical a chemical derived from petroleum or natural gas; **petrochemistry** the study of the chemical properties of oil [27.3 Oct. 1952]

phantom limb a false consciousness of a limb after amputation [22.2 Apr. 1947]

phase microscope a microscope for viewing living cells as they function [28.4 Dec. 1953]

philanthropee a beneficiary of philanthropic action [44.2 May 1969 *illus. s.v.* philanthropoid]

philanthropoid a person who assists in giving away a philanthropist's money [44.2 May 1969]

Philippine-based [20.2 Apr. 1945 forematter]

phillumenist one who collects matchboxes and matchbook covers [26.2 May 1951]

phone-sit *v.* [31.3 Oct. 1956]

phoney war [23.2 Apr. 1948 forematter]

phonogenic speaking well over the telephone [24.4 Dec. 1949]

photobiography a person's life revealed through photographs [28.1 Feb. 1953]

photo op a photo opportunity, an event arranged for photographs and publicity, esp. of politicians; **photo opportunist** one who arranges or takes photographs at a photo op [64.3 Fall 1989]

photo reconnaissance the seeking of information from aerial photographs [28.4 Dec. 1953]

physia *British* a physiotherapist [63.2 Summer 1988]

physical vigorous, physically active, rough [54.3 Fall 1979]

phytotron a laboratory for the study of plant growth under controlled conditions of temperature and light [40.3 Oct. 1965]

pianothon [31.1 Feb. 1956 *illus. s.v.* rockerthon]

piat projector infantry antitank, an antitank weapon [21.3 Oct. 1946 forematter]

pickaback, pick-a-back *see* piggyback [32.2 May 1957]

pickleburger [18.2 Apr. 1943 forematter]

pickled (of airplanes) treated with a protective coating and stored [25.2 May 1950]

pierced (of earrings) designed for pierced ears [45.3–4 Fall-Winter 1970]

pierced look (of earrings) having clip fasteners but looking as though designed for pierced ears [45.3–4 Fall-Winter 1970 *s.v.* look]

pig-a-back *see* piggyback [32.2 May 1957]

pigboat a submarine [17.4 Dec. 1942; 22.2 Apr. 1947]

pigeoneer a keeper or trainer of homing pigeons [18.1 Feb. 1943 forematter]

piggyback, piggy-back, piggy back; piggybacking carrying one freight vehicle on another, as a small seaplane on a larger plane, or a truck trailer on a railroad flat car, or a barge on a scow [32.2 May 1957]

pillow tank a flexible rubber-nylon container for storing or transporting liquids that can be rolled and packed when not in use [36.3 Oct. 1961]

pilotless plane a Robot Bomb, *also* P-plane [19.4 Dec. 1944 forematter]

pin *British* a paper fastener, such as a staple; to fasten pieces of paper together [63.2 Summer 1988]

pinch effect the confinement of a hot gas into a narrow column by magnetic lines of force (a Magnetic Bottle), so that the gas does not touch or affect the sides of its material container [34.1 Feb. 1959]

pinchhit *v.* [31.3 Oct. 1956]

ping-pong to bounce back and forth, be discussed in several quarters; to bat around, discuss (a matter) without reaching a decision; two-channel sound recorded with exaggerated shifts from one loudspeaker to another, usu. with the primary aim of demonstrating the capabilities of the equipment; *attrib.* pertaining to the improved relations between the United States and mainland China as a result of ping-pong diplomacy; showing Chinese influence, as a result of or subsequent to the initiatives of ping-pong diplomacy [46.3–4 Fall-Winter 1971]; to refer (a patient, esp. one on Medicaid) to other doctors, particularly if such referral is not medically necessary [54.3 Fall 1979]

ping-pong diplomacy the first step toward normalized relationships between the U.S. and mainland China, initiated by an invitation to a U.S. table-tennis team to compete in the People's Republic of China, *also* table-tennis diplomacy [46.3–4 Fall-Winter 1971]

ping-pong diplomat a member of the U.S. table-tennis team that visited the People's Republic of China in April 1971 [46.3–4 Fall-Winter 1971]

ping-ponger a table-tennis player [46.3–4 Fall-Winter 1971]

ping-ponging referring a patient, esp. one on Medicaid, to other doctors, particularly if such referral is not medically necessary [54.3 Fall 1979 *s.v.* ping-pong *v.i.*]

ping-ping-pong-pong four-channel sound recorded with exaggerated shifts from one loudspeaker to another, usu. with the primary aim of demonstrating the capabilities of the equipment [46.3–4 Fall-Winter 1971]

pinpoint, pin-point to aim, direct, or determine with great exactness and accuracy; **pinpointing, pin-pointing** [24.3 Oct. 1949]

pin-point bomb to bomb a particular preidentified target [20.4 Dec. 1945 *illus. s.v.* pattern-bombing, precision bombing]

pin-upper a pin-up model [34.2 May 1959]

pistol-whip to beat with a pistol; **pistol-whipping** [30.4 Dec. 1955; 31.3 Oct. 1956]

pitch-hitter a DESIGNATED HITTER [46.1–2 Spring-Summer 1971]

plane-crash *v.* [31.4 Dec. 1956]

plastic made of plastic; something made of plastic [18.1 Feb. 1943]

plastic bomb an explosive the consistency of putty that combines TNT and hexogen; **plastic bombing** the use of plastic bombs [40.3 Oct. 1965]

plastinaut a life-sized plastic dummy astronaut used for biological studies of radiation above the atmosphere [39.2 May 1964; 40.3 Oct. 1965 *s.v.* -naut]

plastique *see* plastic [18.1 Feb. 1943]

plastiqueur *French* one who uses a plastic bomb [40.3 Oct. 1965]

platinum a record album with sales of a million copies; **platinum-selling** (of recording artists) producing records that sell a million copies [57.2 Summer 1982]

playaholic *British* an individual who plays a great deal [63.1 Spring 1988]

play-in a demonstration for integration at a segregated park or pool [38.3 Oct. 1963 *s.v.* in]

playsuit a light sports suit for women, usu. with a skirt that may be fastened over shorts [17.4 Dec. 1942 forematter; 18.2 Apr. 1943]

playwrite *v.* [31.4 Dec. 1956]

plea-bargain to carry on negotiations with the aim of permitting or inducing the accused to plead guilty or give testimony in exchange for reduced charges; specif. to agree to plead guilty to a less serious charge if a more serious charge is waived or give testimony in return for a lighter charge, or to agree to reduce the charges against a defendant in return for testimony or a plea of guilty; to plead guilty in return for some special concession by the prosecution other than reduced charges; **plea bargain,** a defendant's waiving of the constitutional right to trial in exchange for lenient sentencing [49.1–2 Spring-Summer 1974; 49.3–4 Fall-Winter 1974]

plea bargainer [49.3–4 Fall-Winter 1974]

plench (from *pliers* + *wrench*) a tool for use in space by weightless astronauts, a kind of ZERT [40.3 Oct. 1965]

plexipave *British* a kind of surface for a tennis court [63.2 Summer 1988]

ploughperson's *British* a ploughman's lunch, typically cheese, bread and butter, pickles, and crudités [63.2 Summer 1988]

plumber a member of a special investigative team within the White House created to stop security leaks and investigate other sensitive security matters; **plumbing** stopping security leaks; **plumbing crew** a group charged with stopping information leaks; **plumbing union** *stunt* organization of those engaged in stopping information leaks [54.4 Winter 1979]

plushy complacently opulent [18.2 Apr. 1943]

pluto-democracy (used by totalitarian propagandists) a democracy tainted with plutocracy [18.1 Feb. 1943]

plutonium the 94th element on the atomic chart [21.4 Dec. 1946]

police state a state in which individual liberty – social, economic, and political – is suppressed [24.1 Feb. 1949]

pollee one polled by a public-opinion institute [16.4 Dec. 1941 forematter]

polltaxer one in favor of the polltax [34.2 May 1959]

polyunsaturate an organic compound containing double or triple bonds between carbon atoms, hence a vegetable fat supposed to be particularly healthful in the diet [40.3 Oct. 1965]

Pontiac fever a nonfatal illness similar to LEGIONNAIRE'S DISEASE [56.2 Summer 1981 *illus. s.v.* Legionella pneumophila, Legionellosis]

poolathon [31.1 Feb. 1956 *illus. s.v.* rockerthon]

pool it to drive or ride in a car pool, *also* carpool (it); **pooler** a CARPOOLER; **pooling** participating in a CAR POOL; **poolmate** a fellow member of a CAR POOL [51.3–4 Fall-Winter 1976]

pop art a form of art that makes wide use of objects and imagery drawn from popular culture [41.2 May 1966]

pop-ism either extreme harshness or extreme feebleness in the father as a cause of psychoneurosis among American men [32.4 Dec. 1957]

Popsicle *trademark* (from *icicle*) [18.4 Dec. 1943 forematter]

popster one who produces or is a fan of pop art [41.2 May 1966]

popular frontism, Popular Frontism ideas and practices associated with an antifascist coalition of leftist and liberal or centrist groups, esp. in France [32.4 Dec. 1957]

Pop Warner football organized football for youngsters [48.1–2 Spring-Summer 1973]

porky pie *British* (riming slang) lie [63.2 Summer 1988]

Pornogate a scandal involving erotic films purportedly made with equipment used for filming the Quebec National Assembly sessions [59.2 Summer 1984 *s.v.* -gate]

portal-to-portal pay pay for underground miners including the time spent traveling from the mouth of the mine to the place where the substance is to be mined [21.4 Dec. 1946]

pose-happy [22.3 Oct. 1947 *s.v.* happy]

positively vet *British* to check a person's suitability for security clearance [63.2 Summer 1988]

post the shaft of a stud earring [46.1–2 Spring-Summer 1971]

post-family-hour after the FAMILY HOUR [51.3–4 Fall-Winter 1976 *s.v.* family hour]

post-ping-pong following the resumption of contacts between the United States and the People's Republic of China [46.3–4 Fall-Winter 1971]

postwar the period after World War II [21.4 Dec. 1946]

post-Watergate existing or occurring after the Watergate revelations; characteristic of the mood or climate of American public life after the events of the Watergate scandal became known, typified by the public's decreased willingness to tolerate activities it regards as wrong, the anxiety of those in positions of power or prominence that their actions might be considered morally wrong, and a sincere desire for behavior that is morally right [54.4 Winter 1979]

potato a COUCH POTATO; **potatophernalia** commercial objects with a couch-potato theme [63.3 Fall 1988]

pot bust an arrest for the use, possession, or sale of marijuana; **pothead** a marijuana user; **pot hound** a dog trained to detect marijuana; **pot likker** tea brewed with marijuana; **pot-phobe** one strongly opposed to the use of marijuana; **pot plane** an airplane on which marijuana is smuggled; **pot-prone** predisposed to the use of marijuana; **pot sniffer** a dog trained to detect marijuana, a pot hound; **Pots' People Partier** a member of an ad hoc group of protesters at the 1972 Democratic Convention; **pot-struck** under the influence of marijuana; **pot-vague** disoriented as a result of smoking marijuana [57.4 Winter 1982]

Poujadism [32.4 Dec. 1957]

pousada-hop [48.1–2 Spring-Summer 1973 *s.v.* hop]

POW, P.O.W. prisoner of war [21.2 Apr. 1946; 21.3 Oct. 1946 forematter]

powder room a women's rest room [18.1 Feb. 1943 forematter]

power associated with, conducive to, or emblematic of power, esp. political or economic; involving powerful people, *as in* ~ user, ~ breakfast, ~ lunch, ~ suit, ~ flier, ~ tie, ~ suspenders, ~ walking, ~ color, ~ game, ~ writing [63.4 Winter 1988]

power-happy [19.1 Feb. 1944 forematter]

powerhouse something very strong [18.4 Dec. 1943]

power-intensive [60.1 Spring 1985 *s.v.* intensive]

power-pile *v.* [31.4 Dec. 1956]

power politics international politics exerted through military might [32.2 May 1957 *illus. s.v.* ICBM]

power zert a battery-powered space tool, such as a wrench anchored to keep it from spinning [40.3 Oct. 1965 *s.v.* zert]

P-plane (from *pilotless plane*) a ROBOT BOMB [19.4 Dec. 1944 forematter]

pratfall, prat-fall; prattfall, pratt-fall a fall on the posterior, *also fig.* uses [18.1 Feb. 1943]

pray-in a demonstration for integration involving public prayer [38.3 Oct. 1963 *s.v.* in]

pre-atomic before the atomic bomb, prior to 6 August 1945 [21.3 Oct. 1946]

precision bombing PATTERN BOMBING of a group of related objects, with an effort to PIN-POINT BOMB the most important object [20.4 Dec. 1945; 26.2 May 1951]; **precision bomber** [20.4 Dec. 1945 *s.v.* precision bombing]

pre-echo an echo in a phonograph record caused by excessively close grooves [36.3 Oct. 1961]

prefab prefabricated; **prefabricator, pre-fabricator** a builder of prefabricated houses [21.3 Oct. 1946]

pre-gavel to post-gavel beginning before the formal opening of a meeting and lasting until after the formal closing [57.1 Spring 1982]

premiere to show for the first time, give a premiere of; to have a premiere [19.1 Feb. 1944; 24.4 Dec. 1949]

prepackaged (esp. of meat and produce in a supermarket) packaged before offered for sale; (of anything) prepared in advance; **prepackaging, pre-packaging** packaging goods before they are offered for sale [27.1 Feb. 1952]

presentism [32.4 Dec. 1957]

preset missile, pre-set missile a missile fired, like a shell, at a target [31.1 Feb. 1956]

presidentiad the term of office of a president [29.3 Oct. 1954]

pressure to exert pressure or force (on) [18.2 Apr. 1943]

pressure pattern a pattern made by various barometric pressures [31.1 Feb. 1956]

pressurize to provide with air under pressure, as an aircraft for breathing purposes to compensate for low natural pressure at high altitudes [18.4 Dec. 1943]

Pretoriastroika *stunt* a restructuring of the political policies of the South African government [65.3 Fall 1990]

pre-Watergate before the Watergate revelations, hence insensitive to issues of political morality [54.4 Winter 1979]

price fix *v.* [31.3 Oct. 1956]

primo (esp. of marijuana) first-class, top-quality, *also* el-primo [57.4 Winter 1982]

printed circuit; printed wire a circuit etched on an insulated base [28.4 Dec. 1953]

priority *euphemism* rationing [17.2 Apr. 1942 forematter; 17.4 Dec. 1942 forematter]

private enterprise business activity under private as opposed to public (government) control, *also* free enterprise [24.3 Oct. 1949]

private enterpriser one engaged in private enterprise, esp. a small-business person [34.2 May 1959]

privateer an operator or advocate of private ownership of a public utility [18.1 Feb. 1943 forematter]

privilege *suffixal form* a right to do as one wishes by virtue of a position held and esp. to be free from the authority of another [48.3–4 Fall-Winter 1973]; *cf.* Crown privilege, executive privilege

prizeworthy [16.2 Apr. 1941 forematter]

probable a supposed casualty, esp. referring to military craft [20.4 Dec. 1945]

product mix, product-mix the relative proportion of the different products to all products of a company, normally expressed in terms of dollar sales or individual units [33.2 May 1958]

profiler [34.2 May 1959]

profit center an organizational unit of a business enterprise for which data about expenses and revenue are gathered; any highly profitable unit or activity of an enterprise, source of profit, moneymaker [56.2 Summer 1981]

Promin a drug used in the treatment of malaria, tuberculosis, and leprosy [23.2 Apr. 1948]

prong to hang up (a telephone receiver); to move in a prong-like formation [18.1 Feb. 1943]

propeller-stop; prop-stop *attrib.* political campaigning by airplane trips [28.1 Feb. 1953]

protective surveillant, alleging to provide protection, *esp. in* ~ custody [17.4 Dec. 1942 forematter; 18.2 Apr. 1943]

protodweeb early instance of a dweeb [65.3 Fall 1990 *s.v.* dweeb]

prototype an object (esp. a vehicle) manufactured in small numbers for experimental purposes [16.2 Apr. 1941]

proximity fuze; proximity fuse a tiny radio set device in the nose of a missile that causes the shell to explode at a position where maximum damage will occur [21.3 Oct. 1946]

proxy war brushfire war; a war fought by a client state to which a patron state lends support but not active participation [33.2 May 1958]

psychodrama a therapeutic type of drama in which the patient/actors do not learn parts, but make them up spontaneously to meet the situation being enacted [23.1 Feb. 1948]

psychohistory the study or treatment of historical subjects from the standpoint of psychology or psychoanalytical theory; a work of psychohistory; **psychohistorian** one who treats historical subjects from a psychological or psychoanalytical viewpoint [47.3–4 Fall-Winter 1972]

psycholinguistics the study of psychological aspects of language [28.1 Feb. 1953]

psychological warfare [23.2 Apr. 1948 forematter]

PT boat [21.3 Oct. 1946 forematter]

PTFP prime time family programming, the family hour [51.3–4 Fall-Winter 1976]

pubcrawl *v.* [31.4 Dec. 1956]

publicitor press agent [31.1 Feb. 1956]

publisher-hop [47.3–4 Fall-Winter 1972 *s.v.* hop]

Pulitzergate [56.4 Winter 1981 *s.v.* -gate]

pulpateer one who writes for the pulps [18.1 Feb. 1943 forematter]

pump-primer [17.4 Dec. 1942 forematter]

punch-out the beating of a randomly selected victim by a gang of teenage boys as sport, *esp. in* play ~, *also* wilding [65.2 Summer 1990]

punch-drunk [22.3 Oct. 1947 forematter]

punkette *British* (of clothing style) pertaining to a female punk [63.2 Summer 1988]

punk out to go back on a promise [31.1 Feb. 1956]

pupil; pupil barrister *British* a newly called barrister serving in the chambers of an older member of the bar [63.2 Summer 1988]

purgee a victim of a political purge [16.4 Dec. 1941 forematter]

Purple-Heart Circuit [24.4 Dec. 1949 forematter]

purple market legalized prices formerly characteristic of the black market [25.2 May 1950 forematter]

purpose-bred animal an animal bred specifically for research use [64.2 Summer 1989]

pushbutton, push-button remote-controlled [24.2 Apr. 1949]

PV *British* positive vetting; positively vetted [63.2 Summer 1988]

PW *see* POW [21.2 Apr. 1946; 21.3 Oct. 1946 forematter]

P-word please [63.4 Winter 1988 *s.v.* word]

Q fever [21.3 Oct. 1946 forematter]

quackupuncture acupuncture performed by unqualified persons [49.3–4 Fall-Winter 1974]

quad quadiphony, four-channel sound; equipment for the playback of four-channel recordings; quadriphonic, four-channel [48.1–2 Spring-Summer 1973]

quadminium a four-unit structure in which the tenants own their apartments [47.3–4 Fall-Winter 1972]

quad-quad discrete four-channel sound [48.1–2 Spring-Summer 1973]

quadracast *see* quadricast [48.1–2 Spring-Summer 1973]

quadraphonic four-channel sound; equipment for the playback of four-channel sound; *see* quadriphonic; **quadraphonically** *see* quadriphonically; **quadraphonics** *see* quadriphonics; **quadraphony** *see* quadriphony [48.1–2 Spring-Summer 1973]

quadrasonic four-channel sound; quadriphonic [48.1–2 Spring-Summer 1973]

quadricast the transmission of four-channel sound by radio; to transmit four-channel sound; **quadricasting** four-channel broadcasting [48.1–2 Spring-Summer 1973]

quadriminium a quadminium [47.3–4 Fall-Winter 1972]

quadriphonic four-channel; **quadriphonically; quadriphonics** the theory or techniques of four-channel sound reproduction; **quadriphony** the use of four-channel sound [48.1–2 Spring-Summer 1973]

quadrophonic *see* quadriphonic; **quadrophonics** *see* quadriphonics [48.1–2 Spring-Summer 1973]

quadrosonic *see* quadrasonic [48.1–2 Spring-Summer 1973]

quarterback (of any activity) to lead, direct, or guide [27.3 Oct. 1952]

quasar quasi-stellar object, the most distant object so far discovered in space and the most powerful source of radiation of both light and radio waves [40.3 Oct. 1965]

quasi-quad derived four-channel sound [48.1–2 Spring-Summer 1973]

queer-bashing *British* beating up homosexuals [62.4 Winter 1987 forematter]

question *suffixal form* (used after the initial letter of a word under real or pretended taboo to make a jocular euphemism) [63.4 Winter 1988]

queue happy affected by waiting in long lines [22.3 Oct. 1947 *s.v.* happy]

quickie; quicky something done quickly, esp. without ceremony, forethought, or preparation; specif. a movie made quickly and cheaply [17.4 Dec. 1942]

quisling a traitor; **quisle** to act as a traitor [16.2 Apr. 1941]

quizmaster [18.2 Apr. 1943 forematter]

quizzee [16.4 Dec. 1941 forematter]

raceway a track for harness racing [29.4 Dec. 1954]

racket buster, racket-buster a fighter against organized crime [18.1 Feb. 1943 forematter; 23.3–4 Oct.-Dec. 1948 *s.v.* buster]

radar radio detecting and ranging, a vacuum-tube device for detecting and locating planes [19.1 Feb. 1944; 21.3 Oct. 1946 forematter]

radar fence a protective network of radar stations surrounding an area [24.2 Apr. 1949]

radar island one of a series of floating platforms serving as radar stations against enemy aircraft, *also* Texas tower [31.4 Dec. 1956]

radar screen *see* radar fence [24.2 Apr. 1949]

radar-track *v.* [31.4 Dec. 1956]

radioastronomy a branch of astronomy utilizing high-frequency radio waves [24.4 Dec. 1949]

radiobotage (from *sabotage*); **radioboteur** (from *saboteur*) [18.4 Dec. 1943 forematter]

radiocast [18.2 Apr. 1943 forematter]

radiofication the replacement of wireless radio sets by wired or telephonic radio [31.4 Dec. 1956]

radiogenic (from *photogenic*) [18.4 Dec. 1943 forematter]

radio-poison *v.* [31.4 Dec. 1956]

radio star a star of low luminosity detectable by shortwave radio signals [28.3 Oct. 1953]

radio telescope a device that gathers short wave radio signals from outer space [28.3 Oct. 1953]

rah-rah accent *British* upper-class speech, with associations of the hunting crowd [63.2 Summer 1988]

railroad-buster [23.3–4 Oct.-Dec. 1948 *s.v.* buster]

ramjet, ram-jet an engine operating on a continuous jet of hot gases [23.3–4 Oct.-Dec. 1948]

R&D-intensive with a high level of research and development [60.1 Spring 1985 *s.v.* intensive]

ranger a member of an organization of American soldiers, created December 1941, formed of volunteers and trained in close-range fighting for raids on enemy territory, the U.S. counterpart of the U.K. COMMANDO [18.4 Dec. 1943]

rank-and-filer, rank and filer a member of the rank and file [16.2 Apr. 1941]

rank-happy [22.3 Oct. 1947 *s.v.* happy]

Rashogate [56.4 Winter 1981 *s.v.* -gate]

rat-borne [20.2 Apr. 1945 forematter]

rat race a mounted military review; a dance; mad, confused scramble; vicious circle; whirl [24.3 Oct. 1949]

raunch (of broadcasting) vulgarly sexual in language and subject; **raunch radio; raunch television** [65.1 Spring 1990]

R-day the anniversary of the Russian Revolution; the day for the official start of redeployment [21.3 Oct. 1946 forematter]

RDX an explosive with greater force than TNT [22.2 Apr. 1947]

reactor an apparatus for producing atomic energy by the interaction of fissionable material and neutrons, *esp.* in atomic ~, nuclear ~ [25.2 May 1950]

reader-alouder one who reads aloud [34.2 May 1959]

read-in a demonstration in a library protesting an administrative rule; a segregation demonstration in a public library [38.3 Oct. 1963]

Reaganaut a supporter of Ronald Reagan and his policies; **Reaganesque** characteristic or supportive of Ronald Reagan or Reaganism; **Reaganism** the political, social, and eco-nomic ideas espoused by Ronald Reagan as Governor of California and President of the U.S.; **Reaganite** a supporter of Ronald Reagan or his policies; a member of the Reagan staff or administration; **Reaganize** to deal with in the manner of Ronald Reagan; to bring under the influence of Ronald Reagan and his principles; **Reaganometrician** one who supports and assesses the results of Reaganomics; **Reaganomic** pertaining to Reaganomics; **Reaganomics** the economic ideas of Ronald Reagan; **Reagan red** a shade of red favored by Nancy Reagan [57.3 Fall 1982]

reality; reality-based (of TV) purporting to be realistic, but emphasizing the crude, vulgar, and violent; **reality-based show; reality-based television; reality show; reality television; reality TV** [65.1 Spring 1990]; **reality programming** [60.4 Winter 1985 *illus. s.v.* docu-schlock *s.v.* docu-]

real time time when the report of an event is simultaneous with the event; (of computers) a speed sufficient to permit control of an operation in process; *attrib.* simultaneous, instantaneous [40.3 Oct. 1965]

Rebelgate an incident at the University of Mississippi, from its nickname, *Rebel* [59.2 Summer 1984 *s.v.* -gate]

re-bop BEBOP music [24.1 Feb. 1949]

recap to resurface a tire; a tire so resurfaced [17.4 Dec. 1942 forematter; 19.1 Feb. 1944]

recession-speak euphemisms for losing one's job [59.4 Winter 1984 *s.v.* speak]

recycle to invest in the United States and other oil-importing countries (the surplus foreign exchange earned in those countries through the sale of oil) [49.1–2 Spring-Summer 1974]; to reuse previously published material with little or no change [58.2 Summer 1983]

Red Crosser a Red Cross worker [34.2 May 1959]

redeploy, re-deploy to reorganize military forces, move personnel and materials to a different theater of war, esp. from Europe to the Pacific after the collapse of Germany; **redeployment, re-deployment** [21.4 Dec. 1946]

red feather pertaining to the Community Chest [23.3–4 Oct.-Dec. 1948]

red-hot pants HOT PANTS for East Germans [46.1–2 Spring-Summer 1971 forematter]

red light any signal to stop action [26.2 May 1951]

red market the sale of an inferior grade of meat for red ration points [25.2 May 1950 forematter]

redshirt a player with one more year of college eligibility; **red shirt, red-shirt,** to hold (a college athlete) out of competition to prolong eligibility; **redshirting** the practice of holding athletes out of competition to prolong their eligibility [45.3–4 Fall-Winter 1970]

red sweat red-colored sweat on Eastern Airlines' flight attendants, caused by red ink on life jackets, but for a time believed to be a mysterious illness [57.1 Spring 1982]

reed buster, reed-buster a saxophone [23.3–4 Oct.-Dec. 1948 *s.v.* buster]

reefer (pronunciation spelling of *refr.*) refrigerator car [21.3 Oct. 1946 forematter]

reexaminist, re-examinist one who wishes to reconsider existing policies for the covert purpose of changing them, esp. an isolationist [26.4 Dec. 1951]

reflag to register a foreign ship to permit it to fly the flag of the registering nation and thereby bring it under the diplomatic and military protection of that nation; **reflagging** [64.4 Winter 1989]

regular *euphemism* small in size [17.2 Apr. 1942 forematter]

rehab rehabilitation [57.3 Fall 1982]

Reich-Buster RAF plane bombing Germany [23.3–4 Oct.-Dec. 1948 *s.v.* buster]

reindustrialize to revitalize the American economy through modernization of obsolescent and inefficient means of production in basic industries such as steel and transportation; **reindustrialization** [57.1 Spring 1982]

reliefer [34.2 May 1959]

REM rapid eye movement, a sleep stage during which dreams occur [44.2 May 1969]

repechage (of boat races) a second-chance heat [33.2 May 1958]

republicrat; republocrat a member of the Democratic or Republican Party who votes with the opposition [24.3 Oct. 1949]

research-intensive [60.1 Spring 1985 *s.v.* intensive]

restaurant-hop [48.1–2 Spring-Summer 1973 *s.v.* hop]

rest cabin [24.2 Apr. 1949 forematter]

restore to bring back (a food) to the original nutritive value of its ingredients [18.4 Dec. 1943]

retread to resurface a tire; a tire so resurfaced [19.1 Feb. 1944]

retrorocket, retro-rocket, retro rocket a decelerating rocket used to brake the descent of a rocket landing on the moon [36.3 Oct. 1961]

returnee a military person who returns from an overseas assignment for further training and reassignment [21.3 Oct. 1946]

rev to increase (the revolutions of an engine) [17.4 Dec. 1942]

revenue enhancement *euphemism* a tax increase; **revenue enhancer** a means of increasing the amount of monies available to a government [58.4 Winter 1983]

reversed discrimination discrimination in favor of a group formerly discriminated against; **reverse discriminatory** pertaining to or promoting discrimination in reverse [57.1 Spring 1982]

reverse integration the attendance of white students at previously all-black schools [40.3 Oct. 1965]

rev it up to increase the revolutions of an engine [17.4 Dec. 1942 *s.v.* rev]

revolutioneer *v.* [18.1 Feb. 1943 forematter]

rhochrematics (in manufacturing) the flow from raw materials through production to the distribution of the finished product; the management of material flows [40.3 Oct. 1965]

rhubarb a scuffle or squabble, usu. amusing to witnesses [24.2 Apr. 1949]

ribbon happy having an extreme interest in military decorations [22.3 Oct. 1947 *s.v.* happy]

rice happy (of a prisoner of war) hoarding one's rice allowance for several meals in order to enjoy the sensation of one large meal [22.3 Oct. 1947 *s.v.* happy]

right-wingism extreme political conservativism [39.3 Oct. 1964]

ripple a quick succession of fired rockets [27.1 Feb. 1952]

rivet buster, rivet-buster a tool for knocking off rivetheads [23.3–4 Oct.-Dec. 1948 *s.v.* buster]

roadblock, road-block, road block any barrier or obstruction to events [27.1 Feb. 1952]

road-borne [19.3 Oct. 1944 forematter; 20.2 Apr. 1945 forematter]

Roadmaster Brakes [18.2 Apr. 1943 forematter]

road test, road-test *v.* [31.3 Oct. 1956]

rob to empty (something) of its contents [31.1 Feb. 1956]

robomb a robot bomb [19.4 Dec. 1944]

robot bomb; robot plane; robot a self-propelled bomb, shaped like an airplane, operated by jet propulsion and piloted by gyrocompass control, *also* Bob 'Ope, bumble bomb, doddle(bug), flitter bomb, pilotless plane, P-plane, rocket bomb *or* plane, V-1, whirley, winged comet, Wuwa [19.4 Dec. 1944]

robot airplane; robot bomber; robot raider a robot bomb [19.4 Dec. 1944 forematter]

rock (in baseball) a boner, blunder, mistake, *in* pull a ∼ [27.3 Oct. 1952]

rocker, Rocker (from *rock 'n' roll*) a leather-jacketed, long-haired, motorcycle-riding member of a British teenage gang [41.2 May 1966]

rockerthon *Canadian use* a cash-prize contest for the jobless who try to keep rocking chairs in motion [31.1 Feb. 1956]

rocket bomb; rocket plane a ROBOT BOMB [19.4 Dec. 1944 forematter]

rock happy affected by a long stay on an island [22.3 Oct. 1947 *s.v.* happy]

rock 'n roller, rock 'n' roller [34.2 May 1959]

rockoon a balloon-borne rocket [32.2 May 1957]

rockumentary a documentary movie, or one in that style, about rock music and musicians [60.4 Winter 1985]

roid rage violent behavior resulting from the excessive use of anabolic steroids, *also* steroid rage [64.4 Winter 1989]

ROK, Rok, R.O.K. Relief of Korea; Republic of Korea; *pl.* soldiers of the Republic of Korea [26.3 Oct. 1951]

roll (in railroading) bump or displace in a job [22.3 Oct. 1947 forematter]

rollaway ramp a portable stairway on wheels for boarding an airplane and deplaning [64.2 Summer 1989]

rollback, roll-back a forcible return (of prices) to a former, lower level [19.1 Feb. 1944]

Roller *British* a Rolls Royce automobile [63.2 Summer 1988]

rolling adjustment a period during which some industries are in recession while others are prospering, with changes in the status of each kind [30.2 May 1955]

rolling four-ten a work pattern that alternately schedules two teams of workers for four ten-hour workdays followed by four days off so that each week, in an eight-week cycle, a crew begins its four workdays one day later than in the preceding week, hence "rolling" [57.1 Spring 1982]

rolling vote (of a legislator) judgment on a legislative matter in the press without deliberation [63.3 Fall 1988]

Roosevelt-baiter [17.2 Apr. 1942 *s.v.* baiter]

rubber room a room padded with foam rubber for violent, mentally deranged persons; a tedious, routine, pointless, or stressful job, esp. in cramped, unpleasant working conditions [64.4 Winter 1989]

rubia (de la costa) a strain of Colombian marijuana, *also* blonde from the coast [57.4 Winter 1982]

rugged tough, difficult or grueling [23.1 Feb. 1948 forematter]

ruggedization making equipment sturdier [28.3 Oct. 1953 *illus. s.v.* miniaturization]

ruin-hop [48.1–2 Spring-Summer 1973 *s.v.* hop]

ruly English a synthetic language created from English by the United States Patent Office to be accessible to computers by systematizing the inherent inconsistencies in every day "unruly English" [39.3 Oct. 1964]

rumble a fight between teenage gangs, *cf.* fair one [30.2 May 1955]

rumptaske a FANNY PACK [65.1 Spring 1990]

run (a red light or stop sign) drive through without stopping [29.4 Dec. 1954 *s.v.* run]

run-around an evasion [17.4 Dec. 1942]

rundown, run-down a summary listing of the high points, *esp. in* quick ~, latest ~ [26.1 Feb. 1951]

run-through a rehearsal, esp. of songs [25.1 Feb. 1950]

ruptured duck the button insignia for discharged service people [21.3 Oct. 1946]

rushee [16.4 Dec. 1941 forematter]

Russia-based [20.2 Apr. 1945 forematter]

Rutgers 612 a repellent [22.2 Apr. 1947 forematter]

RV a recreational vehicle; to travel in a recreational vehicle; **RV-cationer** one who vacations in a recreational vehicle [56.3 Fall 1981]

Sad Sack [21.4 Dec. 1946 forematter]

safe computer practice an operation to protect computers against contamination by electronic viruses [64.3 Fall 1989]

Safespeak the language of consensus journalism reflecting market research, opposed to personalized journalism [59.2 Summer 1984 *s.v.* speak]

Sage Semi-Automatic Ground Environment, a radar network to give warning of attack [31.1 Feb. 1956]

sailorette a member of the women's naval auxiliary [17.4 Dec. 1942 forematter; 18.2 Apr. 1943 forematter]

Saipan-based [20.2 Apr. 1945 forematter]

saki-happy [22.3 Oct. 1947 *s.v.* happy]

salad sandwich *British* a sandwich made with salad ingredients: lettuce, tomato, cucumbers, onion, and salad cream, i.e., a thick mayonnaise dressing [63.2 Summer 1988]

salariat (used in Japan of a type of employee) [18.1 Feb. 1943 forematter]

sampy *British* sexually active, multiple-partnered youth [62.4 Winter 1987]

sand happy, sand-happy psychologically affected by desert campaigning [19.1 Feb. 1944 forematter; 22.3 Oct. 1947 *s.v.* happy]

sandwich generation a person or persons with the responsibility of caring for both children and parents [65.3 Fall 1990]

sandwich junction *British* a multilevel intersection of major roads [63.2 Summer 1988]

sanitary dressing *British* a sanitary napkin [63.2 Summer 1988]

Santa Marta gold a high-quality marijuana from Santa Marta, Colombia [57.4 Winter 1982]

sap-happy drunk [19.1 Feb. 1944 forematter]

Sarong Circuit [24.4 Dec. 1949 forematter]

satelloid a manned, powered, reusable craft that orbits the earth like a satellite but, when its propellants are exhausted, can return to the earth like an airplane [31.4 Dec. 1956]

saturation bombing AREA BOMBING, CARPET BOMBING; **saturation attack** an assault of saturation bombing; **saturation raid** a saturation attack; **saturation raider** a plane participating in a saturation raid [20.4 Dec. 1945]

sausageburger [18.2 Apr. 1943 forematter]

scatter-bomb [17.4 Dec. 1942 forematter]

schnorchel; schnorkel; schnorkle an apparatus for underwater breathing in submarines submerged at moderate depth; specif. a pipe or tube of about periscope height, extending from the ventilating system of the engines to the surface and fitted at the end with a valve that closes automatically when submerged [21.4 Dec. 1946]; *also* snorkel

scholar's privilege [48.3–4 Fall-Winter 1973 *s.v.* privilege]

sciencespeak scientific-sounding prose, esp. in cosmetic advertising [59.4 Winter 1984 *s.v.* speak]

scientific creationism; science creationism CREATION SCIENCE; **scientific creationist** a CREATION SCIENTIST [58.1 Spring 1983]

Scrantongate the unauthorized acquisition of prepublication copies of H. R. Haldeman's *The Ends of Power* at its bindery in Scranton, PA [53.3 Fall 1978 *s.v.* -gate]

scrapbook-happy interested in collecting clippings about oneself in a scrapbook [22.3 Oct. 1947 *s.v.* happy]

scrap-happy [19.1 Feb. 1944 forematter]

script to write (a scenario); to change (a plot or story) into a scenario [18.1 Feb. 1943 forematter; 19.1 Feb. 1944]

scripter a scriptwriter [20.3 Oct. 1945]

scripteur (from *entrepreneur, connoisseur, coiffeur*, etc.); **scripteuse** (from *danseuse, chanteuse*, etc.) [18.4 Dec. 1943 forematter]

script-write v. [31.4 Dec. 1956]

scrub (of a missile launch) to cancel; a cancelation [35.1 Feb. 1960]

scuba self-contained underwater breathing apparatus [36.3 Oct. 1961]

scubacide death by untrained use of scuba equipment [39.3 Oct. 1964 *s.v.* -cide]

scuttle to destroy or damage severely; to discard [18.1 Feb. 1943]

scuttlebutt, scuttle butt (naval slang) a rumor of doubtful origin [20.3 Oct. 1945]

S-day surrender day; school day [21.3 Oct. 1946 forematter]

seabee CB, a naval Construction Battalion [19.3 Oct. 1944]

sea-borne [19.3 Oct. 1944 forematter]

second banana a supporting comedian [31.1 Feb. 1956]

security blanket; security anything affording one a feeling of security, comfort, or safety; an experimental blanket-like safety device preventing or reducing injury to an automobile driver or passenger in a collision [49.1–2 Spring-Summer 1974]

seed money a relatively small amount of money used to start a project and to attract larger funds [49.3–4 Fall-Winter 1974]

see-through (of clothing) of transparent or semitransparent fabric or with openings; **see-throughness** (of clothing fabric) transparency [46.1–2 Spring-Summer 1971]

segregated practicing or maintaining segregation [31.1 Feb. 1956]

selectee *euphemism* draftee, one conscripted for military service through the selective service program [16.4 Dec. 1941 forematter; 17.2 Apr. 1942 forematter]

self-spin the analysis of a political event in which the analyzer is involved [63.3 Fall 1988]

self-standing *British* independent, self-contained, capable of being used alone [63.2 Summer 1988]

seller something offered for sale [16.4 Dec. 1941]

sell platinum to sell a million copies of a record album [57.2 Summer 1982 *s.v.* platinum]

semiballistic excited, angry, upset [65.2 Summer 1990]

semi-porno a motion picture that, while daring or erotic in content, is less explicit in its treatment of the subject than a pornographic film, soft porn [46.1–2 Spring-Summer 1971]

sencit senior citizen [45.3–4 Fall-Winter 1970 *illus. s.v.* sitcom]

send-in *British* a submission, as for an exhibition of pictures [63.2 Summer 1988]

senior bowler a university senior who has played in a bowl game [34.2 May 1959]

senior citizen an older person; retiree [48.1–2 Spring-Summer 1973]

sensorialism the theory of Jean LeGrand that only sense experience is valid and therefore sex, as the most intense of sensory experiences, is the most valid [32.4 Dec. 1957]

separate *in pl.* an outfit with parts intended to be worn with one another or with other articles in various combinations [25.1 Feb. 1950]

serf suburban early retired folk [60.1 Spring 1985 forematter]

service mark a distinguishing mark for services (e.g., Greyhound), as distinct from the trademark for products [27.3 Oct. 1952]

set shot a deliberate, unhurried basketball shot made from a still position some distance in front of the basket by a player who, momentarily unguarded, has time to get set [24.2 Apr. 1949]

Sewergate a scandal concerning the failure of the EPA to clean up sites contaminated by hazardous wastes [59.2 Summer 1984 *s.v.* -gate]

sex kitten a young motion picture actress whose chief asset is sex appeal [39.3 Oct. 1964]

shackmaster an American sailor who takes a native woman as a mistress [21.4 Dec. 1946 *illus. s.v.* bamboo American *s.v.* bamboo]

shack (up) with engage in sexual relations with [23.1 Feb. 1948]

shadow *British* unreported, unrecorded, *in* ~ economy; skeleton, *as in* ~ management [63.2 Summer 1988]

shadow factory; shadow plant [18.1 Feb. 1943 forematter]

SHAEF Supreme Headquarters Allied Expeditionary Force [19.4 Dec. 1944]

shambled littered up, reduced to rubble [28.3 Oct. 1953]

shambles any disorder [21.4 Dec. 1946]

Shangri-La an imaginary or secret military (esp. air) base [18.1 Feb. 1943 forematter; 19.1 Feb. 1944]

shaped charge a form of explosive packed with a hollow cavity at the front to produce a more concentrated blast [26.3 Oct. 1951; 27.1 Feb. 1952]

shape-up a system by which a foreman chooses longshoremen to hire from a semicircular line in front of him [29.4 Dec. 1954]

sharecrop *v.* [31.3 Oct. 1956]

shirt-sleeve diplomacy [46.3–4 Fall-Winter 1971 forematter]

shmoo (from the comic strip "Li'l Abner" by Al Capp) a small, gourd-shaped mythical animal with a face somewhat like that of a seal, whose productivity and generosity satisfy all human needs [24.2 Apr. 1949]

shock (of entertainment) lurid, violent, vulgar, sexually explicit; **shock artist; shock-cabaret; shock jock; shock-jocking** hosting a shock radio program; **shock photojournalism; shock radio; shock TV; shock video** [65.1 Spring 1990]

shock frock a bare-bosomed cocktail dress [40.3 Oct. 1965]

shoe-leather routinely investigative [64.2 Summer 1989]

shoo-in (in horse-racing) a race in which the winning horse has no serious competition; any winner without serious competition [25.3 Oct. 1950]

shooterie a film with gun fights [16.4 Dec. 1941 forematter]

shooting war a war involving actual participation of armed forces, not merely propaganda and sanctions [18.1 Feb. 1943; 23.2 Apr. 1948 forematter; 23.3–4 Oct.-Dec. 1948]

shootout any hotly fought contest between evenly matched rivals [57.2 Summer 1982]

shop *v.t., esp.* ~ a store, *but also* ~ the majors, ~ wares [26.4 Dec. 1951]

shopping network a system of advertising on cable television for products and services to be ordered by telephone; **shopping show** a TV program for home-shopping [64.1 Spring 1989]

shore-based [19.3 Oct. 1944 forematter; 20.2 Apr. 1945 forematter]

short to dispense fewer pills than prescribed but charge the price of the prescribed quantity [54.3 Fall 1979]

short cuts HOT PANTS [46.1–2 Spring-Summer 1971 forematter]

shorthand circuit secretarial schools [24.4 Dec. 1949 forematter]

shortpants; short shorts HOT PANTS [46.1–2 Spring-Summer 1971 forematter]

shotgun marry v. [31.3 Oct. 1956]

shovel-pass v. [31.3 Oct. 1956]

shriek alarm British a compressed-air canister carried by women as a defense against mugging or rape [63.2 Summer 1988]

shrink-wrap; shrink-wrapped (of computer software) wrapped in cellophane, the removal of which binds the purchaser to legal restrictions on the use of the software; hence, commercially available but with legally restricted use [64.2 Summer 1989]

shuttle base one of two bases between which a plane flies shuttle bombing missions [20.4 Dec. 1945 s.v. shuttle bombing]

shuttle bombing bombing done by a plane flying between two bases [20.4 Dec. 1945]

shuttle diplomacy negotiations between two or more countries conducted by a mediator who frequently flies back and forth between the nations involved in the dispute, cf. space-shuttle diplomat [49.1–2 Spring-Summer 1974]

shuttle flight a flight on which a plane performs shuttle bombing; **shuttle plane** a plane flying between two bases, esp. for shuttle bombing; **shuttle raid** an aerial attack made by planes flying between two bases [20.4 Dec. 1945 s.v. shuttle bombing]

side-armer a sidearm ball in baseball [34.2 May 1959]

sideline (in sports) to force out of play because of illness or injury [24.1 Feb. 1949]

Siegfriedism a quotation from a book by André Siegfried [32.4 Dec. 1957]

signature beer a MICROBREW [65.4 Winter 1990]

silent virus a COMPUTER VIRUS that escapes detection, leaves no trail, and causes random errors [64.3 Fall 1989 s.v. virus]

silver cord mother fixation [24.4 Dec. 1949]

simulated euphemism artificial, imitation [17.2 Apr. 1942 forematter]

simulcast to broadcast by radio and television simultaneously [25.2 May 1950]

sin buster, sin-buster a preacher [23.3–4 Oct.-Dec. 1948 s.v. buster]

singing shoulder a road shoulder with corrugated paving that gives off a loud hum when a car drives on it [36.4 Dec. 1961]

sitcom a TV situation comedy [45.3–4 Fall-Winter 1970]

sitdown a sit-in, esp. at a lunch counter [36.4 Dec. 1961]

sit-in a demonstration against segregation by blacks sitting in public service areas formerly restricted to whites, esp. in restaurants; integrated attendance in a court room [36.4 Dec. 1961 also s.v. in]; v. **sits-in, sat-in** to protest insufficient civil rights by sitting in a segregated area to which one would not be legally allowed access [39.3 Oct. 1964]

sitting duck an easy target [24.3 Oct. 1949]

sitting park a small park intended for sitting, with benches and tables [36.4 Dec. 1961]

sitting pigeon see sitting duck [24.3 Oct. 1949]

sitzkrieg inactive warfare, or an inactive war [16.2 Apr. 1941; 23.2 Apr. 1948 forematter]

Siwash a jerkwater college [16.4 Dec. 1941]

6-2-2 a repellent [22.2 Apr. 1947 forematter]

skiing [54.3 Fall 1979 forematter]

skilled-labor intensive [60.1 Spring 1985 s.v. intensive]

skip-bombing low-level bombing with delayed-action bombs that ricochet into the target [20.4 Dec. 1945]

skippie school kid with income and purchasing power [64.2 Summer 1989]

skirting socket British an electric socket at a baseboard [63.2 Summer 1988]

skort a mid-thigh pleated skirt with a matching pair of shorts attached inside [36.4 Dec. 1961]

skull-buster a detective [23.3–4 Oct.-Dec. 1948 s.v. buster]

skunk, Skunk an unidentified or enemy surface ship [33.2 May 1958]

sky prefixal form [20.4 Dec. 1945]

sky artillery [20.4 Dec. 1945]

sky bends [20.4 Dec. 1945]

sky block British a sky scraper, a tall apartment building [63.2 Summer 1988]

sky-borne [20.2 Apr. 1945 forematter]

skybridge an overhead suspended walkway across an enclosed court within a building such as a hotel [57.2 Summer 1982]

skybus a postwar plane designed esp. for feeder-line operation; a high-wing twin-engine all-metal monoplane with a tricycle landing gear [20.4 Dec. 1945]

sky-cab [20.4 Dec. 1945]

sky car [20.4 Dec. 1945]

sky clipper [20.4 Dec. 1945]

skyfighter [20.4 Dec. 1945]

sky freighter [20.4 Dec. 1945]

skyglow a glow in the sky caused by the reflection of city lights [18.4 Dec. 1943]

skyhook a device for dropping supplies [20.4 Dec. 1945]

sky jeep [20.4 Dec. 1945]

skylander [20.4 Dec. 1945]

skymarker bomb the M87 bomb, which trails colored smoke through the air [20.4 Dec. 1945]

Skymaster the Army C–54 Combat Transport, manufactured by Douglas [20.4 Dec. 1945; 21.2 Apr. 1946]

skyport [20.4 Dec. 1945]

sky-prodder an antiaircraft gun [20.4 Dec. 1945]

sky road [20.4 Dec. 1945]

skyrocket to cause to soar swiftly like a skyrocket [18.1 Feb. 1943]

sky scout a chaplain [20.4 Dec. 1945]

sky soldier [20.4 Dec. 1945]

sky train a troop carrier [20.4 Dec. 1945]

sky truck [20.4 Dec. 1945]

skytyping, sky typing a method of skywriting [39.3 Oct. 1964]

skywalk a suspended walkway [57.2 Summer 1982]

sky warrior [20.4 Dec. 1945]

skyway a suspended walkway [57.2 Summer 1982]

sky winder a member of the air corps [20.4 Dec. 1945]

sky wire an antenna [20.4 Dec. 1945]

slab happy [22.3 Oct. 1947 *s.v.* happy]

slap-and-yell *nonce* KISS-AND-TELL by children about parents [64.1 Spring 1989 forematter]

slap-happy [22.3 Oct. 1947 forematter]

Slaughtergate an Australian scandal involving the substitution of inferior meat in exports [59.2 Summer 1984 *s.v.* -gate]

sleaze television; sleaze TV TV programs in bad taste because of their subjects and treatment [65.1 Spring 1990]

slit wing plane a plane with an air-inhalation system increasing flight range and cargo capacity [39.3 Oct. 1964]

Sloaneish *British* having the characteristics of a Sloane Ranger: upper-middle class, young, with country connections [63.2 Summer 1988]

sloganeer to attempt to exert influence by the use of slogans [18.1 Feb. 1943 forematter; 30.4 Dec. 1955]

sloganeering using slogans for propaganda [30.4 Dec. 1955]

sloganize to express in slogans; to influence by slogans [30.4 Dec. 1955]

slotting allowance; slotting fee a charge made by a grocery store to a manufacturer for the use of shelf space to stock a product [65.4 Winter 1990]

slowdown, slow-down an intentional decrease in work speed, used as a weapon in labor disputes [16.2 Apr. 1941]

slug (of guns) to fire; (of submarines, airplanes, tanks) to fight; (of writing) to work industriously [23.1 Feb. 1948]

slumlord the landlord of a slum, a landlord who does not maintain rental property adequately [36.4 Dec. 1961]

sluppy *British* Sloane yuppy, a person combining characteristics of a Sloane Ranger and a yuppy [63.2 Summer 1988]

small-fry football; small-time football organized football for youngsters [48.1–2 Spring-Summer 1973]

small magazine *see* little magazine [23.2 Apr. 1948]

smarm *British, in* ~ school [63.2 Summer 1988]

smart-type [23.2 Apr. 1948 forematter]

smaze a combination of smoke and haze [29.4 Dec. 1954]

smist a combination of smoke and mist [29.4 Dec. 1954 *illus. s.v.* smaze]

smoke jumper a forest-fire fighter who parachutes into a fire area [23.1 Feb. 1948; 30.4 Dec. 1955]

smokeless cigarette a cigarette that produces no ash and little sidestream smoke [64.2 Summer 1989]

smokestack based on manufacturing, in contrast to high-technology or service-oriented [58.2 Summer 1983]

smokey ((the) bear), Smokey ((the) Bear) a state trooper or other law enforcement officer; **Smokey report** a CB radio report on the location of police cars [51.3–4 Fall-Winter 1976]

smoothie; smoothy a smooth-mannered person; an attractive person [18.4 Dec. 1943]

smug-buster [23.3–4 Oct.-Dec. 1948 *s.v.* buster]

smurk a combination of smoke and murk [29.4 Dec. 1954 *illus. s.v.* smaze]

smuttery *British, stunt* comic smuttiness [63.2 Summer 1988]

SN 7618 an antimalarial drug [22.2 Apr. 1947 forematter]

snafu, SNAFU situation normal, all fouled up [21.2 Apr. 1946]

snake-belly *v.* [31.4 Dec. 1956]

snap *British* (in newsrooms) a news flash [63.2 Summer 1988]

snap-happy exhilarated about taking snapshots [19.1 Feb. 1944 forematter]

snap tin *British* a container for a packed meal, lunch box [63.2 Summer 1988]

snazzy stylish and somewhat flashy [18.4 Dec. 1943]

snickerer [34.2 May 1959]

sniffer *British* (from riming slang *sniffer and snorter*) a reporter [63.2 Summer 1988]

snifter a compact radio direction finder used to locate short-range radio transmitters [26.2 May 1951]

sniperscope an infrared mechanism enabling snipers to see their quarry in the dark, also used for the study of fossils [23.3–4 Oct.-Dec. 1948]

snooperscope an infrared device similar to the sniperscope [23.3- 4 Oct.-Dec. 1948]

snoozamorooed drunk [16.4 Dec. 1941 forematter]

snorkel an underwater breathing device [24.3 Oct. 1949]; *also* schnorchel

snort(s) *see* schnorchel [21.4 Dec. 1946]

snow skiing [54.3 Fall 1979 forematter]

SN 13,276 an antimalarial drug [22.2 Apr. 1947 forematter]

soap a radio or TV soap opera [36.4 Dec. 1961]

soaper a radio soap opera [34.2 May 1959]

soaperatic pertaining to soap opera [36.4 Dec. 1961]

soap opera a radio serial, usu. highly emotional and melodramatic [20.2 Apr. 1945; 22.2 Apr. 1947]

social ecology the study of ecological issues in the light of social and political factors [63.4 Winter 1988]

socialwise socially [63.2 Summer 1988 *s.v.* -wise]

sockee one socked, i.e., struck [16.4 Dec. 1941 forematter]

sod-buster a rustic; a farmer [23.3–4 Oct.-Dec. 1948 *s.v.* buster]

sofa spud a COUCH POTATO [63.3 Fall 1988]

soft (of detergents) readily broken down by bacteria in soil and water, *also* biodegradable [40.3 Oct. 1965]

soft-land to land (an object), specif. on the moon, without being destroyed on impact; **soft landing** the landing of an object without destruction on impact [40.3 Oct. 1965]; an end, esp. of a business boom, without undesirable consequences such as a recession [47.3–4 Fall-Winter 1972]

soft sell an unaggressive sales technique [31.1 Feb. 1956]

software virus a COMPUTER VIRUS [64.3 Fall 1989 *s.v.* virus]

soggy-ballad circuit Chicago night clubs [24.4 Dec. 1949 forematter]

soggy-trick a DIRTY TRICK [49.3–4 Fall-Winter 1974]

sonarman Naval rating of a sonar operator [25.3 Oct. 1950]

song buster [23.3–4 Oct.-Dec. 1948 *s.v.* buster]

sonic barrier; sonic wall the sound barrier [23.1 Feb. 1948]

sonic boom; sonic explosion shock waves and a cannon-like noise produced by a plane breaking the sonic barrier [30.2 May 1955]

sophisticated (of machines and equipment) complex and versatile; **sophistication** [35.4 Dec. 1960]

sorority-hop [48.1–2 Spring-Summer 1973 *s.v.* hop]

sortie a flight by a military aircraft [19.4 Dec. 1944]

sound bite a short, striking, and memorable quotation useful for TV news programs [64.3 Fall 1989]

sound off a competition of automobile stereo sound systems [65.4 Winter 1990]

souvenir happy [22.3 Oct. 1947 *s.v.* happy]

space opera a science fiction work involving interplanetary travel, episodic adventures, and extraterrestrial dangers met and overcome [26.2 May 1951]

spacecraft earth spaceship earth [54.2 Summer 1979]

spaceman economy an economy based on conservation and recycling [54.1 Spring 1979]

spaceport an airport for spaceships [33.2 May 1958]

Spacer (in a science-fiction novel) a descendant of humans who settled the stars [34.2 May 1959]

spaceship, space ship an aircraft for traveling between planets or in outer space [22.2 Apr. 1947]

spaceship earth Earth viewed as a spaceship, as a body moving through space and carrying limited resources that must be conserved, esp. through international cooperation [54.2 Summer 1979]

space-shuttle diplomat *stunt* Henry Kissinger or a similar diplomat conducting SHUTTLE DIPLOMACY around the world, suggestive of an astronaut circling the earth [49.1–2 Spring-Summer 1974]

Space-speaк [59.2 Summer 1984 *s.v.* speak]

spacewalk, space walk the maneuvering of an astronaut outside a capsule in space; **spacewalker, space walker** one who performs a spacewalk; **spacewalking, space-walking, space walking** the act of maneuvering outside a capsule in space [44.2 May 1969]

spa-hop [47.3–4 Fall-Winter 1972 *s.v.* hop]

SPAMburger [18.2 Apr. 1943 forematter]

spammer space hammer, a tool with a spring triggered to bang like a riveter, for use in space by weightless astronauts, a kind of ZERT [40.3 Oct. 1965]

Spamwich (from *sandwich*) [18.4 Dec. 1943 forematter]

spark to incite or arouse [23.1 Feb. 1948]

SPARS [21.3 Oct. 1946 forematter]

speak *suffixal form* a jargonish or idiosyncratic style of speech associated with a particular person, group, register, or style [59.2 Summer 1984; 59.4 Winter 1984; *British* 63.2 Summer 1988]

spearhead to act as a spearhead (leader of a thrust or attack) for [18.4 Dec. 1943]

spectacular a long, high-cost, star-filled television program [30.2 May 1955]

speed climb *v.* [31.4 Dec. 1956]

speeder-upper a small truck used in heavy traffic by the NY Post Office [34.2 May 1959]

speed-zone *v.* [31.4 Dec. 1956]

spell out to explain simply or in detail [24.4 Dec. 1949]

spelunker one who explores caves [24.2 Apr. 1949]

spending tax a tax on spending [18.2 Apr. 1943]

S-people socialists [63.4 Winter 1988 *s.v.* people]

spin an interpretation of an event for public presentation; **spin control** an interpretation of events that is favorable to the party of the interpreter; specif. the efforts of campaign officials to convince reporters of their candidate's ability and popularity; **spin doctor** one who interprets political events for public dissemination, *also* Dr. Spin; **Spin Hall of Fame** *facetious* a record of outrageous distortions of events for political purposes; **spinner** a spin doctor [63.3 Fall 1988]

spin off, spin-off (in economics) to give (the stock of a subsidiary company) to the stockholders of the parent company as a dividend; create (subsidiary companies whose stock is to be distributed to the stockholders of the parent company as a dividend); *also* **spinoff** a transfer by a corporation of a portion of its assets to a newly formed corporation in exchange for the latter's capital stock, which is distributed as a property dividend to the stockholders of the original corporation [36.4 Dec. 1961]

spiral to rise disproportionately (said of prices, rates, etc.); a rise of such a nature [18.4 Dec. 1943]

spirit of ping pong rapprochement of China and the United States following the 1971 invitation for a U.S. table-tennis team to visit China [46.3–4 Fall-Winter 1971]

spirit of Watergate, Spirit of Watergate an awareness of the need for morality in public affairs [54.4 Winter 1979]

splashdown the landing of a spacecraft in the ocean [39.3 Oct. 1964]

splat gun *British* a gun that shoots blood-colored dye pellets [63.2 Summer 1988]

splice-edit *v.* [31.3 Oct. 1956]

splinter a subgroup split off from a larger group [24.3 Oct. 1949]

splurge gun [63.2 Summer 1988 *s.v.* splat gun]

spook an incompetent, erratic motorist [25.2 May 1950]

sportcast; sportcaster; sportscaster [18.2 Apr. 1943 forematter]

sportspeak the language of sportswriters and announcers [59.2 Summer 1984 *s.v.* speak]

sports shorts HOT PANTS [46.1–2 Spring-Summer 1971 forematter]

spot check a quick, rough sampling [23.1 Feb. 1948]; **spot-check** *v.* [31.4 Dec. 1956]

spot-mark *v.* [31.4 Dec. 1956]

spud a COUCH POTATO; **spudismo** the fashion for the couch-potato theme; **spud suit** a garment for wear while watching TV at home; **spud-ucopia** *stunt* an abundance of commercial products on the couch-potato theme [63.3 Fall 1988]

sputnik an artificial satellite, esp. Russian [33.2 May 1958; 33.4 Dec. 1958 forematter]

spy-buster [23.3–4 Oct.-Dec. 1948 *s.v.* buster]

spy in the sky a plane or satellite that gathers intelligence information through flights over foreign territory, *also attrib. as in* ~ satellite [40.3 Oct. 1965]

spymaster [18.2 Apr. 1943 forematter]

squack a native woman of the Pacific taken as a mistress by a sailor [21.4 Dec. 1946 *illus. s.v.* bamboo American *s.v.* bamboo]

squadrol a type of police vehicle [35.1 Feb. 1960]

square-bashing *British* military drill [62.4 Winter 1987 forematter]

squeaky-clean ethically or morally beyond reproach [60.4 Winter 1985]

squeezee [16.4 Dec. 1941 forematter]

squirt a military jet plane [26.3 Oct. 1951 *illus. s.v.* blow job]

sro *British* a self-regulating organization, an association of businesses that regulates their operation [63.2 Summer 1988]

SST supersonic transport; a jet plane that reaches speeds faster than the speed of sound [44.2 May 1969]

stack buster, stack-buster [23.3–4 Oct.-Dec. 1948 *s.v.* buster]

stagette [17.4 Dec. 1942 forematter]

Stakhanovism a Russian technique of speed-up and efficiency for increasing industrial production; **Stakhanovist, Stakhanovite** an adherent of Stakhanovism [18.4 Dec. 1943]

Stalinoid pertaining to or influenced by the thought of Josef Stalin [24.2 Apr. 1949]

stall-in [39.3 Oct. 1964 *s.v.* in]

standard *euphemism* second-rate [17.2 Apr. 1942 forematter]

standard-setter that which sets a standard [34.2 May 1959]

standee [16.4 Dec. 1941 forematter]

stand-in a protest against segregation by attending a segregated event, such as a theater performance [36.4 Dec. 1961]

stand-up (of a comedian or comedy) done without costumes, props, action, or assistance; a stand-up comedy routine [48.1–2 Spring-Summer 1973]

starlet a new or young movie actress [18.1 Feb. 1943; 21.4 Dec. 1946]

starry-eyed visionary [28.1 Feb. 1953; 28.3 Oct. 1953]

starter-upper [34.2 May 1959]

state of altered consciousness an ALTERNATE STATE OF CONSCIOUSNESS [60.3 Fall 1985]

stateside; states-side relating to, in the direction of, or in the United States [21.3 Oct. 1946]

States' Righter a member of the 1948 States' Rights Democratic Party [24.1 Feb. 1949]

station-hop to ride slower trains, getting off at each interesting town along the way for sightseeing [54.1 Spring 1979 *s.v.* hop]

stay-downer [34.2 May 1959]

stay-put *British* hose with an elastic top, *also* hold-up [63.2 Summer 1988]

stealth auto bra; stealth car bra a NOSE MASK [65.4 Winter 1990]

steel-collar worker a reprogrammable automatic machine, sometimes called a robot [59.1 Spring 1984]

steel curtain [25.3 Oct. 1950 forematter]

steel intensive [60.1 Spring 1985 *s.v.* intensive]

steer to send (a patient) to a particular pharmacy, esp. one connected with the referring agency [54.3 Fall 1979]

step dance a synchronized, athletic African-American dance characteristic of black college fraternities and sororities; **step dancing** performing a step dance; **stepping** a step dance; step dancing; **stepping out** [65.4 Winter 1990]

steppingstone hypothesis the belief that marijuana use may or, in the view of some, must lead to heroin addiction, *also* domino theory [57.4 Winter 1982]

step show a performance of step dance [65.4 Winter 1990]

steroid rage ROID RAGE [64.4 Winter 1989]

stick-handle *v.* [31.3 Oct. 1956]

stirrer-upper one who stirs up (e.g., racial prejudice) [34.2 May 1959]

Stockmangate a purported scandal involving David Stockman, director of the Office of Management and Budget [59.2 Summer 1984 *s.v.* -gate]

stockpiler one who stockpiles [34.2 May 1959]

stock-take *v.* [31.4 Dec. 1956]

STOL, S.T.O.L. short take-off and landing, a plane that can operate from confined areas with negligible sacrifice of forward speed; **STOL-ing** using STOL aircraft; **stolport, STOLPORT, STOL-port** an airport or runway for STOL planes; **stolstrip** an airstrip for STOL planes [44.2 May 1969]

stomp (sometimes incorrectly labeled dialect) to beat down forcibly, as with the foot [30.4 Dec. 1955]

stonewash stonewashed, *also* acid [65.1 Spring 1990]

straiten-outer (error for *straighten-outer*) one who straightens out problems [34.2 May 1959]

strategic bombing the bombing of targets like factories and refineries, with the aim of crippling the enemy's industrial and economic power [21.2 Apr. 1946]

strato- *prefix* stratosphere [20.4 Dec. 1945]

strato-chamber [20.4 Dec. 1945]

stratoclipper [20.4 Dec. 1945]

stratocruiser the Boeing Model 377, equipped with four 3500-horsepower engines and a pressurized cabin, cruising at 340 mph, operating at 30,000 feet, and carrying about 80 passengers [20.4 Dec. 1945]

strato equipment [20.4 Dec. 1945]

stratoliner [20.4 Dec. 1945]

stratopen a fountain pen that does not leak at high altitudes [20.4 Dec. 1945]

stratopower [20.4 Dec. 1945]

strato-suit flexible pressurized suit of rubberized fabric for use in high-altitude flying [20.4 Dec. 1945]

stratotrainer [20.4 Dec. 1945]

stratovision television rebroadcast from airplanes flying at a level of 30,000 feet [20.4 Dec. 1945; 21.2 Apr. 1946]

strawhat, straw-hat, straw hat pertaining to summer theater [24.4 Dec. 1949]

straw hatter, straw-hatter a summer theater or a play performed in summer theater [34.2 May 1959]

streak to run naked in public; to run naked in front of (an audience); an instance of running naked in public; a streaker; **streaker** one who streaks; **streaker alert** radio reports of streaking in progress; **Streakers (Party)** a student political organization at Florida State University, Tallahassee; **streak-in** an arranged event of group streaking; **streaking** the act of running naked; **streak-watcher** a spectator at a streak [48.1–2 Spring-Summer 1973]

streetspeak trendy, up-to-the-minute jargon [63.2 Summer 1988 *s.v.* speak]

strike-happy [22.3 Oct. 1947 *s.v.* happy]

string (bikini), The String a small bikini bottom with front and back cloth triangles held by thin strings and worn with a minibra [50.1–2 Spring-Summer 1975]; *cf.* g-string

strip a landing strip [20.2 Apr. 1945]

stripe happy, stripe-happy (of a soldier) eager for promotion [19.1 Feb. 1944 forematter; 22.3 Oct. 1947 *s.v.* happy]

strippeuse; stripteuse (from *danseuse, chanteuse*, etc.) [18.4 Dec. 1943 forematter]

strip show a radio soap opera [20.2 Apr. 1945 *s.v.* soap opera]

structural unemployment unemployment due to technological change, esp. improvement, in the economic system [48.1–2 Spring-Summer 1973; 54.3 Fall 1979]

study-in integrated attendance at a segregated school [36.4 Dec. 1961 *s.v.* in]

stuffer *British* (customs office jargon) a drug runner who inserts a contraceptive sheath packed with heroin into the anus or vagina [63.2 Summer 1988]

sub-buster [23.3–4 Oct.-Dec. 1948 *s.v.* buster]

subminiature (in aviation) an extremely small component; **subminiaturization** (in aviation) the reduction of electronic parts in size and weight [26.4 Dec. 1951]

suborbital, sub-orbital pertaining to a space flight with a short, steep trajectory without entering orbit around the Earth [36.4 Dec. 1961]

subsatellite, sub-satellite a large aluminum-clad balloon deployed as an earth satellite; a satellite circling a satellite, such as the moon; an object carried into orbit inside an artificial earth satellite [36.3 Oct. 1961]

subterranean economy a segment of the economy in which transactions are based on cash or barter and are not reported to the Internal Revenue Service, including both legal activities and illegal ones such as drugs, gambling, and prostitution, *also* underground economy *or* economic activity [58.1 Spring 1983]

subway circuit the legitimate theaters accessible by subway in Greater New York [24.4 Dec. 1949]

subway silver NEW YORK CITY SILVER [57.4 Winter 1982]

sug *British* selling under guise, an ostensible survey actually taken to discover the telephone number of a prospective buyer, esp. for investment schemes [63.2 Summer 1988]

superbazooka, super-bazooka a recoilless rocket launcher more powerful than a normal bazooka [26.2 May 1951]

Superdumbo, Super-Dumbo a B-29 accompanying a strike mission as a rescue plane [21.2 Apr. 1946]

superfortress, super fortress; superfort a B-29 heavy bomber made by Boeing [20.2 Apr. 1945]

superhighway, super-highway, super highway a highway for high-speed traffic; any four-lane highway, esp. a divided one [20.3 Oct. 1945]

supermarket a new-automobile dealership that carries cars of several makes [32.2 May 1957]

supermarket TV TABLOID TV [65.1 Spring 1990]

superseniority, super-seniority the requirement that veterans be rehired for at least one year, even if it is necessary to lay off nonveteran employees with greater seniority on the job [21.3 Oct. 1946]

Superstreak *stunt* a streaker [48.1–2 Spring-Summer 1973]

suppie Southern yuppie [64.2 Summer 1989]

supply-side pertaining to a view of economics advocating monetary restraint, reduction of the role of government in the economy, and a cut in the tax rate to stimulate investment and increase the production of goods and services; **supply-sider** a proponent of supply-side economics [56.4 Winter 1981]

surround-sound discrete four-channel sound heard through four loudspeakers, each of which provides primary musical sound [48.1–2 Spring-Summer 1973]

SU-3 theory [40.2 May 1965 *illus. s.v.* eightfold way]

swallower *British* (customs office jargon) a drug runner who swallows a contraceptive sheath packed with heroin [63.2 Summer 1988]

sweat shopper [34.2 May 1959]

sweepswinger a member of the crew of a racing shell [27.1 Feb. 1952]

swim-in swimming at an undesignated beach [36.4 Dec. 1961 *s.v.* in]; a demonstration for integration at a segregated park or pool [38.3 Oct. 1963 *s.v.* in]

swindletron (from *swindle* + [*elec*]*tron*) a small atom smasher that accelerates the same particle twice with one source of voltage [29.4 Dec. 1954]

swing shift (in industry) a shift from about 4 pm to midnight [18.4 Dec. 1943]

swingster; swingstress one who plays or sings swing music [18.4 Dec. 1943]

switcheroo a switch [17.4 Dec. 1942 forematter]

S-word socialism; sex [63.4 Winter 1988 *s.v.* word]

sword(s) and sorcery fantasy fiction having as its theme knightly quests, magic, and mythical creatures, and set in a past or future era resembling the Middle Ages [60.4 Winter 1985]

Symingtonism [32.4 Dec. 1957]

symphonic drama a historical pageant with music, dancing, spectacle, and dramatic episodes, esp. one by Paul Green [27.1 Feb. 1952]

synchrocyclotron, synchro-cyclotron a cyclotron in which the frequency can be varied to keep the electric field synchronized with the rotating particles [23.2 Apr. 1948]

synchronous (of a satellite) with orbital speed matching that of the earth's rotation so that the satellite seems to hover over one spot [39.3 Oct. 1964]

synchrotron a type of cyclotron [25.3 Oct. 1950 *illus. s.v.* cosmotron]

Syncom a synchronous communications satellite [39.3 Oct. 1964]

synthetic four-channel [48.1–2 Spring-Summer 1973 *s.v.* four-channel *n.*]

table hop, table-hop *v.* [31.3 Oct. 1956; 47.3–4 Fall-Winter 1972 *s.v.* hop; 48.1–2 Spring-Summer 1973 *s.v.* hop]

table hopper, table-hopper one who moves from table to table to converse with others in a restaurant or bar [34.2 May 1959]

table-tennis diplomacy PING-PONG DIPLOMACY [46.3–4 Fall-Winter 1971]

tabletop fusion COLD FUSION [65.2 Summer 1990]

tabloid (of television) combining investigative stories, celebrity interviews, and a lurid treatment of taboo subjects; **tabloid show; tabloid talk show; tabloid television, tabloid TV** *also* trash television, me TV, supermarket TV [65.1 Spring 1990]

tailgate [56.4 Winter 1981 *s.v.* -gate]

take a dim view (of) to regard (something) skeptically or unfavorably; **take a poor view** to disapprove [21.3 Oct. 1946 *s.v.* view]

take-home pay; take home, take-home the pay remaining after deductions [21.3 Oct. 1946]

take it to endure a challenge, hardship, or punishment [23.1 Feb. 1948 *s.v.* take]

takeover, take-over the occupation, expropriation, or assumption of ownership or authority [28.4 Dec. 1953 *s.v.* take over]

talk down; talk in to give directions to a pilot as assistance in landing, esp. in adverse conditions [22.2 Apr. 1947]

talking book a phonograph recording of a book [21.3 Oct. 1946; 22.2 Apr. 1947; 23.1 Feb. 1948]

talky-type [23.2 Apr. 1948 *s.v.* type]

Talmadgeism [32.4 Dec. 1957]

tank-buster antitank (corps) [23.3–4 Oct.-Dec. 1948 *s.v.* buster]

tank circuit a minor circuit playing small (i.e., tank) towns [24.4 Dec. 1949 forematter]

tank-dozer a medium-sized tank fitted with a bulldozer blade [20.3 Oct. 1945]

tape recording the recording of sound on tape [24.2 Apr. 1949]

taper relief *British* reduced rates of taxation, as for gifts made several years before the giver's death [63.2 Summer 1988]

tap-happiest exhilarating because of its tap dancing [19.1 Feb. 1944 forematter]

target-buster a trapshooter [23.3–4 Oct.-Dec. 1948 *s.v.* buster]

target virus a computer virus that attacks programs from a particular manufacturer [64.3 Fall 1989 *s.v.* virus]

task force a group of different types of naval vessels ordered to carry out a specific task, sometimes applied to land operations [19.3 Oct. 1944]; (nonnaval use applied to other operations) [20.3 Oct. 1945]

Tass [21.3 Oct. 1946 forematter]

tattle-tale KISS-AND-TELL [64.1 Spring 1989 forematter]

tavern-hop [47.3–4 Fall-Winter 1972 *s.v.* hop]

taxflation the effect of inflation on taxes [58.4 Winter 1983 *s.v.* -flation]

T-ball *see* tee ball [64.2 Summer 1989]

TBS a talk-between-ships radio or phone [21.4 Dec. 1946]

TD [21.3 Oct. 1946 forematter]

T day Tax day [21.3 Oct. 1946 forematter]

teaching machine a small box into which are loaded preprogrammed lessons that appear through a frame when a knob is turned [39.3 Oct. 1964]

Teapot Domegate [56.4 Winter 1981 *s.v.* -gate]

technology-intensive [60.1 Spring 1985 *s.v.* intensive]

tee ball a variety of baseball played by young children, in which the ball is not pitched but is hit from a stationary position atop a stake or tee [64.2 Summer 1989]

teen-ager a youngster between 13 and 19 years of age [20.2 Apr. 1945; 21.4 Dec. 1946]

Teflon; Teflon-coated; Teflon-skinned free of criticism for or unfavorable effects from one's own actions [64.3 Fall 1989]

telecast [18.2 Apr. 1943 forematter]

telecaster a television broadcaster [18.4 Dec. 1943]

telecon a teletype machine that uses radio or underwater cable to send over very long distances messages that are flashed on a screen [27.1 Feb. 1952]

teleconferencing group communication by telephone or television [58.4 Winter 1983; *British* 63.1 Spring 1988]

telecourse a course carrying college credit, taught by television [29.4 Dec. 1954]

telegenic (from *photogenic*) [18.4 Dec. 1943 forematter]

teleporn sexual subjects treated luridly on TV [65.1 Spring 1990]

teleprompter, Teleprompter, TelePrompTer *trademark* an electronic device that rolls a large-lettered script for a television performer, *also* idiot board [28.4 Dec. 1953]

telespud a COUCH POTATO [63.3 Fall 1988]

telethon a television show organized to raise a sum of money for some charitable cause [28.4 Dec. 1953]

tenant-farm *v.* [31.3 Oct. 1956]

tendentious dissident, trouble-making [16.4 Dec. 1941]

Tenderoni (from *macaroni*) [18.4 Dec. 1943 forematter]

1080 a rat poison, sodium fluoroacetate [21.4 Dec. 1946]

tenigue tension and fatigue, esp. on the highways [29.1 Feb. 1954]

tenniser tennis player [34.2 May 1959]

terminal leave accrued, unused leave granted an officer in the services between relief from an assignment and separation from the service (relief from active duty, retirement, or discharge) [21.3 Oct. 1946]

terror bombing bombing designed to hasten the end of a war by terrorizing the enemy population [21.4 Dec. 1946]

test drive *v.* [31.3 Oct. 1956]

test-fire *v.* [31.3 Oct. 1956]

test fly, test-fly to test an airplane in actual flight [21.4 Dec. 1946; 31.3 Oct. 1956]

test-freeze *v.* [31.3 Oct. 1956]

test-pilot *v.* [31.3 Oct. 1956]

test-sit *v.* [31.3 Oct. 1956]

test-tube produced by artificial insemination [23.3–4 Oct.-Dec. 1948]

Texas tower a radar station built on a floating platform, stationed along the Atlantic coast, resembling the offshore oil rigs in the Gulf of Mexico, *also* radar island [31.4 Dec. 1956]

thalamotomy an operation involving the lowering of a needle through the skull to the thalamus [24.4 Dec. 1949]

theatre-in-the-round; theater in the round, theater-in-the-round a seating arrangement in which the audience sits on all sides of the acting area, *also* area staging, area theatre, central staging, circle staging, circle theatre [26.4 Dec. 1951]

theatrical privilege [48.3–4 Fall-Winter 1973 *s.v.* privilege]

theme park an amusement park organized around a specific theme or group of themes [47.3–4 Fall-Winter 1972]

thermoboot, thermo boot an antifrostbite shoe issued to UN forces in Korea [30.4 Dec. 1955]

thermonuclear, thermo-nuclear pertaining to the fusion process in the interior of stars, converting hydrogen into helium, and in the hydrogen bomb, involving extremely high temperatures [27.1 Feb. 1952]

thinifer *British* one thin by nature, an intolerant, antagonistic person [62.4 Winter 1987]

thinkism [32.4 Dec. 1957]

third force a third, intermediate party or power between two opposing groups [26.4 Dec. 1951]

third placer one who takes third place in a contest [34.2 May 1959]

third termer an advocate of a presidential third term [16.2 Apr. 1941 forematter]

third zero complete elimination of nuclear missiles from Europe [65.2 Summer 1990]

thirtysomething characterized by or of the thirties in age, the generation of baby boomers, preoccupied with personal problems and approaching middle age, yuppie; **thirtysomethingish** [65.2 Summer 1990]

thobber (said to be from *thinking out the opinion that pleases one and believing it*) one who prefers guesswork to investigation and reinforces beliefs by asserting them frequently [34.2 May 1959]

thoroughbredism qualities and behavior of the upper classes [32.4 Dec. 1957]

three-hander *British* a play for three actors [63.2 Summer 1988]

throttle-happy [22.3 Oct. 1947 *s.v.* happy]

throw-weight the capacity (of a rocket) to deliver military payloads [51.1–2 Spring-Summer 1976]

thumb buster, thumb-buster a mechanic; a spinning steering wheel on four-wheel drive trucks when driven on rough ground or in mud; an old-fashioned, single-action revolver [23.3–4 Oct.-Dec. 1948 *s.v.* buster]

till point *British* a cash register desk [63.2 Summer 1988]

tilt (esp. of one who is or claims to be neutral) a tendency to favor one alternative over another, bias; to favor one alternative over another; to cause to favor one alternative over another [54.2 Summer 1979]

Timbergate a Chinese scandal in which officials accepted bribes for scarce lumber [59.2 Summer 1984 *s.v.* -gate]

time-intensive [60.1 Spring 1985 *s.v.* intensive]

Time Manager *trademark, British* a PERSONAL ORGANISER [62.4 Winter 1987]

time-of-day (of a proposed price structure for electricity) charging according to the time at which the electricity is used, with the highest rates set for electricity consumption at times of greatest demand [55.1 Spring 1980]

Tinman a triathlon that is not so grueling as Hawaii's Ironman [58.2 Summer 1983]

Tinseltown, tinseltown, TinselTown, tinsel-town, Tinsel Town, tinsel town Hollywood [60.4 Winter 1985]

tiptank (from [*wing*]*tip tank*) an auxiliary fuel container in an airplane [30.4 Dec. 1955]

tirelegger [18.1 Feb. 1943 forematter]

tissue curtain [25.3 Oct. 1950 forematter]

Titoism the political principles and practice of Marshal Tito of Yugoslavia, combining communism and independent nationalism; **Titoist** pertaining to Titoism; one who favors Titoism [25.2 May 1950]

Toastmaster [18.2 Apr. 1943 forematter]

TOFC, T-O-F-C, t.o.f.c. trailers on flat cars, a method of transporting freight [32.2 May 1957]

tokenism partial or minor accessions to a demand as an appearance of satisfying it, a token response, esp. for integration [38.3 Oct. 1963]

toll plaza, toll-plaza a widened area on a toll highway with booths for paying tolls [35.1 Feb. 1960]

tommy-buster a man who takes women by storm [23.3–4 Oct.-Dec. 1948 *s.v.* buster]

top drawer the highest in rank, quality, authoritativeness, or importance [21.3 Oct. 1946]

topectomy a brain operation in which a portion of the frontal lobes is removed [24.1 Feb. 1949]

top secret, top-secret of the greatest secrecy [21.3 Oct. 1946]

top-up *British* pertaining to a second mortgage on one's primary residence, which has tax advantages and is supposed to be used for home improvement, but is often taken as a source of cash for other purposes [63.2 Summer 1988]

tossing revealing the homosexuality of celebrities, *also* outing [65.4 Winter 1990]

total diplomacy coordination of all branches of government and all aspects of national life in foreign relations [26.1 Feb. 1951 *s.v.* total]

total war [23.2 Apr. 1948 forematter]

Totegate a British scandal concerning the Tote, a government-run horse-racing concession [59.2 Summer 1984 *s.v.* -gate]

tot lot a playground for small children, usu. part of the facilities of an organized recreation program [50.1–2 Spring-Summer 1975]

tot-yard a fenced-in play area adjoining a private residence [50.1–2 Spring-Summer 1975 forematter]

touch dance to participate in touch dancing; **touch dancing** ballroom dancing, *also* body-dancing, close dancing, partner dancing [50.1–2 Spring-Summer 1975]

tourist *euphemism* (in travel) second class [17.2 Apr. 1942 forematter]

tourist camp; tourist park [24.2 Apr. 1949 forematter]

tourist court a motor court [24.2 Apr. 1949]

town-buster a large bomb [23.3–4 Oct.-Dec. 1948 *s.v.* buster]

toyboy, toy boy a handsome young man, esp. the lover of an older woman, supported by her, gigolo; a young man supported by an older homosexual lover [65.4 Winter 1990]

tractor brush *British* a tractor with an attached brush for cleaning the ground [63.2 Summer 1988]

tractorette female operator of power farm equipment [18.2 Apr. 1943 forematter]

trade *euphemism* second-rate; **trade gin** *euphemism* bathtub gin [17.2 Apr. 1942 forematter]

trailerite one who lives in a trailer [18.4 Dec. 1943]

trainasium (from *gymnasium*) [18.4 Dec. 1943 forematter]

trainbuster [23.3–4 Oct.-Dec. 1948 *s.v.* buster]

traincard *British* a pass for use on the underground railway [63.2 Summer 1988]

transaxle a common housing of the transmission and the differential of a car, connected to the axle [39.3 Oct. 1964]

trapdoor a code for gaining access to a computer system devised by a programmer to sidestep normal entry procedures and security safeguards [64.3 Fall 1989]

trash-sport pertaining to luridly presented TV reports of concocted sports events [65.1 Spring 1990]

trash television; trash TV TABLOID TELEVISION [65.1 Spring 1990]

traxle *see* transaxle [39.3 Oct. 1964]

trial subscribe *v.* [31.3 Oct. 1956]

triathlete a participant in a triathlon [58.2 Summer 1983]

triathlon an athletic event, usu. consisting of a swim, a bicycle ride, and a distance run, done without a break [58.2 Summer 1983]

trigger to set off or cause to begin [24.3 Oct. 1949]

trigger happy, trigger-happy prone to fire a weapon [19.1 Feb. 1944 forematter; 22.3 Oct. 1947 *s.v.* happy]

triple platinum sales of three million copies of a record album [57.2 Summer 1982 *s.v.* platinum]

triskaidekaphobia; triskedekaphobia fear of the number 13 [29.4 Dec. 1954]

troutgate [56.4 Winter 1981 *s.v.* -gate]

Trumanism governmental and political policies associated with Harry Truman [32.4 Dec. 1957]

trust-buster [23.3–4 Oct.-Dec. 1948 *s.v.* buster; 24.4 Dec. 1949 forematter]

truth serum the drug sodium pentothal, which promotes uninhibited speech [23.1 Feb. 1948]

truth squad a group of Republicans who trailed President Truman on his campaign for re-election in 1952 and took issue with statements that they claimed to be untrue; any group who point out mistakes, oversimplifications, or errors of judgment in the work of another [54.3 Fall 1979]

TSO *British* trading standards officer, a supervisor of regulations, such as for the load weight of trucks [63.2 Summer 1988]

tuber a couch potato [63.3 Fall 1988]

tunnel-buster [23.3–4 Oct.-Dec. 1948 *s.v.* buster]

turbofan, turbo-fan an engine with large fan blades near the air inlet supplying air to the engine and moving a larger mass of air at a slower velocity than a turbojet [35.1 Feb. 1960]

turbojet, turbo-jet an engine run by air taken in at the front, compressed, and heated so it expands with great force through a turbine operating the compressor and finally escapes from the rear in a jet with powerful propulsive thrust [23.3–4 Oct.-Dec. 1948]

turf an area in a city controlled by a teenage gang [35.1 Feb. 1960]; a location that one considers to be one's own; any field, discipline, subject, or area of responsibility that one claims as one's own [54.3 Fall 1979]

turkeyfurter (from *frankfurter*) [18.4 Dec. 1943 forematter]

turkeymallies (from *tamale*) [18.4 Dec. 1943 forematter]

turkeywich (from *sandwich*) [18.4 Dec. 1943 forematter]

turnaway, turn-away top-capacity, so large that some of the persons wishing to attend must be denied admission [26.1 Feb. 1951]

turn over to lose (the ball) to the opposing team through an error or misplay; **turnover** a loss of ball possession to an opposing team through an error or misplay [46.3–4 Fall-Winter 1971]

tutu (perh. from *too too* [*much*] with a pun on the ballet skirt) outrageously exaggerated [40.3 Oct. 1965 *illus. s.v.* monokini]

TV television [24.2 Apr. 1949]

T-V day total victory day [21.3 Oct. 1946 forematter]

twee (with a ref. from *Time* mag. 1964 to British use, but not in the current British sense) (of a monokini) excessively chic [40.3 Oct. 1965 *illus. s.v.* monokini]

tweeter a treble speaker for a stereo set [25.3 Oct. 1950; 26.3 Oct. 1951]

20-20 perceptive, accurate [31.1 Feb. 1956]

twilight-night; twi-night (in baseball) pertaining to two sequential games, the first of which begins during twilight, *in* ~ doubleheader [25.3 Oct. 1950]

two-bit word a long or pretentious word [17.3 Oct. 1942 *s.v.* dollar]

two-digit DOUBLE-DIGIT [49.1–2 Spring-Summer 1974]

twofer a pair of theater tickets sold for the box-office price of a single ticket [25.2 May 1950]

2-4-D, 2,4-D; 2,4-Di; 2,4-dichlorophenoxyacetic acid a synthetic hormone used as a weed killer [21.4 Dec. 1946]

two-partyism [32.4 Dec. 1957]

T-word taxes; tornado [63.4 Winter 1988 *s.v.* word]

type *suffixal form* (adjective forming) [23.2 Apr. 1948; 24.3 Oct. 1949]; *cf.* cafeteria-type; *prefixal form* **type blouse; type character; type limb; type person; type scripter** [23.2 Apr. 1948 forematter]

U-Drive [21.4 Dec. 1946 forematter]

ultimate weapon a weapon against which there is no defense [32.2 May 1957]

ultraconsciousness a consciousness superior to the normal [63.3 Fall 1988]

Umtee; Umptee Universal Military Trainee [23.2 Apr. 1948]

uncybernated not automated or computerized [41.2 May 1966 forematter]

under-achiever one who expends little effort and makes lower grades in school than intelligence tests predict [35.1 Feb. 1960]

underbelly any weak or vulnerable spot, *esp. in* soft ~ [25.3 Oct. 1950]

undergraduette [17.4 Dec. 1942 forematter]

underground in secrecy, *in* go ~ 'to act or operate in secrecy or concealment' [21.4 Dec. 1946]

underground economic activity; underground economy *see* subterranean economy [58.1 Spring 1983]

under-sixer a child below the age of six [34.2 May 1959]

underworlder a criminal [16.2 Apr. 1941 forematter]

un-flation reduction in prices to counteract some effects of inflation [58.4 Winter 1983 *s.v.* -flation]

unfriendly (of computer software) not easy to use without scientific or technical expertise [60.1 Spring 1985 forematter]

union-buster [18.1 Feb. 1943 forematter; 23.3–4 Oct.-Dec. 1948 part II]

unioneer [18.1 Feb. 1943 forematter]

united fronter one who favors cooperation with Communists [34.2 May 1959]

UNIVAC *trademark* Universal Automatic Computer [25.2 May 1950]

UNO United Nations Organization [21.2 Apr. 1946]

unpierced (of earrings) designed for unpierced ears [45.3–4 Fall-Winter 1970]

UNRRA, U.N.R.R.A. United Nations Relief and Rehabilitation Administration [21.2 Apr. 1946; 21.3 Oct. 1946 forematter]

up-day a day on which average stock values increase [63.3 Fall 1988]

upgrade to bill the agency administering Medicaid for more services than were provided Medicaid patients [54.3 Fall 1979]

upper-bracketeer [18.1 Feb. 1943 forematter]

uraniumaire one who is a millionaire through uranium mining [32.2 May 1957]

uranium curtain [25.3 Oct. 1950 forematter]

urban enterprise zone *see* enterprise zone [58.2 Summer 1983]

urbiculture care of cities and city people [32.2 May 1957]

U.S.-baiting [17.2 Apr. 1942 *s.v.* baiter]

user-friendly (esp. of computer hardware and software) easy to operate, even without scientific or technical expertise; **user-friendliness** a quality of ease of use even without scientific or technical expertise [60.1 Spring 1985]

usherette female movie usher [18.2 Apr. 1943 forematter]

USO, U.S.O. United Service Organization [22.2 Apr. 1947]

ustabie a has-been [65.3 Fall 1990]

vaccination program; vaccine program a program to protect computers from computer viruses [64.3 Fall 1989]

V-A day victory in Asia day [21.3 Oct. 1946 forematter]

Valgirl a female teenager from the San Fernando Valley, CA [59.4 Winter 1984 *illus. s.v.* Valspeak *s.v.* speak]

Valley Girlspeak; Valspeak the language spoken by teenage girls in the California San Fernando Valley [59.2 Summer 1984 *s.v.* speak]; **Valleyspeak; Valley talk** [*illus. s.v.* Valspeak]

van pool a car pool in a van supplied by the employer; **van pooling** participating in a van pool [51.3–4 Fall-Winter 1976]

Vatergatski (pseudo Russian) the Watergate scandal [54.4 Winter 1979]

V-bomb any German V-1, V-2, etc. bomb [21.2 Apr. 1946]

V day, V-day the day of final victory over the Axis powers [21.2 Apr. 1946; 21.3 Oct. 1946 forematter]

VE-Day, V-E (Day), V-E day the day on which the WWII Allies were victorious in Europe, specif. 8 May 1945 [21.2 Apr. 1946; 21.3 Oct. 1946 forematter]

veep, Veep a vice president [26.1 Feb. 1951]

velocitization a driver's unconscious increase in the speed of a vehicle on an open highway; **velocitized** (of motorists) accustomed to high-speed driving and therefore unable to judge speed accurately in a lower-speed zone [29.1 Feb. 1954]

velvet curtain [25.3 Oct. 1950 forematter]

veto-proof (of legislation) so important that the President would not veto it, or supported by enough legislators to override a veto; (usu. of the U.S. Congress) able to override a veto [51.1–2 Spring-Summer 1976]

vibaroo Vibraphone [16.4 Dec. 1941 forematter]

vibratese language coded information received through vibrations on the skin [36.3 Oct. 1961]

vichyate, vichy-ate *also cap.* to subject (France) to the regime of Vichy [17.2 Apr. 1942]

Victory Circuit [24.4 Dec. 1949 forematter]

victory girl a young woman soliciting or sexually favoring enlisted men [21.3 Oct. 1946]

videoconferencing *British* a meeting conducted by television [63.1 Spring 1988 *illus. s.v.* teleconferencing]

videot *pejorative* a COUCH POTATO [63.3 Fall 1988]

vidspud a COUCH POTATO [63.3 Fall 1988]

view *in* take a dim *or* poor view (of) [21.3 Oct. 1946]

viewing the custom of looking at a body before burial, esp. at a funeral parlor [22.2 Apr. 1947 forematter]

VIP, V.I.P. a very important person [22.2 Apr. 1947]

virus a program maliciously inserted into a computer to alter or destroy other computer programs, *also* computer virus, electronic virus, software virus; **virus attack** the activity of a computer virus; **virus epidemic** a large number of computer virus attacks in a brief time; **virus program** a computer virus [64.3 Fall 1989]

virus pneumonia pneumonia caused by a filtrable virus [23.3–4 Oct.-Dec. 1948]

vitamin B12, B-12, B$_{12}$ a biological chemical that aids anemia and oversecreting thyroid glands [24.4 Dec. 1949]

V-J Day the day on which the WWII Allies were victorious in Japan, specif. 2 September 1945 [21.2 Apr. 1946; 21.3 Oct. 1946 forematter]

V-mail microfilmed letters, enlarged for delivery [18.1 Feb. 1943 forematter; 19.3 Oct. 1944; 21.3 Oct. 1946 forematter]

vocumentary (coined by Peter Tamony) a documented analysis of words and expressions in song lyrics, a study of a song for its verbal information [36.3 Oct. 1961]

V-O day victory on Okinawa day [21.3 Oct. 1946 forematter]

Vodka Circuit [24.4 Dec. 1949 forematter]

Volgagate a facetious account of officials in the USSR creating a scandal by not practicing deception and trickery [53.3 Fall 1978 *s.v.* -gate]

volleyball diplomacy the potential normalization of relations between the U.S. and Cuba as a result of a U.S. volleyball team's competing in Cuba [46.3–4 Fall-Winter 1971]

Volscan an electronic system to control aircraft landings [30.2 May 1955]

V-1 a ROBOT BOMB [19.4 Dec. 1944]

votelegger [18.1 Feb. 1943 forematter]

V-P day victory in the Pacific day [21.3 Oct. 1946 forematter]

V-R day victory over Russia day [21.3 Oct. 1946 forematter]

VT fuze; VT fuse a variable time or proximity fuze [21.3 Oct. 1946]

V-2 a German rocket 30–50 feet long and 5 feet in diameter, with a bomb load estimated at 1 ton or more [20.2 Apr. 1945]

V-weapon *see* V-bomb [21.2 Apr. 1946]

V-word videotape [63.4 Winter 1988 *s.v.* word]

WAAF [21.3 Oct. 1946 forematter]

WAAS [21.3 Oct. 1946 forematter]

WAC [21.3 Oct. 1946 forematter]

wackaroo an object sold to be broken, or whacked against a wall [16.4 Dec. 1941 forematter]

wade-in a demonstration for integration at a segregated pool or beach [36.4 Dec. 1961; 38.3 Oct. 1963 *s.v.* in]

wait-in a gathering of persons waiting for an event to begin [47.3–4 Fall-Winter 1972]

wait state a brief pause in the performance of a computer's central processing unit to match it to the speeds of memory subsystems [64.3 Fall 1989]

walkathon [31.1 Feb. 1956 *illus. s.v.* rockerthon]

Walkergate the events surrounding the signing of Herschel Walker to play professional football [59.2 Summer 1984 *s.v.* -gate]

walkie-lookie a portable TV camera, *also* creepie-peepie, peepie-creepie [28.3 Oct. 1953]

walkie-talkie; walky-talky; walkee-talkee a portable radio receiving and sending apparatus [19.3 Oct. 1944]

walk-in an interracial visit to an art gallery or museum [36.4 Dec. 1961 *s.v.* in]

Walter Winchellism [18.2 Apr. 1943 *illus. s.v.* infanticipate, forematter]

wannabe, wanna-be, wanna be; wannabee, wanna-bee; wannabie one who imitates and identifies with another; one who aspires to hold a position or fill a role [65.3 Fall 1990]

warehouse (grocery) store; warehouse (super)market a large grocery store that lowers its operating costs and its prices by reducing or eliminating many of the services, products, or facilities available in traditional stores [57.1 Spring 1982]

war of nerves [23.2 Apr. 1948 forematter]

Warrenism political policies associated with Earl Warren [32.4 Dec. 1957]

war time daylight saving time [19.4 Dec. 1944]

war-weary (of aircraft) too badly damaged to repair overseas, sent back to the U.S. for rehabilitation or junking [21.2 Apr. 1946]; frequently used and depreciated during wartime [28.4 Dec. 1953]

WASP [21.3 Oct. 1946 forematter]

wasp waist an airplane shape resulting from the area rule, designed to respond to the effects of air at speeds approaching that of sound, *also* coke bottle, Marilyn Monroe [31.4 Dec. 1956]

waste-watergate a scandal involving the EPA clean-up of hazardous wastes [59.2 Summer 1984 *s.v.* -gate]

water-borne [19.3 Oct. 1944 forematter]

Waterbugger one arrested for the Watergate break-in to plant concealed microphones; **Waterbuggery, Waterbugging** the planting of concealed microphones in Watergate [54.4 Winter 1979]

Waterbungler one of the group that bungled the Watergate break-in [54.4 Winter 1979]

Waterfallout political or commercial consequences of the Watergate scandal [54.4 Winter 1979]

Watergaffe a bungled attempt to plant listening devices in the offices of a French humor magazine [54.4 Winter 1979]

Watergateana things associated with Watergate [54.4 Winter 1979]

Watergate fallout *see* Waterfallout [54.4 Winter 1979]

Watergateite one of the forty-eight persons implicated in the Watergate scandal [54.4 Winter 1979]

Watergateless having no references to Watergate [54.4 Winter 1979]

Watergateman one involved in the Watergate scandal [54.4 Winter 1979]

Watergater a participant in or one associated with the Watergate scandal [54.4 Winter 1979]

Watergatese language associated with the Watergate hearings, e.g., "at that point in time" [54.4 Winter 1979]

Watergatish characterized by the corrupt values of those involved in the Watergate scandal [54.4 Winter 1979]

Watergatism attitudes and practices associated with the Watergate scandal [54.4 Winter 1979]

Watergative affected by or concerned with the Watergate scandal [54.4 Winter 1979]

Watergatology the implications of the threat of a presidential impeachment on U.S. foreign policy [54.4 Winter 1979]

Watergimmick a novelty such as a sign or poster containing derogatory remarks on the Watergate affair [54.4 Winter 1979]

Watergoof a failed French government attempt to plant listening devices in the offices of a humor magazine [54.4 Winter 1979]

water-intensive [60.1 Spring 1985 *s.v.* intensive]

water people those who live on junks, *also* boat people [55.2 Summer 1980]

water skiing [54.3 Fall 1979 forematter]

wave recorder an instrument for measuring wave characteristics in a fluid medium [24.3 Oct. 1949]

WAVES [21.3 Oct. 1946 forematter]

waxed *British* waterproof, *as in* ~ coat, ~ cotton, ~ garment [63.2 Summer 1988]

way-following guidance [30.4 Dec. 1955 *illus. s.v.* beam-rider guidance]

weaponeer one who readies an atomic bomb preparatory to launching by the bombardier [22.2 Apr. 1947]

weasel an army cargo and personnel carrier that moves over various kinds of terrain, officially designated as the M-29 [24.4 Dec. 1949]

weather buster [23.3−4 Oct.-Dec. 1948 *s.v.* buster]

weather ship a boat used to retrieve and relay meteorological data [23.3−4 Oct.-Dec. 1948]

wedgie a sports shoe with a wedge-shaped piece serving as the heel and connected to the sole [22.2 Apr. 1947]; *see* wedgy [65.3 Fall 1990]; to give (someone) a wedgy or tug on the underpants [65.3 Fall 1990 *s.v.* wedgy]

wedgie attack a surprise infliction of a wedgy as a practical joke [65.3 Fall 1990 *s.v.* wedgy]

wedgiemaster one who organizes a wedgie patrol [65.3 Fall 1990 *s.v.* wedgy]

wedgie patrol a group of college dormitory residents who make a wedgy attack as a form of hazing [65.3 Fall 1990 *s.v.* wedgy]

wedgy a tug on someone's underpants, pulling the cloth tight between the buttocks, *usu. in* give someone a ~; the pulling may be sudden or gradual, deliberate or accidental, malicious or playful, often done as a practical joke, with a result that is uncomfortable and undignified, but also painful if the testes are squeezed by the tightened cloth, *also* fishbite, melvin, murphy [65.3 Fall 1990]

weekend a weekend party; to attend a weekend party [18.2 Apr. 1943 forematter]

welfare statism the policies and practices of a welfare state [32.4 Dec. 1957]

welfarism policies identified with a welfare state [28.4 Dec. 1953]

we-never-had-it-so-gooder an optimist, the opposite of a Jeremiah [34.2 May 1959]

werewolf a Nazi underground or guerilla fighter [23.3−4 Oct.-Dec. 1948]

wet-bag *British* a plastic- or rubber-lined container for toiletries, toilet kit [63.2 Summer 1988]

whackaroo a whack [17.4 Dec. 1942 forematter]

whamfartbananas extremely BANANAS [51.3−4 Fall-Winter 1976]

wheeling transmitting (electric power produced by one agency or company to another) [31.4 Dec. 1956]

whirley a ROBOT BOMB [19.4 Dec. 1944 forematter]

whirlybird, whirly-bird a helicopter [28.1 Feb. 1953]

whistle stop a small town; *also* **whistlestop, whistle-stop** to campaign politically (in an area), originally on a train making brief stops at many small towns; **whistle stopper, whistle-stopper** one who campaigns by whistlestopping; **whistle stopping, whistle-stopping** campaigning, originally on a train making brief stops at many towns [28.1 Feb. 1953]

white market the legal sale of commodities [25.2 May 1950 forematter; 47.3−4 Fall-Winter 1972]

Whitespeak hypocritical language used by whites of and to blacks, reflecting ambivalent attitudes of which the speakers would be ashamed [59.2 Summer 1984 *s.v.* speak]

whodunit; whodunnit detective fiction [18.4 Dec. 1943]

whole-foodie *British* one who eats unprocessed or lightly processed health food [63.2 Summer 1988]

whore-hop [47.3−4 Fall-Winter 1972 *s.v.* hop]

wienergate [56.4 Winter 1981 *s.v.* -gate]

wiglet a small wig [45.3−4 Fall-Winter 1970]

wilding teenage gang violence directed against a randomly chosen victim, impulsive theft, mugging, rape, and terrorizing by a marauding band [65.2 Summer 1990]

Willkieite a follower of Wendell Willkie [17.2 Apr. 1942]

windfall born between 1911 and 1916 and therefore entitled to higher Social Security benefits than those born later; **windfall baby** one born between 1911 and 1916 and therefore entitled to higher Social Security benefits than those born later, *also* bonanza baby; **windfall group** all those born between 1911 and 1916 and therefore entitled to higher Social Security benefits than those born later [64.4 Winter 1989]

window-shop *v.* [31.3 Oct. 1956]

wind shear a weather phenomenon in which adjacent masses of the atmosphere move at different speeds or in different directions, exerting deforming and sometimes destructive forces at the boundary between the atmospheric currents [54.2 Summer 1979]

wind-up *British* a practical joke, put-on, leg-pull [63.2 Summer 1988]

Windy a fan of *Gone with the Wind* [65.2 Summer 1990]

Winegate a scandal concerning a fraudulent scheme to peddle cheap wine as expensive French Bordeaux [53.3 Fall 1978 *s.v.* -gate]

winged comet a ROBOT BOMB [19.4 Dec. 1944 forematter]

wing-happy [22.3 Oct. 1947 *s.v.* happy]

wingman, wing man the pilot of the second of two planes, flying to the side and staggered from the flight path of the lead plane in order to protect it [21.2 Apr. 1946; 21.4 Dec. 1946]

winkie-wiggling *British* an imaginary contest on a TV comedy show involving close-ups of athletes' crotches [63.2 Summer 1988]

winkle *British* to wriggle, force (one's way) [63.2 Summer 1988]

winterize to equip or prepare for winter use; **winterization** the act or process of winterizing [16.2 Apr. 1941]

winter-spot-hop [48.1–2 Spring-Summer 1973 *s.v.* hop]

wire an EAR WIRE [46.1–2 Spring-Summer 1971]

wire around to circumvent (opposition) [63.3 Fall 1988]

wire TV CABLE TV [47.3–4 Fall-Winter 1972]

-wise *suffix, British* (after nouns) with respect to, regarding; (after adjectives) in a – way, –ly [63.2 Summer 1988]

witch-hunting political persecution [19.1 Feb. 1944]

within the ball park feasible or possible [51.1–2 Spring-Summer 1976 *s.v.* ball park]

WLB National War Labor Board [21.3 Oct. 1946 forematter]

wolf a member of a wolfpack, a roughneck teenager [65.2 Summer 1990]

wolf-pack (of teenagers) to congregate, esp. by sitting on cars in shopping-center parking lots [65.2 Summer 1990]

wolf-whistle *v.* [31.4 Dec. 1956]

wonder drug a drug with miraculous curative powers [23.3–4 Oct.-Dec. 1948]

word *suffixal form* (used after the initial letter of a word under real or pretended taboo to make a jocular euphemism) [63.4 Winter 1988]

workshop an informal study group organized to permit teachers to apply the principles of progressive education to their own educational problems [19.3 Oct. 1944]

world-buster [23.3–4 Oct.-Dec. 1948 *s.v.* buster]

worthy *suffixal form* [16.2 Apr. 1941 forematter]

Worzel Gummidge *British* (from a character in children's books and a television series) a scarecrow [63.2 Summer 1988]

WOWS Women Ordinance Workers [21.3 Oct. 1946 forematter]

WPAer a WPA worker [16.2 Apr. 1941]

write-in pertaining to the method of proposing a person for office by writing the candidate's name on the ballot [23.3–4 Oct.-Dec. 1948]

wussy; wuss a weak, ineffectual person, wimp [65.3 Fall 1990]

Wuwa (from German *Wunderwaffe* 'wonder weapon') a ROBOT BOMB [19.4 Dec. 1944 forematter]

W-word wimp [63.4 Winter 1988 *s.v.* word]

xeriscape a landscape with plants requiring little water; **xeriscaping; xericscaping** landscaping with xeric plants [65.2 Summer 1990]

xerography a process for the reproduction of printed matter using static electricity and dry powders [24.2 Apr. 1949]

yah-boo *British* name-calling, shouting, disorderly, *as in* ~ affair, ~ politics [63.2 Summer 1988]

Yap young aspiring professional [60.1 Spring 1985 forematter]

yappie young arctic professional, a yuppie in the Northwest Territories of Canada who is environmentally concerned and dresses in native fashion [64.2 Summer 1989]

Yarg *British* a type of Cornish cheese [63.2 Summer 1988]

yellow market an illicit worldwide trade in gold in Middle Eastern and Latin American markets [25.2 May 1950 forematter]

yellow rain a mycotoxin used in chemical warfare, yellowish in color and sprayed from aircraft, thus falling from the sky like rain [58.2 Summer 1983]

yuca young upwardly mobile Cuban-American [64.2 Summer 1989]

yumpishness the quality characterizing a young upwardly mobile professional [60.1 Spring 1985 forematter]

yumpo *British* youngish upwardly mobile property owner [62.4 Winter 1987]

yup a yuppie; to behave like a yuppie [64.2 Summer 1989]

yuppie, Yuppie young urban *or* upwardly mobile professional [60.1 Spring 1985; *British* 62.4 Winter 1987 forematter]

yuppieback a paperback work of fiction aimed at a yuppie audience, a quality fiction paperback [64.2 Summer 1989]

yuppiecide the killing of yuppies [64.2 Summer 1989]

yuppie disease Epstein-Barr syndrome, an illness causing chronic fatigue and striking primarily young adults [64.2 Summer 1989]

yuppiedom *British* an area associated with yuppies [62.4 Winter 1987]

yuppieism the values and lifestyle of yuppies [64.2 Summer 1989]

yuppification *British* gentrification for yuppies [62.4 Winter 1987]

yuppify *British* gentrify for yuppies [62.4 Winter 1987]

yuppily *British* in a manner suitable for or associated with yuppies [62.4 Winter 1987]

yuppism a characteristic of yuppie behavior; specif. relating to others only as superiors, competitors, or inferiors [64.2 Summer 1989]

yuppy *British* [62.4 Winter 1987 forematter]

yuppy-bashing *British* criticism of yuppy values [62.4 Winter 1987]

yup-scale upscale in a yuppie manner [64.2 Summer 1989]

zany clownish, foolish, idiotic [19.1 Feb. 1944]

Z day zero day, a code term for the date fixed for an important military operation [21.3 Oct. 1946 forematter]

zero-coupon (of a bond or other certificate of indebtedness) offered at a discount, paying no annual interest, and redeemable at face value upon maturity, yielding to the investor the difference between the price at the time of purchase and the face value of the security [57.3 Fall 1982]

zero hour [19.4 Dec. 1944 forematter]

zero in to have the bearings (of a target); aim accurately, *as in* ~ on [21.4 Dec. 1946]

zero wait state a lack of pauses between the issuing of instructions by a computer's central processing unit, thus increasing its speed of operation [64.3 Fall 1989]

zero-zero pertaining to an arms-reduction proposal for each side to eliminate all weapons of a given type [64.2 Summer 1989]; *also* double zero

zert zero reaction tool, a tool for use in space by weightless astronauts, constructed so that its operation will not produce a counter movement in the operator's body [40.3 Oct. 1965]

zinjanthropus a prehistoric primate [39.3 Oct. 1964]

zip to close with or as with a slide fastener [18.4 Dec. 1943]

ZIP code, zip code, Z.I.P. code zone improvement plan code, a number given to a postal district by the U.S. Post Office [39.3 Oct. 1964]

zip gun a homemade pistol, often a small lead pipe mounted on a block of wood with a crude firing pin such as a nail [26.2 May 1951]

zippered equipped with a slide fastener [18.4 Dec. 1943]

INDEX OF CONTRIBUTORS

(by volume and issue numbers)

AMONG THE NEW WORDS

DWIGHT L. BOLINGER
Washburn College

GAINING in favor among the recognized combining forms is the suffix *-worthy*, which of late has cast loose from such oldsters as *seaworthy* and *trustworthy*, giving rise to the following new words: *newsworthy* (see below); *courtworthy* (reported in *Words*, May 1938); *credit worthy* ('holding companies . . . in such shape that nothing but a drastic use of the wringer could ever make them credit worthy,' *Nation*, 150:3, Jan. 20, 1940, p. 75a); *ear-worthy* ('In terms of radio entertainment they may not be ear-worthy,' *Reader's Digest*, 33:197, Sep. 1938, p. 12b); and *prizeworthy* ('the fellowships were not offered as prizes to lucky—even prizeworthy—reporters as such,' *Nation*, 151:10, Sep. 7, 1940, p. 195a).

Seemingly also applied with greater freedom is the suffix *-er* used with nouns to denote 'someone or something associated with' the noun to which it is affixed. I have observed the following: *beefer*, a football player (*Collier's*, 107:1, Jan. 4, 1941, p. 20a); *first termer*, one serving his first term in public office (Pearson and Allen col., Topeka *Journal*, 66:302, Dec. 17, 1940, p. 4d); *bottlenecker*, one guilty of obstructing national defense (*American Guardian*, 24:10, Dec. 6, 1940, p. 4a); *party-liner*, one who adheres to the party line (*Common Sense*, 9:2, Feb. 1940, p. 21b); *inner circler*, a member of the inner circle of government (Pearson and Allen col., Topeka *Journal*, 66:72, Mar. 23, 1940, p. 4c); *third termer*, an advocate of a presidential third term (*ibid.*, 66:74, Mar. 26, 1940, p. 4c); *WPAer* (see below); *Dust-bowler*, an inhabitant of the Dust Bowl (*Saturday Evening Post*, 211:52, June 24, 1939, p. 10; also *Cooperative Consumer*, 7:7, Apr. 15, 1940, p. 5d); *low-incomer*, a recipient of a low income (Topeka *Journal*, 66:275, Nov. 15, 1940, p. A9e); *rank-and-filer* (see below); *Guilder*, a member of the American Newspaper Guild (*New Republic*, 103:19, Nov. 4, 1940, p. 624b); *underworlder*, a criminal (Winchell col., Topeka *Journal* 66:302, Dec. 17, 1940, p. 4d); *Merry-Go-Rounder*, an editor of the column 'Washington Merry-Go-Round' (Pearson and Allen col., Topeka *Journal*, 66:306, Dec. 21, 1940, p. 4c); *lifer*, a life-insurance man (Topeka *Capital*, 64:310, Dec. 20, 1940, p. 14b); and *midnighter*, one abroad at midnight, a regular caption in Winchell's column.

ALERT n. An air-raid alarm. Defined in a glossary in the *Outpost*, reprinted in Topeka *Journal*, Dec. 23, 1940. 'Sirens sounded London's first daylight alert . . . today,' Kansas City *Star*, 61: 69, Nov. 25, 1940, p. 6e; 'my "uneventful night" had seen two or three "alerts,"' Manchester *Guardian*, quoted in Topeka *Journal*, 66: 306, Dec. 21, 1940, p. 4b.

APPEASE v.t. To bribe (an aggressor or potential aggressor): 'While England is appeasing Franco in this strictly limited sense, Franco is certainly not appeasing world opinion,' *New Republic*, 103: 26, Dec. 23, 1940, p. 852b.

APPEASER n. One who appeases (in the sense above): 'Wouldn't it be better to make our own country impregnable. . . ? People who say so are being called "fifth columnists" and "appeasers,"' Hugh Johnson col., Topeka *Capital*, 64: 311, Dec. 21, 1940, p. 4e; 'the Save America Committee (which has become the Politburo of the isolationists and the appeasers),' *New Republic*, 103: 27, Dec. 23, 1940, p. 854b. (Instances of this are the commonest just now of the *appease* family.)

APPEASEMENT n. The practise of appeasing (in the sense above). Defined in *Words*, Sept. 1939.

BLACKTOP n. A macadam or similar black road-surface (used generally of the cheaper grades): 'strewed some of the victims on the blacktop,' AP desp., Topeka *Journal*, 66: 97, Apr. 22, 1940, p. 3f. (This term has been in common use in Missouri and Kansas for at least seven years.)

BLITZ v.t., v.i. To attack in the manner of the blitzkrieg: 'Blitz Poor Little Town Hall Mouse,' Topeka *Journal*, 66: 162, July 6, 1940, p. 1e; 'Let's blitz 'em, gals!' [on the last day of leap year], Topeka *Capital*, 64: 321, Dec. 31, 1940, p. 1f; 'British steel city blitzed,' *PM*, Dec. 13, 1940, cover. (See *American Speech*, Feb. 1940, p. 110b for an intransitive use.)

BRA n. A brassière or article of clothing resembling a brassière, as a detached section of a bathing suit: 'the newest thing in feminine bathing suits . . . featuring a grass skirt cut to ballerina length, with even briefer shorts beneath it. The bra is of cotton printed in a California version of Tahiti tapa cloth,' AP photo, Topeka *Capital*, 64: 249, Oct. 20, 1940, p. 7Be; 'an interesting new play suit. The Bra top is fashioned after a Javanese temple dancer's bodice,' Central Press photo, Topeka *Journal*, 66: 265, Nov. 4, 1940, p. 6g. (In W-sup.[1] only as brassière or waist.)

BRASS HAT n. A military official. Observed at least as early as 1939 as a favorite expression in the Pearson and Allen column. 'If certain leading advertising agencies can sell the idea to army brass hats, the boys in camp this winter will see star radio shows,' Pearson and Allen col., Topeka *Journal*, 66: 261, Oct. 30, 1940, p. 4c; '"Just paint a horse's head on the front and a tail on the rear [of a new armored car]—and the brass hats down on Constitution Avenue will go for it,"' *Harper's*, 182: 1087, Dec. 1940, p. 1a. (The W37[1] definition is 'a general or staff officer,' British soldiers' slang.)

BURP n., v.i., v.t. A belch, etc. Defined in *Words* (noun only), Feb. 1939. 'It was so chastely devised that Brother Will Hays blessed it without a burp,' *New Masses*, 30:10, Feb. 28, 1939, p. 28a; 'He was puffing and looked as if he might burp and she hoped he wouldn't. If a man burped Nig would hardly think he had a charming daughter,' *Writer's Forum*, 1: 5, March 1940, p. 26b; 'Chronic air swallowers should be "burped" three or four times . . . during each feeding because if not "burped" until the feeding is completed, the baby may bring up much of the feeding,' Clendening col., Topeka *Journal*, 66: 93, Apr. 17, 1940, p. 4c; 'Burping at the New Deal?' *Literary Digest*, 122: 18, Oct. 31, 1936, p. 48b.

CAR HOP n. A waiter or waitress who serves customers in parked automobiles: 'Car hops are instructed to be friendly but not familiar with patrons,' AP Dallas, Tex., desp., Topeka *Journal*, 66: 99, Apr. 24, 1940, p. 1b–c; 'each has a car-hop job. Three drug stores employ the boys,' Topeka *Capital*, 64: 123, June 16, 1940, p. 6Be.

CORRIGAN n., adj. Something done backwards; one who so acts, etc. Defined in *Words*, Nov. 1938. 'Youth Locked in Freight Car Going Wrong Way . . ., the "boxcar Corrigan,"' Topeka *Journal*, 65: 38, Feb. 14, 1939, p. 2a; 'doing a Corrigan, eh?' [of a parachute-landing in mid-ocean], Dick Tracy cartoon, Topeka *Capital*, 63: 84, May 9, 1939, p. 13; 'Comes now the "wrong way" or "Corrigan" Calendar' [for barber-shop use, to be read by reflection in a mirror], AP New York desp., Topeka *Capital*, 64: 298, Dec. 8, 1940, p. 1h.

COVENTRIZE, COVENTRYIZE v.t. To bombard (an open city) into ruins. Reported in Winchell col. about Nov. 25, 1940, as in use by the Germans to describe aerial attacks such as that carried out on the night of Nov. 14–15, 1940, against the English city of Coventry; used in Winchell broadcast Dec. 1, 1940. 'The Germans used the bombing of Coventry as their yardstick—"To Coventrize," their propaganda called it—to boast of what they did to nearby Birmingham in the next heavy raid," *Newsweek*, 16: 23, Dec. 2, 1940, p. 27a; '"Conventryize" Is Fighting Word in Britain,' *PM*, 1: 122, Dec. 4, 1940, p. 6a–d (with article explaining the word). Defined in legend of NEA photo, Topeka *Capital*, 64: 302, Dec. 12, 1940, p. 1b–d.

CURVACEOUS adj. Showing curves, used of the human figure: 'Curvaceous and emote have their place as Lucille Neville uses them in a feature article: "Miss Sothern is curvaceous,"' Elizabeth Bahl in *Better English*, 6: 2, Oct. 1940, p. 54a; 'The woman who entered was plump and curvaceous,' *Inside Detective*, 11: 6, Dec. 1940, p. 24b.

EGG, TO LAY AN. To fail, esp. referring to commercial entertainment: '"Pinocchio," I hear, is laying a financial egg,' Winchell col., Topeka *Journal*, 66: 91, Apr. 15, 1940, p. 4f; 'I'm upset enough just being in Chicago. I once laid an egg here,' *Collier's*, 107: 1, Jan. 4, 1941, p. 24.

FELLOW TRAVELER n. 'The new phenomenon is the fellow-traveler. The term has a Russian background and means someone who does not accept all your aims but has enough in common with you to accompany you in a comradely fashion part of the way. In this campaign both Mr. Landon and Mr. Roosevelt have acquired fellow-travelers,' Max Lerner, 'Mr. Roosevelt and His Fellow-Travelers,' *Nation*, 143: 17, Oct. 24, 1936, p. 471a; 'Merwin K. Hart, whom he described as an energetic "fellow-traveler" of the Christian Front,' Topeka *Journal*, 66: 19, Jan. 22, 1940, p. 1a.

FRONT ORGANIZATION n. An organization, esp. political, which intentionally or unintentionally lends its offices to some insidious purpose, giving the latter an air of respectability: '"The plan . . . contemplates thoro [*sic*, intending 'thru'] cultural academic associations . . . the cooperation of the professional and academic world banded together in typical 'front organizations,'" the report said,' AP Washington desp. on Dies Com. Report, Topeka *Journal*, 66: 280, Nov. 21, 1940, p. 6h; 'foreign "isms" . . . masquerading behind "front" organizations,' *Inside Detective*, 11: 6, Dec. 1940, p. 4b.

FUDDIE-DUDDIE, FUDDY-DUDDY n., adj. A fussy, ineffective person, etc.: 'these well-meaning intellectual fuddie-duddies [members of Peace Pledge Union in wartime England] have no remote conception of what is in store. . . . Because mercy and tenderness and love of fellow man, with which these fuddie-duddies are overflowing, aren't in the Nazis,' W. L. White in Topeka *Capital*, 64: 58, Apr. 12, 1940, p. 8a; 'a great many people . . . regard the American Army as backward and resistant to new ideas. They believe its officer class is caste-ridden and fuddy-duddy,' *Harper's*, 182: 1087, Dec. 1940, p. 1a. Used of a busybody in the film 'Personal Secretary.'

G-STRING n. A breechcloth, esp. one used by a strip-tease dancer; observed at least as early as spring, 1940: 'wears her final G-string,' verse entitled 'Strip-Tease Girl' in Winchell col., Topeka *Journal*, 66: 246, Oct. 12, 1940, p. 4f. (Generalized from W37, which limits to savages.)

HIPPY adj. Having prominent hips: 'HIPPY GIRLS WELCOME THE FORM-CONCEALING FLATTERY OF HOOPSKIRTS,' *Life*, 5: 10, Sept. 5, 1938, p. 43; 'I thought how busty and hippy some of us looked in these ski pants and tight sweaters,' *Writer's Forum*, 2: 1, Nov. 1940, p. 17a.

JUL OTTA n. 'JUL OTTA (Christmas Morning Service),' adv., Topeka *Journal*, 64: 306, Dec. 23, 1938, p. 14. 'In the [Swedish-American] churches are held the children's festivals and the "Jul otta" (early morning matins on Christmas morn) when the old, traditional Swedish Christmas hymns and songs are sung once again,' *Writer's Forum*, 1: 11, Sept. 1940, p. 12a.

LEG-UP, LEG UP n. A boost: 'The capture of Gibraltar was to have given Mussolini a leg-up in his attack on Egypt,' DeWitt Mackenzie in N.Y. desp., Topeka *Journal*, 66: 237, Oct. 2, 1940, p. 2c; '"Marrying Merton, he'd feel, was perhaps a kind of leg up for me,"' Agatha Christie, *Thirteen at Dinner*, © 1933, Red Arrow ed., Milwaukee, 1939, p. 52.

LUFTWAFFE, pl. LUFTWAFFEN n. The German air-force: 'Nazi luftwaffe raiders touched off London's first alarm of the day late this afternoon,' AP desp., Topeka *Journal*, 66: 217, Sep. 9, 1940, p. 1g–h; 'If the Luftwaffe succeeds in destroying a considerable part of Britain's port facilities,' *New Republic*, 103: 17, Oct. 21, 1940, p. 546b; 'A little over a year ago the Polish Army foundered under the speed-and-steel avalanche of the *Panzer* divisions and *Luftwaffen*,' *Harper's*, 182: 1087, Dec. 1940, p. 1b.

MOSQUITO BOAT n. A motor-torpedo boat: 'TRIAL RUN FOR "MOSQUITO BOAT"—The PT3, one of two U.S. torpedo boats nearing completion. . . , gets a test run. Its cost: about $100,000,' AP photo, Topeka *Journal*, 66: 103, Apr. 29, 1940, p. 2a–c; 'the Elco Company . . . put up a . . . plant extension . . . to manufacture motor-torpedo ("mosquito") boats,' Pearson and Allen col., *ibid.*, 66: 217, Sept. 9, 1940, p. 4c.

NEWSWORTHY adj. Worthy of figuring in the news: 'The Nazi offensive . . . is, judging from our newspapers, apparently the only newsworthy topic on Latin America,' *Harper's*, 181: 1086, Nov. 1940, p. 588a; 'With great glee the cameramen went into action at the sight of this newsworthy haul,' *Collier's*, 107: 1, Jan. 4, 1941, p. 26d; 'newsworthy information,' *Saturday Evening Post*, 213: 27, Jan. 4, 1941, p. 64a; 'If the dispatch is news-worthy,' *ibid.*, p. 65c. (Note for the current uncertainty of spelling that the last two examples are from the same article.)

NYLON n. Nylon hose: 'Dunk your nylons in rich suds of neutral soap,' *The Woman*, 5: 2, Aug. 1940, p. 68; 'Nylons are harder to get than blood out of a turnip,' adv., Topeka *Capital*, 64: 311, Dec. 21, 1940, p. 3.

PANZER adj. Armored, used of mechanized troops, esp. tanks; also figurative: 'One-fifth of the 2,000-tank panzer armada used by the Nazis . . . has been blasted into inactivity,' AP Paris desp., Topeka *Journal*, June 7, 1940, p. 1g–h; 'How U.S. "Panzer" Divisions Will Be Equipped,' NEA photo, Topeka *Capital*, 64: 284, Nov. 24, 1940, p. 14Db–d; 'Delegations Deploying To Stop Willkie's "Panzer" Wire Attacks,' AP Philadelphia desp., *ibid.*, 64: 131, June 24, 1940, p. 1b.

PROTOTYPE n. 'The prototype is a plane designed in detail and manufactured in very small quantities for experimental purposes,' *New Republic*, 103: 24, Dec. 9, 1940, p. 782b; 'great air and tank fleets can spring from a few prototypes, if the prototypes are good,' *Harper's*, 182: 1087, Dec. 1940, p. 2b.

QUISLE v.i. To act as a traitor (see *Quisling*, below): 'To Quisle, or Quisling, now being used as a verb,' University of Chicago Round Table broadcast, May 5, 1940; 'The idea [of the Italian invasion of Greece] was to attain a pushover, a super-Quisling, a grand entrance and no

1. 'W37' signifies the Merriam *Webster*, Second Edition, 1937 printing; 'W-sup.,' the new-words supplement of the same, as of 1939.

fight,' Topeka *Capital,* 64: 311, Dec. 21, 1940, p. 4a. (Note the gerund in the last example, identical in spelling with the root word.) *American Speech,* Dec. 1940, p. 437b, reports that *quisle* was discussed in the Decatur, Illinois, *Herald,* Sep. 9, 1940, p. 7.

QUISLING n. A traitor. Explained in Ed Murrow's broadcast, CBS, Apr. 19, 1940, from London, as a new antonomastic use. 'I don't think there were many Quislings in the Norwegian Army or Navy,' W. L. White in Topeka *Capital,* 64: 76, Apr. 30, 1940, p. 8Ad; 'even Laval is not quite a Quisling,' *Nation,* 151: 12, Sep. 21, 1940, p. 248a.

RANK-AND-FILER, RANK AND FILER n. A member of the rank and file: 'Others assert he [Bioff] never in his life toiled as an active rank-and-filer,' *Saturday Evening Post,* Jan. 27, 1940, p. 82a; 'Merry Christmas to you rank and filers, good, decent, peace-loving Americans,' *American Guardian,* 24: 13, Dec. 27, 1940, p. 4a.

SITZKRIEG n. Inactive warfare, or an inactive war. Used by Kaltenborn, Radio Station WBBM, Dec. 4, 1939. 'Blitzkrieg or Sitzkrieg?' caption *Time,* 35: 14, Apr. 1, 1940, p. 22a; 'Eight months of sitzkrieg on the western front,' *Newsweek,* 15: 23, June 3, 1940, p. 27c; observed in *Newsweek,* 15: 19, May 6, 1940, p. 24a; *Propaganda Analysis,* 3: 2, Sep. 1, 1940, p. 1b; and *Common Sense,* 9: 11, Nov. 1940, p. 12b.

SLOW-DOWN, SLOWDOWN n. An intentional decrease in speed of work, used as a weapon in labor disputes: 'The slow⸗down is criminal,' Defense Commissioner Knudsen in Topeka *Capital,* 64: 238, Oct. 9, 1940, p. 7a; 'Another consequence [of labor difficulties in the defense program] is the "slowdown" on the job,' Pearson and Allen col., Topeka *Journal,* 66: 314, Dec. 31, 1940, p. A6a.

WINTERIZATION n. Act or process of winterizing (see below): 'PLUS COMPLETE WINTERIZATION,' used car adv., Topeka *Capital,* 64: 298, Dec. 8, 1940, p. 2A.

WINTERIZE v.t. To equip or prepare for winter use: 'Winterize Your Car,' Sears, Roebuck adv., Topeka *Capital,* 64: 291, Dec. 1, 1940, p. 13B; 'winterized tent [suitable for winter use],' *PM,* Nov. 29, 1940. (In W37 only as 'to convert into winter oil.')

WPAer n. A W. P. A. worker: 'put the most competent of the WPAers back into private work,' *Harper's,* 177: 1061, Oct. 1938, p. 480b; 'Fort Wayne leaders got a lot of the WPAers hooked up with the housing problem,' *Collier's,* 105: 20, May 18, 1940, p. 74a.

[Note: Where a word is divided at the end of a line, the double hyphen [⸗] indicates a hyphen in the original.]

AMONG THE NEW WORDS

DWIGHT L. BOLINGER
Washburn College

WHETHER sped by times in which human beings are becoming accustomed to having more and more done to, for, and at them, it would be difficult to prove; but the fact is that the suffix *-ee,* denoting passivity, has gained a flexibility never before seen. Most, but not all, of the new derivatives have to do with the war, or, in this country, with military conscription. Of the latter we have the following: 'the war department . . . said men inducted into the army through the selective service program are "trainees" or "selectees" but never "draftees"' (Topeka *Journal,* January 31, 1941, p. 4b, quoting Salina *Journal*). Of these three, *draftee* and *trainee* are older words, but *selectee* is new; the three are discussed in an article referred to in *American Speech,* April, 1941, Bibliography, p. 137b. *Time* adds *conscriptee,* March 31, 1941, p. 43; this appeared also in the *Saturday Evening Post,* December 14, 1940, p. 28b. Other *-ee* derivatives figuring in the news are: *bombee* (*Time,* March 31, 1941, p. 21c; *Time,* June 9, 1941, p. 30a); *purgee,* a victim of a political 'purge' (*New Republic,* December 9, 1940, p. 788b); *pollee,* one polled by a public-opinion 'institute' (*Propaganda Analysis,* November 11, 1940, p. 4b); *sockee,* one socked, i.e., struck (*PM,* December 4, 1940, p. 11a-c). *Evacuee* (Topeka *Capital,* January 12, 1941, p. 1g; *Time,* March 31, 1941, p. 43) is interesting in that the endings *-é* and *-ée,* denoting gender, formerly current in this word, have been assimilated to the more general *-ee* suffix. *Deportee* has been revived (leaflet 'Must They Starve?' issued by National Committee on Food for the Five Small Democracies, about January 20, 1941). *Words,* October, 1940, recorded *rushee, crack-upee, standee, quizzee,* and *squeezee.*

Spanish, which gave us the prolific *-teria* of *cafeteria,* has provided another suffix which is fast gaining in popularity: *-aroo,* from *buckaroo,* 'vaquero.' Much of its success is undoubtedly due to the coincidental support[1] of *kangaroo,* the image of the animal's antics contributing to the festive tone of all the *-aroo* words, and of words ending in the sound *-aree,* such as *charivari* (cp. 'He made the first [feature picture] I remember, a wild shooterie called "Cheyenne Harry."' *American Speech,* February 1941, p. 16a). I have observed the following: *jivaroo, vibaroo* ('jivaroo on the vibaroo [Vibraphone],' Alec Templeton broadcast, February 7, 1941); *wackaroo* ('a New York department store is now offering a "wackaroo"—a surrealistic chalk figure sprayed with brilliant colors. Seized with one of those uncontrollable urges for breakage, you grab your "wackaroo," dash it against the wall and you have the prettiest mess, plus a nice loud pop when it bursts,' Topeka *Journal,* February 5, 1941, p. 1g); *kissamaroo* ('the old Ohio kissamaroo,' MGM film 'Third Finger Left Hand,' seen July 17, 1941; *babyroo* ('Marlene, the secret-service babyroo,' *Liberty,* May 31, 1941, p. 18b); *snoozamorooed,* 'drunk' (*American Speech,* February 1941, p. 70a); *gageroos,* 'gags,' in comic sense (*American Speech,* April 1941, p. 158a).

1. 'Coincidental support' is a term invented by Peter Tamony to describe the phenomena discussed in 'Word Affinities,' *American Speech,* 15: 62-73 (Feb. 1940).

A. A., ACK-ACK, ARCHIE n., also as adj. Anti-aircraft gun; anti-aircraft: 'A. A. guns firing a hundred miles away,' *Magazine Digest,* August 1940, p. 46b; 'A. A. Fire Takes Edge Off Air War,' Topeka *Journal,* November 21, 1940, p. A3h; 'the puffs of A. A. bursts,' *Harper's,* January 1941, p. 117b. 'Still, one or two [Dorniers] a week got it. Marked up on the board to the credit of the Ack-Ack gunners,' *Saturday Evening Post,* January 11, 1941, p. 12c; 'plane . . . set afire by German ack-ack,' *Time,* July 14, 1941, p. 19a. 'Debunking an "Archie" Myth,' caption, Topeka *Journal,* January 22, 1941, p. 2c. (*Archie* and *ack-ack* treated in *Better English,* December 1940, p. 8a; *American Speech,* Bibliography, s.v. 'War words,' February 1941; s.v. 'Guns,' April 1941. *Archie* is well treated in OEDS.)

BATHINETTE n. A portable bathtub for infants (term probably coined on the analogy of *bassinet,* an infant's cradle): 'GENUINE BABY BATHINETTE,' adv., Topeka *Capital,* November 25, 1938, p. 3; 'Pedal Converts the Bathinette into Baby's Dressing Table,' *Popular Mechanics,* March 1939, p. 416b; 'BABY BATHINETTES. Combination bath and table. The dressing table locks automatically when drawn over the tub for use and baby is safe. In a choice of hand or foot operated,' adv., Topeka *Journal,* April 26, 1940.

BURN n., v. i. Anger, a showing of anger; to show anger: 'The Saga of the Slow Burn Man, or "Killer" [Edgar] Kennedy,' Los Angeles *Daily News,* August 2, 1938, p. 18; 'Right about now I bet the Major's doing a slow burn [with chagrin]!' Maj. Hoople cartoon, Topeka *Capital,* September 15, 1940; 'He's burning,' Charlie McCarthy, January 12, 1941; 'Boy, wait until she saw him squiring Violet Medaris around. Would she burn!' *Saturday Evening Post,* January 11, 1941, p. 70d. (W37 recognizes the figurative use referring to anger, but does not explain this new use implying anger without specification; older metaphors are on the order of 'to burn with rage.')

CASE v.t. To study or plan (a crime, esp. the setting of a crime) so as to preclude accidents: 'There's a pretty good chance this is an inside job. Tuesday's an odd day for pay rolls and this job must have been cased pretty thoroughly to have been carried out so rapidly,' *Dynamic Detective,* January 1941, p. 38a; 'It's my guess that he cased this job first—that he must have visited you once before or had a confederate visit here, just to get the layout,' *True Detective,* June 1941, p. 56; 'The crime itself had been too carefully cased for the thugs' arrival at the particular moment when the officer was gone, to have been accidental,' *Master Detective,* July 1941, p. 6c.

CEILING n. An upper limit (extended from the aeronautical use, in OEDS from 1917; not used here of material objects): 'The Ceiling Over the Head of Industry,' *Reader's Digest,* September 1938, p. 1; 'Even fair price ceilings and quality floors won't answer real needs unless an adequate supply of goods is made available,' *Consumer's Union Reports,* May 1941, outside back cover; 'If Leon Henderson were to answer these Latin floors [on price of coffee] with a U.S. ceiling, Brazilians would yell,' *Time,* June 23, 1941, p. 76c.

CELL n. A nucleus within a larger organization, intriguing for a special interest; fraction (no longer limited, as in W34, to communists, nor, as in Wsup., to Buchmanites): 'Black Shirts . . . meeting furtively in underground "cells,"' *Nation,* November 18, 1939, p. 549a; '[the Nazis] organizing revolutionary cells [in Mexico],' Pearson-Allen broadcast, January 26, 1941. Reported in *Words,* December 1939.

EFFECTIVE n. An agency which successfully effects a desired result (extended from the military sense, in OED from 1722): 'home-made bombs, smoke screens and other delaying effectives,' *New Republic,* October 14, 1940, p. 511b; 'The isolationist press last week lost a major effective: the . . . Detroit *Free Press,*' *Time,* June 9, 1941, p. 44b.

FELLOW-TRAVELING n., adj. An act or acts characteristic of fellow travelers (see ANW[2] April, 1941); pertaining to fellow travelers: 'his [Broun's] "fellow traveling,"' *Common Sense,* February, 1940, p. 19c; 'his fellow-traveling had done him no good with the brass hats,' *Time,* June 30, 1941, p. 42b; 'Davis . . . ran the American Federation of Teachers as a fellow-traveling agency of the Communist Party until he was displaced in 1939,' *Saturday Evening Post,* Feb. 15, 1941, p. 88b; 'the Communist fellow-traveling American Peace Mobilization,' *Time,* March 31, 1941, p. 42.

FLASH adj. and combining form. Sudden and violent (earlier examples, of *flash-flood,* recorded in *Words,* April, 1940; possibly stems from radio use, as in 'flash bulletin'): 'Our post-war gyrations from flash-booms to deep and continued depression,' Hugh Johnson col., Topeka *Capital,* October 2, 1940, p. 4f; 'Glimpsing "Flash" Prosperity,' Topeka *Journal,* January 20, 1941, p. 4a; 'It must have been a flash fire. . . . The people in the sleeping rooms . . . didn't have a chance,' *True Detective,* June, 1941, p. 70a.

FLOOR n. A lower limit (see *ceiling,* above, for antonym and examples of *floor*): 'Excuse for the silver-buying program and its artificial price floor . . . was to keep Western miners at work,' *Time,* July 21, 1941, p. 70c. (In Wsup.)

GUINEA PIG n. Any object of experimentation, esp. if conceived as victimized (reported in *Words,* November, 1939; but note esp. the first of the following examples, preceding the book *100,000,000 Guinea Pigs,* probable source of the present use): 'And may I ask . . . the nature of this *treatment* of yours, these experiments of which we are to be the—guinea pigs, so to speak? Is it to be anything in the nature of a vaccination?' H. G. Wells, *Men Like Gods,* N.Y., Macmillan, 1923, cop. 1922, p. 180; 'the success of the pie-projector on our young guinea pig!' NEA Maj. Hoople cartoon, Topeka *Capital,* April 15, 1940, p. 11: 'the Allis-Chalmers Company is to be a CIO guinea pig, in defiance of the national defense program,' *Reader's Digest,* June, 1941, p. 90b.

HIGH-PRESSURE v.t. To exert high pressure upon, esp. in order to make a sale; to obtain by high-pressure methods: 'I did not attempt to high-pressure the man too much,' *Saturday Evening Post,* February 8, 1941, p. 54c; 'photographers . . . hipressuring portrait sales,' Fidler col., Topeka *Journal,* May 4, 1940, p. 2Ad.

JOAD n. A migratory worker, generally in plural (from the family of this name in Steinbeck's *Grapes of Wrath*): 'one family of "Joads" which came to California from Arkansas,' *Christian Science Monitor,* June 14, 1940; 'Help for the Joads,' caption *Nation,* December 21, 1940, p. 622a. (Reported in *Words,* February, 1940.)

LIFELINE n. A commercial, esp. British maritime, route: 'cut what Britain calls her "life line,"' *Literary Digest,* October 17, 1936, p. 13c; 'Captain B. H. Liddell Hart . . . has expressed concern for the "life-line of the Empire" . . . (*Manchester Guardian,* of April 15, 1937),' Louis Fischer, *Why Spain Fights On,* London, Union of Democratic Control [1937?], p. 31; 'The Burma Road is China's lifeline, principal link with the outside world, despite Japan's encirclement,' Kansas City *Star,* June 8, 1941, rotogravure sec., p. 4; 'The concept of the Mediterranean as the Empire's commercial life line has been dead since Italy's entrance into the war forced merchant ships to sail around the Cape of Good Hope,' *Time,* June 9, 1941, p. 36b.

NEW DEALISM n. 'New Dealism . . . is nothing but the American form of communism,' *Nation,* June 10, 1939, p. 677, quoting N. Y. Economic Council letter of April 3, 1939; 'We must be careful not to identify . . . New Dealism with Franklin Roosevelt and his acts,' *Time,* May 19, 1941, p. 98c, quoting Burnham's *Managerial Revolution.*

2. ANW, this department.

OKIE n. (Reported in *Words*, November, 1939; note for origin:) 'Lewis Delaney Offield . . . changed his name to Jack Oakie' (footnote: 'It meant the same thing to the comic, who had attended school in Muskogee, Okla., that it meant to Author John Steinbeck: an itinerant Oklahoman.') *Time*, May 19, 1941, p. 56c.

SELLER n. Something currently offered for sale: 'Reg. 5c Sellers,' Thrifty Drug Stores handbill, distributed in Los Angeles August 26, 1940, p. 1; 'Regular $2.49 Sellers,' adv., Topeka *Capital*, September 20, 1940, p. 8. (Wrongly defined in W37 as 'a thing which sells readily'.)

SIWASH n. A jerkwater college: 'from fresh water Siwashes to the greatest universities,' Hugh Johnson col., Topeka *Capital*, May 9, 1940, p. 4d; 'all the usual arguments about the value of team play and high ideals and die-for-dear-old-Siwash,' *Collier's*, January 4, 1941, p. 48c.

TENDENTIOUS adj. Dissident, trouble-making: 'The Nazis . . . are very careful now about whom they let into the country. And they warn the ones who are there against being "tendentious." It's a new crime; it means being too firmly and outspokenly pro-democratic in your attitude,' W. L. White in Topeka *Capital*, May 6, 1940, p. 10a; 'The German colony in Uruguay is deeply hurt . . . by the tendentious and unfounded attacks to which it has been exposed,' petition to Pres. Baldomir carried in *Christian Science Monitor*, June 13, 1940, p. 2a; 'Those French teachers' organizations, which, in the hope of securing educational reforms, took up a tendentious position on all political, social and economic issues, invited the strong opposition of reactionary forces,' A. A. U. P. *Bulletin*, February, 1941, p. 91. (Undoubtedly a naturalized word, the W41 definition being neutral; the cognate words in French, German, and Spanish are all pejorative.)

AMONG THE NEW WORDS

DWIGHT L. BOLINGER
Washburn Municipal University

VICHYATE is a perfect example of spontaneous generation in words. This writer suggested it to the editors of *Time* in a letter, September 1, 1941, after following some of the *Vichy* compounds of which *Time* is so fond just at present. The examples below show its use.

Needle, in the two senses 'goad, vex' and 'thread (one's way),' is either a curious oversight on the part of *Webster*, or has enjoyed a recent and very thorough revival. Both senses are in the OED, and the first in particular, as the examples show, has been very popular of late.

A great deal has been written about the tendency toward euphemistic expressions in our national defense effort, such as *selectee* for *draftee*, *priorities* for *rationing*, and *detainees* in place of *prisoners* for Italians interned at Missoula, Montana (*Time*, 18 Aug. 1941 24/1). A writer in the *American Guardian* (18 Apr. 1941 2/3) elaborately uses the verb *coordinate* in place of *censor*, copying the government release on the appropriation given to Lowell Mellett for 'coordinating government reports'; *coordinate* is of course the eulogistic counterpart of *regiment*, which we use when speaking of the other fellow's coordination. Other fields have their minced expressions, too. The mounted state police in Colorado call themselves the 'Colorado Courtesy Patrol.' In the trade it is practically impossible to find plain words for *small*, *artificial*, and *second-grade*. *Small* is disguised as *regular* ('Giant, family or regular size package of White King'–handbill distributed in Los Angeles, 8 Aug. 1940), *guest* (guest-size cake of Ivory soap), *medium* (the dental liquid *Cue* divides itself into *medium*, *large*, and *giant*), and the megalogisms indulged in by the ripe-olive industry, not to mention many others. *Artificial* and *imitation* appear as *simulated*, and, in jewelry, as *costume*; the same intent to deceive is seen in *feminine hygiene* for *contraception*. *Second-rate* has long been transformed into *trade* and *standard* (*Better English*, May, 1941, records *trade gin* as a synonym of *bathtub gin*, and 'standard pack' canned goods are advertised daily). The railroads prefer *tourist* and *coach* to *second* and *third* class. Dairies in most localities innocently use only the first two letters of the alphabet for grades of milk. The American meat industry, which would of course not refer to itself as a *trust*, appears in the magazines under the academic toga of the 'American Meat *Institute*,' which, along with the 'American *Institute* of Public Opinion,' the 'American Iron and Steel *Institute*,' the 'American Petroleum *Institute*,' and the inter-American '*Instituto* del Café,' is giving a commercial turn to a pedagogical word. Even the teaching profession avoids the appearance of receiving forbidden favors by asking its publishers not for *free* copies but for *desk* copies.

Readers are asked to send to the editor any interesting data which they may have on the following words, to be treated in this column. Dates earlier than those given are especially solicited. Credit will of course be given for all material used.

Backstage, covert, concealed: 4 May 1940. *Belt*, assembly-line: 1937. *Bitchy*. *Blitz buggy*: 22 Sep. 1941. *Call girl, call house, call woman*, ref. to prostitution: Apr. 1940. *Clipper*, to fly or send in a clipper plane: 8 Sep. 1941. *Contact lens*: May 1939. *Creative pause*: June 1941. *Cuff, off the*, informal, etc.: Aug. 1941. *Cuff, on the*, on credit: 1936. *Droop*, a languid person: 22 Apr. 1940. *Dunkirk*, a defeat (in general): 9 June 1941. *Flak*, ack-ack: Sep. 1941. *Front*, noun, in political sense: 1927. *Front*, to act as a political front for: 5 Aug. 1939. *Gun*, to accelerate (an automobile): Jan. 1941. *Hit*, to indulge in: 1939. *Hitleristic*: 6 Jan. 1941. *Horsefeathers*. *Jeepers*. *Juco*, a junior college: 26 Aug. 1939. *Lackey*, as popularized by Communist Party: 1939. *Lug*, a political assessment: 1936.

SYMBOLS: The symbol + before a word or definition indicates an Americanism. A date immediately following a word or definition indicates the time of evidence shown in the DAE, or, if so stated, in another publication. Dates in brackets indicate the time, etc., of British usage. An asterisk after a word indicates that the word is illustrated in British usage before 1600.

+ALL-OUTER. An advocate of an all-out policy, as of aid to Britain or of national defense.—1941 *Saturday Evening Post* 25 Jan. 26/2 Do the all-outers remember what they said then? *Common Sense* Nov. 346/1 If fate smiles . . . , the slack between all-outers and non-belligerents need never be taken up.

+BACK-TO-WORK, *a*. Of a plan or movement: Involving a return to industrial employment, esp. in the face of union opposition.—1937 Topeka *Capital* 20 Nov. 1/5 Slusser announced the back-to-work plans, . . . relented in an earlier decision to bar . . . workers. 1941 *Reader's Digest* June 92/1 Many of us who do not join a back-to-work movement.

BAITER. One who heckles. [1611–] +Common as the second element in combinations, esp. ref. to politics or religion: *Roosevelt-, Catholic-baiter*. Hence *boob-, U.S.-baiting*, etc. [*Jew-baiter, Jew-baiting*, 1883–].—1941 *Time* (Air Exp. Ed.) 18 Aug. 4/1 Republican isolationists and Roosevelt-baiters. *Ibid.* (Air Exp. Ed.) 22 Sep. 28/3 Catholicbaiter Thomas Watson. 1926 Haldeman-Julius *Big Blue Book No. B-28* 13 Her [Aimee Semple McPherson's] mastery of boob-baiting. 1941 *Time* 14 Apr. 74 Editor Grey . . . has injected into his technical publication noisy U.S.-baiting ('the civilized world and the United States of America').

+BAR-FLY. An habitué of drinking-places.—1940 *Common Sense* June 11/2 There was a name for this General Krivitsky. It was 'Schmelka Ginsberg,' a barfly. 1941 *Time* (Air Exp. Ed.) 13 Oct. 34/2 This will cut whiskey production by only 12-15%, not enough to worry barflies.

BEACH-HEAD. A military invasion point established on a beach in a territory being invaded; a fortified position on a beach.—1940 *Common Sense* Sep. 18/1 The second theory [of the Germans], to harass communications and airports and beachheads so effectively that landings could be undertaken. 1941 *Time* (Air Exp. Ed.) 25 Aug. 12/2 Marines and soldiers trained in the terrible job of establishing a beach-head, would appear off Martinique. Sta. KECA (Los Angeles) newscast 21 Dec. The [Japanese] invaders are trying to filter inland from their [Luzon] beachheads.

BLACKOUT. 1939 (*Words*, Jan., p. 13). +*fig.* A lapse of consciousness.—1941 *Inside Detective* Oct. 4/2 A crime committed during a mental blackout. *Time* (Air Exp. Ed.) 6 Oct. 29/1 Except for a momentary blackout when he pulled the ripcord, his mind was sharper and quicker than when his feet were on the ground. *Inside Detective* Nov. 12/inset The slaying of McCain occurred while Young was in a 'mental blackout.'

BLOOD-BATH. [Cf. German *Blutbad*.] A massacre; a bath of blood.—1939 G. E. R. Gedye *Fallen Bastions* (London, Gollancz) 35 The workers had replied to the blood-bath in the streets [of Vienna] by the final weapon of the unarmed masses—the General Strike. 1941 *Time* (Air Exp. Ed.) 22 Sep. 13/1 To baptize the decree in the usual blood bath, Nazis sentenced and shot Vigo Hansteen . . . and Rolf Vickstroem.

BLUEPRINT, *n*. 1909 (W.) +*fig.* Any detailed plan.—1941 *American Mercury* Apr. 475/1 Plato's *Republic*, first blueprint of a totalitarian world. *Kenyon Review* Autumn 460 Accept the categories of science as potentially adequate blueprints of all reality. 1942 *Reader's Digest* Jan. 35/1 We must lay out a blueprint of how we will meet the postwar crisis.

+BLUEPRINT, *v. tr.* To devise (a measure).—1941 *Common Sense* Sep. 284/1 Blueprinting the measures necessary for the waging of 'total' economic warfare.

BRIDGE-HEAD. [1812–] A military salient in hostile territory.—1938 Kansas City *Star* 22 Apr. 1/1 Counterattacks had reduced [Spanish] insurgent bridgeheads. 1940 *Better English* Dec. 8/1 *Bridge-head*—Defense position dominating or covering extremity of bridge nearest [*sic*] enemy; in a figurative sense successful landing of Germans in England would be the establishment of a *bridgehead*. 1941 Chicago *Sunday Tribune* 23 Nov. 10/2-3 Parachute troops, who captured Maleme air field and other points, establishing bridgeheads for air transportation of troops.

BUDGET*. [1733, as noun.] +*a.* Conducing to economical spending of household funds.—1941 Minister's Life and Casualty Union *Call* Dec. 3/2 The Union has a monthly budget plan for members who carry both life and casualty insurance. 1941 Le Roy's Jewelers (Los Angeles) 1941-42 *Gift Book* America's largest budget jewelry store. 1942 *The Family Circle* 2 Jan. 6 Budget Dinners.

+CONVENTIONEER. One who attends a convention.—1940 American Association of University Professors *Bulletin* Dec. 643 Professional conventioneers. 1941 *Time* (Air Exp. Ed.) 26 May 3/1 The men of radio, 1,100 strong (and younger and sleeker than most conventioneers), met . . . in St. Louis.

+CURTAINS. Finis, esp. death by violence.—1931 Ben Ames Williams *Pirate's Purchase* (Milwaukee, Red Arrow Books, 1939) 161 Will you play? If you do, you'll get your cut; and if you don't—curtains for you. 1940 *Detective Tales* Mar. 71/1 It was curtains for Alice. 1941 *Time* 11 Aug. 57/1 The commandeering [of silk] meant curtains for most of the 500 U.S. silk-hosiery manufacturers.

+DOCUMENTARY, *a.* [1802–] +*absol.* A documentary film.—1940 *Common Sense* Nov. 8/2 There can be no essential line of demarcation between a documentary and any other kind of picture. 1941 *Time* (Air Exp. Ed.) 13 Oct. 15/2 German propaganda floods Japan with war documentaries and . . . 'culture' magazines.

DECONTAMINATION. Removal of destructive gas and chemicals launched in an air attack.—1938 *Saturday Evening Post* 3 Sep. 23/2 He held forth on the perils of mustard gas and stressed the vital necessity of prompt decontamination. 1941 *Time* (Air Exp. Ed.) 6 Oct. 21/1 The decontamination squad, dressed in rubber suits and gloves, went after the gas bombs, sprinkling chloride of lime everywhere.

+HAMMY. Characteristic of a ham actor.—1939 *New Republic* 11 Jan. 281/1 The acting is consistently hammy. 1941 *Time* (Air Exp. Ed.) 1 Sep. 26/1 [Spencer Tracy's acting in 'Dr. Jekyll and Mr. Hyde' is] hammy when he chuckles fiendish 'Heh, heh, hehs' at his lecherous face in the mirror.

HERRENVOLK. [German.] The dominant class or race in a society.—1941 *Kenyon Review* Summer 338 The destiny of the German people to be the *Herrenvolk* of the western world. *American Guardian* 15 Oct. 6/1 Hitler's . . . race program was stolen from the White Trash Herrenvolk of Dixie.

+IFFY. Contingent, doubtful.—1940 Lavine and Wechsler *War Propaganda and the U.S.* (New Haven, Yale Univ. Press) 59 Questions about the board's work were 'iffy.' 1941 *Time* 14 July 15/3 His chances of pulling out a plum were rather iffy.

+JANIZARIAT, JANISSARIAT. The body of New-Deal advisers and officials about Pres. F. D. Roosevelt.—1940 H. Johnson in Topeka *Capital* 23 Apr. 4/4 Certain Kibitzers—Columnists—Get Information From Janissariats Without Taking Both Sides. 1941 *Time* 10 Mar. 15/2 Justice Douglas still has a finger in all Janizariat pots, sees the President at least weekly. . . . The Janizariat generally believes that . . . Hughes . . . may retire.

JANIZARY*. +A member of the Janizariat.—1941 *Time* 10 Mar. 15/3 Some of the Janizaries wanted La Guardia as the U.S. Beaverbrook of air production.

JIM CROWISM. Discrimination against negroes.—1939 *Nation* 7 Jan. 27/1 His [Justice Black's] vote against Jim Crowism. 1941 *Propaganda Analysis* 26 Aug. 1/2 The Negro organizations . . . want an end to 'Jim Crowism.'

LOYAL OPPOSITION. Toward a party in power, opposition not verging upon disloyalty to fundamental national principles. +Used esp. of the Willkieites (q.v.).—1941 *Nation* 25 Jan. 89/2 The 'Loyal Opposition' [of Wendell Willkie]. *Time* (Air Exp. Ed.) 18 Aug. 3/3 The Republican Party . . . now divided in two great masses—one moving toward Wendell Willkie and 'loyal opposition,' and the other toward isolationism.

+LUCITE.—1939 *Reader's Digest* Feb. 81/1 Light flows through rods made of Lucite, a du Pont plastic, as water flows through a pipe. 1941 Topeka *Capital* Jan. 4/2 Beads of lucite [on clothing].

+MASTERMIND, *v.* [1720, as noun] *tr.* To engineer, or expert, in the capacity of a master mind.—1941 *True Detective* June 18/3 Often suspected but never convicted of masterminding some of the plots hatched in his grog shop. *Time* 26 May 24/2 The *Telegram* hired a series of detective storytellers to mastermind the [Rudolph] Hess case. *Ibid.* (Air Exp. Ed.) 4 Aug. 36 Lilienthal . . . masterminded the tie-in with OPM.

NEEDLE, *v. tr.* 1. To goad, vex [1812–].—1940 Pearson and Allen in Topeka *Journal* 2 Feb. Lewis bitterly resented this pressure, and . . . developed considerable personal heat against Roosevelt for 'needling' him. 1941 *Time* 7 Apr. 22/3 Some 20 Manhattan reporters gave the Ambassador a going-over for 50 minutes. . . . He did not let it appear that he knew he was being needled.

2. To thread (one's way) [1866–].—1940 Mallon in Topeka *Journal* 21 Mar. 4/2 While Mussolini has been losing influence with Franco in Spain, Hitler has been needling in rapidly.

+VICHYATE. *v. tr.* [*Vichy* + *ate,* punning on *vitiate.*] To subject (France) to the regime of Vichy.—1941 American Association of University Professors *Bulletin* Dec. 570 French Civilization Vichyated. *American Speech* Dec. 314 n. Ever since the French government was Vichy-ated. 1942 *Time* 12 Jan. 14 Will sympathy be vichyated?

+WILLKIEITE. A follower of Wendell Willkie.—1940 *American Guardian* 20 Dec. 2/6 The Willkieite, who is heading the Willkie Clubs hereabouts. 1941 Topeka *Journal* 22 Jan. 4/3 They were blocked by a Willkieite.

AMONG THE NEW WORDS

DWIGHT L. BOLINGER
Washburn Municipal University

OF THE words on which information was requested in the April, 1942, instalment of ANW, the following have appeared in the new *American Thesaurus of Slang* with as much information as could have been given here, and are hence not treated below: *on the cuff, gun, horsefeathers,* and *jeepers.* The department is still eager, however, for examples of *jeepers* from about 1933 and before.

Bombardier (see below) is an interesting adaptation of an obsolete word to modern warfare; it also points to the shift in meaning of *bomb,* now something dropped but once synonymous with *shell.*

Professor Maurer of the University of Louisville states that *call-house* (see below) 'is hardly a new word, since it is at least as old as the telephone and the type of brothel of course much older; I strongly suspect that the word goes back to England.' He also reveals that *bar-fly* has come up a notch in the world, apparently having once carried the connotation of one addicted to bumming free drinks (another recent citation: 'Chick was never a bar-fly, but Old Overholt used to be able to depend on him to take a pint a week,' *Writer's Forum,* May 1942, 3/3). And he gives a 1931 reference to *curtains* in his own Dec. 1931 article in *American Speech,* 'Argot of the Underworld,' p. 103.

-dollar word, et al., has been spreading of late to other expressions (see below). Professor Hard of Newcomb College writes that of twenty persons whom he queried, all but one regarded *-dollar* in these combinations to have begun with radio use in spelling and other quiz programs; and that one Chicagoan remembered *five-dollar word* from his school days. Professor Marckwardt of the University of Michigan also favors *five-* or *ten-dollar* as the original form, *five* being preferred by more than half of thirty people whom he queried.

Mr. Julius Rothenberg comments that *droop* may have antecedents in the expressions 'droopy guy' and 'droopy drawers.' Certainly there is coincidental support for *drip* in the consonance of the two words, as there also appears to be for *flak* in the older *flack* ('a blow, slap, or stroke particularly with something loose and pliant,' OED, 1825) and in related *fl-* and *-ck* words (*slack, flip, fling,* etc.).

The data offered for *lug* are not given as final. There are cant senses (e.g. that of *American Speech,* Apr. 1940, p. 119/2, or 'shill,' given by Partridge, or taking *lug* as equivalent to *screw* in 'putting the screws on') which may be the answer to its origin, wholly or in part. The older sense of 'pull,' however, seemed most promising. The term in its political use has not come to my attention from outside the Kansas City area, where it has long been used of the Pendergast machine.

Besides the persons mentioned above, the following others have supplied material used here: Professor N. E. Saxe and Miss Doris Allison of Washburn Municipal University; Mr. Charles V. Stansell of the Kansas City *Star;* and Professor R. M. Duncan of the University of New Mexico.

Please comment: *Anchor,* a key position for a military operation, 1 July 1940. *Chutist,* abbr. of *parachutist,* 11 Dec. 1941. *Firepower,* force of firearms, Apr. 1942. *Full-dress,* in military and other extensions besides 'full-dress debate,' 24 Jan. 1942. *Futurama,* in fig. uses not connected with World's Fair, Feb. 1942. *Hooverville,* a shanty-town, 24 May 1933. *Infanticipate* (or *anticipate* used of expectancy) outside Winchell's column, Autumn 1941; or early instances in the column. *Job,* any large powered machine, Jan. 1938. *Juicer,* a juice-extractor, 1938. *Know-how,* a specific skill in a complicated operation, 13 Apr. 1942. *Lend-lease, v. tr.,* June 1941 (or *lease-lend*). *Longtime,* recent attrib. uses not in *Time.*

SYMBOLS: The symbol + before a word or definition indicates an Americanism. A date immediately following a word or definition indicates the time of evidence shown in the DAE, or, if so stated, in another publication. Dates in brackets indicate the time, etc., of British usage. An asterisk after a word indicates that the word is illustrated in British usage before 1600.

+AMERICA FIRSTER. A member of the America First Committee.—1941 *Time* (Air Exp. Ed.) 22 Sep. 23/2 It exploits all the emotions aroused in the U.S. by the war—even to political gags at which America Firsters clap. 1942 *New Republic* 5 Jan. 7/2 America Firsters and the numerous American-fascist outfits.

+BACKSTAGE, *adv.* 1934 (W.). +*fig. and attrib.* Under cover, not claiming attention.—1940 Pearson and Allen in Topeka *Journal* 4 May 4/4 Berle . . . does a lot of backstage speech writing and economic research for Roosevelt. *Ibid.* 11 May 4/3 There are several backstage factors which have not been discussed. 1942 *Reader's Digest* Jan. 50/2 The cashier feeds her tape into automatic machinery [at a new supermarket] that uses the punched holes to activate sorting apparatus backstage.

BELT. A means for conveying power. [1795–] +A moving assembly line.—1937 Upton Sinclair *Flivver King* 98/2 I'd rather take my chance on the belt. 1938 *Reader's Digest* Jan. 123/2 Automobiles leaving the belt as finished products.

+BLITZ-BUGGY.—1941 *Time* (Air Exp. Ed.) 22 Sep. 20/3 Around the great River Rouge plant, newsmen spotted Army Blitz-buggies everywhere. 1942 Kansas City *Star* 11 Jan. 10A/1 'Blitz buggies,' the highly-maneuverable little 40-inch-high vehicles which Ford and other manufacturers already are producing.

BOMBARDIER*. One who bombs, esp. from aircraft.—1942 *Time* 2 Feb. 35/2 At 30,000 feet, flying 200 m.p.h., a bombardier at best has only about 60 seconds in which to locate his target. A. P. desp. in Topeka *Capital* 26 Feb. 1/4 American pilots and bombardiers fighting in the Netherlands Indies sank two large Japanese transports.

CALL. Used as the first element in combinations ref. to prostitution, esp. where telephone is used to make engagements: *call girl, call house, call woman.*—1940 *Detective Tales* Apr. 68 Call Girls Die Young. 1941 *Time* (Air Exp. Ed.) 15 Sep. 26/3 A crowd of sleepy-eyed 'town girls,' 'call girls,' 'party girls,' juke-joint dames and dance-hall hostesses. 1939 D. W. Maurer, 'Prostitutes and Criminal Argots,' in *American Journal of Sociology* Jan. 547 Or, if she is more fortunate, she may work in a 'call-house,' living to herself, but being constantly and exclusively available to one proprietor by telephone. 1940 *Detective Tales* Apr. 76/2 A photographer who photographs girls for call-house madams. *Inside Detective* Dec. 27/2 Her husband persuaded her to 'work the hotels' as a call woman to 'fill dates with men.'

+CLIPPER. A type of ship, 1823–. +A flying boat, 1939 (W.). +*v. tr.* To ship by Clipper plane.—1941 *Time* (Air Exp. Ed.) 8 Sep. 23/1 The first copy of his latest book was Clippered to TIME. *Ibid.* 29 Sep. 36/3 Manila doctors Clipper x-ray films to U.S. specialists. 1942 C.B.S. broadcast 30 June [The Japanese] even went to the length of Clippering a special envoy here. +*v. intr.* To go by Clipper plane.—1941 *Collier's* 20 Dec. 52/1 Wang and I clippered over [to Hawaii] to handle it ourselves. *Ibid.* 53/2 Wharton immediately clippered to San Francisco.

+CONTACT LENS.—1939 *Reader's Digest* May 65/1 Attached by suction to the eyeball itself, a paper-thin shell of glass or bakelite, its center a tiny lens made to optical prescription. These 'contact lenses' move with the eye. 1941 *ibid.* Dec. 83/2 The aged Kane [portrayed by Orson Welles] even has eyes veined and rheumy to match—delicately designed contact lenses, fitted to the eyeballs.

+CUFF, OFF THE. Informally, extemporaneously (*also attrib.*)—1941 *Time* (Air Exp. Ed.) 4 Aug. 1/1 Day before the freezing [of Japanese funds] order the President had explained why in the simplest vernacular. Talking off the cuff to a group of civilian-defense volunteers he made them a little homily. *Ibid.* 8 Sep. 4/2 A powerful off-the-cuff orator. 1941 Walter Wanger film 'Foreign Correspondent,' at end: I'll have to tell it off the cuff [after bomb has destroyed lights and notes cannot be read]. 1942 *Time* 16 Feb. 84/1 Stevens learned his cinema technique on the roughhouse, two-reel comedy lots, where everyone from prop boy to producer had a hand in the story and no one knew how it was going to end. That is known as 'shooting off the cuff.'

+DIM-OUT, *n.* [For *dim down,* an analogy of *blackout.*] A lowering of lights as a protective measure in wartime.—1942 *Science News Letter* 21 Feb. 123/1 Modified blackouts or 'dimouts' for American cities were suggested by S. G. Hibben, electrical engineer . . . , at a military protective lighting symposium in New York. New York *Times* 3 May 2E/3 In New York City the dim-out recalled the 'lightless nights' caused by the coal shortage in 1917. *Time* 1 June 12/2 The Army clamped down harder on dim outs.

+DIM-OUT, *v. tr.* To dim as a protective measure in wartime.—1942 Green Hornet radio program 31 May The city was dimmed-out.

+DOLLAR. Common as the second element (preceded by a numeral) in combinations ref. to important or pretentious words; by extension, to other important things; by analogy, *-cent* in similar combinations: *two-, four-, five-, ten-, fifteen-dollar, seventy-five-cent, two-bit word; sixty-four-dollar question, -problem; five-dollar question.*—1940 Radio Guild play 18 May Two-dollar word. *American Freeman* Aug. 1/6 It doesn't need many pages of $4 words to convince me this story is funny. Private conversation 28 Dec. Four-dollar word. *American Speech* Oct. 314 What not so many years ago were dubbed 'five dollar words' by the irreverent. 1942 *Life* 25 May 89 'Geopolitics' . . . This five-dollar term. 1940 University of Chicago Round Table broadcast 5 May Ten-dollar word. Pearson and Allen in Topeka *Capital* 21 Sep. 4/3–4 Claude Wickard . . . Avoids $10 Words. 1942 *Time* 26 Jan. 17/1 Mr. Lewis is fond of $15 words. *Ibid.* 58/3 Physicians use 75¢ words to describe minor ailments. *Progressive* 28 Mar. 9/1 Mundabullinganda (a 75 cent word meaning . . . 'end of the mountain country'). 1940 query at Univ. of Michigan 15–25 Nov. Two-bit word. 1942 *Time* 18 May 22/3 The Jap . . . could still sweat over the $64 question: Where did they [the planes that raided Japan Apr. 18, 1942] come from and where did they go? Philip Morris Playhouse (in *The Man Who Came to Dinner*) 10 July That's the sixty-four-dollar problem. *It's Here* (Washburn Municipal Univ. anonymous publication) 2 Apr. 2/2 The five dollar question of the week is why in the h—— does Jack Myers insist upon using that cigarette?

DROOP, *n.* [1647–] +A person disliked for his languidness.—1940 Etta Kett cartoon in Topeka *Journal* 23 Apr. 10 Don't be a droop. Chase and Sanborn program 26 May A room full of old droops. 1941 'Subdebese' in *Life* 27 Jan. 79 [a term used in San Antonio to denote a girl who fails to ask why in order to provide an opening for the point of a joke]. [New York schoolboy slang in] *American Speech* Oct. 190 *Drip, Droop, Schloomp.* A stupid, mopy person.

DUNKIRK. A defeat similar to that suffered by the British at Dunkirk, Belgium, June, 1940.—1941 *Time* 9 June 9/2 In far too many items we are still lagging behind and . . . there may well be more Dunkirks. 1942 *Reader's Digest* Jan. 5/1 We stand an excellent chance of suffering a series of terrible Dunkirks.

FLAK, FLACK.—1941 New York *Times* quoted by *Better English* Sep. 4/1 Ever since the active stage of the war started anti-aircraft fire ceased to be known as 'ackack.' It is always 'flak.' This actually is not slang for it is derived from the German 'fliegerabwehrkanone'—a gun to drive off aircraft. *Collier's* 20 Dec. 59/1 'Flak' is specifically the abbreviation of *'Fliegerabwehr Kanonen'*—cannon warding off fliers. 1942 *Time* 9 Mar. 14/3 Rumors were as thick as flack. *Ibid.* 6 Apr. 23/1 She had sunk a Nazi *flak* ship . . . [footnote:] Small tug or trawler equipped with anti-aircraft guns.

FRONT*, *n.* [1350–, in military sense] 1. A political or other similar alliance arraying diverse forces. 1939 (W.).—1927 Dorothy Sayers *Clouds of Witness* (N.Y., Pocket Books, 1940) 140 A thin, eager young woman . . . looking like a personification of the United Front of the 'Internationale.' 1937 *Harper's* 7 July 211/1 Sanctions had smashed the Stresa Front. 1939 Kansas City *Star* 28 Oct. 1/1 Asked Curran if the National Maritime union was a 'Communist-front organization.' 1941 *Common Sense* June 183/1 The political expression 'front' was borrowed from the armies.

2. An outwardly respectable agent serving as façade of a disreputable activity. 1939 (W.).—1939 Topeka *Capital* 1 Feb. 1/5 4259 gallons came to thirteen Shawnee County major bootleggers or their 'fronts.'

+3. [Probably combining senses 1 and 2.] An individual or group serving as real or nominal head or representative of an enterprise or movement (sense 1) to lend it prestige, concealment, etc. 1939 (W.).—1941 *Time* (Air Exp. Ed.) 26 May 31/1 With committees on which the Fairlesses, Graces and Girdlers are represented by themselves instead of by front men, Washington can deal more realistically. *Common Sense* July 196/1 The following organizations are the principal 'fronts' set up by totalitarian elements within the United States. . . . While strictly speaking the Coughlin-Reynolds-Dilling outfits are not 'fronts' (in the sense that a 'front' is deliberately set up by a political party controlled from abroad), they are included here. 1942 *Mexican Labor News* 29 May 3 Sinarchist Fuehrer-in-Chief Manuel Torres Bueno (really a front).

FRONT* *v. tr.* To serve as a front to (+in sense 3 of *n.*).—1941 *Common Sense* Mar. 88/1 Catholic clergymen are even more adamant in their refusal to 'front' committees. *v. intr.*—1939 *Nation* 5 Aug. 134/2 *America,* accusing us of 'fronting' for the Semites and Communists. . . . We are not 'fronting' for anybody. 1942 *Time* 27 Apr. 82 Mexico . . . has been fronting [in Latin America] for the U.S.

+GAS HOG. One who uses too much gasoline, esp. one who abuses gasoline-rationing privileges.—1942 Topeka *Capital* 16 May 7/2 The Office of Price Administration made things unpleasant for 'gas hogs' tonight. *Progressive* 6 June 4/1 Gas hogs provided with the proper cards can roll up to side street stations where they are unknown and buy what they like.

+HIT. To go at something vigorously. 1888 (OEDS.) +To indulge in, take to greedily.—1939 Private conversation, Bill is hitting cigarets some. 1942 *American Thesaurus of Slang* Hit the booze, hooçh, bottle, grub, gow or hop.

HITLERISTIC. Pert. to or characteristic of Adolf Hitler.—1941 *Common Sense* Jan. 30/1 For the Hitleristic reason of grabbing everything in sight.

+JUCO. Junior College (abbr.)—1939 Topeka *Capital* 26 Aug. 11/2 Dodge City Juco Will Have Aviation Course. 1942 Kansas City *Star* 5 Jan. 10/2 El Dorado . . . appears . . . to be the top Juco basketball team in Kansas.

LUG*, *v. tr.* To give a pull to. +To make an exaction from (in sense of *n*).—1940 Topeka *Journal* 21 Mar. 3A/3 McGivern is charged with lugging the Avenue Shop . . . $50 a month. 1942 *American Thesaurus of Slang* 370.3 [Lug:] Beg; Request for a Loan or Gift.

+LUG, *n.* An exaction, esp. in phrase 'to put the lug on,' to exact money for political purposes.—1936 Kansas City *Star* 15 Oct. 6/1 Indiana Uses the 'Lug.' 1938 Kansas City *Times* 14 Feb. 1/6 The Democratic organization's lug on all city and county employees . . . for its campaign fund . . . has been started. 1940 Topeka *Capital* 27 Jan. 2/8 FRANCO REPEALS LUGS [prison sentences]. *Ibid.* 15 Feb. 4/2 Mayor Steps on Cops' Lug [plea for public subscription to get new uniforms]. *Ibid.* 8 Mar. 4/5 Putting Lug [pressure brought by advertisers to force change in policy] on Newspaper. Topeka *Journal* 26 Mar. 1/8 Shakedowns in Topeka are known to have ranged from $20 to $50 monthly, depending on the amount of illegal business done by the individuals on whom the lug was put.

+NIACIN.—1942 *Cooperative Consumer* 28 Feb. 5/3 'Niacin' is the new name for 'nicotinic acid,' the ingredient of enriched bread which was first discovered as a potent preventive and cure for pellagra. The new name was found to be necessary because some anti-tobacco groups warned against using enriched bread because it would foster the cigaret habit. . . . Federal Security Administrator Paul McNutt, who has charge of making standards for enriching flour, approved the name.

AMONG THE NEW WORDS

DWIGHT L. BOLINGER
Washburn Municipal University

Now that women are being drawn even more than in the first World War into positions ordinarily filled by men, the feminine suffix *-ette* is due for a strong revival. A few uses are already on the scene: 'One of Chief Loar's achievements has been the training of the country's first corps of volunteer women firefighters . . . known far and wide as the North Kansas City "Firettes" ' (*Cooperative Consumer* 31 Aug. 1942 10/2); 'The official crew of sailorettes' (*American Speech* Apr. 1942 88/2). Other recent examples show more usual occupations of women: *American Speech* has recorded separately *laughettes, bachelorettes, glamorettes, Latin Quarterettes,* and *stagette.* A few more are: 'A paragraph in one of the more foolish London dailies about an "Undergraduettes' Rag," informing the world that somebody had made a bonfire of gowns [at Oxford]' (Dorothy Sayers *Gaudy Night,* N.Y., Harcourt Brace, 1936, p. 73); 'The Centaurettes in "Fantasia" ' (*New Republic* 5 Jan. 1942 17/2); 'The Cooperette [singing] Sextette, composed of girl employees of CCA in North Kansas City' (*Cooperative Consumer* 31 Mar. 1942 10/1); 'The Topeka Co-operettes . . . , which is the women's auxiliary of the Co-operative Club (Topeka *Capital* 15 May 1940 9/3); 'Who wouldn't become a confirmed traveler if hotels were staffed with comely "bellehops" like Pearl Pearson? But she doesn't actually tote baggage—just acts as greeterette during Chicago's celebration of National Hotel Week' (NEA photo in Topeka *Capital* 9 June 1940 5B/2); 'The Salina Legionette Band' (*ibid.* 17 Sept. 9/5); 'In a pirate number, the folliettes duel with cutlasses as they skim the ice' (*Saturday Evening Post* 14 Dec. 1940); 'That "nice-pussy-pussy" tone, designed to put frightened dudettes [female patrons of a dude ranch] at their ease' (*Collier's* 9 Sept. 1939 20/1).

Here are a few *-aroos* to add to Mr. Wentworth's list in the February 1942 *American Speech: jugaroo,* for 'jail' (used in short film on Hollywood Club Pirate's Den, seen 9 Aug. 1941); 'jive-mad congaroos'—dancers of the Conga (advance trailer to movie 'Hellzapoppin,' seen 4 Jan. 1942); 'I know a couple of pepperoos [peppy stories]' (Thin Man radio program, 4 Mar. 1942). Other citations for two words in his list: 'Lois coming! That calls for a lightning-fast switcheroo!' (Superman comic, 30 Apr. 1942); *whackaroo,* 'whack' (in film 'You Can't Cheat an Honest Man,' seen 9 Aug. 1941).

Infanticipate, though attributed (I hope correctly) below to Walter Winchell, does not seem to be one of his earlier coinages. Paul Robert Beath in his 'Winchellese' (*American Speech* Oct. 1931, pp. 44-45) records *baby-bound* and three other synonyms, but does not mention *infanticipate.*

The evidence for *job* (below), though having to do in most cases with vehicles, seems to show that it stems directly from 'piece of work' rather than from *job* as short for *job-carriage, job-horse* (OED 1819-). The suggestion is that of 'a job of work turned out by a factory' instead of 'something with which to do a job.'

Please comment: *Bracketeer,* 1939. *Commando,* in current sense, 9 Feb. 1942. *Document,* something documented, 1941. *Fox hole,* in military sense, 15 June 1942. *Freeze,* as in 'freeze funds,' 'freeze models,' 1941. *Gangbuster,* July 1940. *Garrison finish,* 1910 or thereabouts. *Highball,* to speed, Feb. 1942. *Jerk,* epithet, Feb. 1942. *Jigaboo,* negro, 1942. *Miss the boat,* non-nautical, 1939. *Nip,* Japanese, 5 Jan. 1942. *Pancake,* to crush, 6 Oct. 1941. *Peel off,* of an airplane, Sep. 1941. *Playsuit,* May 1941. *Priority,* in current sense, 1941. *Protective,* surveillant, Mar. 1939. *Pump-primer,* 1940. *Recap,* of a tire, 1942. *Scatter-bomb,* 21 Nov. 1940.

SYMBOLS: The symbol + before a word or definition indicates an Americanism. A date immediately following a word or definition indicates the time of evidence shown in the DAE, or, if so stated, in another publication. Dates in brackets indicate the time, etc., of British usage. An asterisk after a word indicates that the word is illustrated in British usage before 1600.

ANCHOR. A means of holding fast or giving security [1855–]. *specif.* A military position used as a base for operations.—1940 *Time* North anchor of the British blockade is Iceland. 1942 AP desp. in Topeka *Journal* 3 Apr. 1/6 The Japanese had cracked the right wing anchor at Prome, key to Burma's vital oil fields. 1942 AP desp. in Topeka *Capital* 20 July 1/5 Rostov, the key Red Army southern anchor protecting the Caucasus.

AXIS. 1. A politico-military alliance between two or more powers. 1936– (W.)—1938 *Newsweek* 8 Jan. 20/2 Central Europe regards the Rome-Berlin axis as an artificial structure. 1941 *Time* 21 Apr. 34/3 The London-Washington Axis.

2. *specif.* The Rome-Berlin alliance, and later the Rome-Berlin-Tokyo alliance. 1936– (W.) [This is prob. the exclusive meaning after 1941].—1939 Central Press photo in Topeka *Journal* 5 May 2A/2-3 Heavy artillery, said to have been installed by the Axis. 1941 *Time* (Air Exp. Ed.) 4 Aug. 17/1 Cuba rounded up 62 Axis agents, German, Japanese, Italian, Spanish.

3. *fig.* Something detrimental to the anti-Axis powers. 1942 *Bread and Butter* 21 Aug. 4/3 The Inner Axis of inflation.

BATTLEWAGON. A battleship. 1942 (Berrey and Van den Bark, *Thesaurus of Slang*).—1942 *Reader's Digest* Mar. 6 The battlewagon can perform its mission only if protected by its own air force. *Ibid.* Oct. 120/1 I don't know what the battlewagons are doing, . . . but if the Heinies don't get wise, there won't be any subs left.

+BITCHY. Sex-appealing, used of a woman.—1939 private letter 16 Dec. A bitchy, flirtatious young woman. 1941 *Time* 13 Oct. 36/1 Two bitchy strip queens are murdered.

BURMA ROAD. The road from Burma to China, used as a military supply-route. +*fig.* A supply-route of similar nature or importance.—1942 AP desp. in Kansas City *Times* 13 Jan. 6/1 Congress was urged today by its Alaskan delegate, Anthony J. Dimond, to expedite construction of a 'Burma Road' linking the United States with the territory. *New Republic* 2 Mar. 292 An Alaska-Siberia 'Burma Road.' *Progressive* 22 Aug. 7 China's New Burma Road [cargo planes].

+CHUTIST. A parachutist.—1941 Los Angeles *Herald Express* 11 Dec. 1/5-6 Chutists Land at Filipino Airport. 1942 *Time* 2 Feb. 38 To military 'chutists a painful fall or stunning bump in landing may mean the difference between success and capture. 1942 Topeka *Capital* 24 Feb. 1/8 Nazi Chutists Used First Time in Leningrad Area.

CREATIVE PAUSE. A term coined by German propagandists to describe the lull in fighting after the Nazi conquest of Crete; and applied to other similar cessations of fighting.—1941 *Common Sense* June 181/1 What are the causes of this unexpected 'pause' [the fact that the United States was still out of the war]? *Time* (Air Exp. Ed.) 14 July 2/1 The creative pauses of Adolf Hitler.

FIREPOWER. The relative force and intensity of an army's explosive weapons. —1942 *Common Sense* Apr. 122/2 Their plans are laid in terms of men, materials, and firepower.

FULL-DRESS. Involving a display of activity for which full preparations are made. [*fig.*, as in *full-dress debate*, 1888–]. —1942 *Progressive* 24 Jan. 2/1 In London, where Prime Minister Winston Churchill faces a full dress debate in Parliament. 1942 Justice J. S. Dawson at Saturday Night Club, Topeka, Kan., 14 Feb. It amounted to a full-dress war before it was finished. *Time* 23 Feb. 16/1 WLB's first full-dress act last week had shown promise. *Saturday Evening Post* 26 Sep. 17/2 A full-dress rehearsal of censorship.

+FUTURAMA. [*Future* + Gr. *horama*, or +*-rama* by anal. with *panorama, diorama*, etc.] The General Motors exhibit at the World's Fair, 1939–40, portraying the future; a similar portrayal.—1939 *Nation* 10 June 682/1 The General Motors futurama. 1940 *Harper's* Dec. 30/2 The most publicized attraction of the entire Fair was General Motors' Futurama, which caused nearly 10,000,000 persons to stand in line for countless hours during 1939 and '40. 1942 *Free America* Feb. 5/1 After five years, and again after ten years, another community pageant was held, the latter being a 'futurama,' picturing the possible future.

+HOOVERVILLE. [Herbert *Hoover*, U.S. Pres. 1929–33]. A temporary, ramshackle town, inhabited usually by migratory workers.—1933 *New Republic* 24 May 39–40 Welcome! You are now entering Hooverville. Settled during the Great Crisis. Named for the Great Engineer. . . . Hoovervilles are in a separate nation, with separate codes. . . . No one profits from Hooverville tenants. 1939 Steinbeck, *The Grapes of Wrath, passim.* 1941 *American Guardian* 24 Jan. 1/4–5 While the children on whose hunger the rich man's plenty is built cough in slums and Hoovervilles.

+INFANTICIPATE. [*Infant* + *anticipate*, coined by Walter Winchell]. To be expectant (of childbirth). 1942 (Berrey and Van den Bark, *Thesaurus of Slang*.)—1941 Los Angeles *Times* 30 Nov. §IV 14 advt. 'Storkettes' for 'Infanticipating' friends of yours. *Cf.* 1941–42 Montgomery Ward fall-winter catalog 234 Anticipating? Here's your wardrobe for the blessed-event.

JOB. A piece of work. [1627–]. +A large powered (and usually locomotive) machine, esp. an automobile or airplane. 1942 (Berrey and Van den Bark, *Thesaurus of Slang*).—1938 *Harper's* Jan. 141/2 There was an antiquated high-wing monoplane job. 1941 *Saturday Evening Post* 18 Jan. 13/1 The presses were special jobs for printing this particular magazine. *Ibid.* 73/2 No use . . . sending our pilots up against him in our 400-mile jobs. *Reader's Digest* Oct. 26/1 A clean-swept boardwalk led up to the small secondhand job [an automobile trailer] in which Lily, her husband and their two boys lived. *Ibid.* June 31/2 A steam locomotive is available for duty only about one third of the time, although on some of the new jobs an availability of 60 percent is claimed.

+JUICER. A machine to extract fruit or vegetable juices.—1938 Cooperative Distributors catalog 28/2 A well constructed juicer for oranges. 1940 Topeka *Journal* 14 May 1A advt. $1.50 Vegetable Juicers, 69¢. 1941–42 Montgomery Ward fall-winter catalog 789 Vita-Juicer—For Health. *Ibid.* Electric Juicer.

+KNOW-HOW. The faculty of knowing how. 1934 (W.) *specif.* Special skill, acquired through practise, in carrying through a complicated process or operation.—1942 *Nation* 18 Apr. 451/1 Standard Oil . . . would not permit an agent of the Department of Justice to go into its laboratories and make sure that the 'know how' on its rubber and toluol patents was made fully available to other companies. *Progressive* 20 June 12/2 Elmer Davis, . . . one possessed of the all-important 'know-how' [to direct news and propaganda activities]. *Time* 11 May 28/1 All AVG's battle-won know-how on the technique of destroying Japs.

LACKEY. One who is servilely obsequious. [1588–]. *specif.* One subservient to capitalists or to capitalistic society (an epithet used by communists).—1939 G. E. R. Gedye, *Fallen Bastions* (London, Gollancz) 37 The Communists did not hesitate to condemn them [the Austrian Socialist leaders], as 'Social Fascists' who did 'lackey service' to capitalist reaction. 1941 *American Mercury* Apr. 417/2 American bankers . . . have already stepped into the role of lackeys of British Imperialism.

+LEND-LEASE, LEASE-LEND, *a.* Pertaining to the bill, later enacted into law, providing for the leasing or lending of American military supplies to foreign powers.—1941 *Business Week* 18 Jan. 15 Despite fireworks, Congress will pass President's lease-lend plan substantially as it is. *Life* 3 Feb. 17 Congressmen Haggle Over Lease-Lend Bill as New British Ambassador Arrives. *Time* 3 Feb. 13/1 On behalf of the Lend-Lease Bill.

+LEND-LEASE, *n.* The act of supplying military goods (in sense of *a.*).—1941 *New Republic* 27 Jan. 103/2 Is Lend-Lease a Step to War?

+LEND-LEASE, LEASE-LEND, *v. tr.* To supply (military goods, in sense of *a.*, or in an analogous sense).—1941 *Common Sense* June 181/2 Japan might even 'lend-lease' subs and warships to her brothers in the Axis. *Time* 18 Aug. 29/3 Leased-lent Flying Fortresses. *Time* 1 Sep. 16/2 The Ecuadorians are angry with the U. S. for not lease-lending them arms. 1942 *Time* 29 June 45/1 Some of these carriers will probably be Lend-Leased to Britain.

+PEARL HARBOR. The Japanese attack at Pearl Harbor, Hawaiian Islands, Dec. 7, 1941; a similar attack or danger.—1942 *Progressive* 31 Jan. 12/3 Compare these recently abandoned myths in Britain with the pre-Pearl Harbor folklore about the Japanese which prevailed in the United States. *Time* 16 Feb. 63 *Liberty's* classic embarrassment in printing a lead article shortly after Pearl Harbor which began: 'Hawaii is ready.' 1942 James M. Landis, quoted in Topeka *Capital* 20 Mar. 15/3 Delay along this line is the delay that spells Pearl Harbor to the vital industrial nerve centers of our economy.

PIGBOAT. A submarine.—1942 *Time* 20 Apr. 62/2 Venezuelan editors heard with dismay that a ship with a supply of [comic strip] mats had been sent to the bottom by a pigboat. *National Geographic* Oct. 555 A Captured Japanese Midget Submarine . . . such tiny two-man pigboats.

+QUICKIE, QUICKY. 1937 (1938 *Words*, Jan.), 1942 (Berrey and Van den Bark, *Thesaurus of Slang*). Something done quickly, esp. without ceremony, forethought, or preparation; *specif.* a movie made quickly and cheaply; *also attrib.*—1939 *Saturday Evening Post* 1 Apr. 11/1 He made a picture of her, and she returned the courtesy by snapping a couple of quickies of him. *Collier's* 23 Dec. 19/1 He wasn't even picking up the quickie stuff [odd jobs, prob. at short movies or in small parts as an actor] he used to pay the rent with. 1940 *Common Sense* Mar. 20/1 [Cordell Hull] found his way to a quicky law school in the county, and developed a scholarly passion for politics. *Detective Tales* Mar. 71/1 She couldn't get a contract except maybe with a quickie [movie] producer. *Writer's Digest* Apr. 18/1 A small-budget movie outfit filming a mob scene for a quickie. 1941 AP desp. in Topeka *Journal* 4 Jan. 1/7 Britain has already begun to invade the continent—giving the Germans a quickie preview of the mass attack British generals have promised to deliver. 1941 Rinso broadcast 5 Feb. Our contestants sometimes ask me quickies [spontaneous questions]. *Time* (Air Exp. Ed.) 22 Sep. 14/1 Admiral Nomura's first call on . . . Cordell Hull lasted only four minutes; it was an all-time quickie. 1942 Topeka *Journal* 2 May 1/1 There was a growing practise of giving army and navy 'quickie' commissions to unqualified civilians.

REV, *v. tr., v. intr.* To increase (the revolutions of an engine) [ca. 1916 (Partridge, *Dictionary of Slang*)]; to make or do revolutions [1923–]; *to rev it up*, to go faster.—1942 *PM* 11 Feb. 20/2 The pilot revs his engine. *Saturday Evening Post* 5 Sep. 22/1 Jimmy revved up and the engine burst into a deep-throated roar. 1942 Innes and Hammond, *Attack Alarm* (N.Y., Macmillan) 1 The din of revving engines. *Time* 9 Mar. 40 Built to make non-stop, coast-to-coast flights for TWA, the Constellation has a range of 4,000 miles. . . . Her four 2,500-h.p. motors can boost her along at 283 m.p.h. cruising speed . . ., can rev it up to 350 m.p.h.

+RUN-AROUND. An evasion. 1937 (1938 *Words*, Feb.), 1942 (Berrey and Van den Bark, *Thesaurus of Slang*).—1934 Erle S. Gardner *The Case of the Lucky Legs* (N.Y., Pocket Books, 1941) 166 A small-town dentist . . ., and you think that fits you to give me a run-around in a murder case, which is *my* specialty. 1941 *Consumers Union Reports* June 144/2 When FTC catches up with it next time, the old run-around [of legal evasions] can begin again. 1942 *Nation* 25 Apr. 480/2 Last year the Truman committee heard of the run-around given to a man named Gaudy who held a patent for making aluminum from common clay.

AMONG THE NEW WORDS

DWIGHT L. BOLINGER
Washburn Municipal University

THE SUFFIX *-ariat*, proper to *proletariat* and *secretariat* (where the suffix is really *-at*), has reappeared in other words: the *Nation* (30 Apr. 1938 p. 491/2) has *infantariat;* the *Literary Digest* reported in 1931 (3 Aug. 15/2) the term *salariat*, used in Japan of a certain type of employee; ANW reported (Apr. 1942) *Janizariat.*

Trust-buster and *gang-buster* are the pivotal examples of *-buster*, which might be defined as 'one who seeks to destroy an organization regarded as undesirable.' It appears also in the Warner Brothers film 'Racket Busters,' released in 1938, and in *union-buster* (*Nation* 22 June 1940 p. 746/2).

Recent examples of *-eer* show for the most part the tendency of this form of *-er* to cluster about it words suggesting 'excess' or 'energetic action'; because of the latter, nouns readily become verbs; coincidental support from *engineer* is not infrequent. Compare *aeroneer* (legend of a picture of a man with a model airplane, in Agfa Ansco store-window advertisement seen 13 May 1942); 'Dyer-Bennet . . . learned the Swedish lute and some *balladeering* tricks' (*Time*, Air Exp. Ed., 13 Oct. 1941 p. 21/3); *balloteer* (noted by a student, 2 Apr. 1940); *basketeer* (*American Speech* Apr. 1941 p. 159/1); *batoneer* (*ibid.*, p. 158/2); *blacketeer*, a black-market operator (*Time* 9 Mar. 1942 p. 29/1 and 30 Mar. 1942 p. 28/2); *black-marketeering* (*Progressive* 23 Nov. 1942 p. 4/3); *bracketeer*, a member of a certain social 'bracket' as regards income, esp. in *upper-bracketeer* (*Nation* 2 Sep. 1939 p. 237/2, *Progressive* 16 May 1942 p. 4/1); 'It hasn't leaked outside the cabinet yet, but some of Roosevelt's *cabineteers* are putting up a fight against the navy for commandeering the one lone trans-Atlantic plane' (Los Angeles *Daily News* 2 Dec. 1941 p. 33/3); '*Concerteers* like a cuffo concert once in a while' (*PM* 5 Jan. 1942 p. 24); *conventioneer* (ANW Apr. 1942); *dandelioneer*, a state employee delegated to dig dandelions (Topeka *Capital* 23 Apr. 1940 p. 1/5); 'The science of *kitcheneering*' (Topeka *Journal* 11 June 1940 p. 5/4); *pigeoneer*, a keeper or trainer of homing pigeons (AP story in Topeka *Journal* 20 Jan. 1941 p. 5/5); *privateer*, an operator or advocate of private ownership of a public utility (*American Guardian* 5 Apr. 1940 p. 4/3-4, 26 Apr. 1940 p. 2/7); *pulpateer*, one who writes for the pulps (*Writer's Digest* 20:8, front cover); *revolutioneer*, verb (*American Speech* Apr. 1941 p. 158/1); *sloganeer*, verb (*Reader's Digest* June 1941 p. 109/1); *unioneer*, a Peglerism (*Consolation* 21 Sep. 1938 p. 16/1 and *American Speech* Apr. 1941 p. 158/2, both quoting Westbrook Pegler; *Time*, Air Exp. Ed., 22 Sep. 1941 p. 4/3).

Now that rationing and other restrictions make some articles hard to get, illegal selling has revived *-legger*, which, as Achsah Hardin pointed out in 'Volstead English' (*American Speech* Dec. 1931 p. 83) was once an abbreviation of *bootlegger*. Compare *foodlegger* (caption of an article on food racketeers in wartime England, *Time*, Air Exp. Ed., 2 June 1941 p. 18/1); *gas 'legger* (N.Y. *Daily News* quoted by *Progressive* 6 June 1942 p. 4/1); *tirelegger* (*Progressive* 18 July 1942 p. 3/2). *Votelegger* (*American Guardian* 22 Mar. 1940 p. 4/1) is somewhat older.

Please comment: *Airgraph*, for V-mail, 21 Mar. 1942. *Cavalry* in gen. sense of 'mounted soldiery,' 2 Nov. 1938. *Coke*, for Coca-Cola. *Cook*, as in phrase 'What's cooking?' *Corny*, 16 July 1938. *Exton*, Feb. 1939. *Hit the ceiling. Jeep*, 21 Dec. 1940. *Lunatic fringe*, 1928. *Man-tailored*, 1940. *Microfilm*, esp. verb. *Nacelle*, in aeronautical sense. *Para-ski*, 1942. *Paraskier*, 1942. *Percentage*, profit in general, 1940. *Powder room*, ladies' rest room. *Script*, verb, 1940. *Shadow factory, shadow plant. Shangri-la*, metaphorical uses, 1941. *V-mail*, Oct. 1942.

SYMBOLS: The symbol + before a word or definition indicates an Americanism. A date immediately following a word or definition indicates the time of evidence shown in the DAE, or, if so stated, in another publication. Dates in brackets indicate the time, etc., of British usage. An asterisk after a word indicates that the word is illustrated in British usage before 1600.

BEAM. A constant unidirectional radio signal transmitted from a flying field for the guidance of pilots. 1939 (W.). +*fig.*: *on the beam,* on the right track, right, sane; *off the beam,* off the track, wrong, insane.—1941 *Daring Detective* Nov. 7/2 'Now we know we're on the beam,' said Brubach. 'Sex maniacs and drinking companions are definitely eliminated.' 1942 Post Toasties radio program 16 July Get him back on the mental beam. 1941 *American Speech* Oct. 238/2 Expressions disparaging a person's mental state: . . . *off his beam* (airplane), perhaps the strongest of these locutions at the present time. 1942 *Life* 31 Aug. 34 advt. I was 'way off the beam when I thought all cola drinks tasted alike.

+CATCH FLAT-FOOTED. To catch (one) in such a way that a prompt defense or other suitable reaction is impossible. 1942 (Berrey and Van den Bark, *Thesaurus of Slang*).—1940 AP desp. in Topeka *Journal* 14 Nov. 1/4 The Italians were caught flat-footed . . ., and from that moment the story was one of deadly Greek bayonet charges. 1942 AP desp. in Topeka *Capital* 25 Jan. 1B/7 Reasons why the Japanese caught Oahu flat-footed in the December 7 raid. *Time* 27 Apr. 96/1-2 advt. Caught Flatfooted! I haven't got the figures!

DOODLER. [<*doodle,* to trifle. [1880-]]. 1. A trifler, dawdler. 1942 (Berrey and Van den Bark, *Thesaurus of Slang*).—1942 Topeka *Capital* 21 Feb. 4 The whole regime of doodlers, including dancers and other entertainers, ought to be pushed . . . off the pay roll.

+2. One who idly draws nonsense figures, as when speaking over a telephone. [A sense popularized by the film 'Mr. Deeds Goes to Town,' 1936.]—1938 Topeka *Journal* 29 Oct. 3A/2 Howard Hughes is an inveterate doodler with a preference for little inter-locking squares.

+DREAM UP. To improvise, originate in an imaginative way. 1942 (Berrey and Van den Bark, *Thesaurus of Slang*).—1942 *Time* 23 Mar. 60/2 Pondering Stanford's lack of a liberal arts school, Professor Dodds dreamed up one which would avoid the failings of most liberal arts colleges.

FLASHBACK. An interruption in the sequence to introduce an event prior to those being presented. 1942 (Berrey and Van den Bark, *Thesaurus of Slang*).—1941 caption of a biographical item in *Time* (Air Exp. Ed.) 8 Sep. 9/3. 1941 B.B.C. broadcast 11 Sep. 9:10 P.M., C.S.T. The news in flashback will be presented.

+GOOSE, *v. tr.* To feed (gasoline) in irregular spurts. 1942 ('Truck Driver Lingo,' *Amer. Speech* Apr. 103/2).—1933, heard in central Arizona. 1942 Berrey and Van den Bark *Thesaurus of Slang* 759.12 *s.v.* Flying (aviation slang) *Goose ('er)* to open and close the throttle quickly.

+INTERPHONE. The telephone system in an aircraft.—1942 *Time* 20 Apr. 25/2 During the same fracas, the pilot inquired over the [Flying] Fortress interphone: 'Are you firing at the enemy?' *American* Oct. 18/3 It was very quiet on the interphones now [in a bombing plane].

+JAPANAZI, *a.* Pertaining to Japan and to Nazi Germany, esp. as military allies. —1942 Walter Winchell in Topeka *Journal* 17 Mar. 4/7 Sympathetic to Japanazi groups. *Time* 27 July 71/2 Japanazi submarines keep all but the most daring fishermen close inshore.

NAME. A famous or notorious person; one whose name is well known. [1611]. +*attrib.* Famous, esp. in phrase *name band.* 1938 (*Words,* Oct.), 1940 (*Words,* Jan.).—1938 *Saturday Evening Post* 2 Apr. 9/1 We are to have an orchestra—'a name band by all means.' 1940 Station WDAF 31 Mar. 6:50 P.M., C.S.T. All name orchestras. *Writer's Digest* May 39/1 There's no ruling that it should be by a 'name' author. Ussher col. in Los Angeles *News* 8 Aug. 27/5 Columbia is making important 'name' additions to the catalog. Pearson-Allen col. in Topeka *Journal* 7 Dec. 4/4 Today, next to Mc-Nary, Vandenburg is the biggest-name Republican in the senate.

+NAZIPHILE, *n.* One who favors National Socialism or National-Socialist Germany.—1941 *Time* (Air Exp. Ed.) 1 Sep. 6/1 The French seem to be turning ever more violently against Darlan's Naziphiles.

+OLD-HAT. Something old-fashioned or trite. 1942 (Berrey and Van den Bark, *Thesaurus of Slang*); *also attrib.*—1941 *Time* (Air Exp. Ed.) 20 Oct. 28/3 A passel of furtive folk vigorously committing homicide to get hold of a bejeweled statuette of a falcon may sound old-hat to present-day cinemagoers, but Director John Huston makes their . . . activities . . . immediate. 1942 Exploring Music program, Station KMBC, 28 Sep. It's all old-hat by now.

+ONE-STOP, *a.* Supplying all the shopper's (esp. the motoring shopper's) needs, so as to remove the necessity of shopping at more than one place; used orig. of filling stations.—1942 *Cooperative Consumer* 17 Mar. 6/1 [The Columbia, Mo., cooperative grocery store] is a one-stop store. Topeka *Capital* 4 Apr. 2/6-8 advt. The complete one-stop [grocery-] store. 1942 Station WREN 15 Nov. 10 P.M. advt. Josky's your one-stop store for the family.

PARATROOP. [*Parachute* + *troop*] 1. A parachute troop (gen. in plural); *also attrib.*—1940 *English Digest* Sep. 43 Copford, East Anglia, has a nasty lesson in store for any paratroops who may land there. 1941 *Illustrated London News* 10 May 594 Paratroops training at Fort Benning. *Time* 14 July 19/2 Boys and girls . . . were organized as paratroop detectors. 1942 *Time* 17 Aug. 38 He was transferred to paratroop service.

2. A paratrooper.—1942 legend of NEA photo 8 Feb. George Hopkins had made 2,300 parachute jumps . . . before enlisting as a paratroop.

PARATROOPER. A member of a parachute troop.—1941 *Time* (Air Exp. Ed.) 4 Aug. 20/1 The paratroopers . . . had never been in an airplane when it was landed. 1942 *Progressive* 24 Jan. 2/3 Thousands of paratroopers landing behind the German lines.

PLASTIC, PLASTIQUE. 1. Any one of a class of substances, such as celluloid or viscose, which are worked into shape for use by molding or pressing when in a plastic condition. 1909 (Century). +*attrib.* —1940 *Consumers Union Reports* 29 Nov. 24/2-3 Plastic (molded) cabinet. 1941 *McCall's* Aug. 71/2 And, of course, Miss Carstairs, very high-heeled slippers. These plastique ones are the newest. *American Weekly* 9 Nov. 2/2 The entire output [of methyl alcohol] has been taken over as a basic part of many plastic products.

2. Something made of a plastic.—1940 Topeka *Capital* 15 Nov. 22 advt. 4-Tube A.C.-D.C. Plastics [radio sets].

PLUTO-DEMOCRACY. A democracy tainted with plutocracy (a term used by totalitarian propagandists).—1940 *Common Sense* Aug. 6/2 The absolute power of a Stalin or a Hitler is seen to be even worse than the economic exploitation and political ineffectiveness of a 'pluto-democracy' with its checks and balances.

+PRATFALL, PRATTFALL, PRAT-FALL, PRATT-FALL, *n.* A fall on the posteriors. 1942 (Berrey and Van den Bark, *Thesaurus of Slang*); *also fig.*—1940 *Time* 19 Feb. 4/1 For parallel usage [ref. to *pratfall*], cf. Hamlet, grave-digger scene: 'Quite chop-fallen.' 1941 Stephen Longstreet Last Man Around the World, N.Y., Random House 344 Like a vaudevillian taking a pratt-fall. *Common Sense* Sep. 265/1 More Pratt-falls [punning ref. to a man named Pratt, whose blunders are described]. *Time* (Air Exp. Ed.) 18 Aug. 4/2 In one skirmish after another they routed the Lewis-Addes side. By week's end it was plain that Mr. Lewis was taking a pratfall. *v. intr.* To fall on the posteriors.—1940 *Time* 29 Jan. 41/1 The sight of Sonja (for the fourth time in her professional career) pratt-fallen. 1942 *Time* 3 Aug. 74/2 On the way to the plate he prat-falls on the carefully laid-out row of bats in front of the dugout.

+PRONG, *v. tr.* To hang up (a telephone receiver).—1940 *Detective Tales* Apr. 55/1 He pronged the phone. *v. intr.* To move in a prong-like formation.—1941 *Time* 30 June 8/1 Four columns of the Second Division pronged down on the flank and rear of the . . . 27th and 30th Divisions.

+SCUTTLE. To destroy or damage severely; discard. 1940 (*American Speech* Oct. 327f.).—1941 *Collier's* 20 Dec. 50/1 Bruce, in a heavy sedan, had come banging out of his driveway to a collision. No one was hurt, but the flivver was scuttled. 1942 AP desp. in Topeka *Capital* 20 Jan. 1/3 The ill-concealed Axis maneuver, apparently part of a . . . scheme to scuttle the [Rio de] Janeiro conference.

+SHOOTING WAR. A war which involves actual participation of armed forces, and not merely propaganda, sanctions, etc.—1941 *Time* (Air Exp. Ed.) 4 Aug. 5/3 55% . . . are ready to risk some kind of shooting war at once. *American Guardian* 29 Aug. 1/3 It is inconceivable that even actual participation in a 'shooting' war could force any reduction in civilian oil supply. 1942 *Christian Science Monitor* 13 Apr. 9/6 Long before the Americas were drawn into the shooting war, Costa Rica had been loyally cooperating.

SKYROCKET, *v. intr.* To soar swiftly like a skyrocket. 1889 (Century). +*v. tr.* To cause to soar swiftly.—1940 Topeka *Journal* 4 Mar. 1/4 War . . . skyrocketed food prices. 1941 *Consumers Union Reports* June 144/2 Advertising appropriations could not be skyrocketed to avoid surplus-profit taxes. *Time* (Air Exp. Ed.) 15 Sep. 19/2 Costs were skyrocketed by high wages.

STARLET. A small star [1830-]. +A young, or coming, female movie star.—1942 AP desp. in Topeka *Journal* 25 Jan. 8B/2 Linda Darnell, screen starlet. *Time* 2 Feb. 10 In Hollywood, Starlet Marilyn Hare said she had kissed 709 soldiers. *American Magazine* Oct. 102 Beverly Hills Hotel pool lures Studio Club movie stars and starlets.

AMONG THE NEW WORDS

DWIGHT L. BOLINGER
Washburn Municipal University

ANW for December, 1942, predicted more words in *-ette* as women are called into new occupations. Here are some: 'Roosevelt Signs "Sailorette" Bill. . . . President Roosevelt signed today legislation creating a women's auxiliary in the Navy' (AP desp. in Topeka *Capital* 31 July 1942); 'Usherette in the . . . movie theater' (Counter Spy radio program 14 Dec. 1942); 'Women Join the "Field Artillery" as International Harvester Dealers Teach Power Farming to an Army of "Tractorettes"' (advt. *Saturday Evening Post* 12 Sep. 1942 p. 37); 'Chicago tries "Copettes"' (*Inside Detective* Dec. 1942 p. 6).

More rationing extends the application of *-hog,* recorded in *gas-hog* in the October ANW: 'Don't be a heat hog!' (Gas Company advt. Topeka *Journal* 16 Nov. 1942 A3/5-8); 'Coffee Hog' (label on figure in cartoon, *Progressive* 16 Nov. 1942 11/3).

Besides the trade names *Mixmaster, Toastmaster,* and *Moist Master,* recorded in *Words,* May 1940, *-master* now appears in at least three more: 'Roadmaster Brakes' (observed advertised in Los Angeles 1 Sep. 1940); 'Chevrolet Trucks with "Load-Master" Engine' (advt. *Collier's* 29 Nov. 1941 p. 40); 'Electromaster Range' (advt. Topeka *Capital* 1 Feb. 1942 2A/7). It also appears in the more literal sense of 'leader': 'Phil Baker, Quizmaster of the CBS program' (*Look* 3 Nov. 1942 p. 28); 'The jump-master [leader of parachute jumpers] . . . cries, "Stand in the door!"' (*Look* 3 Nov. 1942 p. 43); 'The Nazi spymaster and Naval Attaché, Captain Dietrich Niebuhr' (*Time* 18 Jan. 1943 38/2).

The *-cast* of *broadcast* long since cast loose to attach itself in *newscast* (*Words* Feb. 1939, with the derived verb: 'To guarantee unbiased newscasting,' *Common Sense* Mar. 1940 10/1, and the agent *newscaster*), *radiocast* ('This Radiocasting Structure' [a type of antenna], *Christian Science Monitor* 16 Mar. 1940 mag. sec. 3), and *telecast* ('Easter Services . . . were telecast today,' Topeka *Capital* 25 Mar. 1940 1/4). Now we have *sportcast* as noun and verb ('At lunch . . . before the sportcast came on,' *Writer's Forum* July 1940 19/1; 'Adam has sponsored the sportcasting of big-time bouts,' *Time* 31 Mar. 1941 50/1); *sportscaster* ('Sportscaster Walter Lanier . . . Barber, official announcer over Mutual's WOR of all games of the Brooklyn . . . Dodgers,' *Time,* Air Exp. Ed., 11 Aug. 1941 28/2) with the variant *sportcaster* (*American Speech* Oct. 1939 p. 238); *bombcasting* (in title of an article. 'Bombcasting—Thumbs Up for the British!' *Radio Craft* June 1941 p. 714, in *Words* Dec. 1941 97/1; *gridcaster* (for an announcer of football contests, *American Speech,* Apr. 1942 88/1); and *dogcaster* and *gamecaster* ('Dogcaster No. 1. . . . Dog-lovers for a decade have faithfully tuned in on his [Bob Becker's] expert *Chats About Dogs.* . . . Last week Dogcaster Bob . . . became Gamecaster Bob. On his new program, Sportsmen's Spotlight,' *Time* 28 Sep. 1942 p. 55).

Wartime quick-lunches provided just the spur that *-burger* needed to keep it going. *American Speech* has already published lists of these compounds (Dec. 1940 452/1 and Apr. 1942 p. 132). A few more are: *gluten-burger* (*Words* Jan. 1940); 'Gee, Aunt Jenny, these *barbecue 'burgers* taste swell!' (Spry advt. Topeka *Capital* 22 June 1940 p. 5); *Meet-the-People-burger* (musical comedy 'Meet the People' Los Angeles 1940); *SPAMburgers* (advt. *Saturday Evening Post* 18 Jan. 1941 p. 77); *Huski-burgers* (in sign on shop on Western Ave., Los Angeles, observed 21 Dec. 1941); *Cheeseburger* (in sign on shop in Burbank, Calif., observed 23 Dec. 1941); *Bar-B-Burger* (sign on Katz Drug Store, Kansas City, Mo., observed 4 Apr. 1942); 'How to cook a "BURGER" six different ways! . . . cheeseburgers . . . lamburgers . . . sausageburgers . . . nutburgers . . .

pickleburger . . . burger barbecue [with recipes]' (full-page Heinz advt., *Better Homes and Gardens* Aug. 1942).

Mr. Harold Wentworth confirms the opinion (ANW December 1942) that *infanticipate* is not an early Winchell coinage. 'This word,' he says, 'does not appear in my study, *Blend-Words in English* (MS. thesis, Cornell, 1934, 326 pp.). Though I have never read Winchell regularly, the likelihood is that if the word had been used much from 1931 to mid-1933, it would appear in *Blend-Words*.' He sends three examples: 'Walter Winchellism: The Browns are infanticipating' ('Patter' in *Reader's Digest* Aug. 1934 p. 66); *infanticipation* (reported from a Univ. of Tenn. professor as used as title of verse in Syracuse, N.Y., *Post-Standard* 30 July 1934); and ' "Big Rosie [an elephant]," . . . is elephanticipating—in April' (Winchell in Syracuse, N.Y., *Journal* 24 Dec. 1935 p. 9).

PLEASE COMMENT: *Bite, n.* and *v.*, as applied to a propeller, Oct. 1942. *Blimp*, etymology. *Crashdive, v.*, Mar. 1942. *Decolonization*, 1941. *Molotov cocktail* (or just *Molotov*), 1942. *Pass candy*, 1926 or earlier. *Weekend, n.* and *v.*, 'a weekend party,' 1934.

SYMBOLS: The symbol + before a word or definition indicates an Americanism. A date immediately following a word or definition indicates the time of evidence shown in the DAE, or, if so stated, in another publication. Dates in brackets indicate the time, etc., of British usage. An asterisk after a word indicates that the word is illustrated in British usage before 1600.

ANDERSON, ANDERSON SHELTER. A small air-raid shelter.—1941 Topeka *Journal* 1 Feb. 10/8 Any person [Englishman] making less than $20 a week is supplied free with the material for an Anderson. . . . An Anderson shelter is formed of walls of sheet iron, heavily banked on the outside with dirt. . . . But four people are miserably cramped in an Anderson shelter. *Time* (Air Exp. Ed.) 22 Sept. 35/2 He also explained how to put up an Anderson steel shelter.

BUNA. A synthetic rubber developed in Germany, made by polymerization of butadiene. 1941 (W.)—1940 Commodity Research Bureau, *Commodities in Industry* (N.Y.) p. 23 The term Buna comes from the word Bu, for butadiene, and Na for natrium (Latin word for sodium) which was used to polymerize or 'build up' at one phase of the German synthetic rubber development. 1942 *Time* 6 Apr. 16/1 The cartel also gave the U.S. its buna knowledge, except the process of making rubber from coal, a NaziGovernment-sponsored program.

DEGAUSS. [*De*+*gauss*, unit of magnetic intensity.] To neutralize or offset a magnetic field. *specif.* DEGAUSSING, *p.a.*, applied to de-magnetizing equipment.—1941 *Time* (Air Exp. Ed.) 15 Sep. 3/2 More than 320 merchant ships and 30 naval vessels have been repaired, outfitted with guns, degaussing equipment in U.S. yards. *Ibid.* 29 Sep. 36/2 Roebling . . . was turning out huge harbor-defense nets, degaussing cable, wiring for battleships. 1942 *Reader's Digest* Sep. 39/2 The knowledge thus acquired [about magnetic mines, in 1939] enabled scientists to provide two protective devices: the 'degaussing girdle'—wire wound around ships to create an artificial magnetic field.

+DEGLAMORIZE. To deprive of glamor or charm.—1941 Lincoln, Nebr. *Journal and Star* 2 Nov. (quoted *American Speech* Apr. 1942 131/1) Paulette Goddard recently became the first Hollywood glamour girl to de-glamorize herself in the interest of national defense. 1942 *Time* 27 Apr. 16/3 Miami window-display mannequins are being deglamorized for War.

+DEGLAMORIZATION. Act of depriving of glamor or charm.—1942 *Time* 27 Apr. 68/3 Deglamorization of the week was performed by an alert news photographer at Sun Valley, who caught the handsome face of Cinemactress Norma Shearer registering desolation after she had missed a clay pigeon.

DOCUMENT. To prove or support (something) by documentary evidence. [1711–]. +*specif.* Something thus supported, as a film or novel (*cp. documentary*, ANW Apr. 1942).—1941 *Common Sense* Sep. 282/2 The growing importance of the 'document' both cinematic and literary. *Ibid.* 283/1 This little book . . . is the most moving document out of England since the war began. In the sense that it is a deeply-felt record of human suffering and courage, it is more than a document.

EXPENDABLE. That may be expended. [1805–]. +*specif. mil.* That may be expended, or sacrificed, as in order to preserve more valuable equipment or to delay an enemy.—1942 W. L. White *They Were Expendable.* N.Y. Harcourt Brace 14 Sep. *Reader's Digest* Oct. 40/1 These bombers . . . would be considered in part as expendable ammunition much as the Navy considers its PT boats. +*absol. and fig.*—1942 Pearson col. in Topeka *Journal* 9 Nov. 4/4 When an army is retreating, a small force is left behind to cover the retreat and be sacrificed to the enemy. They are 'expendables.' The 'expendables' proposed by the Roosevelt advisers were not valuable shock troops, but the men who had been responsible for economic, political and diplomatic Pearl Harbors. . . . These, they said, are the 'expendables.'

FOX HOLE. A hole in the ground where troops may hide, for protection or ambush.—1942 Union for Democratic Action circular letter received 15 June. Men who would begin defending America, if at all, at the beachheads of Coney Island and in the foxholes of San Diego. *Look* 16 June p. 25 Two grim Aussies in fox holes during training. *Reader's Digest* Oct. 125/2 Smoke-begrimed men, covered with the marks of battle, rise out from the fox-holes of Bataan.

+GANGBUSTER. An officer engaged in breaking up organized crime. 1942 (Berrey and Van den Bark, *Thesaurus of Slang*). *also attrib.*—1940 *Common Sense* July 9/1 The boys with leather boots who liked to act as a combination of Army, vigilantes, Ku Kluxers, gangsters, gangbusters and defenders of the pure Italian or German way of life. 1941 Winifred Johnston *Visual 'Education'* (Norman, Okla., Cooperative Books) p. 27 The release of these gang-buster pictures . . . coincided with a trial in New York City which provided the national Republican press new material for publicizing Dewey.

+GOON. A ruffian, esp. a thug employed in labor disputes. 1939 (W.) Commonest in phrase *goon squad.* 1942 (Berrey and Van den Bark, *Thesaurus of Slang*).—1937 *Nation* 4 Sep. 239/2 The 'goon squad,' as it is commonly called, consists of at least twenty picked thugs and ex-convicts. 1940 *American Guardian* 15 Mar. 1/2 Henry's Goons Confess Bloody Attacks. . . . Everett Moore, assistant to Harry Bennett, Ford's goon squad superintendent. *Saturday Evening Post* 28 Dec. 42/1 'If we raised the goals,' Phog [Allen] says, 'these mezzanine-peeping goons [tall basket-ball players] wouldn't be able to score like little children pushing pennies into gum machines.

+HOT. Rapid. [*cp. hot-foot*, 1300–, and *hot haste*, 1553–].—1940 *PM* 6 Dec. p. 14 The ship came in hot just before dawn. [footnote:] Fast—as used here, 'too fast for a safe landing,' showing something was wrong. 1941 *Words* Dec. 99/1 *Hot-switch*—A rapid program transfer from one point of origin to another.

+HOTSHOT. Rapid; offering through or non-stop service (a truck-freighting term from about 1929); by extension, snappy, excellent, important. *also attrib. and absol.*—1940 *Saturday Evening Post* 9 Nov. p. 4 Battle of the Hotshot. . . . After taking it and disliking it for years, the railroads are at last fighting back at the cross-country truck lines. Door-to-door delivery started it, and now the hotshot freight, which paces the fastest of the passenger expresses, has entered the picture. 1941 advt. Topeka *Capital* 16 Jan. p. 14 Griggs-White's 'Hot Shot' Dollar Day Bargains. *Saturday Evening Post* 1 Feb. 13/2 Everyone knows that its [a motor trucking company's] hot-shot service over the Rockies is the tops in trucking. *Ibid.* 8 Feb. 22/1 My old apprentice mate . . . working up from a boomer machinist . . . to a hot-shot job as works manager of Superaviation Motor Company. 1942 'Truck Driver Lingo' in *American Speech* Apr. 103/2 HOT SHOT. Through schedule. *True Detective* Oct. 79/1 Officers throughout Kentucky were advised to be on the lookout for the local boy who went south and became a 'hot-shot' criminal. 1943 paper read by Kansas State Highway Commissioner 2 Jan. Hot-shot spot [a high-speed intersection between a railroad and a highway].

+JERK. To move the limbs or features in an involuntary spasmodic manner. [1874-]. Hence, to masturbate; by extension, one who hangs about burlesque or strip-tease shows for erotic stimulation (1930 or earlier); hence, a stupid person or anyone viewed with dislike.[1]—1942 *New Republic* 9 Feb. 207/1 Now, Now, Let's Keep Our Tempers.—Aussies Meet Japs; Drive Jerks to Halt.—*Headline in The New York Daily News.* 1942 Fred Allen program 11 Feb. That nasal jerk I was talkin' about. 1942 advt. for RKO film 'Ball of Fire' in *Stardom* Feb. p. 3 I love him because he don't know how to kiss, the jerk!

MONAD. The number one, unity. [1615-]. +*specif.* The S-shaped insignia of the Technocrats, signifying unity, balance, growth, and dynamic functioning for the security of the life processes; also, dynamic equilibrium between production and distribution.

MONOLITHIC. Formed of a single block of stone. [1825-]. +*fig.* Showing solidity or cohesion plus great size.—1937 *Nation* 10 July 32/1 The monolithic corporation. 1941 *Time* (Air Exp. Ed.) 8 Sep. 26/3, quoting Vaillant, *Aztecs of Mexico* (N.Y., Doubleday Doran) The Inca Empire was a 'benevolent monolithic state.' *Common Sense* Dec. 379/1 The CIO includes John L. Lewis's monolithic rule of the United Mine Workers. 1942 *New Republic* 9 Nov. 598/2 The monolithic power structure of the totalitarian state.

+NIP, *n. a.* Japanese. [*Nippon, Nipponese*].—1942 John Van der Cook in NBC 'News of the World' broadcast 12 Jan. *Time* 9 Feb. 23/3 I visited a command post in one sector where they had just rounded up a bunch of Nips. . . . The Nip dead are piled high.

PANCAKE. To flatten. [nonce-word 1879-].—1941 *Time* (Air Exp. Ed.) 6 Oct. 17/1 A . . . near-hurricane . . . that killed three people, leveled grain fields, pancaked buildings, blocked highways. *Ibid.* 20 Oct. 2/1 Starting the bill in the House, with a steam roller set to pancake all opposition. 1942 Our Boarding House cartoon in Topeka *Capital* 15 Mar. Sure! He's pancaked 17 guys in a row! Hits like a train at a grade crossing.

PEEL OFF. [*pill off*, 1545-]. +*fig.*—1941 *Better English* Sep. 4/1, quoting N.Y. *Times* To 'peel off' is to curve away from another aircraft—the movement as one machine comes up close to another and then slants away is supposed to resemble the act of peeling off the skin of a banana. *Reader's Digest* Dec. 59/2 Our fighters seemed to be doing a good job on the Huns because only one peeled off to attack us. 1942 AP desp. in Topeka *Journal* 1/5 We peel off to the left in a dive that makes me gasp.

+PLAYSUIT. A light sports suit for women, usually having a skirt that may be fastened over the shorts.—1941 *Real Detective* May p. 18 I roamed about in a little playsuit. 1942 legend of AP photo in Topeka *Capital* 3 Feb. 5/6-7 Ilyana Yankwich wearing a California-made playsuit; it's in vivid green and brown tones with a gay leaf motif. *Life* 30 Nov. p. 126 Rita in an attractive playsuit.

PLUSHY. Of the nature of or resembling plush. [1611-]. +*fig.* Complacently opulent.—1941 *Time* 9 June 24/3 A Manhattan audience, looking unseasonably plushy, last week cooed and clapped its way through the revival of a cockeyed opera—*Four Saints in Three Acts.*—1942 Atcheson L. Hench in *American Speech* Dec. 250/1-2 [definition of *plushy*] In the sense of 'sumptuous,' 'richly adorned,' 'wealthy,' or 'elegant.'

+PRESSURE. To exert pressure, force.—1942 *Time* 27 Apr. 29/1 Then and there began the German pressuring for Laval's restoration which culminated last week. 1942 Pearson col. in Topeka *Journal* 28 Sep. 4/5 An effort to pressure congress into accepting.

PROTECTIVE. Having to do with, or providing, protection. [1661-]. Surveillant, alleging to provide protection, esp. in phrase *protective custody.*—1940 AP desp. in Topeka *Journal* 19 Apr. 1/8 De Geer in his broadcast declared The Netherlands would resist with arms any attempt by a foreign power to extend protective help to her. *Nation* 27 Apr. 530/1 Milan Stoyadinovich, the pro-German ex-Premier, has been put under protective arrect. 1940 AP desp. in Topeka *Journal* 8 May 3/1 When I was asked to take some letters . . . I agreed readily, thinking they might be an open sesame for sleeping quarters. They were—under British 'protective arrest' in Spillum. 1939 *Nation* 11 Mar. 292/2 Bag and baggage these rights have been taken into 'protective custody' and dumped into a concentration camp. 1940 AP desp. in Topeka *Capital* 10 May 1/3 Great Britain took protective custody of Iceland today. 1941 *Time* 7 Apr. 19/2 The President . . . put all Danish ships in protective custody.

SPENDING TAX. A tax on spending. —1942 *PM* about 4 July. *Time* 7 Sep. 94/3 Pondered a new Treasury proposal for a 'spending tax' designed to encourage war savings. 1943 *Nation* 9 Jan. 47/1 Professor Wallis of Stanford University has advocated a steeply progressive spending tax.

---

1. Derivation suggested by Mr. Elrick B Davis.

AMONG THE NEW WORDS

DWIGHT L. BOLINGER
Yale University

Long lists have been compiled of words formed out of what Harold Wentworth calls neo-pseudo-suffixes. ANW has commented on a number of these, including *-cast, -burger, -legger, -aroo*, and others. How deeply the habit of dissecting words is ingrained in American English may be seen perhaps better, however, in those suffixes of which there are but a few scattered examples and which have yet to become popular. Herewith are listed a number of them, which also meet the condition of not being independent words used in some nonce-combination (such as *busting* or *fest*):

Word of origin	*Coinage*	*Source*
gymnasium	trainasium	*Amer. Speech* Feb. 1943 p. 76/1
philatelist	pencilatelist	Topeka *Capital* 10 Jan. 1940
sabotage	radiobotage	*Words* Dec. 1941 p. 97/1
saboteur	radioboteur	*Ibid.*
icicle	Popsicle	(A trade name long in use.)
hydraulic	magdraulic	*Scient. American* Mar. 1943 p. 124
entrepreneur, connoisseur, coiffeur, *etc.*	scripteur[1]	*Time* (Air Exp. Ed.) 25 Aug. 1941 p. 24/2
danseuse, chanteuse, *etc.*	scripteuse	*Time* (Air Exp. Ed.) 23 June 1941 p. 32/2
	strippeuse	*Life* 2 Jan. 1939 p. 15; *Time* (Air Exp. Ed.) 13 Oct. 1941 p. 36/1
	stripteuse	*Time* 28 Sep. 1942 (play on *tease*)
frankfurter	turkeyfurter	*Words* Jan. 1940
photogenic	radiogenic[2]	Sinclair Lewis, *Gideon Planish,* 1943, p. 418
	telegenic	*Good Housekeeping* Feb. 1941 p. 19
succotash	Bean-o-tash	*Collier's* 13 Apr. 1940
cellophane	Clari-phane[2]	Topeka, Kan. newspaper 17 Nov. 1939
elastic	Perma-lastic	Observed in Los Angeles 4 Dec. 1941
chandelier	Fleur-o-lier	*Sat. Eve. Post* 13 July 1940
tamale	turkeymallies	Observed in Los Angeles 7 Aug. 1940
macaroni	Tenderoni	Van Camp's adv., 13 May 1942
ersatz	hairsatz	*Time* 16 Feb. 1942 p. 32/3
landscape, seascape	lipscape	Los Angeles *Downtown Shopping News* 28 Aug. 1940 p. 2
	contourscape	*Kenyon Review* Spring 1942 p. 255
advertising	bookvertising	*Amer. Speech* Feb. 1943 p. 42/2
advertiser	bidvertiser	*Ibid.* Dec. 1942 p. 283/1
sandwich	Spamwich	*Sat. Eve. Post* 18 Jan. 1941 p. 77
	turkeywich	*Words* Mar. 1941 p. 13/1
	duckwich	*Ibid.*

Of the citations in the following list, seven were supplied by Mr. John Bethel, three by Miss Mamie Meredith, and one each by Mr. Jerry Shaw, Mr. Atcheson L. Hench, Mr. I. Willis Russell, Mr. Allen Walker Read, and Mr. N. E. Saxe.

SYMBOLS: The symbol + before a word or definition indicates an Americanism. A date immediately following a word or definition indicates the time of evidence shown in the DAE, or, if so stated, in another publication. Dates in brackets indicate the time, etc., of British usage. An asterisk used after a word indicates that the word is illustrated in British usage before 1600.

+ANGLO. [*Anglo*-American, 1828-, *American Speech* Apr. 1943 p. 120/1] An American of English-speaking descent. A term used especially in New Mexico.—1943 *New Mexico Quarterly Review* Spring p. 33 Native Anglos and Spanish Americans of New Mexico.

ANTIPERSONNEL MINE.——1942 *Reader's Digest* Dec. p. 83/1 The antipersonnel mine . . . was dramatically introduced by the Germans in the fall of 1939. . . . Its chief feature was an arrangement whereby the mine, on being tripped, was boosted out of the ground to about the height of a man's waist before exploding. It was really a bomb, which sprayed a wide area with shrapnel. 1942 P. W. Thompson *What the Citizen Should Know about the Army Engineers* (Norton) p. 137 The antipersonnel mine usually operates on a hair-trigger trip-type of mechanism, and usually explodes with a shrapnel effect.

BYPASS. [Perh. from engineering sense, 1886-]. To pass up, disregard; *specif.*, to outflank.—1942 *Time* 2 Feb. p. 63/3 Reclaimed rubber, ordinarily bypassed by manufacturers because it wears out faster than natural [= virgin] rubber. 1943 Station WQXR newscast 9 Oct. To . . . bypass Kolombangara.

+CAMELBACK.—1942 *Manual of Retreading and Recapping* (Rubber Mfg. Ass'n, Inc., New York City, 1st ed. copyright 1940) p. 1 The term 'camelback,' broadly used, refers to the uncured rubber applied to the worn tire to make the new tread. More specifically, when this uncured tread has tapered wings extending from the shoulders it is called 'camelback,' whereas if it has an abrupt bevel at the shoulders it is called 'capping stock.' Camelback is used for both retreads and full recaps. Capping stock is used on top-caps only.

+CAR POOL. An arrangement for sharing transportation in private automobiles.—1942 *Reader's Digest* Dec. p. 138 I don't believe I care for anything, thank you. I'm just in their car pool. 1943 *McCall's* Apr. p. 15 On a master map of the city car pools are plotted.

CHEESECAKE*. +A display, esp. photographic, of girls' legs. 1942 (Berrey and Van den Bark, *Thesaurus of Slang*). —1942 *Time* 24 Aug. p. 14/1-2 The Supreme Empress of Cheesecake, the very Marlene Dietrich herself. 1943 *Life* 3 May p. 104 You can see the photographer isn't as interested in her dress as he is in her legs. Cheesecake hasn't been rationed.

+GRAVEYARD SHIFT. In mining, the last shift, when three daily shifts are employed. 1934 (W.) +A shift (in industry generally) from about midnight to about 8 A.M. 1942 (Berrey and Van den Bark, *Thesaurus of Slang*).—1943 *Reader's Digest* Aug. p. 98/2 This child wandered the streets every night until her parents, who work on the 'graveyard' shift, vacated a bed in the crowded home. *Ibid.* Sep. p. 49/1 The graveyard or late night shift.

HANDIE-TALKIE, HANDY-TALKIE.—1942 *National Geographic* Nov. p. 680 Churchill . . . is holding a 'handie-talkie' radio used for conversation between ground points and planes in the air. 1943 *Fortune* Oct. p. 62 Walkie-talkie, weighing about thirty pounds, has given rise to other units, one of which is the five-pound, eleven-ounce 'transceiver,' designed for paratroops and also used by infantry, which looks like a French telephone and is called handie-talkie. *Time* 27 Sep. p. 83 Don't worry about Johnny. He'll talk his way out—summon ground support, tanks, or planes—with his two-way 'handy-talkie.'

+MEATLEGGER. [*Bootlegger*]. One who sells meat contrary to rationing restrictions.—1943 A.P. desp. in Topeka *Journal* 20 Jan. p. 8/5 A typical report, this spokesman added, was of 'meatleggers' going to farmers and buying cattle at higher than market prices, taking the cattle to hidden slaughterhouses for butchering, and peddling the meat at extra-legal prices, either direct to the public or thru retail stores. Baltimore *Sun* 10 Feb. p. 6/2 The hunt for 'meatleggers.'

MOLOTOV BREADBASKET. [*Breadbasket*, a large bomb that explodes in midair releasing many smaller bombs. c.1941 (W.)]—1942 *Britannica Book of the Year* p. 455. 1943 Robert Considine, ed., *Thirty Seconds over Tokyo* (N.Y., Random House) p. 40 Doolittle also told us that we would carry another bomb, a 500-pound incendiary, something like the old Russian Molotov Breadbasket.

PARITY. Equivalence in another currency. [1886-]. +—1941 *Time* (Air Exp. Ed.) 2 June p. 2/3 'Parity' is a political concept which holds that the farmer should receive prices for his products which will give him a purchasing power (in terms of other commodities) equal to that which he had in the period 1909-14. 1937 McIntosh and Orr *Practical Agriculture for High Schools* (Amer. Book Co.) p. 15 Show the actual and parity prices of the major farm products.

+POWERHOUSE. A building which houses machinery for furnishing power. 1881-. +Something very strong. 1942 (Berrey and Van den Bark, *Thesaurus of Slang*).—c.1928 Edgar Wallace *Captains of Souls* (London, John Long) p. 31 He is like a power-house. When I shake hands with him I feel as though I'm going to get a bad burn! 1941 *Saturday Evening Post* 1 Feb. p. 54/3 A thresher is one of the few powerhouses in the shark family. *Time* (Air Exp. Ed.) 15 Sep. p. 25/3 In the final, Powerhouse Kovacs was too much for Riggs in the first set, 7-5. *Ibid.* 29 Sep. p. 2/1 The American Legion struck Isolationism a ruinous blow last week—a ponderous, powerhouse, meat-ax crusher.

+PRESSURIZE. To provide with air under pressure, as an aircraft for breathing purposes to compensate for low natural pressure at high altitudes.—1938 *Time* 23 May p. 33 Without pressurized cabins, planes now fly as high as 14,000 feet; with them, passengers will feel no discomfort at *DC-4's* service ceiling, 22,900 feet. 1942 *ibid.* 2 Mar. p. 50/2 With pressurized cabins, the Constellation is expected to fly comfortably at 30,000 feet.

+RANGER. A member of a body of armed men, usually mounted, employed to range over an area for its protection. 1670-. +A member of an organization of American soldiers, created in December, 1941, formed of volunteers, and trained in close-range fighting for raids on enemy territory. The American counterpart of the British *commando*.—1942 New York *Times* 20 Aug. 1/5 The first American troops to receive a baptism of fire in Europe in this war were the men of the United States Ranger Battalion who fought in the Dieppe raid today. It was the first time the name Rangers had appeared in a war communiqué anywhere.

RESTORE. To bring back to the original state. [1679-]. +To bring back (a food) to the original nutritive value of its ingredients.—1943 Lone Ranger broadcast 6 Sep. Restored cereal.

+SKYGLOW. Glow in the sky caused by reflection of city lights.—1942 *Progressive* 1 Aug. p. 9/3 Newport. . . . This city will have a Dimout Ball. . . . Brown, chairman of the Newport Civilian Defense Council, has approved the event after being assured that the plans will conform with all the Army's dimout regulations and that there will be no skyglow. 1943 New Haven *Evening Register* 7 Aug. p. 5/2 Some communities had so far relaxed their dimout regulations that they were providing a dangerous skyglow.

+SMOOTHIE. A smooth-mannered person; an attractive person. 1942 (Berrey and Van den Bark, *Thesaurus of Slang*). —1933 *Reader's Digest* Dec. p. 66/2 (A type of university student). 1937 Jennifer Jones *Murder-on-Hudson* (Milwaukee, Red Arrow Books 1939) p. 143 She's a smoothie, if there ever was one. 1940 *New Republic* 17 June p. 819/1 The American people are tired of the smoothy in politics. 1941 *Time* (Air Exp. Ed.) 1 Sep. p. 19/2 (Caption of item on the very diplomatic Gen. Andrews).

+SNAZZY. Stylish and somewhat flashy.—1938 Whitman Chambers *Once Too Often* (New York, Mercury Books) p. 9 It was indeed a very snazzy setup and I wondered how many months he was in arrears with his rent. 1942 Sears, Roebuck circular 9 July Snazzy colors that boys like.

SPEARHEAD, *n.* A person or body of persons chosen to lead a thrust or attack. [1929-]. + *v.* To act as a spearhead for.—1938 Los Angeles *Daily News* 27 July p. 8/1 Liberal leader who spearheaded the debate. 1942 *Mexican Labor News* 24 Mar. p. 3 Mussolini's warriors were routed by Spanish Republicans spearheaded by an anti-fascist Italian battalion. *Time* 18 May p. 23/2 Marines and Commandomen . . . spearheaded by light tanks.

SPIRAL, *v.* To wind or move in a spiral manner. [1834-]. +To rise disproportionately (said of prices, rates, etc.)—1941 *Time* (Air Exp. Ed.) 20 Oct. p. 35/1 Even if import and farm prices resist all controls, processors' and retailers' prices will rise but not spiral with them. 1942 Edwin W. Kemmerer *The A B C of Inflation* (McGraw-Hill) p. 156 If wages and the prices of farm products are not adequately restricted but are permitted to spiral upward . . . the whole price situation will get out of control. *n.* A rise of such a nature.—1943 *Reader's Digest* Sep. p. 50/2 The Administration and the leaders in business and in labor must . . . bring the whole menacing spiral to a halt.

STAKHANOVISM. A Russian technique of speed-up and efficiency for increasing industrial production.—1939 *Nation* 16 Dec. p. 67/2 The Stakhanov movement of 1936 was part of this economic offensive. The real significance of Stakhanovism has been buried under a confusion of arguments as to whether or not it was speed up.

STAKHANOVIST, STAKHANOVITE. An adherent of Stakhanovism; *also attrib.*—1940 *New Republic* 18 Nov. p. 685/1 NDAC officials estimate that, in many industries, skilled workers are obliged to spend as much as 85 percent of their time on unskilled routine tasks. Under the 'up-grading' program, each skilled worker is to be provided with a sufficient number of helpers so that all his time can be given to his specialty. This is the 'gang-system'; its resemblance . . . to the Stakhanovist technique of Soviet Russia is marked. 1943 *National Geographic*

1. The suffixes *-eur* and *-euse* seem to be the 'artistic' forms of *-or* and *-oress.*
2. Bona fide suffixes, but not in the senses used.

May p. 537 Because he exceeded his normal output, Butuzov earns big bonuses and is a *stakhanovite*. The name is applied to those who follow the technique of Stakhanov, a coal miner who perfected the Soviet speed-up system. *Saturday Evening Post* 8 May p. 63/2 Before me was an elderly woman turning the handle of a stamping machine. . . . She was the best Stakhanovite of the works and all were proud of her.

+SWING SHIFT. In industry, a shift from about 4 P.M. to midnight.—1941 Baukhage newscast 14 Dec. 1943 *Reader's Digest* Sep. p. 49/1 The swing (or early night) shift.

+SWINGSTER, SWINGSTRESS. One who plays or sings swing music. 1940 Pearson and Allen col. 1 May His [Jerry Sadler's, candidate for governor of Texas] swingsters now rival O'Daniel's family radio act. 1941 *Time* (Air Exp. Ed.) 13 Oct. p. 26/1 Swingstress Ella Logan swung *Tipperary*. 1942 *Time* 20 Apr. p. 47 Swingster Gene Krupa. 1943 Lincoln *Star and Journal* 29 Aug. Swingstress of the nation Dinah Shore.

+TELECASTER. A television broadcaster.—1940 *Nation* 6 Apr. p. 448/1 No telecaster will want to operate on a system incapable of reaching the full potential audience. 1940 Ed. J. Porterfield and K. Reynolds *We Present Television* (Norton) p. 47 Television standards in the United States must be uniformly adopted by all telecasters.

+TRAILERITE. One who lives in a trailer.—1940 A. P. desp. in Topeka *Capital* 28 Jan. p. 16B/5 Many trailerites, caught unprepared by Florida's worst cold spell. 1941 *Reader's Digest* Oct. p. 25/1 A six-acre camp occupied by about 400 trailerites.

+WHODUNIT, WHODUNNIT. Detective fiction.—1941 *Time* (Air Exp. Ed.) 11 Aug. p. 10/3 Paper-covered libraries ranging from Shakespeare to whodunits. 1942 advt. Topeka *Capital* 1 Mar. p. 6C The season's wackiest who-dun-it! 'No Hands on the Clock' [a movie]. 1943 *Writer's Digest* Apr. p. 15/1 Magazines use twice as many straight serials as whodunnits.

ZIP. To move briskly or with a zip. [1907-]. +To close with or as with a slide fastener.—1942 advt. *Time* 23 Feb. p. 78 Zips flawlessly. . . . CONMAR, the MAJOR Zipper. 1942 Green Hornet broadcast 8 Aug. Zip your lip.

+ZIPPERED. Equipped with a slide fastener.—1941 *Time* (Air Exp. Ed.) 25 Aug. p. 2/3 His zippered ankle-high shoes. 1943 Topeka *Journal* 21 Apr. p. 1A/4 The latest in bathing suits . . . with rigid front and zippered elastic back.

AMONG THE NEW WORDS

DWIGHT L. BOLINGER
Yale University

SLAP-HAPPY appears to have been the first of a now very numerous progeny of *happy*, 'dizzy, exhilarated,' used as a combining form. The allusion to intoxication is obvious in that *slap-happy* is a synonym of *punch-drunk*. The earlier extensions usually contrived to rime with *slap*: 'Police thought he was just *sap-happy*' (i.e., drunk; Los Angeles *News* 27 July 1940 p. 2/1-2); *'Scrap-happy*, slap-happy' (movie ad, Topeka *Journal* 28 Sep. 1940 p. 2A); 'I'm *snap-happy* since I discovered Kleenex cleans the . . . lens of my camera' (*Saturday Evening Post* 212:38 p. 46); *'Tap-Happiest*, Swing-Singiest, Melodic Miracle' (movie ad, 30 Oct. 1941, quoted in *American Speech* Apr. 1942 p. 131/2).

Later examples, as well as some early ones, are more versatile: *'Hate-happy* bond-salesmen' (*Nation* 13 Apr. 1940 p. 469/1); *'Hitler-happy'* (in film 'Confessions of a Nazi Spy,' 1940); 'This now *power-happy* intelligence, representing itself to be your Government' (*Saturday Evening Post* 12 Oct. 1940, cited Sargent *Bulletin* 92 p. 4); 'A girl who is a good girl but *footlight-happy*' (i.e., stage-struck; *New Republic* 9 Dec. 1940 p. 789/2).

Now the Army has taken over: *'Bar happy, stripe-happy'* (*American Speech* Oct. 1942 p. 183); 'The [Signal] Corps prefers stable, medium-speed [telegraph] operators, is suspicious of *"dit-happy"* men who break world records' (*Life* 15 Feb. 1943 p. 82).

Examples from Miss Meredith are all military: 'As we went through this campaign we have lived in everything but a building. There have been Cactus Patches, Grain Fields, Waddies . . . , Sand Dunes . . . and many other places which would give us cover and concealment. Living in the above named places along with the conditions that we had to endure started a phrase of *"Cactus"* or *"Olive Happy"*' (General Motors *News and Views*, letter dated July 1943); *Flak Happy* (name of a Flying Fortress; Omaha *World-Herald* 17 Oct. 1943): 'After really bad nervous cases have undergone treatment—they have become what soldiers call *"bomb happy"*—they are tested for their reactions to battle noises' (London *Daily Express*, reprinted in *Britain* Oct. 1943): 'Advancing British captured numerous prisoners from the German 65th infantry division, described as *"bomb happy,"* indicating they were shocked and demoralized from the heavy bombing and shelling' (A.P. desp. 30 Nov. 1943); 'Cadets are taught here to be *"trigger happy"*: to shoot at anything any time' (*Life* 1 Nov. 1943); 'In camp, a man conspicuous for his odd behavior. . . . If he was a British Tommy on the North African desert, he may have gone "lurgy lurgy" or *"sand happy."* . . . In Iceland he is *"glacier happy"*' (*Fortune* Dec. 1943 p. 268).

Besides that given in the body of the text, credit goes to the following: Mr. John P. Bethel, four citations including the earliest for *Molotov cocktail* and *radar* (the latter disclosing the term to have been public property almost two years before it was officially 'released'); Miss Mamie Meredith, three citations; Corp. A. W. Read, two citations including the earliest for *lunatic fringe;* Ensign Bill Carter, the earliest citation for *boot;* Mr. D. W. Maurer, the proposed etymology of *corny;* Mr. Jerry Shaw, the technical information on *recap* and *retread;* Miss Dorothy Vilven, the earliest citation of *man-tailored.*

SYMBOLS: The symbol + before a word or definition indicates an Americanism. A date immediately following a word or definition indicates the time of evidence shown in the DAE, or, if so stated, in another publication. Dates in brackets indicate the time, etc., of British usage. An asterisk used after a word indicates that the word is illustrated in British usage before 1600.

+ALCAN. The Alaska Highway.—1943 letter from Mr. Lawrence J. Burpee, International Joint Commission, Ottawa, Canada 31 Mar. This name was adopted by the Chief of Engineers of the United States War Department early in April, 1942, purely as a short and convenient name for the highway that had been undertaken. The highway was at first known as the Canadian-Alaskan Military Highway, which was found too cumbersome. The name Alcan has never been formally adopted by either the United States Government or the Canadian Government and has no official standing. 1943 Topeka *Journal* 15 Jan. p. 1/6-7 A six months' job on the Alcan highway.

+BOOT.—1901 Austin M. Knight *Modern Seamanship* p. 784 [*Boot*] a recruit. 1940 *Time* 11 Nov. p. 22 To mold 'boots' (Navy lingo for recruits) into the indefinable likeness of a Marine takes hard work on a rigid regimen. 1943 *Saturday Evening Post* 8 May p. 26/3 The officers, many of them reservists, and the crew, 60 per cent boots, were honing for action.

+COKE. A drink of Coca-Cola.—1938 Whitman Chambers *Once Too Often* (Mercury Books) p. 79 I killed ten minutes drinking two cokes. 1942 *Life* 16 Feb. p. 38 Beverly . . . has dates with the boys at camp, dances and drinks Cokes with them.

+CORNY. [*Cornfed*, countrified]. Old-fashioned, sentimental, stale, yokelish, esp. as applied to music. 1939 (W.)—1938 *Collier's* 16 July p. 13/1 He can go corny or classical, and make 'em jump for the rafters. 1941 *Time* (Air Exp. Ed.) 19 May p. 27/3 Corny as a back-country bumpkin, [Jack] Oakie has turned his corniness into a salable commodity. *Ibid.* 8 Sep. p. 1/2 The corny annual get-together of the Franklin Roosevelt Home Club.

DECOLONIZATION.—1941 Richard F. Behrendt *Economic Nationalism in Latin America* (University of New Mexico Inter-Americana Short Papers I, Albuquerque) p. 2 We see today all over Latin America a virtually universal, and in some cases violent, reaction to foreign ownership of important productive enterprises, a movement which in its essence is aiming at . . . a kind of economic independence of those countries, through the nationalization of foreign-owned enterprises and what is sometimes described as 'DECOLONIZATION' of those countries. . . . [*Footnote*] The term is used by W. Feuerlein and E. Hannan, *Dollars in Latin America* (New York: Council on Foreign Relations, 1941), and has been used before by M. J. Bonn, *The Crumbling of Empire* (London: Allen and Unwin, Ltd., 1938).

+ESSENTIALISM. An educational doctrine which stresses time-proven techniques and disciplines, esp. as opposed to the practises of progressivism.—1943 *Time* 13 Sep. p. 74/1 Essentialism . . . would give pupils systematic training in traditional subjects; discipline is stressed and informal learning strictly subordinated.

+ESSENTIALIST. An adherent of essentialism in education.—1938 W. C. Bagley in *Educational Administration and Supervision* April An Essentialist's Platform for the Advancement of American Education. 1943 *Time* 13 Sep. p. 74/1 Progressive education was enjoying a boost last week from the ranks of its professional enemies—the Essentialists.

+EXTON. A Du Pont plastic.—1939 *Reader's Digest* Feb. p. 81/2 Toothbrush bristles that will not soften in water or saliva are made from Exton, a plastic. 1941 Montgomery Ward Fall-Winter Catalog p. 516 Brushes are made with . . . Exton bristles.

FREEZE. To make immobile or inflexible. 1934 (W.). +To arrest, at a given stage, the development or evolution of; used esp. of the standardization of industrial design so as to make mass production possible.—1937 *Harper's* July p. 192/1 With the excessive costs freezing taxes on poverty. 1937 John Gunther *Inside Europe* (Harper and Bros.) p. 123 It would, by 'freezing' the present borders, prevent Anschluss, union of Germany and Austria. 1941 *Time* (Air Exp. Ed.) 26 May p. 22/3 General Electric . . . had . . . frozen its models of receivers and tubes. 1942 *Time* 20 Apr. p. 56/2 The Otter [a small merchantman] was only experimental, was never intended to be a frozen design.

+HORSE CAVALRY. Mounted soldiery using horses rather than motorized conveyances.—1940 A.P. desp. in Topeka *Journal* 3 Apr. p. 13/2-3 General Herr said . . . 'the precise methods of employment as well as the scope of action of horse cavalry has been affected . . . by air and mechanization. *Harper's* Dec. p. 4/2 An extended defense of horse cavalry before a Congressional committee. 1941 *Time* (Air Exp. Ed.) 13 Oct. p. 19/2 [Discipline] could be seen in the achievements of the engineers, in such outfits as the Armored Force and horse cavalry.

+LUNATIC FRINGE. The extremist or unbalanced minority of an organization or movement.—1928 Arthur M. Schlesinger *New Viewpoints in American History* (reprinted in Platt and Perrin *Current Expressions of Fact and Opinion* 1941) p. 367 Advocates for new advances must employ the militant and fantastic methods which mark the 'lunatic fringe' of a new crusade for reform [phrase attributed to Theodore Roosevelt]. 1938 *Nation* 20 Aug. p. 167/2 Their [the pro-fascists'] behavior [toward Jews] was dismissed as a product of reaction's lunatic fringe. 1942 *PMLA Supplement* Part 2 p. 1374 Members of the 'lunatic fringe' among educationists.

+MAN-TAILORED. Of women's clothes, tailored after the manner of men's clothes.—1940 Sears, Roebuck and Co. *Spring and Summer Catalog* p. 58 Man-tailored suits . . . have won. 1940 adv. Topeka *Journal* 27 May p. 5/1 gray, man-tailored Sports Suit.

MICROFILM. To photograph on microfilm.—1942 *Reader's Digest* Nov. p. 80 Most of the letters are microfilmed.

MOLOTOV COCKTAIL.—1940 *Life* 21 Oct. p. 13 'Molotov cocktails' are empty pint beer bottles, scored so that they will easily break, filled with explosives and corked. A fuse is then attached to each bottle. 1943 *Reader's Digest* June p. 17/1 *Der Russe* has also shown an ingenuity displeasing to the Germans. He devised the Molotov cocktail out of an empty vodka bottle, gasoline siphoned from a crippled tank, and cotton batting from his own quilted uniform.

+PARA-SKI. Of parachute troops, equipped with skis.—1942 Topeka *Capital* 8 Mar. p. 7C/1 'Let 'er Buck,' Shouts U. S. Para-Ski Troop. 1942 *Christian Science Monitor* 26 Mar. p. 3 inset Para-ski troopers of the 503rd Parachute Battalion.

+PARA-SKIER. A member of a para-ski troop.—1942 *Christian Science Monitor* 26 Mar. p. 3/4-6 'Let 'Er Buck' Is War Cry of Para-Skiers.

+PERCENTAGE. A share of winnings or profits; a rake-off. 1934 (W.). +Profit in general.—1940 *The Woman* Sep. p. 69/1 Marge was courageous and a straight shooter but there was no more percentage in taking her out than one of the other guys. 1941 *Saturday Evening Post* 22 Mar. p. 101/3 There wasn't no percentage in tryin' to get the pilot. He was barbecue, anyway.

+PREMIERE, *v.* To give a premiere of; to have a premiere.—1938 letter from W. W. Blancké 22 Feb. To première (pronounced prĕmyĕr)—announcer of some radio station . . . 'This composition was premièred (or *premièred*) at such a time and place.' 1940 Winchell col. Topeka *Journal* 11 Dec. p. 4/6 There's irony in the request of Grinnell college's alumni that Frank Capra should premiere 'Meet John Doe' there. 1943 *Newsweek* 13 Sep. p. 101 Keepsakes, a new Sunday program . . . premièred on Blue Sep. 5, 8–8:30.

RADAR. [*Radio detecting and ranging*].—1942 *Britannica Book of the Year* p. 558 Another important wartime development was the 'Radar,' a new application of newly developed vacuum tubes which were capable of generating surprisingly large amounts of ultrahigh frequency power. The British disclosed in the press that this device was exceedingly effective in the detection and location of enemy planes. 1942 *Army Regulations 615-26,* 15 Sep. p. 597 Radar operator, designated set, under direction of a radar repairman, performs various duties as a member of a team which operates a designated radar set. Sets up a designated radar set; sets up radar equipment and operates it in accordance with prescribed procedures.

RECAP. To put a cap on (a thing) again. [1856-]. +To re-surface a tire [see first citation for process]; a tire so resurfaced.—1940 Rubber Manufacturers Assn. *Manual of Retreading and Recapping* (N. Y., 2nd ed. 1942) In recapping, it is necessary to make a distinction between a full recap and a top-cap. . . . In full recapping the old tread is not removed as in retreading. Instead, the worn tire is rasped across the top of the tread and over the shoulders as far as the new rubber is to be extended. . . . In top capping, only the top of the old tread is rasped. . . . All the new rubber is applied just to the top of the tread. 1942 sign observed in Kansas City, Mo., 3 Jan. Jobbers of high-grade recap tires.

+RETREAD. To re-surface a tire [see first citation for process]; a tire so resurfaced; *also fig.*—1940 Rubber Manufacturers Assn. *Manual of Retreading and Recapping* (N. Y., 2nd ed. 1942) p. 1. The term 'retreading,' broadly used, refers to applying a new tread to a worn tire. For instruction purposes it is necessary to know whether the new tread is to be a retread, a full recap or a top-cap. . . . *Retreading* . . . refers to the process of removing all the old tread including the breaker, and replacing with new material. 1943 *Fortune* Oct. p. 240 The men Borum called upon when he formed his general staff were largely chosen among civilians who had flown in the last war, and who had since maintained contact with aviation. Going back into uniform and calling themselves 're-treads.'

+ROLL-BACK, ROLLBACK. A forcible return (of prices) to a former, and lower, level.—1942 *Time* 11 May p. 80 OPA had denied their [retailers'] plea for a 'roll-back' of ceiling dates that would recognize the lag between rising wholesale and retail prices. 1943 *Newsweek* 16 Aug. p. 16 Price rollbacks through payment of subsidies to process are one phase of the program. *Time* 27 Sep. p. 88 A new cost of living rollback.

+SCRIPT. To write (a scenario); to change (a plot or story) into a scenario.—1940 *Writer's Journal* Oct. p. 8/1 Charles Martin is again scripting for radio. 1941 *Time* (Air Exp. Ed.) p. 29/1 Hammett . . . has been scripting his thrillers for Hollywood. 1943 *New Masses* 30 Nov. p. 28/1 John Howard Lawson, who scripted the film.

+SHANGRI-LA. [The setting of James Hilton's *Lost Horizon,* 1933]. An imaginary, or secret, military (esp. air) base.—[Cp. 1939 Van Wyck Mason *The Singapore Exile Murders* (N. Y., Pocket Books 1941) p. 18 Looks like the movie set of Shangri-La. 1941 *Time* (Air Exp. Ed.) 23 June p. 31/3 The Captain operates an insular Shangri-La.] 1942 A.P. desp. in Topeka *Capital* 22 Apr. p. 1/6 President Roosevelt said today [21 Apr.] that American planes reported to have bombed Japan last Saturday came from a new secret base in Shangri La, a fictional Utopia in Tibet. 1943 *Reader's Digest* Jan. p. 120/1 As soon as plans for moving troops overseas are made—to Shangri-la, let's say—requests for data on Shangri-la come to Medical Intelligence. 1943 newscast Station WEAF 26 Nov. Based on some Central Pacific Shangri-La.

WITCH-HUNTING. Political persecution.—1940 *Nation* 20 Jan. p. 74/2 Political motives and witch-hunting. 1941 *Time* 7 Apr. p. 55 The present wave of U.S. jitters will pass, as did four other waves of 'witch-hunting.' 1942 *Reader's Digest* Feb. p. 12/1 Our men do their jobs without the brutality and witch-hunting which has scourged the authoritarian countries. 1942 *Christian Science Monitor* 25 Mar. p. 6/1 Whether innocent persons have been persecuted . . . or whether it all adds up to 'witch-hunting' . . . will have to be left to . . . the facts [concerning the Oklahoma 'book trials']. *Time* 10 Aug. p. 78/2 The witch-hunting First New Deal. 1943 *Progressive* 4 Jan. p. 12/2 The general condition is far better than in World War I in terms of freedom of debate and criticism, lack of witch-hunting.

ZANY. Clownish; foolish; idiotic. [1616-]. *Obs.* 1934 (W.)—1943 letter from C. C. Mish 2 Apr. To prevent the use of 'zany' as an adjective. *Saturday Evening Post* 10 Apr. p. 15/1 Spike Jones and his zany band.

AMONG THE NEW WORDS

I. WILLIS RUSSELL
University of Alabama

In response to the query in ANW (Apr. 1943, p. 148) for information on the etymology of *blimp,* Mr. Harold Wentworth has made a careful search and written an interesting reply. Many of the sources he checked have no material on the word. The term apparently came out of the last war and is recorded in the OED Sup. as early as 1916. For the etymology, the OED Sup. refers to its 1918 quotation, which reads: '*Illustr. Lond. News* 27 July 96 Nobody in the R. N. A. S. ever called them anything but "Blimps," an onomatopoeic name invented by that genius for apposite nomenclature, the later Horace Shortt.' A more likely etymology, thinks Mr. Wentworth, is suggested by a citation from the Ithaca (N. Y.) *Journal-News,* 14 Jan. 1932: '[*Blimp*] is said to have originated from "B" for "balloon" and "limp."' '"B.limp,"' remarks Mr. Wentworth, 'seems a reasonable shortening, such as might be used in military records.' The 1943 Webster's NID says the word was 'Prob. suggested by *limp* adj.' Thus far Mr. Wentworth's material. To it should be added a citation furnished by Mr. Bolinger from an article in the *Reader's Digest,* Sept. 1942, p. 67: 'Experimenting with lighter-than-air craft of the nonrigid type during the first World War, the British found that Model "A-limp" did not stand up in battle. "B-limp" did and became the Blimp.'

The compounding of nouns and past participial adjectives is common in English. Sometimes, as with *-fed,* the adjective acts like a suffix; for example, *corn-fed, milk-fed, bottle-fed.* The war has brought forward two others, *-based* and *-borne,* which are being freely used in the formation of compounds. In the examples which follow no attempt has been made to obtain early dates. 'Britain-based heavy craft were grounded . . .' (AP. in B'ham *News* 27 May 1944 p. 1/6); '. . . the Allies hurled 6,000 British-based planes . . .' (AP. in Tuscaloosa *News* 21 May 1944 p. 1/6); '. . . carrier-based planes . . .' (AP., *ibid.,* 15 Dec. 1943 p. 4); '. . . Nimitz announced Sunday that fleet-based bombers thumped rockets and bombs into Guam's railway facilities' (AP. desp. in B'ham *News* 17 July 1944 p. 1/3); 'The attack was preceded by a diversionary raid . . . by India-based American Liberator bombers' (AP. in Tuscaloosa *News* 23 Apr. 1944 p. 1/1); '. . . Fortresses and Liberators participated in today's Italy-based onslaught . . .' (AP., *ibid.* 13 Apr. 1944 p. 1/2); '. . . Mitscher's planes took Japanese by surprise and wiped out most of their land-based air-power' (*Life* 17 July 1944 p. 19); '. . . I'd been flying PBY's in a patrol squadron shore-based since early in 1942 in Australia' (*Sat. Eve. Post* 27 May 1944 p. 10/1).

The first of the compounds with *-borne* is *air-borne,* which will merit glossarial treatment in a later issue. Some others are '. . . carrier-borne fighter' (Lond. *Times* 19 May 1944 p. 6/2); 'Fourteen men of the first glider-borne force on Sicily . . .' (N.Y. *Times* 13 July 1943 p. 3/4); '. . . mule-borne food and ammunition follows French forces . . .' (*Life* 29 May p. 32); '. . . road-borne supplies to support what he gets by air' (Maj. G. F. Eliot in B'ham *News* 7 Apr. 1944 p. 9/2); 'Naval losses for the sea-borne forces were described . . . as "very, very small" . . .' (AP. in Tuscaloosa *News* 6 June 1944 p. 1/8); 'The water-borne invasion completed, [tanks] tend to replace landing craft on the essentiality list' (AP. in B'ham *News-Age-Her.* 2 July 1944 p. 4-A/4).

First among the acknowledgments for this issue must come that to Mr. Dwight L. Bolinger. His extensive files, now in my keeping, contain a number of words already checked and ready for publication. Some of these are in the present glossary, though additional examples sometimes have been cited. Other words will be drawn upon for future issues. Citations from individuals are distributed as follows: Mr. Bolinger nine; Mr. John P. Bethel four, including the earliest for *flat-top* and *seabee;* Miss Mamie Meredith three; and Mr. Harold Wentworth two. Mr. Harold F. Cotter contributed the earliest citation for *cutback,* Mr. A. T. Hench the earliest American illustration of 'obliteration bombing,' and Mr. J. B. McMillan the earliest for *airgraph.* Thanks are also due Miss Meredith and Mr. Wentworth for helpful checking, and Mr. S. W. Tyler for technical information on *grasshopper.*

In order to present as much evidence as possible in the glossary, references are frequently included in their proper places without the actual citations.

Symbols: The symbol + before a word or definition indicates an Americanism. A date immediately following a word or definition indicates the time of evidence shown in the DAE, or, if so stated, in another publication. Dates in brackets indicate the time, etc., of British usage. An asterisk after a word indicates that the word is illustrated in British usage before 1600.

AIRGRAPH. (British term for V-Mail, q. v.)—1941 Talladega (Ala.) *Daily Home* 22 Apr. p. 1 (INS.) Science and the postal service have developed a new type of mail—'airgraph.' 1942 *Chr. Sci. Mon.* 21 Mar. p. 4/6 (CP.). N. Y. *Times* 26 June p. 18/7 The 10,000,000 airgraph letter . . . was recently dispatched . . .

BABY FLAT-TOP. (See quot. 1944 Feb.). See *Flat-top.*—1943 Time 22 Nov. p. 26/3 That beats a previous high scorer: the escort carrier 'B' . . . , another 'baby flat-top' . . . 1944 *ibid.* 24 Jan. p. 27. Tuscaloosa *News* 21 Feb. p. 1/7 (AP.). . . . American shipyards have turned out scores of escort carriers which represent conversion of cargo-type ships into 'baby flat-tops' . . .

BANGALORE (TORPEDO). [Prob. after Bangalore, India.] 'A device for clearing a pathway through a barbed wire entanglement. . . . Introduced on the Western Front early in 1915.' 1925 (Fraser and Gibbons *Soldier and Sailor Words and Phrases* Lond. Routledge). (See also quots.) —1941 *Pop. Sci.* Aug. p. 79. To blast a path through enemy wire, a Bangalore torpedo—a length of pipe filled with explosive, is shoved under it . . . 1942 *Read. Dig.* Dec. p. 82/1-2. 1943 *Fortune* Feb. p. 124/1 The bangalore, named for the city in India where a clever British officer invented it, consists of sections of pipe about six feet long and packed with TNT. One section fits in the end of another, so that soldiers can push a continuous length of 200 feet through a mine field and barbed-wire entanglement. When the bangalore goes off most of the mines for three feet on each side of it explode, and the barbed wire is blasted away. 1944 B'ham *News* 25 Apr. p. 9 (AP.) *Ibid.* 7 July p. 4/3-4 (AP.).

BLOCKBUSTER, BLOCK-BUSTER, BLOCK BUSTER. 'An air bomb large enough to knock down a whole block of houses' 1944 (Mencken *Am. Sp.* Feb. p. 8/1); from one to four tons in weight.—1942 *Time* 14 Sept. p. 56. *Newsweek* 21 Sept. p. 25 The first group of mighty four-engined Lancasters hit Düsseldorf with 2-ton 'block-busters.' 1943 *Nebraska*

Alumnus Oct. (Adv.) It takes a block-buster only a few seconds to fall from a high-flying U.S. bomber to its bull's eye on Berlin . . .

2. *Fig.* A bombshell (*fig.*).—1943 *Read. Dig.* Mar. p. 25/2 The board's refusal to defer such men hit the railroads with the force of a triple block-buster. *Sat. Rev. Lit.* 30 Oct. p. 40/1. 1944 *Time* 12 June p. 11/1 The President then quietly dropped his blockbuster. *b.* 1943 *Lad. Home Jour.* Nov. p. 116 The day was an emotional block buster for them all. 1944 Tuscaloosa *News* 7 July p. 4/3 (AP.) . . . they are now starting to wonder openly if the administration isn't supplying the opposition with a few political block-busters in the handling of foreign policy. *Time* 17 July pp. 22/3.

CUT-BACK, CUTBACK. *'Gardening.* A plant which has been pruned by cutting off shoots close back to the main stem.' OED [1897-]. + 'A sharp cut in the production of raw materials or manufactured goods, as for the armed services, due to a sudden or unforeseen lessening of demand.' 1944 (*New Intern. Yearbook for 1943*).—1943 *The Iron Age* 6 May p. 152 More than 90 per cent of prime contractors holding Army ordnance contracts are now operating . . . below capacity because of recent cut-backs in ordnance contracts . . . 1944 *Cur. Hist.* Jan. p. 14. *Time* 12 June p. 14/1. B'ham *News-Age-Her.* 2 July p. 4-A/3 (AP.) Sharp cut-backs in war contracts . . . will be paralleled by cut-backs in the war-swollen membership lists of the labor unions.

DRY RUN. Something done for practice only, as a dress rehearsal. 1942 (Colby *Army Talk*).—1941 *Am. Sp.* Oct. p. 165/1. 1943 New Haven *Register* 1 Aug. p. 9/1. *Sat. Eve. Post* 27 Nov. p. 12 She had to locate his pulse, get her watch ready and make a couple of dry runs. 1944 *Lad. Home Jour.* June p. 31/1 . . . hundreds of dry runs—simulated bombings in which no bombs are actually dropped.

FESTUNG EUROPA. (*Ger.* Fortress Europe, q. v.)—1942 *Nation* 19 Dec. p. 682/1 Before long Fortress Europe (*Festung Europa*) will be as familiar a term as Blitzkrieg or the second front. *Newsweek* 28 Dec. p. 44/1. 1943 *Time* 20 Sept. p. 34/1. 1944 *Sat. Eve. Post* 27 May p. 12/1. *Harper's* July (Adv.) 100 hours before the dawn of D-Day, . . . Murrow . . . made the first broadcast from a bomber over Festung Europa.

+FLAT-TOP. An American perennial herb. 1817-8–. +An aircraft carrier. Also attrib.—1942 Pratt *The Navy Has Wings* (Harper & Bros.) p. 190 'Scratch one flat-top,' Commander Dixon's voice had shouted . . . through the ship's radio . . . 1943 Tuscaloosa *News* 15 Dec. p. 4 (AP.). *Sat. Eve. Post.* 18 Dec. p. 100/2. 1944 Tuscaloosa *News* 21 Feb. p. 1/1 . . . the navy has accumulated enough flat-top strength for a . . . two-day assault . . .

FORTRESS EUROPE. Europe within its outer defences, described by Nazis as a fortress. Goebbels hoped the idea might help discourage the Allies and force them into a peace. See *Festung Europa.*—1942 *Nation* 19 Dec. p. 682 . . . it was the Italian press which first launched the idea of *Fortress Europe* . . . 1943 New Haven *Eve. Regist.* 7 Aug. p. 5/4 The so-called fortress of Europe is threatened . . . 1944 *Sat. Eve. Post* 27 May p. 12/1 . . . we shall still face the real problem of Fortress Europe, the penetration of the German mind.

GRASSHOPPER*. +Name given to high-winged cabin monoplanes of the tandem type. Low landing and take-off speeds enable them to be operated from small fields. They are equipped with two-way radio. (See quots.)—1942 *Pop. Sci.* Jan. p. 63 Grasshoppers, new odd-job army planes (quoted *Read. Guide*). 1943 Colby *Army Talk* PUDDLE JUMPER. Slow airplane used for observation of limited areas and for message carrying between headquarters, and for checking positions of front-line troops. Its low flight gives it this name, but it is also called a 'grasshopper,' and this more widely. 1944 Tuscaloosa *News* 17 Feb. p. 4/4 (AP.). B'ham *News—Age-Her.* 19 Mar. p. 14-A. *Sat. Eve. Post* 1 Apr. p. 6 Grasshoppers Over the Caissons.

+LIE DETECTOR. Popular name for the polygraph, used as an aid in obtaining confessions from those suspected of crimes. When one lies, his fear of detection is recorded on the machine. Great skill and care are required in its use.—1931 *Lit. Dig.* 26 Dec. p. 35 The Lie-Detector. [¶] An interesting device, with great possibilities . . . 1935 *Forum* Jan. p. 15/1. 1938 *Amer. City* May p. 15. 1944 *Sat. Eve. Post* 15 Apr. p. 9/3 Keeler calls the machine the 'polygraph'. . . . He and other scientists don't like the name 'lie detector.' . . . But the term 'lie detector' is here to stay.

MAE WEST, *n.* Also attrib. (See quots.)—1940 *Read. Dig.* May p. 39 . . . Mae West for a life jacket. 1941 N. Y. *Times Mag.* 27 July p. 21/2 One can understand much more easily why an airman's life-belt should be a 'Mae West.' It fits over the shoulders and gives the wearer a somewhat feminine figure. 1942 Parry *War Dict.* . . . the bulging padded uniform used by U. S. aviators. Also a life preserver. 1943 *Read. Dig.* June p. 125/1. 1944 *Life* 12 June p. 117 Airman is kept afloat by his 'Mae West' life belt . . .

OBLITERATION BOMBING. Blotting out by concentrated bombing.—1943 Lond. *Spect.* 24 Sept. p. 289 'Obliteration' bombing. H. J. C. Grierson *ibid.* 8 Oct. p. 337. 1944 Balto. *Sun* 9 Mar. p. 8/2 The most frequent answer . . . is that even 'obliteration bombing' is morally justifiable if it serves to shorten the war and to save human lives . . . Tuscaloosa *News* 20 Mar. p. 6/1 (AP.). *Sat. Rev. Lit.* 8 Apr. p. 14/1 . . . Vera Brittain, has become the spearhead of a movement . . . directed against the mass air attacks of enemy cities, which she describes as 'obliteration bombings.'

OPEN CITY. [Cf. OED s. v. *open* adj. 3 and quot. *c.* 825 *Urbs patens*, open burh.] 'A city declared to be unfortified or undefended and hence, under international law, exempt from enemy bombardment.' 1942 (Parry *War Dict.*)—1939 N. Y. *Times* 18 Sept. p. 5/5 (AP.) President Moscicki said his message was in reply to Mr. Roosevelt's message, 'in which you recommend that open cities must not be bombed.' 1940 *ibid.* 14 June p. 1/6-7. 1942 *Time* 5 Jan. p. 20/3. 1944 *Newsweek* 12 June p. 24/1-2 Lt. Gen. . . . Clark . . . reached the outskirts of Rome and then held his fire for three hours to permit the Germans to withdraw in accordance with their self-proclaimed designation of Rome as an open city.

+SEABEE. (See quots.)—1942 Springfield *Eve. Union* 18 Mar. p. 24 The word 'seabees' will be used by the Navy to designate newly-formed construction battalions. 1943 *Look* 6 Apr. p. 32 These white-capped Builders are the Seabees (C. B.'s—Construction Battalions) . . . they're all specialists—mechanics, welders, carpenters, metalsmiths, skilled in some 60 trades. 1944 *Harper's* May p. 567/2 That night our transports left the bay, which tells its own story of how fast and well the Seabees had worked to unload them.

TASK FORCE. A group of different types of naval vessels ordered to carry out a specific job or task. Sometimes applied to land operations.—1942 Harsch *Germany at War* (N. Y.: For. Pol. Ass'n) p. 43 Another important . . . ingredient of German military success is the system of organizing an offensive. It begins on the planning sheets with a particular campaign. The High Command . . . selects the man it considers best qualified for the particular operation. That man then proceeds to gather around him what is called a 'task force.' He becomes responsible for the whole operation . . . Such operations usually require naval and air forces as well as land forces. 1942 *Time* 6 Apr. p. 25/1 The task force crept up before dawn . . . 1943 *Fortune* Feb. p. 124/1 Now is the time for the assault squad—the small task force . . .—to play its part. 1944 *Life* 8 May p. 22/3 The Americans just did not have enough carriers to defend a task force and attack at the same time.

WALKIE (-EE, -Y)-TALKIE (-EE, -Y). 'Portable radio receiving and sending apparatus.' 1941 (*Am. Sp.* Oct. p. 169/2). See *handie-talkie*, *Am. Sp.* Dec. 1943 p. 303/1.—1940 *Newsweek* 18 Nov. p. 40. 1941 *Nat. Geog. Mag.* July p. 31 Smaller outfits carried by one soldier are known in Army slang as *'walkee-talkees.'* 1942 *Time* 28 Sept. p. 46/2. 1943 Tregaskis *Guadalcanal Diary* (Random House) p. 209. 1944 *Life* 3 July p. 12/1 Above the noise of hundreds of bombs . . . , his voice barked through the walkie-talkie . . .

WORKSHOP*, *n.* Also attrib. +An informal study-group organized to permit teachers to apply the principles of progressive education to the solution of their own educational problems. (See first quot.) —1937 N.Y. *Times* 1 Aug. VI p. 5/3 The major requirement for admission to this Summer workshop is an approved project for which the applicant seeks aid and advice. Under the guidance of twenty-five personal advisers, trained in the arts of curriculum designing and evaluation, the teacher-students meet daily from 8:30 to 10 each morning for group discussions and later in the day for private conferences. *Ibid.* p. 5/4 Regarding the importance of the workshop idea to American education, Wilford M. Aikin . . . said . . . 1944 *Mus. Amer.* 25 Mar. p. 28. B'ham *News* 24 May p. 18/2 Language teachers . . . met in the language workshop at Birmingham-Southern College . . . *Ibid.* 30 May p. 16/1.

+V-MAIL. (See quot. 1944.)—1942 N.Y. *Times* 13 June p. 17/6 The new V-Mail for United States overseas forces, patterned after the British microfilm postal system, was started when letters were delivered to President Roosevelt today . . . *Fortune* Nov. p. 72 Last March the War Department launched V-Mail Service . . . 1944 *Sat. Eve. Post* p. 37 (Adv.) What's the secret of V-Mail? By photography on micro-film, your hand-written letter shrinks from page to postage-stamp size. Now a miniature—it crosses the ocean. Enlarged overseas, the letter becomes readable V-Mail . . .

AMONG THE NEW WORDS

I. WILLIS RUSSELL
University of Alabama

AMONG THE several outstanding events of 1944, the invasion of Europe and the Germans' first secret weapon are especially noteworthy. The first event has acquainted a large portion of the English-speaking world with two new terms: *D day*, which is discussed in the glossary; and *H hour*. Some readers may be surprised to learn that *H hour* is recorded in the 1934 NID (*Webster's*): *'Mil., U. S.* The time at which a planned operation is to be begun;—used when the exact clock hour is kept secret till the latest moment. See ZERO HOUR.' Indeed *H hour* is found as early as the 1927 New Words Section of NID, though there the discussion is under *zero*. For some reason *H hour* was popularized much earlier than *D day;* the beginnings of this popularizing can be seen in a passage cited by C. Alphonso Smith in his *New Words Self-Defined* (New York: Doubleday, Page, 1919, pp. 104-5): 1918 Baltimore *Star* 17 Sept. ' "Zero hour" and "over the top" are expressions which have passed from the American Army after long popularity with the British. [¶]America's attack in the Lorraine sector has brought out typical American expressions. [¶]"Over the top" is now "the jump off" and "zero hour" has changed to "H hour." '

When, about ten days after D day, the first buzz bombs hurtled over the English Channel into southern England, the fearful amazement as to what the 'things' were was accompanied by equal puzzlement as to what the 'things' should be called. Now that the names *buzz bomb, flying bomb, robot, robot bomb, robomb,* and *V-1* seem pretty well established, it may be interesting and instructive to look at some of the first reactions. Only a few days after the first onslaught of the robot bombs, an AP dispatch in the Birmingham *Age-Herald* of 20 June 1944 stated:

> Adolph Hitler's new 'secret weapon'—the pilotless plane or rocket bomb—already has more names than . . . Goering has medals, and others are being added daily. . .
> 'Buzz bomb' and 'winged comet' seem to be the catchiest names offered in Britain thus far, though London headline writers have contributed such descriptive titles as 'Bumble Bomb,' 'Flying Bomb' and 'Whirley.'
> 'Robot raider' is a favorite with some who like alliteration, while P-Plane also has attained some popularity.
> German propaganda broadcasts have come up with some fetching names such as 'Hell Hound,' 'Hell Dog,' 'Dynamite Meteor,' and 'Kivik Rocket.' Just what the latter means is not clear.

According to *Newsweek* (26 June 1944 p. 24), 'Officially, the British called them pilotless planes.' 'The German public,' it added, 'continued to use the term *Wuwa*, short for *Wunderwaffe*, or wonder weapon.' Other terms used were *doodle* (*Newsweek* 14 Aug. 1944 p. 35/1) and *doodlebug*, though the latter, in the words of *Time* (24 July 1944 p. 26/1), 'was frowned on as too flippant. Most Londoners called the bombs "those things." '

One of the remarks of the AP writer already quoted suggests an analysis of the names. Those who like alliteration, he wrote, use the terms *Robot raider* and *P-Plane*. To this group of alliteratives should be added, of course, *pilotless plane, bumble bomb,* and *buzz bomb*.

Evidently one of the most distinctive as well as most awe-inspiring characteristics of the bomb is its low humming sound. As one correspondent wrote, 'The planes have a distinctive rhythmic note, giving the effect of a pulsating, low throb.' Hence the onomatopoeic names *bumble bomb, buzz bomb,* possibly *Whirley,* though the latter sounds more like an attempt to laugh it off. *Rocket bomb, rocket plane,* and *winged comet* seem to have been suggested by the speed of the bomb. The shape of the buzz bomb likewise accounts for those terms containing the word *plane* or *airplane* (*Read. Dig.* Sept. 1944 p. 86/1).

Most influential on the imaginations of the name-givers, however, have been two facts: these things are destructive bombs and they are automatically piloted. From the first there was an impersonality, an inhumanity, an irresponsibility about the bombs that angered the British public. Whether or not any of the word coiners knew of the robots in Capek's play makes interesting speculation. At any rate, this aspect of the bomb is frequently expressed in the names *robot bomb, robot bomber* (*Time* 26 June 1944 p. 66/3), *robot raider, robot airplane,* and *robot plane.* The word *bomb,* as is to be expected, appears in several combinations: *buzz bomb, flying bomb, robot bomb,* and *flitter bomb* (*Ladies' Home Journal* Oct. 1944 p. 13/1).

Several other types of word formation are illustrated. Shortening appears in *fly-bomb* (from *flying bomb*), *doodle* (from *doodlebug*), and *P-Plane* (from *pilotless plane*). *Robot* (for *robot bomb*) illustrates ellipsis. It is perhaps worthy of comment that *robot* is never used unless one of the other terms, usually *robot bomb,* has been employed. This crop of names has produced only one blend, which is *robomb.* It seems possible that several of the terms reveal attempts not to appear over-awed. *Doodle* (*doodlebug*), *Whirley, Bob 'Ope,* and *Beeloo* may all exemplify this state of mind. *Beeloo* appears in a letter from Dorothy Black in England: 'Hitler's flying Beeloo's come whiffling over from time to time' (*Ladies' Home Journal* Sept. 1944 p. 13/2). As for Bob 'Ope: 'London cockneys called the robots "Bob 'Opes." Grown-ups . . . learned the derivation: "Bob down and 'ope for the best"' (*Newsweek* 7 Aug. 1944 p. 29).

Acknowledgement is made for citations used in the preceding section and in the glossary. Mr. Henry Alexander has provided three, including the earliest for *robomb;* Mr. Dwight L. Bolinger four; Mr. James B. McMillan one (the AP dispatch on names for the robot bomb quoted above); Miss Mamie J. Meredith six; and Mr. Peter Tamony three, including the earliest citations for *featherbed* and SHAEF.

The practice of sometimes giving references without the citation is limited to those sources readily available.

Although John Gunther's *D Day* (New York and London: Harper and Brothers) is dated 1944 in the *Cumulative Book Index* and in the Library of Congress file, the copy from which citations in the glossary have been drawn bears two copyright dates, 1943 and 1944. The earlier date, 1943, has been used.

SYMBOLS: The symbol + before a word or definition indicates an Americanism. A date immediately following a word or definition indicates the time of evidence shown in the DAE, or, if so stated, in another publication. Dates in brackets indicate the time, etc., of British usage. An asterisk after a word indicates that the word is illustrated in British usage before 1600.

AIRPARK, AIR PARK. See first two quots.—1944 Tuscaloosa *News* 26 July p. 2/7 (AP) 'Airparks,' the ATS said, would be small landing fields in or near communities for the use of private flyers. Two runways, approximately 2,000 feet long and 300 to 500 feet wide, would be arranged in 'L,' 'T,' or 'X' form. Birmingham *News* 26 July p. 10/1 As the name suggests, the airparks would be attractively landscaped to add to the beauty of the community rather than detract from it. Tuscaloosa *News* 27 Aug. p. 3/2 Cities and towns should begin with an airpark and 'let it grow in keeping with community needs,' he said. *Time* 28 Aug. p. 62 (Adv.) . . . Your Cessna travel will be facilitated by air parks . . . which most wide-awake communities are already planning. Tuscaloosa *News* 1 Sept. p. 8/1 'To sell, service and maintain [450] airplanes at one airpark would require four salesmen, six dispatchers, six gas- and oil-service men, 23 mechanics and other employees . . . *Sat. Eve. Post* 7 Oct. p. 70/3 The CAA is beating the drum for 3000 new airports, most of them 'air parks,' for private fliers.

BUZZ-, BUZZ, FLYING BOMB. A robot bomb. (Also attrib.)—1944 Birmingham *News* 17 June p. 1/1 (AP) RAF Spitfire pilots . . . were diving through terrific fire from their own ack-ack guns in bids to destroy these new German buzz-bombs. *Ibid.* 17 June p. 1/1 (AP) At least three persons were killed and others injured by one of the flying bombs . . . *Newsweek* 21 Aug. p. 31/3 Then the buzz bombs sped in again . . . Lond. *Spectator* 7 July p. 4/1. *Sat. Eve. Post* 30 Sept. p. 34/3 He dropped to the ground as the buzz bomb exploded fifty feet away . . . Birmingham *News* 5 Aug. p. 1/2 [Headline] Buzz Bomb Assaults on England Resumed. *Read. Dig.* Sept. p. 86/1 The robot airplane or flying bomb unleashed by Hitler against England is neither a mere 'new weapon' nor yet an irresistible weapon which will decide the war. Tuscaloosa *News* 10 July p. 1/8 (AP) The evacuation of women and children from London and various cities in southern England continued in orderly fashion today as the German flying bomb offensive went into its 26th day.

D-DAY, D DAY. (The capitalization of this term varies: *D-Day, D-day, D Day.*) See quot. 9 May 1944. (Also attrib.)—1. *General.* 1942 Parry *War Dictionary.* 1943 Gunther *D Day* p. 165 Already people are talking about when the next D Day is to be. 1944 *Time* 27 Mar. p. 68 (quoting Hanson W. Baldwin) '. . . inefficient leaders [must be replaced] with good leadership . . . to build up a pride of outfit in . . . the divisions that on the war's greatest D-day will hold the future in their hands.' Birmingham *News* 9 May p. 1/8 (AP) The term 'D-Day' . . . is an army expression used to refer to, but not reveal, the time fixed for a military action such as an attack on a local front or the start of an invasion. *Life* 26 June p. 26.

2. *Specific.* 1918 Field Order No. 8, First Army, A. E. F. 7 Sept. The First Army will attack at H-Hour on D-Day with the object of forcing the evacuation of St. Mihiel salient (quoted 1944 *Time* 12 June p. 2). 1942 *Newsweek* 23 Nov. p. 27 And this weakening of the line in the east may bring about a major Russian offensive long in preparation abiding the eventful D-day. 1943 Gunther *D Day* p. 57 *Malta, Saturday,* July 10.— . . . it is D Day at last. 1944 *Sat. Rev. Lit.* 18 Mar. p. 13/2. *Newsweek* 22 May p. 22/1 But the atmosphere behind Allied lines was electric, for May 11 was D day . . . Tuscaloosa *News* 22 June p. 1/7 (AP) Secretary Stimson reported today that army casualties through June 6 (which would include D-Day) totaled 178,677 . . . *Sat. Eve. Post* 8 July p. 22/1 That would mean that McCook would be transferred from the D-day first team . . .

3. *In combinations.* a. D(-day) minus one (1), etc. The day before *D Day,* etc.—1944 *Time* 12 June p. 85/3 On D-day minus one, a happy Wall Streeter cried . . . 1943 Gunther *D Day* p. 114 'My God,' uttered Poole, 'I haven't seen bread since D Minus 1!'

b. D-day plus one, D-day-plus-one, etc. The first day after D Day, etc.—1944 *Life* 19 June p. 34 By the afternoon of D-day plus one the battle of this beachhead was already the most desperate of the invasion. *Sat. Eve. Post* 30 Sept. p. 6/2 The time is D-day-plus-one off the beach of Provence.

DUCK. See quot. Oct. 30, 1943.—1943 *Time* 21 June p. 68 The soldiers' name for this is the 'duck.' *Sat. Eve. Post.* 30 Oct. p. 7 Christened 'Ducks' by soldiers, these new vehicles are actually 2½-ton trucks, propeller-driven in the water, with six-wheel drives which carry them at high speeds on land. Gunther *D Day* p. 73 We slid down the ladder and this time boarded a duck . . . 1944 *Newsmap* 21 Feb. Vol. II 44 F. Duck—Amphibian truck (2½-ton) is popularly known as the 'Duck' . . . Birmingham *News* 25 Apr. p. 1 Amphibious 'Ducks' ply between this Allied ship and shore . . .

FEATHERBED, *adj.* [cf. DAE, *featherbed soldier,* a soldier who has a soft or easy time. {1837-}]. Pertaining to featherbedding. See also first 1943 quot.—1938 San Francisco *Examiner* 3 June p. 25/1 But he does feel that 'featherbed jobs'—he cites one involving wages at the rate of $4.37 per hour, equal to $10,920 a year for a 48-hour week—should be abolished. 1941 *Traffic World* 7 June p. 1435/2 It is to be made by men . . . who are also the beneficiaries of many so-called 'featherbed' rules by reason of which they secure large payments for doing very little work and in many instances for doing no work at all. 1943 *Newsweek* 20 Sept. p. 74/3 Featherbed rules are, for the most part, the result of organized labor's attempts to protect itself against unemployment resulting from technological advancements. In the railroad industry they are directed, for instance, against reduced employment resulting from faster trains. 1943 *Read. Dig.* Mar. p. 26/2 The so-called 'featherbed' rules are written into labor contracts enforced by the National Railroad Adjustment Board. *Newsweek* 20 Sept. p. 72/3 Earlier McNear himself had issued a report contrasting the difference between the government's featherbed operation of T.P. & W. in 1943 and the road's non-featherbed operation under private management in 1941. 1944 *Britannica Book of the Year* FEATHERBED RULES. Union regulations to accomplish featherbedding.

FEATHERBEDDING, *n.* See 1944 quot.—1943 *Read. Dig.* Mar. p. 26/2 For the unions, featherbedding has become an established business procedure; it makes more jobs for more members who pay more dues. *Ibid.* June p. 114/2 . . . arbitrary union rules limit workmen's output; 'featherbedding'—making work for more employees—is rampant [in shipyards]. *Newsweek* 20 Sept. p. 72/2 And what was Eastman's record since he restored featherbedding on McNear's tiny T.P. & W? 1944 *Britannica Book of the Year* FEATHERBEDDING. The limiting of work or output in order to spread jobs and thus prevent unemployment.

FLYING BOMB. See BUZZ BOMB.

MOMENTARILY. For a moment [1654-66]. Momently, at any moment.—1944 *Musical America* 25 Mar. p. 7/4 An addition to the family . . . is expected momentarily. *Time* 22 May p. 66/2 Captain Robert Johnson . . . momentarily expected home on leave . . . Tuscaloosa *News* 6 July p. 1/6 (AP) . . . Mitchell . . . said two high speed drills were expected momentarily. Birmingham *News* 29 July p. 1/7 (AP) The message came as a great shock to the flier's parents, . . . who had been expecting word momentarily that their son . . . was on the way back to the United States. *Time* 9 Oct. p. 27/3 China's exhausted, tattered soldiers fingered their last handfuls of cartridges, momentarily expecting attack by enemy patrols.

OSCAR. 1. A small gold statuette awarded annually by the Academy of Motion Picture Arts and Sciences for the best performance, production, direction, photography, and similar accomplishments of the year.—1936 *Time* 16 Mar. p. 56/2-3 Awkward moments occurred at last week's ceremony when neither Director Ford nor Screenwriter Nichols appeared to claim their prizes—small gold statuettes which Hollywood calls 'Oscars.' 1937 *Time* 15 Mar. p. 33/1 Oscars of 1937. 1940 *Newsweek* 11 Mar. p. 34/1 . . . the English Vivien Leigh won an Academy statuette—known as an 'Oscar'—for the best performance by an actress. 1944 *Ladies' Home Journal* Sep. p. 97/2 When Greer Garson was given the coveted gold Oscar for the ripe charm she loaned the cinematic Mrs. Miniver, a newspaper in London announced: 'English girl wins Hollywood award.'

2. *Fig.* A symbol of excellence.—1941 *Time* (Air Exp. Ed.) 2 June p. 25/3 That these trials . . . did not keep [movie-] producer Gabriel Pascal from turning out a polished and distinguished product is a transcendent Oscar in the onetime cavalryman's lap. 1944 *Ladies' Home Journal* Jan. p. 94 Stir in the drama, toss in the glamour, and you can produce [salad] 'bowls' at home that will rate you four stars if not an Oscar. *Woman's Day* June p. 53/1 If I had to select one performance out of all the excellent ones given, I suppose I would have to give the Oscar to Roman Bohnen . . .

ROBOMB. [*Robot* + *Bomb*]. A robot bomb.—1944 Toronto *Saturday Night* 22 July Germany's robombs another case of 'too little and too late.' *Time* 7 Aug. p. 26/1 But by now most Londoners were convinced that they were in for something infernally worse: a rocket-propelled robomb . . . Baltimore *Sun* 17 Aug. p. 3/4-5 [Headline] Robomb Lands in Street Scene . . . *Time* 21 Aug. p. 28.

ROBOT. 'Any automatic apparatus or device that performs functions ordinarily ascribed to human beings, or operates with what appears to be almost human intelligence; esp. such an apparatus that is started by means of radiant energy or sound waves.' 1934 (NID). *Specif.* A robot bomb. (Also attrib.)—1944 Birmingham *News* 17 June p. 2/5 While everyone is speculating about the robots, this much seems to be agreed—that they have high speed, a bright red light tail, spit flames from their exhaust, fly on a straight low course, and hum rhythmically like a motorboat. *Newsweek* 10 July p. 30/2 The robot attackers . . . now came in incendiary form . . . *Read. Dig.* Sept. p. 86/1 The German robot is no surprise to military men and engineers. *Sat. Eve. Post.* 30 Sept. p. 34/1 The metal casing of the robot was so light that there was no fragmentation worth mentioning.

ROBOT BOMB, PLANE. A self-propelled bomb, shaped like an airplane, with a wing spread of 16 feet and a small tail surface, operated by a jet propulsion engine and piloted through a gyrocompass control box. Launched like a rocket from specially constructed installations, it has a speed of over 300 m. p. h. and a maximum range of 150 miles. When the fuel of the bomb burns out and it hits something, the one ton or more of explosive loaded in the iron tube which composes its main body is set off. (*Robot bomb* is used attrib.).—1944 N. Y. *Times* 25 June p. 4E/1-2 [Headline] Germans' Robot Bomb Is a Potential Menace. Birmingham *News* 17 June p. 1/1 (AP) Germany's new explosive robot planes . . . struck blindly in parts of Southern England . . . Montgomery *Advertiser* 2 July p. 1/7 (UP) Observers here who have dodged the robot bombs . . . are convinced now that a second type of bomb has been launched by the Germans. Tuscaloosa *News* 10 July p. 1/8 (AP) It was a noisy night as the Germans took advantage of overcast skies over Dover stait [*sic*] to sneak their robot planes through the defense wall. *Newsweek* 10 July p. 30/3 The preventive demolition cut down the effectiveness of the robot-bomb attack when it materialized . . . *Read. Dig.* Sept. p. 86/1 Lawrence Sperry made encouraging tests with a robot plane . . . in 1918.

SHAEF [ʃef]. See quots. (Also attrib.) —1944 San Francisco *Call Bulletin* 14 June p. 1/7-8 SHAEF, June 14 (AP). Lincoln (Nebr.) *Evening Journal* 12 May (Ernie Pyle). The newest and most frequently heard [new term] is SHAEF . . . It is SHAEF that is planning and will direct the invasion. *Life* 12 June p. 100 SHAEF stands for Supreme Headquarters Allied Expeditionary Force, is pronounced 'Shafe' and in practice is both a place and a command. Birmingham *News* 5 Aug. p. 1/7 (AP) She is secretary to a general in SHAEF headquarters . . . *Ibid.* 9 Aug. p. 1/6—SHAEF Report.

SORTIE. A dash or sally by a besieged garrison upon an investing force. [1795-]. See quots., esp. 1944 *Britannica Book of the Year.*—1943 *Time* 17 May p. 27/1 In two days Allied bombers and fighters flew 3,700 sorties (a sortie is one mission by one plane). Tuscaloosa *News* 10 Sept. p. 1/7 (AP) More than 1,000 sorties—individual plane flights—were flown by Flying Fortresses, Liberators, Marauders and Thunderbolts . . . Gunther *D Day* p. 88 There were one hundred and eighty Nazi sorties yesterday and they did some damage. 1944 Tuscaloosa *News* 26 Mar. p. 2/2 (AP) In those 60 hours nearly 7,000 sorties (individual flights) have been flown against Germany from the west . . . *Britannica Book of the Year* SORTIE. An operational flight by one military aircraft. Each return to base for replenishment is counted as the end of one sortie.

V-1. A robot bomb. See first quot.—1944 *Newsweek* 10 July p. 30/1 The Germans officially call the robots V-1—*Vergeltungswaffe, Ein*, or Vengeance Weapon 1. Tuscaloosa *News* 11 July p. 4/5 (AP) . . . Hitler is known to have other vengeance weapons than the V-1. *Life* 24 July p. 20. *Time* 7 Aug. p. 26/1 The worst that one V-1 flying bomb could do was done in London last week. Lond. *Spectator* 18 Aug. p. 144/1.

WAR TIME. See quot. 1942 *Time.*—1942 Topeka *Capitol* 6 Feb. p. 9 Crown Drug Store . . . will operate on WAR TIME (Daylight Saving). *Time* 9 Feb. p. 12/3 Franklin Roosevelt decided what he will call wartime daylight saving when it starts next week. Official name: War Time. 1944 Birmingham *News* 18 July p. 1/8 (AP) One medium-sized cargo vessel being loaded went up with a thundering roar at 10:19 p. m., Pacific War Time. Tuscaloosa *News* 19 July p. 1/4 (AP) U. S. government monitors said that Domei . . . had instructed the Japanese press to 'be certain to receive' the important news at 9:30 a. m., Eastern War Time, today.

AMONG THE NEW WORDS

I. WILLIS RUSSELL
University of Alabama

In 'Among the New Words' for October, 1944, attention was called to the adding of a past participial adjective to different nouns to form various combinations used as adjectives. Then came the sentence, 'The war has brought forward two others, *-based* and *-borne*, which are being freely used in the formation of compounds.' This statement, a friend recently commented, unfortunately implies that these two past participial adjectives are new in the ranks of those regularly used in combinations. It seems advisable, therefore, at the risk of some repetition, to return to the subject and modify this implication. It is also possible to add some new combinations.

Though *borne* is not entered in either NID or Funk and Wagnalls, it is discussed in the OED, s. v. *borne*, ppl. a., where it is defined as 'Carried, sustained, endured, etc. Used attrib. chiefly in such constructions as "patiently borne injuries," the "breeze-borne note".' The only citation is 'The shard-borne beetle' from *Macbeth*, 1605, and no additional citations occur in the OED Sup. The OED's citations for *airborne, seaborne,* and *water-borne,* however, suggest a continuous history down to the present.

Following is a revised list of combinations with *borne: airborne* (OED 1641-), *beetle-borne* (*Life* 11 Sept. 1944 p. 225), *carrier-borne* (*Am. Sp.* Oct. 1944 p. 225), *chairborne* (*Yank* 12 Nov. 1943 p. 15/3), *footborne* (Gunther *D Day* 1943 p. 81), *glider-borne (Am. Sp. loc. cit.), insect-borne* (*Time* 6 Mar. 1944 p. 62/3), *mule-borne (Am. Sp. loc. cit.), rat-borne* (*TN* 4 Dec. 1944 p. 3/4 AP), *road-borne (Am. Sp. loc. cit.), seaborne* (OED 1823-), *sky-borne* (NID *sky-born*), *water-borne* (OED 1702-).

In its sense of 'established as a base, *based* is not in the OED, the NID, or Funk and Wagnalls. The OED Sup. includes it with one citation from 1925. No mention is made of its use in combinations in this sense, though there is an entry for *shore-based* with a citation from 1927. The recorded evidence for this sense of *based* in combinations, therefore, is comparatively recent. Its popularity seemingly dates from the present war.

A revised list of combinations with *based* follows. As with the combinations with *borne,* two or more citations for some of them are on file. *Aleutian-based* (B'ham *News–Age-Her.* 24 Dec. 1944 p. One-A/1 AP), *Australia-based* (*Time* 19 Feb. 1945 p. 88/3), *Britain-based* (*BN* 27 May 1944 p. 1/6 AP), *carrier-based* (*Am. Sp.* Oct. 1944 p. 224), *fleet-based (ibid.), homebased* (*TN* 3 Aug. 1944 p. 1/6 AP), *India-based* (*Am. Sp. loc. cit.*), *Italy-based (ibid.), land-based (ibid.), Leyte-based* (*BN* 25 Nov. 1944 p. 1/1 AP), *Marianas-based* (*BN* 19 Jan. 1945 p. 1/2 AP), *Marshalls-based* (*TN* 30 July 1944 p. 1/3 AP), *Mediterranean-based* (*TN* 12 Nov. 1943 p. 1/6 AP), *Panama-based* (*Sat. Eve. Post* 2 Dec. 1944 p. 90/3), *Philippine-based* (*TN* 22 Jan. 1945 p. 1/1AP), *Russia-based* (*BN* 27 June 1944 p. 1/6), *Saipan-based* (*Time* 11 Dec. 1944 p. 66/2), *shore-based* (OED Sup. 1927).

In 'Among the New Words' for December, 1944, *momentarily,* in the sense of 'momently, at any moment,' was listed with several 1944 citations. But this sense of the word is older. Professor Atcheson L. Hench has already called attention to his note on this sense of the word in *American Speech* 4:187-188, where he lists a citation under date 1928. He notes, among other matters of interest, that *momentarily* in this sense occurs with the verb *expect.*

A belated acknowledgment is owed Professor Hench for a citation used in 'Among the New Words' for December, 1944. For the present issue thanks for citations are due the following: Dwight L. Bolinger (2), H. F. Cotter (1), Ralph Hagedorn (1), Mamie J. Meredith (8), Allen Walker Read (2), Peter Tamony (4). The definitions of *airstrip* and *fighter strip* were derived from material kindly supplied by Mr. Kent Cooper, of the Associated Press. Col. Elvin R. Heiberg, AAF, Washington, supplied the information on *landing strip* and *strip.* According to Col. Heiberg, *airstrip* is not an AAF term, but *landing strip* is.

To conserve space, the abbreviation *'BN'* is used for the Birmingham (Ala.) *News* and *'TN'* for the Tuscaloosa (Ala.) *News.*

SYMBOLS: The symbol + before a word or definition indicates an Americanism. A date immediately following a word or definition indicates the time of evidence shown in the DAE, or, if so stated, in another publication. Dates in brackets indicate the time, etc., of British usage. An asterisk after a word indicates that the word is illustrated in British usage before 1600.

ACTIVATE. 'To make active, move to activity.' [1626-]. +See quots.—1941 Springfield *Republican* 15 Jan. p. 1 Numerous air corps squadrons . . . will be 'activated' at Langley field . . . this morning . . . 1942 *Time* 23 Feb. p. 45 When the Sixth Armored Division was activated (Army for 'hatched') at Fort Knox last week, the Army let it be known that the Armored Force now has two armored corps. . . 1943 N. Y. *Times* 24 Oct. p. 8E/4 . . . activate . . . It means to get busy, to go into action, or, more simply, to begin. 1944 *Time* 25 Dec. p. 21/1 Basic unit of the Volkssturm is the four-company battalion, but brigades and divisions may be activated when it becomes capable of disposing bigger units.

AIR STRIP, AIRSTRIP. A hurriedly-prepared strip of land for temporary use by landing aircraft, usually fighter planes. —1942 *Newsweek* 7 Dec. p. 27 Then . . . further airstrips for landing the transport planes were built by the troops as they went along the jungle trails . . . 1944 *Time* 7 Feb. p. 85. *Sat. Eve. Post* 29 April p. 23/3 . . . the Seabees went into the lagoon, laid four causeways for repairing the air strip. *BN* 25 July p. 1/1 (AP) Marines and Army Infantry met stronger opposition on Guam, . . . but isolated an airstrip . . . Lincoln (Neb.) *Telephone News* Dec. p. 5 On this island it was the Sea Bees who took and held the main air strip.

AMTRAC, AMPHTRACK. See first quot.—1944 B'ham *News–Age-Her.* 2 April p. 9-A (AP) A small American force . . . moved ashore . . . in amtracs (amphibious tractors) and boats. *Nat'l. Geog.* July p. 11. *Newsweek* 7 Aug. pp. 29, 30 Now amphtracks (amphibious tractors) thrashed through the water toward us. *BN* 7 Dec. p. 1/1 (AP) Al Dopkins . . . said the cavalrymen . . . came around the southern horn of Leyte on a 125-mile three-day trip, the longest ever made by amtracs under their own power. 1945 *BN* 22 Jan. p. 9/3-4 (Headline) Amtrac Knocked Out By Luzon Japs.

BAZOOKA. 'A type of horn invented by Bob Burns' (1942 Berrey and Van den Bark *American Thesaurus of Slang*). + See quot. 1944 *Britannica Book of the Year.*—1943 *Newsweek* 5 April p. 18 However, the Allies have a surprise in store for the Axis in the shape of the 'bazooka.' *Time* 5 April p. 74/3 Major General Levin H. Campbell Jr. . . . last week stripped some of the mystery from one secret U. S. weapon, the rocket-firing anti-tank gun which soldiers have dubbed the bazooka. *TN* 15 Sept. p. 1 (AP) The army's secret weapon is a secret no longer —the Bazooka made its first public appearance today at an army show on the Washington monument grounds. Named 'Bazooka' by soldiers, it is an anti-tank rocket gun . . . 1944 *Sat. Eve. Post* 8 July p. 21/2 All of a sudden, one of our boys got his bazooka on his shoulder and let go with a tremendous, crashing 'Boom!' . . . 1944 *Britannica Book of the Year* p. 769/2 BAZOOKA. A firearm, consisting of a metal tube slightly over 50 inches long and under 3 inches in diameter, with a shoulder stock, front and rear grips, sights, electric battery to set off the charge, and trigger, designed to launch rocket projectiles. . . .

BROWNOUT. See quots.—1942 Parry *War Dictionary* . . . brown-out . . . used in Australia to denote semidarkening a city as distinguished from the complete darkening of a blackout. Also a complete blackout. *Business Week* 26 Dec. p. 7/2 'Brownout' is the word for this douse-lights program to distinguish it from blackout and dimout. The term blackout used during power curtailment in southeastern states a year ago, has taken on a harsher meaning since Pearl Harbor. 1943 *Advertising Age* 13 Sept. p. 61 The suggested conservation measures for electricity involve a national 'brownout,' the extinguishing of all ornamental and display lighting and signs after 10 P. M. N. Y. *Post* 1 Nov. p. 34/1 The dimout ends officially tonight and the 'brownout' begins—but you may not be able to detect the difference immediately. *Time* 8 Nov. p. 14/2 Washington suggested that a 'brownout' (midway between total darkness and every marquee ablaze) would help save electricity and fuel . . .

BUZZ, '. . . *rare.* a. To assail, din, or molest by buzzing.' [1679-]. *v. i. & t. Aviation.* To fly close to an object on the ground, to fly close to the ground, esp. in a spirit of frolic or showing-off.—1941 *American Speech* Oct. p. 164/1 BUZZING A TOWN. To do the town; in Air Corps, to fly over it. 1942 *Time* 14 Dec. p. 82/2 They said he could buzz the camouflage off the top of a hangar without touching it. 1943 *Sat. Eve. Post* 18 Dec. p. 11/3 He had to buzz. 1944 *Life* 5 June p. 96 Shortly before McAvoy took this paragraph he sighted a family of hippos disporting in Chad's muddy waters. The plane buzzed them and they submerged. *Sat. Eve. Post* 19 Aug. p. 34/2 He buzzed everything from the pure joy of being alive and up where he loved to be, in an airplane in the sky. He buzzed, magnificently fought and dare-deviled three crews into combat-stress screw-ups, as war neurosis victims are called in the Air Force.

BUZZER, *n.* One who buzzes. (Also attrib.)—1943 *Sat. Eve. Post* 18 Dec. p. 11/2 . . . Johnny was an incorrigible 'buzzer.' 1944 San Francisco *Examiner* 26 May p. 11/4 'Buzzer' Pilots Fined $5,000. *This Week* 12 Nov. p. 6/2 'Are you boys all buzzers?' I ask the flyers. 'No sir!' they come back at me. 'It's just the young, inexperienced ones that dive low over houses an' put on stunts over crowds.'

BUZZING, *n.* The act of flying an

airplane dangerously close to the ground. See also last quot. See *buzz, v.* (Also attrib.)—1943 *Sat. Eve. Post* 18 Dec. p. 44/2 Buzzing seemed ridiculous in his slow, staid, tremendously steady nature. *Ibid.* 18 Dec. p. 11 Buzzin' Johnny Gets His Medal. 1944 *This Week* 12 Nov. p. 6/2 'Poor ol' Art got grounded after he crashed on that buzzin' expedition,' one of 'em said to the rest. San Francisco *Examiner* 11 June p. 3/8 Two Army flyers must pay $1,000 fines for 'buzing' [sic]—flying low over residential areas—. . . . *This Week* 12 Nov. p. 6/2 Well, here about 40 years after comes this word 'buzzin'.' It's how you describe a young airplane pilot showin' off before his family or his girl friend.

DDT. See quots.—1943 *Soap and Sanitary Chemicals* Dec. p. 117/1 An insecticide material of similar type is now being made in the United States by Geigy & Co., New York, under the name 'DDT.' 1944 *Time* 6 Mar. p. 62/3. *The DuPont Magazine* Apr.-May p. 23 The Department has also recently started the manufacture of a new and remarkable insecticide, 'DDT.' This is a new synthetic organic insecticide—the basis for the louse powder now used by the armed forces. *Read. Dig.* May p. 45. *Newsweek* 12 June p. 96. 1945 *Harper's* Feb. p. 265/1 Most spectacular of these weapons, of course, is DDT—dichloro-diphenyl-trichloroethane, or more accurately, 2, 2bis-(parachloro-phenyl) 1, 1, 1-trichloroethane—which really isn't new at all.

DITCH. 'To throw into the "ditch," or sea; to discard' (1942 Berrey and Van den Bark *American Thesaurus of Slang*). *v. i.* & *t.* To bring a disabled aircraft down on the water.—1943 Redding & Leyshon *Skyways to Berlin*, p. 213. *Popular Science* Nov. p. 84. *Life* 29 Nov. p. 75/2 Didn't see her ditch. 1944 B'ham *News—Age-Her.* 27 Aug. p. 5-D/7 (AP) Terry prepared to 'ditch' the plane in the sea. *Read. Dig.* Dec. p. 6/2 We knew about 15 minutes ahead of time we'd probably have to ditch.

DITCHING. (Also attrib.) 1943 Gunther *D Day* p. 12. *Life* 29 Nov. p. 83/3 The prospect of ditching as we approached North Africa seemed trivial after the vicious nightmare of the long trip across southern Germany. 1944 *Ibid.* 1 May p. 112 Ditching is primarily the art of getting a big, fast plane down on the water in one piece. Lincoln (Neb.) *Evening Journal* 2 June Lieutenant White had everybody get in 'ditching position.' *Sat. Eve. Post* Oct. p. 24/3 Krantz had to order the crew to prepare for ditching.

EARTHQUAKE BOMB. Six-ton bomb which penetrates into the earth so deeply that when its delayed-action fuse explodes, the result is 'earth quaking.'—1944 *TN* 3 Oct. p. 1/4 (AP) The 'earthquake' bombs of 12,000 pounds tore gaps in the dike . . . *Time* 23 Oct. p. 28/3. CBS Newscast 7:55 C. W. T. 29 Oct. . . . and the Tirpitz was hit by at least one six-ton earthquake bomb. *PM* 14 Nov. p. 7/3-5 The British Air Ministry announced that 29 RAF Lancaster bombers dropped armor-piercing, six-ton 'earthquake' bombs on the vessel Sunday. 1945 *TN* 8 Feb. p. 1/1 (AP) RAF Lancasters blasted German E-Boat shelters at Ijmuiden on the west coast of Holland with 12,000-pound earthquake bombs today . . .

FIGHTER STRIP. An airstrip.—1944 *BN* 25 April p. 1/1 (AP) Australian Royal Air Force engineers worked at night under floodlights . . . to repair the bomber and fighter strips . . . *Sat. Eve. Post* 8 July p. 32/3 The bus stopped in a village which was hardly more than a mile from the fighter strip . . . *Time* 11 Dec. p. 66/3.

JET AIRPLANE, JET PLANE. Plane operated by jet-propulson.—1944 *Collier's* 22 Apr. p. 13/1 Few standard conveniences for upper stratosphere flying had yet been built into the jet airplane . . . *Sat. Eve. Post* 6 May p. 20/1-2 The British had flown a jet plane successfully . . . *This Week* 9 July p. 9/5 The jet plane has cut out the need for a propeller by providing its own, 'built-in' slipstream. *TN* 21 Aug. p. 3/5 (headline) Nazi Jet Plane Tops In Speed. *Sat. Eve. Post* 2 Dec. p. 35/3 (adv.).

JET PROPULSION. 'The act or method of propelling a vessel or an airship by ejecting water or air from the stern in a powerful jet' (1942 Funk and Wagnalls *New Standard Dictionary*). Also applied to airplanes which run without propellers and use exhaust gases. (Also attrib.)—1932 (Hermann Oestrich) Prospects for jet propulsion of airplanes with special reference to exhaust gases . . . [translation by J. Vanier from] *Jahrbuch 1931 der Deutschen Versuchsanstalt für Luftfahrt*, Washington, May (cited in *Catalog of the Public Documents . . . for the Period from January 1, 1937 to December 31, 1938* . . . Washington, 1942, p. 1573/1). 1944 *TN* 12 Jan. p. 8 The 'rocket' or jet-propulsion method is basically simple. Lond. *Spect.* 14 Jan. p. 26. *Time* 24 Jan. p. 66 This cutaway drawing illustrates in simplified form the operation of a propellerless, jet-propulsion airplane. *Life* 26 June p. 68. *Sat. Eve. Post* 6 May p. 20/1 He'd been interested in jet propulsion for a long time. *Read. Dig.* Sept. p. 86/1.

LANDING STRIP. 'The cleared, drained, and graded strip used by planes in landing and taking off.'—1943 Gunther *D Day* p. 29 . . . on one emergency landing strip a wrecked P-38 on its back . . . 1944 *BN* 16 May p. 3/6 (AP) The Japanese . . . are seeking to disrupt . . . the reinforcement of Allied landing strips . . . *Sat. Eve. Post* 3 June p. 50/4 . . . on the walls were jumbo photographs . . . of memorable days at the base, such as the time a dozen fliers linked arms coming in from the landing strip . . . *Time* 10 July p. 76 (adv.) Sailors and soldiers have laid millions and millions of feet of [landing mat] into airfield landing strips . . . *BN* 1 Dec. p. 8/7 (AP) The Morris Field public relations office said the Fort, which over-shot a landing strip in foggy weather, was based at McDill Field . . .

+SOAP OPERA. A radio serial, usually highly emotional and melodramatic. See also quots. (Also attrib.)—1940 *Harper's* April p. 498/1 These sob-in-the-throat radio dramas are known to the trade as 'soap operas' or 'strip shows.' 1941 Waldo Abbot *Handbook of Broadcasting* (N.Y.: McGraw-Hill) p. 35 Perhaps the newest and most interesting innovation in style in commercial announcing is the announcing technique used on one of the 'soap operas' . . . 1943 *Sat. Eve. Post* 13 Nov. pp. 22/3, 44/1 I sit through innumerable soap operas to keep the atmosphere from being polluted by unintentional obscenity. 1944 *Sat. Rev. Lit.* 19 Feb. p. 26 . . . it is inevitable that he come up with the soap opera number one on the no-hit parade. *Life* 11 Sept. p. 67/2 Like most soap operas (so named because one soap manufacturer spends $15,000,000 a year on the 16 it sponsors), *Mary Marlin* is based on the assumption that the American woman likes to be reminded that it is always darkest before dawn. *Life* 11 Sept. p. 67/1 Mary Marlin, one of radio's longest-suffering soap-opera heroines, is successfully surviving another crisis.

STRIP. 'A long, narrow tract of territory, of land, wood, etc.' [1816-]. See *Landing Strip.*—1942 *Time* 3 Aug. p. 48/3 They learned first to come in on a flood-lighted strip . . . *Newsweek* 21 Dec. p. 20 Originally built by the Japanese, its five strips are now as familiar to the pilots as the floors of their own family living rooms. 1943 *Time* 18 Jan. p. 28/3 . . . Kenney had to find new strips for his supply planes. 1944 *TN* 11 June p. 1/3 (AP) They landed on one of the three strips built since last Wednesday . . . *Sat. Eve. Post* 24 June p. 80/3 And there was apt to be a cross wind over the Tarawa strip. . . .

SUPERFORTRESS, SUPER FORTRESS, SUPERFORT. The B-29 heavy bomber made by Boeing.—1944 *TN* 15 June p. 1/8 The army threw a new fighting giant into the war in the Pacific today, turning loose the new B-29 superfortress in an air attack. . . . *TN* 16 June p. 1/7 (AP) We are in the forefront of scores of Super Fortresses . . . *Time* 26 June p. 63/1-2 . . . to the public at large the Superfortress was a nebulous thing of mystery and hope. *Life* 31 July p. 38. *TN* 21 Aug. p. 1/1 (AP) In the first daylight operation . . . the Superforts of the 20th Air Force got 'good' results in a strike at the industrial area. . . . *Newsweek* 13 Nov. p. 5 (adv.). *Time* 4 Dec. p. 29/2.

TEEN-AGER. One of teen age.—1943 *Good Housekeeping* May p. 58 The right cotton dress can turn a gangling Teen-Ager into a glamour girl. *Recreation* Aug. pp. 275-284+. Cited *Readers' Guide.* 1944 *TN* 17 Feb. p. 10/1 (AP) Georgia, first to enact legislation giving 'teen-agers the right to vote and soldier-vote legislation, has had little response so far from either group. *Harper's* May p. 518/2 A recent article in the *New York Times* described a number of juke joints organized by teen-agers in various parts of the country . . . *Life* 14 Aug. p. 62. *Sat. Eve. Post* 23 Sept. p. 74/2 'You should see the teen-agers who hang around the USO.' *Ladies' Home Journal* Dec. p. 6/1 Too many of our teen-agers have missed the chance to grow in usefulness.

V-2. [Ger. *Vergeltungswaffe Zwei*= Vengeance Weapon 2]. A rocket 30-50 ft. long and 5 ft. in diameter, with a bomb load estimated at 1 ton up. Jet-propelled some 70 miles into the superstratosphere, it falls 800-1000 m.p.h. about 200 miles from its place of launching. (Also attrib.) —1944 *Life* 21 Aug. p. 17/1 It seems probable to me that the V-2, successor to the V-1 robot bomb, will be a heavy rocket . . . *Newsweek* 10 July p. 30/3 V-2 may be the giant rocket with which the Nazis are known to have been experimenting. *Time* 7 Aug. p. 26/2. London *Spectator* 18 Aug. p. 144/1. *BN* 21 Sept. p. 1/7 (AP) Citizens of neutral countries who claim to have seen the Nazi 'V-2' secret weapon, believed to be a rocket bomb, say it looks 'like a flying telegraph pole with a trail of flame' . . . *PM* 12 Nov. p. 10/2 . . . V-2's accuracy is hard to judge. *Life* 25 Dec. p. 48/2 V-2 launching site on Baltic coast was photographed by RAF.

AMONG THE NEW WORDS

I. WILLIS RUSSELL
University of Alabama

When parachutes began to be so widely used early in the recent war, one may say that the linguistic conditions were present for the shortening of *parachute* to *para-* in the many words which have since been formed with this element. The form *para-* was already familiar both as a prefix from the Greek and as a combining form from the Italian, the latter being that form which, combined with *chute,* made *parachute* in the first place. The shortened form seems to have arisen in England, but it has been popular on both sides of the Atlantic. It was first used in the word *paratroops* in 1940. Since then there have been many others, some well established, others occurring in only one citation, apparently nonce forms (see H. L. Mencken, *Am. Sp.,* 19:12, n. 22). Nevertheless, it seems worth while to list as many of the *para-* words as are available, regardless of whether they may be nonce forms or not. We will at least have a record of the popularity of the form.

The list that follows has been made up from published as well as unpublished material. Of the unpublished citations, three were supplied by Professor Henry Alexander and one each by Professor Dwight L. Bolinger and Miss Mamie J. Meredith. The order is chronological.

1940 *paratroops, parashooter, parashot, paraspotter* (*Am. Sp.,* 19:12); 1942 *para-ski, para-skier* (*ibid.,* 19:63); 1943 *parapup, paraspy* (*ibid.,* 19:12, n. 22); 'Parabombs burst above the ground, spray their fragments with telling effect' (*Time* 18 Oct. p. 36/2); 1944 *parapants* (*ibid.,* 10 Apr. p. 12); *parapooch* (dog dropped in a parachute; cited *Sat. Rev. Lit.* 10 Mar. 1945 p. 26/1); *parapup* (*This Week* 14 May p. 18); 'He is one of six paradoctors attached to the Search and Rescue Station of the Second Air Force' (*Time* 10 July p. 92/3); *parafemmes* (Frenchwomen sent down by parachute; Lond. *Eve. Stand.* Aug.); 'Nazi para-mines nearly blocked supply lines' (Kingston *Whig-Stand.* Sept.); 'This . . . Jap Sally plane went up in smoke a few seconds after this picture was taken—destroyed by parafrag bombs. . .' (*TN* 5 Oct. p. 1/1-2); 'The Royal Canadian Air Force has especially trained a group of "para-searchers"' (parachutists who bring help to stranded aviators; Kingston *Whig-Stand.* 3 Nov. p. 7); 'Oliver N. Magee, paramarine, son of War Dad and Mrs. . . . Magee. . .' (*Veterans' Weekly* [Lincoln, Neb.] 15 Dec. p. 2); 1945 '. . . Allied Airborne troops and parapacked supplies are shown as they plummeted down five miles beyond the Rhine. . .' (*BN* 27 Mar. p. 1/5-6); 'And Happy As Larks in Hego Paratwill raincoats! Tailored for the Young by Aquatogs in that shiny, sturdy, rain-defiant fabric paratroopers prize—Paratwill' (adv. in N. Y. *Times Mag.* 8 Apr. p. 37).

Para- in these words is a bound form; and since it is always added at the beginning of the word, it tends to act like a prefix. It is so described by Mr. Allen Walker Read, 'to denote something sent down by parachute' (*Sat. Rev. Lit., loc. cit.*). In some ways, however, these words appear to be compounds (note the presence of a hyphen in some of them), in which case *para-* may be thought of as a special combining form.

Booby trap in the military sense dates from the end of the first World War. The *OED* Sup. lists the term s. v. *booby* and cites a 1918 quotation. Fraser and Gibbons defined it in their *Soldier and Sailor Words and Phrases* in 1925, but it seems not to have gained currency enough for inclusion in the general dictionaries. It is missing, for example, from Wyld's *Universal* (1932), *NID* (1934) and latest 'New Words Section,' and the *New Standard* (c. 1942). The 1944 *New Century* defines it but relates it to 'the World War.' Since 1939, however, citations in general usage have been so numerous, especially with the retreat of the Axis powers, that the term will most likely be assured of a permanent place in the general dictionaries. And the restriction to World War I can now be dropped.

ACKNOWLEDGMENTS: Mr. Joseph Prescott for the earliest citation of *soap opera* in the April (1945) issue. For this issue: Mr. Henry Alexander (2); Mr. Dwight L. Bolinger (1); Mr. A. L. Hench (2); Mr. J. L. Kuethe (1); Mr. J. B. McMillan for the earlier illustration of *dollar word;* Miss Mamie J. Meredith (14); Mr. G. P. Shannon (1); Mr. Peter Tamony (3), including the citation for *milk wagon run;* Mr. Harold Wentworth (1).

The abbreviation *'BN'* is used for the Birmingham (Ala.) *News* and *'TN'* for the Tuscaloosa (Ala.) *News.*

SYMBOLS: The symbol + before a word or definition indicates an Americanism. A date immediately following a word or definition indicates the time of evidence shown in the DAE, or, if so stated, in another publication. Dates in brackets indicate the time, etc., of British usage. An asterisk after a word indicates that the word is illustrated in British usage before 1600.

BLACK MARKETEER, BLACK MARKETER. Operator of a black market. —1942 *New Repub.* 13 Apr. p. 490 The most skilled black marketeer . . . is the sort of man who used to be a confidence man or other City hanger-on. 1944 *BN* 12 Mar. p. 3/4 Philadelphia is the new scene for black marketeers from N. Y., because the Big Town's probe hit too many legal reefs. *Time* 4 Dec. p. 84/3 Some three weeks ago, the French government made its first cautious attempt to curb this inflation by sopping up some of the currency, much of it in the hands of war profiteers and black marketeers.

+BOBBY-SOCK, BOBBY SOCKS, BOBBY-SOX. [Cf. *bobby-pin.*] Anklets, esp. when worn by teen-age girls. (Also attrib.)—1943 *Time* 5 July p. 76/1 . . . hundreds of . . . girls in bobby socks sat transfixed. 1944 *Life* 4 Sept. p. 73/2 The movie scout who discovered Linda Darnell first noticed that future star wandering around in bobby socks in Dallas . . . *BN* 22 Nov. p. 8/4 Bobbysox Rage Is To Shoplift During School. 1945 *Newsweek* 1 Jan. p. 12. *This Week* 15 Apr. p. 21/2 . . . scarcely one per cent of these letters . . . have included comments on teen-age bobby-sock girls afflicted with dementia-Sinatra.

+BOBBYSOCK, BOBBY-SOCKS, BOBBY SOCKS, BOBBY-SOX, BOBBY SOX BRIGADE. See quots.—1944 *Newsweek* 6 Mar. p. 88 In New York City last week, the 'Bobby-sox Brigade' had swelled to such alarming proportions (within a year the Wayward Minors' Court had had nearly 100 per cent increase in delinquent-girl cases) that police imposed an unofficial curfew. Lincoln (Neb.) *Eve. Jour.* 22 Mar. Police in Hartford, Conn., are on the alert for members of the 'bobby socks brigade'—girls of school age found loitering around drug stores, taverns, military installations, movies, and railroad and bus terminals. *TN* 23 Nov. p. 10/5 (AP) The bobbysock brigade seems to be doing its Christmas shoplifting early . . . 1945 *Read. Dig.* Jan. p. 13/1 Almost all those present belong to the bobby-socks brigade, age perhaps 12 to 16. U. of Ala. *Crimson-White* 2 Feb. p. 3/4 . . . one of the highest contestants would probably be a certain professor . . . who affects his predominately [*sic*] female class like Sinatra does the Bobby Sox Brigade . . .

+BOBBY SOCKER, BOBBY-SOCKER, BOBBY-SOCKSER, BOBBY SOXER, BOBBY-SOXER. A girl 12-17 years old. —1944 *Life* 27 Nov. p. 76/2 When bobby-socker squeals, sound is carried to loud-speaker . . . B'ham *News-Age-Herald* 19 Nov. p. 11-A/4 (AP) About 6,000 bobby soxers attended the concert . . . 1945 *Newsweek* 1 Jan. p. 74. *Read. Dig.* Jan. p. 13/1. *Harper's* May (Personal and Otherwise) . . . we think the bobby-soxers ought to sick . . . someone on Mr. Harburg. *This Week* 6 May p. 16/3 We've got to give bobby-soxers a bigger part in this greatest of wars. *Time* 4 June p. 90/3.

CANNIBALIZE. See quots.—1944 Gunther *D Day* (N. Y. and Lond.: Harper and Bros.) p. 7 Here were two ships being 'cannibalized.' This odd expression means that these ships are being torn apart to provide spare parts for other aircraft. *Newsweek* 28 Aug. p. 34 [Jeeps] wrecked or unserviceable are to be 'cannibalized' for repair parts. B'ham *News-Age-Her.* 3 Sept. p. 10-A/3 The government is 'cannibalizing' jeeps. That is, it is using all the jeeps it has by interchanging parts as needed. 1945 *News and Views* (Gen. Motors Acceptance Corp.) Feb. p. 36. *Time* 4 June p. 32/1.

CUT-BACK, CUTBACK. See *Am. Sp.*, 19: 224/2. Add: 2. *Transf.*-1944 *BN* 20 Apr. p. 15/5 (AP) Gen. Giles . . . made this statement in a letter to Sen. Andrews . . . explaining the recent cutback in the AAF flying training program. B'ham *News-Age-Her.* 2 July p. 4-A/3 (AP) Sharp cut-back in war contracts . . . will be paralleled by cutbacks in the war-swollen membership lists of the labor unions.

CUT BACK, *v.*—1943 *Sat. Eve. Post* 6 Nov. p. 112 . . . the day will approach when, if the Army cuts back a program, it will not need the steel for some other program . . . 1944 *Time* 26 June p. 18/3 Before long the Navy . . . expects to cut back this program . . . *TN* 15 Nov. p. 4/2 Labor will have to understand that there will be some unemployment as we terminate contracts and cut back production. 1945 President Roosevelt 6 Jan. Broadcast . . . because their war production has been cut back . . .

DOLLAR. See *Am. Sp.*, 17: 204-5. In phr. *ten-dollar word.* Add earlier illust.—1935 Mark Sullivan *Our Times*, VI, 38n. I doubt whether . . . Ethan Allen . . . ever put his demand on the British commander in any such ten-dollar words. In phr. *sixty-four dollar ($64) question.* Add to def.: Difficult, frequently the climactic question. Add later illust.—1944 Fred Allen Program 12 Mar. I was as hard as the sixty-four-dollar question. *Newsweek* 20 Mar. p. 23 The reply to that $64 question 'Where is the Jap fleet?' thus lies in an analysis of Tokyo's present strategy. *Time* 8 May p. 44 (adv.) . . . —and now for the $64 question—'List the contents of your home.' Almost impossible to do from memory!

+GOBBLEDYGOOK. See second quot. (Also attrib.)—1944 *Time* 10 Apr. p. 57/1 Maury Maverick . . . railed against what he called Washington's 'gobbledygook' language. N. Y. *Times Mag.* 21 May p. 11/1 (Maury Maverick); (cited A. W. Read *Sat Rev. Lit.* 10 Mar. 1945 p. 7/1) . . . 'gobbledygook' . . . talk or writing which is long, pompous, vague, involved, usually with Latinized words. It is also talk or writing which is merely long, even though the words are fairly simple, with repetition over and over again, all of which could have been said in a few words. *Chr. Sci. Monitor Weekly Mag.* 9 Sept. p. 3/1 After many a despairing struggle . . . with official 'gobbledygook,' the Government has finally hammered out provisions . . . 1945 *Harper's* Apr. (John Chamberlain in 'The New Books') He is an enemy of professorial gobbledygook . . .

JEEP, *v. i.*—1942 *Time* 28 Sept. p. 57 Yanks: Drinking English Tea; Jeeping in the Middle East. 1944 Balto. *Sun* 17 Apr. p. 2/3 (AP) Earlier . . . I had flown over and jeeped through a fair portion of the present battleground. *Sat. Eve. Post* 12 Aug. p. 96/3 . . . I jeeped back to camp to break the news. 1945 *Newsweek* 8 Jan. p. 23. Lond. *Picture Post* 14 Apr. p. 7 Sometimes, it took us hours to jeep a few miles.

+JUNIOR MISS. A girl 13-16 years old. (Also attrib.)—1927 *Vogue* 15 Jan. p. 106/2 Junior Misses' Frock No. 8820 . . . 1932 *Harper's* Jan. p. 206 Junior Miss . . . 1941 S. Benson *Junior Miss* (N.Y.: Random House). 1944 *Life* 21 Aug. p. 59/3 Her clean, junior-miss charm and her ability to capture the bewilderment of adolescence contribute to one of the year's pleasantest performances. *TN* 31 Aug. p. 6/3 The junior miss can team up the jacket of this plaid suit with a pair of matching slacks . . .

MAQUIS. [Fr., cf. Larousse.] See quots. (Also attrib.)—1944 *This Week* 30 Apr. p. 4/3 I met one of the maquis soldiers . . . *Time* 29 May p. 36/1 Until invasion lifts the curtain, the many elements which make up French resistance —groups still bearing the old party names, saboteur bands, the maquis . . . —cannot be seen as a clear whole. Lond. *Spectator* 16 June p. 538. B'ham *News-Age-Her.* 16 July p. 16-C/3 (AP) The Maquis—patriots who have taken to the woods to fight—are composed mainly of young men seeking escape from labor service in Germany or sought by the Germans for resisting them one way or another. *Time* 24 July p. 28/3.

+MILK (WAGON) RUN. See quots.—1943 San Francisco *Call-Bulletin* 17 July p. 2/2-5 Loaded with bombs and guns primed, this Marine Corps dive bomber passes over Henderson Field . . . at the start of what is called the 'milk wagon' run. 1944 *Newsweek* 12 June p. 6 The usually accepted definition of a 'milk run' is a sortie against a target that is hit daily. There is no connotation of more or less danger. N. Y. *Times Mag.* 2 July p. 24/4 Milk-run—Routine mission flown repeatedly. *Time* 4 Dec. p. 65/1 In winter the North Atlantic airway to Europe is no 'milk run.' 1945 *Life* 5 Feb. p. 47/3 (adv.) Flying North American B-25 Mitchell bombers, these pilots have boxed the compass in Burma, distributing tokens for Tojo and turning hot spots into milk runs.

+SCRIPTER. A script writer.—1939 Chicago *Herald Examiner* 28 July p. 5 (Pt. 4) The scripters who turned out the story 'Alexander Graham Bell' were so carried away with the quality of the dramatic material available that they forgot about comedy relief. 1941 *Time* 7 July p. 66/3. 1944 *The Matrix* July pp. 10-12 The curator of the University Gallery liked my column . . . and took me on as a radio scripter . . . *Newsweek* 7 Aug. p. 83 Top Scripter. 1945 *Sat. Rev. Lit.* 14 Apr. p. 31/1 No question but that the expert scripter, dialogician, and screen playwright is the future king of Hollywood.

SCUTTLE BUTT, SCUTTLEBUTT. See quot. *Brit. Book of the Year.*—1939 *Am. Sp.*, Feb. p. 77/1 SCUTTLE BUTT. (1) Drinking fountain. (2) Rumor of doubtful origin. 1941 *Time* 14 July p. 32 A great joke to cadets a few weeks ago was the scuttlebutt (rumor) that the Bureau of Supplies and Accounts . . . had stocked the station with a large surplus of caskets . . . 1943 Tregaskis *Guadalcanal Diary* (N. Y.: Random House) p. 47. *Sat. Eve. Post* 8 May p. 26/3 But [Adm.] Halsey knew the 1942 capital ship to be as fast and handy, . . . and scuttlebutt had it that he was curious to see how the Japs would like having sixteen-inch shells around their ears. 1944 *Brit. Book of the Year* p. 770 SCUTTLEBUTT, *naval slang.* Gossip; a rumor. (-1938. Scuttle-butt story, -1901; scuttle butt, drinking fountain on board ship, -1843.) 1944 *Harper's* Feb. p. 232/2. 1945 *Time* 2 Apr. p. 16/2.

SUPER-HIGHWAY, SUPER HIGHWAY, SUPERHIGHWAY. A specially designed highway for high-speed traffic (see 1925, 1938 quots.); any four-lane highway, esp. with an island in the middle.—1925 *Amer. City Mag.* Apr. p. 373/1 The Super-Highway is unique . . . it will furnish an express motor traffic highway upon which automobiles can travel continuously at a maximum speed with safety, because all grade-crossing interference will be eliminated. 1933 *Survey Graphic* Feb. p. 83 Railroads, A Super-Highway And the Unemployed. 1938 *Pop. Mech.* May p. 643 (cited *Read. Guide* 1939 p. 1553/2) Superhighways for 100 mile speed proposed. 1944 *TN* 11 July p. 1/6 (AP) The accident occurred at Ware's station . . . , near the Birmingham-Bessemer super highway. *Sat Eve. Post* 15 July p. 103 (adv.) This is a Super Highway. *Life* 18 Dec. p. 18/2.

TANK-DOZER. See quots.—1944 N. Y. *Times* 4 Aug. p. 3/3 (cited *Sat. Rev. Lit.* 10 Mar. p. 6/3) . . . the 'tank-dozer' . . . consists of a medium sized tank to which is fitted a 3½-ton blade. *U. S. News* 11 Aug. p. 15 . . . the new tank-dozers, a combination of medium tank and armored bulldozer . . . lunged forward . . . *Life* 14 Aug. p. 21 Bulldozers or 'tank-dozers,' tanks equipped with a scraping blade, often cut gaps through hedgerows. B'ham *News-Age-Her.* 27 Aug. p. Two-A/2 The newest member of the family is the tank-dozer . . . This is simply a medium tank with a dozer blade mounted on it.

TASK FORCE. See *Am. Sp.*, 19: 226/2. Add illust. of non-naval sense and revise second part of def. to read: Also applied to other operations.—1945 *Time* 15 Jan. p. 26/1 Near Stavelot a large German armored task force of tanks, tank destroyers, self-propelled guns and trucks snaked northward. *BN* 3 Mar. p. 1/4 (AP) One of the task forces of heavy bombers went 50 miles beyond Leipzig . . . *Time* 16 Apr. p. 77/2 . . . he named . . . Henry P. Nelson . . . to head a special 'task force,' which will recommend to WPB ways to help the industry clear its plants . . . *Sat. Eve Post* 28 July p. 12/1 . . . the 15th Infantry gave Lieutenant von Ripper a small task force to follow up some of his leads. He was after one gentleman in particular.

AMONG THE NEW WORDS

I. WILLIS RUSSELL
University of Alabama

THIS installment of 'Among the New Words' is devoted to words brought into being through the airplane. Since it is planned to devote the next installment to more of these words, extended comment will be reserved till then.

Two words in this glossary deserve brief comment. *Heavy* as an ellipsis is not new in military circles. OED records *heavies* in 1841 to describe 'heavy cavalry,' and the Supplement adds *the heavies* under date 1908 to denote 'heavy artillery.'

Strato- offers a close parallel to *para-*, discussed in the last issue. It already existed as a combining form in another sense; the new combining form is a shortening of *stratosphere,* as *para-* is a shortening of *parachute.* This same process, but with the end of the word retained, is discussed with numerous examples in 'Among the New Words' for December, 1943.

ACKNOWLEDGMENTS. For citations, to C. L. Barnhart (4), Dwight L. Bolinger (5), Atcheson L. Hench (1), Mamie J. Meredith (13), and Harold Wentworth (1). For help in the definitions, thanks are due to the Boeing Aircraft Co. for information on the Stratocruiser, to Lt. Col. Lucius M. Sargent, AAF, Washington, and especially to Dr. John F. Ramsey and Mr. I. E. Alexander.

With the completion of this volume of *American Speech,* the author would like to express his appreciation of aid given him by the University of Alabama Research Committee in the collection and preparation of the material for this department during the year.

The abbreviation '*BN*' is used for the Birmingham (Ala.) *News* and '*TN*' for the Tuscaloosa (Ala.) *News.*

SYMBOLS: The symbol + before a word or definition indicates an Americanism. A date immediately following a word or definition indicates the time of evidence shown in the DAE, or, if so stated, in another publication. Dates in brackets indicate the time, etc., of British usage. An asterisk after a word indicates that the word is illustrated in British usage before 1600.

AREA BOMBING. [Cf. *Area shoot,* 'A widespread bombardment over a whole district to make it untenable by the enemy.' Fraser and Gibbons *Soldier and Sailor Words and Phrases* 1925.] Bombing which attempts to hit every part of a predetermined section of land; saturation bombing.—1944 *Newsweek* 10 Jan. p. 26 So, the Eighth has turned to area bombing, the method of the RAF. 1945 *Collier's* 8 Sept. p. 37/1 They felt that night saturation, or area bombing, was a useful and necessary part of air power, but only as complementary to daylight bombing.

BOMB BAY, BOMB-BAY, *n.* [See NID, s. v. 2 *bay, n.,* 2. b.] That portion of the fuselage where the bombs are lodged. (Also attrib.)—1940 N.Y. *Times Mag.* 30 June p. 6/2 But most of the bombing . . . is done at level flight, bombs being dropped from bomb-bays. . . 1941 David C. Cooke *War Wings* (Robert M. McBride & Co.) p. 66 To drop the explosives, bomb bay doors swing down and out.—1943 *Time* 7 June p. 28/1-2 [Picture of] Halifax Bomb Bay, Loaded for Germany. 1944 *BN* 18 Apr. p. 22/1 (AP) My only uneasy moment came as we neared Matsuwa and I crawled through the dark bomb bay to the waist of the plane. *Sat. Eve. Post* 19 Aug. p. 82/3 . . . her bomb-bay doors squeaked open. . . 1945 *Sci. News Letter* 3 Mar. p. 136.

BOMBER'S MOON. Moon giving light for bombing operation. (Also attrib.) —1944 *Collier's* 1 Jan. p. 23; cited *Read. Guide* 14: 1005/2. *BN* 11 Mar. p. 1/3 (AP) The Air Ministry said three aircraft factories and a small bearing factory . . . were hit in a 'bomber's moon' operation. . . *Sat. Eve. Post* 22 Apr. p. 39 Night of the Bomber's Moon. 1945 *Sci. N. L.* 10 Mar. p. 154/1 Bomber's moons, thunderstorms, fog and ice aren't things that just 'happen.'

BOMB RUN, BOMBING RUN. [Cf. NID, s. v. *run, n.,* 27, '*Bowling.* The clear space, not less than 15 feet in length and immediately back of the foul line, from which the bowler delivers his ball.' Cf. *runway,* 8.] The course from a predetermined point on the ground (called 'initial point' or I.P.) to the point where the bombs are released.—1941 *Sci. Dig.* Nov. p. 53/1 The pilot controls the 'bomb run,' which is the line of flight of the plane and also of the released bomb. 1944 *Scholastic* 3 Apr. p. 24/4 After that, in the 20 to 30 seconds bombing run, no human hand touches the controls. *Harper's* Aug. p. 286/2. 1945 N.Y. *Times Mag.* 25 Mar. p. 38/2 If you make your bomb run upwind . . . you have more time to line up the target because your bomb run is longer.

CRASH-LAND, CRASH LAND, *v. i.* To land a plane with a portion or all of essential landing equipment ineffective.—1942 *Time* 23 Feb. p. 88/1 That time he got away, to crash-land safely. *Read. Dig.* Oct. p. 131. 1944 *Life* 29 May p. 67 He flew day after day over some of the most forlorn and lonely landscapes in the world, where only through an extraordinary coincidence of luck and skill could a flier crash-land safely. *Ibid.* 17 July p. 81/1 Some crash-landed in sea. *BN* 19 Aug. p. 2-B/1 (AP) One crash landed at Saipan after being rammed twice by Jap fighters.

CRASH LANDING, *n.*—1942 *Time* 23 Feb. p. 21/3 The pilot . . . glided in for a crash landing. 1944 *Sat. Eve. Post* 22 Apr. p. 49 (adv.). *Sat. Rev. Lit.* 20 May p. 18/2 He does not know that a broken airscrew, a crash landing in Occupied France . . . lie just a few minutes ahead. B'ham *News—Age-Her.* 27 Aug. p. 5-D/7 (AP) Leaving the wheels of the bomber up, Terry came in for a crash landing.

FIGHTER-BOMBER, FIGHTER BOMBER, FIGHTERBOMBER. See first quot. (Also attrib.)—1942 *Pop. Sci.* Dec. p. 124/1 The fighter-bomber is a regulation pursuit ship fitted with an under-fuselage mounting for carrying a 500-pound delayed-action bomb. 1945 N.Y. *Times Mag.* 25 Feb. p. 11 At a fighter-bomber base in France—Red Cross girls . . . pass out welcome snacks to ground crew members during cold and damp mornings. *BN* 7 Apr. p. 1/7 (AP) . . . the targets they once reached . . . now have come within range of . . . low-flying fighterbombers. *Chr. Sci. Mon. Weekly* 7 Apr. p. 6/2. *BN* 8 Apr. p. 1/1 (AP) Two British destroyers . . . and swarms of American fighter bombers effectively supported the operation. *Harper's* May p. 545/1.

+FLYING BOX CAR, FLYING BOXCAR. See quots.—1941 *Am. Sp.* Oct. p. 165/2 FLYING BOXCAR. A bomber. 1942 *Sat. Eve. Post* 12 Sept. p. 74/2 Flying Boxcars for a Global War. 1943 *Public Affairs,* Pamphlet No. 78, p. 14 Apply this air pick-up system to gliders, and the possibilities of what are romantically called 'flying box cars' and 'aerial trucks' will be immensely increased. 1944 *Newsweek* 22 May p. 76 A flying boxcar . . . was accepted by the Navy last week. . . The Conestoga . . . is a high-wing monoplane 68 feet long with 100-foot wingspread. *Sci. N. L.* 12 Aug. p. 107/1 Giant 'flying box cars' or cargo planes will provide fast . . . service. . . 1945 *Chr. Sci. Mon. Weekly* 5 May p. 19 (adv. of Fairchild) In emergencies, this flying boxcar [the 'Packet'] can be converted *in a few minutes* for the evacuation of the incapacitated from areas of front line danger. . .

GLIDE-BOMB, GLIDE BOMB, *n. & v.* See quot. 1944.—1943 *Time* 25 Oct. p. 23/1 The airmen knew that 1,800 fighters equipped with cannon, machine guns, some with glide bombs . . . are concentrated between Denmark and Belgium. . . *Newsweek* 8 Mar. p. 24 Hollingsworth said a divebomber pilot must be able to glide bomb in certain circumstances. . . 1944 *Brit. Book of the Year* p. 770/1 GLIDE-BOMB. To bomb, from an aeroplane, by descending at an angle of less than 65° from the horizontal when releasing bombs.

HEAVY, *n.* Short for *heavy bomber.*—1943 *Time* 15 Nov. p. 26/2 . . . another coordinated series of punches . . . cost the Allies only ten heavies, two Marauders and five fighters. 1944 *Ibid.* 11 Dec. p. 28/2. 1945 *Newsweek* 1 Jan. p. 19 RAF heavies struck airfields by day, rail yards by night. *Read. Dig.* Sept. p. 35/2.

OBLITERATION BOMBING. See *Am. Sp.* 19: 225/2. Revise def. to read: 'Blotting out . . . by concentrated bombing.'

PATTERN BOMBING, PATTERN-BOMBING. See quot. N.Y. *Times.*—1942 *Coast Artillery Journal* Sept.-Oct. p. 5 Barcelona and other Spanish cities . . . were bombed by German forces . . . to determine once and for all whether dive-bombing and pattern-bombing could be done with devastating effectiveness. N.Y. *Times* 28 Oct. If pattern bombing of an area . . . is tried by a formation of planes, the mathematical chances of obtaining a hit are increased. 1943 *Time* 21 June p. 21/1 'Pattern bombing' crushed gun emplacements one by one. 1944 *Sat. Eve. Post* 4 Nov. p. 107/2 (adv.) For whether it's pattern or pin-point bombing . . . the B-25 takes them all in stride.

+PRECISION BOMBING Pattern bombing of a single group of related objects, with the most important object pinpoint bombed.—1942 *Pop. Sci.* July pp. 102-7; cited *Read. Guide* 13: 222/2 Precision bombing takes team work. 1943 *Time* 7 June p. 29/3 And, according to U.S. testimony, the precision bombing of the American forces is more effective, ton for ton, than the saturation bombing of the R.A.F. 1944 *Newsweek* 10 Jan. p. 26 The greatest achievement of the young Eighth Air Force was precision bombing, the technique of pinpointing with explosive vital points of German industry and communications. . . . 1945 *Life* 4 June p. 22/2. *Collier's* 8 Sept. p. 12/4 This . . . meant adherence to the American faith in daylight precision bombing. PRECISION BOMBER. 1943 *Time* 30 Aug. p. 34/1.

PROBABLE, *n.* 'That which is probable . . .' (NID). See quots.—1942 Topeka *State Jour.* 3 Apr. p. 1/4 A single United States army pursuit squadron . . . destroyed 39 Japanese planes for certain and 26 other 'probables' in fighting over Java. 1943 *Time* 22 Nov. p. 26/3 Their pigboat score: eleven probables, three certains. 1944 *Sat. Eve. Post* 22 July p. 73/3 . . . but I chalked him up with only a probable, because I did not see it crash. *Brit. Book of the Year* p. 770/1 PROBABLE. A supposed casualty, esp. referring to military craft, as 'there were ten destroyed and five probables.'

SATURATION BOMBING. Area bombing.—1943 *Time* 7 June p. 29/3 (quoted under *precision bombing*). 1944 B'ham *News—Age-Her.* 12 Nov p. 1-D/1 The saturation bombing of Rangoon . . . means the tuning up of American and British Far East forces is complete after a year's preparation. 1945 *Collier's* 8 Sept. p. 11/1 The British believed in night area saturation bombing. SATURATION ATTACK. 1944 *BN* 10 Oct. p. 1/7 (AP) The British heavy bombers made a saturation attack on Bochum. . . SATURATION RAID. 1943 *Time* 6 Sept. p. 36/3 Of the 73 raids Berlin had experienced, this was the worst, the first of the kind of saturation raids that had wrecked Hamburg. 1945 *Life* 4 June p. 23/1. *Collier's* 8 Sept. p. 37/1 The British brought great pressure to bear in high places on the American Command to abandon their daylight plan and brigade their bombers with the RAF for night saturation raids. SATURATION RAIDER. 1943 *Time* 30 Aug. p. 33/2 The Allies . . . are using the greatest air force the world has known: a combination of the daylight precision bombing planes of the U S Eighth Air Force and the heavy night-time saturation raiders of the R.A.F.

SHUTTLE BOMBING. [Cf. *shuttle train.*] The bombing done by a plane between two bases.(Also attrib.)—1944 *Newsweek* 10 Jan. p. 27 Last summer the RAF and the Eighth both tried shuttle bombing. Flying from British bases to raid Germany, the bombers instead of returning to their bases, flew south to Africa, fooling German defenses and evading in part the German fighters waiting to catch them on the way home. *TN* 13 Apr. p. 4/3 There we could pick up airfields and ship bases which would bring us nearer to Berlin and enable us to engage in closer shuttle bombing of that harassed capital. *TN* 28 June p. 8/1 (AP) The first three-way shuttle bombing operation of the European war was disclosed today. SHUTTLE BASE. 1944 *TN* 25 June p. 1/3 (AP) While no announcement has been made concerning the sites of the shuttle bases in Russia, it is evident they are located in both northern and southern areas. SHUTTLE FLIGHT. 1944 *TN* 25 June p. 1/3 (AP) Three crewmen also were lost as a result of the attack on the fields, apparently those used by Italian-based and Britain-based bombers in the shuttle flights over Axis targets. 1945 *BN* 13 June p. 3/2 (AP) Durham also was navigator on a shuttle flight to Russia. . . SHUTTLE PLANE. 1944 *Brit. Book of the Year* p. 770/1. SHUTTLE RAID. 1943 *Time* 18 Oct. p. 85/1 . . . the . . . pilot flew on his first mission eight weeks ago, joined the first U. S. shuttle raid on Germany, flew safely to Africa. . .

+SKIP-BOMBING. Low-level bombing with delayed-action bombs which ricochet into the target. (Also attrib.)—1943 *Time* 18 Jan. p. 68/3 . . . a U. S. Flying Fortress thundered into the Jap Harbor at Rabaul . . . to make the first test in the South Pacific of a new technique—'skip-bombing.' *Sat. Eve. Post* 23 Oct. p. 21/2 'Johnson's outfit worked up a kind of dry-land skip-bombing stunt, although they'd never heard the term, "skip-bombing."' *Life* 27 Dec. p. 41 Thus, a new and deadly technique—skip-bombing—had been tried and found not wanting. . . 1944 *Newsweek* 20 Nov. p. 42/2. 1945 Baltimore *Sun* 8 Sept. p. 1/5-6 (AP) . . . the Allied airmen employed . . . skip-bombing tactics in which the bombs were launched at almost sea level into the sides of the vessels.

SKY-.[See OED and Sup. s.v. *sky, sb.*[1], '8. attrib. and Comb.' and '9. Special combs.'] Additional combs.—SKY ARTILLERY. 1941 N. Y. *Times Mag.* 26 Jan. p. 4/2 On land the opponents have used their dreaded dive-bombers as sky artillery. . . SKY BENDS. 1944 *Sci. N. L.* 7 Oct. p. 238. SKYBUS. 1944 *Sci. N. L.* 12 Aug. p. 100 First of the new postwar planes to be designed especially for feeder-line operation is a high-wing twin-engine all-metal monoplane with a tricycle landing gear named the 'Skybus.' SKY-CAB. 1945 *Life* 19 Mar. p. 57/1 You can do it some day in a Helicopter Sky-Cab . . . SKY CAR. 1944 *Newsweek* 29 May p. 59 The Stout Sky Car, a combination airplane-automobile . . . SKY CLIPPER. 1944 *Life* 3 Apr. p. 89 (adv.). SKYFIGHTER. 1942 N Y. *Times Mag.* 11 Jan. pp. 3-4; cited *Read. Guide* 13:151/2. SKY FREIGHTER. 1938 *Rotarian* Apr. pp. 25-8; cited *Read. Guide* 11:31/1. SKY HOOK. 1945 *Collier's* 27 Jan. p. 38; cited *Read. Guide* 14:38/1 . . . skyhook, device for dropping supplies. . . . SKY JEEP. 1944 *BN* 9 Aug. p. 3/1 (AP) The rest had turned tail, and the little 'sky jeep' was waggling home to its landing pasture. . . SKYLANDER. 1944 *Fortune* July p. 165. SKYMARKER BOMB. 1945 *News and Views* (General Motors) May p. 22 Known as the M87 colored streamer smoke bomb, a new sky-marker bomb which trails colored smoke through the air has been developed by the Chemical Warfare Service. . . SKYMASTER. 1945 *Chr. Sci. Mon. Weekly* 21 Apr. p. 3/4 These Constellations and Stratocruisers and Skymaster C-54's are highly believable, because they are here, right now! SKYPORT. 1939 *Travel* May pp. 6-11; cited *Read. Guide* 11:32/1. SKY-PRODDER. 1942 *Time* 16 Mar. p. 57; quoted *Am. Sp.* 18:76/1 Our *Sky-Prodders,* the new U. S. anti-aircraft guns. . . SKY ROAD. 1944 *Newsweek* 11 Sept. p. 11 Post-war 'sky roads'. . . SKY SCOUT. 1941 *Am. Sp.* 16:168/2 SKY SCOUT. The Chaplain. SKY SOLDIER. 1944 *TN* 20 Sept. p. 1/8 (AP) Germans in western Holland had virtually been closed off by the linkup of the British Second Army with sky soldiers at Nijmegen on the Rhine. SKY TRAIN. 1944 Lincoln (Neb.) *Journ.* 20 Nov. Twenty-six American soldiers were killed . . . in the crash Sunday night of a C-47 Skytrain troop carrier. . . 1944 *Newsweek* 19 June p. 31 The skytrain which took the men to France was the greatest ever. Flying nine tow planes abreast, it stretched 200 miles. SKY TRUCK. 1942 *Harper's* July p. 113 (title) Sky Trucks Coming. SKY WARRIOR. 1944 *Woman's Day* June p. 69/3 The sky warrior braided a wreath of tight little white roses for a girl's hair. . . SKY WINDER. 1941 *Am.*

Sp. 16:168/2 SKY WINDER. Air Corps man. 1944 Kendall *Service Slang.* SKY WIRE. 1941 *Am. Sp. loc. cit.* SKY WIRE. An antenna (Signal Corps).

+STRATO-. Combining form for *stratosphere.*—STRATO-CHAMBER. 1942 *Newsweek* 20 July p. 51 (adv.) You can get to the stratosphere in twelve minutes flat . . . without leaving the ground. [¶] Step into the latest type York Strato-Chamber. STRATOCLIPPER. 1940 *Baltimore Sun* 24 Aug. p. 7/1 (AP) The stratoclipper Comet . . . set a . . . record today. . . STRATOCRUISER, q. v. STRATO EQUIPMENT. 1945 *Bus. Week* 10 Mar. p. 41/1 Strato Equipment Co. . . . started two years ago as the outgrowth of research work . . . on high-altitude pressure suits for flyers. STRATOLINER. 1944 *New Century.* STRATOPEN. *Time* 21 Aug. p. 62/2 . . . Stratopen . . . does not leak at high altitudes. STRATOPOWER. 1944 *Harper's* Aug. (adv.) Even the grueling hydraulic test in the 3000-pound pressure range by Wright Field engineers could not lick the Hycon high-pressure 'Stratopower' pump. STRATO-SUIT. 1945 *BN* 24 June p. 1-A/3 (AP) An airman wears a new flexible pressurized 'strato-suit' of rubberized fabric developed here for use in high-altitude flying. . . STRATOTRAINER. 1943 *Collier's* 29 May p. 8; cited *Read. Guide* 13:152/2 Wing talk; Boeing stratotrainer. STRATOVISION. 1945 *Cleveland Plain Dealer* 10 Aug. p. 1/4-6 (AP) 'The stratovision system simply puts the antenna and transmitter in an airplane flying in lazy circles 30,000 feet above the earth. . .

+STRATOCRUISER. The Boeing Model 377, equipped with four 3500-horse-power engines and a pressurized cabin. It cruises at 340 m.p.h. and operates at 30,000 feet. It can carry about 80 passengers; the freight version 35,000 lbs.—1944 *TN* 15 Nov. p. 8/2 (AP) Test flights of the new Boeing military transport, the Stratocruiser, disclosed last night by the Boeing Company as the first of the new postwar planes, were highly successful, test pilots reported today. *Time* 20 Nov. p. 77/1 The new ship is Boeing's postwar superairliner, the 'Stratocruiser,' in a military transport version. *Think* Dec. p. 29 The 'Stratocruiser' . . . is nearest of kin to the B-29 Superfortress . . . 1945 *Chr. Sci. Mon. Weekly* 21 Apr. p. 3/4 The Stratocruiser . . . developed a true air speed of well over 400 miles an hour on its transcontinental hop, Boeing flight personnel said.

AMONG THE NEW WORDS

I. WILLIS RUSSELL
University of Alabama

IN 'Among the New Words' for December, 1945, it was stated that the next installment would contain more words 'brought into being through the airplane.' Consequently, more of these words will be found in the glossary of this issue. To these are added some illustrations of another class of words, abbreviations. The two groups are thrown into one alphabet in the glossary; here it is proposed to make some comments on each group separately.

It is a commonplace that this is an air age, that the war just fought was an air war. One is therefore not surprised at the many coinages reflecting the influence of the airplane. This influence is reflected not only in the names and types of the planes themselves but in the many activities connected with aviation. Thus the many kinds of bombs and of bombing described in this and the preceding installment of 'Among the New Words' may be said to be due to the airplane; most of them, indeed, would be impossible without the plane. Even the atomic bomb, though the first one was not dropped from a plane, by its very nature could hardly have been conceived in a frame of reference that did not assume aircraft. An attempt has been made to include many types of bombing in these two glossaries. Other types, for which there is still insufficient evidence for an entry, include atomic bombing, fire-bombing, pinpoint bombing, scatter bombing, and tactical bombing.

It hardly need be said that these words are but a small selection of the many which have been formed. It is too soon to assess the contribution of aviation to vocabulary, especially during the past five or six years; that must await a more complete dictionary of recent words than is at present available. But there is some suggestive evidence. During the past several years, the *New International Yearbook* and the *Britannica Book of the Year* have published lists of recent word coinages. Of the total number of new terms appearing in the 1945 yearbooks approximately 19% may be said to describe developments due to the airplane. This seems like a high proportion, but many of the words may not survive.

Professor Bolinger noted the use of the combining form *-master* in trade names when he was in charge of this department (*Am. Sp.,* 18:147). Another combination, undoubtedly a trade name, appears in the *Skymaster,* made by the Douglas Aircraft Company. The same company also makes a *Globemaster* (*Time* 17 Sept. 1945 p. 81/3).

Abbreviations have played a part in American English for a long time. 'The characteristic American habit of reducing complex concepts to the starkest abbreviations,' writes Mr. Mencken in *The American Language,* 1936 (p. 92), 'was already noticeable in colonial times, and such highly typical Americanisms as *O. K., N. G.,* and *P. D. Q.* have been traced back to the early days of the republic.' By 1889 the habit was a subject for comment by John S. Farmer, who observed how much more widely abbreviations were used in America than in Europe (*ibid.,* pp. 204-205). Mr. Mencken himself devotes several pages to them in *The American Language,* where he notes the importance of World War I and the New Deal (with its many alphabetical agencies), and he adds to his discussion in *Supplement I* (pp. 410 ff.). Here, drawing on the DAE, he

gives the dates of several (for example, *C. O. D.,* 1863) and distinguishes two types: those which, on the model of the English and the Russians, can be pronounced as words; and those which cannot.

The linguistic importance of abbreviations is thus considerable. Professor Bloomfield (*Language,* p. 488) has shown how 'purely graphic devices lead to novel speech forms,' citing in illustration such abbreviations as *prof.* [prɑf], *lab.* [læb], and *a. m.* ['e'jɛm]. How these new speech forms in turn may be translated back into the written word is shown by *kayo* (K. O.; *Amer. Lang.,* p. 210), *okeh* (O. K.), and, more recently, *Elsie,* for the landing craft, the LC, as it is called (*Life* 19 June 1944 p. 36; *Sat. Eve. Post* 3 June 1944 p. 20/1).

Convenience seems to be a determining factor in the use of abbreviations. This point is made by 'Janus' (Lond. *Spect.* 1 Feb. 1945 p. 108/2), who cites in illustration *UNRRA* and *UNO,* the latter of which he would apparently pronounce [juno]. Some of the acrostics in the glossary must likewise be pronounced as words by those who use them constantly, as: *Jato* ['dʒeto] and *Fido* ['faɪdo]. Convenience would also play a large part in the popularity of abbreviations in the Army (*Am. Sp.,* 20: 262) and in the Navy. The Navy, for example, uses abbreviations for its various commands (*Cincus, Cominch,* etc.); and *Cominch* seems to have supplanted *Cincus* because of the unintended double entendre of the latter ['sɪŋkəs].

What proportion of our vocabulary is supplied by abbreviations? Here are some approximate figures. Webster's table of 5,000 abbreviations is less than 1% of the 550,000 entries stated to be in the dictionary. But of these no more than a third would ever be pronounced as written. An estimate of Mr. Mencken's *Supplement I* gives only .8%; Louise G. Parry's *War Dictionary* (1942) contains 1.8%. A. Marjorie Taylor's *The Language of World War II* (1944), however, contains slightly over 18%, and the two 1945 yearbook lists have about 14.5%. Even if only half of the present crop survives, it would seem that abbreviations are playing a larger part in word formation than ever before.

ACKNOWLEDGEMENTS. For citations, to Henry Alexander (4), C. L. Barnhart (9), Dwight L. Bolinger (1), Margaret M. Bryant (1), Atcheson L. Hench (5), including the 1937 citation of *crewman,* James B. McMillan (1), Mamie J. Meredith (28), and Peter Tamony (4). Thanks are due Dr. Eric Rodgers for the definition of *atomic bomb.*

The abbreviation '*BN*' is used for the Birmingham (Ala.) *News* and '*TN*' for the Tuscaloosa (Ala.) *News.*

SYMBOLS: The symbol + before a word or definition indicates an Americanism. A date immediately following a word or definition indicates the time of evidence shown in the DAE, or, if so stated, in another publication. Dates in brackets indicate the time, etc., of British usage. An asterisk after a word indicates that the word is illustrated in British usage before 1600.

+A-BOMB. Atomic bomb; frequent headline form. (Also attrib.)—1945 Omaha *World-Her.* 15 Aug. p. 2/3 A-bomb Believed to Eliminate Navy. *BN* 16 Oct. p. 20/1 (AP) Maj. Gen. Leslie R. Groves . . . today presented the Army-Navy production 'E' to the University of California, operator of the Los Alamos A-bomb laboratory. 1946 *BN* 3 April p. 11/1-2 A-Bomb Proposal Analyzed.

+AIR-SEA RESCUE. A method of rescuing airmen forced down on the water. A Dumbo (q. v.) locates the men and radios their position. A ship receiving the message will then proceed to the position or an air-sea rescue station will send out a rescue boat. (Also attrib.)—1945 *Time* 9 April p. 62/2 In each carrier plane's air-sea rescue kit is a Celanese rayon-acetate map . . . *BN* 1 June p. 14/1 (AP) In Navy parlance, a 'Dumbo' is any air-sea rescue plane. *Newsweek* 6 Aug. p. 60/1 The PV-3, an experimental helicopter ordered by the Navy for air-sea rescue and transport. . . 1946 *BN* 3 April p. 1/6 (AP) Army and Navy air-sea rescue squadrons searched the waters along the coast of Hawaii Island today for 25 school children. . .

+ANTI-G-SUIT. See *G-Suit.*

+ATOM BOMB, ATOMBOMB. An atomic bomb.—1945 Lincoln (Neb.) *Journal* 12 Aug. p. 2/4 The atom bomb is the most powerful and terrific technical surprise in military history. . . *Life* 20 Aug. p. 17/1 The Atom Bomb and Future War. *Time* 27 Aug. p. 60/2 (quoting *Collier's* newspaper advs.). N. Y. *Daily Worker* 4 Sept. p. 2 Soviet Journal Scores Threats to Use Atombomb for World Mastery.

v. 1945 Lond. *Evening News* 20 Sept. p. 1 The Japanese ship Nagato is to be taken

to the U. S. as a 'show piece' and not atom-bombed 500 miles out to sea. *TN* 12 Dec. p. 12/4 Warships To Be Atom-Bombed. 1946 *This Week* 24 Mar. p. 8/1 I mean the folks who are worried about what is going to happen to Bikini Atoll this May, when the Navy plans to anchor a small fleet there and atom-bomb it.

+ATOMIC BOMB, *n.* A new type of bomb utilizing the atom's nuclear binding energy, which is released by chain bombardment of the nucleus by neutrons. (Also attrib.)—1945 Lincoln (Neb.) *Journal* 6 Aug. p. 1/1 The atomic bomb dwarfs by 2,000 times the blast power of the British 'grand slam' bomb, which weighed approximately 11 tons. *TN* 7 Aug. p. 2/3 The Nipponese have no defense against threatened atomic bomb attack . . . Lond. *Spect.* 31 Aug. p. 197/2. 1946 *Read. Dig.* May p. 125/1 What would have happened if one of the atomic bombs we dropped on Japan had been used on New York?

2. Fig.—1945 *Sat. Rev. Lit.* 29 Sept. p. 13/1 . . . but President Truman himself put an atomic bomb under its thesis . . . *TN* 5 Nov. p. 6/1 A few scathing references to her personal appearance would be atomic bombs that would turn the trick. 1946 *BN* 14 Jan. p. 1/4 Byrnes Tosses Atomic Bomb In Lap of UNO.

+ATOMIC BOMBER, *n.* 1945 *Sat. Eve. Post* 10 Nov. p. 132/3 . . . this is too small an effort to prepare young men for either war or peace. to recruit the basic material for atomic bombers. . . *TN* 15 Nov. p. 4/4 (AP) . . . an American task force of atomic bombers would mean America need not fear atomic bombing. . .

+BOGEY, BOGIE, *n.* [Cf. OED, s. v

bogy, '3. *fig.* An object of terror or dread; a bugbear.' {1865}] See quots.—1944 *Life* 17 July p. 20 Before supper was over this evening, several 'bogeys'—as unidentified planes are called under such circumstances —were seen approaching from different directions . . . *Sat. Eve. Post* 26 Aug. p. 89/2. Chaplain H. M Forgy *And Pass the Ammunition* (N.Y. and Lond.: D. Appleton-Century Co., Inc.) p. 136 'Bogies!' he shouted. . . 'Sky control reports bogies! . . .' 1945 Balto. *Sun* 16 Mar. p. 4-0/6-7 Out here a bogie is an unidentified plane. It may be friendly or unfriendly. *Fortune* July p. 186. *Sat. Eve. Post* 11 Aug. p. 26/2.

BUTTERFLY BOMB. See quots.—1944 *Science N. L.* 14 Oct. p. 247/2 Recently they developed a 'butterfly bomb,' with wings that open up as soon as the bomb is released, and act like a parachute to slow its descent. . . . The small but deadly charge explodes a few feet above the ground, showering bits of hot steel on any soldiers within range. 1945 Lond. *Daily Mail* (Transatlantic ed.) 30 May p. 12/1 Experts said that it was an anti-personnel 'butterfly' bomb dropped during a German air raid on the district. . . *Newsweek* 9 July p. 21/3 . . . one of the Germans' most effective weapons was the butterfly bomb, essentially a booby trap dropped from the air. . . 1946 *TN* 13 Mar. p. 4/6 (AP) The Marine Corps Magazine, 'Leatherneck,' lists some of these as . . . butterfly bombs. . .

CREWMAN, *n.* 'A gang laborer, as at a dock. *Eng.*' (NID 1934). See quots.—1937 Balto. *Sun* 2 July p. 1/6 (AP) Captain Gray . . . will share the 22 3/4-ton Sikorsky flying boat with six other crewmen. 1945 *Science N. L.* 31 Mar. p. 197. *TN* 11 July p. 6/1 (AP) The crewmen changed uniforms for civilian clothing before leaving their planes. . . *Fortune* Aug. p. 207 One crewman was found because a search pilot spotted the man's bare white back as he walked around in a native clearing. *Newsweek* 27 Aug. p. 21/2.

DISPLACED PERSON, DP, D.P., *n.* See esp. quot. from *The Broadcaster.* (Also attrib.)—1944 *Sat. Eve. Post* 22 July p. 14/1 The Symphony of the Refugees . . . , or, as they term these people here, The Symphony of the Displaced Persons. 1945 B'ham *News-Age-Her.* 8 April p. 9-A/2 (NANA) Processing takes some days . . . when German soldiers are discarding uniforms and posing as civilians who are entitled to 'displaced person' status. *Newsweek* 16 April p. 62/1 Tens of thousands of what the Army calls DP's—displaced persons—were sweeping across occupied Germany. *Time* 16 April p. 26/3. *Life* 14 May p. 88A/1 Military authorities know them as DP's, alphabetese for 'displaced person' . . . *The Broadcaster* June p. 7 The real difficulty was and is the care of the slave laborers, men, women and children the Germans had imported from all over Europe to do their work for them. These we call Displaced Persons and for brevity refer to them as DP's. Lond. *Picture Post* 15 Sept. p. 18 I saw an exercise in the registration of D. P.s. 1946 B'ham *News-Age-Her.* 31 Mar. p. 1/7 (Edit. Sect.) Before you see them . . . it is very easy to speak of them as DPs and DP camps.

+DUMBO, *n.* A Navy PBY used for rescue work; any rescue plane. (Also attrib.)—1944 *Sat. Eve. Post* 5 Aug. p. 12/1 Like Walt Disney's elephant with the helicopter ears, its name is Dumbo. 1945 *BN* 1 June p. 14/1 (AP) In Navy parlance, a 'Dumbo' is any air-sea rescue plane. *Time* 16 July p. 22/3 Dumbo rescue planes could save most of the men who hit the water between Iwo and Saipan . . . *Ibid.* 6 Aug. p. 29/3.

EAM, E. A. M. Ethnikon Apeleutherotikon Metopon; see quots.—1944 *Time* 16 Oct. p. 45/3 The Greek resistance forces wore the insignia of E. A. M. (leftwing National Liberation Front) or E. L. A. S. (E. A. M.'s fighting arm). *TN* 5 Dec. p. 1/6 (UP) EAM is a leftist political group dominated by Communists and ELAS is its military arm. 1945 *Life* 5 Feb. p. 28/1 The antiroyalist Greek freedom movement, called EAM, contains a hard core of Communists, but more than half of all Greeks supported it. Lond. *Spect.* 21 Sept. p. 265/1.

E. L. A. S., ELAS, *n.* ['elas, 'eləs]. Ellinikos Laikos Apeleutherotikos Stratos; see quots.—1944 *Time* 16 Oct. p. 45/3 (quoted under EAM). *Newsweek* 4 Dec. p. 60. *TN* 5 Dec. p. 1/6 (UP) (quoted under EAM). 1945 *Christian Sci. Mon. Weekly Mag.* 10 Feb. p. 3/1 Greece has undergone a long series of revolutions and this fighting by ELAS is just the latest revolution in the series. Lond. *Spect.* 21 Sept. p. 265/1.

+ESCORT CARRIER. A small aircraft carrier used in convoys; see quot. 1944 and *baby flat-top* (*Am. Sp.*, 19: 223-4).—1943 *Time* 22 Nov. p. 26/3 That beats a previous high scorer: the escort carrier 'B' . . . , another 'baby flat-top,' and her escorts. 1944 *TN* 21 Feb. p 1/7 (AP) . . . American shipyards have turned out scores of escort carriers which represent conversion of cargo-type ships into 'baby flattops' . . . 1945 *Life* 30 July p. 70/2 An escort carrier and a destroyer were sunk . . . *Read. Dig.* Nov. p. 119/2 The escort carrier was our answer to that. 1946 *BN* 7 Feb. p. 1/2 (AP) Here are the Navy plans for the postwar fleets: Pacific—Nine carriers; nine escort carriers. . .

FACTORY BUSTER, FACTORY-BUSTER, *n.* See quots.—1944 *Every Week* Mar. 13-7 p. 188 The new six ton missiles have been named 'factory busters.' *Time* 7 Aug. p. 26/1. B'ham *News-Age-Her.* 15 Oct. p. 1/6 (AP) 'Even the old-type, 12,000-pound factory buster detonated on the surface. . .' *Time* 11 Dec. p. 28/3.

FFI, F. F. I., *n.* French Forces of the Interior. (Also attrib.)—1944 Balto. *Eve. Sun* 6 Sept. p. 3/2 (AP) . . . FFI leaders said the order for burning the village was not given by the division's own commander . . . *Life* 2 Oct. p. 102. *Sat. Eve. Post* 28 Oct. p. 17/1 He told them he was . . . assigned to work for the FFI within the Gestapo. 1945 *Sat. Rev. Lit.* 16 June p. 14/3 The Germans had . . . unconditionally surrendered to the F. F. I. before any Allied troops reached the city.

FIDO, *n.* See quots.—1945 *Newsweek* 11 June p. 53/2 Fido stands for 'Fog Investigation Dispersal Operation.' It was suggested in 1942 by Prime Minister Churchill to Geoffrey Lloyd. . . *Life* 2 July p. 86/2 Fido, which stands for Fog Investigation Dispersal Operation, is a system of gasoline-filled pipes laid around an airfield. When ignited, vaporized gasoline burns from hundreds of jets, dissipates the fog by heating the air. *Think* July p. 30 The experiment, conducted by Fog Investigation Dispersal Operation, affectionately known as 'Fido,' took place . . . at the Christmas season. . . *Read. Dig.* Sept. p. 35. B'ham *News-Age-Her.* 9 Dec. p. 1/1 (Edit. Sect.) The process is known as 'FIDO' which means 'fog investigation dispersal operation.'

+FLYING JEEP, *n.* Name applied to the Aeronca L-3 Defender, the Piper L-4B-4, and the Taylorcraft L-2A (Winter *War Planes of All Nations*, N.Y., Crowell, p. 104); see also 1944 *Sat. Eve. Post* quot.; see *grasshopper* (*Am. Sp.*, 19: 225/1).—1943 Winter *loc. cit.* The Army has found nothing to touch these 'flying jeeps.' 1944 *TN* 17 Feb. p. 4/4 (AP) A cargo of frozen blood rushed by Cub airplane, those flying jeeps of the battle front, saved at least a dozen lives. . . *Sat. Eve. Post* 26 Feb. p. 39 (Vultee adv.) SENTINEL. . . 'Flying Jeep' 1945 *Life* 29 Oct. p. 69/1 Officially designated L-4s, they were known to GIs as 'grasshoppers,' 'puddle jumpers,' 'flying jeeps' and 'putt-putts.'

+GI, G.I., GI JOE, G.I. JOE, *n.* See quots.—1943 *Time* 15 Nov. p. 11 (letter) I am surprised that you ask for 'a name for soldiers who also serve—behind the front.' . . . That term, of course, is 'G. I.' 1944 *Britannica Book of the Year* p. 770/1 GI, GI Joe, *n.* An American soldier. *GI* is to the army as a whole what *doughboy* is to the infantry. (Short for *GI soldier*, -1941.) *adj.* Pertaining to the army services, or ministering to its needs, as 'GI food,' 'a GI dance.' (General issue.) Lond. *Spect.* 5 May p. 400/2 Relations between British other ranks and their equivalents, the American G. I., notoriously vary. . . 1945 *Science N. L.* 3 Feb. p. 74. *Time* 26 Feb. p. 7/1 (Lt. Dave Breger) In the first issue of *Yank*, June 17, 1942, the comic strip G. I. Joe made its debut. . . If anyone can offer documentary evidence of publication of the term 'G. I. Joe' before June 17, 1942 I will cheerfully withdraw my claim. 1946 *Sat. Rev. Lit.* 6 April p. 6/3. It is not news that thousands of GI's made a handsome profit out of selling watches, clothes, and PX items to the Russians. . .

+G-SUIT, *n.* See quots. Also called *Anti-G Suit*.—1945 *TN* 9 Jan. p. 6/2-3 (NEA) G-suits (the G stands for gravity) have been adopted by the Army Air Forces to prevent fighter pilots from 'blacking out' . . . in steep dives. The anti-gravity pneumatic pants apply pressure to the pilot's abdomen and legs, preventing the blood from pooling in the lower extremities. The pants may be inflated . . . by lung-power or mechanically. *Science N. L.* 1 Jan. p. 57. Balto. *Sun* 1 Mar. p. 1/5 The pilot of the P-80 also will be equipped with the pneumatic 'G-suit' designed by Air Forces engineers to combat the discomforts caused by sharp turns. . . *Read. Dig.* May p. 41/1 The secret was a bit of medical engineering that a few Navy and Army doctors and old fliers had been working on for years, called the G suit. It consisted of five small bladders, a few lengths of hose, and a little trick valve, all weighing less than five pounds. *Ibid.* May p. 42/2 . . . when the first Anti-G suits were developed fliers would not wear them.

HUMP, *n.* See quots.—1944 *TN* 16 June p. 2/1 (AP) Now every drop [of gasoline] must be flown over the Himalayan 'hump' by the Super Fortresses themselves. *Time* 26 June p. 52/1 They're flying it over 'The Hump'—the towering Himalayas between India and China. It's the most treacherous 500-mile air route in the world. *Life* 11 Sept. p. 81 A China-Bound C-46 Starts Over The Stormswept Himalayan Hump Which Begins In Burma East of The Salween River With A Cluster Of 18,000-Foot Peaks. 1945 *BN* 25 June p. 7/4 Most used air route in the world is . . . over 'The Hump' between China and India. *Sat. Eve. Post* 11 Aug. p. 21/1.

ISLAND.* 'Anything regarded as resembling an island in position, isolation, etc. . . .' (NID 1934). +See quot. *Life* 30 July.—1945 Richmond (Va.) *News Leader* 19 Mar. p. 22/1 It's [flight deck] so narrow that when planes take off they use the left side of the deck, in order that their right wing tip won't come too close to the 'island' as they pass. *Read. Dig.* May p. 125/1 The carrier's huge looming island blotted out the sky as he brushed past it. *Life* 9 July p. 28/1. *Ibid.* 30 July p. 68/1 Jap Pilot Makes Perfect Hit on 'Suwannee's' Island (Superstructure), The Nerve Center Of The Ship.

+JATO, *n.* See quots. (Also attrib.)—1944 *Science N. L.* 7 Oct. p. 229/3 Of particular value on the restricted area of carrier flight decks, JATO, as jet-assisted takeoffs are known in the Navy, will also be extremely useful for lifting heavily-laden flying boats from the water. 1945 *Sci. Amer.* Jan. p. 25; cited *Read. Guide* 14: 858/1 Jato rocket units being tested for assisted take-offs. Balto. *Sun* 24 Feb. p. 2/1 Jato is navy lingo for 'jet assisted takeoff.' *Sat. Eve. Post* 19 May p. 26/1 With the help of a new flying wrinkle called jatos—jet-assisted take-offs—Navy planes are now leaping out of some spectacularly tight spots. *Newsweek* 4 June p. 90.

+JET, *n.* Short for jet-propelled plane. (See *Am. Sp.*, 20: 144-5)—1944 *Collier's* 22 April p. 13/3 . . . the jet . . . is capable of faster flight at low altitudes than any airplane with conventional engines and propeller. Lond. *Eve. Stand.* 28 Oct. p. 2 Battle of the jets is on. *Science N. L.* 28 Oct. p. 277. 1945 *Newsweek* 26 Nov. p. 76/1 A midget jet, small enough to fit in the wing of a regular plane. . .

+LCI, *n.* See quot. *Newsmap*.—1943 *Time* 22 Nov. p. 24/3 The broad wake of a PT, plus the outline of the LCI, must have looked like bigger game. 1944 *Newsmap* 21 Feb. 2: 44/6 LCI—The landing craft for infantry is one of the larger troop landing types. Troops disembark on the extended ramps on both sides of the bow. Length 155 ft. *Ladies' Home Jour.* June p. 20/1 Mike Bradley was on the bridge of his LCI (Landing Craft, Infantry) dreamily smoking his pipe. . . 1945 *Science N. L.* 10 Feb. p. 90.

+LCM, *n.* See quots.—1943 *Time* 4 Oct. p. 63/2 As early as 1936 the Navy experimented with tank lighters, and from these tests emerged the LCM (Landing Craft, Mechanized), a 50-footer which carries a crew of four and a medium tank. 1944 *Ibid.* 3 April p. 66/3 LCM (Landing Craft, Medium), in 50- and 56-ft. lengths, for a bulldozer or medium tank. . . 1945 N.Y. *Times Mag.* 7 Jan. p. 9/2 LCM's bear to the trucks metal drums containing vital airplane gasoline.

+LCR, *n.* See quots.—1944 *Newsmap* 21 Feb. 2: 44/6 LCR—Landing craft-rubber are light, quickly-inflated types used with oars, outboard motors, or towed. Length 12 ft. 1944 *Time* 3 April p. 66/3 LCR (Landing Craft, Rubber), in 12- and 16-ft. sizes, to land patrols of seven to ten men. *Life* 15 May p. 99.

+LCT, *n.* See quots.—1943 *Newsweek* 27 Sept. p. 23/2 The row of LCT's on the beach belching vehicles looks like a long line of stranded, gasping whales. *Time* 4 Oct. p. 63/2 As an intermediate step between this small boat [LCM] and the ocean-going LST, the Navy designed a 100-ft. LCT (Landing Craft, Tank), which can be carried to zones of operation on the deck of an LST or a cargo vessel. 1945 *Science N.L.* 10 Feb. p. 90.

+LCVP, *n.* See quot. *Newsmap*.—1944 *Newsmap* 21 Feb. 2: 44/6 LCVP—This landing craft for vehicles and personnel is one of the smaller types carried aboard an LST. Length 36 ft. *This Week* 7 May p. 23/2 One by one the LCVP's moved onto the coral shelf and filled themselves with the wounded, and then pulled off and transferred them to larger LCM's. . . *Sat. Eve. Post* 3 June p. 20/1 The Elsie was an LCVP—landing craft, vehicle, personnel—an open box some thirty-five feet long by nine feet broad. . . 1945 *Time* 2 April p. 26/1.

+LORAN, *n.* See quots. (Also attrib.) —1945 *Newsweek* 20 Aug. p. 42/3 Loran (Long-Range Navigation) which through radar impulses sent from ground stations, permits the pilot to calculate his position and guide him to the target. *TN* 18 Oct. p. 5/2-5 (NEA) Loran employs pairs of transmitting stations, each of which sends out radio impulses. In the airplane, a loran receiver measures the difference in radio wave travel time in millionths of a second, permitting the navigator to chart his exact position. *Science N. L.* 3 Nov. p. 275/2 Loran gets its name from the fact that it is a long range aid to navigation (*lo* from long, *r* from range, *a* from aid, and *n* from navigation).

+LST, *n.* See quots.—1943 *Life* 11 Oct. p. 34/2 The first is the LST (Landing Ship, Tank), 327 ft. long and displacing 5,500 tons. This is about the length of a destroyer and the tonnage of an average freighter. 1944 *Sat. Eve. Post* 3 June p. 20/1 . . . a fleet of LST's had gathered to launch the amphibious LVT's. . . *Science N. L.* 4 Nov. p. 295. 1945 *Read. Dig.* June p. 12/1. 1946 *BN* 3 April p. 1/6 (AP) An LST picked up two school children. . .

+MVA, *n.* See quots.—1944 *New Rep.* 4 Sept. p. 266/2 The antagonisms that flared over the Battle of the Missouri, fought in Washington in a fantastic array of men and bureaus, argued in essence for an MVA. 1945 *Life* 13 Aug. p. 71 MVA stands for Missouri Valley Authority. . . *Collier's* 22 Dec. p. 82/1 Is an MVA—Missouri Valley Authority—on its way into existence? Omaha (Neb.) *World-Her.* 30 Dec. p. 7-A/6 MVA Given Wallace Plug.

+PAC, P. A. C., *n.* The Political Action Committee of the Congress of Industrial Organizations. See *Life* quot. (Also attrib.)—1944 *BN* 8 Aug. p. 1/5 (AP) He also asked an inquiry to determine whether some government officials active in PAC work had violated the Hatch 'no politics' act. *Life* 11 Sept. p. 91/3 Accordingly, at a C. I. O. executive meeting July 7, 1943 they set up P. A. C. as a committee to support labor's interest within the established two-party system. 1945 *Time Index* 1 Jan.–25 June p. 37/3.

+POW, P. O. W., PW, *n.* [pi ˈdʌbəljə] Prisoner of War. (Also attrib.)—1944 *BN* 1 April p. 1/5 Missing Guns Sought In Nazi Colorado Prison; PWs Strike. *Harper's* Nov. p. 541/2 But some of the poems and prose pieces that came in from the 'P. O. W.'s' (Prisoners of War) tear your heart out. . . 1945 *Time* 19 Mar. p. 20/3.

+SKYMASTER, *n.* See quots.—1943 *Aviation* June p. 377 A pair of 'Wings for Victory' by Douglas, the new 'Skymaster'—Army C-54 Combat Transport. 1945 *Newsweek* 25 June p. 30/2. *Fortune* Aug. p. 164/1 Twenty per cent are the C-54, the Douglas Skymaster, whose four engines can take a load of three tons across the Atlantic with only one stop for refueling. *Time* 26 Nov. p. 86/2. San Francisco *News* 27 Dec. p. 18/5-8 First of the new, postwar Douglas Skymaster transports will soon be placed in service by Western Air Lines on its San Francisco-Los Angeles-San Diego route.

+SNAFU, *n.* [ˈsnæfu] See quots.—1942 *Time* 15 June; cited *Am. Sp.*, 18: 77/1 . . . *snafu*, situation normal; all fouled up. 1943 *Am. Mercury* Nov. p. 555/2. 1944 *Life* 16 Oct. p. 20/2 It is a symbol of SNAFU (Situation Normal; All Fouled Up), and a star is rated for each snafued campaign after Guadalcanal. 1945 *TN* 5 Aug. p. 4/3 (AP) The Marines are said to have coined the expression 'SNAFU' (abreviation [sic] for 'situation normal: all fouled up').

STRATEGIC BOMBING, *n.* [Cf. OED, s. v. *strategy*, 2: '. . . the art of projecting and directing the larger military movements and operations of a campaign.' {1810-}] See second quot.—1941 *Nineteenth Cent.* Sept. p. 163 Bombing of cities . . . is a true example of strategic bombing. . . 1944 *Scholastic* 3 April p. 24 American bombing is *strategic* bombing. Its aim is to cripple the enemy's industrial power, and destroy much of his economic strength. To do this we must bomb specific targets such as factories, oil refineries, aircraft plants and the like. 1945 *Read. Dig.* May p. 82/2 Consequently, any plan of strategic bombing to destroy Japan's capacity to make war . . . must include the destruction of these thousands of family factories. *Life* 20 Aug. p. 32/2 From the very concept strategic bombing, all the developments—night, pattern, saturation, area, indiscriminate—have led straight to Hiroshima. . . *Sat. Eve. Post* 1 Sept. p. 23/1.

+STRATOVISION, *n.* [*strato-* (see *Am. Sp.* 20: 303) + *vision*]. See quots. (Also attrib.)—1945 Cleve. *Plain Dealer* 10 Aug. p. 1/5 (AP) The stratovision system simply puts the antenna and transmitter in an airplane flying in lazy circles 30,000 feet above the earth, out of sight of human eyes. The short waves sent out from this air-borne antenna would blanket the earth's surface like a great inverted ice cream cone, covering an area 422 miles across. . . *Time* 20 Aug. p. 67/1 Westinghouse estimates that it would cost $1,000-an-hour to operate each such stratovision station. . . Stratovision, which is Westinghouse's name for the scheme, will probably be tested in the fall. Balto. *Sun* 2 Sept. p. 15/5 The 'stratovision' system developed jointly by the Westinghouse Electric Corporation and the Glenn L. Martin Company will place television on a sound business footing for the first time. . . *The Spiral* Oct. p. 4 STRATOVISION—Soon you will hear about television rebroadcast from planes flying 30,000 feet up.

+SUPER-DUMBO, SUPERDUMBO, *n.* See *Dumbo;* see quots.—1945 *BN* 1 June p. 14/1 (AP) A Super-Dumbo is the name given a B-29 which accompanies a strike mission in the role of shepherd, observer, and rescuer to any Superfort which might hit trouble. *Time* 6 Aug. p. 29/3 A B-29 Superdumbo, assigned to keep radio and visual watch for airmen going down, spotted three life rafts in the water.

UNO, *n.* See quots. (Also attrib.)—1945 *TN* 15 Nov. p. 4/4 (AP) The ideas range like this . . . let the United Nations Organization (UNO) handle it. . . *Newsweek* 26 Nov. p. 25 Even though UNO headquarters may be in San Francisco, its success or failure lies in Europe. 1946 Lond. *Spect.* 1 Feb. p. 109.

UNRRA, U. N. R. R. A., *n.* [ˈʌn,rɑ]. See quots. (Also attrib.)—1943 Lond. *Spect.* 26 Nov. p. 494/2 U. N. R. R. A. at Work 1944 *Newsweek* 25 Sept. p. 36 Twice the United Nations Relief and Rehabilitation Conference had been held up. . . On Sept. 16 . . . at Montreal . . . the second meeting in the UNRRA came to order at last. 1945 *Time Index* 1 Jan.–25 June, inc. p. 58/2 UNRRA See United Nations Relief and Rehabilitation Administration. 1946 *BN* 6 April p. 4/5 Such a program has been urged by UNRRA officials. . .

V-BOMB, -WEAPON, *n.* General terms to describe V-1, V-2, etc. See *Am. Sp.*, 19: 307/2, 20: 146/2. (Also attrib.)—1944 Balto. *Eve. Sun* 13 Sept. p. 1/6 (AP) The Germans, after toning down their 'V' weapons threat for a few days, are now making new threats. *Time* 4 Dec. p. 30/3 Into Britain's book of reckoning went another V-bomb tragedy. . . 1945 *TN* 3 Jan. p. 2/2 Danish Patriots Blow Up V-Weapon Plant. *Harper's* June (Brief Reviews) . . . the V-bombs were falling. . .

+V-DAY, *n.* The day of final victory over the Axis powers. (Also attrib.)—1942 *Time* 16 Mar. p. 11 V-day must bring opportunity. 1944 *Current Hist.* Jan. p. 13. Balto. *Eve. Sun* 18 Sept. p. 1/2 There will be no V-day celebration in Hawaii the day Germany is defeated. 1945 *Sat. Rev. Lit.* 10 Mar. p. 5/1 (Allen Walker Read) Through the early part of the year the term *V-Day* sufficed to refer to the anticipated day of victory, but in September, at the suggestion of James F. Byrnes, Director of War Mobilization, the newspapers began using *V-E Day* and *V-J Day*. *BN* 11 April p. 13/2 (AP) 'The war won't be over on V-Day.'

+V-E, V-E Day, VE-Day, *n.* See quots.—1944 *Newsweek* 18 Sept. p. 72 James F. Byrnes . . . backstopped all agencies with an omnibus report to the President predicting 40 per cent cutback in war production on 'V-E,' (Victory Day in Europe, as distinguished from 'V-J,' Victory Day in Japan). 1945 *BN* 30 Mar. p. 11/1 That's a mighty important question which should be settled now, in advance of VE-Day. *Musical America* 25 April p. 11/1.

2. *Specific.* See quots.—1945 *TN* 9 May p. 1/5 (UP) Britain observed the second day of the V-E celebration in comparative calm. . . *Time* 14 May p. 18/3 Thus, for the history books, May 8, 1945, became V-E day. *Sat. Rev. Lit.* 19 May p. 6/1 Here is the first part of the text of a radio verse-drama by Carl Carmer which was presented over the CBS network on the evening of V-E Day, May 8, 1945. 1946 *Sat. Eve. Post* 6 April p. 114/4 Shortly after V-E Day, the division arrived in Austria. . .

+V-J DAY, *n.* See first quot.—1944 *Newsweek* 18 Sept. p. 72 (quoted under V-E). *Ibid.* 2 Oct. p. 24 Planning for America's between-victories period—V-E Day to V-J Day—centers on two main problems. 1945 *TN* 12 Aug. p. 1/1 (AP) V-J Day in Alabama will be observed as a 'day of rejoicing.'

2. *Specific.* See first quot.—1945 Balto. *Sun* 2 Sept. p. 1/1 (AP) President Truman tonight proclaimed Sunday, September 2, as V-J day. . . *Time* 10 Sept. p. 19/3 When V-J day finally came, it was an anticlimax. The war had been over for 18 days. . . 1946 *BN* 3 April p. 1/3-4 (AP) Employment, which slumped after V-J Day, is 'building up steadily. . .'

+WAR-WEARY, *n.* See quots. (Also attrib.)—1945 *Sat. Eve. Post* 17 Mar. p. 20 Thousands of once-precious B-17's are now 'war-wearies.' Not worth salvaging, they clutter up foreign and domestic airfields. *Fortune* Aug. p. 208 . . . five war-weary Liberators, described with horror by their pilots as 'clunkers.' *Am. Sp.* Oct. p. 227/2 *War-weary.* Applied to aircraft too badly damaged to repair overseas, sent back to this country for rehabilitation or junking. 1946 *Time* 11 Feb. p. 86/3. . . Paul Mantz is no novice at making money on war-weary aircraft.

WINGMAN, WING MAN, *n.* See second quot.—1945 *Read. Dig.* May p. 43/2 Perhaps no flier loves the Zoot Suit more than the vitally important wingmen. *Sat. Eve. Post* 23 June p. 6/2 . . . a wingman . . . is the second man in a team of two, each flying a fighter plane. When you see two planes flying along, one of them just to one side of and staggered back from the leader, then you have seen a wingman. The basic job of the wingman is to protect the leader when the leader is going after a Jap or is in a tangle with one. *BN* 17 Sept. p. 7/1 His two wing men were so close behind and to either side of him that I ran between them with no shots traded.

AMONG THE NEW WORDS

I. WILLIS RUSSELL
University of Alabama

IN THE April, 1946, issue 'Among the New Words' contained some observations on the part abbreviations have played and are playing in the American language especially. The appearance of the 1945 Webster's New Words Supplement (*NID Sup.* 1945) suggests some additional remarks.

A comparison of the Supplements of 1939 and 1945 reveals that, in the opinion of the editors of *NID*, some 72 abbreviations have become a part of the general American vocabulary since 1939. These can be divided into two groups according to whether they are pronounced (53) or not (19). Among the latter we find *FM* (frequency modulation), *MTB* (motor torpedo boat), the more familiar *AMG,* and the government bureaus *OCD, ODT, OPA, OWI,* and *WLB.* It seems strange that no pronunciations are indicated for at least some of these bureaus. Surely few say 'Office of Price Administration,' even 'Office of War Information'; rather they are [ˈoˈpiˈe] and [ˈoˈdʌbljuˈaɪ]. Even in writing, *OPA* and *OWI* seem to be the usual forms, whether or not the full form has previously been used in a given article, though the Webster treatment would indicate otherwise.

For 53 of the abbreviations pronunciations are given. As might be expected, initials occupy the largest group (31): *AA, AT, DE, DNB, E, GI, PABA, POW, PW, TD* are a few. The semi-abbreviations include *D day, E-boat, M day, PT boat, Q fever,* and *V-mail.* Then come 14 combinations of initials which make actual words: *flak, Ovra, piat, radar, reefer* (this is really *refr.*, refrigerator car), *Tass, UNRRA,* and *WAVES.* Of this latter group, six are pronounced not only as words but also by their initials: *SPARS, WAAF, WAAS, WAC, WASP,* and *WOWS.*

Several of these abbreviations form a type which may be called 'initial plus day': *D day, M day,* and *V day* (s. v. *V* in *NID Sup.* 1945). This type is of interest because it seems to be responsible for a considerable progeny of combinations, many of which are doubtless nonce forms. Though the vogue seems to be recent, the type is fairly old. In a specific sense, it goes back at least to 1916, when *A*[labama] *day* occurs in the University of Alabama *Crimson-White* (6 Apr. p. 1/2): 'That each class will be well represented in the inter-class meet to be held on "A" day, April 14, seems assured.' *A day* is well established now at the University. According to the Army, *D day* dates from 7 September 1918 (*Time* 12 June 1944 p. 2/2; *Am. Sp.* 19:305/1), but its great popularity seems to stem from World War II. According to an entry in Fraser and Gibbons (*Soldier and Sailor Words and Phrases*, 1925, s. v. *Z Day;* I am indebted here to Mr. Peter Tamony), *Z day* was used in the same way as *D day* during the first World War. Their entry deserves to be quoted in full:

> *Z DAY:* The official term for the date fixed for any important operation, the letter 'Z,' as a contraction for 'Zero,' being adopted for secrecy in lieu of naming beforehand the exact date. The days immediately preceding were indicated by the preceding letters of the alphabet—*e.g.,* The opening of the main attack of the Somme was fixed for June 29th, and notified beforehand as 'Z Day.' The four days for the preliminary bombardment, June 25th to 28th, were referred to in communications simply as 'V,' 'W,' 'X,' and 'Y' days, no calendar dates being given.

This system seems not to have become general.

The present vogue of *-day* combinations seems to date from 1943, possibly under the influence of the increasing use of *D day.* 'Attack day' in the Pacific was named *A day,* a variant of *D day* in Europe (*Newsweek* 30 Oct. 1944 p. 28; *Time* 30 Oct. 1944 p. 21/3). In Jefferson County, Alabama, the Fifth War Loan opened on *B*[ond] *day* (*BN* 27 May 1944 p. 1/1). Clarion radio had a *C*[larion] *day* in an advertisement (*Chr. Sci. Mon. Mag.* 28 Oct. 1944 p. 10); in a Conoco advertisement it became *C*[ar] *day,* the day when new cars would again be available (*Sat. Eve. Post* 16 Dec. 1944 p. 53). An editorial writer in the Tuscaloosa (Ala.) *News* referred to *D day* in Japan as *DJ-day* (13 July 1945 p. 4/2). *E-day* has been used for 'Education Day' (*TN* 3 Dec. 1945 p. 7/3) and 'Eisenhower Day' (*ibid.* 22 June 1945 p. 1/3). *F*[light] *day* was employed by Elsa Maxwell (N. Y. *Post* 29 Nov. 1944 p. 12/2; cited *Sat. Rev. Lit.* 10 Mar. 1945 p. 5/1). *H-day,* a counterpart of the University of Alabama *A day,* is used by Howard College in Birmingham (*BN* 30 May 1944 p. 9/3). There have been several *M days.* Not only is there the seemingly permanent, generalized *M*[obilization] *day* (defined in *NID Sup.* 1945) but such apparently vogue uses as *M*[oving] *day* in Canada (*Time* 1 May 1944 p. 22/3) and *M-day*, 'the day when the butcher's meat safe will be filled with the cuts we used to buy and can't buy now' (N. Y. *Times Mag.* 1 Apr. 1945 p. 24/2). *R-day* has been employed not only for the 'anniversary of the Russian revolution' (*PM* 19 Nov. 1944 p. 11) but as 'the day for the official start of redeployment' (*Am. Sp*, 21:150/2; *Sat. Rev. Lit.* 22 June 1946 p. 6/2). *S-day* has been used for 'surrender day' (*Time* 24 Jan. 1944 p. 14/1; cited *Sat. Rev. Lit.* 10 Mar. 1945 p. 5/1) and for 'school day' (*Time* 25 Sept. 1944 p. 64/3), *T*[ax] *day* has been used several times (*ibid.* 23 Mar. 1942 p. 15/3; B'ham *News–Age-Her.* 14 Jan. p. 1-B/6; *Printer's Ink* 11 May 1945 p. 11). 'Total victory day' was called *T-V day* in a letter in *Newsweek* (25 June 1945 p. 14; see also *Sat. Rev. Lit.* 22 June 1946 p.6/2). *V-E day* and *V-J day* are evidently permanent additions to the language. These combinations may be partly responsible for *V-A* [victory in Asia?] *day* (*Time* 11 Dec. 1944 p. 25/3; *Fortune* May 1945 p. 194), *V-O* [victory on Okinawa] *day* (Lincoln [Neb.] *Jour.* 24 June 1945 p. 8/3), as well as *V-P day* and *V-R day* to describe the days of victory in the Pacific and over Russia respectively (*Sat. Rev. Lit.* 22 June 1946 p. 6/2). An *L-day* and an *O-day* have been recorded, but what the initials stand for is not clear.

Other readers will have doubtless noted other illustrations of *-day* combinations. The progeny must be even larger than indicated here.

Acknowledgments: For citations, to the American Dialect Society and to members of its Committee on New Words as follows: Henry Alexander (4), Clarence L. Barnhart (4), Atcheson L. Hench (2), Mamie J. Meredith (26), Peter Tamony (5); also Dwight L. Bolinger (3) and Margaret M. Bryant (1). Dr. G. Burke Johnston kindly supplied the definition of *terminal leave*. Thanks are due the University of Alabama Research Committee for secretarial help.

The abbreviation '*BN*' is used for the Birmingham (Ala.) *News* and '*TN*' for the Tuscaloosa (Ala.) *News*.

Symbols: The symbol + before a word or definition indicates an Americanism. A date immediately following a word or definition indicates the time of evidence shown in the DAE, or, if so stated, in another publication. Dates in brackets indicate the time, etc., of British usage. An asterisk after a word indicates that the word is illustrated in British usage before 1600.

+AEROSOL BOMB. See quot. 1946.—1944 *Read. Dig.* May p. 45 Today every soldier in mosquito country is armed with an 'aerosol bomb'—a specially designed container about twice the size of a hand grenade... *TN* 2 Nov. p. 2/4 (AP) When used in the new automatic spraying device called the aerosol bomb . . . the product promises to become an effective postwar weapon against flies in homes... 1945 *Harper's Mag.* Feb. p. 266/2. 1946 *Sci. N. L.* 30 Mar. p. 204 The contents of the Army insect-killing device known as the aerosol bomb included 3% DDT, 2% of a 20% pyrethrum concentrate, 5% cyclohexanone, 5% lubricating oil, and 85% Freon gas as carrier.

+ATOMIC AGE. The period after August 6, 1945, when the first atomic bomb was publicly dropped.—1945 *TN* 8 Aug. p. 1/2 (UP) Forty-eight hours after the historic announcements proclaiming the dawn of the atomic age, officials felt soberly constrained to point out that the new era has yet to reach its zenith. *Life* 27 Aug. p. 29/2 During the last week of World War II and the first of the so-called Atomic Age, lively celebrations, prayerful thanksgivings . . . were in evidence. 1946 *Time* 29 July p. 22/3 Atomic Age.

+DENAZIFICATION, DE-, *n.* The eradication of that which is associated with Naziism.—1944 *Sat. Rev. Lit.* 19 Aug. p. 10 That 'more' makes for a swift-moving, action-packed, and at the same time poignant story which keeps the reader well in suspense and is likely to satisfy his hope for a de-Nazification of Germany's killers. N. Y. *Times Mag.* 8 Oct. p. 2/2 'Denazification' is a sudden new word in the language. 1945 Lincoln (Neb.) *Jour.* 5 Aug. p. 3-A/5 (AP) Denazification of German names of places has brought some strange new signs to streets and squares of old Bavaria. *Time* 8 Oct. p. 31/1 General Eisenhower himself realized that 'de-Nazification' was easier said than done. 1946 *Sat. Eve. Post.* 3 Aug. p. 18/1.

+FOX-, FOXHOLE CIRCUIT. [See *NID Sup.* 1945, s. v. *foxhole*.] A theater circuit at the fighting fronts played by American troupes.—1944 *Newsweek* 31 July p. 60 The performers who were selected to make up the first entertainment . . . wave, as part of USO-Camp Show's 'Foxhole Circuit,' are not famous in the ordinary sense. 1945 *Musical Amer.* 25 Jan. p. 7/1 (headline) Marjorie Lawrence Brings Wagner to Fox-hole Circuit in Australia. *Amer. Leg. Mon.* May p. 42 The show was requested for an immediate tour of the foxhole circuit 'up front' in Italy. 1946 *Life* 18 Feb. p. 49/1 The Lunts' show is a cheerful comedy . . . which they have been playing since 1944, first in London . . . then on the 'Foxhole Circuit' from Paris to Nürnberg. . .

+GENOCIDE. See first quot.—1945 London *Sunday Times* 21 Oct. p. 7 The United Nations' indictment of the 24 Nazi leaders has brought a new word into the language—genocide. It occurs in Count 3, where it is stated that all the defendants 'conducted deliberate and systematic genocide—namely, the extermination of racial and national groups.' [¶] The word was coined from the Gk. *genos* (race) and the Latin *cide* (killing) by Prof. Raphael Lemkin of Duke University. *BN* 27 Dec. p. 14/2 World War II brought several new words into the English vocabulary . . . and a London report points to a new one, 'genocide' . . . 1946 *This Week* 17 Feb. p. 21/1 The United Nations indictment against Nazi war criminals has brought a new word into the English language... The word is *genocide*...

+ISLAND-, ISLAND HOPPING. See quot. *Time*. (Also attrib.)—1944 *Newsweek* 17 July p. 9 Between major actions Bill fills in by island-hopping about the Pacific... *Sat. Eve. Post* 28 Oct. p. 98/3 Another conceded that American air power won the battles for Attu, Kwajalein and Tarawa, and has made possible island hopping. 1945 *Time* 25 June p. 69/2 A cartoon called *Island Hopping* shows a steel-spring mannikin stepping triumphantly toward the Jap home fortress over Pacific islands which are not all terra firma. *Chr. Sci. Mon. Mag.* 10. Nov. p. 12. 1946 *Sat. Rev.. Lit.* 23 Feb. p. 33/1 . . .' Cant takes us along on the island-hopping campaigns. . .

+LUNATIC FRINGE. See *Am. Sp.* 19: 62/2. Add earlier illust.—1913 Theodore Roosevelt *History as Literature* (C. Scribner's Sons) p. 305; quoted by C. A. Smith *New Words Self-Defined* (Doubleday, Page, 1919) p. 52 It is vitally necessary to move forward and to shake off the dead hand, often the fossilized dead hand, of the reactionaries; and yet we have to face the fact that there is apt to be a lunatic fringe among the votaries of any forward movement. In this recent art exhibition the lunatic fringe was fully in evidence, especially in the rooms devoted to the Cubists and the Futurists, or Near-Impressionists.

MOMENTARILY. See *Am. Sp.* 20: 142. Add earlier illust.—1847 Brönte *Jane Eyre* (Nelson ed.) p. 169 During the early part of the morning, I momentarily expected his coming; he was not in the frequent habit of entering the schoolroom, but he did step in for a few minutes sometimes, and I had the impression that he was sure to visit it that day.

+PRE-ATOMIC, *adj.* Prior to August 6, 1945; see *atomic age*.—1945 N. Y. *Times* 12 Aug. p. 8E/4 To talk about limited, almost parochial pre-atomic subjects, there is the important war of 1914-18... *New Yorker* 25 Aug. p. 16 We . . . affectionately hailed a pre-atomic taxi, and went home . . . *Life* 17 Sept. p. 40/1. *BN* 10 Dec. p. 7/5 (headline) Pre-Atomic Explosive Known As 'RDX' Also Made In Tennessee.

+PREFAB, *n.* Short for *prefabricated* (see *NID Sup.* 1945 s. v. *prefabricate, v. t.*). (Also attrib.)—1942 *Bus. Week* 24 Jan. p. 17/2 (title) Break for Prefab. *Time* 16 Mar. p. 77/3 This year 20% of all new houses may be prefabs. . . 1944 *Arch. Rec.* Dec. p. 69/1 Expansible Prefab House for Postwar. 1946 Balto. *Sun* 8 Feb. p. 4/2 (AP) Wyatt told the committee that 'prefabs' would 'play a very considerable part' in the housing problem. Omaha (Neb.) *World-Her.* 21 April p. 6-A/3 (AP) Basic Prefab Code May Speed Building.

+PRE-, PREFABRICATOR. See quots. —1940 *Read. Dig.* July p. 99 Gunnison Housing Corporation, largest of prefabricators, recently sold several factory-built houses in Springfield, Ill. 1942 *Bus. Week* 24 Jan. p. 17/3 Capacity of present prefabricators plus some 200 woodworking shops that can be converted to house manufacturing is believed to be about 8,000 to 12,000 houses a month. 1946 *Time* 11 Feb. p. 79/2 The nation's prefabricators have answered: maybe.

+PROXIMITY FUZE (FUSE). See quots.—1945 *Sci. N. L.* 6 Oct. p. 214/1 The proximity fuze, a tiny radio set device in the nose of the projectile, is rated as the U. S. A. No. 2 secret weapon. *Life* 22 Oct. p. 99/1 One of the war's great secret weapons was the radio proximity fuze which in importance ranks with the atomic bomb and radar. *Time* 31 Dec. p. 51/2. 1946 N. Y. *Times* 10 Mar. p. E9. Johns Hopkins *Alumni Mag.* Mar. p. 76 The function of the [proximity] fuze is thus to cause the shell to explode at a position where maximum damage will ensue, for example at a certain position with respect to an airplane or a certain height above ground.

+RETURNEE. See quots. (Also attrib.) —1944 *Newsweek* 17 July p. 62 The biography of a returnee fits into a regular pattern. 1945 *Chr. Sci. Mon. Mag.* 17 Mar. p. 10/2 A Launch Filled With Returnees and Their Wives Sets Out on Exploration Tour of the Coves. . . *Life* 16 Apr. p. 110/2 Many of the fliers were 'returnees,' men who had already been overseas and had come back for further training and reassignment. 1946 *New Yorker* 23 Mar. p. 53 They may have lists of returnees.

+RUPTURED DUCK. See quots. (Also attrib.)—1945 *Time* 29 Oct. p. 11/1 . . . the design of the present discharge button is not popular (G. Is know it as the 'ruptured duck'). *TN* 26 Dec. p. 4/4 Neither would admit they were patronizing the same press agent, who didn't like the ruptured duck insignia for discharged servicemen. 1946 *Ladies' Home Jour.* Feb. p. 13/2 But since then we have won our wars, returned home and have been given the ruptured duck (discharge emblem—Ed.). *Newsweek* 18 Mar. p. 34/1 n. *Am. Sp.* Apr. p. 153/2 RUPTURED DUCK. . . The 'ruptured' must have come from the fact that one wing of the eagle is underneath and extends beyond the circular design of the button. *Sat. Rev. Lit.* 25 May p. 16/2.

+STATESIDE, STATES-SIDE, *adj. & adv.* Relating to the United States; in the direction of, in the United States.—1944 Karig and Kelley *Battle Report* (Farrar & Rinehart, Inc.) p. 151 . . . it occurred to him that Stateside newspapers might carry stories of the air attack. . . 1945 *Sat. Eve. Post* 16 June p. 21/1 There was just this States-side skirt frisking around. San Francisco *News* 28 July p. 7/1 . . . nobody thought about that possibility when Joe got back stateside... *Newsweek* 13 Aug. p. 101/1. *Life* 29 Oct. p. 40/2 The Navy . . . was going stateside. 1946 *Sat. Rev. Lit.* 16 Mar. p. 8 (title) Stateside, 1941-5.

+SUPER-, SUPERSENIORITY. See quots. (Also attrib.)—1944 *Fortune* Oct. p. 260/2 It would also protect the seniority principle, on which, labor argues, veterans will want to rely if cutbacks occur after their one-year period of superseniority... *Nation* 11 Nov. p. 594/2; cited A. W. Read in *Sat. Rev. Lit.* 10 Mar. 1945 p. 5/3 Veterans must not be set apart, but the Veterans' Personnel Division expounds an interpretation of the Selective Service Act which directs the firing of any worker, even with greater seniority, to make way for the veteran with his 'super-seniority.' 1945 *Newsweek* 10 Sept. p. 71 In the first clear-cut decision on veterans' 'superseniority,' Judge Matthew T. Abruzzo . . . ruled that Fishgold was entitled to his job 'in preference to anyone else except a veteran in the same category.' 1946 *TN* 27 May p. 2/3 (AP) The Supreme Court today decided veterans do not have 'superseniority' rights to their prewar jobs. *Time* 10 June p. 82/3 To businessmen, one of the prickliest of personnel problems is superseniority. As defined by Selective Service, this means that World War II veterans must be given their old jobs for at least one year, even if it means laying off workers with greater seniority, including World War I veterans.

+TAKE-, TAKE HOME (PAY). What remains after deductions have been made. —1943 *Newsweek* 17 Apr. p. 72 Although the 70-year-old president . . . received remuneration of $427,349 in 1943, his actual take-home pay was less than nothing. *The Office Economist* Dec. p. 14 The details of the incentive scheme itself should meet the long-established criteria of a good plan: it must be easily understood by the employee so that he can compute his earnings and know where his effort stands in 'take home' at all times. 1944 *Fortune* Jan. p. 210 The average take-home pay for Jahco production workers, however, is probably the highest in the U. S. for this kind of company. 1945 *Time* 4 June p. 77/1 Maintaining the Take-Home. 1946 *Ladies' Home Jour.*, July p. 22/2 Factory take-home pay has toppled since the war. . .

+TALKING BOOK. An album of recordings of the oral reading of a book. See also quots. (Also attrib.)—1944 *Sat. Eve. Post* 16 Dec. p. 6/2 But she knew that it contained six twelve-inch recordings, the last chapters of A Tree Grows in Brooklyn, one of the many 'talking books' produced by the American Foundation for the Blind, under a grant of the Library of Congress. 1945 *Sat. Rev. Lit.* 8 Dec. p. 17/1 Talking Books reach blind people without cost to them. 1946 *BN* 3 June p. 20/3 He keeps up with the latest in modern fiction and follows the classics through 'Talking Books' furnished weekly by the Library of Congress.

+TERMINAL LEAVE. Accrued, unused leave granted an officer in the services between his relief from assignment and his separation from the service (relief from active duty, retirement, or discharge).—1945 *BN* 11 Oct. p. 20/1-2 On terminal leave now prior to his discharge next Saturday, Maj. Evans is in New York. . . San Francisco *Call-Bulletin* 21 Nov. p. 3/2 Rogers Jr. . . . is still in the Army on terminal leave as a lieutenant colonel. . . Omaha (Neb.) *World-Her.* 25 Nov. p. 1-E The lieutenant, who is on terminal leave. . . *Time* 24 Dec. p. 92/3 Now a major on terminal leave, he will take on his new job in June. . .

+TOP DRAWER. 'a. The highest drawer in a dresser or cabinet. b. *Slang.* The upper class or classes.' (*NID* 1934), [1905]. Hence, the highest in rank, quality, authoritativeness, importance. (Also attrib.)—1943 *Time* 20 Sept. p. 86 BBC countered with what amounted to a top-drawer shake-up. 1945 *TN* 8 Aug. p. 1/7 (UP) In his first interview since the military made public its top-drawer secret, Nichols said that the Oak Ridge plant had been given its production schedule in 1942. . . *Time* 24 Sept. p. 71/1 To judge by last year's furore over Ballerina Alicia Markova, she was the only occupant of ballet's top drawer. *Sat. Eve. Post* 10 Nov. p. 132/3 . . . the many-sided problem of how to keep nourished while traveling at eighty miles an hour deserves some top-drawer thinking. 1946 Omaha (Neb.) *World-Her.* 7 July p. 18-C/4 I think it is sufficient to say that he has pretty well covered the top drawer of our writing talent. . .

+TOP-, TOP SECRET, *adj.* Of the greatest secrecy; confidential to the highest degree.—1945 *Chr. Sci. Mon. Mag.* 13 Oct. p. 5/2-3 When wraps were lifted from that top secret weapon, the atomic bomb, veteran B-24 Liberator crews . . . learned . . . the full meaning of an almost forgotten mission over northern Europe. *Life* 26 Nov. p. 63/2 Certain messages are so top-secret that, after they have been read and noted, they are burned. *TN* 2 Dec. p. 1/5 (AP) Gerhard Gesell . . . told Keefe that the Clark report . . . contained some 'top secret' information. . . 1946 *Time* 1 Apr. p. 62/2 The magazine world buzzed with rumors about various 'Projects X,' all being guarded as top-secret. . .

+VICTORY GIRL. See quots.—1942 San Francisco *Call-Bulletin* 19 Nov. 2nd front page/3-4 'They label themselves the victory girls,' she asserted. 'They think that the boys are here today but may be dead tomorrow, and they reason: "We'll give them all they want."' 1943 *Common Sense* May p. 147/1 They aren't professional bad girls, these 'victory girls' and 'cuddle bunnies' who raise the truancy rate in high school, go uniform hunting in every railroad station, wander arm-in-arm down Main Street late at night looking for pick-ups. 1944 Kendall *Service Slang* victory girls. . . 'teen age girls who are khaki-wacky. . . *Sat. Eve. Post* 2 Sept. p. 20/1 Here, the professional prostitute and the amateur 'victory girl' solicit the soldier and sailor. 1945 *Time* 26 Feb. p. 18/1. *Life* 23 Apr. p. 64/2 The victory girl, Alice (Judy Holliday), tries to make people think she is an intellectual by carrying *Fortune* around with her. 1946 Richmond (Va.) *Times Dispatch* 11 Feb. p. 2/8 The 'victory girl' or patriotute is still an unsolved problem with victory. . .

VIEW.*—*take a dim (poor) view.* To regard skeptically or unfavorably.—1941 *Newsweek* 7 July p. 27 Take a dim view—disapprove. N. Y. *Times Mag.* 27 July p. 5/4 An enterprising airman 'organizes' the wanted article, and if he is caught at it the senior N. C. O. would be reported as having taken a 'poor view.' 1943 *Time* 22 Mar. p. 51/1. 1944 *Sat. Rev. Lit.* 4 Nov. p. 7/3 Of our participation in World Wars I and II one gathers that the Beards still take a poor view. 1945 *Newsweek* 8 Jan. p. 68. 1946 *Sat. Eve. Post* 20 July p. 21/1 Ham took a dim view of night flying. Impractical, he said.

+VT FUZE (FUSE). The variable time or proximity fuze (which see).—1945 *Newsweek* 1 Oct. p. 57/3 But inside its black plastic nose lay the new VT fuse—a miniature five-tube radio receiving and sending set no larger than a pint milk bottle. *Time* 1 Oct. p. 48. *TN* 14 Oct. p. 4/5 (AP) Such data is required . . . in order to make VT fuses for various types of missiles. 1946 *Sci. N. L.* 2 Feb. p. 68 Navy shells carrying the proximity fuze or as it is more technically . . . known, the VT fuze. Johns Hopkins *Alumni Mag.* Mar. p. 76/2 As contrasted with a time fuze the great advantage of the VT fuze is its automatic adjustment of the instant of detonation.

AMONG THE NEW WORDS

I. WILLIS RUSSELL
University of Alabama

THE PRELIMINARY remarks in this issue of 'Among the New Words' will be restricted to comments on two of the entries in the glossary.

The recognition of *bamboo* as a combining form meaning 'native' I owe entirely to information supplied me by my colleague, Professor George Pope Shannon, who resided in Manila in 1919-1920 and again in 1926-1929. He is well acquainted with the terms *bamboo American* and *bamboo English* from his days in Manila. To the combinations in the glossary he is able to add two others. He has heard the term *bamboo ferry* applied (in contrast with the Navy ferry) to a civilian ferry which carried natives, produce, etc., from Manila to Cavite. A *bamboo railroad* is a native-run, native-operated railroad running through rural districts. It implies a jerk-water line, like the one running from Manila to Cavite. Two other combinations, not known to Professor Shannon but listed in Berrey and Van den Bark's *American Thesaurus of Slang,* seem to belong here. A *bamboo fleet* is 'a fleet assigned to Philippine waters' and *bamboo government* refers to the 'Philippine civil government.' The following citation, supplied by Miss Mamie J. Meredith, possibly should have been included under *bamboo* in the glossary: 'We get used to Tiger Brand Whiskey which is a cross between sorghum, kerosene, cylinder oil and turpentine! We call it "Bamboo Juice" and one drink will put you in never-never land' (letter to *News and Views,* July 1945, p. 30).

It will be observed that the *OED* Sup. has a 1923 citation of *mass-produced* as an adjective. The quotation (*Daily Mail,* 22 Jan. p. 5) is as follows: 'All cars made in the United States are not necessarily mass-produced.' Even with the test of Professor Fries (*American English Grammar,* p. 189) before me, I find it difficult to determine whether we are dealing here with an adjective or a passive verb. Perhaps the evidence in the glossary of unmistakable verb uses may suggest that even as early as 1923 the verb form was in existence.

PLEASE COMMENT. Earlier dates are requested for the following. *4F* (1944), *Jaycee* (1940), *Sad Sack* (1943), *U-Drive,* n. & adj. (1938).

ACKNOWLEDGEMENTS. For citations, to the American Dialect Society and to members of its Committee on New Words as follows: Henry Alexander (3), Clarence L. Barnhart (2), Atcheson L. Hench (2), Mamie J. Meredith (10), Harold Wentworth (1), and Peter Tamony (1); also Dwight L. Bolinger (2) and Joseph Prescott (1). Thanks are due the University of Alabama Research Committee for secretarial aid.

The abbreviation *'BN'* is used for the Birmingham (Ala.) *News* and *'TN'* for the Tuscaloosa (Ala.) *News.*

SYMBOLS: The symbol + before a word or definition indicates an Americanism. A date immediately following a word or definition indicates the time of evidence shown in the DAE, or, if so stated, in another publication. Dates in brackets indicate the time, etc., of British usage. An asterisk after a word indicates that the word is illustrated in British usage before 1600.

+AIRBRASIVE, *n. & adj.* [*air + ábrasive*]. See quots.—1945 *TN* 1 Aug. p. 6/1 (UP) It was developed by a Texas dentist, Dr. Robert B. Black, Corpus Christi, who said in his report that his method, named 'airbrasive,' employs for its action a very fine, almost pinpoint, stream of compressed air into which a suitable finely divided abrasive agent has been introduced.' [*sic*] *Time* 6 Aug. pp. 75-6 Dr. Black's new method, which he calls 'airbrasive,' is something like sandblasting, *i.e.,* he wears hard surfaces away with an abrasive propelled by fast-moving air. *Sci. N. Letter* 11 Aug. p. 87 'Airbrasive' is the name . . . coined for the new instrument. It operates somewhat on the principle of a sandblast. . . Instead of sand, aluminum oxide is used as the abrasive. 1946 *Sat. Rev. Lit.* 29 June p. 21/2.

+AMVETS. See quot. 1946 *Harper's.*—1944 *TN* 11 Dec. p. 1/8 (UP) The organization, which will be known as 'Amvets,' was founded yesterday. . . 1945 Omaha *World-Her.* 30 Dec. p. 2-A/5 Amvets Get License for Downtown Club. 1946 *Harper's Mag.* Sept. p. 251/1 These are the American Veterans of World War II (familiarly known as Amvets). . .

+ATOM, ATOMIC BOMBING, *n. & adj.*—1945 *TN* 9 Aug. p. 1/6 (AP) Although the second atomic bombing was carried out on the same day Russia declared war, there was no indication these two great blows were planned to coincide. *Ibid., loc. cit.* General Spaatz' U. S. Army Strategic Air Force headquarters said Nagasaki . . . was even more vulnerable to an atom bombing. 1946 *Collier's* 11 May p. 69/3 Vulnerability of surface craft to atomic bombing does not necessarily mean that they have become obsolete. *Sat. Eve. Post* 8 June p. 18/1 Air crews of the 509th were training for atom bombing without knowing there was an atom bomb. *BN* 25 June p. 2/2 (AP) Shortly after daylight on July 1 . . . the atomic-bombing B-29 of Maj. . . . Swancutt will lead the sky train from Kwajalein to Bikini. . .

BAMBOO. Combining form meaning 'native,' 'pertaining to natives.' *Colloq.* or *Dial. Pacific Area.*—BAMBOO AMERICAN. 1940 *Life* 28 Oct. p. 99/1 *Squacks* are the native girls of the Pacific sometimes taken to mistress by sailors who assume the title of *Shackmaster,* and become *Bamboo Americans.* BAMBOO ENGLISH. 1942 Berrey and Van den Bark *American Thesaurus of Slang* ¶181.5 . . . bamboo English, *broken English spoken in the Philippine Islands.* . . BAMBOO TELEGRAPH, WIRELESS. 1945 *Read. Dig.* Mar. p. 107/1 The bamboo telegraph carried the news of this event all over the island. . . Ira Wolfert *American Guerrilla in the Philippines* (N. Y.: Simon, Schuster) p. 104 Bamboo telegraph usually brought word to one American of the existence of another. *Chr. Sci. Mon. Week. Mag.* 2 June p. 17/1 Just as the McKinleys were about to complete their surrender the bamboo telegraph brought them a message from Filipino friends. *Sat. Eve. Post* 3 Nov. p. 107/2 In addition to runners, warnings came by bamboo wireless. News seemed to travel by itself, jumping the space between barrios as if by magic.

+COOK WITH GAS (ELECTRICITY, RADAR). *Slang.* See quot. 1943 *Am. Sp.*—1941 Kansas City *Star* 23 Feb. Now you're cooking with electricity! 1942 *Time* 27 Apr. p. 84/3 Many a student of U. S. patent law and practice figured that, at that point, Thurman Arnold was cooking with gas. 1943 *Am. Sp.* Apr. p. 154/1-2 *Now you're cooking with gas.* 'Now you're getting somewhere.' *Sat. Eve. Post* 20 Nov. p. 12/3 The little yellow lights in the cockpit indicating 'bombs away' flashed, the interphone came to life and a moment after Gardner and Mitchell spoke, Jim Moberly remarked, 'We're sure cookin' with gas today, Dry.' 1946 *Time* 20 May p. 6/2 Now you are cooking with gas. Frederic Wakeman *The Hucksters* (N. Y.: Rinehart & Co.) p. 209 Vic said, 'Good boy, Georgie. Now you're cooking with radar.'

DE-, DENAZIFY. To eradicate Nazi doctrines and adherents.—1944 *BN* 8 May p. 1/6 (AP) The Army added that it was carrying on an educational program designed to 'de-Nazify' the prisoners by giving them a chance to see for themselves the advantages of democracy. Lond. *Spect.* 28 July p. 72/2 . . . whenever the problem of . . . de-Nazifying the young Nazis, [sic] is being seriously approached, some encounter or incident turns up to make the hopelessness of the situation inescapable. 1945 *TN* 20 June p. 6/1 (UP) 'Denazify the country,' he said, 'but leave Germany her skilled laborers to work for the good of all nations under Allied guidance.' 1946 B'ham *News–Age-Her.* 16 June p. 1/6 (editorial sec.) . . . some may recall that at the Crimean and Potsdam conferences the principal Allies agreed to denazify Germany.

FIRE-, FIRE BOMB. An incendiary bomb. (Also attrib.)—1941 *Read. Dig.* Mar. p. 6 By cable to the Reader's Digest comes this vivid firsthand account of the experiences of an American reporter on the night that fire-bombs rained on the ancient city of London. 1942 *House Beautiful* Sept. p. 84; cited *Read. Guide* 13: 223/1 Latest facts about fire bomb protection. 1944 *BN* 10 Oct. p. 1/7 (AP) The British heavy bombers made a saturation attack on Bochum . . . , dumping thousands of fire bombs. . . 1946 *Sat. Eve. Post.* 8 June p. 135/1 Veteran fliers who'd been commuting from Tinian to Japan with fire bombs asked loudly, 'Why all the secrecy?'

+INCENTIVE PAY. See quots. (Also attrib.)—1943 *Read. Dig.* Aug. p. 11/1 Mr. Charles E. Wilson . . . is urging war industries to adopt 'incentive pay'—that is, to pay workers more if they *produce* more. *Fortune* Nov. p. 141 In the latter, labor finds the speed-up worse than ever, and a constant effort to introduce piecework rates, renamed 'incentive pay.' 1944 *Time* 14 Feb. p. 12 Incentive Pay. In Los Angeles a restaurant hung a sign in its window: 'Waitress Wanted: Good Wages—Free Meals—Free Bobby Pins!' 1945 *TN* 22 Aug. p. 1/4 (UP) The Bureau of Internal Revenue today modified its salary stabilization rules to permit . . . incentive pay and other types of compensation. 1946 *Life* 16 Sept. p. 73/1-2 Studebaker is only auto manufacturer with incentive pay system, making its workers highest paid in auto industry.

ISLAND. See *Am. Sp.* 21: 142/2. Add earlier illust.—1941 *Life* 31 Mar. p. 60/1 The 'Island' is the superstructure.

MASS-PRODUCE. 'mass-produced, *adj.*' 1934 (NID). [1923]—*v. t. & i.*—1940 *Life* 9 Dec. p. 84/2 U. S. Now Mass-Produces. 1944 *Time* 26 June p. 104/3 But commercial manufacturers expropriated the designs of the Guild's hand-tooled products, mass-produced them cheaply. *Sat. Eve. Post* 21 Oct. p. 15/1 In response to Government requests, they bagged powder, they mass-produced 3-inch anti-tank cannon, mass-produced tank tracks, mass-produced subassemblies for Martin bombers and finally mass-produced complete airplanes. . . 1946 *This Week* 10 Mar. p. 5/1 This and similar work set Russia to mass-producing ACS. . .

MOLOTOV BREADBASKET. See *Am. Sp.* 18: 303/2. Add earlier illust.—1940 *Illust. Lond. News* 6 Apr. p. 446 The 'Molotov Breadbasket' . . . appeared to consist of two types.

NEPTUNIUM. See quots.—1911 *Century Dict. and Cycl.* neptunium . . . a supposed new element announced by Hermann in 1877 as present in columbite and ferro-ilmenite. Its existence has not been confirmed. 1945 *Warren (Ohio) Tribune Chronicle* 12 Aug. p. 1/4-5 (AP) The race brought discovery of two new elements, neptunium, No. 93, and plutonium. . . *Sci. N. Letter* 18 Aug. p. 103/3 Borrowing the names of the planets in our solar system, the new elements were named Neptunium (symbol Np) and Plutonium (symbol Pu). *Life* 20 Aug. p. 106 The investigators called it 'neptunium,' from the fact that it is beyond uranium—the heaviest natural element—in the table of the elements just as Neptune lies beyond Uranus in the solar system. 1946 *Brit. Book of the Year* p. 82/2 One important result of these studies was the discovery that with neutrons of certain speeds U-238 exhibited a high probability for neutron capture, becoming an unstable isotope, U-239, which by emitting a beta particle became a new element, No. 93, to which the name of 'Neptunium' was given. But this was also unstable and by emitting another electron became No. 94, named 'Plutonium.'

PEDAL PUSHER(S). 'A bicycle rider, especially in a race; a bicycler; a bicyclist.' 1934 (Weseen *Dictionary of Amer. Slang*).+ See quots.—1944 *Life* 28 Aug. p. 65/2 When college girls took to riding bicycles in slacks, they first rolled up one trouser leg, then rolled up both. This whimsey has now produced a trim variety of long shorts, called 'pedal pushers.' 1945 *Liberty* 1 Sept. p. 68 Miss McCardell . . . borrowed little-boy pants for 'pedal pushers,' the knee-length shorts . . . and started a new campus fashion. 1946 *Sears, Roebuck Catalogue* Fall and Winter 1946-7 p. 207B/1 Checked Pedal Pusher . . . the smart below-the-knee pants for cycling and all sorts of high-jinks and fun.

PLUTONIUM. See quots.; also those under *neptunium*. (Also attrib.)—1945 *Life* 20 Aug. p. 106/2 But neptunium also is radioactive and in turn changes to 'plutonium'—Pluto being beyond Neptune. 1946 *N. Y. Times* 31 Mar. p. E11 When very small amounts of U-235 or plutonium are used . . . there is no necessity to denature them. *Sat. Eve. Post.* 29 June p. 20/1 Atomic armchair strategists are inclined to count out the Ground Forces in this new age of plutonium pulverization. . .

PORTAL-TO-PORTAL PAY. See quots.—1943 *Time* 25 Oct. p. 21/3 He emerged with proposed Contract No. 3: an intricate formula which cagily skirts any mention of increased hourly wages or 'portal-to-portal' pay. 1944 *BN* 27 Mar. p. 1/5 The Supreme Court ruled Monday that underground iron ore miners are entitled to 'portal-to-portal' pay for the time spent traveling between the mouth of the mine and the place where the ore is actually mined. 1945 *Mueller Clipper* June p. 2 Additional compensation is taking various forms—time differentials, . . . portal-to-portal pay . . . 1946 *B'ham*

News-Age-Her. 15 Sept. p. 5A/4 The attorneys represented miners who recovered $557,488.25 in portal-to-portal pay, representing the time they traveled to and from the mouth of a mine.

POSTWAR. '. . . *adj.* After the war, esp. the World War.' 1934 (NID). [1908]—*n.*—1944 *Arch. Rec.* Dec. p. 69/1 Expansible Prefab House for Postwar. 1945 *TN* 8 May p. 4/3 (UP) Railroads Make Lavish Plans For Postwar. *Time* 24 Sept. p. 15/2 'Management-labor unity . . . must be continued in the postwar.' 1946 *Chr. Sci. Mon. Week. Mag.* 25 May p. 2 Farmer in the Postwar.

RE-, REDEPLOY, *v. t. & i.* To reorganize the war machine; move men and materials to a different theater of war, *specif.* from the European to the Pacific Theaters in World War II after the collapse of Germany.—1945 *Lond. Sunday Times* 27 May p. 7 Re-deploying to crush Japan. *Sat. Rev. Lit.* 16 June p. 12/1 Others stated that the plan to redeploy troops from Europe was a great mistake. . . *Time* 16 July p. 42/2 Some were waiting to be re-deployed to the Pacific.

RE-, REDEPLOYMENT, *n. & adj.*—1945 *Time* 12 Feb. p. 17/2 The new blueprint for U. S. re-deployment calls for an army of 6,500,000 men to defeat Japan. *Newsweek* 28 May p. 28/3 In the redeployment of three and four star generals from the European theater, the best estimates are: . . . *N. Y. Times* 24 June p. 10 Redeployment traffic moves west. 1946 *Life* 19 Aug. p. 116/2 Fraulein strolls by ogling GIs from Marburg redeployment center.

SCHNORCHEL, -KEL, -KLE. Also SNORT(S). See quots. (Also attrib.)—1944 *Richmond News Leader* 11 Dec. p. 1/4 Meanwhile it is a matter of official knowledge that Germans have developed a submarine equipped with radical new devices for underwater breathing and it is possible that some of the craft may even now be at sea. Known as the Schnorkel spirall submarine the new vessel has been dubbed the 'snorts' by the British. 1945 *Time* 19 Feb. p. 66/1-2 The Germans call it the Schnorkel (spiral); the British, the 'snort.' *Illust. Lond. News* 3 Mar. p. 229/2 The most recent move in this never-ceasing battle was the introduction, last year, of the 'Schnorkel' apparatus (described in 'The Illustrated London News' of December 23), enabling U-boats to remain submerged for several weeks at a time. *Chr. Sci. Mon. Week. Mag.* 15 Sept. p. 10/2 Of prime interest . . . was the 'schnorkle,' a device which permitted the submarines to 'breathe' while submerged at moderate depth, so named because in operation it sounded like a lusty snorer. 1946 *Collier's* 11 May p. 69/2 The other [part] the Germans called the *Schnorchel.*' That was a pipe or tube of about periscope height, that extended from the ventilating system of the engines to the surface and was fitted at the end with a valve that closed automatically when the sub submerged. *Newsweek* 13 May p. 31/3.

SHAMBLES. See *Am. Sp.* 16: 19-20. Add *Fig.*—1940 *Time* 8 Apr. p. 69 (cited *Am. Sp., loc. cit.*). 1941 *Read. Dig.* Mar. p. 130/2 When the time came, the theory was, world shipping could thus be turned into a shambles at a signal. 1945 *TN* 15 Oct. p. 7/2 (AP) Pre-season predictions . . . have been blasted to a shambles. 1946 *B'ham News-Age-Her.* 8 Sept. p. 1/3 Clothing manufacturers have charged mill owners with cut-throat business practices that have made a shambles of distribution. . .

STARLET. See *Am. Sp.* 18: 65/2. Add earlier illust.—1940 *Life* 29 Jan. p. 37/3 Starlets Are World's Most Envied Of Girls.

TBS. See quots. (Also attrib.)—1944 *Harper's Mag.* June p. 38/1 . . . it seemed this morning as if we were a part of a huge, grim square dance on the open seas . . . as the tired, imperturbable man aboard the carrier flagship called his orders over the gravelly-voiced TBS (talk between ships). 1945 *Read. Dig.* May p. 111/1-2 . . . another scout pilot was also

reporting, and the TBS (Talk Between Ships) phone announced: . . . 1946 *Sat. Eve. Post* 26 Oct. p. 66/3 The astounded admiral grabbed the TBS radio and shouted, 'What ship is that under way?'

TEEN-AGER. See *Am. Sp.* 20: 146. Add earlier illust.—1941 *Read. Dig.* Apr. p. 72/1 'I never knew teen-agers could be so serious.'

1080. [So called because the 1080th substance tested in a search for a rat poison was found to be effective.] See quots.—1945 *Time* 17 Sept. p. 68/2 But '1080,' a chemical known as sodium fluoro-acetate, fools the cagiest rat. . . And a pinpoint of it kills a half-pound rat. *Sci. N. Letter* 10 Nov. p. 297 Chemically, 1080 is sodium fluoroacetate; the number is simply a convenience designation. 1946 *BN* 12 Feb. p. 10/5 It was Ickes' men who developed the deadly new rat poison, 1080. . . A Polish chemist discovered 1080 while working on poison gas.

TERROR BOMBING. Bombing designed to hasten the end of a war by terrorizing the enemy population.—1941 *Read. Dig.* June p. 58/2 . . . it must be remembered that this government today is Hitler, Göring, Goebbels, Himmler and a few others—men who . . . ordered the terror bombing of Rotterdam last summer and of London last winter. 1945 *BN* 18 Feb. p. 1/3 (AP) The Allied air bosses have made the long-awaited decision to adopt deliberate terror bombing of the great German population centers as a ruthless expedient to hasten Hitler's doom. *Time* 26 Feb. p. 32/1 . . . terror bombing of German cities was deliberate military policy.

TEST-, TEST FLY, *v.t.* To test an airplane in actual flight.—1944 *Brit. Book of the Year* p. 31/2 It was known that machines were extensively test-flown both in England and in America. *Life* 19 June p. 11/2 Since your story has appeared the plane has been test flown and delivered to the Army. 1945 *Time* 5 Nov. p. 74/2 They had been test flown 'somewhere in the U. S.' *N. Y. Times* 18 Nov. sec. 1 p. 4/1; quoted *Am. Sp.* 21: 150/2. 1946 *Free World* Feb. p. 21 1st Lieut. William W. Skinner . . . was killed . . . while test-flying a P-47. *Collier's* 11 May p. 8/3.

2,4-D, 2.4-D, 2.4-Di(chlorophenoxy-acetic acid). See quots.—1945 *Time* 19 Feb. p. 67/1 It is a synthetic hormone, called 2.4-D by the U. S. Department of Agriculture, which helped develop it. *Science* 22 June pp. 642-4; cited *Read. Guide* 10 Oct. 1945 p. 133/2 Bacteriostatic and bactericidal properties of 2,4-dichlorophenoxyacetic acid. *Du Pont Mag.* Aug. p. 5 Another still newer compound has not as yet been given a trade-mark name, and still bears its laboratory nick-name—2·4-D. *Sat. Eve. Post* 10 Nov. p. 17/3 It is a promise as exciting as the new insecticide,

DDT, or the unexcelled weed killer, 2,4-D. 1946 *This Week* 17 Mar. p. 19/2 Besides being a weed-killer, what else will the new chemical called '2,4-Di' do? Hasten the ripening of bananas, apples and pears; kill ragweed which causes 90 per cent of the country's hay fever; make apples cling to the tree longer than usual.

UNDERGROUND, *adv.* '2. *fig.* In secrecy or concealment; in a hidden or obscure manner.' [1632].—*n.* 'The aggregate of suppressed political parties and factions forced into hiding but actively engaged in organizing for resistance to an autocratic regime.' 1945 (NID Sup.)—*adv.* See quots.—1943 *Time* 8 Nov. p. 20/3 The Swedish newspaper *Ny Dag* said that extremist Nazis . . . are planning methodically to go underground, and are establishing secret radio stations, arms dumps, sabotage material. 1944 *TN* 30 Apr. p. 1/6 (AP) Himmler's Schutzstaffel . . . has elaborately detailed plans to go underground in the event of German defeat. . . 1945 *TN* 23 Aug. p. 7/2 (NEA) . . . authorities fear the black market won't disappear, but will simply go underground. *Life* 19 Nov. p. 112/1 . . . he . . . went underground and got to Moscow. 1946 *Warren (Ohio) Tribune Chron.* 19 Aug. p. 17/2 (AP) The national KKK broke up or at least went underground in 1944. . .

WINGMAN. See *Am. Sp.* 21:145/2. Add earlier illust.—1943 *Sat. Eve. Post* 6 Nov. p. 86 I looked to both sides of us. Our two wing men were gone.

ZERO(ED) IN, *v. & ppa.* 'Zero, *to:* A marksman's term. To ascertain by experimental testing the peculiarities of a rifle at known ranges and set the sights to suit the marksman's individual idiosyncrasies in aiming. Zero being known, allowances for deflection, etc., at various ranges would be calculated readily.' 1925 (Fraser and Gibbons *Soldier and Sailor Words and Phrases*). See first 1945 quot.—1944 *Newsweek* 8 Jan. p. 45 . . . don't you know the Jerries have that road zeroed in?—a phrase meaning the Germans had sighted their guns on the road and needed only to pull their triggers. *Life* 14 Aug. p. 57/1 Germans who had retreated out of town 'zeroed in' mortar shells among troops and light tanks which tried to follow. . . 1945 *B'ham News-Age-Her.* 8 Apr. p. 9-A/2 (NANA) Kraut gunners saw him [observation plane] circling overhead, saw one ranging shot land long by 500 yards and then a second ranging shot fall 50 yards short. They knew they were zeroed in, and before the whole salvo hit them they spread white cloths on the ground. *Sat. Eve. Post* 7 July p. 57/2 'It'll be suicide,' Wes protested. 'They've got the place zeroed in.' 1946 *Time* 28 Jan. p. 24/2 German artillery, high in the hills, were zeroed in on the river banks.

AMONG THE NEW WORDS

I. WILLIS RUSSELL
University of Alabama

THE FOLLOWING observations have been prompted by the comment of a recent writer on the tendency to employ numbers in the naming of some of the new products. 1080 and 2-4-D were treated in the glossary of the December, 1946, issue of 'Among the New Words.' A few more will be treated briefly here.

A-10 and A-105 are germicides that may be useful in the treatment of such diseases as typhoid and cholera (*Newsweek* 17 June 1946 p. 64/2). NIH-204 has some of the properties of Atabrine (*Sci. N. L.* 24 Nov. 1945 p. 329), and NMRI-448 is an insecticide whose name is derived from 'the fact that it was the 448th of many compounds developed by the [Naval Medical Research] Institute' at Bethesda, Maryland (*ibid.* 14 Sept. 1946 p. 168). SN 7618 is an antimalarial drug, so called because that number of substances were tested (Lincoln [Nebr.] *Journ.* 4 Jan. 1946). According to *Life* (22 July 1946 p. 57/1), 'The name of SN 13,276 is derived from the fact that it was the 13,276th drug to be classified by the Office of the Survey of Antimalarials at Johns Hopkins.'

Some of the new repellents still in an experimental stage are NMRI 201 (*Sci. N. L.* 20 Oct. 1945 p. 247), NMRI 407 (*loc. cit.*), Rutgers 612 (*Collier's* 13 July 1946 p. 51/1), and 6-2-2, the last named deriving from the proportions of the three substances used in it (*loc. cit.*).

Three other names in which numbers are used are G-410, a 'convenience designation' of penta-chlor-phenol (*Sci. N. L.* 11 Aug. 1945 p. 94); GR-S-10, a synthetic rubber (*ibid.* 14 Oct. 1945 p. 233); and LL 30, an anesthetic (*Newsweek* 4 Mar. 1946 p. 56).

Though the Addenda in the 1944 edition of the *Shorter Oxford English Dictionary* defines *brains trust* in the general sense, it uses the plural *brains,* which is not the customary American form, and gives no date; hence the inclusion of *brain trust* in the glossary of this issue. Readers of *American Speech* will recall the discussion of this term some seven years ago, a discussion which was concluded when the late General Hugh Johnson stated that it was an Army term referring to the general staff and that it went back to 1901 (15: 79). This meaning of the term is noted in the glossary of Eugene S. McCartney in the *Papers of the Michigan Academy of Science, Arts, and Letters,* 1929, p. 281/2.

Please Comment. Verbal and printed evidence (two citations) indicates that in the Philadelphia, Pa., area the custom of looking at a body before burial, especially if the body is at a funeral parlor, is known as a *viewing.* Is this usage found outside Philadelphia?

Acknowledgments. For citations, to the American Dialect Society and to members of its Committee on New Words as follows: Clarence L. Barnhart (9), Mamie J. Meredith (15), and Peter Tamony (2); also Dwight L. Bolinger (2). Most of the citations used in the preliminary remarks on numbers were supplied by Mr. Barnhart and Miss Meredith.

Special mention should be made of the contributors of the earlier datings in the glossary. The majority of them were furnished by Miss Mamie J. Meredith: *Anderson shelter, battlewagon, blueprint, dime store, documentary, open city, pigboat, soap opera,* and *Talking Book.* Professor Atcheson L. Hench contributed the earliest citations of *brain trust* and *brain truster,* Mr. Peter Tamony the 1936 citation of *brain trust,* and Professor D. L. Bolinger that for *atomic bomb.*

Symbols: The symbol + before a word or definition indicates an Americanism. A date immediately following a word or definition indicates the time of evidence shown in the DAE, or, if so stated, in another publication. Dates in brackets indicate the time, etc., of British usage. An asterisk after a word indicates that the word is illustrated in British usage before 1600.

AIR-SEA RESCUE. 1945 cited in *Am. Sp.* 21: 139/1. Add earlier illust.—1942 *Flying* Sept. p. 152-4+; cited *Read. Guide* 13: 150/1 Air-sea rescue.

ANDERSON SHELTER. 1941 cited in *Am. Sp.* 18: 149/1. Add earlier illust.—1939 *Newsweek* 21 Aug. p. 20/1 In back of his house . . . most Britons will soon have an Anderson—sometimes called 'dog house'—shelter.

ATOMIC BOMB. 1945 cited in *Am. Sp.* 21: 139/2. Add earlier illust.—1914 *The Century Mag.* 87: 571/2 His companion . . . sat with his legs spread wide over the long coffin-shaped box which contained in its compartments the three atomic bombs, the new bombs that would continue to explode indefinitely and which no one so far had ever seen in action.

BATTLEWAGON. 1942 cited in *Am. Sp.* 17: 270/2. Add earlier illust.—1938 *Newsweek* 14 Nov. 11/2 The Navy had sent out bids . . . for three new 35,000-ton battlewagons. . . .

BLUEPRINT, *n.* 1941 cited in *Am. Sp.* 17: 122/1. Add earlier illust.—1939 *Newsweek* 5 June p. 16/2 The decision of Grover Cleveland Bergdoll . . . to end his nineteen-year exile in Germany and return to the United States to 'face the music' came as a timely blessing to the Army High Command, whose grim preparations for 'Mobilization Day' include blueprints for a draft.

BOMBARDIER. 1942 cited in *Am. Sp.* 17: 203/2. Add earlier illust.—1940 *Life* 5 Aug. p. 22/3 . . . up front in the nose the bombardier is signaling the ground crew with his Adlis blinker.

BRAIN TRUST. 'A group of college teachers acting as advisers to President F. D. Roosevelt.' 1934 (NID)—Any group acting in an advisory capacity. (Also attrib.)—1933 Balto. *Sun* 17 Aug. p. 8/6 The 'brain trust' of the gang chooses a city for the 'operation' located within a hundred miles of a State boundary line. 1936 *Esquire* Sept. p. 160/2 An executive meeting is a confab, a powwow, a brain-trust huddle, or a heart-to-heart. 1945 *Sat. Eve. Post* 27 Oct. p. 27/1-2 This is the Crisler brain trust.

BRAIN TRUSTER. A member of a brain trust.—1934 Balto. *Sun* 28 Mar. p. 3/3 William A. Wirt . . . will rely on his word as against that of the Roosevelt 'brain trusters' he accuses to substantiate his charges that efforts are being made to turn the nation to communism, he admitted today. 1944 *Life* 11 Sept. p. 50/1 Bell is Dewey's . . . chief brain truster. 1945 *Sat. Eve. Post* 21 July p. 22 The author . . . looks and listens while his Number 1 Brain Truster . . . works out a strike plan in their flagship plotting room.

DEHUMIDIFICATION. See quots. (Also attrib.)—1944 *Sci. N. L.* 1 July p. 9 A new rust-proofing technique, called 'dehumidification,' is being used by the Bureau of Ships of the Navy to keep ships that are in reserve or inactive in readiness for sea. 1945 *Newsweek* 1 Oct. p. 56/2 The Navy's Bureau of Ships has perfected a new rust-preventing technique called 'dehumidification' . . . 1946 *Life* 9 Sept. p. 32/1 Dehumidification machines, which turn on automatically whenever air gets damp and by which the sleeping ship will breathe dry air for years after, are installed. *Sat. Eve. Post* 13 July p. 35/1.

+DIME STORE. A store dealing in low-priced commodities. (Also attrib.)—1938 *Newsweek* 31 Jan. p. 36/1 'Best buy' was a dime-store product, which cost 5 cents a gram. 1940 *Life* 21 Oct. p. 4 I work in a dime store . . . 1941 *Read. Dig.* Jan. p. 25/2. 1942 Berrey and Van den Bark *Amer. Thesaurus of Slang* ¶21.14 Cheap; Paltry . . . dime-store. 1946 *Time* 30 Sept. p. 50/2 The dime-store heiress . . . was all excited about her purchase.

DOCUMENTARY. 1940 cited in *Am. Sp.* 17: 122/2. Add earlier illust.—1939 *Newsweek* 29 May p. 27/1 Even down to the recent Chicago fair in 1933-34 the celluloid contribution was relatively unimportant; the usual dry-as-dust travelogues, documentaries, and other institutional fodder.

FIRE-POWER. 1942 cited in *Am. Sp.* 17: 271/1. Add earlier illust.—1932 *Cong. Record* (Proceedings and Debates) 72 Congress 1 Session Vol. 75 Part 9 p. 9930/1 The purpose of a mechanized force is to provide a powerful, fast-moving weapon, capable of wide maneuverability, which combines fire-power, speed, and shock to a much higher degree than now exists in the older arms or in any one combatant arm.

FRATERNIZATION. '. . . fraternal association' (OED) [1792].—See *fraternize.* —1945 *Life* 2 July p. 26 . . . the word fraternization has taken on a meaning in Germany which you won't find in any dictionary. Lond. *Spect.* 10 Aug. p. 130/1. *Newsweek* 3 Sept. p. 44/3 Fraternization has taken place on a large scale, and the average GI likes the average German girl. . . . 1946 *Life* 2 Dec. p. 107/3 . . . in view of the Japanese enthusiasm for their conquerors it is not surprising that 'fraternization' seems an even more inappropriate euphemism for what goes on in Nippon than it is for similar activities elsewhere.

FRATERNIZE. 'To associate or sympathise *with* as a brother or as brothers . . .' (OED) [1611]—See quot. 1946.—1945 Omaha *World-Her.* 29 July p. 12-c/3 It's awful to think of it and still some boys fraternize. *Time* 16 July p. 62/1 The town of ornately painted, deep-eaved houses where G.I.s stroll, lounge and (officially) do not fraternize is Oberammergau. . . . 1946 *Am. Sp.* 21: 251 *Fraternize.* To have close relations, usually sexual, with a female enemy national. By extension it is used also with respect to the female population of allied countries and even American girls. . . .

FRATERNIZING.—1945 *Newsweek* 7 May p. 39/2 Fraternizing, Plain and Fancy. . . . *Time* 2 July p. 25/1. Tuscaloosa *News* 24 July p. 1/1 *Fraternizing In Germany.*

FREE ENTERPRISE. See quot. 1943. —1932 *Read. Guide* 8: 953/2 Free Enterprise. See Laissez faire. 1938 *Newsweek* 3 Oct. p. 37/3 Management leaders representing the world's democratic countries agreed that free enterprise, not government control, is the key to better times. . . . 1943 Lincoln (Neb.) *State Journ.* 16 Aug. 'Free enterprise is the right of every man to work (or trade) where he likes, save and invest according to his own judgment, run his business as he thinks wise, and take the consequences of gain or loss.' 1946 B'ham *News* 14 Oct. p. 11/2 He talks about regimentation, the end of free enterprise. . . .

G. C. A. See quots. (Also attrib.)—1946 *Time* 14 Jan. p. 63/1 G. C. A. is a fairly complicated radar system for guiding aircraft in for blind landings. *Life* 26 Apr. p. 93/1 The U. S. Civil Aeronautics Authority is trying out a radar blind-landing system called G. C. A. (Ground Controlled Approach). *Sat. Eve. Post* 26 Oct. p. 20. 1947 *Illust. Lond. News* 15 Feb. p. 203 Perhaps, too, there will be a development of the G. C. A. system, whereby the pilot can be 'talked down' by experts on the ground who, by means of radar, watch the aircraft coming in and guide it on to the runway.

+(HOTEL) DE GINK. See quots.—1944 *Life* 3 Jan. p. 57/2 . . . C. O.'s are forewarned . . . to arrange no special favors and to provide him only with regulation board and lodging in the local 'Hotel De Gink' (visiting officers' quarters). 1945 *This Week* 25 Mar. p. 19/1 . . . ATC accommodations are known all over the world as De Ginks. . . . *Ladies' Home Journ.* Apr. p. 176/2 The Hotel d'Gink in Iceland was in a Quonsett hut. . . . *Chr. Sci. Mon. Week. Mag.* 7 Apr. p. 3/3 'Hotel de Gink' is the popular name for billeting accommodations at many bases. *Fortune* Aug. p. 210/2 Vips are . . . then whisked off by limousine to the local 'Hotel de Gink,' as the best quarters available for ATC transients are called.

LOVELY, *n.* 'A very pretty girl: from ca. 1930 . . .' (Partridge *Dict. Slang and Unconventional Eng.* N.Y.: Macmillan 1937).—*U. S.* Usually applied to motion picture actresses; see also quots.—1941 *Screen Romances* Oct. p. 6/3 Betty Bryant . . . is about the loveliest lovely ever seen on the screen. 1943 *Time* 4 Oct. p. 73/2 Aircooled Motors Corp.'s . . . current advertising illustration of a lithe and leggy aircooled lovely clad in little or nothing. 1944 *Sat. Eve. Post* 12 Aug. p. 81/2 When Ginger Rogers, Lucille Ball and other sleek lovelies appear. . . . 1944 B'ham *News* 3 Oct. p. 3/5-6 The Alan Young premier . . . will bring a new singing lovely to a regular spot of this kind. . . . 1947 Leslie Waller *Show Me the Way* (N. Y.: The Viking Press) p. 176 'Twelve, count 'em, twelve gorgeous lovelies in poses you will enjoy.'

NEAR MISS. See quot. 1944.—1940 *Life* 9 Sept. p. 120/2 . . . the other was a near miss amidships. *Illust. Lond. News* 28 Dec. p. 829/2 They came back with direct hits on a mine-sweeper and a supply ship, and a near miss on a destroyer to their credit. 1944 *Shorter OED* Addenda s. v. Near, *a.* 6 *N. miss,* not a hit but aimed close enough to damage the target.

OIL BOMB. See quots.—1940 *Illust. Lond. News* 5 Oct. p. 435/2 The oil bomb, which may be of various sizes, is filled in some cases with petrol, thus becoming a tremendously powerful incendiary bomb. In other cases it is filled with crude oil, which is ignited by a small petrol charge. . . . 1941 *Read. Dig.* Feb. p. 108-9 The oil bomb is a large sphere filled with crude oil. . . . The core consists of high explosive which ignites the oil and blows it out in all directions . . . 1947 *Illust. Lond. News* 25 Jan. p. 117/1 The magnificent hammer-beam roof of Westminster Hall . . . was extensively damaged by an oil bomb in 1941. . . .

OPEN CITY. 1939 cited in *Am. Sp.* 19: 225/2. Add earlier illust.—1938 *Newsweek* 4 July p. 9/3 . . . the State Department was represented as viewing with favor the suggestion advanced by Norman H. Davis . . . : neutralized hospital zones, a pact restricting bombing of 'open' cities. . . .

PHANTOM LIMB. See quots.—1940 *Sci. N. L.* 4 May p. 281/1 The wholesale maiming of human bodies in the present European conflict is seen by the psychologist as an unfortunate opportunity for study of a curious phenomenon—the 'phantom limb.' 1944 *Newsweek* 24 Apr. p. 105/1 Both are suffering from 'phantom limb,' a false consciousness of a limb after it has been amputated. 1946 B'ham *News-Age-Her.* 22 Dec. p. 21A/4 (AP) A new operation to get rid of phantom limbs, the imaginary arms and legs of amputees, which nevertheless are really painful, has been reported to the American College of surgeons [sic].

PIGBOAT. 1942 cited in *Am. Sp.* 17: 272/2. Add earlier illust.—1939 *Newsweek* 9 Jan. p. 20/1 Presumably Germany will now build up to this by constructing ocean-going pigboats.

RDX. See quots.—1941 *Newsweek* 8 Dec. p. 43; cited Taylor *Lang. of World War II* p. 58 One [explosive], developed in cooperation with the British and identified with the stuff used in Britain's 'super-bombs,' is known as RDX and credited with 40 per cent more bursting power than TNT. 1944 *Life* 4 Sept. p. 49 It is called RDX—its code name in the war research laboratories . . . it has demonstrated in action a destructive violence 20% greater than that of standard TNT. 1945 *Sci. N. L.* 27 Jan. p. 55. 1946 Tuscaloosa *News* 26 Mar. p. 2/2 (AP) Dr. Raymond Boyer . . . testified today that he gave information to Fred Rose regarding the new explosive, RDX.

SOAP OPERA. 1940 cited in *Am. Sp.* 20: 145. Add earlier illust.—1939 *Newsweek* 13 Nov. p. 44/2 Transcontinental Network bubbled up out of the 'soap operas.' . . .

SPACE SHIP, SPACESHIP. See quots. —1942 *Sci. N. L.* 24 Oct. p. 266/1 Ever since the public learned that rocket propulsion would function in a vacuum, . . . space ships traveling from planet to planet have been envisioned as part of the future world. 1946 B'ham *News* 25 Jan. p. 1/1 (AP) Far-roving space ships were listed as one of the 'less likely' applications. 1946 *This Week* June p. 4/3 The drawings on these pages show my version . . . of what an earth-to-moon space ship of the future might look like.

TALK (DOWN, IN). Give directions to a pilot that enable him to land; see quots.—1943 Plane Talk June p. 28/3 The bombardier talks the pilot 'in,' telling him which way to turn. . . . 1945 *Sci. N. L.* 25 Aug. p. 127 A blindfolded pilot . . . was 'talked-down' to the runway. 1946 *Fortune* Aug. p. 196/2 T. W. A. is training pilots in the ground-control approach system, in which ground radar operators locate and then 'talk in' fogbound planes. *Sat. Eve. Post* 26 Oct. p. 20 Operators inside watch planes on radar screens, talk them down through the overcast. 1947 *Illust. Lond. News* 15 Feb. p. 203 [quot. given s. v. G. C. A.].

TALKING BOOK. 1944 cited in *Am. Sp.* 21:225/1. Add earlier illust.—1939 *Newsweek* 24 Apr. p. 32/3 . . . the American Foundation for the Blind in 1935 began publishing 'Talking Books'—long-playing phonograph records of standard literary works. . . . 1940 *Read. Dig.* Sept. p. 93/2.

USO, U. S. O. United Service Organization. (Also attrib.)—1941 *Time* 13 Oct. p. 43/1 . . . U. S. O. has been carrying on as best it could. . . . 1944 *This Week* 12 Nov. p. 4/1 But . . . USO Unit 130 was never completely defeated. 1945 *Sat. Eve. Post* 10 Nov. p. 37/3 . . . the New York World-Telegram called him a one-man USO. 1946 *Tuscaloosa News* 1 Aug. p. 5/2 (AP) . . . property used as a USO center is not subject to city ad valorem taxes.

VIP, V. I. P. See quots.—1944 *Collier's* 26 Feb. p. 73 (adv.) VIP is Army slanguage for 'very important people.' 1945 *Fortune* Aug. p. 161 Very important persons, or 'Vips,' usually travel in plush C-54's. . . . Lincoln (Nebr.) *Journ.* 12 Dec. p. 4 (UP)

Other revelers . . . stolidly refused to make a stir above the vips—very important persons—in the king's English. 1946 *Sat. Eve. Post.* 27 Apr. p. 100/4. *Life* 2 Dec. p. 124/2 One of the hardships of life for the resident personnel in an occupation capital is the constant swarms of V. I. P.s sent out. . . .

WEAPONEER. One who readies an atomic bomb preparatory to launching by the bombardier.—1945 *Tuscaloosa News* 8 Aug. p. 3/2 (UP) Here are the names of the Superfortress crew which carried the atomic bomb to Japan: . . . naval observer and 'weaponeer,' Capt. William S. Parsons. . . . 1946 *Brit. Book of the Year* p. 85/2 Capt. Parsons . . . went along as the 'weaponeer.' N. Y. *Times* 1 July p. C2/3 . . . in addition to the crew of nine will be two weaponeers to take personal care of 'Gilda' until the bombardier thumbs the release. *Newsweek* 8 July p. 20/1 In the bomb bay, two 'weaponeers' from the Manhattan District worked over the 6-foot atom bomb, preparing to arm it.

WEDGIE(S). A sports shoe with a wedge-shaped piece serving as the heel, the whole resting on a single sole.—1940 *Mademoiselle* Apr. p. 13 Your wardrobe is . . . without a pair of wedgies. 1943 *Consumers' Research Bull.* Dec. p. 20/2 Brown leather 'wedgie' with bottom-sole of thin leather. . . . 1946 *Sat. Eve. Post.* 31 Aug. p. 39/4 (adv.) A heel manufacturer attaches felt lifts to the heels of 'wedgies.'

AMONG THE NEW WORDS

I. WILLIS RUSSELL

University of Alabama

THE WORD *bump*, in the glossary of this issue, seems originally to have been a railroad term. The citation from *American Speech* gives a good description of how bumping works, omitting only the very beginning. The first step in bumping is usually the abolishing of a job. If the job is a high-ranking one requiring seniority, then the individual out of a job is entitled to bump one with lower seniority. The person who finds himself without a job will probably go on a preferred waiting list. I have found no uses of the word before Partridge. His suggested date of -1920 I can verify only from memory, which would put the date around 1915. But it was in such common use then on the Western Maryland that it would be surprising indeed if earlier (printed) evidence did not turn up. It was a matter of some interest to me that the Southern Railway employee with whom I discussed the term seemed to prefer *roll*, though he was acquainted with *bump*. *Bump*, as applied to airplane travel, whereby a preferred traveler can obtain the seat of another in the plane, is defined in the 1947 *New College Standard Dictionary*, and labeled 'Popular.'

The beginnings of *-happy* as a combining form have already been given by Professor Bolinger (*American Speech*, 19: 60-61). The adjective *happy*, in its sense of 'dizzy, exhilarated,' seems to have become attached to *slap* to describe some one 'drunk' from 'slaps' or 'punches' (Bolinger notes that *punch-drunk* is synonymous with *slap-happy*). 'The earlier extensions,' writes Professor Bolinger, 'usually contrived to rime with slap,' but after that they became 'more versatile,' especially as they developed in the Army. He lists some twenty illustrations.

In view of the way in which this combining form has caught on, it has seemed fitting to add to the illustrations already cited by Professor Bolinger the many listed in the glossary below. With a few exceptions, these illustrations have not, so far as I know, been cited, nor am I aware of any other place where a large group of these combinations is available. Several additional remarks may be made. A partial morphological description of *-happy* as a combining form includes these facts: *happy*, an adjective, joins with nouns to form compounds of which it is the second member. These compounds are usually hyphenated and are adjectives. Semantically, the compounds fall into two distinct but closely related groups. A third group was finally rejected because of the uncertainty of their meaning. Indeed with so many of the compounds nonce-forms, completely accurate ascription to a group is not always possible.

The word *mother* as used in the terms *mother plane* and *mother ship* in the glossary has an interesting history. As 'A woman who exercises control like that of a mother . . .' the OED traces it back to around 1366. In the compound *mother ship*, 'a ship having charge of one or more torpedo boats'—I still follow the OED—it first occurs in 1890. Later on, according to the OED Sup., it was extended to include 'a ship (or airship) having charge of submarines or aeroplanes'; the dates given are 1922 and 1926, the latter for the airship. From here it is but a step, of course, to the

notion of a control exercised through an electro-magnetic wave. The first instance of the latter I am aware of—though it is not at all certain—arose in connection with the small German Goliath tank which was said to be 'herded by a mother tank several hundred yards to the rear' (*Tuscaloosa News*, 9 April 1944, p. 2/3), but whether the tank was remote-controlled or cable-controlled was not known.

ACKNOWLEDGMENTS. For citations, to the American Dialect Society and to members of its Committee on New Words as follows: Clarence L. Barnhart (1), Atcheson L. Hench (1), Albert H. Marckwardt (1), Mamie J. Meredith (11), and Peter Tamony (2); also Dwight L. Bolinger (1) and Allen Walker Read (3). Thanks are due the University of Alabama Research Committee for secretarial aid.

SYMBOLS: The symbol + before a word or definition indicates an Americanism. A date immediately following a word or definition indicates the time of evidence shown in the DAE, or, if so stated, in another publication. Dates in brackets indicate the time, etc., of British usage. An asterisk after a word indicates that the word is illustrated in British usage before 1600.

BAKA (BOMB). See quots.—1945 *Time* 7 May p. 47 The strange little men of Japan turned up in the Pacific with a strange little aircraft—a man-controlled rocket plane that carried its pilot to certain death. . . . U. S. soldiers promptly dubbed it the 'baka' (Japanese for 'foolish') bomb. *Newsweek* 7 May p. 46 American forces have officially designated this bomb as 'baka,' baka being Japanese for foolish, silly or stupid . . . San Francisco *Examiner* 2 June p. 2/6 Effectiveness of the antiaircraft fire aboard United States Naval vessels forced the airmen of the Rising Sun in desperation into the use of human rocket (Baka) bombs . . . *Life* 30 July p. 74/2 *Baka* is carried to within a few miles of the target at heights up to 27,000 feet and then released to glide to the target.

+BALDING, adj. See quots.—1941 *Time* (Air Express ed.) 25 Aug. p. 26/1 Moonfaced, balding, bespectacled, Mort broods a great deal about his health. 1946 *This Week* 22 Sept. p. 15/2 Balding Fred Astaire and . . . Ginger Rogers became the boy-and-girl team of the century. 1947 *Tuscaloosa News* 14 May p. 3/1 (AP) The gray and balding jailer said he was unable to identify any member of the mob. *This Week* 20 July p. 8/2 Although now well along in his sixties, this grizzled and balding waterdog still likes to plunge into the water . . .

BUMP,* *v. t.* + See 1934 quot.—1934 Eric Partridge *Slang To-day and Yesterday* (N.Y.: Macmillan) p. 427 Bump, to. To displace, esp. on railways, a junior (-1920). 1941 Boston *Daily Globe* 3 Jan. p. 20; quoted in *Am. Sp.* Apr. 1941 p. 159/2 Bumping seems a popular pastime down in Onawa, Piscataquis County, Maine, where, according to a newspaper item, 'Joe Begin is working on the section for the C. P. R. here, having bumped Romeo Lavallee. Romeo then bumped Henri Carrier, who was working at Camp 12, and Henri, having no one to bump, is out of work pro temps. 1944 *Fortune* Oct. p. 260/2 According to this plan, a veteran with one year's shop seniority and three years' service credit could 'bump' a veteran who had three years' shop seniority, but he could not bump one who had five years' shop seniority. *Tuscaloosa News* 23 Oct. p. 4/3 (AP) But the right of a returned veteran to 'bump' a non-veteran with greater seniority has not been determined by the courts. 1946 *B'ham News* 4 Apr. p. 24/4 (NANA) This caused thousands to be 'bumped' from jobs . . .

+CONTACT, *n.* & *adj.* See quots.—1940 *Life* 16 Sept. p. 65/2-3 But most of the trip was flown 'contact' . . . 1942 Jordanoff *Aviation Dictionary*, s. v. 'contact flying.' 1944 *Tuscaloosa News* 23 Apr. p. 8/1 (AP) Instead, he [the private flier] flies by 'contact,' that is, within sight of the ground and with a safe margin of visibility and ceiling. *Harper's* Sept. p. 307/1 The Russians' flying often seems to be all contact, following the good old iron compass—the railroads. 1947 *Harper's* Apr. p. 324/1 When you can see any trace of the ground . . ., that's 'contact'—because you are visually in touch with the world.

+DOWNGRADING, *n.* Placing in a lower grade or rank. (Also attrib.)—1941 *Am. Sp.* Dec. p. 319/1 . . . distinct 'downgrading' is to be observed . . . in the designation of places of particularly unsavory reputation as *jouks*. 1944 *The* (San Francisco) *Labor Herald* 8 Dec. p. 6/1-3 Aircraft Union Join To Fight Downgrading Pay Cut Drive. 1945 N. Y. Nat'l City Bank *Report* Nov. p. 119 Another point is that costs will be reduced by re-classification of jobs, or 'downgrading' . . . 1946 *B'ham News* 6 Feb. p. 1/2 (AP) By downgrading, McCarthy referred to suggestions that millers be required to divert a larger portion of the wheat kernel into flour.

DREAM UP. 1942 cited in *Am. Sp.* 18: 64/1. Add earlier illust.—1941 *Life* 3 Mar. p. 23/2 . . . aside from being well-born and well-to-do, Ambassador Winant is about as far from the conventional picture of a . . . diplomat as Franklin Roosevelt could have dreamed up.

DRONE.* One who avoids work at the expense of others [-1529].—See quots. (Also attrib.)—1946 *B'ham News* 25 June p. 2/2 (AP) The Navy's drones will be sent into the cloud by one mother ship, then taken over other ships and led—by radio control, of course—to a landing field at Roi. *Life* 1 July p. 41 Remote-control 'Drone' will fly into atomic cloud. Cleveland *Plain Dealer* 20 Aug. p. 8/1 The 2,500-mile over-water flight of the drone planes . . . revealed how an atomic bomb attack could be launched against this country, or from it.

FLIGHT TESTING, *n.* & *adj.*—1943 *Sci. N. L.* 30 Jan. p. 73/3 Flight Testing Advances Win Award for MacClain. *Aviaion* May p. 118. 1946 Benson Hamlin *Flight Testing* (N.Y.: The Macmillan Co.). 1947 *Newsweek* 7 July p. 35 Today the first Boeing Stratocruisers are being prepared for rigorous flight testing . . .

GOBBLEDYGOOK. See *Am. Sp.* 20: 224/1. Add variant spelling *gobbledegook*.—1945 *Tuscaloosa News* 7 Aug. p. 4/3 (UP) The trouble is that the explanations sound like gobbledegook to me. Los Angeles *Times* 11 Aug. Pt. II p. 1. 1947 *Tuscaloosa News* 25 May p. 4/3 Gobbledegook did it . . .

GUIDED MISSILE. A weapon guided by remote-control. (Also attrib.)—1945 *Newsweek* 27 Aug. p. 25 The other was the 'guided missile'—a rocket projectile that can be aimed accurately over great distances. *Sat. Eve. Post* 15 Sept. p. 22/2 . . . but now we've developed 'guided missiles' and the atomic bomb . . . 1946 *Collier's* 11 May p. 66/2 Subs carrying guided missiles will be able to roam the seven seas . . . N.Y. *Times* 9 July p. 23C/1 The center will coordinate all anti-aircraft artillery and guided missile activities of the Army Ground Forces . . . 1947 *B'ham News* 19 June p. 40/3 Primarily, the five-wing structure is intended for work in applied research on rockets, including all components such as fuses, high-power explosives and guided missiles.

-HAPPY.* See preliminary remarks.— 1. Bored, fed-up, slightly 'goofy,' jittery.— BARK-HAPPY. 1945 *Sat. Eve. Post.* 4 Aug. p. 23/3 Bark-happy watchdogs and sore feet make the fugitives' path through France miserable. BATTLE-HAPPY. 1944 *Life* 9 Oct. p. 60 Next morning two thoroughly frightened battle-happy guys go down to the beaches to try to find our ship. COOP HAPPY. 1943 *Am. Sp.* Apr. p. 153/2 Coop Happy. To be out of one's mind from being shut up. DOUGH-HAPPY. 1946 *Sat. Eve. Post* 20 July p. 22/3 But the joint is jumping with dough-happy amateurs . . . ELECTION-HAPPY. 1945 U. of Ala. *Crimson-White* 4 May p. 2/6 Last week when it was revealed that election-happy campaigners had done considerable damage to the walls of Morgan and Graves halls, most of the student body condemned the people who had done it. FIGHT-HAPPY. 1944 *Sat. Rev. Lit.* 10 June p. 9 If you are not punch-drunk and fight-happy after you have gone the distance with Mr. Stern's relentless battle sequences, you are a stout fellow. FLAK HAPPY. 1944 *Newsweek* 29 May p. 68 The soldiers call it [sodium pentothal] 'flak juice' and refer to their condition as 'flak happy.' N.Y. *Times Mag.* 4 June p. 12/2 Airmen who say they don't mind flak are termed 'flak happy' by airmen who do mind it. *Ibid.* 2 July p. 24/4 Flak happy—Condition resulting from combat fatigue. *Read. Dig.* Dec. p. 5/1 'I couldn't believe my eyes,' the American pilot said later. 'I thought I was flak-happy.' HARBOR HAPPY. 1944 *Life* 10 Apr. p. 6 All hands at Dutch Harbor were 'Harbor Happy' to some degree. *Family Circle* 27 Oct. We get so harbor-happy looking at faces with beards and whiskers that we'll probably go hog-wild at the sight of a wisp of a veil and a party dress. HEADLINE-HAPPY. 1947 U. of Ala. *Crimson-White* 29 Apr. p. 3/5 Headline-Happy C-W Staff Holds Picnic At Deal's Lake. HEAT-HAPPY. 1945 *Sat. Rev. Lit.* 10 Mar. p. 26/1 The adjective *happy* has developed into a formative element, as in *saki-happy* and *heat-happy*. HUMP HAPPY. 1944 *Time* 19 June p. 59/1 It was named from a form of war neurosis peculiar to the region where the hazards of flying the Hump are in every man's mind—*Hump-Happy*. *Life* 11 Sept. p. 88/2 When they do they are declared to be 'Hump happy,' a phrase loosely used to describe any number of neurasthenic disorders. ISLAND HAPPY. 1947 *Am. Sp.* Feb. p. 55/1. JAP-HAPPY. 1945 *Criticism, Suggestion, and Advice* 14 Apr. (publ. by *Sat. Eve. Post*) Alec is 'the old Jap nemesis' who is obviously 'Jap-happy.' JUNGLE-HAPPY. 1944 *Yank* 9 June p. 5 The Marauders and the Japs they fought each had at least one jungle-happy poet laureate among them. 1947 *Am. Sp.* Feb. p. 55/1. KHAKI-HAPPY. 1944 *Letters* Oct. p. 4 There's something about having a khaki-happy tailor that denies you the civilian right to write a letter saying: . . . QUEUE HAPPY. 1945 Tuscaloosa *News* 6 May p. 2/3 They were tired and 'queue happy' from months of waiting in line for bread, meat, fish . . . which Nazis doled out . . . ROCK HAPPY. 1946 Richmond *Times Dispatch* 9 May p. 12/1 Rock Happy Roger turned up on half a dozen islands . . . to commiserate GI's who were growing rock happy from too long internment on a coral island. SAKI-HAPPY. See *heat-happy*. SAND-HAPPY. 1944 John Gunther *D Day* (N.Y. and Lond.: Harper and Bros.) p. 129 . . . many are what the officers call 'sand-happy'; this is a phrase almost equivalent to punch-drunk, except that it does not mean lack of fighting instinct. STRIKE-HAPPY. 1946 *Time* 28 Jan. p. 27/3 Strike-happy Americans could take comfort . . . THROTTLE-HAPPY. 1944 Lt. Fred Harms in *Prairie Schooner* p. 129 . . . throttle-happy bum . . . TRIGGER-HAPPY. 1944 *Life* 19 June p. 94 All nerves are on edge, eyes are haggard and everybody, German or American, is trigger-happy *Time* 4 Sept. p. 64/3 There were no Japs there, but the Force made the most of it, learned more about living and marching in the field, refused to be tempted into 'trigger-happy' firing. 1945 *Sat. Eve. Post* 29 Sept. p. 6/2 . . . trigger-happy soldiers . . . fired twice in quick succession. *Life* 29 Oct. p. 112/2. *Time* 5 Nov. p. 22/3. 1946 *Sat. Eve. Post* 6 July p. 106/1 He made possible glittering funerals for deceased gangsters by restoring their remains to their trigger-happy pals. SLAB HAPPY. 1944 *Am. Sp.* Oct. p. 232/1. WING-HAPPY. 1945 *New Yorker* 2 June p. 19/3 'From now on, Artie, I'm washing my hands offa writers . . . They're all wing-happy from them bats flappin' aroun' loose up in their belfries.'

+2. See *ribbon-happy*.—AUTO-HAPPY. 1946 *Newsweek* 10 June p. 86/2 On Memorial Day, more than 175,000 auto-happy spectators made their way by foot . . . to the Indianapolis Motor Speedway. BAR-HAPPY. 1942 *Am. Sp.* Oct. p. 183. CAB HAPPY. 1945 *Ibid.* Apr. p. 147/2. DEFENSE-HAPPY. 1946 *Time* 11 Nov. p. 54/3 Some defense-happy coaches even thought that the unstoppable T . . . was on the way to being stopped . . . GADGET HAPPY. 1946 *Consumer's Guide* May p. 16/1 Job-hungry GI's and gadget happy housewives make shining targets for swindlers, postwar tickers indicate. HOBBY-HAPPY. 1946 *Time* 28 Jan. p. 8/1 You'll sell not one, not two, but three or four to hobby-happy Venusians. HYPO-HAPPY. 1941 *Am. Sp.* Oct. p. 166/2. JIVE-HAPPY. 1946 U. of Ala. *Crimson-White* 29 Mar. p. 1/5 Sharp-looking vocalist, jive-happy instrumentalists . . . this is Bobby Adair's new campus orchestra. PARADE-HAPPY. 1945 *Yank* 16 Mar. p. 5/2 A bunch of parade-happy guys had moved in ahead of you, and for awhile it seemed as if that was all you were doing—marching up and down the damn streets. POSE-HAPPY. 1946 Tuscaloosa *News* 15 Apr. p. 1/5-6 A pose-happy clown places his arm on the shoulder of Mrs. Harry Truman . . . RANK-HAPPY. 1945 *Yank* 9 Mar. p. 9/1 'But every officer starts as a private so they're not rank-happy.' RIBBON HAPPY. 1944 N.Y. *Times Mag.* 2 July p. 24/4 Ribbon happy—Airman with extreme interest in his decorations or in collecting them. RICE HAPPY. 1946 B'ham *News* 27 May p. 3/6 A prisoner who would hoard his rice allowance for several meals in order to enjoy the sensation of one large meal was referred to as 'rice happy.' SCRAPBOOK-HAPPY. 1945 *Sat. Eve. Post.* 1 Dec. p. 18/3 His lack of ego was unique in Madry's experience with a succession of scrapbook-happy athletes. SOUVENIR HAPPY. 1945 *This Week* 22 Apr. p. 15/1 'Anyway, they was just as "souvenir happy" as the marines.' STRIPE HAPPY. 1942 *Am. Sp.* Oct. p. 183. 1945 *Sat. Eve. Post* 1 Dec. p. 132/1 'Stripe happy' in the Army refers to a soldier's itch for promotion—a compelling drive to get a stripe added to his sleeve.

+JAMPACKED, JAM-PACKED, *adj. Colloq.* Filled full; tightly packed.—1929 'Haircut,' from *Round Up—Stories of Ring Lardner* (Charles Scribner's Sons); reprinted in *The Pocket Book of Short Stories* (Pocket Books, Inc., 1945) p. 177 This place is jam-packed Saturdays . . . 1940 *Time* 1 Jan. p. 18/2 Ahead was a Berlin-Cologne Christmas special, jam-packed with third-class passengers. 1944 Wentworth *American Dialect Dictionary*. *Sat. Rev. Lit.* 2 Dec. p. 21/3 During a long jampacked troop-train ride to his post . . . , Lieutenant Karski noted the mood of his countrymen. 1945 *Ibid.* 14 July p. 37/2 If you like secrets and gossip, here are 7200 pages jampacked with the stuff . . . Tuscaloosa *News* 9 Aug. p. 1/6 (AP) General Spaatz' U. S. Army Strategic Air Force headquarters said Nagasaki, with its houses jampacked probably was even more vulnerable to an atom bombing. *Life* 24 Dec. p. 3 (adv.) Jam-packed with entertainment! 1946 B'ham *News* 26 Jan. p. 4/6 One hundred thousand troops jam-packed on the island get in each other's way . . . *Sat. Eve. Post* 1 June p. 70/3 Today's New Orleans . . . is a prosperous jam-packed city of some 600,000 souls.

MOTHER PLANE, SHIP. A plane which controls another plane (drone) by means of electro-magnetic waves.—1945 *Time* 19 Nov. p. 52/2 Everything it sees is projected by radio on a screen in a mother plane or on the ground. 1946 B'ham *News* 25 June p. 2/2 (AP) The Navy's drones will be sent into the cloud by one mother ship . . . N.Y. *Times* 30 June p. L3/4 . . . pilotless drones herded through the air by mother planes to record the turbulence and radio-activity of the cloud mass . . . Cleveland *Plain Dealer* 20 Aug. p. 8/1 The mother planes, following at a distance of 50 miles, could have guided them to their targets and exploded the atomic charge by radio.

+ NAME CALLING. The attempt to put a person or thing in a bad light by attaching to him or it a word with unpleasant connotations.—1937 *Propaganda Analysis* Nov. (Institute for Propaganda Analysis); reprinted in *Essays of Three Decades* (ed. A. L. Bader and C. F. Wells, N.Y. and Lond.: Harper & Bros., 1939) p. 46 'Name Calling' is a device to make us form a judgment without examining the evidence on which it should be based. 1940 *Sci. N. L.* 24 Feb. p. 126/1 'One reason for the disappointment of propaganda in the present war . . . is that "name-calling" had been so early developed by early summer that it lost its effectiveness as the crisis heightened.' 1944 B'ham *News* 3 Nov. p. 1/3-4 (AP) The new surge of name calling poured openly into the political campaign Friday . . . 1947 *Sat. Eve. Post* 21 June p. 6/2 Mere name calling is the last resort of a mental vacuum.

AMONG THE NEW WORDS

I. WILLIS RUSSELL
University of Alabama

THE CONVENTION of naming awards, popularized by the Oscar of the motion pictures (see *Am. Sp.* XIX, 306) has spread. During the war there were several modifications of the term *Oscar* itself. From General MacArthur's troops Humphrey Bogart and Greer Garson received 'the first "Fuzzy Wuzzy" Oscars: effigies of Fiji Islanders mounted on fragments of Jap airplane metal' (*Time* 3 July 1944 p. 44/3). This particular award was also called a *GI Oscar* (B'ham *News* 10 July 1944 p. 4/4), a term which crops up again the following year (*Life* 16 July 1945 p. 30/1-2). Still another modification of *Oscar*, this time a derivative, is *Oscarette*, used to describe the award Bob Hope gave the young Margaret O'Brien in 1945 (B'ham *News* 22 Mar. 1945 p. 9/3).

All these awards relate to preeminence in motion pictures. Several awards in other fields have likewise been given names, doubtless in imitation of the Oscar. One of these, the *Gertrude*, is a small sterling silver kangaroo which is given those authors the Pocket edition of whose books has sold a million copies (*Publ. Weekly* 13 Jan. 1945 p. 151; *Ladies' Home Journ.* Apr. 1946 p. 87/2). An *Edgar* is an award for writers of detective stories and consists of a porcelain bust of Edgar Allan Poe (*Am. N. & Q.* July 1946 p. 53/2; *This Week* 15 June 1947 p. 19/2). Finally may be mentioned the *Barney*, the award for cartoonists of merit: 'The Barneys are silver cigaret boxes with sketches of Barney Google and Snuffy Smith engraved on them' (B'ham *News* 13 May 1947 p. 2/3).

It is interesting that *slug* (see glossary), so widespread during the war, has virtually disappeared (if my collections are a reliable index). Nevertheless, it seems as if the word should be treated, if only because of its great popularity during the war. Another word popularized by the war was *rugged*, which virtually became a counter word. At first glance it seems to be adequately covered by such a definition as 'severe, hard, trying,' but that in the *American Thesaurus of Slang Sup.* 1947 ('tough, difficult, gruelling') gives the proper connotation of the new usage. This sense dates from at least 1943: 'The war here is still pretty rugged, as the boys say' (*Newsweek* 27 Sept. p. 23/1).

To take it is included in the glossary, even though it is in the 1944 Addenda to the *Shorter Oxford*, because it is also well established in American usage (which incidentally gives us an earlier date than the *Oxford*, where it is undated) and not covered by the general American dictionaries. The Oxford labeling is correct for American usage now.

ACKNOWLEDGMENTS. For citations, to the American Dialect Society and to members of its Committee on New Words as follows: Atcheson L. Hench (3), including those for *talking book* and the earliest for *truth serum*, Mamie J. Meredith (7), and Peter Tamony (1); also Clarence L. Barnhart (7). Thanks are due the University of Alabama Research Committee for secretarial aid.

SYMBOLS: The symbol + before a word or definition indicates an Americanism. A date immediately following a word or definition indicates the time of evidence shown in the DAE, or, if so stated, in another publication. Dates in brackets indicate the time, etc., of British usage. An asterisk after a word indicates that the word is illustrated in British usage before 1600.

+ABLE-DAY. [From *able*, the signaler's word for *a*, + *day*.] Atom bomb day. (Also attrib.)—1946 N.Y. *Times* 30 June p. L3/5 . . . the Able Day atom bomb is now resting inside a fenced enclosure in a restricted section of this island . . . *Time* 8 July p. 20/3 It was Able-Day for Operation Crossroads . . . *Am. N. & Q.* July p. 53/1 'Able Day': the day of the Bikini atom bomb test, June 30, 1946.

ACS. Initials of 'anti-reticular-cytotoxic serum.' See quots.—1944 *Time* 17 Jan. p. 42/1 Because of his serum, which he calls 'anti-reticular-cytotoxic serum' and mercifully abbreviates to ACS, the professor was decorated last week . . . 1945 *Ladies' Home Journ.* Dec. p. 136/2 In simpler language, ACS is a serum to stimulate the reticular cells of the connective-tissue system, which, rejuvenated, resumes its original role of rejuvenating the rest of the organism. 1946 N.Y. *Times* 16 June p. B7/1 . . . it is known as 'antireticular cytotoxic serum,' . . . shortened to ACS. It is made from the reticulo-endothelium which is associated with connective tissue. *Time* 17 June p. 92/2 This recipe, with variations, seems to be the starting point of many a medical marvel . . . the life-prolonging serum 'ACS'—with which Russian physicians bemuse their foreign colleagues and astound the public . . .

+A-DAY. Able-Day (which see). (Also attrib.)—1946 *Sat. Eve. Post* 8 June p. 18 . . . mere experts were washed out by the brutally rugged standards as the 509th Composite Group trained for A-day. B'ham *News–Age-Her.* 30 June p. 1-A/2 . . . scientists and military men alike felt the growing tension as the probable A-day deadline . . . approached.

+BAKER DAY. [From *Baker*, the signaler's word for *b*, + *day*.] The day the second (hence B) atomic bomb was exploded during Operation Crossroads. See quots. (Also attrib.)—1946 N.Y. *Times* 19 July p. C8/2 . . . the Baker Day atomic bomb on July 25 will be suspended and detonated by radio impulses from outside the lagoon. Omaha *World-Her.* 21 July p. 21-A Here's what will happen on Baker Day—second climax of the Navy's Operation Crossroads . . . The bomb will be slung beneath a specially-adapted barge placed amid the warships . . . Tuscaloosa *News* 30 July p. 2/1 (UP) The battleship Nagato . . . sank to the bottom of Bikini Lagoon today to bring the Baker Day atomic bomb total to five ships . . .

BATTLEWAGON. 1938 cited in *Am. Sp.* 22: 146/1. Add earlier illust.—1934 Weseen *Dictionary Amer. Slang.* p. 125.

+BUSH PILOT. A commercial pilot who flies over relatively uninhabited country, as Alaska.—1945 Hamann *Air Words* p. 13/1. 1946 *Coronet* Jan. p. 53 The postwar air age is old stuff to the ingenious bush pilots of the Far North. *Sat. Eve. Post* 19 Jan. p. 114. 1947 *Time* 16 June p. 26/3 The bush pilot is still making medicine with his light plane, still landing passengers and freight in improbable corners of the country.

CHAIN REACTION. Tech. sense in NID 1934.—+*Fig.*—1947 Balto. *Sun* 25 Jan. p. 4/2 (Editorial) The chain reaction to Government farm price policy which the poultry people started in November has now reached the congressional agricultural committees by way of warning testimony from the Secretary of Agriculture. *Sat. Eve. Post* 22 Mar. p. 140/3 Other writers have told me that if you publish a candid article about any community, giving actual names of people and telling what you think of them, you are sticking your neck way out, and braving a chain reaction of lawsuits, riots and civil commotion. *Time* 7 July p. 9/2 It set up a chain reaction among our readers that is still snapping and crackling around these offices.

ETO. European Theater of Operations. (Also attrib.)—1943 N.Y. *Times Mag.* 11 July p. 16/2 (cited Taylor *Lang. of World War II* p. 26) Artie arrived in the ETO on Jan. 31. 1945 Balto. *Sun* 29 Aug. p. 11/3-4 (headline) 15,274 ETO Veterans Return . . . 1947 *Am. Thes. Slang. Sup.* *Time* 29 Sept. p. 104/1 . . . Allen . . . was Patton's G-2 operations executive . . . in the ETO campaign.

FLIGHT,* *n.* 'In titles of officers of various ranks in the Royal Air Force.' [1916] (OED S). +FLIGHT ENGINEER. See first quot.—1942 *Trade Winds* (Wright Aeronautical Corp.) Feb. p. 3 The flight provided an ideal demonstration of the flight engineer's value . . . his specialized job is the operation of the power plants . . . 1947 B'ham *News* 11 Aug. p. 1/7 (AP) These included . . . the previous flight of the Bombshell with Odom, Milton Reynolds . . . and Flight Engineer T. Carroll Sallee . . . *Time* 6 Oct. p. 61/1 (Reports said nothing about the flight engineer, who probably nursed his engines as usual.)

+LANDING MAT. A section of meshed steel 12 by 3 feet containing fasteners so that a number can be joined together to form a surface of any desired area. So called because used as a landing surface for aircraft during the war. Peace-time uses include reinforcing for concrete.—1944 *Time* 10 July p. 76 (adv.) Since then a hundred thousand tons of steel have steamed into Butler factories to be made into steel landing mat. 1947 Tuscaloosa *News* 25 June p. 12/8 (adv.) Just Received Another Carload Landing Mats—For Fences, Trellis, and other uses. Balto. *Eve. Sun* 4 Sept. p. 1/7-8 The previous complaints alleged overcharges . . . on the hauling of steel and aluminum airplane landing mats and other items.

MACH [NUMBER]. [mɑk] See quots. —1945 B'ham *News–Age-Her.* 21 Oct. p. 18-A/3 (AP) The Mach number, named for Dr. Ernest Mach . . . represents the speed at which air flowing past a given part of an airplane attains the speed of sound. 1947 *Aviation* June p. 79 (Title) Speeds and Mach Numbers. *Sci. N. L.* 6 Sept. p. 146/3 The procedure followed was to fly the plane in each testing program first at a six-mile altitude at a designated 'Mach Number.' This is the ratio of its speed to that of sound at the particular altitude. *Time* 8 Sept. p. 76/2 During both flights it reached 'mach .828.' This means that both times it moved at 82.8 per cent of the speed that sound would travel through the same air.

+PARKING METER. A device to charge for parking. The insertion of a coin into a mechanism placed at the curb permits the moving of a handle, which causes a flag to disappear. A clock mechanism is then released which allows the flag to return to full view as the time runs out.—1936 *Am. City* Jan. p. 95/3 In July of this year there came to the attention of the officials in Dallas a device known as the parking meter. 1943 *Read. Guide* 13:1409-10 and references there cited. 1947 *Chr. Sci. Mon. Mag.* 27 Dec. p. 14/4 It is heavenly, they say, with no squeezing into a too narrow space, no parking meters . . .

+PSYCHODRAMA, *n.* See quots. (Also attrib.)—1945 *Sci. N. L.* 22 Dec. p. 396 . . . psychodrama, a therapeutic type of drama, in which the actors do not learn parts, but make them up spontaneously to meet the situation being enacted . . . 1946 *Collier's* 16 Feb. p. 6/3 A new type of therapy for mental patients known as psychodrama is helping many veterans at St. Elizabeth's . . . On the stage of a small theater, servicemen are relieved of the fear of facing certain future situations by enacting them spontaneously before an audience of other patients. *Time* 19 Aug. p. 68/2 It includes . . . a 'psychodrama' theater . . . B'ham *News* 6 Nov. p. 16/2 The acting is called psychodrama . . . The players solve their problems by acting them out.

SHACK (UP) WITH. *Slang.* See *Am. Sp.* XXI, 198, 252, 304; XXII, 56.—1947 Leslie Walker *Show Me the Way* (N. Y.: Viking Press) p. 191 'She wanted me to shack with her tonight . . .'

SLUG, *v.* 'To strike . . . heavily or violently . . .' {1862} (OED).—+*Fig.*—1943 *Fortune* Feb. p. 122/1 . . . guns slugging at close range. *Time* 10 May p. 98/3 Twice it screens exciting action: once when the sub slugs it out with a disguised German raider . . . *Newsweek* 9 Aug. p. 27/1 This found them . . . still slugging along at a point between the coastal villages of Tetere and Zovi. 1944 *Harper's Mag.* Aug. p. 283/1 . . . in attacking others we know we will have to fight our way all the way in, flying through heavy barrages of flak over the target and then slugging our way all the way out. *Read. Dig.* Nov. p. 62/1 But always he was slugging away at novel writing on the side. 1945 *Time* 2 Apr. p. 20/1 Ranking Armored Force officers never believed the tank's function was to slug it out toe-to-toe with other tanks.

+SMOKE JUMPER. A forest-fire fighter who parachutes into a fire area.—1940 *Read. Dig.* July p. 70 The 'smoke jumpers' wear specially designed suits, helmets, steel-mesh masks, ankle braces and heavy gloves, and use a new type of parachute . . . 1943 *Family Circle Mag.* 22 Oct. p. 8. 1945 *Sci. N. L.* 26 May p. 332 U. S. Forest Service 'smoke jumpers' and their flame-fighting tools are parachuted to forest fires in regions inaccessible by roads. 1947 *Chr. Sci. Mon. Mag.* 6 Dec. p. 8/3 Parachute smoke-jumpers . . . operated on 202 fires . . .

+SONIC BARRIER, WALL. See quots. (Also attrib.)—1947 Tuscaloosa *News* 7 June p. 1/2 (UP) Army Air Force sources indicated that the AAF probably will take over the sonic barrier tests with one of its own pilots. *Time* 30 June p. 52/3 Well below these speeds, the 'sonic barrier' makes itself felt, jamming an airplane's controls, destroying the lift of its wings. *Pop. Sci.* Aug. p. 134/1 (Title) Test Planes Tooled to Tap Sonic Wall. *Time* 24 Nov. p. 31/1 Douglasmen hoped that it would make air history by breaking through the sonic wall—*i.e.*, by flying faster than the speed of sound . . .

+SPARK, *v.* Short for *sparkplug* (see 1939 *NID Sup.*)—1944 Information, Please! radio program 3 Apr. It really does what good food always does, spark the appetite. Tuscaloosa *News* 26 Apr. p. 2/1 Clark . . . is chairman of the Senate finance subcommittee which sparked the omnibus World War Two veterans' aid bill to unanimous Senate passage . . . 1946 *Newsweek* 18 Nov. p. 28/3 A current move in Henry Wallace's transformation of the New Republic—sparked by the public-relations firm of Edward L. Bernays—is a Washington-bureau expansion . . . 1947 *Sat. Rev. Lit.* 12 July p. 7 His own predilection for Periclean culture was sparked by . . . Prentice . . . B'ham *News* 16 Nov. p. 4C/1-2 (AP) Southern Methodist went ahead . . . on an 81-yard drive sparked by the passing of Gilbert Johnson . . .

+SPOT CHECK. A quick, rough sampling.—1945 Tuscaloosa *News* 31 Oct. p. 1/7 (AP) A spot check of the House ways and means committee indicated the president's jobless pay liberalization bill . . . will stay on the shelf . . . 1946 N. Y. *Times* 30 June p. L25/2 Spot checks are made but many of these slaughter houses go as long as five weeks without a check. 1947 B'ham *News* 28 Sept. p. 1/7-8 (AP) A spot check of representative cities from coast to coast disclosed fresh meats, butter or eggs—or all three items—were down from the record retail price peaks in most sections.

TAKE,* *v.*—*to take it.**+See last quot.—1934 Weseen *Dict. of Amer. Slang.* pp. 176, 317 can't take it. 1940 *Read. Dig.* Oct. p. 134/2 Some of the boys wondered if a movie actor could 'take it.' *Sat. Rev. Lit.* 16 Nov. p. 13 . . . a novel about the dust bowl has a queer air of being post-dated in a world which is wondering whether Great Britain can take it. 1943 *Nation* 15 May p. 699 (title) The Farmers Can Take It. *Harper's Mag.* Sept. p. 341 . . . when the treaty of non-aggression between Germany and the Soviets not only filled the sanitariums with literary idealists who couldn't take it . . . 1944 *Sat. Eve. Post* 8 Jan. p. 19/1 One of the things a severe neurotic cannot do is 'take it.' Sh OED Add. *to take it:* to endure punishment, affliction, etc. with fortitude (*colloq.*).

TALKING BOOK. 1939 cited in *Am. Sp.* 22:149/2. Add earlier illust.—1934 N. Y. *Times* 13 Mar. p. 20/3 The perfected 'talking book' is a combination phonograph and radio set.

+TRUTH SERUM. See quots.—1935 Balto. *Sun* 4 Dec. p. 15/1 'Twilight sleep' . . . was advanced as a 'truth serum' in 1923 by Dr. R. E. House . . . 1946 B'ham *News* 18 July p. 1/4 (AP) Some of the reports said the youth made the disclosures while under the influence of sodium pentothal, the so-called 'truth serum.' *Life* 29 July p. 31/2-3 Chicago stories say he was given sodium pentothal, Army-developed 'truth serum,' in order to make him confess. 1947 B'ham *News* 6 Dec. p. 1/4 (AP) Under the influence of a truth serum, she indicated her home was in Ohio . . .

AMONG THE NEW WORDS

I. WILLIS RUSSELL
University of Alabama

THE WAR JUST COMPLETED gave us a number of terms for various types and shades of war: 'bacteriological warfare' (1937), 'total war' (1937), 'blitzkrieg' (1938), 'phoney war' (1939), 'psychological warfare' (1939), 'sitzkrieg' (1939), 'war of nerves' (1939), and 'shooting war' (1941) (see article 'Words and Meanings, New,' *Ten Eventful Years* [Encyclopaedia Brit., Inc., 1947] and *Am. Sp.* 18:65/2). A glance at the glossary below will reveal two new terms, 'cold war' and 'hot war.' Several of these are of especial interest. According to the dating, we have this progression: 'blitzkrieg,' 'phoney war' and 'sitzkrieg,' and finally 'shooting war.' Notice that the two middle terms imply the absence of the essential element in our concept of war; what that element is is made explicit in the last term, '*shooting* war.' A similar progression is seen in 'war,' 'cold war,' 'hot war.'

On the basis of findings he reported in *Am. Sp.* 20: 21, Professor A. R. Dunlap concluded 'that the *type person* construction is current colloquially in all the larger divisions of the American speech area.' This locution Professor Dunlap calls the 'adjunct noun equivalent' of a 'prepositional genitive phrase,' that is, to use his examples, 'the type person that I dislike' equals 'a person of the type that I dislike.' Written examples of this construction do not seem to be as plentiful as the colloquial evidence Professor Dunlap offers. I have noted 'the type characters' (N. Y. *Times Book Rev.* 31 May 1942 p. 4), 'type blouse' (*Time* 9 Apr. 1945 p. 90/2), 'type scripter,' (*Sat. Rev. Lit.* 14 Apr. 1945 p. 31/1), and 'type limb' (Tuscaloosa *News* 23 Aug. 1945 p. 6/5). Another one of Professor Dunlap's examples of this construction is 'women of the smart type' beside 'smart-type women.' Since the dictionaries and the grammars which I have consulted seem to be silent on the *-type* construction, the citations below may prove useful additions to Professor Dunlap's material. A lighter note is supplied by the following remark of a correspondent of the N.Y. *Herald Tribune* (quoted *Time* 22 Mar. 1943 p. 52/3): 'Everybody is a "type" of some sort: "good type," "bad type" or "good-bad type" . . . and there are innumerable other classifications: melancholy type, backward type, insistent type.'

ACKNOWLEDGMENTS. For citations, to the American Dialect Society and to members of its Committee on New Words as follows: Atcheson L. Hench (2), Mamie J. Meredith (8), and Peter Tamony (4); also O. B. Emerson (1), Gladys Nichols (2), and Mrs. Bonita Thomas (1). Dr. G. P. Shannon kindly supplied the definition of *cold war.* Thanks are due the University of Alabama Research Committee for secretarial aid.

SYMBOLS: The symbol + before a word or definition indicates an Americanism. A date immediately following a word or definition indicates the time of evidence shown in the DAE, or, if so stated, in another publication. Dates in brackets indicate the time, etc., of British usage. An asterisk after a word indicates that the word is illustrated in British usage before 1600.

AIR LETTER. 'Air-mail letter' (*Amer. Thesaurus Slang* 1942). See quots. —1947 *Friends Intelligencer* 22 Mar. p. 142/1 A new air letter that may be sent anywhere for ten cents will become available soon—a peacetime use of V-mail that has been developed by the Post Office Department. *This Week* 30 Mar. p. 30/2 How much will the 'air letter' to be issued by the post office cost? *Newsweek* 14 Apr. p. 77/1 On April 29, the Post Office Department will authorize use of a single sheet 'air letter' which folds into an envelope and may be sent to any part of the world for ten cents.

BATHYSCAPHE, *n.* See quots.—1947 *Time* 18 Aug. p. 44/2 Last week 63-year-old Scientist Piccard told the North American Newspaper Alliance about the 'bathyscaphe' (from the Greek for 'depth ship'), his submarine balloon which will descend into the sea suspended from a steel and aluminum 'gas bag' full of lightweight gasoline. B'ham *News* 20 Nov. p. 30/4 (NANA) When Prof. Auguste Piccard makes a 2½-mile dive to the ocean bed in his bathyscaphe soon, he will transmit a minute-by-minute account of his experiences and observations to a parent ship on the surface.

BENELUX. See quots. (Also attrib.) —1947 *Foreign Affairs* July p. 692 The Secretariat prepared a common tariff for the 'Benelux Union,' . . . Lond. *Spectator* 10 Oct. p. 454/1 Success would make 'Benelux' (BElgium, NEtherlands, LUXembourg) the third trading power in the world . . . Lincoln (Neb.) *Journ.* 23 Oct. p. 6/1 Follow the Benelux Trail *Sat. Eve. Post* 22 Nov. p. 26/1 This suggestion has astounded the originators of Benelux, for they intended their concoction to be merely an economic association between Belgium, the Netherlands and Luxembourg—the three nations whose names were contracted to form that word 'Benelux.'

COLD WAR. A prolonged contest for national advantage, conducted by diplomatic, economic, and psychological rather than military means.—1946 Baltimore *Sun* 11 Mar. p. 2/6 After stating that Russia began a 'cold war' on Britain and the British Empire after Russian diplomacy believed it had separated the two western powers from each other at the Moscow conference, the *Observer* expert sums up the situation which Churchill undertook to confront . . . 1947 N. Y. *Times* 17 Apr. p. 21/4 'Let us not be deceived—we are today in the midst of a cold war.' San Fran. *Chronicle* 8 July p. 14/6 Best description of what's going on in Europe today was given by elder statesman Bernie Baruch when he said we are in a 'cold war.' *Fortune* Sept. p. 38/1 Facets of a cold war . . . 1948 Tuscaloosa *News* 5 May p. 5/4 (AP) . . . the number one issue of the period is whether the cold war will develop into a shooting war or whether it can be kept within bounds.

FROZEN FOOD. Quick-frozen food that retains its flavor and nourishment.—1935 *Readers' Guide* 9: 848/2 Frozen food . . . 1942 *Sci. N. L.* 20 June p. 391/2 Frozen Foods With Flavor Produced By New Method. 1947 Tuscaloosa *News* 9 Apr. p. 6/5-6 (adv.) And Now—Frozen Food.

GERONIMO. Name of an Indian chief, used as a battle cry by the U. S. paratroops during World War II.—1942 *Newsweek* 30 Nov. p. 20/1; cited Taylor *Lang. of World War II* (H. W. Wilson Co., c. 1944) A defiant yell, 'Geronimo!' echoed over North Africa last week. 1947 Berrey and Van den Bark *Amer. Thesaurus Slang: Sup.* 1948 B'ham *News* 14 Mar. p. 5C/2 . . . at Troy State Teachers College the new yell is 'Geronimo,' adopted from the U. S. paratroops of World War II. *Time* 10 May p. 90/2 Geronimo!

GLEEP, *n.* See quots.—1947 Tuscaloosa *News* 17 Aug. p. 2/5 (UP) The United Kingdom's forst [sic] atomic pile is called 'gleep' (graphite low energy experimental pile) and was built primarily for experiments in nuclear physics. *Time* 25 Aug. p. 74 (note) Britain's first pile . . . began operation last week. Officially it is a 'gleep' (graphite *l*ow energy *e*xperimental *p*ile).

GRAY (GREY) MARKET. [See *black market, s. v.* 'black,' *adj.* in NID Sup. 1945.] The market where goods can be bought, but at prices considered exorbitant. (Also attrib.)—1946 *Life* 1 Apr. p. 32/1 In the Rocky Mountain region there is a gray market in toilet paper. *Time* 17 June p. 84/3 What was shocking was the grey market in cars . . . 1947 B'ham *News* 29 May p. 6/3 (AP) He will tell his version of a $50,000,000 'gray market' steel transaction. 1948 *Time* 26 Jan. p. 82/3 The Joint Congressional Committee on Housing had padded from coast to coast, sniffing for the scent of a grey market in building materials.

HOT WAR. See *cold war* and Preliminary Remarks. See quots.—1947 *Newsweek* 17 Nov. p. 25/2 'The ideological war of the Communists is as ruthless and as determined . . . as a hot war.' *Sat. Eve. Post* 6 Dec. p. 236/2 Thus it is a little premature to talk about our supposed triumph in the cold war; a triumph, incidentally, which will be meaningless if we cannot prevent the cold war from boiling up into a hot war. 1948 Tuscaloosa *News* 25 Apr. p. 1/5 (AP) Secretary of State Marshall returned yesterday from the inter-American conference and the brief outbreak of 'hot war' at Bogota to resume direction of American strategy in the global 'cold war' with Russia.

IMAGE ORTHICON. A highly sensitive television camera tube; also see quots. (Also attrib.)—1945 B'ham *News* 29 Oct. p. 9/1 The product of RCA engineers . . . the device is known as an 'image orthicon,' . . . *Time* 5 Nov. p. 72/2 Then R.C.A.'s new 'image orthicon' pickup tube went into action . . . 1946 *Collier's* 30 Mar. p. 28/4 The new eye, called the 'image orthicon,' will pick up the soft lighting effects that set the dramatic mood for a love scene, or the eerie half-light that goes with murder mysteries . . .

LITTLE (SMALL) MAGAZINE, REVIEW. See quot. 1946.—1914 The Little Review . . . Mar. 1914-May 1929 . . . ; quoted Huffman, Allen, Ulrich *The Little Magazine* (Princeton University Press, 1946) p. 245/1. 1930 *Bookman* Jan.-Feb. p. 657/1 In the bright morning of the little magazine, which broke upon the world somewhere around the year 1912, the pioneers stood out against the vermillion sky in very bold relief. *Eng. Journ.* Nov. p. 689; cited Huffman, Allen, Ulrich, *op. cit.* p. 402 Small Magazines. 1943 Baker *Little Reviews* . . . (George Allen & Unwin Ltd.) p. 5 The little review or small magazine is an integral part of literature. 1946 Huffman, Allen, Ulrich, *op. cit.* p. 2 A little magazine is a magazine designed to print artistic work which for reasons of commercial expediency is not acceptable to the money-minded periodicals or presses. 1948 *Sat. Rev. Lit.* 15 May p. 19/1 . . . he writes esoteric essays for little magazines . . .

MOMISM. [*mom,* from *mama,* + *ism.*] See quots.—1942 Philip Wylie *Generation of Vipers* (Rinehart & Co., Inc.) p. 185 Hitherto, in fact, man has shown a considerable qui vive to the dangers which arise from momism . . . 1946 *Sat. Eve. Post* 26 Oct. p. 15/3 Furthermore, momism is the product of a social system veering toward a matriarchy in which each individual mom plays only a small part. *Sat. Rev. Lit.* 7 Dec. p. 21 (Philip Wylie) . . . I was glad to see this quasi-official sanctioning of [my] terms. The war had proved that Momism is the deadliest disease of the nation . . . 1947 *Life* 6 Jan. p. 78/2 While I do not agree altogether with Mr. Philip Wylie's outbursts against 'mom' and 'momism,' there is no question that a matriarchy is developing in the U. S. *This Week* 30 Mar. p. 4/1-2 During the war, when almost everyone was glorifying her [the American Mother] Wylie turned on her savagely, described her at her worst and, inventing the word 'momism,' held her responsible for a vicious, smothering influence that all but ruins American men.

1947N. See first quot.—1947 San Fran. *News* 13 Dec. p. 14/1 The new comet got its name '1947N' because so many astronomers saw it simultaneously and no one's name could be assigned to it. The letter 'N' is added to the year of discovery because it is the 14th comet discovered this year . . . *Time* 29 Dec. p. 40/1 Last week a bright but furtive comet called 1947-N was already 100 million miles from the earth . . . 1948 Lond. *Spectator* 9 Jan. p. 44/1 A new comet can . . . go into the stud-books as 1947N . . .

PROMIN. See quots.—1941 *Sci. N. L.* 4 Oct. p. 212/1 Promin and sulfadiazine, two of the newest sulfa drugs, may be regarded as 'important substitutes' for quinine or atabrine in treatment of malaria . . . 1942 *ibid.* 28 Feb. p. 131/2 A derivative of di-amino-di-phenyl-sulfone, named promin, is being tried in human tuberculosis cases . . . 1946 Omaha *World Her.* 1 Jan. p. 7 (UP) The little-publicized discovery of promin . . . will enable hundreds of lepers to thank 1945 scientists for improved treatment of their disease . . . 1948 San Fran. *Call-Bull.* 12 Apr. p. 3/6 (AP) Diasone and two companion drugs, promin and promizole, have shown promise against both tuberculosis and leprosy but they have some disadvantages.

SYNCHRO-CYCLOTRON, SYNCHROCYCLOTRON. A cyclotron (see NID Sup. 1945) in which the frequency can be varied to keep the electric field synchronized with the rotating particles. —1947 *Time* 27 Oct. p. 65/1 When the great new 'synchro-cyclotron' at the University of California was first turned on last fall, a powerful beam of unidentified radiation shot from its circular chamber. *Sci. N. L.* 25 Oct. p. 260/1-2 'It is, therefore, understandable that as soon as the synchrocyclotron was well launched on its operating career, W. M. Brobeck, who was chiefly responsible for the engineering design of the great machine, should give some thought to the next step up the energy scale.' 1948 *World Almanac* p. 787/1 Elements were transmuted 16 steps down the periodic table and 22, possibly 30, particles were knocked out of an atomic heart or nucleus with the new 4,000-ton synchro-cyclotron.

-TYPE. Combining form of the noun *type,* added to nouns and adjectives with or without hyphen, to form compound adjectives.—1945 *Sat. Eve. Post* 2 June p. 93/1 . . . some even have British-type mustaches . . . 1946 Tuscaloosa *News* 2 Aug. p. 1/7 (AP) Although it was a record for a conventional type plane, fast pursuits have crossed the nation in better time. 1948 B'ham *Post* 5 Mar. p. 1 (headline) Red Finns Open Coup-Type Move. 1948 *Christ. Sci. Mon. Week.* 21 Feb. p. 2 (Picture caption) Discussion-Type Classes Are Backed by Frequent Examinations. 1947 *Life* 24 Nov. p. 75/1 Accordingly Nimitz turned over to Kinkaid . . . a huge force of old battleships, escort-type aircraft carriers . . . 1948 B'ham *News* 23 Apr. p. 14/3 The position of the receiver on French-type handset . . . is with the openings on the 'down side.' *Ibid.* 16 Apr. p. 12 He has a clock made of 150 pieces of wood . . . two horse-drawn-type hearses . . . 1940 *Lond. Illust. News* 28 Dec. p. 821 The outbreak of the war found the Fleet Air Arm using for the most part adapted land-type machines . . . 1928 Odell 'Traditional Examinations and New Type Tests'; cited *School & Soc.* 35: 100/2, note. 1935 Bossing *Prog. Meth. of Teaching in Sec. Schools* p. 479 The examination was of the new type objective form. 1937 N. Y. *Times* 1 Aug. VI p. 5/1 (headline) 'Progressives' Hail New Type School. 1941 *Newsweek* 29 Sept. p. 40; quoted Taylor *Lang. of World War II* p. 62 A new type cargo ship . . . 1944 *Time* 12 June p. 53/3 This baler forms a new type rolled bale . . . 1947 B'ham *News* 18 Dec. p. 24/2 (AP) Here are some of the claims made for the new-type plane . . . 1948 *Time* 16 Feb. p. 73/1 Together they improvised a talky-type song . . .

UMTEE, UMPTEE. ['ʌm ti, from UM (Universal Military) + T (Trainee).] See quots. (Also attrib.)—1947 *Time* 3 Mar. p. 19/2 At Fort Knox the experimental 'Umtees' were treated as human beings. *Life* 10 Mar. p. 43/2-3 He is one of 664 teen-age 'Umtees' (Universal Military Trainees) . . . B'ham *News* 21 May p. 2/2 Some have been unkind enough to refer to the 'Umptees' as 'beardless wonders,' 'senior Boy Scouts,' . . . Richmond *News Leader* 8 July p. 3/2 . . . 'Umtees,' they call themselves.

AMONG THE NEW WORDS

I. WILLIS RUSSELL
University of Alabama

I

IN A LETTER to me, Professor Atcheson L. Hench made some observations on the extension in meaning of *deep* and *depth* (treated in the glossary) which cannot well be worked into an etymology and which, therefore, find a better place here. He points out that Webster's *deep, adj.,* 2b, 'deals with physical depth—depth measurable by feet or human bodies (4 rows deep) or some other physical measurement.' The extended sense, however, 'deals with reserves in supply, substitutes in some activity.' He recalls seeing the extension first in such military uses as 'The general had deep reserves as he attacked the Rhine,' in which the reference is to the 'many military units in reserve.' Then comes the extension to sports. After quoting two definitions of the military sense of *depth,* Professor Hench continues:

> Neither of these definitions recognizes what actually happened to the word—that its meaning got transferred from the space these troops or tanks occupied to the troops or tanks themselves. *Depth* came to refer to the reserves themselves and not to the space they occupied. And *deep* followed along immediately. Then it was not long before the word was used in non-military senses.

I am indebted to Professor Hench for these comments.

ACKNOWLEDGMENTS. For citations, to the American Dialect Society (1), Atcheson L. Hench (the earliest for *depth*) and Mamie J. Meredith (2), including the earliest for *eager beaver*). I should like to record a continuing obligation for the generosity and patience of those of my colleagues whom I am continually seeking for help in technical definitions (for example, *air lift* and *atom-smasher* in this issue). Thanks are also due the University of Alabama Research Committee for secretarial aid.

SYMBOLS: The symbol + before a word or definition indicates an Americanism. A date immediately following a word or definition indicates the time of evidence shown in the *DAE*, or, if so stated, in another publication. Dates in brackets indicate the time, etc., of British usage. An asterisk after a word indicates that the word is illustrated in British usage before 1600.

ACRONYM, *n.* [Gr. *akro-*, comb. form of *akros* 'extreme, tip,' + Gr. *onyma* 'name']. See quots.—1943 *Amer. N. & Q.*, Feb. p. 167/1 Your correspondent who asks about words made up of the initial letters or syllables of other words may be interested in knowing that I have seen such words called by the name *acronym*, which is useful, and clear to anyone who knows a little Greek. 1947 *Word Study: a Publication of G. & C. Merriam Co.* . . . May p. 6/2 The word [*snafu*] is an English *acronym*, that is to say, a word formed from the initial letters of other words. *Ibid.*, Dec. p. 11/2 The article on 'Acronyms' . . . has aroused much interest.

AIR LIFT, AIRLIFT. 'A form of displacement pump . . .' (*NID* 1934). *Mil.* Air service for the transportation of personnel and/or cargo, sometimes supplemental to other forms of transport such as rail and water.—1945 *Life* 17 Dec. p. 112/2 General Ho Ying-chin used the American air lift to pass four crack American-equipped and American-trained armies over the heads of the Communists into Shanghai . . . 1947 Tuscaloosa *News* 26 Oct. p. 14/6 The 'Air Lift' is a service unit just extended to Tuscaloosa by the Air Reserve Training Unit in Birmingham. Any four or more air reservists may use the service by notifying Birmingham one day in advance. 1948 B'ham *News—Age-Her.* 11 July p. 1A/8 (AP) Allied officials expressed confidence that the airlift would allow them to keep the food ration at its present level. *Life* 9 Aug. p. 15/1 (title) The Great Airlift Sustains Berlin.

ATOM-SMASHER, *n.* Any machine such as the cyclotron and betatron that furnishes the projectiles which are used to bombard the nuclei of atoms.—1937 *Lit. Dig.* 12 June p. 17/3 The Westinghouse atom-smasher will look like a gigantic aluminum pear . . . 1943 *Sci. Dig.* May p. 75/1 Scientists are now applying the 'atom-smasher'—the cyclotron—to the solution of many of the riddles of physiology and medicine. 1948 *Britannica Book of the Year* p. 86/1 More than $10,000,000 was spent in the U. S. during 1947 on new 'atom-smashers.' *Science News Letter* 8 May p. 291 Atom-Smasher.

BACITRACIN, *n.* [*bacillus* + *Tracy* + *-in*; see quots.] See quots.—1945 *Science* 12 Oct. p. 376/1 We named this growth-antagonistic strain for the patient, 'Tracy I.' When cell-free filtrates of broth cultures of this bacillus proved to possess strong antibiotic activity and to be non-toxic, further study seemed warranted. We have called this active principle 'Bacitracin.' 1946 *Collier's* 14 Sept. p. 6/2 The newest antibiotic, or germ-inhibiting drug, is bacitracin which . . . promises to be even more useful than penicillin in certain types of infection. The strain of micro-organism which formed its original culture was discovered in the leg wound of a seven-year-old girl, Margaret Tracy . . . and the drug was named in her honor. 1947 *Woman's Home Companion* May p. 126/2 Its name is bacitracin. 1948 *Science* 27 Feb. p. 228 (title) Assay of Bacitracin in Body Fluids.

BAT BOMB. [After the bat, which locates, and thus avoids, objects by emitting supersonic sound waves which are reflected back to it from the objects.] A bomb which is guided to its target by radio waves sent out by a mechanism in its nose; see also etymology and 1946 quot.—1945 B'ham *News—Age-Her.* 16 Dec. p. 1/6-8 (Editorial Sect.) Navy reveals that its radar-guided 'Bat' bombs, carried under wings of mother ship, accounted for many Japanese ships during war's last year. 1946 *Senior Scholastic* 8 Apr. 11/2 The Navy's Bat Bomb [column heading] Because it works on the same principle that enables a bat to fly in the dark, the latest bomb developed by the Navy is called 'The Bat.' . . . Instead of the bat's sound wave 'feelers,' the bomb sends out short radio wave 'feelers.' 1948 Tuscaloosa *News* 31 July p. 1/1 (UP) The Navy's newest weapons, radar-guided bat bombs, proved 'a disappointment' when tried out on the veteran battleship Nevada, Navy officers said today.

CABINETEER, *n.* 1941 in *Am. Sp.* 18: 62. Add earlier illust.—1934 Weseen *Dict. Amer. Slang* p. 316.

CHLOROMYCETIN, *n.* [Gr. *chloro-*, comb. form, 'green,' + Gr. *mycet-*, comb. form, 'fungus,' + *-in*]. See quots.—1947 B'ham *News* 2 Nov. p. 8c/1 This material, chloromycetin, was obtained from a minute organism, closely related to that from which streptmycin [sic] is secured . . . *Sci. N. L.* 8 Nov. p. 291/1 Epidemic typhus fever, Rocky Mountain spotted fever, scrub typhus and parrot fever . . . are among the serious diseases which may be conquered by this newest member of the penicillin-streptomycin family of drugs. Chloromycetin is its name. 1948 B'ham *News* 29 July p. 24/3 (AP) Payne decided he'd take along with him a little of the still experimental drug 'chloromycetin' which his firm, Parke, Davis & Co., was developing.

CONVENTIONEER. 1940 in *Am. Sp.* 17: 122/2. Add earlier illust.—1934 Weseen *Dict. Amer. Slang* p. 322.

DEEP*, *adj.* 'Having extension backward of specified measure: as, . . . soldiers 4 rows deep' (*NID* 1934, s. v. *deep, adj.*, 2b). Hence, *Sport.*, pertaining to substitutes, amount of reserve strength.—1942 B'ham *News* 10 Nov. p. 8/3-4 The Jackets aren't knee deep in reserves . . . 1947 Tuscaloosa *News* 11 March p. 8/1 (AP) Both fives are deep in material . . . B'ham *News* 23 Oct. p. 42/6 (AP) Three-deep in Talented [sic] material at every backfield post, Michigan has powered its way to 222 points . . . *Ibid.* 20 Nov. p. 43/4-5 L. S. U. has backs three and four deep at every position. 1948 *Sat. Eve. Post* 20 Mar. p. 34/1 . . . but the U. S. C. coach is a great one for making sure that his teams are two deep in an event—sometimes even three deep.

DEPTH*, *n.* '. . . *spec. (Mil.)* The distance from front to rear of a body of soldiers as measured by the number of ranks.' *OED* {1667}. *Sport.* See *deep, adj.*—1945 Radio broadcast 6 Oct. over WCHV 'Coach —— has a pretty good first team but he lacks depth. 1947 B'ham *News* 23 Oct. p. 42/6 (AP) Few who saw the Gophers tumble in a 40 to 13 licking last week at the hands of Illinois believe that Minnesota has the depth to press the Michigan steamroller . . . *Sat. Eve. Post* 20 Dec. p. 24/3 Almost everywhere there were squads of unusual depth and skill.

DIXIECRAT, *n.* Usually in the plur. [*Dixie* + *Democrat*]. Name popularly applied to one of those Democrats who opposed first the civil rights program of the Truman Administration and later the civil rights plank of the 1948 platform of the Democratic Party; a group of these Democrats convened at Birmingham, Alabama, and nominated their own candidates on a platform of states' rights. See also last quot. (Also attrib.)—1948 B'ham *News* 22 May p. ‑/5 (headline) Truman Finds Some Dixiecrats Supporting Him on A-Veto Stand. *Ibid.* 22 July p. 11/2 (AP) Baltimore . . . Maryland voters who want to cast their ballots for 'Dixiecrat' candidates . . . will have to use the write-in method . . . Tuscaloosa *News* 27 July p. 3/3 (UP) Marion Junction—(UP)—Alabama Dixiecrats reportedly will gather in their first major state meeting tomorrow . . . *States' Rights* (Birmingham, Alabama) 26 July p. 1/1 Former Governor Frank M. Dixon of Alabama . . . proposed 'Constitutional Democrats' as the proper name for the opponents of the Truman federalist-centralization program. He said: [¶] 'States' Righters is all right, but the term, "Dixiecrats," leaves the wrong impression. Our contention is that we are returning to the original concepts of the founding fathers of our nation and the Democratic Party. This is not just a Dixie movement . . .'

EAGER BEAVER. *Slang.* See quots.—1943 *Daily Nebraskan* 7 Nov. Eager Beaver —Anyone who has the slightest conception of what physics is all about. 1945 *Am. Sp.* Oct. p. 226/2 *Eager beaver.* Same as *busy beaver.* . . . Used in a derogatory or spiteful manner of an industrious worker. 1947 *Sat. Eve. Post* 16 Aug. p. 122/1 Before photostating my application, some eager beaver . . . helpfully typed the address . . . *Ibid.* 18 Oct. p. 137/1 (adv.) Eager Beaver —Is he ambitious, hard-working, anxious to get ahead in the world? *Time* 29 Dec. p. 58/2 Its hands were so full collecting quarters that it established a franchise system to sell machines to the eager beavers who wanted to get into the business. *Amer. Thesaurus of Slang. Sup.* 1948 Tuscaloosa *News* 24 June p. 1/4 (NEA) Other claims and rumors of delegate switch-overs, started by the eager beavers on the Dewey psychological warfare team, didn't sit well with the anti-Dewey forces.

FACT-, FACT FINDER.—1926 De Kruif *Microbe Hunters* (Pocket Book ed. 1945) p. 46 He believed in an all powerful God, but while he believed, the spirit of the searcher, the fact finder, flashed out of his eye . . . 1945 *Time* 31 Dec. p. 13/2-3 (picture caption) Fact-Finders Stacy, Garrison, Eisenhower. 1946 *Life* 21 Jan. p. 29/3 (picture caption) Fact Finders in G. M. strike . . . 1947 *Time* 26 May p. 44/2 Parliamentary fact-finders last week finished adding up the cost to Canada of World War II . . .

FLYING STOVEPIPE. *Slang.* See quots. —1947 *Time* 23 June p. 70/2 A simpler type . . . is the ram jet or 'flying stovepipe,' which has no moving parts at all. *Sat. Eve. Post* 6 Sept. p. 95/3 . . . the ram-jet, widely known as the flying stovepipe. 1948 *Sci. N. L.* 22 May p. 323/3 The ram-jet has been called the flying stovepipe because of its simple shape.

GRAY-, GRAY, GREY MARKETEER. —1948 *Life* 12 Jan. p. 34/1 . . . for every ton of steel that actually exists in the gray market there are a dozen gray-marketeers trying to cut in on the deal. *Time* 26 Jan. p. 84/3. *Life* 2 Feb. p. 6/2 (caption) The Case for the Gray Marketeer. *Britannica Book of the Year* p. 125/1 Gray marketeers also were active in the purchase and sale of automobiles.

RAM-, RAMJET, *n.* See quots. (Also attrib.)—1945 *Sci. N. L.* 17 Nov. p. 317/3 It is a ramjet motor of new and unusual design. 1946 *Cleveland Plain Dealer* 30 Aug. p. 1/7 (AP) He predicted that the ramjet—an engine which has no moving parts and operates on air from the atmosphere—will take the place of the gas turbine in high-speed planes. 1947 B'ham *News* 19 June p. 40/2 The ram-jet's advantage is in its ability to ram air through its nose under compression, thus eliminating the necessity of carrying oxygen inside the weapon, as in the V-2. B'ham *News* 9 Oct. p. 1/5 (AP) A ram-jet engine has no moving parts, except itself. The compression of air needed to burn fuel is attained by the engine's own forward speed. Because of that, it cannot operate below 400 miles an hour. 1948 *Sci. N. L.* 22 May p. 323/3.

RED FEATHER. Pertaining to the Community Chest.—1946 B'ham *News* 5 Nov. p. 1/7-8 The Red Feather Man Says . . . 1947 Tuscaloosa *News* 4 June p. 2/1 . . . the speaker said that the Association's brooms are marketed through regular trade channels, and that a 'red feather' trade-mark is placed upon the handle. 1948 *Sat. Rev. Lit.* 10 July p. 31/2 When you give . . . give generously . . . enough for all Red Feather services . . . for a full year through your Community Chest.

SHOOTING WAR. See *Am. Sp.* 18: 65/2. Additional illust.—1947 *Friends Intelligencer* 8 Nov. p. 600/2 . . . 'This award emphasizes the original purpose of the founders of the American Friends Service Committee to find a constructive way to wage peace even in the midst of a shooting war.' 1948 B'ham *News* 5 March p. 9/1 (AP) I don't believe a shooting-war is imminent . . .

SNIPERSCOPE, *n.* 1. An attachment for a rifle which operates on the principle of the periscope (*NID* 1934). 2. An infra-red mechanism which enables snipers to see their quarry in the dark and which also makes possible the study of very old fossils; see quots.—1946 Tuscaloosa *News* 16 April p. 3/5 (UP) A fighter hears a sound. He points the sniperscope into the darkness, peers into the eyepiece and turns on his power supply. He swings the weapon back and forth like an invisible searchlight until he sights the enemy. *Time* 29 April pp. 89/3-90/2 The U. S. sniper, looking through a fat telescope ('sniperscope') mounted on his carbine, saw a bright green picture of everything in front of him. *Harper's Mag.* Oct. p. 331/2 As a sniperscope it enabled German riflemen to pick off a man in total blackness. 1948 B'ham *News* 12 Aug. p. 6/1 (*NANA*) The sniperscope and snooperscope, used by both Americans and Germans in World War II to 'see in the dark,' now have been adapted to penetrate slices of opaque minerals and allow study of the structure of 5,000,000,000-year-old fossils imbedded in rock.

SNOOPERSCOPE, *n.* [*snooper* + *scope*]. An infra-red device similar to the sniperscope; see also quots.—1946 Tuscaloosa *News* 16 April p. 3/5 (UP) The sniperscope, mounted on a .30 calibre carbine, and the snooperscope, a hand model, made it possible for fighters to shoot an invisible beam of light into the night. B'ham *News* 18 April p. 32/4 This is a snooperscope fitted over a special helmet in position used by American soldiers starting in the summer of 1944 . . . 1948 *Sci. N. L.* 1 May p. 279/2 The infra-red radiation that enabled soldiers to see enemies in the dark by use of the snooperscope is now ready to combat frost in fruit orchards. B'ham *News* 12 Aug. p. 6/1 (s. v. *sniperscope*).

TEST-TUBE, attrib. {1886}. Pertaining to that produced by artificial insemination.—1937 *Sci. Amer.* Jan. p. 40/2 Is a 'test-tube baby' legitimate or illegitimate? 1939 *Newsweek* 8 May p. 29/2 Dr. G. Pincus . . . is studying artificial fertilization but isn't interested in test-tube babies. 1940 *Bus. Week* 30 Nov. p. 36; cited *Read. Guide* 12: 997/2 Test-tube cows; rapid growth of artificial insemination. 1945 *Sci. Dig.* Jan. p. 16 (title) Test-Tube Cows Produce Extra Quart Each Day. 1947 *Friends Intelligencer* 7 June p. 290/2 Dr. Mary Barton . . . said 300 'test-tube' babies have been born in England during the last five years as the result of artificial insemination by strangers, and 'thousands' after artificial insemination by husbands. Tuscaloosa *News* 21 Oct. p. 1/2 (UP) Justice Henry Clay Greenberg will be asked in Manhattan Supreme Court tomorrow to decide whether a test-tube baby legally and physically can have only one parent.

TURBO-, TURBOJET, *n.* [*turbo-*, comb. form of *turbine*, + *jet*]. An engine which, in flight, is run by air taken in at the front, compressed, and heated; the air expands with great force through a turbine which operates the compressor and finally escapes from the rear in a jet with powerful propulsive thrust. (Also attrib.) —1945 *Sci. N. L.* 10 March p. 147/2 The airplane is powered by General Electric's turbo-jet engine installed in the tail of the sleek plane. 1946 *Sat. Rev. Lit.* 22 June p. 6/1. 1948 *Sci. N. L.* 22 May p. 323/3 The afterburner being installed is a cylindrical device eight feet long which is attached on the exhaust nozzle of the Westinghouse turbo-jet engine which powers this plane. *Time* 9 Aug. p. 54/1 The coming of the turbojet does not mean that the engine in use since the first days of the Wright brothers (pistons and propellers) is done for.

VIRUS PNEUMONIA. See quots.—1943 *Am. Mercury* April p. 475/1 In the last ten years, a new type of pneumonia has appeared . . . known as virus pneumonia because it is caused by a filtrable virus . . . 1948 B'ham *News* 15 July p. 4/4 Stricken with virus pneumonia a 9-year-old Central Park boy today lay on his sick bed and called for his dog. *Time* 9 Aug. p. 73/1 Died. Susan Glaspell . . . of virus pneumonia.

WEATHER SHIP. See quots.—1947 B'ham *News* 21 Oct. p. 4/1-2 (picture caption) Horror seized the 69 passengers and crew aboard the flying boat Bermuda Sky Queen when it was forced to set down in mountainous seas near a weather ship in the North Atlantic. *Time* 27 Oct. p. 28/3 . . . he doubled back toward the U. S. Coast Guard cutter *Bibb*, which was on station as a weather ship about 900 miles northeast of Newfoundland. *Sat. Eve. Post* 29 Nov. p. 36/1 Life is rugged and perilous on the weather ships—those floating weather bureaus that squat in the North Atlantic and save the passengers of a doomed ship or plane. *Ibid.* 29 Nov. p. 61/2 The weather ships also make themselves exceedingly useful as radio-relay stations. . . . Most important of all is their air-sea-rescue activity.

WEREWOLF*, *n.* [*OED*, s. v. werewolf, 1. β. fig. 1902 *Spectator* 5 July p. 17/1 When from that underworld. . . . The werwolves of the darkness pour by night And show . . . their misery and their guilt.] See quots. (Also attrib.)—1945 B'ham *News* 8 April p. 1/3 (AP) Hitler decreed the splitting of state and Nazi party officers Saturday in a drastic move enabling topflight Nazi leaders to abandon their posts . . . and take up underground stations in the 'werewolf war.' *Time* 9 April p. 40/1 It boasted that . . . underground killers—'Werewolves'—had carried out the sentence. Tuscaloosa *News* 11 April p. 4/3 The partisans who have decided to fight

on and who recently made themselves known as the 'Werewolf' must also be considered as Nazis. 1948 *Life* 19 July pp. 26-27 American and British armored cars and jeeps with mounted machine guns keep a slow, steady prowl through the rain—on guard, not for the Nazi 'werewolves' of three years ago but for Red revolutionaries in Soviet army trucks.

WONDER DRUG. A drug with miraculous curative powers.—1940 *Sci. N. L.* 17 Feb. p. 105/3 Other uses of metallic sodium: . . . for use in preparing such new wonder drugs as sulfapyridine for pneumonia. 1947 *Time* 10 Nov. p. 54/3 What excites researchers most: in animal tests it has proved a potent cure for certain rickettsial diseases, caused by tiny, bacteria-like organisms that have resisted previous 'wonder drugs.' 1948 *Life* 9 Aug. p. 87/2 Methadon is not a wonder drug.

WRITE-IN, *adj.* 'Write in. To insert (a fact, statement, etc.) in writing . . .' (*OED*, s. v. write, *v.*, 14) {*c.* 1425}. *Specif.* Pertaining to the method of proposing a person for office by writing his name on the ballot.—1934 J. P. Harris *Election Administration in the United States* (Washington: The Brookings Institution) p. 176 Write-in candidacies are usually put forward under one of several contingencies . . . 1944 Tuscaloosa *News* 26 April p. 1/5 (AP) But Dewey took a big early lead in the GOP write-in voting . . . 1946 B'ham *News* 26 June p. 12/6 . . . Ellis Patterson . . . may run for the House of Representatives again as a write-in candidate. 1948 B'ham *News* 22 July p. 11/2 (AP) Maryland voters who want to cast their ballots for 'Dixiecrat' candidates in the November presidential election will have to use the write-in method . . .

II

The second part is devoted to combinations of *-buster* (agent noun of the verb *bust*, 'to smash'), which has been active recently. But because the history of the form has not, so far as I am aware, been treated with any great completeness, I have attempted to place the new compounds in their historical setting by bringing together as many combinations, old and new, with their dates, as I have been able to find. Many of them, to be sure, are already in dictionaries, but since they are not listed under *-buster*, they are not easy to come by. Included here, for example, are the *-buster* compounds scattered throughout the indexes of the slang compilations of Weseen and of Berrey and Van den Bark. A search of other indexes would doubtless yield additional, perhaps earlier, compounds, but even so I believe that the examples assembled here make a fairly imposing array and will give a view of the form hitherto impossible.

The better to exhibit the history of the form, let us list the compounds chronologically from the earliest recorded through 1942. Selection of the last date as a stopping point will permit the inclusion of the many combinations taken from Berrey and Van den Bark, who, presumably, had earlier citations.

1888 broncobuster	1936 gang-, jam-b.
1890 belly b.	1938 cloud-, fence-, racket-b.
1907 middle b.	1940 balloon-, brush-, union-b.
1911 trust-b.	1941 knuckle-, mollybuster
1933 bush-b.	1942 banjo-, beak-, block-, bog-, brownie-,
1934 chin-, clay-, company-, contract-,	button-, conk-, cop-, ghost-, joint-,
rivet-, skull-, sod-, target-, thumb-b.	keister-, kidney-, knuck-, reed-, sin-,
1935 bull-, tommy-b.	spy-, stack-, tank-b.

In view of the length of time *-buster* has been used as a combining element, one would expect this function to have been recognized some time ago. Yet it was not until 1943 that Professor Bolinger noted (*Am. Sp.* 18: 62) that '*Trust-buster* and *gang-buster* are the pivotal examples of *-buster*, which might be defined as "one who seeks to destroy an organization regarded as undesirable."' He cited in addition the film 'Racket Busters' (1938) and *union-buster*. A year later, in 1944, the Addenda to the *Sh OED* recognized *-buster* 'As the second element of an objective compound' and 'in familiar designations of guns, bombs, etc.,' citing in illustration *broncho-buster* and the war-born *block-buster, dam-buster,* and *tank-buster.* The many examples assembled here show that Professor Bolinger's definition can be generalized and that *Oxford* can add to its illustrations.

How should *-buster* compounds be labeled? It seems to me that lexicographers may have tended to give such compounds a low usage level

because of the association of *-buster* with *bust,* 'to smash,' itself considered vulgar (the *OED* calls *buster* a 'vulgar corruption of *burster*'). How should, for example, *trust-buster* and *block-buster* be labeled? The latter is labeled *colloq.* by the *ACD* and slang by *Webster's*; but since I have never seen the bomb referred to by any other name, it is hard for me to see why *block-buster* should be labeled at all. On *trust-buster* specifically and the whole question generally, Mr. Mencken had something pertinent to say years ago. In his 1919 *American Language* (p. 143, and note), he commented on the rise in the usage level of *bust,* which he said tended to supplant the more proper *burst* in figurative uses, and asked this question: 'Who, in America, would dare to speak of *bursting* a broncho, or of a *trust-burster?*' If *-buster,* therefore, is established as a standard combining element, then the only question is to determine in each case the actual usage level of a given *-buster* compound.

ACKNOWLEDGMENTS. For citations, James B. McMillan (1), Mamie J. Meredith (9), Allen Walker Read (1), and Peter Tamony (5). Thanks are also due the Research Committee of the University of Alabama for secretarial aid.

-BUSTER. See preliminary remarks.—ATOM-B. 1946 *Time* 22 July p. 65/1 To the American Physical Society, U. S. atom-busters described carefully laid plans for further busting. BALLOON B. 1940 *Life* 2 Sept. p. 29/1 German 'Balloon Busters' Attack the Dover Barrage. BARGE B. 1944 San Fran. *Examiner* 1 Oct. (Amer. Weekly Sec.) p. 11 (adv.) Barge Busters! . . . the Navy's versatile PTs are taking a terrific toll of Jap troopcarrying barges. BATTLESHIP B. 1943 *ibid.* 6 June (Sec. 1) p. 1/8 Carrying giant 2,000 pound 'battleship busters'—bombs that can smash through armor—the Flying Fortresses made the longest operational flight of the North African campaign. BEAK B. 1942 Berrey and Van den Bark *Amer. Thesaurus of Slang* (N.Y.: Crowell, 1943 printing) ¶ 695.1 Boxer . . . beak bender *or* buster. BIKEBUSTER. 1944 *GM Folks* Dec. p. 24 [Beneath a picture of two boys taking apart a velocipede is the caption] Bikebusters Tom McNamara and Robert Cook . . . BLOCKBUSTER. 1942 cited in *Am. Sp.* 19: 224/1. BRIDGE B. 1944 *Newsweek* 20 Nov. p. 42/3 In all, Captain Boutselis, home last week after two tours of duty with the 'Burma Bridge Busters,' as the 490th is called, collected five bridges . . . 1946 *Sat. Eve. Post* 23 March p. 4/3 Bridge-Buster. BRUSH-B. 1940 *Read. Dig.* Sept. p. 84/2 They are using gigantic brush-busters . . . , leviathans that bowl through the thickest, roughest brush and crush and tear and uproot all in their path. CHIN B. 1934 Weseen *Dict. Amer. Slang* (N. Y.: Crowell) p. 231 Chin buster—A boxer . . . CLAY B. 1934 *ibid.* p. 250 Clay buster—A trapshooter. CLOUD B. 1938 *Newsweek* 21 Feb. p. 10/1 (picture caption) Cloud Buster: . . . flying fortresses will attend the inauguration . . . DAM B. 1944 *Time* 11 Dec. p. 28/3 He was the famed 'Dam Buster' (so dubbed by Winston Churchill after the spectacular Möhne and Eder dam-breaching raids . . . FACTORY B. 1944 cited in *Am. Sp.* 21: 141/1. FORTBUSTER. 1945 *Pop. Sci.* June p. 95 A little fuse—no bigger than a hen's egg—crumbled the concrete of the German West Wall and the Siegfried Line, and will do smashing duty wherever there is tough concrete or similar resistance on the road to Tokyo. It's the Army's Fortbuster. HURRI-B. 1943 Hunt and Pringle *Service Slang* (Lond.: Faber and Faber) p. 33 The Flying tin-opener. A name for the Hurricane tankbuster, or Hurri-Buster. KEISTER B. 1942 *Amer. Thes. Slang* ¶ 461.16 Safecracker . . . keister buster. LINE B. 1948 Tuscaloosa *News* 4. Nov. p. 10/4 Line buster—Wade Farris, Holt's hard hitting fullback . . . MIDDLE B. 1907 Hunt *Forage & Fiber Corps* p. 352; quoted *OED Sup. s. v. middle,* B *sb.* b. By means of a 'middle buster,' which is a double moldboard plow. 1934 *New Inter. Dict.* s. v. *lister.* RAILROAD-B. 1944 B'ham *News* 1 May p. 1/8 Targets of the RAF's Railroad-Busters . . . were Acheres . . . and Somain . . . RIVET B. 1934 *New Inter. Dict.* rivet buster. *Mach.* A tool for knocking off rivetheads. SOD-B. 1934 Weseen *op. cit.* p. 399 Sod-buster—A rustic; a farmer [see also p. 197]. 1942 *Amer. Thes. Slang* (Index). SUB-B. 1943 A. D. Rathbone *He's in the Sub-Busters Now.* 1944 *Time* 24 April p. 17 (picture caption) . . . A Coast Guard Sub-Buster Is Loaded for Europe. TANK-B. 1942 San Fran. *News* 11 Dec. p. 2/3-5 (heading) Tank-Buster Corps Is Really Tough. 1944 *Sh OED Add.* TARGET B. 1934 *op. cit.* p. 269 Target Buster—A trapshooter. TRAINBUSTER. 1944 B'ham *Age-Her.* 1 Nov. p. 12/3 (AP) And across No-Man's Land . . . the boys behind the guns of a certain artillery battalion are grinning at their new role as 'trainbusters.' 1945 *Time* 19 March p. 32/1 (caption). TUNNEL-B. 1944 *ibid.* 8 May p. 20/1 Ace of tunnel-busters is Major William Benedict . . .

Fig.—BAND-B. 1946 *ibid.* 4 Nov. p. 58/3 He organized his first orchestra—15 kids who called themselves the Band-busters . . . BANJO B. 1942 *Amer. Thes. Slang* ¶ 576.10 . . . banjo buster, *a banjo player.* BEACH B. 1945 *News and Views* (Gen. Motors) May p. 6 The Navy's newest tracked amphibious vehicle . . . known as the LVT-3 or 'Beach Buster' easily handles 10,000 pounds of cargo or fifty men, fully equipped. BELLY B. 1890 cited in Wentworth *Amer. Dial. Dict.* (N. Y.: Crowell). BLOCK-

BUSTER. 1943 cited in *Am. Sp.* 19: 224/1-2. 1945 Omaha *World Her.* 30 Dec. p. 3-A/2 blockbuster [an intoxicating drink]. BOG-B. 1942 *Time* 31 Aug. p. 78/2 Captain Hampton Green's bog-busters chewed switchbacks down a steep hillside of ice-hard dirt . . . BOOZEBUSTER. 1945 *Time* 12 Feb. p. 78/2 . . . Boozebuster Johnson . . . BOTTLENECK B. 1944 *Sat. Eve. Post* 8 July p. 59 (adv.) . . . C. T. C. is a bottleneck buster which helps us make the existing trackage carry maximum traffic. BRAIN B. 1944 *Sat. Rev. Lit.* 8 April p. 23 (adv.) *The Nation's* Cross Word Puzzle Book; 55 Brain Busters . . . 1944 'Quiz Kids' radio program 16 April. BRONCO-B. 1888 cited in *DAE.* BRONZE B. 1947 *Time* 8 Dec. p. 74/1 Bronze Buster [a sculptor]. BROWNIE B. 1942 *Amer. Thes. Slang.* ¶ 461.15 brownie buster, . . . *a freight car burglar* [also ¶ 772.5]. BRUSH-B. *ibid.* ¶ 913.10 brush buster . . . *a cowboy in brush country.* BULL-B. 1935 *Am. Sp.* 12: 13/1 Bull-Buster. A crook who habitually resists arrest. 1942 *Amer. Thes. Slang* ¶ 461.30. BUSH-B. 1933 cited in Wentworth *op. cit.* . . . bush-buster . . . hillbilly. BUSTLE B. 1947 B'ham *News* 25 Aug. p. 1 (picture caption) Long Skirt Haters and Bustle Busters. BUTTON B. 1942 *Amer. Thes. Slang* ¶ 281.4 . . . joke . . . belly buster . . . button buster ¶ 583.12 Comedian. Belly buster . . . button buster. CITY-B 1943 *Time* 13 Dec. p. 36/2 Between these city-busters, heavy bombers in lesser force hit seven times at industrial targets . . . 1945 Hamann *Air Words* p. 15/1 City buster. Atomic bomb. CLOUD-B. 1943 *Am. Sp.* 18: 104 Fly balls include the *sky-scraper,* the *cloud-buster* . . . COMPANY B. 1934 Weseen *op. cit.* p. 78 Company buster—An employee of a mining company who works above ground. 1942 *Amer. Thes. Slang* ¶ 514.7. CONK B. 1942 *Amer. Mercury* July p. 94/1 Conk buster—cheap liquor; also an intellectual Negro. CONTRACT B. 1934 Weseen *op. cit.* p. 95 Contract buster—A professional horse breaker. 1942 *Amer. Thes. Slang* ¶ 913.12. COP B. 1942 *ibid.* ¶ 461.30 bull *or* cop buster. CRIME B. 1943 *Coronet* Feb. p. 119 (title) Crime Busters on Wheels. DOORBUSTER. 1948 B'ham *News* 10 Oct. p. B-2 (adv.) Monday Morning Doorbusters. ELEPHANT B. 1947 *This Week* 7 Dec. p. 20/2-3 (title of an article on those who break elephants) Elephant Busters. FENCE B. 1938 *Newsweek* 10 Oct. p. 30/3 When big Red Ruffing pitches, the Yanks have nine potential fence busters [home run hitters]. 1942 *Amer. Thes. Slang* ¶ 670.10. GANG B. 1936 N. Y. *Times* 18 March p. 24/2 Gang Busters—Sketch. 1945 Mencken *Amer. Lang. Sup. I* (N. Y.: Knopf) p. 370 *Gangbuster* appeared . . . *c.* 1935. GHOST B. 1942 *Amer. Thes. Slang* ¶ 327.10 . . . ghost buster, *an exposer of spiritualistic mediums.* GUN B. 1943 Hunt and Pringle *op. cit.* p. 38 Gun Buster. An artificer of the Royal Army Ordnance Corps; a Tiffy. HIGHWAY-B. 1947 *This Week* 19 Oct. p. 22/2 'Since when,' I ask 'em, 'did you highway-busters [truck drivers] get so tongue-tied you can't each one speak for himself?' HURRICANE-B. 1947 B'ham *News* 12 Oct. p. 1/8 (AP) A hurricane-buster plane—especially equipped B-17 Army bomber—with scientists aboard left Schenectady . . . for Mobile . . . JAM-B. 1936 Mencken *Amer. Lang.* (1945 printing) p. 583 . . . a yardmaster is a *dinger* . . . his assistant is a *jam-buster* . . . 1943 *Am. Sp.* 18: 166. JOINT B. 1942 *Amer. Thes. Slang* ¶ 461.15 Burglar . . . joint buster. KETTLE B. 1944 *Am. Sp.* 19: 231/1 Kettle buster. Boilermaker. KIDNEY B. 1942 *ibid.* 17: 104/1 Kidney buster. Hard-riding truck. 1947 *Amer. Thes. Slang Sup.* . . . kidney buster, *an army truck.* KNUCK-B. 1942 *Amer. Thes. Slang* (Index only). KNUCKLE B. 1941 *Am. Sp.* 16: 166/2 Knuckle buster. Crescent wrench. 1942 *Amer. Thes. Slang* (Index). 1943 Colby *Army Talk* p. 227. LAW B. 1947 Fred Allen radio program 26 Jan. MOB B. 1945 *ibid.* 11 Nov. MOLLYBUSTER. 1941 *Am. Sp.* 16: 156/2 Mollybuster. A tamp for expanding anchors. NUT B. 1945 *Am. Sp.* 20: 148/1 Nut buster. Mechanic. OMNIBUSTER. 1946 *Time* 15 April p. 14/2 Omnibuster. In London, Ernest Meadow leaped into the driver's seat of an idling bus, caromed off through traffic . . . RACKET B. 1938 *Newsweek* 1 Aug. p. 8/1 . . . 'Racket Buster' Dewey was concerned mainly with ridding the city of extortionists. REED B. 1942 *Amer. Thes. Slang* ¶ 577.12 Saxophone . . . reed buster. REICH-B. 1945 N. Y. *Daily News* 15 March p. 3/1 RAF Using 11-Ton Reich-Busters. SIN B. 1942 *Amer. Thes. Slang* ¶ 327.7 Preacher . . . sin buster. SKULL-B. 1934 *Am. Sp.* 9: 27/2 Skull-Buster. A detective. 1942 *Amer. Thes. Slang* ¶ 460.17, 18. SMUG-B. 1945 N. Y. *Post* 10 Sept.; quoted by A. W. Read in *Sat. Rev. Lit.* 1946 *Sat. Eve. Post* 19 Jan. p. 34 (title) Song Buster. SPY-B. 1942 San 22 June 1946 p. 48/3 'You can be a smug-buster,' he declared. SONG B. Fran. *News* 2 Dec. p. 17/7 New kinds of soldiers, these: Spy-busters. STACK B. 1942 *Amer. Thes. Slang* (Index). THUMB-B. 1934 Weseen *op. cit.* p. 109 Thumb-buster—An old-fashioned, single-action revolver. 1942 *Amer. Thes. Slang* (Index). *Am. Sp.* 17: 105/1-2 THUMB BUSTER. Mechanic or grease monkey . . . a spinning steering wheel on four-wheel drive trucks when driven on rough ground or in mud. TOMMY-B. 1935 *ibid.* 10: 22/1 Tommy-buster. A man who makes short shrift with women; one who takes them by storm. 1942 *Amer. Thes. Slang* (Index). TOWNBUSTER. 1945 *Time* 2 April p. 73/2 Called variously 'volcano bomb,' 'townbuster,' . . . it carves an enormous crater, tossing up divots weighing five tons apiece. TRUST-B. 1911 *Cent. Dict. & Cy.* 1919 Mencken *Amer. Lang.* p. 310 Nor was there any other satisfactory word for *graft* when it came in, . . . nor for *trust-buster.* WEATHER B. 1944 *Time* 4 Dec. p. 65/2 Their reports . . . now enable the 'weather busters' of the A. T. C. to forecast the weather across the North Atlantic mile by mile . . . WORLD-B. 1945 *Sat. Eve. Post* 8 Sept. p. 4/3 Which still wouldn't get some of us far enough away, if the new world-buster fulfills its youthful promise as a new and far fancier method of extinction.

AMONG THE NEW WORDS

I. WILLIS RUSSELL
University of Alabama

ACKNOWLEDGMENTS: For citations, C. L. Barnhart (1), Dwight L. Bolinger (1), Atcheson L. Hench (4), James B. McMillan (1), Mamie J. Meredith (13), and Peter Tamony (8). Thanks are also due the Research Committee of the University of Alabama for secretarial aid.

SYMBOLS: A date immediately following a word or definition indicates the time of evidence shown in the *DAE,* or, if so stated, in another publication. Dates in brackets indicate the time, etc., of British usage. An asterisk after a word indicates that the word is illustrated in British usage before 1600.

AEROBEE, *n.* [*aero-* + *bee* (see 1949 quot.)] See quots. (Also attrib.)—1948 *Time* 15 March p. 78/3 The Army & Navy announced last week that a rocket called the Aerobee had risen 78 miles above White Sands . . . and reached a speed of 3,000 m. p. h. . . . *Sci. N. L.* 20 March p. 178/3 . . . the aerobee climbed to 78 miles altitude and reached a speed of 4,400 feet per second . . . Unlike the V-2, the new liquid-fueled missile is designed primarily for carrying instruments into the upper atmosphere. 1949 B'ham *News—Age-Her.* 9 Jan. p. A-4/7 (NANA) The present device, known as the Aerobee because of its buzzing sound, was worked out especially for this purpose.

AMINOPTERIN, *n.* See quots.—1948 *Newsweek* 26 April p. 48/2 Dr. Farber emphasized that aminopterin is not a cure for acute leukemia. *Sci. N. L.* 21 Aug. p. 126/2 The chemical, aminopterin, was used to treat leukemia at Children's Hospital . . . after it had been successfully tested against the disease in animals. B'ham *News* 2 Oct. p. 1/7 And today the administration of aminopterin began.

BABY SIT, BABY-SIT, *v.i.* To mind one or more children while their parents or guardians are out.—1947 *The Matrix* Sept. p. 8/3 . . . offer to 'baby sit' with her little boy . . . 1948 *Life* 7 June p. 148/2 The college students who live in the veterans' housing project . . . have an ideal neighbor who can baby-sit for seven families at a time. *Ibid.* 4 Oct. p. 66 . . . Joan Pederson . . . baby-sits with the Fords' daughter while mother sticks close to desk.

BE-BOP, BEBOP, *n.* See quots. (Also attrib.) See *re-bop.*—1945 *Down Beat* 1 Aug. p. 8/2 BE-BOP 1946 Omaha *World-Her.* 17 March p. 8-E/1 (UP) We didn't even give it a name—it got that because when you hum it, you just naturally say 'Be-bop, be-de-bop.' *Harper's Mag.* Oct. p. 325/1 . . . if this girl happened to be interested in be-bop music, . . . he could talk about Harry the Hipster . . . 1947 *Sat. Rev. Lit.* 30 Aug. p. 18 This offshoot from the so-called 'real jazz' bears the name *bebop,* an onomatopoetic term derived from the sounds the instruments make as they negotiate the characteristic curt phrasing and tortuous unison passages of this new music. 1948 *Life* 11 Oct. p. 142/2 Experts say bebop is a form of discordant jazz in which notes are played at breakneck speed with accents more on the upbeat than the downbeat.

BELLYLAND, -LAND, *v. t.* and *i.* To land a (in a) plane without using its landing gear.—1944 Balto. *Sun* 10 June p. 2/3 . . . Johnson bellylanded his plane safely near the spot where he had seen Allied troops from the air. 1947 B'ham *News* 17 Nov. p. 2/7 (headline) Pilot Belly-Lands . . .

CARETAKER, *adj.* See quots.—1945 Tuscaloosa *News* 23 May p. 1/8 (AP) Churchill is expected to lead a new 'caretaker' government into Commons when it reassembles Tuesday. 1946 B'ham *News* 13 Nov. p. 20/4 . . . dope is that a stopgap or caretaker operation will be established to carry on at the state's biggest college. 1948 B'ham *News—Age-Her.* 7 Nov. p. E-3/2 No one believed that the Truman administration was anything more than an interim, caretaker government.

COMINFORM, *n.* Acronym formed from *Com*munist *Inform*ation Bureau; see quots.—1947 Tuscaloosa *News* 3 Nov. p. 1/1 (AP) The American Communist Party, however, approves strongly of the announced purpose of the cominform, an information bureau set up by the Communist parties of nine European countries, an official party statement declared yesterday. San Fran. *News* 17 Nov. p. 4/3 A Chinese press dispatch said today that representatives of Communist parties from China, Korea, Japan, India, Mongolia, the Philippines and Indo-China met last month . . . and decided to form an Oriental Cominform. San Fran. *Examiner* 22 Nov. p. 2/1-2 European Communists were reported today to be considering both Mexico City and Montevideo . . . as headquarters for a 'Cominform' in the Western Hemisphere. 1948 *Sat. Eve. Post* 12 June p. 168/1 This happened last autumn, two weeks after the setting up of the Cominform, which was founded in order 'to facilitate the exchange of information between the Communist Parties in Eastern and Western Europe.'

COPTER, *n. Slang.* A heli*copter.* (Also attrib.)—1947 Balto. *Sun* 28 June p. 9/2 The 'copter stepped out of the test tunnel into a wartime job. 1948 *Wall St. Jour.* 3 April p. 1/1 They're interested in the copter line as an experimental prototype for similar projects . . . Chicago *Tribune* 19 May p. 27/5 Non-scheduled passenger copter charter services also have been approved. 1949 B'ham *News—Age-Her.* 9 Jan. p. 13A/2-3 (AP) The tips of the whirling rotor are equipped with lights which give this grotesque appearance as the 'copter' ascends.

CRYPTO-COMMUNIST, *n.* [Gr. *kryptos* 'hidden, secret' + *communist*] See quots.—1946 *Newsweek* 10 June p. 44/3 To . . . Ernest Bevin these extreme left-wingers with their demands for 'working class unity' appear as fellow travelers. He has denounced them as 'crypto-communists.' 1947 B'ham *News* 18 April p. 10/4 (AP) 'A crypto-communist,' he declared, 'is one who has not got the courage to explain the destination for which he is making.' *Life* 28 April p. 45/3. *Friends Intelligencer* 24 May p. 265/2 . . . he was called a crypto-communist . . . 1948 *Word Study* (Springfield: G. & C. Merriam Co.) Oct. p. 3 Sidney Hook's suggested word makes it possible to distinguish three groups of pro-Sovieteers (to coin another word): the open Communists, the fellow-travelers . . . , and the crypto-Communists—probably the most dangerous.

CRYPTO-FASCIST, CRYPTOFASCIST, *n.* See quot. *Sat. Rev. Lit.* (Also attrib.)—1940 *Time* 22 Nov. p. 110 The *Daily Worker* has suggested that he may be a 'crypto-Fascist,' . . . 1945 *New Rep.* 29 Jan. p. 156/2 From the reviews of these plays it doesn't seem that they could be described as more than crypto-fascist . . . *Sat. Rev. Lit.* 10 Mar. p. 6/1 The terms *cryptofascist,* referring to a covert type of fascist . . . , and *parafascist* . . . have also appeared. 1948 *Sat. Eve. Post* 17 July p. 115/1 The readers of the Slogan were being told that when the last imperialist power had been defeated in the Far East, lovers of progress would have to turn their attention to the crypto-Fascists, the armament kings and the preachers of patriotism in our midst.

DO-GOODER, *n.*—1927 cited in Mencken *Amer. Lang. Sup.* I p. 327, n. 10. 1936 Mencken *Amer. Lang.* p. 187 Many of the most popular of American compounds are terms of disparagement, e.g., . . . *do-gooder* . . . 1943 *Time* 25 Oct. p. 2 (letter) Go find yourself out something about Charles P. Taft before dismissing him as famed do-gooder . . . 1947 *Sat. Eve. Post* 18 Oct. p. 8/2 . . . he knows better than ever that the way of the do-gooder is hard. 1948 *ibid.* 20 March p. 18/3 Mrs. Matthews was the street's do-gooder.

DRUNK-O-METER, DRUNKOMETER, *n.* See quots.—1939 *Newsweek* 16 Jan. p. 15/3 Drunk-O-Meter . . . an apparatus containing a solution of potassium permanganate and sulphuric acid. 1948 *Sci. N. L.* 22 May p. 332/1 'Drunkometers' are devices now used by several American cities with persons charged with drunk-driving; the suspect blows a measured quantity of breath into a rubber bag within which is a series of tubes containing chemicals which determine the alcoholic content. Lincoln (Nebr.) *Journ.* 18 Aug. p. 9/1 (UP) After each shot of bourbon, Scotch or gin, beer or brandy, the newsmen will breathe into a little gadget known as a drunkometer . . .

52-20 CLUB. See quots. (Also attrib.) —1946 *Time* 26 Aug. p. 17/3 . . . General Omar Bradley had sharp words for the ex-doughboys who would rather stay in the '52-20 clubs' (drawing $20 a week up to 52 weeks) than take low paid jobs. *This Week* 8 Sept. p. 29/3 The captain . . . lived with his wife and mother-in-law as he looked for a decent job, then deserted his family to join the 52-20 Club—vets' unemployment compensation. 1947 *Sat. Eve. Post* 22 March p. 23/2 I've also heard those civilian critics who mutter that 'the 52-20 Club is a loafer's paradise,' . . . 1948 B'ham *News* 31 Jan. p. 3/4 In another similar '52-20 Club' case, a Negro was placed on probation for a year.

FLYING DISCS, -DISKS, -SAUCERS. Strange objects sighted at different times over different parts of the United States. See quots. (Also attrib.)—1947 B'ham *News* 12 July p. 3/5 'Flying Saucers' Not Part of Any Secret Project, Say Scientists. *Ibid.* 12 July p. 3/5 'Flying disks' have no connection with any secret weapons now being developed by the Army or Navy . . . *Ibid.* 22 Dec. p. 2/3 Rep. Ellsworth . . . revived reports today that last Summer's 'flying saucer' epidemic may have stemmed from Russian rocket experiments. 1948 B'ham *News—Age-Her.* 29 Feb. p. 32D/3 (AP) The flying discs of last Summer reflected part of the vague public fears over mysterious pushbutton war. Tuscaloosa *News* 11 Oct. p. 2/5 (AP) The flying disc business shows no signs of fading out.

FREEWAY, *n.* A thoroughfare; express highway.—1939 Balto. *Sun* 16 Jan. p. 5/7 C. S. Mullen . . . expressed the opinion that construction of freeways, either elevated or on the ground, would be necessary to facilitate movement of traffic in and out of Washington. 1940 San Fran. *News* 13 Aug. p. 1/2 When completed, the road would be a 100-foot divided highway, connecting with the Bayshore Freeway proposed by the State Highway Commission . . . 1943 *Life* 22 Nov. p. 118/2 Almost everybody in Los Angeles has some pet plan for rebuilding large parts of the city after the war and opening up new 'freeways' (express auto highways) . . . 1947 *Harper's Mag.* Jan. p. 34/1 Relief from city traffic jams, then, and particularly any relief from the widespread and expensive traffic jams of today and the immediate future, cannot be expected from this large-scale planning of mammoth highways, expressways, trunk lines, and—newest word of all—freeways. 1948 Tuscaloosa *News* 1 Oct. p. 9 Workmen prepare to pave Washington's first elevated highway, Whitehurst Freeway . . .

GUPPY, *n.* A small fish. (*NID* 1934) —See quots. (Also attrib.)—1948 B'ham *News* 13 Oct. p. 12/6 However, the Tigrone was not streamlined into the high speed 'guppy' class with which the Navy is experimenting. Tuscaloosa *News* 8 Nov. p. 3/5-6 Vice Admiral D. B. Duncan . . . said the speedy snorkel submarines, called 'guppies,' had far outclassed the Navy's wartime anti-submarine devices. B'ham *News* 9 Dec. p. 23/6 But our success in pushing the Germans' snorkel development way beyond their maximum achievement, in our new 'guppy' submarines, suggests that already we may well have overcome the disadvantages of the Walter engine.

HIT,* *v. t.* To strike an object one is aiming at. {c. 1205} *Football.* To complete a forward pass.—1947 Tuscaloosa *News* 23 Nov. p. 1/5 (UP) . . . for Kentucky had pushed 58 yards in eight plays midway of the first period as Blanda hit Jack Farris on a screen pass play that went 10 yards for a touchdown. B'ham *News* 25 Dec. p. 12/4 Hoffman hit Shipkey with an 18-yard aerial to the Crimson eleven. 1948 B'ham *News—Age-Her.* 31 Oct. p. 2-C/1 Ranch failed to hit Walston in the flat.

HOT,* *adj.* Charged with electricity. {1930}—See quots.—1946 *Sci. N. L.* 10 Aug. p. 84/1 . . . a large part of Bikini lagoon remained too 'hot' with radioactivity to permit anything but the quickest dashes into the contaminated area . . . 1947 *Life* 11 Aug. p. 85 On Submarine That Is Still 'Hot' Navy Workmen in Hoods Spray Acid to Remove the Radioactive Paint. *Time* 10 Nov. p. 82/2 'Hot' (radioactive) atoms have already caused plenty of trouble in laboratories. 1948 B'ham *News* 15 Oct. p. 35/3-4 (AP) A dozen of the 76 ships used in the 1946 Bikini atomic bomb tests are still a[f]loat, three still dangerously hot with radioactivity.

HYPOSPRAY, *n.* [Gr. *hypo-* 'under, beneath' + *spray*] See quots.—1947 San Fran. *Call-Bull.* 11 Oct. p. B/7-8 Dr. Edward B. Tuohy of Georgetown University demonstrates the 'hypospray'—an airgun he developed to inject drugs without breaking the skin, thus circumventing use of hypodermic needle. *Time* 27 Oct. p. 82/2 The revolutionary gadget, called the 'hypospray,' is a kind of airgun that shoots an injection under the skin in a spray so fine that the patient usually does not feel it. *Life* 24 Nov. p. 65 Known as the Hypospray, this new device 'blasts' a microscopically small jet of medicinal fluid into the body tissues. 1948 *Sci. N. L.* 11 Sept. p. 169/3 Thousands of injections by the needleless 'hypospray' method have shown it therapeutically effective, Dr. James M. McKibbin and Robert P. Scherer . . . declared.

ISRAEL,* *n.* Ancient kingdom of the Jews. {1388}—See quots.—1948 Tuscaloosa *News* 14 May p. 1/5 (AP) 'Accordingly, we, the members of the National Council representing the Jewish people in Palestine and the Zionist movement of the world, met together in solemn assembly by virtue of the natural and historic right of the Jewish people and of the resolution of the General Assembly of the United Nations hereby proclaim the establishment of the Jewish state in Palestine, to be called 'Israel.' San Fran. *Examiner* 15 May p. 1/4-8 (headline) U.S. Recognizes 'Israel.' *Life* 31 May p. 21/2 . . . 'The name of our state shall be Israel,' he [Prime Minister David Ben-Gurion] intoned, and a new nation was born. 1949 B'ham *News* 14 Jan. p. 6/4 (AP) Eytan said Egypt and Israel have no natural cause for enmity . . .

ISRAELI, [ɪz'relɪ] *n. & adj.* See quots. —1948 B'ham *News—Age-Her.* 19 Sept. p. 21A/5 'The Israeli Army liaison officer was riding in the car ahead . . .' *Ibid.* 7 Nov. p. A1/2-3 (headline) Arabs Advised to Make Peace Soon with Israeli. Tuscaloosa *News* 29 Nov. p. 8/6 (UP) Israeli officials here announced they would file formal application for Israeli membership in the United Nations . . . N.Y. *Times Mag.* 5 Dec. p. 4/3 Shortly after the proclamation of the new State of Israel in May of this year, Moshe Shertok announced that its citizens would be called Israelis. B'ham *News* 28 Dec. p. 16/7-8 (headline) Britain Demands Israeli Quit Negev . . . 1949 B'ham *News—Age-Her.* 9 Jan. p. 1A/7 (AP) Britain accused the Israelis Saturday of shooting down five RAF planes . . . B'ham *News* 14 Jan. p. 6/4 (AP) These are the topics Egyptian and Israeli delegates will discuss . . .

LP. Initials of Long Playing, usually attrib.; see quots. Trademark.—1948 *Musical America* July p. 19/3 The new disc, called LP (long playing) Microgroove, requires a new pickup. *Life* 26 July p. 39/1 To the record collector the LP (for Long Playing) disk means not only a vast saving in space . . . and improved tonal quality . . . , but also a saving in money. 1949 *Sat. Rev. Lit.* 22 Jan. p. 33/2 The record, again, works on present LP equipment . . .

MICROGROOVE, -GROOVE, *adj.* [Gr. *mikro-* + *groove*] Pertaining to a phonograph record with a much larger number of grooves than the conventional type.—1948 *Musical Amer.* July p. 19/3 The new disc, called LP . . . Microgroove, requires a new pickup. *Life* 26 July p. 40/2 However, they may all get on the Long Playing bandwagon soon since the micro-groove feature of LP records is not an exclusive patent. Tuscaloosa *News* 18 Aug. p. 4/4 But last month I finally unbelted and bought a television, plus a thingamananny called a 'Long-playing Microgroove Record-Player.'

POLICE STATE. A state in which individual liberty—social, economic, and political—is at a minimum. (Also attrib.) —1947 *Newsweek* 1 Dec. p. 72 Back to Police-State Controls? *Time* 29 Dec. p. 25/1 If the Russian worker got ten times as much instead of a tenth as much, he might—just possibly—consider that living in a police state was worth the price. *Life* 7 June p. 37/1 They have failed in France and Italy because the peoples have had a chance to show their preference for Western democracy over a police state. 1948 Tuscaloosa *News* 10 Aug. p. 1/2 The former governor urged students 'to be the shock troops in this battle for freedom and against the police state' . . .

RE-BOP, *n.* See quots. (Also attrib.) See *be-bop.*—1945 *Down Beat* 1 Sept. p. 3/3 Much controversy has arisen of late over the claims of altoist Charlie Parker and trumpeter Dizzy Gillespie to the origination of their fantastic and exciting 're-bop' style . . . 1947 *Time* 1 Sept. p. 32/3 Re-bop (according to Jazz Pedant Rudi Blesh): 'Healthy jazz distorted into frantic rhythms, fantastic harmonic *non sequiturs,* a psychosomatic heterophony.' 1948 *Language* Mar. p. 132 . . . people in Chicago use *rebop* and *bop* for the same kind of music . . .

SIDELINE, *v. t. Sport.* To force out of play because of illness or injury.—1946 B'ham *News* 9 Sept. p. 15/3 . . . several other lettermen are sidelined with minor hurts. 1947 Balto *Sun* 15 Sept. p. 12/4 Heine points out that his protege has been sidelined since that scrap by an injured nose. B'ham *News—Age-Her.* 20 July p. 1B/7 Charley Keller . . . is recovering . . . from an operation to relieve the back ailment that has sidelined him for several weeks . . . 1948 Tuscaloosa *News* 1 Oct. p. 10/5 (headline) Fractured Skull Sidelines Hirsch.

STATES' RIGHTER. A member of the 1948 States' Rights Democratic Party.—1948 *States' Rights* (Birmingham, Ala.) 26 July p. 1/1 'States' Righters is all right, but the term, "Dixiecrats," leaves the wrong impression.' *Time* 20 Sept. p. 25/2 The States' righters crowed . . . Tuscaloosa *News* 22 Nov. p. 1/2 The issue arose in connection with a suit . . . to force Electors . . . to vote for President Truman instead of States Righter, J. Strom Thurmond.

TOPECTOMY, *n.* [Gr. *top-*, comb. form of *topos* 'place' + *-ectomy* 'a cutting out'] See quots.—1948 *Newsweek* 29 Mar. p. 47/3 In the new operation, called a topectomy, the brain fibers are not cut. *Time* 5 April p. 50/2 Some thought that the new operation, called topectomy, was the best yet. *Think* June p. 21/1 Topectomy, it is claimed, removed certain areas of the brain in the 'front top side' of the head, without affecting the personality of the patient or impairing his intellectual ability. *Life* 16 Aug. p. 57/2 In the recent past, two other principal surgical methods have been used to interrupt the nerve impulses: 1) prefrontal lobotomy . . . and 2) topectomy, in which a portion of the frontal lobes is removed.

AMONG THE NEW WORDS

I. WILLIS RUSSELL
University of Alabama

CLUSTERING ABOUT an idea or object are sometimes many variant terms. These may represent rival forms, especially if the idea or object is new, most of which may eventually disappear. Or they may represent a deliberate stylistic device for obtaining variety. Whatever the reasons for their creation, the job of the linguist is to collect them where possible. It is with this thought in mind that I have attempted to bring together here a group of words used for 'overnight accommodations for automobile tourists.' Three of the more important unrecorded terms *(auto court, motor court,* and *tourist court)* are treated in the glossary below. In this preliminary section I wish to make a few remarks on the whole group.

These variant terms fall into two semasiological groups which reflect, in turn, two stages in the development of the object they denote. The first stage will be recalled to most readers by an illustration in one of the early articles I consulted for these comments. Several 1920-vintage automobiles (no closed cars, of course!) were parked haphazardly in a wooded area containing cabins. This, as most older readers know, was an *auto camp,* defined by the 1934 Webster's *New International Dictionary* as 'A camping ground, often provided with cabins or tents, for the accommodation of automobile tourists.' Incidentally, Webster's is the only general dictionary of those I have consulted which contains this term; it was not in the 1927 New Words Supplement, though the term dates from at least 1922 (*American City* March p. 242/2). Virtually all the variants of this stage suggest the 'camp' idea. *Tourist camp,* which is as old as 1923 (*Out-*

look Aug. p. 591/3), is defined by the 1947 *College Standard* (the only general dictionary including it) as 'A roadside group of cabins for the accommodation of transients, usually automobilists.' The term *motor camp* seems to be unrecorded (for citations see 1925 *Sat. Eve. Post* 10 Oct. p. 98/1, and 1934 *Lit. Dig.* 9 June p. 40/2), though the 1934 *New International* lists *motor-camper* and *motor-camping*. Two other variants connoting 'camp' are *rest cabin* (1934 *Lit. Dig.* 9 June p. 40) and *tourist park,* which occurs in one of the citations quoted below. One term is without the 'camp' connotation: *auto inn* (1923 *Sunset* May p. 62; cited *Read. Guide* 6: 240/1).

Many of the preceding terms, I suspect, will soon be of interest only to the historical lexicographer. For some time around 1930, there began to develop on the West Coast a new type of tourists' accommodation which promises to supplant the old camp even though designed primarily for a different group of travelers (see 1936 *Pop. Mech.* 66: 118A/2 'This indicates that a different class of motorists is attracted to the courts, also called "motels," "autels," and "autotels," than patronizes auto camps and tourist parks'). This new type of accommodation was described by the word *motel,* noted, along with *autel,* in 1932 *American Speech* (7: 233). What the *motel* is may be seen from the 1936 citation under *motor court* in the glossary. Its early history is of interest. According to Frank J. Taylor, the word was coined by Oscar T. Tomerlin, who, with his brother, set up a motel in 1930 (*Sat. Eve. Post* 5 July 1947 p. 33/1). Though the brothers copyrighted the term for their sole use locally, they allowed it to be used elsewhere, with the result that when their right even for local exclusive use was questioned, the word had, in the opinion of their lawyers, become a common noun and was thus incapable of restriction. Taylor quotes one of the brothers to the effect that they did not desire ownership of the word: they merely wished 'to make it mean something' (*ibid.,* p. 93/1). *Motel* was recorded by Berrey and Van den Bark in their 1942 *American Thesaurus of Slang* (along with *automotel, autotel, jungle,* and *jungles,* all of which are included under *tourist camp*). Three years later it found a place in the 1945 Webster's New Words Supplement; it is still absent from the other general dictionaries.

The variants of *motel* are not found in any of the general dictionaries. In addition to those already quoted and those treated in the glossary, there are *cottage court,* a less expensive variety, and *motor lodge* (1936 *Pop. Mech.* 66: 118-20). The following are from the *Post* article by Taylor already cited: *highway-hotel* (attributive use only), *highway inn, horizontal hotel, motor-hotel* (attributive use only), and *motorist(s') inn.* Though some of this latter group may be only nonce forms for artistic variation, they seem worth recording.

In connection with the entry for *do-gooder* in the February issue, it may be observed that the *OED* lists *do-good,* marked obsolete, illustrated by one citation dated 1654. My colleague, Professor James B. McMillan, has turned over to me the following: 1923 *Nation* 21 Nov. p. 569/2 'There is nothing wrong with the United States except . . . the parlor socialists, uplifters, and do-goods.' It may be recalled that the earliest date cited for *do-gooder* (from Mencken) was 1927.

PLEASE COMMENT: *four-letter word* 1936.

ACKNOWLEDGMENTS. For citations: Clarence L. Barnhart (1), Dwight L. Bolinger (1), Atcheson L. Hench (3), James B. McMillan (3), Mamie J. Meredith (7), Peter Tamony (3). Thanks are also due the Research Committee of the University of Alabama for secretarial aid.

SYMBOLS: The symbol + before a word or definition indicates an Americanism. A date immediately following a word or definition indicates the time of evidence shown in the *DAE,* or, if so stated, in another publication. Dates in brackets indicate the time, etc., of British usage. An asterisk after a word indicates that the word is illustrated in British usage before 1600.

+AUTO COURT. A motel.—1940 *Architectural Record* July p. 98 (title) Auto Court Is Planned for Privacy. 1947 *Sat. Eve. Post* 5 July p. 33/2 We think of the auto court as the modern version of the stagecoach inn . . . 1949 *This Week* 30 Jan. p. 5/1 When I told him my wife and I had to live in a small auto court . . . he was flabbergasted.

+BOP, *n.* Short for *be-bop, re-bop.* See quot. *Lang.* (Also attrib.)—1948 *Lang.* March p. 132 . . . people in Chicago use *rebop* and *bop* for the same kind of music . . . *Sat. Rev. Lit.* 25 Dec. p. 48/2 It is, in the words of bop hepsters, real crazy. 1949 N.Y. *Times* 23 Jan. Sec. 2 p. 4/4 To this listener the bop school still is a mixture of good points. *Sat. Rev. Lit,* 29 Jan. p. 64/1 Nevertheless, the resulting dissonances made some exhilarating listening, a cacaphonous product that was the beginning of bop.

+BOPPER, *n.* See quots.—1948 *Life* 11 Oct. p. 139/2 Boppers go gaga over such bebop classics as *OO Bop Sha Bam, Oop Pop A Da* and *Emanon* . . . 1949 *Time* 21 Feb. p. 55/1 The boppers . . . tend to speak of him in the past tense.

+ENIAC, *n.* See quots.—1946 *Time* 25 Feb. p. 90/2 The huge gadget was known as the 'electronic numerical integrator and computor.' Its inventors . . . called it 'eniac.' *This Week* 8 Sept. p. 6/1 (adv.) Perhaps the most uncanny development along these lines is the ENIAC, a massive, 30-ton computing and calculating machine . . . 1948 *Science News Letter* 21 Aug. p. 123/2 The ENIAC, which was also designed by Dr. Mauchly and Mr. Eckert, could store in its internal memory 20 numbers of 10 digits each and could multiply these numbers 300 times a second.

+GO-SHOW. See quots.—1941 *Collier's* 27 Sept. p. 4/3 In airplane parlance, he is known as a 'Go-Show.' 1946 *This Week* 21 April p. 13/2 Go-Shows . . . Would-be passengers who fail to get reservations, yet are sent to airports in the hope they may replace 'no-shows,' or prospective passengers who do not pick up their reservations. *Time* 5 Aug. p. 84/2. *Fortune* Aug. p. 76/2 'go-show' . . . Airline jargon for the passenger without a reservation who takes his chances on getting aboard at the last minute in place of the 'no-show.'

+MOTOR COURT. See 1936 quot. (Also attrib.)—1936 *Pop. Mech.* 66: 674/1-2 The motor court is a recent development of the motor age. . . . It's not a tourist park, it's not an auto camp. . . . It's a collection of miniature homes clustered around a central service and administration building . . . 1940 *Bus. Week* 15 June p. 19 (title) America Takes to the Motor Court. 1947 *Sat. Eve. Post* 5 July p. 33/1 In the mushrooming motor-court business, nearly everybody points to the Tomerlin team . . . 1949 *This Week* 30 Jan. p. 5 (caption) Oregon's handsome new capitol . . . Contrasts sharply with cheap motor court . . .

+NO SHOW, NO-SHOW, NOSHOW. See quots. (Also attrib.)—1941 *Collier's* 27 Sept. p. 67 He's what the Airlines call a 'no show.' 1942 TWA timetable July Please don't be a no-show. 1946 Balto. *Sun* 3 Sept. p. 6/6-8 The travelling public has long been aware of the so-called 'no-show.' He is the person who reserves airline space, buys a ticket and then neglects to cancel his reservation when he decides not to go. *Time* 21 Oct. p. 92/2 These 'no-shows' cost the lines an estimated $8 million a year . . . 1948 *ibid.* 10 May p. 89/3 Last week ship lines were still accepting tentative bookings—but only to replace last-minute no-shows. 1949 B'ham *News* 17 Feb. p. 40/3 (NANA) Many passengers who were denied seats could have occupied those left empty by 'no-shows.' The airlines are in the red largely because of 'noshow' passengers.

PUSH-BUTTON, *n.* A small button, the pushing of which completes an electric circuit. {1878}—+ *adj.* Remote-controlled. See also quots.—1945 *Life* 20 Aug. p. 17/1 There may be devastating 'push-button' battles. 1946 B'ham *News* 3 Feb. p. 1/3 (AP) The Army Air Forces came forth Saturday with a real push-button plane. Balto. *Sun* 15 Feb. p. 10/1-2 'Push-button' flight is completely controlled by automatic devices . . . 1947 *Life* 6 Oct. p. 87 (adv.) Push-button telegraphy. . . . Now Western Union switching clerks just push buttons and, in a flash, telegrams are speeded onward to their destinations. 1948 *Sci. N. L.* 14 Feb. p. 112/1-2 Push-button telegraphy has entered the airline communications field. It is a switching center. . . . Each message is typed only at the point of origin; pushing a button gives an incoming message a route to its destination. B'ham *News—Age-Her.* p. 32D/3 (AP) The flying discs of last Summer reflected part of the vague public fears over mysterious pushbutton war. B'ham *News* 16 July p. 6/3 (AP) The Air Force's push-button plane, a four-engined C-54 transport, has ended its third long-distance automatic flight.

+RADAR FENCE, RADAR SCREEN. A protective network of radar stations surrounding an area; see also quots. (Also attrib.)—1948 *Sat. Eve. Post* 21 Aug. p. 27/1 There are wide gaps in the Soviet radar fence. Russia is too huge to be rimmed completely with twirling antennas. 1949 B'ham *News—Age-Her.* 9 Jan. p. 1A/4 (AP) . . . A 'radar fence' around the country to warn of air attack and direct the defense. B'ham *News* 10 Feb. p. 1/2 (AP) Maj. Gen. . . . Saville . . . urged swift approval of a . . . plan to throw an effective radar screen around the U.S., with outposts at sea and around the Air Force. Tuscaloosa *News* 13 Feb. p. 1/6-7 (headline) Radar Screen Plans Pushed.

RHUBARB*, *n.* '. . *fig.,* as a type of bitterness or sourness' (*OED* {1526}).—+ See quots.—1943 *A. N. & Q.* Dec. p. 134/2 Rhubarb. . . . Another definition, seemingly advanced by 'Red' Barber, . . . is 'squabbling, scuffling, wrangling.' 1944 *ibid.* March pp. 184/2-185/1 Rhubarb . . . I would call it: a messy but hilarious disturbance that leaves its participants the object of slightly derisive yet sympathetic laughter. 1946 cited in Mencken *Amer. Lang. Sup. II* p. 737. 1947 *Time* 22 Sept. p. 70/1 Next inning, at the plate, there was a face-to-face exchange of hot words between Robinson and Garagiola—the kind of rough passage that fans appreciatively call a 'rhubarb.' *Life* 15 Dec. p. 40/2 Last week Petrillo . . . was engaged in a characteristic rhubarb. 1948 Tuscaloosa *News* 28 Dec. p. 10/2 (AP) In the opening game . . . the play caused a rhubarb between the rival champs . . .

+SET SHOT. *Basketball.* A deliberate, unhurried shot made from a still position some distance in front of the basket by a player who, momentarily unguarded, has time to get set. (Also attrib.)—1940 N.Y. *Times* 21 Jan. p. S1/3-2/6 The cadets, their set shots hitting the mark with a remarkable degree of accuracy, gained the upper hand at the outset . . . 1948 Tuscaloosa *News* 18 Jan. p. 5/1 Hayden Riley sank a beautiful set shot from 15 feet . . . *Time* 29 March p. 55/1 They were missing their star set-shot artist . . . 1949 Tuscaloosa *News* 4 Feb. p. 10/1 The six-one sophomore can really handle the ball, and has that Kentucky eye when it comes to set shots . . .

+SHMOO, *n.* A small, gourd-shaped mythical animal, with a face somewhat like that of a seal, whose productivity and generosity do away with man's wants; see also quots.—1948 *Time* 13 Sept. p. 29/2 The shmoo was discovered by Al Capp's Li'l Abner. When, last month, he began to hear strange music which sounded like 'shmoooooooooooo!', his eager pursuit of the lilting sound was barred by an amazon of fierce and busty aspect. *Newsweek* 11 Oct. p. 62 . . . cartoonist Al Capp told *Newsweek* that 'the Shmoo is a creature that can do what no other creature on earth can do' . . . B'ham *News* 13 Oct. p. 1/4 (UP) Their creator, Al Capp, . . . handed a carton of 12 inch plastic shmoos to the crew of an overseas airlines flagship . . . 1949 *ibid.* 6 Jan. p. 11/1 The objective which these experiments are designed to achieve sounds remarkably like the scientific counterpart of L'il Abner's famous Shmoo.

+SPELUNKER, *n.* With spelling *-car,* pertaining to a cave. {1855}.—See quots.—1946 N.Y. *Times* 16 June p. M 26/1 The 'spelunker' (from the Latin word *spelunca,* a cave) is one who hunts and crawls into caves for the sport of it . . . *Life* 4 Nov. p. 143 Cave exploring, . . . which bears the scientific name of speleology, has a group of amateur followers who like to call themselves 'spelunkers.' *A. N. & Q.* Dec. p. 135/2. 1948 *Pop. Mech. Mag.* Sept. p. 163/1 Real cave hunters, named speleologists, are the backbone of the society and lend it the dignity of a genuine scientific approach. The hobbyists . . . are called spelunkers.

STALINOID, *adj.* [From Joseph *Stalin* + *-oid*] See 1948 quot.—1941 *American Mercury* April p. 498/2 But merely for the record, let us make note of what is perhaps the most extraordinary example of the Soviet aberration that has come to my attention in years of careful reading of the Stalinoid literature of hallucination. 1945 *Sat. Rev. Lit.* 10 March p. 26/1 Words using other suffixes are . . . *Stalinoid.* 1947 Balto. *Sun* 4 Nov. p. 10/3 Food prices [in Italy] have come down—to the consternation of Stalinoid cohorts. 1948 *Sat. Rev. Lit.* 6 March p. 20/1-2 'Stalinoid' is a term of the author's own coining. . . . The author defines his brainchild as indicating 'a general adherence to the Communist Party line of the moment,' and says it embraces 'Party members, fellow travelers, and the vast army of "innocent dupes."'

+TAPE RECORDING. The recording of sound on tape; see last quot.—1941 *Quart. Jour. Speech* 27: 377 The advantages of magnetic tape recording over other types were variously listed. 1945 *Radio News* July pp. 32-34; cited *Read.*

Guide 15: 1865/2 Magnetic tape recording. 1948 *Sat. Rev. Lit.* 31 July p. 42/3 There are those who consider it a mere detour en route to such higher objectives as tape or wire recording of infinite length . . . *Read. Guide* 48 (No. 4): 237 Tape recording. See Sound—Recording and reproducing—Magnetic recording.

+TOURIST COURT. A motor court (which see). (Also attrib.)—1937 *American City* Oct. p. 115 (title) House Trailer and Tourist Court Regulations. 1940 *Arch. Rec.* July p. 100 (title) Attractive Setting Helps Tourist Court Set Income Record. 1948 B'ham *News—Age-Her.* 15 Aug. p. 5E/4 (AP) Convicted of the holdup of a St. Augustine (Fla.) tourist court, he was assigned to a road gang . . . 1949 *Sat. Rev. Lit.* 5 Feb. p. 36/3 You can rent a hotel room, a tourist court . . .

+TV. ['ti 'vi] *Television.* (Also attrib.) —1948 *Fortune* May p. 83/1 The average capital investment for a TV station is about $375,000 . . . B'ham *News* 21 June p. 17/3 Birmingham and Alabama, of course, will not be in on the TV . . . *Time* 13 Sept. p. 84/2 Even the inventive U.S. had been unable to think up anything better than video or TV. 1949 *ibid.* 28 Feb. p. 17/1 Radio & TV . . .

+XEROGRAPHY, *n.* [zɪ 'ɑgrəfɪ] [Gr. *xeros* 'dry' + *-graphy* (Gr. *graphos*)]. See quots.—1948 San Fran. *Call-Bulletin* 23 Oct. p. B/3-5 (AP) Xerography, a revolutionary process for the reproduction of printed matter . . . was demonstrated publicly yesterday for the first time. *Sci. N. L.* 23 Oct. p. 263/1 Static electricity and dry powders take the place of the familiar chemical solutions used in photography, in the new process called 'xerography.' *Time* 1 Nov. pp. 82-83 The 'revolution' was electronic 'dry writing,' or Xerography. *Fortune* Dec. p. 9 The Haloid Co. of Rochester . . . has announced the development of Xerography . . .

AMONG THE NEW WORDS

I. WILLIS RUSSELL
University of Alabama

Acknowledgments. For citations: Clarence L. Barnhart (1), Dwight L. Bolinger (1), James B. McMillan (2), Mamie J. Meredith (2), George Pope Shannon (1), and Peter Tamony (1). The etymology of *sitting duck* was supplied by Peter Tamony. I am indebted to Scott Barr for aid in the etymology of *bevatron* and to Russel C. Larcom and Marcus Whitman for help in locating early illustrations of *free enterprise* and *private enterprise.* Thanks are also due the Research Committee of the University of Alabama for secretarial aid.

Symbols: The symbol + before a word or definition indicates an Americanism. A date immediately following a word or definition indicates the time of evidence shown in the *DAE*, or, if so stated, in another publication. Dates in brackets indicate the time, etc., of British usage. An asterisk after a word indicates that the word is illustrated in British usage before 1600.

+BEVATRON, *n.* [*b*illion *e*lectron *v*olts + *a* + *-tron*] See quots.—1947 San Fran. *Examiner* 16 Oct. p. 13 In the same report Doctor Lawrence revealed plans for a super atom smasher, to be called a 'bevatron,' capable of hurling protons and neutrons at ten billion electric volt capacity . . . *Science News Letter* 25 Oct. p. 259/1 A new monster atom-smashing 'bevatron' to attain 10 billion electron volts was also shown in preliminary design by Prof. Lawrence. 1948 *World Almanac* p. 786/1 Bevatron, atom smasher that can speed up electrons to a billion electron volts, was designed. 1949 *Sci. N. L.* 19 Feb. p. 114 Bevatrons will have energy ranges measured in billions of electron volts compared with hundreds of millions of electron volts for the most powerful types of cyclotrons . . .

BLUEPRINT, *n.* 1939 cited in *Am. Sp.* 22:146. Add earlier illust.—1931 *Business Week* 24 June p. 44/2 (editorial) The capacity for coördinated creative activity ultimately resides in the individual. Not blueprints or a Big Boss, but only common objectives, clearly conceived, generally agreed upon, vitalized by effective leadership, are needed to mobilize it.

+FAX, *n.* Short for facsimile transmission, *specif.* facsimile newspaper. (Also attrib.)—1948 *Time* 12 Jan. pp. 60-62 But time and mass production might take care of all that; the big news about 'fax' was that, technically, the bugs were pretty well worked out of it. *New Yorker* 28 Feb. p. 21/3 The facsimile newspaper, or 'fax,' as it is beginning to be called, travels through the air. *Time* 21 June p. 77/1 On July 15 any FM station that is ready for the job may start printing 'fax' newspapers by radio. 1949 *Banking* Jan. p. 24 (title); cited 1949 *Industrial Arts Index* Feb. p. 101/1 Fax in the bank lobby; Columbia savings bank . . . provides customers with a daily facsimile newspaper.

+FLYING LABORATORY. An experimental airplane equipped with various testing instruments.— 1937 *Newsweek* 20 March p. 27 Amelia Earhart moved her 'flying laboratory' from Los Angeles to Oakland airport . . . 1939 *ibid.* 4 Oct. p. 42/3 The individual air lines boosted research budgets, set tasks for their flying laboratories . . . 1947 *This Week* 2 Nov. p. 4 (picture caption) The Air Force's experimental, bullet-shaped XS-1 is really a 'flying laboratory.' 1949 N. Y. *Times* 29 May p. 6E/3 The first of the actual flying laboratories, the Bell X-1, startled the world by breaking successfully through the sonic barrier.

FREE ENTERPRISE. 1932 cited in *Am. Sp.* 22:147/2. Add earlier illust.—1890 Alfred Marshall *Principles of Economics* (London: Macmillan and Company) 1:30 We may then return to trace with somewhat more detail the growth of free enterprise in England.

+HOT ROD. See quots. (Also attrib.) —1945 *Life* 5 Nov. p. 87 A 'hot rod,' also called a 'hot iron,' or a 'hop-up' or 'gow job,' is an automobile stripped for speed and pepped up for power until it can travel 90 to 125 mph. Most hot rods are roadsters. . . . 1946 *Sat. Eve. Post* 14 Sept. p. 14/2 Ten years ago a hot rod was a stolen gun, wanted by the police; today a hot rod is a hopped-up, stripped-down flivver used by teen-agers to terrify parents and frustrate the police. 1948 *Life* 5 Jan. p. 2 At Farmington . . . last summer a boy was driving his first hot-rod race. 1949 B'ham *News* 30 May p. 2/6 Despite their respect for the youngsters' ability, track officials gave the hot rod and midget specialists a stern lecture yesterday.

PINPOINT, -POINT, *n.* '. . . usually *fig.* as a type of something extremely small or sharp' (*OED* {1849-}); 'used attrib. of precision bombing or bombardment concentrated on a small target; hence as vb.' (Addenda to 1944 *Sh OED.* s. v. *pin*).—+Hence, *v. t.,* to aim, direct, determine with great exactness and accuracy (*NID* Sup. 1945 defines *adj.* as 'Directed with extreme precision . . . ; as, *pinpoint* bombing.').—1945 B'ham *News* 26 May p. 1/6 (AP) The Jewish boy led Yank patrols through heavy fire to a hill where they could pin-point the guns. *Readers Digest* June p. 101/1 Soon after war ends, the psychological know-how accumulated from the AAF's tests of three quarters of a million young men will be available to schools and colleges to pinpoint the training of students, and to industry for fitting the right jobs to the right people. *Sat. Eve. Post* 14 July p. 13 (picture caption) Vice Admiral McCain . . . pinpoints the details . . . 1946 B'ham *News* 5 Jan. p. 1/6 (AP) The Pearl Harbor committee called for photographs of the Navy's ship location board today to pinpoint movements of the Pacific Fleet in the days just before the Japanese attack . . . 1947 *Time* 2 June p. 89/2 It can pin-point its cargo onto a busy unloading dock . . . B'ham *News* 7 Nov. p. 36/3 (AP) Who committee [sic] the error . . . is hard to pin-point. *Sat. Eve. Post* 29 Nov. p. 62/2 And the ship's electrician . . . was almost lyrical about his radio installations, which can . . . pinpoint the exact spot from which a distress signal comes. 1949 B'ham *News* 14 May p. 1/8 (AP) However, the cause of the blast could not be pinpointed in the welter of debris.

+PINPOINTING, -POINTING, *n.*— 1944 *Newsweek* 10 Jan. p. 26 The greatest achievement of the young Eighth Air Force was precision bombing, the technique of pinpointing with explosive vital points of German industry and communications . . . 1945 Tuscaloosa *News* 23 Aug. p. 1/1 (AP) . . . newsmen asked Presidential Secretary Charles G. Ross again today about prospects for pin-pointing the date. 1947 *Am. Thes. Slang Sup.* ¶53.2 pin-pointing . . . precision focusing of a specific landmark . . .

PRIVATE ENTERPRISE. *Specif.* Business activity under private as opposed to public (government) control; free enterprise.—[1844 H. H. Wilson *Brit. India* III. 310; quoted *OED* s. v. *enterprise, sb.* I. b. *abstr.* That position of the trade . . . which the Company relinquished to private enterprise.] 1871 John Stuart Mill *Principles of Political Economy* (text of seventh edition. Ed. Sir W. J. Ashley. London: Longmans, Green, 1923) p. 978 Government aid, when given merely in default of private enterprise, should be so given as to be as far as possible a course of education for the people in the art of accomplishing great objects by individual energy and voluntary co-operation. 1887 Francis A. Walker *Political Economy* (N. Y.: Holt, 1888) pp. 520-21 Protectionism is purely and highly socialistic. Its purpose is to operate upon individual choices and aims, so to influence private enterprise and the investments of capital, as to secure the building up, within the country concerned, of certain branches of production which could not be carried on, or would grow but slowly, under the rule of competition and individual initiative. 1924 *Sat. Eve. Post* 20 Sept. p. 28/2 . . . but at the same time there is a very grave objection to bureaucratic regulation of private enterprise. 1949 *Sat. Rev. Lit.* 5 March p. 11/1-2 (title) Product of Private Enterprise.

+RAT RACE. 1. *Mil.* See quots.— 1941 *Newsweek* 7 July p. 30/2 Rat race—mounted review. *Am. Sp.* 16:168/1. 1947 *Am. Thes. Slang Sup.*

2. See first quot.; a dance; mad, confused scramble; vicious circle; whirl.— 1940 *Life* 26 Aug. p. 57/1 A cadet's first flight comes in 'rat race' (great swarm of planes) at Corry field. *Time* 16 Dec. p. 26/3 Veteran fliers blanched when they saw the hourly, crowded 'rat race' at Randolph—the close-packed stream of trainers, gliding in to land and take on fresh cadets and instructors. 1942 *Am. Thes. Slang* ¶366.3 dance; ball . . . rat race. 1945 *Time* 1 Jan. p. 46/2 'Old Darwin men knew they would never see the real scramble again or . . . the close-quarter hairy old rat races above the field.' 1947 *Sat. Eve. Post* 6 Sept. p. 95/3 And so a sort of mathematical rat race is started—more fuel means more weight, which means more power, which means faster fuel consumption. 1948 *ibid.* 7 Feb. p. 102/2 On Saturday we swelled the highway rat race to Ann Arbor to watch Michigan trounce Michigan State . . . *Ladies' Home Jour.* Sept. p. 183/1 'Furthermore,' she was declaiming, 'to get a meal in this kitchen is a rat race. The dishes are roughly one half a mile from the sink.' Mencken *Am. Lang. Sup. II* p. 707 A dance is a *rat-race* . . . *Time* 22 Nov. p. 63/3 With unlimited substitutions . . . the game has become a 'rat race.' *Sat. Eve. Post* 18 Dec. p. 69/1 But his mind was a rat race. Time was ticking against him, and the busted belt was . . . an awkward article to repair in a hurry.

+REPUBLI(O)CRAT, *n.* [*Republ(i)can* + Dem*(o)crat*] See quots.—1935 cited by Miss Mamie J. Meredith in 'Words and Meanings, New,' *Ten Eventful Years* 4:634/2. 1940 *Better English* Oct. p. 55/1 A republocrat, as 'Time' uses it, is a republican or a democrat who will have anyone but Mr. Hoover. 1942 *Am. Thes. Slang* ¶856.4 democrat-republican . . . Republicrat. 1946 *Time* 22 April p. 11/1 Would you be good enough to give us the names of the 'republocrats' in the House and Senate who have organized for the purpose of defeating President Truman's legislative program . . . ? 1949 *Southern Farmer* July p. 3 In return, all we ask is that the Hindu philosophers tell us how to make the Southern Republicrats climb up a rope and disappear.— republicratic, *adj.* 1944 cited by A. W. Read in *Sat. Rev. Lit.* 10 March 1945 p. 5/3.

+SITTING DUCK (PIGEON). [Prob. derived from fact that marksmanship in duck hunting is determined by the ability to hit ducks in flight and not while they are sitting.] *Fig.* An easy mark. (Also attrib.)—1944 *Read. Dig.* May p. 53 (title) Why Tankers Are No Longer Sitting Ducks. 1945 *ibid.* May p. 84/2 A plane making only 100 miles is a sitting pigeon for ground flack. *Time* 4 June p. 32/3 A bomb jammed the rudder, and the ship heeled in a sitting-duck circle. B'ham *News* 17 Sept. p. 7/3 And I hesitated to pull up over its line of fire since I was already going so slow that I would be left hanging in mid-air at almost a sitting duck for stalling speed . . . 1948 *Harper's Mag.* April p. 290/2 Ever since Sinclair Lewis gave the first lessons in marksmanship, men of the Senator's type have been sitting ducks for the opposition. 1949 *Sat. Eve. Post* 16 July p. 23/3 (picture caption) Rescuing downed aviators sometimes got a sitting-duck submarine fired on by our own quick-triggered forces.

SNORKEL. Variant spelling. For spelling *schnor-*, see *Am. Sp.* 21:298-9.— 1948 *Life* 9 Aug. pp. 42-3 The snorkel, from the German *Schnörkel,* is a breathing device . . . *Ibid.* 13 Dec. p. 61 (title) Snorkel.

SPLINTER*, *n. Fig.* {1606-} Add American illusts. (Also attrib.)—1948 Dwight Griswold in address at the University of Neb. 5 Oct. Splinter parties developed in Greece—splitting off from the regular political parties. B'ham *News* 20 Oct. p. 14/3 (letter) States' Righters, a Democratic splinter, insist they . . . are the real Democrats. *Ibid.* 10 Nov. p. 12/5 So, making allowance for the two splinter parties, Bean's calculation . . . was close to the mark. 1949 N. Y. *Times* 20 Feb. Sec. 2 p. 10/6 If stations go out of business, the remaining outlets will inherit the 'splinter' audiences . . .

TRIGGER, *n. Fig.* {1706-} *v.* See quots.—1942 *Am. Thes. Slang* ¶236.5 scheme . . . trigger . . . 1946 N. Y. *Times* 3 July p. 47C/5 These beacons are 'triggered,' or caused to locate themselves clearly on the screen of the plane's set by impulses sent from the plane. 1947 *This Week* 23 Feb. p. 5/1 . . . grandmother's beads 'triggered' the boiling process by breaking up the even distribution of heat on the bottom of the kettle . . . 1948 *Sat. Eve. Post* 20 Mar. p. 39/3 There is certainly no lack of evidence that the typical glaucoma patient has a nervous temperament and that emotional episodes will increase the pressure within the eyeball and even trigger off acute attacks.—triggering, adj.—1947 *This Week* 23 Feb. p. 5/1 . . . Nature's own 'triggering' agent is still unknown . . .

-TYPE. (See *Am. Sp.* 23:251ff.) 1928 cited in *Am. Sp.* 23:150/2. Add earlier illusts.—1924 *Sat. Eve. Post* 13 Sept. p. 80 (adv.) Has the car you have in mind a European type, high compression motor? *Ibid.* 27 Sept. p. 47 (adv.) There are very real reasons why the new Gabriel Balloon-Type Snubbers are needed with balloon and low-pressure tires.

+WAVE RECORDER. See quots.— 1948 *Sci. N. L.* 27 March p. 204/3 Wave studies of seaplane landing areas and har-

bors may be important uses for the wave recorder . . . *Time* 29 March p. 84/2 What he is looking for are long slow 'swells' . . . that cannot be detected except with the wave recorder. *Sci. N. L.* 31 July p. 72/2 Wave recorders . . . will register wave characteristics and the information gained will be of benefit in erecting waterfront structures . . . Records from the wave recorders also provide means of checking the method of forecasting waves from weather charts . . . 1949 N. Y. *Times* 19 June p. 9E/7 Wave recorders are being installed on the California and Washington coasts and at Guam.

AMONG THE NEW WORDS

I. WILLIS RUSSELL
University of Alabama

AT THIS writing *straw-hat circuit* and *subway circuit* (both entered in the glossary) appear to be permanent members of a group of analogical formations many of which can best be described as mere vogue forms. *Circuit* in the sense used in these formations is, of course, not new. Not new, either, is the qualifying of *circuit* with a noun in a figurative sense: Berrey and Van den Bark record *Borscht circuit* (*American Thesaurus of Slang* 1942), a circuit described by a writer in the Birmingham *News* (29 July 1948 p. 15/1) as 'A fabulous new type of show business . . . developed in the big hotels strung through the Catskill Mountain resorts . . .' The writer further observes that this term, which has 'sneeringly' been used 'for years,' derives from the fact that *borscht* (beet soup) is one of the favorite dishes of those who frequent these hotels. Also recorded by Berrey and Van den Bark is *tank circuit,* 'a minor circuit playing small [tank] towns.'

But according to my collections, the vogue of these formations on *circuit* as a base dates from the recent war. Four of them are entered in Miss Marjorie Taylor's *The Language of World War II* (1948), where she cites as her source an article in the *Newsweek* of 31 July 1944. The first of these formations, *Foxhole Circuit,* has already been treated in this department (*Am. Sp.* 21:223/1). This circuit was for USO shows, as were *Victory Circuit, Blue Circuit,* and *Hospital Circuit.* Two more of the circuits for the entertainment of soldiers were the *Purple-Heart Circuit* (*This Week* 22 Oct. 1944 p. 11/1) and the *Sarong Circuit* (ibid. 12 Nov. 1944 p. 4/1).

For the year 1945 my file yields *chocolate circuit* and *high-school-football-and-milk-shake circuit.* The first is described in a UP dispatch: 'When their efforts go unrewarded . . . the officers disappear to the more lucrative chocolate circuit and the nurses are left to walk home alone' (Tuscaloosa *News* 27 Sept. 1945 p. 3/3). The second occurs in an article in the *Sat. Eve. Post* (10 Nov. 1945 p. 20/1): 'Kids from our high-school-football-and-milk-shake circuit made up the 32nd Infantry Division . . .' These are vogue indeed!

Two illustrations turn up in 1946. The August issue of *American Notes & Queries* (p. 71/2), citing the New York *Times Magazine,* reports: ' "Citronella Circuit": summer theaters; coined by Tallulah Bankhead' (also used by *Time* 20 June 1949 p. 44/3). This citation brought forth the further observation that 'The Mississippi showboats play the "catfish circuit" ' (*Amer. N. & Q.* Aug. 1946 p. 92/2).

The extent to which *circuit* has become vogue becomes increasingly clear from now on. The rounds of a newspaper society reporter are given the name *ladyfinger circuit* by a writer in the *Sat. Eve. Post* (15 Nov. 1947 p. 31/2). A variant term for the summer theaters, *cowbarn circuit,* appears in the *Sat. Rev. Lit.* the following year (10 April 1948 p. 18/1), and later in the same year we find *cocktail circuit:* 'The buzz of gossip and speculation along the cocktail circuit was set off by the release of the 1949 social list of Washington' (B'ham *News–Age-Her.* 10 Oct. 1948 p. 22D/3). Early in the next year, Miss Dorothy Thompson quotes the term *chicken-patty circuit,* to describe speaking tours sponsored by women's clubs in the smaller cities and towns of the United States (*Ladies' Home Jour.* Jan. 1949 p. 146/3), and in the same month a writer in *Time* refers to someone who 'got on the chicken à la king and mashed potatoes circuit': Kiwanis, Rotary, the Elks' (17 Jan. 1949 p. 14/3). The week preceding a writer in *Life* had used the term *fellow traveler circuit* (10 Jan. 1949 p. 24/2).

Three more -*circuits* appear in February, 1949. In an article in the *Sat. Eve. Post* (12 Feb. 1949 p. 30/3) the writer states that a certain 'chain of four swanky secretarial schools' is 'sometimes described by jealous competitors as "the Ivy League of the shorthand circuit." ' '. . . the soggy-ballad circuit around Chicago night-clubs' is mentioned in an article in *Time* (14 Feb. 1949 p. 77/3), and the following title is used in *Newsweek* (21 Feb. 1949 p. 30): 'On the Vodka Circuit.'

Two more of these formations during the remaining half of the current year bring us virtually up to the time of writing. 'Shakespeare on the Gymnasium Circuit' is the title of an article in *Reader's Digest* (March 1949 p. 95); and *Time* employs the term *campus theater circuit* (25 July 1949 p. 61/1).

As the citations in the glossary show, *free wheeling* in its figurative senses is old enough to be labeled 'popular' rather than 'slang' (only the slang dictionaries have included it; see James B. McMillan in *College English* 10:217/1).

The word *free wheel(ing)* raises several interesting questions. First, what is its origin? Is it an extension of the technical sense or is it a fresh coinage? The conditions apparently surrounding both the technical coinage and that pertaining to traffic are similar, namely, the presence of a fixed and a free wheel. Additional, earlier citations may throw light on the etymology. Another interesting question raised by this term involves its locale. When I sent a copy of the *American City* citation to Professor Atcheson L. Hench, he replied by sending me the three citations from Baltimore newspapers that made an entry possible. But the *American City* citation is from an article carrying a Baltimore date line; hence, the term seems to be a local one. Since, however, it has a local history of some fifteen years, publication of an entry seems worth while. Other readers may have some information on this use of *free wheel(ing).*

It was with great regret that I recently found among some unfiled slips a reference to *buster* material in H. L. Mencken's two Supplements which might well have been utilized in my discussion (*Am. Sp.* 23:290 ff.). According to Mr. Mencken, 'The first *trust-buster* appeared in 1877' (*Sup. I* p. 300).

ACKNOWLEDGMENTS. For citations: Dwight L. Bolinger (1), Margaret M. Bryant (one in the October issue), Atcheson L. Hench (4), Mamie J. Meredith (8), and Peter Tamony (3). George Pope Shannon supplied the definition of *spell out.* Thanks are also due the Research Committee of the University of Alabama for secretarial aid.

SYMBOLS: The symbol + before a word or definition indicates an Americanism. A date immediately following a word or definition indicates the time of evidence shown in the *DAE,* or, if so stated, in another publication. Dates in brackets indicate the time, etc., of British usage. An asterisk after a word indicates that the word is illustrated in British usage before 1600.

+AEROPOLITICS, *n.* [*aero*- 'air' + *politics*] See quots.—1943 *Time* 4 Oct. p. 66/2 Gas within pipe-spurt of the northern take-off fields, aviation gas which need not be trucked or flown in, is vital in the Army's aeropolitics. 1944 *Britannica Book of the Year* p. 769/1 aeropolitics. Political and economic development as influencing, and as influenced by, the development and application of aviation . . . *New International Year Book for 1943* p. 1. 1948 A. G. Renstrom *Aeropolitics; a selective bibliography on the influence of aviation on society* (Washington: Library of Congress); cited 1949 *Industrial Arts Index* Feb. p. 5/2.

+ATLANTIC COMMUNITY. See first quot.—1944 Walter Lippmann *U. S. War Aims* (Boston: Little, Brown and Co.) p. 80 In addition to the United States, the United Kingdom, and France . . . the Atlantic Community includes . . . [the South American countries], . . . Australia, Belgium, . . . Canada, . . . [the Central American countries], Cuba, [the Scandinavian countries], Dominican Republic, . . . Eire, . . . Haiti, . . . Iceland, Liberia, Luxembourg, Mexico, the Netherlands, New Zealand, . . . Commonwealth of the Philippines, Portugal, . . . Union of South Africa, Spain, . . . Italy, . . . Greece . . . , and Switzerland . . . *Sat. Rev. Lit.* 8 July p. 7/2 Once more . . . [Mr. Lippmann's] emphasis is on the commitments the United States . . . has developed with respect to other nations—China, Britain, Latin America, what Mr. Lippmann calls the Atlantic Community . . . 1945 *Fortune* May p. 266 If her rehabilitation results in prosperity, western Europe will merge with what Walter Lippmann, for lack of a better word, baptized the Atlantic Community. 1949 *Time* 18 April p. 21/1 So, too, were two other events last week in Washington: the move to arm the Atlantic community . . .

+BW. See quots.—1946 *Life* 18 Nov. p. 118/2 (title) BW. 1949 B'ham *News–Age-Her.* 13 Mar. p. 1/4 In military jargon, this form of warfare is called simply 'BW.' *Newsweek* 30 May p. 52 Biological warfare, . . . 'B W,' as the scientists call it . . .

+CYBERNETICS, *n.* [Gr. *kybernetes* 'stecrsman' + -*ics*] See quots.—1948 *Newsweek* 15 Nov. p. 89 . . . Prof. Norbert Wiener . . . believes that the machine and the brain have so much in common that they should be brought under the heading of a single science. He has a name for that science—cybernetics—from the Greek equivalent for the word 'governor.' 1949 *Sat. Rev. Lit.* 23 April p. 24/2 'Cybernetics' is the name given to the entire field of control and communication theory, whether in the machine or in the animal. . . . The name, coined in 1947, is as new as the science which, in 1943, had been 'fairly born.' *Britannica Book of the Year* p. 786/1-2 It [the calendar year 1948] would also go down in history as the birth year of two new sciences—radioastronomy and cybernetics.

+DOUBLE-PARK, *v.* To park on a street outside the curb area provided for parking, usually when this area is occupied.—1936 *Amer. City* Jan. p. 95/1 . . . it was a frequent occurrence for an exasperated motorist in desperation to double-park his vehicle . . . 1948 Tuscaloosa *News* 21 April p. 1/4-6 (picture caption) Notice that 13 cars are double-parked in the portion of the block on the south side of the street.

+DOUBLEPARKING, -PARKING, *n.*— 1936 *Amer. City* Jan. p. 95/3 . . . Double parking has been eliminated. 1939 *Mass Transportation* Jan. p. 12 Double parking is not only extremely selfish but creates real hazards to safety. 1941 *Balto. Sun* 27 Nov. p. 14/1 Double parking on the wider streets is almost as bad. 1948 Tuscaloosa *News* 21 April p. 1/4-6 (picture caption) The City Commission has authorized preparation of an ordinance designed to forbid double-parking downtown.

FREE WHEEL(ING), *n.* Tech. sense. {1899-} +*Adj. trans. & fig.* Pertaining to vehicles not confined by tracks.—1929 *Amer. City* July p. 144/1 Before the ban [on parking], free wheel traffic moved at the rate of 6.18 miles per hour . . . 1936 Balto. *Sun* 26 Aug. p. 20/1 Tracks will be removed from the span and it will be re-decked and made available for free-wheel traffic only. 1945 *ibid.* 3 Nov. p. 4-0/1 In approaching the latest plan to give Baltimore an elaborate one-way street system and drastically to reduce the number of streetcars by the substitution of free-wheel vehicles—trackless trolleys and busses—it should be distinctly understood that the plan is the product of the Baltimore Transit Company. *Ibid.* 3 Nov. p. 10-0/3 In connection with the inauguration of all free-wheeling service . . . the transit announced that it intends to inaugurate through service . . .

+FREE WHEELING, *n.* Tech. sense (1934 *NID*).— +*Fig. N.* See quots.; *adj.* free, easy, open, unrestrained. (Also attrib.)—1934 Weseen *Dict. Amer. Slang* p. 254 Free wheeling—Easy sailing; an easy road to victory. 1935 Odets *Awake and Sing* Act. I His hands got free wheeling . . . 1942 Berrey and Van den Bark *Amer. Thes. Slang* Index. 1946 *Read. Dig.* Jan. p. 124/1 Kelly is careful not to make free-wheeling Chicago a more sanctimonious town than it wants to be . . . 1947 Tuscaloosa *News* 9 May p. 8/6 (AP) College athletics . . . have also attracted many of the free-wheeling manners of professional sports spectators . . . 1948 *Time* 15 March p. 118/3 . . . *Henry Wallace* has a free-wheeling frankness that is the product of an independent and irreverent mind. 1949 B'ham *News—Age-Her.* 14 Aug. p. A-19/2 Folsom's innercircle members say reversals at the hands of the Legislature have made him all the more determined to put over, if not all, [*sic*] of his free-wheeling, tax-and-spend program.

+GIVEAWAY SHOW, PROGRAM; also GIVEAWAY. *giveaway, n.* A game employing the principle of giving away tricks, etc. (1934 *NID*); a prize (1942 *Amer. Thes. Slang* ¶373.2).—An audience-participation radio program in which the successful contestants receive prizes.—1948 *Time* 4 Oct. p. 42/2 Plugged as a give-away show . . . *Split the Atom* was even endowed with a sponsor . . . Tuscaloosa *News* 11 Nov. p. 4/6 He denies that 'audience participation' shows—he dislikes the term 'giveaways'—are only nuisance programs that attract morons. *Sat. Eve. Post* 13 Nov. p. 184/2 That twelve-year give-away show doesn't count. 1949 N. Y. *Times* 19 June p. X9/6 . . . the Friday night schedule . . . will offer a full two hours of audience-participation giveaway shows . . . B'ham *News* 19 Aug. p. 1/8 (AP) The government today slapped stringent new rules on radio and television giveaways.

+PHONOGENIC, *adj.* [Gr. *phono-* 'voice' + *-genic* (see 1949 *New Web. Col.* s. v. *-genic*, 2)] See quots.—1947 *Bell Tel News* Jan. Are you 'phonogenic?' A Jamestown, N.Y., publication has coined this word to describe the 'ideal' telephone personality, just as 'photogenic' describes the person who photographs well. *Red Barrel* Feb. p. 22 She shows how to be phonogenic by what not to do. 1949 *Sat. Rev. Lit.* 26 Feb. p. 49 (title) On Being Phonogenic.

PREMIERE, *v.* See *Am. Sp.* 19:63/1. Additional illus.—1944 B'ham *News* 13 March p. 9/4 Top of the Evening . . . will premier on WSGN . . . 1945 Mencken *Amer. Lang.: Sup. I* p. 387. 1946 *Omnibook* Jan. p. 45/1. 1948 *Sat. Eve. Post* 16 Oct. p. 40/3 In Europe it was not unusual for a new Molnar play to be premièred at the same time in six different capitals.

+RADIOASTRONOMY, *n.* See quots.—1948 *Science News Letter* 1 May p. 279/1 Radioastronomy is a new branch of astronomy only recently announced, Dr. Shapley stated. By use of high-frequency radio waves meteors are tracked in their flight across the heavens through clouds and even in full sunlight. 1949 *World Almanac* p. 759/2 Radioastronomy . . . used radar and other high frequency waves to study meteors, the sun and distant stars. *Britannica Book of the Year* p. 786/1-2 It [the calendar year 1948] would also go down in history as the birth year of two new sciences—radioastronomy and cybernetics.

+SILVER CORD. *Fig.* Mother fixation.—1926 Sidney Howard *The Silver Cord.* 1942 Philip Wylie *Generation of Vipers* (New York: Rinehart & Co., Inc., 1946) p. 185 Our land, subjectively mapped, would have more silver cords and apron strings criss-crossing it than railroads and telephone wires. 1946 *Sat. Eve. Post* 26 Oct. p. 15/2 A mom does not untie the emotional apron string—the Silver Cord—which binds her children to her. 1949 *Time* 21 Feb. p. 105/1 But Herbert's young bride wants him with no kite strings—nor silver cords—attached.

SPELL OUT, *v.* '. . . to enunciate or write letter by letter' {1750-}; with *out* {1867-} (*OED.* s. v. *spell*, *v*². 3 and 3*b*).— + Explain simply and/or in detail.—1940 San Fran. *News* 31 Dec. p. 11 In the interest of clarifying public opinion, these opponents should spell out their position fully. 1945 *Time* 3 Dec. p. 40/1 The new, vigorous U. S.-Latin American policy forged by Assistant Secretary of State Spruille Braden was spelled out by one of his appointees last week. Mencken *Amer. Lang.: Sup. I* p. 417. 1948 *Trends in Education-Industry Cooperation* Dec. p. 1 (headline) Wason Spells Out Over-all Program to Curb Inflation. 1949 N. Y. *Times* 31 July p. 2E/2 He spelled out the demands . . .

STRAW-HAT.* + A summer theater. (Also attrib.)—1939 cited in *Ten Eventful Years* 4:635/1. 1945 Mencken *Amer. Lang.: Sup. I* p. 337. 1946 *Life* 5 Aug. p. 81/1 More than 125 straw-hat theaters now adorn the eastern seacoast . . . 1947 *Time* 7 July p. 54/3 To the straw-hat circuit, *Henry* is worth every C-note of it. 1949 N. Y. *Times* 12 June p. 1X/2 Returns from the straw hat circuit indicate that there will be a brisk activity in summer theatres this season. *Time* 20 June p. 38/2 He was given a bit part in a strawhat production of *The Corn Is Green.*

+SUBWAY CIRCUIT. See quots.—1944 *Amer. Notes & Queries* Dec. p. 135/2 Subway Circuit: phrase describing legitimate theaters accessible by subway in Greater New York region. 1947 N. Y. *Times* 20 July Sec. 2 p. 1/6 Subway Circuit. 1948 Mencken *Amer. Lang.: Sup. II* p. 693 Subway circuit. All the theatres within reach of the New York subways. *Sat. Rev. Lit.* 11 Dec. p. 14/2 Something more from the subway circuit. 1949 N. Y. *Times* 26 June p. 1X/6 Subway Circuit.

+THALAMOTOMY, *n.* [Gr. *thalamo-*, comb. form of *thalamos* 'inner room' + *-tomia* 'a cutting'] See quots.—1948 *Time* 21 June p. 76/2 Last week they announced first results of their new operation, called thalamotomy. *Life* 16 Aug. p. 57/1 The operation, known as a thalamotomy, involves the lowering of a needle through the skull to the thalamus . . .

+VITAMIN B_{12}. See quots.—1948 San Fran. *Examiner* 16 April p. 32/1 The new substance is tentatively called Vitamin B-12 . . . *Sci. N. L.* 24 April p. 259/2-3 A single shot of B_{12}, chemical extracted from liver, promptly started formation of new red blood cells in patients with pernicious anemia. Omaha *World-Her.* 5 Dec. p. 8/6 (UP) The new vitamin B12 . . . now has been found in a mold . . . 1949 B'ham *News* 18 Aug. p. 32/2 (NANA) Vitamin B-12—most powerful biological chemical yet discovered, which in doses measured by billionths of ounces as [*sic*] capable of arresting pernicious anemia—also is proving an effective remedy for oversecreting thyroid glands.

WEASEL,* *n.* + *Transf. Colloq.* See quots.—1944 *Life* 25 Sept. p. 14 (adv.) This versatile new cargo and personnel carrier, nicknamed the Weasel, is officially designated by the Army as the M-29. Like a weasel in stealth and swiftness, in sure-footed movement on all kinds of terrain . . . 1947 Berrey and Van den Bark *Amer. Thes. Slang. Sup.* 1948 *Sat. Eve. Post* 31 Jan. p. 31 (picture caption) Designed to meet every rigid test, moving across drifts where army weasels bog down, this Sno-Cat was developed after 24 years of experiment. 1949 *Time* 7 Feb. p. 12/1 . . . more welcome was the fact that Army & Navy snow-moving equipment, bulldozers, weasels, and other heavy machinery was being moved into the battle . . .

AMONG THE NEW WORDS

I. WILLIS RUSSELL
University of Alabama

ACKNOWLEDGMENTS: For citations, Atcheson L. Hench (3), Mamie J. Meredith (3), and Peter Tamony (1). Thanks are also due the Research Committee of the University of Alabama for secretarial aid.

SYMBOLS: A date immediately following a word or definition indicates the time of evidence shown in the *DAE*, or, if so stated, in another publication. Dates in brackets indicate the time, etc., of British usage. An asterisk after a word indicates that the word is illustrated before 1600.

AIRBOAT, AIR BOAT, *n.* {1913} See quots.—1946 *Christian Science Monitor Mag.* 30 Nov. p. 8/4 The airboat, a small boat equipped with an airplane motor and rudder, is used in very shallow water to locate oil on the ocean floor. 1949 B'ham *News—Age-Her.* 9 Oct. p. C-8/5-6 'An innovation in fighting out-breaks in Canada is the use of an air boat—a flat-bottomed aluminum shell propelled by a light plane engine—in patrolling the shallow lake and picking up dead and dying waterfowl.'

ATOMIC CLOCK. A clock in which the nitrogen atom of a molecule of ammonia is utilized to obtain virtually perfect accuracy.—1949 *Science News Letter* 7 May p. 301 (adv.) You will hardly want an 'atomic clock' to get to the office promptly. . . . But scientists and engineers who must split seconds into millions of parts need this more accurate way of *telling time. Industrial Arts Index* June p. 57/1 Atomic clock.

BIZONE, *n.* See quots.—1949 *Foreign Commerce Weekly* 31 Jan. p. 20/1 (title) 1948 Foreign Trade of Bizone Shows Marked Recovery. B'ham *News* 5 Feb. p. 9/3 (AP) New mines cannot be opened until conveying equipment can be got from the (British-American) bizone . . . *Ibid.* 18 Feb. p. 19/5 (AP) The British control commission for Germany reports 'The peaceful industry of the bizone is rapidly getting on its feet again.'—BIZONAL, *adj.*—1948 Balto. *Eve. Sun* 10 Sept. p. 1/6 (AP) He was asked what was the attitude of his agency toward Bizonal Germany. B'ham *News—Age-Her.* 12 Dec. p. 11A (headline) Bizonal Germany's Partisan Press Keeps Hot Fight at Floodstage. 1949 *Manchester Guardian Weekly* (Air ed.) 7 April p. 13/2 Certainly the German bi-zonal offices have published figures of cost-of-living indices which have since been proved to have been widely optimistic.

CHANGE-UP, *n. Baseball.* An unexpected, slow pitch designed to throw off a batter's timing.—1948 B'ham *News* 7 May p. 46/4 (AP) 'He's got everything—speed, curve, change-up and plenty of heart!' 1949 *ibid.* 23 June p. 49/1 The Change-Up. . . . This pitch is popularly called the 'change of pace' ball. MBS Broadcast of World Series game 9 Oct.

COLD RUBBER. See quots. (Also attrib.)—1948 *Pop. Mech. Mag.* Sept. p. 146/2 You'll get up to 30 percent more wear out of that set of synthetics when 'cold rubber' is used. *Newsweek* 11 Oct. p. 75 The Reconstruction Finance Corp. is putting up $3,500,000 to raise 'cold-rubber' output from 21,000 to 183,000 tons a year at government-owned synthetic-rubber plants. *Sci. N. L.* 18 Dec. p. 389/1 Chemists rejoice over . . . 'cold rubber' synthetically made at near-freezing temperatures that is better than the natural material. 1949 *Time* 6 June pp. 86-88 Cold rubber (so called because it is cooled at 41° Fahrenheit, compared to 122° for regular synthetic) has been the sensation of the U. S. synthetic industry.

DRESS OUT, *v. t.* '. . . to deck out with dress.' *OED* {1766-}—*v. t. & i. Sport.* To put athletic garb on (someone).—1947 B'ham *News* 23 Nov. p. 2C/1 L. S. U. dressing out 45 players in gold jerseys and gold pants with purple numerals, came on the field at 1:30. *Ibid.* 18 Oct. p. 1/3 They made the trip from Tuscaloosa by bus, and went straight to the stadium to 'dress out' for the job ahead. 1949 *ibid.* 19 Oct. p. 23/5 Roy Smalley . . . was the only man who did not dress out.

FALSIES, *n. pl.* [*OED* enters an obs. v. *falsy;* cf. *OED false, n.* '. . . false appearance. *Obs.* exc. *arch.*' {1584}]—*Specif.* See quots.—1947 *Life* 15 Dec. p. 114/2 This includes a litter of facial tissues, powder puffs . . . eye shadow and 'falsies' . . . 1949 Balto. *Sun* 18 April p. 2/1 Trixie turned out to be Gene Kelley, in a wig and falsies. B'ham *News* 12 Aug. p. 8/4-5 (AP) She has been quoted on many things—falsies, French bathing suits, morals and so on . . . *Time* 15 Aug. p. 28/1 . . . Bebe came out foursquare against false bosoms . . . 'Falsies aren't honest.'

FIVE,* *adj.* 'In parasynthetic sbs. with suffix -er¹ (chiefly *colloq.*), denoting individuals of a certain rank or size, as *five-boater* . . .' *OED* s. v. *five* C. 1. c. {1887-}—FIVE (5) PERCENTER. See quots.—1949 N.Y. *Times* 14 Aug. Sec. 4 p. 1/5 How closely these were linked with 5 percenters was never firmly established . . . *Ibid.* 28 Aug. Sec. 4 p. 1/1 . . . 'five percenters.' These are men who, in return for a percentage fee, help businessmen get Government contracts and otherwise deal with the Government. *Life* 24 Oct. p. 97/2 . . . Be unswervingly loyal to all his party friends, even if they turn into five-percenters . . . *Sat. Eve. Post* 5 Nov. p. 32 (title) Are Five-per-Centers Necessary?

FIVE (5) PERCENTISM. See first quot.—1949 N.Y. *Times* 14 Aug. Sec. 4 p. 1/3 The subject of '5 percentism'—the practice of charging fees for obtaining government contracts—was under investigation on Capitol Hill . . . *Ibid.* 4 Sept. p. 1E/4.

FRINGE PARKING. Vehicular parking on the outskirts of a city's business district. (Also attrib.)—1947 *Harper's Mag.* Jan. p. 35/2 . . . he was suggesting a parking solution that has been found practical in a number of cities: 'fringe parking,' it is called. Balto. *Sun* 4 April p. 4/2 Purpose of the survey was to determine how much 'fringe-parking' was contributing to solution of the downtown parking problem. San Fran. *Examiner* 13 Nov. p. 4/4-5 'Fringe' Parking Urged to End City Congestion. 1949 *Public Utilities Fort.* 28 April p. 538 Baltimore was either the first or one of the very first cities in the United States to set 'fringe parking' lots in connection with shuttle busses as a method for solving the terrific postwar traffic problem which has swept through virtually every city of the nation.

MOTION SICKNESS. See first quot.—1942 *Sci. N. L.* 12 Dec. p. 378/1 Air sickness can be prevented or cured if you know how. So can seasickness and the other kinds of motion sickness that attack men lurching over battlefields in tanks and jeeps . . . 1949 *ibid.* 2 July p. 9/1 Not all persons who take this new medicine for motion sickness get drowsy. Balto. *Eve. Sun* 6 Sept. p. 14/1 Capital Airlines reports on over a million passengers showed that .89 per cent of the travelers experienced motion-sickness. N.Y. *Times* 25 Sept. p. 16X/3 . . . a three-month test of that line's passengers . . . helped prove the effectiveness of [D]rama-mine, the new drug that relieves and prevents motion sickness.

NONSKED, NON-SCHED, n. *Aviation.* See quots. (Also attrib.)—1946 *Harper's Mag.* Oct. p. 324/1 The non-scheds naturally look with envy at the mail subsidies now granted to the big airlines . . . 1949 *Aviation Week* 30 May p. 7/1 . . . the nonsked may barely break even as a result. *Industrial Arts Index* June p. 7/2 (sub 'Air carriers: Non-scheduled operations').

OFF-STREET, adj. See quots.—[1851 Mayhew *Lond. Labour* II. 423/2 Friar-street is one of the smaller off thoroughfares; quoted *OED s. v. off*[1] C. 3] 1929 *Amer. City* Sept. p. 133 (title) Off-Street Loading Facilities. 1947 *Balto. Eve. Sun* 12 Sept. p. 2/5 Fringe parking on the perimeter of the business district would help relieve traffic congestion whereas providing more off-street space for automobiles in the heart of a city would actually aggravate the problem . . . 1949 *B'ham News* 30 May p. 8/1 This bill would authorize Alabama municipalities to condemn property for off-street parking. *N.Y. Times* 11 Sept. Sec. 1 p. 59/1 Five of the off-street sites located at strategic spots are providing space for 450 automobiles.

PARADOCTOR, n. See *Am. Sp.* 20: 220.—1944 quoted in *Am. Sp. loc. cit.* 1947 *B'ham News* 30 May p. 1/7 (AP) Authorities of Morrison Army Air Field

. . . have disclosed that Capt. . . . Holliday . . . , a paradoctor from Athens . . . parachuted into the jungle . . . 1949 *B'ham News* 7 Aug. p. 1/7 (AP) Dr. . . . Little . . . , former Army paradoctor, gave first aid to the injured . . .

RUN-THROUGH, n. 'A hasty perusal or rehearsal.' *OED Sup.* {1929}—Add American ills.—1949 *Musical Amer.* 1 Jan. p. 14/2 Not every soprano would have cared to change places with Nadine Conner . . . without the assistance of any preliminary rehearsal with the orchestra or full run-through on the stage. *N.Y. Times* 10 July p. 1X/1 After the first run-through, Mr. Berlin casually tossed out three songs . . .

SEPARATE, n. {1612}—*n. pl.* See quots.—1945 *Britannica Book of the Year* p. 276/2 These 'separates' were outfits of which the several parts could be interchanged to form many combinations. As an example: a short black skirt, a black jacket lined in stripes, a striped shirt, a striped halter, a striped long skirt. 1947 *Ten Eventful Years* 2:312/2 'Separates,' something new and characteristically U.S. in fashion, often substituted for dresses. 1949 *N.Y. Times* 11 Sept. Sec. 1 p. 26 (adv.) Your favorite Fall separates, a blouse and skirt in easy-to-care-for nylon. *Life* 29 Sept. p. 89/1 By combining 'separates' in different ways and with clothes she already owns, she can make two old dresses look like four new ones.

AMONG THE NEW WORDS

I. WILLIS RUSSELL
University of Alabama

THE TERM *black market* has given rise to several interesting analogical formations. Two of them represent specializations. In 1944 there arose a 'red market,' which, in the words of Allen Walker Read (*Sat. Rev. Lit.* 10 March 1945 p. 6/1), sold 'an inferior grade of meat in return for red ration points.' A 'yellow market,' dating from 1946, was defined in *This Week* (29 Sept. 1946 p. 14/5) as 'An illicit worldwide trade in gold that has sprung up in Middle East and Latin American markets.' *Time* also used this term two years later (26 July 1948 p. 11/2-3).

Another group of -*market* formations behave somewhat differently. Probably the best known of these is *gray market*, already treated in this department in the issue of April, 1948, where it was defined as 'The market where goods can be bought, but at prices considered exorbitant' (*Am. Sp.* 23:149/1). A 'purple market' occurred in 1946: 'Fiorello LaGuardia tells what emasculated bill will mean in higher prices, says it will bring purple market (legalized black market)—"it is rigged against the consumer" ' (*PM* 30 June 1946 p. 1/2). Finally, with *white market*, we return to the idea of *market* on which *black market* was originally set up as a base: 'The British ministry has announced sufficient stores of food in that nation to meet rationing quotas in all lines, even butter and cheese which are practically non-existent in white markets here' (Tuscaloosa *News* 10 May 1946 p. 4/6); 'The term "black market" is a misnomer . . . When there is no "white market"—and there is not a "white market" worthy of the name in Germany today—the so-called black market becomes the normal free market . . .' (Balto. *Sun* 9 June 1948 p. 12/3).

Something of the progression just noted occurred in French. According to Joseph E. Tucker (*French Rev.* 20:230), the French *marché noir* had a contrasting term, *marché légal.* To the illegal market was applied the euphemistic *marché parallèle.*

The word *chichi*, treated in the glossary, looks like a French borrowing and is probably older in American usage than the citations indicate. It will not be surprising to find earlier examples, possibly with the word italicized or in quotes.

ACKNOWLEDGMENTS: For citations: Clarence L. Barnhart (1), Dwight L. Bolinger (3), O. B. Emerson (2), Atcheson L. Hench (5), James B. McMillan (2), Mamie J. Meredith (5), and Peter Tamony (3). Thanks are also due the Research Committee of the University of Alabama for secretarial aid.

SYMBOLS: A date immediately following a word or definition indicates the time of evidence shown in the *DAE*, or, if so stated, in another publication. Dates in brackets indicate the time, etc., of British usage. An asterisk after a word indicates that the word is illustrated before 1600.

ANTI-TITOIST, n. See *Titoism, Titoist* below.—1949 *N. Y. Times* 4 Dec. p. E1/5-7 (picture cap.) ANTI-TITOISTS—In Sofia Tito in effigy, bearing the slogan 'The State—am I.'

BIKINI, n. See quots.—1948 *Newsweek* 14 June p. 33 This . . . French beauty (left) shows the 1948 countertrend against the skimpy 'Bikini' style (right) which swept French beaches and beauty contests

last year. *Life* 13 Sept. p. 132 Scanty Bathing Suit of Girl in White Is Known as a 'Bikini.' 1949 *ibid.* 12 Sept. p. 65/2. *B'ham News* 13 Dec. p. 11/2 But it isn't because their women aren't built to fill the wispy bikinis . . .

BINAC, n. See first quot. Trademark.—1949 *Sci. N. L.* 2 April p. 222/2 The new computer is called BINAC because it uses a binary system, distinguishing between one and zero. San Fran. *Examiner* 22 Aug. p. 12/7 (INS) An electronic 'brain' which can calculate 12,000 times faster than a human being was being demonstrated today. . . . The remarkable engineering development . . . has been christened 'Binac' by its inventors . . . *Sci. N. L.* 24 Sept. p. 198.

BLIMPCASTING, n. [blimp + broadcasting] See quots.—1948 *B'ham News* 26 April p. 1/6 The latest news reports were flashed in letters 12 feet high. This is common procedure for the blimp and is known as blimpcasting. *Ibid.* 10 Nov. p. 1/1 The new system transmission is known as 'blimpcasting,' Goodyear officials have pointed out.

CHI-CHI, CHICHI, adj. 'Shabby . . . not in good taste . . . arrogant' (1942 *Am. Thes. Slang*)—Smart, pretentious, affected.—1940 *Nation* 3 Feb. p. 128/1 In the dark it was of course impossible to get a clue to the reaction of Mr. Zanuck's chichi guests. 1947 *Sat. Eve. Post* 8 March p. 126/2 It was a nice voice, not chi-chi, natural. 1949 *Time* 25 April p. 62/1 Still, he couldn't quite see his reddish-brown hair at Carnegie-Hall length either; the audiences there were 'too special, too chichi.' *N. Y. Times Mag.* 11 Dec. p. 14/4 They distrust it . . . because its audiences are chi-chi . . .—*n.*—1940 *Topeka Jour.* 10 Dec. p. 3/3 (AP) Some chi-chi survives. But nowadays the audience contains a high percentage of burghers and their wives, of students and of ordinary people. 1950 *Mademoiselle* Jan. p. 24/2 Another Chinese delicacy which would add extraordinary chichi to any party is the already famous butterfly shrimp . . .

COMMUNITY, n. As attrib. {1919-} —*Community college*, see quots.—1949 *Nat. Ed. Assn. Jour.* Oct. p. 502 (title) The Community College [*community* is written above the word *junior*, through which several lines are drawn] *N. Y. Times* 13 Nov. p. E9/1 What, then, is a community college? . . . It is a college that meets the needs of the population within the community. *Ibid.* 27 Nov. p. E9/2 On the other hand, community colleges show a substantial growth in enrollment.

CRASH*, attrib. Employed prepositively to designate that which protects from a crash {1923} or that which is used to rescue those involved in a crash.—CRASH BOAT. 1944 Tuscaloosa *News* 20 Oct. p. 1/7 (AP) Third Air Force headquarters at Tampa said the men took to a dinghy when their crash boat apparently got into difficulty and search crews had found no trace of them. 1945 *Am. Sp.* Oct. p. 226/2 *Crash boat.* A marine rescue boat, for rescuing aircraft personnel and sometimes planes making forced landings at sea. 1947 *College Stand. Dict.* CRASH-CUSHION. 1949 *Consumers' Research Bull.* June p. 9/1. CRASH PAD. 1944 *Time* 25 Dec. p. 1/1 (adv.) But rubber burns, so B. F. Goodrich developed crash pads of Koroseal—it will not flame even if hit by a shell. 1947 *College Stand. Dict.* CRASH TRUCK. 1943 *Sci. N. L.* p. 387/2-3 (picture cap.) Crash Truck—Built for Army Air Forces, this truck is ready to rush to the scene of a crash and shoot hundreds of gallons of water on a burning plane, blacking out the fire and rescuing pilot and crew. 1947 *Sat. Eve. Post* 5 July p. 59/1-2 I had expected the ambulance and crash truck, of course, but scooting along the roads toward the landing strip came racing jeeps, trucks, command cars and even the admiral's own car . . . 1948 *Life* 8 Nov. p. 99/1-2 (picture cap.) The crash truck being tested here is a new model developed to fight fires at airports. CRASH WAGON. 1938 *Time* 5 Sept. p. 51/2-3 (adv.) Known to the Navy as 'Crash Wagons,' these three White trucks represent the last word in modern emergency equipment . . . 1948

Mencken *Am. Lang.: Sup. II* p. 719 Crashwagon. An ambulance.

DEEP FREEZER. A food locker maintaining a very low temperature, around 0° F.—1949 *Time* 18 July p. 34/1 Helen Hayes stuck a hand into her deep freezer . . . *Sat. Rev. Lit.* Sept. p. 39/1 The antidote I mean is the knowledge that there still exists another America, hidden away under the avalanche of billboards and Betty Grables, atom bombs and soap operas, superfortresses and deepfreezers . . .

ELECTRONIC BRAIN. Electronically operated device that seems almost to think; applied especially to mathematical calculators, such as BINAC (q.v.) and UNIVAC (q.v.)—1947 *Spring Book Catalogue* (Macmillan) Professor Hartree speaks [in *Calculating Machines*] from his experience with . . . the ENIAC at the University of Pennsylvania, which has been lately (though rather misleadingly as he shows) described as the 'electronic brain.' 1948 *Sci. N. L.* 13 Nov. p. 311/3 The electronic 'brain' which turns street lights on and off automatically at dusk or dawn is in the center transparent tube being demonstrated by a GE engineer. 1949 *N. Y. Times* 3 July p. E7/6 So many 'electronic brains' have made their appearance in the last ten years that this department finds it hard to keep up with them. *Sci. N. L.* 24 Sept. p. 198 A half dozen electronic brains are being used to attempt the solution of some of civilization's major problems . . .

FOUR-LETTER WORD. [Partridge (*Dict. Slang and Unconventional Usage* 1937) cites *four-letter man*—1923] An obscene word, specifically one consisting of four letters. (Also attrib.)—1936 Mencken *Am. Lang.* (1945 printing) p. 301 There arose there . . . a fashion for using openly the ancient four-letter words that had maintained an underground life since the Restoration. 1944 *Sat. Rev. Lit.* 1 April p. 14 The question is whether the time has not come to end the bootlegging of the so-called four-letter words. 1948 *New Yorker* 23 Oct. p. 52/3 In both World War I and World War II, they depended mainly upon a couple of four-letter words that are obscene but not profane . . . 1949 *Ladies' Home Jour.* Jan. p. 106/4 I would not advise parents to use four-letter words as their only means of talking about sex with children. *Sat. Rev. Lit.* 8 Jan. p. 7/2 What could be added to them by the four-letter-word or anatomical approach?

HYPERSONIC, adj. [hyper- + sonic, adj. 2 in 1949 *Web. New Col.*] See last quot.—1946 *Jour. of Math. and Physics* Oct. p. 247 Hypersonic flows are flow fields where the fluid velocity is much larger than the velocity of propagation of small disturbances, the velocity of sound. 1949 *Jour. Aeronautical Sciences* Jan. p. 22 Hypersonic flows are flow fields where the fluid velocity is much larger than the velocity of sound. *B'ham News—Age-Her.* 4 Dec. p. A1/5 They speak of things transsonic, super-sonic and hyper-sonic, the latter meaning anything that can fly at a speed higher than 2,700 [m.p.h.].

ME-TOOISM, n. ['. . . me-tooing the President's statements' (WREN newscast 11:05 A.M. C.S.T. 17 Jan. 1941]; *me too* (attrib.) and *metooistic* 'imitative' cited in 1942 *Am. Thes. Slang*] See quots.—1949 *N. Y. Times* 18 Dec. p. E7/6 Arthur E. Summerfield . . . called for an end of 'me-tooism.' *B'ham Age-Her.* 22 Dec. p. 11/1 (David Lawrence) The idea that the three Republican campaigns were waged on the claim that the Republicans favored the same objectives as the Democrats but hoped to execute the policies more efficiently and better in detail has come to mean 'Me-Tooism.' *B'ham News* 26 Dec. p. 18/6 (Drew Pearson) When Vandenberg got wound up on GOP politics and 'me-tooism,' a reporter commented: . . .

NUCLEAR REACTOR. See *reactor.*

PARLAY, v. t. 'To wager (money) on a horse race, cards, etc., and to continue to wager the original stake plus the winnings on subsequent races, cards, etc.' 1892 (*DAE*).—*Fig. & transf.* To make a small possession, endowment, etc., yield a large return.—1942 San Fran. *Examiner* 5 May p. 18/5 As far as the girl who was kicked off the '36 Olympic team . . . and parlayed it into a million dollars or so, water these days is strictly for drinking and bathing. 1945 *Time* 5 Feb. p. 46/2 Supplying a heavy piece of change was . . . Webb . . . who . . . parlayed a saw and hammer into a million-dollar construction business. 1948 Charlottesville (Va.) *Daily Progress* 23 Feb. p. 9/3 (AP) Assault, the Texas thoroughbred that parlayed a club foot and a champion's heart into a $626,620 fortune, will be retired from racing . . . 1949 B'ham *News—Age-Her.* 20 March p. A3/5 Hospital officials said the man [Joe E. Brown] who parlayed a big grin into fame is feeling fine. B'ham *Age-Her.* 17 Oct. p. 13/7-8 (AP) The Chicago Bears parlayed Johnny Lujack's deadly passing into a 38-21 upset of the Philadelphia Eagles . . . N. Y. *Times* 18 Dec. p. F3/3 In exactly ten years of whirlwind streamlining, effective planning and organizing, he parlayed an interest in a faltering Baltimore grocery wholesaling house into the giant company.

PICKLED, *ppa.* 'Preserved in pickle; steeped in some chemical preparation . . .' {1552-} (*OED*).—See quot. *Am. Sp.*—1945 *Time* 4 June p. 32/1 At Wheeler Field . . . there are more Liberator heavy bombers withdrawn from combat, either to be cannibalized for parts or 'pickled' for future disposition, than there were in combat in the entire Central and South Pacific commands two years ago. *Am. Sp.* Oct. p. 227/1 *Pickled* (motor). One prepared with a rustproof oil or corrosion preventive compound. 1948 B'ham *News* 31 July p. 2/3-4 (picture cap.) These B-29 Superfortresses 'cocooned' and 'pickled' at Davis-Monthan Air Force base . . . are being stripped of their protective coatings and being readied for flight.

REACTOR, *n.* 'An apparatus possessing electrical reactance.' {1926} (*OED Sup.*)—See quots. (Frequently with attrib., as *atomic r., nuclear r.*)—1947 *Newsweek* 8 Sept. p. 52/1 It is the first atomic reactor which, by employing undiluted fissionable material triggered with fast neutrons, can truly be called 'a controlled version of the atomic bomb itself.' *Ibid.* 8 Sept. p. 76/3 The tight-lipped Atomic Energy Commission did not tell all it knows about the new 'reactor.' The active substance is plutonium . . . 1948 *Time* 27 Dec. p. 27/1-2 This is the first atomic pile, or 'nuclear reactor,' known to be in operation outside the Anglo-Saxon world. 1949 *Readers' Guide* 10 March p. 59/2 Nuclear reactors. See Atomic piles. *Time* 21 March p. 80/2 . . . two big plutonium reactors are now close to completion. *Sci. Dig.* March back cover. The two reactors . . . are creating radiation and particles for research purposes. N. Y. *Times* 4 Dec. p. E13/6 What we used to call an 'atomic pile' or 'furnace' is now called a 'reactor.'

SIMULCAST, *v. i.* [*simul*taneous + broad*cast*] See quots.—1948 *Am. N. & Q.* May p. 26/2 'To Simulcast': 'to broadcast by radio and television simultaneously'... 1949 Richmond (Va.) *News Leader* 30 Aug. p. 12/1 (AP) The first commercial show 'to be simulcast by NBC will be the Howard Barlow . . . concerts . . . N. Y. *Times* 23 Oct. Sec. 2 p. 11/2 Much the same complaint can also be voiced in the case of the Firestone Hour . . . which also is 'simulcast' at 8:30 P.M. . . .

SPOOK, *n.* 'A ghost or specter.' 1801 (*DAE*)—See quots.— 1947 *Sat. Eve. Post* 16 Aug. p. 15/2 In the professional lingo of state highway patrolmen, an incompetent, crazy-driving motorist is called a 'spook,' a term which aptly implies that the specter of death slides in beside him whenever he gets behind a wheel. *Ibid.* 6 Dec. p. 20/2 That does not mean only the drunks, . . . the 'spooks' who cut in and out of traffic . . . 1949 *ibid.* 1 Jan. p. 12/2 The 'spooks' who drive so irresponsibly, the chronic speeders and the drunken drivers are all pedestrian killers.

TITOISM, *n.* [Marshal *Tito* + *-ism*] See quots.—1949 *Newsweek* 15 Aug. p. 9 Titoism has now infected the Communist Party in the Middle East, a split is developing between Stalinists and Titoists in Beirut . . . Balto. *Sun* 22 Aug. p. 10/3 Thus Hoxha has his troubles at home putting down Titoism . . . N. Y. *Times* 6 Nov. Sec. 1 p. 35/1 The determination of international Communism to crush national Communism, or Titoism, is the root cause for the troop movements . . . B'ham *News* 11 Nov. p. 19/1 (Marquis Childs) 'It is not correct to speak of Titoism,' the marshal [Tito] said firmly . . . 'We here in Yugoslavia are following the true Marxism science both in principle and application and as it relates both to our internal affairs and our relations with other nations.'

TITOIST, *n. & adj.*—1949 *Newsweek* 15 Aug. p. 9 (quoted s. v. *Titoism*). N. Y. *Times* 30 Oct. Sec. 1 p. 17/1 The delegation denied any intention of starting a Titoist 'movement' in Italy. *Ibid.* 4 Dec. p. E1/2 The major problems facing the party are similar to those in Italy: how to combat the papal edict and what to do about those Communists . . . who are now going Titoist. *Ibid.* 4 Dec. p. E1/2-4 (picture cap.) TITOISTS—In Belgrade the portrait of the Marshal dominates the street scene. B'ham *News* 14 Dec. p. 14/4 There are unconfirmed rumors he may be tried as a Nationalist or Titoist (the words are synomous [sic] in Cominform vernacular).

TWOFER, *n.* [*two for* one (nickel, etc.; see quots.)] See quots.—1936 Mencken *Am. Lang.* p. 143 Among the coinages of the first half of the century that are still in use today [is] . . . *two-fer* . . . 1948 N. Y. *Times* 30 Aug. p. C13 To commemorate the entrance of Joe E. Brown into the cast of 'Harvey' tonight, 'Twofers' (two for one tickets) will be dispensed with for the longest run attraction of Broadway's present crop. *Musical America* 1 Nov. p. 11/3 Two-for-ones, or 'twofers,' in theatre jargon, are pairs of tickets sold at the box-office price of a single seat.

UNIVAC, *n.* An acronym formed from *Univ*ersal *A*utomatic *C*omputer. Trade-mark.—1948 *Sci. N. L.* 3 April p. 213/2 A mercury 'memory' slightly larger than the one reported here is used in the UNIVAC (Universal Automatic Computer) . . . *Newsweek* 5 April p. 53/3 Two of the Eniac's builders, J. Presper Eckert Jr. and J. W. Mauchly, having gone into private business as the Eckert-Mauchly Computer Corp., issued a catalogue for a machine called the UNIVAC. *Sci. N. L.* 21 Aug. p. 123/2 The earlier ENIAC [see *Am. Sp.* 24:145/1] was pretty smart but the UNIVAC is even smarter.

AMONG THE NEW WORDS

I. WILLIS RUSSELL
University of Alabama

IN THE February issue of *American Speech* (p. 40), Paul Fussell, Jr., contributed a most interesting note on the phrase *iron curtain,* which he found used twice in a story by H. G. Wells in 1904, many years before the famous use of it by Winston Churchill 'in 1946 to describe the line of demarcation between western Europe and the Russian zone of influence' *(ACD).* Moreover, the figure was to be repeated, again long before Churchill's use of it. A NANA press release (B'ham *News* 7 April 1949 p. 50/4-5) quotes George Crile's *A Mechanistic View of War and Peace* (1915), p. 69: 'France (is) a nation of 40,000,000 with a deep-rooted grievance and an iron curtain at its frontier.' (Incidentally, in my check of this reference [ed. Amy F. Rowland. New York: the Macmillan Co., 1915, p. 69], I find only the following sentence: 'Suppose that Mexico were a rich, cultured, and brave nation of forty million with a deep-rooted grievance, and an iron curtain at its frontier.')

Several interesting questions arise. Are these citations part of the history of the Churchillian phrase? Is Churchill or Wells the originator? What are the conditions under which a figure of speech—or any innovation, for that matter—becomes a lexical item? In answer to the first question, it seems likely that we are dealing with independent creation rather than with continuous history. The second question, closely related to the first, may be answered by listing Wells as the first user and Churchill as the popularizer, though such a solution is not entirely satisfactory. Apropos of question three, a few suggestions may be made. When he uttered the phrase, Churchill was a man of greater prominence than either of the other two, at least when they used the phrase. For another thing, Churchill's use of the figure was much more widely disseminated (through the press) and seen by a larger number of people. Finally, and possibly of greatest importance, when Churchill used the figure, he had a real, not a supposititious, frame of reference. In this latter connection, it is worth noting that the earliest recorded use of *atomic bomb* is found in an H. G. Wells story (*Am. Sp.* 22:146). The term caught on, of course, just as soon as there was a real bomb.

Almost as interesting is the number of analogical formations that have stemmed from *iron curtain.* Though they might be classified according to whether they are humorous or serious, a better picture of the linguistic phenomenon may be had if they are presented chronologically.

The first of these formations is not, strictly speaking, analogical at all. James Marshall, writing in the *Saturday Review of Literature,* observes that 'We too have a curtain, not of iron but of nylon . . . our women stand in line for hours to get nylon stockings . . .' (29 June 1946 p. 5). More serious is the term *velvet curtain:* 'Pravda accused Great Britain today of hanging up a "velvet curtain" over the Pacific and the Middle East where, it declared, there is "neither peace nor order" a year after the war' (Balto. *Sun* 16 July 1946 p. 8/4). Still another formation is due to the Russians, who 'would admit their "iron curtain," but pointed out that there was also the Anglo-U. S. "uranium curtain" ' (London *Spectator* 13 Sept. 1946 p. 257/2). A final phrase for the year 1946 is worth recording only quantitatively: 'Even Uncle Sam's uniformed Lotharios, successful nearly everywhere else, failed to break through Niihau's iron nonfraternization curtain' (*Sat. Eve. Post* 2 Nov. p. 29/2).

To the year 1947 belong three *-curtain* formations, whose meaning is revealed in the citations. They follow without further comment: 'The verdant subtropical screen which lies between the two cultures seems to act as a sort of ideological Green Curtain' (*Life* 10 March p. 34/1); 'Said one Lithuanian recently: "We don't speak of the Iron Curtain, as that is not a strong enough expression. Our country lies behind the Steel Curtain" ' (*Time* 14 April p. 33/1); 'Maj. Gen. Bryant Moore . . . formally denied the charge . . . that an army "brass curtain" had concealed news of numerous American casualties in the Trieste area' (Balto. *Sun* 1 Nov. p. 1/5).

Early in the next year we pick up *atomic curtain* in a Li'l Abner cartoon: 'So thass th' atomic curtain! ! Once Ah Dives into it—No One'll be able t' see who ah is . . .' (*ibid.* 7 Jan. p. 10/4-6). Here occurs the first of three uses of *paper curtain,* all different: 'However, to take for granted that we can block Communist infiltration by a paper curtain of United States currency would be a pathetic fallacy' (Richmond *Times Dispatch* 13 Jan. p. 10/1-2); 'With the long-awaited Customs Simplification Act of 1950 now before Congress, foreign traders last week felt that one of the most important moves in years, aimed at cutting customs red tape and piercing the "paper curtain" affecting imports, has been started' (N. Y. *Times* 30 April 1950 p. F1/1); 'But instead of being a window through which we can see Soviet reality, these [Soviet newspapers and magazines] constitute rather a paper curtain' (N. Y. *Times Mag.* 4 June 1950 p. 17/1). To the year 1948 belongs also *golden curtain:* 'Few readers will share Author Matthiessen's sense of the abominations "behind the golden curtain" of the U. S. . . .' (*Time* 20 Sept. p. 114/3).

Time has thrice used the phrase *bamboo curtain* to refer to Communist China; only one citation, the earliest, need be quoted: 'The Communist bosses of Peiping dropped a bamboo curtain, cutting off Peiping from the world' (*Time* 14 March 1949 p. 55/1-2; see also 27 June 1949 p. 25/2 and 7 Nov. 1949 p. 33/3). This formation was also used by the press: 'Christian missionaries behind the "bamboo curtain" of Communist China are facing what appears to be a highly problematical future' (B'ham *News—Age-Her.* 20 March 1949 p. E1/3).

Of the four remaining citations, only one is a serious analogical formation: 'At the same time ex-Judge Dawson . . . plans to sue Lewis "every day" if necessary to get past his coal dust curtain and discover what's happening to the fund's muddled millions' (B'ham *News* 8 Nov. 1949 p. 2/6). Those that remain illustrate the extent to which the formations have become vogue, such as the 'curtain, iron or silk or smoke' used by a writer in *Look* (29 Sept. 1949 p. 25/2), the *tissue curtain* in a poem in the New York *Times Magazine* (18 Dec. 1949 p. 53), and the *Hollywood silk screen* of Bennett Cerf (*Sat. Rev. Lit.* 23 April 1949 p. 4/1).

ACKNOWLEDGMENTS: For citations, Henry Alexander (1), C. L. Barnhart (1), Atcheson L. Hench (9), Mamie J. Meredith (7), and Peter Tamony (13); to Mr. Tamony I am indebted for virtually all the material in the entry on *shoo-in*. Thanks are also due the Research Committee of the University of Alabama for secretarial aid.

SYMBOLS: A date immediately following a word or definition indicates the time of evidence shown in the *DAE*, or, if so stated, in another publication. Dates in brackets indicate the time, etc., of British usage. An asterisk after a word indicates that the word is illustrated before 1600.

AFTER-, AFTERBURNER, *n.* [1911 *Cent. Dict. and Cy. afterburning, n.* In gas engines, combustion or burning off of the gases after the explosion has taken place which should have made all the gas unite at once with the oxygen present.] See quots. (Also attrib.)—1948 *Sci. N. L.* 22 May p. 323/2-3 A ram-jet-like device called an afterburner, which is attached on the exhaust of a jet-engined airplane to give special spurt when needed, will be installed on Navy Pirate fighting planes . . . 1949 B'ham *News* 5 July p. 5/1 . . . the XF-94 has two features which convert it into a specialized interceptor type: . . . an 'afterburner' device to boost the normal power of the jet engine and thus enable the airplane to climb rapidly to the altitude of the attacking bomber. *Newsweek* 11 July p. 55 The plane features the long secret 'afterburner'—a ram-jet engine coupled to the rear of the conventional turbojet engine—for added power. 1950 N. Y. *Times* 5 March p. X21/5 . . . the J-42, with a dry thrust rating (without use of either a water injection system or an afterburner) of 5,000 pounds, is the American version of the British engine.

AIR-, AIR BRIDGE, *n.* An established airline, formerly across water; *specif.*, the Berlin airlift of 1948-1949.—1939 Balto. *Sun* 17 April p. 9/1 The New Zealand service will constitute the air line's second 'air bridge' of the Pacific. 1948 *Newsweek* 9 Aug. p. 27/1 The Berlin 'air bridge'—as the Germans call it—claimed its first American victims on July 9 . . . 1949 Balto. *Sun* 11 Jan. p. 11/3 Only 25 people a month can take the air bridge [from Berlin to Western Germany], so the waiting list is long. *Friends Intelligencer* 9 July p. 379/2 . . . it is safe to assume that England and America contributed together about 170 million dollars to the maintenance of the 'air-bridge.'

AUTOMATION, *n.* [*automatic* + *-tion*] See first quot.—1949 *Mech. Engr.* May p. 389/1 Mr. Bricker had asked for means of handling parts in process of manufacture, without some of the delays often incurred due to the human element. [¶] 'That's right . . . , what we need is more automation,' remarked Mr. Harder. . . . A new word was coined and an engineering section devoted entirely to automation has become a reality. *Indust. Arts Index* June p. 25/1. San Fran. *Examiner* 1 July p. 10/1-2 The Ford Motor Company . . . coined for the new manufacturing science the word 'automation,' and has set up a new Automation Section of Mechanical Design.

AVIONICS, *n.* [*aviation* + *electronics*] See first quot. (Also attrib.)—1949 *Aviation Week* 17 Oct. p. 28/2 'Avionics' is a new word, coined by *Aviation Week* as a simple and much needed term to describe generically all the applications of electricity to the field of aeronautics. 1950 *Indust. Arts Index* March p. 25/2 Altitude brings avionics challenge . . . *Aviation Week* 52:28 + Ja 9 '50.

BENTHOSCOPE, *n.* See quots.—1945 *Am. N. & Q.* Sept. p. 87/1 BENTHOSCOPE: new deep-sea diving device, designed by Otis Barton; two great wheels enabling it to roll along the ocean's bottom are said to do away with the great hazard of the bathysphere dives—striking projecting rocks that smash the windows. *Sci. N. L.* 20 Oct. p. 248/1 . . . a benthoscope . . . is intended for work among the fantastic animals that crawl on the ocean bottom, or are even grown fast to it, like plants. 1949 Tuscaloosa *News* 13 Aug. p. 1/4 The new steel ball is called a benthoscope from the Greek *benthos* (depth of the sea) and *scopein* (to view). Balto. *Sun* 15 Aug. p. 3/1 (AP) Otis Barton . . . sent his steel benthoscope 6,000 feet below the ocean surface today with cameras and floodlights . . .

COSMOTRON, *n.* See quots.—1949 *Britannica Book of the Year* p. 787/1 One, named the cosmotron . . . would hurl protons at energies of 2,500,000,000 to 3,000,000,000 ev, and would thus become the most powerful atom smasher in the world. *Newsweek* 7 Feb. p. 51 . . . foundations have been laid for a giant 'cosmotron' of record voltage. *Sci. N. L.* 19 Feb. p. 114/2 The bevatron, a sort of giant cyclotron, is also known as the 'cosmotron' or 'proton synchrotron.' 1950 B'ham *News* 9 July p. A5 (pict. cap.) This is the first picture of the Cosmotron . . .

DIXIEGOP, *n.* [*Dixiecrat* + *G.O.P.*] See quots.—1948 *Am. N. & Q.* Oct. (Not issued till mid-spring 1949) p. 105/2 (quoting N. Y. *Times* 20 March 1949) 'DIXIEGOP' . . . 1949 Tuscaloosa *News* 27 March p. 1/7 Dr. McMillan . . . referred to the linguistic history of American politics which [*sic*] many unofficial names for parties such as . . . Hoovercrat, and just recently Dixiegop . . . *Time* 28 March p. 20/1 A C.I.O. propagandist coined an angry name for the coalition: 'Dixiegop,' a nightmare animal with 'the front legs and face of a donkey [and] the trunk and rear end of an elephant,' . . . *Ibid.* 11 July p. 15 Then when Republicans and Southern Democrats ganged up to kill Harry Truman's civil rights program, an angry C.I.O. official said that (the 81st) Congress was run by the 'Dixiegop.'

DOL, *n.* [dol] [*dolorimeter*] See quots. —1949 *Sci. N. L.* 7 May p. 300/3 Units of pain in the new scale are called dols. Top of the scale [10 dols] is the point where a further increase in the intensity of the heat rays [on the forehead] fails to add any to the pain felt. . . . Bottom of the scale, one dol, corresponds with the amount of heat which produces a just barely perceptible prick. *Sat. Eve. Post* 3 Dec. p. 29/3 The term 'dol' was created to designate a unit of pain, each dol representing two gradations.

DOLLAR GAP. See quot. *Brit. Book of the Year.*—1949 Balto. *Sun* 25 Aug. p. 14/2 (edit.) In a little more than a fortnight, Mr. Ernest Bevin and Sir Stafford Cripps will arrive in Washington to discuss with Mr. Snyder . . . and the State Department just what to do about the famous 'dollar gap.' *Life* 12 Sept. p. 51/2 Yet the so-called 'dollar gaps' increase, and no conceivable amount of direct ECA relief will close them. 1950 *Brit. Book of the Year* p. 739/2 dollar gap. The shortage in dollar-exchange existing when a country's essential imports from a dollar area, such as the United States, exceed its exports to that area. N. Y. *Times* 13 Aug. p. 1F/2-3 A warning against short-term thinking on the dollar gap in international trade was voiced here last week . . .

DOLORIMETER, *n.* An instrument for measuring pain.—1949 *Sat. Eve. Post* 3 Dec. p. 29/3 The insttument they developed has been christened a 'dolorimeter.' The name is derived from the Latin word for pain and 'meter,' meaning a measuring device.

HASSEL, HASSLE, *n.* [Cf. Wright *Eng. Dial. Dict.* and Wentworth *Am. Dial. Dict. s. v.*] See quot. 1946 *Sat. Eve. Post.*—1945 *Down Beat* 15 Feb. p. 1/5 Building bands is getting to be a habit with Freddie Slack. He broke up his last few after booking hassels but is currently planning another . . . 1946 *Sat. Eve. Post* 31 Aug. p. 72/2 'Hassle' is a gorgeously descriptive word which lately has won wide usage in show business. It means a quarrel, a fuss, an argument, a struggle or a mess. San Fran. *Examiner* 10 Sept. p. 18/2 The hassel went on and on . . . 1948 *Sat. Eve. Post* 3 April p. 17/3 He completely forgot . . . the recent hassle with the Imperial Japanese Empire. San Fran. *Examiner* 9 May p. 23/8 Because she accepted a $2,500 automobile from grateful citizens of Ottawa, . . . Canada's 18 year old figure skating champ . . . is in what might be described as a hassel or fine kettle of fish. 1949 B'ham *News* 27 Jan. p. 1/5 (AP) Before the wedding, Power told friends earnestly he hoped it wouldn't turn into a 'hassle,' a word he learned in the Marines which, freely translated means something like a three-ringed circus. 1950 *Sat. Eve. Post* 25 Feb. p. 148/3 I remember one fearsome hassle . . . in which, by way of illustrating one of Einstein's ideas, you were invited to imagine two moving rods, hung from beginning to end with clocks. B'ham *News* 30 June p. 24 ('Mary Worth's Family') My department always handles those meet-the-genius hassles![1]

SHOO-IN, *n.* [See quot. 1935. Shoo-ins are generally arranged by a 'jockey ring,' who plan the race beforehand and bet on the shoo-in; literally, the winner or shoo-in is 'chased in' by the others. Cf. 1908 *Racing Maxims and Methods of 'Pittsburgh Phil'* (N. Y.: Prosperity Institute) p. 124 There were many times presumably that 'Tod' would win through such manipulations, being 'shooed in,' as it were.] 1. *Horse Racing.* See quot. 1935.—1928 *National Turf Digest* (Baltimore) Dec. p. 929/2 A 'skate' is a horse having no class whatever, and rarely wins only in case of a 'fluke' or 'shoo in,' or by some accident, except when among its own kind. 1935 A. J. Pollack *The Underworld Speaks* (San Francisco: Prevent Crime Bureau) not paged. Shoo-In, a horse race in which the winner is the only horse trying.

2. Hence, a certainty, a 'sure thing.'—(Also attrib.) 1939 San Fran. *News* 30 Jan. p. 15/5-6 (headline) Bear Cagers Appear Shoo-In for Southern Division Title. 1942 *ibid.* 6 Nov. p. 21/6 (headline) Cal 'Shoo-In' over Trojans . . . 1948 *ibid.* 27 Dec. p. 18/1-2 (headline) Taft Appears to Be Shoo-In for Top Senate G. O. P. Job. Tuscaloosa *News* 30 July p. 4/2 Yet this type of registration might endanger their balloting in the local elections, where Democratic candidates are usually chosen on a 'shoo-in' basis. *Life* 18 Oct. p. 44/1 . . . Dewey looks like a shoo-in for the presidency. 1950 N. Y. *Times* 5 March p. 2S/5 The Cleveland Indians . . . looked a shoo-in to repeat.

SONARMAN, *n.*—1949 N. Y. *Times* 18 Dec. p. 66/4 'The sonarman in the Navy is the key to the anti-submarine effort,' a Navy statement explained today. 1950 N. Y. *Times Mag.* 11 June pp. 12/2-24/2 They were striking for a variety of ratings —boatswain's mate, . . . sonarman . . .

TWEETER, *n.* See quots.—1949 *Harper's Mag.* March p. 106/2 And you ought to get a set of two tiny, treble speakers ridiculously known as 'tweeters.' . . . An ordinary twelve-inch speaker lets the double-basses rumble the floor, but the tweeters double the range up into the high notes . . . *Pop. Science* March p. 233 (title) Bring out high notes with a tweeter; cited *Read. Guide* 10 March 1949 p. 69/1.

TWI(LIGHT)-NIGHT, *adj. Baseball.* Pertaining to a double-header, the first game of which begins during twilight.—1948 B'ham *News* 15 July p. 36/3 (AP) The badly crippled . . . Athletics may reach the crossroads of a thus-far amazing season in a twi-night double-header with the league leading Cleveland Indians. Tuscaloosa *News* 28 Aug. p. 4/4 (UP) . . . The Philadelphia A's came to life to win a twi-night double-header from the Browns . . . 1949 B'ham *News* 5 Aug. p. 31/1 Cleveland pulled another long game out of the fire, trimming Washington, 6-3, in 12 innings to take the first of their twilight-night doubleheader. 1950 Balto. *Sun* 17 Aug. p. 17/1 (AP) Manager Lou Boudreau's pinch single . . . drove in the winning run as the Cleveland Indians defeated the St. Louis Browns . . . in the second game of a twi-night double-header.

UNDERBELLY, *n.* U. of a kangaroo {1607}. 2. 'The lower part of the body' (*Sh OED Add* 1944).—*Fig.* A weak, vulnerable spot or point; see also quots.—1944 *Sh OED Add* The soft u[nderbelly] of the Axis [*sc.* Italy] 1942 (W. S. Churchill). 1944 Gunther *D Day* p. 166 (chap. heading) Across the Underbelly. B'ham *News* 15 Aug. p. 1/8 (AP) The great stab into the 'underbelly of Europe' . . . was backed by more than 800 ships . . . 1947 *Sat. Rev. Lit.* 24 May p. 17/2 Churchill's aim was to strike at the 'underbelly' of Europe with a view to keeping the Red Army out of the Balkans, Poland, and Czechoslovakia. 1949 *Life* 31 Oct. p. 36/2 Winston Churchill, recalling a famous wartime phrase, sounded the keynote: an all-out attack on the 'soft underbelly' of socialism. 1950 *This Week* 15 Jan. p. 5/1 Instead of a single giant thrust across Western Europe, [Churchill] favored a supplementary attack on the Nazis through the 'soft underbelly' —southeastern Europe and the Balkans. *Sat. Rev. Lit.* 22 April p. 11/3 In this volume, at least, Mr. Churchill by no means appears as the defender of the attack on the 'soft underbelly' of the Axis and the opponent of a direct landing in Northern France.

1. Mr. W. L. McAtee, Chicago, supplies the following note on this word:

In the magazine *Headquarters Detective*, VIII (January, 1950), 48, appears a word not discoverable in any of a considerable collection of dictionaries. It is *hassel* and is defined as 'a minor irritation. . . . What a hassel!' Search for further information resulted in a letter from Elwin G. Greening, city editor of the *News-Dispatch*, Michigan City, Indiana, from which is quoted: 'We've bandied about the word for a number of years here, and I can't give it any more authority than our circle of "breakfast club" members. I have seen it in print in a magazine, however . . . that caused quite a few laughs . . . because we thought we were alone in using it. . . . We've attached it to anything which is more of a minor irritation than a major problem.' Another instance of its usage may be found in the New York *World-Telegram* for February 2, 1950. Robert C. Ruark writes: 'This was the year of the big hassle in Congress.'

AMONG THE NEW WORDS

I. WILLIS RUSSELL
University of Alabama

ACKNOWLEDGMENTS: For citations, T. J. Crowell (3), O. B. Emerson (1), Atcheson L. Hench (3), Mamie J. Meredith (3), and Grant Turnblom (1). Thanks are also due the Research Committee of the University of Alabama for secretarial aid.

SYMBOLS: A date immediately following a word or definition indicates the time of evidence shown in the *DAE*, or, if so stated, in another publication. Dates in brackets indicate the time, etc., of British usage. An asterisk after a word indicates that the word is illustrated before 1600.

APPARATUS, *n.* 'The things collectively in which [a certain] preparation consists, and by which its processes are maintained . . .' (*OED s. v. apparatus* 2. {*a.* 1628}).—*Transf. and fig.* See quots.—1946 N. Y. *Times* 7 July p. 1/6 For the Soviet government 'apparatus,' as the Russians use the word, is a political machine . . . 1949 *Time* 5 Dec. p. 26/3. N. Y. *Times* 11 Dec. p. 2E/2. 1950 *Time* 13 Feb. p. 23/1-2 He had had them photographed on microfilm and had turned over the films to the Soviet spy apparatus. B'ham *News* 11 Aug. p. 1/6 You may wonder just why the pro-Soviet apparatus picked this Pennsylvania town as an assignment for its key operatives . . .

BEST-SELLERDOM. 1928 and 1939 cited by Wentworth *PMLA* 56:297. Additional illus.—1946 *Sat. Rev. Lit.* 19 Jan. p. 7/1 . . . it is one of those rare books which, fated for bestsellerdom, will at the same time interest . . . the serious, adult reader. 1947 *ibid.* 10 May p. 5/1 Some day there may be a couple of shorts made to show . . . how a book is . . . promoted to best-sellerdom . . . 1950 N. Y. *Times Book Rev.* 9 July p. 3 With their first work some [authors] . . . reached best-sellerdom . . .

COLD WAR. See *Am. Sp.* 23:148/2. Political sense in *NID Add* 1950.—2. Implacable and militant opposition.—1950 N. Y. *Times* 5 Feb. p. 42L/2 A 'cold war' was in progress today on the banks of the Chattahoochee as the police of Phenix City, Ala., dared Georgia's revenue agents to invade Alabama. *Ibid.* 2 April p. 3L/1 A 'cold war' was proclaimed today by members of the faculty of the University of California in their 'loyalty oath' controversy with the Board of Regents. *Ibid.* 16 April p. 67L/2 A warning that 'the "cold war" is on in health and welfare as well as in political and international affairs,' was sounded today . . . *Ibid.* 1 Oct. p. 92L/3 The plenary session devoted to psychiatric genetics and eugenics indicated no abatement in the 'cold war' between the genetic and environmental schools of thought.

CORTISONE, *n.* See quots.—1949 N. Y. *Times* 1 June p. 33/8 The hormone . . . was named yesterday by its discoverer, Dr. Edward C. Kendall . . . as 'cortisone,' an abbreviation of its long chemical name, 17-hydroxy-11 dehydrocortico-sterone. *Ibid.* 2 June p. 29/2 Studies at the Harvard Medical School suggesting the possibility that cortisone, the recently synthesized hormone of the cortex (outer layer) of the adrenal gland, may prove useful in the treatment of epilepsy were reported yesterday at the International Congress on Rheumatic Diseases at the Waldorf-Astoria Hotel. *Sat. Eve. Post* 23 July p. 28/2 And, finally, there is the new chemical, Compound E, or cortisone, which in experimental trials has held rheumatoid arthritis symptoms in check so effectively that the experts are in a rare glow of enthusiasm. 1950 *Read. Guide* July p. 49/2 *s. v.* cortisone.

DOVAP, *n.* An acronym; see quots.—1949 *Scientific Monthly* March p. 172 (title) DOVAP—A Method for Surveying High-Altitude Trajectories. *Ibid.* March p. 172/2 DOVAP uses continuous-wave radio signals to determine missile distances by a Doppler effect. *Time* 21 March p. 80/2 What kept track of it [WAC corporal] was DOVAP (DOppler Velocity and Position), a new instrument designed for rocket-tracking by the Army's Ballistic Research Laboratories . . .

FLYBOY, *n.* See quots.—1946 *Am. Sp.* 21:248 . . . airforce flying personnel are sometimes labelled *birdmen* or *flyboys* . . . 1948 *Life* 1 Nov. p. 87/2 But the generals are no full-throttle 'flyboys.' 1949 N. Y. *Times Mag.* 24 July p. 5/4 'And who's gonna carry that atom bomb, if and when? . . . A flyboy.' 1950 *This Week* 29 Oct. p. 11/4 'You know how it is with us flyboys. . . . A girl in every airport.'

GHOST, *n.* A secondary image in a telescope. {1867}—*Television.* See quots.—1942 Berrey and Van den Bark *Amer. Thesaurus of Slang* ¶ 618.3 . . . ghost, *a double image on a television receiver.* 1946 *Radio Alphabet* (N. Y.: Hastings House) p. 37 GHOST—An unwanted image appearing in a television picture, as a result, for example, of signal reflection. 1948 Mencken *Amer. Lang. Sup. II* p. 731. 1949 *Time* 28 Nov. p. 52/2 They may show 'dot crawl' too, and have incurable trouble with 'ghosts.' 1950 *House Beautiful* Aug. p. 110/3 *Ghost:* This is a second image on your television screen produced when the signal from the transmitter reaches your receiver by two paths.

GUEST-CONDUCT, *v. t.* To conduct an orchestra as a guest.—1945 *Time* 16 April p. 58/3 From the podium of Oklahoma City's Municipal Auditorium he will guest-conduct the Minneapolis Symphony. 1946 *Life* 18 Feb. p. 57/2 The Greek moved on to New York and Philadelphia, guest-conducting other orchestras. 1949 N. Y. *Times* 23 Oct. p. X7/5 He is not carrying the full burden alone, for Sir Thomas Beecham, George Szell, Ernest Ansermet and Dimitri Mitropoulos will each guest-conduct a concert . . . 1950 *New Yorker* 15 April p. 50 I guest-conducted it [a concerto] myself with the Boston Symphony . . .

GUPPY, *n.* See *Am. Sp.* 24:74/2. Add illus.—1949 *Harper's Mag.* Feb. pp. 63-64 For the U.S.S. *Dogfish* is a 'guppy,' a transitional, experimental type, a herald of things to come, altered from one of the big fleet-type submarines that saw so much service during the war . . . (The first four-fifths of the name, incidentally, are supposed to stand for 'Greater Underwater Propulsive Power'; what the *Y* is for nobody knows—possibly 'Yoicks.')

H-BOMB, H. BOMB. Short for *hydrogen bomb* (*q.v.*). (Also attrib.)—1950 Tuscaloosa *News* 19 Jan. p. 1 (headline) President Remains Silent on H-Bomb Manufacture. N. Y. *Times* 22 Jan. p. El/7 (An analysis of scientific aspects of the H-bomb is printed on page 13 of this section.) *Fortnightly* March p. 173 Moreover, it cannot be considered apart from . . . the popular terror stimulated by unceasing announcements and conjectures concerning the A. and H. bombs.

HELL BOMB. The hydrogen bomb (*q.v.*).—1950 B'ham *News-Age-Her.* 29 Jan. p. 1B/1 Several major questions must be answered before President Truman can come to any sound decision on whether this country should attempt to make a hydrogen bomb—the so-called 'Hell Bomb' whose potential destructive power has been variously estimated at from 5 to 1,000 times as great as that of the plutonium bombs dropped on Japan at the end of World War II. N. Y. *Times* 5 Feb. p. 39L/2 . . . Warning Issued on 'Hell Bomb.' *Friends Intelligencer* 25 March p. 163/1 *The Catholic Worker* . . . calls the hydrogen bomb a 'hell bomb.'

HYDROGEN BOMB. See quots.—1948 *Sci. N. L.* 17 July p. 35/1 It would be made principally from the double-weight variety of the lightest chemical element, hydrogen. This isotope . . . is called heavy hydrogen or deuterium. . . . This is the 'hydrogen bomb' that certain high officials in past months have vaguely . . . hinted may be made. 1950 B'ham *News* 11 Jan. p. 8/6-8 (heading) If Terrific Hydrogen Bomb Is in Offing Truman Hasn't Yet Asked for Funds. N. Y. *Times* 5 March p. E1/5 One month has passed since President Truman announced that he had ordered work on the 'so-called hydrogen or super-bomb.' *Read. Guide* 10 May p. 19/1 *sub* 'atomic bombs.'

LOON, *n.* See quots.—1947 *Newsweek* 17 March p. 64/2 The Navy also displayed a 'bat bomb' and a 'loon,' two hitherto secret radio-controlled missiles. 1949 N. Y. *Times* 6 Nov. p. L55/3 The missiles in the maneuver will be 15,000-pound 'loons,' which will be fired from launching platforms of the submarines Cusk and Carbonero. 1950 *This Week* 12 March pp. 4-5 (picture cap.) . . . the *U. S. S. Carbonero* firing a 'loon' during Pacific fleet exercises.

MIDDLE-, MIDDLEBROW, *n. & adj.* {1929 and 1928 respectively}.—Add American illus.—1942 Berrey and Van den Bark *Amer. Thesaurus of Slang.* 1946 Richmond *News Leader* 30 July p. 15/1 Romberg is a 'middlebrow composer,' he told me . . . 1949 *Harper's Mag.* Feb. p. 19 (title) Highbrow, Lowbrow, Middlebrow. N. Y. *Times Mag.* 12 June p. 10/4 Culturally, '34 combines high-brow musical tastes with middle-brow liking in literature. 1950 *Time* 20 March p. 102/2 More middlebrows than highbrows have applauded Viereck's efforts . . .

NEOMYCIN, *n.* See quots.—1949 *Sci. N. L.* 2 April p. 211/1 Christened neomycin, the new antibiotic comes from the same general kind of microscopic organism that produces streptomycin. *Time* 4 April p. 42/3 Last week Scientist Waksman . . . announced a new . . . antibiotic which he called neomycin. Like streptomycin, it is derived from actinomycetes . . . N. Y. *Times* 26 June p. 1/2-3 Neomycin was isolated last March from a soil mold, related to the organism producing streptomycin . . .

OFF-LOAD, *v. t. S. Africa* {1850}.—Add American illus.—1949 *Sat. Eve. Post* 12 March p. 130/2 . . . but we could off-load gasoline and load on fifteen hundred more pounds of fire bombs . . . 1950 B'ham *News* 15 Jan. Comic Section 'Terry and the Pirates,' by George Wunder. Soon as we get in, the underground's local men off-load the bales . . . *Sat. Eve. Post* 1 April p. 46/2 Her weight made a vast difference and I thought we'd never reach the spot where I'd off-loaded our gear.

RUN-, RUNDOWN, *n.* A summary listing of the high spots.—1949 Edward R. Murrow over CBS 15 April. Give us a quick run-down on the films you are showing. Tuscaloosa *News* 8 Oct. p. 1/8 (AP) Here's a quick run-down of major disputes which already have made idle more than a million workers . . . 1950 *ibid.* 10 Oct. p. 10/1 (AP) Here's the latest rundown of gridiron might, with every section represented . . .

TOTAL, *adj.* 'Co-ordinating the activities of all citizens and agencies and the use of all resources and methods in a concentrated national program . . .' *NID Add* 1950).—Add *total diplomacy.* See quots.—1950 N. Y. *World-Telegram-Sun* 14 March p. 12 He [Acheson] defines 'total diplomacy' as the full use of Congress, the Department of Defense, the Treasury, Agriculture, Commerce and Interior, various other government agencies, as well as business, labor and agriculture —in short, all segments of American life. N. Y. *Times* 19 March p. E3 (heading) Acheson Begins Applying 'Total Diplomacy.' *Ibid.* 23 April p. L27/1 'Total diplomacy,' said Mr. Acheson, means that 'there is no longer any difference between foreign questions and domestic questions,' and that both are parts of the supreme question of preserving the nation's existence.

TURN-, TURNAWAY, *n.* {1858}; 1942 *Amer. Thes. Slang.*—*adj.*—1943 *Life* 1 Nov. p. 76 In the few weeks since the beginning of her radio show she has enlarged her audience 34%, business at the Persian Room is turnaway . . . 1950 Tuscaloosa *News* 8 Jan. p. 7/3-4 The New York club walloped Philadelphia, 81-59, before a turn-away crowd of 18,000. N. Y. *Times Mag.* 21 May p. 24/2 Although today's children know Charlie Chaplin only as a name as bygone as Christopher Columbus, the showing was a turn-away sell-out. B'ham *News* 27 Oct. p. 45/1 (AP) In death, as in life, Al Jolson drew a turn-away crowd.

VEEP, *n.* [from V [vi] + P [p]; cf. *jeep,* prob. derived in part from G [dʒi] + P [p] (see *NID Add* 1950)] See quots.—1949 B'ham *News-Age-Her.* 12 June p. 24/2-4 (heading) 'Veep' Barkley's Name Now Often Tied with Some Eligible Widow's. *Life* 1 Aug. p. 32/2 (picture cap.) Senator Lucas . . . and 'Veep' Barkley also look on . . . B'ham *News-Age-Her.* 25 Sept. p. D28/7 . . . some of the Washington gossips insist that the veep's daughters oppose a marriage which would focus the social spotlight on a new second lady . . . 1950 B'ham *Age-Her.* 16 Feb. p. 15/2 (heading) Crax Veep Says Deal for Eskimo Lofty News to Him.

AMONG THE NEW WORDS

I. WILLIS RUSSELL
University of Alabama

ACKNOWLEDGMENTS. For citations, to Clarence L. Barnhart (1), O. B. Emerson (2), Atcheson L. Hench (5, including the earliest for *nerve gas*), Mamie J. Meredith (4), Peter Tamony (7, including the earliest for *fireman, lox,* and *red light*), and Paul W. Terry (1). Grant Turnblom supplied all the material for the entry *zip gun.* Thanks are also due the University of Alabama Research Committee for secretarial aid.

SYMBOLS: A date immediately following a word or definition indicates the time of evidence shown in the *DAE*, or if so stated, in another publication. Dates in brackets indicate the time, etc., of British usage. An asterisk after a word indicates that the word is illustrated before 1600.

AREA BOMBING. 1944 quoted in *Am. Sp.* 20:299. Additional illus.—1939 cited in *Ten Eventful Years* 4:633/2. 1950 N.Y. *Times Mag.* 27 Aug. p. 52/2 The object of this type of bombing—known as 'area bombing'—is to destroy cities and to cause the greatest possible destruction of civilian life and property.

CEASE-FIRE. *'Mil.* The signal to cease firing . . .' (*Shorter OED Addenda* 1944 {1859})—Add American illus.—1949 *New Words and Words in the News* (Funk and Wagnalls Co.) Sup. No. 2 (Spring) p. 1/2. 1950 Tuscaloosa *News* 5 Aug. p. 1/4 (AP) Soviet Delegate Jakob A. Malik . . . introduced a resolution calling for a cease-fire . . . B'ham *News* 7 Aug. p. 12/5 . . . a cease-fire now would prevent them from conquering the whole country.

CLUTCH,* *n.* 'Critical situation' (1942 Berrey and Van den Bark *Am. Thesaurus of Slang;* also 1950 *NID Addenda*).—Add attrib. illus.—1950 B'ham *News* 14 Sept. p. 56/1 But two tragic Baron blunders and the lack of a clutch base hit with runners begging for transportation home enabled the Vols to stagger in. N. Y. *Times* 8 Oct. p. S 1/1 (AP) All American Bob Williams, the great clutch shooter, tried 20 passes and completed only seven. *Time* 16 Oct. p. 51/1 In the tenth, Joe Di Maggio stepped up and demonstrated his old specialty: winning ball games with clutch home runs.

DECLASSIFY, *v. t.* [*de-* + *classify* '*Mil.* to mark or otherwise declare (a document, paper, etc.) of value to the enemy and limit and safeguard its handling and use' (*ACD*)] See quots.—1948 B'ham *News* 21 Dec. p. 14/6 However, Forrestal asked Adm. Souers and Gen. Gruenther to 'declassify' it (make it non-secret) immediately. 1950 N. Y. *Times* 12 March Sec. 1 p. 39/3-4 (UP) 'He may have made the confession in the hope that we would go ahead and declassify important secrets.' *Ibid.* 16 April p. 8E/3 Despite all the protests of men such as

Dr. Bronk the government agencies show no sign of abandoning unnecessary restrictions, of 'declassifying' information which is no longer of military consequence, or of realizing the long-range consequences of their restrictions. *Time* 7 Aug. p. 49/2 'Project Cyclone' operated in secret until last week when the Navy declassified some of its activities.

DEPTH INTERVIEW. Depth psychology (s. v. psychology, depth) defined in 1945 Carter V. Good *Dict. of Educ.* (N. Y. and Lond.: McGraw-Hill Book Co.) p. 318/1.—See 1949 *Fortune* quot.—1948 *Jour. of Applied Psychol.* Oct. p. 550 To orient ourselves to the problem and sketch in its broad outlines we began with a series of a hundred 'depth interviews' of television families. 1949 *Sat. Rev. Lit.* 26 March p. 8/2-3 They do not seem to be aware of the extensive use of depth interviews (a qualitative type of interview which is used extensively even before a questionnaire is written); . . . *Industrial Arts Index* June p. 152/2. *Fortune* Sept. Sup. p. 2/2 A depth interview is really nothing more than a long conversation in which the interviewer thoroughly explores the subject with the respondent. There is no questionnaire and the interviewer is not allowed to take notes; like the great Boswell he sets it all down afterward as nearly verbatim as possible. *Time* 10 Oct. p. 54.

DEVIATIONISM, *n.* Divergence from a certain line of thought.—1949 N. Y. *Times* 30 Oct. p. 2E/2 It was reported that he might be charged with 'deviationism' when he returns to Prague from Lake Success. 1950 *ibid.* 22 Oct. p. 31/1 Slovak separatism, too, has lately proved troublesome to the Communists; it is called 'bourgeois nationalist deviationism' and consists in this case more in resentments against Prague than against Moscow.

DEVIATIONIST, *n.*—1946 San Francisco *Examiner* 14 May p. 17/3 Communist words now in common use are 'deviationist,' 'capitalistic contradiction,' 'mass base,' 'revisionist.' 1950 Memphis *Commercial Appeal* 1 Jan. Sec. IV/C p. 2 It [America] took its old enemies Japan, Germany, and Italy to its heart, and found room to welcome the first great 'deviationist'—Tito and his truculent Yugoslavia.

DIXIECRATISM, *n.*—1949 Tuscaloosa *News* 17 Dec. p. 4/3 And Truman sent him in reply a significant letter which ignored the issue of why Byrnes resigned, and dwelt instead on Byrnes' conversion to Dixiecratism. 1950 B'ham *News* 15 April p. 4/3 (repr. from Anniston [Ala.] *Star*) Dixiecratism then can take its place in history alongside the Populists, the Know-Nothing-Party, the Hoovercrats, the Socialists and the score or more of other splinter parties that have plagued the American people from time to time.

FIREMAN, *n.* 'One who is employed to extinguish fires' (*OED* {1714-}).—*Fig. and transf.* See quots.—1940 San Francisco *Chronicle* 27 Aug. p. 1H/2-4 (heading) Fireman Feller Saves Game . . . 1941 San Francisco *Call-Bulletin* 2 Oct. p. 1H/4 The starting pitcher begins 'to lose his stuff' and the manager flashes a sign. Up gets the fireman and starts to warm up. 1942 San Francisco *News* 14 July p. 16 Mons. François Joseph O'Doul . . . realizes the value of a fireman, as a relief pitcher is called. 1948 Balto. *Sun* 18 Feb. p. 13/7 He declares . . . that if he is to be the club fireman again he's got to have more dough. 1950 N. Y. *Times* 1 Oct. p. 2E/7 Nonetheless, until about a year and a half ago, his chief claim to fame so far as the public was concerned was that his brother was Fireman Johnny Murphy, former New York Yankee relief pitcher.

FROGMAN, *n.* See quots. (Also attrib.).—1949 N. Y. *Times* 25 Dec. p. E7/5 'Frogmen,' as they are called, wear self-contained breathing apparatus and web-like rubber shoes, used in the war, and swim like fish without stirring up mud, so that fish can be stalked with cameras. 1950 Tuscaloosa *News* 13 Jan. p. 1/4-5 (UP) A naval 'frogman' swam into the smashed British submarine Truculent on the bottom of the Thames Estuary late today and found the entire craft flooded. B'ham *News* 14 Jan. p. 9/7 (AP) Frogmen are expert swimmers who go down in black rubber suits with rubber fins attached. They carry portable oxygen machines and lights. N. Y. *Times* 5 Nov. p. X1/8 And 'Paysages du Silence' is a magical trip with 'frog men' divers under the Mediterranean . . .

GLIDE PATH. The path of descent of an airplane described by a radio beam. (Also attrib.).—1946 *Sci. N. L.* 23 Feb. p. 120 . . . a second signal indicates that it has intersected an additional or 'glide path' beam which is also necessary for instrument approach. 1948 *National Geog.* Feb. p. 252 The other . . . is an Instrument Landing System (ILS), in which the pilot follows a radio beam 'glide path' down to the field . . . 1950 *Aviation Week* 9 Oct. p. 44/1 In the one instrument, a pilot is provided a continuous picture of his heading, course, reciprocals, wind drift, and glide path.

HAND-, HANDOFF, *n.* '*Rugby Football.* . . . the action of pushing off an opponent' (*OED* 1922-).—*Am. Football.* A handing of the ball from one player, usually the quarterback, to another; a ball so handled.—1945 N. Y. *Times* 7 Oct. p. 1S/7 (AP) Mathews slipped end for 16 and on a fake handoff, Holtsinger ran around the weak side to score . . . 1947 Charlottesville (Va.) *Daily Progress* 8 Nov. p. 5/4 . . . on a handoff from Quarterback . . . [he] ran squarely against a stone wall . . . 1949 B'ham *News—Age-Her.* 13 Nov. p. C5/4 On his long jaunt, after taking a handoff from Dick Raklovits who took the kick, Karras was hemmed in at least three times on the side-lines by Ohio tacklers. 1950 Tuscaloosa *News* 8 Jan. p. 8/6 (UP) The 175-pound T-formation quarterback passed for the South's first two touchdowns, set up the third with another toss and in between was keeping defenders dizzy with hand-offs to an adept crew of half-backs . . .

INTERCHANGE, *n.* '. . . *attrib.* in reference to the passage of traffic from one railway line to another, as *interchange service, station,* etc.' (*OED* {1887}).—*Specif.* A place on the Pennsylvania Turnpike where vehicular traffic can enter or leave the pike.—1940 *Life* 29 July p. 56/2 Interchanges are equipped with acceleration and deceleration lanes 1,200 ft. in length. 1947 Esso Road Map of Pennsylvania. 1950 N. Y. *Times* 12 Nov. p. X19/1 Eighteen interchanges connect with all important national and state highways leading to numerous historic Pennsylvania sites, shrines and mountain vacation spots.

JITTEROPTERA, *n.* See last quot.—1946 *Time* 15 April p. 73/1 . . . Decca announced that Heifetz' next album will be *Hexapoda*—'five studies in Jitteroptera.' 1950 *Richmond Times Dispatch* 19 Feb. p. 14D/3 Highlighting the program will be Carpenter's rendition of 'Hexapoda' or five studies in 'jitteroptera.' . . . According to the composer, 'jitteroptera' is a new music which he hopes 'has all the quality of American folk music and is yet erudite enough for sober consideration by serious musicians.'

LOX, *n.* Acronym for *l*iquid *ox*ygen.—1940 San Francisco *News* 3 Oct. p. 19/4 . . . and that liquid is called liquid oxygen, or 'L-O-X,' as the mining men say. 1949 *Time* 18 April p. 65/1 Behind him . . . were thick-walled tanks of 'lox' (liquid oxygen) and alcohol. *Ibid.* 6 June p. 72/3.

NERVE GAS. See quots.—1940 Balto. *Sun* 13 May p. 1/5 A specialist in nervous diseases and a chemist . . . said tonight that a 'nerve gas,' reported possibly used by the Nazis . . . was 'entirely within the range of possibility.' 1948 *ibid.* 24 March p. 13/3 Researchers also point out that, unlike any drug used in such cases in the past, the 'nerve gas' [di-isopropyl-fluorophosphate] has a long continued effect. 1950 *Britannica Book of the Year* p. 466/1 This new gas uses Tabun, first of the G series, as a base. This series is also known as 'green ring three' and includes the deadly nerve gases, sometimes referred to as psychological gases since they cause irresponsible action or behaviour among their victims. 1950 N. Y. *Times* 23 April p. E11/6 The so-called 'nerve gases' are hydrocyanic acid (prussic acid), cyanogen bromide and cyanogen chloride . . . all are highly volatile, and all cause death by paralysis of the central nervous system.

PHILLUMENIST, *n.* [? Gr. *phil-* 'loving' + L. *lumen* 'light' + *-ist*] See quots.—1949 *This Week* 23 Oct. p. 24/2 Phillumenists (the word properly fits those who collect labels from wooden-match boxes, but also is applied to the paper-book fans) are outnumbered among hobbyists only by stamp collectors. 1950 *Friends Intelligencer* (Philadelphia) 11 Nov. p. 662/1 Do you have phillumenists among your strange classes of collectors? We do, and they have just been holding in London the annual exhibition of matchbox and booklet labels, which are the objects they collect.

PRECISION BOMBING. 1942 quoted in *Am. Sp.* 20:301. Add illus.—1939 cited in *Ten Eventful Years* 4:633/1. 1950 N. Y. *Times Mag.* 27 Aug. pp. 50-52 To be sure, strategic bombing as carried out by the American 8th and 15th Air Forces in Europe was 'precision bombing' directed, so far as operational accuracy permitted, against specific military targets.

RED LIGHT. *Fig.* A blocking of action.—1938 *Mag. Dig.* (Ontario) Jan. p. 66 (title) A Red Light for the Pugnacious. 1939 San Francisco *News* 14 Aug. p. 13/1-2 By snapping the red light on the Beesemyer parole, Governor Olsen may have pinned a 'Kick Me' sign on his coat-tails . . . 1946 Balto. *Sun* 29 Jan. p. 11/1 'What in fact the Associated Press has done is to put up the red light,' . . . 1950 Tuscaloosa *News* 18 Sept. p. 1/4-5 (headline) Red Light Flashed on Over-easy Credit.

SNIFTER,* *n.* See quots.—1944 *Sci. N. L.* 12 Aug. p. 103 'The snifter' . . . is a portable, one-man direction finder that 'smells out' by radio the very room in which an illegal radio transmitter is hidden. 1946 *Collier's* 5 Oct. p. 6/3 When searching for illegal radio transmitters, operatives of the Federal Communications Commission sometimes use a miniature 'snifter,' a receiver for short-range detection that arouses no suspicion as it can be carried in a vest pocket or held in the palm of the hand and set to register the strength of the signal by a low hum or silently on a dial. 1949 *Life* 5 Dec. p. 166/2 At the start hunters with radio direction finders, called 'snifters,' collect at Brookfield Zoo.

SPACE OPERA. See quots. (Also attrib.).—1949 *Sat. Rev. Lit.* 24 Dec. p. 7/3 No less than eight of this year's crop of science-fiction novels are what is known in the trade as 'space operas'—books built round the theme of interplanetary travel. 1950 *ibid.* 17 June p. 32/2 He tells a better story and tells it better than any of the other three writers who have entries in the 'space opera' category this spring . . . *Ibid.* 30 Dec. p. 16/2 All these appurtenances and a couple of new ones are present in the three examples of 'space opera' on the current list. . . . All are alike in being serials from the science-fiction pulps and therefore in being episodic chronicles and extra-terrestrial dangers met and overcome.

SUPER-, SUPERBAZOOKA, *n.* See quots.—1945 B'ham *News* 9 Feb. p. 3/2-3 An American soldier demonstrates how easily the 4.5-inch rocket and launcher, the 'Super Bazooka,' which together weigh only a little more than 50 pounds, can be carried. . . . This big brother of the famed Bazooka is more than two inches larger and packs all the destructive punch of a 105-mm. howitzer. 1946 Tuscaloosa *News* 31 March p. 20/2 (UP) There are also: A superbazooka, newest version of the foot soldier's famed tank-buster . . . 1950 N. Y. *Times* 16 July p. 1E/4 But the new 'super-bazooka,' of 3.5-inch caliber, is now believed to be in action. *Life* 7 Aug. p. 31/1-3 It is the new 3.5-inch recoilless rocket launcher, the 'superbazooka.' . . . Made of aluminum, it weighs only 15 pounds. . . . Your loader . . . rams an 8.5-pound rocket into the back of the 'stovepipe' . . . can penetrate up to 11 inches of armor.

ZIP GUN. A homemade pistol, often a small lead pipe mounted on a block of wood with a crude firing pin, *e.g.,* a nail; it usually takes .22 caliber ammunition.—1950 *Time* 12 June p. 22 Before the cops broke up the war, two boys had been wounded by bullets from a homemade .22 caliber 'zip gun' . . . N. Y. *Post* 29 Sept. p. 2 Three Bronx schoolboys were held by police today after admitting shooting off a home-made 'zip' gun. . . . It was fashioned of a 6-inch stainless steel tube taped to a wooden block with an ordinary closet bolt for a 'trigger.' By means of a rubber band, a long .22 caliber bullet could be shot from it. N. Y. *Mirror* 27 Nov. p. 2 The zip guns, knives, blackjacks and brickbats will be turned over to the police . . .

AMONG THE NEW WORDS

I. WILLIS RUSSELL
University of Alabama

ACKNOWLEDGMENTS. For citations, Edward Artin (2), Atcheson L. Hench (2), Mamie J. Meredith (5), and Peter Tamony (2). Thanks are also due the University of Alabama Research Committee for secretarial aid.

SYMBOLS: A date immediately following a word or definition indicates the time of evidence shown in the *DAE*, or, if so stated, in another publication. Dates in brackets indicate the time, etc., of British usage. An asterisk after a word indicates that the word is illustrated before 1600.

BLOW JOB, TORCH. See quots.—1945 San Fran. *Examiner* 26 July p. 9/5 A P-59 jet propelled Airacomet, affectionately called the 'blow job' by flyers, will make several flights . . . 1946 *Brit. Book of the Year* p. 832/1. *Sat. Rev. Lit.* 22 June p. 6/1. 1948 Tuscaloosa *News* 29 April p. 1 (pict. caption) BLOW TORCHES—In echelon formation . . . are four of the 78 Thunderjets . . . they form the first USAF unit completely outfitted with jet fighters. Their pilots . . . call . . . their planes 'blow torches' or 'squirts.' 1950 *Popular Mechanics* May pp. 110-11 (title) Strait Jacket for a Super Blowtorch.

CAPTIVE*, *adj.* '*transf.* Said . . . of things restrained from escaping, as *a captive balloon*' (*OED, s. v. captive, a.* and *sb.*, A. 1. *b.*).—*captive audience. Fig.* Audience so situated that it must listen involuntarily; see quots.—1949 Omaha *World-Her.* 6 Nov. p. 3-A It [tram radio] gives a radio station what is referred to in less polite circles as a 'captive' audience. 1950 *Newsweek* 26 June p. 18/3 But not until last week did the Corps finally get the captive audience it had wanted. The President went to the Quantico base for a six-hour visit. *Sat. Rev. Lit.* 18 Nov. p. 4/2 Daily newspapers and magazines are delivered to a man's door; radio and television are his to enjoy in his home by simply turning a knob. In some places he cannot escape them; he is part of a captive audience. 1951 N. Y. *Times* 3 June p. 8E/3 (editorial) This issue of the 'captive audience' was raised in our own city when passengers waiting to board trains in the Grand Central Station were bombarded during some turbulent weeks with commercial loud-speaker programs.

CARPET BOMBING, RAID. Also *carpet*. See quots.—1945 Balto. *Sun* 23 Feb. p. 3/5 Several ministries were laid in ruins that Saturday as a result of the American carpet bombing . . . *Rich. Times Dispatch* 16 March p. 1/8 The United States Seventh Army . . . swept into the Saar basin at a new point behind a tremendous carpet of bombs. *Life* 4 June p. 25 A carpet raid is an effort to pulverize an area in front of ground troops to facilitate a breakthrough . . . *Sat. Eve. Post* 20 Oct. p. 52/2 The planes kept coming overhead . . . and the bomb carpets came down . . . 1946 *Brit. Book of the Year* p. 832/1. *Sat. Rev. Lit.* 22 June p. 6/1. 1951 *Read. Dig.* April p. 29/2 Or 'atom bombing' might replace 'carpet bombing' as employed in the St.-Lô break-through in the Normandy invasion. At St.-Lô hundreds of planes unloaded 5200 tons of ordinary bombs in an area roughly one and a half by four miles to clear the way for ground troops.

CHEMOSPHERE, *n.* [*chemo-* 'chemic' + *-sphere*] See second quot.—1950 *Newsweek* 16 Oct. p. 53 Physicist J. Kaplan . . . revealed that a region 26 to 70 miles above the earth (he called it the 'chemosphere') appears to be rich in the hydroxyl molecule, a highly combustible compound of hydrogen and oxygen. *Sci. Dig.* Dec. Inside back cover. The word 'chemosphere' is a new term coined by Dr. Kaplan and associates to designate that layer of space 26 to 70 miles above the earth's surface, so rich in photo-chemical activity.

COMPATIBILITY, *n.* '. . . mutual tolerance, . . . congruity' (*OED* {1611-}).—*Specif. television.* See quot. N. Y. *Times* (Also attrib.)—1950 *Tele-Vision Engineering* Sept. p. 5/2 They doubted the compatibility prospects of the system . . . *Tele-Tech* Oct. p. 26/2 The report states that compatibility 'is too high a price to put on color.' 1951 N. Y. *Times* 3 June p. 2E/6 The first factor is 'compatibility'—whether color signals will show up on present television sets in black and white.

COMPATIBLE*, *adj. Specif. television.*—1949 *Time* 28 Nov. p. 51/1 But the worst thing about the CBS system, says RCA, is that it is not 'compatible.' 1950 *Tele-Vision Engineering* Sept. p. 5/1 . . . perhaps it would only be possible to consider compatible systems. B'ham *News* 1 Nov. p. 10/3 (AP) The rival systems rejected by the FCC . . . are compatible. The colorcasts could be picked up in black and white on present type sets with no adjustment or added equipment. 1951 N. Y. *Times* 3 June p. 2E/6 If it is a compatible color system, then the owners of old sets will at least be able to see the evening programs in black and white . . .

DEATH SAND, DUST. See quots.—1950 *Sci. N. L.* 5 Aug. p. 83/1 An invisible dust of radioactive 'death sand' could spread over cities of the earth and kill their populations by radioactivity without the noisy warning of an atomic bomb. *Time* 7 Aug. p. 50/3 This 'death sand' (containing .05% of radioactive material) would be applied at a rate of 12 milligrams (1/2500 oz.) per square meter and would be entirely invisible. *New Yorker* 26 Aug. p. 17/1 We pushed the little girl for a few minutes, then returned to the house and settled down to an article on death dust, or radiological warfare, in the July *Bulletin of the Atomic Scientists*, Volume VI, No. 7.

DIANETICS, *n.* [Gr. *dianoētikós* 'having to do with thought'] See quots.—1950 N. Y. *Times Book Rev.* 2 July p. 9/1 On the first page of *Dianetics* L. Ron Hubbard states that as a result of the theories presented in this book the 'hidden source of all psychosomatic ills and human aberration has been discovered and skills have been developed for their invariable cure.' . . . dianetics—the author's name for his 'science of the mind' . . . 1951 *Read. Guide* Vol. 50, No. 18, Jan. 10 p. 364/1 *s. v. psychoanalysis.*

FRONT-RUNNING, *adj.* Also *front. Sport.* Being in the lead all through a race; leading.—1950 N. Y. *Times* 11 June p. S3/2 Tuning up for a possible shot at the N.C.A.A. half-mile crown next Saturday, Wade beat Pearman by nine yards in the 880 with a front-running race. Balto. *Sun* 27 Aug. Sports Sec. p. 1/2 (AP) . . . Detroit's front-running Tigers scored four unearned runs in the ninth inning today . . . 1951 B'ham *News* 20 May p. D4/2 Jud Webster . . . made a terrific bid for the 880 against front-running John Paris . . . N. Y. *Times* 3 June p. S1/2 Wearing down Army's Dick Shea with a powerful front race, Fred Wilt set a Travers Island record . . . today . . .

FURNACE*, *n.* 'An apparatus consisting essentially of a chamber to contain combustibles for the purpose of subjecting minerals, metals, etc. to the continuous action of intense heat' (*OED* {*a.* 1225-}).—See quots.—1950 N. Y. *Times* 8 Jan. p. E9/7 The 'furnace' or nuclear reactor . . . will be cooled with natural air . . . *Ibid.* 16 July p. E9/6 (A reactor is the 'furnace' where uranium atoms are split after they have been bombarded by neutrons.) *Sci. N. L.* 5 Aug. p. 83/1 What would be done would be to collect the debris of smashed uranium atoms from atomic 'furnaces' in which fissionable material is being 'burned.'

LETTRISM, LETTRISME, *n.* See quots.—1946 *Time* 2 Dec. p. 31/2 Lettrism, founded by Isidore Isou . . . is a theory of poetry as 'rhythmic architecture.' The rapidly growing hordes of Lettrists . . . prefer meaningless combinations of letters to dictionary words. 1947 *New Yorker* 8 Feb. p. 21/1 The *very* latest literary movement in France . . . is Lettrism. The Lettrists are outdoing Dada and Surrealism by creating not only new word combinations but new letters for the alphabet. So far they have invented eighteen new letters. 1948 Lond. *Spectator* 9 April p. 432/2 I have been reading this week some poems written in the new mode of '*lettrisme.*'

MONITOR(ING) SCREEN. *Television.* A screen on which appears the telecast as it goes to the home viewer.—1950 N. Y. *Times* 5 March p. xii/2-3 (pict. caption) On the right is the monitor screen which shows him what the home viewer is seeing. N. Y. *Times Mag.* 30 April p. 16 (pict. caption) He must worry about: . . . (6) monitor screen . . . N. Y. *Times* 12 Nov. p. x13/3 In the studio, Mr. Maugham did not witness much of the actual performance as it went on the air and showed no inclination to watch it on a monitoring screen.

ROK, R. O. K., *n.* Relief of Korea. Republic of Korea. In plur., soldiers of the Republic of Korea. (Also attrib.)—1950 N. Y. *Times* 2 July p. E1/6 The man who took over direction of Operation ROK—Relief of Korea—in these dire circumstances was General MacArthur. *Life* 11 Sept. p. 52/1 The Durable Roks [title] . . . But the Rok (for Republic of Korea) army was more durable than anybody thought. N. Y. *Times* 8 Oct. p. 2/3 R. O. K. Republic of Korea. Tuscaloosa *News* 9 Oct. p. 1/8 (AP) The South Koreans (Roks) may be preparing to turn at Wonsan . . . 1951 N. Y. *Times* 20 May p. E3/6 . . . the psychological inferiority of the Koreans vis-a-vis the Chinese . . . is evidenced on the battlefield by the tendency of the R. O. K.'s to break or panic when heavily attacked by the Chinese.

SHAPED CHARGE. See quots. (Also attrib.)—1950 *Time* 31 July p. 27/1 (pict. caption) The Big Bazooka (3.5 in.) shoots an 8½-lb. rocket whose shaped charge can penetrate about eleven inches of armor . . . N. Y. *Times Mag.* 6 Aug. p. 14/3-4 The shaped charge shell's explosives are so packed that a hollow cavity is left at the front; that is, an empty cone is shaped out in the charge. When the shell strikes, the explosive gases and material rush into this hollow space, which is the point of least resistance, and then emerge in a concentrated and mighty blast. *Life* 18 Sept. p. 78/2 The shaped charge gets its name from the inverted cone hollowed out into the explosive. . . . The inverted cone acts as a funnel, directing all the force of the blast through one small area. *Ibid.* 23 Oct. p. 67/1 The startling picture below . . . shows a thin jet of steel particles coming through the armor plate and reaching 30,000 feet per second. . . . This steel jet driven through the nose of a shaped-charge shell is what was used to stop the Red tanks in Korea.

TWEETER, *n.* 1949 cited in *Am. Sp.* 25:229. Add earlier illus.—1939 *Broadcast Receivers and Phonographs for Classroom Use* (N.Y.: Committee on Scientific Aids to Learning, Sept.) In order to reproduce more of the high frequencies, small speakers are sometimes added. These speakers commonly go under the name of 'tweeters.' 1948 *Consumers' Research Bulletin* Oct. p. 21.

AMONG THE NEW WORDS

I. WILLIS RUSSELL
University of Alabama

ACKNOWLEDGMENTS: For citations, Rossiter Bellinger (1), Dwight L. Bolinger (1), Atcheson L. Hench (4), Mamie J. Meredith (15), Allen Walker Read (3), George Pope Shannon (2), Peter Tamony (5), and Grant Turnblom (1). Thanks are also due the University of Alabama Research Committee for secretarial aid.

SYMBOLS: A date immediately following a word or definition indicates the time of evidence shown in the *DAE*, or if so stated, in another publication. Dates in brackets indicate the time, etc., of British usage. An asterisk after a word indicates that the word is illustrated before 1600.

ARENA STAGING, ARENA THEATRE. Also *arena* (attrib.) [Cf. *OED*, *s. v. arena* 'The central part of an amphitheatre . . . {1627-}] See quots. See *central staging, circle staging, theatre-in-the-round.*—1948 *Theatre Arts* June p. 58; cited *Read. Guide* 16:1992/1 (title) Round and round; central staging, theatre-in-the-round, or arena theatre. 1950 N.Y. *Times* 11 June p. X1/1 For arena staging or central staging or theatre-in-the-round, as it is variously known, is a practical form of theatre producing and just as logical as the proscenium or picture-frame stage. *Theatre Arts* June p. 52 (picture cap.) The Lambertville (N.J.) Musical Circus, a tent show operated by St. John Terrell, presents revivals of light operas, arena style, on the banks of the Delaware River. N.Y. *Times* 16 July p. X1/2 Nor are the outdoor scenes especially difficult in arena staging. *Ibid.* 1 Oct. p. X3/3 The two most solid dramatic theatres in Houston are non-professional, community-type organizations—the twenty-six-year-old Little Theatre and the four-year-old Alley, a so-called 'arena' establishment. 1951 *ibid.* 10 June p. X1/1 For purposes of Broadway simplicity, theatre-in-the-round, circle or central staging, is here going to be called arena theatre, and it refers to the increasingly prevalent form in which the actors perform the play in the centre of a room.

BALTIC WALL. See quots.—1950 *Newsweek* 24 April p. 28 From what Western intelligence has learned, the Russians are bulwarking the Baltic seacoasts of East Germany, Poland, and the Soviet Union itself with a Baltic Wall which may make Hitler's Atlantic Wall look like sand dunes. B'ham *News* 10 Oct. p. 25/1 (AP) These indicate that with its iron hand Russia has. . . . Replaced Nazi Germany's 'north wall' with a still more extensive 'Baltic Wall' of defense.

BERKELIUM, *n.* [*Berkeley* + *-ium*] See quots.—1950 San Fran. *Examiner* 15 Jan. p. 1/4 The new element No. 97 in the atomic scale with a weight in the atomic scale above 242, probably will be named Berkelium in honor of the university's home town. N.Y. *Times* 22 Jan. p. E13/5 The new element has been provisionally named 'berkelium' and given the chemical symbol Bk . . . *Time* 30 Jan. p. 73/3 Proposed name for No. 97: 'berkelium' (pronounced berklium), in honor of Berkeley . . . *Sci. N. L.* 25 March p. 182/2.

CALIFORNIUM, *n.* [*California* + *-ium*] See quots.—1950 Lincoln *Journal* 17 March p. 2 (UP) Scientists have created a new element—Californium—carrying the heaviest atom ever known, it was announced Friday. Balto. *Sun* 18 March p. 3/1 Element 98 is the sixth new substance to be found by atom smashing methods. The discoverers has [sic] suggested 98 be named californium *Sci. N. L.* 25 March p. 182/1 Creation of the 98th and heaviest chemical element through atomic bombardment in the University of California 60-inch cyclotron has been made known. It has been christened californium, honoring the university and state . . . N.Y. *Times* 26 March p. E9/5 Recently discovered element 98, named californium after the University of California and the state, is the heaviest atom known, standing six steps up the periodic table from uranium, the most massive atom in nature. *Time* 27 March p. 80/3.

CALL-UP, *v.* '. . . to summon to the colours according to military status or grade' (*OED Sup.*, *s. v. call*, 35 {1830-}).—CALL-UP, *n.*—1941 D. Reed *Prophet at Home* p. 264 I had suggested . . . that the rate of the call-up was too slow. 1945 *Strand Mag.* Nov. p. 25/1 The blitzes, the call-up of drivers, and the impossibility of replacing either men or material, have reduced London's cab fleet to less than half its pre-war strength. 1950 N.Y. *Times* 27 Aug. p. 10E/3-5 (under chart) Additions shown in the chart are based on the call-ups announced thus far by the three services. *Ibid.* 29 Oct. p. L46/1 (AP) It said the same system would be used in determining the order in which additional enlisted reservists were ordered to active duty in any future call-up.

CENTRAL STAGING. See *arena staging* and quots. there cited.—1949 *Theatre Arts* March p. 60/1 Because of the tremendous success of central staging in this country there is a tendency to consider it the be-all and end-all of the experimental theatre movement. 1950 N.Y. *Times* 16 July p. X1/1-2 (title) Central Staging.

CIRCLE STAGING, CIRCLE THEATRE. See *arena staging*.

CLUTCH, attrib. 1950 cited in *Am. Sp.* 26:143. Add earlier illus.—1948 Tuscaloosa *News* 7 July p. 12/4 But another reason not generally recognized has been the clutch hitting of shortstop Eddie Joost . . .

DEMOTH(BALL), *v.* See first quot.—1950 *Life* 27 Feb. p. 28 Earth-bound bombers, old B-29's, . . . are preserved in webby plastic coverings and are stored in scattered areas. Some have been demothed for shipment to England. Lincoln *Journal* 2 Aug. p. 8 Navy's Major Need Said Men to Demothball. *Time* 16 Oct. p. 19/3 Phase by phase . . . , here is how U.S. preparedness would probably look . . . [¶] Navy: By next June, 500,000 men and more than 900 ships, including . . . two battleships (the *Missouri* . . . and the *New Jersey*, now being demothballed) . . .

DISPOSABLE INCOME. See quots.—1948 *Nebraska Resources Bull.* vol. 1, no. 3 (Aug.), p. 3 'Disposable income,' then, represents the money actually available for consuming power, for savings and for investments. B'ham *News—Age-Her.* 15 Aug. p. 1B/8 (AP) The increase plus the cut in income tax payments boosted disposable income—the amount available to consumers for spending after taxes are paid—more than 4 per cent over first quarter figures. Lincoln *Journal* 28 Nov. p. 5-B Each month an enlarging proportion of disposable income goes toward payments on past purchases of automobiles . . . furniture, etc. 1951 N.Y. *Times* 6 May p. 2E/6 The country's total meat bill generally runs to about 5½ to 6½ per cent of the disposable income . . .

FRAME OF REFERENCE. [*OED, s. v. frame*, sb., 4, 'An established order, plan, scheme, system, *esp.* of government' {1599-}; *OED Sup., s. v. frame*, sb., 4.d. '*Frame of reference:* a set of coordinates by means of which the movements of a body or group of bodies are described.' {1929}]—See quot. 1944.—1935 *Harper's Mag.* Feb. p. 345/1 They are cast, as the physicists say, in different frames of reference, and their conclusions cannot be compared without considerable violence to both logic and statistics. 1942 Anne Cleveland and Jean Anderson *Vassar—a Second Glance* (Poughkeepsie) When we consider the integral relationships unquestionably inherent in such a frame of reference, it becomes apparent that certain basic characteristics hitherto attributed by scholars to external influences, or assumed to have been superimposed at a later date, must of necessity . . . 1944 Henry P. Fairchild (ed.) *Dictionary of Sociology* (N.Y.: Philosophical Lib.) p. 123/2 frame of reference . . . a connected set of 'facts' and 'axioms' in reference to which members of a group do their thinking, their defining of situations, their conceiving of personal and group rôles in such situations, and their communicating of such thoughts and attitudes. 1950 *Antioch Rev.* Summer p. 253 And his theories indicated that, while he was a relativist, he more or less held that a fact had the character of factualness within its proper frame of reference. 1951 *Sat. Rev. Lit.* 27 Jan. p. 16/2 Yet I am less impressed with the novel than I would have been if Mr. Bates had furnished somewhere in it some frame of reference for these shocking events. N.Y. *Times Book Rev.* 20 May p. 7/3 And Mr. Blanshard's 'frame of reference' for his whole discussion is secular.

MCCARTHYISM, *n.* [Joseph R. *McCarthy* + *-ism*] See quots.—1950 N.Y. *Post* 5 April p. 44/1 (Max Lerner) To call McCarthyism a fascist atmosphere would be descriptive enough. . . . The atmosphere surrounding McCarthyism is this atmosphere of decay. B'ham *News* 27 April p. 21/2 (Marquis Childs) Over all is the screaming obbligato of McCarthyism, like a distracting blast on a steam calliope. *Ibid.* 3 May p. 27/3-4 (M. L. Arrowsmith) Right off, he [Owen Lattimore] struck out at what he called threats to academic freedom from 'McCarthyism.' *Ibid.* 9 May p. 14/5 (Walter Lippmann) If that were to become the practice, if McCarthyism were to become recognized as legitimate or even tolerable senatorial behavior, then the great principle of the constitution would be in jeopardy. *Ibid.* 18 June p. E3/1 (Marquis Childs) You hear the question frequently asked in Washington: when will McCarthyism end? It is asked by those who feel . . . that the technique of smear and countersmear is doing infinite harm to the political and moral life of the nation. *Newsweek* 26 June p. 12 Democrats are confident the tide of 'McCarthyism' is ebbing. *Sat. Rev. Lit.* 30 Sept. p. 38/3. 1951 B'ham *News* 3 March p. 4/6 (Drew Pearson's staff) The real danger of McCarthyism is summed up in an eye-opening editorial in The St. Louis Post-Dispatch of Feb. 18: 'Gloomy Washington prophets are forecasting a period of "the big lie," of the furtive informer, of the character assassin, of inquisition, eavesdropping, smear and distrust. They lump the whole under the term McCarthyism, a common noun derived, as in the past other expressions have been taken, from personalities such as Judge Lynch, Capt. Boycott and Vidkun Quisling.' *New Republic* 26 March p. 7/2 The Tennessee state legislature has tossed out two stringent antisubversive bills, introduced by Sen. Frank Taylor and modeled after Maryland's Ober law. The fight showed how McCarthyism can be met and routed when active opposition is advanced. N.Y. *Times* 15 April p. E1/6 This conflict was intensified by the long-drawn-out controversy over 'McCarthyism'—the charge by Senator Joseph R. McCarthy that the Communists' gains in the Far East have resulted from 'softness' toward communism in the Administration, particularly in the State Department under Secretary Acheson.

MAMBO, *n.* See quots.—1948 San Fran. *Call-Bull.* 17 Sept. p. 11/1 Tony DeMarco predicts the new dance fad will be 'The Mambo,' which was introduced at Havana-Madrid last week. A zingier form of rhumba. 1950 N.Y. *Daily Mirror* 14 March p. 5 No special talent is required to learn the tango, fox trot or the exotic rumba, samba and mambo. *Newsweek* 4 Sept. p. 76 Basically speaking, the difference between the rumba and the mambo is the difference between the regular foxtrot and the jitterbug. 1951 *Time* 9 April p. 38/3 Part rumba and part jive, with a strong dash of itching powder, the mambo had left unstormed only the tango strongholds of Argentina and the sambaland of Brazil.

RE-, REEXAMINIST, *n.* See quots.—1950 N.Y. *Times* 19 Nov. p. 36/3 Secretary Acheson, noting that isolationists were supposed to be extinct, said 'there is a new species that has come on the horizon and this new species I call the "re-examinist": because the re-examinist says, "I want to re-examine all our policies and all our programs."' Balto. *Sun* 23 Nov. p. 1/2 Dean Acheson . . . today softened his previous remarks about the 're-examinists' and asserted that he intends to continue consulting with Republican congressional leaders about foreign policy. *Newsweek* 27 Nov. p. 20 To the already overloaded *lexicon* of politics, Secretary of State Dean Acheson last week added a new epithet—'reexaminist.' . . . 'The re-examinists' were a new breed of isolationists, Acheson declared, comparing them with 'a farmer who goes out . . . and pulls up all his crops to see how they've done during the night.' *Time* 27 Nov. p. 16/1.

SHOP*, *v. i.* {1764-}—*v. t.*—1943 *Read. Dig.* Aug. p. 124/2 We shopped drugstores, restaurants, and clothing stores. Tuscaloosa *News* 22 Dec. p. 10 (adv.) Its [sic] Never Too Late to Shop Sokol's! 1947 B'ham *News* 1 July p. 8 (adv.) Shop Sears Wednesdays. 1950 Tuscaloosa *News* 25 Oct. p. 11/5 (AP) The 41-year-old Appling . . . indicated he may shop the majors to play 'three or four more years.' 1951 B'ham *News* 7 June p. 2/2 (Sylvia Porter) Many of us will prefer to shop his wares . . .

SUBMINIATURE, *n.* (Also attrib.)—1949 *Aviation Week* 11 April p. 18 (title) Subminiatures Call for New Skills. *Ibid.* 11 April p. 18/1 Since both research and tactical missiles are expendable, it is essential that subminiature electronic equipment have a high producibility. 1950 *Sci. Dig.* Sept. p. 36/1 The vice-president of one flight instrument concern thinks subminiature parts will be hitting the commercial market on a large scale 'within five years.'

SUBMINIATURIZATION, *n.* See quots.—1949 *Aviation Week* 11 April p. 18/1 Not content with 'miniaturization' of electronic equipment for airborne installations, engineers are now utilizing 'subminiaturization' of this material to reduce its size and weight. 1950 *Sci. Dig.* Sept. p. 35/1 The experts call it 'subminiaturization.' Break down the tongue-twister and it means something like the process of making something smaller than small. . . . [¶] They're turning out radio tubes no bigger than paper clips, and fingernail sized transformers . . .

THEATRE(-ER)-IN-THE-ROUND, THEATER IN THE ROUND. See quots.; see also *arena staging*.—1949 N.Y. *Times* 31 July p. X1/3-7 (picture cap.) Mr. Hirschfeld renders his impression of theatre-in-the-round as it is being practiced in the novel summer tent theatre started this season at Lambertville, N.J. 1950 *Newsweek* 1 May p. 71/1 And he would be the last to claim that theater in the round is a new idea. N.Y. *Times* 11 June p. 22/1-2 What, exactly, is theatre-in-the-round? It is theatre in which the audience surrounds the stage and becomes, to some degree, a participant in the action. There are no footlights, no curtain (a blackout indicates breaks), and, as a rule, no scenery. Some stage properties are used and lighting is from the top. Balto. *Sun* 26 July p. 10/2 The Arena, New York's first theatre-in-the-round, has been as successful with its initial musical attraction as it was with a modern comedy and with Shakespeare. *Life* 14 Aug. p. 65/1-2 But the audiences that have been crowding into the tiny Circle Theater in Hollywood (a 'theater in the round,' where the spectators sit on all sides of the square stage) have reported that the illusion of an older and courtlier day is kept up for surprisingly long stretches.

THIRD FORCE. See quots. (Also attrib.)—1948 Washington *News* 23 Feb. A phrase has come into use here which may have political significance in days ahead—the 'third force.' It is borrowed from Europe and is used to describe the non-Communist left. 1950 *Sat. Rev. Lit.* 25 Feb. p. 11 The 'third force' represents a decision to avoid a clash within and a war between countries. Balto. *Sun* 22 June p. 1/2 The 'Third Force' movement, calling for a united western Europe standing between the United States and Russia in support of world peace, was reported today to be gaining momentum in western Germany. *Sat. Rev. Lit.* 18 Nov. p. 33 I don't think we should expect angelic standards of democracy, but we must avoid what would be a stench in the nostrils to the decisive Third Force (anti-Communist, anti-Fascist) marginal peoples all over the world who will swing the balance of the struggle, whether in peace or war. 1951 *Brit. Book of the Year* pp. xxvii-xxviii Presently certain Asiatic powers together with Arab states, who looked upon themselves as a neutral third force in this conflict [between free and totalitarian nations], offered their mediation. N.Y. *Times* 14 Jan. p. 1/4 (AP) The Yugoslav Communist leaders are prepared to collaborate with all Socialist and progressive movements in the West as a third force to help preserve peace. *Fortune* Feb. p. 113 In Europe, especially in France, there has developed an important political philosophy referred to as the Third Force, whose admirable aim is to segregate out the extremes of left and right, to create a middle-of-the-road democracy, free of totalitarian control, whether Communist or Fascist. *Atlantic Monthly* March p. 45. *Specif.* See quots. (Also attrib.)—1947 San Fran. *Chronicle* 14 Dec. p. 5/3-4 There is widespread public interest in the birth of a 'Third Force' to cushion the test of strength between the followers of General de Gaulle and Communist Maurice Therez. 1948 *Nation* 10 Jan. p. 44 (title); cited *Read. Guide* 16:1574/2. 1949 France's third force. 1950 N.Y. *Times Book Rev.* 9 July p. 5/5-24/5 'Third Force' Socialism, as he [Professor Robert Brady] calls the peculiar British variety, adds up to 'a highly unstable set of compromises,' which is a good way of putting it. 1951 N.Y. *Times Mag.* 10 June p. 10 Of these, fifteen parties might be called nationally important, but only five have captured the international spotlight: the authoritarian Gaullists, the Communists, and the three major parties of the 'Third Force'—the Socialists, Popular Republicans and Radical Socialists. *Life* 18 June p. 36/3.

AMONG THE NEW WORDS

I. WILLIS RUSSELL

University of Alabama

ACKNOWLEDGMENTS: For citations, O. B. Emerson (1), Atcheson L. Hench (2, including the earlier illustration of *shaped charge*), Mamie J. Meredith (3), and Peter Tamony (3, including the earliest illustrations of *beef up* and *litterbug*). Thanks are also due the University of Alabama Research Committee for secretarial aid.

SYMBOLS: A date immediately following a word or definition indicates the time of evidence shown in the *DAE*, or, if so stated, in another publication. Dates in brackets indicate the time, etc., of British usage. An asterisk after a word indicates that the word is illustrated before 1600.

BEEF,* *v.* 'To put more muscle into, to drive harder. *U. S.* (College slang.)' {1860} (*OED Sup.*)—'beef up! Pull especially hard!, "put some beef into it": nautical (-1903)' (Partridge *Dict. of Slang and Unconventional Eng.*, Macmillan, 1950).—BEEF UP, *v. t.* Build up strongly; see quots. under *adj.*— 1944 *Time* 24 Jan. p. 22/3 This time the Eighth proved that it had beefed up its reserves. . . 1945 *ibid.* 12 March p. 30/2 For four weeks the Germans had nervously watched as Marshal Georgo K. Zhukov beefed up a tremendous force for the assault aimed at Berlin. 1946 *Think* Oct. p. 11/2 Up to this stage [in aviation] the only problems had been how to 'beef up' the structure, cut down air resistance and pile in the power. 1947 *Time* 5 May p. 22/3 Army troops at parade rest, Scouts (boy & girl), and high-school cadets were to line the route of march from the airport to the White House, and Government workers were to be dismissed at 4 P.M. on arrival day—to beef up the sidewalk crowds. 1951 Tuscaloosa *News* 20 Aug. p. 1/8 (UP) Three more aircraft carriers will be beefed up to handle atomic bombers. . . the Navy announced today. BEEFED-, BEEFED UP, *adj.* 1942 Baughman *Aviation Dict.* p. 44/2. 1945 *Time* 2 April p. 24/2 Lieut. General Courtney Hicks Hodges' First Army had begun to burst the seams of its beefed-up bridgehead along a 35-mile front. 1947 *College Standard* beefed up. . . . Strengthened or reinforced to increase load capacity; said of an aircraft. 1951 *Bus. Week* 17 March p. 88 (adv.) Beefed-up Plastics Move in on Metals. BEEFING UP.—1945 *Time* 10 Sept. p. 92/2. 1951 *Bus. Week* 28 April p. 44 (title) Beefing up Planes by Integral Ribs.

BRAINWASHING, BRAIN WASHING. See quots.—1951 *Am. Jour. of Psychiatry* Feb. p. 595/2, n. 1 In the newly authoritarian countries the term 'brainwashing' is born to indicate this systematic breaking down of old loyalties and paternal ties. N.Y. *Times* 11 March p. E9/6 In totalitarian countries the term 'brainwashing' has been coined to describe what happens when resistance fighters are transformed into meek collaborators. Dr. Meerloo cites S. K. Swift's 'Cardinal's Story' to show

how Mindszenty was spiritually softened until he became putty in the hands of his persecutors. *Time* 8 Oct. p. 39/1 From Hong Kong last week, *Time* Correspondent Robert Neville cabled a survey of brain washing in Red China: . . .

CARPET BOMBING, RAID. See *Am. Sp.* 26:208/2. Delete 'Also *carpet*,' and enclose in square brackets quots. from *Rich. Times Dispatch* and *Sat. Eve. Post.*

FILL-IN, *v.* {1840}—*n.* A brief sketch of the background.—1946 *Sat. Rev. Lit.* 20 July p. 24/3 . . . George Holmes . . . had given the President a fill-in on Stimson's literary background. 1948 B'ham *News* 19 July p. 1/8 (AP) 'They gave the president a fill-in on the Berlin situation,' Eben Ayers . . . said. 1950 *ibid.* 9 Nov. p. 49/4 (AP) If you're wondering what Tuesday's elections mean in Congress, here's a brief fill-in. 1951 Tuscaloosa *News* 8 March p. 1/7 (UP) Steelman arrived here late yesterday to give the president an up-to-date fill-in on the domestic situation.

GARRISON STATE. See quots. —1950 N.Y. *World-Telegram and Sun* 30 Dec. p. 2/8 (UP) 'How long could we survive holed up in a "garrison state" without an ally in the world?' he asked. 1951 *Time* 15 Jan. p. 12/3 The Administration's military program would cost $20 or $30 billion more a year, turn the U. S. into a garrison state . . . 1951 N.Y. *Times Mag.* 30 Sept. p. 9/2 Orators with greater eloquence than discriminating judgment announce that we are already living in a police or garrison state . . .

LITTER-, LITTERBUG, *n.* See quots.—1947 N.Y. *Her.-Trib.* 13 Feb.; quoted *Am. N. & Q.* 6:183/2 'Litterbug': New York City subway rider who drops newspapers and other litter on the platforms and tracks of the underground system. 1950 Jackson (Tenn.) *Sun* 12 Feb. p. 4 (edit.) The 'Litter-Bug' 1950 *Am. N. & Q.* March p. 189/1 'Litter-Bugs' . . . The New York City Sanitation Department did not invent this word. Several years ago it won a prize contest in San Francisco. 1951 B'ham *News* 4 Feb. p. A1/1 I'm happy to see that a good many folk around here are at war with the litterbug. *Ibid.* 15 Aug. p. 19/4 (headline) New York litterbugs pose major problem, give you red eye.

MENTICIDE, *n.* [menti- + -cide] See quots.—1951 *Am. Jour. of Psychiatry* Feb. p. 595/1 (original passage in italics) Such an organized system of psychological intervention and judicial perversion, in which a powerful tyrant synthetically injects his own thoughts and words into the minds and mouths of the victims he plans to destroy by mock trial, may well be called menticide. *Sci. N. L.* 3 March p. 140/2 Menticide is now the stock-in-trade of all police states. Use is made of the most modern psychiatric techniques to impress the

will of the dictator on his victims. N.Y. *Times* 11 March p. E9/6 This breaking down of the mind Dr. [Joost A. M.] Meerloo calls 'menticide,' a crime worse than genocide, in his opinion.

NEO-FASCISM, *n.* See *neo-fascist.* —1949 *New Repub.* 25 April p. 10/2 From Bavaria, Drew Middleton of the New York *Times* reports 'a political situation in which neo-Fascism and authoritarianism are winning and democracy is losing.' 1951 *Current Hist.* April p. 215/1 . . . for Neo-Fascism, as yet, is a typically European phenomenon just as the arguments of the Neo-Fascist writers are typically European arguments.

NEO-, NEOFASCIST, *adj.* See quots.—1944 B'ham *News* 28 June p. 8/5 (AP) The Swiss Telegraphic Agency Tuesday quoted 'reliable frontier reports' to the effect that the Germans had dissolved the Neofascist movement in Northern Italy and taken over complete administration of all public functions. 1948 *Time* 26 April p. 40/3 She had lost her right to vote, but the fancy villa she occupied was plastered with posters for the neo-Fascist M. S. I. party . . . 1950 N.Y. *Times* 12 March p. 2/2 (headline) Neo-Fascist Group in Austria Recedes. 1951 *Current Hist.* April 213/1 As will be seen later, the designation Neo-Fascist is in itself inaccurate and misleading, yet I shall, for the sake of simplicity, use this adjective in its present and broadly accepted sense. I shall apply it to those who believe and maintain that it would have been better, had National Socialist Germany and Fascist Italy won the last war; who believe that the outcome of that war went against the grain of justice, human progress and history.

OUT - OF - TOWNER, *n.* See quots.—1941 *Read. Dig.* May p. 29/1 Sometimes out-of-towners leave no tip at all. 1942 *Am. Thes. Slang* ¶386.1. 1951 N.Y. *Times* 22 April p. E1/3 Police reported that 7,500,000 New Yorkers and out-of-towners hung out of windows and lined the streets of his nineteen-mile parade route . . . *Bus. Week* 2 June p. 120. B'ham *News* 13 Aug. p. 19/2 (N.Y. date line) Out-of-towners who come to New York City to take a job often decide they'd rather live anywhere except in New York City.

PREPACKAGED, *adj.* See last quot.—1945 *Bus. Week* 18 Aug. p. 91 Swift & Co. and a few smaller packers 15 years ago burned their fingers on union meat cutters' prejudices in an ill-timed effort to market prepackaged frozen meat. 1948 *Christian Sci. Monitor Mag.* 8 May p. 4 (title) Presto! Prepackaged Circus. 1951 N.Y. *Times* 1 April p. F11/2 Prepackaged items have been making considerable headway as super markets gained in size, speeding store traffic by preparing in advance food ordinarily cut or weighed to order.

PRE-, PREPACKAGING, *n.* See

prepackaged. (Also attrib.)—1947 *Printers Ink* 3 Jan. p. 70 (title) Produce marketers survey pre-packaging to stem competition from frozen foods. *Bus. Week* 7 June p. 47 (title) Prepackaging Sells Glassware. 1949 N.Y. *Times* 14 Aug. p. 6F/5 More general adoption of pre-packaging processes for meat and other products can be speeded through demonstrating the technique's value as a competitive cost and price-cutting factor, it was recommended yesterday by packaging industry officials. 1951 *ibid.* 1 April p. F11/2 Food industry sources say that prepackaging, a new method of selling meat, fruit and vegetables, is likely to be curtailed.

RIPPLE, *n.* 'A sound as of rippling water' {1859-} (*OED*).—See quots. (Also attrib.)—1944 *Sh OED Addenda* Ripple, *sb.*[2] Applied to a method of firing torpedoes in succession 1940. 1951 *Life* 18 June p. 54/3 (pict. cap.) Using six rocket launchers with 24 tubes each, the platoon in a matter of seconds blasted Red positions with 144 rounds—a barrage which rocketmen call a 'ripple.' *This Week* 5 Aug. p. 18/2 In ripple fire, the rockets are shot in quick succession, about a tenth of a second apart; the first touch on the pilot's trigger sets off the whole string.

ROAD-, ROADBLOCK, ROAD BLOCK. A barrier across a road (1950 Addenda to *NID*).—*Fig.* See quots.—1945 Tuscaloosa *News* 19 June p. 4/5 . . . the French general is probably the only remaining roadblock to Communism in France. 1949 Richmond *Times Dispatch* 24 Nov. p. 11/1 (headline) Titoism Seen as Road Block to Soviet Plans. 1950 B'ham *News* 1 Dec. p. 1/5 (AP) Senate Democratic Leader Lucas . . . said he held no hope a coalition of Republicans and Southern Democrats would remove the roadblock they set up to stall the measures. 1951 *Christian Century* 14 March p. 323/2 Ratification by the necessary 36 states of the 22nd amendment to the United States Constitution belatedly sets up a roadblock against dictatorship. B'ham *News* 23 May p. 12/6 (Drew Pearson) Wilson's alibi for the roadblock was that his counsel . . . were opposed. N.Y. *Times* 3 June p. E7/7.

SHAPED CHARGE. 1950 cited in *Am. Sp.* 26:210/2. Add earlier illus.—1948 Balto. *Sun* 2 Jan. p. 1/3 The airborne tanker's principal weapon, he holds, should be a light but potent recoilless gun of the new type, using a 'shaped charge' like that of the bazooka.

SWEEPSWINGER, *n.* A member of the crew of a racing shell.—1949 N.Y. *Times Mag.* 12 June p. 48/4 It is for such a moment that hundreds of sweepswingers are sweating it out this week at Gales Ferry and Red Top on Connecticut's Thames River . . . 1951 N.Y. *Times* 18 March p. 45 (pict. cap.) The Oxford Sweepswingers Preparing for Race with

Cambridge. *Ibid.* 8 April p. S3/5-7 (pict. title) Cambridge and Yale Sweepswingers Get Acquainted.

SYMPHONIC DRAMA. See quots.—1950 *Theatre Arts* July p. 54/3 Paul Green calls these plays of his (which combine pageant, drama, music, and festival) symphonic dramas and he says they seem to be fitted to the needs and dramatic genius of the American people. N.Y. *Times* 13 Aug. p. X1/1 Like its predecessors, 'Faith of Our Fathers' is what Mr. Green describes as a 'symphonic drama' with music, dancing, spectacle, brief dramatic episodes and links of historical information spoken by two narrators who stand in a box at one end of the enormous stage. *Ibid.* 1 Oct. p. 1X/7 Down in Washington yesterday the initial season of Paul Green's third symphonic drama, 'Faith of Our Fathers,' came to an end.

TELECON, *n.* [*teletype* + *conversation*] A teletype machine which, by utilizing radio or underwater cable, can send over very long distances messages that are flashed on a screen. (Also attrib.)— 1950 N.Y. *Times* 2 July p. 8E/1 This was the 'telecon' room, equipped with machines that enable officers in Washington to confer with headquarters overseas. Throughout the week, all day long, two-way 'conversations' with General MacArthur's Tokyo headquarters continued. . . . The telecon, essentially, is just a teletype machine, but it has certain modifications which make it especially useful for military communications . . . *Ibid.* 2 July p. E1/3 They sit before the 'telecon' screens . . . 1951 *ibid.* 1 July p. E1/3 They were talked over by telecon with General Ridgway in Tokyo. B'ham *News* 16 Sept. p. A11/4 (NANA) Its huge message center sends and receives communications to and from Korea, Europe, ships at sea, wherever American forces go. Conferences can be held by telephone and teletype—the famous 'telecons'—with participants in far-flung places such as London, Tokyo, and Berlin.

THERMO-, THERMONUCLEAR, *adj.* See quots.—1948 *Time* 30 Aug. p. 56/1 Inside the stars, where the temperature may reach a 'scorching' 20 million degrees centigrade, thermonuclear reactions are constantly at work changing hydrogen into helium. 1950 N.Y. *Times* 22 Jan. p. E13/6 Here the physicist deals with what he calls a 'thermo-nuclear reaction.' *Ibid.* 5 Feb. p. 1/1. 1951 *ibid.* 27 May p. E2/4 'Thermonuclear' is the term applied to the fusion process that would take place in the H-bomb. . . . The fusion process requires fantastic temperatures. *Ibid.* 24 June p. E9/7 Though new information and understanding of the basic phenomena underlying thermonuclear reactions were collected at the recent Eniwetok test, a hydrogen bomb is not even in sight.

AMONG THE NEW WORDS

I. WILLIS RUSSELL
University of Alabama

Acknowledgments: For citations, Clarence L. Barnhart (3), T. L. Crowell (2), O. B. Emerson (2), Atcheson L. Hench (2), Mamie J. Meredith (12), Peter Tamony (1), and Grant Turnblom (1). Thanks are also due the University of Alabama Research Committee for secretarial aid.

AVGAS, *n. Aviation gasoline.* (Also attrib.)—1945 *The Lamp* (Standard Oil of New York) Aug. p. 11/2 When 'avgas' is being pumped, the smoking lamp is off throughout both ships. 1950 *Newsweek* 9 Oct. p. 74 ... the 'avgas' problem stole the show. 1950 *Industrial Arts Index* p. 64/2 (two citations). 1951 *New Words and Words in the News* (Funk & Wagnalls Co.) Sup. No. 7 (Fall) p. 1/1. 1952 *Britannica Book of the Year* p. 741/2.

BIG, GREAT LIE. See quots. (Also attrib.)—1948 *San Francisco News* 30 July p. 2/5 This is a continuation of the Nazi theory of the 'big lie,' expounded by Hitler and Goebbels, that the bigger the lie and the more frequently it is told the more people who would accept it. 1950 *Balto. Sun* 7 Nov. p. 4/2 It was recognized, however, that the Communist charges were part of the now-familiar 'big lie' technique ... *N. Y. Times Book Rev.* 31 Dec. p. 1 (title) How the Big Lie Grows and Grows. 1951 *Friends Intelligencer* 9 June p. 330/1 Dr. Ronald Bridges ... warned that 'the worst weapon of war today is the *great lie*—not just ordinary, old-fashioned lies, but the magnified, increased and stepped-up *lie*.' 1952 *Britannica Book of the Year* p. 741/2.

BIRD*, *n.* '4. In various *fig.* applications ...; as in reference to the winged or noiseless flight, or soaring of birds ...' {1588-} (*OED*)—*Slang.* A guided missile.—1948 *Wall Street Jour.* 23 March p. 1/6 One of the newer uses is in 'birds,' military jargon for guided missiles such as the 'Gargoyle' glide bomb with an auxiliary rocket motor. 1951 *Time* 21 May p. 84/1 These 'birds' (so the missilemen call them) are the heirs presumptive of war. 1952 *N. Y. Times* 9 March p. 4/1 When completed, these stations, together with the launching base and supporting activities here, will provide a completely calibrated and instrumented flight range 1,000 miles long for the 'birds' of weird sizes and shapes that the guided missile designers are now developing.

COOK*, *v. t. Fig.* {1588-}—To make (a substance) radioactive by putting it in a 'furnace' (atomic pile).—1950 *Time* 27 Feb. p. 65/1 Others are formed in aluminum cans of raw material 'cooked' by the pile's neutrons. 1951 *ibid.* 19 Nov. p. 56/2 More cobalt is being 'cooked' for the first U. S. units.

DEPURGE, *v. t.* [*de-* +*purge* (see *NID Add.*)] See last two quots. *s. v. depurgee.*

DEPURGEE, *n.* See quots.—1951 *Time* 2 July p. 34/1 Home from the political wilderness last week came 69,000 Japanese who were banned from public office by General MacArthur 5½ years ago. The 'depurgees' (as they were labeled in army gobbledygook): former leaders of certain nationalistic organizations and onetime 'undesirables' from the press, radio and motion picture industries. *Sat. Rev. Lit.* 18 Aug. p. 23/1 ... Miss Telberg frequently used the terms 'depurge,' 'depurged,' 'depurgee,' a common usage in occupied countries both in Europe and Asia to denote persons once purged for anti-democratic or other acts hostile to the Allies and now restored to good standing. 1952 *B'ham News* 25 Feb. p. 1/4 (AP) The government today depurged 290 war-time leaders, some of them dead. The live depurgees may seek public office.

DIXIECRATIC, *adj.* [*Dixiecrat* (in *NID Add.*)+-*ic*]—1948 *Tuscaloosa News* 14 July p. 4/1 (editorial) It also appears that he will be the choice of States Rights' walkout delegates who apparently will meet Saturday in Birmingham to select a 'Dixiecratic' nominee for President. 1951 *B'ham News* 29 May p. 12 (title) Dixiecratic Debit.

FANZINE, *n.* [*fantasy* +*magazine*] See quots.—1950 *Am. N. & Q.* March p. 184/2 'Fanzines': fantasy magazines, or magazines for fantasy fans; term cited in an article on California writers in the *New York Times Magazine*, May 7, 1950. 1951 *Life* 21 May p. 130/2 Between fanferences they communicate by means of 'fanzines,' or fan magazines, which are usually small mimeographed publications devoted to amateur STF, criticism and gossip.

GLOBAL BOMBER. See quots.—1951 *Balto. Sun* 7 Jan. p. 2/6 (AP) Six American 'global bombers'—giant B-36's which can carry an atom bomb 10,000 miles—roared into this air base today from Texas. *Newsweek* 25 June p. 30. 1952 *Tuscaloosa News* 13 May p. 1/2 (UP) The Air Force today partially lifted the secrecy surrounding its eight-jet B-52 'global' bomber.

GRAY MOBILIZATION. [*gray.* '1. The adjective denoting the colour intermediate between black and white ...' (*OED*); cf. *gray market.*] Incomplete mobilization.—1950 *N. Y. Times* 29 Oct. p. 2E/6 He declared indirect controls are adequate for the country's present 'gray mobilization'. ... Thus much depends on what happens when the gray of mobilization grows darker and the weight of the defense effort ... is more fully felt in industry. [1950 *Newsweek* 11 Dec. p. 67 In Symington's words, the nation would shift from a 'light-gray' to a 'dark-gray' mobilization ...] 1951 *Atlantic Monthly* March p. 6 Wilson has further sharpened the Marshall point by explaining that the significant word in our gray mobilization is industrial capacity.

GROUND ZERO. See quots.—1946 *N. Y. Times* 7 July p. E10/1 The intense heat of the blast started fires as far as 3,500 feet from 'ground zero' (the point on the ground directly under the bomb's explosion in the air) ... 1950 *Time* 21 Aug. p. 16 A mile from 'ground zero' (the point directly under the burst), the speed of the wind drops to 200 m. p. h. ... 1951 *N. Y. Times* 30 Sept. p. E9/7 With two or more such reports, a headquarters unit can determine ground zero and the height of the explosion. *Life* 12 Nov. p. 38/2 Animals were tethered at varying distances from ground zero ... 1952 *N. Y. Times* 27 April p. E2/4 Two thousand troops crouched in fox-holes and open trenches four miles from 'ground zero' ...

HOT*, *adj.* or *adv.* [Cf. 'hotte haste' {*a* 1553}, 'In hot pursuit' {1870}; also 'hot rod,' a rebuilt jalopy capable of high speed.] Fast, with reference to an airplane's landing speed.—1944 *Sat. Eve. Post* 24 June p. 80/2-3 PV's can outrun all but the fastest of Jap fighters, but they pay for their speed by landing hot, with the same steep, whistling plunge as fighter planes. 1951 *N. Y. Times Mag.* 21 Oct. p. 59/2 Certainly, the pure jet does land a little 'hotter' than the propeller plane.

HYDRO-JET, *n.* See quots. (Also attrib.)—1946 *N. Y. Times* 1 July p. C4/3 Other marine engineering developments, ... and a modified hydro-jet (water jet) form of propulsion, are pending. 1951 *ibid.* 26 Aug. p. 2E/4 Or, the reactor might be used in a hydro-jet, in which sea water sucked into a cylinder would be heated; the resultant pressure would thrust the submarine forward in the same way that air thrusts an unclosed toy balloon forward.

INFLUENCE PEDDLER. See quots.—1949 *N. Y. Times* 14 Aug. p. E7/5 The Investigations subcommittee of the Senate Committee on Expenditures in the Executive Departments which is inquiring into the activities of the 'five percenters' and the 'influence peddlers' has discovered that selling influence may be unethical, but it is not always illegal. 1951 *Newsweek* 2 April p. 13. 1952 *B'ham Post-Her.* 7 Jan. p. 4/1 When he took over the Reconstruction Finance Corp., after it had been riddled by influence peddlers and favor-givers, Mr. Symington said he wanted the office to 'bristle with integrity.'

INFLUENCE PEDDLING.—1951 *Tuscaloosa News* 15 March p. 2/3 (AP) Nixon said he will continue to insist that a Senate committee investigating 'influence peddling' get to the bottom of the matter. *B'ham News* 9 Dec. p. 17A/5 (NANA) It's a matter of 'influence peddling' in obtaining steel applied to an industry basis.

PARA-MEDIC, *n.* [*para-* (see 1950 *NID Add.*)+*medic*] See first quot. (Also attrib.)—1951 *N. Y. Sunday Mirror* 8 April p. 3 Para-medics from air-sea rescue squadrons based at March Air Force Base were in the search planes, ready to parachute with medical aid should there be any sign of life around the wreckage. 1952 *B'ham News* 21 Jan. p. 12/2-3 (AP) Three other men, presumably thrown from the plane during its plunge, were listed as missing. A para-medic team of four pressed a search for them.

PETRO-, PETROCHEMICAL, *n.* [*petroleum*] See quot. from *Du Pont Mag.*—1948 *Industrial Arts Index* (two citations). 1949 *New Words and Words in the News* (Funk & Wagnalls Co.) Sup. No. 2 (Spring) p. 3/1. 1950 *N. Y. Times* 19 Nov. p. 1F/3 Petrochemicals, which are derived from the vast supplies of petroleum and natural gas available in the South, are the bellwether of the country's chemical economy, according to Frank J. Soday ... 1952 *Du Pont Mag.* March p. 25 Similar as they sound, petroleum chemicals and petrochemicals are opposites. Petrochemicals are made by the oil men and used by the chemist. Petroleum chemicals ... are made by the chemical industry for use in the oil industry's gasoline and lubricants.—*adj.*—1948 *Industrial Arts Index* (two citations). 1949 *New Words and Words in the News* Sup. No. 2 p. 3/1. 1952 *N. Y. Times* 13 July p. 4F/6 Continental stated that the plant will be operated by its petrochemical department ...

PETROCHEMISTRY, *n.* See quots.—1949 *New Words and Words in the News* Sup. 2 p. 3/1. 1951 *The Lamp* (Standard Oil of N. J.) June p. 4 Some chemists are bothered by the name (petrochemistry) because the root 'petro' means rock, not oil. 1952 *Service* Jan. p. 13 This record ... indicates something of the speed with which petrochemistry has been growing ... *N. Y. Times* 3 Feb. p. F5/4 What is petrochemistry? [¶] Simply the study of oil—petroleum, its components and its uses and its possibilities.

QUARTERBACK, *n.* 1879.—*v. t.* Direct, plan, guide.—1945 *Life* 1 Oct. p. 118/2 Joint meetings are held regularly and Young Henry quarterbacks them. 1952 *B'ham News* 24 Jan. p. 10/2 (AP) Sen. Russell ... who usually quarterbacks filibusters for his Southern colleagues, has declared repeatedly he would fight any move to change the rule. *Ibid.* 24 June p. 14/6 ... Sen. Pat McCarran has quarterbacked many a fast one in the Senate ...

ROCK*, *n. Baseball.* A boner.—1951 *B'ham News* 31 July p. 16/3 (AP) How does a guy who has been labeled 'the perfect player' feel after pulling his first 'rock' in a long and brilliant baseball career? 1952 *This Week* 20 April p. 15/1 Manager Casey Stengel said, 'I may have pulled a rock last year when I played him in right field ...' *B'ham News* 20 July p. B-3/2 (AP) Even in winning, a baseball manager can pull a rock.

SERVICE MARK.—1945 *Bus. Week* 30 June p. 86/2 A separate register would be authorized for 'service' marks to identify services rather than merchandise. This register would include 'names, symbols, titles, designations, slogans, character names, and distinctive features of radio or other advertising used in commerce.' 1946 *ibid.* 20 July p. 82/2 The new law [Lanham Act] will also admit 'service marks' (those applied to services rather than goods) . . . 1949 *Fortune* Feb. p. 147/2 In 1947 Congress passed the Lanham Act, which covers all sorts of marks used in commerce 'over which Congress has control'—trademarks (e.g., Kodak), service marks (e.g., Greyhound), and certification marks (e.g., the Good Housekeeping seal). 1950 *Radio Age* April p. 29 'Service mark' is a relatively new term in the Trade Mark Division of the Patent Office.

AMONG THE NEW WORDS

I. WILLIS RUSSELL

University of Alabama

As a glance at the glossary in this issue will reveal, the term *whistle stop*, recorded as early as 1934, was extremely active linguistically during the presidential campaign just passed. A few additional points can be better treated here.

When asked by a commentator on a CBS television program last October 18 what he knew about the term *whistle stop*, a railroad man replied that it was a political term, that railroad men said *flag stop*. Sure enough, reference to the *Official Guide of the Railways* soon turns up two examples of *flag stop* (July, 1952, pp. 518, 582). How old the word phrase is I do not know; Mencken (1936) has it, and it would doubtless show up in earlier issues of the *Official Guide*, none of which is available to me. But the general and slang dictionaries I have consulted are curiously silent on the phrase; only the 1950 *Webster* Addenda Section has it. The more common term seems to be *flag station*, which appears in all the dictionaries. It is an Americanism dating from 1849, and is defined by the *DAE* as 'a railroad station at which trains stop only when signaled' and by the *ACD* as 'a railroad station where trains stop only when a flag or other signal is displayed or when one or more passengers are to be discharged.'

Even though railroad men use *flag stop* rather than *whistle stop*, the two are connected and have a similar origin. According to an editorial writer in the Jackson (Tenn.) *Sun*,

A 'whistle-stop,' in railroad terms, is a community too small to enjoy regular scheduled service. Customarily, the passenger trains whiz right by. But if there are passengers to be discharged, shortly before the train approaches the station, the conductor signifies that fact by pulling the signal cord. The engineer responds with two toots of the whistle. Naturally enough, such unscheduled pauses became known as 'whistle-stops.' The communities were 'whistle-stop towns,' shortened in the course of time to 'whistle-stops.'

This practice is similar to that on the Western Maryland Railway, as I recall it some thirty-five years ago. At a designated place about a mile from a flag station, the engineer would blow one long blast on his whistle. If he saw a green flag displayed at the station (indicating a passenger to get on) or if he heard his cab signal whistle three times (indicating a passenger to get off), he would acknowledge by giving three toots on his locomotive whistle. (I have even seen a conductor repeat his signal when the engineer failed to make an acknowledgment.) It would appear, then, that from one point of view,

such a station is a *flag station* or *flag stop*; from another, it is a *whistle stop*. In either case, it is a small town where a given train 'stops on flag' or 'stops on signal to take or leave passengers' (typical explanations of the *f* preceding an arrival time found in *Official Guide*, pp. 1093, 991).

An INS dispatch (printed in the Denver *Post*, 29 Sept. 1952, p. 35/2) runs in part as follows: 'President Truman said Monday that Senator Taft (Rep.) of Ohio invented the phrase, "whistle-stop." The president told a crowd at Fargo, N.D.: "You know, that phrase was invented by Senator Taft on Oct. 8, 1948. The Republicans were trying to make fun of my efforts to take the issues in that campaign directly to the people all over the country." ' As is shown by the citations below of the *DA*, Weseen, and Berry and Van den Bark, the term was in use before the 1948 campaign and Senator Taft cannot have invented it in that year. It is not impossible, however, that he may have been the first to give it currency as a political phrase.

Not specifically noted in the glossary but implied by some of the citations is a semasiological development of *whistle stop* pointed out by the Jackson *Sun* editorial writer already quoted. He writes:

As applied to modern political campaigning, the term is quite inaccurate. Campaign trains now pause only at relatively populous centers. These stops are carefully charted and precisely timed well in advance. Everyone concerned has known for days when the train will arrive and the moment it is due to depart. Advance bulletins have been dispatched to the local party leaders, thus assuring that The Right People will be at the right place at the right time.

If the reader will turn to the first quotation under *whistle stopper* in the glossary, he will see a reference to 'the biggest "whistle stop" of them all': this was New York City, hardly a whistle stop in the usual sense of the term.

Acknowledgments: For citations, Henry Alexander (1), T. L. Crowell (1), O. B. Emerson (4), Atcheson L. Hench (2), Mamie J. Meredith (7), and Peter Tamony (2). Elliott V. K. Dobbie supplied the material for the etymology of *apartheid*, and O. B. Emerson pointed out the editorial in the Jackson *Sun*. Thanks are also due the University of Alabama Research Committee for secretarial aid.

AEROPAUSE, *n.* See quots.—1951 *Time* 19 Nov. p. 68/3 Last week the Air Force School of Aviation Medicine held a symposium at San Antonio on the dangers that will crowd around explorers of the aeropause. [Footnote:] Variously defined, but meaning in general the region above the present ceilings of 'inhabited aircraft,' *i.e.*, above 75,000 feet. 1952 *N.Y. Times* 27 July p. E9/5 At an altitude of 79,000 feet, which has been attained by a supersonic plane, there is only about 4 per cent as much air as at sea level, and at a height of 250 miles, a record made in 1949 when the WAC Corporal was fired from the nose of a V-2 rocket, there is virtually a vacuum. Drs. Konrad J. K. Buettner and Heinz Haber, physicists in the University of California at Los Angeles, Calif., suggest that this region be called the 'aeropause.'

APARTHEID, *n.* [Du. separation; Du. *apart, adj.*, separate + *-heid*, -ness] See quots. (Also attrib.)—1949 *Christian Cent.* 16 Nov. p. 1348/2 A recent dispatch from Johannesburg to Religious News Service tells of three national denominational conferences just held, in each of which condemnation of *apartheid* (segregation) measures occupied the top spot on the agenda. *New Words and Words in the News* (Funk & Wagnalls Co.) Sup. No. 3 Fall p. 1/1. 1950 *Life* 18 Sept. p. 114/1–2 Under *apartheid*, each group (white, black, Asiatic and Coloured, or half-caste) must live apart from others, except in a master-and-servant or trade relationship. 1952 *N.Y. Times* 23 March p. 2E/2 The key plank in its program was *apartheid*—pronounced apart-hate—meaning literally apartness, in effect, separation of all races. *Friends Intelligencer* 16 Aug. pp. 467–68 Today the policy of *Apartheid* as defined by the National Party in power 'accepts the Christian guardianship of the European race as the basic principle of its policy with regard to the non-European races and desires to furnish them with the opportunity to develop themselves in their own areas in accordance with their natural genius and capacity, and to ensure for them fair and just treatment in the administration of the country. It is definitely opposed to any miscegenation between European and non-European races and favors the territorial, political, residential, and, as far as possible, industrial separation of Europeans and non-Europeans.'

DRUG-, DRUGFASTNESS, *n.* See 1952 quot.—1946 *Time* 15 July p. 94/2 Though bacterial 'drug-fastness' is a serious problem for medical researchers, Dr. Molitor believes there is yet no cause for public anxiety. 1952 Omaha *World-Her.* 6 Jan. p. 10-B It soon became evident that the organisms or germs which the antibiotic controlled had the ability to alter themselves so that the drug was no longer effective against them. This is called drugfastness.

GRAYOUT, GREY OUT, *v. i.* To become semiconscious.—1945 *Read. Dig.* May p. 43/2 Formerly a pilot had only two choices: . . . or go in all the way and turn sharply, incurring enough G to grayout or blackout. 1952 *Time* 28 April p. 72/2 And at 4.2 Gs the average man begins to 'grey out.' Blood drains from his head. His sight begins to blur.

HACKIE, *n.* See 1950 quot.—1949 Tuscaloosa *News* 25 July p. 4/3 If you don't know a good, clean reasonably-priced one [hotel], ask the hackie. 1950 *Read. Dig.* June p. 103 I've been a New York hackie for almost 30 years now, mostly on the night shift. I *like* driving a cab. . . .

IN-, INFIGHTING, *n.* 'In pugilism: Fighting or boxing at close quarters . . .' {1816} (*OED*)—*Fig.* Contention usually among members of the same group.—1948 *Time* 2 Feb. p. 54/3 Mrs. Scott is understandably possessive and protective of her daughter, but does her best to avoid the infighting among 'skating mamas.' 1950 Tuscaloosa *News* 30 April p. 10/4 (NEA) The in-fighting on the negro issue is heavy. *Life* 30 Oct. pp. 30–31 (heading) Candidates Get Down to Infighting in the Battle to Control Congress. 1951 Tuscaloosa *News* 25 April p. 2/4 (AP) In the oratorical infighting here, Senator Wiley . . . proposed that the United Nations be asked to approve aerial attacks on the Manchurian base 'sanctuaries' about which MacArthur complained before Mr. Truman fired him as Pacific commander. 1952 *N.Y. Times* 15 June p. E1/1 Senator Taft's political assault marked the start of the period of intricate infighting—with no holds barred and an occasional thumb in the eye—that will be waged all during the three weeks remaining before the Chicago convention. *Time* 21 July p. 15/1 Through that eye [TV] during the last two days millions of Americans saw political infighting in its most instructive form. . . .

MUDDER, *n. Sport.* Person or thing that performs well under muddy conditions.—1905 cited in *DA* and *OED Sup.* in reference to a race horse. 1942 Berrey and Van den Bark *Amer. Thesaurus of Slang* ¶ 120.39 . . . mudder . . . a horse that runs well in mud. . . . *Ibid.* ¶ 683.1 . . . mudder . . . a [football] player for whom a wet field is no great handicap. . . . 1950 *New Yorker* 11 Nov. p. 121/2 Cornell's last one [fumble] gave Columbia, a remarkably good mudder, the chance to tie the score in the fourth quarter. . . . 1952 *Time* 5 May p. 71/1 But Gehrmann and Druetzler proved no mudders and, though Wilt sloshed along valiantly, Purdue's Denis Johansson, 23, splashed past the leaders on the last lap, all but floated across the finish line to win by 10 yards over Wilt.

PHOTOBIOGRAPHY, *n.* A person's life as revealed through photographs.—1944 Lond. *Spectator* 3 March p. 188/1 . . . a 'photobiography,' consisting of 250 scenes from Woodrow Wilson's life, with 150 pages of letterpress by Gerald W. Johnson . . . is in an advanced stage of preparation . . . 1951 *Publishers' Weekly* 21 April p. 1729 Cecil Beaton has done what he calls 'a photobiography' for Doubleday . . . *Vogue* June p. 72. 1952 N.Y. *Times Book Rev.* 1 June p. 12 In more than 250 skillfully selected and arranged pictures, Editor Hicks has brought out . . . Ike's life from his boyhood . . . to . . . NATO. A 'photobiography' that does not seem likely to lose the general votes in the future.

PROP(ELLER)-STOP, *attrib.* See second quot.—1952 N.Y. *Times Mag.* 12 Oct. p. 11/2 Speech conference with writer Stanley High . . . occupies Eisenhower between 'prop-stop' appearances. Tuscaloosa *News* 21 Oct. p. 1/2 (UP) For his final campaign tour Stevenson dropped his airplane 'propeller-stop' technique and aimed an old-fashioned railroad 'whistle-stop' trip at 12 eastern states with a lucrative total of 206 electoral votes.

PSYCHOLINGUISTICS, *n.* See first quot.—1946 N. H. Pronko 'Language and Psycholinguistics: A Review,' *Psychological Bull.* May p. 213 Theory in Psycholinguistics . . . [Yet, despite a wealth of interest and of work, there seems to be no corresponding increase in our understanding of linguistic responses.] 1951 N.Y. *Times* 19 Aug. p. 59/2 A new field of study, 'psycholinguistics,' has developed out of a meeting at Cornell University of psychologists and linguists from five universities. *The CEA Critic* Oct. p. 4 At Cornell, an eight-week summer seminar on psychological problems of language helped articulate the field of study called 'psycholinguistics.'

STARRY-EYED, *adj.* Visionary.—1948 *Time* 21 June p. 112/3 He was a leader of such starry-eyed, leftish setups as the League for Industrial Democracy and the League of American Writers. 1949 B'ham *News* 28 Sept. p. 3/6 He warns against the belief held by many that the commies are nothing more than starry-eyed theorists or warped disgruntles. 1951 N.Y. *Times* 24 June p. X1 /1 I now come quickly to two major disappointments, lest all this seem a trifle starry-eyed.

WHIRLY-, WHIRLYBIRD, *n.* A helicopter.—1951 *Read. Dig.* Sept. p. 86. *Newsweek* 5 Nov. p. 35 To those who fly it, the helicopter is a whirlybird or a puddle jumper . . . *Life* 29 October p. 36/2 For a year small copters have been used to evacuate wounded, ferry generals, rescue pilots and to carry emergency supplies but this was the first time in history that the 'whirlybirds' had transported a unit as large as a full battalion into a combat area. 1952 *People Today* Jan. p. 3 Thus whirlybirds airlifted almost 11,000 troops to safety . . .

WHISTLE STOP, *n.* [See Preliminary Remarks.] See quots. 1944 (*DA*)—1934 Weseen *Dict. of Amer. Slang* p. 418 Whistle stop—A small town. 1942 Berrey and Van den Bark *op. cit.* ¶776.2 Small Station or Town . . . whistle stop.

WHISTLE-, WHISTLESTOP, WHISTLE STOP, *v. t. & i.*—1952 B'ham *News* 26 July p. 1/3 (AP) In a sort of swan song to the Democratic Party as its leader, he offered to whistle-stop the country for his successor. *Ibid.* 27 Sept. p. 1/5 (headline) Truman leaving tonight to whistle-stop nation. *Ibid.* 6 Oct. p. 1/6 (AP) Whistle-stopping eastward through Utah in behalf of the Stevenson-Sparkman Democratic ticket, the president hit anew at the GOP and its presidential candidate . . . *Time* 13 Oct. p. 23/3 In Michigan last week, nearly 100,000 people turned out to see Eisenhower as he whistlestopped across the state. Nashville *Tennessean* 14 Oct. p. 2/1 (AP) Thursday afternoon he will whistle stop through Windsor Locks and Thompsonville . . . Jackson (Tenn.) *Sun* 20 Oct. p. 1 (headline) Ike Whistlestops in New England.

WHISTLE-, WHISTLE STOPPER, *n.*—1952 B'ham *News* 11 Oct. p. 1/4 (AP) Whistle-stopper Harry S. Truman lent a hand to Adlai Stevenson here Saturday in the biggest 'whistle stop' of them all. Nashville *Tennessean* 11 Oct. p. 2 (headline) Whistle-Stopper Cites General's 'Betrayal.' *This Week* 26 Oct. p. 4 (title) Whistle Stoppers.

WHISTLE-, WHISTLE STOPPING, *vbl. n.*—1952 B'ham *News* 23 Sept. p. 14/5 Ike Eisenhower had settled down to whistle-stopping . . . *Ibid.* 28 Sept. p. D3/1 If this bothers Gen. Eisenhower, or, indeed, occurs to him, there is no sign of it in his current whistle-stopping. Nashville *Tennessean* 14 Oct. p. 2/1 (AP) Then comes more whistle stopping through Exeter and Plaistow . . . B'ham *News* 19 Oct. p. E2/6 In the wake of Gen. Eisenhower's whistle-stopping, his political crew has left behind a blueprint for winning the independent and Democratic vote.

AMONG THE NEW WORDS

I. WILLIS RUSSELL
University of Alabama

ACKNOWLEDGMENTS: For citations: Henry Alexander (1), Clarence L. Barnhart (2), Dwight L. Bolinger (2), Thomas L. Crowell (2), O. B. Emerson (1), Atcheson L. Hench (2), Howard E. Kasch (1), Mamie J. Meredith (11), Porter G. Perrin (1), George Pope Shannon (1), and Peter Tamony (6). Thanks are also due the University of Alabama Research Committee for secretarial aid.

BAFFLEGAB, *n.* [*baffle* + *gab;* see quots.] See quots. — 1952 San Fran. *Call-Bulletin* 4 March p. 8G/1–2 Milton Smith, the assistant general counsel of the U.S. Chamber of Commerce, has coined a new word 'bafflegab' designed solely for Washington bureaucrats, or for UN bureaucrats, for that matter. B'ham *News* 25 March p. 16/2 I still can't swallow it. 'And,' Reeves confessed, 'is just a sample the "bafflegab" our industry uses.' [*sic*] *Ibid.* 26 Oct. p. 20/3–4 'I decided we needed a new and catchy word to describe the utter incomprehensibility, ambiguity, verbosity and complexity of government regulations,' Mr. Smith said. . . [¶] So he set to work. . . First he scribbled down 'legalfusion,' 'legalprate,' 'gabalia,' and 'burobabble.' Then 'gab,' 'prate,' and 'baffling.' [¶] Still weary and ill at ease, he suddenly struck on [*sic*] mighty chord—bafflegab. 1953 *Ibid.* 9 Feb. p. 19/4 Even I—and I've been exposed for an awfully long time to financial bafflegab—squirmed uncomfortably. . .

BUCK ROGERS, *attrib.* [from the comic strip character of the same name.] Fantastically ingenious; see also quots. — 1946 *Life* 2 Sept. p. 100/2 Alongside the 'Buck Rogers stuff' being bandied about by supposedly feet-on-the-ground military men, the new 10,000-mile B-36 bomber and the B-17 'drones' that flew devoid of crew from Hawaii to the West Coast seem scarcely more spectacular than a 1946 motor car. 1950 B'ham *News* 8 Oct. p. 2E/6 This guided-missile section could become the nucleus of a separate armed service in any Buck Rogers era of the future. . . 1952 N.Y. *Times* 2 March p. 28/1 This base and its complex of auxiliary fields and supporting installations—the largest Air Force reservation in the country—is a 'Buck Rogers' empire. Here the weird, the strange and the wonderful come to life and cavort about the skies from tree-top level to the stratospheric realms of cold and silence 45,000 feet above the earth. 1953 *Sat. Eve. Post* 13 June p. 31/1 It can panic us into going off half-cocked, and foolishly scrapping things still vital to the national defense because of wild rumors about Buck Rogers type weapons.

CREEPIE-PEEPIE, *n.* A walkie-lookie (which see). Cf. *peepie-creepie.*—1952 *Life* 21 July p. 18 When it worked, the walkie-lookie (a new NBC hand camera which was promptly dubbed a creepie-peepie) did for the visual audience what the roving candid microphone had done for radio listeners.

DEBRIEF, *v.* See *Am. Sp.* 25:74/1.—DE-, DEBRIEFING, *n.* (Also attrib.)—1945 London *Picture Post* 31 March p. 9 Crump and his men go through a medical test, immigration and security formalities, de-briefing and customs. 1951 *Life* 17 Dec. p. 31/2 He went to the debriefing shed and made a routine report on the railroad bombing mission . . . and on MIG activity . . . 1952 *Sat. Eve. Post* 19 July p. 92/2 At the post-mission debriefing in Combat Operations, jaws were wagging a mile a minute.

DECELERON, *n.* [deceleration + aileron. Cf. in *WNID Add.* 1950 *elevon* (*elev*ator + aileron) and *adrenergic* (*adren*aline + en*ergic*).] See quots.—1949 *Sci. N.L.* 2 July p. 3/3 AIR BRAKES—The jaw-like control surfaces shown above at the outer end of the wing trailing edge on a Northrop Scorpion, twin-engine, jet-propelled, all-weather fighting airplane are known as 'decelerons' because they combine the functions of ailerons, fighter brakes and landing flaps. 1952 Tuscaloosa *News* 6 March p. 14 (pict. capt.) The brakes, known as 'decelerons,' make it possible for the plane to descend from 40,000 feet to land in a phenomenally short time while maintaining full control of its speed.

DRAG*, *v.* '3. *intr.* To hang behind with a retarding tendency; to lag in the rear' {1494–1530} (*OED*); '2. To draw along heavily or wearily; as, to *drag* the feet along slowly' (Funk and Wagnalls *New Stand. Dict.*)—*to drag one's feet, elbows. Fig.* To hold back, delay, slow up.—1946 *Life* 20 May p. 69/1 . . . and the Soviets are frankly 'dragging their feet' in making the European peace in order to prolong chaos and thus promote the Communist parties in other European nations. 1952 *Read. Dig.* March p. 93 A good many people are dragging their feet in the fight against inflation. . . *Wall St. Jour.* 13 June p. 1 The senator said we should 'drag our feet' in Korean truce talks until the South Koreans can be armed with U. S. weapons. Cleveland *Plain Dealer* 29 Aug. p. 1/2 (AP) A federal judge said today the Justice Department . . . dragged its feet in investigating last year's tax fraud scandals in St. Louis. Omaha *World-Her.* 31 Aug. p. 3-*A* And what's more, the surplus exists partly because French wine drinkers are dragging their elbows. N.Y. *Times* 14 Sept. p. E3/6 Senator McCarthy is 'their man,' and any affront to him may cause them to drag their feet all the harder.—*Gerund phr.*—1946 San Fran. *News* 27 May p. 8 'There will be no dragging of heels,' a spokesman said. 1952 *Newsweek* 30 June p. 17 . . . he was accused by the Administration of dragging his feet unduly on meeting the union demands. *Ibid.* 30 June p. 21 . . . there will be a lot of heel-dragging right through the campaign.

FIX-, FIXIT SHOP. A repair shop.—1951 N.Y. *Times Book Rev.* 6 May p. 11 (title) Fixit-Shops Are Frequent. 1952 B'ham *News* 27 July p. E1/3 . . . The fourth will open a fix-it shop in a small town . . .

FLY-PAST, *n.* {1914}—Add American illus.—1951 N.Y. *Times Mag.* 1 July p. 7 (pict. cap.) . . . Members of the royal family watch the 'fly-past' of the Royal Air Force, following the King's Birthday ceremony. 1953 B'ham *News* 17 March p. 7/2 In brief, at the air show given on Red Army Day two years ago in Moscow, foreign observers identified one plane in the fly-past which was certainly bigger and seemed to be faster than the TU-4s which also took part.

FOURTH FORCE. *French politics.* See quots.—1951 N.Y. *Times* 24 June p. E1/7 Moreover during the election campaign, some of the Radical deputies allied themselves with the rightist independents in a new group called the Fourth Force. *Ibid.* 1 July p. 2E/3–4 On the far left the Communists have 103 seats. Between them lie the Third Force [See *Am. Sp.* 26:294–95]—Socialists, Radicals and Popular Republicans—283 seats—and the an [*sic*] amorphous collection of centrist and rightist deputies, some of whom call themselves the Fourth Force.

FRONT-, FRONT RUNNER. A leader. — 1952 B'ham *News* 5 May p. 12/1 (edit.) Not a front runner, he is a dark horse who might come in first should Taft and Eisenhower cancel each other out. *Ibid.* 24 June p. 1/7–8 (AP) Such a move reportedly was under discussion by some supporters of Ohio's Sen. Robert Taft, a front-runner with Gen. Dwight Eisenhower in the GOP presidential race. Walter Cronkite over CBS Television Network 25 July All the other front runners . . . picked up strength . . . N.Y. *Times* 27 July p. E1/2 The front-runners all followed the same strategy with regard to the phantom Stevenson challenge . . . 1953 *Ibid.* 25 Jan. p. S1 (pict. cap.) It is evident McCreary's mount had to come from way back to win — front runners stay clean.

FRONT-RUNNING, *adj.* See *Am. Sp.* 26:209/2; revise definition to read '1. *Sport.*

Being in the lead all through a race. 2. Leading.' Additional citations.—1951 *Life* 1 Oct. p. 32/1 Taft is the strongest single Republican and the front-running candidate for the '52 nomination. 1952 B'ham *News* 14 June p. 1/4 (AP) And he swung a punch at Gen. Dwight D. Eisenhower, one of the front-running candidates for the Republican presidential nomination. *Ibid.* 17 Dec. p. 8/3-4 (AP) Of Stevenson, who headed off Kefauver's front-running bid for the party nomination and then lost in the election, Kefauver had this to say. . .

(GOLD) FISH BOWL, GOLD-FISH BOWL. '. . . the room in which the third degree is administered' (1942 Berrey and Van den Bark *Am. Thesaurus of Slang* ¶ 466.11). — *Transf. & fig.* That which is open to public view. (Also attrib.) — [1904 Saki 'Innocence of Reginald' in *'Reginald' and 'Reginald in Russia'* (N.Y.: Viking, 1929) p. 79 'After that, I might have been a goldfish in a glass bowl for all the privacy I got.'] 1935 Mark Sullivan *Our Time* (N.Y.: Scribners) 6:150 The situation was the more trying because it was as plain to the newspapers as to Harding and Daugherty — their relations for several months were carried on in a goldfish bowl. 1944 Balto. *Sun* 24 Feb. p. 15/4 We intend . . . to conduct this business in a gold-fish bowl with every record and every transaction open to the whole wide world for examination. 1945 San Fran. *Examiner* 16 March p. 4/3 A 'goldfish bowl' policy for the San Francisco conference of the United Nations was outlined today by Secretary of State Edward R. Stettinius, Jr., in recognition of widespread world interest in its developments. 1950 N.Y. *Times* 11 June p. X7/5 His reputation for rectitude, his dignified behavior in the Hollywood fish bowl, his stature as an actor, were just the attributes that the . . . company wanted . . . *Time* 31 July p. 9/3 After three weeks of fish-bowl mobilizing, the Defense Department was tightening up on security. 1951 *Sat. Eve. Post* 22 Dec. p. 44/4 From the hump the cars roll, sometimes four or five to a minute, to a series of switches controlled by the towermen in their elevated air-conditioned goldfish bowls . . . 1952 B'ham *News* 9 March p. A2/3 (AP) Parliament was plunked into a teachers academy overlooking the Rhine River. The parliamentarians work in a goldfish bowl. In the summer there's a beer garden just outside the glass-walled chamber where they meet. 1953 Berrey and Van den Bark *op. cit.* ¶ 617.6 Broadcasting Station . . . fish bowl, aquarium, *the clients' studio observation booth* . . .

GUES(S)TIMATE, *n.* [see quot. Berrey and Van den Bark] An estimate. — 1937 *Am. Sp.* 12:157/2 'The various estimates of unemployment are nothing more than that, "guestimates" is the word frequently used by the statisticians and population experts.' 1942 Berrey and Van den Bark *op. cit.* ¶ 168.2 Estimation. . . *Spec.* guesstimate, *blend of 'guess' and 'estimate.'* *Time* 18 May p. 23/3 One reasonably informed guesstimate came . . . from Peter Masefield. 1943 New Haven *Register* 24 Oct. Mag. Sec. Various 'guesstimates' place its extreme range as 600 to 800 yards. 1950 N.Y. *Times* 7 May p. E5/4 . . . the best appraisal that can be made of Russian progress in the development of new arms is, at best, a 'guestimate.' 1952 *Ibid.* 15 June p. E5/1.

JET STREAM. See quots. — 1950 *Time* 29 May p. 70/2 Six miles up, where the air is thin and cold, a fearful wind zigzags round the earth at 200 m. p. h. Meteorologists call it the 'jet stream.' 1951 N.Y. *Times* 8 April p. 69/1 (AP) Called the 'jet stream' by the University of Chicago scientists who discovered it, it is a narrow wind with speeds up to 300 miles an hour. It rides six to ten miles above the earth, always moving from west to east, near the top of the atmospheric envelope. 1953 *Blackwood's Mag.* Jan. p. 4/2 I glanced at my watch: in London they would be taking afternoon tea, and I, dozing as we flew over the gold-dusted ribs of the Mediterranean below, had been wafted between Athens and Rhodes on a westerly jet stream at a speed of five hundred and sixty-five miles an hour. Atlanta *Constitution* 17 April p. 1/2 (AP) It did so while flying eastward from Albuquerque, N.M., toward Wichita, Kan., at an altitude of 40,000 feet, by hooking onto a jet stream — one of the recently discovered mysterious 'rivers' of high winds in the upper skies. B'ham *News* 11 June p. 15/3 (AP) This high-riding air current—called the 'planetary wave train' by scientists—begins at about 10,000 foot altitude and extends upward at least 30,000 feet more. It is believed to be thousands of miles in width. [¶] Its central core is a high-speed wind, called the 'jet stream' which sometimes attains a speed of 300 miles an hour.

KILOTON, *n.* [F. *kilo-* 'thousand' + *ton*] See quots. — 1952 B'ham *News* 24 April p. 14/5 According to informed forecasts, the new bomb will have an explosive power of between 200 and 300 kilotons. *Sat. Eve. Post* 25 Oct. p. 150/2 The accepted measure of power of atomic weapons is the 'kiloton.' A kiloton equals 1000 tons of high explosive. 1953 B'ham *News* 4 June p. 10/4 (AP) A kiloton is the AEC scientists' term for the equivalent of 1000 tons of TNT. The nominal or Hiroshima bomb contained the equivalent of 20,000 tons (20 kilotons) of TNT.

METHODOLATRY, *n.* [*method* + *-o-* + *-latry*] Overconcern with method; see second quot. — 1948 *Sewanee Rev.* Summer p. 478 (subtitle) Methodolatry. 1951 *New Repub.* 22 Jan. p. 21 (rev.) Chief among them, perhaps, is the need to prove itself [sociology] a lusty young science; hence its excessive concern with what Aiken and Quine call methodolatry, and its elaborate protestations of moral neutrality.

MINIATURIZATION, *n.* See quots. (Also attrib.) — 1949 *Sci. N.L.* 23 April p. 268/3 Miniaturization is a big word which means, of course, making things smaller. 1951 N.Y. *Times* 15 April p. 94/2 (NANA) Impetus for the 'miniaturization' program was the success in perfecting tiny electron tubes for the receiver-transmitter of the proximity fuse . . . *Sci. Am.* Aug. p. 14 As the equipment grows in complexity, it grows more and more bulky. This has led to an attempted solution rather inelegantly called 'miniaturization.' *Time* 13 Aug. p. 52/3 'Special emphasis,' it announced, 'has been placed on miniaturization and ruggedization.' Meaning: the equipment will be smaller and tougher. 1952 *Wall St. Jour.* 26 March p. 1 Playing a major role is what the electronics men call 'miniaturization'— which means, in simplest terms, reducing different electronic parts to miniature size.

OZONER, *n.* See quots. — 1948 *Time* 26 April p. 96/2 As spring's gaudy carpet rolled north last week, the drive-in theaters were opening as fast as the daffodils. This week, New York City will get its first 'ozoner': a 600-car, $300,000 affair on Staten Island. 1952 N.Y. *Times* 9 March p. 2X/7 In the movie trade, drive-ins—or ozoners, as Variety calls them—are 'passion pits with pix.'

PARA-, PARADROP, *v. t.* To drop by parachute. — 1950 B'ham *News* 27 Nov. p. 28/3 An Iuka man was one of the pilots who para-dropped more than 4,000 men of the 11th Airborne on an arc between the North Korean cities of Sukcon and Sunchow. 1951 *Newsweek* 6 Aug. p. 78 To date the United States Air Force has parachuted more than 16,000 tons of weapons, ammunition, food, and other supplies . . . . This is more than was para-dropped during the entire second world war. 1952 *Time* 31 March p. 71/2 (adv.) Here, it paradrops vital supplies 'up front.'

PEEPIE-CREEPIE, *n.* A walkie-lookie (which see). Cf. *creepie-peepie.* — 1952 *Time* 14 July p. 22/3 Most startling TV innovation was a portable camera known as the walkie-lookie, or peepie-creepie, with which the enterprising TV reporter could sneak up to Mr. Delegate and catch him yelling his head off or scratching his nose. *Newsweek* 21 July p. 53 NBC's walkie-lookie, or 'peepie-creepie,' was not a singular success in its debut.

RADIO STAR. See quot. *Brit. Book of the Year.* — 1950 N.Y. *Times* 27 Aug. p. E9/6 It may be that the radio stars are a special type that can be detected only by means of radio receivers. Balto. *Sun* 12 Oct. p. 3/2 They are called radio stars because they send short-wave radio signals. 1951 *Sci. N.L.* 3 Nov. p. 277/1 Astronomical highlights for the past year picked by Dr. Harlow Shapley . . . are: . . . [¶] 3. Raising to over a hundred the number of known 'radio stars' . . . *Brit. Book of the Year* p. 742/2 radio star. A star whose luminosity is so low that its existence is known only through short-wave radio emanations

RADIO TELESCOPE. See quots. — 1948 *Newsweek* 18 Nov. p. 98/2 The newer radio telescope, employing a parabolic mesh of wire instead of an aluminum mirror, is designed to gather radio static in the microwave region. 1950 N.Y. *Times* 20 Aug. Sec. 1 p. 56/3 (AP) Delicate 'radio telescopes' are helping scientists to investigate the mysteries of the outer atmosphere. *Ibid.* 27 Aug. p. E9/6 Now there are radio telescopes that look like parabolic saucers and that catch the stellar radio signals. The saucers may be as much as 200 feet in diameter. . . 1953 *Ibid.* 19 April p. E9/5 The foundations of Britain's million-dollar radio telescope . . . are now being built at Jodrell Bank, Cheshire.

SHAMBLED, *adj.* [**shamble, v.* 'To reduce to rubble' (f. *shambles, n.* 'A ruin'; see *Am. Sp.* 16:19-20) + *-d*] Littered up; rubbleized. — 1940 *Newsweek* 17 June p. 21 (pict. cap.) Nazis photographed the shambled Dunkerque's water front. 1952 *Time* 11 Aug. p. 25 (pict. cap.) Reconstruction of the shambled town . . . is expected to take at least five years. . .

STARRY-EYED, *adj.* See *Am. Sp.* 28:50. Substitute the following. — STARRY-EYED, *attrib.* ['Figuratively, influenced by stars; aspiring to starlike heights. . .' (1934 *WNID*, *s. v. starry, adj.* 5; *WNID* lists *starry-eyed* among the combinations of *starry*.)] *Fig.* Visionary.

WALKIE-LOOKIE, *n.* See quots. — 1946 *Sci. N.L.* 30 March p. 195 'Walkie-lookie,' the picture equivalent of the small remote voice instrument known as 'walkie-talkie,' will come from the 'block' system's light-weight, easily portable television camera. . . 1948 *New Inter. Yearbook* p. 657/2. 1951 *Bus. Week* 24 March p. 72 Walkie-Lookie Is TV's Latest [title]. That's the meaning of RCA's new experimental portable, battery-powered transmitter. The whole unit, camera and back-pack transmitter, weighs just 53 lb. [col. 3] 1952 *Wall St. Jour.* 26 March p. 1 The heart of the walkie-lookie is a midget camera tube called the vidicon. The brain child of Radio Corporation of America technicians, the tube measures six inches long and one inch in diameter. N.Y. *Times* 20 July p. X9 (pict. cap.) . . . in the center is that network's [NBC's] walkie-lookie . . . *Life* 21 July p. 18 (quot. *s. v. creepie-peepie*). *Sci. Dig.* Aug. p. 3/1 The Walkie-Lookie is described in RCA's technical journal, *RCA Review*.

AMONG THE NEW WORDS

I. WILLIS RUSSELL
University of Alabama

ACKNOWLEDGMENTS. For citations, to Clarence L. Barnhart (2), John H. Christian (1), Thomas L. Crowell (2), O. B. Emerson (2), Atcheson L. Hench (9), Mamie J. Meredith (17), Verner M. Sims (1), and Peter Tamony (5). Thanks are also due the University of Alabama Research Committee for secretarial aid.

ANZUS, *n.* Acronym of Australia, New Zealand, and United States; see quots. (Usually attrib.)—1952 San Fran. *Chronicle* 3 Aug. p. 1/2 He said that Australia, New Zealand and the United States were holding the first meeting of the ANZUS Council at Honolulu to work on the organization and procedures of their mutual defense treaty. San Fran. *News* 6 Aug. p. 16 The current Honolulu foreign ministers conference of Australia, New Zealand and the United States (ANZUS) is very important . . . *Chr. Sci. Mon.* 8 Aug. p. C-1 Foreign ministers of the ANZUS countries during the three-day conference in Hawaii decided it was 'premature' to establish relationships with other states or regional organizations at this time. N.Y. *Times* 12 Aug. p. 18/2 An immediate practical outcome of the ANZUS conference in Honolulu is the invitation to the United States naval and air forces to again use the Manus Island base. Tuscaloosa *News* 16 Dec. p. 1/5 (AP) . . . Anzus—Australia, New Zealand, United States—originally was formed as a barrier against any resurgence of Japanese militarism.

COOK-, COOKOUT, *n.* See first quot. — 1949 *Am. Sp.* 24:233/1 To the list in 'Verb+Adverb=Noun,' . . . may be added *cookout*, meaning the cooking of a meal out of doors, as by a group of children at a camp. 1952 *Friends Intelligencer* 3 May p. 256/1 Wallingford, Vermont, summer apartment, 6 rooms and bath, completely furnished. Water-front privileges for swimming, boating and outdoor cook-outs. *U. S. A.* July p. 22 Cook-outs and other purely recreational activities are welcomed by the youngsters . . . 1953 Memphis *Commercial Appeal* 23 May p. 6/3 It [substance for cooling] . . . will come in handy for picnics, cookouts, etc.

DOUBLETHINK, *n.* [Cf. *doubletalk*] See first quot. — 1949 George Orwell *Nineteen Eighty-Four* (N.Y.: Harcourt, Brace and Co.) p. 36 His mind slid away into the labyrinthine world of doublethink. To know and not to know, to be conscious of complete truthfulness while telling carefully constructed lies, to hold simultaneously two opinions which canceled out, knowing them to be contradictory and believing in both of them, to use logic against logic, to repudiate morality while laying claim to it, to believe that democracy was impossible and that the Party was the guardian of democracy. . . 1952 *Sat. Rev.* 28 June p. 8 (title) History in Doublethink. B'ham *News* 13 Sept. p. 4/3 (title) Mossadegh 'Doublethink'? *Sat. Rev.* 20 Sept. p. 23/3 If totalitarian 'doublethink' ever takes over, we may have to hide this series in some subterranean vault so that our children's children may recover their superb heritage. *Newsweek* 6 Oct. p. 94 (Henry Hazlitt) 'Doublethink,' according to the late George Orwell, who coined the word, means 'the power of holding two contradictory beliefs in one's mind simultaneously, and accepting both of them.'

EGG-, EGG HEAD, EGGHEAD, *n.* [Cf. *highbrow;* see third quot.] See quots. (Also attrib.) — [1920 W. Deeping *Second Youth* iv, A little egg-headed pedant (cited in *OED Sup.* s. v. *egg, sb.* 6. c).] 1952 N.Y. *Times* 19 Oct. p. E1/7 Some pro-Eisenhower papers said the mail was running generally pro-Stevenson—though it was pointed out that writers of letters to editors tend to be in the intellectual or 'egg-head' category where Stevenson sentiment is strong. Omaha *World-Her.* 26 Oct. p. 2-G (Louis Bromfield) Egg head. A person of intellectual pretensions, often a professor or the protege of a professor. Fundamentally, trivial and superficial in approach to any problem. . . Balto. *Sun* 27 Nov. p. 14/6–7 . . . writers on the lower levels of the trade have sought in vain for a new way of saying 'highbrow.' . . . 'Loftydome' was about the best they could do, until 'egghead' came along. 1953 *Mueller Clipper* Feb. My, how the scientific egg-heads strive to make it hard for us work-a-day fellows! Balto. *Sun* 13 Feb. p. 1/1 They complain because the new Government no longer gives high priority to the theories of foreign socialists or to the notions of local eggheads. Lincoln *Evening Jour.* 18 Feb. p. 6 . . . while the Eisenhower administration has undoubtedly drawn more heavily from the ranks of business than from college faculties, labor unions and the ranks of professional intellectuals—or eggheads—there is nothing 'experimental' about it.

IN-, INFLIGHT, *attrib.* See quots. — 1945 *This Week* 25 March p. 20/3 . . . the Air Transport Command furnished quarters . . . and provided another 2,000,000 'inflight' meals. 1950 *Sci. N. L.* 1 April p. 197; cited *Read. Guide* 10 May 1950 p. 7/2 Details of in-flight refueling system revealed. 1952 N.Y. *Times* 21 Dec. p. X27/3 Thousands of in-flight refueling operations have been completed without a single accident. . .

INFRA-, INFRASTRUCTURE, *n.* [L. *infra-* + *structure*] See quots. — 1950 N.Y. *Times* 2 July p. 2E/7 Mr. Winston Churchill: 'In this debate we have had the usual jargon about "the infrastructure of a supranational authority". . .' 1951 *Newsweek* 30 July p. 27 One of NATO's most serious problems is agreeing on an over-all financial program, especially for features such as 'infra-structure.' This is a word used to cover the whole network of supranational communications and services necessary for the establishment of new military bases. *Ibid.* 1 Oct. p. 26 [Gen. Norstad] admitted that progress had been painfully slow toward building the infrastructure—the complex of bases—that Allied Air Forces, Central Europe, will need before it can be fully effective. *Time* 1 Oct. p. 30/3 . . . Got a U. S. promise of half a billion dollars for NATO's 'infrastructure,' i.e., defense installations built in one country but shared by all. 1952 Balto. *Sun* 26 Feb. p. 1/1 The most immediate action resulting from the Lisbon decisions will be to start work on $500,000,000 worth of 'infrastructure,' the NATO word for airfields, communications and headquarters needed to back up their armies. 1953 *ibid.* 25 April p. 1/5 Then came the budget for infrastructure, those semi-permanent installations needed by modern armies.

PHASE MICROSCOPE. See quots. — 1948 *Sci. N. L.* 8 May p. 295/1 This new kind of microscope, a further development of the phase microscope, will permit man to spy upon cells as they grow, multiply and carry on their important life functions. 1949 Omaha *World-Her.* 4 Dec. p. 19-A . . . the phase microscope can see the interior of a cell in bright or dark contrast to bring hidden parts into view. 1951 *Sci. Am.* Aug. p. 5 (adv.) Many living cells, cancer tissues, bacteria, are too transparent to be seen clearly under a microscope. Now the *phase microscope* reveals things eyes could not see before. AO [American Optical Co.] scientists spent years helping to develop the basic phase theory into a workable microscope for research use.

PHOTO RECONNAISSANCE. The seeking of information from aerial photographs; see first quot. (Also atrtib.) — 1944 *Sci. N. L.* 19 Aug. p. 117/3 Photo reconnaissance supplies information regarding the strength of enemy troops, the placement of enemy weapons. . . 1950 *Time* 24 July p. 57/1 The money problem was licked by getting a Government order to build a new photo-reconnaissance plane. N.Y. *World Tel. and Sun* 30 Dec. p. 2/4 There were four of us aboard this old B-26—the Hot to Go . . . Hot to Go is a photo reconnaissance plane.

PRINTED CIRCUIT (WIRE). See quots. — 1946 *Sci. N. L.* 2 March p. 133 'Printed wire,' the new development that reduces wiring radio circuits to a two-dimensional lithographic process . . . 1950 *ibid.* 29 April p. 259 TV tuning improved by printed circuit. 1952 *Wall St. Jour.* 26 March p. 1 Getting about as much attention as miniaturization in the electronic laboratories these days is use of what the lab men call the 'printed circuit.' [¶] This is a method of eliminating bulky wires, coils and other component parts in electronic gadgets by 'printing' or etching their functional equivalents on an insulated base.

TAKE OVER, *v.* {1916}. — TAKE-, TAKEOVER, *n.* — 1946 Balto. *Sun* 10 Aug. p. 4/7 Sobolev said special consideration was being given to the planning of a smooth take-over of UNRRA facilities . . . 1948 Lond. *Spectator* 6 Feb. p. 178/2 (headline) Gas Take-Over Terms. 1951 N.Y. *Times* 24 June p. 1E/4 Iran's long-heralded takeover of British oil properties in the country was put in motion last week . . . 1952 *ibid.* 13 April p. 1E/3 . . . Attorney General Robert Jackson justified the takeover . . . B'ham *News* 11 Nov. p. 10/5 The time elapsing between the presidential takeover was longer then . . .

TELEPROMPTER, *n.* See quots. Trademark. — 1951 *Life* 12 March p. 131 Set at the eye level of performers, the Teleprompter unrolls a script whose inch-high letters, printed by special typewriter, can be read 25 feet away. 1952 Nashville *Tennessean* 8 July p. 7/4 Speakers read their speeches from a gadget called a 'teleprompter' which rolls it off in big type about four feet in front of the microphones. N.Y. *Times* 20 July p. X9/1 The Teleprompter, the electronic gadget used to unfold prepared speeches in giant letters in front of a speaker, also is expected to be eliminated in the interest of neatness. *Ibid.* 24 July p. 14 A teleprompter is an electronic gadget normally on a standard before a speaker, that rolls up his speech in big block letters, line by line, at whatever pace the operator requires. *Newsweek* 4 Aug. p. 51 Four years ago the TelePrompTer Corp. started when president Fred Barton, then playing one of the sailors in 'Mr. Roberts,' got the idea of a machine that could roll a TV script in front of actors but away from the eyes of the home audience.

TELETHON, n. [*tele*cast + mara*thon*] A television show which is organized to raise a sum of money for some charitable cause and which closes only when the money has been subscribed. — 1949 San Fran. *Examiner* 10 April p. 22/5 (heading) 'Telethon' Nets $702,000. *Red Barrel* May p. 4 Telephoned pledges poured into NBC stations in these cities all day and night and some 9,000 calls were answered personally by Berle who manned a battery of nine busy phones during the 16-hour 'telethon.' 1951 San Fran. *Progress* 26–27 June (24th Street Edition) p. 4/3 The telethon will be staged in the Marines Memorial Theatre . . . *Variety* 14 Nov. p. 36 WJZ-TV . . . has scheduled a 14-hour telethon on behalf of the United Cerebral Palsy fund. 1952 Balto. *Sun* 23 June p. 1/6 (AP) Bing Crosby and Bob Hope, in a 14½-hour coast-to-coast telethon today raised more than $1,000,000 in contributions and pledges for the United States Olympic fund . . . B'ham *News* 23 June p. 19/3 The U. S. Olympic team will travel to Helsinki in style now, thanks to a coast-to-coast fund-raising telethon . . . . The marathon telecast . . . began Saturday night and ended Sunday morning. 1953 Ellery Queen *The Scarlet Letters* (Little, Brown) p. 78 . . . they had both attended the all-night telethon emceed by a round robin of TV comedians in the interest of the recent blood-plasma drive.

WAR-WEARY, *n.* See *Am. Sp.* 21:145/2. Additional illust. — 1952 Tuscaloosa *News* 14 Oct. p. 5/2 (NEA) King's goal was to turn thousands of war-weary planes into missiles. . .

WELFARISM, *n.* [*welfare* state + *-ism*] Policies identified with a welfare state. —1949 *Life* 25 July p. 17/2 Taft replies that he is as much concerned as any man, but there must be safeguards so that welfarism does not end in economic or political tyranny. *Ibid.* 14 Nov. p. 42 With the rise of Welfarism, maybe the unions will be themselves. 1952 *Harper's Mag.* Jan. p. 28 The gigantic apparatus of government built up to promote welfarism . . . is still the dispensary of money . . . Balto. *Sun* 31 March p. 10/4 And yet the prospects raised by the 1933-type welfarism and its British models do not stop with mere one-partyism.

AMONG THE NEW WORDS

I. WILLIS RUSSELL
University of Alabama

ACKNOWLEDGMENTS: For citations: Thomas L. Crowell (2), O. B. Emerson (1), Dorothy H. Eshleman (1), Atcheson L. Hench (1), Mamie J. Meredith (6), Porter G. Perrin (1), John F. Ramsey (1), and Peter Tamony (5). Thanks are also due the University of Alabama Research Committee for secretarial aid.

AISLE-SITTER, *n.* A dramatic critic. — 1950 N.Y. *Times* 1 Jan. p. X1/5 Although Betty Field, the aisle-sitters said, was excellent, eight of the nine couldn't say anything close to that for 'The Rat Race,' in which Miss Field is starred. *Ibid.* 22 Jan. p. X1/6 . . . Three of the aisle-sitters were satisfied with 'Alive and Kicking,' the new revue. *Ibid.* 30 July p. X1/7 . . . A careful dissection of the reports rendered by the aisle-sitters indicates that they came to the Festival Theatre's début last week full of midsummer good-will. N.Y. *Times Book Rev.* 8 Oct. p. 8/1 An aisle-sitter at the Sadler's Wells ballet observes that . . . a publishing house and a poet get a choreographic assist at the Met.

ATOMIC COCKTAIL. 1. See quots. — 1945 *Life* 27 Aug. p. 32/3. 1946 *Sat. Rev. Lit.* 22 June p. 5/3 Other uses [of *atomic*] have been more trivial still. Bars have shaken up 'atomic cocktails'. . .

2. See quots. — 1949 Lincoln *Journal* 7 April p. 16 (AP) A . . . girl drank her second 'atomic cocktail' Wednesday hoping to cure a rare glandular ailment. . . . drank a glass of radioactive phosphorus . . . 1953 N.Y. *Times* 22 Feb. p. 32/1 The new unit requires fifteen rooms. One is a heavily shielded 'hot laboratory' where radioactive materials received three times a week in thickly insulated containers from the Atomic Energy Commission's Oak Ridge, Tenn., center, are compounded into medicine—principally tasteless 'atomic cocktails' that patients drink from paper cups just like water. Atlanta *Journal* 16 April p. 77/3 (UP) A soft-spoken young naval veteran, once doomed to death by cancer, Thursday praised an 'atomic cocktail' for apparently saving his life.

BINAURAL, *adj.* {1881} — See quots. — 1953 N.Y. *Times* 17 March p. 1 The availability of two channels on which to transmit from the same station, Dr. Armstrong said, would make practical 'three-dimensional sound' on radio, also known as binaural transmission. *Musical Amer.* 15 April p. 15/1 The word 'binaural,' which designates two-eared hearing, has been detached from its quiet nook in the textbooks of experimental psychology to name a new approach in recording, designed to restore the sense of space to reproduced sound.

BINAURALITY, *n.* [*binaural* + *-ity*] See quots. — 1953 *Musical Amer.* 15 April p. 15/2 On one side are those who assert that the two-channel two-speaker system produces true binaurality, and on the other are those whose stand is that this can only be obtained with headphones and that any system using speakers must be called 'stereophonic.' *Sat. Rev.* 29 Aug. p. 65/2 . . . Columbia has announced an additional 'XD' speaker unit . . ., and by means of its separate room location (and some frequency-spectrum division) provides a '3-D' effect of sound dispersion that perhaps comes as close to 'binaurality' as is possible with single channel recordings and reproducers.

BLOODMOBILE, *n.* See last quot. — 1948 *Sci. N.L.* 10 July p. 26/2–3 (pict. cap.) Red Cross Bloodmobile. 1949 Omaha *World-Her.* 11 Nov. p. 1 (UP) Schuyler donors set a new record by giving 156 pints of blood when the bloodmobile stopped here. 1950 *Brit. Book of the Year* p. 739/1. 1951 *New Yorker* 29 Aug. p. 27 Five bloodmobiles . . . of the American Red Cross received blood from donors yesterday. *New Words and Words in the News* (Funk & Wagnalls Co.) Sup. No. 7 Fall p. 1/2. 1953 Berrey and Van den Bark *Am. Thes. Slang* ¶ 81.9 . . . bloodmobile, *a mobile Red Cross blood-donor unit.*

CONCUSSION GRENADE. See quots. — 1952 B'ham *News* 23 May p. 1/4 (AP) A concussion grenade is a cardboard and tin covered explosive containing TNT. It is designed to give shock, but not to wound or kill. San Fran. *Examiner* 10 June p. 1/7 (AP) (A concussion grenade is an explosive aimed at stunning, rather than killing, persons in an area where it is thrown. It is about the size of an ordinary hand grenade, but does not shoot out death-dealing fragments when it explodes . . .) San Fran. *Chronicle* 11 June p. 7/5 (AP) The Army's new concussion grenade . . . is a cardboard container holding a quarter of a pound of TNT. . . . General Mark W. Clark's headquarters said the official name is 'Grenade, Hand, Offensive.'

CONELRAD, *n.* [See quots.] See quots. — 1953 San Fran. *Call-Bull.* 4 May p. 8G/1–2 The system, known as 'Conelrad,' will go into effect as of that date. San Fran. *Examiner* 17 Aug. p. 32/7–8 The term 'conelrad' comes from the phrase 'plan for control of electro-magnetic radiation.' N.Y. *Times* 13 Sept. p. 3/4 (AP) So Conelrad was developed, a joint effort by the F. C. C., the Civil Defense Administration, the Air Defense Command and the broadcasting industry. . . . the system requires that as many stations as possible be kept on the air, with the largest stations sharply reducing power and every station shifting promptly to a frequency not its own. Thus an approaching enemy plane would be provided with not one beam but more than it could handle. . . . Only two broadcasting frequencies will be used during the emergency period—640 kilocycles or 1240 kilocycles . . . B'ham *News* 14 Sept. p. 20/3 (AP) Conelrad, short for 'Control of Electro-magnetic Radiation' . . . is a 'planned confusion' approach to befuddling enemy bombers which might try to follow radio broadcasting beams to American cities. In Wednesday's test, some 1250 standard radio stations will shift their frequencies and power while 20 Air Force bombers try their luck at finding large cities with theoretical bomb loads. Omaha *World-Her.* 17 Sept. p. 5 (AP) Heavy Air Force bombers posing as 'enemy attackers,' sought to ride scrambled broadcasting beams to American cities early Wednesday in the first national civil defense test of CONELRAD.

CROSS-CHECK, *v. t. & i.* To check from many points of view. — 1951 N.Y. *Times* 24 June p. E9/7 According to Dr. Alvin C. Graves, director of the test division of Los Alamos laboratory and deputy commander for scientific operations at Eniwetok, the instrumentation for a carefully planned program may provide for hundreds of experiments designed to cross-check important results. 1953 *Harper's Mag.* Sept. p. 22/2 Dr. Kinsey and his three research associates . . . rechecked later . . . and cross-checked in over three times as many cases as in the first book reports from husbands and wives. — *n.* — 1953 N.Y. *Times* 18 Jan. p. S3/6 An Associated Press cross-check yesterday of the men in the press boxes showed them lined up, 5 to 1, in support of the Football Rules Committee action this week in throwing out the free substitution rule.

DURABLE*, *adj.* 'Denoting a lease that gives the tenant a permanent interest. Also absol. *Obs.* . . .' (*DA.* Date of absol. use 1846) — *n.* Something durable. — 1951 N.Y. *Times* 14 Oct. p. 1F/1 (headline) Production Eases on Some Durables. *Bus. Week* 17 Nov. p. 158 (title) Consumer Durables Slash. 1952 N.Y. *Times Book Rev.* 28 Sept. p. 40/3 During the Nineteen Twenties, and particularly in that decade's second half, real wages . . . had stopped growing so that consumer durables could be purchased only by an extraordinary and unhealthy expansion in installment selling . . .

DUST-, DUSTUP, *n.* 'Disturbance, uproar; a brisk bout in rowing, boxing, etc. . .' (*OED Sup.* {1897}) — Additional def. (see first quot.) and U.S. illus. — 1942 *Am. Sp.* 17:5/2 (Allan F. Hubbell) DUST-UP. A quarrel, a row. 'There was a *dust-up;* and she ran away and married him in Scotland.' [G. D. H. and M. Cole *Double Blackmail* (1939) p. 233.

This ref. from Hubbell.] 1948 *New Yorker* 27 March p. 23/1 He has been making a considerable dustup over the matter... 1949 *Time* 26 Sept. p. 23/1 The whole dustup was hardly calculated to win much sympathy for the rebellious Navy. 1952 N.Y. *Times Mag.* 18 May p. 16/2 The dust-up on the House floor was precipitated when someone read into the Congressional Record an article from The Binghamton Press of April 22 . . .

FALL OUT, *v. phr.* {1577} — FALL-, FALLOUT, *n.* See last quot. — 1952 N.Y. *Times* 17 Aug. p. E9/6 Nevertheless, a good deal of radioactive stuff is picked up and carried by the wind and deposited all over the country. . . . So far there have been no dangerous concentrations of radioactive 'fall-out,' as it is called, that is outside of the proving grounds in Nevada. 1953 B'ham *News* 23 Jan. p. 11/2–3 (NANA) One trouble caused by the radioactivity sifting down from the clouds after a test is that for a short while after a test it may effect [*sic*] the calculations of these planes. The excited buzz of the counters ordinarily indicates that they have made a 'strike,' but the fuss is actually caused by a minute amount of 'hot dust' from the 'fallout.' *Time* 2 Feb. p. 42/2 According to AEC, no dangerous 'fall-out' of radioactive dust has occurred outside the test area. *Bull. of the Atomic Scientists* April p. 87/1 Fall-out—the descent of the [radioactive] particles back to earth—may occur in the immediate vicinity of the detonation or as far as several thousand miles away, although it is heaviest near the site.

FULL-DRESS, *adj.* See *Am. Sp.* 17:271. Additional illus. — 1952 Tuscaloosa *News* 17 May p. 1/6 (AP) The President spoke extemporaneously at the dinner after Secretary of State Acheson had delivered a full-dress speech on the theme that only the combined efforts of the United States and its allies can prevent Russia from 'engulfing the world.' 1953 Atlanta *Constitution* 17 April p. 1/8 (UP) The United Nations agreed to resume full-dress Korean truce talks according to a formula that would ban forced repatriation of war prisoners.

HELIBUS, *n.* [*heli*copter + *bus*] See last quot. — 1949 B'ham *News-Age-Her.* 13 Nov. p. A18/3 But there is much work yet to be done before the combination of the jetliner and the helibus can be fully utilized. 1953 N.Y. *Times Mag.* 13 Sept. p. 44 Opening of a passenger helicopter line, the 'helibus,' serving the city's airports, was recently hailed as the start of a new air-taxi era.

TENIGUE, *n.* [See quots.] See quots. — 1951 Balto. *Sun* 9 Nov. p. 3/2 A new national disease called tenigue was reported today. It's something almost any motorist may catch once he gets on the highway. Tenigue is a made-up word—from tension and fatigue. 1953 Omaha *World-Her.* 28 May p. 33 After we've gone that way for a while we also fall victim to what Mr. Harris calls 'tenigue'—tension and fatigue. This makes for a near-hypnosis in which we do not react promptly to an emergency that would have been dangerous even at 50.

VELOCITIZATION, *n.* [*velocity* {c. 1550} + *-ization*] See quots. — 1952 *This Week* 1 June p. 8/2 Another thing about speed. After miles of driving with your foot to the floor, you get used to it. You're driving 70, but you feel and act as if it were 40. The experts call it 'velocitization.' 1953 N.Y. *Times* 4 Jan. p. 31/4 'Velocitization . . . refers simply to deceptive speeds possible on a modern expressway. Motorists who normally drive on the open road at forty to fifty miles an hour suddenly find their speedometers reading seventy on a superhighway.'

VELOCITIZED, *adj.* See quot. — 1953 *This Week* 30 Aug. p. 5 The American Automobile Association has coined a new word, 'velocitized.' . . . It describes the condition of motorists who, after driving long stretches at 50 m. p. h. or more, misjudge speeds while passing through towns or cities.

AMONG THE NEW WORDS

I. WILLIS RUSSELL
University of Alabama

Acknowledgments: For citations: Clarence L. Barnhart (1), Thomas L. Crowell (4), Joe H. Gardner (2), Atcheson L. Hench (3), Mamie J. Meredith (6), Porter G. Perrin (3), Helen Sparks (1), Peter Tamony (2), and E. Neige Todhunter (2). James B. McMillan suggested the etymology of *lead time*. Thanks are also due the Research Committee of the University of Alabama for secretarial aid.

APPESTAT, *n.* [*appe*tite + thermo*stat*] See first quot. — 1952 Norman Joliffe *Reduce and Stay Reduced* (N.Y.: Simon and Schuster) p. 2 As a thermostat will automatically adjust the furnace, so as to keep the temperature of the house relatively constant in spite of changes in outside temperature, so will the normal weight-regulating mechanism adjust the appetite and keep the weight constant in spite of considerable changes in total energy expenditure. As a convenient term by which to refer to this mechanism, we have coined a word for it — the *appestat*. *New Yorker* 9 Aug. p. 18 The father of the appestat! That's what the fellows down at the New York City Department of Health have been calling Dr. Norman Joliffe . . . ever since . . . he coined the word . . . to describe an appetite-regulating mechanism located at the base of the brain. *New Words and Words in the News* (Funk & Wagnalls Co.) Sup. No. 8. Spring and Fall p. 1/1. 1953 N.Y. *Times Book Rev.* 4 Jan. p. 23/4 (adv.) This is because of what Dr. Joliffe calls the Appestat — the Appetite Regulating Mechanism in the hypothalmic region of your brain.

AQUASCOPE, *n.* See quot. — 1953 N.Y. *Times* 25 Jan. p. 9E/7 The National Geographic Society is lowering a strange new diving chamber called the 'aquascope' into the sea off the Florida Keys for experiments in underwater color photography at night at depths of fifty to 100 feet. This aquascope is a 2,700-pound tank of armor plate steel with wide plastic windows. Inside are two men with color cameras, high voltage power equipment and bright lights.

BEV. See first quot. — 1952 N.Y. *Times* 21 Dec. p. E7/6 After 2,500,000 trips around the circle, this push has accumulated until the protons are traveling close to the speed of light, with an energy of close to 2,500,000,000 electron volts, usually abbreviated as 2.5 BEV. 1954 B'ham *News* 1 Feb. p. 24/7 (NANA) . . . and before you can do a thorough job of batting an eye the protons have reached 2.3 BEV . . .

BIT, *n.* See quots. — 1950 *Science* 4 Aug. p. 143/2 To express the capacity of the ear in the conventional informational units of 'bits' (binary digits)/ sec, it is necessary to inquire how many of the distinguishable tones are independent of each other. 1952 *Sci. N.L.* 5 April p. 217 Even a poor telephone circuit can transmit about 20,000 bits per second, a 'bit' being the mathematical unit of information. 1953 *Sat. Rev.* 27 June p. 53 Primarily Dr. Jacobson's study is an application of the quite recently developed 'information theory' to analyses of the informational capacities of the human ear and of various recording media. Using the theory's basic counter, the binary unit, or 'bit,' and what seem to the layman like monstrously complex calculations, Dr. Jacobson finally emerges from his heavy sea of equations and graphs with some unmistakably plain numerical estimates.

BOOK BURNER, BOOKBURNER. *Fig.* See first quot. — 1953 Balto. *Sun* 18 June p. 1/5 What he was trying to express at Dartmouth, he said, was his opposition to the suppression of ideas — and he was using the term 'book-burners' to describe suppressors of ideas. N.Y. *Times* 5 July p. 2E/2 *President Eisenhower* . . . In a speech at Dartmouth last month he said bluntly, 'Don't join the bookburners.' *Sat. Rev.* 8 Aug. p. 27/2 This discussion with Mr. MacLeish seemed considerably more organized and brought forth the argument that 'book burners' attacked, in truth, neither books nor their authors, but rather their readers, the people, and held, in effect, that our citizens were incapable of judging things for themselves.

BOOK-, BOOK BURNING. *Fig.* — 1952 *Time* 21 July p. 61/1 . . . Matthew . . . Josephson discovered 'book-burning' in schools and libraries. 1953 Balto. *Sun* 18 June p. 1/5 Today's presidential comments on 'book-burners' and 'book-burning' did not issue voluntarily. N.Y. *Times* 28 June p. 6E/1 The situation . . . was that the actual book burning had, from all accounts, stopped, but the purge of books suspected of Communist taint goes on with the expectation of continuing. N.Y. *Times* 5 July p. 2E/2 The controversy over 'book burning' kept simmering last week . . . *Sat. Rev.* 5 Sept. p. 4/1 So it was that two of America's greatest newspapers . . . printed an extraordinary advertisement by one of America's leading publishers — and printed it when the furor over 'book-burning' was at its height in July.

CAPSULIZE, *v. t.* [*capsule, v. t.* (in *WNID Add.* 1950) + *-ize*] — 1950 *Sat. Rev. Lit.* 11 Nov. p. 17/1 This is a brief, almost capsulized account of postwar USSR . . . 1953 B'ham *News* 27 March p. 3/2–3 These fabulous little tales capsulize the fabulous history of the latest boom in fabulous Florida . . . *Ibid.* 1 April p. 8/4–5 If I had to select a slogan that above all others capsulizes Washington's economic thinking and hopes today, this would be it: Balance the Budget!

CHOPPER, *n.* See first quot. — 1952 *Life* 28 July p. 96 He decided to leave the raft there, climb the cliff and find a clearing where he could signal with his radio, then wait calmly for a rescue 'chopper' (helicopter) to come right over and get him. N.Y. *Times Mag.* 17 Aug. p. 16/4 . . . the record of the helicopter is no less impressive. . . . Oil and gas producers use the 'chopper' to patrol long and rugged gas and oil pipelines. 1953 *Harper's* Sept. p. 68 . . . he walked over to the little landing strip where the Marine chopper stood waiting for him . . .

COMPLETER, *n.* See quots. — 1949 *Sat. Rev. Lit.* 24 Dec. p. 7/1 This public has bought at $6 each a large number of copies of the 'Checklist of Fantastic Literature,' which is merely a directory of books in the field, and the word 'completer' is well known in the trade to designate a reader so avid that he must buy a copy of every single book of the kind published. 1953 *Sat. Rev.* 7 March p. 26/1 . . . as one of the fans remarked recently: 'I used to be a completer (philological note: one who obtains a copy of every science-fiction book published), but now I find it hard to be a completer on even one author.'

COUNT-, COUNT DOWN. 1. An audible counting off of a certain length of time. 2. See second quot. — 1953 B'ham *News* 4 June p. 1/6 (AP) Observers on the mountain were able to hear the count-down on the drop from the control tower via AEC short wave radio at the Angel's Peak Station at the 9000-foot level. *Monsanto Mag.* July p. 4 *The time is X minus 210!* The loudspeaker booms again, telling those working at the . . . launching site that they must have the [flying] missile ready to fire in 210 minutes. . . . Time on the range is expressed in minutes before a missile is to be fired. This is called a 'count down.'

CRASH, *adj.* [Cf. *OED, crash, sb.*,[1] 2 *b:* '*fig.* The action of falling to ruin suddenly and violently; *spec.* sudden collapse or failure of a financial undertaking, or of mercantile credit generally' {1817}; '3. A bout of revelry, amusement, fighting, etc.; a short spell, spurt. *Obs.*' {1549–1767}] Done, carried out in the shortest time possible. — 1915 Partridge *Dict. Slang and Unconventional English* (N.Y.: Macmillan, 1950) p. 189/2 crash dive. 'The sudden submersion of a submarine on being surprised, or in imminent danger of being rammed'; naval coll.: 1915. Fraser and Gibbons *Soldier and Sailor Words and Phrases*, 1925. 1922 quoted in *OED Sup.* 1934 *WNID* (repr. 1940) p. 619/2 crash dive. *Nav.* In the handling of submarines, a dive made in the least possible time. 1952 Balto. *Sun* 28 Feb. p. 1/1 . . . the construction of the bases was undertaken as a 'crash' job, that is, a job to be done with all possible speed. 1954 N.Y. *Times Mag.* 3 Jan. p. 39/2 One year, two years, or even three; the time is uncomfortably short in view of the enormous task we face in erecting defenses against atomic attack. That is why many eminent scientists are urging immediate 'crash' programs in defense to arrest the swing of the weapons pendulum, now far to the side of 'offense,' and restore it to a more neutral position.

DOWN-, DOWN RANGE STATION. See second quot. — 1952 N.Y. *Times* 9 March p. 4/1 'Down-range' stations at Jupiter Inlet on the Florida coast and on Grand Bahama Island already provide instrumentation 200 miles from the missile launching sites on Cape Canaveral. 1953 *Monsanto Mag.* July p. 3 When Army engineers came to Cape Canaveral, Fla., in 1949 to build this proving ground for the most modern of weapons, they seized upon the light house as a reference point. From it they worked 'down range' to establish a series of stations from which to observe the flight of missiles. . . . A typical down range station is a little electronic city set up to track missiles, predict weather, receive telemetry signals from missiles. . .

EISENHOPPER, *n.* See quots. — 1953 *Inside the ACD* Feb. p. 4/2 During the campaign, President Eisenhower was reported as sending high-hopping plastic grasshoppers flying through the air while talking with visitors. These secret weapons against tension were promptly termed Eisenhoppers. B'ham *News* 19 March p. 14/6 . . . Presidential burdens haven't changed Ike's engaging sense of humor. He still uses his mechanical grasshopper (the Eisenhopper) to relieve tension at staff meetings.

4 PERCENTER. One who engages in influence peddling with the Government for a fee of four percent. — 1953 N.Y. *Times* 13 Sept. p. 2E/1 (heading) 4 Percenter. B'ham *News* 25 Sept. p. 14/3 (Herblock cartoon) Influence Peddling! G.O.P. Aide Admits Trying to Be 4 Percenter.

HIDDEN HUNGER. See quots. — 1945 Icie G. Macy and Harold H. Williams *Hidden Hunger* (Lancaster, Pa.: the Jaques Cattell Press) p. 75 The consequences of misfeeding are frequently designated as 'hidden hunger.' p. 74 Consumption of an inadequate diet over a prolonged period of time will lead to disease and physical degeneration. This condition has been called 'hidden hunger.' 1951 *Harper's* Sept. p. 78 . . . the food problem is likely to be one of quantity rather than quality—of frankly 'hollow hunger,' rather than 'hidden hunger.' 1954 B'ham *News* 22 Jan. p. 7/1 Hidden hunger is tissue hunger which leads to a nagging, unsatisfied feeling and so you continue to overeat.

HOLLOW HUNGER. See first quot. — 1945 Macy and Williams *op. cit.* p. 73 Poverty is the greatest contributor to underfeeding, commonly designated as 'hunger' ('hollow hunger' by some). 1951 *Harper's* Sept. p. 78 (quoted under *hidden hunger*).

HOMOGENEOUS REACTOR. See quots. — 1952 Tuscaloosa *News* 14 Feb. p. 8/3 (UP) It will be a 'homogeneous reactor,' energized by splitting atoms in a sort of hot soup from which, it is expected, a continuous flow of power can be produced. 1953 N.Y. *Times* 15 March p. E9/6 The homogeneous reactor is so called because a single solution serves as fuel, moderator and cooling agent. 1954 *Life* 4 Jan. p. 89 (pict. cap.) 'Homogeneous' reactor uses liquid fuel . . . a uranium compound dissolved in water, which is held in a steel sphere about size of a basketball. Fuel acts as its own coolant, circulates from core through heat exchange boiler.

JETOMIC, *adj.* [*jet* + *atomic*] — 1952 *Steel* 13 Oct. p. 131 (title) Metals in the Jetomic Age. *Ibid.* 3 Nov. p. 98 (title) High Temperature Metallurgy: Jetomic Age Demands It.

LEAD TIME. [Cf. *OED. Sup., lead, v.*[1]: 'To aim in advance of.' {1892}] See quots. — 1945 B'ham *News* 19 May p. 8/1 Both automotive manufacturers and thousands of automotive workers are familiar with the 'lead-time' normally required to bring out new models. 1953 Tuscaloosa *News* 1 May p. 12/1 (AP) This, the President said, was possible because of a shortening up of lead times — the period between the designing of a weapon and the start of volume production — and concentration on critical areas and items. 1954 *Life* 18 Jan. p. 80/2 That gave the designers, engineers and production men a head start on the 21-month-plus 'lead time' which is General Motors' minimum for development of new body lines, delivery of the dies to stamp them out and retooling of the assembly lines to make the new cars. *Read. Dig.* Feb. p. 21/2 Wilson called the top aircraft manufacturers together last spring. Purpose: to cut the 'lead time' on aircraft-contract renewals. . . . He demanded that one manufacturer cut the time between contract signing and delivery from 30 to 16 months. . . . This manufacturer had previously wired the Air Force that 30 months' lead time was essential to national safety.

MEGADEATH, *n.* [*mega-* 'a word element meaning "great," and, in physics, 1,000,000 times a given unit' (*ACD*) + *death*] See quots. — 1953 B'ham *News* 21 June p. E3/1 He does not deal in numbers of atomic bombs or precise methods of delivery, in kilotons or megadeaths. Seattle *Times* 24 June p. 6 What is a megadeath? It is the death of a million human beings — as in the phrase, 'a saturation attack resulting in eight megadeaths.'

MEGATON, *n.* See quots. (Also attrib.) — 1952 *Sat. Eve. Post* 25 Oct. p. 150/3 A 1000-kiloton bomb — or one-megaton bomb, as the specialists call it — is a true hydrogen bomb. 1953 B'ham *News* 16 Jan. p. 11/1 As previously reported in this space, the H-bomb tested at Eniwetok developed the totally unexpected and unprecedented power of three to five megatons — which is the explosive force of three to five million tons of TNT. Seattle *Times* 24 June p. 6 What is a megaton? It is a measure of the explosive power of an atomic thermonuclear weapon — a bomb of one megaton has the explosive power of a million tons of TNT. 1954 N.Y. *Times Mag.* 3 Jan. p. 12/4 An island in the Eniwetok group disappeared below the surface of the water, smashed by the colossal punch of the world's first H-bomb. Reliable reports put the explosion as equaling the blast of five million tons of TNT, i.e., a 5 megaton bomb.

NAME-, NAME DROPPER. One who tries to impress by interlarding his conversation with the names of prominent people he knows. — 1947 San Fran. *Examiner* 7 Sept. Pictorial Rev. Sect. Not paged. Our Newest Menace. The Name Dropper. 1953 N.Y. *Times* 16 April p. 28 He can spot humbug in any guise. He is generally willing, though, to let name-droppers and braggarts expose themselves . . . *Freeman* 4 May p. 568 An inveterate name-dropper and a consummate sycophant, he liked to tell stories of the great and the celebrated, usually with himself in the scene as a victorious participant.

PRESIDENTIAD, *n.* — 1936 Mencken *The Amer. Lang.* p. 75. 1945 Mencken *Amer. Lang.: Sup. I* p. 125. 1953 N.Y. *Times Book Rev.* 25 Jan. p. 5/3 When the United States Government began its new Presidentiad on St. Agnes Eve, officers . . . were too busy to remember an eightieth anniversary coming up.

AMONG THE NEW WORDS

I. WILLIS RUSSELL
University of Alabama

ACKNOWLEDGMENTS: For citations: Clarence L. Barnhart (1), Dwight L. Bolinger (1), Thomas L. Crowell (5), Robert J. Geist (1), Atcheson L. Hench (2), John Luskin (1), Mamie J. Meredith (10), Porter G. Perrin (4), and Peter Tamony (3). Mamie J. Meredith and Peter Tamony both called my attention to the material on *catbird seat* in *American Speech.* James B. McMillan made several useful suggestions for the etymologies. Thanks are also due the University of Alabama Research Committee for aid.

BAKE-OFF, *n.* [By analogy with *fightoff, playoff, runoff, shootoff*] See quots.— 1950 *Am. N. & Q.* Jan. p. 151/2 'Bake-off': term applied to the recipe-and-baking competition sponsored by Pillsbury Mills, Inc., in early December; all the contestants worked under one roof . . . and produced their own specialities within a given period . . . each was provided with an electric range, utensils, and ingredients . . . *New Words and Words in the News* (Funk & Wagnalls Co.) Sup. No. 4 Spring p. 1/1. *Am. Sp.* 25:150/1–2 (with spelling *bakeoff*). 1953 Seattle *Times* 16 Dec. p. 25 (AP) The winner was among 100 finalists who came here to demonstrate their cooking ability in a 'bake-off' at the Waldorf-Astoria Hotel.

BEEFCAKE, BEEF CAKE, *n.* [By analogy with *cheesecake.*] See first quot.—1949 Richmond *News Leader* 25 Oct. p. 30/6 Alan Ladd has a beef—about 'beefcake,' the new Hollywood trend toward exposing the male chest. 1953 Berrey and Van den Bark *Am. Thes. Slang* ¶ 522.16. 1954 Tuscaloosa *News* 29 July p. 7/4 (UP) Mae West . . . made her night club debut . . . by introducing 'beef cake' to saloon shows.

CATBIRD SEAT. See quots.—1942 *New Yorker* 14 Nov. p. 17/2 . . . 'sitting in the catbird seat' meant sitting pretty, like a batter with three balls and no strikes on him. 1943 *Am. Sp.* 18:278/1 'Is *sitting in the catbird seat* a current expression or a nonce formation?' asks a contributor. 'Red Barber, the baseball radio announcer, uses it frequently . . .' 1944 *ibid.* 19:152/1 'The Catbird Seat' was the title of a short story by James Thurber published in the *New Yorker* magazine of November 14, 1942. The story fully explains the usage. 1948 *Newsweek* 10 May p. 12/3 CBS sports broadcaster Red Barber is doing a book about his radio career. He'll call it 'The Catbird Seat,' his term for the announcers' box at sports events. 1950 *Harper's Bazaar* Nov. p. 74 From this catbird seat he has just delivered a third of his new novel to his agent. 1952 *Wall St. Jour.* 3 June p. 11 This month of brides is being ushered in with a week of homage to secretaries, whom a public poll already had indicated are in the catbird's seat at the business of snaring a spouse. 1953 N. Y. *Times Book Rev.* 14 June p. 8 'Desiree' and 'The Silver Chalice' . . . were still in the catbird seat.

DISCOUNT HOUSE. {1863}—A store where prices are cut.—1952 *Fortune* June p. 210 The trim exterior of N.Y.'s Masters, Inc. . . . illustrates the climb of the once furtive discount house toward respectability. 1954 N.Y. *Times* 3 Jan. p. 48/3 A 'discount house' . . . has offered to 150,000 National Guardsmen all models of 1954 Fords at delivered prices only slightly above the wholesale cost to dealers. 1954 *Life* 9 Aug. p. 52/1 It began nine years ago, when the great postwar shopping spree set off a series of border incidents between the nation's big, manorial department stores and a small, night-riding band of price cutters operating establishments known as discount houses.

DOOR-KEY CHILDREN, KIDS. See quots.—1942 *Sci. N. L.* 10 Oct. p. 230 'Door-key' children of war workers are a new problem in many communities. . . . Children whose parents are at work or war, often come to the playgrounds in the morning bringing the front door key with them. Children who used to stay only a short while now remain all day until mother returns from work. 1943 *Harper's Mag.* April p. 461/2 Well, there were health problems, security problems, juvenile delinquency problems, children left alone all day (they called them door-key kids) . . . 1944 *New International Year Book* p. 763/1. 1945 *Ladies' Home Jour.* Oct. p. 133/1 We have heard a great deal about 'door-key' children whose parents left them unsupervised in order to work in war industries. Mencken *The Am. Lang. Sup. I* p. 593 One of the best of recent coinages is *doorkey children* . . . 1947 *Ten Eventful Years* 4:641/1. 1954 N.Y. *Times Mag.* 6 June 56/2 'Door-Key Kids' are children of working mothers who come to school with door keys hung around their necks and who go home after school to empty apartments.

EISENCRAT, *n.* [*Eisen*hower + Demo*crat*] See quots.—1952 N.Y. *Times* 28 Sept. p. 58/5 The Louisiana 'Eisencrats,' a name applied by the neighboring pro-Stevenson Democrats of Mississippi, are staying severely away from the few Republicans who are active in the state. 1953 *Christian Sci. Mon.* 11 Sept. p. 9 'Actually, it gives the young Democrats an opportunity to rise against the mistake of the "Eisencrats" and rally support to the true Democratic Party.'

ESCAPE SPEED, VELOCITY. That speed that overcomes the pull of gravity.—1951 Tuscaloosa *News* 16 Oct. p. 4/6 The problem of reaching the moon is basically that of getting rockets to fly fast enough to attain an 'escape' speed—an escape speed being about 23,000 miles an hour—sufficient to escape from the pull of the earth's gravity. 1952 N.Y. *Times* 13 April p. E9/7 To get back to their home planet the visitors would have to overcome the gravitational clutch of the earth, which means that an 'escape velocity' of seven miles a second must be attained. *Sat. Rev.* 5 July p. 15/1 The galaxies are speeding faster than the escape velocity . . . 1954 N.Y. *Times* 4 April p. E9/7 The escape velocity from the earth is 25,000 miles an hour, yet astronauts talk glibly of achieving it, though they are fully aware of the heat that will be generated.

EXPLOSIVE DECOMPRESSION. See quots.—1947 *This Week* 2 Nov. p. 26/2 ' "Explosive decompression," they call it. Your insides feel as if they're being pumped up with gas. Air rushes out of your nose and mouth. You cough. Perhaps bubbles form in the blood stream. That's painful, like having a penknife jabbed into you time and again.' 1948 *Time* 6 Sept. p. 66/2 Dr. Samuel Gelfan of the Yale University School of Medicine explained that the pressurized cabin, which has solved many of the problems of high-altitude flying, has in turn created a new and equally tough problem: explosive decompression. 1952 N.Y. *Times Mag.* 16 Nov. p. 40/4 If the space station were punctured there would be a blowout—what the engineers call 'explosive decompression.' In other words, the compressed air of the cabin would rush out through the holes like air in a cut tire. 1953 N.Y.*Times* 26 July p. E7/7 In a space station or interplanetary ship all that separates the crew from outer space is a wall which, relatively speaking, is about what a shell is to an egg. If there is a puncture there is an 'explosive decompression,' a sudden event, comparable with the bursting of a toy balloon.

FAIR-TRADE, *v.t.* [See *Fair-Trade Agreement* in *WNID. Add. Sect.* 1950]—1947 *Pub. Wk.* 24 May p. 2592 . . . When we phoned the publisher he advised us that this book was fair traded in Ohio and that we were required to sell it at the $2.75 price until June 30. 1949 *Red Barrel* July p. 17 He had no cut price on the popper. It was fair traded. 1952 N.Y. *Times* 30 March p. 1F/2 Nothing short of airtight legal compulsion will halt the Chicago appliance concern's continuing relentless fight to 'fair trade' effectively its Mixmasters and other small appliances.

FAIR TRADING. (Also attrib.)—1952 N.Y. *Times* 31 Aug. p. 1F/1 They appear to be inviting court tests of their position and so far few 'fair trading' manufacturers have moved against the larger and more powerful violators. *Ibid.* 12 Oct. p. F1/2 The principal barrier to 'fair trading' of phonograph records is ceiling prices.

FIRE STORM. {1581.} — See quots. — 1946 N.Y. *Times* 7 July p. E10/1 In Tokyo, in the terrible fire storm which devastated almost sixteen square miles of the city, 279 planes dropping 1,667 tons of incendiaries and conventional high explosives caused only 5,300 deaths per square mile. 1952 B'ham *News* 3 Feb. p. B1/2 (AP) The engineers foresee fire of terrific proportions—they call it a 'fire storm' in the ¾-mile ring just outside ground zero —up to one mile from the blast. 1953 *ibid.* 9 Jan. p. 12/3 The report also attempts to introduce to a wide audience the concept of 'fire storm' . . . Such a storm essentially is a man-made tornado, or hurricane. It occurs when there is such an intense fire over such a large area that the heat rising from the center of the fire pulls in cooler air from near the surface of the earth. The rising air over the bombing center thus becomes a huge sort of flue.

FLY-IN, *n.* [By analogy with *drive-in*] See quots. (Also attrib.) — 1948 *Newsweek* 19 July p. 82 With space for 25 planes, Brown's 'Fly-In' provides jeeps to tow its winged clientele to a ramp facing the screen and has loudspeakers to pipe the soundtrack into closed cockpits. 1952 N.Y. *Times* 9 March p. 2XX/7 (Not eligible for this prize are small planes landing at a combination drive-in and fly-in.) 1953 N.Y. *Times Mag.* 20 Sept. p. 30/4 A fly-in theatre established in St. Ansgar, Iowa, has a ramp equipped to handle eight planes, for the convenience of cinema-loving aeronauts.

GRAY*, *adj.* '1. The adjective denoting the colour intermediate between black and white . . .' {*a* 1000} (*OED*). — Hence, intermediate; indicating a stage between extremes; indeterminate. — [1941 S. I. Hayakawa *Lang. in Action* (N.Y.: Harcourt, Brace & Co.) p. 168 But the opposition between 'white' and 'black' is another kind of opposition. White and black are the extreme *limits of a scale*, and between them there is a continuous range of deepening shades of gray . . .] GRAYOUT, *v. i.* To become semiconscious. 1945 cited in *Am. Sp.* 28:49. GRAY MARKET. The market where goods can be bought, but at prices considered exorbitant. 1946 cited in *Am. Sp.* 23:149/1. (Cf. *WNID Add. Sect.*: 'A market using irregular channels of trade and undercover methods not actually or explicitly illegal [as in a *black market*], chiefly in scarce materials at prices far above list prices.' See also *white market* in *Am. Sp.* 25:143.) GRAY MOBILIZATION. Incomplete mobilization. 1950 cited in *Am. Sp.* 27:205. 1951 *Atlantic Monthly* March p. 17 India does not follow the classic neutrality principle of strict non-participation and impartiality. In a period of gray wars, it moves one way or the other to maintain an even grayness. 1952 B'ham *News* 29 Oct. p. 15/2 Ruml himself divides contributors into three categories: 'White,' those who really expect nothing in return; 'gray,' those who have a hankering for an ambassadorship or other post of honor, but expect no flat commitment; and 'black,' those who expect a flat (and profitable) commitment from the future administration. 1953 N.Y. *Times Mag.* 12 July p. 10 (pict. cap.) Scene in one of the 'Gray Areas'—Soviet tanks are used to break up German demonstrations in East Berlin. *Loc. cit.* Up to now the resentments have seldom been translated into open, and suicidal, rebellion. Instead, they have found expression in the 'gray war'—an immense flood of one-man protests through sabotage, wrecking, malingering, absenteeism and cheating that has been playing havoc with the satellite economies to a degree seldom realized in the West. 1953 B'ham *News* 28 July p. 23/4–5 (AP) Nothing is quite as black or white as it used to be. We live in a gray time, where one thing merges inconclusively into another thing. You don't know when war ends, because you don't know when peace begins. And that is the point upon which the world teeter-totters today. Both sides insist they went to war to preserve peace—a peace that (to show how gray even language has become) was known as 'the cold war.'

HARD NEWS. [Cf. *OED Sup. s. v. hard, 7.b*: 'Of facts: Incapable of being denied or explained away, "stubborn" ' . . . {1887}] See quots. — 1948 *Newsweek* 16 Aug. p. 51/1 The bulk of the broadcast time is given over to so-called 'hard news'—that is, straight newscasts of what is going on in the world and in the United States. 1952 Frank L. Mott *The News in America* (Cambridge, Mass.: Harvard University Press) p. 32 'Hard news' refers to the less exciting and more analytical stories of public affairs, economics, social problems, science, etc.; and 'soft news' is that which any editor immediately recognizes as interesting to his readers and therefore 'important' for his paper. 1953 *Harper's Mag.* Sept. p. 87/2 Another thing that got in our way was the American liking for 'hard' news—facts, figures, and direct quotations.

HIGH-SPEED HYPNOSIS. See quots. — 1952 *This Week* 1 June p. 8/1 A second danger on the superhighways is something called 'high-speed hypnosis'—a trance-like state induced by mile after mile of effortless driving. 1953 N.Y. *Times* 4 Jan. p. 31/4 As to high-speed hypnosis, the institute said it was a psychological phenomenon peculiar to the modern expressway. 'The road is straight and flat and seemingly endless. . . . Directly ahead of the driver is the ever-present "wet-spot" glare. . . . Nothing but mile after mile of repetition. Under such circumstances these drivers are prone to become literally hypnotized and drift into a trance. High speed does the rest.'

PANELIST, *n.* See quot. *Brit. Book of the Year.*—1952 N.Y. *Times* 14 June p. 13 Bennett Cerf . . . television panelist and anthologist, has compiled another book of humor . . . *Time* 1 Sept. p. 74/3 . . . the BBC's *What's My Line?*, like its U.S. counterpart, has four sharp-witted panelists. 1953 *Sat. Eve. Post* 1 Aug. p. 48 There are now about 150 men and women in New York, Philadelphia, Chicago and Los Angeles who are professional panelists . . . *Brit. Book of the Year* p. 752/2 panelist, *n.* A member of a discussion panel. N.Y. *Times* 4 Oct. p. 13/2 Mr. Stassen and six teen-age panelists appeared with Moderator Dorothy Gordon . . . 1954 *Newsweek* 8 Feb. p. 84/1 The other night . . . a television panelist, said thoughtfully: . . .

RACEWAY, *n.* {1868}. — A track for harness racing. — 1953 N.Y. *Times* 4 Oct. p. 1/8 The raceway was shown to have paid large sums to union officials to insure 'labor peace.' *Ibid.* 1 Nov. p. 84/5 Stock ownership in the two raceways by prominent Republicans and a county judge's association with a concern set up to print programs for Roosevelt Raceway have provided a wealth of campaign material for the Democrats.

RUN*, *v.t.* '*Run the* (or *a*) *blockade . . .*' {1869} (*OED* s. v. *run*, 40. b). — RUN (A RED LIGHT, STOP SIGN). — 1935 *Harper's Mag.* June p. 60/2 Perhaps we even 'ran' a light, relying on the waiting cars to continue to wait until we were out of their way. 1953 B'ham *News* 8 Aug. p. 1/8 Wilson told officers the brakes on his . . . truck failed, causing him to run a red light at the intersection. — RUNNING, *n.* — 1951 Tuscaloosa *News* 28 Jan. p. 1/7 (AP) Mitchell . . . had been arrested on charges of reckless driving and running a stop sign. 1954 *ibid.* 8 Aug. p. 3/4 Other charges made in the traffic division were classified as follows: . . . running stop signs, 5; running red lights, 16 . . .

SHAPE-UP, *v. phr.* (*Cent. Dict. Cyc.* 1909) — SHAPE-UP, *n.* [See first quot.; cf. *line-up*] See quots. (Also attrib.) — 1942 *PM* 11 Feb. p. 5/1 At 8 A.M. . . . they form in a rough semi-circular 'shape' around the hiring foreman for the stevedore company. He picks the men he wants to work that day. That's the barest outline of the shape-up system. 1953 N.Y. *Times* 10 May p. E2/7 Every morning outside New York's piers, longshoremen form a semicircle and the pier 'hiring boss' picks those who are to work cargo that day. The bosses . . . have arbitrary power. This hiring system, known as the 'shape-up,' has been the root cause of the evils besetting the docks for years . . . Tuscaloosa *News* 6 Dec. p. 4/5 Hitherto, these hiring bosses have operated the 'shape-up,' which means that longshoremen line up in front of them and are picked by the bosses for work. Berrey and Van den Bark *Am. Thes. Slang* ¶ 528.5.

SMAZE, *n.* [See quots.] See quots. — 1953 Charlottesville, Va. *Daily Progress* 21 Nov. 1/6–7 Called 'smog' by most people, the smoke-haze combination might more aptly be termed 'smaze,' according to weather observers. N.Y. *Times* 21 Nov. p. 1 Smaze is what it should really be called. . . . Dr. Morris B. Jacobs . . . explained that the gray pall overhanging this area was a blend of smoke and haze. Smog, he said, is a combination of smoke and fog. Berrey and Van den Bark *op. cit.* ¶ 71.9. 1954 *Christian Century* 7 April p. 425/1 They classified four kinds of these wicked things that contaminate the air, resulting in four kinds of city 'air'—'smog, smurk, smaze and smist.'

SWINDLETRON, *n.* [*swindle* + *electron*] See quots. — 1953 B'ham *News* 6 Nov. p 9/1 (AP) A poor man's atom smasher, called a swindletron because it seems to get something for nothing, is being built at the University of California. This relatively small instrument will produce a beam of atomic particles bearing charges of one million volts each, even though it uses only a half-million volt power source. N.Y. *Times* 22 Nov. p. E9/5 The University of California has a new atom smasher that the physicists there call the 'swindletron,' which is a good deal easier to say than 'charge-exchange accelerator,' the technical name. The swindletron makes it possible to accelerate the same particle twice with one source of voltage, which accounts for the name.

TELECOURSE, *n.* See quots. — 1952 *Pleasures of Publishing* (Columbia University Press) July p. 1 In keeping with the 'what's next' attitude of the modern world, some colleges like the University of Michigan and Western Reserve are allowing course credits for study at home via TV. These telecourses apply as full credit toward degrees since regular instructors are used for the telecasts. 1953 Seattle *Times* 28 June p. 24 Dr. George Horton . . . reports all applicants who registered for the first two telecourses completed their studies . . . 1954 *Univ. of Wash. Daily* 5 Jan. p. 1 The causes of weather conditions . . . are being taught to television viewers in the University's sixth Telecourse on KING-TV.

TRISKAIDEKAPHOBIA, TRISKEDEKAPHOBIA, *n.* [See last quot.] See quots. — 1951 N.Y. *Sunday Mirror* 8 July p. 14 Thirteen superstitions about artists . . . will be debunked by 13 crusaders against triskedekaphobia (fear of 13) . . . 1953 N.Y. *Times Mag.* 8 Feb. p. 32 Experts have labeled people who react to the '13' superstition as victims of triskaidekaphobia (fear of the number 13). N.Y. *Times* 8 Nov. pp. E2, E9. . . . A discussion in the U.N. last week on the number of members on a committee raised the question of triskaidekaphobia. What's that? [p. E9] . . . Fear (phobia, in Greek) of the number thirteen (triskaideka).

AMONG THE NEW WORDS

I. WILLIS RUSSELL
University of Alabama

ACKNOWLEDGMENTS: For citations: Dwight L. Bolinger (1), Thomas L. Crowell (1), Atcheson L. Hench (4), Mamie J. Meredith (13), Porter G. Perrin (11), Thomas Pyles (1), and Peter Tamony (2). Martha Jackson contributed to the definition of *belt out*. Thanks are also due the University of Alabama Research Committee for aid.

ANTI-ANTI-COMMUNIST, *n.* See quots. (Also attrib.)— 1953 Los Angeles *Examiner* 22 Nov. p. 1 For ease of reference we might call them anti-anti-communists, or members of the AAC, because they always seem to attack anybody who is trying to make it tough for Communist infiltrators. Tuscaloosa *News* 24 Nov. p. 4/4 The phrase, anti-anti-Communist, is cumbersome and does not quite convey the idea that while those who follow this line say that they are as violently opposed to Communism as anybody else, they always, without exception, come to the defense, if not of Marxist ideas, certainly of Communist personalities when they get into trouble. *Time* 7 Dec. p. 24 Harry Truman gave the Wisconsin Senator the opening by using a well-worn anti-anti-Communist technique; he denounced Attorney General Herbert Brownell's handling of the White case as 'McCarthyism.' 1954 *Life* 26 July p. 20/3 The Communists and the anti-anti-Communists are delighted.

ANTI-FLUORIDATIONIST, *n.* One who disapproves of the fluoridation of water.— 1954 B'ham *News* 25 April p. 2E/6 Would you please permit these few lines to call attention to efforts of anti-fluoridationists to use the 'guilt by association' technique to smear the chemical compound, sodium fluoride, which exists in fluoridated water? N. Y. *Times* 5 Sept. p. E2/7 The editorial cites a list of authorities who favor fluoridation and challenges 'the small but vociferous group of anti-fluoridationists' to provide scientific evidence in support of their views.

BARRIER CREAM. See quots.—1950 N.Y. *Times* 16 April p. E9/5 A British chemical firm protects workers who handle dyestuffs, chemicals, explosives, oils, acids, alkalis and grease by means of 'barrier creams.' The cream is spread over the hands until an invisible 'glove' is formed. 1954 *This Week* 10 Oct. p. 31/1 Next the demonstrator applied a white cream to his hands. He washed in cold water, explaining that this would 'set' the now invisible cream. He dried, and then with a calm smile, plunged his hands into the acid. They came out intact. . . . It was a demonstration of a remarkable 'barrier cream' . . .

B-, Short for *bar* (in combinations).—1953 *This Week* 26 July p. 7/1 And a gal that's good with the B-drink tricks can run it up to two hundred or three hundred dollars. *Loc. cit.* THIS WEEK MAGAZINE assigned girl reporter Edan Wright to get an inside story on how 'B (for Bar) joints' really work. 1954 B'ham *News* 22 June p. 1/4 The 'B-girls' . . . were leaving by car, bus, or by foot . . . *Ibid.* 17 Aug. p. 8 (heading) Guardsmen set trap for ring carrying B-girls to Aiken, S.C.

BELT OUT, *v. phr.* [Cf. *OED*, s. v. *belt*, *v.* 4: 'To thrash with a belt . . .' {1649}; *ACD*, s. v. *belt*, *v.* 11: '*Colloq.* to give a thwack or blow to'; 1942 Berrey and Van den Bark *Amer. Thesaurus of Slang* ¶703.3: *belt out*, 'knock out' (boxing); *belt out* (baseball), 'to belt out a three-bagger.'] To sing with great energy and with a strongly accented rhythm ('to give it all you have').—1953 *Sat. Rev. Lit.* 12 Dec. p. 55/1 Standing there in the dim haze, with her feet apart, belting out the sophisticated sweetness of Porter's 'Get Out of Town' or 'You Better Go Now' . . . the piano trickling along behind her, Bricky has a way of covering the place with great misty clouds of Scott-and-Zelda nostalgia. 1954 N. Y. *Times Mag.* 24 Jan. p. 50 (caption) Belting It Out—Above and at left Miss Garland tears into one of the eight songs she sings in the picture. B'ham *News* 10 Nov. p. 27/4 But it's all Ethel, who really comes over as she belts out 'Make It Another Old Fashioned, Please,' 'Let's Be Buddies' and 'Ridin' High.' BELTER, *n.*—1953 *Time* 20 July p. 90 With a voice that can be a shy soprano but is more often a belting baritone, Joyce Bryant seems to have trouble relaxing on-stage. . . . And so, almost automatically, she became a belter. She found herself 'living' every song she sang . . .

BLOW-, BLOWOUT, *n.* {1826}—See quots.—1954 N.Y. *Times* 4 April p. E5/4–5 Similar reasoning applies to the H-bomb, though in this case it is the dissipation of energy upward that limits what is called 'blowout.' Seattle *Times* 11 April p. 6/4 A phenomenon known as the 'limit of blow-out' curtails the lateral destruction of the hydrogen bomb; after about 50 megatons, there is no appreciable increase in lateral destruction, because all additional power is dissipated in the relatively nonresistant upper atmosphere . . . which probably reduces to well below 'the limit of blow-out' the power of a bomb . . . *Ibid.* 19 April p. 6/4 . . . a phenomenon known as 'the limit of blow-out' limits the lateral destructive effect of the bomb to less than 20 miles.

BRUTALITARIANISM, *n.* [*brutalitarian* {1904}+*-ism*]—1940 *Am. Freeman* Sept. p. 1/4 I am prejudiced against every manifestation of Brutalitarianism. 1954 Tuscaloosa *News* 16 April p. 9/4 (AP) In the past five years McCarthy has: 1. Accused Army officers of extracting war crimes confessions from German SS troopers in such a manner that 'our government had been placed in a position of condoning a brand of brutalitarianism worse than that practiced by the most morally degenerate in either Hitler's or Stalin's camps . . .'

BUILT-IN, *adj.* Lit. sense in *WNID* 1934.—*Fig.*—1951 *World Almanac* p. 261 The increase in consumer buying and costs brought higher prices; the N.Y. *Times* called this 'built-in inflation' and declared further inflation inevitable under the system. 1953 Berry and Van den Bark *op. cit.* ¶ 757.10 . . . built-in head wind, *said to be possessed by a plane with a slow cruising speed.* B'ham *News* 18 Oct. p. B2/1 But a house with automatic built-in weather is the latest word in luxurious living. 1954 N.Y. *Times* 31 Jan. p. 30/1 Officials say, however, that 'built-in' barriers of the law have caused most of the seeming delay in getting the program 'off the ground.' *Life* 19 April p. 26/1 Without specifically brandishing the H-bomb, they insist on the futility and built-in sinfulness of all human achievements. *Ibid.* 19 July p. 11/2 There was a built-in controversy on the salad question even before Life appeared this week.

CAFETORIUM, *n.* [*cafe*teria+*auditorium*] See quots. (Also attrib.)—1954 Tuscaloosa *News* 28 Feb. p. 1/5 It will have approximately 14,550 square feet of space with eight classrooms, a cafetorium, or a room that can be used for an auditorium or cafeteria, work rooms, offices, and a multipurpose room. Gainesville (Fla.) *Sun* 1 Sept. p. 1 Controversy seemed to be the order of business for the day, with the Board faced with bids on the Sidney Lanier cafetorium project which exceeded by more than $14,000 the estimated figure . . .

CONILLUM, *n.* [See quots.] See quots.—1954 N.Y. *Times* 18 July p. 10/1 (UP) The plan, also called 'conillum' (control of illumination), calls for restrictions on outdoor advertising signs and floodlights. Lincoln (Nebr.) *Sunday Jour.* 18 July p. 1 (AP) Military and civil defense authorities Saturday night announced a plan for controlling 'sky glow' in event of enemy attack—a system of dimming city lights but not blacking them out as in World War II days. Called 'Conillum,' for controlled illumination, it is a companion measure to 'Conelrad' . . .

DESEGREGATE, *v.t.* To bring about the condition in which all races, especially Negroes, can avail themselves of the same facilities, such as motion picture theaters and public schools. —1953 *Life* 13 July p. 36/1 It is hoped that this decision of the court will help to desegregate the white movie theaters, which all still draw the color line except a few small houses of the 'art' type. 1954 N.Y. *Times Mag.* 13 June p. 4 [His] article was a case history concerned with the impacts, happy or otherwise, on the adults and children of . . . a Southern-minded . . . community, when it desegregated its public schools. *Time* 27 Sept. p. 60/2 . . . plans were afoot to desegregate the whole school system by next year.

DE-, DESEGREGATION, *n.*—1952 N.Y. *Times* 14 Dec. p. E9/2 A 'statement of experts' . . . has been filed in behalf of the NAACP, citing the effects of segregation and the consequences of de-segregation.' 1953 *Ibid.* 14 June p. E12/3 . . . it seems likely that only in proportion to Negro political strength will there be any 'de-segregation' in this area. *Sci. N. L.* 29 May p. 338/1 Desegregation has already been put into effect in elementary and secondary public schools within the past five to ten years in local communities of 12 states . . . Charlottesville (Va.) *Daily Progress* 31 May p. 1/5 (headline) Suits Will Press De-Segregation. *Newsweek* 19 July p. 84 Desegregation . . . *School and Society* 21 Aug. p. 53/2 Many of those resisting de-segregation via court order object to the element of compulsion. [Five later citations not used have *desegregation* (without hyphen).]

EUROVISION, *n.* [*Euro*pean tele*vision*] See quots. (Also attrib.)—1954 N.Y. *Times* 6 June p. 85/3 Europe's leading television engineers will twirl dials with crossed fingers tomorrow when they tune in the first eight-nation 'Eurovision' hook-up through Lille. Balto. *Sun* 8 June p. 14/1 'Eurovision' went off smoothly. This is a European television network which embraces transmitters in Italy, France, Britain, West Germany . . . *Variety* 14 July p. 2 Members of the recently-established European Television Network (Eurovision) are now considering closed-circuit tv as a means of further strengthening their inter-country communications setup . . . N.Y. *Times* 31 Oct. p. F7/5 'Eurovision,' the European TV network that blankets the Continent, 'has a bright future' . . .

FLY-IN, *n.* See *Am. Sp.* 29:284. Additional quot.—1954 *Family Weekly Mag.* 19 Sept. p. 6/2 We had drive-in theaters for automobiles, so now there is a fly-in theater for airplanes.

HONEST JOHN. See quots. (Also attrib.)—1954 Balto. *Sun* 17 Feb. p. 1/2 'This country's first successful adaptation of the rocket principle to a tactical missile with medium-to-long-range capability . . . put into position much more quickly than conventional artillery . . .' (This is 'Honest John.') B'ham *News* 7 March p. A24/4–5 The Army is stockpiling the plane-killing Nike units, and semi-guided field artillery rockets designated as the 'Honest John.' *Aviation Week* 19 July p. 7/1 Honest John missile blasted off from its self-propelled launcher at Ft. Bragg, N.C., last week in the first public showing of Army's three-ton operational artillery weapon, designed to carry a nuclear warhead (*Aviation Week* April 6, p. 12).

LYTIC COCKTAIL. [See second quot.] See quots.—1954 *Time* 14 June p. 80/3 He found that it [chlorpromazine hydrochloride] worked against shock and produced the effects of hibernation. Laborit promptly organized a research team to make the most of these effects, and from its combined efforts came the 'lytic cocktail.' In this, chlorpromazine is combined with Phenergan and Dolosal to block the automatic nervous system. *Harper's Mag.* Sept. p. 62/2 Three years ago, he [Laborit] found a combination that lowered body temperature, provided a remarkable simulation of hibernation in other ways, and also . . . made it easy and safe to chill patients into a still deeper state. His drug combination included the synthetic narcotic demerol; chlorpromazine . . . and phenergan . . . . This combination has been dubbed the 'lytic cocktail' because, when injected, it 'dissolves' the nervous system's regulatory mechanisms.

MOUSE, *n.* [See first quot.] See quots.—1954 Seattle *Times* 15 April p. 10/4 The 'new look' in proposed satellites has been named 'Mouse.' The name stands not only for its size, but for 'Minimum Orbital Unmanned Satellite, Earth.' Omaha *World-Her. Mag.* 23 May p. 11/7 (repr. from *Time*) The Mouse will be a sphere, weighing one hundred pounds and packed with instruments, that will be carried up by a three-stage rocket. The third and final stage will enter an orbit 190 miles above the earth's surface. . . . Mr. Singer believes that the Mouse will stay up long enough to send back a wealth of information. *Sci. N. L.* 12 June p. 381/1 It would cost less than $1,000,000 for each 'shot' of the MOUSE, or minimum orbital unmanned satellite, earth, Dr. S. F. Singer of the University of Maryland has estimated.

ROLLING ADJUSTMENT. See quot. N. Y. *Times Mag.*—1953 B'ham *News* 4 Dec. p. 39/2 Only the word 'recession' is too strong to describe the series of relatively mild 'rolling adjustments' which we're now experiencing. 1954 *Newsweek* 15 Feb. p. 69 . . . is the current business dip a 'recession' or a 'rolling adjustment'? . . . Treasury Secretary George Humphrey disagreed sharply. 'We've not got a recession in every industry,' he said. 'I use rolling adjustment because some things are operating at the same levels . . .' N. Y. *Times Mag.* 28 March p. 14/4 A rolling adjustment is a period in which one or a few major industries are taking a beating at a time when others are really prospering. Then when the industries which have suffered come out of their valley of momentary despair, others drop down. [N. Y. *Times* 13 June p. E7/1 Last January's phrase to describe the economic outlook, 'rolling readjustment,' has been succeeded by an equally picturesque bit of jargon, 'saucering out.']

RUMBLE, *n.* [Cf. *OED*, s. v. *rumble, sb.* 2: 'Commotion, bustle, tumult, uproar. *Obs.*' {*c.* 1386–1682}; '3. *Sc.* A severe blow. *Obs.*' {1375–1434}; 1953 Berrey and Van den Bark *op. cit.* ¶ 496.1, s. v. *rumble, n.* (*v.* in 1942 ed.): '. . . a disturbance in order to distract attention from confederates . . .'] See quots.—1948 Jack Lait and Lee Mortimer *New York: Confidential!* (Chicago: Ziff-Davis Pub. Co.) p. 121 Their [activities] now range from fighting each other for the pure love of bloodshed (called 'rumbles') to highway robbery. Often fights are faked so that in the confusion and the crowd a quick job of larceny is inconspicuous. 1950 *Time* 4 Dec. p. 40/3 Each gang had a . . . war counselor who arranged the time and place for gang 'rumbles' (wars) . . . 1952 *Sat. Eve. Post* 5 July p. 21 A 'rumble' is East Harlem for gang—or perhaps we should say ganglet—war. 1953 N.Y. *Times* 7 June p. 1/2 A 'rumble' or fight was also averted at 189th Street and Croton Avenue, the Bronx. 1954 N.Y. *Times Mag.* 21 March p. 17/1 He had had to cope with confidences involving hold-up plans, impending 'rumbles'—the teen-age wars that produced ten murders in New York City in a single year—and a variety of other crimes.

SONIC BOOM, SONIC EXPLOSION. See quots.—1954 *Aviation Week* 8 March p. 13 (title) Sonic Boom: a Potential Weapon? NAA study finds shock waves can knock light planes out of air, batter ground structures and create panic. [col. 2] . . . The North American study of shock waves is one of the most complete undertaken in this country and the first to indicate publicly that the increasingly familiar 'sonic boom' may be potentially dangerous. B'ham *News* 16 May p. A13/2 It's all because of a man-made headache becoming increasingly troublesome—the veritable claps of doom called sonic explosions. Omaha *World-Her. Mag.* 16 May p. 5/7 (title) Those Sonic Booms. *Loc. cit.* The cannon-like booms are caused by planes breaking the sonic barrier. . . . Discovery of the sonic explosions came by chance. B'ham *News* 13 Oct. p. 6/1–2 (AP) Witnesses said it exploded with a terrific blast and plummeted to the ground like a ball of fire. But officials at North American Aviation, Inc., where Welch was chief test pilot, said the blast might have been a 'sonic boom' caused when a jet pulls out of a dive at high speed. *Sat. Eve. Post* 4 Dec. p. 27/1 This sonic boom is created whenever an airplane pierces the sound barrier. . . . Not only is it caused by a diving jet pointed toward the earth; a supersonic plane traveling straight and level parallel to the earth can propagate a constant boom which, under certain atmospheric conditions, will trail along the ground in its wake like a following shadow.

SPECTACULAR, *n.* [Cf. *OED*, s. v. *spectacular, a.* and *sb.* 4: 'A spectacular display' {1890}.] *Specif.* See quots.— 1954 N. Y. *Times* 28 March p. X13/1 Its [NBC's] big feature . . . will be a series of costly and lavish ninety-minute 'spectaculars'—opera, drama, musical comedy, circuses, ice shows, etc.—that will show color off at its best. *Sat. Rev.* 17 April p. 24 The imaginative Mr. Pat Weaver in charge of the NBC network has come up with the announcement that next season he will inaugurate a series to be known as 'spectaculars.' They will be hour or hour-and-a-half shows designed as something off the beaten path of television fare. B'ham *News* 14 May p. 43/1 Announcements are beginning to come out about next Fall's color 'spectaculars' on NBC-TV. Balto. *Sun* 27 May p. 16/1 Now that NBC-TV has announced its series of 'color spectaculars,' CBS-TV has replied with news of a series with which they hope to top them. Lincoln (Nebr.) *Sunday Jour. and Star* 22 Aug. p. 10D. One of the reasons is the 'spectaculars'—lengthy, high cost, top-talent shows. . . . Variety . . . tagged these proposed superdoopers as 'spectaculars.' Seattle *Times* 7 Oct. p. 54/5 In the Betty Hutton spectacular on N.B.C. the dub-in was so poor her lips didn't always keep exact time with her voice.

VOLSCAN, *n.* See quots.—1953 N.Y. *Times* 8 Dec. p. J2/7 The system, called 'VOLSCAN,' . . . is a combination of radar and electronic tracking and computing devices that sort out and memorize a selected plane's flight path. *Newsweek* 21 Dec. p. 54 Volscan's electronic brain had perceived the B-29 and noted its speed and direction. From that moment, the plane was under the steady surveillance of Volscan's complex sensory organ, a . . . computer called Antrac. This robot fed its knowledge to . . . Datac, which continuously calculated the plane's correct heading, air speed, and altitude. Datac posted the results . . . on a bank of dials. 1954 *Think* Jan. p. 26 'Volscan,' U.S.A.F.'s new electronic control system to speed aircraft landings, can handle 120 planes an hour. 1955 N.Y. *Times* 30 Jan. p. X33/3 One of the more promising [traffic-control devices] is Volscan, an application of the electronic calculator to the business of safely guiding a heavy flow of planes through bad weather to an airport.

AMONG THE NEW WORDS

I. WILLIS RUSSELL

University of Alabama

ACKNOWLEDGMENTS: For citations: Walter S. Avis (1), Dwight L. Bolinger (1), T. L. Crowell (5), Atcheson L. Hench (6), Albert L. Marckwardt (1), Mamie J. Meredith (18), Porter G. Perrin (10), George Pope Shannon (1), and Peter Tamony (6). James B. McMillan contributed the etymology of *back-to-back;* Atcheson L. Hench and Mamie J. Meredith contributed to the definitions of *ground* and *hard sell* respectively. T. L. Crowell suggested the declassification of *stomp* as dialect.

A-B-C, *adj.* See quots.—1951 N.Y. *Times* 12 July p. 23 Civil Defense in Modern War: a Text on the Protection of the Civil Population against A-B-C Warfare (Atomic-Bacterial-Chemical), by Brig. Gen. Augustin M. Prentis . . . 1954 Irving R. Levine over NBC 3 Oct. in the phrase 'A-B-C weapon.' B'ham *News* 3 Oct. p. A-1/8 (AP) West Germany guaranteed to outlaw the manufacture of the A-B-C weapons—atomic, bacteriological and chemical—and other heavy war equipment . . .

AEROCAB, *n.* See last quot.—1953 *Harper's Mag.* May p. 29/1 It predicts helicopter aerocabs by 1954 . . . 1955 R. Mueller 13 Jan. (letter to Mamie J. Meredith) 'Aerocab' has appeared in print for a 'taxi' to and from the airport to a downtown helistop.

AUTOMOBILIANA, *n. pl.* [*automobile* + *-i-* + *-ana*] Things having to do with automobiles considered collectively. (Also attrib.)—1950 *Hobbies* July p. 38 Attention: Automobiliana Fans 1953 *Musical Amer.* 15 April p. 8/1 James Melton is transferring his fabulous collection of old cars and automobiliana . . . from New England to . . . Florida. 1954 *Hobbies* March p. 118 (title) Automobiliana on Stamps.

BACK-TO-BACK, BACK TO BACK, *adj.* [Cf. back-to-back aces in stud poker. Since the ace in the hole is face down and the one on top face up, they are back to back, hence consecutive.] One after the other; consecutive.—1952 N.Y. Times 24 Aug. p. S1/8 Back to back doubles by Gene Woodling and Joe Collins off Early Wynn in the fourth inning produced the only tally of the day. 1954 B'ham *News* 6 Aug. p. 15/5 (AP) Back-to-back home runs in the eighth by Ernie Banks and Eddie Miksis boomed the Cubs to victory over the Giants. Schenectady *Union-Star* 28 Aug. p. 11/3 (UP) Maglies [sic] conquest of the Braves last night marked the sixth time this season and the fourth time since July 20 that the Maglie-Antonelli combination has produced back-to-back victories.

BASCART, *n.* [*basket* + *cart*] See first quot.—1949 Reported by Albert H. Marckwardt in use in Ann Arbor 'for the kind of basket on wheels in use in the supermarkets.' 1952 *Am. Sp.* 27:229–30. 1954 *Life* 2 Aug. p. 49/1 But the pint-sized consumers confounded the experts almost as soon as they began filling their 'bascarts' . . .

BEAM-RIDER GUIDANCE. See first quot. (Also fig.)—1951 *Johns Hopkins Mag.* Nov. p. 7/2 In beam-rider (or way-following) guidance, an artificial path—such as a radar beam tracking the target—is marked out in space. Missile has a mechanism for sensing its position continuously with respect to the axis of this path, knowing when it deviates and correcting its course accordingly. 1953 *Sat. Eve. Post* 5 Sept. p. 99/2 '. . . They're the sort a self-respecting girl can lead to the altar before you can say Jack Robinson and apply beam-rider guidance the rest of his natural life. Which every man needs.'

BOOTLEG, *adj.* [Cf. Mathews, *DA*, s. v. *bootleg, n.* b.: 'Used attributively for anything that is inferior or illegal . . .' (1895)] See quot.—1954 *Changing Times* May p. 20 'Bootleg' automobiles are brand-new cars which secondhand-car dealers buy from new-car dealers who are overloaded with stock, and resell for just a few dollars more than the original dealer paid for them. 1955 *U.S. News* 11 Feb. p. 27 Suppliers of the 'bootleg' market are regular dealers who find themselves overloaded with cars.

BOOTLEGGING, *n.* See quots.—1954 N.Y. *Times* 7 Feb. p. 2F/3 (AP) In some instances the dealers have blamed this development for the revival of new-car 'bootlegging.' In this practice an overstocked new-car dealer sells his surplus stock at a little more than cost to a used-car dealer. The latter takes the cars into another territory and sells them at less than list price. *Time* 12 July p. 82/1 One of the most damaging of the sales tricks is auto bootlegging. Spokane *Spokesman-Rev.* 23 July p. 34 (AP) 'Bootlegging,' he [president of the National Automobile Dealers Assn.] said, 'has become a definite big business.' 1955 N.Y. *Times* 6 Feb. p. 32X/4–5 The National Automobile Dealers Association . . . takes a very dim view of General Motors Corporation's attempt to curb passenger-car bootlegging by offering to take back from dealers their unsold cars or to have such cars transferred to territories where they will sell more readily. *U.S. News* 11 Feb. p. 27 'Bootlegging,' so called, is said to be flourishing this year as it was in 1954. This is the practice of selling new cars at cut prices through used-car dealers who do not hold factory franchises.

CARLEGGING, *n.* [*car*+*bootlegging*] See quot.—1954 Tuscaloosa *News* 4 March p. 4/1 It is explained 'carlegging' works something like this: A dealer has to accept and pay for a certain number of cars in order to retain his franchise. In order to move those cars, or certain slow moving models, he sells them to a person at a discount with the understanding that this car, or cars, will be taken from his trade area. In turn, the cars are sold, at a profit, but still under the normal price for new cars.

CHURNING*, *n.* [Cf. *OED*, s. v. *churn*, *v.* 2: 'To agitate, stir, and intermix any liquid, or mixture of liquid and solid matter . . .' {1697}] *Fig.* See second quot.—1953 N.Y. *Times* 22 Nov. p. F1/6 The 'churning' caused by tax selling and buying, it must be remembered, is a factor contributing to the mixed pattern of the market. 1954 San Fran. *Call-Bull.* 29 March (financial page, cols. 1–3) The main characteristic was 'churning,' meaning large blocks of stock turned over with little or no change in price.

COLOMBO, *adj.* [See quots.] See quots.—1954 N.Y. *Times* 27 June p. E5/2 The task of enlisting the help of the new Asian states, more recently known as the 'Colombo powers'—India, Pakistan, Ceylon, Burma and Indonesia—was taken over by Anthony Eden . . . Irving R. Levine over NBC 28 Dec. . . . Colombo powers, so called because they had their first meeting . . . at Colombo, Ceylon. 1955 N.Y. *Times* 2 Jan. p. E5/3 The Colombo powers—Pakistan, India, Ceylon, Burma and Indonesia—have enhanced their influence in world affairs . . . *Ibid.* 9 Jan. p. 6E/1 A variety of motivations figured in the decision of the Colombo Prime Ministers last week to sponsor the conference of Asian and African nations . . .

COLONIZE, *n.* [Cf. *OED*, s. v. *colonize*, *v.* 1: '. . . to plant or establish a colony in' {1622}; *DA*, s. v. *colonize*, *v.*: '1. *tr.* To place or register (hired political supporters) in doubtful districts where their votes may decide a closely contested election . . .' (*Vbl. n.* 1842; *v.* 1903)] See *colonizer* below.—1949 B'ham *News* 8 April p. 22/1 (AP) Communist plans to 'colonize' key U.S. industrial plant [*sic*] were described yesterday by an undercover man who fed the FBI with secrets from his strategic position in the Red underground.—COLONIZING, *adj.* {1805}—1949 *ibid. loc. cit.* Philbrick's declarations followed previous government testimony that a postwar 'colonizing' program was started by the U.S. Communist politburo on orders from Moscow.

COLONIZER, *n.* {1781} See second quot.—1949 *ibid. loc. cit.* col. 2 The witness quoted Blum as saying 'the status of a colonizer' is 'a high honor in the party.' 1954 San Fran. *News* 3 Sept. p. 7/8 (UP) Nearly 100 Red 'colonizers' have been sent into Michigan by the Communist Party to infiltrate the auto industry, the House un-American activities committee warned last night. The committee said in a report 27 of these Communist 'colonizers' were found 'holding positions of influence' in Flint.

COMMAND*, *adj.* [Cf. *OED*, s. v. *command*, *sb.* 4: 'Power of control, disposal, or direction . . .' {1642}] See quots.—1947 *Time* 23 June p. 70/3 'Command' missiles follow orders (radio signals) from the ground, a ship, or a piloted aircraft. 1949 *Newsweek* 21 Feb. p. 52/2 *Command guidance*. . . . In this system the missile only needs to carry enough mechanism to receive and obey commands from the ground. 1951 *Johns Hopkins Mag.* Nov. p. 6/1 In command guidance, a ground station tracks both the missile and the target. It computes what adjustments should be made to the missile's course and then transmits instructions to the missile which cause it to alter its course accordingly. 1954 *N.Y. Times Mag.* 29 Aug. p. 49/2 The 'command-guidance' type of missile can be altered in course by electronic impulses from the ground, from an accompanying plane or from a ship. The Nike . . . is a command-guidance missile . . .

CREEPER-, CREEPER LANE. See first quot.—1953 Balto. *Sun* 12 Jan. p. 6/6 'Creeper lanes,' which have proved very successful in promoting a free flow of highway traffic, are third lanes built to accommodate vehicles that must creep up the hills. Seattle *Times* 26 Jan. (Same quot. as preceding). 1954 Roy C. Foster Eh 388 (Univ. of Wash.) term paper on truckers' vocabulary: The highest and lowest gears are spoken of most affectionately. Low gear and low range is known as *the little one*, *the grannie hole*, and *the creeper*. The new truck lane over Snoqualmie Pass automatically becomes the *creeper lane* to drivers who go over the *pass*—the *hump*—with a load. *Life* 9 Aug. p. 4 By eliminating steep grades Thruway engineers have avoided the necessity of 'creeper' lanes for trucks which turnpikes in more mountainous terrain require.

DO-IT-YOURSELF, *n.* The practice of doing oneself such things as working with wood and finishing. (Also attrib.)—1953 *Harper's Mag.* May p. 94 By the time *Business Week* got to it, however, the do-it-yourself business had already expanded beyond home workshop tools. *Ibid.* Oct. p. 6 If economy were the real incentive to what its promoters call do-it-yourself, the boom would have come in the thirties, when people had to make do on so little. 1954 Balto. *Sun* 25 March p. 27/1 Manufacturers . . . are packaging items especially to lure do-it-yourself trade. *Business Week* 27 March p. 122 (cited *Read. Guide* 54: 140/1. May 10, 1954) Sap is running in do-it-yourself. N.Y. *Times* 5 Sept. p. F1/4–7 (pict. cap.) Preparing a Favorite Material for Do-It-Yourself Enthusiasts. *Life* 25 Oct. p. 87/1 They are now applied professionally only but may wind up as a do-it-yourself package.

DO-IT-YOURSELFER, *n.*—1954 N.Y. *Times* 5 Sept. p. F1/7 To the do-it-yourselfer, plywood is as essential as paint, tools, plastics and ordinary lumber. *Wall St. Jour.* 13 Oct. p. 8 Now . . . mass volume has enabled the company to serve the do-it-yourselfer handsomely . . . 1955 *This Week Mag.* 1 May p. 25 (pict. cap.) . . . Granddaughter stars as do-it-yourselfer. *McCall's* July p. 98/4 . . . do-it-yourselfers may purchase from certain prefab companies houses with no interior finishing.

DO-IT-YOURSELFING, *n.*—1954 Omaha *World Her.* 2 Nov. p. 1 Do-it-yourselfing interests Mom.

DO-IT-YOURSELFISM, *n.*—1954 N.Y. *Her. Trib.* 21 March Sec. 4 p. 17 There are other reasons, too, for the tidal wave of do-it-yourselfism . . . 1955 *Life* 25 July p. 99/1 'Now you *admit* Do-It-Yourselfism is a deadly business.'

FACELESS, *adj.* 1. See quots.—1953 N.Y. *Times* 4 Oct. p. 5/1 The 'faceless men'—about 15,000 anti-Communist Chinese and 7,000 anti-Communist North Koreans—have assumed a role relatively new to military history. In all their wars the Communists have regarded prisoners not as human beings but as hostages and pawns, as means to a Communist end. 1955 *N. Y. Times Book Rev.* 20 Feb. p. 10/5 And there are many things worth pondering over in the eloquent last paragraphs of this book which briefly state the democratic answer to Marxist philosophy with its disdain for individuals while it trumpets its concern for faceless collectives.

2. Of secret identity.—1953 *Friends Intelligencer* 19 Dec. p. 691/2 Men are adjudged on the whispered accusations of faceless people not known to the accused.

GIRLIE, GIRLY, *adj.* {1886} [Cf. Berrey and Van den Bark *Am. Thes. Slang* ¶ 590.9: *girly burly* 'burlesque show'; ¶ 590.13: *girlie; girly* or *girly-girly show* 'chorus show'] See quots. (Also absol.)—1949 *This Week* 23 Oct. p. 24/2 Favorites of the collectors are hotels . . . 'bridge' covers . . . 'girlies' (mostly by well-known calendar artists) . . . 1950 *Time* 26 June p. 71/1 *Liberty* . . . was being sold to 'one of those awful girlie books.' *Capitol News* (house organ of Capitol Records, Hollywood) July Vol. 8, No. 7 Midsummer Girlie Issue [White on black banner strip across front page illustrating a girl in dark glasses and a bikini mounting recordings on a portable player.] 1951 *Newsweek* 30 July p. 63. 1952 *Pub. Weekly* 13 Dec. p. 2318 The committee indicated it would turn over these books . . . including some 'girlie' magazines . . .to post office inspectors . . . B'ham *News* 21 Dec. p. A12/2 (AP) Miss Banning said there are 1,231 magazines being published and all but about 100 are classified as 'girlies' which she regards as 'vicious and provocative.' 1953 *Sat. Rev.* 24 Jan. p. 10 In Washington, novelist Margaret Culkin Banning righteously proclaimed to the Gathings House Investigating Committee that only about 100 of the country's 1,231 magazines escaped her classification as 'girlies' . . . *Life* 16 Feb. p. 105/1–2 Nightclub owners . . . snatch up bright new stars . . . and surround them with gaudy girlie acts. *Harper's Mag.* April p. 42/2 The Committee studied comic books, 'cheesecake or girlie magazines,' and 'pocket-size paper-bound books.' 1955 N.Y. *Times* 19 June p. 40/3 Advertisements in 'girly' magazines were 'come-on' material, replies to which brought a group of pin-ups.

GROUND*, *v.* 'To place or set on the ground; to cause to touch the ground . . .'{?1650} (*OED*); 'To restrict (a pilot, passenger, or airplane) to the ground' for various reasons (*WNID Add. Sect.* 1954).—To suspend one's license; as, to ground a jockey, an automobile driver; to forbid (a person) to drive a car.—1939 *Turf Dict. for Racing Fans* (Los Angeles: Scientific Publications) GROUNDED. When a jockey is suspended or disqualified, he is said to be 'grounded.' 1942 *Am. Sp.* 17: 103/2 Grounded. License revoked. 1948 Mencken *Am. Lang.: Sup. II* p. 719. 1952 B'ham *News* 19 Sept. p. 11/4 (AP) Proving that the law which went into effect last January has teeth that can bite, the State Department of Public Safety has already 'grounded' more than 2000 drivers for varying periods of time. 1953 *Time* 12 Jan. p. 66/2 But he rode so badly in his first race that the stewards grounded him and advised him to give up riding entirely. 1954 Balto. *Sun* 4 Jan. p. 12/7 'We're all grounded.' It took only another question or two to discover that for these youths 'grounded' meant not having the use of the family car.

HARD SELL. Vigorous, high-pressure salesmanship.—1952 William H. Whyte, Jr. *Is Anybody Listening?* (N.Y.: Simon and Schuster) p. 59 Want to mark yourself as a comer in the advertising field? Speak, then, of fun stories, sweet guys, the hard sell . . . 1954 *Newsweek* 15 Feb. p. 70 The 'hard sell' is back, as everyone knows, and a Newsweek survey showed this week that business is using every device it knows to move merchandise. 1955 *Sat. Rev.* 2 April p. 32/2 In the movie's many sermons Peter Marshall gives the gospel the 'hard sell,' and Henry Koster's direction combined with Eleanore Griffin's script gives the 'hard sell' to Peter Marshall.

HIGHWAY HYPNOSIS. See second quot. (Cf. *high-speed hypnosis*, *Am. Sp.* 29:285).—1952 *This Week* 1 June p. 9/1 No one knows how many accidents are caused by highway hypnosis. 1954 Omaha *World-Her.* 1 Aug. p. 2-F . . . highway hypnosis is one of the many hazards that confront the long-distance driver. This is a condition where a driver unconsciously hypnotizes himself while driving for long periods of time.

NOMINAL, *adj.* [Cf. *OED*, s. v. *nominal*, *a.* and *sb.* A. 4: '. . . merely named, stated, or expressed, without reference to reality or fact.' {1624}] See quots.—[1953 N.Y. *Times* 22 March p. E9/6 The A-bomb of 1945 had a rating of 20,000 of TNT, which is still the standard.] 1953 *Bull. of the Atomic Scientists* April p. 86 'A nuclear detonation releases tremendous energy, equivalent in a so-called "nominal" burst to approximately 20,000 tons of TNT.' B'ham *News* 4 June p. 10/4 (AP) The nominal or Hiroshima bomb contained the equivalent of 20,000 tons (20 kilotons) of TNT. 1955 B'ham *News* 5 May p. 1/6 (AP) The device being tested packed twice the wallop of the nominal A-bomb that devastated Hiroshima and Nagasaki.

PISTOL-WHIP, *v. t.* To beat with a pistol.—1942 Berrey and Van den Bark *op. cit.* ¶ 322.5. 1950 *Time* 27 Nov. p. 21 'I never pistol-whipped anyone.' 1953 B'ham *News* 24 Feb. p. 1/7 (AP) . . . in one sequence, two deputy sheriffs arrest a meek American miner of Mexican descent and proceed to pistol-whip the miner's young son. 1954 *New Repub.* 25 Jan. p. 23 (quoting Memphis *Commercial Appeal*). Seattle *Times* 3 March p. 8/1 Zilbauer testified he made a date with Kmiec, intending to pistol-whip Kmiec . . . *Sat. Eve. Post* 13 March p. 37/1 Hart, the charge went, had brutally pistol-whipped the doctor with a gun for which he had no permit . . .

PISTOL-WHIPPING, *n.*—1949 Tuscaloosa *News* 19 Sept. p. 1/7 (AP) . . . Maxey may be sentenced today for pistol-whipping the nurse . . . 1953 San Fran. *News* 21 Nov. p. 1 . . . after pistol-whipping two janitors working there. 1954 B'ham *News* 11 Aug. p. 1/2–4 (pict. cap) Questioned about pistol-whipping . . .

SLOGANEER, *v. i.* [Noun (in *WNID*) goes back to 1932 (Mencken *Am. Lang.: Sup. II* p. 360, n. 3)] 1948 *Time* 24 May p. 27/2 Both sides picketed, sloganeered, glowered.

SLOGANEERING, *n.*—1941 *Read. Dig.* June p. 109/1 We are . . . getting all ready . . . with hardly a variation in timing sequence or superficial sloganeering. 1949 Balto. *Sun* 13 Oct. p. 18/3 Eastern Germany's tireless Communists, still a bit breathless from the ten-day marathon of sloganeering over the new 'East German Republic,' are faced with another chore . . . 1955 N.Y. *Times* 17 April p. 10E/5 It has been the press and not the leaders of the Democratic party who have drawn the attention of the country to the sloganeering of the Administration in the field of foreign policy . . . *Time* 25 April p. 70/3 (quoting the preceding quot.)

SLOGANIZE, *v. t.*—[1948 *Sat. Rev. Lit.* 21 Aug. p. 15/2 It is perhaps the only collection of speeches by a public man in this world of sloganized glibness which can be read as a book.] 1954 Balto. *Sun* 22 Feb. p. 4/2 (AP) The Americans for Democratic Action today accused Administration spokesmen of trying to 'sloganize' the country out of an economic decline.

SMOKE JUMPER. 1940 cited in *Am. Sp.* 23:67/1. Add earlier and later illus.—1938 Marjorie Allee *Smoke Jumper* (Houghton Mifflin). 1953 Berrey and Van den Bark *op. cit.* ¶ 850.4. 1954 Seattle *Times* 30 Nov. p. 46 Russia Boasts Smoke Jumpers.

STOMP, *v.* (The dictionaries generally label as dialect, and it is entered in Wentworth's *ADD*. Many of the quots. in the latter, however—e.g., *W. Va. Rev.*, Carl Carmer, *Downbeat*, *Time* (9 quots.), *New Yorker*, *Sat. Eve. Post*—hardly seem dialectal. These plus those that follow indicate that the label *dial.* should be removed. See esp. first quot. and *ADD* quot. 1914 c. Mass. Cape Cod.)—1948 Mencken *Am. Lang.: Sup. II* p. 76 *To stomp*, in the sense of to beat down forcibly, as with the foot, is only provincial in England, but in the United States it is in relatively good usage, though no American would ever speak of a *postage-stomp* or of *stomping* a letter. 1952 N.Y. *Times* 28 July p. 10 The man . . . apparently was stomped to death. 1953 Tuscaloosa *News* 24 June p. 4/6 'My ambition was to stomp all over it.' *This Week* 27 Sept. p. 31/2 Before I'd finished my Barbara Frietchie oration, Grimes and Durocher had stomped out . . . 1953 *Musical Amer.* Oct. p. 9/3 'In Luxembourg we first met the custom of hearing the audience stomp their feet in addition to applauding for numbers they really liked.' 1954 *Ladies' Home Jour.* Oct. p. 116/3 He noticed that the upper half of the door consisted of four panes of glass, and thought that was sensible in a vocational high school, where any passerby could look through the glass and see if the teacher inside were perhaps being pinned to the wall or stomped into the floor. 1955 B'ham *News* 14 July p. 55/2 . . . she stomped her feet in the manner in which she testified she saw Colin walking toward the car to take the battery.

THERMOBOOT, THERMO BOOT. See quots.—1953 N.Y. *Times* 18 Jan. p. 80/1 'We use the basic principle of the thermoboot,' Mr. Gianola said. That anti-frostbite footgear, of which Mr. Gianola was co-inventor, is now standard issue to all United Nations forces in Korea. 1954 Balto. *Sun* 26 April p. 13/3 The outside layer kept the wind out, the insulation kept the body heat in and the inner waterproof layer kept perspiration from permeating the materials. A vapor-absorbing vest worn next to the skin was added for the wearer's comfort. 'Thermo boots' were perfected along the same moisture barrier principle.

TIPTANK, *n.* [wing*tip tank*] See quots.—1952 *Wall St. Jour.* 15 April p. 5 First conceived in 1938, tiptanks became standard as auxiliary fuel containers for the early-day F-80 jet fighters ... 1954 N.Y. *Times* 19 Sept. p. 28X/5 The airline will also make other changes in the planes, in addition to the tiptanks, to be able to avoid the usual refueling stop at Gander, Nfld.

AMONG THE NEW WORDS

I. WILLIS RUSSELL
University of Alabama

ACKNOWLEDGMENTS: For citations: Walter S. Avis (2), Atcheson L. Hench (1) Evelyn McMillan (1), Mamie J. Meredith (10), Porter G. Perrin (6), Peter Tamony (1). Thanks are also due the University of Alabama Research Committee for aid.

AUTOMATED, *adj.* [**automate* (underlying form of *automation* in *Am. Sp.* 25:227/1) + *-ed.* Cf. *shambled* in *ibid.* 28:212] Characterized by automation.—1952 *Cleveland Plain Dealer* 13 April p. 12 Another 'automated' line, less spectacular than the block line, machines the cylinder heads. 1954 Omaha *World-Her. Mag.* 7 March p. 2-G The major 'automated' operation in a modern auto plant involves engine production. 1955 B'ham *News* 4 Jan. p. 13/2 Therefore, the argument goes, a guaranteed annual wage and a shorter work week are essential to insure insufficient [*sic*] purchasing power to buy the products of these 'automated' plants. *Time* 7 Feb. p. 56. B'ham *News* 3 Nov. p. 59/3 (AP) The Ford Motor Co.'s plant at Cleveland has a 500-foot automated production line for making engine blocks.

BEERCASTING, *n.* [*beer*+broad-, tele*casting*] See first quot.—1952 *Time* 16 June p. 71 They charge that brewers have taken over TV with their 'beercasting' because 'they need a new crop of drinkers to replace chronic alcoholics.' 1955 *Chr. Sci. Mon.* 7 May p. 7 (headline) 'Beercasting' Spotlighted.

BLOOD CHIP, BLOOD CHIT. See quots.—1944 *Life* 10 July p. 81/2 They also carried 'blood chips,' notices offering Chinese peasants a reward for return of downed airmen. 1945 Tuscaloosa *News* 7 Jan. p. 10 B-29 crews, wearing 'Blood Chips' to insure help from the Chinese if forced down, are ready. 1955 *Newsweek* 7 March p. 15 U.S. pilots from now on will carry 'blood chits' to help them escape if shot down in enemy territory. The chits guarantee payment of a reward, in gold, to any who help them elude capture.

CAR-, CAR PARK, CARPARK. An automobile parking area.—1945 Mencken *Am. Lang.: Sup. I* p. 477 and n. 6 (quoting 'An unidentified London paper') Many of the large houses were pulled down and the sites converted into *car-parks*. 1952 *Friends Intelligencer* 15 March p. 146/1 ('Our London Letter') According to a board on its front, William Penn preached to a large crowd from a little window in this building . . . and on this account, as much as for the intrinsic interest of an old . . . building, the Preservation Society of the city of Wells is up in arms because the City Council has decided to pull it down and put a car park and flower beds on its site and that of another old house adjoining. 1954 *Life* 28 June p. 93/1 Crossing a neighbor's asphalt carpark one recent Monday morning, Keith Vining . . . noticed a small but curious bulge in its thick surface . . .

CERTIFIED MAIL. See quots.—1955 *U.S. News* 25 Feb. p. 4 Latest wrinkle in postal service is certified mail, which must be signed for by the recipient. . . . Certified letters will go on record in post offices, but will not be guarded at every handling post, as registered mail is. If a sender wants a return receipt, he will have to pay 7 cents additional for it. *Seattle Times Mag.* 13 March p. 21 Certified mail will be used for first-class and air mail and will be cheaper than registered mail. . . . The difference is that certified mail is not insured. B'ham *News* 1 May p. A-9/1 Certified mail . . . will go into effect around June 1.

CIVILIANIZATION, *n.* The adding of civilians to the services.—1954 *N.Y. Times Mag.* 5 Dec. p. 56 Civilians are running the military services to a far greater degree than ever before in our history. The overextensive 'civilianization' that has taken place during and since World War II is one of the causes of poor service morale. 1955 N.Y. *Times* 30 Oct. p. 37/1 The move is part of an Air Force program to replace military personnel with civilians in training and support units. 'Civilianization' is one of three ways by which the Air Force plans to raise its operational strength . . .

CLASSIC CAR. See quots. (Also attrib.)—1955 Omaha *World-Her.* 10 June p. 11 (UP) 'The Classic Car Club of America' started in 1952 with eighty members. . . . Their constitution specifies that the classic is one of the super-fine cars built between 1925 and 1942. *N.Y. Times Mag.* 17 July p. 14 A classic car is difficult of definition, but it is usually taken to mean an automobile of outstanding beauty and engineering, produced between the years 1925 and 1942.

CRACKPOT(T)ISM, *n.* [*crackpot (WNID* 1934)+*-ism*] Eccentric and extreme ideas.—1953 *Sat. Rev.* 18 April p. 46/1 Extremism, crackpottism, fellow travelling, whether Fascist or Communist, have a hard time surviving when faced by a succession of gusty challenges. 1955 *Harper's Mag.* Feb. p. 34/2 Crackpotism finds it hard to get a foothold in the warm Florida sands . . .

CRONYISM, *n.* [*crony*{1665}+*-ism*] The appointment of close friends to government posts.—1950 *Collier's Mag.* 24 June p. 78/1 . . . [he] sets a heap of store by the solemn vows of cronyism. 1952 N.Y. *Times* 17 Aug. p. 8E/1 (edit.) Governor Stevenson's personal integrity, no matter how great, is inadequate to cope with the amount of politically entrenched bureaucracy that has earned for Mr. Truman's regime its sorry reputation for corruption, cronyism, extravagance, waste and confusion. B'ham *News* 5 Sept. p. 20/3–4 (Walter Lippmann) . . . the Truman administration appeared to be foundering in the mess it was making of corruption, cronyism and so forth. 1955 N.Y. *Times* 18 Sept. p. 1E/6 . . . once-loyal Peronista officers have become increasingly disturbed by mounting 'cronyism' in the army . . .

MILEAGE, *n.* [Cf. *ACD*, s. v. *mileage*, 3: 'an allowance for traveling expenses at a fixed rate per mile . . . ' and *OED*, s. v. *mileage*, b. *fig.*: '1860 Russell *Diary India* I. x. 155 It has been a heavy mileage of neglect for which we have already paid dearly.'] *Fig.* 'Percentage'; see quot. *Brit. Book of the Year.*—1954 N.Y. *Times* 14 Feb. sec. 2 p. 1 (caption) Making Mileage at the Belasco. *Sat. Rev.* 15 May p. 5/1 . . . Weisberger . . . has certainly gotten a lot of mileage out of his announcement that he was closing down his combination Peabody Bookshop and Bierstube . . . *New Republic* 12 July p. 2/2 All of which means that Ike will be left in his noble posture while the GOP tries to counter the disagreeable loss of Indo-China by getting more political mileage out of 'Acheson.' B'ham *News* 21 Oct. p. 19/2 The situation is not without humor but the politicians say there is no mileage in it either way. 1955 *Brit. Book of the Year* p. 814/2 *mileage, n. Fig.* Publicity; kudos. N.Y. *Times* 13 March p. E1/6–7 The Democrats were not particularly disheartened by this news because they felt the Johnson bill was designed for maximum political mileage—if the President vetoed both a cut for the small taxpayer and refused to consider repeal of last year's concessions to corporations and stockholders, then, the Democrats felt, they might make some headway with the cry of 'rich man's tax policy.' *This Week Mag.* 10 July p. 26/5 In brief, while we have much to learn about guarding our hearts, the simple rules of our ancestors—reasonable amounts of exercise, rest, and a sensible diet—are still the best ways to get the greatest mileage from your heart.

PARAPACK, PARAPAK, *n.* See second quot.—1950 K. E. Larsen, USAFR, Historical Rept. 90th T. C. Szd. Aug. A resupply mission was flown in the afternoon—with a drop of parapaks and other supplies simulated. 1954 N.Y. *Times Mag.* 6 June p. 79/2 In less time than it takes to write (or read) this, the door bundles were pushed out; Captain Schweiter slapped the switch controlling the parapacks (belly bundles), bellowed: 'Follow me,' and jumped.

PRE-, PRESET MISSILE. See quots.—1953 *Sat. Eve. Post* 13 June p. 152/2 The only kind of missile which is not vulnerable to jamming is what the experts call a 'preset missile.' This is one which receives no outside help or intelligence from its operators or its target after it is fired. . . . It is set to hit a fixed geographic point on the earth. 1954 N.Y. *Times Mag.* 29 Aug. p. 49/1 The pre-set missile is not guided; it is fired, like a shell, at a predetermined trajectory. . . . The Honest John free-flight artillery rocket is this type of missile . . .

PRESSURE PATTERN. A pattern made by various barometric pressures. (Also attrib.) —1947 *Time* 10 March p. 72/2 The answer is 'pressure pattern flying.' 1954 N.Y. *Times* 6 June p. X31/2 During the past eight years Trans World Airlines pilots flying over the Atlantic between the United States and Europe have mastered the techniques of getting maximum range from their planes by flying 'pressure patterns.' Instead of simply following a Great Circle course from New York to Gander, Nfld., to London . . . the eastbound pilots fly complex varying courses that enable them to make the shortest possible flights to Europe in terms of time. These courses, chosen to give maximum tailwinds at all points on the trips, carry the planes from the outskirts of one barometric pressure to another.

PUBLICITOR, *n.* See last quot.—1951 Lincoln (Nebr.) *Jour.* 8 Dec. p. 6 . . . O . . . who rose from the job of sports publicitor . . . was assailed by Judge . . . 1952 Cleveland *Plain Dealer* 30 Oct. p. 26 John Cox, the publicitor of the Naval Academy . . . said . . . 1954 B'ham *News* 14 Oct. p. 18/1 We were startled . . . yesterday by a dispatch fresh from American League offices stating that news of the Athletics' move to Kansas City was given in an announcement by the league's 'publicitor.' We take this to mean press agent.

PUNK OUT, *v. phr.* To go back on a promise.—1954 N.Y. *Times Mag.* 21 March p. 66/3 Well, the boy had said, wavering, he had promised B . . . that he would go through with the hold-up. He didn't want to 'punk out.' 1955 *Life* 11 July p. 34/3 'Nono got the B but he punked out. He said "Count me out on this one".'

ROB, *v. t.* [Cf. *OED*, s. v. *rob*, *v.* 3: 'To plunder, pillage, rifle (a place, house, etc.)' {*c*1230}] *Slang.* To empty of its contents.—1953 Berrey and Van den Bark *Am. Thes. Slang* ¶853.7 . . . rob the box, *to collect mail from a street box* . . . 1954 B'ham *News* 27 June p. B7/2 The pickup man who serviced and robbed the machines outside Phenix City made the rounds once each week.

ROCKERTHON, *n.* [*rocker*+mara*thon*] See quot. *Life.*—1955 Kingston *Whig-Stand.* 7 March The Rokerval [Quebec] rockerthon . . . ended Saturday afternoon in a dead heat. . . *Life* 4 April p. 51/1 . . . the jobless contestants were competing for cash prizes in a rockerthon. The idea, most bizarre twist in Canada's epidemic of walkathons, pianothons and poolathons, was to see who could keep a rocking chair going the longest.

SAGE, *n.* [See first quot.] See quots.—1955 N.Y. *Times* 25 Sept. p. 2E/2 Some time in 1954—the exact date has not been disclosed—the National Security Council gave the Air Force the go-ahead on a project to link up thirty-two radar centers of the continental warning system and eight air combat centers in an intricate, semi-automatic communication network. The project is called Sage, an abbreviation of its technical name—Semi-Automatic Ground Environment. *Ibid.* 2 Oct. p. 34/1 Sage is a project designed to shorten the time interval between discovery of an attacking enemy aircraft and the use of planes and missiles to bring it down.

SECOND BANANA. [By analogy with *top banana.*] *Slang.* See quots.—1953 N.Y. *Times* 24 May p. X11/2 In television and radio, Mr. Carnay has played second banana to many star comedy performers . . . 1955 *Newsweek* 28 March p. 53 Known to the trade as 'supporting comedians' or 'second bananas,' they get their laughs and paychecks . . . with a carefree regularity . . .

SEGREGATED, *adj.* {1652} Practicing, maintaining segregation.—1954 N.Y. *Times* 23 May p. E1/5 Three of the nine were from segregated states. 1955 *Harper's Mag.* Oct. p. 53/1 'I wonder,' he said finally, 'if there is anything convincing we can say about brotherly love and racial understanding, when the church itself is the most segregated institution in America.'

SOFT SELL. [By analogy with *hard sell.*] See first quot. and cf. *hard sell* in *Am. Sp.* 30:286—1955 *Life* 25 July p. 21/1 Sometimes they ran into the 'soft sell'—'Sit down, we don't want you to order anything, just get acquainted.' N.Y. *Times* 25 Sept. p. F1/5 Soft sell, sociology and movies.

20–20, *adj*. [Cf. *WNID Add. Sect.* 1954, s. v. *twenty-twenty* or *20/20, adj*.: 'Designating the visual acuity of the normal human eye that . . . can distinguish at a distance of 20 feet characters one-third inch in diameter.'] *Fig*. See quots.—1951 *Sat. Rev. Lit.* 22 Sept. p. 31/1 *SRL Recommends . . . A Streetcar Named Desire*: Tennessee William's [*sic*] prize-winning drama remolded for screen with 20–20 insight by Director Elia Kazan and unexcelled cast. . . 1954 N.Y. *Times Mag.* 22 Aug. p. 13/3–4 (pict. cap.) Interpreting the flood of statistics—It helps to have 20–20 insight.

AMONG THE NEW WORDS

I. WILLIS RUSSELL

University of Alabama

In the May, 1956, issue of *American Speech* there appeared an interesting and provocative article by Professor Robert A. Hall, Jr., entitled 'How We Noun-incorporate in English.' In the course of his remarks Professor Hall emphasized the need for additional attestations of this type of formation. This installment of 'Among the New Words,' devoted to noun-incorporating verbs, will supply further examples. Possibly a more systematic search of my file of quotations will uncover other illustrations, which can be published in a subsequent installment.

For the noun incorporations already in print, I have given the earliest date known to me. For example, though a noun incorporation may be entered in the 1934 *Addenda Section* of the 1934 *Webster's New International Dictionary* (I have used the 1940 printing), if it was entered in the 1945 *Addenda Section* I have used the earlier date.

AIR CONDITION, *v.t. WNID Add. Sect.* 1939.

AIR-COVER, *v.t.*—1951 B'ham *News* 18 May p. 31/3 At 3:45 P.M. Atmore will be air-covered with formations of three T-33s and six F-51s.

AIR DROP, *v.t. WNID Add. Sect.* 1954.

AIR-EVACUATE, *v.t.*—1951 B'ham *News* 17 June p. C-4/3 'He was air-evacuated to Japan.'

AIRLIFT, *v.t. WNID Add. Sect.* 1950.

AIRMARK, *v.t.*—1948 *Britannica Book of the Year* p. 804/2; *WNID Add. Sect.* 1954.

BABY-SIT, *v.i.* Though the entry in *WNID Add. Sect.* 1954 implies an inflected form *baby-sat*, Professor Hall's question (p. 87) indicates that the following citations may be useful.—1948 *Time* 13 Dec. p. 75/1 . . . Drew baby-sat for 25c an hour to eke out a scholarship. 1951 N.Y. *Times Mag.* 13 May p. 19/1 Who was the young girl from Nantucket who baby-sat for a Boston widower . . . ? 1952 *ibid.* 2 Nov. p. 23 (pict. cap.) . . . the Twentieth [precinct] 'baby-sat' for her three children until morning.

BABY-TEND, *v.i.*—1953 N.Y. *Times Mag.* 7 June p. 12 (pict. cap.) Constant baby-tends while reading l'Equipe.

BARGAIN-HUNT, *v.i.* [*bargain-hunting* {1792}; *bargain-hunter* {1868}]—1956 B'ham *News* 24 May p. 13/6 (Sylvia Porter) But millions of Americans can't bargain-hunt.

BELLYLAND, *v.*—1944 cited in *Am. Sp.* 24:72/1.

BONUS-SIGN, *v.t.*—1952 B'ham *Post-Her.* 8 Nov. p. 11/1 The Red Sox recently bonus-signed Dave Sisler. . .

BOOBY-TRAP, *v.i. WNID Add. Sect.* 1945.

BOOK-MATCH, *v.t. WNID Add. Sect.* 1954.

BORE-SIGHT, *v.t.* To have under direct aim or fire.—1944 *Sat. Eve. Post* 22 July p. 73/3 Just about that time a Zero bore-sighted us from fifty feet. *Ibid.* 12 Aug. p. 11/2 They had him bore-sighted. He couldn't turn without flying into cannon fire.

BOUNCE-PASS, *v.t. Basketball.*—1948 Basketball broadcast over Alabama Basketball Network 21 Dec. . . . bounce-passes one to [name of player].

BRAINWASH, *v.t. WNID Add. Sect.* 1954.

BREAST FEED, *v.t.* {1928}—1946 *Time* 4 Feb. p. 68/2 Until an Okinawan baby is three, his mother breast feeds him . . .

CARHOP, *v.i.*—1942 *Am. Thes. WNID. Add. Sect.* 1954.

CHAIN-SMOKE, *v.t.*—1946 cited in *Am. Sp.* 21:148/1. [*chain smoker* {1890}]

CHAIN-WHIP, *v.t.*—1953 *Sat. Eve. Post* 20 June p. 36/1 Rioters chain-whipped convict [name given] . . .

CHRISTMAS-SHOP, *v.i.*—1951 *Sat. Eve. Post* 24 Nov. p. 67 (title) He Christmas-Shops for Men Who Can't.

CITY-EDIT, *v.t.* [*city editor* 1870 (*DA*)]—1950 *Life* 13 March p. 130/2 Why, the guy is city-editing the *Press* out in the middle of the Atlantic!

COLORCAST, *v. WNID Add. Sect.* 1954.

COMBAT-LOAD, *v.t.*—1950 *Time* 24 July p. 13/2–3 Transports were combat-loaded, *i.e.*, 'backwards,' kitchen gear put aboard first because it probably would be needed last; assault vehicles loaded last so they would be on top and could be spewed out onto the grey ships.

CONTOUR-PLOW, *v.t.* [n. 1941 (*DA*)]—1941 *Life* 13 Jan. p. 68/1 . . . they . . . contour-plowed 600 acres of land. . .

COPYREAD, *v.t.*—1945 cited in *Am. Sp.* 21:148/2. [*copyreader* 1892 (*DA*)]

CRASH-LAND, *v.*—1942 cited in *Am. Sp.* 20:300/1. *WNID Add. Sect.* 1950.

CUSTOM-MAKE, *v.t.* [*custom-made* 1855 (*DA*)]—1949 N.Y. *Times* 11 Dec. p. 99/5–8 (adv.) Edith Lances custom-makes an enchanting evening bra.

DEEP-FAT-FRY, *v.t.*—1956 (conversation) 10 June If you deep-fat-fry a small bream . . .

DEWBATHE, *v.i.*—1945 cited in *Am. Sp.* 21:149/1.

FIELD TEST, *v.t.*—1950 B'ham *News* 20 Nov. p. 15/1 (AP) Early this year the results were field tested in the Yukon . . .

FINGER-CATCH, *v.t.*—1950 Gordon McLendon over Liberty Broadcasting System and AFRS 19 Nov. . . . in his efforts to finger-catch the ball.

FLAG PLOT, *v.i.* ?Plot with flags on a map.—1947 *Sat. Eve. Post* 5 July p. 59/2 Finally I . . . went back to flag plot.

FLASH-PHOTOGRAPH, *v.t.*—1949 N.Y. *Times* 3 July p. E7/6–7 The selector's photo-electric eyes . . . automatically select the desired frames and flash-photograph them on a separate film.

FLIGHT DELIVER, *v.t.*—1940 *Sci. N. L.* 25 May p. 326/2 These can also be flight delivered by filling up the cabin with gasoline tins.

FLIGHT TEST, *v.* [*flight testing* 1943 (*Am. Sp.* 22:228/1)]—1946 *Britannica Book of the Year* p. 832/2. 1950 Tuscaloosa *News* 24 Feb. p. 3/2. The breakaway cockpit will be flight tested late this year. . . .

FLOUR-PASTE, *v.t.* [n. {1806}]—1945 *Read. Dig.* Nov. p. 29/2 The War Department and the Navy Department . . . had to be flour-pasted into a makeshift unity . . .

FORMULA-DIET, *v.i.*—1956 *Ladies' Home Jour.* July p. 44/2 'I plan to formula-diet any time the scales begin to warn or worry me.' *Ibid.* p. 44/3 On the opposite page is the story of one teen-ager who formula-dieted and lost 50 pounds . . .

GANG-TACKLE, *v.t.*—1953 N.Y. *Times* 25 Oct. p. S2/6 When he's gang-tackled, the system is quite helpful.

GIFT-LOAN, *v.t.*—1952 Tuscaloosa *News* 16 March p. 4/6 'We gift-loan to foreign countries money to enable them to outbid us in the world market . . .'

GIFT-PRICE, *v.t.*—1939 cited in *Am. Sp.* 14:316/1.

GIFT-WRAP, *v.t.*—1948 Rexall Radio program 19 Dec. . . . are ready to gift-wrap your package . . . 1951 *Read. Dig.* Oct. p. 107/1 Butcher to housewife: 'Two pounds of steak! Would you like it gift-wrapped?'

GRASS-FEED, *v.t.*—1947 *Time* 15 Dec. p. 96/2 He has the vast acreage to grass-feed his cattle the year round . . .

GROUND TRANSPORT, *v.t.*—1955 Tuscaloosa *News* 6 July p. 1/3 From here they plan to move on to Birmingham, and ground transport the boat to Decatur where they will enter the water again on the return trip.

GUEST-CONDUCT, *v.t.*—1945 cited in *Am. Sp.* 26:52/1.

HAND-FIGHT, *v.i.*—1950 *Life* 6 Nov. p. 143/1 'Gives ground and hand-fights well.'

HAND-RIDE, *v.i.*—1942 *Am. Thes.* ¶ 739.5. 1947 B'ham *News-Age-Her.* 4 May p. 1B/7 But apparently he'd learned about the colt as though he were reading it from a book, because he never had to do more than hand-ride today.

HAND-SIGN, *v.t.*—1949 *This Week* 6 Nov. p. 23/2 Whether to imprint or to sign the card by hand puzzles many people. Don't do both on the same card. That is, don't try to make your imprinted cards more personal by hand-signing over your printed name. It's better if you carefully select extra cards for your personal friends and hand-sign them.

HAND-WHIP, *v.t.*—1953 Tuscaloosa *News* 25 July p. 1/5 (UP) B . . . . said she told him to hand-whip a bowl of cream for icing.

HEDGEHOP, *v.* {1928}

HOUSEPAINT, *v.i.*—1945 cited in *Am. Sp.* 21:149/2.

JUMP-PASS, *v.i.*—1948 *Britannica Book of the Year* p. 805/1.

JUMP-SHOOT, *v.i.*—1950 sportscast over WTBC 13 Feb. . . . he jump-shoots . . .

KICKTURN, *v.i. WNID Add. Sect.* 1945.

LIBEL-SUE, *v.t.*—1944 *Time* 27 Nov. p. 62/3 He has been . . . libel-sued for $1,750,000 . . .

LIP-READ, *v.t.* {1927} [*lip reader* {1912}]—1946 *Sat. Eve. Post* 9 March p. 10/2 (pict. cap.) Tele addicts contend they see football better than from any seat in the stadium, and can lip-read the signals.

NOUN-INCORPORATE, *v.*—1956 *Am. Sp.* 31:83.

PATCH-FARM, *v.t.*—1954 *Britannica Book of the Year* p. 752/1.

PATTERN-BOMB, *v.*—1944 *Britannica Book of the Year* p. 770/1.

PHONE-SIT, *v.i.*—1954 *Sat. Eve. Post* 16 Oct. p. 160/4 . . . she phone-sits while writing stories with a Middle East flavor like her Post debut on page 34 . . .

PINCHHIT, *v.i.*—1931 (*DA*) [*pinchhitter* 1912 (*DA*)]

PISTOL-WHIP, *v.t.*—1942 *Am. Thes.* Index. 1954 *Sat. Eve. Post* 4 Dec. p. 64/3 A . . . . had pistol-whipped one guard.

PRICE FIX, *v.t.* [n. {1920}]—1949 *Time* 25 July p. 22/2 Bread was price fixed . . .

ROAD, ROAD-TEST, *v.t.* [n. 1934 (*WNID*)]—1946 *Time* 29 July p. 80/2–3 When this 60-ft. aluminum-magnesium bus was road-tested in California last week a startled by-stander yelled . . . 1952 N.Y. *Times* 13 July p. 1F/4 While this speculation is going on many new models are being road tested in various parts of the country.

SHARECROP, *v.t.*—1937 (*DA*) [*share cropper* 1929 (*DA*)]

SHOTGUN MARRY, *v.t.* [*shotgun marriage* 1929 (*DA*)]—1955 B'ham *News* 23 Oct. p. 18-A/6 (Drew Pearson) The committee was questioning . . . on charges he had 'shotgun married' a Colorado power co-op to the Western Colorado Power Company . . .

SHOVEL-PASS, *v.i.*—1948 B'ham *News-Age-Her.* 31 Oct. p. 5C/1–2 Frank Tripucka . . . then shovel-passed to Sitko.

SPLICE-EDIT, *v.t.*—1950 *Sat. Rev. Lit.* 27 May p. 67/1 . . . I read with interest Mr. Gelatti's remarks concerning the splicing in the Toscanini recording . . . especially since I was the one who splice-edited it.

STICK-HANDLE, *v.i.*—1953 N.Y. *Times* 8 March p. S2/3 Taking off at full speed, he skated through the entire varsity team and whipped the disk past the surprised goalie. 'From there on I didn't give a hang whether he could lift the puck or not,' Rogers says. 'Anybody who could stick-handle like that belonged on our team.'

TABLE HOP, *v.i.*—1953 *Am. Thes.* ¶ 363.7. 1955 *Sat. Eve. Post* 26 March p. 36/2 It was up to me to do a lot of mixing, wasn't it? So I got up and started to table hop.

TENANT-FARM, *v.t.* [n. {1861}]—1949 *Time* 27 June p. 84/2 . . . Joe Acosta directed the 150 pickers on the 1,600 acres he tenant farms . . .

TEST DRIVE, *v.t.*—1950 B'ham *News* 13 Feb. p. 7 (adv.) 'Test Drive' the one *fine* car in the low price field . . .

TEST-FIRE, *v.t.*—1947 B'ham *News* 27 Oct. p. 1/2 O . . ., the officers related, told them he stole the automatic pistol from an automobile and test-fired it twice before calling for the cab. 1952 N.Y. *Times* 27 April p. E5/2 The atomic gun-fired shell . . . will probably be test-fired in the course of the next year or so. *Sat. Eve. Post* 19 July p. 90/1 I flipped on my gun switch and pressed the trigger on my joy stick to test-fire my guns.

TEST FLY, *v.t.*—1944 cited in *Am. Sp.* 21:299/2. See also *ibid.* 21:150/2.

TEST-FREEZE, *v.t.*—1949 *Harper's Mag.* June p. 40/1 At least 1,200 to 1,300 different foods have now been test-frozen.

TEST-PILOT, *v.t.*—1947 *Sat. Eve. Post* 6 Dec. p. 78/2 They reminded him of the fiery trail left by the high-altitude jet plane he had test-piloted in the last week of the war.

TEST-SIT, *v.i.*—1955 *Sat. Eve. Post* 19 March p. 19 (pict. cap.) Customers 'test-sit' a new Cadillac.

TRIAL SUBSCRIBE, *v.i.*—1949 *Harper's Mag.* Aug. p. 14/3 I have only recently subscribed—'trial subscribed'—to your publication.

WINDOW-SHOP, *v.i. WNID* 1934.

AMONG THE NEW WORDS

I. WILLIS RUSSELL
University of Alabama

ACKNOWLEDGMENTS. For citations, Woodrow W. Boyett (1), O. B. Emerson (1), Atcheson L. Hench (4), Mamie J. Meredith (2), Porter G. Perrin (1), and Peter Tamony (2). Robert K. Johnson helped with the definition of *area rule*. In addition to the aid already acknowledged, Mr. Boyett gave substantial and valuable help in processing the entries in this issue.

In the October installment of 'Among the New Words,' devoted to noun-incorporating verbs, I wrote that a search of my file might uncover more examples. Thanks chiefly to the aid given by my colleague Mr. Boyett, that search has been made and the results are given in Section I below. To these have been added some terms only recently found (cf. Robert A. Hall, Jr., 'How We Noun-incorporate in English,' *American Speech*, XXXI (1956), 88, n. 11) as well as several illustrations of terms entered in the last issue, e.g., *deep-fat-fry* and *field-test*.

In his article on noun-incorporating verbs in the issue of last May, Professor Hall stated that many of these verbs arose as back formations from agent nouns in *-er* and action nouns in *-ing*. I think that there may be a third possibility, namely, the adjective composed of a noun plus a past participle. The type is numerically very strong. *Jet-propel* below seems to have arisen this way. (See *Am. Sp.* XXI (1956), 295, ¶3)

I

BATTLE-TEST, *v.t.*—1945 *Read. Dig.* May p. 42/1 Although the Navy originated this air suit and was the first to battle-test it, the Army Air Forces supplied important simplifications . . .

BED-MAKE, *v.t.* [*bedmaker* {*c* 1500}; *bedmaking* {1670}]—1954 Tuscaloosa *News* 1 March p. 14/3 He had a little pamphlet showing how to bed-make a car and had the back end open, all set for sleeping except for making of the bed.

BODY-PLANE, *v.i.*—1948 *This Week* 13 June p. 14/4 Don't indulge in horseplay; don't race; don't body-plane; don't call the lifeguard needlessly.

BOOK-KEEP, *v.t.* [*book-keeping* {1689}]—1942 Berrey and Van den Bark *Amer. Thes. Slang* ¶558.6. 1945 Mencken *Amer. Lang. Sup.* I p. 396. 1956 Conv. 20 July They'd book-keep themselves to death.

CHICKEN-FRY, *v.t.*—1943 *Sat. Eve. Post* 23 Oct. p. 110/3 'I taught him to chicken-fry meat Southern style, dipping it in egg batter like mom did back home.'

CLIFF-HANG, *v.i.* [*cliff-hanger* (1942 *Am. Thes. Slang*)]—1946 *Time* 26 Aug. p. 58/1 'The only thing I will admit is wrong with most soap opera is cliff-hanging. I never, never, cliff-hang.'

DEEP-FAT-FRY, *v.t.*—1956 Conv. 30 July Fritters are deep-fat-fried.

DEPTH-CHARGE, *v.t.* [*depth charge, n.* {1917}]—1918 *Daily Mail* 23 Sept. (quoted

Eng. Studies 4:63) From the captain of a U-boat . . . came to me the following description of what it is like to be depth-charged.

EAR-CONDITION, *v.t.* [By analogy with *air-condition*]—1947 *The Q from WMAQ* (Chicago, Jan.); quoted *Am. Sp.* 22:157/1 Miss [Frances] Langford . . . is continuing to *ear-condition* her audience to beautiful music—beautifully sung.

FACT-FIND, *v.i.* [*fact-finding, adj.* (*WNID* 1934)]—1953 N.Y. *Times* 8 Feb. p. E1/4 Ostensibly their mission was to fact-find on the problem of speeding the rearmament of Europe.

FACTORY-SHIP, *v.t.*—1956 N.Y. *Times* 29 July p. X31/3 Wet batteries are factory-shipped with electrolyte added as a final step in manufacture.

FELLOW-TRAVEL, *v.i.* [*fellow-traveller* {1665}; *fellow traveler* (*WNID Add. Sect.* 1939)]—1949 *Life* 4 April p. 39/1 Its host was the U. S.'s own National Council of Arts, Sciences and Professions, dominated by intellectuals who fellow-travel the Communist line.

FIELD-TEST, *v.t.*—1955 N.Y. *Times Mag.* 23 Oct. p. 78/4 All equipment developed by the laboratory is field-tested by Cornell's team.

HAND-TRIM, *v.t.*—1955 *Sat. Eve. Post* 8 Oct. p. 34/1 He was hand-trimming the edges of the front lawn . . .

JET-PROPEL, *v.t.* [*jet-propelled, adj.* (1944) on file; *WNID Add. Sect.* 1950]—1950 B'ham *News* 2 Jan. p. 17/1 (AP) They have learned to jet-propel bodies, but they haven't taken the first step in jet-propelling the human spirit.

LINE-CHECK, *v.t.*—1946 *Collier's* 16 March p. 8/3 On one occasion in South Dakota I took off a Stinson Voyager that had just been line-checked and pronounced okay by a mechanic and when I was less than two hundred feet off the ground, the left side of the engine cowling came loose and plastered itself all over the windshield on my side.

MOTOR-HAUL, *v.t.*—1941 *Read. Dig.* June p. 31/2 The Union Pacific and the Burlington motor-haul trains out of Chicago to Denver . . .

NIGHT-DRIVE, *v.i.*—1956 *This Week* 29 July p. 11/2 But if you must night-drive, keep the dash-lights as dim as possible—this particular glare is hypnotic.

PLANE-CRASH, *v.i.*—1946 *Time* 8 Oct. p. 69/1 Four years before Knute Rockne plane-crashed to death in Kansas, Irishman Frank Leahy came to Notre Dame.

PLAYWRITE, *v.t.*—1949 *Sat. Rev. Lit.* 24 Dec. p. 24/3 One of the unique and beckoning characteristics of his plays was that they were written no less than playwritten.

POWER-PILE, *v.t.*—1950 *Time* 6 Nov. p. 44/1 . . . Davison got up his speed well back, power-piled his way into the Cornell line the way fullbacks used to do.

PUBCRAWL, *v.i.* [*pub-crawl, n.* {1915}; *pub-crawler* {1910}]—1949 *Sat. Rev. Lit.* 29 Jan. p. 15/3 They would have to wear scarlet breeks . . . pubcrawl with Robert Burns . . .

RADAR-TRACK, *v.t.*—1956 Tuscaloosa *News* 31 July p. 11/6 (AP) The Italian Line said the Doria radar-tracked the oncoming Stockholm before the fatal crash.

RADIO-POISON, *v.t.*—1956 B'ham *News* 25 July p. 37/4 Exploded near the surface, the three mile fireball of a 'dirty bomb' scoops out vast quantities of material, radio-poisons it, and sucks it into the upper atmosphere . . .

SCRIPT-WRITE, *v.t.* [*script-writer* (*WNID Add. Sect.* 1939)]—1941 *Life* 10 March p. 30/1 No Hollywood movie was ever more carefully script-written . . . than Germany's conquest of western Europe.

SNAKE-BELLY, *v.i.*—1944 *Nat'l. Geog. Mag.* July p. 8 Then they 'snake-bellied,' or crawled on hands and knees, through the jungle . . .

SPEED CLIMB, *v.t.*—1956 N.Y. *Times Mag.* 29 July p. 19/2 . . . Stan Lyon and Johnny Kaelin speed climb hundred-foot spars.

SPEED-ZONE, *v.t.*—1952 B'ham *News* 1 April p. 17/2 (AP) Before Gov. . . . Persons took matters into his own hands and speed-zoned the roads, the only thing resembling a state-wide ceiling on fast driving was a 'reasonable and proper' limitation.

SPOT-CHECK, *v.t.* [*n.* 1945 (*Am. Sp.* 23:67/2)]—1946 *Time* 6 May p. 92/2 . . . they spot-checked hundreds of recently treated syphilis cases. 1948 Balto. *Sun* 8 April p. 1/7 The bureau now has only enough money to spot-check 3 percent of all income-tax returns.

SPOT-MARK, *v.t.*—1949 *Sat. Eve. Post* 1 Jan. p. 44/3 The Switzers' fluorescent panels spot-marked our troops' advances in the North African campaign . . .

STOCK-TAKE, *v.t.* {1892} Add American illust.—1951 Tuscaloosa *News* 31 May p. 18/7 (UP) 'Sir . . . there are some things we will not stock-take.'

WOLF-WHISTLE, *v.i.*—1955 Balto. *Sun* 2 Sept. p. 1/5 (AP) The Governor of Mississippi today called for a complete investigation of the kidnap-killing of a Negro youth who allegedly wolf-whistled at a white woman. N.Y. *Times* 25 Sept. p. 1/7 They were accused of kidnapping Emmett Till . . . and beating and shooting him dead because he allegedly had 'wolf-whistled' at B——'s young wife.

II

ANTI-, ANTIPROTON, *n.* See quots.—1951 *Sci. N. L.* 12 May p. 293/1 The latest and fifteenth elementary particle of matter is the anti-proton, or the negative counterpart of the heart of the hydrogen atom. 1954 *Life* 19 July p. 31/1 He guessed that the mysterious particle was an antiproton, whose presence in outer space has been postulated but never proved. 1955 N.Y. *Times* 23 Oct. p. E9/6-7 (heading) Discovery of the Anti-Proton Ends a Long Search, Confirms Einstein's Equation. B'ham *News* 3 Nov. p. 54/2 (NANA) Official discovery announcements call it an 'anti-proton' because it is like the proton, but carries a negative electric charge. . . . Scientists with the Atomic Energy Commission today are calling the new particle 'the anti-proton,' but they agree that the name is unwieldy. Some scientists outside government call it 'the negatron.' 1956 *Science* 24 Feb. p. 318 The antiproton, newly discovered particle of negative matter . . . is twice the size scientists expected . . .

AREA RULE. (*WNID* 1934) *Aerodynamics.* Given a theoretically ideal design for an airplane fuselage for minimum air resistance, the area rule states that the increased drag caused by the addition of wings can be kept closer to this ideal minimum by reducing the area of the fuselage at any point along the root of the wing by an amount equal to the area of the wing at that point, or by adding in front of or behind the wings an area equal to that of the wings.—1955 N.Y. *Times* 2 Oct. p. 20/4-5 Similarly, the tests proved, shock waves produced by the wings of an equivalent plane can be eliminated by removing an area of fuselage equal to the area of the bulge. The slimming is done along the section where the bulge had been trimmed—that is, the section where wing joins the fuselage. The principle is known as the 'area rule.' *Life* 21 Nov. p. 150/2 The basis of Area Rule concerns the areas of cross sections of the plane. If those areas have the proper relationship to each other, they will obey the rule and the resulting design will have a minimum of drag.

BEAM-, BEAM PAD. See quots. (Also attrib.)—1952 N.Y. *Times* 8 June p. E11/5 E. B. Dye . . . has developed a so-called 'beam pad' principle for aircraft helmets to protect the head against severe blows. 1955 N.Y. *Times Mag.* 23 Oct. p. 78/3-4 . . . one of the essential features of the new helmet is the so-called 'beam-pad,' an invention now patented by Cornell Laboratory. Its action is described by its name. Seated inside the helmet's shell, the beam-pad combines the structural advantages of a beam, which distributes the load, with the force-absorbing characteristics of a true pad material.

BIOPIC, *n.* [*biographical picture*] See quots.—1951 Memphis (Tenn.) *Commercial Appeal* 22 Dec. p. 6/3 . . . 'Variety' coins another word for show biz—'biopic,' meaning a biographical picture. 1955 *Sat. Rev.* 11 June p. 26/2 What *Variety* calls 'the biopics,' movies based on the lives of famous people, have certainly come a long way . . .

BUG, *n.* See quots.—1952 B'ham *News* 18 Dec. p. 1/5 (AP) He said, 'They got me dead to rights. They must have a bug (microphone) in the room.' *Time* 29 Dec. p. 16/3 . . . the mayor had wept on his shoulder, and moaned: 'They've got me dead to the rights—they must have had a bug [microphone] in the room.'

BUGGING, *n.* [See *bug*, above] See quots.—1955 *The Reporter* 10 Feb. p. 22/1 'Bugging,' or the installation of concealed microphones, has undergone the same revolution in recent times as wiretapping . . . B'ham *News* 6 Oct. p. 36/5 (AP) The Justice Department is investigating the planting of a microphone in a federal jury room. . . . The *Times* reported that the 'bugging' of the jury room and recording of jury deliberations was done with the consent of U. S. District Judge . . . Balto. *Sun* 13 Oct. p. 1/6 A Senate subcommittee investigating jury 'bugging' spent a good part of its time today investigating the political views and association[s] of the two law-school professors who directed the 'bugging.'

DRY DRUNK. See quot.—1955 *Sci. N. L.* 4 June p. 358/2–3 The 'dry drunk,' they explained, is a term used by alcoholics to describe an emotional state they must cope with while keeping sober over an extended period. Depression, impatience, intolerance, irritability, nervousness, occasional confusion and an irrational desire to resume drinking are symptoms of this state. *Sci. Dig.* Aug. p. 35 (title) Dry Drunks

FILL IN, *v. phr.* [*n.* in *Am. Sp.* 27:50 and in *Web. New World Dict.* (1956), where it is defined as 'a brief summary of the pertinent facts.'] See quots.—1951 *Time* 19 March p. 46/3 Later, he felt chipper enough to spend an hour and 45 minutes with General MacArthur 'filling him in' on U. S. affairs. 1953 Bill Fitzgerald over NBC 8 Nov. To fill us in, we shift to London . . . 1955 N.Y. *Times* 31 July p. 1/3 'We talked about a good many things. . . . I filled him in on a lot of details of the President's recent Geneva conference. Lincoln (Nebr.) *Eve. Jour.* 13 Oct. p. 1 (AP) Still unissued—and unsighted—was the long-forecast official public statement which is supposed to fill the nation in on the prospects of another marital alliance between the royal house and the common people.

MAU-, MAU MAU. [See quots.] See quots.—1952 San Fran. *Chronicle* 26 Oct. 'This World' (section) p. 5/2–3 . . . the natives' resentment finally crystallized in the Mau Mau, a blood-brotherhood dedicated to driving Europeans from Africa. 1953 N.Y. *Times Mag.* 3 May p. 14/2 Mau Mau is openly anti-white and anti-Christian. Its purpose is, by intimidation and murder, to drive all Europeans and other foreigners out of Kenya. . . . It is not certain exactly when the movement started, nor how it got its name, which seems to have no particular meaning. San Fran. *Examiner* 17 May 'The American Weekly' (section) pp. 10–11 One theory of the origin of the word Mau-Mau is that it is a distortion of 'Uma-uma,' the Kikuyu phrase for 'Get out.' 1955 N.Y. *Times* 3 July p. 8/5 No one in Kenya is able to give a reliable estimate of the extent of serious infiltration of the Kikuyu, who originated the anti-white terrorist Mau Mau.

RADAR ISLAND. A Texas tower (which see).—1955 B'ham *News* 16 Feb. p. 2/5–7 There is . . . the latest type of radar 'gadget.' It is an off-shore manmade island—a platform riding the waves somewhat like the floating oil wells used off the Gulf Coast. These floating towers will make up a warning net to flash news of invading enemy aircraft. . . . The Navy is contracting for 30 of the 'radar islands' . . . *Ibid.* 11 July p. 21/4 The 6000 ton radar island is the first in a circle of outer warning stations proposed to protect 1500 miles of coast from Newfoundland to Norfolk, Va., against enemy planes. Balto. *Sun* 21 Nov. p. 1/6 A storm of hurricane violence is slamming this radar island today with 35-foot waves . . .

RADIOFICATION, *n.* See second quot.—1950 Balto. *Sun* 19 July p. 13/1 (AP) . . . *Izvestia* says: 'The movement for complete radiofication has taken on a nation-wide character . . . 1954 *The Reporter* 30 Dec. p. 3/3 (letter) The author says [George Clay in *The Reporter* of 18 Nov. 1954]: 'With every month that passes, RFE, the Voice of America, and the British Broadcasting Corporation are being rendered more and more obsolete by what the Communist regimes call radiofication—a widespread program to replace wireless sets by wired or telephonic radio.'

SATELLOID, *n.* [Cf. *WNID*, s. v. *satelloid*, *adj.*: 'Resembling a satellite . . .'] See quots.—1955 N.Y. *Times* 7 Aug. p. E9/7 Moving in reduced gravity and low air resistance, a satellite already at 300 miles' altitude traveling at 18,000 miles an hour could be driven with little additional energy. Then it might become a 'satelloid,' capable of some directed motion. *Aviation Week* 26 Sept. p. 23/1 The satelloid, proposed by Mr. Krafft Ehricke of Convair, is a hybrid and manned vehicle—half airplane, half satellite. Small rocket motors boost to a matter of days the orbit lifetimes . . . the satelloid is to be manned, powered, reusable and able to glide safely back to Earth with its occupant(s) when the propellants are exhausted. 1956 Seattle *Times* 23 April p. 40/3 (AP) Man must build a satelloid—a vehicle midway between an airplane and a space ship—before he can venture safely beyond the pull of the earth, says Krafft A. Ehricke . . .

TEXAS TOWER. [See quots.] See quots.; also those s. v. *radar island*, above.—1954 Tuscaloosa *News* 13 Aug. p. 3/4–6 (AP Wirephoto) Platform in the Sea—Here is a closeup of a section of one of the 'Texas Towers,' newest device in our far flung radar and air raid warning network, being built offshore along the Atlantic coast. Towers, named for oil rigs in the Gulf of Mexico, will be built along the continental shelf, some of them as far as 125 miles out at sea. 1955 N.Y. *Times* 10 April p. 28/1 The radar stations are named 'Texas Towers' because they resemble the offshore rigs drilling for oil in the Gulf of Mexico. They are 6,000-ton steel platforms, equal in weight to a fair-sized merchant vessel, and triangular shaped, 200 feet on each side and 20 feet deep.

WASP WAIST. See first quot. (Also attrib.)—1955 Balto. *Sun* 12 Sept. p. 4/5 NACA labelled the design principle 'area rule,' and said it produces the airplane shape known variously as coke bottle, wasp waist and 'Marilyn Monroe.' N.Y. *Times* 2 Oct. p. 20/3 The wasp-waist style was made necessary by the difficult behavior of air when planes approached the speed of sound . . . 1956 *Flying* March p. 36 (title) Wasp Waist. [p. 36/1] . . . it was he who first uncovered the basic clue leading up to the recent announcement concerning the development of the 'Wasp Waist' plane.

WHEELING*, *n.* [Cf. *OED*, s. v. *wheel*, *v.*, II, 8, b, *fig.*: 'To pass or convey easily or smoothly, as if on wheels. *rare.*' {1658}] See quots.—1949 *Fortune* July p. 22 By 'wheeling' (i.e., transmitting) the government's power, they argued, the T. P. & L. was just hurting itself and the other utilities. 1955 B'ham *News* 13 Oct. p. 24/5 (AP) The dispute has centered over ways of 'wheeling'—or transmitting—the power to co-ops and public agencies given preferences to public power by law.—*adj.*—*Ibid.* 22 March p. E1/8 (AP) If private power came into the valley, it presumably would have to go over TVA lines in a 'wheeling' arrangement.

AMONG THE NEW WORDS

I. WILLIS RUSSELL
University of Alabama

ACKNOWLEDGMENTS: For citations: Ruth I. Aldrich (1), Walter S. Avis (1), Clarence L. Barnhart (2), S. V. Baum (1), Dwight L. Bolinger (1), Joseph S. Hall (3), W. D. Halsey (1), Atcheson L. Hench (3), Mamie J. Meredith (8), Porter G. Perrin (2), Frances Rucks (1). Richard F. Bauerle contributed all the citations of *hard top*. W. D. Halsey and Jerome W. Schweitzer contributed the etymology of *brouhaha*.

BROUHAHA, *n.* [Fr. *brouhaha* (see Oscar Bloch, *Dictionnaire etymologique de la langue française*. Paris, 1932)] To-do, fuss.—1934 C. O. Sylvester Mawson *Dict. of Foreign Terms* (N.Y.: Thomas Y. Crowell Co.). 1943 *Time* 27 Sept. p. 104/2 But the true sources of this fantastic brouhaha are not literary. 1955 N.Y. *Times Mag.* 23 Oct. p. 42/2 'Why do they make all this fuss?' (*Brouhaha* was the word he used.) *Life* 5 Dec. p. 139/1 Brancusi was amazed by what he called the 'brouhaha' over his bird. 1956 N.Y. *Times Book Rev.* 4 March p. 8/2 'The great trouble with this kind of brouhaha is that Oxford is packed with the kind of people I call *hedgers* and *ditchers*.' *Ibid.* 25 March p. 1/4 In the face of all this *brouhaha* the observer can only wonder, Is it worth it? *Ibid.* 20 May p. 8/1 What's right now is a small brouhaha caused . . . by the future Grushenka of 'Brothers Karamazov.'

BUBBLE CHAMBER. [By analogy with *cloud chamber* (see *Am. College Dict.*)] See quots.—1954 *Sci. Am.* Jan. p. 39 A new detector for high-speed sub-atomic particles may soon appear in physics laboratories. Like the cloud chamber, it produces a visible track in the wake of an ionizing particle. But the track is produced in a liquid instead of in a vapor. Called a 'bubble chamber,' the instrument was conceived by Donald A. Glaser, a physicist at the University of Michigan. 1955 N.Y. *Times* 30 Jan. p. 28/1 A six-inch 'bubble chamber' . . . is equivalent to a cloud chamber 140 feet long. Photographs of the bubbles provide information on the masses and the energies of the particles colliding with the nuclei in the liquid, and also of the particles, such as mesons, created as the result of the nuclear collisions. *Sci. Am.* Feb. p. 50/3 It appears that the bubble chamber will become a standard detection instrument for work with the high-energy particle accelerators in laboratories . . .

CLEAN*, *adj.* [Cf. *OED*, s. v. *clean*, *adj.* 5 c: 'Free from the pollution of leprosy or other contagious disease' {1382}] See quots.—1956 B'ham *News* 25 July p. 37/2–3 It could mean that the Atomic Energy Commission has succeeded in achieving a 'clean bomb'—a bomb with little or no radioactive side effects. *Life* 29 Oct. p. 44/1 The H-bomb . . . is a relatively 'clean' bomb unless it is made 'dirty' (more radioactive) by using the tremendous heat of fusion to set off another fission process . . . N.Y. *Times Mag.* 9 Dec. p. 58/3 The development, for example, of a 'clean' hydrogen bomb—one in which the area of serious contamination resulting from an explosion can be reduced from thousands to only tens of square miles—can radically change our concepts of nuclear defense and warfare.

DIRTINESS*, *n.* {1561}—1956 *Life* 29 Oct. p. 44/2 To have any meaning, the ban would not be limited to the *size* of bombs . . . but to the amount of radioactivity they would be allowed to generate—their 'dirtiness.'

DIRTY*, *adj.* See quot. from *Life* s. v. *clean* above.—1956 B'ham *News* 25 July p. 37/3 Previous efforts to make a 'clean bomb' (which would be a fusion bomb rather than a fission-fusion-fission bomb, like the 'dirty' bombs now in American and Soviet stockpiles) have met a 'technological blank wall.' *Life* 29 Oct. p. 44/1 (quoted s. v. *clean* above).

ELECTRO-, ELECTRONUCLEAR, *adj.* See first quot.—1948 *Sci. N. L.* 8 May p. 291/1 Two new gigantic 'atom smashers' or electronuclear machines, both of which promise to operate at billions of electron volts in the energy range of the cosmic rays, will be built in the next few years . . . 1956 N.Y. *Times* 26 Aug. p. 36/2 Construction of France's first electro-nuclear power plant for peaceful uses will begin soon in the Loire Valley.

FILIPIN, *n.* [See first quot.] See quots.—1955 N.Y. *Times* 2 Oct. p. E9/5 A potent new antibiotic which is called 'filipin' and which combats plant diseases is described in the current issue of the Journal of the American Chemical Society. . . . Filipin apparently belongs to a new family of antifungal agents. It was obtained from a previously unreported organism, named streptomyces filipinensis, discovered in soil from the Philippines. *Sci. N. L.* 22 Oct. p. 265/1 Filipin appears to belong to a new family of antifungal agents, the scientists said, though it closely resembles another fungicide, fungichromin, which was recently announced.

FISHY-, FISHYBACK, *adj.* [By analogy with *piggyback* below.] See quots.—1954 *Wall St. Jour.* 10 Nov. p. 24 McLean Trucking Co. . . . pushing hard before the Interstate Commerce Commission for approval of its new . . . 'fishyback' proposal for coordinated land-water transportation of freight along the Atlantic Coast . . . loaded highway truck-trailers on specially-designed ships. . . . It derives its nickname from a land-based cousin, 'piggyback' . . . 1955 Balto. *Sun* 30 Sept. p. 16/2 (edit.) . . . the piggyback service and its twin, the 'fishyback' service, are capable of achieving the very desirable end of getting a large number of these monster trailer trucks off the crowded highways. *Barron's* 21 Nov. p. 1/1 . . . For TMT Trailer Ferry operates a unique transportation service known as 'fishyback,' the hauling of loaded truck trailers on ocean-going ships. 1956 Los Angeles *Times* 14 Jan. Sect. I p. 23/2 He described 'piggybacking' (loading truck-trailers on railroad flat cars) as an excellent example of 'truck trailers in automation' and forecast a 'tremendous future for this operation' as well as for two new similar operations, i.e., fishyback shipping and birdieback shipping. *Forbes* 15 Oct. p. 60 (adv.) 'Fishy-Back' [—] What Is It? . . . T. M. T. Trailer Ferry, Inc. . . . picks up general and frozen cargo from loading platforms of shippers anywhere in U. S. and carries it in same trailer to the doors of overseas consignees.—FISHYBACKING, *n.*—1954 *Wall St. Jour.* 10 Nov. p. 24 McLean's 'fishybacking' would be on a larger scale . . . . their sea-land service would take longer than overland routing but would be cheaper.

GROUND CUSHION. See quots. (Also attrib.)—1954 *Life* 25 Jan. p. 52 Moreover, a conventional, piston-driven plane is helped into the air by what is known as the 'ground cushion,' a buoyancy created in part by the propeller slipstream and by compression on the air beneath the wing surfaces. 1956 N.Y. *Times* 8 Jan. p. X41/5 The issue revolves about a phenomenon peculiar to helicopters known as ground cushion effect. What it means is this: Up to ten or twelve feet off the ground, or over water, a helicopter receives added buoyancy by the packed mass of air churned downward from the overhead rotors.

HARDTOP, HARD TOP. See quots.—1956 *Sat. Rev.* 7 April p. 40/2 Meanwhile, though the number of enclosed theatres now colloquially known as 'hard tops' declines and art theatres scarcely hold their own, drive-ins continue to prosper and multiply until there are now close to 5,000. Delaware (Ohio) *Gazette* 27 July p. 9/2 One expert predicts within five years the nation's 19,000 movie theaters (4,000 drive-ins and 15,000 'hardtops') will dwindle to 10,000. *Variety* 1 Aug. p. 7/4 Among the 17,385 houses listed by 20th as being equipped for CinemaScope, 3,602 are drive-ins and 12,967 are regular hardtops.

I.B.M. See quots.—1954 B'ham *News* 27 July p. 13/1 In the year 1960, by the agreed estimate of the Pentagon's official analysis, the Soviet Union will fly its first intercontinental ballistic missile. That missile, or I.B.M. as the experts call it, will be an accurately guided rocket, comparable to a giant V-2, capable of carrying a hydrogen warhead over a range of 4000 to 5000 miles. 1955 *Ibid.* 23 Jan. p. A13/1 The I.B.M., married to a hydrogen warhead, is the true ultimate weapon. N.Y. *Times* 13 March p. 8E/5 . . . theoretically it may even be possible sometime hence to produce a missile-hunting missile which could intercept an I.B.M. (intercontinental ballistic missile).

ICBM, See quots. and s. v. *ultimate weapon* below.—1955 *Newsweek* 30 May p. 13 The Air Force is now calling the Intercontinental Ballistic Missile the ICBM instead of the IBM.

Too many people got the missile confused with International Business Machines Corp. . . . 1956 N.Y. *Times Mag.* 3 June p. 9/1 The ICBM—the intercontinental ballistic weapon—has become, even before its first test flight, part of the language of power politics. 1957 B'ham *News* 1 Feb. p. 1/1–3 The first test of the international ballistic missile, or ICBM, will be comparable in significance to the first test of the atomic bomb.

ISOLATION BOOTH. A glass-enclosed booth to which contestants on a quiz program may retire to consider the answer to a question.—1956 B'ham *News* 15 Feb. p. 8/3 The two shoemakers . . . could be seen conferring at points with lively gestures through the window of the isolation booth. *Woman's Day* Nov. p. 8/3 We have a dilly of a giveaway here in New York that could use a couple of isolation booths (with iron bars and a padlock) from *$64,000 Question* or *Challenge*.

LARYNGECTOMEE, *n.* [*-ectomy* {1888}]—1956 *Sat. Eve. Post* 1 Sept. p. 21/1 Pupils in these classes are called 'laryngectomees.' They had been silenced by life-saving surgery for cancer of the larynx—the voice box. *Vogue* 15 Oct. p. 127/2 A laryngectomee breathes air through the stoma [the hole in the throat left after the operation] directly into the lungs.

PIGGY-, PIGGYBACK, PIGGY BACK, PIG-A-BACK, PICKABACK, PICK-A-BACK, *adj.* & *adv.* [Cf. *OED*, s. v. *pick-a-back*, *adv. phr.* (*a.*, *sb.*); *pick-a-back* {1823}; *Dial. pig-aback; piggy-back* {1888}: 'On the shoulders or back like a pack or bundle; said in reference to a person (or animal) carried in this way.'] See quots. (Also absolute.)—1936 Balto. *Sun* 6 July p. 9/1 Progress on the pick-a-back airplane, a combination in which a 'mother' plane will carry on its back a smaller long range seaplane for 'launching' at high altitude, is more secret. 1952 *New Standard Dict.* (1955 printing) pick-a-back plane. 1953 Lincoln (Nebr.) *Eve. Jour.* 3 Nov. p. 6 No sooner had 'piggy back railroading' (hauling truck trailers on flat cars) been hailed by various railroads and one major automotive manufacturer as a strikingly simple idea for abating highway congestion and cutting the high price of trucking, than the organized truck operators rose to denounce it. N.Y. *Times* 25 Oct. p. 8E/2 (edit.) Will the Government help promote railroad 'piggy-back' operation—the hauling of loaded truck trailers on railroad flat cars? Chicago *Tribune* 4 Nov. Sect. II p. 8/1 The North Western railroad next Tuesday will start carrying loaded truck trailers on flat cars between Chicago and St. Paul-Minneapolis and between Chicago and Omaha in an extension of its coordinated rail-highway or 'piggyback' service . . . 1954 *Sat. Eve. Post* 9 Jan. p. 90/2 'Then we lay our scows alongside the bank here; an' wid blocks an' rollers we'll nudge them barges on board our scows an' carry 'em downstream piggy-back.' Tuscaloosa *News* 7 Feb. p. 12/5 'The piggy back trains would not be locals . . . and they would be 50 car trains with the cars being 75 feet in length.' *Time* 19 July p. 69/3. *Railway Age* 26 July p. 3/2 Further expansion of piggyback by the Chicago & North Western took effect on July 15 . . . Seattle *Times* 21 Sept. p. 16/1 Railroads throughout the country are studying or instituting limited pickaback service. *Ibid.* 10 Oct. p. 2/1 The Union Pacific Railroad announced yesterday it has completed schedules on a new 'pick-a-back' freight service in the Pacific Northwest. 1955 *American* July p. 47 She also set up the piggy-back mail plan—truck trailers loaded with mail which are hauled on railroad flatcars. N.Y. *Times* 23 Oct. p. F1 (pict. cap.) . . . 'Pig-a-back' or trailer-on-flatcar freight service. 1956 *Bus. Week* 28 April p. 26 (title) Chessie Shows Stockholders One Answer to Piggyback. PIGGYBACKING, *n.*—1954 Los Angeles *Times* 2 July Sect. II p. 6/1 One of the most important developments in freight transportation in a great many years is the pronounced trend to 'piggybacking' . . . 1955 *Railway Age* 5 Dec. p. 38 (heading) 'Piggybacking'—the Plan is Growing.

ROCKOON, *n.* [*rock*et+ball*oon*] See quots. (Also attrib.)—1953 N.Y. *Times* 27 Sept. p. E9/6 Physicists of the State University of Iowa have returned from East Canadian and Greenland waters, where for the second successive summer they have sent up 'rockoons,' combinations of balloons and rockets, to establish new records for altitude and to gather information about cosmic rays. 1954 *New Words and Words in the News* (Funk & Wagnalls Co.) Sup. No. 9 & 10 p. 2/2. 1956 Kingston (Ontario) *Whig-Stand.* 17 Oct. p. 25/2 U. S. Navy Goes Rockoon Hunting. *Sci. N. L.* 3 Nov. p. 276/1 Rockoons are balloon-borne rockets fired about 15 miles above the earth's surface to zoom to 60 miles in the atmosphere. Dr. Wexler . . . said the rockets will be used to observe cosmic ray intensity, the air glow caused by aurora, and electrical currents in the atmosphere.

SUPERMARKET, *n.* [Cf. *supermarket* in *WNID Add. Sect.* 1954] See quots. (Also attrib.)—1955 *Bus. Week* 1 Oct. p. 104 (title) Supermarkets: Dealers in Surplus Cars Go Big Time. N.Y. *Times* 6 Nov. p. 51/1 A high-volume 'supermarket' has appeared. It gives the shopper a choice of makes—Ford, Chevrolet, Nash—all on the same lot. The dealer has no loyalty to any particular factory. 1956 *Harper's Mag.* Aug. p. 70/1 A new kind of enterprise—the new car supermarket—has sprung up on highways near big cities. While more conventional auto dealers sell one or two makes produced by the same manufacturer, the supermarket operator sells every make he can get.

T-O-F-C, T.O.F.C., TOFC, Trailers on flat cars. (Also attrib.)—1954 *Railway Age* 13 Dec. p. 49/1 . . . most of the roads which established T-O-F-C for rail-billed freight found at first that volume fell far short of their expectations. 1955 *Bull. of the Public Affairs Information Service* 41:342/2 The case for t. o. f. c. . . . movements . . . *Railway Age* 26 Sept. p. 3/1 The tariff has been a key in the development of railroad-operated trailer-on-flat-car service. It has produced a growing volume of TOFC tonnage . . . *Ibid.* 5 Dec. p. 37 (heading) A Look at TOFC Service Today.

ULTIMATE WEAPON. See quots.—1953 Oleg Anismov *Ultimate Weapon* (Chicago: Henry Regnery Co.). 1955 B'ham *News* 23 Jan. p. A13/1 The I.B.M., married to a hydrogen warhead, is the true ultimate weapon. *Ibid.* 17 July p. A-19/1 A deadly, unseen race is going on, in fact, to produce the first workable models of the true ultimate weapon—the intercontinental guided missile with atomic or hydrogen warhead. Los Angeles *Times* 11 Dec. Sect. I p. 31/1 (UP) Military men call the ballistic missile the 'ultimate weapon' because there is, at present, no known defense against it. 1956 N.Y. *Times* 4 March p. 3/1 Dr. von Braum described the ultimate futuristic weapons, a space ship and a satellite platform 1,075 miles above the earth. From the platform guided missiles could be fired upon earth targets with greater accuracy than he expects of the weapon of the nearer future now referred to as the 'ultimate' weapon—the intercontinental ballistic missile (ICBM). 1957 B'ham *News* 1 Feb. p. 1/3 The ICBM is called the ultimate weapon simply because it cannot be intercepted by any means now known.

URANIUMAIRE, *n.* [*uranium*+million*aire*] See quots.—1953 *Newsweek* 28 Dec. p. 41 The Uranium Industry Association has coined a new word for its twentieth-century prospectors who have struck it rich. . . . It calls them 'uraniumaires.' 1955 *Sat. Eve. Post* 1 Jan. p. 35/1 'Why not? Seems a fitting place for uraniumaires.' *Field and Stream* (Colorado Springs: Atomic Research Corp.) p. 47 (adv.) Uncle Sam Wants to Make You a Uraniumaire.

URBICULTURE, *n.* [*urb*an+agr*iculture*, by analogy with *agriculture*] 1954 N.Y. *Times* 25 July p. 25/2 (UP) 'Now' . . . said [Rep. J. Arthur Younger] 'About 75 per cent live in cities. Problems such as slums, dope, juvenile delinquency, housing and smog are problems originating in the cities. And they are national problems. Mr. Younger said he believed the new word 'urbiculture' covered the matter. *New Words and Words in the News* (Funk & Wagnalls Co.) Sup. No. 9 & 10 p. 3/2 urbiculture . . . term coined on the analogy of *agriculture* . . . 1955 Mary Reifer *Dict. of New Words* (N.Y.: Philosophical Lib.) p. 218. 1956 *This Week* 5 Aug. p. 8 'Urbiculture' is a newly coined word. Just as 'agriculture' refers to farms and farmers, so 'urbiculture' means care of cities and city people. Below are examples of some of the things a Department of Urbiculture could do.

AMONG THE NEW WORDS

I. WILLIS RUSSELL AND WOODROW W. BOYETT
University of Alabama

ACKNOWLEDGMENTS: For citations: Dwight L. Bolinger (2), T. L. Crowell (1), O. B. Emerson (4), Atcheson L. Hench (1), Mamie J. Meredith (5), G. P. Shannon (2), Peter Tamony (1).

This issue is devoted to what Mencken (*Am. Lang.: Sup. I*, p. 364) has called the 'plentiful offspring' of the suffix *-ism*. Admittedly included among our collection are some nonce formations, to which *-ism*, as the *OED* points out, is particularly susceptible. It is quite possible, however, that some, which may be regarded today as mere coinages for convenience at the moment, may, like *Hooverism*, of the late twenties and early thirties, come to be well-respected additions to our dictionaries.

In a future issue we hope to consider many other new *-ism* formations, not only those in our own files, but those which have been noted in various collections and word lists as well. With these numerous examples we hope to obtain a clearer picture of the behavior of this ancient suffix in present-day English. We would be grateful if readers would send examples from their files.

AGAINST-ISM, *n.*—1950 *Sat. Rev.* 28 Jan. p. 38/2 It supplements those liberal writings which define the liberal attitude too much in terms of what may be called 'against-ism,' too little in terms of 'for-ism.'

ANTI-WOGGISM, *n.* [*wog* (*WNID Add. Sect.* 1954)]—1957 N.Y. *Times* 27 Jan. p. 19/1 (Drew Middleton) The 'anti-woggism,' which 'embraces Indians and Americans as well as Arabs, can only do us damage—it neither frightens nor impresses its victims,' . . . 'Wog' is a generic term for Arabs and other natives of the Middle East employed by the British Army and other services in the two world wars.

BEST-SELLERISM, *n.* [*best seller* (*WNID* 1934)]—1943 *Fortune* Nov. p. 281 It takes elaborate pains to escape being labeled a publicity outfit; because its periodic selection of one book as an 'imperative' smacks too much of best-sellerism, it is now considering dropping the term altogether.

BIG-SHOTISM, *n.* [*big shot* (*WNID* 1934)]—1952 *Time* 24 March p. 56/2 The brutalization through big-shotism and the defeat through victory of Joe Bonaparte, who becomes a prizefighter and breaks his violin-playing hands, is given a copy-book patness. B'ham *Post-Herald* 23 May p. 18/5 I should like to see a rebellion against pressure groups and lobbies. I should like to see a rebellion against big-shotism in every field—take your pick.

BRANNANISM, *n.*—1949 B'ham *News* 26 Dec. p. 18/1–2 (editorial head) Farm Bureau rejects Brannanism.

CAUDLEISM, *n.*—1951 Tuscaloosa *News* 26 Dec. p. 4/6 (Drew Pearson) And when the country boys have large families to support, and when they don't suspect that the nice people are so very, very nice, not because they like them but because they want something, then the result is 'Caudleism.'

COMMUNITARIANISM, *n.* [*communitarian* {1841}]—1952 N.Y. *Times Book Rev.* 31 Aug. p. 6/1 In the section on American socialism, Stow Persons writes on what he calls Christian communitarianism, paying particular attention to the Shaker settlements and John Humphrey Noyes' perfectionist experiment at Oneida. . . .

COMPANY TOWNISM, *n.*—1943 *Sat. Rev.* 4 Dec. p. 52 (Benjamin Appel) Can the old-stock Americans depend on a man who sees values in company townism. . . .

CONCILIATIONISM, *n.* [*conciliation* {1543}]—1951 *Time* 26 Feb. p. 30/3 (heading) Conciliationism.

CONSUMERISM, *n.* [*consumer* {1535}]—1956 Ernest H. Gaunt *Consumerism and Independent Small Business* (*Reports on Independent Private Enterprise*, No. 1).

COSMOTARIANISM, *n.*—1945 *Time* 24 Sept. p. 42/2 Before a healthy audience of some 2,000, he [Bernarr Macfadden] flailed clerical prudery, plumped for the healthy life and for good clean sex ('The sexes were never made to be separated.') and explained cosmotarianism, 'the Religion of Happiness.'

DE VOTOISM, *n.*—1955 *Harper's Mag.* Nov. p. 16/3 (Bernard DeVoto) The Chicago *Tribune* put me on its list long ago and invented the word 'DeVotoism' to classify one entire order of its phobias.

DIVERSIONISM, *n.* [*diversion* {1600}]—1955 *Reporter* 16 June p. 3/1 Will *Pravda's* rash critic now be found to have indulged in right-wing diversionism and petty-bourgeois wrecking?

EASTLANDISM, *n.*—1956 B'ham *News* 25 May p. 1/2 (AP) 'The forces of reaction, obstruction, segregation, White Citizens Councils, Eastlandism, have reached out with the tentacles of his own palace guard and stopped his progress. . . .'

EDITORIAL-ISM, *n.* [*editorial* {1744}]—1944 B'ham *News-Age-Herald* 23 April p. 2-D/3 (quoting Sylacauga *News*) The currently popular and much discussed 'progressive education' is gradually reaching into the higher brackets, before the inevitable swing-back of the pendulum, and in that we might be in vogue—this, coupled with the fact that our force is continually becoming more acutely short—we are going into 'progressive editorial-ism' in a big way.

EDUCATIONISM, *n.* [*education* {1540}]—1953 *Sat. Rev.* 12 Sept. p. 61 (G. K. Chalmers) The real villain of the piece is Educationism itself: its establishment as an autonomous operation, its growth into a tremendous monopolistic enterprise whose inflated course requirements and artificial standards deflect the prospective teacher from genuine educational interests . . . 1956 *Key Reporter* Jan. p. 6/2 Their 'educationism' did not spring, like some strange anti-Minerva, full accoutered from the brow (or whatever it would be) of whoever-it-was (schools were rather modern in my time, too).

EGGHEADISM, *n.* [*egghead* 1952 (*Am. Sp.* 28:294–5)]—1956 N.Y. *Times Mag.* 9 Sept. p. 68/3 'People said it was "eggheadism" or "moderation" . . . oh, well.'

EISENHOWERISM, *n.*—1952 N.Y. *Times* 2 Nov. p. L84/1 (AP) 'They damn . . . Eisenhowerism.' 1953 Balto. *Sun* 20 Aug. 16/2 With the immediate press of the legislative session out of the way, a clearer pattern of what might be called essential Eisenhowerism in the field of political theory is beginning to emerge. The main Eisenhower theme seems more and more clearly to be a wish to work the Federal Government back into the community life as just one strand of the national enterprise . . .

FLYING SAUCERISM, *n.* [*flying saucer* 1947 (*Am. Sp.* 24:74)]—1952 B'ham *News* 29 July p. 10/5 (heading) Although Flying Saucerism Once Belittled, Regular Study, Watch-Out Program Carried On.

FOLSOMISM, *n.*—1951 B'ham *News* 22 July p. C7/1–2 For one thing, the public got another insight into the workings of the so-called parole racket during the last 15 months of Folsomism on Capitol Hill.

FOOTNOTARIANISM, *n.*—1951 *Time* 19 Feb. p. 104 Schuyler Cammann travels in the tradition of the scholar-adventurer, and his book, *The Land of the Camel*, cleaves to the best in its tradition (truthfulness, a sense of moral involvement, good humor) while shunning the worst (bad writing, political or sectarian tirade, excessive footnotarianism).

FOR-ISM, *n.*—*See* against-ism.

GAULLISM, *n.*—1951 *Twent. Cent.* Nov. p. 400 (title) Aspects of Gaullism.

GOBELISM, *n.* See quot.—1954 *Life* 27 Dec. p. 69/1 (Loudon S. Wainright) The *George Gobel Show* . . . a low-keyed blend of monolog, song and spoof, reaches an audience estimated at 25 million and is literally driving a competing network's comedy show off the air. All over the country adults are parroting such Gobelisms as 'Well, I'll be a dirty bird' and 'Cri-mi-nentlies.'

GO-IT-ALONEISM, *n.*—1954 *Sat. Rev.* 26 June p. 9 (part of subheading) Anti-Americanism is on the increase in Europe, go-it-aloneism on the increase in the United States.

HALSEYISM, *n.*—1947 *Time* 6 Oct. p. 28/1 Last week such Halseyisms drew down the wrath of the Methodist Board of Temperance.

HUCKSTERISM, *n.* [*huckster* (*WNID Add. Sect.* 1950)]—1951 *Newsweek* 27 Aug. p. 80 Robert Saudek, a three-time Peabody Award winner for documentaries. Saudek, a soft-spoken man without a hint of hucksterism . . . 1952 Nashville *Tennessean* 8 Oct. p. 25/4 (heading) Hucksterism Clouds Issues, Black Says. 1957 N.Y. *Times* 6 Jan. p. E11/4 An attack on Southern schools of journalism for 'kicking the humanities around' while emphasizing 'hucksterism' and 'quick turnover' in education is the theme of the main article in a recent edition of the South Atlantic Bulletin, published by the South Atlantic Language Association.

ISMATISM, *n.*—1951 Washington *Times-Herald* 10 April p. 12/8 (Westbrook Pegler) But then these platitudes incarnate got infected with acute, compound, galloping ismatism, and a lot of bailbond lawyers and lipstick magnates got into a scramble to see who could hang most medals on the First Lady of the Universe in the names of their private 'foundations.'

JOLLY-DOGGISM, *n.*—1953 *Sat. Rev.* 18 April p. 26/2 (letter) The notion that this 'wrong side of the tracks' bad-breath attack on the locution by the learned ignorance of pedants (even those who exhibit a good deal of jolly-doggism and ghastly gayety in their reviews) may banish it fills me with dismay.

KHRUSHCHEVISM, *n.*—1956 N.Y. *Times Mag.* 27 May p. 22 (subtitle) With remarkable sang-froid, the party has switched from Stalinism to Khrushchevism.

MCGEORGE BUNDYISM, *n.*—1952 *Sat. Eve. Post* 16 Feb. p. 10/1 Thus when William F. Buckley, Jr., charged in God and Man at Yale (Henry Regnery Co.) that Yale undergraduates had been getting some strange religious and economic instruction at Old Eli, his reward was to be sawed in two by McGeorge Bundy in the November, 1951, Atlantic Monthly. . . . The point is that the young writer of today may ignore 'McCarthyism,' but 'McGeorge Bundyism' poses a problem. Despite the alleged reactionary terror, the McGeorge Bundyites still hold the fort in most of the sectors commanded by book reviewers, radio commentators and other propagandists.

ME FIRSTISM, *n.*—1956 B'ham *News* 12 Aug. p. A-8/5–6 (Roger Price) Interposition—This principle, recently re-discovered by the South, refers to a State's Right to ignore Federal Law and set itself up as an Independent Island of Me Firstism completely apart from the United States (and everything else).

ME-NEITHERISM, *n.*—1952 *Time* 4 Aug. p. 9/2 Me-neitherism, not me-tooism, is the Republican pitfall.

NEO-DEWEYISM, *n.*—1957 N.Y. *Times Book Rev.* 27 Jan. p. 20/5 Mr. Morison will disappoint some persons when he doesn't blame business men trustees or politicians so much as he does the 'mediocrity' of teachers and abuses in university administration. Exponents of 'neo-Deweyism' and loyal alumni of Columbia Teachers College should take due warning: a Rear Admiral (Ret.) with the verbal equivalent of a belaying pin is on their trail.

NEO-TOMISM, *n.* See quot.—1944 *Time* 13 March p. 54/2 (title of article reporting criticism of proposal to film *Uncle Tom's Cabin*) Neo-Tomism.

NEW YORKERISM, *n.*—1951 *Time* 22 Oct. p. 102/2 Many a New Yorkerism (e.g., Cartoonist Carl Rose's 'I say it's spinach, and I say the hell with it') has become a part of the language.

NICE-NELLIEISM, *n.* [*nice Nellie* (*Am. Thes.* 1945 ¶434.2)]—1956 N.Y. *Times Book Rev.* 30 Sept. p. 2/2 In fact, none of the words which Ned Sheldon and his medical friend found so obnoxious seems to me acutely distasteful, with the exception of 'funeral parlor,' which carries nice-nellieism to the nth degree.

NIXONISM, *n.*—1952 *Life* 29 Sept. p. 4 Agreed: we must renew our fight against Communism. Let's do it with Nixonism. 1953 B'ham *News* 22 March p. E2/4 A good lawyer of unquestioned integrity, Martin was recommended by the GOP State Central Committee. But he was tinged with Nixonism, and Knowland said no.

ONE-WORLDISM, *n.*—1950 Tuscaloosa *News* 2 July p. 4/2 (AP) The United Nations is preparing to go ahead indefinitely without Russia. This means, of course, that one-worldism is a dead duck.

PEGLERISM, *n.*—1940 *Nation* 9 March p. 323 He coined new Peglerisms.

PENDERGASTISM, *n.*—1952 *Read. Dig.* June p. 44/1 There were other early signs that the nation was in for another era of Pendergastism. Ralph de Toledano *Spies, Dupes, and Diplomats* (N.Y.: Duell, Sloan, & Pearce—Little, Brown) p. 176 This the pundits of Pendergastism could not do . . .

POP-ISM, *n.*—1948 *This Week* 18 Jan. p. 4/3 Going further, Dr. Johan H. W. van Ophuijsen, a New York psychiatrist, asserts that there is a parallel condition of 'pop-ism'—either extreme harshness or extreme feebleness in the father—which he holds equally responsible with 'Momism' for much of psychoneurosis among American men.

POPULAR FRONTISM, *n.* [*popular front* (*WNID Add. Sect.* 1939)]—1938 *Nation* 14 May p. 555/1 'He [Philip F. La Follette] wants no more to be tied to trade unionism, as the British progressives are, than he wants to be tied to popular frontism, as the French progressives are.' 1957 *New Rep.* 7 Jan. p. 14/2 What kind of liberals will you find in the average large university? A handful of ADA people, most of them far from firebrands; *perhaps* one liberal of the sort who feels a nostalgic attachment to Popular Frontism . . .

POUJADISM, *n.*—1955 *Life* 18 April p. 63/1 The mushrooming political strength of Poujadism last month forced Premier Edgar Faure's government to promise sweeping exemptions to the small shopkeepers.

PRESENTISM, *n.* [*present* {*ca.* 1600}]—1956 N.Y. *Times Book Rev.* 8 Jan. p. 22/3 (letter) I think Mr. Nevins' review underscores the danger of 'presentism'; I suggest historians would strengthen their position by applying the chief test of their profession—perspective and caution in contemporary analyses.

SENSORIALISM, *n.* [*sensorial* {1768}]—1946 *Time* 2 Dec. p. 31/2 Sensorialism was founded by 35-year-old Jean LeGrand. . . . His theory: nothing is valid except sense experience, in which sex experience, being the most intense, is the most valid.

SIEGFRIEDISM, *n.* A quotation from a book by André Siegfried.—1955 *Sat. Rev.* 11 June p. 12/1–2 Siegfriedisms.

SYMINGTONISM, *n.*—1952 B'ham *Post-Herald* 3 Jan. p. 5/6–7 (heading) In Singapore Tin and Rubber 'Symingtonism' Is a Bad Word.

TALMADGEISM, *n.*—1948 Balto. *Eve. Sun* 9 Sept. p. 33/2 The triumph of Talmadgeism in Georgia yesterday is comparable to the restoration of the Long dynasty in Louisiana.

THINKISM, *n.* [*think* {*ca.* 800}]—1953 *Sat. Eve. Post* 6 June p. 12 (title of edit.) The Kremlin Takes Dim View of Thinkism.

THOROUGHBREDISM, *n.* [*thoroughbred* {1701}]—1955 *Sat. Rev.* 2 April p. 30/3 It does this despite the fact that of the cast only Peggy Maurer's Irina and Leonardo Cimino's Solyony really have the kind of useless thoroughbredism that lies at the root of Chekhov's tragic inertia.

TRUMANISM, *n.* See quots.—1950 Lincoln *Journal* 3 Dec. p. 2-D (Louis Bromfield) A new word—'Trumanism'—has come spontaneously into being from one end of the country to another. I think anyone on the street could tell you what it means. It means indecision, compromise, inefficiency, extravagance, high taxes, big bureaucracy, a confused and improvised foreign policy and above all a cheap political motive for every citizen. 1951 *Time* 27 Aug. p. 18/3 The policy of pretending that Communist influence on the Government didn't exist can be called 'Trumanism.' 1952 B'ham *News* 5 Sept. p. 20/4 (W. Lippmann) Except in military and foreign affairs—which are outside this discussion—the Democratic Party under 'Trumanism' had become a calculated combination of blocs for carrying the pivotal states. *Time* 27 Oct. p. 27/3 Point by point, Byrd ripped into Trumanism, which he called the campaign's main issue—'usurpation of power by the Executive . . . trends to socialism . . . inefficiency . . . profligate spending . . . fiscal irresponsibility . . . high and oppressive taxes . . .' 1953 B'ham *News* 16 Sept. p. 11/1 Trumanism was interpreted in the election of last November as meaning a pseudo-liberalism that got caught in a 'Washington mess'—special privileges for the tax-fixer, failure to prosecute Communists inside the government, and a profligate spending program that threatened the solvency of the nation's finances.

TWO-PARTYISM, *n.*—1952 B'ham *News* 5 Oct. p. E2/4 (heading) Sign of Two-Partyism.

WARRENISM, *n.*—1953 N.Y. *Times Mag.* 11 Oct. p. 10/5 In California he applied his philosophy to a peculiar brand of unpartisan, personalized politics—something his friends, and foes, termed 'Warrenism.'

WELFARE STATISM, *n.* [*welfare state* (*WNID Add. Sect.* 1950)]—1949 Lincoln *Journal* 16 Dec. p. 6 Welfare statism advanced slowly and gradually, but steadily, from 1893 to this time. 1957 B'ham *News* 4 March p. 9/2–3 (NANA) The trend is so marked among some sections of British society . . . that even the Labor Party has found it expedient to protest against some of the 'bureaucratic excesses' of welfare statism.

AMONG THE NEW WORDS

I. WILLIS RUSSELL AND WOODROW W. BOYETT
University of Alabama

ACKNOWLEDGMENTS. For citations: Walter S. Avis (5), R. F. Bauerle (5), Margaret M. Bryant (1), Edith Thompson Hall (1), Atcheson L. Hench (2), Mamie J. Meredith (7), Porter G. Perrin (4), Frances Rucks (1), Peter Tamony (2), Wiley Williams (1). R. F. Bauerle supplied all the citations of *exposure.* James Clark supplied the definition of *product mix.*

ASIALATIONIST, *n.* [*Asia* + *isolationist*] A person advocating concentration on Asian rather than European affairs.—1950 B'ham *News* 16 Dec. p. 4/3 [Herblock cartoon showing in the foreground a man labeled 'Asialationists' tugging at the arm of Uncle Sam holding a paper marked 'World Strategy' and in the background Stalin with a self-satisfied smile. Caption: 'Forget about Europe—I'll Take Care of That.'] 1953 *Sat. Rev.* 13 June p. 14/3 'Nothing short of the establishment of an American military protectorate in fact if not in name could have saved China.' Even the 'Asialationists' were never willing to advocate that on the scale that would have been necessary.

ATOMIC GARDEN. See quots. (Also attrib.)—1950 N.Y. *Times* 15 Jan. Sec. 1 p. 59/5 One of the spectacular developments during the year was the planting at the Argonne National Laboratory near Chicago of an atomic garden, in which every plant is radioactive, serving at the same time as a tree of knowledge and a tree of life. This was accomplished by making the plants grow in greenhouses in an atmosphere containing radioactive carbon dioxide, which the plants use in the creation of sugars, fats, proteins, vitamins, and a large number of other substances, all of which are thereby produced in radioactive form. 1954 *ibid.* 20 June p. 42/1 (AP) The answer to these medical puzzlers may be growing in the University of Chicago's 'atomic garden' project where plants breathe radioactive carbon dioxide gas.

AUTOMATE, *v.t.* & *i.* [Back formation from *automation* or *automated*. Cf. etymology s.v. *automated* in *Am. Sp.* 31:61] See quots.—1954 N.Y. *Times* 4 May (heading) Huge Sums to Be Spent to Automate Plants. 1955 *Controller* Dec. 602/2 PanAm Automates. 1956 N.Y. *Times* 8 Jan. p. E11/5 A real drama is planned. In the drama, an imaginary company is considering whether to automate its factory. . .

BRAINSTORM, BRAIN STORM, *attrib.* [Cf. *DA*, s.v. *brain-storm:* 'a succession of sudden and severe phenomena, due to some cerebral disturbance' (1894); Weseen *Dict. Amer. Slang*, p. 175: 'A sudden thought, especially one that is considered brilliant' (1934). Cf. also *OED Sup.*, s.v. *brain-storm:* '1907 N.Y. *Eve. Post* 23 May 4 Referring to Mr. William's discussion . . . [he] declares "it is the result of a brain-storm." '] See *brainstorming*.—1953 San Francisco *Examiner* 15 March (Sunday Pictorial Rev. Sect.) p. 4/2–3 Alex Osborn . . . has contributed to American business a new technique and terminology—the 'brain storm session.' 1956 *New Repub.* 20 Feb. p. 8 The pioneer thinkers christened their early efforts at creative collaboration 'brainstorm sessions,' according to Mr. Osborn, 'because, in this case, "brainstorm" means using the brain to storm a creative problem . . .'

BRAINSTORMING, *v.i.* & *t.* To participate in brainstorming (which see).—1955 N.Y. *Times* 6 Nov. p. F3/5 They are being taught, by specialists far removed from their own specialties, how to brainstorm their way to conclusions concerning subjects ranging from world affairs to specific engineering puzzles. 1956 *New Repub.* 20 Feb. p. 8 BBD & O itself has brainstormed all sorts of big and little problems for its very big clients . . . *This Week* 9 Dec. p. 8/2 Five of the session members had brainstormed before . . .

BRAINSTORMER, *n.*—1956 *Life* 11 June p. 20 (pict. cap.) Better mousetrap is compared by Brainstormer Clark to the traditional snaptop trap . . . 1957 *This Week* 14 Jan. p. 8/2 Speaking as fast as they could think, the brainstormers rattled off their ideas for marketable auto safety gadgets.

BRAINSTORMING, *n.* See first quot.—1955 *Business Week* 6 Aug. p. 158/1–2 The students credit Alex F. Osborn, one of the founders of Batten, Barton, Durstine and Osborn advertising agency, with drawing attention to the whole concept of teaching management people how to come up with fresh ideas for solving business problems. His system has been tabbed 'brainstorming,' free-wheeling sessions that encourage wild ideas but prohibit any evaluation or discussion until the session is over. 1956 N.Y. *Times* 20 May p. 52/2 Sluggish Federal brains are in for some peppy pummeling in the months to come if Charles H. Clark, the high apostle of 'brainstorming,' has his way in Washington. *Life* 2 July p. 18/4 . . . the process of brainstorming was originated in 1938 by Alex Osborn, 67-year-old founder of Batten, Barton, Durstine & Osborn. 1957 Chicago *Daily News* 25 March p. 7 (heading) 'Brainstorming' Transit Issue. 1957 *Sat. Rev.* 31 Aug. p. 27/1 In the 'technique of ideation' known as 'brain storming' the play tendency may also be discovered.

BRUSH-, BRUSH FIRE WAR, BRUSHFIRE WAR. [*brushfire* 1850 (*DA*)] A small controllable localized war. See *proxy war*.—1955 N.Y. *Times* 9 Jan. p. 8E/5 . . . the terrible words . . . were immediately interpreted all over the world as a threat that the United States would instantly retaliate with atomic weapons against the heart of the Communist world if the Commies started another proxy or brush-fire war. Balto. *Sun*, 2 Feb. (Edition B) p. 2/5 (AP) A fleet of air transports will be built to fly the streamlined units to 'brush-fire wars' caused by Communist penetration along the perimeter of the Red world. 1956 Omaha *World-Herald* 27 Nov. p. 14/1 This same United States Air Force which boasts a superb strategic arm is also readying its Tactical Air Command for bigger tasks—namely, the fighting of 'brush fire' wars, as in Korea. 1957 B'ham *News* 3 Jan. p. 24/6 'The U. S. should be prepared to use military force where a so-called brushfire war gives evidence of extending its consequences to our vital interests.' Tuscaloosa *News* 7 April p. 1/7 (AP) 'Britain's land power is virtually disappearing,' he declared. 'Suppose a brush fire war breaks out somewhere. Are we going to have to police it alone?' *Ibid.* 11 Aug. p. 1/6 (AP) However, the belief that any East-West atomic conflict would lead to total devastation is giving way here to the idea that the existence of small nuclear weapons will make a limited military clash or 'brush fire' conflict, entirely conceivable in the coming years. *Wall St. Jour.* 14 Nov. p. 1/6 The hydrogen warhead will no longer be reserved for intercontinental bombing and missile attacks, but in its midget form will be available for American use in any small 'brushfire' war. N.Y. *Times* 22 Dec. p. 2E/2 The money would go not only for missile defenses but for beefing up 'conventional' forces so that a brushfire war could be kept from spreading into a big war.

BUSHING, *n.* See quots.—1954 N.Y. *Times* 24 Jan. p. X29/3 According to the bureaus' analysis, 'such offers are often just tricks to get a prospect into a salesroom.' Once there, the prospect may be subjected to what is commonly termed 'bushing,' extra-slick high pressure selling. When the sale is practically complete, the prospect often discovers he cannot get as much allowance as the card said he could, or there may be other fancy financial double-talk. Omaha *World-Herald* 6 March p. 12 (quoting the St. Louis *Post-Dispatch*) The automobile business, under increasing sales pressure, has produced several neat dodges. One is called 'bushing.' A car owner finds a card on his windshield offering more than his car is worth on a trade-in for a new auto. When he looks into the offer, the dealer accuses the salesman of quoting a ridiculously high figure. The two stage a dramatic and persuasive argument which culminates in offering the buyer a 'compromise.' 1957 N.Y. *Times* 16 June p. XX25/3–4 Then the sales manager went into the act that the trade calls 'bushing' a customer. The origin of this term is as clouded as the ethics it represents, but in this instance the bushing consisted of an attempt to convince the customer that the deal could still be saved if he would be willing to take the power steering and windshield wipers.

CIRCUITRY, *n.* A system of electronic circuits; such circuits considered collectively.—1954 Cleveland *Plain Dealer* 4 Sept. p. 19/5 (AP) . . . R.C.A. . . . will demonstrate its new 21-inch tri-color tube . . . which Sarnoff said embodies major simplifications in circuitry. 1956 N.Y. *Times* 29 July p. 2E/1 These [drawbacks] include partial failure during severe storms when the 'sea return' caused by high waves confuses the picture on the radar scope; difficulty in keeping the intricate electronic circuitry in working order, and the failure to interpret radar data properly . . . 1957 *Newsweek* 8 July p. 58/3 Though bigger than the tiny transistor, the solion will eventually make equipment even smaller since it requires a much simpler circuitry, and can perform the work of several transistors or vacuum tubes. *Sat. Eve. Post* 20 July p. 64/2 We are pretty darn sure the bomb won't go off when we arm it, but with the complex circuitry involved there is always the one chance in a million that something might go wrong.

EXPOSURE, *n.* {1606} See quots.—1956 St. Louis *Post-Dispatch* 23 Aug. p. 2F/1 There is a word for this sort of thing that has come into great fashion in the last couple of years. It's 'exposure.' The very use of the word and its wide popularity in the upper echelons of television is indicative of what is happening in show business. Years ago an entertainer was hired for a performance. Then as the extent of his performance dwindled, he was said to make an appearance. Now it's exposure—a word heretofore associated with the click of a camera shutter. And that's about all you get, too. *Harper's Mag.* Nov. p. 30/1 The next step is exposure on camera. . . . Then if she goes, there'll be a series of exposures. 1957 *Variety* 5 June p. 1/4 Global Exposure for Khrushchev's Interview on CBS [heading]. Communist Party boss Nikita Khrushchev's precedental television interview on CBS-TV's 'Face the Nation' will get wide exposure beginning this week. St. Louis *Post-Dispatch* 27 June p. 2F/1 Simply by using their beans, British comedians have avoided the trap our comedians have fallen into—namely overexposure. British comedians refuse to appear once a week.

IDIOT BOARD. See quots.—1952 *Newsweek* 4 Aug. p. 51 The Republicans and the Democrats got their 'idiot boards' free. 1955 *New Repub.* 2 May p. 8 A more tangible aid to orators was the TelePrompTer, an invention provided the politicians *gratis* by its promoters. Otherwise known as the 'idiot board,' this contrivance permits a candidate to appear to be talking from memory while he reads his script off a concealed screen. *Harper's Mag.* June p. 42/1 The first test of this came when it was suggested that I use a teleprompter or a set of 'idiot boards' for an appearance on television. *Sat. Eve. Post* 24 Sept. p. 29 (pict. cap.) 'Idiot boards' are held out of camera range to prompt forgetful performers. Girls who hold them up are called 'idiot girls.'

IDIOT GIRL.—See last quot. s.v. *idiot board*.

JIFFY, *n.* [Cf. *OED*, s.v. *jiffy:* 'A very short space of time; only in such phrases as *in a jiffy* . . .' {1785}] See quots.—1951 N.Y. *Times Mag.* 22 April p. 35/4 JIFFY: Not yet accepted officially, this term has been popular since it was invented at Oak Ridge after a need arose for a name for an extremely small unit of time. It refers to the time it takes something moving with the velocity of light to travel one centimeter. 1956 *This Week* 6 May p. 19/2 Terminology. . . . What new scientific term, a measure of time, has been showing up lately in technical papers by nuclear physicists? A jiffy—it is the length of time it takes a beam of light moving 186,000 miles per second to travel one centimeter—about two-fifths of an inch.

LUMBERJILL, *n.* [By anal. with *lumberjack* with association of 'Jack and Jill.'] See first quot.—1946 *Sat. Rev. of Lit.* 22 June p. 49/1 (Allen Walker Read, 'The Word Harvest of '45.') The 'lumberjills,' in gay plaids, represent a feminized form of the lumberjack. 1956 Tuscaloosa *News* 11 June p. 9/8 (pict. cap.) LUMBERJILL—The Redwood Region Logging Conference at Ukiah, Calif., has come up with a 'lumberjill.'

MOONLIGHTER, *n.* [Cf. *WNID*, s.v. *moonlighter:* 'One who follows an occupation or pastime by night' (1934).] A person who holds two or more jobs.—1957 Chicago *Sunday Tribune* 18 July, Part 1, p. 14R/1 There is a new word in the vocabulary of labor statistics and employment—moonlighting. The moonlighter, unlike the moonshiner, is not conducting some illicit trade under the faint lunar beams. He is a respectable citizen, a thrifty citizen bent on achieving the better things of life—a guy who holds two jobs. . . . The department of commerce published a report on multiple employment—moonlighting—a few months ago. *Maclean's* 31 Aug. p. 3/1 . . . ten percent of its clients are moonlighters.

MOONLIGHTING, *n.* [Cf. *OED*, s.v. *moonlighting*, 1: 'The performance by night of an expedition, or of an illicit action' {1881}] See quots.—1957 *Maclean's* 31 Aug. p. 3/1 'More time to relax' has become both a promise and a creed in this age of automation—labor unions fight for it—but more and more Canadians are defeating it by 'moonlighting,' a new addition to the language meaning to work at a second job after the normal day's work is done. *The Reporter* 8 Aug. p. 11/3 Accordingly he takes two or three hours off and then, refreshed by a nap and an early dinner, departs for a second job. . . . The practice is known as 'moonlighting.' *Time* (Canadian ed.) 2 Sept. p. 11/3 The doubling-up produced a spate of editorial grumbling. But moonlighting was also popular among the Liberals; Workhorse C. D. Howe carried two heavy departments from 1951 on. 1958 Lincoln *Evening Jour. and Nebraska State Jour.* 7 Jan. p. 4/3 'Moonlighting' is the practice of holding a second regular job after a work shift. According to a report issued by the Commerce Department one out of every 20 employees—a total of 3.5 million—worked at more than one job.

PRODUCT-, PRODUCT MIX. The relative proportion of the different products to all products of the company, normally expressed in terms of dollar sales or individual units.—1953 Franklin G. Moore *Manufacturing Management* (Homewood, Ill.: Richard D. Irwin) p. 85 Valid comparisons of over-all figures sometimes become almost meaningless because variations in the 'product mix'—the quantities of different items produced—occur continually. 1954 Phil Carroll *Timestudy for Cost Control* (N.Y.: McGraw Hill, 3d ed.) p. 298 (Index) product mix. [The pages referred to in the Index do not use the term but discuss the problem as, 'We need common denominators because most plants turn out several products or several sizes of one product' (p. 9).] 1956 *Fortnightly Rev.* (Anderson & Strudwick, Richmond, Va.) 13 Nov. p. 3 The postwar period witnessed the change of the industry's product-mix from predominantly heavy to primarily light steels. 1957 Donald R. Longman and Michael Schiff *Practical Distribution Cost Analysis* (Homewood, Ill.: Richard D. Irwin, Inc.) p. 72 It provides an indication of the effect on costs and profits of any change in the product mix or in the ratio of customers of different types. [p. 379] The change in product mix increased the extent to which productive facilities of the plant were employed, thus yielding additional savings. 1957 N.Y. *Times Mag.* 1 Dec. p. 125/3 It is quite clear that Americans—and the American economy—have up to now been able to afford both tail fins and defenses, TV sets and education. If the 'product mix' has been such as to leave us a little less well-defended and well-educated than perhaps we should be, the underlying reason does not appear to be a special American wish for more consumption.

PROXY WAR. See first quot.—1955 N.Y. *Times* 9 Jan. p. 8E/5 . . . the terrible words . . . were immediately interpreted all over the world as a threat that the United States would instantly retaliate with atomic weapons against the heart of the Communist world if the Commies started another proxy or brush-fire war. 1956 *ibid.* 18 Nov. p. 12E/5 The second was in Korea, where the Soviet Union, reaching this time toward the other great industrial complex on its flanks—Japan—resorted to a proxy war in the belief that America would not fight, and in the hope of extending Communist power throughout the Korean peninsula to the gateway of Japan.

REPECHAGE, *n.* [French *repechage* '(fig.) . . . supplementary examination for candidates who have previously failed, consolation race.' (*Concise Oxford French Dict.*)] See quots.—1948 San Francisco *Call-Bulletin* 3 July p. 5/3 Harvard, upset by Cornell in the first trial heat, got back into the running by the 'repechage' or second-trial system. Yesterday the well-balanced Crimson boatload got square by beating Cornell by a full length in the semi-final. 1956 *Life* 10 Dec. p. 44/1 Surprisingly and badly beaten in its first race, the U. S. eight-oared entry still could qualify for the semi-finals by winning a repechage, or second-chance heat.

SKUNK, *n.* See quots.—1952 N.Y. *Times Mag.* 19 Oct. p. 14/4 The cruiser is a jack of many trades, important as a floating anti-aircraft battery, and useful at times for coastal bombardment or to seek out and destroy enemy 'skunks' (surface craft). 1957 *ibid.* 19 May p. 22/3 A Skunk is an unidentified surface ship, as opposed to a Bogie, which is an unidentified aircraft.

SPACEPORT, *n.* An airport for spaceships.—1950 *Time* 14 Aug. p. 88/2 *Spaceman's* hero may live in the 22nd century, serve as third mate on a 200,000-m.p.h. Earth-to-Venus spaceship, and burble endlessly about ray guns and spaceports, but Lancelot himself is an old stand-by. 1955 Omaha *World-Her. Mag.* 14 Aug. p. 4G Vast 'spaceports' will be set up on Earth, according to Arthur C. Clarke in his book, 'The Exploration of the Moon.' They will be located far from human habitation and it is from these stations that the rockets will be launched. 1957 Tuscaloosa *News* 27 May p. 6/5 (NEA) The spot [Cape Canaveral] will probably go down in history as the world's first spaceport. Cape Canaveral is the shooting end of the Patrick Air Force Base long range missile test center. From its huge, thick concrete launching pads are being test-fired the first series of intermediate range ballistic missiles and intercontinental ballistic missiles.

SPUTNIK [ˈspatnɪk, ˈsputnɪk], *n.* [Russian *sputnik* 'fellow traveler'; see also quot. *Newsweek* 14 Oct.] See quots. (As the quots. indicate, the word is employed both as a common and as a proper noun.)—1957 N.Y. *Times* 6 Oct. p. 43/7 To a Russian, the earth satellite launched by the Soviet Union is 'something that is traveling with a traveler.' That is the literal translation of 'sputnik,' the Russian word for the satellite. *Newsweek* 14 Oct. p. 38/3 What did this, the Russian '*Sputnik*' (short for *Iskustvennye Sputnik Zemli*, or 'Artificial Fellow Traveler Around the Earth') actually consist of? *New Repub.* 14 Oct. p. 4/2 Those members of both parties who are dedicated to voting the voters a tax cut before the 1958 election will scream about the cost and predict bankruptcy if we start building those new-fangled 'sputniks.' *Time* 14 Oct. p. 27 The Russians called it *sputnik* . . . [Three other uses on the page, e.g., '*sputnik's* signals,' '*sputnik's* success,' and 'firing of the *sputnik*.'] *Commonweal* 18 Oct. p. 60/2 But the scientific world's elation over the success of *Sputnik* has to be tempered by a recognition that this has been achieved at forced draft by a nation whose leaders are openly bent on the domination of the world. Lincoln *Jour. and Star* 20 Oct. p. 8A/3 In I. A. Smirnitsky's Russian-English dictionary, a standard Soviet work, published in 1952, 'Sputnik' is defined as 'a companion, a concomitant . . .' *Friends Jour.* 26 Oct. p. 691/1 At this writing Sputnik is still spinning her not altogether flattering circles around our . . . world . . . N. Y. *Times* 27 Oct. p. 6/5 Dr. Levitt declared that the launching of the sputnik is man's first step toward the moon. *Ibid.* 3 Nov. p. 22/2 (UP) 'But we know right now . . . that sputnik has at least modified some of our notions about conditions in the upper atmosphere.' *Ibid.* 3 Nov. p. 10E/2 The Russian sputnik, of which we learned on Oct. 5, is still going round and round. Tuscaloosa *News* 20 Nov. p. 4/5 Presumably the Sputniks have altered this mood. *Ibid.* 24 Nov. p. 1/4 (AP) The carrier rocket of Sputnik I circled closer and closer to the earth tonight . . . *Ibid.* 4 Dec. p. 4/5 Russia has the Sputnik, but we still don't have a name for our own satellite. 1958 *Nation* 25 Jan. p. 65/2 The current recession, falling market prices and rising sputniks are combining to discourage donations . . . *Friends Jour.* 25 Jan. p. 51/1 Mr. Rao pointed to Sputnik . . . Tuscaloosa *News* 5 Feb. p. 4/5 (Drew Pearson) Two military men . . . rejoiced when the American sputnik 'Explorer' sailed into outer orbit.

AMONG THE NEW WORDS

I. WILLIS RUSSELL AND WOODROW W. BOYETT
University of Alabama

OVER FIFTEEN YEARS AGO, Dwight L. Bolinger made some remarks in this department on the activity of the noun-forming suffix *-er* and cited a number of illustrations (*American Speech*, XVI [1941], 144). This present installment of 'Among the New Words' and a subsequent one will be devoted to additional illustrations of *-er* derivatives which, according to our checking, have not yet appeared in standard references or in such lists as appear in the yearbooks.

Indeed, it seems likely that a number of them will never reach the standard dictionaries. Many of them certainly look like nonce forms; besides, a large number are so self-explanatory that entering them in a dictionary, whether slang or standard, would seem to be unnecessary. Since, however, the activity of any affix can be measured only by all of its derivatives, whether nonce or not, it seems worth while to record as many as are available. Additional citations of any of the terms for which we have only one citation will be welcomed.

Whenever possible we indicate as an etymology the underlying form of the derivative with a date. For several we have not been able to find bases, and it may well be that such forms are not properly derivatives at all. For example, given *America firster*, the forms *Asia firster* and *Germany firster* are possible without assuming **Asia first* and **Germany first*. Nevertheless, with this caution, we include them here. Additional evidence may clarify their status. Since all the derivatives are nouns, part-of-speech labels have been omitted. The meaning of most of them is self-evident from the quotations. On the type *backer-upper*, *cleaner-upper*, *ear-pinner-backer*, *flattener-outer*, with the suffix added to both elements of a verb-adverb combination, see Mencken's *American Language: Supplement I*, pp. 380–81, and the references there cited.

We are indebted to Eric P. Hamp for the following communication on our entry *sputnik* in *American Speech*, XXXIII (1958), 129:

> Because of the technical meaning acquired in English by the term *fellow traveler*, it might be well to point out that besides this literal morpheme-by-morpheme meaning, *sputnik* is well translated by 'satellite,' for which it is the ordinary Russian technical astronomical term. Thus, despite the New York *Times* and *Newsweek* [citations given here], the Russians were simply talking about an 'artificial earth satellite.' A 'fellow traveler' is of course *popútchik*.

Apropos of the pronunciation, Professor Hamp observes: 'I have heard (and I think I myself say) [ˈsputnɪk]; maybe that occurs mainly in academic circles.'

ACKNOWLEDGMENTS. For citations: Dwight L. Bolinger (3), John H. Christian (1), Thomas L. Crowell (1), and Mamie J. Meredith (3).

A.D.A.-ER. [*ADA* 1947 on file]—1955 *Reporter* 16 June p. 2/1 It also appears that the A.D.A.-ers do not do their work in catacombs. . .

AIR-MAILER. [*air mail* (*WNID* 1934)] A person who tosses garbage out of windows. —1950 *Life* 4 Dec. p. 44/2 Its cops pounded up tenement stairways, putting the arm on mop-shakers and air-mailers.

AIRTROOPER. [*air troops* (*U.S.A.F. Dict.* 1956)]—1942 *Time* 17 Aug. p. 53/3 Now the Army is ready to add airtroopers, who swoop in after the paratroops, help them hold and exploit the gain.

ANTHOLOGER. [*anthologist* (*WNID 1934*)]—1953 *Sat. Rev.* 7 March p. 13/2 This puzzled me, for after reading more, I found that the anthology is by no means all bad. A few pages of unadulterated Twain are inserted in the end, and there are unsimplified pieces by James Thurber and Dorothy Canfield, as well as many other selections, both contemporary and classic, which show that the anthologers set about their task with imagination and taste.

ASIA FIRSTER.—1951 N.Y. *Times* 3 June p. E3/3 There are some people here now in both parties who sincerely believe that the resignation of Mr. Acheson would change the attitude of the America Firsters and the Asia Firsters on Capitol Hill. 1952 *Reporter* 19 Aug. p. 16/3 He has voted with the 'Asia Firsters' and he has voted with the 'Europe Firsters' . . . 1953 N.Y. *Times Mag.* 16 Aug. p. 1/3 Anyway, say the Asia-firsters—following the lead of Spengler—Europe is a static and perhaps a dying continent; Asia is a teeming, virile, undeveloped continent where the future will be made. N.Y. *Times* 20 Sept. p. E3/4 His critics among the Asia-Firsters were pleased.

BACKER-UPPER. [cf. *back up* (a) (*WNID* 1934)]—1946 *Sat. Eve. Post* 23 Nov. p. 28/1 Midway through the first quarter, he scribbled a note: 'Backer-upper trailing left half in motion to right. Run 29.' 1947 B'ham *News* 21 Oct. p. 20/4–5 Pat O'Sullivan . . . was tried out at end and tackle before being tried out as line backer-upper . . . 1948 N.Y. *Times Mag.* 29 Oct. p. 7. 1950 B'ham *News* 26 Sept. p. 27/5 In addition, Oscar Wolfe, an ace backer-upper from Warren Eastern High School in New Orleans, has joined the Tulane center ranks. . .

BETWEEN-AGER.—1957 N.Y. *Times Mag.* 24 Feb. p. 40 (heading) The Between-Agers: 11 to 14.

BUBBLE-GUMMER. [*bubble gum* (*WNID Add. Sect.* 1945)]—1947 Tuscaloosa *News* 13 March p. 7/2–4 Fourteen-year-old . . . A . . . is a serious bubble-gummer, ambitious to blow the biggest and best bubbles in town.

BY-LINER. [*by-line* (*WNID* 1934)]—1944 B'ham *News* 7 April p. 9 A few years ago he discovered a young writer and launched him in the newspaper business, where he soon became a popular sports by-liner. 1949 *Newsweek* 2 May p. 56 Though a by-liner whose daily Washington column . . . appears in some 600 papers, he is a crack legman himself.

CCFER. [*Cooperative Commonwealth Federation*]—1945 *Time* 2 April p. 42/3 Then bumptious Liberal Leader . . . H . . . had upset the applecart by teaming with teacherish . . . J . . . and his 32 socialist CCFers.

CHANNELER. {1897} A swimmer attempting to swim across the English Channel. —1955 *Life* 29 Aug. p. 121 (caption) Checkup on Channelers.

CIOER. [*CIO* (*DA* 1936)]—1941 *Reader's Dig.* June p. 91/1 As they were about to leave the plant in an automobile on the night of December 18 they were set upon by a crowd of CIOers.

CLEANER-UPPER. [*cleaner up* (*WNID* 1934)]—1939 *Topeka Cap.* 24 July p. 4/4–6 (cartoon) The Dandy Little Cleaner Upper.

CLUBMOBILER. [*Clubmobile* (*Am. Sp.* 19:78/1)]—1944 *This Week* 20 Aug. p. 5 Pat Rey . . . tells of a fellow who slipped off a 'clubmobiler's' torn glove . . . 1946 *Am Sp.* 21:148/1.

DAVIS CUPPER. [*Davis Cup* (*DA* 1901)]—1947 *Time* 1 Sept. p. 46/3 He is the U.S. singles champion, the Wimbledon champion, and the No. 1 U.S. Davis Cupper in both singles and doubles. 1956 Balto. *Sun* 26 Aug. p. 4D (pict. cap.) New U.S. Davis Cuppers . . .

DCER. [*Double Crostic*]—1944 *Sat. Rev. Lit.* 4 March p. 27 It was Miss Toms who some six years ago invited me for an interview with Emma Bagby, feature writer of the *Herald Tribune*, and a meeting with Geoffrey Parsons, editor, all DCers.

DEAD ENDER. [*dead end* (*WNID* 1934)]—1947 *Time* 11 Aug. p. 62/2 The most effective talk came from the Dead Enders themselves. 1950 N.Y. *Times Book Rev.* 11 June p. 5/1 (pict. cap.) Deadender—In his brief acceptance speech when he was given the National Book Award for his novel, 'The Man With the Golden Arm,' Nelson Algren warned that he might one day take his 'oscar' to the nearest pawnshop. Here he is, ready for a new novel, sitting under a viaduct in his home town, Chicago, 'just feeling around, just feeling around in the dark.'

DEBARKER. [*debark* {1744}]—1945 B'ham *News* 4 Oct. p. 16/2 Some pulp mills are using a new debarker said to result in an estimated 20 percent saving of wood.

DE-FUZZER.—1944 *Time* 18 Sept. p. 84/2 (pict. cap.) Peach De-fuzzer. *Ibid.* 16 Oct. p. 6/2 Time may have been be-fuzzed about de-fuzzers, but not about goofer feathers.

DIM-VIEWER. [*dim view* 1943 on file]—1949 B-ham *News-Age-Herald* 18 Sept. p. B1/1 Foreign Secretary Ernest Bevin, with an eye to dim-viewers in America, forthrightly declares: 'The United States is just as much a welfare state as we are.'

DISC-ER. [cf. *Amer. Thes.* ¶581.1]—1947 B'ham *News* 1 July p. 13/5 (pict. cap.) Jazz Dean Disc-er. . .

DISCOGRAPHER. [*discography* 1941 on file]—1946 *Sat. Rev. Lit.* 5 Jan. p. 22/3 (signature on record column).

DRAFT-AGER.—1951 *U.S. News* 11 May p. 19 (heading) Draft Agers' Odds for Survival.

EAR-PINNER-BACKER.—1944 *Sat. Rev. Lit.* 7 Oct. p. 22/2 Mr. L . . .'s rash assumption prompted the following blast from that veteran ear-pinner-backer . . . S. . .

ELASER. [*ELAS* (*Am. Sp.* 21:141/1)]—1945 Tuscaloosa *News* 10 Jan. p. 3/3 (AP) But the Greeks are chuckling over the way the British and the ELASers played football with each other amidst the battle. . .

ENROUTER. [*en route* (*WNID* 1934)]—1952 B'ham *News* 17 Feb. p. 1F/1 (caption) Enrouters.

EYEWITNESSER. [*eyewitness* {1539}]—1945 *Time* 27 Aug. p. 60/3 From Guam he filed what may have been the last eyewitnesser of the war.

FEEDERLINER. [*feeder line* {1858}]—1950 *Aviation Week* 21 Aug. p. 33 (title) Soviet's Newest Feederliner: Yak 16. 1951 *ibid.* 8 Jan. p. 21.

FIFTY-ONER. [*fifty-one* (*WNID* 1934)]—1951 N.Y. *Times Mag.* 11 Nov. p. 22/1 The 'fifty-oners,' like the forty-niners of the last century, carry picks, drills and other conventional equipment for digging up the earth.

5-INCHER. [See *OED*, s.v. *five*, C.c.: 'In parasynthetic sbs. with suffix -er¹ (chiefly colloq.), denoting individuals of a certain rank or size, as five-boater, -master, -rater.' {1887}]—1944 *Life* 30 Oct. p. 29/1 Their main armament is nine 16-inch guns, their secondary batteries twenty dual-purpose 5-inchers.

FLATTENER-OUTER. [*flatten out* (*Am. Thes. Slang* 1942)]—1939 *Sat. Eve. Post* 13 May p. 118/2.

FOUR-PLACER.—1949 *Aviation Weekly* Feb. p. 35 (title) Lightplane Trend to Four-Placers.

FOURTH TERMER.—1944 *Life* 30 Oct. p. 60/2 Reinhold Niebuhr, a fourth termer, admits in the London *Spectator*. . .

FREE-ENTERPRISER. [*free enterprise* (*Am. Sp.* 24:226/1)]—1943 Lincoln (Nebr.) *Jour.* 16 Aug. Free enterprisers in this country include the big industrialists. 1949 *Life* 24 Oct. pp. 97–98 . . . *Believe to the death in the party platform*, even if the platform . . . turns him from a free-enterpriser into a socialist. 1949 *Time* 5 Dec. p. 32/3 (pict. cap.) Free-Enterpriser Erhard.

GAWKER. [*gawk* {1785}]—1951 *Harper's Mag.* July p. 96 The simple gawker and head-turner is changing into something that looks suspiciously like a historian on wheels.

GEE-WHIZZER. [*gee whiz* {1888}]—1954 *Time* 12 July p. 82/3 Lockheed Aircraft Co. last week took some of the wraps off its new entry in the lightweight jet plane race. Called the XF-104 by the Air Force and the 'Gee-Whizzer' by Lockheed, the new ship is a small, relatively simple dayfighter designed to win local air superiority over the battle-field. *Newsweek* 19 July p. 66 (photo) This is an artist's conception of the Air Force's new 'Gee Whizzer'. . .

GERMANY FIRSTER.—1953 N.Y. *Times* 6 Sept. p. E5/4 Chancellor Adenauer's chief opponents are . . . the Social Democrats. They might be described as the 'Germany firsters.'

GET-RICH-QUICKER. [*get-rich-quick* (*DA* 1902)]—1957 *Sat. Rev.* 8 June p. 25/1–2 As a businessman, yes; as a private enterpriser, a get-rich-quicker, of course; but as an upholder of the sacred tradition of the humanities in the country, decidedly no.

GLOBALER. [*global* {1892}]—1943 *Time* 18 Oct. p. 84/3 The Lower the Globaler.

GOP-ER. [*G. O. P.* (*DA* 1887)]—1944 *Life* 23 Oct. p. 106/2 Some of the new Republicans were old-fashioned GOP-ers. . .

GRACE-HOPER.—1955 *Sat. Rev.* 12 Nov. p. 22/1 Any serious author is a grace-hoper. The grace he hopes for is that his readers will treat his books with understanding and appreciation, perhaps even admiration and affection.

GRASS ROOTER. [*DA* 1947]—1935 *Harper's Mag.* Sept. p. 484/1 'We believe,' the embattled Republican Grass Rooters resolved, 'that the maintenance of the independent sovereignties of the Federal Government and the several States, as guaranteed by the Constitution, is vital to the maintenance of our American System of government, and we reaffirm the wisdom of our forefathers who reserved to the States their power over matters of intra-state and local concern.' *Ibid.* p. 489/2 Do we hear the Grass Rooters, the financial interests, and the industrialists raising their voices in protest against this usurpation?

GUM BUBBLERS.—1947 *Sat. Eve. Post* 1 Nov. p. 21/1 At least three members of Congress are known to be surreptitious gum bubblers. . .

HAIR-DOER. [*hairdo* (*WNID Add. Sect.* 1939)]—1944 B'ham *News* 9 Oct. p. 11/6 (headline) Wacs and Hair-Doers Compromise on Style for Tresses of Lana.

HALL OF FAMER. [*Hall of Fame* (*DA* 1901)]—1948 B'ham *Age-Herald* 24 March p. 15/6 (AP) 'It looks as if I'll be here for awhile,' the baseball hall of famer explained. 1958 Tuscaloosa *News* 27 July p. 10 (heading) I. L. Hall of Famer in 'Oldtimers' Tilt.

IKE-LIKER. [*I like Ike*]—1952 B'ham *News* 14 July p. 1/4 He made this statement, after a crowd of Ike-likers from Birmingham and other parts of Alabama whooped it up at a welcoming party for the state chairman and Mrs. Vardaman upon their return late Sunday.

IN-BETWEENER. [*in-between* {1815}]—1958 N.Y. *Times* 16 Feb. p. X1/8 This much is evident now, however: the average or mediocre films—the ones without any sharp distinctions—are generally doomed nowadays along Broadway. The old familiar first-run theatres simply cannot make out with such films, as they managed to do in the past, when things were different. The 'in-betweeners' die quickly on Broadway.

KAMIKAZER. [*kamikaze* 1945 on file]—1945 Tuscaloosa *News* 14 Aug. p. 6/3 (headline) Destroyer Drexler Sunk by Kamikazers.

M.G.ER.—1945 *Time* 26 March p. 20/3 But M.G.ers . . . knew that their next mood would be profound depression.

MIDDLE-AGER.—1956 N.Y. *Times Mag.* 29 July p. 5 (title) America's Unknown Middle-Agers.

MID-SEASONER. [*mid-season* {1882}]—1951 N.Y. *Times* 1 July p. 37/5 (adv.) Nylon Mid-Seasoner for misses and women.

MODELER. One interested in model airplanes.—1950 *Sat. Eve. Post* 4 Nov. p. 152/2 The latter [contestants] are housed in Navy barracks and fed Navy food during the five-day meet, with the idea of attracting modelers to naval aviation.

AMONG THE NEW WORDS

I. WILLIS RUSSELL
University of Alabama

ACKNOWLEDGMENTS. For citations: Ruth Aldrich (2), Walter S. Avis (3), John R. Conover (1), Jane Crist (1), Virginia Foscue (1), Mamie J. Meredith (10), Porter G. Perrin (1), and Anne B. Russell (4). S. V. Baum contributed the five citations of *asphalt jungle*.

ADENO-, ADENOVIRUS, *n.* [See first quot.] See quots.—1956 *Sci. News Letter* 4 Aug. p. 68/1 Instead of calling the boss to tell him you are staying home today because you have caught the 'bug,' or a 'virus,' you soon may be able to tell him you are suffering with an 'adenovirus.' . . . The name was chosen because the 13 strains of the virus first reported were located in the adenoids of humans. *Time* 19 Nov. p. 96/2 (Canadian ed.) Researchers at the National Institutes of Health in Bethesda, Md. chose cancer of the cervix to study, picked some odd particles called adenoviruses to attack the tumors. 1957 N.Y. *Times Mag.* 24 March p. 56/1. N.Y. *Times* 22 Sept. p. E11/6 . . . some are caused by adenoviruses, the agents of grippe-like diseases. 1958 *Harper's Mag.* Feb. p. 62/2 (note) In 1953 scientists succeeded in isolating a group of new viruses from patients with respiratory infections which have been named adenoviruses.

ASPHALT JUNGLE. See first quot.—[1920 cited in *Am. Sp.* 33:78, where it is defined as 'a big city.'] 1949 W. R. Burnett *The Asphalt Jungle* (N.Y.: A. A. Knopf). [This is the story of the underworld of a large Midwestern city and traces the conflict between an honest police commissioner and a notorious criminal and his gang.] 1956 *Atlantic* March p. 54 . . . the 400,000 indigenous Americans still living in reservations and small communities are being turned loose upon the asphalt jungles of metropolitan centers in one of the most extraordinary forced migrations in history. N.Y. *World-Telegram Sun* 14 May p. 1/5 A native of the steaming topical [*sic*] jungles, Emily [an elephant] succumbed last night in the teeming asphalt jungle of East Harlem. *Newsweek* 28 May p. 106 Summing up [of the motion picture 'Crime in the Streets']: Anthropology in the asphalt jungle.

ATARACTIC, *n.* [See first quot.] See quots.—1957 N.Y. *Times* 23 June p. 4E/7–8 Tranquilizers, or ataractics (from the Greek ataraxia, 'not disturbed'), are the latest in a long series of attempts by man, from the dawn of history, to alter his mood. *Harper's Mag.* July p. 21/2 To tense, excited, and agitated patients the new drugs bring a most welcome serenity without somnolence. In this way they earn their name, 'tranquilizers,' or the neo-Hellenic one of 'ataractics.' ATARAXIC, *adj.*—1956 *Time* 26 Nov. p. 52/3 To the fast-swelling ranks of ataraxic (tranquilizing) drugs, another was added last week . . .

BLAST-, BLASTOFF, *n.* [Cf. *OED*, s.v. *blast*, *sb.* 8: 'A "blowing up" by gunpowder or other explosive . . .' {1635–1853}; Reifer, *Dict. of New Words* (N.Y.: Philosophical Library, 1955), s.v. *blast-off*: '*Rocketry*. Energy expended during take-off of a rocket or a space-ship . . .'] See second quot.—1958 N.Y. *Times Mag.* 26 Jan. p. 61/1 The camera . . . will record the blast-off in color from far closer than any human eye. *Life* 10 Feb. p. 16 At instant of take-off launching pad is blanketed with billowing clouds of flame spewed out by space-bound Jupiter. . . . After blast-off, higher, higher . . . Tuscaloosa *News* 16 Feb. p. 1/4 (AP) A mechanical 'bug' halted the test launching of an Atlas intercontinental ballistic missile today a split second before the blastoff. *Ibid.* 17 Aug. p. 1/8 (AP) If the initial blastoff toward space is successful, the world will have to wait 2½ days for an announcement on the results.

BLAST AWAY, BLAST OFF, *v.i.* [Cf. Reifer, *op. cit.*, s.v. *blast off*, *v.*: '*Slang*. To depart; take one's leave . . .']—1958 Tuscaloosa *News* 16 Feb. p. 1/4 (AP) On Feb. 7, the fifth Atlas to be test flown blasted away. *Ibid.* 17 March p. 1/7–8 (AP) The three-stage rocket had blasted off from Cape Canaveral, Fla., at 7:16 A.M. *Ibid.* 13 Aug. p. 1/2 (AP) . . . the three-stage rocket . . . may blast off . . . around 7 A.M. . . .

BLAST-DOWN, *n.* The landing of a space ship.—1957 *Time* 14 Jan. p. 41/3 (Canadian ed.) If Captain Dart gets to the Whirlpool Galaxy while he is still young enough to make a safe blast-down on some hospitable planet, he will thank, in part, Albert Einstein and the theory of relativity.

BLOCKHOUSE, *n.* [Cf. *OED*, s.v. *blockhouse*, b: '. . . An edifice of one or (formerly) more storeys, constructed chiefly of timber, loop-holed and embrasured for firing.' {1512–1878}] See quots.—1953 *Monsanto Mag.* July p. 4 (pict. cap.) This blockhouse is as close as anyone gets to a missile at take off. Two large ports, arranged like periscopes, permit observation of the launching pads from a position of safety. Loudspeakers, lights and weather instruments are mounted atop the blockhouse. 1958 N.Y. *Times Mag.* 26 Jan. p. 60/2 The blockhouse itself is a compact array of clocks, panels, dials, timers and oscillographs. *Life* 17 March p. 30/1 (pict. cap.) In the blockhouse at Cape Canaveral, Army missilemen . . . turned from the window where they had been watching firing preparations on Explorer II to cast worried looks at instruments. Tuscaloosa *News* 4 June p. 4/5 (NEA) . . . the blockhouse . . . is a hemispherical shelter 800 feet from the pad. It has 9 feet of concrete, 16 feet of sand and four inches of reinforced gunite for a roof. The blockhouse has no windows overlooking the pad. But it has four periscopes and four closed circuit television cameras. Its console of instruments can record some 300 measurements. In the center of six control desks sits the test director in a swivel chair at his console panel with start and stop push buttons.

CAR PARK. See *Am. Sp.* 31:60. Additional illus.—1955 *Sat. Eve. Post* 29 Jan. p. 65/2 (Max Murray). *Ladies' Home Jour.* Sept. p. 110/4 (Alec Waugh). *Ibid.* Nov. p. 218/2 (Queen Alexandra of Yugoslavia). 1957 *Sat. Eve. Post* 27 April p. 128/1 Today's 'car parks' or 'parking stations' are cleaned up, paved and well lit . . .

COTTAGE COLONY. See quots.—1956 *Chr. Sci. Mon.* 25 May p. C5/3 After visiting Ellinor Village in Florida—a huge, self-sufficient cottage colony . . . vacation resort . . . has own store, movie house . . . keyed to entire family. 1957 *Mademoiselle* April p. 101/1 In the Stroudsburg, Pa. area alone there are nearly 200 resorts, ranging from relatively primitive camps to elaborate dude ranches and cottage colonies. 1958 N.Y. *Times* 3 Aug. p. X19/1 Essentially a cottage colony is a small group of cabins or cottages equipped for what is elastically defined as light housekeeping and clustered about a body of water where parents can pool their offspring for purposes of communal diversion.

ELECTRO-, ELECTROJET, *n.* [Cf. *jet stream* in *Am. Sp.* 28:210–11.] See quots.—1957 *Fortune* June p. 167/1–2 Many [U. S.] stations are clustered near the geomagnetic poles and the magnetic equator so that scientists can observe the effect of the magnetic field and the three atmospheric 'electrojets' on auroras . . . and other phenomena. The equatorial electrojet, a current of about a hundred thousand amperes that flows in the ionosphere . . . moves westward with the sun. N.Y. *Times* 25 Aug. p. 34/1 The Electrojet seems to be part of a globe-enveloping system of electric currents generated by tidal movements of the earth's atmosphere. 1958 *ibid.* 19 Jan. p. E11/3 (pict. cap.) The existence of an 'electrojet,' a river of electric energy that girdles the geomagnetic equator in the upper air, has been confirmed.

ELECTROLUMINESCENCE, *n.* See first quot.—1956 *Sat. Rev.* 6 Oct. p. 55/1 This new form of light is called electroluminescence. The glow comes from a powdered phosphor bound in a plastic and sprayed on the surface of a glass plate as thin as an ordinary window. On the side that emits the light the glass is coated by Corning with a transparent stuff that conducts electricity . . . 1957 Milwaukee *Sentinel* 21 Sept. III/4/1 In their constant research in the field of electroluminescence, a method by which specially coated sheets of glass can be made to produce light, Westinghouse scientists are experimenting with producing phosphors.

ELECTROLUMINESCENT, *adj.*—1956 *Life* 24 Sept. p. 18 Arranged horizontally, 120 of the electroluminescent panels give off a mottled glow because of structural variations . . . N.Y. *Times* 30 Sept. p. 38/4 Electroluminescent materials, which emit light on the application of an electric current, show promise—when combined with other new materials—of making possible mural television. 1957 Milwaukee *Sentinel* 21 Sept. III/4/1 An area light source, electroluminescent lamps are basically a two dimensional source.

FISSION-FUSION-FISSION, *adj.* See last quot.—1956 N.Y. *Times* 29 July p. 19/1 It appears highly probable that the so-called fission-fusion-fission bomb came about by pure accident. 1957 *ibid.* 10 Nov. p. E5/5 The early 'fission-fusion-fission' devices with a jacket of uranium (heavier than lead) were about as compact and easy to carry as a railroad locomotive. 1958 N.Y. *Times Book Rev.* 23 Feb. p. 1/1 The bomb set off at Bikini that morning was neither an ordinary atom bomb nor a hydrogen bomb, but a city-buster beyond either—a U- or fission-fusion-fission bomb. In the U-bomb, an ordinary plutonium or U-235 (fission) bomb triggers a hydrogen (fusion) explosion; fast neutrons from the latter in turn fission a mantle of ordinary uranium (U-238) wrapped around the entire device.

GHANA, *n.* See quots.—1957 N.Y. *Times* 10 March p. 2E/4 Last week Ghana, a merger of the British crown colony of the Gold Coast and Togoland protectorate, became the nineteenth nation to arise since the war. . . . The new nation, which derives its name from the Negro empire of Ghana which flourished in West Africa a thousand years ago, has a population of 4,500,000, covers almost 100,000 square miles and produces more than one-third of the world's cocoa. *Life* 18 March p. 31/1 The name Ghana was derived from a great African empire of the Third Century . . . GHANIAN, *n.*—1958 N.Y. *Times* 4 May p. 12/1 (heading) Ghanians Enlist Aid from Israelis.

MICROMETEOR, -ITE, *n.* See quots. (Also attrib.)—1957 N.Y. *Times* 26 May p. 15/1–2 The scientific effort will include studies of ocean currents . . . micrometeorites and other long-standing problems. Seattle *Times* 10 Nov. p. 16/5 (AP) . . . density of micrometeors and meteoric dust, and the like. 1958 Tuscaloosa *News* 4 May p. 12/6 (AP) Only seven hits by micrometeorites—tiny, speeding particles of space dust which might present another hazard to space travel—were recorded by Explorer I during a period of a month . . . N.Y. *Times* 3 Aug. p. E9/7 *Micrometeorite Density*.—Data obtained to date have given evidence that a satellite will not be seriously endangered by the impact of small meteors traveling at the speed of 25,000 miles per hour.

PARK-RIDE, *adj.* See quots.—1947 *Harper's Mag.* Jan. p. 35/2 Atlanta . . . has a big municipal parking lot a mile and a half from the business center, with a 'park-ride' service for thirty-five cents that includes both parking charges and round-trip fare. 1957 N.Y. *Times* 22 Sept. p. 61/1 Under the Philadelphia plan existing rail lines would be used, but they would be bolstered with adequate park-ride lots and be provided with proper connections with existing bus routes.

PINCH EFFECT. See quots.—1956 *Sci. News Letter* 15 Sept. p. 174/1 Generating the high heat in a controlled manner requires containers that will not melt or be otherwise affected. Using the 'pinch effect' would seem to eliminate the container problem, since the reacting gas column would contract to contain itself, thus not touch any walls . . . .The 'pinch effect' was first noted by E. Northrup in 1907. 1958 N.Y. *Times* 26 Jan. p. E9/7 Instead of a material vessel, scientists have devised what they call a 'magnetic bottle.' This is made possible by the fact that an electrical current creates around itself a magnetic field, with magnetic lines of force which prevent the electrified hydrogen particles from crossing. These magnetic lines of force create what is known as the 'pinch effect,' pinching the gas into a narrow column inside the material container, thus preventing the hot gas from touching the walls of the container and thus losing its energy.

AMONG THE NEW WORDS

I. WILLIS RUSSELL AND WOODROW W. BOYETT
University of Alabama

THIS INSTALLMENT of 'Among the New Words' is devoted to the remainder of the *-er* derivatives in our files. For general comments, see *American Speech*, XXXIII (1958), 280.

ACKNOWLEDGMENTS. For citations, Walter S. Avis (1), Dwight L. Bolinger (3), O. B. Emerson (1), Atcheson L. Hench (1), Mamie J. Meredith (2), and Porter G. Perrin (1).

NO-GOODER. [*no good* (*DA* 1924)]—1944 *This Week* 22 Oct. p. 21/2 . . . any newspaper reader of the late '20's would remember this no-gooder.

OBSTETOGRAPHER.—1948 *Sat. Rev. Lit.* 21 Aug. p. 21/3 (letter) Has not obstetographer R. B. Hall . . . thought of this passage on 'childbirth from the point of the observer'?

OPMER. [*OPM* Jan. 1941 on file]—1941 *Collier's* 29 Nov. p. 4/4 We've been talking to a top-flight OPMer.

OUT-OF-STATER. [Cf. *out-of-towner* (*Am. Sp.* 27:51/2)]—1954 N.Y. *Times* 10 Jan. p. X19/1 But Georgia fortunately has come to the realization that more out-of-staters travel the route near the coast, en route to and from Florida . . .

PACIFIC-FIRSTER. [Cf. *America firster*]—1953 N.Y. *Times Mag.* 16 Aug. p. 1/2 Asia is the continent where the bullets have been flying and American boys have been dying; our efforts should be concentrated there, say the Pacific-firsters.

PIN-UPPER. [*pin-up* (*WNID Add. Sect.* 1945)]—1944 Tuscaloosa *News* 27 April p. 8/3 (NEA) Miss G. . . . also was worried about what effect becoming a mama would have on the gents in the armed forces who seem to prefer her as their No. 1 pin-upper.

POLLTAXER. [*poll tax* (*WNID* 1909)]—1944 B'ham *News* 10 May p. 9/4 (AP) The polltaxers and the anti-polltaxers will tip their hats to the constitution . . .

PRIVATE ENTERPRISER. [*private enterprise* 1844 (*Am. Sp.* 24:226–27)]—1952 N.Y. *Times Mag.* 20 July p. 13/2 But it is from the furiously bubbling melting pot that the Democratic Party was spawned and has since been nourished. From the days of Jefferson and Jackson . . . it has drawn to its ranks the masses of the discontented, the wage-earners, the frontiersman and the farmer, the immigrant and the private enterpriser in conflict with the 'money interests.'

PROFILER. [*profile* {1656}]—1949 N.Y. *Times* 4 Sept. p. 4/7–8 (adv.) Everitt's Needlepoint profiler is a saucy pom-pon hat with a wonderful windswept brim.

READER-ALOUDER.—1952 *Sat. Rev.* 13 Sept. p. 6/3 Hemingway is a reader-alouder, it appears.

RED CROSSER. [*Red Cross* (*WNID* 1909)]—1946 *Time* 20 May p. 72/2 Married. Captain Harry C. Butcher . . . and Mary Margaret Ford, 34, ex-Red Crosser.

RELIEFER. [*relief* {*c* 1400}]— 1936 *Harper's Mag.* Jan. p. 203/2 Reliefers don't of course live by themselves and form a compact group with relief as their only topic . . . [1937 cited in *Ten Eventful Years*, ed. Walter Yust, IV, 629/1.]

ROCK 'N ROLLER, ROCK 'N' ROLLER. [*rock-and-roll* 1955 (*1956 Brit. Book of the Year* p. 751/2)]—1956 *Time* (Canadian ed.) 24 Sept. p. 67/1 '*My Boy Elvis* . . . is a real rock 'n roller . . .' N.Y. *Times* 4 Nov. p. X13/1 Or is their destiny just to be culture's rock 'n' rollers?

SENIOR BOWLER.—1952 B'ham *Post-Her.* 7 Jan. p. 9 (headline) Pro Scouts Scramble for Senior Bowl-ers after North Victory.

SIDE-ARMER. [*sidearm. Baseball.* (*WNID* 1934)]—1948 Balto. *Sun* 15 March p. 17/8 'I used the side-armer against right-handed hitters only . . .'

SNICKERER. [*snicker* {1694}]—1951 *Time* 19 Nov. p. 32/1 (caption) The Snickerers.

SOAPER. [*soap opera* (*WNID Add. Sect.* 1945)]—1946 *Time* 26 Aug. p. 56/3 The result: *Pepper Young's Family*, one of radio's most popular soapers.

SPACER. [*space* {1667}]—1954 N.Y. *Times Book Rev.* 7 March p. 16/3 The Earth of the far future is plagued with many problems: what to do about its conquerors, the 'Spacers,' descendants of the men who settled the stars; where to employ people thrown out of work by robots; why mankind prefers to live in a few gigantic megalopoles, and how to discover the murderer of an eminent Spacer.

SPEEDER-UPPER. [*speed-up* {1923}]—1955 N.Y. *Times Mag.* 27 Nov. p. 56 (pict. cap.) Speeder-Upper—A small truck handy in traffic, put into service by the New York Post Office this year.

STANDARD-SETTER.—1947 *Sat. Rev. Lit.* 19 July p. 26/2 Meanwhile passengers can whet their appetites with GM's standard-setter as it slips noiselessly around the country.

STARTER-UPPER. [*start-up* {*c* 1205}]—1939 Billboard adv. observed 27 May.

STAY-DOWNER. [*stay-down strike* 1952 (*1953 Brit. Book of the Year* p. 752/2)]—1952 *Time* 28 April p. 24/1 All of the 'stay-downers' . . . are reserve officers . . .

STIRRER-UPPER.—1941 *Time* (Air Exp. Ed.) 13 Oct. p. 40/2 Mr. L. . . . has been revealed as a prime stirrer-upper of racial prejudice.

STOCKPILER. [*stockpile* (*WNID Add. Sect.* 1945)]—1951 *Bus. Week* 24 Nov. p. 26 (subheading) Stockpilers are dipping in now and then to keep both civilian and military industry going.

STRAITEN-OUTER.—1951 Seattle *Times* 19 July (T. L. Stokes column) So, for deliverance from our worries, the tendency now is toward a military man rather than the traditional businessman straiten-outer [*sic*]—or at least it is so with many.

STRAW-, STRAW HATTER. [*straw hat* 1939 (*Am. Sp.* 24:306/2)]—1949 N.Y. *Times Mag.* 21 Aug. p. 24/4 The trick of operating a successful straw-hatter is to build up a steady clientele—a sizable number of people who get the habit of regular attendance because they have learned that the general average of production is good. 1954 *Wall St. Jour.* 4 Aug. p. 9 The Howard Lindsay-Russell Crouse straw hatter ('Life with Father') subsequently made Broadway . . .

SWEAT SHOPPER. [*sweat shop* (*DA* 1895)]—1946 Tuscaloosa *News* 22 April p. 4/2 But to take the lower standards and apply them the other way around would simply play into the hands of the 'sweat shopers' [*sic*].

TABLE-, TABLE HOPPER. [*table hop* (*Am. Thes. Slang* 1953)]—1944 *Life* 16 Oct. p. 11/2 Table hopper constantly leaves his companion to swap stories with anybody. 1953 *News & Views* (Gen. Motors) Feb. p. 23 By definition, a table-hopper is a man, woman or ex-child who, during the height of the meal in a crowded restaurant, springs from table to table without visible means of propulsion.

TENNISER. [*tennis* {*c* 1400}]—1951 B'ham *News* 13 March p. 22/5–6 (headline) Touring tennisers play here tonight.

THIRD PLACER.—1958 Tuscaloosa *News* 13 July p. 24 (pict. cap.)—Runner-up Lynne Galvin . . . and third placer Lucille Strazza . . . took the news happily . . .

THOBBER. [*thob* (*WNID* 1934)]—1945 *Time* 24 Sept. p. 48/3 A thobber is a person who prefers guess-work to investigation and reinforces his beliefs by asserting them frequently. [footnote] Grammarian Charles Henshaw Ward . . . coined the word from the phrase: thinking out the opinion that pleases one and believing it.

UNDER-SIXER.—1949 B'ham *News Age-Her.* 9 Oct. p. 1/2–3 (headline) 'Under-Sixers' Are Teacher Headache. Most 5½-Year-Olds Lag behind in Rudiments of School Conduct.

UNITED FRONTER.—1948 Tuscaloosa *News* 26 July p. 4/5 He is a 'united fronter'—one who believes in co-operation with the Communists.

WE-NEVER-HAD-IT-SO-GOODER. [Cf. the expression *You never had it so good.*]—1957 N.Y. *Times Book Rev.* 8 Sept. p. 18/4 There are many Jeremiahs . . . and many we-never-had-it-so-gooders . . .

AMONG THE NEW WORDS

I. WILLIS RUSSELL
University of Alabama

THE EARLY CITATIONS OF *featherbed* in the glossary are made possible by the kindness of James G. Lyne, who recently sent the editors of *American Speech* two tearsheets of his column, 'Railroading after Hours,' in *Railway Age*. In his column for July 27, 1959 (p. 66/1–2) Mr. Lyne raised the question of who had first employed the word in its new sense, citing F. J. Lisman's use of it, quoted below, and expressing the suspicion that Lisman was the coiner. In his column of September 7, 1959 (p. 21/1), however, he was able to push the date farther back on the strength of a reference from Robert Hicks, of the New York Central Railroad. Mr. Hicks's reference is to the 1922 edition of the Loree work cited in the glossary, which unfortunately is not available to me, though the 1929 edition, from which I have quoted, is. My thanks to Mr. Lyne for sending us these tearsheets.

ACKNOWLEDGMENTS: For citations, Ruth I. Aldrich (3), Clarence L. Barnhart (1), Joseph S. Hall (1), Atcheson L. Hench (3), Mamie J. Meredith (6), Arthur Minton (6), Porter G. Perrin (2), Anne B. Russell (4), and Peter Tamony (1). The entry *maître d'*, except for a few minor changes, was prepared by Arthur Minton. Ruth I. Aldrich supplied the citations of *squadrol* and suggested the etymology. To the foregoing and to Woodrow W. Boyett thanks are also due for help in checking.

AFTERBURNER, *n.* [See *Am. Sp.* 25: 226/1.] See quots. (Also attrib.)—1955 Los Angeles *Times* 18 July p. I 17/1–4 Wallace Linville . . . said perhaps the greatest promise has been shown by so-called after-burner controls. These are chambers in which exhaust gases are mixed with air to provide oxygen for burning up the average 7% of gasoline left unburned after cylinder combustion. If improvements are adequate, the afterburner may prove suitable for installation on gas-burning trucks and busses. 1956 Seattle *Times* 8 Feb. p. 21/5 Tail-Pipe Afterburners May Reduce Smog Source. 1959 N.Y. *Times Mag.* 18 Jan. p. 32/4 The chief aim has been the development of an 'afterburner'—a device to be attached to the exhaust pipe to complete the oxidation of gasoline to harmless products.

BIOASTRONAUTICS, *n.* [*bio-* + *astronautics*] See first quot.—1957 N.Y. *Times Mag.* 20 Oct. p. 12/1 The third phase has a wholly new name, 'bioastronautics'—the study of man's capabilities and needs, and the means of meeting those needs, for travel in outer space. 1958 *ibid.* 23 March p. 24/1 A more realistic portrait emerges from the young science of bioastronautics, the newest and strangest of medical disciplines.

BOATEL, BOTEL, *n.* [*boat* + *motel*] See first quot.—1958 Washington *Post and Times Herald* 24 Aug. p. C 7/6 Chalk's 'Boatel' with its restaurants, swimming pools, parks and parking space would certainly be a boon to both power and sailboating in Washington. [Boatel sign observed by Anne B. Russell 4 Sept. on U. S. 19 in Florida near the Suwanee River.] 1959 *Brit. Book of the Year* p. 752/2. *Woman's Day* July p. 28/2 The area is accessible only by boat or seaplane, and there are no automobiles on the island. Hence the Inn at Windigo Harbor and the Lodge at Rock Harbor are referred to as botels rather than motels.

BROAD-, BROAD SPECTRUM, *adj.* [Cf. *OED*, s.v. *spectrum*, 3: 'The coloured band into which a beam of light is decomposed by means of a prism or diffraction grating.' {1671}] See first quot.—1952 *Scientific Am.* April p. 49 They are known as the broad-spectrum drugs, because each of them attacks a wide range of infections. 1957 N.Y. *Times* 18 Aug. p. E 9/6 Antibiotics themselves are not believed to be effective against influenza viruses. The broad-spectrum antibiotics are being tried, but in general experience has shown the modern 'miracle' drugs do not affect virus-caused diseases. 1958 *ibid.* 3 Aug. p. 1/1 The complaint involves the 'broad spectrum' drugs, so designated because they destroy or inhibit the growth of a wide range of micro-organisms that breed disease. 1959 *ibid.* 21 June p. E 9/5 Drs. . . . Hirsch and . . . Finland . . . reported . . . that a new antibiotic of the broad-spectrum tetracycline family has been found to be more effective against test bacteria than any of its predecessors.

COMETOID, *n.* [Cf. *OED*, s.v., b: 'A name proposed by Prof. Kirkwood of Indiana for luminous meteors.' {1871}] See quot.—1959 *Sat. Rev.* 5 Sept. p. 52/3 I shall introduce the word 'cometoid' at this point to give a name to what I believe is the next phase in a comet's decline. I define cometoid as a chunk of ice too small to be observed as a comet but too large to be entirely melted before it glides into the last few miles of air above Earth.

COWFETERIA, *n.* (*cow* + ca*feteria*] See quots.—1950 *Mademoiselle* Jan. p. 74/2 . . . Also making life easier, but for cows, is the cowfeteria, a serve-yourself barn. . . . 1957 N.Y. *Times* 25 Aug. p. 31/2 Mr. Haggins has designed and contructed a 'cowfeteria' that lets the cows select and eat as much feed as they want.

FEATHERBED, *adj.* 1938 cited in *Am. Sp.* 19: 305/1. Add earlier quots.—1922 L. F. Loree *Railroad Freight Transportation* (N.Y., London: D. Appleton and Co.) p. 625 (see preliminary remarks). 1929 *ibid.* (2d ed.) p. 625 No reliable data have been collected that would enable an estimate to be made of the annual cost of these so-called 'feather-bed' practices. 1934 *Railway Age* 97: 858/2 (F. J. Lisman) While it may not be reasonable to expect railroad labor to admit that their pay is greatly in excess of the rate of pay in similar occupations, the fact is that earnings will no longer support both the high wage rates and the restrictive rules, sometimes called 'featherbed rules,' which the unions with the aid of legislators have gradually compelled the carriers to concede.

HEADACHE BAND. [See first quot.] See quots.—1958 *Life* 28 April p. 103 Rather surprisingly the style was also taken up by Mrs. Cornelius Vanderbilt III, who was rarely seen without a band. Someone said it made her look as if she had a chronic headache and from this came the name, headache band. Tuscaloosa *News* 13 Aug. p. 17/3 (pict. cap.) The Headache Band. Newest headpiece to go with the revolutionary change in fashions. It's a circlet of chiffon enterwined [*sic*] with pearls. Holds your curls in place, or a pony tail if you please! Use it as a collar on a basic date dress.

INDUSTRIAL PARK, INDUSTRIAL DISTRICT. See quots.—1953 San Francisco *Examiner* 28 March p. 1/2 The area . . . is to become a carefully planned and controlled 'industrial district.' 1956 Baltimore *Sun* 22 June (Edition B) p. 31/8 A growing demand is reported for sites in well situated and designed . . . 'industrial parks' . . . that have come into prominence here in recent months. 1959 Tuscaloosa *News* 9 Jan. p. 9/1 Such a site becomes an industrial park when a developmental group, civic or private, has it zoned for industrial building and installs adequate facilities—access roads, water and gas mains, electricity and sewer lines. Railroad facilities often are stressed. N. Y. *Times* 30 Aug. p. 51/1 (headline) Fairfield Weighs Industrial Park. *Industrial Development and Manufacturers Record* (Oct.) p. 14/3 In northwestern Staten Island a new industrial park is underway.

JAZZOPHILE, *n.* [*jazz* + *-o-* + *-phile*]—1947 *Time* 15 Sept. p. 80/2 . . . (it would take an undaunted jazzophile to tell where one began and the other ended). 1959 *Look* 21 July p. 76/2 But 3,000 brave jazzophiles sat patiently through three hours of liquefied jazz. *Family Week* 13 Sept. p. 16/3 And for the jazzophiles, Dot's 'Gilbert & Sullivan Revisited' by Manny Albam and the Jerry Duane Singers, and MGM's 'The Seven Ages of Jazz,' featuring an all-star cast, are both well worth your listening time.

MAÎTRE D', MAITRE D'., MAITRE D'. [Cf. *A. D. C.* 'aide-de-camp' (*Am. Thesaurus of Slang*, *Sup.* 1947, ¶ 9.18) and *maitre de bar* ('The autobiography of the maitre de bar of the Pierre'—a description of *Nothing Lasts Forever* by Oscar Haimo [privately printed,

1953], N.Y. *Her. Trib.* 2 Nov. 1953 p. 17/3).] Clipped form of *maître d'hôtel* {1540}.—1950 Polly Adler *A House Is Not a Home* (N.Y. and Toronto: Rinehart and Co.) p. 27 Hatcheck girls, waiters, the matire d', some nicely dressed people at one of the tables—they all spoke to Harry and smiled at me. *Ibid.* pp. 318–19 Moreover, just as in top restaurants it is the personality of the maitre d' which gives a place its particular cachet. . . . 1951 N.Y. *Her. Trib.* 10 Feb. p. 9/8 Louis Pellegrini, Maitri [*sic*] D', is an oldtime Friend of the Family. . . . 1953 *Cue* 28 March p. 29 . . . the new management (Clinton Mello, maitre d'., Peter Bodo, chef, and Renato Traversi, bartender). . . . 1954 N.Y. *Her. Trib.* 13 March p. 11 (pict. cap.) Here Maitre d' Charles Kozonis samples the pickled marrons. *Ibid.* 16 Oct. p. 9 (pict. cap.) Here Maitre d' Louis carves the caneton a l'orange. . . .

OPEN OCCUPANCY. [Cf. *OED*, s.v. *open*, *a.* (*adv.*), II, 14: 'Not confined or limited to a few, generally accessible or available . . .' {1460}] Racially unrestricted housing. (Also attrib.)—1953 *U. S. Housing and Home Finance Agency*. Open occupancy in public housing; a bulletin based upon local experience in the administration of federally aided low-rent public housing projects occupied by more than one racial group. [Washington]; cited in *National Union Catalogue* (1953–57) XXIV (1958), 606/1. 1954 *Friends Intelligencer* 18 Dec. p. 700/2 In Bucks County . . . is going up an attractive new housing development. . . . It will be occupied by both white and Negro families. . . . Concord Park is planned for open occupancy. It thus provides a test of the belief that the best community is one open to all qualified persons. 1958 N.Y. *Times* 30 Nov. p. 60/2–3 These steps of procedure are contemplated: . . . Stimulating the sale and rental of dwellings on an open occupancy basis . . . 1959 *ibid.* 8 Feb. p. 7/4 But some . . . find in the local easing of the situation . . . hope that New York will eventually become an 'open occupancy' city.

SCRUB, *v.t.* See quots.—1944 Ted Malone from European Theater over NBC. 30 Oct. 1956 W. A. Heflin *U. S. Air Force Dict.* p. 458/2. 1958 N.Y. *Times Mag.* 26 Jan. p. 60/3 Recently, the lowering of the ball ceased to be a reliable indication that a test had been 'scrubbed' or canceled, anyway . . . *Newsweek* 10 Feb. p. 29/1 The same day Vanguard sprung a leak in its second stage nitric-acid fueler just fourteen seconds before firing time. The shoot was scrubbed, in the parlance of missilemen. —*n.*—1958 N.Y. *Times Mag.* 16 March p. 10/1–2 The backstage crew is made up of engineers and technicians who work themselves to a frazzle during the long countdown . . . which may end not in a firing but in a series of 'holds' or a 'scrub'—cancellation.

SQUADROL, *n.* [*squad* + ?*patrol*]—1954 Chicago *Trib.* 24 June Sec. IV p. 12 (pict. cap.) Police squadrol on its side at Wabash and Grand avs. as a CTA wrecker truck prepared to right it yesterday following collision of the squadrol and taxicab. *Ibid.* 2 Sept. Sec. I p. 12/7 In less than 3 minutes there were three squad cars and one squadrol at the scene. 1957 Milwaukee *Sentinel* 24 Oct. p. I 4/5 The manufacturer of 47 police squadrols and station wagons is falling behind on a promise to restore their brakes to satisfactory operating condition . . .

TOLL-, TOLL PLAZA. A widened area on a toll highway where booths for paying toll are located.—1948 Balto. *Sun* 20 Nov. p. 14/2–7 (under diagram) All tolls for travel across the Chesapeake Bay Bridge will be paid at booths on the 1000-foot toll plaza on the Western Shore approach to the bridge. 1957 N.Y. *Times* 18 Aug. p. 68/4 There will be two traffic tubes, each with two lawns [*sic*], and only one toll plaza . . . *Sat. Eve. Post* 16 Nov. p. 90/2 Only one painter has died as the result of an accident in the twenty years since the bridge opened, and he was injured in an eight-foot fall in the Toll Plaza, not on the bridge.

TURBO-, TURBOFAN, *n.* [*turbofan* in *WNID* 1934; cf. *U. S. Air Force Dict.* 1956, s.v.] See quots. (Also attrib.)—1959 Seattle *Times* 17 May p. 40 A turbofan engine has large fan blades near the air inlet which not only supply air to the basic engine but send one and a half times that air volume around the engine. A turbojet engine moves a relatively small mass of air at high velocity, a turbofan a larger mass at a slower velocity. N.Y. *Times* 18 Oct. p. 1/5 The new engine, called a turbo-fan, is said to be quieter and more powerful than the turbojet. The engine will go into use early next year.

TURF, *n.* [Cf. *OED*, s.v. *turf*, sb.[1] d: 'A sod cut from the turf of an estate, etc., as a token or symbol of possession . . . *Obs.*' {1585}; Eric Partridge, *A Dict. of the Underworld*, s.v., who cites the meaning 'the road' from 1899; *Am. Thes. Slang* (1942), ¶ 486.2: 'Trampdom. . . . the road to roam, turf, vagabondia.'] An area in a city controlled by a teen-age gang. —1956 N.Y. *Times* 19 Aug. p. E 2/6 The agreement they reached, couched in youth gang terms, pledged a truce (no 'rumbles') until September 4 and, to avoid further provocation, no invasions of the 'turf' of the opposing side by more than three persons at a time. 1958 *Sat. Rev.* 18 Oct. p. 60/2–3 He was afraid to move more than three or four blocks from home, even to go to the moving pictures because he would have to pass through the 'turf' of another gang. 1959 N.Y. *Times Mag.* 8 Feb. p. 68/2 It is 9:30 in the morning, on an average day, when Pete leaves the second-story headquarters of Unit VIII on Meyer Square and heads south on Amsterdam Avenue toward the Sharks' 'turf.' It is a four-block-long area the Sharks have cut out as their own, an area which, by gangwar tradition, a member of any other gang trespasses if he is not particularly anxious to come home intact. *Ibid.* 16 Aug. p. 13/2 The more 'rep' a gang has, the more 'good things' come to it, such as girls or the ability to control public places or a 'turf' (a series of city blocks).

UNDER-ACHIEVER, *n.* See quots.—1950 N.Y. *Times* 29 Oct. p. E 9/1–2 One is the 'under-achiever': 'He is the able lad who drifts through college, passes his courses and enjoys the life around him, but never acquires any of the training, skills, discipline, insights or interests that education should give.' 1951 *What the Colleges Are Doing* (Ginn and Co.) 5 Jan. p. 5 (N.Y. *Times* passage, above, quoted). Warren (Ohio) *Tribune Chronicle* 8 Sept. p. 14/3 An over-achiever makes better grades than one would expect from his intelligence tests and entrance exams. An under-achiever is just the opposite. 1958 *Johns Hopkins Mag.* Oct. p. 30/3 Yet it is quite simple to overlook these intelligent under-achievers. 1959 N.Y. *Times Mag.* 4 Jan. p. 38/5 Even more significant to the average family, however, is the amount of attention being given to smoking out and stimulating the efforts of the under-achievers. N.Y. *Times* 13 Sept. p. E 11/1 Amherst has begun a scheme which would eliminate the drifters, academically dubbed 'under-achievers.' These are able students who, though their grades may be within the 70 to 80 range, are not running their intellectual motors on all cylinders.

AMONG THE NEW WORDS

I. WILLIS RUSSELL
University of Alabama

ACKNOWLEDGMENTS: For citations, Walter S. Avis (2), R. F. Bauerle (2), Atcheson L. Hench (6), Mamie J. Meredith (7), Porter G. Perrin (2), Thomas Pyles (1), Anne B. Russell (3), Peter Tamony (2), and Robert N. Whitehurst (1). E. Scott Barr aided with the definition of *sophisticated*.

ABLATE, *v.t.* [Cf. *OED Sup.*, s.v.: '*Obs.* in general sense; in recent scientific use as back-formation from *ablation*, 3, 4.' {1902}] See *ablation*.—1952 *Astrophysical Jour.* 116:203 In the meteor work . . . only the parameter (where Γ is the retardation coefficient and ζ the energy to ablate unit mass of meteor material) . . . could be determined from the observations. 1959 Woodford A. Heflin, ed. *Aerospace Glossary* (Maxwell Air Force Base, Ala.: Research Studies Institute, Air University) p. 1/1.

ABLATING, *vb. n.*—1959 *Sat. Rev.* 5 Sept. p. 53/1 The calculations here at Astronautics show that a solid sphere of frozen water, entering the atmosphere at that speed, can survive and slow down to terminal velocities without completely ablating. Heflin, ed. *Aerospace Glossary* p. 1/1.

ABLATION, *n.* [Cf. *OED*, s.v., 4 *Geol.*: 'The wearing away or superficial waste of a glacier by surface melting, or of a rock by the action of water.' {1860}] See last quot. (Also attrib.)—1951 *Astrophysical Jour.* 114:460 Particularly, more direct methods of determining actual surface losses by ablation should be developed. 1952 *ibid.* 116:204 . . . the paper compares fusion and vaporization as the ablation source. 1958 *Space Talk* (Republic Aviation Corp.) p. 4 *Ablation*. Melting of nose cone materials during reentry of space ships or vehicles into the earth's atmosphere at hypersonic speeds. 1959 *Sat. Rev.* 5 Sept. p. 54/2 During this period of its travel, when the pressure would be inadequate to produce melting, the cometoid would undergo a preliminary shaping by ablation processes. Heflin, ed. *Aerospace Glossary* p. 1/1 *ablation*, *n. Specific*. The melting or vaporizing of an outer surface so as to keep an inner part cool.

ABLATIVE, *adj.* {*c* 1440} Descriptive of material with a high heat-vaporization point.—1959 N.Y. *Times* 30 Aug. p. 42/4 Special ablative material on the capsule's nose would burn away from the heat of friction as the gradually thickening atmosphere slowed the vehicle.

AGRIBUSINESS, *n.* [*agriculture* + *business*] See quots.—1955 *Harvard Bus. School Bull.* Autumn p. 41 Dr. John H. Davis, Director of the Program in Agriculture and Business . . . with the assistance of Dr. Ray Goldberg '50, is in the midst of preparing some new publications analyzing 'Agribusiness'—a term coined to define the many diverse enterprises which produce, process, and distribute farm products or which provide supporting services. 1956 N.Y. *Times* 8 Jan. p. E9 (adv.) *From Agriculture to Agribusiness* by John H. Davis . . . 1958 *Am. Sp.* 33 (May, Part 1), 157 The word *agribusiness* refers to fields related to agriculture but not to farming operations *per se*. Examples of agribusiness are the manufacture and sale of farm machinery, farm and crop research and experimentation, and the work of agricultural colleges. Gainesville (Fla.) *Sun* 13 July p. 5 The word agribusiness was first used publicly by John H. Davis in a paper presented at the Boston Conference on Distribution, Boston, in October 1955. 1959 *Virginia Record* April p. 8/1 Agribusiness has produced the same sort of pressures on farm suppliers, farmers and farm marketers.

AUDING, *n.* [L. *audio* + *-ing*; cf. *audile* and *audist* in *OED Sup.*] See quots. (Also attrib.)—1956 *CEA Critic* Sept. p. 6 Professor Donald Brown . . . has given English a new word—auding—for the ability to listen with retentive understanding. [It] distinguishes auding from just hearing . . . 1957 *ibid.* Feb. p. 7/1 The school must provide a crossover from the child's command of speech and auding patterns to reading and writing . . . 1959 *ETC.* Autumn pp. 114–15 Auding is important enough in its own right as a language process to take its place with reading, speaking, and writing in the language curriculum.

BACK-, BACKUP, *n.* [Cf. *OED*, s.v. *back*, *v.* 8: '*To back up:* to stand behind with intent to support or second, to uphold or support materially or morally . . .' {1865}] See quots. (Also attrib.)—1956 Woodford A. Heflin, ed. *U. S. Air Force Dict.* (Maxwell Air Force Base, Ala.: Air University) p. 67/2 *backup communications equipment*. Alternate communications equipment. . . . [Ed.: ' . . . "backup," as used in this context, is obsolescent in the USAF.'] 1958 *Space Talk* (Republic Aviation Corp.) p. 5 *Backup*. A substitute rocket or missile, or alternate procedure, to save time in the event of a delay or failure in launching. 1959 *Life* 14 Sept. p. 38/3 There are back-up systems, redundancies for every system in the capsule. If something fails, the pilot will have a sound alternative to fall back on. N.Y. *Times Mag.* 11 Oct. p. 19/2 (pict. cap.) Every component has a 'back-up,' or alternate.

BLUE-, BLUE COLLAR, *attrib.* [By analogy with *white-collar* (*DA* 1921).] Descriptive of an industrial or manual employee who works for hourly wages; see also quots.—1950 Tuscaloosa *News* 25 Nov. p. 1/5 (AP) The Navy estimated today that about one-half of its 175,000 'blue collar' workers will receive pay increases. . . . Most of the employes getting such raises will be mechanics. 'Blue collar' workers also include helpers, laborers, and supervisors. 1952 San Francisco *News* 28 Feb. p. 25 The Navy has asked the Wage Stabilization Board to approve a new pay system for its 14,500 supervisors of per diem (blue collar) employes. *Ibid.* 13 Aug. p. 23 The blue-collar boys are the ones who intend to seek careers as skilled workers in industry via actual job experience. 1956 Seattle *Times* 23 Jan. p. 17/1 The government has more than 700,000 'blue-collar' workers who are paid by the day like industrial employes. Balto. *Sun* 7 Sept. (Edit. B) p. 1/2 . . . the bureau found that 'white-collar' workers bore fewer children than 'blue-collar' or manual workers. 1958 *Harper's* Aug. p. 22/1 I pointed out that labor's present inability to organize successfully can be explained by the revolutionary shifts in occupation which are replacing many blue-collar jobs with white, and so are changing both the status and the loyalty of the mass of workers. 1959 *New Repub.* 20 April p. 2 The 7,000 present were mostly blue-collar 'respectable' unemployed.

CAREERISM, *n.* [Cf. *careerist* {1910} in *OED Sup.*] See def. in *Webster's New World Dict.*—1946 Eric Bentley *The Playwright as Thinker* (N.Y.: Reynal & Hitchcock) p. 58 It shows the other side of Faustian living, the striving of modern careerism with all its vast implications. 1952 N.Y. *Her.-Trib.* 16 Aug. (Late City ed.) p. 6/6 But the fragility of the bubble 'careerism' in the Communist world was well illustrated by a tale . . . 1953 *Webster's New World Dict.* (College ed.).

COMMON MARKET. See quots.—1957 *Barron's* 28 Jan. p. 1/2 Benelux has become the pattern for the proposed common market. *Time* (Canadian ed.) 18 Feb. p. 26/2 Said he: 'On the day when the [European] Common Market . . . has been created, [France] would like to promote the formation of a Eurafrican whole . . .' *Sat. Eve. Post* 29 June p. 10/3 (edit.) N.Y. *Times* 14 July p. 2E/6 Under the *common market*, all customs barriers between the participating states will eventually be scrapped, and the six will maintain a common tariff toward the outside world. 1958 *ibid.* 23 Nov. p. 2E/1 The *common market* is an agreement among six O.E.E.C. members—France, West Germany, Italy, Belgium, the Netherlands and Luxembourg—that on Jan. 1 they will begin gradually reducing tariffs toward each other while maintaining a common tariff against goods from outside. 1959 *Harper's* July p. 39/2 In India, Puerto Rico, the United Kingdom, in Europe's coal-steel community and the Common Market, in all the Communist nations, men have turned from reliance on impersonal market forces to some conscious and public planning of investment, prices, and wages. 1960 N. Y. *Times* 22 May p. 6E/1 By the end of this year six states will have altered their tariffs as a first move toward the setting up of a common tariff wall around the Common Market.

COUNTDOWN, *n.* See *Am. Sp.* 29:215. Add 3. The period immediately preceding a critical decision or turning point.—1959 Russ Ward over NBC 1 March (quoting Lyndon B. Johnson) 'The countdown has started . . .' 1960 Tuscaloosa (Ala.) *News* 2 Feb. p. 3/5 (AP) Medaris has also said he plans to write a book, tentatively titled 'Countdown to Decision.' N.Y. *Times Book Rev.* 14 Feb. p. 3/2–4 (heading) Countdown for the Minds of Men.

4. A roll call of states at a political convention.—1960 Tuscaloosa (Ala.) *News* 8 July p. 1/2 (AP) And if they can't snag the gold ring on the second go-around, they were saying they can outlast any of the other contenders even if a half dozen countdowns are needed. *Ibid.* 9 July p. 1/2 (AP) They professed to believe that Kennedy would lose support in Indiana, Maryland and Ohio on a second countdown.

EURATOM, *n.* [*European* + *atom*] See quots. (Also attrib.)—1956 *Chri. Sci. Mon.* 27 Feb. p. 4/6 Even while Euratom, the projected Western European atomic research and power pool, seemed to be making new headway . . . a cold wind came blowing here . . . N.Y. *Times* 21 Oct. p. 7/2 The foreign ministers of six nations discussed here today the vital question of the control of uranium and other fissionable materials in the proposed West European nuclear pool called Euratom. *Ibid.* 4 Nov. p. 3/4 Herr Strauss clarified the status of negotiations on the Euratom treaty . . . 1957 N.Y. *Her.-Trib.* (European ed.) 10 Feb. p. 1 (AP) The United States 'anticipates active association' in the proposed European Atomic Agency (Euratom), the State Department said today *Time* (Canadian ed.) 20 May p. 24/3 . . . the three experts said that the Euratom countries must do likewise. 1959 N.Y. *Times* 3 May p. W7/4 At the same time the six nations signed another treaty creating Euratom, calling for a pooling of efforts in the joint development of nuclear energy.

EURO-, EUROMARKET, EUROMART, *n.* [*European* + *market*, *mart*] See quots.—1957 B'ham *News* 14 Feb. p. 46/1 The plan, nicknamed 'Euromart,' has yet to be ratified by these six nations . . . N.Y. *Times* 14 July p. 4E/6–7 (heading) Vote on Euromarket and Euratom May Help to Open a New Era. 1958 Lincoln (Nebr.) *Evening Jour.* 15 Feb. p. 6/1 All of the political advantages of the Common Market will evaporate if Euromarket—as the Common Market is called—leads the nations of Western Europe away from the U.S.A. . . . 1959 N.Y. *Times* 15 Feb. p. 4E/1 The European Economic Community—the common market, or Euro-market—[h] as led to controversy . . .

EXOTIC FUEL. [Cf. *WNID Add. Sect.* 1959, s.v. *exotic*, *adj.*: 'Strikingly out of the ordinary; strange; rarely met with.'] See quots.—1957 Nov. 1 *U. S. Air Force Dict. Addenda* (Maxwell Air Force Base, Ala.: Air University) p. 2/12. Fuels that combine hydrogen with boron or lithium are considered to be exotic fuels. 1959 N. Y. *Times* 30 Aug. p. 42/4 They continued: 'No newer exatic [sic] fuels are required . . .' N.Y. *Times Mag.* 1 Nov. p. 59/2 *Exotic Fuel* (A fuel containing chemicals of very high rating.)

FOSDIC, *n.* [See quots.] See quots.—1954 N.Y. *Times* 7 March p. E9/6 . . . FOSDIC, a high-speed electric device that can read census data sheets and tell what to do with them . . . is a contraction for 'Film Optical Sensing Device for Input to Computers.' 1959 *National Geog.* Nov. p. 712/1 Information processing starts with Fosdic (film optical sensing device for input to computers). Fosdic scans microfilmed copies of enumerator's work sheets and converts the marks on each tiny frame into magnetic-tape pulses . . .

FURLOUGH, *v.t.* [Cf. *DA*, s.v.: 'To give (a soldier) leave of absence, also transf.' (1781). Cf. esp. the 1931 quot.: 'He got furloughed at the Sabraton shops last summer.'] See quot. under the adj.—1959 Tuscaloosa (Ala.) *News* 20 July p. 1/4–5 (AP) Approximately 40,000 workers in related industries, chiefly coal and transportation, have been furloughed.—*adj.*—1959 Tuscaloosa (Ala.) *News* 5 Aug. p. 1/4 (AP) An unofficial tally of layoffs in industries depending on steel indicates that nearly 100,000 workers are idle. They are furloughed men who . . . became involved in the dispute because their companies depend on steel to operate at full scale.

INNER SPACE. [By analogy with *outer space.*] The sea.—1958 Edward P. Morgan over ABC 6 Oct. . . . a breakthrough in inner space. 1959 N.Y. *Times Mag.* 14 June p. 48/5 The sea is the limitless realm of inner space.

JUMBOIZE, *v.t.* [*jumbo* 'Anything large of its kind' (*DA* 1883) + *-ize*] See first quot. s.v. *jumboizing*.—1956 N.Y. *Times* 23 Dec. p. S11/7 (heading) Concern to Build Ten and 'Jumboize' Nine. 1957 Balto. *Sun* 4 April (Edit. B) p. 16/4–6 We're 'jumboizing' present tankers by cutting 'em apart and welding the bow and stern to a larger mid-section.

JUMBOIZED, *adj.*—1957 Balto. *Sun* 4 April (Edit. B) p. 16/4–6 Today first completed 'jumboized' oil tanker . . . 1959 *Richfield Oil Corp. 1958 Annual Report* p. 14 (pict. cap.) Trial run of the 'jumboized' tankship S. S. David E. Day.

JUMBOIZER, *n.*—1957 *New Yorker* 14 Sept. p. 33/3 (E. B. White) In language controls, the trend is toward bastardization, if you ask us, and we wish the National Association of Manufacturers would call in all the jumboizers and miniaturizationists and bang their heads together.

JUMBOIZING, *vb. n.* See quots.—1956 N.Y. *Times* 23 Dec. p. S11/7 'Jumboizing' consists of building an entire new center section for a tanker. The existing vessel is then cut off at the bow and stern which are later joined to the new section. 1957 *New Yorker* 9 Feb. p. 23/1 In the annual report of the Irving Trust Company, there's a paragraph, relating to ship loans, that tells how you can increase the capacity of an oil tanker by fitting an old vessel with a brand-new midsection. The bank calls this process 'jumboizing.' Balto. *Sun* 19 Feb. (Edit. B) p. 10/5 The technique of installing midbodies is known as 'jumboizing.' *New Yorker* 14 Sept. p. 33 Some months ago, we took exception to the word 'jumboizing' . . . 1959 *Richfield Oil Corp. 1958 Annual Report* p. 14 'Jumboizing' of the S. S. David E. Day was completed in 1958.—*adj.*—1956 N.Y. *Times* 23 Dec. p. S11/7 Three of the 'jumboizing' jobs will be done at the Bethlehem yard . . .

KNOWLEDGEABLE, *adj.* See *Am. Sp.* 34:71–72. Additional illus.—1949 B'ham *News-Age-Her.* 20 Feb. p. E3/3 'People I have consulted—knowledgeable people—say there is no such thing . . .' *Time* 25 April p. 102/3 The hour is not only Britain's finest, but Churchill's, calling upon him to exert to the full every talent and scrap of wisdom of his 65 knowledgeable years. *Ibid.* 5 Sept. p. 44/2 . . . knowledgeable Marty Marion is the steady man . . . 1956 N.Y. *Times Mag.* 22 Jan. p. 64/2 Mozart's originality and powers of invention were startling even to knowledgeable men. *Life* 6 Feb. p. 50/1 Eva Marie Saint's knowledgeable office appearance . . . rests not on a stint at secretarial school but on her acting ability . . . B'ham *News* 26 March p. 25/5 (Stewart Alsop) . . . at least one knowledgeable Harriman man thinks that Symington . . . presents the real danger to the Harriman candidacy. N.Y. *Times Book Rev.* 21 Oct. p. 1/1 (James R. Newman) He is knowledgeable and honest. *Am. Sp.* 31:299 . . . dissent was expressed by two other knowledgeable people with whom I discussed the matter. 1957 N.Y. *Times Book Rev.* 1 Dec. p. 54/2 A knowledgeable French lady once wrote to a neophyte chef, 'Cooking is a multi-faceted art.' 1959 *CEA Critic* March p. 11/3 I have spoken with some knowledgable [sic] students . . . N.Y. *Times Book Rev.* 2 Aug. p. 7/3 . . . this is a vigorous and knowledgeable interpretation. *Ibid.* 13 Sept. p. 24/4 'The Living Theatre' instead is a collection of workmanlike and knowledgeable essays . . . N.Y. *Times* 25 Oct. p. X1/3 It is a novel . . . that is infused with 'suspense, irony, thoroughly credible characterizations of Russians and knowledgeable sketches of Russian backgrounds.' 1960 *Time* 18 Jan. p. 18/3 But not until all the pieces were reassembled, and all the fragments of bodies examined, were inspectors likely to make a knowledgeable guess about one of the strangest crashes in U. S. aviation history. N.Y. *Times* 28 Feb. p. 19XX/1 He will be in the hands of a guide or tour leader (if one is fortunate, a knowledgeable and experienced one) . . .

SOPHISTICATED, *adj.* {1603} [Cf. *WNID*, 2: 'Deprived of native or original simplicity; made artificial, or, more narrowly, highly complicated, refined, subtilized, etc. . .'] *Specif.* Descriptive of very complicated and versatile mechanisms.—1956 N.Y. *Times* 1 April p. 19/1 Navy scientists are virtually exploring multidimensional space in a time machine in the search for what they call 'sophisticated' high-yield weapons. 1958 N.Y. *Times* 23 March p. 14F/2 (adv.). *Ibid.* 12 Oct. p. E1/2 It is the most sophisticated missile ever fired. March *Interim Glossary of Aero-Space Terms* (Maxwell Air Force Base, Ala.: Air University) p. 28/2. 1959 *Time* 28 Sept. p. 68/3 The Vanguard was a typical product of U.S. space technology: a small, sophisticated bird strained to the utmost to achieve its purpose. N.Y. *Times Mag.* 1 Nov. p. 59/2 SOPHISTICATED MISSILE (a large, complicated missile.) 1960 N.Y. *Times* 3 Jan. p. E9/5 Preliminary findings by the 92.3-pound satellite, the most sophisticated, heavily instrumented space vehicle yet launched by the United States, show that future space travelers will have to contend with sudden sporadic bursts of radiation . . .

SOPHISTICATION, *n.* {*c* 1400} See *sophisticated.*—1959 *Time* 12 Oct. p. 67/3 In the past the usual comment was that Russian space vehicles are big and brawny because of more powerful launching rockets, but that U. S. space vehicles, small and elegant, made up for the Russians' gross size by their sophistication. *Ibid.* 19 Oct. p. 27/3. 1960 *Barron's* 11 Jan. p. 20/2 Capacity of the address reader I.M.R. has been developing for the Department gradually has been raised until it now can recognize 13 capital letters and 17 in lower case. This degree of sophistication enables it to handle the 20 post office names selected for the research project.

AMONG THE NEW WORDS

I. WILLIS RUSSELL

University of Alabama

ACKNOWLEDGMENTS: For citations, Walter S. Avis (2), T. L. Crowell (1), Sarah Kendall Dunn (1), O. B. Emerson (1), Atcheson L. Hench (2), Mamie J. Meredith (8), Porter G. Perrin (8), and Peter Tamony (1). Joseph S. Bolt supplied the definition of *droodle*.

ACTIVE, *adj.* [Cf. *OED*, s.v., 2: 'Opposed to *passive:* Originating or communicating action, exerting action upon others; acting of its own accord, spontaneous. . . .'{*c* 1400}] Of a satellite, provided with instrumentation.—1960 N.Y. *Times* 9 Oct. p. E9/6–7 Courier is an 'active satellite.' It carries some 300 pounds of equipment to receive messages from the earth and to retransmit them either immediately or on signal from the ground after some time. 1961 Seattle *Times Mag.* 19 Feb. p. 17 Active satellites can pick up faint radio signals. . . .

BLOW—, BLOWBY, *n.* See quots. (Also attrib.)—1940 *Sat. Eve. Post* 17 Aug. p. 62/1–2 (adv.) That's why these rings will stop oil waste and prevent blow-by in your car. . . 1959 N.Y. *Times* 6 Dec. p. 67/5 The gasoline vapors, called 'blowby' by automotive engineers, are hydrocarbons forced between the cylinder wall and the piston during the compression stroke. 1960 Seattle *Times* 13 March p. 38 The device proposed by the auto industry deals with 'blowby' losses—vapors blown past the piston rings into the crankcase. 1961 N.Y. *Times* 2 April p. 4A/4 Blowby is unburned gasoline forced by leaky pistons into the car's crankcase. There it accumulates, forming a rich, potent mixture representing between 10 and 40 per cent of all fumes emitted by an automobile.

CASTROISM, *n.* [Fidel *Castro* + *-ism*] Fidelismo (which see).—1960 *U.S. News and World Rep.* 14 Nov. p. 60/3 Three members of the International Staff of 'U.S. News and World Report' have just completed an on-the-spot survey of Castroism in the Caribbean. 1961 Tuscaloosa *News* 24 Jan. p. 14/1 (AP) While the rest of the continent watches, President Romulo Betancourt and his supporters are casting aside their fear of Castroism and its potential for mischief in alliance with communism. *Ibid.* 20 Feb. p. 3/3 (AP) But still the germ of Castroism became deeply imbedded. It infected many in influential places—men and women able to command followings of dissatisfied workers, restless students, resentful intellectuals, all shades of unreasoning anti-Yankeeism. William Benton, 'The Voice of Latin America' p. 31/1–2 (in *1961 Brit. Book of the Year*, Chicago: Encyclopaedia Britannica, Inc.) [Quot. s.v. *Fidelismo.*]

DISKERY, *n.* [*disk* + *-ery*] A company that manufactures records. (Also attrib.)—1951 Birmingham *News* 22 April p. B6/1 Several months back his [Frankie Laine's] musical mentor Mitch Miller, switched to that diskery [Columbia] . . . 1959 Tuscaloosa *News* 29 Nov. p. 37/4 Diskery execs are now keeping a close watch on their LP product looking for signs that will indicate whether they've got a side that can be culled from the package for an additional run in the singles market.

DROODLE, *n.* A witty drawing, more contrived than a doodle, designed to mystify the viewer, who usually comprehends what it represents only after it is explained.—1953 *This Week* 27 Sept. p. 38/2 . . . Roger Price . . . comes up with another set of drawings which you can use to infuriate your friends. The trick is simple: just sketch a Droodle on a scrap of paper and make people guess what it means. 1954 Omaha *World-Herald* 25 April p. 4-A (pict.) Mr. Price says he didn't invent Droodles. He simply formalized and named them. They can be traced back to game called 'What Is It?' that Mr. Price played in boyhood. . . .

Simon & Schuster has published 'Droodles,' a book by Mr. Price . . . 1956 University of Washington *Daily* 9 May p. 4 (adv.) Say, d'ja see these lucky droodles? 1960 E. H. Gombrich *Art and Illusion* (N.Y.: Pantheon Books, Inc.) p. 215 Three lines with a triangle on top 'represent' a Capuchin preacher asleep in his pulpit; the line with semicircle and triangle, the hat of a mason and his trowel on the other side of the wall. This type of picture puzzle has lately gained some popularity under the name of 'droodle,' but the droodle has not become an art form. DROODLING, *vb.n.*—1955 *Sat. Rev.* 19 March p. 7/1 Roger Price has stopped 'droodling' long enough to invent a No-Cal Embalming Fluid.

FIDELISMO, FIDELISM, *n.* [Span. *Fidelismo*] See quots.—1959 Washington *Post* 24 Nov. p. A14/1 Fidelismo has become revolution for revolution's sake. 1960 *Bus. Week* 3 Dec. p. 87 Add a new word to your vocabulary, another 'ism.' This one is 'Fidelism,' or 'Fidelismo,' as the Latin Americans call it. . . . Fidelism is the Castro-style revolution that's followed by a left-wing, Communist-influenced, perhaps Communist-controlled, government. . . . It promises economic and social reform. . . . It means totalitarianism . . . 1961 N.Y. *Times* 22 Jan. p. 8E/4 At the other extreme, and reputedly best organized within the Cuban underground, are the ex-Castro men led in exile by a number of former Castro ministers and army leaders. They want 'Fidelismo without Fidel,' the democratic social revolution for which they say they were fooled into fighting Batista. William Benton, 'The Voice of Latin America' p. 31/1–2 (in *1961 Brit. Book of the Year*) 'Fidelismo' has spread in varying degrees of meaning, intensity and power throughout this . . . region. . . . As a movement, it still has a long distance to go before it attains Castro's stated goal of 'turning the Andes into the Sierra Maestra. . . . But even in its present confused and complex character —a mixture of legitimate aspirations for land and other reforms plus extreme left-wing opportunism and starry-eyed youthful idealism—Castroism is developing an inner life that is so like the Communists' in method, aim and effects as to warrant the fear that they may fuse into a single force.

FIDELISTA, *n.* [fr. Span.] A follower of Fidel Castro; an adherent to his program.—1960 *Bus. Week* 3 Dec. p. 87 . . . the Fidelistas and Communists opposed to Betancourt are trying to provoke a right-wing coup. 1961 Tuscaloosa *News* 5 Jan. p. 1/5 The Fidelistas have learned from the Communists the technique of accusing an enemy of what one plans oneself. William Benton, 'The Voice of Latin America' p. 39/2 (in *1961 Brit. Book of the Year*) In the autumn of 1960 the governments of Guatemala and Nicaragua were shaken by rebel movements which they said were directly inspired by Castro and his 'Fidelistas' . . . .

MONOPHONIC, *adj.* [Cf. *OED*, s.v., *a. Mus.*: 'Homophonic 1,2.' {1885}] Having only one sound track.—1958 *Newsweek* 13 Oct. p. 102/2 Bending an ear to a single-track (monophonic, to hi-fi devotees) record is 'like listening to a concert through a crack in the door,' . . . 1959 *WNID, Add. Sect.* p. cxix/2. N.Y. *Times* 25 Jan. p. X15/2 The record companies are busily engaged in the process of transferring to stereo disks the major items of their monophonic catalogue. *Ibid.* 1 March p. 18/6 The monophonic version was one of Victor's Christmas offerings of 1957; the stereophonic version came out last Christmas. *Ibid.* 4 Oct. p. 20X/1 These reels are played on standard stereophonic tape decks (which will also play back old monophonic tapes); and many companies are supplying kits that will convert monophonic tape decks into stereophonic ones.—*adv.*—1959 N.Y. *Times* 8 Feb. p. 14X/3 . . . the disks are available stereophonically and monophonically.

MOON GARDEN. See quots.—1959 Tuscaloosa *News* 9 Dec. p. 17/6 (AP) Space scientists are using a 'moon garden' in their studies of food problems facing future airmen in orbit. The garden in which ordinary vegetables are grown under reduced air pressure is one of the projects under the direction of Dr. Norman Lee Barr. 1960 *This Week* 26 June p. 8/3 In the 'Moon Garden' developed by the Republic Aviation Corporation, Scientists have been successful in inducing 'nervous breakdown' . . . in plants being tested as possible space foods.

MOONQUAKE, *n.* [By analogy with *earthquake.*] See first quot.—1958 *Sat. Eve. Post* 16 Aug. p. 82/4 Additional information about our natural satellite's composition and structure can then be obtained by setting off artificial explosions or by observing the natural explosions that would result from the fall of moderately sized meteorites. The manner in which waves travel through the substance of the moon as a result of these 'moonquakes' will tell us much of the moon's inner structure. 1961 Elmer Peterson on 'Emphasis' (NBC), 4 Jan., discussed moonquakes and their measurement.

MOON SUIT. See quots.—1958 *Life* 6 Jan. [p. 56] (under picture) 'Moon suit' is worn by men erecting transmitter to show flexibility. Inflatable suit, developed by Navy for altitude flight, would work on moon. 1961 Seattle *Times* 22 Feb. p. 49 A 'moon suit' for spacemen is undergoing development testing. The model consists of a two-piece cylindrical aluminum tunic and torso with legs and arms attached. It is big enough for an occupant to lower a tripod stand, pull his legs out of the suit's legs, and sit on a shelf in the cylinder.

PASSIVE, *adj.* [Cf. *OED*, s.v., 2: 'Suffering action from without . . .' {1613}] See quots.—1959 Woodford A. Heflin (ed.) *Aerospace Glossary* (Maxwell Air Force Base, Ala.: Research Studies Institute, Air University) p. 74/2 *passive satellite.* A satellite without instrumentation. 1960 N.Y. *Times* 9 Oct. p. E9/6 Echo, a 'passive' satellite, reflects or bounces radio signals sent from one station back to another point on the earth. 1961 Seattle *Times Mag.* 19 Feb. p. 17 . . . it appears highly desirable that the Air Force undertake a fool-proof passive-satellite system.

PILLOW TANK. [See quots.] See quots.—1951 *Sci. News Letter* 10 Feb. p. 93/1 A new synthetic rubber-nylon 'pillow' tank for gasoline that lies flat on the ground and provides 10,000 gallons of storage in ten minutes will soon be servicing U.S. fighting tanks and trucks at the front. 1959 Washington *Post and Times Herald* 5 Aug. p. B7/3–5 (under picture) With a pillow like this, you don't need a bed. It's a rubber-coated nylon container, manufactured by the Aviation Products Division of Goodyear Tire and Rubber Co. The pillow tanks can be used to transport virtually all types of liquids on trucks, railroad cars and barges. When not in use, the collapsible containers can be rolled up and packed in a box.

PRE-ECHO, *n.* An echo in a record caused by having the grooves too close together.—1956 N.Y. *Times* 22 Jan. p. 16X/4 BEETHOVEN: Piano Concertos Nos. 2 and 4; Rudolf Serkin and Philadelphia Orchestra conducted by Ormandy (Columbia). Hearty, large-scale performances, but some annoying pre-echo is present. 1957 *ibid.* 24 Feb. p. X15/1 When LP first came out the maximum was about twenty minutes to a side. Engineers say that a disk should not contain much more music than that; that the grooves will have to run too closely together with additional minutes; that there will be pre-echo, damage and results too ghastly to contemplate.

RETRO-, RETRO, RETROROCKET, *n.* [L. *retro-* 'backward'] See quots.—1958 N.Y. *Times Mag.* 17 Aug. p. 12/4 . . . the moon shot, right up to the tricky retro-rocket supposed to brake the instrument package sideways into weak lunar gravitation, will take care of itself. Seattle *Times* 12 Oct. p. 2 The retro rockets are intended to slow down the space ship so it can enter the gravitational field of the moon. *Life* 27 Oct. p. 126/2–128/2 It had two parts: a so-called 'retrorocket' to act as a kind of brake for Pioneer and, around it, a package of instruments in a Fiberglas and plastic shell. 1959 N.Y. *Times* 12 April p. E9/8 But in order to make a 'soft' landing, a manned satellite vehicle would have to include, as part of its payload, decelerating rockets to bring it out of orbit and down to earth. Such 'retro-rockets' are still in a rather preliminary stage of development . . . *Ibid.* 13 Sept. p. E11/5 Retrorockets slow capsule for return.

SCUBA, *n.* [See third quot.] See third quot. (Also attrib.)—1957 *Time* 25 Feb. p. 55/1 (Canadian ed.) Most types of scuba are of the open-circuit design which supply air on demand, and discharge exhaled air into the water. . . . *Mademoiselle* April p. 100/3 Snorkels and scubas will be an essential part of your wardrobe if you take an active part in Pan America's Undersea Safari to the Virgin Islands. N.Y. *Times* 23 Aug. p. 16 The word scuba was coined and it meant self-contained underwater breathing apparatus. 1958 *Am. Sp.* 33:238. 1959 Seattle *Times Pictorial* 11 Oct. p. 45 Sport diving—underwater exploring for fun as opposed to commercial diving—usually is classed in two ways. There is skin diving and another form called scuba diving.

SUB-, SUBSATELLITE, *n.* See quots.—1956 *Time* 24 Dec. p. 53/1 (Canadian ed.) Developed by William J. O'Sullivan, Jr. . . . the inflated sub-satellite is a balloon of Mylar plastic .0025 in. thick covered with an aluminum film .0006 in. thick. 1958 N.Y. *Times* 30 March p. 35/3 A 12-foot spherical balloon has been built to be floated in space by a future Explorer satellite of the Army. The aluminum-clad balloon—or subsatellite as it is officially described—would be much larger than scientific satellites now planned, and thus far more visible in space. *Ibid.* 13 April p. E9 Officially termed a 'subsatellite,' the aluminum-clad balloon would be much larger than the scientific satellites now planned. . . *Sat. Eve. Post* 16 Aug. p. 82/4 A harmless way of obtaining additional information is to circle the moon with a small subsatellite, a moon's moon. 1959 Heflin (ed.) *Aerospace Glossary* p. 100/2 *subsatellite, n.* An object designed to be carried into orbit inside an artificial earth satellite but later ejected to serve a particular purpose.

VIBRATESE LANGUAGE. [See quots.] See quots.—1959 Chicago *Daily News* 30 Dec. p. 5/6–8 A psychologist said Wednesday a new form of silent communication—through the skin—has been accomplished. . . . A subject . . . has learned to receive coded information through skin vibrations at the rate of 38 five-letter words a minute. . . . The 'vibratese language' was described to the American Association for the Advancement of Science by Dr. Frank A. Geldard, professor and chairman of the department of psychology, University of Virginia, Charlottesville. 1960 *Sat. Rev.* 2 July p. 48/3 (F. A. Geldard) A simple alphabetic code was devised and applied so successfully that a subject who had invested a total of thirty hours in learning the alphabet of 'vibratese' language could, after a further training period of only thirty-five hours, receive sentences with ninety per cent accuracy when these were transmitted at the rate of thirty-eight five-letter words per minute.

VCOUMENTARY, *n.* [*vocal* + *documentary*] See quots.—1959 Peter Tamony 'Bessie: vocumentary' *Jazz* (Fall) pp. 281–85; cited *Am. Sp.* 36:67. 1960 *Caravan* July p. 25 (Peter Tamony) The term *Vocumentary* is a coinage of the writer. 1961 *Am. Sp.* 36:67 Mr. Tamony . . . has coined the word *vocumentary* for the documented analysis of words and expressions in song lyrics. *Brit. Book of the Year* p. 753/1 A study of a song for its verbal information.

AMONG THE NEW WORDS

I. WILLIS RUSSELL

University of Alabama

ACKNOWLEDGMENTS. For citations, Walter S. Avis (1), Richard F. Bauerle (2), Thomas L. Crowell (1), Mary Fischer (2), Joseph S. Hall (1), Atcheson L. Hench (4), Joseph E. Lane (2), Raven I. McDavid, Jr. (1), Mamie J. Meredith (9), Stephen L. Mooney (1), Porter G. Perrin (2), Frances B. Rucks (1), Anne B. Russell (2), and Peter Tamony (1).

D.I., DISCOMFORT INDEX. See quots.—1959 Los Angeles *Times* 8 March I, p. 8/1 (AP) The Weather Bureau said tonight it will try its hand this summer at computing and announcing, on a regular basis, the discomfort index. San Francisco *Chronicle* 9 March p. 1 (AP) And what's the discomfort index? It is a term coined by a bureau scientist, Earl Thom, for a mathematical indication of the human discomfort caused by the combined effect of temperature and humidity. Tuscaloosa *News* 24 March p. 4/5 (NEA) Something new may be added to U.S. Weather Bureau reports and forecasts on an experimental basis in some localities this summer. It will be a 'Discomfort Index,' or 'D.I.' *Newsweek* 2 June p. 65/1 Over much of the U.S. last week, the Weather Bureau's new 'discomfort index' (compounded of temperature and moisture readings) hovered for hours at a sticky 80 . . . Tuscaloosa *News* 10 July p. 4/4 The howls set up over the Weather Bureau's use of the phrase 'discomfort index,' and its abandonment of the term, tell a good deal about the kind of life we lead in the mid-20th century.

FREEZE-DRIED, *adj.* See second quot.—1952 N.Y. *Times* 6 July p. E9/6 The Naval Medical School at Bethesda, Md., is now experimenting with freeze-dried bone. 1961 *Fortune* June p. 45/1–2 (adv.) New Armour freeze-dried foods keep their fresh meat flavor and texture right on your kitchen shelf. . . . The process both freezes and dries food. By extracting moisture while food is frozen, the moisture is removed as vapor without going through the liquid state. So the food keeps its normal shape and size.

FREEZE-DRYING, *n.* See quots. (Also attrib.)—1949 *Fortune* Sept. p. 127 In the laboratory marvelous products were achieved by freeze-drying. . . . In this process meat, fish, and vegetables (or biologicals) are first frozen rapidly, and then placed on heated shelves in a vacuum cabinet. . . . The transformation is analogous to the way Dry-Ice turns directly from a solid to a vapor. 1950 *McCall's* Aug. p. 16/2 New freeze-drying equipment makes possible the production of ACTH . . . 1952 N.Y. *Times* 6 July p. E9/6 Blood plasma, proteins, enzymes, vitamins, glands have been preserved for months, even years, by a process known as 'freeze-drying.' *Ibid.* 29 Oct. p. E9/7 In freeze-drying, a material is dried in vacuum by reducing its water content as ice instead of evaporating it as a liquid. 1957 *Newsweek* 20 May p. 131 Food that will keep indefinitely without being refrigerated is the promise held out by a new 'freeze drying' process developed by the Raytheon Manufacturing Co. of Waltham, Mass. Meats, fish, fruits, and vegetables are dehydrated by microwave energy in a below-freezing vacuum. The food can be restored to its original fresh condition in a matter of minutes (with no loss of flavor, texture, or nutrient value) simply by immersing in water.

FUEL CELL. See quots.—1958 San Francisco *News* 17 Nov. p. 4/4 L. Eugene Root, Lockheed vice president, today disclosed development of a 'fuel cell,' which he said may revolutionize conventional propulsion theories. 1959 *Chr. Sci. Mon.* 27 Aug. p. 1c/1 To an engineer, a fuel cell is a far more elegant and efficient way of turning the energy of fuels into electricity than is a conventional steam-powered generating plant. 1960 N.Y. *Times*

6 March p. 27/1 This new heart will be a fuel cell—a revolutionary device for generating electricity directly from chemicals at an efficiency that even beats the biggest, fanciest power house in the world. 1961 *Ibid.* 15 Jan. p. 38/1 Engineers defined the fuel cell as a primary battery. Chemicals are fed from the outside source into the cell where they react and produce an electric charge and a chemical by-product.

-IN. Illustrations of additional analogical formations of *sit-in* are brought together here. The terms have been italicized.—1961 *Ibid.* 18 May p. 2/3 (AP) Bruised 'freedom riders' disbanded here today after a Negro minister urged renewed efforts to smash segregation barriers—including '*marry-ins* in the race you find your lover.' Knoxville *News-Sentinel* 31 May p. 6 In Miami, 25 Negro teen-aged boys in an impromptu *swim-in* at an undesignated beach drew a crowd of 300 shoving, shouting Memorial Day bathers and boaters yesterday. Tuscaloosa *News* 18 May p. 2/3 (AP) He called for *walk-ins* in art galleries and museums, *drive-ins* at segregated motels and roadside ice cream stands, *sit-ins* in court rooms, *study-ins* at segregated schools, and *bury-ins* to integrate cemeteries.

KNEEL-IN, *n.* [By analogy with *sit-in.*] See first quot. (Also attrib.)—1960 Tuscaloosa *News* 8 Aug. p. 2/2 (AP) Negro college students have initiated a new 'kneel-in' campaign in the South by attending services at white protestant Atlanta churches. 1961 N.Y. *Times* 29 Jan. p. 64/3 There have been stand-ins at theatres, kneel-ins at churches and wade-ins at public beaches.

METER MAID, METERMAID. See quots.—1957 Lincoln *Even. Jour.* 4 Feb. p. 3/1 Surveys conducted in cities using 'meter maids' have found that their meter revenue increased, fewer complaints about tickets were received, and the general ticket program was more efficient. Seattle *Times* 12 Sept. p. 38 Spokane—The City Council today authorized the Police Department to hire ten 'meter maids,' uniformed women who will patrol the streets and write tickets for overparking. 1958 Washington *Post and Times Herald* 1 Aug. p. A18/1 [The Deputy Chief of Police of Washington] proposes, simply, that the city employ 'meter maids' . . . 1960 *N.Y. Times Mag.* 10 Jan p. 21/1 It will soon be taught to New York City's 'meter maids,' the newly formed division of women assigned to enforce parking meter regulations.

SINGING SHOULDER. See quots.—1956 *This Week* 29 July p. 10/2 They have constructed 'singing shoulders' which give off a loud hum when touched by a car's tire and deliberately put curves in a new highway that could have been absolutely straight. 1959 *Lamp* (Standard Oil of N.J.) Jan. p. 22/3 Artificial curves, rest areas, and even 'singing shoulders' are being built. 1961 N.Y. *Times* 16 April p. 21xx/3 Also, thirty-nine miles of Parkway are equipped with what are known as 'singing shoulders.' Once a tire hits this corrugated pavement, which has been installed along curves or where the road drops off sharply, the driver immediately becomes aware that he is on anything but smooth macadam. A slight veer to the right or to the left, whichever the case may be, and he is out of trouble.

SITDOWN, *n.* [See *sit-in*, below, and *sit-down strike* (*DA* 1936)] A sit-in (which see). (Also attrib.)—1960 Washington *Post* 24 Feb. p. B3/7 White college students joined Negroes today in 'sitdown' lunch counter protests in Winston-Salem. . . N.Y. *Times* 3 April p. 7E/1–2 Negro students at Southern University in Louisiana apply at registrar's office to withdraw from the university to protest expulsion of classmates for lunch-counter sitdowns.—SIT-DOWNER, *n.*—1960 N.Y. *Times* 15 May 12E/1 (heading) Sit-Downers Score a Quiet Victory.

SIT-IN, *n.* [Cf. *WNID*, 'New Words Sect.,' 1939: = *sit-down, n., sit-down strike.*] See quot. *Brit. Book of the Year.* (Also attrib.)—1960 *Chr. Sci. Mon.* 15 Feb. p. C5/3 The North Carolina Negro college students who have been demanding lunch-counter service on the same basis as white patrons are using a technique that has been partly successful in the Middle West, a spokesman for the Southern Regional Council here points out. It is known among racial groups as the 'sit-in.' N.Y. *Times* 6 March p. 1/7 (heading) Rallies Here Back Sit-Ins in the South. *Reporter* 31 March p. 17/2 For the sit-in demonstrations at a lunch counter have turned Nashville into one of the South's most explosive racial areas. *Time* 30 May p. 69/1 How much have the sit-ins and picketing hurt business? N.Y. *Times* 26 June p. 6E/1 All this followed some brief student demonstrations, beginning with a sit-in a week ago today at a Woolworth's lunch counter. 1961 *Brit. Book of the Year* (Chicago: Encyclopaedia Britannica, Inc.) p. 753/1 *sit-in, n.* The act of one or more Negroes sitting down at a restaurant or similar place where before only whites have sat down. N.Y. *Times* 25 June p. 13/1 Salisbury in the last weeks has been the scene of African sit-in demonstrations at cafes, snack bars, hotels and hair-dressing establishments.

SITTING PARK. A park designed chiefly for sitting; see second quot.—1954 *New Yorker* 31 July p. 12/3 . . . she said . . . that what she liked best about the proposed bust and sitting park was that they would be right next to a playground full of swings and slides. 1958 Tuscaloosa *News* 5 May p. 11 (under picture) Sprucing up the grounds of the City's newly-purchased Old Junior High School has already begun to provide what Mayor George Van Tassel has called a 'sitting park.' The Park and Recreation Board yesterday installed four benches and a picnic table on the school grounds. . . .

SKORT, *n.* [*skirt* + *short*] See quots.—1957 *Life* 10 June p. 71/1 Fashion has given the English language a new word to contend with: 'skort,' a hybrid garment consisting of a mid-thigh-length pleated skirt with a matching pair of short bloomers attached underneath. 1958 N.Y. *Times* 2 March p. 91 (adv.) the 'skort' goes asleeping 1961 *Ibid.* 24 July p. 56/1 A cross between Bermuda-length shorts and a tennis skirt, the skort is a natural to storm campuses from coast to coast.

SLUMLORD, *n.* [By analogy with *landlord.*] See quots.—1954 *New Words and Words in the News* (Funk & Wagnalls Co.) Sup. No. 9 & 10 p. 3/1. 1957 N.Y. *Times Mag.* 12 May p. 36/3 The landlord had bitterly protested to the Buildings Commissioner that he was not a 'slumlord' and avowed that he was ready to put the building in condition *if* he could get a guarantee that it would stay that way; otherwise he had no alternative but to demolish it. 1960 *Barron's* 29 Aug. p. 1/3 To prevent the enrichment of slumlords, for example, the General Accounting Office, in fixing property values, would rule out all income earned in defiance of local ordinances.

SOAP, *n.* [*soap* opera; cf. *soaper* in *Am. Sp.* 34:132.] Short for *soap opera.*—1956 *Sat. Rev.* 14 July p. 24/2 Writing soaps is actually helpful to a would-be serious author, states Mr. Karp. 1958 Delaware (Ohio) *Gazette* 8 May p. 4/5 NBC-TV has picked two 30-minute soaps . . . to fill the one-hour 'Matinee Theatre' slot beginning June 30. 1960 N.Y. *Times Mag.* 4 Dec. p. 111/1 Some of the new plot developments in television would never have happened in radio soaps.

SOAPERATIC, *adj.* [*soaper* (*Am. Sp.* 34:132) + -*atic*; cf. *operatic*] Having to do with soap opera.—1954 N.Y. *Times* 16 Oct. p. 15 But he has bathed it in extravagant quantities of soaperatic lore.

SPIN-, SPINOFF, *n.* See quots.—1951 Joyce Stanley and Richard Kilcullen *The Federal Income Tax* (New York: Tax Club Press) p. 182. Sec. 112(*b*) (11), added by the 1951 Act, permits the distribution of stock in a spin-off without recognition of gain to the stockholders, subject to certain restrictions designed to prevent the use of spin-offs to distribute earnings and profits. 1954 N.Y. *Times* 1 Aug. p. 1F/3 The company then carried each of these stocks through all its split-ups, spin-offs and other corporate adventures. *Wall St. Jour.* 29 Nov. p. 12 Stockholders . . . approved the 'spin-off' of the oil and gas business of the corporation into a new company . . . 1957 Eric L. Kohler *A Dictionary for Accountants* (2d. ed.; Englewood Cliffs, N.J.: Prentice-Hall, Inc.) p. 443/2 *spinoff:* (Federal income taxes) The transfer by a corporation of a portion of its assets to a newly formed corporation in exchange for the latter's capital stock, which is thereupon distributed as a property dividend to the stockholders of the first corporation. . . . 1958 *New Internat'l Year Book* p. 564/2. 1960 *Accounting Rev.* Jan. p. 83/1 A 'spin-off' takes place when the stock or securities of a corporation controlled by a transferor corporation are distributed to the shareholders of such parent company without a surrender by the shareholders of stock or securities in that distributing corporation.

SPIN-, SPIN OFF, *v.t.*—1957 N.Y. *Times* 9 June p. F1/3 Right now, there is considerable speculation that du Pont will 'spin off' its G. M. stock—that is, give it to its own stockholders in the form of a dividend. 1959 *Wall St. Jour.* 13 May p. 32/3 They claimed the stock should have been spun-off to Lackawanna shareowners . . . *Time* 20 July p. 94/2–3 He transformed the corporation from a sprawling holding company with dozens of subsidiary corporations into an integrated corporate unit, spun off businesses, *e.g.*, shipping, that did not fit into the company's basic pattern.

STAND-IN, *n.* [By analogy with *sit-in.*] See last quot. (Also attrib.)—1961 Tuscaloosa *News* 16 March p. 25/8 (AP) The father of a Chattanooga, Tenn., Negro stand-in demonstrator says his son's life has been threatened and a crude cross burned in their yard. *Ibid.* 18 March p. 6/3 (AP) Among those taking part was a Negro Episcopal rector who was slugged by a white man Thursday while watching a stand-in that led to the arrest of nine Negroes. *Ibid.* 21 May p. 1/2 At first, he said, he just watched the lunch counter demonstrations and theater stand-ins staged in Nashville by students of the predominantly Negro college.

SUB-, SUBORBITAL, *adj.* See third quot.—1959 N.Y. *Times Mag.* 11 Oct. p. 18/1 (under pict.) . . . The moment has come, after months of training, testing and short, suborbital flights, when one of seven carefully chosen men climbs into a space capsule perched high on the nose of an Atlas rocket. 1960 *Life* 22 Aug. p. 19/2 Still to come in 1960: more weather, navigation, communication and 'spy-in-the-sky' satellites, two moon orbiters, another deep space probe, two Mercury Atlas orbital shots with man-sized capsules, and three suborbital shots—the last one with a man in it. N.Y. *Times Mag.* 11 Sept. p. 22/3 ['Sub-orbital' means several things and is expected to prove several things. In the Project Mercury program, suborbital flights mean firing astronaut capsules—first unmanned, then manned—into space but returning them at once. It will be a short, steep trajectory—500 miles up, but landing in the Atlantic only 200 miles from Cape Canaveral . . . . —*Times Mag. Ed.*] 1961 Tuscaloosa *News* 17 July p. 1/3 (AP) For all practical purposes, Grissom's suborbital flight will be identical to the rocket ride taken by Navy Cmdr. Alan B. Shepard Jr. on May 5.

WADE-IN, *n.* [By analogy with *sit-in.*] See quots. (Also attrib.)—1960 *Newsweek* 16 May p. 34/1 Into the already-roiled waters of the South, Negroes will wade this summer in a campaign to break down segregation at public beaches—a wade-in counterpart to the widespread lunch-counter sit-ins of recent weeks. Letter from Raven I. McDavid, Jr. 8 June Has the term *wade-in* (the public beach analogy of the lunch counter *sit-in*) hit the press yet? It is apparently freely used in conversation among those not currently allowed on the beaches. 1961 Tuscaloosa *News* 9 July p. 2/1 (AP) A group of Negroes and white persons staged a 'wade-in' demonstration Saturday at a public beach in Chicago's South Side. B'ham *Post-Herald* 10 July p. 7/3 (AP) Nine persons were arrested today as 80 Negroes and whites staged a four-hour long 'wade-in' for the second day at largely white Rainbow Beach.

AMONG THE NEW WORDS

I. WILLIS RUSSELL
University of Alabama

ACKNOWLEDGMENTS. For citations, Woodrow W. Boyett (2), Thomas L. Crowell (1), Atcheson L. Hench (1), James Macris (1), Mamie J. Meredith (10), Porter G. Perrin (5), Peter Tamony (4), and Robert M. Wallace (1). Boyett framed the definition of *contour couch.*

Webster's Third New International Dictionary is abbreviated *WTNID.*

BIRCHER, *n.* [John *Birch* + -*er*] One who belongs to the John Birch Society; see also *John Bircher.*—1961 San Francisco *Chronicle* 28 March p. 8/1–4 (heading) 'Birchers' Active in S. F. San Francisco *Examiner* 19 July p. 18/1–2 (heading) Birchers Want War, Russ Claim. N.Y. *Times Mag.* 10 Dec. p. 9/2–3 The Birchers will fight back—as is their right.

BIRCHISM, *n.*—1961 *Time* 10 March p. 22/3 . . . one Chicago conservative who backed away from Birchism . . . Lincoln (Nebr.) *Even. Jour.* 7 April p. 4/4 Birchism is the antithesis of conservatism. San Francisco *Examiner* 16 April Sec. I p. 14/1–5 (heading) U.S. General Meets with Boss on 'Birchism.'

BUS-BACK, *adj.* See quots.—1960 *Moody's Transportation Manual* 7 June p. 1390 New bus-back service is being tested under agreement with Transcontinental Bus System, Inc. which provides for container shipping on 1½ ton trailers hauled by inter-city buses on regular routes. *Newsweek* 20 June p. 91/1 Joining the piggyback, fishyback, and birdyback freight-shipping trend is a new 'bus-back' cargo-carrying service inaugurated by Railway Express. Compact, 1½-ton 'pup' semi-trailers are hitched behind regularly scheduled intercity passenger buses. The tag-along highway trailers are delivered to and picked up at the bus terminals by Railway Express.

COM-, COMSYMP, *n.* [*com*munist + *symp*athizer] See quots.—1961 *Nebraska State Jour.* 12 April p. 11/3–4 He [Robert Welch] defined a 'Comsymp' as a 'Communist or a sympathizer with Communist purposes.' Seattle *Times* 6 July p. 12 (UPI) The founder of the John Birch Society has asked its members to help compile 'the most complete and most accurate files in America on the leading Comsymps (Communist Sympathizers), Socialists and liberals.' Tuscaloosa (Ala.) *News* 9 July p. 16/1 (AP) . . . the right-wing nationalist group called on its members to help build up 'the most complete and most accurate files in American [*sic*] on the leading "comsymps" (Communist sympathizers), Socialists and liberals.' *Life* 17 Nov. p. 6/1 (edit.) . . . Welch . . . declared that 'one-half of one percent of all Catholic priests are Comsymps.' *Nation* 16 Dec. p. 482 . . . for in Birchite circles both Mr. . . . and Mr. . . . are at the moment regarded as 'com-symps.'

CONTOUR COUCH. [Cf. *contour chair* in *WTNID.*] A couch in a space vehicle especially designed to fit the form of the astronaut's body.—1959 N.Y. *Times Mag.* 11 Oct. p. 18/1 (caption) He is sealed into the container and, after a multitude of checks, lies there in his 'contour couch' and waits out the long countdown. Tuscaloosa (Ala.) *News* 26 Dec. p. 6/1–3 (caption) In the center is the pilot, strapped to a contour couch. 1961 N.Y. *Times Mag.* 10 Dec. p. 10/2–3 (caption) Crowded with instruments and safety gear, it barely allows room for the astronaut in his 'custom-made' contour couch.

COSMONAUT, *n.* See quots.—1959 N.Y. *Times* 27 Nov. p. 26/1 Then last month Ogonek, the Soviet magazine, carried an article and pictures of the 'Cosmonauts' in training. . . 1960 *Newsweek* 11 July p. 59/1 The Russian 5-ton 'satellite ship' sent into orbit in May . . . could accommodate two cosmonauts (the Russian term) for several days of scientific observation. . . . 1961 N.Y. *Times* 22 Jan. p. E9/7 Will he be one of the seven American astronauts. . . ? Or will he be one of the Russian Cosmonauts. . . ? Cleveland

Plain Dealer 13 April p. 1 The Soviet Union put the first human 'cosmonaut' into orbit around the earth yesterday in a five-ton space vessel . . . *Sci. News Letter* 13 May p. 290/1 The first U.S. astronaut is not just a spectator watching the view as was the first Russian cosmonaut. N.Y. *Times* 8 Aug. p. 28 The safe landing of the Soviet cosmonaut . . . marked the climax of man's greatest single adventure so far. COSMONAUTICAL, *adj.*—1961 *Life* 21 April p. 35 (heading) Some Cosmonautical Questions.

JOHN BIRCHER. [*John Birch* + *-er*] See quots.—1961 Lincoln (Nebr.) *Even. Jour.* 6 April p. 4/4 We have a lot of near John Birchers right here in Nebraska. *Newsweek* 10 April p. 62/2 What the John Birchers do not deny, however, is a violent distaste for the social concerns of the nation's churches, the use of certain well-tried Communist tactics (such as 'front' groups) to achieve their goals, and an antipathy toward all the social and economic legislation of the past 30 years . . .

MOLECULAR ELECTRONICS. See quots. esp. *Brit. Book of the Year*.—1960 N.Y. *Times* 3 Jan. p. 1F/2 . . . the chief executive officer . . . disclosed that Westinghouse was actively engaged in 'molecular electronics.' . . . Mr. Cresap said that Westinghouse had been able to rearrange molecules in various components that made up an electronic end product in a single unit instead of an assembly of these components. *Time* 1 Feb. p. 54/1 The amplifier is made by a new technique called molecular electronics. Westinghouse treats the molecules of germanium or silicon crystals in such a way that different parts of the same tiny block acquire different electrical properties. These 'domains' and the 'interfaces' between them act like the components of complicated electronic circuits. *Chri. Sci. Mon.* 11 Feb. p. 3c/3 The second new wonder is 'molecular electronics,' a concept that is expected to extend man's reach into space by making equipment 1,000 times smaller and vastly more reliable than before. 1961 N. Y. *Times* 26 March p. 1F/6 Thousands of products . . . eventually may be much smaller, more reliable and cheaper as a result of molecular electronics. *Brit. Book of the Year 1961* (Chicago: Encyclopaedia Britannica, Inc.) p. 753/1 *molecular electronics*. The use of certain properties of molecules in devices for amplification and control, as distinguished from solid state electronics and vacuum tube electronics. The molecules might be either free or incorporated as impurities in other metals.

MOON SHOOT, MOONSHOOT. A moon shot (which see).—1958 Tuscaloosa (Ala.) *News* 13 Aug. p. 10/2 Moonshoot. *Ibid.* 15 Aug. p. 1/1 (heading) Moon Shoot Tricky Business. 1959 N.Y. *Times* 8 March p. F1/4 Astronomical expenditures and grinding effort by thousands for almost a full year preceded last Tuesday's 'moon shoot.'

MOON SHOT, MOONSHOT. See last quot. (Also attrib.)—1958 Tuscaloosa (Ala.) *News* 13 Aug. p. 1/3 (AP) Those are the three most favorable days this month for a moon shot. N.Y. *Times Mag.* 17 Aug. p. 12/4 . . . the moon shot . . . will take care of itself. Washington *Post and Times Her.* 18 Aug. p. A8/4 . . . 'the fact that the moon shot failed is not too significant' in itself. Seattle *Times* 12 Oct. p. 2 . . . spreading around the world the story of the successful moonshot launching. *Sat. Eve. Post* 8 Nov. p. 34/1 (caption) Above is the lunar probe Pioneer as it blasted off its pad at Cape Canaveral in last month's historic moon shot. 1959 Woodford A. Heflin (ed.) *Aerospace Glossary* (Maxwell Air Force Base, Ala.: Research Studies Institute, Air University) pp. 67–68 *moon shot*. The launch of a probe vehicle aimed at placing a lunar probe on course toward the moon.

NEATNIK, *n.* [By analogy with *beatnik*.] One who is neat in his personal habits; see quots.—1959 N.Y. *Times* 30 Aug. p. 67/1 The beatniks and the neatniks had at each other this week . . . *Ibid.* 6 Dec. p. 128 (adv.) . . . Beatnik goes Neatnik . . . Seattle *Times* 16 Dec. A neatnik is the opposite of a litterbug. 1960 N.Y. *Times* 3 Jan. p. 48 (adv.) Seeing how you're a Neatnik, you'll be buying things like soap and ties and stuff from now on . . . 1961 Tuscaloosa (Ala.) *News* 13 Feb. p. 9/1–4 (heading) It Pays to Be a 'Neatnik' When It Comes to Figures.

NEUTRON BOMB. [See *neutron* in *WTNID*.] See quots.—1959 Washington *Post* 19 July; cited in *U. S. News & World Report* 30 May 1960 p. 57/1. 1960 *ibid.* 30 May p. 56 The weapon—in one possibility being discussed—could be built as a 'light-weight' device able to send out streams of poison radiation greater than those produced by today's big 'conventional' nuclear bombs. . . . A team of saboteurs could carry a small neutron bomb into an enemy territory to destroy men at essential nerve centers. 1961 *Life* 5 May p. 34/2 The AEC has a variety of new weapons and improvements which are stalled for lack of testing, including the small all-fusion or 'neutron bomb' which could radically change the whole nature of tactical warfare . . . 1961 N.Y. *Times* 25 June p. 1/1 As now conceived, the neutron bomb would be radically different from any nuclear or thermonuclear bomb now in the atomic arsenal. Tuscaloosa (Ala.) *News* 2 Nov. p. 1/5 (AP) The underground test caverns in Nevada may be the site for the first tentative experiments on the theory of a neutron bomb—sometimes referred to as a 'death ray' bomb—which would kill without leaving wide destruction.

PARKING ORBIT. See first quot.—1961 Tuscaloosa (Ala.) *News* 24 July p. 1/6 (AP) NASA said the 675-pound Ranger will be fired first into a brief 'parking orbit' 115 miles above the earth. For about 13 minutes Ranger I will zoom along at 18,000 miles an hour, high above the Atlantic Ocean, as though it were a regulation earth satellite. Then its Agena-B second-stage rocket will fire up for a second time to accelerate Ranger I to a velocity of 23,800 miles an hour and start it on a trajectory 685,000 miles out into space. Seattle *Times* 23 Aug. p. 1/1 (AP) The Agena second stage rocket spun into a 'parking orbit' from which the 675-pound payload, Ranger I, was to have been flung far into space.

PARKINSONISM, *n.* [G. Northcote *Parkinson* + *-ism*] See first quot. and *Parkinson's Law*.—1957 *Life* 15 April p. 57/1 (edit.) But fat there is—and maybe where the squeeze ought to be applied hardest is on 'Parkinsonism,' that trend for every bureau to proliferate . . . 1960 N.Y. *Times* 31 Jan. p. 56/3 Professor Parkinson's book, 'Parkinson's Law,' expounding this and other Parkinsonisms, was published in 1957.

PARKINSON'S LAW. [See quots.] See quots.—1957 N.Y. *Times* 5 May Sec. 3 p. 1/7 . . . Parkinson's Law is that British Government employes multiply by about 5 per cent a year even though their total work output does not increase in proportion. 1958 *Sat. Rev.* 17 May p. 12/1–2. N.Y. *Times Book Rev.* 13 July p. 8/1 This will be 'Parkinson's Law,' . . . This law says . . . that subordinates multiply at a fixed rate, regardless of the amount of work done. N.Y. *Times Mag.* 12 Oct. p. 10/3 Apparently the 'law' set forth by . . . . . . C. Northcote Parkinson, in . . . 'Parkinson's Law'—which shows how continuous growth in administrative personnel occurs, regardless of its contribution to the main task or need for such personnel—operates in higher education in the United States even as it does in government and industry. 1960 *Time* 29 Feb. p. 115/2 Put in its now classic form, *Parkinson's Law* . . . holds that 'work expands so as to fill the time available for its completion' . . .

AMONG THE NEW WORDS

I. WILLIS RUSSELL
University of Alabama

ACKNOWLEDGMENTS: For citations, Walter S. Avis (1), Thomas L. Crowell (1), E. E. Ericson (4), Mary P. Fischer (1), John Luskin (1), Mamie J. Meredith (6), Porter G. Perrin (1), Anne B. Russell (1), and B. J. Wells (1).

The editor of this department records with sorrow the death of two individuals whose names have frequently appeared among the contributors. The contributions of both Thomas L. Crowell and Porter G. Perrin will be missed.

A-O.K., A-OK, A-OKAY, *adj.* See quots.—1961 Omaha *World-Her.* 8 May p. 12m/2 "A-okay," as everybody now knows, means all's well, everything functioning perfectly. *Newsweek* 31 July p. 19/1 A-Okay—Almost All the Way. N.Y. *Times* 29 Oct. p. 2E/5 (heading) Saturn A-O.K. 1962 Tuscaloosa *News* 18 Aug. p. 1/4 (AP) The A-OK words for this month are parameter, definitize and interface.

BIONICS, *n.* [*biology* + *electronics*] See quots.—1960 *Time* 3 Oct. p. 54/1–2 Sciences, like animals, can reproduce when placed together under the proper circumstances. In Dayton, at a symposium sponsored by the Air Force, an infant science born of biology and electronics has made its appearance. Its name: bionics. Its aim: to study living creatures in hope of gaining knowledge to improve man-made mechanisms. 1961 *Science* 24 Feb. p. 588/1 (heading) Bionics. 1962 *Life* 14 Sept. p. 58/2–3 Now scientists are studying nature's biological solutions to see whether these principles can be applied to man's own inventions: to computers, for example, or to devices like television cameras which must perceive. The new field is called "bionics." At Servomechanisms, Inc. in Santa Barbara, Redemske, a specialist in the field, is studying the structure of insects to see what he can learn about possible ways of changing the structure of machines.

BRANCHING, *vbl. n.* [Cf. *OED*, s.v. *branching*, *vbl. sb.* 1: "diverging in the manner of branches" {1578}] See first quot.—1960 *Fortune* Oct. p. 259 (pict. cap.) A distinctive feature of Crowder's programs is what he calls "branching." If a student's answers indicate the need for review of material already covered, the student may be diverted temporarily to a "branch"—i.e., a sequence of frames that a more knowing student can bypass. 1961 *Barron's* 30 Oct. p. 14/2 Raymond C. Hagel of Crowell-Collier, who is setting up at the company's New York City headquarters what he says will be the biggest programming center in the trade, avers: "We are disciples of neither Crowder nor Skinner. Our programs will make use of either branching or linear techniques, depending on which seems best suited to the subject matter."

CRYOBIOLOGY, *n.* [See quot.] See quot.—1962 *Business Week* 16 June p. 72/1 Essentially, cryobiology is the marriage of two separate sciences: cryogenics, or extreme low-temperature physics, and biology. . . . They are studying the effects of extreme cold—hundreds of degrees below freezing—on living systems, both plant and animal.

CRYOBIOLOGIST, *n.*—1962 *Business Week* 16 June p. 72/1 Actually, cryobiologists have come up with two ways to preserve cells by freezing.

CRYOSURGERY, *n.* [Gk *kryo-* 'icy cold'] See quot.—1962 *Union Carbide Stockholder News* Dec. p. 1/1 Many people crippled by Parkinson's disease, as well as other disorders causing exhausting tremors or rigidity, have been given a chance for a more normal life as a result of an unusual new brain surgery technique. It makes use of freezing as a surgical tool. The new technique was developed at St. Barnabas Hospital in New York. Engineers of Linde Company, Division of Union Carbide, have been working closely with the hospital in designing and building equipment to deliver and control the super cold required for this cryosurgery, as it is called.

CUSTOMIZER, *n.* [*customize* (*NID 3*) + *-er*]—1959 N.Y. *Times* 29 Nov. p. 83/1 Customizer, he found, was a youngster who delighted in changing the appearance of the family car. He had been allowed to "dechrome" the hood and put decals on it, but his family had rejected further alterations . . ., such as lowering the roof, dechroming the trunk and lowering the body of the car on the chasis. 1960 *ibid.* 17 Apr. p. 20A/2 Thus a "customizer" who is intensely interested in changing the appearance of the family car can be expressing his own restlessness and discontent with his own image.

CYBORG, *n.* [See first quot.] See quots.—1960 N.Y. *Times* 22 May p. 31/1 A cyborg is essentially a man-machine in which the control mechanisms of the human portion are modified externally by drugs or regulatory devices so that the being can live in an environment different from the normal one. The word "cyborg" is a hybrid of two others: "cybernetics" . . . and "organism." *Life* 1 Aug. p. 9/4 Cyborgs would be humans with some organs only temporarily altered or replaced by mechanical devices. On returning to earth the devices would be removed and normal body functions restored. Seattle *Times Mag.* 11 Dec. p. 17 These doctors propose to create what they call "Cyborgs." These men will have devices deliberately incorporated in them to extend the unconscious self-regulatory control, permitting the Cyborg to adapt to new and, perhaps, hostile environment. By doing this, scientists believe they can provide a unified system in which physiological problems are taken care of automatically, leaving the man free to perform his specified duties.

DOUBLE-BLIND, *adj.* See quots.—1957 *Harper's* July p. 24/1 Accordingly, in the best controlled test, neither patient nor physician knows which patients receive which pill. This secret remains in a code broken only at the end of the experiment. We call this the "double-blind" experiment. 1960 N.Y. *Times* 14 Aug. p. 77/3 After the first few cases of improvement with griseofulvin therapy were noted, a research method known as the "double blind" was used. With this technique the pills look the same, but one of them is the real drug and the other is an inert substitute. Neither the patient nor the physician knows which is which.

FLY-BY-WIRE, *nominal.* See quots. (Also attrib.)—1962 Tuscaloosa *News* 20 Feb. pp. 1/5–2/1 (AP) He immediately switched to what the astronauts call a "fly-by-wire" mechanism, in which the craft is controlled by pushing a button on the flight stick to send electronic signals to the jets—18 of which are located on the capsule surface. N.Y. *Times* 27 May p. 44/3 Now he tried a third control method. He switched to the manual part of the so-called "automatic" system. Its technical name is "fly-by-fly." Manual movements of the control stick operate the jet thrusters electronically. But here is where he made his mistake in the pressure of getting squared away for that vital moment—"retro" firings. In changing to "fly-by-wire" he neglected to turn off the manual system. *Life* 26 Oct. p. 41/1 I immediately switched to "fly-by-wire"—the control system in which the pilot uses the manual stick to operate fuel jets that are normally automatic—and turned the capsule around for the long ride.

-IN. See *Am. Sp.* 36: 282. Additional illusts. The terms are italicized.—1962 Tuscaloosa *News* 7 Jan. p. 2/2 (AP) An official of the Congress of Racial Equality (CORE) said Saturday the integrationist group would stage a mass "*join-in*" at white churches in Baton Rouge next month. The Rev. B. Elton Cox . . . said in an interview 100 Negroes in groups of two would go to the white churches Feb. 11 on "race relations Sunday." 1963 *ibid.* 28 May p. 2/8 Jesse Turner . . . said, however, that *wade-ins*, *swim-ins*, and *play-ins* will be seen if the city park commission goes ahead with intentions to open still-segregated parks and pools June 13. B'ham. *Post Her.* 14 June p. 3/6 (UPI)—A white Ohio State University graduate student and a Negro minister today chained themselves to seats in the gallery of the State Legislature vowing to stay there until the lawmakers passed a satisfactory fair housing bill. . . . The two, both members of the Congress of Racial Equality, apparently staged the *chain-in* because earlier this week, CORE members were blocked from entering the House chamber to stage a "*pray-in*."

MAGNETOSPHERE, *n.* [*magneto-* 'magnetic'] See quots.—1962 N.Y. *Times* 28 Jan. p. 103/7 The news about the single radiation belt, which has been named the magnetosphere, followed another discovery, announced the day before Christmas, that the earth has a corona of helium gas forming a 900-mile thick layer in the upper atmosphere, beginning at an altitude of 600 miles. This layer was revealed by Explorer VIII, launched Nov. 3, 1960. *Sat. Rev.* 3 Feb. p. 42/2–3 (pict. cap.) The magnetosphere of earth, sketched above, is now known to trap electrical particles in varying densities to a distance of 60,000 miles. Dark arcs suggest original conception of Van Allen Belts. Note spiraling along magnetic lines.

OVERKILL, *v.i.* [*over-* (*OED*, s.v., II, 22 {1582}) + *kill*] See quots., esp. those under the noun.—1958 Lincoln *Even. Jour.* 8 Aug. p. 4/4 What then is this theory of "overkill?" In essence it is the argument that you do not need the power to "overkill," if you already have H-bombs and the means to deliver them in quantities sufficient to destroy the Soviet Union. . . . 1959 N.Y. *Post* 6 April p. 14/2 There was a lot of talk in high places about the power to "overkill," a word that has lately achieved a unique place in the ghoulish lexicon of war. 1963 *World Book Encyclopedia Dict.*

OVER-KILL, OVERKILL, *n.* See quots. (Also attrib.)—1958 *Time* 17 March p. 25/2 A word coming more and more into Pentagon usage is "overkill"—a blunt but descriptive term implying a power to destroy a military target not once but many times more than necessary. N.Y. *Times* 30 March p. 6E/4 They also point to what is to them the futility of further nuclear weapons tests. Our strategy of deterrence already has a tremendous "overkill" capability; that is we have far more than enough bombs—if they could be delivered—to devastate every sizeable city in Russia several times over. 1960 St. Louis *Post-Dispatch* 10 Feb. p. 1 "Overkill equals total non-surviveability plus." N.Y. *Times* 22 May p. 21/1 . . . the Army and the Navy have insisted . . . that it is wrong to create a huge stockpile that, if ever used, would wreak destruction beyond an enemy's probable surrender point. This has been called a policy of "overkill." N.Y. *Post* 9 Sept. p. 48/1 New words of frightening significance keep popping into the language. . . . the latest I've heard is "overkill," which, I learn, means the capacity to kill more people than there are. 1962 N.Y. *Times Mag.* 10 June p. 38/4 And quite sane and sober Americans must now adjust their moral sensibilities to the language of "overkill" . . . 1963 *World Book Encyclopedia Dict.*

PARARESCUEMAN, *n.* [*pararescue* (*NID 3*) + *man*] See second quot.—1961 Lincoln *Sun. Jour.* 3 Sept. p. 2A (photo) On the stabilizing wing at bottom of the raft is . . . Vargas . . ., who, with . . . Vigare . . ., aboard other raft, and another "pararescueman" picked up capsule after its return from outer space. 1962 N.Y. *Times Mag.* 11 March p. 88 (pict. cap.) The space-age vocabulary has acquired another new word—"pararescuemen." It denotes some remarkable Air Force teamworkers whose job it is to snatch men, space capsules and nose cones from the ocean. Each is a parachutist, frogman, medic and mechanic.

READ-IN, *n.* [See third quot.] See quots. (Also attrib.)—1961 *Newsweek* 10 April p. 27/1 The Read-In. N.Y. *Times* 9 Nov. p. 37 Last night, twenty-four students gathered in the campus library for an all-night "read-in" demonstration [to protest an administrative ruling]. 1962 *Brit. Book of the Year* p. 743/1 *read-in, n.* [By analogy with *sit-in.*] A protest demonstration of Negroes in a city library.

TOKENISM, *n.* [[2]*token, adj.* (*NID 3*) + *-ism*] See first quot.—1962 N.Y. *Times Mag.* 5 Aug. p. 11 The Case against Tokenism [heading] The current notion that token integration will satisfy his people, says Dr. King, is an illusion. 1963 N.Y. *Times* 7 June p. 18/2 "We're through with tokenism and gradualism and see-how-far-you've-comeism." *Ibid.* 16 June p. E1/3 . . . the time when "tokenism" could satisfy Negroes is long past.

AMONG THE NEW WORDS

I. WILLIS RUSSELL
University of Alabama

ACKNOWLEDGMENTS: For citations, Thomas L. Crowell, Jr. (1), E. E. Ericson (2), Mamie J. Meredith (5), and Porter G. Perrin (1).

AUTOMANIA, *n.* [*auto*mobile + *mania*] See quots.—1963 N.Y. *Times Mag.* 11 Aug. p. 18/1 A Nassau County judge recently charged that suburban teen-agers suffer from a "serious malady—automania." He defined the term as "an overobsession with the automobile as a status symbol, as a means of getting someplace in a hurry, as a vehicle for a flight from tensions, or to indulge in a craving to show off." N.Y. *Times* 15 Sept. p. 118/4 "The rose-colored glasses show a city come to its senses; a city that has outreasoned the follies and foibles of the smog-laden metropolis 400 miles to the south; a city that has discovered automania to be incurable because its treatment aggravates the disease. . . ."

AUTOMANIAC, *n.* See quot.—1963 N.Y. *Times Mag.* 29 Sept. p. 50/1 An automaniac is herewith defined as one who, clad in the goggles and duster of a bygone age, mounts an antique automobile and goes pop-popping about the landscape, squeezing the bulb of a serpent horn, twirling his false mustachios, and living some dream of himself as a gay, sly dog, happy as a child in Never-Never land. . . . the automaniac not only drives old cars, but also collects old junk—the older, the better. . . . He speaks a special language, as all hobbyists do.

BILLBOARD, BILLBOARD ANTENNA, *n.* A large rectangular antenna of billboard proportions, mounted on tall uprights.—1955 *M.I.T. Observer* Oct. p. 4 This transmission uses the giant billboard antenna (120′ high x 130′ wide) that dominates the picture. 1963 *Life* 1 March p. 20/1 Dye Main's 60-foot-high radio antennas—the technicians call them "billboards"—make sure these warning signals get through.

BIO-, BIOACOUSTICS, *n.* See second quot.—1955 Monitor broadcast 25 Dec. 1959 *Sat. Rev.* 26 Sept. p. 43/2 A relatively new area of scientific research—bio-acoustics—is concerned with the impacts on human beings, and animals, of sound impulses.

BIOCIDE, *n.* [By analogy with *genocide.*] See quots.—1947 *Sat. Rev. Lit.* 30 Aug. p. 21/3 (letter by E. M. Greenberg, M.D.) "Biocide," or destruction of the tissues of the human body, is caused by all the unphysiologic habits that civilization has imposed upon the human race. 1948 *Brit. Book of the Year* p. 804/2. 1963 *Sat. Rev.* 19 Jan. p. 23/1–2 (letter by Wallace G. Holbrook) It seems to me that somewhere in my literary travels I have encountered the term "biocide" used in a context similar to genocide . . . namely, the destruction of living species by indirect chemical, or, for that matter, nuclear, poisons. *Ibid.* 2 Feb. p. 18/1 (Eds. reprint Dr. Greenberg's original letter.)

BUG, *n.* [Cf. *NID 3*, s.v. [1]*bug, n.*, 11: 'a light usu. two-seater stripped-down automobile.'] See quots.—1962 N.Y. *Times* 15 July p. E7/8 From this vehicle [an Apollo spacecraft], a small two-man lunar excursion vehicle commonly known as the "bug" would be detached from the mother craft for the trip to the lunar surface. Tuscaloosa *News* 11 Oct. p. 17/4 (AP) From a garage, in Apollo's midsection perhaps, there will be released a small two-man "bug" with two crewmen aboard. 1963 N.Y. *Times* 11 Aug. p. 2/4 In Project Apollo, under present plans, a two-man vehicle known as a "bug" will descend to the moon's surface from a command capsule orbiting around the moon. The two men will explore the moon for a few days, then re-enter the bug and rejoin the orbiting capsule for the return trip to the earth.

BURMA BRIDGE, *n.* See quots.—1961 N.Y. *Times* 10 Sept. p. 29 (pict. cap.) . . . A "Burma bridge" is a training aid. 1962 *The Johns Hopkins Mag.* Nov. p. 12/1 (pict. cap.) One of the first challenges faced by a student is the rope course through the trees, which includes climbs, swings, "Burma bridges," and other hazards.

CONTRONYM, *n.* [See first quot.] See quots.—1962 *Word Study* Oct. p. 8/2 The name *contronym* (meaning: any word which is used in two senses which seem to contradict each other) is particularly suitable as a label for a word possessing this peculiarity. The *-onym*, of course, parallels the same element in . . . "antonym," "homonym," and "paronym." The *contr-* . . . is an element also found in "contraband," "contradict," . . . and other words. *Amer. Sp.* Oct. p. 219 (Bibliography) Herring, Jack. 'Contronyms.' *Word Study*, 37:8. Feb. 1962. [Proposes *contronym* as a name for 'any word which is used in two senses which seem to contradict each other.'] [Preceding square brackets are in the original. IWR.]

EURODOLLAR, EURO DOLLAR, *n.* [*Euro*pean + *dollar*] See quots.—1961 Lincoln (Nebr.) *Sun. Jour.* 19 March p. 10 A/4 A Euro dollar is a dollar deposit owned by a European, or somebody operating from the continental money markets. It may be deposited either in the U.S. or in a European branch of a U.S. bank. Generally it is a demand rather than a time deposit. . . . 1963 N.Y. *Times* 8 Sept. p. F1/8 Eurodollars are dollar deposits of foreigners—not only Europeans—outside the United States.

EXO-, EXOSOCIETY, *n.* [*exo-* 'external, outside' + *society*] See quots.—1961 *Harper's* March p. 60 Here we use the new term exo-society to designate intelligent life beyond our solar system. 1963 Cedar Rapids (Iowa) *Gazette* 4 Jan. p. 2/1 . . . recently a word was coined to describe an intelligent social order outside our solar system. The word, "exo-society."

FAIR ONE, *n.* See quots.—1954 N.Y. *Times Mag.* 21 March p. 66 Sometimes, instead of a "rumble," they arranged for a "fair one," in which one or several boys from each gang battled it out to avenge a real or fancied grievance. 1963 N.Y. *Times* 15 Sept. p. 121/3 A technical change included a technique known as the "fair one." This involved choosing a member from each of two gangs to settle differences openly in front of other gang members with their fists.

FAMILY, *n.* [Cf. *NID 3*, s.v. [1]*family, n.*, 1b: 'the retinue or staff of a nobleman or high official.'] See first quot. (Also attrib.)—1963 N.Y. *Times* 29 Sept. p. E5/7 The ruling commission [of Cosa Nostra] has until recently consisted of twelve men, each called the "capo" or "boss." Each boss is in charge of a "family," the generic name for the operating unit in a specific geographic area. Each family is supreme in its region. *Ibid.* 6 Oct. p. 6E/3 The syndicate, or "family," chief has other protections.

GHOST, *n.* See quots. (Also attrib.)—1952 B'ham *News* 19 Sept. p. 1/5 (heading) Mississippi "ghost" students cost millions. 1959 *Harper's* Feb. p. 46/1 If even Harvard has "ghosts" (admitted applicants who do not show up on registration day), the smaller colleges must expect to be roundly haunted, and they are.

HOOPSTER, *n.* [*hula hoop* (*NID 3*) + *-ster*] A person operating a hula hoop.—1958 *Life* 8 Sept. p. 38 (pict. cap.) Relaxing hoopsters at an Atlanta motel practice rotating at the pool during the cocktail hour. N.Y. *Times Mag.* 28 Sept. p. 8/2 (pict. cap.) Hoopsters. . . .

KREMLINOLOGIST, *n.* [*Kremlin* + *ologist* ('specialist' (*NID 3*))] See last quot.—1962 St. Louis *Globe-Dem.* 30 March p. 6A/6 . . . the Kremlinologists . . . warned that the United States must be frightfully careful not to rock the boat of diplomacy. 1962 Tuscaloosa *News* 8 Nov. p. 4/5 Not myself being a Kremlinologist, I do not know what will be the effect of the two great crises on the international situation of the Soviet Union. 1963 N.Y. *Times Mag.* 14 July p. 9 That experience now adds up . . . to establish Averell Harriman as the leading "Kremlinologist" of this Administration. He has spent more time in direct consultation with Stalin, Khrushchev and other leaders of Communist Russia, living and dead, than any other American official.

KREMLINOLOGY, *n.* See quot.—1960 *Sat. Rev.* 15 Oct. p. 37/1 The Kremlinology he discussed is the pseudoscientific method by which one scans Russian literature and infers attitudes which guide today's Communist leaders in the Soviet Union.

PLASTINAUT, *n.* [*plastic* + *astronaut*] See quots.—1961 Lincoln (Nebr.) *Even. Jour.* 14 Aug. p. 5/1 The Air Force is building three mansize plastic dummy astronauts—it calls them plastinauts—for biological studies of radiation above the atmosphere. 1963 Atlanta *Jour. and Constitution* 20 Jan. p. 8/1 (NANA) Newest American "airman" is the plastinaut . . . a dummy man made of material resembling human flesh which has a base of isocyanate rubber, plus various additions designed by Air Force chemists. . . . He is 5 feet 9 inches tall and weighs 162 pounds. . . .

AMONG THE NEW WORDS

I. WILLIS RUSSELL
University of Alabama

ACKNOWLEDGMENTS: For citations, S. V. Baum (1), Colgan H. Bryan (1), Mary Fischer (4), Atcheson L. Hench (1), Raven I. McDavid, Jr. (1), Mamie J. Meredith (7), Porter G. Perrin (1), A. B. Polsgrove (1), Edward F. Richards (1), Anne B. Russell (3), and Peter Tamony (2). Thanks are due to Mary Fischer, who prepared the typescript.

BIOSATELLITE, *n.* See quots.—1958 *Newsweek* 17 Feb. p. 95/1 The NACA sphere could be ready within a year as a biosatellite to test space stresses on small laboratory animals. 1959 Woodford A. Heflin (ed.) *Aerospace Glossary* (Maxwell [Ala.] Air Force Base: Research Studies Institute, Air University) p. 18/1 BIOSATELLITE, *n.* A satellite designed to carry an animal or plant, or a satellite that carries an animal or plant. (Ed. note: "The word *animal* as used here includes man.") 1964 N.Y. *Times* 23 Feb. p. 7E/7–8 Fourteen biological specimens have been chosen for the first flight, in 1965, of National Aeronautics and Space Administration's biosatellite. Its purpose is to study the effects of radiation, weightlessness and the absence of earth's rotation, combined, on living things. *Ibid.* 8 March p. 1/6 Because all these effects [e.g., atrophied muscles, softened bones] of extended space travel are possible, the National Aeronautics and Space Administration has scheduled six "biosatellites" to probe such dangers.

BLACK NATIONALIST, *n.* [Cf. *white supremacist*] A believer in the supremacy of the Negro.—1963 *Life* 24 May p. 4/2 The Negro's feeling that the white man's law has failed him is polarized by extreme black nationalists. . . . 1964 *Friends Journal* 15 Jan. p. 39/2 That organization would not tolerate an out-spoken black nationalist.

CARTNAP(P)ER, *n.* [*cart* + kid*naper*] See quots.—1958 Tuscaloosa *News* 8 Jan. p. 1/7 (AP) A cartnaper? He's the person or persons who make off with those four-wheeled carts used by the customer to haul groceries. 1960 Lincoln (Nebr.) *Sun. Jour. and Star* 11 Sept. p. 7A/1 Cartnapers take off with $1,259,000 worth of carts a year in greater New York, store owners report. 1963 *Wall St. Journal* 18 July p. 1/4 (heading) "Cartnappers" Beware: Stores Strive to Cut Shopping Cart Losses."

CARTNAPPING, *vb. n.*—1957 N.Y. *Times* 22 Sept. p. F1/2 (pict. cap.) Driving hazards are one result of "cartnapping." Hundreds are borrowed each week and left in streets or parking lots.

CHUNNEL, *n.* [*ch*annel + t*unnel*]. See quots.—1957 N.Y. *Times Mag.* 17 Nov. p. 55/1 A channel tunnel? Of course. As quickly as possible. Britain has needed one for a century. My newspaper christened the project "The Chunnel." The word has stuck in the minds of the British people. 1964 *Reader's Digest* July p. 35/2 The Channel tunnel—or "Chunnel," as the British have dubbed it—will owe its realization in part to the circumstance that an American lawyer . . . had a rough Channel crossing in the summer of 1956.

-CIDE. The new terms are italicized.—1964 Montgomery *Advertiser* 1 April p. 4/6 There are people who consider this to be a nation "bent on self destruction by *autocide*". . . . 1963 *Today's Health* June p. 18/2 A new word—"*scubacide*"—has been coined to describe such a situation. The scubacide victim is the person who tries to become a scuba diver in one fatal lesson (self-taught).

FAN-JET, FAN-JET ENGINE, *n.* See quots.—[1959 F. D. Adams *Aeronautical Dict.* (National Aeronautics and Space Administration, Washington, D.C.: U.S. Gov't Printing Office) pp. 71, 62 FAN ENGINE . . . DUCTED-FAN ENGINE . . . a jet engine in which a ducted fan or ducted propeller is used to take in air to augment the gases of combustion in the jet stream.] 1963 *Sat. Rev.* 20 July p. 14 (adv.) In 1961, American Airlines introduced a new engine called the fan-jet—with 30% more power than ordinary jets. So much power that the plane itself had to be changed. This was the birth of our Astrojet. N.Y. *Times* 15 Sept. p. XX7/3 The fan-jet engines—they were built for this plane and for a minimum of engine noise—have turbine blades spaced for a minimum of sound. They also have a ring of sound-absorbent material just inside the air intake to smother the air and turbine scream.

GO-NO GO, GO-NO-GO. 1. *Attrib.* See first quot. 2. *Nominal.* See first quot. (Also attrib.)—1. 1959 Heflin (ed.) *Aerospace Glossary* p. 43/2 GO-NO-GO, *adj.* Of a rocket missile launch: So controlled at the end of the countdown as to permit an instantaneous change in decision on whether to launch or not to launch. 1961 B'ham *Post-Her.* 18 July p. 1/7 (UPI) The "go-no go" decision was made by Walter Williams, the Cape's Project Mercury chief, on the basis of weather information he received just before a conference on the Cape at 11 p.m. 2. 1963 *Am. Sp.* May p. 118 GO-NO-GO, *n.* A specified point on the runway, normally 4,000 feet from the end of the runway, used as a decision point for aborting. If trouble develops on the take-off roll before go-no-go, it is possible to abort and stop the aircraft on the remaining runway. If trouble develops after go-no-go, the aircraft is committed to take-off because it is not possible to stop the plane on the remaining runway. Very simply, it is the point where you make up your mind either to go or not to go. N.Y. *Times* 19 May p. 1E/1 *Orbit.* [*sic*] 16. The "go-no-go" point for 22 orbits was reached. "You have a go for 22 orbits," Control told him. "Roger. Very good," Cooper replied.

HIGH-RISE, *attrib.* See quots.—1957 *Fortune* Sept. p. 213/2 What kind of people . . . prefer "high-rise" apartment buildings, what kind of people prefer two-to-five-story "low-rise" houses? 1960 San Francisco *News* 14 June p. 15/1–2 . . . about modern architecture as a cover-up for almost compulsive jerry building of high-rise structures. . . . 1961 San Francisco *Examiner* 8 May p. 33/1–2 . . . you should familiarize yourself with planners' jargon: What you're moving into is not just a tall building, it is a "high rise" apartment. N.Y. *Times* 30 April p. E9/2–3 (pict. cap.) Architect's model of Boston University's sixteen-story Law-Education Building—first structure in "high-rise" campus. 1963 *Business Topics* Autumn Vol. 11 No. 4 p. 18/2 The pressures of population and shortages of usable land fostered construction of high-rise buildings. 1964 *U.S. Steel News* April p. 14 (pict. cap.) Design concepts, prepared by U.S. Steel, illustrate steel's versatility for high-rise apartments and office buildings.

-IN. See *Am. Sp.* 36: 282, 38: 229. Additional illusts. The terms are italicized.—1964 B'ham *Post-Her.* 3 March p. 2/3 (AP) B . . . and . . . Y . . . were arrested as they took part in an Indian protest "*fish-in*" on the Puyallup Ricer [*sic*]. The state had banned off reservation fishing and the Supreme Court uphld [*sic*] the law. The two cast a net into the river from an Indian canoe and caught two steelhead trout. N.Y. *Times* 19 April p. 1/1 The proponents of the *stall-in*, who say they are convinced that other civil rights groups will not be able to penetrate the fairgrounds with a meaningful demonstration, are extending their tactics. They plan marches, sit-ins and possible "*pedal-ins*" (with bicycles) near the fairgrounds. Tuscaloosa *News* 20 April p. 1/8 As the reported demonstration plans grew—from an auto *stall-in* on access roads to the fair to sit-ins, *lie-ins* and alike on other major highways, bridges and in tunnels throughout the city—reverberations sounded in Congress.

MEGACORPSE, *n.* [See quots.] See quots.—[1958 Tuscaloosa *News* 4 Sept. p. 4/5 (AP) The eeriest new word coined in the space age is "Megacorpse." It means one million dead, waiting for disposal after a nuclear attack. 1963 H. L. Mencken *The Amer. Lang.* . . . abridged, with annotations and new material, by Raven I. McDavid, Jr. With the assistance of David W. Maurer (N.Y.: Alfred A. Knopf) p. 232 Nuclear physicists talk . . . of . . . the anticipated carnage in *megacorpses* or *megadeaths*.

OGO. See quots.—1961 *Sat. Rev.* 6 May p. 71/3 (adv.) Each spacecraft in the OGO series will be capable of carrying up to 50 selected scientific experiments in a single flight. 1963 N.Y. *Times* 24 Nov. p. 16/3 OGO is the family name for Orbiting Geophysical Observatories, being built for the National Aeronautics and Space Administration. . . . Each compact OGO—only 6 feet long by 3 feet square—costs about $18,000,000. The 1,000-pound research satellite will carry aloft about 150 pounds of scientific instruments to study the Van Allen radiation belts and other space phenomena. 1964 *ibid.* 5 Jan. p. E11/6–7 (pict. cap.) Artist's concept of one of the Orbiting Geophysical Observatories, or OGO satellites, to be launched during the I.Q.S.Y. 1964–65. The wing-like panels convert sunlight into electronic power. Long arms hold sensing devices far enough apart to avoid mutual interference. Antenna transmits data to earth.

OLIGOPITHECUS, *n.* [*Oligo*cene + *-pithecus* 'monkey'] See quot.— 1962 N.Y. *Times* 6 May p. 80/2–4 (pict. cap.) Thickened lines show probable region on tree where newly discovered "Oligopithecus," oldest known Zinjanthropus [see separate entry] and other early primates arose.

OPEN, *adj.* Racially nonsegregated.—1960 *Am. Sp.* Feb. p. 58 OPEN OCCUPANCY [entry in "Among the New Words."]. 1964 N.Y. *Times* 12 Jan. p. E11/1 Thus . . . no Negro child would be kept out of any school, if his parents moved into the school's area. Moreover—taking realistic cognizance of housing barriers which usually make such moves impossible—the New York system in 1960 inaugurated a policy of "open enrollment" which permitted youngsters from designated predominantly non-white schools to apply for transfer to designated predominantly white schools.

PALEOMAGNETISM, *n.* [*paleo-* 'old,' 'ancient' + *magnetism*] See second quot.—1960 *Supplement to the Glossary of Geology and Related Sciences.* Prepared by the Glossary Review Committee, J. Marvin Weller, Chairman. (Washington, D.C.: The American Geological Institute operating under the National Academy of Sciences—National Research Council.) p. 47/2. 1963 N.Y. *Times Mag.* 21 July p. 15/1–2 More substantial still, there is now evidence provided by the new geophysical science of paleomagnetism (the study of the magnetization of ancient rocks) to show that at least some of the continents were once closer together than they are today. Working from the knowledge that many rocks become magnetized when they are formed and that their magnetism is in the direction of the earth's magnetic field at that time, the geophysicists have been able to get "fixes" on the position of the North and South Poles relative to the continents in different geological periods.

RIGHT-WINGISM, *n.*—1962 Tuscaloosa *News* 12 Feb. p. 4/6 A little over a week ago, . . . W . . . was called to the phone from a meeting of the American Jewish Congress which had been discussing right-wingism in the USA. 1964 *ibid.* 3 May p. 4/5 There has been a lot of talk lately about right-wingism on college campuses. . . .

RULY ENGLISH. [Cf. *OED*, s.v. *ruly*, *a.*[2] 1: 'Observing or amenable to rule or good order; law-abiding, disciplined, orderly.' {*c* 1400}; *NID 3*: '*archaic:* obedient, orderly.'] See quots.—1958 N.Y. *Times* 16 Nov. p. 84/3: Washington, Nov. 15—The Patent Office has discovered that the English language is too complex and ambiguous to be understood by modern computers. So it is creating a new vocabulary with sounds, which if alien to the human ear, will still fit well on a magnetic tape. The new language is called "ruly English" in contrast to everyday "unruly" English. The man in charge of its development is Simon M. Newman, an engineer in the Patent Office. *Time* 17 Nov. p. 68 To leap this communication barrier, Engineer-Lawyer Simon M. Newman of the Patent Office has been working out a synthetic language called Ruly English that is especially adapted to a computer's huge but simple brain; unlike ordinary, 'unruly' English, it gives one and only one meaning to each word. 1959 N.Y. *Times Mag.* 8 Mar. p. 32/4 The work of turning this unruly verbiage into "Ruly English" suitable for electronic minds is being done by Simon M. Newman. . . .

SEX KITTEN, *n.* A young motion picture actress whose chief asset is sex appeal; see second quot.—1958 Washington *Post & Times Her.* 1 Aug. p. D8/1 The rather lavish production offers the little French "sex kitten" such starry support as Charles Boyer. . . . 1960 Tuscaloosa *News* 24 April p. 22/5 At the same time, she may learn whether she really is an actress or just a world-famous "sex kitten." *Time* 10 Oct. p. 48/2 At week's end the aging "Sex Kitten" of French moviedom was recovering. 1964 N.Y. *Times Mag.* 1 March p. 73/1–2 (heading) A sex kitten in boots . . . wows Britain's males by knocking them out.

SIT-IN, *v.i.* [Cf. *sit-in*, *n.* in *NID 3*.]—1961 *Brit. Book of the Year* p. 753/1 SITTER, *n.* *Specif.* A Negro demonstrator who sits-in at a restaurant. *Look* 25 April p. 46/2 Our expressions in the public prints, at meetings and in resolutions are, certainly, still countered by outcries of segregationists who support this tottering political regime and excoriate Negroes who picket, sit-in, crowd our jails, advance on white schools and otherwise approach prevailing privilege. Tuscaloosa *News* 10 July p. 4/6 (Drew Pearson) This pretty well intimidated Negro troops stationed at Fort Hood until April 22 of this year, when Curtis and one other Negro soldier again sat-in at Craig's restaurant.

SKY TYPING, SKYTYPING, *n.* [*sky* + *typing*; cf. *skywriting.*] A method of skywriting.—1949 N.Y. *Times* 2 Oct. p. E9/5 (heading) Sky Typing 1961 N.Y. *Times* 9 June p. 44/3 If the weather is good, the company will collect a minimum of $400 for a single job and about $3,500 for skytyping, the latest development in aerial advertising.

SLIT WING PLANE. See quots.—1963 N.Y. *Times* 26 May p. E9/7 The Air Force announced last week the first successful flight test at Edwards Air Force Base in California of its "slit wing" plane with a revolutionary air-inhalation system. The system, called Laminar Flow Control, or LFC, aims to increase a plane's range or cargo load up to 50 per cent by greatly reducing the drag caused by friction. *Ibid.* 29 Dec. p. E7/7 *Aviation*—The Air Force announced the first successful flight test of its "slit wing" plane with a revolutionary air-inhalation system, called Laminar Flow Control, or LFC, which is expected to increase a plane's range or cargo load up to 50 per cent.

SPLASHDOWN, *n.* [Cf. Harold Wentworth and Stuart Berg Flexner *Dict. of Amer. Slang* (N.Y.: Thomas Y. Crowell Co., 1960) s. v. *splash* 5: 'A military plane shot down in combat. . . .'] The landing of a spacecraft in the ocean.—1961 *Newsweek* 31 July p. 20/3 Recovery ships and cameras picked up the orange and white chute one minute before splashdown. 1962 Frank McGee speaking on NBC 20 Feb. 1963 Tuscaloosa *News* 16 May p. 1/1–3 (heading) 'Splashdown' due tonight near Pacific's Midway Isle *Life* 24 May p. 32/1 Milk for Buttons. After news of her father's safe splashdown thousands of miles away in the Pacific, Jan Cooper, 13, gives her cat a special saucer of milk. *Ibid.* 31 May p. 36/3 Word of the splashdown was the most exciting—Gordon was actually back on earth.

SYNCHRONOUS, *adj.* [Cf. *NID 3*, s. v. *synchronous*, *adj.* 2: '. . . marked by strict and exact coincidence in time, rate, or rhythm . . .'] See quots. See also *syncom.*—1961 N.Y. *Times* 30 July p. L9/8 Synchronous satellites will require bigger boosters to reach their higher altitudes. *Ibid.* 8 Oct. p. M15/4–5 The third approach is the synchronous active repeater satellite, orbited 22,300 miles above the equator. At this altitude, the satellite would make a complete trip around the earth in exactly the time it takes the earth to turn on its axis. So the satellite would appear to remain motionless over a given spot. 1962 *ibid.* 15 July p. 5E/3 A second, more advanced type of active communications satellite is known as the high-altitude synchronous system. 1963 *ibid.* 21 July p. E7/7 The National Aeronautics and Space Administration is scheduled to launch another communications satellite of the Syncom class into near synchronous orbit from Cape Canaveral next week.

SYNCOM, *n.* [*syn*chronous *com*munications] See quots. See *synchronous*, *adj.*—1962 N.Y. *Times Mag.* 12 Aug. p. 16/3 Something better called Syncom is said to be in the offing. 1963 Tuscaloosa *News* 14 Feb. p. 1/6–7 (AP) A program official reported in midmorning, several hours after launching, that radio signals were lost 13 seconds after a small payload motor fired with the intention of kicking Syncom into a synchronous orbit—one in which the vehicle appears to hover over one spot on earth because its speed matches that of the earth's rotation. N.Y. *Times* 28 July p. E7/7 Syncom may be said to be the prototype of the global communications satellite of the future, though a number of years may pass before it becomes operational.

TEACHING MACHINE, *n.* See quots. (Also attrib.)—1958 *Science* 24 Oct. p. 971/2–3 (B. F. Skinner) Fig. 2. Student at work on a teaching machine. 1960 *PMLA* Sept. (Part 2) p. 1 (title of art. by F. Rand Morton) The Teaching Machine and the Teaching of Languages: A Report on Tomorrow. Tuscaloosa *News* 20 Nov. p. 4/4 There are several types of teaching machines being manufactured. The most frequently seen of these resemble an oblong or rectangular metal box which sits on a table or desk in front of the student. The student fits teaching material into the box and then uses them [*sic*] at his own speed. He looks through one small window at a question pertaining to text which he has studied. He answers [t]he question in space provided and then rolls the material forward so that the answer is exposed in another small window just above the question. 1961 *Brit. Book of the Year* p. 580/2 The interest in "teaching machines" continued to gain momentum. *Sat. Rev.* 6 May p. 8/2 But there was also a lot of news here at home, especially about thinking machines, teaching machines, and even machines that write books. *Barron's* 30 Oct. p. 3/3 The teaching machine is just three years old. . . . However, not until October, 1958, when an article on teaching machine techniques by Harvard psychologist B. Frederick Skinner appeared in "Science" magazine, did the current furor begin. 1962 *Wall St. Journal* 8 Feb. p. 1/5 Teaching machine methods invade the security markets. 1963 *Family Weekly* 8 Sept. p. 1/1–2 The so-called "teaching machines" are usually no more than a box about the size of a portable record player. The preprogrammed lesson, on paper or microfilm, is loaded into the machine, which brings each "step" of the lesson into view at the turn of a knob. The student then writes in the answer to the question in the frame and pulls a lever to uncover the correct answer so he can compare it with his own.

TRANSAXLE, TRAXLE, *n.* [See quots.] See quots.—1958 N.Y. *Times* 1 June p. X21/4 The engineers call the new system a "transaxle" or a "traxle." 1960 *ibid.* 16 Oct. p. 10A/1–2 In a sense Corvair too has a transaxle, for the term is applied to any combination, in a common housing, of the transmission and differential. Engineers define transaxle as a word coined from "transmission" and "axle." In Detroit parlance this refers not only to the rear axle but to the differential housing which is an integral part of it. *Family Weekly* 16 Oct. p. 20/4 Happily, the pesky floor hump is on its way out. The Tempest, by Pontiac, is the forerunner of that welcome news. Front-engined, it has a level floor, thanks to its combination transmission and axle at the rear. This transaxle is America's first on a front-engine car.

ZINJANTHROPUS, *n.* See quots.—1959 *Newsweek* 14 Dec. p. 110/1 Last summer, British anthropologist Louis S. B. Leakey uncovered in British East Africa the remains of zinjanthropus which he considers "the first unquestionable man." Zinjanthropus had a long face, massive shoulders, spindly legs, and lived perhaps a million years ago. 1961 *NID 3*.

ZIP CODE, Z.I.P. CODE. [Zoning *I*mprovement *P*lan] A number given a postal district by the U.S. Post Office Department.—1963 N.Y. *Times* 5 May p. 86/3–4 Z.I.P. codes, for the present at least, are for big business, and more particularly big users of the mails such as publishers, banks, insurance companies and mail-order houses. Chicago *Daily News Magazine Sect.* 16 Nov. p. 7/3 (Raven I. McDavid, Jr.) "Zip code" was too late for us. . . . 1964 N.Y. *Times Book Rev.* 5 April p. 3/2 Among his petty peeves are . . . zip codes and automatic telephone dialing.

AMONG THE NEW WORDS

I. WILLIS RUSSELL
University of Alabama

ACKNOWLEDGMENTS: For citations, Clarence L. Barnhart (2), Julie Cound (2), Peggy Ann Daniels (1), E. E. Ericson (1), Stephanie Grand (1), Preston Grover (1), Ernest H. Hawkins (1), William P. Head (1), Norman R. McMillan (7), Mamie J. Meredith (7), Martha Nelson (1), Anne B. Russell (2), Jo Ann Schanbacher (1), and May L. Sims (1). Thanks are due to Edward D. Terry for the etymology of *bossa nova*. Thanks are also due to my assistant, Norman R. McMillan, who performed most of the routine, did a large part of the checking, contributed to the etymologies and definitions, and, finally, carefully prepared the typescript.

ATOMIC ROCKET, *n.* See quots.—[1949 *New Yorker* 19 March p. 25/1 . . . we're now pushing an improved model, called the Atomic Rocket. The crown of the beanie, see, is shaped like an airplane, with a pinwheel mounted in the nose.] 1950 *Fortnightly* March p. 163 Numerous theoretical studies of the "atomic rocket" have now been made, and several organizations in the United States (including the Fairchild Corporation under a contract from the Atomic Energy Commission) are working on the problem. 1958 *Think* July p. 16/1 . . . there can be little doubt that the energy needed for interplanetary operations will come from nuclear sources. Much theoretical and some practical work has been carried out on the development of the so-called atomic rocket. . . . 1964 *Sci. News Letter* 28 Nov. p. 343/1 An atomic rocket—a rocket engine powered by a nuclear reactor—could be ready to fly by 1975.

BOSSA NOVA, *n.* [Brazilian Port., 'New style.'] See quot. *Sat. Rev.*—1963 *Brit. Book of the Year* p. 855/2. 1963 *Sat. Rev.* 27 July p. 46/1 . . . I have recently been asked by several eager people: "What is this bossa nova music?" In an effort to be helpful, I have begun by saying that the term "bossa nova" was applied during the past few years to certain Brazilian musical performances characterized, among other things, by romantic atmosphere and a delicate use of propulsive rhythms in the general area of *samba rhythms*. 1964 *World Book Year Book* p. 608/2 BOS.SA NO.VA . . . a dance music of Brazil that combines the rhythm of the samba with jazz music. *Playboy* Sept. p. 46/3 *Herbie Mann/Latin Fever* (Atlantic) continues the flutist's close association with the bossa nova and kindred rhythms.

BOSSA NOVIST, *n.*—1964 *Sat. Rev.* 11 July p. 42/2 . . . but Astrud Gilberto and other bossa novists maintain that thinking is not singled out by the compliment, but, rather, the active expression of simple but inventive taste. 1965 *Encyclopedia Year Book* (N.Y.: Gaché Publishing Co.) p. 357/2 BOSSA NOVIST. One who plays bossa nova music.

BRAIN DRAIN, *n.* See quots.—1964 N.*Y. Times* 16 Feb. p. 2/3 The "brain drain," as the departure of scientists is called here, is not new to Britain. For decades, foreign universities and other institutions of learning and research, especially in the United States, have been drawing scientific talent from Britain. Newscaster on CBS 23 Feb. N.Y. *Times* 1 March p. 22/1 British scholars and scientists are leaving their country by the country [*sic*] for better paying jobs in the United States. Professor Lattimore represents something of a "brain drain" in reverse. N.Y. *Times Mag.* 22 March p. 13 (heading and subheading) A British "Brain" Explains the "Brain Drain" An eminent scientist examines the reasons why so many of his colleagues are emigrating to the United States—to the consternation of Britain's scientific community. Tuscaloosa *News* 8 July p. 8/5 (AP) Part of the problem, one of the major factors, is that there is a "brain drain" from the farms into the cities where life is better.

CAP COM, *n.* A capsule communicator (which see).

CAPSULE COMMUNICATOR, *n.* See quots.—1961 Seattle *Times* 17 July p. 1 (UPI) Shepard will be the capsule communicator (the man who talks to the pilot in the capsule during flight). 1962 *Life* 26 Oct. p. 41/1 Deke Slayton, that cool and reassuring expert on the booster's operation who was now reacting as my Cap Com (Capsule Communicator) in the control center, came through on the radio with a joke almost immediately. 1965 Montgomery *Advertiser* 1 June p. 3/2 (AP) A capsule communicator—the man who actually talks with the astronauts—is stationed at the command communicator console. Tuscaloosa *News* 17 June p. 17/1 "CAPCOM" is an abbreviation of "capsule communicator." Normally, he is an astronaut, but in some cases an engineer, stationed in the flight control center in the tracking stations along the worldwide network. CAPCOM is the only individual designated to talk with astronauts orbiting overhead.

CHASE, (AIR) PLANE, AIRCRAFT, *n.* [Cf. *OED*, s.v. *chase*, *sb.*[1]: '1. The action of chasing or pursuing with intent to catch. . . .' {1297}; *OEDS*, s.v. *chaser*, *sb.*, 6: 'A small, light, usually single-seated military aeroplane of great speed and climbing power, used in repelling hostile aircraft.' {1915}] See 1956 quot.—1949 *Time* 18 April p. 64/3 Followed by two F-80 "chase airplanes" (to observe the X-1 in flight), the B-29 circled to 7,000 ft. above the lake. *Ibid.* 18 April p. 65/1 Cardenas called the last warning to all radio listeners: "B-29 eight zero zero to NACA radar, Muroc Tower, F-80 chase aircraft. One minute warning." 1956 *Life* 18 June p. 78/2 The F-86s are not of course undergoing tests, having been in the Air Force for some years. They are used as 'chase planes': when a new aircraft is tested, one or two F-86s will follow it very closely through the air, their pilots radioing observations and advice to the test pilot. 1963 Hugh Downs on "Today" on NBC 26 Sept.

COMPLEX, *n.* [Cf. *OED*, s.v. *complex*, *sb.*: '1. A whole comprehending in its compass a number of parts, *esp.* (in later use) of interconnected parts or involved particulars. . . .' {*a* 1652}; *NID* 3, s.v. [3]*complex*, 1, a-e.] *Specif.* See quots.—1952 N.Y. *Times* 6 May p. 2/6 Ten medium bombers . . . using electronic techniques, last (Saturday) night dropped 100 tons of high explosives on to the rail bridge complex at Chongju . . . 1955 *ibid.* 20 Feb. 20/3–4 Although most of the details of the pipeline construction are secret, it is understood that six vast storage areas are planned along its route . . . Each of these storage areas, known as complexes, consists of a series of smaller units known as farms. Each farm, in turn, consists of several storage tanks with a pump house. 1964 *ibid.* 26 Jan. p. 1XX/2 . . . and soon I was slipping along at 60 miles an hour (the speed limit) through the industrial complex of metropolitan New Jersey. *Ibid.* 17 May p. E9/1 Elementary schooling would continue to take place in the children's immediate neighborhood, even if this meant segregation. But beginning with middle school, an attempt would be made, through the establishment of "complexes" or clusters of schools, to feed youngsters from both white and Negro neighborhoods into these larger campus-type institutions. Cleveland *Plain Dealer* 26 May Rocky River City Council last night approved zoning changes for construction of an $8-million complex of apartments and a $20 million shopping center. 1965 N.Y. *Times Book Rev.* 3 Jan. p. 23/1 On a highway complex as big as this one it is hard to get turned around.

DINOSAUR, *n.* [See second quot.] See quots. (Also attrib.)—1961 N.Y. *Times* 16 April p. E9/7 Because of its very short half-life, element 103, according to one theory, is a "dinosaur" element which was formed at the birth of the universe but which decayed out of existence in a few weeks. *Think* Sept. p. 2/2 . . . heavy elements, not existing since the earth was formed 5,000,000 years ago. (Such elements, according to one theory, are "dinosaurs" of matter. They were created with the universe, but were decayed out of existence within a few weeks time.) 1963 *World Book Year Book* p. 396/1 DINOSAUR ELEMENT. An element that came into being when the universe originated and which deteriorated almost immediately.

DISCO, *n.* Short for *discotheque*. (Also attrib.)—1964 *Playboy* Sept. 55/3 Los Angeles has emerged with the biggest and brassiest of the discos . . . *Glamour* Oct. The dress is black wool crepe, and Nicole wears it dancing with Pipart at Paris's disco of discos, the New Jimmy's.

DISCOTHEQUE, DISCOTHÈQUE, *n.* [Cf. *Nouveau Petit Larousse Illustré* (Paris, 1952) s.v. *discothèque*, *n. f.*: 'Collection de disque de phonographe; meuble destiner à la contenir.'; 'a dance hall the music for which is supplied by recorded music' (reported by my colleague C. Beaumont Wicks as being in use in Paris 1961–62).] **1.** See quots.—1964 *Playboy* Sept. 54/2 As if you didn't know by now, the most dynamic development on the U. S. nightclub scene in years is the discothèque—a place in which to dance to both live and recorded music. *Mademoiselle* Sept. p. 164 What's it like in the discothèques these nights? There's a new dance, the Ska—like The Game set to music. A new jukebox, the Scopitone—like a sight-track for sound. And a new way of dressing—like, wild! . . . *TV Guide* Dec. 12–18 p. 19/1 A discotheque is a small, intimate night club that plays recorded music for dancing—and discotheque dresses make dancing the frug, the monkey, and the Watusi a delight because they move with the beat. *Look* 15 Dec. p. 37/1 Nightclub proprietors, by installing record players to replace live bands and adopting the French name "discothèque," have created the legend that this is where the action is. N.Y. *Times Mag.* 27 Dec. p. 12/2–3 (pict. cap.) L'interdit—"The Forbidden," at the Gotham Hotel, is one of New York's pioneer discotheques. It operates on the theory that if it attracts young people who know all the dances, and dance them expertly, others will come to watch. So records are played, one drinks, and one dances or looks on—depending upon age. N.Y. *Times Mag.* 27 Dec. p. 12/2–3 (pict. cap.) El Morocco—For 33 years, Morocco has been the heart beat of New York cafe society. This is the Champagne Room on the second floor; downstairs are the main room (with the well-known zebra-striped banquettes) and the newly opened Garrison Club, a discotheque, following the current trend to places that offer only a record player for entertainment. 1965 N.Y. *Times Book Rev.* 31 Jan. p. 42/4 (adv.) The gorgeous Go-Go girls are your escorts to the discotheque that swings with the latest in dance crazes—see them all in color. **2.** *Attrib.* See quots.—1964 N.Y. *Times* 26 July p. F 11/3 Ensembles are doing well, the buying offices report, and the "discotheque look," a dressy cocktail-type dress, is gaining favor. Tuscaloosa *News* 9 Aug. p. 29/4 The discotheque dress is almost always black, often crepe (but sheer wool, velvet, chiffon or brocade will fill the bill too), and must have a daring neckline. Skirts are mobile to dance in, the smartest have something going at the hemline. Flounces, fluting, ruching, petals, beading or embroidery all make a focal point of legs and feet. These dresses are worn a mite shorter too—right in the middle of the kneecap. It's the new young way to look atter [*sic*] dark.

DISCOTHEQUENIK, *n.* [*discotheque* + *-nik* (*Am. Sp.* 37: 41, n. 1)] See quot.—1964 *Playboy* Sept. p. 54/2 The menu is French and pleasant, but hardly distinguished, which matters little, since sustenance is the last thing on most discothequenik's minds.

EIGHTFOLD WAY. See quots.—1965 N.Y. *Times* 31 Jan. p. 6E/6–7 It was then found, in 1961, that a more complex form, SU (3), could be used to arrange the particles into symmetrical groups of eight (and, in one case, ten). The patterns predicted the existence of another particle, the Omega minus, and its characteristics. The announcement of its discovery, a year ago, gave added weight to the arrangement, popularly known as the "eightfold way." *Sci. News Letter* 6 Feb. p. 85/1 Discovery of the new theory, reported to the American Physical Society meeting in New York, follows less than a year after the confirmation of the SU-3 theory, or eightfold way. *Sci. News Letter* 6 Feb. p. 85/1 Early in 1964 order was brought to the nuclear "jungle" by the SU-3 theory under which the 100 or so known nuclear particles are grouped into families, or multiplets, of eight and ten members. Each eight-fold way multiplet consists of several sub-groups of particles having the same mass, hypercharge and isotopic spin. A rule explaining how the masses of the sub-groups differ binds them together into a multiplet.

FREEDOM, *attrib.* [Cf. *freedom fighter.*] Concerning an organized protest of racial segregation or one who takes part in such a protest.—FREEDOM RIDE.—1961 N.Y. *Times* 20 Aug. p. 2E/6 Civil-rights leaders say that the "stand-ins" will be an addition to, not a substitute for, sit-ins and Freedom Rides. The latter are expected to continue until bus-terminal segregation ends, whatever the outcome of current legal efforts by the U. S. and by civil rights organizations. *1963 ibid.* 5 May p. E1/3–4 The weapons are sit-ins, demonstrations, boycotts, protest parades, freedom rides. *1964 World Book Year Book* p. 609/1. FREE-DOM RIDER.—1961 *Tuscaloosa News* 21 May p. 1/1–2 (AP) A young white ministerial student from Wisconsin who said he came south only as an observer was one of the "Freedom Riders" most severely beaten Saturday by a mob in Montgomery. *Life* June p. 46 The Freedom Riders were deliberately and knowingly asking for trouble. . . . The ride was another weapon in the Negroes' nonviolent—and carefully planned—fight for civil rights, a fight that was reminiscent of Gandhi's passive resistance in India. N.Y. *Times* 4 June p. E10/1 (edit.) The demonstrations of the Freedom Riders have already resulted in a major advance. *Friends Journal* 15 June p. 251/2 The Freedom Riders will not wait for administrative initiative to support the Constitution. FREEDOM STAY-OUT.—1964 *Tuscaloosa News* 26 Feb. p. 25/1 Leaders of the movement call it a "freedom stay-out." FREEDOM WALKER. —1963 N.Y. *Times Mag.* 9 June p. 80/4–5 (pict. cap.) In Alabama—A Freedom Walker is arrested at the state line.

GEM, *n.* [Cf. *NID* 3 s. v. *ground effect.*] Short for *ground effect machine.*—1961 N.Y. *Times* 2 April p. 6A GEM means Ground Effect Machine. These devices, which are still under study, skim over the ground or water on streams of air, which propel them at speeds up to 175 miles an hour. *1965 Sci. News Letter* 16 Jan. p. 38/1–2 (pict. cap.) Called a ground effect-machine (GEM), it was designed by Vickers, England, and is being marketed by Republic Aerospace, New York.

GOLDWATERISM, *n.* [Barry M. *Goldwater* + *-ism*] See quots.—1964 *Tuscaloosa News* 12 July p. 4/3 A really through-going Goldwaterism at home would not, however, be merely amiable and picturesque nostalgia, like rebuilding Williamsburg or the Wayside Inn. Without doubt, Goldwaterism applied rigorously at home would provoke some social disorder. For the congested urban masses cannot live in a loose 19th-century social order. *Ibid.* 12 July p. 4/4 (Walter Lippmann) Yet Goldwaterism at home, the longing to restore America as it was before this century, makes sense only if we can also restore the world as it was before the great wars and the great revolutions and the population explosion and the technical developments of the 20th century. N.Y. *Times* 30 Aug. p. 10E/1 (edit.) . . . the more important aspect of Goldwaterism lies in another direction. This is its essentially negative, almost nihilistic, approach—a kind of reactionary radicalism of the right, which has nothing to do with genuine conservatism and is totally out of consonance with the political, social and economic philosophy on which American institutions have been built in this century and under which they are flourishing today. *Ibid.* 13 Sept. p. 12E/5 (letter) Goldwaterism uses liberty as a weapon against any effort by the Federal Government to oblige the affluent to help the needy—all it suggests is "voluntary" schemes to which the rich would not have to contribute and to which the poor could bring only their poverty. *Ibid.* 18 Oct. p. 10E/2 (edit.) His [Senator Keating's] re-election, if accompanied—as we hope it will be—by an overwhelming electoral victory for President Johnson in this state, will represent the most forceful rebuff New Yorkers can administer to Goldwaterism, with all its corrosive impact on the centrist tradition of American politics. *New Republic* 31 Oct. p. 4/2.

GOLDWATERITE, *n.* [Barry M. *Goldwater* + *-ite*] An adherent of *Goldwaterism* (which see).—1964 N.Y. *Times* 13 Sept. p. 12E/5 (letter) Goldwaterites talk as if a gang of left-wingers—altogether bleeding hearts, softheads, and devilishly tricky operators—had for thirty years perverted our Constitution and corrupted our traditions. *Newsweek* 16 Nov. p. 35 Across the nation, indeed, it was GOP moderates who profited most by ticket-splitting—and the Goldwaterites who gained the least. *Time* 9 Oct. p. 30/3 (pict. cap.) Goldwaterites in Paris.

HARDLINER, *n.* See second quot.—1963 *Sat. Rev.* 25 May p. 22/2 The fact that war has now become an instrument of mutual suicide and possibly even global disaster has made no dent in the thinking of hardliners. *1964 Encyclopedia Year Book* p. 365/2 HARDLINER, *n.* One who persists in a line of thinking, regardless of the consequences. Wells Hangen NBC News London 15 Oct.

HOMO HABILIS, *n.* [See first quot.] See quots.—1964 N.Y. *Times* 5 April p. E7/8 A name was given last week to the creature that many consider the oldest known ancestor of man. It is Homo habilis, based on the Latin word that indicates skillfulness. Fossil remnants of Homo habilis have been found during recent years, by Dr. Louis S. B. Leakey and his wife. Homo habilis is thought to have lived in East Africa 1,750,000 years ago. *Ibid.* June p. 40 A British specialist doubts that the creature, named Homo habilis, should be classed as a distinct early species of man at all. He believes it should probably be classed as a sub-species of the African man-apes, or near-men called Australopithecines. *1965 World Book Year Book* p. 546/1 HOMO HABILIS. Name given to fossil remains of what has been asserted to be an ancestor of man who lived about 2,000,000 years ago.

HOMO TRANSVAALENSIS, *n.* See quots.—1965 *Nature* 9 Jan. p. 123/2 (J. T. Robinson) The first [species] could be *H. transvaalensis* and would include the tool-using phase of the lineage involving small-brained forms which were primarily tool-using, had relatively poor communication and comparatively simple social structure. *Sci. News Letter* 30 Jan. p. 73/1 In reassessing material presented by Dr. Louis S. B. Leakey, British anthropologist who discovered in eastern Africa the skull of a new species which he named *Homo habilis*, Dr. Robinson proposes a new name: *Homo transvaalensis*.

LATCHKEY, *attrib.* [Cf. *OEDS*, s. v. *Latch-key*: 'Freq. allusive, with reference to the use of a latchkey by a younger member of a household or a lodger.' {1902}] See quots.—1944 NBC *Bulletin of Public Service Broadcasting*, Jan. Program No. 5, Feb. 12 in a series entitled 'Here's to Youth' is 'Latchkey Children.' Ten important national voluntary agencies concerned with young people and their problems are cooperating in this series of dramatized programs directed towards promoting the most intelligent thinking to deal effectively with present conditions. *1946 Life* 8 April p. 90/2 His was a latchkey existence, a world of unsympathetic schools, truancy. . . . *1955 Sat. Eve. Post* 12 March p. 18/3 The chief emphasis of Bob's missionary endeavor was help for the "latchkey kids," the social work term for youngsters who roam without supervision, rear themselves, are chiefly from indifferent or broken homes and are either a problem or a burden to their guardians. *1959 N.Y. Daily News* 7 June p. B24/2 Half of the new students speak no English. Many are "latchkey children" who must carry keys because their mothers are at work when school lets out. *1961 N.Y. Times* 5 Feb. p. 53/1–2 Almost half a million "latchkey" children under 12 are completely on their own during their mother's working hours.

LEM, *n.* [See quots.] See quots.—1964 Reported by Frank Blair on "Today" on NBC 2 March. N.Y. *Times* 2 Aug. p. 10E/3–4 (pict. cap.) LEM: Three men will orbit moon in Apollo. Two of them will transfer to Lunar Excursion Module for trip to moon, then rendezvous with Apollo for return to earth. *1965 Newsweek* 8 March p. 57/1 At first, it looks hardly suitable for landing a 15-ton Lunar Excursion Module and its two passengers. But the LEM has four "feet" which are spread wide enough apart to keep it from tipping over. . . .

MICROELECTRONICS, *n.* See quots.—1961 *Life* 10 March p. 60/1 The housefly below has been put in a world where it looms like a giant, a world where even light bulbs are smaller than its tiny eye. This strange Lilliput is the creation of a new science, micro-electronics, which is already out-moding the revolutions wrought by vacuum tubes and transistors. Through microelectronics, the inside of a TV set may in a decade or two be wonderfully simplified—no tangle of wires and tubes, just two or three chips of crystal engraved and etched like jewelry.—1964 N.Y. *Times* 6 Dec. p. F1/3 It moves under various descriptions—microelectronics, modular electronics, integrated circuits and many other names.

MICROMETEOROID, *n.* See quots.—1959 Woodford A. Heflin (ed.), *Aerospace*

Glossary (Maxwell [Ala.] Air Force Base: Research Studies Institute, Air University) p. 64/2 MICROMETEOROID, *n.* A very small meteoroid, esp. as encountered by earth satellites, probes, or the like. 1961 *Tuscaloosa News* 27 Aug. p. 1/3 (AP) NASA officials said the wider spread means the satellite has more of an opportunity to check on the tiny space bullets called "micrometeoroids" at different altitudes. *1964 World Book Year Book* p. 610/2. 1965 *Time* 26 Feb. p. 58/1 So frail that it can hold its shape at weightless, airless altitudes, that wide wing is the working element of a satellite . . . for detecting micrometeoroids.

AMONG THE NEW WORDS

I. WILLIS RUSSELL
University of Alabama

(With the assistance of Norman R. McMillan)

Reference to the entry *chimp(o)naut* and the citations under *-naut* will disclose an interesting new formative element. It may have become implicit in the word *astronaut*, formed, according to the *NID* 3, from "*astr-* + *-naut* (as in *aeronaut*)" and defined in one sense as 'a traveler in interplanetary space.' *Aeronaut* itself is generally considered to be a borrowing from the French *aéronaute* (Gr. *aēr(o)-* + *nautēs* 'sailor'). It is defined by the *OED* as 'one who sails through the air, or who makes balloon ascents,' by the *NID* 3 as 'one that operates or travels in an airship or balloon.'

Though perhaps the astronauts began as 'travelers in interplanetary space,' they have more and more become explorers, and with the word in this connotation is almost immediately associated another, *Argonaut*, one who, if not an actual explorer, came to be considered 'an adventurer or traveler engaged in a particular quest' (*NID* 3, b). Hence we arrive at the use of *-naut* added to another word element to denote 'one who explores or investigates; that which is employed in exploration or investigation.' It is, possibly, to be described as a combining form.

Despite the fact that *plastiqueur* is apparently not yet an English word, the two citations in English publications perhaps justify its inclusion in the glossary along with *plastic bomb* and *plastic bombing*. Its formation would presumably parallel that of English agent nouns, viz., *plastique* + *-eur*. No French dictionary available to me lists *plastique* in the sense given in the etymology of *plastic bomb* in the glossary. The *Larousse Modern French-English Dictionary* (N. Y.: McGraw Hill Book Co., 1960) has the sense 'plastic goods.'

The number of citations of *megabuck* may seem disproportionate for such a simply defined term. They are included for the light they throw on attitudes. Even after nineteen years, a writer still regards the term as slang. In this connection there comes to mind a remark that James B. McMillan once made (*Coll. Eng.*, 10: 217/1) to the effect that the slang label might better be used only for "short-lived novelties."

ACKNOWLEDGMENTS: For citations, H. Alexander (1), T. L. Crowell (1), O. B. Emerson (1), E. E. Ericson (1), Rex Everage (1), Ernest H. Hawkins (2), Alice C. Kingery (1), Raven I. McDavid (2), James Macris (1), Mamie J. Meredith (7), Porter G. Perrin (7), Anne B. Russell (3), and R. M. Wallace

(2). C. Beaumont Wicks contributed to the remarks on *plastiqueur*, and Charles L. Seebeck, Jr., composed the definition of *real time*.

BIODEGRADABLE, *adj.* [*bio-* + ¹*degrade* (cf. *v.t.* 6 and *v.i.* 4 in *NID 3*) + *-able*] See quots.—1964 Texize Chemicals, Inc. "Interim Report on Operations for Six Months Ended May 2, 1964," 29 May. We are now preparing to market a remarkable new light-duty liquid detergent product that is biodegradable, referred to as a "soft" detergent. 1965 *Encyclopedia Year Book* (N.Y.: Gaché Publishing Co.) p. 357/1 BIODEGRADABLE, *adj.* Said of a detergent whose chemicals are quickly destroyed or broken down by the bacteria found in soil and water.

BIOTRON, *n.* [Cf. *OEDS*, *s.v. Biotron 'Wireless Telegr.'* {1926} The biological term seems more likely to be formed by analogy with *phytotron*, as suggested by the first quot.] See quots.—1958 *Science* 5 Sept. p. 510/3 (S. B. Hendricks and F. W. Went) The phytotron has been generally accepted as an experimental tool, comparable to telescopes, particle accelerators, fossil collections, and other tools of science. Interest in such facilities . . . has also been expressed by others experimenting with animals; thus the concept of a "biotron" developed. 1959 *New International Year Book* (New York: Funk & Wagnalls Co.) p. 554/1. 1964 N.Y. *Times* 31 May p. E7/8 Final approval has been given for the construction of a "Biotron" at the University of Wisconsin. The building will be designed for the study of living organisms in a wide variety of environments.

CHIMP(O)NAUT, *n.* [*chimp*anzee + *-naut* (see preliminary remarks and *-naut* in the glossary)] See quots.—1961 Des Moines *Register* 30 Nov. p. 6/2 Chimpnaut Enos has said very little about his experience in orbit, but for solid information, his report is about as enlightening as those of the Russian cosmonauts at that. 1962 N.Y. *Journal-American* 14 May p. 8/5–7 (heading and subheading) [Dr. James A.] Van Allen downgrades spacemen[.] Prefers chimponauts. Tuscaloosa *News* 17 June p. 26/6–7 Because of the close similarity between chimpanzees and men, the chimponauts are expected to keep pioneering the way for man in space—perhaps all the way to the moon. 1965 *World Book Year Book* p. 546/1.

COUNTER-ESCALATION, *n.* See *escalation.*—1965 *Newsweek* 7 June p. 55/3 However, the Soviets now begin to take a more active role in the defense of North Vietnam, simultaneously hinting at counter-escalations against the West elsewhere in the world. . . .

ESCALATE, *v.t. & i.* [Cf. *escalate* and *escalation* in *NID 3*.] See last quot.—1964 Chet Huntley over NBC 8 June The war in Laos has been escalated. . . . Tuscaloosa *News* 27 June p. 4/2 No, it is not 1914 in the Far East. The present unacknowledged war might indeed be "escalated." But—again assuming rationality in Peking—it could hardly "escalate" too violently. *World Book Year Book* p. 608/3. 1965 Tuscaloosa *News* 15 Feb. p. 2/2 (AP) The fact that the Viet Nam crisis did not escalate into anything worse over the weekend was a reassuring factor. N.Y. *Times* 11 April p. 14E/3 "Escalate" means "step up the war," but again anybody can say, "We've stepped up the war in Asia," without giving the impression that all he knows is what he reads in the newspapers.

ESCALATION, *n.*—1961 *Nation* 4 March p. 181/2 But wars, large or small, are fought for victory. That means you pound the enemy with every available lethal assistance, with the inevitable result—to use the fancy new term—of escalation to all-out war. Limited war is a contradiction of terms. It is an illusion of limited minds. 1965 *Newsweek* 7 June p. 54/3 Kahn's odd brand of liberalism strongly colors his latest book, "On Escalation: Metaphors and Scenarios" (*308 pages. Frederic A. Praeger. $6.95*), a searching exploration of modern nuclear strategy.

GOLDWATERISM, *n.* See *Am. Sp.* 40: 144. Add earlier quots.— 1960 *Nation* 9 July p. 25/2 (letter from Barry M. Goldwater) A bit further along Mr. Spivack asks [*Nation* 18 June p. 531/3]: "How deep is Goldwaterism? And what does it portend for the future of the GOP?" That is the end of any discussion of my Republican philosophy. What he has done here is to resort to a word—"Goldwaterism"—hoping that, without explanation, it will mean something to the general public.

HARD, *adj.* [Cf. *OED*, s.v. *hard, adj.*, 14.a: 'Applied to water holding in solution mineral, especially calcareous, salts, which decompose soap and render the water unfit for washing purposes' {1660–}] See quot.—1964 N.Y. *Times* 2 Aug. p. E7/7–8 An end may be in sight to the pollution of the nation's underground water supplies by the foamy "hard" detergents. Those chemicals, which are not easily degraded by natural biological processes in the soil they pass through, have been putting heads of foam on lakes and streams, blowing as froth over the countryside and even streaming sudsily out of drinking faucets.

INNER SPACE, *n.* [Cf. *inner space*, 'the sea' (*Am. Sp.* 35: 285)] See quots.—1958 *Sat. Rev.* 13 Sept. p. 28/2 Must this inner space continue to be peopled with imaginative dragons of strange color and dropping off places that confine the moral venture to the shallow water of one's own mainland or adjacent islands of narrow self-interest? Must the haunting emptiness of inner space isolating man from man and nation from nation continue to be the dominant theme of poet, prophet, and philosopher in our time? 1961 N.Y. *Times Book Rev.* 14 May p. 7/1–2 In "Exploring Inner Space," "a nationally known writer chose to use the pseudonym Jane Dunlap" for the purpose of relating her "personal experiences under LSD-25," lysergic acid diethylamide, a drug that induces psychotic-like reactions. 1962 N.Y. *Times* 1 July p. E7/2 (cartoon cap.) "Anybody worried about inner space?" 1963 *Friends Journal* 1 Feb. p. 53/1 Fifth, exploring "inner space" of the "beyond within" appears to be no armchair diversion for the timorous. It takes uncommon audacity to venture into the unknown. Outer space has captured the public fancy, but probing the beyond within is just as daring a pursuit as piloting a space ship, with as many rigors, demanding every ounce of a person's courage, skill, and determination. *Ibid.* 1 Nov. p. 465/1 An article in the Friends Journal of February 1, 1963, "Exploring Inner Space," by G. M. Smith, tells of a group of people who met at Pendle Hill with a Japanese Zen Buddhist to learn oriental ways of meditation. The article suggests that this sort of training might be given to groups of Friends to deepen the spiritual life of our Meetings. I would like to point out that the new depth psychology, coming to us from Europe, offers a method of spiritual growth that is more suited to our western minds. 1964 *Encyclopedia Year Book* p. 365/2 INNER SPACE. The limitless depths of the personality.

MEGABUCK, *n.* [*mega-* 'million' + *buck* 'dollar'] See quots. (Also attrib.)—1946 London *Picture Post* 7 Dec. p. 10 They have laughingly coined the term 'megabuck'—one megabuck equals a million dollars. 1950 *Sat. Eve. Post* 18 Feb. p. 111/1 The Mark trio, which cost more than $1,000,000—a "megabuck" or "kilogrand," as mathematicians say facetiously—work twenty-four hours a day, seven days a week. 1951 N.Y. *Times Mag.* 22 April p. 35/4–5 Megabuck: Today this unofficial term is as frequent in modern physics as its predecessor, "kilobuck," which is a scientist's idea of a short way to say "a thousand dollars." A fifty-megabuck ($50,000,000) laboratory is today a common-place. Mega means "great" in Greek, "million" as used here. *Fortune* July p. 138 It has recently been estimated that all that would be required to build a pilot model of a completely electronic record-keeping system is one 'megabuck'—$1 million. 1952 N.Y. *Times* 21 Dec. p. E7/7 (The cosmotron cost about three and one-half "megabucks"—a megabuck being physicist's slang for $1,000,000.) 1953 Seattle *Times* 24 June p. 6 And what is a megabuck? It is a million dollars—as in the sentence, "it will cost so and so many thousand megabucks to deliver (or to prevent) an attack of X-megaton power, which may be expected to result in Y-megadeaths." 1954 *Life* 12 April p. 27 Scientists, preparing to measure the force of the explosion in megatons (1 megaton is 1 million tons of TNT), measured the cost facetiously in megabucks. 1956 N.Y. *Times* 18 Nov. p. 46/3 This, with other equipment, including the half-mile tunnel, the subterranean target building, the building for the remote control of the machine, a large administration building and a power house with a 30,000-kilowatt generator, will bring the total cost of the machine to $26,000,000, or 26 "megabucks" in the terminology of the scientists. 1958 *New Republic* 27 Jan. p. 10 We are living in what Von Neumann called the Megabuck or Kilogrand era. 1963 Mencken-McDavid *The American Language* (N.Y.: A. A. Knopf) p. 232 Nuclear physicists talk cheerfully of . . . the cost of apparatus in *megabucks*. . . . 1965 Tuscaloosa *News* 16 June In atomic age slang, $1 million is a megabuck.

MONOKINI, *n.* [*mono-* + *bikini*] Skimpy bathing trunks for men.—1964 *Time* 7 Aug. p. 36/3 Betweentimes, they had themselves a ball sunbathing at Beirut's Saint Simon Beach, she in a bikini that was utterly tutu, he in a monokini that was, as they say in London, utterly twee. 1965 *Encyclopedia Year Book* p. 357/2. *Newsweek* 7 June p. 80/1 The monokini already had gone the way of the bikini.

MOON SHIP, MOONSHIP, *n.* See quots.—1951 Tuscaloosa *News* 21 Oct. p. 25/6 (UP) Actually, he said, there probably will be three types of space ships—a ferry or "local" ship to take man outside the atmosphere, a moon ship sent up to the artificial satellite or even built there to make the flights to the moon where another tanker might refuel it for the trip back, and deep space ships which would be built in space and stay there. 1958 *Life* 6 Jan. p. 65 The moon ship, designed for exploration trips around the moon, is composed mainly of a cluster of chemical fuel tanks. [Remainder of quot. fully describes the moon ship.] 1959 Woodford A. Heflin (ed.), *Aerospace Glossary* (Maxwell [Ala.] Air Force Base: Research Studies Institute, Air University) p. 67/2 MOONSHIP, *n.* A spacecraft designed for travel to the moon. 1964 N.Y. *Times* 16 Aug. p. 9/4 The Saturn will carry a dummy Apollo moonship into orbit for the second time.

NAB, *n.* [*nut* + *and* + *bolt*] See quots.—1963 *Life* 27 Sept. p. 37 The other idea is to outfit him with a weird, new array of tools . . . a technician . . . tries out a NAB (Nuts and Bolts) which works very much like a ZERT. . . . (which see) 1964 *National Geographic* March p. 380/1–2 At right, a special wrench called nab (short for nut and bolt) allows him to apply twisting force to the bolt without moving his body. 1965 *Newsweek* 14 June p. 34/3 Some of the hardware is small, like the tool called nab (a contraction of nut and bolt), for use in weightless space.

-NAUT. See quots. and preliminary remarks.—ALUMINAUT. 1964 N.Y. *Times* 30 Aug. p. 81/1 Hamilton, Bermuda, Aug. 29—An important new weapon will be added to man's armory for exploration and research exploitation of ocean depths on Wednesday when the Aluminaut is launched at Groton, Conn. The Aluminaut, being built by the Electric Boat Company, is 50 feet long and designed to descend 15,000 feet and travel underwater for 100 miles. In Bermuda at the moment is the father of the vessel, Louis Reynolds, chairman of the board of Reynolds Metals, owner of the submarine. BATHYNAUT. 1961 N.Y. *Times Book Rev.* 5 Feb. p. 7/5 As the deep-ship crept down into its last fathom—its dangling guide rope coiling on the red ooze, its lanterns wan in the primordial dark—the bathynauts saw a fish, not a nightmare of a creature suited to the place but a prosaic flatfish like a sole, with a pair of normal-looking and wholly unaccountable eyes. Slowly, too, Piccard and Walsh shook hands. HYDRONAUT. 1961 N.Y. *Times Book Rev.* 25 June p. 20/4 *130 FEET DOWN: Handbook for Hydronauts.* By Hank and Shaney Frey. Illustrated. 274 pp. New York: Harcourt, Brace & World. $6.50. Basic information for those who wish to explore the underwater world. PLASTINAUT. [See quots. s.v. in *Am. Sp.* 39: 146.] 1964 *Missiles and Rockets* 10 Feb. p. 35/3 . . . the Air Force "plastinaut," a plastic dummy whose tissue characteristics simulate man's, could be orbited in the early unmanned check-out of the MOL [Manned Orbiting Laboratory] to get exact radiation data. (1965 *Encyclopedia Year Book*, p. 357/2.)

NERVA, N.E.R.V.A., *n.* [See first quot.] See quots. (Also attrib.)—1961 Seattle *Times Mag.* 2 July p. 17 Research results will be used in the fabrication of the first flyable nuclear-rocket engine, called N.E.R.V.A. (an acronym for Nuclear Engine for Rocket Vehicle Application). 1962 *Brit. Book of the Year* p. 742/2. N.Y. *Times* 7 Oct. p. E7/8 A major step in the development of NERVA, the A. E. C. states in its 1962 report to Congress, will be the initial inflight test series "which may reasonably be anticipated in the 1966–67 period." It is presently planned to test a NERVA engine in an upper-stage of a Saturn launch vehicle. The flight-test vehicle would be lifted off the ground by the chemical booster and the nuclear engine would start as the chemical booster finished firing. 1964 *Sci. News Letter* 28 Nov. p. 343/1 Tests for the Westinghouse-developed NERVA reactor (Nuclear Engine for Rocket Vehicle Application) have already shown a specific impulse—the rocket equivalent of miles-per-gallon or efficiency—better than twice as great as that of equally powerful chemically-powered engines.

NEUTRON STAR, *n.* See quots.—1952 *Time* 14 July p. 51/1 But when the excitement was over, the only thing left would be a "neutron-star": a ball of peculiar matter made largely or entirely of neutrons. 1964 N.Y. *Times* 12 Jan. p. E11/7 The new technique of rocket astronomy has disclosed what seem to be the most "solid" objects ever observed. They are thought to be stars composed entirely of closely packed neutrons, weighing from 10 to 100 billion tons per cubic inch. It has been calculated that such neutron stars must be from five to ten miles in diameter, with a weight comparable to that of the entire sun. Tuscaloosa *News* 27 April p. 1/5–6 (AP) . . . the novel experiment is designed to prove or disprove this theory: That mysterious, celestial X-rays, discovered last summer by another rocket flight, are generated "neutron stars." These are believed to be the ultimate remnants of supernovae, or exploding stars.

NUKE, *n.* [From *nuclear*.] See quots.—1959 N.Y. *Times Mag.* 1 Feb. p. 46/3 . . . soon there may be 5-inch nuclear shells and portable Davy Crockett "nukes" for the infantryman. 1960 *Time* 4 July p. 52/1 But the nuclear submarines—called "nukes"—can cruise underwater for weeks at top speed. 1964 *Time* 25 Sept. p. 16/2 G . . . has described these tactical "nukes" as "conventional—any weapon carried by an infantryman or a team of infantrymen." *U. S. News & World Report* 19 Oct. p. 46 All the "tactical nukes" now are said to require a personal go-ahead from the President before they can be fired.

OP-, OP ART, *n.* See quots.—1964 *Life* 11 Dec. p. 133 Op-art is short for "optical art," a paradoxical movement dedicated to the practice of fascinating deceptions. *Reporter* 14 Jan. p. 46/3 But they do have the beginnings of Pop Art and Op Art (Optical Art), and since a copy of *Art International* mailed from Zurich will reach Tel Aviv in ten or twelve days, there is no reason for any lag. 1965 *Sat. Rev.* 29 May p. 29/3 Though Albers has been called the father of op art, I find this an unjust label. His delicately balanced paintings are not based on obvious optical rules, nor is he trying to shock our eyes merely by illusive tricks. *Ibid.* 5 June p. 6/2 Well, we've had pop art and op art, and we suppose it's only simple computer logic to expect the next step . . . Tuscaloosa *News* 4 July Sunday Comics ("Buzz Sawyer" by Roy Crane) What's "op" art? It's a new movement, Sir. "Op" stands for optical. It's intended to dazzle the eye and give illusion of motion.

OPSTER, *n.* [*op* art + *-ster*]—1965 *Sat. Rev.* 29 May p. 29/3 It would seem that two older artists have been curiously misunderstood—Albers by the "opsters" and Duchamp by the "popsters."

PHYTOTRON, *n.* [*phyto-* 'plant' + *-tron* (see *NID 3* and first quot. s.v. *biotron*)] See quots. and *biotron* above.—1949 *New Words and Words in the News* (Funk & Wagnalls Co.) Supp. No. 3 Fall p. 3/1. *Newsweek* 20 June p. 54 The laboratory, called the 'phytotron,' . . . creates 'weather' by closing switches and pushing buttons on an intricate control board. 1950 *Brit. Book of the Year* p. 740/1. 1958 *Science* 5 Sept. p. 510/2–3 The first facility for the study of plant growth under a wide range of controlled conditions was constructed at California Institute of Technology in Pasadena, in 1948–49. This facility was dubbed a "phytotron" in a humorous moment, but the term was so appropriate that it has endured. The variables under control are chiefly ranges of temperature, light intensities, and cycles of these variables.

PLASTIC BOMB, *n.* [Fr. *plastique*, *Specif.* An explosive the consistency of putty that combines TNT and hexogen (1962 N.Y. *Times Mag.* 4 Feb. p. 10/1; *Newsweek* 5 Feb. p. 37/2)]. See etymology and quots. (Also fig.)—1962 Douglas Edwards on CBS News 22 Jan. /plæstɪk bam/ *Newsweek* 5 Feb. p. 37/2 The French language has gained several new words from the plastic bombs that rock Paris every night. *Life* 23 Feb. p. 41 (pict. cap.) The night before, the O.A.S. had flung here and there the plastic bombs that have become the dread of Paris. *Harper's Mag.* April p. 26 It is thus a kind of French "ultra" movement, lobbing ideological plastic bombs into the national marketplace. 1964 *World Book Year Book* p. 611/1.

PLASTIC BOMBING, *n.*—1962 N.Y. *Times Mag.* 4 Feb. p. 11/1–2 A wave of plastic bombings . . . has led to widespread belief in the danger of a Fascist coup.

PLASTIQUEUR, *n.* See quots.—1962 *Newsweek* 5 Feb. p. 37/2 The French language has gained several ominous new words from the plastic bombs that rock Paris every night. The men who plant the explosives are *les plastiqueurs*. . . . Seattle *Times* 13 May p. 8 I cannot help but wonder if "plastiqueur" may not soon find its idiomatic equivalent in Spanish and Portuguese.

PLENCH, *n.* [See quots.] See quots.—1963 *Life* 27 Sept. p. 37 PLENCH. Combination pliers and wrench, it works like a ZERT to install or remove nuts and bolts. 1964 *National Geographic* March p. 380/1–2 Astronaut's tool kit includes new devices for making repairs in the weightless environment of space—spammer (space hammer), plench (pliers and wrench), and zert (zero reaction tool).

POLYUNSATURATE, *n.* [*poly-* + *unsaturate*, *n.* (*NID 3.* Cf. *ibid.*, s.v. *unsaturated, adj.* b: '*of a chemical compound or mixture:* used esp. of organic compounds containing double or triple bonds between carbon atoms. . . .')] See quots.—1962 Seattle *Times Pictorial* 25 March (adv.) Polyunsaturates Make Beauty News[.] It's a face cream that contains essential polyunsaturates. That's right—polyunsaturates, the natural elements you've been reading so much about that are so important to your health. Chicago *Sun-Times* 20 July p. 28/3 Maybe, so current thinking goes, we would be better off in the long run to reduce our costly animal fats and substitute the vegetable (polyunsaturate) fats and oils. 1965 *Newsweek* 24 May p. 56/1 (adv.) Medical studies now suggest great possible advantages in diets low in saturated fats and high in polyunsaturates.

QUASAR, *n.* [*quasi*-stellar object.] See quots.—1964 N.Y. *Times* 6 Sept. p. E9/7 The recent discovery of "quasars"—objects at extreme distances radiating light and radio waves with almost incredible intensity—has revived Dr. Ambartsumian's theory. Some at the meeting suggested that there may be no essential difference between the energy source at the core of our own galaxy and that which powers the radio galaxies of the quasars. 1965 *Sci. News Letter* 2 Jan. p. 7/3 Combined optical and radio studies of the universe increased the observed number of "quasars," short for "quasi-stellar objects," to 13. Quasars are the most distant objects so far discovered in space and the most powerful sources of radiation, both light and radio waves, yet known. *Newsweek* 21 June p. 62/2 Sandage and other astronomers have found about 60 quasars—a unique class of starlike objects that give off more light and radio noise than a galaxy of 100 billion stars. N.Y. *Times* 13 June p. 1/3 They resemble the strange, recently discovered "quasars," except they are not sources of strong radio emission, and are so numerous that they should enable astronomers to determine the nature of the universe.

REAL TIME, *n.* The term used when a computer is processing data so that its results can be immediately utilized in an experiment being conducted. Also see quots. (Also attrib.)—1959 Woodford A. Heflin (ed.) *Aerospace Glossary* (Maxwell [Ala.] Air Force Base: Research Studies Institute, Air University) p. 84/1–2 REAL TIME. Time in which reporting on events or recording of events is simultaneous with the events. *Systems Mag.* (Remington Rand) Feb. p. 17/2 (pict. cap.) The objective is data reporting on missile test flights in 'real time' (instantaneously). When the system is completed, information will be read back from a missile immediately, telling the scientists how it is reacting to speed, friction, how the guidance system is performing, and many other details. 1960 N.Y. *Times* 17 July p. 13/4 As an experiment, Air Force and Weather Bureau meteorologists attempted to use the pictures to make "real time" forecasts of the weather—forecasts fresh enough to be useful. 1961 *ibid.* 28 Feb. p. 13S The airline said it recently signed an order for two Remington Rand Univac "real time" computers and their auxiliary equipment. The term "real time" refers to computer operation that takes place simultaneously with an event, such as a sale of a seat or a change in an airliner's arrival time. Such systems are used in the control of missiles in flight. 1964 *ibid.* 22 Nov. p. 10F/3 A process computer accepts data directly from measuring devices used in industrial processes. It acts upon the data in "real time," or at a speed sufficient to make effective changes in the process. 1965 *Newsweek* 14 June p. 32/3 This "real-time flight planning"—deciding what to do according to the occasion—pleased Kraft.

REVERSE INTEGRATION, *n.* See quots.—1954 N.Y. *Times* 30 May p. 34/5 Fisk officials cite her case as being possibly an example of "reverse integration," a phrase enunciated in the light of the recent Supreme Court decision prohibiting segregation in the public schools. There are two others at Fisk who offer comparable examples. They are white students in the undergraduate school. 1957 N.Y. *Times Mag.* 6 Jan. p. 20 (title) Reverse Integration 1963 N.Y. *Times* 7 April p. 63/4 Hundreds of white students are attending educational institutions that were once Negro, according to the Associated Press. "Reverse integration," this development is called. Tuscaloosa *News* 8 Sept. p. 14/7 (AP) Little Rock, scene of violent integrationist movements six years ago when Negro students sought entrance to all-white schools, is the scene today of reverse integration.

RHOCHREMATICS, *n.* [See second quot.] See quots.—1960 Seattle *Times* 15 May p. 19 The subject is "Rhochrematics—A Scientific Approach to the Management of Material Flows." *Rhochrematics, A Scientific Approach to the Management of Material Flows.* Management series, no. 2 (Seattle: Bureau of Business Research, College of Business Administration, University of Washington) p. 3 Today's business literature is replete with references to "total distribution costs," "landed cost management," and other words and phrases which refer to different aspects of the management of material flows. To avoid the stigmas and manifold impressions attached to new terms a new word broad enough to encompass those areas of business activity yet precise to the point of being exclusive in connotation has been developed. This word is Rhochrematics ["Created by Professor William C. Grummel and Mr. William Royal Stokes of the Department of Classics, University of Washington."] It comes from the Greek "rhoe" meaning to flow as a river or a stream; "chrema" meaning products, materials, or things; and the abstract ending "ics" for any of the sciences. 1961 *Advanced Management* Feb. p. 16/1 (Richard A. Johnson) Rhochrematics is defined to include the flow from raw materials, through the processing stages, to the distribution of the finished product, and was coined specifically to eliminate the confusion among terms. It incorporates all of the other concepts—to produce to satisfy the needs of the consumer—to organize the distribution of finished goods in terms of the consumer—to integrate the functions of production and marketing into an effective total system.

SHOCK FROCK, *n.* See quots.—1964 Nashville *Tennessean* 25 June p. 15/4 (AP) The makers of Britain's first bare-bosomed cocktail dresses said yesterday they have had second thoughts about their shock frocks. 1965 Tuscaloosa *News* 13 Feb. p. 4/3 (quoting Charleston *Daily Mail*) Now comes the ultimate—the topless swim suit and the "shock frock" or (why not come right out and say it) the bare-bosom look.

SOFT, *adj.* [Cf. *OED*, s.v. *soft, adj.*, 25.a: 'Applied to water, such as rain or river water, which is more or less free from calcium and magnesium salts . . .' (1775–)] See quots.—1963 *Union Carbide Stockholder News* Sept. p. 1/1 Facilities are now being built at Union Carbide's Texas City, Texas, and Institute, West Virginia, plants for producing 150 million pounds or more a year of an alkylate for making "biologically soft" detergents. Most of today's detergents resist breakdown by bacteria present in soil and water, and as a result create voluminous foam in sewage treatment systems. However, the detergents that can be produced from the new Union Carbide chemicals can be quickly destroyed or degraded in sewage systems and waterways to non-detergent-like products, which show little surface activity and do not produce foam. 1964 Texize Chemicals, Inc. 29 May [Quot. s.v. *biodegradable*.]

SOFT-LAND, *v.t.* & *i.* To land (an object) on the moon in such a manner as to prevent its being destroyed on impact.—1960 Seattle *Times Mag.* 29 May p. 22 . . . the first lunar vehicle may be a small robot to be soft-landed on the moon within the next five years. 1963 *Family Weekly* 7 April p. 5/1 You've soft-landed on the uneroded, airless surface of the moon. 1964 *Time* 7 Aug. p. 42/3 Later, J.P.L.'s unmanned Surveyor spacecraft will soft-land on the moon. . . . 1965 *Newsweek* 21 June p. 24/3 . . . the latest Lunik probe, dispatched on Tuesday to "soft land" on the moon and perhaps steal some of the spotlight from the Gemini 4, failed to make a needed mid-course maneuver and missed its target by 100,000 miles.

SOFT LANDING, *n.* See last quot.—1958 *Think* July p. 6/1 Moon explorations will involve three distinct levels of difficulty. The first would be a simple shot at the moon, ending either in a 'hard' landing or a circling of the moon. Next in difficulty would be a 'soft' landing. And most difficult of all would be a 'soft' landing followed by a safe return to earth. 1959 Seattle *Times Mag.* 25 Oct. p. 10 In a soft landing it is necessary to take the payload down to the surface with retro-rockets firing near the approach. . . . 1960 N.Y. *Times* 31 July p. E7/8 The Surveyor craft will be used for "soft" landings, designed to place equipment on the moon, with the craft presumably still able to function. 1965 Tuscaloosa *News* 8 July p. 7/2 In a soft landing the spacecraft comes down so slowly and gently that delicate scientific instruments are able to survive the impact and relay their measurements back to earth.

SPAMMER, *n.* [See quots.] See quots.—1963 *Life* 27 Sept. p. 37 SPAMMER. Short for space hammer, it uses a spring which is triggered to bang away like a riveter. 1964 *National Geographic* March p. 380/1–2 [Quot. s.v. *plench*.]

SPY IN THE SKY, SPY-IN-THE-SKY, *n.* **1.** See quots.—1960 N.Y. *Times* 12 June p. 6E/2 The U-2 reconnaissance "overflights" provided, by aerial photography and tape recording of Soviet radio and radar emissions, the most important intelligence gathered by the C.I.A. The "spy in the sky" more than compensated for the very few spies on the ground that the United States has been able to infiltrate into Russia. 1961 *World Book Year Book* p. 160/2. 1963 N.Y. *Times Mag.* 10 Nov. p. 96/4 The argument about so-called "spies in the sky" serves to illustrate how military-political issues act as roadblocks to progress in reaching agreement on practical legal questions. **2.** *Attrib.* See quots.—1960 *Life* 22 Aug. p. 19/2 Still to come in 1960: more weather, navigation, communication and "spy-in-the-sky" satellites, two moon orbiters, another deep space probe, two Mercury orbital shots with man-sized capsules, and three suborbital shots—the last one with a man in it. 1965 *Sat. Rev.* 22 May p. 16/2 The notorious U-2, the most effective spy ever invented, was developed, and a start was made with the spy-in-the-sky satellites—though their value may have been exaggerated.

ZERT, *n.* [See quots.] See quots.—1963 *Life* 27 Sept. p. 37 POWER ZERT. Battery-powered wrench does work. It is anchored in place to keep it from spinning. *Ibid.* 27 Sept. p. 37 HAND ZERT. The word stands for Zero Reaction Tool, and you must squeeze the handles to turn a bolt. 1964 *National Geographic* March p. 380/1–2 [Quot. s.v. *plench*.]

AMONG THE NEW WORDS

I. WILLIS RUSSELL
University of Alabama
(With the assistance of Norman R. McMillan)

IN CONNECTION with the term *empty calorie* in the glossary, it is interesting to note a variant term which occurred earlier: 1954 *What's New in Home Economics* June p. 88/3 "What is a naked calorie? It is one that makes no nutritional contribution except for fuel value. This is true of pure fat or any straight carbohydrate food, such as sugar or pure starch." This is the only citation of *naked calorie* in my file. If there was an earlier rivalry between the terms, it seems clear which one won out.

In connection with *cybernation*, a writer in *Fortune* (March, 1962, p. 80/1–2) alludes to "the present uncybernated world."

ACKNOWLEDGMENTS: For citations: William P. Head (1), Mamie J. Meredith (6), Porter G. Perrin (5), Anne B. Russell (3), Jo Ann Schanbacher (1), Roger W. Shuy (1), Ethel Strainchamps (1), and Peter Tamony (2). Thanks are also due to Captains Ira F. Allen and Charles R. Eckerly and Theodore E. Klitzke for aid in the definitions of *hot line* and *pop art*.

CYBERNATED, *adj.* [See quots. s.v. *cybernation*.] See quots.—1962 *New Republic* 26 March p. 25 In a cybernated society, what will be needed most are sophisticated trouble-crews to repair breakdowns. . . . *Fortune* March p. 80/1 Michael warns darkly that "most of our citizens will be unable to understand the cybernated world in which they live." 1965 *Sat. Rev.* 15 May p. 68/3 While we are training hundreds in the advanced techniques of a cybernated society, thousands of others are being left behind on a human slag heap, victims of inadequate preparation.

CYBERNATION, *n.* [See quots.] See quots. (Also attrib.)—1962 St. Louis *Post-Dispatch* 10 Feb. p. 4A/2 At least one expert is now covering the field with a new word, cybernation, derived from cybernetics, which in turn pertains to the process of communciation and control in men and machines. *Newsweek* 12 Feb. p. 78/2 The title "Cybernation: The Silent Conquest" sounds perfect for a science-fiction chiller about the robot-minded computer taking over man and his world . . . it is a carefully reasoned warning that the threat of cybernation (a neologism for thinking machines and automation) is frighteningly real. *Fortune* March p. 80/1 Donald N. Michael, who uses "cybernation" as the title and theme of a report published a month ago by the Center for the Study of Democratic Institutions, says he derived the term from "cybernetics," which M.I.T. professor Norbert Wiener coined out of the Greek word for "steersman." *Sat. Rev.* 3 March p. 5/3 On the cybernation front, the telephone company scaled new peaks in modern horrors—it now takes ten numbers of their beloved "direct dialing" to reach, for an out-of-town call, just "Information." 1965 *Sat. Rev.* 5 June p. 53/1 Most production jobs and many services are being automated out of existence. Cybernation is replacing the traditional jobs, leaving as work only those jobs that deal with human beings and values: poetry and politics.

EMPTY CALORIE, *n.* See quots.—1956 Birmingham *News* 23 March p. 33/4 (AP) 2. Eat fewer "empty calories" such as fats, oils, sugar and syrups. 1957 Chicago *Sunday Trib.* 25 Aug. Part 1 p. 14/3 From now on you can expect to hear more about empty calories. These are foods that contain no or few proteins, minerals, and vitamins. Whiskey, sugar, and cooking fats are the best examples. The empty calorie is packed with energy, which is used immediately. It is that 'quick energy' food that was advertised so widely a decade ago. These calories count in the daily diet so far as weight is concerned but they contribute to malnutrition because they leave nothing for the body to use.... These products should be used only as a supplement to meats, fish, eggs, milk, vegetables, cereals, and fruits. 1958 N. Y. *Times Mag.* 2 March p. 28/2 Snacks nibbled between meals are frequently made up of what many nutritionists call "empty calories"—calories like those in sweetened coffee and unenriched pastries that carry with them few or none of the additional nutritive values that are necessary to a balanced ration. *Brit. Book of the Year* p. 752/1. 1959 *U. S. Depart. of Agriculture. Food, the Yearbook of Agriculture 1959* p. 307/2. Here is an example of changing food habits for the worse, as they now eat the "empty calories" of sweet bakery goods in place of fruit, milk, and other foods of high nutritive value. 1962 N. Y. *Times Mag.* 30 Sept. p. 30/2 And in view of the fewer calories most of us live on, does it not become more necessary than ever before that we avoid empty calories and make each calorie count nutritionally? 1966 *Ladies' Home Journal* Feb. p. 46/2 Pediatricians and nutritionists would also like to see American children eat less empty calories. These are the foods that are high in calorie value, but low in nutrients, and leave a youngster feeling hungry again in a few hours—potato chips, popcorn, candy, pastry, soft drinks. The experts are heartily in favor of between-meal snacks, but suggest instead an apple, a thin slice of ham, tomato juice, carrot sticks.

EVA, n. /ȉy vȉy éy/ Extravehicular (which see) activity. (Also attrib.)—1965 *Science Year; The World Book Science Annual* (Chicago: Field Enterprises Educ. Corp.) p. 321/1. *Newsweek* 14 June p. 30/3 [Quot. s.v. *extravehicular.*] 1966 *World Book Year Book* (Chicago: Field Enter. Educ. Corp.) p. 565/2. *Encyclopedia Year Book* (N. Y.: Gaché Publishing Co.) p. 336/2 Woodford A. Heflin, ed., *The Second Aerospace Glossary* (Maxwell [Ala.] Air Force Base: Documentary Research Division, Aerospace Studies Institute, Air University) p. 47/1. [/ȉy vȉy éy/ was referred to frequently during the televising of the Gemini 10 Mission July 18–21.]

EXTRAVEHICULAR, *adj.* [*extra-* 'outside: beyond—esp. in adjectives formed from adjectives <extracranial>....' (*NID 3*) + *vehicular*] See quots.—1965 *Newsweek* 7 June p. 54/1 The David Clark Co.... received a contract fourteen months ago to develop extravehicular suits in time for the Gemini 5 flight this fall. *Newsweek* 14 June p. 30/3 White climbed into a new "extravehicular activity" (EVA) suit: thirteen new layers had been added.... *Ibid.* 14 June p. 32/3 He also had to unstow and strap on an extravehicular pack which would both regulate his suit and provide ten minutes of emergency air in case his oxygen line failed him. *Ibid.* 21 June p. 24/3 Empty food bags, scraps of paper, all had to be carefully stored in compartments behind their shoulders, and with the lifeline, space gun and other extravehicular equipment still inside the cabin, there wasn't much room.

FLIP, *n.* [See quots.] See quots.—1962 Seattle *Times* 1 July p. 14 "Flip" is the short way of saying "floating instrument platform." It is the newest thing developed for research on sound waves in the ocean. It also will be used for other research. *Ibid.* 25 June One of the strangest craft ever in Northwest waters was to flip today in Dabob Bay.... The craft, 355 feet long and 20 feet wide, can be towed in a horizontal position. But when in position, the craft can "flip" into a vertical position, so about 50 feet is above water and the rest sticking into the depths. Flip was built by Scripps Institute of Oceanography.... 1963 *Encyclopedia Year Book* p. 362/2. 1964 N. Y. *Times* 12 April p. E7/6 A remarkable research vessel called Flip, that can stand bow-up in the water and float like a buoy, has spent 27 days in its vertical position while making observations 1,500 miles west of San Francisco.

FOLKNIK, *n.* [*folk* singer + *-nik* (*Am. Sp.* 37: 41)] See quots.—1958 *Caravan* Sept. p. 29 On MacDougal Street, in Greenwich Village, ... lies the Folklore Center ... near the door is the lettering "Israel G. Young." ... Invariably, folkniks (to quote Izzy) are present, for this den is the meeting place and home address for New York's up and coming folksingers and hangers on. 1960 *ibid.* Jan. p. 32 American Playparties (Folkways FC 7604)—Pete Seeger ... doing playparties, obviously intended more to teach these wonderful games than to entertain aurally. Folkniks with teachable children should look this one up. N. Y. *Times Mag.* 8 May p. 32/2 Folk-singing, once a rather recondite occupation for a few reedy-voiced guitar-plunkers, has now struck so responsive a chord in the general public that anyone who can master three chords, grow a beard and sit heavily on a stool can be a folknik. There are foreign-language and native-American folkniks, a selection of whom, as depicted in "The Guitar Review," appear applying their tradenik here. 1963 *Time* 26 July p. 39/2 Pablo Casals conducting his own oratorio *El Pesebre* has been followed by Folk Songsters Peter, Paul and Mary conducting 13,934 folkniks into collective rapture. 1964 *ibid.* 7 Aug. p. 74/3 (note) Newport appreciates the business, spokesman announced last week, but wants the folkniks farther out of town.

HOT-LINE, *n.* [Cf. *NID 3*. s.v. *hot, adj.*: '6: showing energy or activity in an unusual degree: as **a:** of intense and immediate interest <~news story>...'] A communications line that is open at all times. (Also attrib.)—1955 N. Y. *Times Mag.* 7 Aug. p. 10/1 To hold this breakthrough to a minimum is "ConAd's" job. It has twelve air divisions, tied in by "hot line" communications with one another and with the Army, Navy and Civil Defense Administration.... 1963 N. Y. *Times* 9 June p. 2E/7. *Ibid.* 25 Aug. p. E11/3–6. 1963 *World Book Ency. Dict.* (Chicago: Field Enterprises Educ. Corp.) p. 955/3.

IMP, *n.* [See quots.] See quots. (Also attrib.)—1963 N. Y. *Times* 1 Dec. p. E9/7–8 The second step was the launching of IMP (interplanetary monitoring platform), first of a new class of unmanned satellites, the dual mission of which is (1) to explore regions beyond the earth's magnetic field, and (2) to help plan measures for protecting astronauts against the perils of radiation in space. 1964 *ibid.* 22 March p. 7/3 The Interplanetary Monitoring Platform, or IMP satellite, has charted the gigantic shock wave produced as gas from the sun pounds at supersonic speed against the barricades of the earth's magnetism. Tuscaloosa *News* 4 Oct. p. 1/6 (AP) An interplanetary monitoring platform (IMP-2) rocketed into a great oval orbit Saturday night to chart radiation hazards along the astronauts' route to the moon. 1965 *Encyclopedia Year Book* p. 357/2. 1966 Heflin *Second Aerospace Glossary* p. 64/1.

JET SET, *n.* [See quots.] 1. See quots.—1951 San Francisco *Examiner* 5 Aug. p. 5/1 You're strictly jet set in Carmel if you stake your claim in the dunes, always in the same spot ... NEVER descend to ocean level except for a quick dunk or a trek to Pebble Beach golf club, sans clubs.... 1955 San Francisco *Call-Bulletin* 30 Nov. p. 28/6–8 The jet-set in New York are men and women in a hurry, who seek to get as much fun out of their nights as they can pay for or get somebody else to pay for. They seek so much and attain so little they are usually bored.... The fastest among them has been designated as the jet-set by Igor Cassini, who knows them well as it is his business to do. He thinks of them as the jet-propelled epigoni of men who made money by hard work and left it to a third generation which is engaged in hard play. 1963 *Am. Sp.* Oct. p. 206 JET SET, *n.* (Analogous to *smart set.*) Rhyming slang term referring to the sophisticated, well-to-do skiers who go abroad by jet just for skiing vacations in the best known resorts. 1964 *World Book Year Book* p. 609/3. 1965 *Life* 2 July p. 17/1 The eccentric originality of his prose, a complex mixture of several vernaculars—teenage, jet set, academic and drugstore modern—made him a big discovery among the folks who discovered chichi things like collecting old Superman comic books. *Newsweek* 19 July p. 42/2 ... by that time R ... had become a wealthy man and was well launched as a member of the jet set long before jets were ever heard of.

2. See quots.—1956 N. Y. *Times Mag.* 4 Nov. p. 14 This is the Soviet 'Jet Set,' an element of the younger generation that is causing great concern to the country's leaders and to the Communist party. The term was originated by a young member of a foreign embassy staff in Moscow and refers to the Soviet youth who are attracted by things foreign—specifically Western things and especially clothing, hair styles, jazz, movies, automobiles—and who go in for restaurants, hard drinking, wild parties and the gay life generally. 1958 N. Y. *Times Mag.* 12 Oct. p. 13/2 (pict. cap.) HIGH LIFE—At the Metropole Hotel, Moscow's "jet set" dances, above, to a six piece band playing a pseudo-jazz considered daring in Russia. The music is at least noisy. The dancing, however, is very sedate. 1959 *Newsweek* 2 Feb. p. 39/1 But little has been done so far to interfere with the antics of the Jet Set [in Russia], for their parents have become indispensable to the regime.... 1964 *World Book Year Book* p. 609/3.

JET-SETTER, *n.*—1965 N. Y. *Times* 13 June p. 17 (pict. cap.) Jet-setter Mrs.... and model ... prepare for ABC's fall special, "The Wild, Wild East."

MLF, *n.* [See quots.] See quots.—1964 *Time* 4 Dec. p. 21/1 In Europe, U. S. diplomats are still trying to promote a multilateral nuclear fleet (MLF) as an alternative to proliferating national forces. *U. S. News & World Report* 14 Dec. p. 44 Right now, an argument over MLF—multilateral nuclear force—is exploding into an international argument that threatens to shake apart the alliance between U. S. and the nations of Europe. 1965 *Newsweek* 26 July p. 36/2 ... F ... has even advised that the U. S. give up its plan for a NATO multilateral nuclear force (MLF) as the price for a Russian agreement on a non-proliferation pact.

MOD, *n.* [See first quot.] See quots. (Also attrib.)—1964 N. Y. *Times Mag.* 7 June p. 72/1 In recent months, the beaches of England have become arenas for rival gangs of teen-agers from the London slums, determined to show their power before the worshiping eyes of the girls who travel with them. On improtant holidays the battle, complete with casualties, property destruction and arrests, is joined between long-haired, leather-jacketed, aggressively masculine, motorcycle-riding Rockers (from "rock 'n' roll") and foppishly dressed (in multihued pastels), meticulously groomed (even to feminine makeup), motorscooter-riding Mods (from "modern"). 1965 *Newsweek* 7 June p. 57/2 "Bill has a young feeling for clothes without making us into mods and rockers"; he is "the perfect extra man for parties." *Ibid.* 19 July p. 58/2 But this summer the thatched cottages, quaint pubs and beefeater guards are drawing fewer worshipers than ... the Mods and Rockers. *Ibid.* p. 58/1 But a Little Orphan Annie dress by Mary Quant or Caroline Charles will do, or for the male, a set of Mod threads. ... Tuscaloosa *News* 11 Aug. p. 15/6–7 More in the mod feeling, there were soft, long-sleeved smock dresses and tight, high-bodiced empire dresses with puffy skirts. 1966 N. Y. *Times* 6 March p. 4E (pict. cap.) MODS, SATELLITE-STYLE: In Nowa Huta, Poland, leather-clad, long-haired youths exhibit the new spirit of "independence" in the satellite nations of Eastern Europe.

MOL, *n.* [See quots.] See quots.—1963 *Aviation Week and Space Tech.* 16 Dec. p. 30/1–2 As described by Defense Secretary McNamara, the system, called MOL for manned orbiting laboratory, will consist largely of hardware already under development.... 1964 *Missiles and Rockets* 10 Feb. p. 35 The Air Force is now pressing for a winged ferry vehicle for rendezvous missions with the *Manned Orbiting Laboratory* (MOL). N. Y. *Times Mag.* 13 Dec. p. 110/5 They will be experiments to determine just what are the military uses of space; Manned Orbital Laboratories (MOL) will be among the results, around 1967. 1965 *Sci. News Letter* 2 Jan. p. 6/2 The most immediate USAF manned space project is the Manned Orbital Laboratory (MOL), scheduled for some time between 1967 and 1969. In the MOL two men will spend 30 days in orbit around the earth, studying both outer space and each other's reactions to it. Tuscaloosa *News* 26 Aug. p. 15/4 (AP). *Time* 3 Sept. p. 51/2. *U. S. News & World Report* 6 Sept. p. 42/1 The Air Force on August 25 won long-sought approval to start work on its own manned space program.... First step: development of a Manned Orbiting Laboratory—or MOL.... 1966 *Encyclopedia Year Book* p. 336/2. Heflin *Sec. Aerospace Glossary* p. 87/2.

NUCLEAR BLACKMAIL, *n.* The attempt of a country to coerce another country into responding to its demands by the threat of using nuclear weapons.—1964 Tuscaloosa *News* 17 Oct. p. 1/5 "This is a major achievement of the Chinese people in their struggle to increase their national defense capability and oppose the U. S. imperialist policy of nuclear blackmail and nuclear threats...." *Ibid.* 19 Oct. p. 3/2 President Johnson referred in his speech to the nation Sunday night to the danger of "nuclear blackmail" and offered assurance to China's neighbors that they will have strong U. S. support if they ever need it in resisting efforts to pressure them into knuckling under to Chinese Communist demands. 1965 *Ibid.* 3 July p. 6/1 (AP) ... B ... accused the United States today of nuclear blackmail by claiming it has more nuclear-armed intercontinental missiles than the Soviet Union. *Ibid.* 4 July p. 1/7 (AP) He accused unnamed American officials of nuclear blackmail by claiming the United States has missile superiority over the Soviet Union.

POP ART, *n.* [*pop*ular + *art*] A form of art, begun in part as a reaction to abstract expressionism with its emotional subjectivity, which makes wide use of specific objects and imagery drawn from popular culture. (Also attrib.)—1965 *Sat. Rev.* 5 June p. 6/2 Well, we've had pop art and op art, and we suppose it's only simple computer logic to expect the next step.... *Newsweek* 21 June p. 70/2 Even though the advertisements in the two editions of the weekly shopper's throwaway were published a full year apart, they seemed exactly the same—familiar pop-art pictures of steaks, asparagus, coffee cans, and egg cartons scattered throughout the boldface thickets of supermarket "specials." Tuscaloosa *News* 4 July Sunday Comics ("Donald Duck" by Walt Disney) POP ART EXHIBIT *World Book Year Book* p. 607/2.

POPSTER, *n.* [*pop* art + *-ster*] One who engages in or is a fan of pop art.—1965 *Sat. Rev.* 29 May 29/3 It would seem that two older artists have been curiously misunderstood—Albers by the "opsters" and Duchamp by the "popsters."

ROCKER, *n.* See quots. s.v. *mod.*

AMONG THE NEW WORDS

I. WILLIS RUSSELL
University of Alabama

ACKNOWLEDGMENTS: For citations: Mamie J. Meredith (2), Porter G. Perrin (1), and Marcus Whitman (1).

Since the beginning of 1968, I have been going through my file of neologisms with the aim of making an analysis of those which appeared during the twenty-five-year period 1940–64. As would be expected, many of these neologisms have not survived and hence are not entered in the recent editions of our dictionaries. I plan, therefore, from time to time to enter in "Among the New Words" some of these recent short-lived terms for which a number of citations are on file. *Balloon bomb*, in this issue, is such a term.

One would have expected the derivative *civil rightist* to show up before now. In this connection, a somewhat earlier citation for *civil righter* may be quoted: ". . .'civil righters will no longer try to use the courts to push integration . . .' " (1959 Tuscaloosa *News* 11 April p. 1/1 [AP]).

ABL, *n.* See quots.—1964 N.Y. *Times* 14 June p. E-7/6-7 Last week the National Aeronautics and Space Administration invited industry to undertake the design of an Automated Biological Laboratory, or "ABL," for the detection of life on Mars. It would be landed by the Voyager vehicles due to fly in the 1970's. 1965 *Time* 7 May p. 81/1 ABL. Final step . . . will be to land an ABL (Automated Biological Laboratory) equipped to search for and analyze anything resembling life, and to send reports back to earth by radio. The ABL must be prepared to select and analyze kinds of life unknown on earth. 1966 [World Scope] *Encyclopedia Year Book* (N.Y.: Gaché Publishing Co.) p. 336/1.

ACID, *n.* [lysergic *acid* diethylamide] See quots. (Also attrib.)—1966 *Life* 25 March p. 30c/1 A bad trip—a sudden vision of horror or death which often grips LSD users when they take it without proper mental preparation—overtakes a teen-age girl at an "acid party" near Hollywood's Sunset Strip. *Life* 25 March p. 33/4 "When my husband and I want to take a trip together," says the psychedelic mother of four, "I just put a little acid in the kids' orange juice in the morning and let them spend the day freaking out in the woods." 1967 *Brit. Book of the Year* (Chicago: Brit. Encyclopaedia, Inc.) p. 802/1. Tuscaloosa *News* 17 Oct. p. 5/3 (NEA) With acid—LSD—and grass—marijuana—to help them, they think lofty thoughts, see splendid visions, hear glorious and profound words. 1968 *ibid.* 2 Dec. p. 1. Lt. S . . . said he . . . asked if he could "score some acid"—purchase LSD.

AEROBAT, *n.* [Cf. Woodford A. Heflin (ed.) *U.S. Air Force Dict.* (Washington: Air Univ. Press, 1956) p. 12/1 s.v. *aerobat*, *v.* Heflin calls it a "Back formation from *aerobatics* [*OEDS* 1917]" and labels it *Brit.* For the noun usage, cf. also *acrobat* (*OED* 1825): *acrobatics* (*OEDS* 1882).] See first quot.—1959 *Life* 22 June p. 96/2 One of her family's friends is a stunt flier and for two years Linda pestered him to make her an aerobat. 1965 N.Y. *Times* 16 May p. 39/2 (heading) BRITISH FLYING CLUB CERTIFIES AEROBATS 1966 [World Book] *Encyclopedia Year Book* p. 336/2.

AQUANAUT, *n.* [*aqua*+-*naut* (*Am. Sp.* 40:208, 211)] An underwater explorer; see last quot.—1960 N.Y. *Times* 11 Sept. p. X23/3-5 (pict. cap.) "Aquanauts"—Sarah Marshall and Keith Larsen explore the ocean depths in a new Wednesday night series from 7:30 to 8:30 over the C.B.S. television network. 1961 Lincoln (Nebr.) *Even. Jour.* 9 Sept. p. 1/10 (pict. cap.) Astronaut or aquanaut, the phraseology and feeling is pretty much the same. 1965 Atlanta *Journal* 7 Sept. p. 34/2 (UPI) Ten days of living underwater around-the-clock has not dampened the enthusiasm of America's 10 aquanauts, . . . N.Y. *Times* 5 Sept. p. 8E/1 (edit.) It is these practical considerations that inspire the Sealab 2 project now begun 205 feet below sea level off the California shore. Here American aquanauts have begun experiments to see how well man can live and work for extended periods under water. Their home is a steel cylinder with an artificial atmosphere consisting mainly of helium. 1966 *World Book Year Book* (Chicago: Field Enterprises Educ. Corp.) p. 565/2. *Random House Dict. of the Eng. Lang.* **aquanaut** . . . a skin-diver . . . .

BALLOON BOMB, *n.* See quots.—1945 Tuscaloosa *News* 30 May p. 8/1 (UP) Conscientious objectors and veteran army paratroopers are standing ready side by side to quell any forest fires started by Japanese balloon-bombs, . . . *Time* 11 June p. 56/3 (heading) Balloon Bombs. Birmingham *News-Age-Her.* 8 July p. 1-D (pict. cap.) Japanese Balloon Bomb. JOURNEY'S END for this Japanese paper balloon was on a rugged hillside in North America. Upper right shows control mechanism governing bomb release, while lower shows incendiary charges. 1949 *Time* 30 May p. 17/3 The kids had stumbled upon one of the 9,000 balloon bombs launched from Japan against the U.S. West Coast.

BALL PARK, *n.* See quots.—1960 Tuscaloosa *News* 15 Nov. p. 1/7 (AP) HONOLULU (AP)—The U.S. Air Force did it again Monday, plucking a Discoverer satellite capsule out of the skies for the second time . . . The Air Force, which calls the gigantic recovery area a "ball park," could point to a climbing fielding average. Lincoln (Nebr.) *Sunday Jour. and Star* 11 Dec., p. 1/4 He had asked, and received a particular spot in the formation of 9 of the Flying Boxcars spread over the farflung 'ball park'—the area where the capsule was expected to descend—of the Pacific. 1961 Seattle

Times 15 Oct. p. 1 (AP) The aerial recovery in an area called the "ballpark" was the sixth in the Discoverer series.

CIVIL RIGHTIST, *n.* [*civil rights* (*DA* 1874)]—1968 N.Y. *Times* 28 July p. 13D/5 The confrontation . . . came during the making of "Cabin in the Sky," which, along with "Stormy Weather," has been retroactively belittled by civil rightists. *Newsweek* 16 Sept. p. 90/1 Three years later he repulsed efforts by K . . . and other civil-rightists to unseat him, gaveling the convention closed before the votes had been tabulated.

CRAWLER-TRANSPORTER, *n.* [Cf. *OEDS*, s.v. *crawler*, '. . . Applied to a kind of tractor, moving on an endless chain,' 1922] See quots.—1965 *Time* 26 March p. 90 (pict. cap.) MOBILE LAUNCH TOWERS give new look to NASA installation on Merritt Island, . . . Crawler-transporter in foreground can pick up 445-ft towers, complete with Saturn V rockets—a total load of 12 million lbs.—and move them to launch pads. *Lamp* (Stand. Oil N.J.) Summer p. 23/1 (pict. cap.) The crawler-transporter in top photo will carry the 6,000-ton load of Saturn V and its launch tower (bottom) 1966 *U.S. Steel News* May–June p. 16/1 Lifting launcher and rocket onto its back, the massive vehicle—a crawler-transporter—clanks out of the building on eight crawler tracks toward the launch pad. . . . It travels a crawlerway—nearly eight lanes wide and stronger than any highway ever built. Its roadbed is about eight feet deep to support the 17.5-million-pound load of crawler, launcher, and space vehicle. [World Scope] *Encyclopedia Year Book* p. 336/2.

CRAWLERWAY, *n.* See quots.—1966 [Quot. s.v. *crawler-transporter*.] Woodford A. Heflin [ed.] *Second Aerospace Glossary* (Maxwell Air Force Base, Ala.: Documentary Research Div., Aerospace Studies Institute, Air Univ.) p. 36/1.

GIVE-UP, *n.* [Cf. *NID 3*, s.v. *give-up, n.*: 'a transaction on an exchange in which the broker reveals the name of his principal who is under obligation to complete the transaction.'] See quots.—1968 *Wall St. Jour.* 26 Jan. p. 26/1 A give-up is the frequently used mechanism whereby a big customer, such as a mutual fund, directs a brokerage firm executing a transaction to yield part of its commission to other brokers who have performed other services for the customer, such as selling fund shares. N.Y. *Times* 6 Oct. p. F1/5 The changes involve volume discounts on large-block transactions and an end to the practice known as the "give-up"—or the splitting of commissions between two or more brokerage houses on a single securities transaction.

PERSONNEL TRANSFER CAPSULE. See first quot.—1965 Tuscaloosa *News* 11 Sept. p. 8/1 Doctors say a swift rise to the surface would probably be fatal. So the aquanauts will enter a special personnel transfer capsule that will take them to the surface where they will enter a decompression chamber on the mother ship's deck. 1965 Newscast over NBC 28 Sept.

AMONG THE NEW WORDS

I. WILLIS RUSSELL
University of Alabama

For this department, a new word is a word or meaning that has not yet been entered in one of the standard dictionaries. Since, however, the commercial dictionaries—and these are the ones that are kept up to date—do not include dated citations, it seems as if it might be useful to publish from time to time the earliest citation in the editor's file of a new word or meaning that is entered and defined in one of the standard dictionaries of recent date but has not been treated in "Among the New Words." *Audible* and *SST* are two such words.

Acknowledgments: For citations: James B. McMillan (2) Norman R. McMillan (5), Mamie J. Meredith (2), Porter G. Perrin (2), Mary Gray Porter (4), and Marcus Whitman (4). Thanks are also due to Marcus Whitman for the definition of *conglomerate* and to Norman McMillan for aid in checking.

AUDIBLE, *n.* See quots.—1965 Tuscaloosa *News* 28 Nov. p. 17/7-8 (AP) Taylor's contention that the huddle, as it now is used, is on the way out stems from the growing use of pro football's latest offensive technique—the so-called automatic, audible or check-off call. . . the maneuver in which the quarterback comes to the line of scrimmage and then changes the play originally called in the huddle in order to combat the defensive alignment. 1966 *NID 3 Addenda Sect. s.v.*

BARIATRICS, *n.* [Gr. *bar*- 'weight' + -*iatrics* 'medical treatment, care' (*NID 3; Random House Dict.*)] See quots.—1967 Cleveland *Press* 23 Aug. p. F8/1 Bariatrics is a word that simply means the study of obesity. 1969 *Family Weekly* 9 Feb. p. 7/1 In 20 years of medical practice and bariatrics—the specialization of treating the overweight—it's obvious to me that the average obese person is not really capable of assimilating carbohydrates properly.

CONGENERIC, *n.* [Cf. *OED*, s.v. *congeneric, adj.* 'Of the same genus, kind, or race; allied in nature or origin.' *a* 1834] See first quot. (Also attrib.)—1968 [See last quot. s.v. *conglomerate, n.*] [1969] *First Jersey Nat'l Bank. Our 104th Annual Report 1968* p. 4/2 1968 also saw the rapid emergence of a "new" form of financial conglomerate, the One-Bank Holding Company. *Ibid.* First Jersey National has taken some long steps down the congeneric road. . .

CONGLOMERATE, *adj.* [Cf. *OED*, s.v.B. 1{1816} and N.Y. *Times* quot.]—1967 John C. Narver *Conglomerate Mergers and Market Competition* (Berkeley and Los Angeles: Univ. of Calif. Press) p. 3 A *conglomerate merger* is any merger that is neither horizontal nor vertical. The products of the acquiring and acquired firms are not competitive nor are they vertically related. Thus, a completely conglomerate merger produces a firm having a number of external markets equal to the sum of the pre-merger external markets of the acquiring and the acquired firms. 1968 *Sat. Review* 15 June p. 65/2 Its trustees. . . oversee the governance of the collection of colleges and graduate schools as though it were a "conglomerate" enterprise dealing in real estate, weaponry, and pharmaceuticals. 1968 N.Y. *Times Mag.* 27 Oct. p. 33/1 To the geologist, a conglomerate is a rock composed of stone fragments held together by hardened clay or some other cement. Analogously, the conglomerate corporation is a group of companies which operate in separate markets and are held together by bonds of financial and administrative authority. *Ibid.* Clearly, a Xerox-CIT union would be of the conglomerate type.

CONGLOMERATE, *n.* A corporate enterprise which achieves product and/or service diversity through the acquisition of existing independent companies, usually in situations where earnings and security price relationships and expectations indicate profitable outcomes for the parties involved. See also quots. (Also attrib.)—1956 Robert A. Bicks "Conglomerates and Diversification under Section 7 of the Clayton Act," *Antitrust Bull.*, II (Nov.–Dec.); cited by John C. Narver *Conglomerate Mergers and Market Competition* (Berkeley and Los Angeles: Univ. of Calif. Press, 1967) p. 146. 1967 *Life* 10 March p. 43/1–2 B. . .'s success results from his ability to exploit a new kind of company called a "conglomerate"—a hodgepodge of different enterprises all roped together under one name. Tuscaloosa *News* 14 April p. 4/4 But there is nothing in the books to say that dissimilar companies shouldn't merge. And so we have the peculiar phenomenon of multi-market companies and so-called conglomerates. 1968 *Value Line* (N.Y.: Arnold Bernhard) 16 Feb. (Part II) p. 117/2 A diversified product line and a policy of expanding through merger and acquisition are the essential ingredients of all conglomerates. Tuscaloosa *News* 13 Oct. p. 4/3 (Art Buchwald) What it boils down to is that if you merge an apple company with another apple company, you're violating the antitrust laws. But if you merge an apple company with a banana company, then you're building a conglomerate. . . . *Bus. Week* 30 Nov. p. 74/1–2 Indeed, the very word "conglomerate" has become so tainted that today very few conglomerate operators will admit to running conglomerates: Fresher fad words such as "congeneric" are now the substitutes.

CONGLOMERATION, *n.* [*OED*, 1626] See quots.—1967 Narver *op. cit.* p. 3 Through internal expansion, the act of conglomeration or "diversification" refers to any act of increasing the number of the firm's external markets. 1968 N.Y. *Times Mag.* 27 Oct. p. 32 (pict. cap.) THE MONEY-SPINNERS [heading] A conglomeration of entrepreneurs heading companies of widely varying resources and operating styles. *Ibid.* p. 144 (pict. cap.) CONGLOMERATION—Why does a corporation seek to acquire other companies in unrelated fields?

CONGLOMERATOR, *n.* See quots.—1968 N.Y. *Times Mag.* 27 Oct. p. 144/4 Conglomerate entrepreneurs—or conglomerators—must raise the price-earnings ratios of their stock if they are to expand, for unless it's loaded with cash, the rising conglomerate must depend on loans to acquire new companies. *Bus. Week* 30 Nov. p. 75/1 Creators rather than curators, the conglomerators often revive competition in settled industries by picking up marginal producers and energizing them with new capital, uninhibited ideas, and fresh expertise.

DECONGLOMERATION, *n.* See *conglomeration.*—1968 N.Y. *Times Mag.* 27 Oct. p. 152/3. When Ling took over Wilson, he decentralized its management by breaking it up into three companies. L.T.V.'s acquisition in short, resulted in a measure of *de*conglomeration, the object of which was to persuade the market that Wilson's P/E's should be higher.

EXPANSION, *attrib.* [Cf. *OEDS*, s.v.: 8 *expansion box* 1838; 1c *expansion drawing* 1869] Descriptive of a professional football team that resulted when the league was expanded.—1967 Tuscaloosa *News* 18 July p. 6/1 "H. . . has a 50–50 chance to play," said [the] coach of the New Orleans Saints, the expansion team that claimed the do-everything halfback in the draft. 1968 *ibid.* 16 Dec. p. 5/1–2 But the Vikings. . . had to sweat out a furious Bear charge in the final minutes before nailing their first division title in eight years as a NFL expansion franchise. 1969 Sportscaster over CBS 5 Jan. . . . takes an expansion team. . . .

MICRO-, MICROSLEEP, *n.* [Cf. *OED*, s.v. *micro-*, 1 {1899}] See quots.—1959 Seattle *Times* 21 June p. 15 (AP) The sleep occurs in the form of very brief lapses of attention. In these flash blackouts, our eyes remain open and we may be moving about, but there is an unawareness of surroundings. . . . The new phenomenon, labeled "micro-sleep," was discovered in the minute-to-minute study of a New York disk jockey who set a record of 201 hours and 13 minutes without sleep. . . . The micro-sleep episodes were not discernible to the eye. . . . But they could be seen on brain-wave tests. 1960 *Brit. Book of the Year* (Chicago: Encyclopaedia Britannica, Inc.) p. 752/2. 1966 N.Y. *Times Mag.* 17 April p. 73/1 They become unreliable at simple tasks, lapsing into infinitesimal blackouts called microsleeps. 1968 *Newsweek* 29 April p. 60/2 Errors on tests. . . coincide with periods of "microsleep" that last only a few seconds.

PHILANTHROPOID, *n.* [*philanthropist* + *-oid* 'resembling, allied to' (*OED*, s.v. *-oid*)] See quots.—1949 *Harper's* March p. 9/1 Edwin R. Embree. . . calls himself a 'philanthropoid,' a term which he and Frederick Keppel of the Carnegie Corporation coined some years ago to describe a person who gives away other people's money. 1955 *New Yorker* 10 Dec. p. 57 A philanthropoid. . . is the middleman between the philanthropist and the philanthropee. . . . 1957 *Brit. Book of the Year* p. 814/1. 1959 *Fortune* May p. 110/2 (pict. cap.) Philanthropoid is what Jonathan King cheerfully calls himself. King has spent most of his adult life giving away money; . . . 1968 *Natural History* June–July p. 66/3 It is only when one takes his patrons seriously that one is lost. Watson's handling of the philanthropoids who supported him should be an inspiration to all students. *Sat. Rev.* 21 Sept. p. 74/3 Only a veteran philanthropoid . . . could have written the section of advice on how to parlay one grant into several overlapping ones . . . .

REM, *n.* See quots.—1966 N.Y. *Times Mag.* 17 April p. 29/4 He is in a special variety of Stage I, known as REM (for "rapid eye movement") sleep. 1967 *ibid.* 12 Feb. p. 27/2 Further investigations with adults showed (1) that these rapid movements (or REM's) could be found in all sleepers . . . . 1969 *Family Weekly* 12 Jan. p. 4/1 ". . . he'll connect the electrodes for an electroencephalograph so that we can monitor the REMs (rapid eye movements) that tell when you're dreaming . . . ."

SPACE, SPACEWALK, *n.* The maneuvering of an astronaut outside of a capsule in space.—1965 *Newsweek* 14 June p. 30/3 . . . thirteen new layers had been added just under the outer nylon covering to protect his torso and legs against micrometeorites and the extreme temperatures on his spacewalk. Tuscaloosa *News* 1 July p. 5/1 In the films showing Maj. White's space walk, what was the object which looked like a sack of potatoes, that flew out of the spacecraft? 1967 *Brit. Book of the Year* p. 804/2 1969 Tuscaloosa *News* 6 March p. 1/1–2 (heading) Space Walk 'Fun Time' For Apollo 9 Astronaut.

SPACE, SPACEWALKER, *n.* One who performs a spacewalk (which see).—1965 *Newsweek* 21 June p. 24/1–3 (pict. cap.) After emerging from the open hatch door over the Pacific, spacewalker White fires his maneuvering gun and glides smoothly away. 1967 *Brit. Book of the Year* p. 804/2. 1969 Tuscaloosa *News* 6 March p. 1/1 SPACE CENTER, Houston (AP)—Astronaut Russell L. Schweickart braved the eerie, empty world of the space walker for about 40 minutes today . . . .

SPACE, SPACE-, SPACEWALKING, *n.*—1965 *Newsweek* 21 June p. 24/1 All White lacked, he added, was a longer tether and more fuel in the maneuvering gun, but he was firmly convinced that spacewalking is an easily mastered art. 1965 *Sat. Rev.* 4 Sept. p. 17/1 Perhaps we *can* afford Major White's joy in space-walking. 1967 *Brit. Book of the Year* p. 804/2.

SST [*s*uper*s*onic *t*ransport] See quots. (Also attrib.) 1961 *Fortune* June p. 161/1 Now in the preliminary design stage is the supersonic transport, or SST. 1966 *Random House Dict.* s.v.

S.T.O.L., STOL, *n.* [See quots.] See quots.—1956 N.Y. *Times* 4 Dec. p. 45/3 An aircraft classification of fairly recent vintage—S.T.O.L.—is attracting increasing and significant attention. The letters stand for "short take-off and landing," but they fall far short of adequately defining this airplane category. A true S.T.O.L. plane is one that not only can operate from confined areas, but can do so with negligible sacrifice of forward speed. 1956 *Aviation Week* 16 April p. 34. N.Y. *Times* 14 Oct. p. X33/3. It is Mr. Curtis' view that, if perfected, the "short take-off and landing" or S.T.O.L. plane will vastly complicate the task of regulating aerial traffic. 1959 *Aviation Week* 9 March p. 191. 1963 *ibid* 18 Feb. p. 67. 1967 *Brit. Book of the Year* p. 804/3. 1968 *Sci. News* 7 Sept. p. 229/1 One of the saddest stories in commercial aviation today is that of the STOL—short take-off and landing aircraft.

STOL-, STOLPORT, *n.* See quots.—1968 N.Y. *Times* 14 Jan. p. 1/1 A stolport would serve planes that make a "short take-off and landing." They use much shorter runways than those required by commercial jets. *Time* 16 Aug. p. 63/1 La Guardia's STOLPORT, as the 1,095-ft. runway has already been dubbed, is first of its kind in the U.S. to offer commercial airplanes those desirable qualities. *Science News* 7 Sept. p. 230 (pict. cap.) Frenetic ground travel to and from New York's main airports may be replaced by STOL-ports along the Hudson river.

STOL-ing, *n.*—1968 *Science News* Sept. p. 230/3 The airlines, manufacturers, airport operators and FAA have been going around in circles, looking for a place to start STOL-ing.

STOLSTRIP, *n.*—1968 N.Y. *Times* 14 Jan. L53/2 The authority is already using three stolstrips at Kennedy and has laid out a stolstrip of 835 feet at LaGuardia, . . .

AMONG THE NEW WORDS

I. WILLIS RUSSELL
University of Alabama

SEVERAL OF THE ENTRIES in this installment of "Among the New Words" are deserving of comment. It is true that *counter-productive* is entered in the new *Supplement to the OED* (*OEDS*-72). Nevertheless, it seems useful to add a definition and U.S. examples, one of which predates the earliest in the *OEDS*-72.

Certainly *ear jewel* is far from being a new term. It may, indeed, have a more continuous history than the widely scattered citations indicate. Yet the evidence at hand suggests that the word never really caught on, that to all intents and purposes the 1967 example was a new nonce word (see *W3*, s.v. *nonce word*).

Wiglet raises an interesting question. Occurring as long ago as 1831, it has only recently been used often enough for dictionary entry and thus seems to be virtually a new word. If the recent illustrations turn out to have originated in the United States, can we describe *wiglet* as an Americanism? Mitford M. Mathews's perceptive discussion of *alcalde* (*DA*, p. vii) will suggest an answer. The same question may well arise with *drop earring*, with no citation in the *OED* or the *OEDS*-72 after 1801.

Acknowledgments: For citations, Eleanore W. Ward (1), David J. Weir (the 1701 citation of *ear jewel*). Thanks are also due Mary Gray Porter for aid in checking.

counter-productive *adj* [*OEDS*-72 enters sv *counter*- 9 without def, with quots from 1964 *Ann. Reg. 1963* and 1969 *Spectator*] Producing results contrary to what was hoped or expected Addit US quots: 1961 Apr 20 *Minneapolis Morning Tribune* 5/5–6 " 'Counter-productive' was first used, so far as memory goes, by President Eisenhower in a press conference. Then GOP chairman Thruston Morton picked it up and used it a few times. Now Bundy. 'Counter-productive' means unwise, worse than useless, contra-indicated, and lousy." 1970 Apr 4 & 11 *New Repub* 37/1 "It is true that 'the Administration proposals are so weak as to be almost counter-productive' but at least the country is beginning to wake up to the serious problems of the environment." 1970 July 17 *Tuscaloosa News* 13/1–2 (NEA) "Trouble is, though, many smokers subjected to the anti-smoking commercials get so nervous their response is counterproductive. They become so worried they relieve the anxiety by—you guessed it—lighting up another 100 mm." 1972 Feb 13 *NY Times* E11/5 (Tom Wicker) "But Mr. Nixon's position—also stated in varying degrees of sharpness by Mr. Haldeman, Secretary of State Rogers, Attorney General Mitchell and Herbert G. Klein—is that while the President's proposal is on the table at Paris, it is at best nonproductive and probably counter-productive and may be even unpatriotic for anybody to propose anything else."

drop earring   n   [OED sv drop sb III 23 a 1778 and 1801]   Later US quots: 1957 Mary Brooks Picken Fashion Dict (NY: Funk & Wagnalls) 105/2   1964 Nov 15 NY Times 75 (ad) "drop earrings, $4."   1966 Sep 18 ibid 64 (ad) "Delicate cameo 14K pendant with matching drop earrings."   1972 Oct 15 ibid (ad) "Drop Earrings."

ear jewels   n pl   Earrings; ear ornaments   [1594–95 Shakespeare Romeo and Juliet ed G L Kittredge 1.5.47–48 "It seems she hangs upon the cheek of night / Like a rich jewel in an Ethiop's ear."   1596–97 Merch of Venice 3.1.92–93 "I would my daughter were dead at my feet and the jewels in her ear!"]   1701 Edward Taylor "Meditation 44. Joh 1.14 'The word was made Flesh'" in Poems of Edward Taylor ed D E Stanford (New Haven: Yale Univ Press, 1961) 161 "Where-with his Oratory brisk he tricks / Whose spicy charms eare jewells doe commence."   1725 Defoe New Voyage Round the World (London) ed Geo A Aitken 14:120–121 (cited by OED sv ear III 15; the OED does not quote the whole passage) "Our men were . . . surprised to see hanging round the ears of both the men . . . large flat pieces of pure gold, and the thread which they hung by was made of the hair of the goats twisted very prettily together, and strong enough . . . he . . . made the other . . . pull off his two ear-jewels also."   1820 Walter Scott Ivanhoe (NY: Dodd, 1941) 498 "Rowena opened the small silver-chased casket, and perceived a carcanet, or necklace, with ear-jewels of diamonds, which were obviously of immense value."   1967 Aug 23 Cleveland (Ohio) Press E11 (ad) "Ear Jewels / Fancy new designs. For pierced, unpierced or pierced-look."

ear jewelry   n   1969 Nov 30 NY Times 96 (ad) "Ear Jewelry."

float   vb   [OEDS-72 enters vi & vt with definitions and Brit quots 1965–71]   Addit US quots: 1971 May 24 Newsweek 10/2 See FLOATING   1971 Aug 29 NY Times 12E/1 (editorial) "President Nixon's new economic policy has scored its first solid victory on the international front with the announcement by the Japanese Government that it would float the yen."   Sep 18 Sat Review 10/2 "The dollar has been gradually sinking for some years. When it started to go down for the third time, our President had the courage to leap into the troubled water, grab G. Washington by the wig, pull him to the surface, apply mouth-to-mouth resuscitation, and put him in condition to float."

floating   pres part, adj, n   See OEDS-72 sense 5c   Addit US quots: 1954 Delbert A Snider Introd to International Economics (Homewood, Ill: Richard D Irwin) 207 "Canada's 'Floating' Dollar. A more recent, and quite different, experience with a freely fluctuating exchange rate is offered by the Canadian dollar. In September, 1950, official support of the fixed par value of the Canadian dollar was abandoned, and the rate of exchange was allowed to fluctuate in response to market forces. In December, 1951, all exchange controls were abolished."   1968 Robert Triffin Our International Monetary System: Yesterday, Today, and Tomorrow (NY: Random) 73 "Freely floating rates—à la Friedman—would 'bottle up' within each country's borders the inflationary or deflationary pressures arising from every expansionist or contractionist error in domestic policies."   1971 May 24 Newsweek 10/1–2 "Instead, he favors 'a general floating of exchange rates to allow currencies to find their own true level.' And last week, following Bonn's decision to 'float' the mark, he commented that 'there was no other alternative.'"

French   adj   [OED sv French A adj 3 "In names of things of actual or attributed French origin"; the quots under 3b include eleven combinations such as French sleeves applied to clothing and dress materials dating from 1592]   1966 Nov 27 NY Times 24/7–8 (ad) "14k gold earrings . . . Specify pierced or French back."   1968 May 5 ibid 17 (ad) "As round stud earrings for pierced ears, or with French backs."   Sep 22 ibid 75 (ad) "both available for pierced ears or with French backs."   Dec 8 ibid 147/4 "DOUBLE CULTURED PEARL EARRINGS Matching 7 mm. size in 14K white gold setting. French back."

-look   As the second element in usually ephemeral fashion terms   —**American look**   1947 Aug 18 Time quoted in 1951 AS 26:231/2   —**bare look**   1972 July 28 Life 59 "Where does the bare look come from? Some say it is an upward development of the hot pants craze of a year and a half ago. No matter; it is a cool, carefree and eye-popping way to dress for hot summer streets."   —**cigar look**   1951 AS 26:231/1   —**ghillie look**   1971 Sep 12 Tuscaloosa News 3C/3–5 "The ghillie look will be in step this fall."   —**guitar look**   1951 Brit Book of the Year 742/1   AS 26:231   —**layered look**   1972 Oct 25 Dinah Shore on "Dinah's Place" NBC "And that layered look is in."   —**new look** (specific)   1948 Brit Book of the Year 805/1   —**pierced look**   1967 Aug 23 Cleveland Press E11 (ad) See EAR JEWEL   1967 Nov 10 (on a tag for earrings that appear to be designed for pierced ears but are not)   1967 Dec 24 Tuscaloosa News 8/6–7 (ad) "Pierced and pierced-look FASHION EARRINGS."   1969 (rec'd Dec 29) Breck Catalog 44 "Pierced-Look Earrings."

non-pierced   adj   Of an earring: designed for unpierced ears   1968 Dec 23 Tuscaloosa News 3 (ad) "Genuine Diamond Earrings . . . Pierced or Non-Pierced."   1972 See PIERCED

pass-fail, pass/fail   attrib   1966 Dec 1 (Univ of Ala) Crimson-White 4/3 "On the last SRI poll, students were asked to give their opinion on a system known as 'pass-fail electives.' Under this system a student could take 2 or 3 electives while he was here at the University and not have to worry about his grade. If he did passing work, he would get three hours (or whatever it was) added to his total hours, but these hours would not be counted when his QPA was computed."   1968–69 Winter Key Reporter 2/1 "The inquiries of the committee have included a review of many detailed studies concerning pass-fail options."   1970 Aug 9 NY Times E7/6 "There has been much discussion of grading reforms; but the only major change, if it can be called that, has been the introduction of some options to take a certain number of courses on a pass-fail basis, without any indication of the actual quality of the work performed."   1972 Mar 4 Sat Review 49/2 "All courses are given on a pass/fail basis."

pierced   adj   [prob short for pierced-ear 'designed for pierced ears'; Mary Brooks Picken Fashion Dict 250/2 enters pierced-ear earring with a cross reference to earring 108/2, where the former is defined]   1965 Oct 15 Time 70/3 "Moreover, they [the girls] argue—with some reason—that pierced earrings are by far the most attractive ones available."   1966 Jan Changing Times (Kiplinger Mag) 30/1–2 "There's no such thing as a pierced earring that pinches or is so loose it falls off."   June 6 NY Times 53 "Variation on the pierced earring theme."   1967 Aug 22 Cleveland Plain Dealer 19/5 "Pierced earrings, a prominent part of the '67 fashion picture."   Nov Consumer Bulletin 7 " 'Pierced earrings' are harder to lose and easier to wear."   1970 Nov 6 letter to I W Russell "I know she did wear pierced earrings."

[1972] offer of Kellogg's mini-package jewelry on a box of Kellogg's Corn Flakes purchased during April "Choice of pierced or non-pierced earrings."

redshirt   n   1955 Dec 5 Life 144/2 "Although he is what the pros call 'redshirt,' a player with one more year of college eligibility, five pro clubs are eyeing him."   1971 W3 addenda

red shirt   vt   1950 Sep 27 Birmingham (Ala) News 35/1 "He coached all the juniors and senior linemen and the boys red shirted."   Nov 19 ibid C1/2 "There are not enough players to have a 'B' squad or red shirt promising sophomores."   1952 Oct 19 ibid C2/1–2 "The Vols red-shirted P . . . S . . . in 1951."

redshirting   n   1958 Jan 8 Tuscaloosa News 6/8 (AP) "An anticipated argument over 'red shirting'—the practice of holding athletes out of competition to prolong their eligibility—failed to develop."   1971 W3 addenda

sitcom   n   [short for situation comedy, which is in 1971 W3 addenda]   1964 Sep 18 Life 24/2 "Even Bing Crosby has succumbed to series TV and will appear in a sitcom as an electrical engineer who happens to break into a song once a week."   1971 Mar 15 Newsweek 68/1–2 (picture caption) "Television's 'hottest' sitcom."   Mar 15 Sat Review 64/3 "the 'hottest' sitcom to hit TV in years."   1973 Mar 17 TV Guide 42/2 "There are two fine senior-citizen actors here, and there's plenty of room on TV for a fine sencit sitcom."

unpierced   adj   Designed for unpierced ears   1967 See EAR JEWEL

wiglet   n   [OED sv wig sb³ 5 "(chiefly nonce-wds.)"   1831 quot]   1964 Oct 4 NY Times 122 (ad) "Wiglets."   1966 W3 addenda   1971 World Book Dict

[Received February 1973]

AMONG THE NEW WORDS

I. WILLIS RUSSELL

With the assistance of Mary Gray Porter
University of Alabama

As FASHION TERMS both *earwire* and *wire* are old, but their earlier referent is quite different from that in the glossary below. *Wire* is defined by the OED (III, 9, b) as "A frame of wire (a) to support the hair; (b) to support the ruff." Except for an 1893 quotation from Georgiana Hill's *History of English Dress*, which is bracketed, all the citations date from the sixteenth and seventeenth centuries: 1583, 1595, 1607, 1612, 1619, and two from 1690. The term in this sense is labeled obsolete by the OED.

Though the OED does not cross-reference it, *earwire* (s.v. *ear*, III, 16) seems to be synonymous with *wire*. For the definition, the OED cites the 1685 quotation from Cooke's *Marrow of Chirurgery*: "The ear-wires worn by women to fix their Headclothes to keep them on." The 1659 quotation for *ear-wire* is less explicit.

Nearly twenty-five years ago in this department, the senior author prefaced some observations on the variants for 'overnight accommodations for automobile tourists' as follows: "Clustering about an idea or object are sometimes many variant forms. These may represent rival forms, especially if the idea or object is new, most of which may eventually disappear. Or they may represent a deliberate stylistic device for obtaining variety. Whatever the reasons for their creation, the job of the linguist is to collect them where possible" (*American Speech* 24:143).

These remarks are particularly relevant to *bikeway* and its variants entered in the glossary below. The fact that only *bikeway* is entered in the 1973 Webster's New Collegiate Dictionary (WNCD8)—the eighth in the Merriam Collegiate series—and the Barnhart Dictionary of New English since 1963 (BDNE)—Bronxville, N.Y.: Barnhart, and Harper and Row, 1973—suggests that, according to their evidence, it is the standard form. Nevertheless, we think it may be of some interest to present to the readers of American Speech the evidence from our files supporting the variants.

Like *bikeway*, *hot pants*, "the accepted generic term" (*Time*, 1 February 1971, p. 48/2; *BDNE* has the full quotation), also has its variants, several of them perhaps facetious. A writer in *Newsweek* (29 March 1971, p. 75/1) points out that hot pants are not new, that "thirty years ago [when] they were known as 'short shorts,' " movie actresses "posed in them." This view is confirmed at the end of the year by a writer in *Life* (31 December 1971, p.

15/2), who observes that "to an untrained eye . . . hot pants looked rather like the old short shorts of 20 or 30 years ago, except that they were a bit skimpier and a lot flashier." The term *short shorts* is also used in the 29 January 1971 *Life*, p. 36/3, along with "Cool Pants, Short Cuts or simply Les Shorts." A propos of the French *les Shorts*, we find in *The Bulletin*, 11 May 1971, p. 118, a picture caption "Hot Lederhosen: A Bavarian designer's gift to the style-minded miss and her public." A month later (22 June, p. 158), *The Bulletin* suggests *Red-hot pants* as appropriate for East Germans (compare the report, amusing, if a little irrelevant here, in the 28 June 1971 *National Observer*, p. 6/4, of the woman who "appeared at work in what were said to be 'the hottest pants in three states' "), while *Hallo Friends* (no. 1, 1971, p. 7/1; Deutsche Welle) gives us *city shorts* and *lukewarm pants*, the latter "a loose type of Bermuda shorts reaching down to the knee" and recommended for those "ladies past thirty and beyond mannequins' measurements." From *Sports Illustrated* (26 April 1971, p. 58/3) comes the term *sports shorts*. We may fittingly conclude with a quotation from the *New Yorker* (3 April 1971, p. 101/1); writes Kennedy Fraser ("Feminine Fashions"): "Some advertisers, perhaps unnerved by reports that the name 'hot pants' has no more 'psycho-social acceptance' than the midi or the Edsel, have chewed their pencils over alternatives. But 'shortpants,' 'short cuts,' and 'minipants' sound teenage or boring, and cannot compete with a more general and a naughtier term that has the weight of *Women's Wear Daily* behind it. That recklessly didactic, supremely fashionable newspaper has insulted the frumpy old English language even more than usual by fixing on the term and the spelling 'HotPants.' "

Acknowledgments: John Algeo (for the first citation of *McGovernomics*) and Paul Vining, who was consulted about several jewelry terms in this and the previous issue.

bicycle boulevard *n* 1963 Apr 28 *NY Times* 79/3 "The 'bicycle boulevards,' for the most part run parellel [*sic*] to main streets. They lead to important commercial and recreation areas and connect residential areas with schools and play grounds." 1964 *World Book Year Book* (Chicago: Field) 430/2 (under "New Words and Phrases")

bicycle lane; bike lane *n* 1973 June 7 *Tuscaloosa News* 4 (editorial) "The Sierra Club's comprehensive plan for bicycle lanes and paths is a fine piece of work." Ibid "A test of the bike lanes is needed on the campus."

bicycle trail; bike trail *n* 1966 Edward C Crafts, May *Parks & Recreation* 437/2 "The Potomac plan proposes a hundred miles of bicycle trails within the District of Columbia and adjacent Virginia, over six hundred miles within the surrounding day-use zone of the capital and over one hundred miles in the more distant valley of the Potomac." 1971 Dec 6 *USN&WR* 84/2 "That means 90 per cent financing by the Federal Government, 10 per cent by the State, for bike trails alongside interstate highways." 1973 June 7 *Tuscaloosa News* 4 (editorial) "The full report . . . cites the need for recreational bike trails, extension of the bike routes to serve schools, to give consideration to bike riders in future improvements of existing streets and construction of new ones."

bicycle way *n* 1973 May *Pop Sci* 63/1 "The 444-mile California Aqueduct will soon be converted into one of the world's longest bicycle ways. It will be a protected path for bicyclists, with a network of protective gates that would even keep motorcycles out. [¶] The bikeway now is open for 67 miles from Bethany Reservoir, east of San Francisco, to San Luis Dam, near Los Banos."

bike path; bicycle path *n* 1971 June 28 *Newsweek* 67/2 "To help the bikers, the U.S. Department of Transportation has already set aside money for building bike paths along new highways." 1973 June 7 *Tuscaloosa News* 4 (editorial) "Purpose of the bike paths or lanes is to separate bicycle riders from automotive and pedestrian traffic on streets and roads." For *bicycle path* see BICYCLE LANE first quot

bike route *n* 1971 June 28 *Newsweek* 67/1 "In Chicago last month . . . Mayor Richard Daley was pedaled around town on a tandem bike by a racing trainer to open a planned 250-mile bike route through his city." 1973 see BICYCLE TRAIL

bikeway *n* [*WNCD8, BDNE*] Earlier quot 1967 *Brit Book of the Year* 802/1 (under "Words and Meanings, New")

cycling trail *n* 1966 Edward C Crafts *Parks & Recreation* 437/3 "There is an acute need for bicycle trails in or near urban areas. To quote one sentence from the National Trails report, 'Perhaps the greatest need in metropolitan areas is for cycling trails.' . . . The report proposes a standard of twenty-five miles of bicycle trail per each fifty thousand urban residents."

designated hitter; dh; designated pinch-hitter; DPH *n also attrib* 1: In the American League, a tenth player who may, if the manager chooses, be named in the line-up to bat for the pitcher, but anywhere in the batting order 1973 Joe Durso, Feb 4 *NY Times* S1/1 "In the baseball box scores this summer, he will be listed as the 'dh,' the designated hitter for the pitcher. . . . [¶] Q. Just who or what is the designated hitter? [¶] A. In an experiment voted by the American League on Jan. 11, he is a player who will be designated by the manager on any given day to bat for the pitcher." Ibid S1–2 "Q. Is the designated hitter the same as the designated pinch-hitter? [¶] A. He's the same fellow. Since the American League adopted the experiment last month, it has been decided that the proper term is 'designated hitter'—he doesn't bat or pinch-hit for the pitcher, but bats instead of the pitcher without forcing him from the game." Mar 7 *Tuscaloosa News* 19/5–6 (AP) "American League owners, faced with dwindling fan interest, created the 'designated hitter' to put more sock into their game. [¶] . . . Minnesota nominated big Larry Hisle for the DH role in Tuesday's first exhibition baseball game and the Twins' 10th man murdered Pittsburgh." Mar 11 ibid 6B/5 (AP) "The AL teams has [*sic*] been using the designated hitter for the pitcher during spring training." Ibid (heading) "DPH Official Debut April 6" John C Smith, Mar 30 *Natl Review* 370/2 "A designated hitter (DH) has been instituted [in the American League]. . . . Each team will pick a tenth man to hit for the pitcher. . . . the designated hitter can appear anywhere in the order." Mar 31 *TV Guide* 30 "This year the American League will try its 'Designated Hitter's Rule' to add power to the manager's line-up." Wells Twombly, Apr 1 *NY Times Mag* 17/1 "Known as the 'designated hitter' rule, the new regulation, in effect for the next three seasons, will permit a manager to add a 10th man to his starting line-up. The sole task of this 'designated hitter,' or 'dh,' will be to hit for the pitcher, or for those who relieve him. The pitcher will not be required to leave the game, as he is when a pinch hitter substitutes for him." Apr 4 *Tuscaloosa News* 15/1–2 (heading) "Bench-warmers Like DPH Rule" Ibid 15/1 (AP) "DH really stands for designated hitter." Apr 7 ibid 6/1 (AP) "Blomberg became the first official designated hitter in major league baseball history." 2: With transferred sense Feb 17 *New Yorker* 31/2–3 (cartoon caption, older member of firm introducing new employee:) "Fenton, I want you to meet Ted Bolton, our new designated pinch-hitter."

dh, DH DESIGNATED HITTER

DPH Designated pinch-hitter (see DESIGNATED HITTER)

ear wire, earwire *n* See quots 1942 William T Baxter and Henry C Dake *Jewelry, Gem Cutting, and Metalcraft* (NY: McGraw-Hill) 112 (The eardrops shown are the screw-on type.) "By the use of pierceless ear wires, many types of eardrops may be made with both faceted and cabochon stones." 1964 Richard T Liddicoat Jr and Lawrence L Copeland *The Jewelers' Manual* (Los Angeles: Gemological Inst of America) 251 "earwire, or earring. An ornament attached to the ear lobe by a small screw or clip or by a wire piercing the ear." 1965? Dec Lorch's *Diamond Shops Catalog* "Sterling Faceted with 14 kt Ear wires" 1971 Dec 31 *Tuscaloosa News* 8/6 "The self-piercers take so long and then when they finally do push through, the hole is so small that only ear wires will fit into it." 1973 Apr 19 ibid 6/3–5 (ad) "a complete wardrobe of pierced earrings . . . all with 14-kt. gold earwires or posts."

electionomics *n* [*election* + *economics*, perhaps by analogy with NIXONOMICS] Economic policies or actions considered primarily from the standpoint of their possible effect on the election of candidates advocating them. 1972 June 16 *Life* 53/2 "Their 'electionomics' is based on something-for-nothing: it promises more service (free medicine, more welfare, money to rebuild the cities) without more taxes, or with some kind of shell game that anticipates enormous benefits if only we 'close the loopholes.' [¶] There is no pinning down an adept practitioner of electionomics." July 10 *Time* 76/2 "Nixon might have tempted foreign ranchers to sell more to the U.S. if he had permanently lifted the protectionist, inflationary import quotas. That action, however, would have been bad electionomics because it would have endangered his farm vote."

fast-food *adj* [*WNCD8, BDNE* as adj] For additional uses see quots 1971 Oct *Reader's Digest* 139/2 (condensed from *NY Times Mag* July 4) "And it tastes pretty much like a dozen other fast-food burgers." Ibid "I consulted a 15-year-old fast-food freak I know." —**fast food** *n* 1972 Oct 16 Ken Ringle (*Wash Post*) *Tuscaloosa News* 5/2 "Fast food is a $1 billion business for McDonald's."

hot pants, hotpants, HotPants *n pl* [*BDNE* suggests an origin and defines as a garment "worn by women."] Also worn by men 1971 Feb 15 *Natl Observer* 8/4 "Hot pants. These short shorts are not as short as the women's version." Sept *GQ: Gentlemen's Quarterly* 126/2 "And when he orders a three-piece suit, the third piece isn't a vest. It's hotpants." 1972 *Brit Book of the Year* 733/2 (under "Words and Meanings, New") "hot pants *n pl*: very short shorts." (For the spelling *HotPants*, see preliminary remarks.)

McGovernomics *n* [George *McGovern* + *economics;* perhaps by analogy with NIXONOMICS] See first quot 1972 July 4 *Atlanta Journal* 6A/2 (NYT) "The term 'McGovernomics [*sic*] is frequently used in a jocular sense to describe McGovern's policies for income redistribution, welfare reform and changes in the nation's tax structure. The word crops up repeatedly in investment advisory reports issued by brokerage houses." Fall *Johns Hopkins Mag* 10–11 (heading) "NIXONOMICS VS. MCGOVERNOMICS by Carl F. Christ"

Nixonian *adj* [Richard M *Nixon* + *-ian*] 1970 David Halberstam, July *Harper's* 30/3 "It was not, after all, critics of the Administration who defined Nixonian language for us—Don't watch what we say, watch what we do—it was the Administration spokesmen themselves." 1971 Nov 1 *Between the Lines* (Newtown Pa) 1/1 "Voluntarism, the theme of the new Nixonian-economics, puts capitalism to its most severe test." 1972 Jan 26 *Tuscaloosa News* 8/1 (AP) "Conservatives have shown rising irritation with the Nixonian economics." May 29 *Newsweek* 30/2 "Connally stepped down at the apogee of his influence in Nixonian Washington." Oct 29 *NY Times Book Review* 46/3 "Herblock analyzes Nixonian techniques such as the Happening or Non-Event in which the Vice President is photographed standing at a podium addressing the President and full Cabinet and telling them what a great job they are doing or the Word-Shaking Event [*sic*] in which the President explains that whatever he has done is the first or greatest or most surprising event ever."

Nixonomics *n* [*BDNE*] 1: Additional quots 1969 Oct 29 *Demo Memo* (Wash DC) 1 "Walter Heller . . . challenges the soundness of 'Nixonomics.' " Dec 4 ibid 2/3 "House Democratic Leader Carl Albert charged that Nixon Administration economics—recently dubbed 'Nixonomics' by Economist Walter Heller—were 'placing this country in dire peril of a recession.' " 2: For the sense of the collocation *new Nixonomics*, see quots 1971 Aug 30 *Newsweek* 3/1 "President Nixon's 180-degree turn in economic policy produced a tumultuous week on many fronts, at home and abroad. . . . Subsequent sections [of *Newsweek*'s cover story] examine the three main components of the new Nixonomics. . . . the wage-price freeze . . . the dollar's new role in international finance and trade . . . the President's program to stimulate the economy." Sept 19 *NY Times* 2E/2 "By way of making more graphic his resolve to move forward aggressively on the activist tack, the President dredged up a term he had always treated with derision as a symbol of economic blundering by his Democratic predecessors and converted it to the dynamics of the new Nixonomics. He was going to use 'jawboning,' he said, but he was going to make it meaningful by putting teeth in the jawbone." 1972 Jan 17 *Newsweek* 61/1 "From the very beginning of phase two of the new Nixonomics, the clamor has been growing for firm and consistent actions by the Pay Board and Price Commission and clarification of the legal tangles surrounding any wage or price increase." Oct 16 *Newsweek* 89/1 "But phase two of the new Nixonomics has changed nearly all the rules—and as one result, quite a few companies these days . . . are going out of their way . . . to cut profits down."

pitch-hitter *n* DESIGNATED HITTER [*pinch-hitter* with substitution of *pitch-* prob from *pitcher*] 1973 Mar 31 *TV Guide* 30 "Next week in TV Guide: . . . THE PITCH-HITTER [¶] . . . This year the American League will try its 'Designated Hitter's Rule' to add power to a manager's line-up."

post *n* Shaft of a stud earring; see 1971 quot 1965? Dec Lorch's *Diamond Shops Catalog* "Cultured Pearls with 14kt Posts." 1966 Dec 11 *Tuscaloosa News* 10/1–3 (ad) "Whatever your earring whim, it's here in 14 kt. Gold or 14 kt. Gold Filled, all with posts of 14 kt. Gold." 1971 Dec 31 *Tuscaloosa News* 8/3–4 "The back of the earring is placed on the earring post, and the simple process is over." 1973 see EAR WIRE

see-through *adj* [*World Bk Dict 71* and *WNCD8* as adj; *BDNE* as adj and n] Additional quot 1966 *Brit Book of the Year* 298/1 "Under the circumstances, it is not surprising that 1965 should have produced its 'see-through' blouses and sweaters, its rib cutouts and midriff transparencies, that shoulders should have been widely bared by cut-out armholes, and that 'peep-a-boo' holes should have been used on casual shoes and sun hats."

see-throughness *n* [*see-through* adj + *-ness*] Transparency 1971 Apr *House & Garden* 104/1 "Almost anything fabric can do, crochet can do, too, plus adding its singular charm of pattern, texture, see-throughness."

semi-porno *n* [*BDNE* sv *porn*] Motion picture that, while daring or erotic in content, is less explicit in its treatment of the subject than a pornographic film 1972 John Ciardi Apr 1 *Sat Review* 12/1 "Glower and grin [the masks of tragedy and comedy above a theater marquee] had made a long grimace of it in their time, looking down successively on traveling drama companies, minstrel shows... foreign art films, and—in a last lost effort to stave off the wreckers—semi-pornos."

wire *n* See EAR WIRE [1965 Klares Lewes *Jewelry Making for the Amateur* (London: B T Batsford; NY: Reinhold) 55 "for pierced ears the attached wire can itself be formed into a hook instead of a ring."] 1967 Aug 9 *Tuscaloosa News* 18A/1–2 (ad) "Monogrammed Earrings... —Available with gold filled, 14 K wires or post." 1973 Mar *Family Circle* 16/1 "Attach your creations to old pierced-ear wires."

[Received June 1973]

AMONG THE NEW WORDS

I. WILLIS RUSSELL and MARY GRAY PORTER
University of Alabama

MANY OF THE ENTRIES in this installment are supported by only one citation; nevertheless, we believe they will be of some interest to readers of this department because of their relationship, in one way or another, to more abundantly attested items.

Ping-pong diplomacy seems to have been the immediate model for *baseball diplomacy*, *table-tennis diplomacy*, and *volleyball diplomacy*. All agree in having the name of a sport as the attribute and, with the possible exception of *baseball diplomacy*, in referring to efforts to ease international tension, but are otherwise analogous to the older phrases *dollar diplomacy* (*DA* 1911), *gunboat diplomacy* (*BDNE* s.v., note) *King Cotton Diplomacy* (the title of a book by Frank L. Owsley, published in 1931 by the University of Chicago Press), and *shirt-sleeve diplomacy* (*DA* 1933; *shirt-sleeve diplomacy* in *Saturday Review of Literature*, 5 Oct. 1929, p. 204).

In the only citation of the phrase in our files, *ping-pong diplomat* denotes a member of the American table-tennis team which visited China, even though the overtures to ping-pong diplomacy came from the Chinese. Compare, however, *U.S. News and World Report*, 17 Apr. 1972, p. 46 (the entire heading is quoted below s.v. *ping-pong diplomacy*): "To warm up relations with the U.S., Peking is sending envoys wielding table-tennis paddles."

The game of table tennis has not only furnished the occasion and a metaphor for the reduction of tensions between the United States and the People's Republic of China, but has also provided *ping-pong* (v.i.) 'to be tossed back and forth for discussion' and *ping-pong* (v.t.) 'to toss (a subject) back and forth for discussion.' The shift of the sound of a Ping-Pong ball from one side of the playing area to the other has given *ping-pong* and *ping-ping-pong-pong* for excessive shifting from one channel to another in the recording and reproduction of stereophonic and quadriphonic sound, respectively.

Designated pinch hitter, an alternate name for the *designated hitter*, seems to have been abandoned soon after the American League's adoption of the designated-hitter rule early in 1973, but it has attained some currency as a synonym for 'substitute.' Although the designated hitter is the only extra player whose specialized activity has been authorized, and that only in the American League, sportswriters have raised the possibility that other

specialists may also be added to the traditional nine-man baseball team: the *designated base runner* or *designated runner*, who would run for the catcher, and a second designated hitter. A writer in *Newsweek* (16 Apr. 1973, p. 52/3), following baseball terminology, uses the verb *designate*, instead of the more obvious *delegate* or *assign*, in a meaning adequately covered by *W3*, definition 4a, but in a context that indicates he is engaging in a form of wordplay. He writes of the persons assigned to perform specific tasks related to the beginning of the new season in major-league baseball: "Forsaking the Presidential pitch-it-yourself tradition, Mr. Nixon designated Air Force Maj. David Luna, a former Vietnam POW, to throw out the first ball at the California Angels' home opener in Anaheim, which he did to thunderous applause. For its part, the National League refused to break with tradition and will not use designated players. But *Newsweek* designated Associate Editor Peter Bonventre to give his predictions for the 1973 season."

We would like to repeat a statement made in a previous installment of "Among the New Words": For this department, a new word is a word or meaning that has not yet been entered in one of the standard dictionaries. Since, however, the commercial dictionaries—and they are the ones that are kept up-to-date—do not include dated citations,[1] it seems useful to publish from time to time the earliest citation in the editor's file of a new word or meaning that is entered and defined in one of the standard dictionaries of recent date but has not been treated in "Among the New Words."

Acknowledgments: O. B. Emerson (*ping-pong* v.i.), Mamie J. Meredith (*comitology*, 1960 Feb. 22, and her comments on C. N. Parkinson's address), and Anne B. Russell (*corn row*, 1973 Feb. 23).

baseball diplomacy *n* 1971 July 17 *Tuscaloosa News* 1/1 (AP) "Hungarian and Polish newspapers, registering the first Soviet-bloc reaction to President Nixon's planned trip to Communist China, have called it 'baseball diplomacy' and a 'shocking somersault.'"

comitology *n* [*committee* + *-ology*] See quots 1960 Jan 3 *NY Times Mag* 25/2 "While this is not in dispute, the fact remains that the discoverer of the law [Parkinson] was also the founder of Comitology—the study of the life cycle and evolutionary development of the Committee—which is the latest of the biological sciences." Feb 22 title of address by C Northcote Parkinson at Univ of Nebr convocation "Comitology—the Life Cycle of a Committee" (Mamie J Meredith, who sent in the citation, added this comment: "Parkinson says he got the idea for his 'law' while serving as a major with the British Army during World War II. While a member of a committee whose jurisdiction was somewhere between the British Army, Navy, and Air Force, he noticed that the executives simply made work for each other, 'reading each other's minutes and criticizing each other's grammar.'" 1961 *Brit Book of the Year* 752/2 1969 Oct 30 *Tuscaloosa News* 4/4 James J Kilpatrick "To judge from internal evidence (the work itself is not dated), Parkinson's preliminary conclusions upon the science of comitology must have appeared in the summer of 1953, not long after the creation in April of the U.S. Department of Health, Education and Welfare. This was the tenth department of our government. Ideally, as Parkinson shows, a Cabinet should not have more than five members, which was how the Republic began."

corn row *n* [*BDNE* vt & i 1972; the literal sense dates from 1769, *DAE*] See quots under vb 1971 Sep 5 *Tuscaloosa News* 6C/3 Aileen Jacobson (*Wash Post*) "They may do it themselves, as Laurel Tucker, a teacher, does, or they may find 'a friend with nimble fingers,' as Ana Maria Covington, a freelance TV journalist and teacher, does when she wants her short hair in corn rows." 1973 Feb 23 "Dinah's Place" NBC "[Cicely Tyson:] 'It stems from what we call corn row.' [Dinah Shore:] 'Is corn-rowing replacing the natural?'"

cornrow *vb* [*BDNE* 1972] Earlier quots 1971 Sep 5 *Tuscaloosa News* 6C/1 Aileen Jacobson (*Wash Post*) "Others are braiding or 'cornrowing' their hair in a return to childhood hairstyles, newly discovered to be a custom for some adult African women." Nov 8 ibid 10/4 Marily Goldstein (*Newsday*) "The first thing little black girls once did when they got to be big girls was to unbraid their 'corn-rowed' hair. Now big black girls borrow back this childhood coiffure. Cornrowing—the process of dividing the hair into geometric sections and braiding the sections flat to the scalp—is high style." Ibid 10/6 "Corn-rowing is different from common braiding because the corn rows do not hang loose. The hair to be corn-rowed is divided into three clumps, just as for regular braiding, but not all the hair is taken up into the clumps. Some of it is left loose and the loose strands are worked into each crossover of the braid, thus anchoring it flat to the scalp."

deck *vt* [*W3*, *RHD* & *WNCD8* define with quots from boxing] Quots from football 1968 Nov 18 *Tuscaloosa News* 5/2 (AP) "Starr gave way to Zeke Bratkowski early in the third quarter after being decked on an 11-yard scramble." 1970 Nov 22 Curt Gowdy over NBC "Unitas was decked after he let the ball go." 1971 Nov 29 *Tuscaloosa News* 7/2–3 (AP) "Namath's nerves got away from him with 10:33 left in the second quarter when Davis was decked and forced out of the game with a sprained right ankle."

designated base runner *n* See DESIGNATED RUNNER

designated homer; designated HR *n* Home run hit by a designated hitter 1973 Aug 7 *Tuscaloosa News* 9/6–8 (heading) "Hank [Aaron] Proves His Point / With Designated Homer" Ibid 11/1 (heading) "Designated / HR Proves / Aaron Point."

designated pinch hitter *n* See *AS* 46 (1971), 145; add under 2: With transferred sense: substitute, replacement, stand-in Additional quots 1973 Mar 26 *Newsweek* 27/3 "[Héctor] Campora himself was the first to admit that his main qualifications for office were an unswerving loyalty to Perón—who tapped him in 1972 as his own designated pinch hitter in the election—and long service in the Peronista cause." May 28 *Newsweek* 15/2 Alden Whitman "Speaking of things to drink, it's 100 to 1 that only a few of you have drunk Maryland rye whisky,

1. The recent *Barnhart Dictionary of New English since 1963* has dated citations, but since, in the editor's view, "it would be fruitless to give a historical account of words whose available attestation in publications spans a mere ten years, the order of the quotations is not necessarily chronological and no attempt is made to give the earliest quotation available. The emphasis is placed instead on the utility of the quotations" (p. 23).

a noble product that has given way to blended booze, a designated pinch hitter of dubious provenance."

designated runner; designated base runner *n* Additional baseball player who may eventually be added to the lineup to run for the catcher 1973 July 16 *New Yorker* 56/3 Roger Angell "The age of the baseball specialist has arrived, and with two specialists already admitted to the lineup—the designated hitter and, in his new capacity, the pitcher—who can doubt that within another season or two there may not be more: the designated base runner, the *second* designated hitter, and, in time, the offensive and defensive teams?" Sep *Esquire* 39/2-3 Roger Kahn " 'The game isn't dying,' [Bing] Devine said. 'In fact good things are happening. I'm in favor of the designated hitter. Like Lou Brock, I'd be in favor of a designated runner. Remember the great excitement Jackie Robinson brought on the bases. Suppose now instead of watching some heavy-legged catcher drag from first to second you could see an Olympic sprinter.' "

designee *n* Designated hitter 1973 July 16 *New Yorker* 56/2 Roger Angell "The designees have hit out a hundred and seven [home runs] so far, as against a full season's total of forty-eight by the 1972 pitchers and pinch-hitters."

empty nest *n* Demographic group composed of parents whose children no longer live in the parental home 1973 Mar *Esquire* 84/2 "[Rip Coalson, president of a film-making company, American National Enterprises, Salt Lake City:] 'We know what kind of movies people want to see, because if our company has a forte at all, it's research. In our test market, we give our audiences quite extensive questionnaires, and we get a socio-economic profile of each one of them. Altogether we have twenty-seven categories, and these are much more subtle than just blue-collar, white-collar, managerial-professional, and youth. For example, one of our categories is "empty nest," and a sub-category of that is "solitary survivor," which is to say widows and widowers.' "

empty-nest depression *n* EMPTY-NEST SYNDROME 1973 Apr *Ladies' Home Journal* 47/2 Letty Cottin Pogrebin "Meaningful employment is one of the best antidotes to the 'empty nest' depression women often experience when their children leave home."

empty nester *n* One who no longer has a child living at home 1966 July 29 *Time* 53/1 "If her children are in their teens, the shadow of becoming an 'empty nester' also falls across her spirit." 1970 Dec 7 *USN & WR* 88/1-2 "Says John Fagan, vice president for marketing of the Housing Guidance Council in Washington: 'They [buyers of condominium units] are the "empty nesters" whose children have flown and who now want something smaller but just as elegant as they had before.' " 1972 Sep *Town & Country* 100/4 "Then there are the 'empty nesters'—people whose kids are out of the big old family home. . . . Empty nesters are a major factor in condominium golf communities." Oct 9 *USN & WR* 62/2 " 'Condos [condominiums] are quite attractive to young persons without children and to empty nesters in the 50-65 age group who do not want to maintain a large house after their children have gone,' said Michael L. Humphreys, a California housing developer."

empty-nest syndrome *n* Changes in the mental and emotional state of parents whose children have grown up and moved away from home; form of depression common in women whose children no longer live at home (see also EMPTY-NEST DEPRESSION) 1972 Feb *Ladies' Home Journal* 124/4 "Even the 'empty nest' syndrome hasn't seemed to hit her. She seems genuinely delighted by both of her daughters' marriages." Dec *McCall's* 132/1 "There is even a depression so common in women of middle age that it is called 'empty-nest syndrome'—the feelings prompted when children leave home." 1973 Jan *McCall's* 138/3 "We knew, of course, about the empty-nest syndrome but were not perceptive enough to recognize it in ourselves. It did not occur to us that to grow gracefully into a new kind of life required an affectionate search for the neglected, unused parts of ourselves."

karate chop *n* [BDNE 1970] Figurative use 1970 Feb 8 *Tuscaloosa News* 37/2 (AP) "President Nixon's $200.8 billion budget submitted the past week to Congress was a karate chop in the fight against inflation, but it will take time to see how well the blow was aimed." 1971 Feb 22 *Newsweek* 56/2 "But although [Norman] Mailer delivers karate chops aplenty, he has never been a man to come through fire without more keenly tempered insights, and he deals fairly, seriously, and even tenderly with the whole emotion-fraught subject—from the exploitative Kinder, Küche, Kirche syndrome (a matter of 'who would finally do the dishes?') to the womb-hating militants who would like to think of themselves as 'men who bore the burden of the reproductive process.' " 1972 July 14 *W* (biweekly published by *Women's Wear Daily*) 6/1 "The young reformer's victory ousted Celler from the seat he has held for 50 years, giving an acutely felt karate chop to the machine that backed the venerable lawmaker."

letter bomb *n* also *attrib* See quots 1972 Sep 24 *NY Times* sec 4 2/4 "After the explosion another deadly letter bomb was found in the [Israeli] embassy and four more were uncovered and rendered harmless at the London post office." Ibid "How secure are Israeli officials here from such letter-bomb attacks?" Sep 30 *National Observer* 5/1 Lawrence Mosher "Enter the letter-bomb, the latest in a lengthening list of terrorist techniques that reflect the apparently limitless depths of Middle East despair and vindictiveness. . . . [¶] Some of the bombs were described as long and thin like pencils. Some were said to consist of thin strips of plastic explosives. Others were reported to look like oversized tea bags, similar to the U.S. 'gravel' mines that used to be scattered over parts of Vietnam to inhibit Viet Cong traffic. Tightly wrapped in cardboard or stiff paper, the explosives were designed to go off when pressure was removed from a spring coiled or folded inside the wrappings." Oct 2 *Newsweek* 30/2-3 "Yet the use of the letter-bombs pointed up once again the seemingly infinite variety of weapons at the disposal of the Arab commandos." 1973 Apr *Reader's Digest* 92/2 "Their [terrorists'] methods are becoming ever more sophisticated. . . . They've perfected the letter bomb." Aug 29 *Montgomery Advertiser* 13/5 (AP) "A British embassy secretary maimed in a letter-bomb explosion was reported 'in good spirits' and recovering satisfactorily at a local hospital." Sep 1 *National Observer* 2/3 "At least 12 letter bombs were received at London offices and department stores, and one was delivered to British Prime Minister Edward Heath's residence."

mail-a-bomb *n* also *attrib* LETTER BOMB 1972 Sep 28 *NY Times* 46/5 (heading and letter) "American-Made / Mail-a-Bombs / To the Editor: / One of the most tragic aspects of the mail-a-bomb campaign against Israeli diplomats, so far overlooked by most observers, is the fact that the bombs used in the campaign are American-made gravel mines, and were first used by American forces in Indochina."

mail bomb *n* LETTER BOMB 1972 Sep 24 *NY Times* sec 4 2/3 (heading) "Mail Bombs: / Death / In an / Envelope."

micro-skirted *adj* Wearing a very short skirt 1969 July 28 *Newsweek* 64/1 "He is accompanied everywhere by a clutch of two, three or more young micro-skirted jet-setters." 1971 July 12 ibid 78/3 " 'This is nothing but out-and-out harassment,' fumed one micro-skirted young Manhattan hooker as she fled from the shutter."

miniskirted [AHD, RHD 1969, BDNE miniskirt *n* 1968, IWR file 1966] Earlier quots 1966 Nov 12 *New Yorker* 53/3 " 'New York is a *rough* town,' said a miniskirted young woman with green eye makeup and hair the color of talcum powder." Dec 4 *Tuscaloosa News* 54/4-5 (AP) "Everything looked 18th century except one thing—the two shapely legs of miniskirted Jutta Morris of the British Travel Association, twinkling from beneath her heavy cloak." Dec 11 ibid 10/2-3 "If women can wear trousers, why can't men wear miniskirts? a Munich, Germany, men's shop reasons. The miniskirted male model at the right dances with a female counterpart at a showing." 1967 Feb 19 *NY Times Book Rev* 50/3 "Its offices, with their valuable collection of half-empty bottles and their mini-skirted decor, provide a welcome goal for a local writer's afternoon amble in the sun of North Beach." 1969 Oct 16 *Tuscaloosa News* 12/4 (AP) " 'I was scared to death,' said miniskirted Kristine Anderson."

ping-ping-pong-pong *n* Four-channel sound recorded with exaggerated shifts from one loudspeaker to another, usually with the primary aim of demonstrating the capabilities of the equipment See quot sv PING-PONG *n*

ping-pong *n* [OED *ping-pong* "parlour game resembling lawn-tennis" 1900; WNCD8 *Ping-Pong* "trademark—used for table tennis"] See quot 1971 Aug *Pop Sci* 20/1 "But you may remember that in the early days of stereo there was a lot of 'Ping-Pong'—sound that jumped back and forth from one speaker to another for no reason except to convince the customer that he was listening to stereo. Unfortunately, most of the people making four-channel recordings now can't seem to resist fooling around, and most of the recordings I've heard could be called Ping-Ping-Pong-Pong."

ping-pong *adj* 1: Pertaining to the improved relations between the United States and mainland China as a result of PING-PONG DIPLOMACY 1971 Apr 26 *Newsweek* 20/1 "If rapprochement between China and the U.S. ever gets past the Ping-Pong stage, the impact on world affairs could be immense—and unpredictable. Even a moderate warming trend could, for example, alter the course of the war in Vietnam." 1972 Apr 29 *National Observer* 7/2 Wesley Pruden Jr "He [President Nixon] thanked Graham Steenhoven of Detroit, the president of the U.S. Table Tennis Association, who led an American team to Peking last year in the celebrated Ping-Pong thaw and who arranged the return visit [of a Chinese table-tennis team to the US]." Dec 9 *New Yorker* 122/2 "Meanwhile, table tennis, which was given a boost by international politics (People's Republic of China division) last year, continues to prosper; sales have risen three hundred per cent in many stores since the great Ping-Pong *rapprochement*." 2: Showing Chinese influence, as a result of or subsequent to the initiatives of PING-PONG DIPLOMACY 1971 Nov *McCall's* 36/4 (heading) "PING-PONG FASHION."

ping-pong 1: *vi* Bounce back and forth; be discussed in several quarters 1952 Aug 21 *Jackson* (Tenn) *Sun* 1/1-2 (heading) "Question of Margaret's Guards Ping-Pongs Across Atlantic." 2: *vt* Bat around; discuss (a matter) without reaching a decision 1970 Nov 22 *Washington Post* B6/3-4 "So while the administration 'ping-ponged' the proposal back and forth, as one spokesman put it, Rep. Thomas L. Ashley (D.-Ohio) and Sen. John J. Sparkman (D.-Ala.) along with other leading Democrats, stepped in and introduced it last March."

ping-pong diplomacy *n* First step toward normalized relationships between the United States and mainland China, initiated by an invitation to a US table-tennis team to compete in the People's Republic of China 1971 June 14 *Newsweek* 106/3 "Whether the recent breakthrough of Ping Pong diplomacy will lead one day to the permanent stationing of American correspondents on Mainland China still remains to be seen." June 21 ibid 33/1 "The trade list began to take shape last April as a part of the Administration's response to Peking's Ping Pong diplomacy." July 31 *New Yorker* 60/2 "The domestic problems that China faces in recovering from the turmoil of her cultural revolution, plus her desire to build up a new trade relationship with the United States, must have led her to make the decision to follow up the earlier stages of ping-pong diplomacy with the invitation to Dr. Kissinger and to President Nixon." Aug 22 *Tuscaloosa News* 10A/1 (AP) "A visit to Communist China by a U.S. table tennis team initiated what was described as 'Ping-Pong Diplomacy' and was followed in July by President Nixon's announcement that he will visit Peking before next May." Sep 18 *Sat Rev* 44/2 "Add to these developments [reductions in US forces in the Philippines and in Thailand] 'Ping-Pong diplomacy,' and it seems reasonable to conclude that the containment of John Foster Dulles is dead even if it has not been replaced by a policy of total disengagement." Dec *Atlas* 27/2 "They may have paid lip service to Mao's line but they want ping-pong diplomacy, the profit motive for the peasant, sound economy, a modern professional Army in the field and political indoctrination kept in its proper place." Dec 11 *New Yorker* 112/2 "And, of course, 1971 was the year that brought 'ping-pong diplomacy' into the language and promised to send the sales of table-tennis sets to new highs." 1972 Jan *Atlantic* 39/2 Ross Terrill "Now he [Chou En-lai] reaches across an epoch of China's modern history to face Richard Nixon in the ping-pong diplomacy of the 1970s." Jan *Atlas* 59/3 (tr from *Münchner Merkur*) "Yet, despite eased travel restrictions since the new ping-pong diplomacy, it is still amazing to find that a German writer has been allowed to travel 3,000 miles through the People's Republic." Apr 17 *USN & WR* 46 (heading) " 'Ping-Pong' Diplomacy / CHINESE ATHLETES / OPEN ANOTHER ROUND / To warm up relations with the U.S., Peking is sending envoys wielding table-tennis paddles." Dec *Harper's* 44/2 Barbara Tuchman "When the break [between Russia and China] developed into open hostility, the need of friends, or at least of new options and new alignments, became crucial, however awkward ideologically. Hence ping-pong diplomacy, rapprochement first with the U.S., then Japan, and fervent patronage of the small Third World nations." 1973 June *Atlantic* 4/3 Ross Terrill "When introduced late in the Cultural Revolution, it [China's 'dual adversary' policy] looked like a closed-door policy for a winter of defiance. But it proved no less serviceable as the basis for a very forthcoming policy during the springtime of Ping-Pong and U.N. diplomacy."

ping-pong diplomat *n* A member of the US table-tennis team that visited the People's Republic of China in April 1971 1972 Feb 5 *TV Guide* A-30 (box) "A veteran China watcher, [John] Roderick covered the Nationalist-Communist civil war in the '40s, and returned last April with the U.S. ping-pong diplomats."

ping-ponger *n* [OED *ping-pong vi, ping-pongist n*, 1901] Table-tennis player 1972 Mar 18 *National Observer* 16/1 "For the chief resident and Ping-ponger extraordinaire is one Dal-Joon Lee."

post-ping-pong *adj* Following the resumption of contacts between the United States and the People's Republic of China 1971 Aug 9 *National Observer* 24/2 "So when Anne Keatley had the opportunity to roam the country in the post-Ping-Pong thaw in international relations, her observations provided a rare insight into the life and moods of modern China." (see also PING-PONG *adj*)

spirit of ping pong *n* Rapprochement of China and the United States following the 1971 invitation to a US table-tennis team to visit China 1971 May 8 *Science News* 313/1 "At a news briefing following the business meeting of the National Academy of Sciences last week, the Academy vice president, Dr. George B. Kistiakowsky of Harvard University, remarked that 'we hope to extend the spirit of Ping Pong to international [scientific] collaboration.' "

table-tennis diplomacy *n* [*OED table tennis n* 1902; see prelim remarks, par 2] PING-PONG DIPLOMACY 1971 May 10 *Newsweek* 43/1 " 'Diplomacy,' some of those in business are fond of saying, 'is frequently the art of making a good impression unexpectedly.' If so, then the diplomats of Mao Tse-tung's China—having just dazzled the world with their championship techniques in table-tennis diplomacy—appear to have mastered the art." June 18 *Tuscaloosa News* 4/2 Jack Anderson "Chinese Quandary—the best intelligence estimate is that Red China would like to restore normal relations with the U.S. in order to counter the Soviet military build-up on the Chinese border. But Peking's table-tennis diplomacy with the U.S. has upset its hard-line camp followers round the world. The most militant communists look to Peking for leadership. There was a backfire, therefore, when Peking appeared to be adopting a softer line toward the U.S."

turn over *vt* [Cf *OED turn* 77,h 1552] Lose (the ball) to the opposing team through an error or misplay 1971 Jan 29 *Tuscaloosa News* 8/5 " 'We knew we could force Kentucky to turn the ball over and we did. The difference is we didn't convert on the turnovers and they did. Kent Hollenbeck got three steals and three baskets and Casey added another while we didn't get many of those.' " Dec 5 Curt Gowdy over NBC "They turned the ball over."

turnover *n* [*WNCD8* def 8; cf *OED* A,1 1660] Earlier quots 1969 Mar 20 Curt Gowdy over NBC "North Carolina has 22 turnovers, Purdue 11." 1971 Jan 25 *Sports Illust* 12 (sub-heading) "Baltimore had seven turnovers and Dallas only four." Sep 27 *Tuscaloosa News* 6/7 (AP) " 'We've averaged six turn over [*sic*] a game for our past four games,' said Florida Coach Doug Dickey, 'and you can't win ball games with that kind of mistake-making, no matter what kind of desire you have.' "

volleyball diplomacy *n* [see prelim remarks, par 2] Potential, but as yet unrealized, normalization of relations between the United States and Cuba as a result of a US volleyball team's competing in Cuba 1971 Aug 22 *Tuscaloosa News* 10A/1 (AP) "The Nixon administration does not rule out the long-range possibility of more normal relations with Communist Cuba, but officials said Saturday they do not anticipate a round of 'volleyball diplomacy.' . . . An American volleyball team has been in Havana this week, competing in an Olympic play-off series, and the traveling party reportedly has been well received."

AMONG THE NEW WORDS

I. WILLIS RUSSELL AND MARY GRAY PORTER
University of Alabama

Since this department is historically oriented, we continue to publish earlier citations for new words that have not been treated here and are now in the standard dictionaries, especially if they contain good defining details or unrecorded variant terms. *CATV* in the glossary below is a good example. If the term for which we supply earlier quotations is entered in one or more recent dictionaries, we cite them with their dates of publication, except in the case of the new *OEDS* and the *BDNE*, for which we use the date of the earliest quotation.

The 1963 quotation for *flipper* in the run-on entry under *flipping* seems especially interesting to us since it may give a clue to the origin of this sense of *flipping*. Do we have here a transfer of *flipper* in the sense of 'one who flips cards' to the individual whose card-flipping is a part of the loan shark's operation and hence is also called a *flipper*? In any case, the *flipper* here seems to be the agent noun formed from the underlying form of the *flipping* dealt with in the entry.

Five of the citations under the entry *-hop*, namely, *booth-hopping, castle-hopping, party-hopping, publisher-hopping*, and *tavern-hopping*, are drawn from the late Mamie J. Meredith's "Radiation of 'Hop' " (*American Speech*, 30, 1955, 72–73). Meredith notices the extension of meaning in this group but does not spell out what it is.

In footnoting Meredith's material for the Mencken-McDavid *American Language* (p. 245n), Raven I. McDavid, Jr., recognizes the suffixal nature of this use of *hop* by employing the form *-hop* in both the index and the note, but he likewise offers no definition. In describing *booth-hopper, castle-hopping, party-hopping* as "derivative nouns in *-er* and *-ing*," he assumes an underlying verb form, just as we do in these and other examples in the glossary below.

As can be seen from the references and quotations in the entry for *-hop*, as early as 1954 (with *Webster's New World Dictionary*), combinations with *-hop* have been appearing in modern dictionaries. With the publication of *Webster's Third* and in later dictionaries, including the *W3 Addenda*, the definitions of the terms entered take the shape that suggests our definition and suggests also, with our additional examples, that *-hop* has become an active combining form. The *BDNE*, it may be observed, recognizes the type in its etymology of *job-hop* as "patterned after *table-hop, island-hop*, etc."

We would like to cite a fairly recent reference book that we are finding extremely useful. It is *Words and Phrases Index: A Guide to Antedatings, New*

Words, New Compounds, New Meanings, and Other Published Scholarship Supplementing the Oxford English Dictionary, Dictionary of Americanisms, Dictionary of American English and other Major Dictionaries of the English Language, compiled by C. Edward Wall and Edward Przebienda, 4 vols., Ann Arbor: Pierian Press, 1969–70.

Acknowledgments: For citations, E. E. Ericson (1), James B. McMillan (1), Norman R. McMillan (1), Mamie J. Meredith (3), Anne B. Russell (1), Eleanor Symons (1).

cable TV *n* [*BDNE* 1970] See 1966 quot sv CATV

cartop *vi* [cf *World Book Dict* 1971 sv *cartop adj* "designed to be transported on the roof of an automobile: *a cartop boat*"] 1: Load and transport a boat on top of an automobile 1972 Jan *Pop Sci* 78/2 See quot sv CAR-TOPPER 2: Of a boat, be loaded and transported on the top of a car 1973 May *Pop Sci* 148/3 "Because it's light, cartops conveniently, can be paddled easily by one person for long periods of time, and can be used in very shallow water—the canoe is ideal for river travel."

cartop *vt* 1: Load and transport (a small boat or other bulky object) on top of an automobile 1971 Sep *Pop Sci* 75/1–2 (photo caption) "For car-topping a sailboat: an easy loader [¶] Sailboats up to 250 pounds can be carried easily atop your car with this loader." 1972 June 10 *National Observer* 9/1-6 (heading) "Shoppers Eagerly Cartop New Sofas Home to Save a Few Bucks" 2: Use a cartop boat on (a body of water) 1972 June *Sports Afield* 128/2 "For cartopping the Pacific, use at least a 12-foot aluminum [boat]."

cartoppable *adj* Of a boat, of such size and weight that it can be loaded and transported on top of a car 1972 Dec *Pop Sci* 82/4 "The 14-foot car-toppable day sailer has 75 square feet of sail, roller-reefing boom, and kick-up rudder for beaching." 1973 Apr *Pop Sci* 93/2 "Weighing only 65 pounds, the craft is easily cartoppable." July *Pop Sci* 77/3 "The 13-footer [canoe] weighs only 60 pounds and is cartoppable."

car-topper *n* [*RHD* and *WNCD8* define as a cartoppable boat] One who cartops 1972 Jan *Pop Sci* 78/2 "Car-topper's friend [¶] Car-topping is easier than ever with the new Cosom one-man boat loader and hitch extender."

CATV *n* [*RHD* 1969; *BDNE* 1970] Earlier quots 1965 Jan *Electronics World* 12/2 "Our first reaction was that CATV is an ideal method of distributing TV signals, particularly in remote areas." 1966 Sept 17 *Sat Rev* 63/1 "A more dramatic way of achieving full set efficiency is Community Antenna Television (CATV), also known as 'cable' or 'wire' TV [see 'The Coming Cable TV War,' *SR*, June 11]. A CATV system operator merely lengthens the wire from your tuner to your antenna to reach a whopping big master antenna atop a high hill in your vicinity, where he pulls in, off the air or by microwave relay, or even by other wires, the signals of stations that you can't receive adequately." (brackets in the original)

condo *n* [*condo*minium] Condominium 1970 Sept *Reader's Digest* 182 (condensed from Sept *Kiwanis Mag*) "A typical 'condo' is a cross between a house and an apartment. . . . Each buyer owns his property as though it were a private home. But he shares with neighbors the costs of a pool, beach house, grounds maintenance." 1972 Oct 9 *USN&WR* 60/2 "In resort areas of Florida and California, multistory apartments once used only on a seasonal basis are 'going condo' and are selling out completely in a matter of weeks." Ibid 62/2 "One developer said the 'condo-conversion craze' was spurred about a year ago when rent controls made it more difficult for owners to meet rising expenses." Oct 14 *National Observer* 9/1 "In warm-weather areas such as Florida and the Southwest, and in many resort communities elsewhere, 'condos' have been rising at a spectacular rate." Nov *Town & Country* 196/2 (ad) "The going market value for these opulent condos is between $80,000 and $90,000." 1973 Aug 20 *Newsweek* 58/1 "As many as three in five new housing starts in Detroit these days are condos, while thousands of Los Angeles landlords are converting their rental apartments into condominiums faster than most tenants can learn to pronounce the word."

condomania *n* [*condo*minium + *mania*] 1973 Jan *Town & Country* 106/2 (ad) "CONDOMANIA—TODAY'S BOOMING MARKET . . . Today the craze is all for condominiums. More than 100,000 such units sprang up across the state [Florida] from 1970 to 1972, and '73 could see another 70,000 units."

CREEP; CRP Committee for the Re-Election of the President 1972 Sept 15 *Life* 29/2 "The CRP—or 'CREEP,' as some members of the Republican National Committee call it—occupies five floors of one building and spills across the street onto three floors [of another]." 1973 May 21 *Time* 34/3 "But during the campaign he [Senator Robert J. Dole] fought many a gallant losing battle with the Committee for the Re-Election of the President; in fact it was he who dubbed it CREEP." June 17 *NY Times* 20XX/2 "The Committee for the Re-Election of the President (known to friend and foe alike as 'Creep') . . . housed a number of principals in the Watergate affair during the 1972 campaign." July 22 *NY Times Mag* 8/1 "It [the election fight] was entrusted instead to the Committee for the Re-election of the President (CREEP)." Aug 13 *Newsweek* 7/3 "The suggestion that CREEP helped nominate George McGovern, a myth arising presumably from the margin of defeat, not only is patently ridiculous but also is controverted by the facts." (see also FIN-CREEP)

drop out *vb* [*OEDS* 1967; *BDNE vi* 1970; *WNCD8* 1973] Additional US quots 1966 July 12 *Tuscaloosa News* 15/8 (from *LA Times*) "Some completely heed Leary's advice and 'drop out' of society." 1967 Feb 19 *NY Times Book Rev* 1/3 "Scathing look for this interruption of the easy flow. Marshalling his McLuhan, the dropped-out, anti-word poet declared no-speech to be a bigger gas than speech."

dropoutism *n* 1964 Aug *Woman's Day* 39/2 "Experts on dropoutism feel that youngsters are too seldom taught the value and dignity of service." 1969 June 23 *Crimson-White* (University, Ala) 6/4 (College Press Service) "Besides the stigma of dropoutism is worse than playing a game at which they are, by now, fairly adept."

eco- [*BDNE* as prefix, *WNCD8* as combining form] Additional illustrations of words with *eco-* as the first element unrecorded in the standard dictionaries checked —**ecoaction** 1970 May *Natural History* 75/1 "Surely, as editor he should have spotted something that seems so contradictory, and then set his readers straight so they know what to expect from so seemingly satisfactory an ecoaction as tree planting." —**eco-award** 1971 Feb *McCall's* 42/3-4 "ECO-AWARDS . . .

Operating through their 14,000 participating clubs, the GFWC [General Federation of Women's Clubs] has just announced an Environmental Responsibility Program; with the help of Shell Oil Company they've set up a generous system of state and national awards." —**eco-awareness** 1973 May *Harper's* 51/1 "And with the growing forces in this country against the blood sports, with the eco-awareness of the '70s, enacting a bounty would only accelerate those forces and hurt the hunter." —**Eco-Bag** 1971 Oct *McCall's* 48/2–3 "Our first shopping spree netted us an Eco-Bag, an oversize natural-canvas tote, stamped with an artful green eco-design and equipped with a roomy pocket. . . . It's designed to carry loose (and even leaky) groceries in order to spare 'wasteful consumption' of paper shopping bags. [¶] . . . The Eco-Bag, by Toni Totes of Vermont, Inc., is sturdy and washable." —**Eco-Commando** See quots svv ECOTAGE, ECOTEUR —**eco-consciousness** 1972 Feb *McCall's* 51/4 "Others are harmless—and just might raise our eco-consciousness a bit." —**ecoconversion** 1970 Oct *Natural History* 82/3 (subheading) "Ecoconversions" —**eco-design** See quot sv ECO-BAG —**eco-detergent** 1971 Oct *Atlas* 64/1 "SOVIET ECO-DETERGENTS: Detergents with germicidal additives will eventually replace most of the Soviet Union's present stock of detergents. The microbes in the new substance not only clean better but are 90% bio-degradable." —**eco-drunk** 1973 Nov 30 *New Times* (NYC) 58/1 "Obviously, all he had ever done was obliterate poisonous snakes, but now he was in the midst of a *new* eco-drunk breed that demanded the land be retained in its present form." —**eco-enthusiast** 1971 Oct *Harper's* 102/2 "This apolitical dream leaves one to wonder just how some eco-enthusiasts really plan to implement coercive measures for which they see an urgent need." —**Eco-Farm** 1971 Oct *Organic Gardening and Farming* 21/1 (letter) "[signed:] LEONARD URBANOWICZ / Leonard's Eco-Farms / Westport, Connecticut" —**Ecogame** 1971 Sep *Atlas* 29/2–3 (from London *Observer*) "'Ecogame' is an application of computing in a social context. . . . The game makes the health of your bank balance depend partly on what you do and partly on what your neighbor does." —**Eco-Gemini** 1970 May *Natural History* 71 (title of review of two books: *Ecotactics: The Sierra Club Handbook* and *The Environmental Handbook*) "Eco-Gemini: Two for the Teach-In" —**eco-house** 1973 ad recd 12 May "[Among the articles in issue No 20 of *The Mother Earth News* is] THE GRAHAME CAINE ECO-HOUSE" Aug 28 *World* 47/2 (box) "Eco-house [¶] A London architectural student is achieving a lot of interest and support for an 'ecological house' of his design, construction, and occupancy. The self-sufficient habitat will have solar heating, rain collection, hydroponic gardening, and waste recycling for the production of methane for cooking and fertilizer." —**eco-journalism** 1971 Feb 22 *Newsweek* 4/3 (letter) "'Eco-Journalism' (THE MEDIA, Feb. 1) rightly describes increased and very uneven treatment of the environment in news media, but I was surprised to see no mention of Environment magazine." —**Eco-land** 1973 Nov 30 *New Times* 58/2 "But as I moved along the river bank in the querulously preserved Eco-land, it soon became apparent that indeed, what I was witnessing was the *real* game—more important than the river." —**ecomanagement** 1971 *Brit Book of the Year* ("Words and Meanings, New") 779/1 —**ecomodel** 1971 *Brit Book of the Year* ("Words and Meanings, New") 779/2 —**Eco-Now** 1971 Aug *McCall's* 44/2–3 (box) "Their fashionable socks now sport decorative buttons, birds, and messages—like the peace symbol, Eco-Now, and SEX." —**econut** 1972 Aug *Analog* 4/1 "But—in a world where the 'econuts' rage against science and technology, and the scientists dither in dignified confusion asking each other what the hell 'science for the people' could mean, we have a conflict." —**eco-palace** 1972 May *Organic Gardening and Farming* 146/1 (caption) "An eco-palace growing out of the land; a central living space surrounded by garden terraces and sound-proofed suites which open onto private walled gardens. This is a project for a rich man or, on a more modest scale, for a do-it-yourself home-builder who can afford the time needed to pour concrete in these complicated but appealing earthy shapes." —**eco-philosophy** 1970 Oct *Natural History* 86/2 (heading) "Ecophilosophy" —**Eco-plastics** 1971 Aug 7 *Science News* 92/1 "Dr. J. E. Guillet of the University of Toronto . . . is a consultant to Ecoplastics Ltd. of Toronto." —**ecopolicy** 1971 *Brit Book of the Year* ("Words and Meanings, New") 779/2 —**ecopolypse** [*eco-* + *apocalypse*] 1971 May 29 *Science News* 364/2 (letter) "For there is nothing but bitter experience on Nader's and our side (those of us outside [hopefully] soon to be cleaned up Muskegon) that tells that all the corporations and all the governmental regulatory agencies will sit around muttering pieties about what is 'technically possible' or 'economically feasible' until the ecopolypse is upon us." —**eco-prophet** 1971 Oct *Harper's* 100/3 "In the same vein, it was announced in the fall of 1970 that there would be a dire shortage of oil and natural gas for heating in the coming winter. The eco-prophets immediately pounced on this further evidence of our technological exhaustion of the earth's resources." —**eco-pundit** 1971 Apr 22 *New Scientist and Science Jour* 186/1 "The next environmental pollutant to hit the headlines looks like being cadmium, which has the advantage for eco-pundits of having even less known about it than mercury, which it in some ways resembles." —**eco-skit** 1972 June 26 *Time* 40/1 "Instead, the students put on gentle 'eco-skits' to dramatize 'eco-catastrophes.' In one, for example, a girl painted as a skeleton and accompanied by drums and cymbals danced a warning about the radioactive fallout from French nuclear-bomb tests in the Pacific." —**ecosteel** 1972 *Christmas 1972* [catalog] The Kenton Collection 25/1 "THE AURORA PEN: . . . Diamond 'ecosteel', with 14 kt. white gold point and an equally graphic presentation case." —**ecotactics** 1970 May 2 *Sat Rev* 67/1 "But between the two is the no man's land of indifference, and it is here that ecotactics, Earth Days, and the like play their part." May *Natural History* 71/1 "ECOTACTICS: THE SIERRA CLUB HANDBOOK FOR ENVIRONMENT ACTIVISTS, edited by John G. Mitchell. *Pocket Books, Inc.*" —**ecotage** 1972 Feb *McCall's* 51/1 "For a year now, Environmental Action has been running a nationwide competition called Ecotage. Ecotage—the word is a clever blend of ecology and sabotage—has been described by its sponsors as a contest for activists. 'We want to know,' they explained, 'what tactics can be used by concerned citizens to stop corporations or institutions from polluting, exploiting, or otherwise threatening the survival of the earth and its inhabitants.'" Ibid 51/2 "The Eco-Commandos, who operate out of Miami, have already engaged in several exploits in the name of ecotage." 1973 *Brit Book of the Year* ("Words and Meanings, New") 732/1 —**ecoteur** [*eco-* + *saboteur*] 1972 Feb *McCall's* 51/2 "The masked figure is a representative of the Eco-Commando Force '70, to whom Environmental Action is awarding first prize—the Golden Fox Trophy. (The trophy is named for The Fox of Kane County, Illinois, an ecoteur who has won national fame for harassing polluters.)" —**eco-unit** 1973 July *Reader's Digest* 12–14 (from *NY Times*) "A garden, I read the other day, is now a 'personalized recreational eco-unit.' This presumably means we'll have to start calling a spade a 'manually operated recreational eco-unit maintenance tool.'" —**eco-version** 1970 Jan *Reader's Digest* 13/1 "In Berkeley, Calif., a group called Ecology Action has developed a kind of street theater to dramatize pollution protests. The movement has its own songs, including an eco-version of 'America the Beautiful.'"

ecofreak; ecology freak *n* [for this sense of *freak*, see *WNCD8 n* 2d, possibly 2c for 1972 *Newsweek* quot] 1970 Aug 31 *National Observer* 10 "Everybody's an ecology freak." Oct *Natural History* 22/2 (letter) "I've been an ecofreak for 30 years." 1971 June 28 *Newsweek* 67/1 "For in recent months the phenomenon of biking to and from work has ceased to be the special province of a few eco-freaks, exercise faddists and professional eccentrics and has become what promises to become a full-blown movement of its own." 1972 *Brit Book of the Year* ("Words and Meanings, New") 733/1 June 12 *Newsweek* 38/2 "Stockholm had never seen anything quite like it. At the railroad and airline terminals last week, motley groups of hippies, radicals and ecofreaks were mingling with scientists, diplomats, politicians and newsmen from 109 nations." June 18 *Charlotte* (NC) *Observer* 21A/4 (NY Times News Service) "Industry, accustomed to carrying some weight in almost any milieu, found itself here almost as far on the sidelines as the Hog Farm 'ecology-freaks' who spent most of the fortnight talking to each other." Sep *Atlantic* 50/2 "The Cellulose, Paper, and Carton Administration of the Ministry of Timber, Paper, and Woodworking in the USSR is going to have its problems too. It has its quotas, and the boys at the ministry get their satisfactions from churning out the stuff, and ecology freaks are everywhere." Oct 14 *TV Guide* 18/1 "This came about because his wife and kids are ecology freaks." Oct 21 *National Observer* 16/5 "Second, he says fishermen don't tend to be 'ecology freaks.'" 1973 Oct 15 *Newsweek* 67/2 "The meet in Michigan drew housewives, ecology freaks, Boy Scout troops, families with children and dogs, a faculty team from Ohio University and the champion Marine Corps team from Quantico."

electronic *adj* [*W3* sense 2] Additional quots with abstract referent 1973 Apr 8 *NY Times* 15E/6 "Perhaps because electronic surveillance is so ineffective, few of the states have adopted the authority to use it, although it has been made available to them by Congress." July 22 *NY Times Mag* 30/3 "Pointing to various charts as he went along, he outlined plans for electronic surveillance and photography of documents." Aug 6 *Newsweek* 47/2 "'Electronic eavesdropping is very unusual in Japan,' explains Kinji Kawamura." Dec 10 *Newsweek* 28/3 "[He] has worked with electronic surveillance and detection devices for more than two decades."

energy crisis *n* [Cf *W3* sv *crisis* sense 3] See quot 1973 Oct 7 for literal and figurative senses 1970 Nov 28 *Science News* 415/1 "The current short-term energy crisis (SN: 11/14, p. 379), the long-term finiteness of fuel resources and the increasing success of environmentalists in stalling the building of new generating plants are causing utility engineers to look more and more to geothermal reservoirs as a possible source of electrical energy." 1971 Jan 10 *Washington Post* F8/1 "Although some progress has been made in dealing with the U.S. 'energy crisis,' the likelihood of more electric power brownouts and even blackouts in the coming year is not being ruled out by top government energy experts." July *Pop Sci* 55/1 "For the truth is this: We are in an energy crisis unique in the history of our nation." Aug 7 *Sat Rev* 50/2–3 (heading) "'THE ENERGY CRISIS' The fundamental question is this: Do we *need* twice as much electricity every ten years?" 1972 Sep *Harper's* 27 (heading of ad) "*America's Energy Crisis*: The Case for a Nationwide Power Network" 1973 July *Intellectual Digest* 4/2 "Jack Shepherd's 'Energy' series (in this issue, 'Energy 8: Sun Power,' page 19), which began last year, well before energycrisis became one word, fits into that category." Aug *Atlantic* 63/2 "Not long ago, the 'energy crisis' was on the front pages regularly." Oct 7 *NY Times* 14F/3 "The real energy crisis is not the shortage of fossil fuels or of power generating facilities or the conflict of energy and environmental objectives. [¶] The real energy crisis for Americans, in my estimation, is the lack of the fire of commitment, inspiration and pride of achievement that once burned fiercely in our national soul." 1974 Jan 5 *TV Guide* 6/1–2 "Crisis there was in abundance: the short-lived gasoline scare of summer was but a portent of the Energy Crisis of the fall." Jan 6 *Tuscaloosa News* 9A/5 (AP) "The first three-day work week in Britain's national emergency ended Saturday with predictions that the energy crisis will become even more serious." *NY Times* 14E/2 (editorial) "Secretary of State Kissinger's warning that worldwide depression and economic suicide lie ahead if the industrial nations persist in dealing separately and competitively with the energy crisis is blunt talk, but long overdue." Jan 7 *Newsweek* 38/1 "A little more than a decade ago, Americans were alarmed by something even more frightening than an energy crisis."

Fin-Creep Financial Committee to Re-Elect the President 1973 Oct 8 *Newsweek* 42/1 "It was the family Bible of the Financial Committee to Re-elect the President—a hefty 5 inches thick, heavy as a millstone and filled to bursting with the names of friends, fat cats and corporate high rollers who bet on Richard Nixon his last time out. Last week, Fin-Creep reluctantly bowed to a court order—won by Common Cause two months ago—and surrendered the books to the clerk of the House of Representatives, then Fin-Creep made the figures public."

flipping *n* Renewal of a loan with additional interest, charging interest on interest 1969 Aug 17 *Tuscaloosa News* 2/1 (AP) "SMALL LOANS—Bill to do away with 'flipping' or the rapid renewal of loans under 175 [dollars] passed in Senate, on calendar in House." 1973 *Brit Book of the Year* ("Words and Meanings, New") 732/2 "flipping *n*: the charging of interest on interest (as by a loan shark)." Sep 24–25 *Graphic* (Tuscaloosa, Ala) 2/2 (editorial) "The notorious practice of flipping—turnover of loans at frequent intervals with interest piling up each time—is prohibited." —**flipper** *n* 1963 Feb 17 *St Louis Post-Dispatch* 8C/5 "The 'flipper' is a man in a small loan office who flips the loan record cards in the filing cabinet to get the hooked borrower to sign another note with added charges."

-hop [cf *W3* sv [1]*hop vi* sense 2b; *RHD* 1969 sv *hop*[1] sense 3 "make a flight or any short, quick trip"] The second element (often as *-hopping*, *-hopper*) in combination with nouns to form intransitive verbs with the meaning 'proceed, go, or move from one to another (referent of the noun)'; the subentry word is the verb, even where it is not attested by a quot —**barhop** 1961 *W3* —**booth-hop** 1952 quot for *booth-hopper* in *AS* 30 (1955): 73 —**boutique-hop** 1972 Apr *Town & Country* 16/2

"You're better off boutique-hopping in town or taking one of the smaller side trips." **—castle-hop** 1953 quot for *castle-hopping* in *AS* 30 (1955):73 **—cemetery-hop** 1971 Sep 4 *Sat Rev* 14/2 "Cemetery-hopping is not one of my passionate pastimes, but over the years I have been to innumerable burial places abroad as well as at home, because often they can be pleasant to visit even if you wouldn't want to live there." **—channel-hop** 1971 May 22 *TV Guide* 21/2 "When one show is over, I channel-hop madly, crying, 'What am I missing?' " Aug *Atlantic* 56/2 "They channel-hop, trying to find something to hold them, but there is nothing; it all slides past until, after nine, on *Carol Burnett*, she and Gomer Pyle do an actually pretty funny skit about the Lone Ranger." **—city-hop** 1972 Oct 6 *Life* 49/1 "Yet, up in his campaign plane, city-hopping across the country, the candidate himself is buoyant with optimism, genuinely convinced by recent fervent rally crowds that the campaign is 'turning.' " Oct 28 *TV Guide* A4/1 "Stuck under strips of mending tape, rows of unreturned hotel keys dangling from their tags like military decorations, tangible evidence of the city-hopping existence of the candidate watchers." **—country-hop** 1973 Aug 27 *Newsweek* 54/1 "Country-hopping with her father, a Boston Brahmin and career diplomat named Robert L. Berenson, and her Franco-Italian mother, Gogo, Marisa and her sister Berry were as familiar a sight on the ski slopes of Gstaad, Mégève and Klosters as they were on the beaches of the Riviera, the Dalmatian coast and Tripoli." **—deck-hop** 1944 July 22 *Sat Eve Post* 73/1 "Looking down, Caldwell saw the Jap ships shoot at one another as his boys deck-hopped cruisers and destroyers, weaving in and out." **—galaxy-hop** 1972 July 29 *New Yorker* 44/3 "Like the peripatetic gunfighter of the old Western, the galaxy-hopping, blaster-toting starship captain of the early space opera has been elevated to the status of an archetypal hero." **—gallery-hop** 1971 Dec 27 *Newsweek* 36/1–2 (heading) "Gallery-Hopping in New York" **—island-hop** 1944 quots for *island hopping* in *AS* 21 (1946):223/1 1954 *WNWD* 1955 quot in *AS* 31 (1956):85 **—job-hop** 1952 Feb 18 *Wall St Jour* 1 "The aircraft industry is one which is being hard hit generally by worker job-hopping." Mar 24 *Wall St Jour* 4 "Job-Hopping: The Salary Stabilization Board announced it has sent investigators into a dozen cities to cut down 'pirating and job-hopping' in the engineering field." 1953 *Brit Book of the Year* ("Words and Meanings, New") 752/1 1970 quot for *job-hop* and 1967, 1971 quots for *job-hopper* in *BDNE* 1971 *W3* Addenda *job-hopping* and *job-hopper* **—male-hop** 1973 June 15 "*W*" (Fairchild Pubs, NYC) 4 "[She] was in excellent form as she male-hopped around the Ground Floor restaurant at the dinner party." **—mansion-hop** 1963 Nov 17 *NY Times* 1XX/1–3 (heading) "The Mansion-Hopping Trail" **—museum-hop** 1972 Aug *House Beautiful* 96/4 "What A Scamp for museum-hopping, window shopping!" 1973 June 17 *NY Times* 14XX (heading) "18 Years of Museum Hopping" **—paddy-hop** 1960 *AS* 35:261 "Thirdly, some terms were probably unique to the situation of a field army, notably the description of illicit nocturnal activity outside the compound as *paddy hopping*." **—party-hop** 1952 quot for *party-hopping* in *AS* 30 (1955):73 **—publisher-hop** 1953 quot for *publisher-hopping* in *AS* 30 (1955):73; the complete second sentence is "He'd spent about three months here, publisher-hopping, trying to establish the same connection with them [publishers] that the printer has." **—spa-hop** 1973 Aug 27 *Newsweek* 53/3 "Spa-hopping from Agadir to Acapulco, the golden progeny of money old and new, of industrialists and aristocrats, royalty and filmmakers make up this generation's group of Visible People." **—table-hop** 1961 *W3* **—tavern-hop** 1953 quot for *tavern-hopping* in *AS* 30 (1955):73 **—whore-hop** 1972 May *Harper's* 63/1 "[Fired employee:] 'Why me?' [he] asks of no one in particular. 'I don't mess in politics, I don't drink, I ain't no whore-hopper.' "

intensive care *attrib* [Cf *BDNE intensive care unit* "medical unit" 1967] Of a section of a city, under special police patrol 1970 June 7 *NY Times* 84/3 "ATLANTA, June 6—This city's so-called 'hippy area' has become an official 'intensive care section' with nightly patrols by 64 policemen." 1971 Mar 14 *NY Times Mag* 63/1 "On the evening of June 4, in a televised address, he [Atlanta's Mayor Sam Massell, Jr] declared The Neighborhood to be 'an intensive care area' and announced he was dispatching a special force of 64 policemen into the locale."

linear park *n* Long narrow park along a riverbank or right-of-way 1971 Apr *Southern Living* 71/2 "Thus the river was saved from oblivion, and its development as a pedestrian-oriented linear park in the heart of the city achieved ignition and lift-off just prior to World War II." May *Pop Sci* 52/3 "Beneath the aerial structure, the BART [Bay Area Rapid Transit] right-of-way has been turned into attractively landscaped linear parks and recreational areas." July *Reader's Digest* 100/1 "Beneath the structure [support for BART's elevated lines], which has won a design award for engineering excellence, landscaped linear parks with walkways, benches, fountains and playground equipment are planned."

moment of truth [*W3* Addenda 1966, *BDNE* 1966] Earlier quot 1962 *Yale Law Jour* 71:903 "Finally, in the moment of truth, the judiciary has a telling advantage over the other branches, the prerogative of interpreting the Constitution."

palazzo *n usu pl* [*BDNE palazzo pajamas* 1968] Long, wide-legged pants for women; usually made of crepe, jersey, or other soft fabric 1972 Sep 9 *New Yorker* 8/1 (ad) "Our haltered palazzos come in champagne beige. . . . The no-waistband, back-zip palazzos." Sep 23 *New Yorker* 111/2–3 (ad) "Sly fox. Showing up over party palazzos now, city classics next." Oct 20 "*W*" (Fairchild Pubs, NYC) 11/1 "Pants are still full but haven't reached palazzo proportions." 1973 Mar 17 *New Yorker* 56 (ad) "We like the palazzo shape as a slashback culotte: shoulders very bare, lace very see-through." Apr *Harper's Bazaar* 5 (ad) "Lollipops loll on a plunging palazzo of luscious Qiana® nylon. Shirring and sashing halt the halter above billowing pyjamas." Oct *Today's Health* 36/1 "On the way home, Linda stopped at the dry cleaners to pick up the flowered silk pallazzo [*sic*] outfit she planned to wear to the theater on Saturday."

palazzo pants *n* Palazzos 1972 Oct 28 *TV Guide* 47 "For languid lounging in the idyllic gazebo, Tracy chooses an at-home diaphanous printed palazzo-pants outfit. . . . The pants are wide and flaring." 1973 Apr *Weight Watchers* 44 (photo caption) "Stand out against this rainbow of yarns in your wide-leg palazzo pants." June *Town & Country* 67/3 (photo caption) "Above: Pale-gray chiffon as soft and light as a cloud, swirling with its own cloud print in extra-full *palazzo* pants matched with a strapless tiny tube top and a shirt jacket." Sep *Woman's Day* 168/1 (ad) "Choose from smashing palazzo pants and clothes with the bare look."

palazzo sleeve *n* Very wide, flowing sleeve 1972 Aug 26 *New Yorker* 55/2–3 (ad) "Our fluid navy wool knit with permanent pleated polyester chiffon palazzo sleeves."

parking deck *n* [cf *W3 deck n* sense 2b] Multistoried structure for parking automobiles 1972 Nov 30 *Graphic* (Tuscaloosa, Ala) 12/3 "The County Commission Tuesday formally adopted a multi-level parking deck to be constructed adjacent to the County Jail at a cost of up to $1,100,000." Dec 17 *Birmingham* (Ala) *News* A4/1 "With two parking deck sites assured . . . the properties surrounding the station could be purchased and the proposed seven-story structure built in an L-shape." 1973 Sep 25 *Tuscaloosa News* 4/4 "The Johnsey plan called for . . . a 280,000 square foot parking deck." 1974 Feb 17 *Tuscaloosa News* 3D/2 "The authority was to build a parking deck for the downtown area."

psychohistorian *n* [*BDNE psychohistorical* 1970] One who treats historical subjects from a psychological or psychoanalytical viewpoint 1972 Apr 29 *Sat Rev* 68/3 See quot sv PSYCHOHISTORY sense 2 1973 Feb 25 *NY Times Book Rev* 36/4 "The psychohistorian's premise is that 'persons who are trained and experienced in both psychological and socio-political fields may be able to make more relevant analyses of political persons and issues than specialists in either field.' " Aug *Psychology Today* 17/1 "Indeed 'death and the continuity of life' has been the energizing concern of [Robert Jay] Lifton's work as a psychohistorian." Sep 24 *Newsweek* 22/3 "Is there a psycho-historian in the house?" Oct 1 *New Yorker* 35/1 "Here one can only speak of transcendence, that wild card that fills the psychohistorian's inside straight."

psychohistory *n* 1: Study or treatment of historical subjects from the standpoint of psychology or psychoanalytical theory 1971 Sep 25 *Sat Rev* 43/3 "In *History and Human Survival* (Vintage, $2.45), accurately subtitled 'Essays on the Young and Old, Survivors and the Dead, Peace and War, and on Contemporary Psychohistory,' Dr. [Robert Jay] Lifton unites a whole battery of disparate disciplines." 1972 Mar *UA Faculty Newsletter* (University, Ala) 2/1–2 "Twenty sophomores . . . delve into the minds of some of the major personalities who have shaped world history. 'Psycho-history,' as the Honors 2 course is called, considers the principles of psychology through the interpretation of history." Mar 25 *Sat Rev* 98/2 "*Psychohistory*, a relatively new literary term, is about to gain greater currency. Next month Basic Books will publish *In Search of Nixon: A Psychohistorical Study*, by Bruce Mazlish. . . . [¶] The roots of psychohistory may go back to Sigmund Freud's *Leonardo da Vinci: A Study in Psychosexuality*, published in Vienna in 1916." Apr *Esquire* 206/1 "Except for an excerpt from Erikson's *Ghandi's* [*sic*] *Truth*, the venturesome discipline of psycho-history has gotten the brush-off [from *NY Rev of Books*]." Apr 29 *Sat Rev* 68/3 "Psychohistory represents a fusion between psychoanalytic theory and the facts of history, using each to illuminate the other." May 29 *Newsweek* 84/2 "At his modest best, he offers this experiment in psychohistory as a 'sketch' that 'might inspire others to further effort.' " 1973 Feb 25 *NY Times Book Rev* 36/4 " 'The Kennedy Neurosis' is what Nancy Clinch calls 'psychohistory,' a term she believes was coined by Erik Erikson. In fact, its more likely inventor is Isaac Asimov, in one of his science-fiction sagas—an appropriate origin in view of the science-fiction characters of most works in the genre." Apr 24 *World* 48/3 "Mr. Payne has made his [biography of Hitler] into highly readable, unexcited prose that occasionally works its way to psychohistory." June *Psychology Today* 94/2 "As its name implies, 'psychohistory' involves an attempt to study the lives of *historical* figures in the light of psychoanalytic theory." Oct *Psychology Today* 12/2 (letter) "I was dismayed at their limitation of psychohistory to figures of the past. Two of the finest recent works of psychohistory . . . deal effectively with living persons." Dec *Esquire* 118/3 "Professor Tucker was on the staff of the American Embassy in Moscow, and knows what he is talking about, but, for me, the narrative is marred by his preoccupation with what Erik Erikson has called 'psychohistory'—more psycho than history." Dec 14 *New Times* 20/1 "Right up through mid-November—until Richard Nixon began campaigning almost insurgently, like some old Bull Mooser, to keep himself a sitting President—I would have said the man and his deeds were all but passing into psychohistory." Dec 17 *New Yorker* 53 (cartoon caption) "[Author at cocktail party:] I've done some soft-core, some as-told-to's, and a few gothics. Right now I'm into psychohistory." 2: Work of psychohistory 1972 Mar 25 *Sat Rev* 98/3 "Another psychohistory to be published by Basic Books next fall is a study of Hitler by Dr. Walter Langer." Apr 29 *Sat Rev* 68/3 "Bruce Mazlish is far too competent a psychohistorian to fall into many of the pitfalls awaiting a naive investigator, but Richard Nixon is far too opaque a subject to provide data for a truly informative psychohistory."

quadminium; quadriminium *n* [*quad*(*ri*-) + condo*minium*] Four-unit structure in which the tenants own their apartments 1972 Oct 14 *National Observer* 9/2 "Another innovation is the 'quadminium'—a cluster of four living units that are sold separately." 1973 June *House Beautiful* 85 "Displayed—and photographed—at the Industrialized Building Exposition (INBEX) in Louisville, this is a prototype single unit of what would in reality be a four-unit 'quadriminium'."

soft landing *n* [*BDNE* sv *soft land vi* 1967] Figurative use 1973 Aug 29 *Tuscaloosa News* 4/1 (editorial) "Today, we're being told by top officials in the Treasury Department that the present business boom will end in a 'soft landing'. There will be a cooling off period without recession." Sep 17 *Newsweek* 65/2 "Even if the President succeeds in pulling in the rampaging economy for a soft landing, of course, the arrival will be nonetheless bumpy for many." Nov 4 *NY Times* 1F/1 "Paris—The high-flying economies of the Western industrialized states face three possibilities over the next 12 to 18 months: a soft landing, bumps, a crash."

theme park *n* Amusement park organized around a specific theme or group of themes 1967 *Brit Book of the Year* 335/2 "American-type theme parks around the world included Edenlandia Fun Park, Naples, Italy; Prater Fun Park, Vienna; and a new park, Centro de Diversion, opened at Puerto Rico's Isla Verde." 1968 ibid 339/2 "Theme parks, kiddielands, playlands, fun parks, zoos, aquariums, and marineland parks continued to outgross all other forms of recreation." 1970 ibid 340/1 "More than 360 million North Americans spent an estimated $500 million at over 1,000 U.S. and Canadian theme parks, kiddielands, and general amusement parks and some 1,500 municipal parks, zoos, and aquariums." 1972 Feb *Southern Living* 51/2 "He's now planning a $22 million theme park to be built on a 161-acre site astride the North Carolina–South Carolina line south of Charlotte." Apr *Better Homes and Gardens* 173/1–2 "The Magic Kingdom theme park is only one of the many lures here [Disney World]." 1973 Apr *Southern Living* 148/3 "Six Flags is a theme park with 95 rides, shows, and attractions on 145 treed acres." May *Amer Home* 30/1 "The old-fashioned amusement park may be obsolete, but in its place we now have 'theme' parks." May *Southern Living* 97 (subheading) "Opryland U.S.A., nestled in the hills of Tennessee, calls itself the home of American music. It's a $28 million theme park that's been built with a song for its foundation." May 21 *Newsweek* 90/1–2 "Corny, kitschy and commercially successful, the Land of Oz is one of the many new 'theme' parks that have opened up across the country. Unlike the traditional amusement park, the new themelands are organized around a unifying idea and deliver a spanking-clean entertainment package for the entire family." May 24 *Rolling Stone* 22 (reprod of ad) "NEW BIBLICAL 'DISNEY-TYPE' THEME PARK NEEDS YOU!! . . . If you want to be associated with the World's Greatest Theme park with the World's Greatest Theme, send your proposal."

wait-in *n* [see *-in* in *BDNE*] Gathering of persons waiting for an event to begin 1966 Aug 1 *Friends Jour* 378/2 "When the Senate adjourned without debate . . . thirty-six Friends remained sitting in a silent 'wait-in' for the debate to begin." 1973 Aug 6 *Newsweek* 24/2 (caption to picture showing a group of young people, some standing in a partly formed line, others sitting on the floor, waiting for the hearings room to be opened) "Wait-in at the Watergate hearings: People 'just want to say they were here.' "

white market *n* Legal sale 1946 and 1948 quots in *AS* 25 (1950):143 1948 Feb 9 *Newsweek* 56 "France's action meant it has merely recognized officially a fact which already existed in the black market, where francs had been selling at 340 to the dollar, compared to the 'white market' rate of 119." 1973 Nov 26 *Newsweek* 83 "Allocate 10 gallons of gas a week to each family. . . . The government would mail coupons to each family, with one coupon good for one gallon of gas. A motorist could buy additional coupons from the government for perhaps 50 cents or redeem unused ones. Government planners dub this one the 'white market.' " Dec 10 *Newsweek* 98/3 "Under one plan, each driver would receive a basic weekly ration of 10 or 15 gallons; if he did not use all his coupons, he could sell them to someone who needed more than the basic ration, probably through private coupon exchanges that would inevitably spring up. 'You're really issuing money,' says one planner, 'so you may as well make the black market legal, make it a white market.' " Dec 10 *Newsweek* 113/2 "Or consider another variant: distribute coupons covering all gasoline that will be available (say 20 gallons per week), fix the price at 45 cents a gallon, but permit the coupons to be sold in a 'white' market." 1974 Jan 6 *NY Times* 14E/3 (letter) "And how about the needs of such people, ranging from TV repairmen to social workers, who must use their cars, often extensively, in their occupations? Will they be forced to buy coupons in the 'white market' (really a whitewashed black market) from persons having more coupons than they really need?"

wire TV *n* See 1966 quot sv CATV

[Received February 1974]

AMONG THE NEW WORDS

I. WILLIS RUSSELL and MARY GRAY PORTER
University of Alabama

IN THE PRELIMINARY REMARKS of the Fall-Winter 1970 "Among the New Words," the statement was made that the word *wiglet*, dating from 1831, "has only recently been used often enough for dictionary entry." The proper statement, of course, should have been "for entry into the commercial dictionaries."

According to our checking, the legal term *fishing expedition* has only recently been entered in the general dictionaries, for example, *W3* 1961, *RHD* 1969, *OEDS* 1972 (without definition, 1961 and 1966 quotations, neither one defining), and the *World Book Dictionary* 1971. The additional quotations in our entry, therefore, may be of some interest.

It is not a little ironical that *island-hop*, which in its military sense seems to have been the first of the *-hop* type, is not entered even in its generalized sense in any recent dictionary examined except *Webster's Third*, which enters both senses. We therefore quote several recent uses of this combination in our supplementary entry in the glossary below.

Though *structural unemployment* in the glossary is presumably covered by the senses of the adjective cited within the square brackets, we are venturing an entry with a definition because our evidence, especially the 1966 quotation, implies that "change" in structure is the critical factor. In view of the wording of Taylor's 1966 definition, it is especially interesting to observe that the colleague in economics who was consulted on our original definition, agreeing with our view and without seeing our evidence, insisted on the necessity of adding the word "fundamental" to "changes in structure."

Acknowledgments: For citations, John Algeo (1), Helen B. Lewis (1), James B. McMillan (1, the earliest citation of *fishing expedition*), Norman R. McMillan (1), Mamie J. Meredith (4, including the two 1956 citations of *check-off*), Porter G. Perrin (2, the earliest citations of *senior citizen* and *structural unemployment*), Mark Reynolds (2), and Gerrie Thielens (1). Thanks are also due Dale L. Cramer for aid in the definition of *structural unemployment*.

blow dead *vb phr* Cause (a football) to be dead (i.e., out of play) by the blowing of the referee's whistle 1964 Nov 14 sportscaster over NBC "But was it blown dead first?" 1966 George Plimpton *Paper Lion* (NY: Harper) 238 "The referee wouldn't allow it. He said he'd blown the ball dead while we were struggling for it." 1973 Nov 25 *NY Times* D19/5 "He goes on to tell his men to get the uprights during a field-goal attempt and to stick with a runner even if the referee's whistle blows the play dead."

body jewelry *n* [*BDNE* body-jewel 1970] Cf EAR JEWELRY in *AS* Fall–Winter 1970 1969 Nov 30 *NY Times* 96 (ad) "Body jewelry [¶] A graceful body bib of simulated pearls to festoon over the simplest costume."

bridge streaking [STREAK *vb*] 1974 Mar 10 *Birmingham* (Ala) *News* A27/5–6 (AP) "Bridge streaking also seemed popular in West Virginia. Nine young men dashed across the toll bridge from East Liverpool, Ohio, to Newell, W. Va., early Saturday."

budget motel *n* Motel, economically built on a simple scale, featuring only the necessities demanded by travelers, and offering rooms at low rates [1966 Aug 27 *Bus Week* 57 "Bedding down the budget-minded" (heading) "At a time when most motels are getting plusher, Motel 6 sticks to basics: clean rooms and baths, good location, and—most important—good beds for a low price."] 1973 Apr 8 *NY Times* F3/1 "The budget motel's rooms are fully furnished, carpeted and air-conditioned. Some have individual phones in the rooms. Budget motels do not have luxurious lobbies, or spacious grounds, and many do not have swimming pools or restaurants." Aug 5 *NY Times* XX1 (picture caption) "If you're willing to dispense with the standard motel frills you stretch your dollars at the new 'back to basics' budget motels springing up around the country." Sep 9 *NY Times* XX4/1 (letter) "[She] glosses over the fact that because 'budget motel rooms cost less to build than conventional motel rooms' and because of other economies they can sell their rooms for less."

checkoff *n* [*DA* sv check 5 "arrangement whereby a labor union receives the union dues, fees, etc., of its members directly from the employer who withholds them from wages"] 1: Arrangement whereby a livestock producer contributes for each animal marketed a fee for a promotional program 1956 Feb 5 *Omaha World-Herald* 12B "The first two of three steps to determine sentiments concerning the check-off system to finance meat promotion will be taken this week." Mar 20 *Lincoln* (Neb) *Evening Jour* 2/1 "Gov. Leo A. Hoegh said he hopes a governors' livestock conference which begins at Omaha Wednesday will come up with a 'yes' or 'no' answer on a proposed 'checkoff' system to finance a meat promotion plan. [¶] The proposal to be offered governors and representatives of 18 states, including Nebraska and Iowa, calls for contributions of 10 cents per marketed beef animal, 5 cents per hog and 2½ cents for sheep. The fee would be paid by the producer for publicity and promotion aimed at creating greater consumption and higher market prices." 2: Arrangement whereby a taxpayer indicates whether he wishes a dollar of his income tax to be used for public financing of political campaigns 1973 Dec 2 *NY Times* 2E/1 "The funds would be raised by using the present check-off system on income tax returns." 1974 Mar 10 *Parade* (*Birmingham* [Ala] *News*) 31/2 "In the meantime, Congress already has given us a handle to turn around the financing of Presidential elections—The so-called $1 checkoff." Mar 15 *In Common: News for Common Cause Activists* 3 "*Tax Check-Off*. . . . The Internal Revenue Service reports that thousands of Americans have designated $1 and $2 of their taxes to finance the 1976 Presidential campaign."

fishing expedition See preliminary remarks Earlier quots 1916 *Dial Notes* 4:323 "*fishing expedition*, go on a, *v. phr.* In law, to ask questions without definite purpose, in hopes of eliciting information. 12 Kansas 451." 1921 *Corpus Juris* 645/1 1940 *S E Reporter* 2 ser 7:863/2 "Nor does it provide the excuse for a fishing expedition." 1940 quot in William Safire *New Language of Politics* (NY: Random, 1968) 147/1 1941 Feb 21 *Fed Rules Decisions* 4:271/1 (1946) "The plaintiff interposed an objection to the interrogatory on two grounds: . . . (2) The interrogatory merely constitutes a 'fishing expedition' on the part of the defendant to ascertain the identity of the government's employee-witnesses and to delve into the government's evidence." 1946 *Federal Sup* 67:626 "[15–17] The Court answers the questions it initially propounded in the affirmative, and holds: . . . (2) That the examination sought here is not such a 'fishing expedition' as is condemned under the law." 1951 *Black's Law Dict* sv *fishing bill* 765/1 1958 *Words and Phrases* (St Paul: West) 17:133–34 sv "fishing expedition" cites 14 cases in which the term occurs.

four-channel *adj* [Cf *channel* W3 Addenda 1971; also *OED sb¹* sense 8 "That through which information, news, trade, or the like passes; a medium of transmission, conveyance, or communication" 1537] QUADRIPHONIC; designed for the recording, broadcasting, or reproduction of sound by dividing the original signal into four distinct segments that the listener hears through four loudspeakers placed so as to provide front-to-rear separation as well as the side-to-side separation of conventional stereo 1961 May *Electronics World* 6/3 "In normal 2-channel operation you use a left and right speaker. In our 4-channel system, we have added two other speakers—both in the center—one near the listener and the other some distance away." 1969 Sep *High Fidelity Mag* 62/1 "We heard rumblings that Acoustic Research was planning a series of four-channel broadcasts in the Boston area this fall using the FM-multiplex signals of stations WGBH and WCRB—and requiring the listener to have two stereo FM systems, one tuned to each of the stations." Dec *Electronics World* 6/3 "The 4-channel disc may or may not be a long way off." 1970 Oct 31 *Sat Rev* 57/1 "And the new development that I found most intriguing—the Electro-Voice/Len Feldman four-channel matrix system—showed up again at AES [Audio Engineering Society (convention)] a few weeks later." Dec 2 *Rolling Stone* 1/3 "The result . . . has been . . . an almost non-stop attack on the senses—four-channel rock specials . . . [and a] live color four-channel broadcast of the opening of Winterland." 1971 Feb 22 *Moneysworth* 2/1 "[The reel-to-reel tape recorder] holds the greatest potential for high-quality four-channel stereo sound." Oct *Pop Sci* 42/2 "CBS, in cooperation with Sony, has introduced a four-channel disc. It does not contain four discrete—entirely separate—channels, but uses one kind of matrixing principle: The four channels are electronically mixed into two; decoding circuitry unscrambles the four channels when the disc is played back." Dec *Playboy* 45/1 (ad) "Both [auto and home models] play 4-channel sound as recorded on 8-track stereo cartridges—the only *true* 4-channel material available today." 1972 *Cat 223* Radio Shack 13/2 "True 4-Channel Sound means 4 different sound sources at the program end (records, tapes, FM) and the playback end. 'True' 4-channel (quadraphonic) sound thus requires true 4-channel program material and 4 channels of reproduction (4 amplifiers, 4 speakers)." 1972 May 27 *Sat Rev* 24/1 "RCA's April announcement of their Quadradisc four-channel record's imminent release temporarily stole the spotlight from Columbia's SQ four-channel disc." 1973 Mar *Pop Sci* 107/2 "This new four-channel decoder . . . decodes all matrix-encoded records presently on the market as well as plays two-channel stereo and stereo FM with a realistic four-channel effect." Fall *Stereo & Hi-Fi Times* 86/2 "The four-channel headphone is a phenomenon that, unbelievably, works." Oct *Better Homes and Gardens* 86/1–2 "Above the audio center you can see one of the speakers of the four-channel sound system that's spaced evenly around the room." Nov *Pop Sci* 125 (box) "Don't mistake 'four-channel effect' for quadraphonic sound." Nov *High Fidelity Mag* 34/1-2 quot sv QUADRIPHONICS.

four-channel *n* 1: Any of several methods or techniques for recording and playing back sound signals so that the listener hears, or has the illusion of hearing, through four loudspeakers, separate elements of the original signal with lateral separation (as in conventional stereo) and also front-to-rear separation. *Discrete four-channel* makes use of four distinct signals in recording and playback; both *matrix four-channel* and *derived* (*synthetic*) *four-channel* require decoding devices to feed parts of the two recorded tracks to the rear speakers. Also, the sound reproduced by any of these techniques 1970 June 27 *Sat Rev* 51 "If four-channel stereo gets popular, what will happen to the equipment and recordings we own now? . . . until that question's answered, four-channel simply can't make it." Nov *High Fidelity Mag* 24/1-2 (ad) "The redesigned transducer in the [earphones] provides a wider band width, greater usable frequency response and more low frequency output to surround you (as 4 channel does) with the ultimate in listening pleasure." Nov *Pop Photog* 21/3 "*What is 'derived' or 'synthetic' four-channel sound?* [¶] Just about every modern stereo disk and tape has the 'out-of-phase' sound of the concert hall, or whatever is used for the recording studio. It is possible—with an inexpensive device—to extract this out-of-phase sound: fed to rear stereo speakers, it will almost simulate the sound of the concert hall in the listener's home. Derived four-channel sound should not be confused with 'discrete' four-channel in which the performance is recorded directly on four separate tracks." Nov 27 *Sat Rev* 91/1 "The phonograph record remains . . . the logical medium for making four-channel truly popular." Dec *Pop Photog* 62/3 "Using four-channel is one thing, getting the correct four-channel equipment is something else." 1973 Jan 20 *New Yorker* 19 (ad) "When you're ready to switch to four-channel, will your stereo be?" Feb *Esquire* 27/1 (ad) "Four-channel isn't somebody's idea of the future . . . it's happening now." Fall *Stereo & Hi-Fi Times* 52/1 "We feel it is time to show just how big four-channel is *now*." Dec *Esquire* inside front cover (ad) "A six-piece home entertainment system that can play everything in discrete 4-channel." 2: [Cf *W3 stereo n* sense 3 b] Equipment for the playback of four-channel sound 1973 Jan *Esquire* 77/3 (ad) "When you buy one of the new Sony compact stereos, you're getting more than a compact stereo. [¶] You're getting half a four-channel."

front four *n* Guards and tackles on the defensive unit of a football team 1966 George Plimpton *Paper Lion* 174 " 'It took me five years before I appreciated that my value as a decoy was important, and I even began to get a kick out of double-teaming and blocking—even trying to hold those monster defensive ends in the front four.' " 1967 Jan 2 *NY Times* 27 "Their fine front four . . . also kept Dawson under pressure." 1969 Dec 25 *Tuscaloosa News* 37/2-3 "Even in this, the Year of the Front Four, the players in the trenches still consider defensive excellence as something more than just sacking quarterbacks." 1970 Jan 4 Curt Gowdy over NBC "He's been the man today with that front four." Jan 9 *Tuscaloosa News* 10/1-2 (*Washington Post*) "There is good, old-fashioned football talk once more, about the front fours, and the pass rush, and the down-and-outs, the quick releases and the inevitable hard-nosed stuff." 1971 Jan 25 *Sports Illust* 12/3 "The rush of the front four was hurrying him." Sep 26 *Tuscaloosa News* 1B/1 " 'I felt like before the game that if we were going to win our front four on defense and the front five on offense would have to play better than they had before all season,' Bryant told a large group of reporters."

hang-up *n* [*BDNE* 1968 sense 2] Earlier quot 1966 Dec 27 *Look* 72/2 "Toward the tenth hour, a few hang-ups were pulled out—sex and the church, fear of being unloved."

hipism, hippism *n* [*W3* Addenda 1971 *hipness*] 1: 1967 Oct 30 *Newsweek* 85/3 "For most straights, press reports of the East Village murders added a sinister new word to their glossary of hipisms." 2: 1968 June 17 *Birmingham* (Ala) *News* 8 "Indeed, this sort of rhetoric approaches outright recklessness, just as [his] voluntary association with the wilder aspects of the youth cult threatens to identify him with a kind of hippism which the ordinary citizen wishes to see repudiated for good and all."

honey shot *n* TV view of a woman spectator, usually young and pretty, at a public event 1968 Oct 28 *Newsweek* 71/2 "But by the time an engineer announced 'we're away,' Arledge had managed to cram nine events into a one-hour show, plus two interviews and three 'honey' shots (ABC lingo for prolonged looks at pretty female spectators)." 1974 Feb 11 *Sports Illust* 14/1 "A chap named Andy Sidaris has an unusual job: he is responsible for the 'honey shots' during ABC telecasts of college football games. A honey shot, if you didn't know, is a quick camera glimpse of a girl in the stands."

Hong Kong flu *n* [*BDNE* 1970] Earlier quot 1968 Dec 8 *NY Times* 10E/3-4 "Thousands stayed home from work suffering from Hong Kong flu, the pesky new variant of the influenza virus that has reached the United States from across the Pacific and was spreading through the hinterland."

-hop See *AS* Fall-Winter 1972 ANW Additional examples and quots —**aisle-hop** 1972 July 22 *TV Guide* A-1/1 "Networkers claimed most phone calls were 'complimentary,' only a few objecting to TV's aisle-hopping and analyzing." —**art-gallery-hop** 1971 Aug 16 *Newsweek* 16/2 "Minority Leader Hugh Scott was ticketed for Helsinki, Moscow and Sofia for chats with Iron Curtain leaders and some art-gallery hopping on the side." —**boulder-hop** 1973 Mar *Sports Afield* 58 "Tightening down on my drag, I began boulder-hopping downstream to save precious line." Ibid 61/2-3 (picture caption) "I hooked what I thought was a smallmouth-dream-come-true in this pool, but because I had to boulder-hop, I lost him." —**canyon-hop** 1971 Apr *Boys' Life* 11/1 "On our canyon-hopping jaunt, we crossed *El Vados de los Padres* on our way to nearby Padre Bay." Ibid 11/4 "And early in the afternoon we started back to Wahweap Marina, canyon hopping all the way." —**chateau-hop** 1971 Jan *House Beautiful* 139/2-3 "Off in a wooded park near Luynes . . . there's . . . a calm and charming place to catch one's breath after the rigors of chateau-hopping." —**city-hop** 1972 Oct 28 *TV Guide* A5/1 "McGovern city-hops six days a week and may even get in a little Sabbath campaigning." —**compartment-hop** 1972 Apr *Atlantic* 116/3 "The train people amuse themselves by compartment-hopping." —**continent-hop** 1973 Dec 14 "*W*" (Fairchild Pubs, NYC) 11 "[She] is deliberately removed from the studied world of the nobility and from the continent-hopping life of her husband." —**country-hop** 1971 Sep 11 *TV Guide* 15/2 "NBC also has *Topaz*, Hitchcock's 1969 thriller with high style and lots of country-hopping to keep you amused—and confused." —**gallery-hop** 1972 July *Atlantic* 65/1 " 'I went gallery-hopping with my wife last night,' he said." —**island-hop** 1946 *Brit Book of the Year* 832/2 1972 Oct 14 *Sat Rev* 7/2 "If they [birds migrating overland] must cross open sea, they will island-hop." 1974 Mar *Sci Amer* 118/3 "Even after island-hopping and some drifting had settled the west, the winds allowed no easy drifts into the core of eastern Polynesia." Mar 16 heard in conversation "Out in the Caribbean island-hopping." —**mountain-hop** 1971 Oct *Better Homes and Gardens* 148/1 "The *Appalachian Trail* . . . mountain-hops 2000 miles through 14 states, eight national forests and two national parks." —**pousada-hop** 1971 Oct 9 *National Observer* 9/1 "And pousada hopping is a particularly economical way to see Portugal, since a night at a pousada costs only about $5 per person, room and meals." 1972 July *Town & Country* 12/2 "If time is pressing, an excellent idea is to see what you can of Lisbon, then go *pousada* hopping. [¶] POUSADAS. Most of these are little gems—government inns scattered all over the countryside. They are manors, monasteries, or castles, now modernized, but with characteristics of each region meticulously retained." 1973 Apr *Family Circle* 194/3 "Or, if you are devout travel bugs, spend the balance of your time pousada-hopping throughout Portugal." —**restaurant-hop** 1972 June *House Beautiful* 136/2 "And restaurant-hopping certainly can be a delight." —**ruin-hop** 1972 July *Town & Country* 52/1 "The enigmatic, jungle-wrapped pyramids . . . have piqued the curiosity of [certain] international ruin-hoppers." Ibid 123/2 "Deliciously succulent, fresh Yucatán fruits . . . are . . . wonderful thirst quenchers while ruin-hopping." —**sorority-hop** 1971 Sep *Harper's* 62/1 "There are also a couple of how-to books covering exam cramming and sorority hopping." —**table-hop** 1944 quot for *table-hopper* in *AS* 31:211 1951 *West Folklore* 10:171 "Table hopper: Waitress. Also a person who goes from table to table to greet friends, thereby picking up free drinks." 1953 *Am Thesaurus* 363.7 table-hopping 1955 quot for *table-hop* in *AS* 34:132 —**winter-spot-hop** 1972 Feb *Southern Living* 26/3 "Winter-spot hopping is the name of the game."

marathon *n* [See *WNCD8* sv *marathon* 2b for general sense] Group therapy of prolonged duration whose aim is to help participants discover their real selves 1966 Dec 27 *Look* 69 (picture caption) "Judy is reached at a 'marathon,' almost 40 hours of emotional poking and probing in a therapy-like group. It is self-discovery talked out under pressure, demanding unblushing honesty under the spotlight." Ibid 72/2 "Planned emotional collisions, like the marathon or the shorter 'encounter,' are turning up, and churning up, people all over the country." 1971 *Brit Book of the Year* 779/2 ("Words and Meanings, New")

nonstreak *n* [*BDNE non-* 2] 1974 Mar 18 *Newsweek* 42/2 "Most *political non-streak*: Some University of Pennsylvania students called a 'streak for impeachment' at the White House on April Fool's Day 'to lay bare the facts about Watergate and give us the naked truth.' Then they hastily explained it was just a gag."

parachute-streak *vi* 1974 Mar 18 *Newsweek* 42/1 "Five students at the University of Georgia, all male, parachute-streaked from a Cessna 182 over the campus while hundreds of spectators cheered."

parastreaker *n* [*W3* ²*para-*, 1 + STREAKER] 1974 Mar 18 *Newsweek* 42/1-2 "The parastreakers landed far from their target—one of them in the playground of the married students' quarters and one in a cesspool."

Pop Warner football *n* Organized football for youngsters See SMALL-FRY FOOTBALL 1965 Dec 6 *Newsweek* 103/1 "But in the not-so-small world of Pop Warner football, more than 600,000 kids between the ages of 9 and 15 struggle through the autumn months in an atmosphere not much different from that of college competition. Formed in Philadelphia in 1929 and named for the Temple University coach, the Pop Warner league is growing at the rate of 15 per cent a year and expects to have 1 million boys in 2-pound shoulder pads by 1970. 'Pops' wear $50 worth of scaled-down equipment, study a guidebook written by Frank Gifford, play in bowls and on television." 1974 Mar 5 participant on "Dinah's Place" NBC TV "They play Pop Warner football." Mar 5 Larry Csonka on "Dinah's Place" NBC TV "Pop Warner football or small-time football, whatever you want to call it."

quad *adj* [*quad*riphonic] QUADRIPHONIC, FOUR-CHANNEL 1970 June 27 *Sat Rev* 56/1 "Their new Quadraphonic Processor is an add-on bringing true (and quite well simulated) quad sound to two-channel systems." Nov *High Fidelity Mag* 76/2 "While this method perforce reduces total playing time to half of what it would be, it provides for quad stereo with no sacrifice in sonic quality." 1971 Nov *Esquire* 227/2-3 "That is why a decoder is an essential building block in transforming your stereo into a quad system." 1972 Nov *Amer Home* 154/2 "All three outfits will be able to accommodate four-channel cassettes, when and if these ever become a quad medium." Dec *Pop Sci* 12/3 "By mid-1973, all RCA discs will be issued in the compatible quad/stereo format." 1973 Fall *Stereo & Hi-Fi Times* 46/1 "To sample Vanguard's various approaches to the quad medium, try its versions of Mahler's *Symphony No. 3*, which re-creates the rich ambience of the Mormon Tabernacle where it was recorded; Berlioz's *Requiem* which is mainly ambient except for the very evident rear directionality of the additional brass choirs used during the blazing *Tuba Mirum* section; and Handel's *Royal Fireworks Music* and Stravinsky's *Petrouchka* for full surround-sound." Nov *Esquire* 236/1 (ad) "Does this quad receiver have *built-in* circuitry to play CD-4 discrete records from Warner, Atlantic, Elektra and RCA?" Nov *Pop Sci* 125/1 "Players have their own power amplifiers, driving two (stereo) or four (quad) speakers directly."

quad *n* 1: QUADRIPHONY, four-channel sound 1971 Nov *Esquire* 228/2 "Nevertheless the necessity of making quad compatible with mono and stereo recordings and broadcasts is probably going to necessitate the use of some system that matrixes the four channels down to one." 1973 Feb 5 *Newsweek* 65/1 "But quad goes beyond putting the listener in the best seat in the hall." July 14 *Science News* 18/2 "[The book] explains the differences between *discrete*, *matrix* and *derived* 4-channel sound, describes the various approaches to quad and what to expect from each individual approach." Fall *Stereo & Hi-Fi Times* 45/2 "The other major classical labels . . . have been recording in quad for some time." Nov *High Fidelity Mag* 34/2 "The nickname 'quad' is, incidentally, presently being pursued through judiciary thickets; Acoustical Manufacturing of England insists that it infringes the company's registered tradename 'Quad'—as in electrostatics—and a judgment from a Washington, D.C., court is awaited at this writing." 2: Equipment for playback of four-channel recordings 1973 Nov *Pop Sci* 125 (box) "Quadraphonic, with speakers in all four corners of the car, brings you four channels of music. Most makers offer quads now."

quad-quad *n* [QUAD *adj* + QUAD *n*] Discrete four-channel sound 1972 Oct 4 *Boll Weevil* (University, Ala) 12/3 "[Derived four-channel sound is] basically an enhancement technique and is sometimes called 'quasi-quad.' Though it has its faults it is much cheaper than quad-quad."

quadraphonic *n* 1: Four-channel sound 1972 June *Esquire* 55/3 (ad) "Should you wait until quadraphonic is perfected?" Nov *Amer Home* 152/1 "This new medium, also called four-channel, quadraphonic and surround-sound, is finally catching on." 2: Equipment for playback of four-channel sound 1973 Nov *Pop Sci* 125 (box) "Quadraphonics for cars may have FM-stereo radios, like this Pioneer model." Dec *Southern Living* 123 (ad) "When the time comes, you're not losing a stereo, you're gaining a quadraphonic."

quadrasonic, quadrosonic [QUADRISONIC *BDNE* 1970] *adj* QUADRIPHONIC 1970 Nov 12 *Rolling Stone* 40/5 "And Phillips of Holland . . . has shown some very promising four-channel tapes and cassette machines, called a 'quadrosonic' system." 1971 Feb 22 *Moneysworth* 2/1 "Quadrasonic sound will hit the market in a big way within the next few months." Nov *Pop Sci* 21/3 "What is the difference between the new quadrosonic recorders and the ordinary stereo models?" 1972 Spring *Tape Recorder Guide* 28/2 "Quadrasonic sound is reproduced through four speakers that surround the listener." 1973 Sep 24 *New Yorker* 113/1 "Be a Part of New York's Newest Disco . . . appreciate the Elite Atmosphere of Total Quadrasonic Sound!"

quadrasonic *n* Four-channel sound 1971 Dec *Playboy* 24/1–2 (ad) "Right now, the only way to get into quadrasonic is with 8-track tape. . . . Even if you just listen to the FM stereo radio, you'll be experiencing a totally new sound because of our unique Quadruplex^{TM} circuitry which transforms regular stereo into the quadrasonic experience. Not true quadrasonic. But almost."

quadricast, quadracast [*quadri-*, *quadra*phonic + broad*cast*] 1:*n* Transmission of four-channel sound by radio 1970 Mar *High Fidelity Mag* 72/1–2 "Like the transmitter, the new receiver-*cum*-adapter would also be compatible—that is, it would respond to quadricasts when they are transmitted, and continue to bring in conventional one- or two-channel signals when those are transmitted." Oct 31 *Sat Rev* 57/3 "He would not compete with the Mikado/Dorren FM four-channel quadracast multiplex system because it was better than his own." 2:*vt* Transmit four-channel sound by radio 1970 Mar *High Fidelity Mag* 72/1 "The progress of quadricast FM would parallel that of two-channel stereo FM." —**quadricasting** *n* 1970 Mar *High Fidelity Mag* 72/1 "The immediate prospect for this form of four-channel broadcasting—let's call it 'quadricasting'—is a system developed by William Halstead and Leonard Feldman. . . . Together, Messrs. Halstead and Feldman have evolved a one-station-four-channel system which they claim will allow a single FM station to transmit four independent channels simultaneously."

quadriphonic [*BDNE* 1970], **quadraphonic** [*WNCD8*], **quadrophonic** [*BDNE* 1971; the only illust is from a Brit journal] *adj* Earlier dates for *quadriphonic*, *quadraphonic*; US quots for *quadrophonic* 1969 Sep *High Fidelity Mag* 63/1 "The four channels might be used for double ping-pong effects—perhaps a quadriphonic version of 'Switched-On Bach.'" 1970 Nov 30 *Rock* 31/4 "We're also working with quadraphonic sound." 1971 Nov *Esquire* 162/1 "You begin to understand quadraphonic sound when you think of having four speakers rather than two speakers in one room." Nov *Pop Sci* 128/3 "I think the quadraphonic concept, if employed sensibly, can add a good deal to musical enjoyment." 1972 Mar 9 *Women's Wear Daily* 5/1 "It's 'the only club in the U.S. with quadrophonic sound.'" Mar 25 *Sat Rev* 34/2 "The quadrophonic sound proves very satisfactory on stereo equipment."

quadriphonically, quadraphonically *adv* 1970 Nov *High Fidelity Mag* 76/2 "In classical music recorded quadriphonically the two front channels serve the same use as the left and right channels of conventional stereo." Nov 30 *Rock* 31/4 "'Cool Water' is recorded quadraphonically."

quadriphonics, quadraphonics, quadrophonics *n* Theory or techniques of four-channel sound reproduction 1970 Nov *High Fidelity Mag* 76/2 (subheading) "The Quadriphonics Sweepstakes." 1971 Feb 18 *Rolling Stone* 16/1 "He's been in New York . . . working with quadrophonics for CBS." 1972 Nov *Amer Home* 152/1 "Pacesetters are already out in front, boning up on quadraphonics and starting to buy." 1973 *Four-Channel Sound 1974 Ed* 5 "Four years ago we began spelling quadriphonics the correct way—with an 'i.' Subsequently, when the audio industry seemed to settle on 'quadraphonics,' we switched. The Institute of High Fidelity has now decided it *should* be spelled with an 'i,' and we decided to follow suit." Fall *Stereo & Hi-Fi Times* 52/1 "Four-channel sound—quadriphonics—is burgeoning at an unexpected rate." Nov *High Fidelity Mag* 34/1–2 "Orthographers—like ornithologists—will go to great lengths in pursuing a specimen of interest; in our industry they are still atwitter over those coined for four-channel sound. We originally chose 'quadriphonics' (used from September 1969, explained in 1971) and—despite its mixed Latin and Greek roots—find it the least bothersome of the specimens we've sighted. But we were chicken; when the majority of the industry seemed to have accepted 'quadraphonics' we went along, preferring to put our emphasis on ready understandability rather than purity of style. Now the Institute of High Fidelity has officially backed our original spelling, and effective with this issue we revert to it."

quadriphony, quadraphony [*WNCD8*] *n* 1970 Jan *High Fidelity Mag* 38/2 "Levels of the rear channels, which carried only ambience and audience sounds, were kept the prescribed 10 dB below front-channel levels. We found that visitors almost invariably faced the front speakers. . . . Conditions were quite different . . . with rear speakers set for relatively high gain. Under these conditions, with musical material emanating from all four corners of the room, we found that visitors stood every which way to listen. Perhaps the most descriptive terminology for these two techniques, therefore, would be polarized and unpolarized quadriphony, respectively." 1971 Nov *Pop Sci* 128/3 "Quadraphony is no substitute for quality." Nov 27 *Sat Rev* 91/1 "But quadraphony raises the price another dollar or two for disc and Q8 cartridges, and jumps open-reel tape up to $15." 1973 *Brit Book of the Year* 732/3 ("Words and Meanings, New") "Quadraphony."

quasi-quad *n* Derived four-channel sound 1972 Oct 4 *Boll Weevil* 12/3 quot sv QUAD-QUAD 1973 Fall *Stereo & Hi-Fi Times* 77 "The Quasi-Quad adapter from BSR is a passive matrix enhancer that comes complete with two rear speakers."

senior citizen *n* [*AHD* 1969 with usage note and *RHD* 1969; cf *W3* ²*senior* 1,b] Earlier and additional quots 1956 May 12 *School and Society* 169 (letter) "As a basis for their education, it is good for the young, the middle-aged, and our senior citizens." (Porter G Perrin, who contributed this quot, notes on the slip that the term is a "euphemism for old(er) people" and that "sentimentality [is] suggested by its frequent use with *our*.") Sep *Harper's* 46/1 "Every community nowadays abounds in activities intended partly or entirely for what the press loves to call Senior Citizens." 1963 Mencken-McDavid *Amer Lang* 354 n 9 "Among favorite euphemisms of the 1960s one must note . . . *senior citizen* for the old." 1971 Jan *Reader's Digest* 134/2 "'Damn it!' he roared, 'I'm *not* a senior citizen! *I am an old man!*'"

small-fry football; small-time football *n* 1970 Oct *Ladies' Home Jour* 147 (title of article by Fran Tarkenton) "Don't Let Your Son Play Small-Fry Football." 1974 Mar 5 Larry Csonka quot sv POP WARNER FOOTBALL.

stand-up 1: *adj* [Both *AHD* 1969 (sense 4) and *RHD* 1969 (sense 6) define in the specific sense for which quots are supplied here] 1959 May 7 *Tuscaloosa News* 9/5 "Because of language barriers, stand-up comedians were immediately eliminated." 1961 Aug 6 *Parade* 4/1 (picture caption) "A stand-up comedienne is a female who stands in front of an audience and tells jokes at which the audience laughs, but *laughs*." 2: *n* [Cf *W3 adj*, 2 and illust "*stand-up* comedy act"] 1971 Aug 1 *NY Times* D13/2 "Writing for Carson's opening stand-up is not exactly as easy as rolling off a monologue."

streak *vb* [Cf *World Book Dict* 1974 *vi* "2. *Informal* . . . go at full speed"; and 1901 quot in *OED* sv *streak sb* 3, c "running like a streak, to use the local phrase"] *Specif* 1: *vi* Run naked in public 1974 Feb 24 *Birmingham* (Ala) *News* 22A/3 "As a last resort, everybody could go naked on college campuses, and force students to streak fully clothed." Mar 10 *Birmingham News* A27/7–8 (AP) "Pan American World Airways said a man described only as 'a short, bearded Turk in his early 30s' streaked through one of the carrier's jumbo jets during a flight from London to New York." Mar 15 *Athens* (Ga) *Banner-Herald* 4/5 "GAINESVILLE, Fla.—The only new activism the early 1970s have developed is that of students 'streaking' across some open space to bedazzle onlookers, clad in their innocence and good spirits. It seems to have started at Tallahassee, on the Florida State campus, followed in a few days by the University of Florida campus here, where I am writing this dispatch as from a war front." Mar 18 *Newsweek* 41/2 "They streaked on motorcycles and on unicycles, in wheelbarrows and in wheelchairs." Apr 15 *Newsweek* 61/1 "Amidst all the cries and whispers that attended Hollywood's annual Academy Awards last week . . . an unexpected guest . . . supplied some American graffiti by shedding his clothes and streaking across the stage." 2: *vt* Run naked in front of (an audience) 1974 Mar 29 Johnny Carson on "Tonight Show" (delayed broadcast) "Yesterday, March 27, will go down in history as the day we were streaked."

streak *n* [Cf *OED sb* 3, b (1781) and *World Book Dict* sense 7 "a flash of lightning"] 1: Instance of running naked in public 1974 Feb 4 *Newsweek* 63/3 "At the University of Maryland, a student who participated with 125 others in a co-educational streak has been suspended from school—not for indecent exposure, but for assaulting a college official who suggested that he cover up." Feb 24 *Birmingham* (Ala) *News* 32A/1 "At Birmingham-Southern College, where the state's first coed streak occurred Tuesday, when two boys and a girl made a nude run, the three streakers plus their getaway car driver have been placed on administrative probation." Mar 10 *NY Times* 49/2 "It was but one of the thousands of 'streaks' run on and off the nation's college campuses in recent days as the country's latest fad—running nude through public places—streaked north with the warm rays of spring." 2: STREAKER 1974 Mar 18 *Newsweek* 41/2 "A Michigan State class was discussing 'Criminal Sexual Deviation,' when—whoosh!—a streak flashed through the classroom."

streaker *n* One who STREAKS 1973 Dec 10 *Time* 14/2 "Streakers generally race nude between two unpredictable points, and the idea is catching on among college students and other groups." Dec 31 *Time* 6/3 (letter) "This place [Notre Dame] may be better known for its other sports, but streakers deserve exposure too." 1974 Feb 2 *National Observer* 6/3 "Last week another 'streaker' crossed the campus [of Florida State University], his passing, reported the campus newspaper, the Flambeau, 'announced by a woman's shriek and followed by laughter and applause.'" Feb 4 *Newsweek* 63/3 "In Detroit, two skinny male streakers recently collided while racing through a fashionable restaurant; one of them was knocked cold and had to be dragged from the scene by his fellow nudist." Feb 24 *Birmingham* (Ala) *News* 22A/3 "Or, better still, everybody could start wearing ski masks, forcing streakers to run around bare-faced if they really want to stand out." Mar 4 (Univ of Ala) *Crimson-White* 2/1 "A streaker was arrested by the Northport police this weekend." Ibid 15/1 (classified ad) "STREAKER GETAWAY CAR. 1967 Chevelle SS396 for sale." Mar 5 *Tuscaloosa News* 6/2 "He was the nearest thing to a streaker in town, zipping quickly to no less than five other fast break opportunities." Mar 6 *Current* (University, Ala) front cover (cartoon) "[One cowpoke to another:] WHO WERE THET MASKED MAN?—THAT, MY FRIEND, WAS THE LONE STREAKER, AND HIS FAITHFUL INDIAN COMPANION, RUNNING BARE." Mar 7 *Tuscaloosa News* 14/7–8 (heading) "Streaker foils no-hitter." Mar 10 *NY Times* 49/2 "But some academics, none of them known streakers, say the fad [streaking] is an innocent asexual flouting of social rules, a 1974 version of wearing long hair or a nonviolent way to demonstrate the generation gap." Mar 10 *Tuscaloosa News* B1/7 "Well, Birmingham Southern left fielder Steve Mayer is still trying to figure out what to say to that pair of streakers who invaded his territory here Saturday as the Panthers clashed with Coach Hayden Riley's Alabama baseballers." Mar 18 *Newsweek* 42/1 "Then the University of Maryland (one of several colleges claiming to be the 'birthplace of streaking') claimed to have mustered 553 streakers at a time." Mar 20 *Current* (University, Ala) 3/5 "Debate over who was the original streaker and where did it occur has apparently been resolved. . . . [¶] Judge [Fred] Pierce, now living in Sacramento, confessed this week that as an 18-year old Stanford student back in 1918 he had accepted a $5 bribe to streak naked in front of sorority row." Mar 23 "Carol Burnett Show" CBS TV "And you're looking as fresh and natural as a streaker in a [blue?]berry patch." Mar 26 *Plain Dealer* 4A/1 "Four male streakers burst across the stage and stole kisses from . . . movie star Linda Lovelace, who was speaking during Sex Week at the University of Alabama in Tuscaloosa." Apr 22 *Newsweek* 70/3 "The Mets lost the opening game to a streaker."

streaker alert *n* 1973 Dec 10 *Time* 14/2–3 "Few streakers are reported to police . . . and no one knows where they might strike next. Richard Kimball, a disc jockey for radio station KMET, is trying to correct that by broadcasting 'streaker alerts' for Angelenos; when a racing nudist is spotted, listeners phone in their reports." 1974 Feb 4 *Newsweek* 63/3 "For a time, one Los Angeles radio station broadcast 'streaker alerts' to warn the populace that naked youths were on the loose."

Streakers; Streakers Party *n* Student political organization at Florida State University, Tallahassee 1974 Feb 2 *National Observer* 6/4 "The Streakers Party has been formed to run candidates for student-government elections. Randy Mutter, who says he is a former Marine running on the party ticket, explained to the

Tallahassee Democrat: 'The idea of Streakers symbolizes that people want to cast off some of the regimentation imposed by society.' "

streak-in n [STREAK vi + -in (BDNE)] 1974 Mar 6 reporter on NBC TV "They [plan] for a massive streak-in."

streaking n Act of running naked 1973 Dec 10 Time 14/2 "In the cool Southern California evening, a Van Nuys housewife last week shed all of her clothes, slipped out of her house, and began running through the San Fernando Valley streets. She was eventually seen loping through a small public park, but before she could be caught she had disappeared into the night, another statistic in a growing Los Angeles-area fad: streaking." Dec 31 Time 6/3 (letter) "Actually the term streaking derives its meaning from the fact that unless one appeared as a streak against the landscape, the Minnesota winter was triumphant and streaker became statue." 1974 Feb 2 National Observer 6/3–4 "What's unusual at Florida State, however, is that 'streaking' may become institutionalized." Quot continues sv STREAKERS; STREAKERS PARTY Feb 4 Newsweek 63/2–3 " 'Streaking'—making Blitzkrieg runs through public areas completely in the buff—has become a fad of epidemic proportions among students from California to Maryland." Mar 10 Birmingham (Ala) News A27/4 (AP) "The San Jose, Calif., streaking fest began Friday night and lasted into the early morning hours on Saturday."

streak-watcher n Spectator at a STREAK (sense 1) 1974 Mar 18 Newsweek 42/3 "But any number of other streak-watchers didn't react at all."

structural unemployment n [Cf W3 sv structural, adj 1c; AHD 1969, 5; World Book Dict 1974 adj 6] Unemployment resulting from fundamental changes in the structure of the economy, such as those enumerated in the 1961 and 1966 quots 1961 Apr 4 Seattle Times 8 "The N.P.A. describes chronic or structural unemployment as not caused primarily by the ups and downs of the business cycle. [¶] . . . caused by inadequate growth, more automation, economic changes abroad, movement of industry to new locations, and 'discriminations against age and racial groups practiced by some employers and in some cases by unions.' " 1962 Jan 3 Lincoln (Neb) Evening Jour 30/4 " 'Structural unemployment' remains at a steep rate in the face of a strong, solid business expansion." Brit Book of the Year 743/1 ("Words and Meanings, New") 1964 Washington Newsletter (Friends Com on Natl Legislation) 2/1 "Two questions of major concern to the Clark Subcommittee were: (1) Is automation creating 'structural unemployment' which the economy finds increasingly difficult to absorb?" 1966 Philip A S Taylor A New Dict of Economics (NY: Augustus M Kelley) 260 "structural unemployment. . . . [pp. 282–83] economists distinguish between several types [of unemployment]: . . . (vi) structural—this due to fundamental changes taking place in the economy, such as the decline of some industries and the rise of others."

Superstreak n [super- after the comic-strip character Superman + STREAK n sense 2] 1974 Mar 18 Newsweek 41/2 "Is it a bird? Is it a plane? No—it's Superstreak! Or so it is likely to be these days, as some bare-bottomed scholar propels himself in a bum's rush through college and beyond."

surround-sound n Discrete four-channel sound heard through four loudspeakers, each of which provides primary musical sound; sometimes called full surround-sound (see last quot); occasionally used for conventional two-channel stereo heard through four loudspeakers (see 1972 quot) 1969 Sep High Fidelity Mag 63/1 "Vanguard's initial offering in what it has termed 'Surround Sound' will include the Berlioz Requiem, which calls for four brass bands to be spread around the cardinal points of the hall." Oct High Fidelity Mag 48/1 "Incidentally, Vanguard's trade name for the four-channel sound system is Surround Stereo—not Surround Sound. We had been led to believe that the latter would appear on the tapes scheduled for issue in September and used that term in our September article. But Vanguard tells us that the original announcement was correct; so Surround Stereo it is." 1972 Nov Amer Home 154/2 "Meanwhile, if you already have a cassette deck or plan to buy one, you can hook it in and enjoy two-channel stereo cassettes in regular sound or in surround-sound." 1973 Fall Stereo & Hi-Fi Times 45/1 "One of the first problems that record producers had to deal with was the question of ambient versus surround-sound. Ambient quad refers to the use of the rear channels for ambient or room information only. . . . Surround-sound implies the use of all four channels for 'primary' information without restrictions as to what one actually hears during a live performance." Ibid 46/2 "Finally for Columbia's full surround-sound try Stravinsky's Rite of Spring (with Bernstein) and Bartok's Concerto for Orchestra (with Boulez)."

[Received May 1974]

AMONG THE NEW WORDS

I. WILLIS RUSSELL AND MARY GRAY PORTER
University of Alabama

IT MUST HAVE BEEN during the summer of 1973 that the senior author became curious to see what dictionaries had to say about the term *executive privilege*, which he was frequently hearing and seeing in print. Since the notion seemed to date from the time of George Washington, he was not a little surprised to find that the first general dictionary he consulted was silent on the subject. He then checked the historical dictionaries, with no better luck. The law dictionaries consulted were likewise silent. He finally found the term in two dictionaries, the specialized *Crescent Dictionary of American Politics* by Eugene J. McCarthy and the general 1974 *World Book Dictionary*, edited by Clarence L. Barnhart.

Since the term is still very much in the news and the *World Book Dictionary* gives only one undated citation, it seems to us that the entry in this installment is justified and may be of interest to our readers.

As already stated, in view of the apparent age of the idea, the comparative newness of the term *executive privilege* is surprising. In his new book on *Executive Privilege*, Raoul Berger also comments on the newness of the term, and he devotes a long footnote (p. 1, n. 3) to the dating of it. He cites testimony of Deputy Assistant Attorney General Mary C. Lawton in 1973 that "the term is of recent origin." His own researches have turned up no usage earlier than the 1958 quotation. And in spite of his disclaimer to any pretense "to an exhaustive search," it does seem, even if earlier dates turn up, that the term became a recognized item in the lexicon during the 1950s.

Interesting corroborative inferential evidence for a first date in the 1950s was called to our attention by our colleague, John Luskin, who found that whereas the term *executive privilege* is used and indexed in the revised 1964 edition of James Russell Wiggins's *Freedom or Secrecy*, it is not indexed in the original edition of 1956. He pointed out the pages containing the Brownell memorandum, which we have used as our second bracketed quotation.

Finally, two of the quotations place the origin of the term in President Eisenhower's time, that is, in the 1950s.

In the last sentence of his footnote, Berger cites two phrases from a litigation, which, though he does not say so explicitly, he seems to imply may be pointing toward the term. We agree and hence place this remark within square brackets as our first quotation.

We have several quotations containing terms that we suspect were suggested by the current frequent use of *executive privilege*. We place them in alphabetical order in an entry *-privilege*.

The late dates of our attestations of the term *bottom line* are also surprising. Several of our colleagues from the University of Alabama School of Commerce and Business Administration have told us that the phrase has been used by accountants for many years. Peter Tamony, who supplied the 1967 quotation, also notes that stock brokers have told him that this usage goes back to the 1930s, if not earlier, and adds that recent usage "seems to derive from voicings on [Louis] Rukeyser's *Wall Street Week* television program on Public Television stations. Channel 9, KQED, San Francisco, has been screening this since 1971–72."

We would like to note two illustrations of the vogue of the expression in addition to those in the glossary. The Bottom Line, a new "rock-and-folk club," has recently opened in New York (*New Yorker*, 25 February 1974, p. 6/1–2). A *Newsweek* caption writer (18 March 1974, p. 42/3) cleverly, if not very meaningfully, combines the vogue term *bottom line* with the streaking fad: "a parastreaker in Atlanta floats to the bottom line"; the photograph shows the rear view of a parachutist descending to earth clad only in shoes, shirt, and parachute harness.

Acknowledgments: For citations: John Algeo (5), Elizabeth Brock (1), John Luskin (2), Evelyn McMillan (1), Eunice Payne (1), Peter Tamony (1), and Loretta M. Thomason (1). For help on the entry *executive privilege*, thanks are due Walter H. Bennett, Jay M. Murphy, John C. Payne, and C. Dallas Sands. Thanks are also due John Algeo for extensive checking of the term *bottom line*.

bottom line n 1: Last line of a financial report *specif* a: Line that summarizes the net profit (or loss) or the earnings per share of a corporation or other organization; also **bottom profit line** (see first 1974 quot) 1970 Robert Townsend *Up the Organization* (Greenwich, Conn: Fawcett Pubs, 1971; c 1970) 57–58 "Therefore, all overheads should be brought down to the bottom line for bonus purposes on principles agreed to in advance." 1971 July 12 Newsweek 68/3 " ' IBM has always been heavy on corporate paternalism,' he adds, '. . . Learson may well be willing to sacrifice some of that for those results on the bottom line.' " 1972 Oct Harper's Bazaar 105/3 "His only interest is in the bottom line. He doesn't know or care about books or art or music or even his own wife—only about the bottom line." 1973 Apr 24 World 52/2 "[He] cited the studio's ability 'to give top quality for the bottom-line dollar.' " July 2 Newsweek 53/1 "And the crucial bottom line will be watched closely by the moneymen who determine the fate of the [Chicago] Tribune's parent company." July 2 New Yorker 42/2 "The second [figure of interest to the average investor in the stock market of the 1960s] was the net profit per share—the famous 'bottom line' of a company's quarterly earnings report." Aug 13 New Yorker 63/1 "So it came to pass that the do-nothing S.E.C. . . . ended the year with its own bottom line showing a net profit." Sep 7 W (Fairchild Pubs, NYC) 11 "He violates the cardinal rule of ambition—fanaticism that turns the Bottom Line into Divine scripture." Sep 24 NY Times F14 (heading) "The

'Bottom Line' Is No Longer Where It's At / An accounting executive lists five considerations for corporate social responsibility." Oct 8 *Newsweek* 42/1 "The bottom lines of the print-outs [records of the Financial Committee to Re-elect the President] were amazing in themselves." Oct 15 *Newsweek* 114/3 "Thirty million investors lost $300 billion in the downdraft of the 'go-go' years—suckered... by chicaneries like 'bottom-line fiction,' 'creative accounting,' 'garbage stock' and 'two-a-week underwriters.' " Nov 2 *New Times* 20 (title of a feature, in this and other issues, devoted to short news items from the business world) "THE BOTTOM LINE." Nov 18 *Atlanta Jour and Constitution* 1E/4–3E/1 "It's the sort of thing that affects the bottom line of building costs." 1974 Jan *Sci Amer* 121 (ad) "We can help you put a smile on your bottom line. [¶] One way to make your bottom profit line look better is to increase the speed and efficiency of your assembly operations." Jan 21 *Newsweek* 44 (ad) " 'Bottom-line' spoken here . . . We're really not interested in getting into a price-bidding contest. But we *are* anxious to compete in terms of long-range *cost*. Because that's the language of the bottom line." Mar 9 *Bus Week* 80/1–2 "Inventory profits, of course, still count as solid profits on the bottom line." Apr 6 *SR/World* 6/2 "Nothing produces more tension and even feuding on a staff than the psychology of a losing magazine. DeVoto felt the pressure of the bottom line."

b: Line of an income tax return on which the taxpayer signs 1974 July 25 Rep Edward Mezvinsky, House Judiciary Comm impeachment debate WTOK-TV (Meridian, Miss) "It wasn't his tax lawyer's name that was on the bottom line. It wasn't his tax accountant's name on the bottom line. It was 'Richard Nixon' on the bottom line." (see also ON THE BOTTOM LINE, WHEN YOU GET DOWN TO THE BOTTOM LINE, below)

2: *Transf senses* a: Definitive argument, statement, or answer; summary; punch line; clincher 1967 Sep 8 *San Francisco Examiner* 35/7–8 "On actors becoming politicians: 'George Murphy and Ronald Reagan certainly qualified because they have gotten elected. I think that's the bottom line.' [¶] On actors becoming friendly: 'It is difficult to be very, very friendly. The definition of success is really to be doing better than your best friend. I think that's the bottom line.' [¶] Despite the vacuity of Tony's bottom line statements . . ." 1972 Feb 12 *National Observer* 17/4–5 "With Mileti, a listener usually knows when the punch line is coming because he'll say in profit-and-loss lingo, 'Now here's the bottom line.' " 1973 Feb *Harper's* 42/3 "But the bottom line on why I wanted to watch the [election] returns with the pinheads, spastics, morons, maniacs, and paranoids . . . is that the ancient advisory nexus between madness and statecraft had been broken, and I wished to view the workings of the latter from the perspective of the former." Apr 10 *World* 8/3 " 'The question is, Do you miss our Havana cigars?' [¶] 'Well, in answer to that, and to get to the bottom line, I don't smoke.' " May *Today's Health* 21/2 [A gynecologist, after citing the arguments most often advanced for and against breast-feeding, adds:] "But the bottom line is simply this: You're the mother. You do whatever you want to do." May 24 *Rolling Stone* 34/4–44/2 "Their emphasis of these discoveries implied this was enough to circumstantially prove [he] was indeed involved in a nefarious dope ring. The implication carried a sneaky bottom line: *Think about it, pal, if the guy was a dope merchant in the business of corrupting your children, his corpse wasn't worth shrieking about.*" May 28 *Newsweek* 45/3 "Perhaps what we need is a new set of seven deadly sins, special ones for our times. . . . Numbness, Dumbness, Beaverism, Euphemism, Riggery, Laundery and Trickery. . . . [¶] And *Trickery* is the name of the game, the Watergate bottom line." Aug 6 *Newsweek* 14/3 "The brusque tone of the letters smarted, but neither Cox nor the committee was surprised by the bottom-line refusal to yield." Sep 24 *Newsweek* 66/2 "By at least trying to reach for an issue's bottom line, 'Maude' defines its own—and the medium's—potential." Oct 1 *Newsweek* 30/3 " 'We cannot accept a Connally, Rockefeller or . . . Reagan,' said one House leader flatly. 'The bottom line over here is: No candidate for 1976 [as vice-presidential nominee].' " Nov 4 "The Embattled President" CBS News Special Report WCFT-TV Ch 33 (Tuscaloosa, Ala) "Integrity is the bottom line in the social contract." Nov 19 *Anniston* (Ala) *Star* 4A "And doesn't it suggest the ultimate bottom line—that even if we think the President is guilty, we shouldn't try him because he's the President?" Dec 18 *SR/World* 13/1 "And the bottom line of the lesson is simple: Throw away your statistics, your figures, and your chart board—get yourself a dart board." 1974 Feb 18 *Newsweek* 25/2 "The message was guardedly drawn, in spots lawyerly to the point of obscurantism. . . . But the bottom line seemed plain: no deal." Mar 6 Richard Nixon, press conference telecast "Then we came to what I considered the bottom line." Mar 12 "One Night in Paradise" (CBS TV special) "Here is the bottom line. I lied when I told you you were exciting." Mar 21 "Ironside" NBC-TV "[Mark:] 'We have six witnesses.' [Ironside:] 'That's the bottom line.' " May 20 CBS News "Now that the story is on the record, the bottom line, as the White House might say, is that the weather war was about as successful as the other war." July 13 *TV Guide* 15/1 "One inquiring into the economic aspects of the television deal is bidding for a complicated explanation, the bottom line of which is that the money is small." July 22 *New Yorker* 23/2 "The Sales Executives Club of New York, as most people know, has far-reaching influence in the area of popular syntax (club members introduced, almost single-handed, the phrases 'bottom line,' 'one-to-one relationship,' and 'very personal rapport' into common usage)." **—on the bottom line, when you get down to the bottom line** In the final analysis 1973 Oct *Viva* 92/2 "I have what it takes on the bottom line to be a fighter, over and above the skills I can cultivate." Ibid 98/2 "One guy's skills may outstrip another guy's skills in the area of bedroom play, but when you get down to the bottom line there are other values to consider."

b: [cf *W3* ³*line* 5a(2) "a bounding restriction (as on personal conduct): limit, restraint"] Lower limit 1973 Aug 20 *Newsweek* 33/3 "He was more than a man with absolute standards; he was a man who lived up to those standards. . . . Like his old customer, J. Edgar Hoover, the old man had a bottom line below which he would not go."

3: [cf *W3* ³*line* 5b "*archaic:* position in life"; 10a "stock of goods"; *top-line*] Lowest rank or quality 1973 Merle Miller *Plain Speaking: An Oral Biography of Harry S. Truman* (NY: Berkley Publ Corp; distrib by Putnam's) 31 (quoting Harry S Truman) "Millard Fillmore's son burned all his father's papers because he was ashamed of his father, who had come from the very bottom line right to the top." 1974 July *Pop Sci* 28/3 "For the bottom-line model, without automatic rewind . . . the take-up reel is scalloped so you can reach a finger in to grasp the film."

bottom-line *adj* Fundamental, ultimate 1974 Mar 22 *New Times* 44/2 "As long as the music thrives . . . the ethnic dance hall will be the bottom-line midtown thrill." May *Esquire* 20/2–3 " 'The same but different!' What is that? A Zen concept? . . . No, no, it is indeed a bottom-line, ongoing principle, unabashedly blessed by all those folks . . . who are responsible for filling infinite prime-time hours . . . which this season has raised network advertising revenues for the first time to over two billion dollars."

bottom-line syndrome (cf BOTTOM LINE 1a) 1974 Mar 25 Paul Garner, Dean Emeritus, School of Commerce and Business Administration, Univ of Ala "The bottom-line syndrome—that's what a lot of the younger middle management have. They look at what effect everything will have on the bottom line—the EPS, earnings per share."

executive privilege [cf *OED*, sv *executive* B1 b "Chiefly U.S., applied to the President (also called *chief executive*), and to the governors of states," 1787→; sv *privilege sb* B4 "The special right or immunity attaching to some office, rank, or station; prerogative," ante 1225→; enumerated are *the privilege* 'the royal prerogative,' *privilege of clergy, privilege of parliament, privilege of peerage* or *of peers*] See quots [1953 Raoul Berger *Executive Privilege: A Constitutional Myth* (Cambridge, Mass: Harvard Univ Press, 1974) 1, fn 3 "So too, in a private litigation, United States v. Reynolds, 345 U.S. 1 (1953), the government claimed an 'executive power to suppress documents,' and the Court referred to the 'privilege against revealing military secrets, a privilege which is well established in the law of evidence'; ibid. 6–7." 1954 May 17 Herbert Brownell quoted in *Freedom or Secrecy* by James Russell Wiggins (NY: Oxford Univ Press, 1956) 68 "Presidents have established, by precedent, that they and members of their Cabinets, and other heads of executive departments have an undoubted privilege and discretion to keep confidential, in the public interest, papers and information which require secrecy."] *Federal Bar Jour* 14:113 (title of article by Conrad D Philos) "Executive Privilege and the Release of Military Records." 1958 *Federal Supp* 157:943/2 "The position taken rests on the claim of executive privilege." (Since Berger, p 1, fn 3, gives only the reference, we supply the quot.) 1959 Mar 13 US Congress, Senate, Committee on the Judiciary, Subcommittee on Constitutional Rights (title) *Executive Privilege and Freedom of Information*, hearings on S Res 62, 86th Cong, 1st sess, pt 2 (Washington: US GPO). 1961 June William H Stewart MA thesis George Washington Univ (title) "The Doctrine of Executive Privilege: A Study of Its Applications during the Eisenhower Administration." 1962 *Yale Law Jour* 71:879 (title of article by Paul Hardin III) "Executive Privilege in the Federal Courts." Eugene J McCarthy *Crescent Dict of Amer Politics* (NY: Macmillan) 56/1 "Executive Privilege The right of the executive branch—a right oftentimes disputed—to withhold information from the legislature." 1963 Apr *NY Times* 4 Nov 1973 E17/2 (quoting a speech by Gerald R Ford in the House) "I shall not attempt here to review the legal problems and precedents involved in the concept of executive privilege." 1964 James Russell Wiggins *Freedom or Secrecy* (rev ed; NY: Oxford Univ Press) 228 "Subordinate executive personnel invoked executive privilege as authority for withholding information from Congress on forty-four separate occasions." 1965 Emmette S Redford et al *Politics and Government in the United States* (NY: Harcourt) 365 "Most presidents since then [1796] have had occasion to invoke 'executive privilege' against the demands of Congressional investigations." 1971 Sep 18 *New Repub* 8/1 "There are many colors to the cloak of 'executive privilege.' " 1972 Peter M Sandman, David M Rubin and David B Sachsman *Media: An Introductory Analysis of American Mass Communications* (Englewood Cliffs, NJ: Prentice-Hall) 154 "He [George Washington] told the Congress that the executive branch of government had a right to withhold any information that might injure the public if disclosed. This is called the doctrine of Executive Privilege." 1973 Robert A Liston *The Right to Know: Censorship in America* (NY: Franklin Watts) 103–4 "A final method of censorship to be discussed here . . . is 'executive privilege.' This is the principle that the president cannot be required by judicial process to perform any given act and cannot, therefore, be required to make information available to the Congress that he does not wish to divulge." Mar 26 *Time* 28/2 "Executive privilege expanded in the cold war. Widening areas of federal activity were removed from congressional—or public—scrutiny. Foreign and defense policies were often deemed too sensitive to be disclosed." Apr 8 *NY Times* E15/1 "The executive and Congress are going to have to compromise on executive privilege, on the Watergate, on the control of inflation and the impoundment of funds and the conduct of the war." Apr 28 *New Yorker* 33/3 "But executive privilege isn't a legal question; it's a political question." July 22 *NY Times* 12E/2 (editorial) "Executive privilege, in one modern formulation, means that 'the inherent constitutional powers of the executive branch give it the legal authority to determine what documents in its possession will be produced'—in court or Congress or the public record." July 22 *NY Times Mag* 41/1 "The doctrine of executive privilege—which holds that communications within the executive branch should be protected from public exposure—quickly became one of the White House's front lines of defense on Watergate." Aug 6 *Time* 16/3 "From the beginning, Presidents have exercised something like Executive privilege, although it did not get that name until Dwight Eisenhower's time." Sep 10 *Time* 14/3 "[Sirica] noted that the Supreme Court in 1953 had recognized an Executive privilege for military secrets. . . . But he made it clear that Executive privilege does not cover conversations relevant to a criminal investigation and not involving performance of official duties." Oct 14 *Birmingham* (Ala) *News* A18/2 "Executive privilege, n. The doctrine that as a function of the separation of powers some information in possession of the federal government may be withheld from disclosure." Nov 18 *NY Times Book Rev* 20/4 "It is true, of course, and it is important, that Eisenhower (through his Attorney General, William Rogers) made the most sweeping claims for 'executive privilege,' and that Mr. Rogers probably introduced the very term into our politics." Dec 10 *Newsweek* 27/3–28/1 "The White House argued on ground of Executive privilege that parts of all three of them [tapes] ought still to be kept secret." 1974 Sam J Ervin, Jr "Controlling 'Executive Privilege' " *Loyola Law Rev* 20, no. 1:11 " 'Executive Privilege' refers to the purported authority of the President in his discretion to withhold information in his possession or in the possession of the executive branch from the compulsory process of the other branches of government. . . . [fn 2] Executive privilege is also used in private litigation involving the Executive Branch." Raoul Berger *Executive Privilege: A Constitutional Myth* (Cambridge, Mass: Harvard Univ Press) 1 "[']Executive privilege'—the President's claim of constitutional authority to withhold information from Congress—is a myth. . . . The very words 'executive privilege' were conjoined only yesterday, in 1958."

gravitational radiation [cf *gravitational wave(s) BDNE* 1970 quot, *W3* 1971 addenda, and *WNCD8*] 1970 Oct *Sci Jour* 15/4 "The first observation of gravitational radiation was announced in June 1969 by Joseph Weber of Princeton University's Institute for Advanced Study." Dec 26 *Sci News* 480/3 "The theorists suppose that an object enters the ergosphere from outside. Here it is split into two pieces, one of which falls into the black hole while the other escapes. In the process the black hole transfers some of the energy associated with its rotation to the escaping body. [¶] In this kind of interaction a strong burst of gravitational radiation would be produced." 1971 Apr 8 *New Scientist and Sci Jour* 75/2 "Earlier in the year, Allen Anderson, University of Uppsala, Sweden, recorded Doppler shift measurements on Mariners 6 and 7 which could have been due to the direct effects of gravitational radiation on the Spacecraft's trajectory (Nature, vol 229, p 547)." May *Sci Amer* 22/1–2 "Of course, the processes by which an atom or a molecule emits light involve the acceleration of particles with mass (electrons), and these particles should in principle generate some gravitational radiation as well. The trouble is that the ratio of electric charge to mass for an electron is extremely large. . . . [¶] As a result I decided at the beginning to search for gravitational radiation from very large masses—on the order of stars or galaxies—with detectors consisting of large numbers of atoms excited coherently, or as an assemblage, rather than individually. At that time [1958] no information existed regarding sources of gravitational radiation." Ibid 22/3 "The sensitivity of any gravitational-radiation detector would be proportional to both its mass and its size." 1972 May *Pop Sci* 192/1 "Our own galaxy is a spiral type with most of the matter in a plane. Gravitational radiation may be emitted by objects in orbits lying in this plane." May 6 *Sci News* 293/1 "One of the theoretically possible antennas for gravitational radiation is the earth itself." June 10 *Sci News* 377/2 "The bursts of gravitational radiation that Joseph Weber of the University of Maryland records apparently come from a source where very violent processes occur." 1973 Feb *Sci Amer* 48/1 "Weber's apparatus was basically a solid aluminum cylinder five feet long and three feet in diameter. Attached to the surface of the cylinder were piezoelectric crystals that could detect changes in the cylinder's dimensions equivalent to as little as a millionth the diameter of an atom. Sudden changes in dimension were assumed to be due to the passage of pulses of gravitational radiation." Aug 18–25 *Sci News* 108/2 "Gravitational radiation is supposed to be detected by vibrations that it causes as it passes through large aluminum cylinders. Weber has been detecting bursts of such vibrations at rates of up to several times a day. Levine and Garwin and Tyson used detectors that they claim are more sensitive than Weber's and found nothing. . . . The conclusions are that either Weber has been observing something other than gravitational radiation, or gravitational radiation he observed in 1969 was not present in 1973." 1974 Mar *Astronomy* 9/1 "'We may [see black hole formation] in six or eight years,' predicts Thorne. 'Not by looking with our eyes through telescopes or cameras, but looking instead at the gravitational radiation that is emitted by the star's collapsing core—gravitational radiation which can fly outward through the outer exploding envelopes with impunity; gravitational radiation that just doesn't care that the outer regions are in the way. It just passes through and hopefully will soon be detected by gravitational radiation detectors that are under development at several institutions in the United States and elsewhere."

-privilege See preliminary remarks **—executive privilege** 1973 Oct 1 *New Yorker* 9 (ad) "The pure enjoyment of wearing Southwick sportcoatings remains one of the last vestiges of executive privilege." Dec *Esquire* 82/2 "Rounding out Mr. Traub's Christmas selections is an item Bloomingdale's calls 'Executive Privilege.' This is an electric paper shredder, with a smoky Plexiglas shell to catch the shreds." **—ex-reporter's privilege** 1971 Aug 9 *Newsweek* 42/3 (heading) "Ex-Reporter's Privilege." **—journalistic privilege** 1974 Feb *Good Food* 84/2 "In collecting booklets for this article, I exercised journalistic privilege and contacted the companies by telephone." **—judicial privilege** 1973 Sep 10 *Newsweek* 21/2–3 (cartoon caption) "Judicial Privilege." (The cartoon by Oliphant, © 1973 Denver Post, shows Judge Sirica holding his gavel over the head of President Nixon, who is sitting in the witness chair clutching an armload of tapes.) **—newsmen's privilege** 1973 Nov *Selected U.S. Government Publications* vol 2, no 21, item 66W "*Newsmen's Privilege* Presents hearings held on various dates between February 20 and March 14, 1973, before the Committee on Constitutional Rights of the Senate Committee on the Judiciary, 93d Cong., 1st sess., concerning whether Government should be permitted to compel the press to reveal the identity of confidential sources of information or the content of unpublished information." Nov 11 *Tuscaloosa News* 15A/2 (AP) "Sixty-two per cent of those polled in the nationwide survey said 'newsmen's privilege' should be protected, compared with 57 per cent in a similar survey in November 1972." **—scholar's privilege** 1972 Dec 2 *National Observer* 17/1 "[Samuel Lewis] Popkin had argued that to answer some of the grand jury's questions would violate his right of free speech and 'scholar's privilege,' which he likened to a reporter's right not to divulge confidential sources of information." **—theatrical privilege** 1973 Nov 11 *Birmingham* (Ala) *News* E1/3 "Eileen Herlie is royalty by theatrical privilege. She was Queen Gertrude, Hamlet's treacherous mother, in the motion picture with Laurence Olivier and on Broadway with Richard Burton . . . [¶] She now plays Queen Mary . . . in 'Crown Matrimonial.'"

[Received August 1974]

AMONG THE NEW WORDS

I. WILLIS RUSSELL AND MARY GRAY PORTER
University of Alabama

In our installment in the Spring–Summer 1971 issue, we commented on some of the variants, several of them probably facetious, of *hot pants*. *Insecurity blanket*, in this glossary, certainly looks like a facetious play on the serious *security blanket*.

It is with some reluctance that we use a quotation with an unverifiable reference, that for *double-figure* from the *New York Times*. But since the writer may have been using it as a variant for the more frequent *double-digit*, we think its inclusion may be justified. Incidentally, if any of our readers happen to have filed this quotation, we would be most grateful for the complete reference.

On his citation slip containing the 1952 quotation of *big labor* appearing in the glossary below, Atcheson L. Hench noted the analogy with *big business*. Indeed, this may be the prototype for the other *big* collocations in the glossary. True, *big money* occurs earlier (*Dictionary of Americanisms*, s.v. *big, a.*, 5 (17); *Oxford English Dictionary Supplement* (1972) s.v. *big, a.*, B, 2, but only the 1947 quotation in the *Dictionary of Americanisms* seems to reflect precisely the sense of *big* illustrated in the glossary. Though this 1947 date predates our evidence, we think that the additional material may be useful.

Acknowledgments: For citations, Clarence L. Barnhart (the two for *double-figure* from the London *Sunday Times*), Atcheson L. Hench (the earliest for *big labor*), Porter G. Perrin (the first for *big steel*). Thanks are also due Dale L. Cramer for the definitions of *petrodollar* and *recycle*.

bargaining chip *n* [Cf *W3* sv *bargain vi* 1 & *vt* 1 a; cf *World Book Dict* 1974 sv *bargain vi* 1; cf *W3* sv [1]*chip n* 5 a] Something, such as an arms program or diplomatic maneuver, that can be used to gain an advantage or effect a concession 1973 Apr *FCNL* (Friends Committee on National Legislation) *Washington Newsletter* (Washington, DC) 3/1 "Regarding the SALT negotiations, 14 Republican Congressmen appealed to President Nixon to go slow on the 'bargaining chip' idea, calling for restraint in development of weapons such as the B-1 bomber and the Trident submarine at this time. The 14 reasoned that research and development is as strong a bargaining point and would save a lot of money." 1974 June 30 *NY Times Mag* 48/1 "In addition, the process of negotiation itself has sometimes provided new justifications for still stronger arms. Bargaining from strength calls for arms programs that can serve as 'bargaining chips' to trade for concessions that the other side might not otherwise make. Naturally, to be credible as bargaining chips, those weapons programs must also serve as hedges against an unacceptable (to military planners) outcome of the negotiations. The pursuit of hedges and chips brings about an intensification of the arms race just to keep 'bargaining-chip gaps' from developing." Sep 29 *NY Times* 16E/2 (editorial) "Granted that the Palestinians have long been unjustly relegated to the status of human bargaining chips—by Arab governments as well as others." Dec 2 *Atlanta Constitution* 4A/5 (Jack Anderson) "The United States, meanwhile, was seriously considering the withdrawal of its consulate in Salisbury. Prime Minister Smith, in desperate need of official recognition, wanted the United States to stay. With this bargaining chip, Washington managed to negotiate the release of one spy, who was delivered to the airport while allegedly en route to prison." Dec 8 Sen Henry Jackson on "Face the Nation" (CBS) "We'll just throw away a bargaining chip."

big *adj* [Though one or more of the dictionaries enter such terms as *big business* (*DA* 1905) and *big labor*, this sense of *big* is reflected in *World Book Dict* 1974 [1]*adj* 1, which uses *big business* as an illustration, and *W3* [1]*adj* 2 d, which uses *big government* as an illustration] Additional examples **—big art** 1974 May *Family Circle* 32/2 "As you can see, besides being big art, posters are big business." **—big banking** 1974 Dec 12 "NBC News" "It is difficult to imagine any decision [that would not impinge in some way on] big oil, big banking, airlines [etc]." **—big broadcasting** 1971 June 19 *Sat Rev* 16/3 "Transcending party lines, big government and big broadcasting may understand each other clearly." **—big education** c1970 Robert Townsend *Up the Organization* (Greenwich, Conn: Fawcett Pubs, 1971) 191 "It's not clear to me exactly when 'free enterprise' became a joke. Was it after the Civil War, when big business, big government and the Supreme Court formed an unholy alliance to exploit the American farmer and laborer? Or was it later, when big labor got a partnership? Or when big military elbowed up to the trough? Or when big education cut itself in on the deal?" **—big labor** [*WBD* 1974] Earlier quots 1952 Sep 13 *NY Times* (late city ed) 6/2 "The protection of the people against any arbitrary excessive power, which may be developed by big business or big labor or other pressure groups, is also essential." 1954 *Brit Book of the Year* (Chicago: Ency Brit Corp) 751/2 "*big labor.* Organized labor. (1952)." **—big military** c1970 See quot sv BIG EDUCATION 1974 Jan 26 *SR/World* 46/1 "Our campuses are Big Government / Big Business / Big Military turf." **—big money** [*DA* 1947; see prelim remarks] 1974 Oct 17 *Birmingham* (Ala) *Post-Herald* A6/1 (editorial) "The new law sets reasonable limits on how much candidates may spend; it reduces the influence of big money by limiting the amounts wealthy individuals and organizations may give, and it creates a six-member elections commission with the power to make the new regulations stick." **—big oil** 1974 Jan 14 *Newsweek* 63/1 "David Freeman, the Ford Foundation's energy expert, added: 'Look at it like a war. Big oil didn't start the war, but they are war-profiteering.'" Feb 9 *National Observer* 14/1 (editorial) "All the flaming populists from Richard Nixon leftward are muttering about the 'windfall profits' that Big Oil is making from the energy crisis." Feb 11 *Newsweek* 71/2 "As a result, Big Oil has come under the most ferocious attack directed at any industry since the Great Depression." Feb 18 *Time* 22/1 "Because it is a symbol of big oil, and its stations dot the country, one company stood to take more than its share of criticism." 1975 Jan 18 *National Observer* 1/2 "These giant multinational corporations . . . make up Big Oil. These six companies absorbed perhaps 10 per cent of all profits earned last year in corporate America." **—big steel** 1954 June 29 *Seattle Times* 1/3 (heading) "Big Steel, Union Agree on 8-Cent Package Raise." 1971 Feb 8 *National Observer*

2/5 "If he can make the plumbers and carpenters behave, while continuing to lean on Big Steel, even the severest critics of 'Nixonomics' would see a rosier glow on the economy."

double-digit 1: *adj* Equaling or exceeding 10, or 10 percent, but less than 100 1974 June 15 *National Observer* 6/1 "Living with double-digit inflation has become a problem for professional economists and politicians as well as for the American consumer." June 24 William E Simon, Sec of the Treasury "double-digit inflation." July 13 *National Observer* 6/1 "We're now in a situation that economists are calling 'double digit' inflation, meaning that prices are rising more than 10 per cent a year." Aug 4 Hobart Rowen on "Meet the Press" (NBC TV) "Does that [remark] imply that we're stuck with double-digit inflation for the rest of the year?" Sep *Progressive Farmer* 13/2 "This year it [the inflation rate] may go to a double-digit figure of 10% or more, which, if continued, could bring recession, even depression." Sep *Reader's Digest* 126/2 (interview with William E Simon, Sec of the Treasury; from June 17 *USN&WR*) "Yes, but in the past we've never had double-digit inflation; it has always been well under ten percent." Sep 1 *Forbes* 12/2 "Depressed tanker rates and double-digit cost inflation are forcing many a tanker owner onto the beach." Sep 26 John Chancellor (NBC TV) "double-digit inflation." Sep 27 Jim Hartz on "Today" (NBC TV) "The current double-digit inflation continues." Sep 28 *Bus Week* 27 "Service prices moved into the double-digit range last May as weekly earnings—which are closely tied to the price of services—have been accelerating." Nov 4 *New York Mag* 18/2 "To continue to live the good life, it turns out, they're contending with inflation rates that are *really* double-digit." Nov 10 *NY Times* 14E/1 (editorial) "Despite the heavy Republican losses in last week's Congressional and gubernatorial elections, the Ford administration seems as confident as ever that the electorate is wrong in demanding a change in White House policies that have helped bring double-digit inflation and high unemployment." Nov 18 *Tuscaloosa News* 4/6 (NEA) "With 5.5 million Americans out of work and double-digit inflation as well as energy and leadership shortages, despair is on the rise." Dec *Psych Today* 31/1 "Prices have risen so fast that double digit inflation is here, leading the experts to an outpouring of terminology that defies understanding." 2: *n usu pl* 1974 Sep 28 *Bus Week* 27 (side heading) "Service costs in double-digits." Dec 9 *Time* 34/2 "As inflation rates reached double digits, the Federal Reserve clamped a stranglehold on the money supply, which choked the housing industry."

double-figure *adj* [*OEDS sv* double *a* 6: "double figures (rarely double figure): a total or score, esp. of runs at cricket" (all the quots 1860–94, exc possibly the last, refer to cricket; only the pl form occurs in the quots)] 1966 London *Sunday Times* 28/7 "Even if the Government had been firmer with the doctors, judges, M.P.s, ministers and senior civil-servants, who have all had double-figure rises—there seems little point in setting a target which invites the splashing of phrases like 'Incomes Policy Failure' in the world's headlines." 1967 Dec 10 ibid 24/3 "I suppose 90 per cent. of golfers with double-figure handicaps qualify under 'using more energy than is necessary' and 'releasing the wrist action too early.'" 1974 *NY Times* "The United States and West Germany apart, most of the western world's industrial economies are now suffering from double-figure inflation."

firestorm *n* [*OEDS sv* fire *sb* B 5 defines literal sense with quots from 1581 (with a cross reference to *OED* B I a) to 1959; cf also *OED sv* storm *sb* I 3 a (a1000–1868)] Figurative use 1970 Aug 30 *Tuscaloosa News* 30 (James J Kilpatrick) "The next revolutionary who strikes a match in Seattle may ignite a political firestorm." 1973 Nov 5 *Newsweek* 20/1 "Richard Nixon clung tenuously to office last week in the face of the most devastating assault that any American President has endured in a century—a nationwide rebuke of such magnitude that one of Mr. Nixon's principal aides described it as 'a fire storm.'" 1974 Jan 13 *NY Times Mag* 48 (title of a story on the dismissal of Archibald Cox as Special Prosecutor and the public reaction) "Firestorm." Ibid 58/4 "In the wake of the 'firestorm' that swept through his [Nixon's] Administration in mid-October, the President set about remaking his image and cultivating his constituency." Apr 1 *Newsweek* 18/1 "It was a full five months since the Saturday-night massacre—the firing of special prosecutor Archibald Cox, the resignation of Attorney General Elliot Richardson and the ouster of his deputy, William Ruckelshaus—touched off the fire storm of public outrage that made the impeachment of a U.S. President a real possibility." Aug 8 *Tuscaloosa News* 3/2 (AP) "White House aides later said no one expected the resulting negative public reaction [to the dismissal of special Watergate prosecutor Archibald Cox]. 'Some kind of nightmare,' it was described. 'A fire storm.'" Aug 9 Bruce Morton (CBS) quoted a Congressman to the effect that he "predicted a firestorm of criticism [apropos of the pardon of Richard M Nixon]." Sep 12 *Wall St Jour* 1/1 "It may well be, as some of Mr. Ford's oldest and closest advisers say privately, that the President will soon recover from the fire storm that followed the Nixon pardon." Sep 15 *NY Times* E3/3 "Then last Sunday, after President Ford announced an unconditional pardon for former President Nixon, the White House just as suddenly became engulfed again in the aura of Watergate. The Ford presidency was under a 'firestorm' only a little less intense than that Mr. Nixon set off last October when he fired special prosecutor Archibald Cox." Oct 21 *New Yorker* 38/1 "The announcement that Sergeant Major Lymo Hascarni, the Premier of Voslymbuc, had tied up the coveted big game (against, it is rumored, keen bidding from Liechtenstein and Bolivia) created an initial firestorm of protest from American basketball fans."

insecurity blanket *n* 1973 Oct 8 *Newsweek* 70/1 (heading of story about the problems of a new television series) "Insecurity Blanket." See also quot from the story *sv* SECURITY BLANKET

Linus blanket *n* [*Linus*, in Charles M Schulz's comic strip *Peanuts*, a child who often finds consolation in his blanket] SECURITY BLANKET 1973 Dec *Esquire* 151/1 "The job is like a 'Linus blanket,' he concedes, an anchor in the 'real world' he has always known." 1974 Oct 12 *TV Guide* 27/1 "It's my Linus blanket, working in bed."

OPEC /ˈopɛk/ (by Sen Henry M Jackson CBS 1974 Oct 8; by Sen Richard C Clark ABC Nov 14, NBC Nov 18; by Rep John B Anderson ABC Dec 15) 1: *n* Organization of Petroleum Exporting Countries; see Dec 29 quot for names of the member nations 1974 June 22 *National Observer* 19/4 "Emboldened by a sellers' market, Iran then led the Organization of Petroleum Exporting Countries (OPEC) in the first of several stunning price hikes on Feb. 14, 1971." Sep 22 *NY Times* 16E/1 (editorial) "With two to three billion dollars flowing to the oil producers *every week* for years to come, the World Bank estimates that the Organization of Petroleum Exporting Countries (OPEC) could accumulate $650 billion within five years and $1.2 trillion by 1985." Sep 28 *Bus Week* 30/2–3 "OPEC is still far more unified than the consuming nations. Our highest card is the two of clubs." Oct 5 *Sci News* 213/1 "Though President Ford's address to the World Energy Conference

in Detroit signaled a new, tougher stance in the face of continued high oil prices from the Organization of Petroleum Exporting Countries (OPEC), Sheikh Ahmad Zaki Yamani of Saudi Arabia responded by patiently explaining why oil producers will not be moved by threats and then lectured the United States on the evils of 'economic imperialism.'" Nov 25 *Time* 36/3 "Then—and only then—can the major consumers and OPEC members sit down with any hope of reaching an accord on price." Dec 29 *Miami (Fla) Herald* E1/3 (Washington Post Service) "Stung by this high-handed treatment, the original five members—Saudi Arabia, Iran, Iraq, Kuwait and Venezuela—met in Baghdad and decided 'to create an organization for regular consultation and for the coordination of oil policies.' . . . Now, in addition to the five charter members, the OPEC roster includes Algeria, Ecuador, Gabon, Indonesia, Libya, Nigeria, Qatar and the United Arab Emirates." 1975 Jan *Reader's Digest* 50/2 "The World Bank has calculated that, if purchasing continues as at present, the Organization of Petroleum Exporting Countries (OPEC—which includes seven Arab states) will by 1980 have amassed currency reserves totaling $653 billion."

2: *adj* Belonging to OPEC 1974 Oct 5 *Sci News* 214/1 "Yamani's response to delegates concerning the progressively more desperate situation in the poorest countries was that several development funds are being established by the OPEC countries." Oct 8 Sen Henry M Jackson on CBS News "OPEC countries." Nov 14 Sen Richard C Clark (ABC) "OPEC nations." Nov 18 Sen Richard C Clark (NBC) "the OPEC nations." Dec 14 *National Observer* 18/3 "If the price of oil remains at anything like its present level—and there are repeated stirrings in OPEC [the oil-producing] countries to move it still higher—there will be a massive redistribution of economic and political power among the countries of the world." Dec 15 Rep John B Anderson "Issues and Answers" (ABC) "We are not the only country affected by the actions of the OPEC countries."

petro- [*petro-* comb form (*World Book Dict* 1974)] —**petrobillions** *n pl* 1974 Oct 7 *Newsweek* 52/3 "Top Arab leaders have now decided not to put their petrobillions into U.S. Treasury bonds . . . but to invest in American industry instead." —**petrodiplomat** *n* 1974 Nov *Town & Country* 209/1–2 (heading) "The Petrodiplomat[:] Sheik Yamani." —**petrodollar** *n usu pl* (*exc attrib or in comb*) 1: Surplus dollars (or dollar claims or assets) that the oil-exporting countries accumulate in the oil-importing countries 1974 Aug 25 *NY Times* F1/2 "While most experts feel that it is a bit early to predict the extent of Arab investment in the American defense industry, what emerged in intensive interviews with them in Washington and New York last week was a growing concern over the swiftly accelerating petrodollar holdings of the Arabs. (Petrodollars are defined as the excess foreign-exchange assets of the oil-producing countries.)" Sep 21 *Bus Week* 40/2 "A $30-billion fund for recycling petrodollars to industrialized countries will be one of the key topics of discussion at the International Monetary Fund annual meeting, which begins in Washington on Sept. 30." Sep 21 *National Observer* 3/1 "The petrodollar impact promises to be momentous . . . Iowa's Rep. John C. Culver, writing in the fall issue of Foreign Policy magazine, predicts that a new economic era has just begun that will require major changes in how the Federal Government operates if the country is to weather the 'petrodollar crisis.'" Ibid 3/4 "These are just a few of the ramifications of the petrodollar." Sep 22 *NY Times* 16E/2 (editorial) "The United States and other major industrial countries which have been treated as a safe haven for the growing hoard of petrodollars could bring additional pressures on the oil-exporting countries by limiting their right to invest in these safe countries beyond the amounts needed to cover the deficits in balance of payments." Sep 28 *Bus Week* 30/2 "At the energy conference in Washington last February, U.S. policy was to leave the issue of oil prices alone for the time being in the belief that financial institutions could absorb and recycle the 'petrodollars.'" Sep 29 *NY Times* E17/2 "On the basis of these staggering figures, the primary questions before the ministers in Washington were how the oil-consuming nations were going to meet these bills, and what the oil-producing countries were going to do with this vast and growing accumulation of petro-dollars." Ibid 4F/6 "David Rockefeller, chairman of the Chase Manhattan Bank, contends that the responsibility for recycling petrodollars has to be shifted from commercial banks to government agencies." Oct 7 *Newsweek* 52/2 "These Arab leaders are quietly working out a new oil-and-monetary strategy that could ultimately lead to lower oil prices and a recycling of billions of 'petrodollars' into the Western economies." Nov 25 *Time* 38/3 "But offering lower prices to other buyers would do little to alleviate the petrodollar crisis, says Oil Economist Walter Levy." Dec 1 *Atlanta Jour and Constitution* 4B/1 (quoting Sen Hubert H Humphrey) "'There is no way to control inflation and to achieve political or economic stability in the world until we solve the problem of excess petrodollars.'" 2: [generalization of sense 1] Any wealth derived from petroleum 1974 Nov *Town & Country* 259/3 "On the other hand, petrodollars will provide a new life for at least one antebellum gem, San Francisco Plantation. Recently sold to Energy Corporation of Louisiana, a firm jointly owned by New Orleans-based Ingram Corporation and Boston-based Northeast Petroleum Industries, the 2,500-acre plantation . . . will become a $300-million refinery producing 200,000 barrels of oil a day." —**petrodollar-rich** *adj* 1974 Nov *Town & Country* 173/2 "But last, if not least, it should be noted that it was an incognito petrodollar-rich Arab who was the first to check into London's posh new Wellington, which is not a hotel but a hospital." —**petropolitics** *n pl* 1973 Dec 3 *Time* 44/1 "The energy crisis . . . may have been artificially imposed, but its implications stretch far beyond petropolitics."

plea bargain *n* [Cf *W3* bargain plea *n* slang] 1974 Jan *Harper's* 8/1–2 "The vast majority of criminal sentences in the United States—between 80 percent and 90 percent in some jurisdictions—are the result of 'plea bargains' in which the defendant 'waives' his constitutional right to trial in exchange for a 'good deal.'" May 13 *Daily Advance* (Lynchburg, Va) 14/1 (Copley News Service) "A more complex situation arises when the defendant enters into a plea bargain." June 15 *National Observer* 3/2–3 (heading) "His Is the Latest in a Chain of Watergate Plea Bargains."

plea-bargain *vi* 1: Carry on negotiations with the aim of permitting or inducing the accused to plead guilty or give testimony in exchange for reduced charges [1926 *The Missouri Crime Survey* (Patterson Smith Repr Ser in Criminology, Law Enforcement, and Social Problems, Pub no 10; Montclair, NJ: Patterson Smith, 1968) 149 "The popular impression is that when an offender enters a plea of guilty he throws himself upon the 'mercy of the court.' As a practical proposition he does nothing of the kind. He has already thrown himself upon the mercy of, or struck a bargain with, the prosecutor, before he takes his plea. The court usually accepts the recommendation of the prosecutor as to the punishment on plea of guilty." 1929 *The Illinois Crime Survey* conducted by the Illinois Association for Criminal Justice (Patterson Smith Repr Ser in Criminology, Law Enforcement, and Social Problems, Pub no 9; Montclair, NJ: Patterson Smith, 1968) 470 "When the plea of guilty is found in records, it is almost certain to have in the background, particularly in Cook County, a session of bargaining with the state's attorney. If the prisoner is charged with a severe crime, which for some reason or other he does not care to fight, he frequently makes overtures to the state's attorney to the effect that he will plead guilty to a lesser crime than the one charged." 1936 *Jour of the Amer Inst of Crim Law and Criminology* 26, no 5 (Jan–Feb) 709 "Prior to October 1, 1930, the administration of criminal justice in Cook County was beset with grave problems. . . . Since it would have required some forty judges to try all the cases by jury, a system developed of bargaining with defendants, offering them lesser penalties than the cases justified in return for pleas of guilty." 1956 *Manual for Prosecuting Attorneys* ed by Morris Ploscowe (NY: Practising Law Inst) 2: 319 "In many cases where the offense charged is a felony, the plea will be taken to a misdemeanor. When the defendant is represented by counsel, these pleas of guilty are usually forthcoming after a bargain has been entered into with the prosecuting attorney. . . . [¶] But while there are many legitimate means for bargaining with defense attorneys for pleas of guilty, there are also plenty of illegitimate ones."] 1963 *Univ of Pennsylvania Law Rev* 112 (1964): 865 n 5 "Some prosecuting attorneys object to the use of the phrase 'plea bargaining.' One prosecutor indicated that 'by labeling the procedure "plea bargaining" you tend to make the procedure sound unethical and improper.' Questionnaire Reply From State Prosecutor, November, 1963." 1964 Ibid 865–66 "The commonplace practice of 'plea bargaining'—compromises by prosecuting attorneys with criminal defendants or their counsel to obtain guilty pleas—is in part responsible for the high incidence of such pleas." 1966 *Atlantic Reporter* 2d ser. Commonwealth v Maroney (15 Nov) 223 (1967): 703/1–2 "Although the subject of considerable criticism, plea bargaining between the prosecution and the defense is a frequently resorted to technique. In exchange for a guilty plea, the prosecutor may agree to recommend a lighter sentence, to accept a plea to a lesser included offense, or to dismiss other pending charges." 1967 *Pacific Reporter* 2d ser. 423: 718/1–2 n 1 "For discussion re advisability and approval of plea bargaining, see, Commonwealth ex rel. Kerekes v. Money, 423 Pa. 337, 223 A. 2d 699 (1966)." 1968 ibid 448: 60/1 "The device used by the county attorney's office is known as 'plea bargaining'. Its ideal purpose is to prevent the necessity of trial if an alternative can result in justice to society and the accused." Ibid 61/1 "While 'plea bargaining' is recognized, a guilty plea procured by 'fraud or duress' is ground for setting aside a judgment on the plea of guilty."

Specif, a: Agree to plead guilty to a less serious charge if the more serious charge is waived; give testimony in return for a lighter charge 1973 Apr 21 *New Yorker* 44–45 "I assumed that a lawyer faced with that kind of calendar would be less tempted to urge clients to go to trial than to suggest that they accept the usual plea-bargaining way out—that is, to urge their clients to plead guilty if the state would reduce the original charges." Oct 8 *Newsweek* 30/3 "Still 'hurt and angry,' according to associates, over misleading reports about his eagerness to plea-bargain like a common criminal, [he] remained outwardly courteous and relaxed." Nov *Reader's Digest* 169/1 "Even then, they'll tell you that plea bargaining—in which a youngster pleads guilty to a lesser offense in return for a lighter sentence—is possible." 1974 Jan 21 *Newsweek* 19/2 "There was a report that his onetime mainstay . . . was plea-bargaining with the special prosecutor." Feb 8 *New Times* (NYC) 8/2 "In a plea-bargaining scramble, witnesses have volunteered more evidence, including tapes from very high levels in the White House staff." Apr 29 *Time* 23/3 "[He] may begin to plea bargain with the special prosecutors and start talking." May 13 *Daily Advance* (Lynchburg, Va) 14/1 (Copley News Service) "Plea bargaining has become a common tactic in today's court system . . . [¶] A drawback . . . however, is the offense admitted to is always less serious than the original charge." May 26 *Tuscaloosa News* 2D/3 "They're Watergate defendants and their lawyers and they're waiting to plea bargain with the special prosecutor." June 15 *National Observer* 3/3 "Leverage for the prosecutor is one purpose of plea bargaining, which is a defendant's agreement to plead guilty to a charge or charges and cooperate in other investigations. In return, other charges against him may be dropped, and he presumably gets a lighter sentence. Plea bargaining and the granting to a defendant of immunity to prosecution as a result of his testimony have played a big part in Watergate." Aug 24 *TV Guide* 29/2 "Another example of 'contraband' that Professor Rosenberg considers especially damaging to the defendant's chances is the report that his lawyers are engaged in 'plea bargaining' with the prosecutors—trying to swap a guilty plea for the promise of a light sentence." Sep 23 character in "As the World Turns" (CBS TV) "Plead guilty to a lesser charge. It's called plea bargaining."

b: Agree to reduce the charge(s) against a defendant in return for his testimony or a plea of guilty 1974 Jan 28 *Newsweek* 14/2 "Jaworski was plea-bargaining with a number of the principals—'dealing up' with reduced charges in return for their testimony against their betters." June 17 ibid 19/2 "For the prosecution, it was another example of plea bargaining with a defendant in hopes of landing bigger game." Aug 11 *NY Times* E5/2 "Its absence [clemency] may speed up the plea-bargaining process that has been used so extensively by the special prosecutor."

2: Plead guilty in return for some special concession by the prosecution other than that in sense 1 1973 Nov 12 *Time* 94/1 "Caught in Canada early last year and finally extradited, [he] pleaded guilty . . . to second-degree murder and arson—but not before an unusual bit of plea bargaining. [He] wanted, as [his attorney] put it, 'a chance to bring to his compatriots what he did and why.' "

recycle *vt* Invest in the United States and other oil-importing countries (the surplus foreign exchange earned in those countries through the sale of oil) 1974 Sep 22 *NY Times* 16E/1 (editorial) "Optimistic economists have contended that the problem of 'recycling' oil dollars can be dealt with by normal capital markets—this on the theory that the oil-producing states must invest their money 'somewhere.' " Sep 28 See quot sv PETRODOLLAR Sep 29 *NY Times* 16E/1 (editorial) "Temporary solutions are required quickly to prevent economic, political and physical disaster to nations unable to pay for oil at its current extortionate price. The annual meeting of the International Monetary Fund and the World Bank in Washington this week will provide a forum for nations to propose plans of vast scope for 'recycling' oil money to those countries in the most desperate straits. One such proposal, to be presented by the British Chancellor of the Exchequer, Denis Healey, will call for the establishment of a fund consisting of $25 to $30 billion drawn from the short-term deposits the Arabs will be making in New York, Frankfurt, Zurich and other hard-money centers." Ibid 4F/6 See quot sv PETRODOLLAR Oct 7 *Newsweek* 52/1 "Petroleum expert Walter Levy . . . has also broached the idea of setting up a new international banking system to recycle OPEC funds into loans to the poorer nations to enable them to pay their fuel bills." Nov 25 *Time* 36/2 "This international institution would recycle the oil money in order to 'help assure the stability of the entire financial system.' "

security *n* [shortened from *security blanket*] SECURITY BLANKET 1973 R A Lafferty "By the Seashore" in *The Best from Galaxy* vol 2 (NY: Award Books, 1974) 66 (repr from *Galaxy* Nov 1973) "Some small boys have toy pandas or bears. But Oliver Murex had this big seashell for his friend and toy and security. He slept with it—he carried it with him always. He depended on it."

security blanket *n* [Cf *Webster's New World Dict*, 2d college ed (NY: World Pub Co, 1970) sv] Figurative use 1: Anything affording one a feeling of security, comfort, or safety [1970 Lee Mendelson in assoc with Charles M Schulz *Charlie Brown & Charlie Schulz: In Celebration of the 20th Anniversary of Peanuts* (NY: World Pub Co) 75/2 "But perhaps the best idea I ever had . . . was Linus and the security blanket. . . . It suddenly made security blankets and thumb-sucking okay all around the world, and if we made parents a little less worried about their kids, then this would have to be one of my biggest thrills with the strip."] 1971 Mar *House & Garden* 37/2 "Her two other security blankets are Dr. Laszlo's famous Sea Mud Soap . . . and also his Active pHelityl Oil, which she can even pronounce." July 19 *Newsweek* 48/1 "It is to ease this dilemma that Beloit and a few other colleges have established deferred-admissions plans—a sort of security blanket that prospective students can carry with them during a year's sabbatical." 1972 Feb *Atlantic* 41/2 "He found Mr. Nixon . . . scribbling notes on one of the two yellow-lined pads that serve him as security blankets (he used to use one pad, but since he became President, he needs two)." Dec 11 *USN&WR* 55/1 "Tenure, the 'security blanket' of the teaching profession, is in jeopardy at U.S. colleges." 1973 June *Esquire* 176/3 "Q. You're so seldom in one place, wouldn't it pay you to sublet?—A. Well, then you lose your grip on your security blanket." Oct 8 *Newsweek* 70/1 "It's not so much his job—supervising a state employment office can be a security blanket for a man who started worrying about old age when he was 9." Nov *Ladies' Home Jour* 27/1 "To be Frank's friend is like one of his songs: 'All or Nothing At All.' It is a total, unconditional commitment, a never-fraying security blanket." Nov *Reader's Digest* 258/1 "Sometimes, when the world crowds in too much, we . . . drive 20 miles from home to our own particular security blanket. It is a piece of the mid-California coast, where a trail takes us to a rocky bluff overlooking the Pacific." Dec *Ladies' Home Jour* 102/4 "A worn, torn, one-eyed teddy bear about a foot long was my 'security blanket.' . . . I slept with it, took it to camp the first summer, hugged it, and loved it without reserve." 1974 Jan 21 *Newsweek* 24/1 "Ziegler instead is, by one in-house assessment, Mr. Nixon's 'security blanket.' " Mar *Harper's Bazaar* 123/1 "I just don't exist without my [false] eyelashes. . . . they're my security blanket." Apr *Atlantic* 23/2 (ad) "And aside from the fact that Dasher is designed to be reliable and easy to maintain . . . it's covered by the most advanced coverage plan of them all, the VW Owner's Security Blanket, which includes free computer analysis." Dec 14 *TV Guide* 29/1 "This is a stock-company series in which Walker is just one of the family ensemble, but it is not possible for him by nature or by looks to be inconspicuous, and he is the comic security blanket of the show. He only has to open his mouth to jolt the studio-audience laugh meter over the red line." Dec 23 "ABC News" "[Ownership of gold can be] a security blanket."

2: Experimental blanket-like safety device to prevent or reduce injury to an automobile driver or passenger in a collision 1970 Nov 16 *USN&WR* 1/3 (ad) "This 'security blanket,' another passive restraint, is also undergoing tests."

shuttle diplomacy *n* [Cf *W2 Add Sect* 1950 sv *shuttle n* 1; also *W3* sv *shuttle n* 5 a] Negotiations between two or more countries conducted by a mediator who flies frequently back and forth among the nations involved in the dispute 1974 Feb 15 *Between the Lines* (Newtown, Pa) 2/3 "So beware of an over-celebration of Kissinger's shuttle diplomacy, heroic as it's been." Mar 4 *Time* 25/1 "At week's end Kissinger was to return to Washington for a day or so before flying once again to the Middle East for another round of 'shuttle diplomacy'—this time to Damascus, Jerusalem and Cairo, where he is expected to announce resumption of full diplomatic relations between Egypt and the U.S." Apr 1 ibid 2/1 "State Department Correspondent John Mulliken, who has gone on three major journeys with the Secretary of State since September and contributed to this week's cover story, notes that a day of shuttle diplomacy often starts at 4 a.m." Ibid 26/1–2 "A classic example: the Egyptian-Israeli disengagement negotiations, which climaxed with Kissinger, in his now famous shuttle diplomacy, making almost daily flights between Jerusalem and President Anwar Sadat's vacation retreat in Aswan." May 20 *Newsweek* 63/3 "He meant that after two weeks of the latest round of shuttle diplomacy, the other major elements of an Israeli-Syrian agreement had been virtually worked out." May 20 *Time* 40/3 "Last week Kissinger was heavily engaged in another round of Middle East shuttle diplomacy, flying not only between Damascus and Jerusalem but also back to Egypt to give Sadat progress reports." June 8 *TV Guide* A74 "The Kissinger style, however, is epitomized by scenes of his 'shuttle diplomacy' meetings with Soviet and Chinese leaders in Moscow and Peking, and the recent month-long peace mission in the Middle East, culminating in an Israeli-Syrian accord to separate their armies on the Golan Heights." June 15 *National Observer* 2/4 "Henry Kissinger's stunning shuttle diplomacy has brought U.S. influence to new heights in the Arab world, while sending Soviet prestige plummeting." June 17 *New Yorker* 92/2 "In April and May, Henry Kissinger flew in thirteen times, as part of the shuttle diplomacy that brought a disengagement between Israel and Syria along the Golan Heights front." June 19 *Tuscaloosa News* 1/6 (AP) "Nixon sent Kissinger on a constant round of shuttle diplomacy, building ties with previously hostile Arab governments while negotiating disengagement agreements."

space-shuttle diplomat *n* [*BDNE space shuttle* 1970] 1974 June 24 *Time* 6/1 (letter) "The only possible accomplishment left for Henry Hercules [=Henry Kissinger] is for him to become an astronaut, and then maybe he could be the first space-shuttle diplomat."

two-digit *adj* DOUBLE-DIGIT 1974 May 6 *Newsweek* 75/3 "Concretely, whatever we do, the odds favor a retreat of inflation by year's end to well below the present two-digit range." June 15 *National Observer* 6/3 "In recent months we've had a two-digit inflation with the rise in consumer price index 10.2 per cent above year-before levels, and in April, which is the most recent month for which we have available information, the CPI was up a yearly rate of over 12 per cent." Aug 1 *Forbes* 57/3 "The resentment of the people against two-digit inflation—anything less than that is a rare exception—has become so universal that one may wonder whether everyone might not prefer a brief deflationary depression to suffering lingering death by inflation, which impoverishes everyone." Sep 21 *Bus Week* 16/2 "It clearly indicated the importance of suddenly erupting shortages of food, raw materials, and oil—combined with the astronomical increases in prices by the oil cartel—in propelling the U.S. to two-digit levels of inflation.''

[Received January 1975]

AMONG THE NEW WORDS

I. WILLIS RUSSELL AND MARY GRAY PORTER
University of Alabama

THE CLASSIFICATION of *dirty tricks* as a new lexical unit is admittedly borderline, but its recent and frequent use, especially in the plural, as a specialized collective in the area of politics and its occurrence as an immediate constituent in *dirty-trickery* and *dirty-trickster* offer a measure of support for considering and defining it as a word phrase.

As its first sense, the *OED* defines *trick*, in part, as ''a crafty or fraudulent device of a mean or base kind . . . esp. in phrase *to play* (*show*) *one a trick* . . . cf. sense 2.'' The quotations are dated from about 1412 to 1888. Sense 2 is, ''A freakish or mischievous act; a frolic . . . a hoax, practical joke.'' The quotations for this sense are dated from 1590 to 1888.

In its concrete sense, *dirty* dates from the sixteenth century; in its figurative, moral sense from 1670. For the latter, the *OED* (2b) has quotations from 1670 to 1888. Three of the quotations for sense 2b are of especial interest. The one containing the phrase *dirty trick* is quoted below. The other two (1764 and 1888) contain the phrase *dirty work* in reference to politics.

It is worth noting that even though the *OED*'s sense 1 of *trick* survives to modern times, its sense 2 is qualified by figurative *dirty* as early as 1674. As the dictionary illustrations show, the phrase has not been thought of as a lexical unit.

Dirty has been used to qualify *work*, in a sense much like that it has in *dirty trick*, since about 1735, when Pope wrote in the ''Epistle to Arbuthnot'' (1. 92): ''The creature's at his dirty work again.'' Webster's *International* (1900, s.v. *dirty*, adj. sense 3) quotes the line and identifies the author. As already noted, quotations with *dirty work* from 1764 and 1888 are in the *OED* (2b). As an entry, it appears, with *dirty work at the crossroads* as a variant, in *Webster's New International* (1934) and Berrey and Van den Bark's *American Thesaurus of Slang* (1942, 1953). Though the entry is dropped from *Webster's Third* (1961), it appears in *Webster's New Collegiate* (1973), with an illustration involving politics. The phrase is also entered in the Wentworth-Flexner *Dictionary of Slang* (1960) and *The World Book Encyclopedia Dictionary* (1963; *World Book Dictionary*, 1971, 1974, 1975).

If stress alone is considered, *dirty wòrk*, as we say it and hear it, fits into the noun phrase pattern of *blúe blòod*, *flýing machine*, *hígh schòol*, and *móving vàn*, which contrast with *blúe blóod*, *flýing machíne*, *hígh schóol*, and *móving ván*. But *dirty tricks* has its parallels: *blâck góld* (petroleum), *blâck lúng* (the disease), *dôuble ágent*, *grêen light*, all of them entered as nouns, but with no indication of stress, in *Webster's New Collegiate Dictionary*.

The quotation containing the phrase *dirty campaign tricks* (1973, Oct. 8, *Newsweek*), indicating the divisibility of *dirty tricks*, suggests that *dirty* may be merely an adjective, but the fact that one can refer to ''an atomic or a hydrogen bomb,'' both terms entered in dictionaries (with a noun label in *Webster's Third*),[1] supports our view that its divisibility does not disqualify it as a lexical entry.

In keeping with our policy of publishing additional quotations for terms already in dictionaries, especially if they supply earlier evidence or throw light on definitions, we are setting up an entry for *seed money*, with quotations that bring out the idea of 'seed,' that is, money that ''would generate a flow'' of money, ''trigger a growth in net capital flow,'' stimulate additional donations. See especially the last quotation.

Acknowledgments: For citations, Dennis E. Barnon (1), Jay W. Murphy (1), John C. Payne (2), and Peter Tamony (5, including the examples of *plea bargain*[*ing*] from newspapers, all predating those from general sources in an earlier issue).

affirmative action [*W3 affirmative* adj 4 'assertive, positive'] Positive action taken toward any goal, opposed to passive failure to take action that would produce the opposite effect; *specif*, positive steps taken to eliminate discrimination against members of minority groups, esp in employment, as opposed to a mere lack of overt discrimination against minorities [1956 Morris Ploscowe *Manual for Prosecuting Attorneys* (NY: Practising Law Inst) 323 ''His position in such a case is that the people expect him to act affirmatively and to go out and look for evidence where it is not already available.''] 1965 Sep 24 Lyndon B Johnson Executive Order 11246 in *Weekly Compilation of Presidential Documents* pub by National Archives and Records Service [for] Week Ending Friday, September 24, 1965 (issue date: 27 Sep 1965) 306/1 ''The contractor will not discriminate against any employee or applicant for employment because of race, creed, color, or national origin. The contractor will take affirmative action to ensure that applicants are employed, and that employees are treated during employment, without regard to their race, creed, color, or national origin. Such action shall include, but not be limited to the following: employment, upgrading, demotion, or transfer; recruitment or recruitment advertising; layoff or termination; rates of pay or other forms of compensation; and selection for training, including apprenticeship. The contractor agrees to post in conspicuous places, available to employees and applicants for employment, notices to be provided by the contracting officer setting forth the provisions of this nondiscrimination clause.'' 1972 Dec 4 George C Roche III report excerpted in 1973 Jan 1 *USN&WR* 49/2 ''Between 1964 and 1972, however, Executive Orders 11246 and 11375 had already directed *all* federal contractors and those receiving federal assistance from HEW to take 'affirmative action to insure that employees are treated during employment without regard to their race, color, religion, sex or national origin.''' Ibid 50/1 ''In Mr. Pottinger's own words: 'The premise of the Affirmative Action concept of the Executive Order is that systematic discrimination in employment has existed, and unless positive action is taken, a benign neutrality today will only preserve yesterday's conditions and project them into the future.''' (J Stanley Pottinger, director of the Office of Civil Rights, Dept of Health, Educ and Welfare) 1973 Apr *Solidus: The Newsletter of the Ala Conf, Amer Assoc of Univ Professors* 3/1 ''Passive nondiscrimination, in which overt bias is avoided, while the usual hiring of Anglo males goes on uninterrupted, is giving way to Affirmative Action, which is, in the Labor Department's phrase, 'result oriented.''' May *Family Circle* 135/3 ''A compliance review undertakes to determine whether the contractor 'maintains nondiscriminatory hiring and employment practices and is taking affirmative action' to rectify any inequities that exist.'' June *Amer Teacher* (Amer Fed of Teachers AFL-CIO) 17/1 ''Prof. Miro Todorovich . . . spoke of what he viewed as reverse discrimination, of instances where white males had been denied jobs 'reserved' for 'affirmative-action' candidates.'' Dec 10 *Newsweek* 123/3 ''In more than 40 cases OCR [Office for Civil Rights, HEW] delayed the awarding of Federal contracts until an 'affirmative-action plan' to increase the hiring and promotion of women was approved. Under such a plan, a university must set a reasonable 'goal' of qualified women to be hired within a certain time; it need not reach the precise goal, but it must show a 'good faith' effort.'' 1974 Office of Fed Contract Compliance, US Dept of Labor poster GPO: 1974 O-528-973 ''Executive Order Number 11246, issued by the President, prohibits job discrimination because of RACE, COLOR, RELIGION, SEX, or NATIONAL ORIGIN, and requires affirmative action to ensure equality of opportunity in all aspects of employment.'' *The Equitable Annual Report 1973* (Equitable Life Assurance Society of the US) 11 ''Our Affirmative Action goals were revised to call for a substantial increase in the number of minorities and women in our sales force and in middle and upper level salaried positions within the next five years.'' [Jan *Atlantic* 65/1 ''Lawyer William Cannon considers the matter of 'pulling the plug' [stopping the use of life-sustaining devices and practices] under American law and comes up with this conclusion: 'If it is concluded to be an omission, the law is murky at best. If, however, it is concluded to be an affirmative act, the law has a ready charge: Murder in the first degree.' ''] Jan 18 *San Francisco Examiner* 21/4 ''The woman chosen to implement equal hiring for women and minorities at the University of California at Berkeley has quit because she feels the university has no commitment to 'affirmative action.''' Jan 29 *San Francisco Examiner* 52/4–6 ''Basic Vegetable Products, Inc., the world's largest dehydrator of onions and garlic . . . has agreed to an 'affirmative action program' to end reported discrimination against women and minorities in its hirings and promotions.'' Mar 9 *National Observer* 4/3 '' 'The hospital, once life support was begun, was committed to it,' Mitchell said. 'To follow the parents' wishes would have been to violate medical precepts. It was the difference between not starting life support at all and terminating it. In other words, inaction versus affirmative action.' '' May 6 *Time* 6/1 ''By whatever name—reverse discrimination, affirmative action or quota system—the emotional issue argued by DeFunis, a white, was whether blacks and others as a class could constitutionally be given preferential treatment.'' May 15 *Wednesday Report* (Univ of Ala) 2/1 ''THE AFFIRMATIVE ACTION PLAN for the University includes objective standards for and measurements of job qualifications to preclude discrimination in hiring and promoting

---

1. The new *OED Supplement*, however, enters *atomic bomb* under *atomic*, A. *adj*. e. ''Of weapons: . . . .''

employees." May 26 Chesterfield Smith, Pres Amer Bar Assoc, on "Meet the Press" NBC TV "We believe in affirmative action programs [to achieve certain goals]." June *Selected US Government Publications* (Sup of Docs, US GPO) 14/3 "AFFIRMATIVE ACTION PLANS FOR STATE AND LOCAL GOVERNMENTS. The course is designed to provide guidance to participants who are responsible for developing or improving their programs of affirmative action to assure equal employment opportunity." June 17 *Newsweek* 76/3 "The consultant will study a company's testing and recruitment program, examine what sort of jobs women and minorities hold and then present an 'affirmative-action plan' to comply with government regulations. . . . In many cases affirmative action requires a horrendous amount of paper work, so much that a new staff may have to be hired simply to keep the program running." Aug 17 *National Observer* 10/4 "A small percentage of white men (small in proportion to the total labor force) believe that they are being treated unfairly by employers who hire blacks and women to satisfy affirmative action guidelines." Sep 1 David Mathews, Pres, Univ of Ala, memorandum to all employees "By its commitment to equal employment opportunity, the University is further committed to a program of affirmative action. Through this program; the University undertakes all necessary and appropriate actions to fully promote the concept of equal employment opportunity and to deliberately ensure its realization." Sep 12 *Wall St Jour* 6/1 "Under a 1965 Executive Order, government contractors must provide equal employment opportunities, and nonconstruction contractors with 50 or more workers and a contract of $50,000 or more must prepare a written affirmative action plan for each facility. Companies failing to meet the requirements face suspension or cancellation of the contract or other sanctions." Oct *Amer Home* 99/1 (editor's note) "There are no legal watchdogs looking out for the homeowner, no vigorous lobby in Washington or in any state capital. . . . Form a committee, write letters, set up a public meeting, challenge local officialdom. You can't simply *expect* affirmative action; you must *demand* it." Nov 29 *St Petersburg* (Fla) *Times* A19/6 "The two main points of dissension as the midterm conference [the Democratic Party's 'miniconvention'] approaches are: A proposed 'affirmative action' plan to assure fair representation for women, youths and racial minorities at national conventions." Dec 1 *NY Times* F13/1–2 "While applauding the proposals [for reducing Federal spending], a former high Republican official called the program a 'fraud' on the ground that there is not the slightest chance that Congress will enact the three-fourths of it that requires affirmative Congressional action." Dec 8 James J Kilpatrick *Tuscaloosa News* D4/6 "These reformers want the [Democratic] party to be 'issue-oriented.' They demand 'affirmative action' to produce greater participation by minorities and women." Dec 8 *NY Times* 47/1 "Several dozen prominent university professors have signed a letter to President Ford opposing the Federal Government's affirmative-action plan for increasing the proportion of women and minority members on the faculties of higher educational institutions." Dec 9 *Time* 24/2 "The commission recommended abolishing mandatory quotas in favor of 'affirmative action' intended 'to encourage full participation by all Democrats, with particular concern for minority groups, native Americans [ie, Indians], women and youth in the delegate selection process and in all party affairs.'" 1975 Jan 16 *NY Times* 22/1 "This is the first judicial decision to state categorically that so-called affirmative action programs at the university level are illegal." Jan 26 *NY Times* E16/1 (editorial) "Since rebuilding a railbed and laying new track require a large number of unskilled laborers, affirmative action now would relieve unemployment." Feb *MLA Newsletter* 7/2 "Be it resolved that the MLA . . . join with local, regional, and national faculty groups . . . to work actively against attrition of affirmative action programs, loss of faculty jobs, cuts in college budgets, and erosion of tenure." Feb 16 Hubert H Humphrey on "Meet the Press" NBC TV "We've got to have affirmative action." (He then went on to enumerate some of the things he would do to aid the sagging economy.)

dirty trick *n* [cf *OED* dirty adj 2b; *W3* 1d & esp 2d; *OED* trick sb I 1–2, *W3* 1a–b; see prelim remarks] A malicious act, usu covert, esp one directed toward a political opponent 1674 *Essex Papers* (Camden) 253 (quoted in *OED*) "To me he called it a dirty trick." 1906 *Century Dict and Cyclopedia* (NY: Century Co) sv *dirty* 4 "Morally unclean or impure; base; low; despicable; groveling: as, a *dirty* fellow; a *dirty* job or trick." 1933 *OEDS* sv *dirty* adj 2b "*To do the dirty*: to play a dirty trick." 1942 Berrey and Van den Bark *Amer Thesaurus of Slang* (NY: Crowell, 1945 printing) sec. 338.1 "Dirty *or* nasty *trick, a malicious act.*" 1967 *Western Folklore* 26: 189 "*Irish trick, dirty*—always, to the best of my recollection, used jocularly. A 'dirty trick' was a scurvy act, but 'Irish' as a modifier carried with it an implication of unwilling amusement or admiration and removed most or much of the sting." 1972 Margaret Truman *Harry S Truman* (NY: Wm Morrow, 1973) 548 "Along with the smears and lies Dad was continually rebutting, the Republicans threw in a few dirty tricks aimed specifically at our campaign train. A 'Truth Squad' followed us around the country, issuing statements that supposedly countered Dad's speeches. In Buffalo they hired a horde of school children who tried to drown out Dad with screams and catcalls, anticipating by twenty years the Students for a Democratic Society." Sep 3 *NY Times Book Rev* 23/1 "Time was when the Central Intelligence Agency was accused of some particularly dirty trick by the press it would reply blandly, 'The C.I.A. neither confirms nor denies the charge.'" 1973 Mar 10 *Natl Observer* 5/1 "Money from the safe, it is alleged, was used to finance Republican 'dirty tricks' during the campaign." Apr 29 *NY Times* E1/5 "Last week, it was disclosed that a third private treasury of about $600,000 [was] used to finance a variety of dirty tricks." May 6 *NY Times* E1/1–2 (heading) "Republican 'dirty tricks' expert indicted." June 4 *Newsweek* 28/1 "[He was] a subcontractor to Ehrlichman's dirty-tricks department." July 23 *New Yorker* 36/2 (Elizabeth Drew quoting John Gardner, founder and head of Common Cause) "Some of the highest officials of this nation carried on a sustained and systematic attempt to destroy our form of government. It wasn't 'dirty tricks' within the system—it was an attempt to subvert the system, an assault on virtually all the checks and balances that protect our system." Sep 23 *NY Times* E1/4–6 (picture caption) "The Ervin committee prepares to go into the 'dirty tricks' and financing of the 1972 election campaign." Oct 8 *Newsweek* 36/1 "Last week, however, the committee finished up the first item on its agenda . . . and moved on to the slippery ground of dirty campaign tricks." Ibid 36/3 "Campaign tactics, he [Patrick J Buchanan] observed, can be divided into four broad categories: . . . dirty tricks (the notorious Muskie 'Canuck' letter in the New Hampshire primary)." Oct 15 *Time* 20/2 "His voice rising in anger, his eyes boring coldly into the face of a defiant witness, Senator Sam Ervin assailed the notion that White House–inspired dirty tricks employed in the 1972 presidential campaign were commonplace practices

in U.S. politics. Regaining some of their lost momentum, even while losing full television coverage for the first time, Ervin's Watergate committee hearings hammered home a key point: there was a humorless, malicious quality in many of these covert activities that carried them well beyond the category of mere pranks." Oct 20 *National Observer* 2/2 "The Watergate committee recessed its hearings until Oct. 30 to analyze the voluminous material it collected on political 'dirty tricks' and to prepare for an investigation into campaign financing." Nov 20 *SR/World* 45/1 "Somewhere in the snake pit there were traces of a department of dirty tricks invented to snuff out the presidential aspirations of former Prime Minister Jacques Chaban-Delmas, who is the mayor of Bordeaux." Dec 18 *SR/World* 70/1–2 (cartoon caption) "[King to wizard:] 'Merlin, I need ten dirty tricks by sunset.'" Dec 30 *NY Times* E4/3 "The vote-siphoning 'dirty trick' that led to [his] indictment . . . has now been attributed to one of Long Island's leading Democrats. It has been charged that in the same race where [he] and others tried to build up the Liberal Party vote at the expense of the Democratic candidate, the Democrats were helping finance a Conservative to hurt the Republicans." 1974 Jan *Newsweek* 71/3 "[He] is the crafty spy who has recently been accused—but not convicted—of such dirty tricks as greasing his offensive players' jerseys and slipping a slightly deflated football to a rival field-goal kicker." Mar 10 *Tuscaloosa News* G1/2 "If Congress wants to find out about 'dirty tricks' in election campaigns, it might take a look at some of the doozies Alabama voters have witnessed in the years gone by." Apr 18 *NY Rev of Books* 33/3–4 (ad) "Stewart Steven's book reveals for the first time the story of this most sinister of the CIA's dirty tricks." May 20 *Time* 22/3 (repr from *Omaha World Herald*) "They will say that dirty tricks and Watergate break-ins and cover-ups are just politics." Sep *McCall's* 120/2 "It wasn't just our Southern heritage; it also was the sympathy we felt for each other as political dirty-tricks victims." Sep 20–21 *Graphic* (Tuscaloosa, Ala) 2/3–4 (editorial) "Spying and trying to topple unfriendly governments in other nations is an ugly business. Sure this activity is 'dirty tricks.'" Sep 21 *TV Guide* A8/2 (Judith Crist) "Jack Palance is grimmer, slicker and viler than ever as head of the oil monopoly's dirty-tricks squad." Sep 22 *NY Times* E1/3 "The mystique is gone . . . and now the CIA's covert activities, the so-called 'dirty tricks' department, are in question." Oct 21 *New Yorker* 114/2–3 "This week, [he] was sentenced to a prison term of from ten to thirty months for perjury before the Watergate grand jury investigating 'dirty tricks.'" 1975 Mar 30 *NY Times Mag* 11 (heading of article by Fred W Friendly) "WHAT'S FAIR ON THE AIR? . . . Democratic dirty tricks."

dirty-trickery [DIRTY TRICK + -ery] 1974 Mar 18 *Newsweek* 26/2 "Before the week was out, Mr. Nixon did a radio speech previewing his campaign-reform package, including proposed ceilings on individual gifts . . . shorter national campaigns and prohibitions against dirty-trickery."

dirty-trickster *n* [DIRTY TRICK + -ster] 1973 May 28 *Newsweek* 38/3 "*Newsweek* has also learned that at least two other Nixon dirty-tricksters were imitating Segretti's tactics around that time." Oct 2 *Tuscaloosa News* 3/1 (AP) "Donald H. Segretti, political dirty trickster financed by Nixon campaign funds, has become the third Watergate figure to plead guilty and agree to cooperate with federal prosecutors." Oct 8 *Newsweek* 42/3 "The report also made public a few campaign expenditures that have interested Archibald Cox and the Ervin committee: $40,000 to dirty-trickster Donald Segretti." Nov 26 *Newsweek* 33/3–34/1 "And in California, dirty-trickster Donald Segretti, pale and nervous, checked into a minimum-security prison camp to start a six-month sentence for political sabotage." 1974 Feb 25 *Newsweek* 55/1 "So pass the more pleasant moments for inmates in the wall-less Federal prison camp near Lompoc, Calif., the current residence of Watergate 'dirty trickster' Donald Segretti and 352 other prisoners." Nov 4 *New Yorker* 42/2 "And, as if all these scandals weren't enough to demoralize the voters in the Twenty-sixth District, we've learned of a one-man political vendetta by an eight-year-old, whose real name is Larry but whom we'll call the Littlest Dirty Trickster. His idea of a neat way to spend an afternoon after school is to go around town tearing down Goodman posters." 1975 Jan 31 *Harper's Weekly* 1/3 "Dirty trickster Donald Segretti and his 'controller' . . . both received jail terms for their escapades."

fishing expedition See *AS* 48 (1973): 132 1874 *Kansas Reports* (St Paul: West, 1886) 12: *453 "It is also said that this permits one to go on a 'fishing expedition' to ascertain his adversary's testimony."

Fordonomics *n* [Gerald R Ford + -ONOMICS] 1974 Aug 24 *Natl Observer* 3/1 "Eventually, he [Pres Gerald R Ford] will evolve a distinctive strategy. No doubt it will be called Fordonomics, just as Richard Nixon's policies, although sometimes contradictory, became known as Nixonomics. [¶] At this early date, however, Fordonomics is a name without content."

miniconvention *n* A small convention usu of a political party set up to consider strategy for the regular convention 1973 June 2 *TV Guide* 5/1–2 (Neil Hickey) "Seldom was heard an encouraging word among the kid-show hosts as they held two days of meetings recently at the Sonesta Beach Hotel in Key Biscayne, Fla. . . . The mini-convention was being held barely four weeks after the National Association of Broadcasters had attached a new rule to its Code, forbidding kiddie-show hosts of member stations to deliver commercials 'within or adjacent to' their programs, or even to do lead-ins to commercials when that might imply any endorsement whatever of the advertised products." Sep 17 *Newsweek* 30/1 "After that, the crucial test will be how well Democrats do in next year's Congressional elections, and whether they can pull themselves together at a proposed 'mini-convention' in 1974." 1974 Jan 6 *NY Times* 34/1 "The main purpose of the so-called miniconvention, to be held Dec. 6 to 8, is to debate and approve a national Democratic party charter." Jan 31 *Tuscaloosa News* 8/6 "The 'mini' convention's formal name is the Conference on Democratic Party Organization and Policy. It is an innovation required by action of the Democratic National Convention of 1972." Feb 24 *Tuscaloosa News* A12/1 "HOUSTON, Tex. (AP)—Supporters of Alabama Gov. George Wallace opened a two-day session Saturday to plot strategy for the September Democratic miniconvention in Kansas City, Mo., where party rules will be adopted. [¶] 'The aim of this conference is to elect as many people as possible (to the miniconvention) who are in accord with the thinking of the people at this conference,' said Hall Timanus, a Houston lawyer who headed Wallace for President efforts in Texas in 1972." Mar 24 reporter on NBC TV ". . . gather at a miniconvention [of Republicans] in Chicago." Aug 26 *Tuscaloosa News* 4 (David S. Broder) "If Mayor Wheeler is, indeed, looking forward to the December miniconvention here [Kansas City], he's about the only Democrat in the Country who is." Dec 9 *Time* 24/1 "After McGovern's disastrous loss to Richard Nixon, the Democrats set about writing a charter that would be fairer to all factions. A special commission was well along with a draft for the miniconvention when it ran into trouble in August over the role of minorities." Dec 13 *New Times* (NYC) 18/1 (Peter Ross Range) "Mickey was trying to get Wallace delegates elected to the Democrats' mini-convention coming up in Kansas City."

-(on)omics Combining form for *economics* (see *electionomics, McGovernomics, Nixonomics* in *AS* 46 (1971): 145–46; FORDONOMICS)

plea bargain *n* See *AS* 49 (1974): 128 Additional quots 1969 *Northwestern Reporter* 2d ser (St Paul: West) 165: 528/1 "Court has proper role of discreet inquiry into propriety of settlement whereby defendant as result of plea bargain agrees to plead guilty to lesser degree of offense than that with which he was charged." 1970 Dec 22 *San Francisco Examiner* 10/7 "90 percent of the criminal cases in San Francisco courts are settled by plea bargains." 1974 *Cumulative Annual Pocket Part* for *Words and Phrases* (St Paul: West) 32A: 39 "'Plea bargain' ordinarily contemplates that accused will plead guilty as quid pro quo for reduction of the charge against him."

plea bargain *vi* See *AS* 49 (1974): 128–30 Additional quots 1970 Dec 14 *San Francisco Examiner* 6/1–8 (heading) "Plea Bargaining Rules at Hall of Justice." Dec 22 *San Francisco Examiner* 10/7 "Plea bargaining—The arrangement in which a defendant, in return for his guilty plea, receives a light sentence."

plea bargainer *n* 1975 Jan 26 "The American Parade: The Case against Milligan" CBS WCFT-TV ch 33 Tuscaloosa Ala "There would be over 60 witnesses. Some were paid informers; some were plea bargainers."

quackupuncture *n* [*quack*ery + ac*upuncture*] Acupuncture performed by unqualified persons 1973 June *Psychology Today* 37/3 "By early 1972, the acupuncture boom in the U.S. was well launched. Entrepreneurs—medical and nonmedical, authorized and unauthorized—had begun to promote, peddle, push and sponsor acupuncture correspondence courses, do-it-yourself acupuncture kits, acupuncture seminars, acupuncture demonstrations, acupuncture books and acupuncture clinics. This, of course, brought on warnings of quackery, or quackupuncture." 1974 week of June 24 Barbara Walters on "Today" (NBC TV) "Is it acupuncture or is it quackupuncture?" Sep 12 (Tuscaloosa, Ala) *Graphic* 16/2 "Dr. Richard Palmer, pathologist from Alexandria, Va., added, 'Unfortunately, when people are in pain they'll try anything. We must make sure that acupuncture doesn't become quackupuncture. It must be regarded in the Western world as experimental and used only by licensed physicians, dentists, and research scientists.' "

seed money *n* [*BDNE* 1968; *W3 Add Sect* 1971; *WNCD8*; *World Bk Dict* 1975] Additional quots (see preliminary remarks) 1966 Aug 21 *NY Times* F15/2 "The bonds would have enabled the state to gain $17-million, to be used as seed money to set up the loan guarantee rotary fund." Sep 17 *Sat Rev* 24/2 "The additional $1.5 billion for soft loans and pre-investment projects would generate a flow of several times that amount of assistance to the developing countries in conventional investments and hard loans. This increase in soft loans and pre-investment seed money could well trigger a growth in net capital flow from the present $6.5 billion to $12 billion or $14 billion annually." 1970 Jan 10 *Sat Rev* 27/1 "This was seed money in the best sense of the term. As President Nixon pointed out to Congress last month, every dollar of Foundation money has stimulated the donation of three dollars from other sources." 1975 Mar *Episcopalian* 15/3 "At a time when it usually takes two dollars to do the work of one . . . THE EPISCOPALIAN is offering readers an opportunity to make one dollar do the work of two. [¶] Here's how. Contribute to the SEED MONEY FUND of THE EPISCOPALIAN to help the Church achieve its goal to reach each Episcopal family with a simple, inexpensive carrier of local, national, and worldwide news each month." May 5 (date received) letter from Stewart L Udall, national campaign manager of the [Morris K] Udall 1976 Committee "Spring is planting time for all of us who have green thumbs. The new election laws make this spring a political planting time as well. I hope you can provide some of the crucial 'seed money' we need for our campaign."

soggy-trick DIRTY TRICK 1973 Sep 24 *Newsweek* 22/2 "Which isn't to say that all White House staffers sign up with the soggy-tricks squad before climbing aboard."

[Received May 1975]

AMONG THE NEW WORDS

I. WILLIS RUSSELL AND MARY GRAY PORTER

University of Alabama

OUR ENTRY *disclosing* in this installment recalls *dirty tricks* in the previous one. In a preliminary draft, we set up separate entries for *disclosing* plus each of the various noun heads, *agent, solution, tablet* (modified also by *disclosure*), and *wafer*. There is, of course, support for this in the / ' / stress pattern and in the *Woman's Day* quotation, but the variation of the head suggests that our present treatment is preferable, perhaps—in the phraseology of mathematics—more elegant. We may even be witnessing a process we discussed in "Among the New Words" for Spring-Summer 1971 in connection with *bikeway* and its variants. Additional evidence will be found in the references at the end of the entry.

All the quotations for *tot lot* except the last, which is ambiguous, refer to a public facility, part of an organized recreation program. A similar term, *tot-yard*, 'fenced-in play area adjoining a private residence,' seems not to have caught on, but the single quotation in our files, contributed many years ago by Mamie J. Meredith, may be of interest to our readers: "Some of the benefits to Park Forest residents: The rental houses with enclosed 'tot-yards' all face streetless malls with rear parking courts" (25 May 1953, *Newsweek*, p. 71). If our readers have in their files additional quotations of *tot-yard*, we would be happy to have them for use in an entry.

Acknowledgments: For citations, Dennis Baron (2), Maria Caliandro (1), Mamie J. Meredith (2), Anne B. Russell (1), and Peter Tamony (1, the earliest for *tot lot*). Thanks are also due Dale L. Cramer for the definition of *indexing*.

architectural barrier *n* Any feature of a building or other construction that prevents or hinders access or use by handicapped persons, BARRIER 1963 July-Aug *Jour of Rehabilitation* 15/1 "Are communities doing anything about removing those troublesome architectural barriers that needlessly complicate the lives of the physically handicapped?" 1964 July *Today's Health* 26/1–2 (picture caption) "There are no special classroom buildings or dorms for the disabled. But the architectural barriers have been removed." 1965 July-Aug *Rehabilitation Record* 39/2 "Plans for all new buildings specifically provided for the elimination of architectural barriers. [¶] Then came redesigning of drinking fountains, telephones, restrooms, and shower facilities, use of cafeteria carts, and recessing and cutting down curbs." Nov 8 Public Law 89-333 in *United States Statutes at Large Containing the Laws and Concurrent Resolutions Enacted during the First Session of the Eighty-Ninth Congress of the United States of America 1965 and Reorganization Plans, Proposed Amendment to the Constitution, and Proclamations,* vol 79 (Washington: US GPO, 1966) 1289 "PUBLIC LAW 89-333—Nov. 8, 1965 . . . 'Sec. 15. (a) There is hereby established in the Department of Health, Education, and Welfare a National Commission on Architectural Barriers to Rehabilitation of the Handicapped, consisting of the Secretary, or his designee, who shall be Chairman, and not more than fifteen members appointed by the Secretary without regard to the civil service laws. . . . [¶] (b) The Commission shall (1) determine how and to what extent architectural barriers impede access to or use of facilities in buildings of all types by the handicapped; (2) determine what is being done, especially by public and other nonprofit agencies and groups having an interest in and a capacity to deal with the problem, to eliminate such barriers from existing buildings and to prevent their incorporation into buildings constructed in the future; and (3) prepare plans and proposals for such further action as may be necessary to achieve the goal of ready access and full use of facilities in buildings of all types by the handicapped, including proposals for bringing together in a cooperative effort, agencies, organizations, and groups already working toward that goal or whose cooperation is essential to effective and comprehensive action.'" 1966 May *Parks & Recreation* 429/1 "It is up to recreation planners to develop facilities in such a way that all potential participants may use them despite their handicaps. [¶] . . . for further information the following are suggested: Architectural Barriers Commission, Vocational Rehabilitation Administration, United States Department of Health, Education, and Welfare, Washington, D.C." 1970 Nov 29 *Tuscaloosa News* D1/1 "'Architectural barriers' can be curbs which are too high for a wheelchair student to negotiate by himself, steps leading into a building, light switches too high for him to reach, restrooms without handrails, too low electrical outlets—the list could go on and on." 1973 Feb 28 *Boll Weevil* (University, Ala) 6/1 "Because the building was designed so that there will be no architectural barriers, the handicapped will have no difficulty navigating the complex." 1974 Mar *Emory Mag* (Atlanta, Ga) 10/1 "One of Mr. Webb's interests is working toward the removal of architectural barriers in the city of Atlanta. He is pushing the city administration into building ramps along with stairs in city buildings and cutting ramps into curbs on city streets." Dec 8 *Birmingham* (Ala) *News* A39/5 "The upshot of Mock's survey was a campuswide campaign to remove architectural barriers on the UNA campus." 1975 Jan 1 George Wallace, public service announcement WBMG-TV Ch 42 Birmingham, Ala "These architectural barriers prevent handicapped people from living where they want to. . . . So, as your governor, I'd like to ask you to join me in making Alabama the leading state in the removal of architectural barriers." Feb 6 *Crimson-White* (University, Ala) 2/1 "Mae Lewis, director of the University Rehabilitation Counseling Service, said that the main problems of the wheelchair student are the architectural barriers around campus." Aug 3 *Tuscaloosa News* 6A/1–4 (picture caption) "Titled project HELP, the club sought to eliminate architectural barriers for the handicapped in the Tuscaloosa community." Additional reference 1975 Feb 23 *NY Times* XX1/6

barrier *n* [*OED barrier* sb "1. *gen*. A fence or material obstruction of any kind erected (or serving) to bar the advance of persons or things, or to prevent access to a place"] *Specif,* ARCHITECTURAL BARRIER 1965 Nov 8 Public Law 89-333 Quot sv ARCHITECTURAL BARRIER 1974 Dec 8 *Birmingham* (Ala) *News* A39/6

"Ramps to defeat barriers of street curbs and lowered water fountains are the results of Flippo's suggestions." 1975 Feb 6 *Crimson-White* (University, Ala) 2/1–2 "None of these students are able to use recreational facilities to the fullest, specifically the wheelchair handicapped and the blind who are our primary concern as far as the barriers go." —**barrier-free** 1973 Feb 22 *Crimson-White* (University, Ala) 1/2 "'The structure is architecturally barrier-free,' said Espy, 'which makes it a lot easier for handicapped students to enjoy the Center facilities.'" 1974 Dec *Emory Mag* (Atlanta, Ga) 1/1–2 "Among the barrier-free design features of the new building are wider doors, ramps for wheelchairs, and bar-type door-handles to permit easy navigation for handicapped persons. Plans call for doors to be easily opened; buttons and equipment within reach; windows that can be looked through in the seated position; non-slippery floors, and access to pleasant, wooded outdoor surroundings."

body-dancing *n* TOUCH DANCING 1973 Dec 10 *Newsweek* 16/1–17/1 "Reporters of social doings now tell us that 'body-dancing' is back and that They are doing it. . . . We never called it 'body-dancing'; it was just a delicious way for males and females to move together on any smooth public or private floor large enough for a small band and free movement. . . . [¶] Yes, the man led and the woman followed, and it was good that way. Surrender *was* voluptuous in a simple physical sense. In this small area of life, a woman leading a man was simply no good for either or for their essential unity. Perhaps that was one reason, along with the emergence of rock, why men and women broke apart by dancing separately. However sensual their writhes and wriggles, there was space between them and the woman was on her own. Direct contact was through intercourse. As for love, although one concedes the thudding excitement, strong visceral response and mass hallucination of rock, it is hard for those not born to it to find the tenderness, the romanticism, and—yes—love that 'body-dancing' could and did evoke."

close dancing *n* TOUCH DANCING 1974 Feb 9 *National Observer* 1/4 "An astonished Lucy is waltzed through a Peanuts cartoon strip by a knowing Snoopy, who proclaims: 'Close dancing is back.'"

disclosing *adj* [*W3 disclose* vt 2a 'expose to view'] *Specif*, revealing, by means of special vegetable dye preparations, the plaque or food particles adhering to inadequately cleaned tooth surfaces 1965 *Dorland's Illustrated Medical Dictionary* (24th ed; Phila: W B Saunders) 1402/2 "disclosing s[olution], a solution which is used for the purpose of making something apparent, such as one to be painted on the surface of a tooth in order to stain, and thus render visible, foreign matter or bacterial plaques." 1972 Jan *Today's Health* 33/3 "In 1961 a tablet of red food-coloring dye was developed that, when chewed, leaves a red stain on plaque and food particles, but not on clean teeth. With this disclosing tablet, a user sees immediately how well he has removed plaque." June *Woman's Day* 114/2 "And you can easily measure your success by means of a small tablet, a solution or a wafer containing a plaque-disclosing dye (usually called disclosing tablets or disclosing solution) that when swished around in your mouth, stains all the plaque you missed." 1974 Mar *Harper's Bazaar* 106/2 "An excellent way to find out if you are getting all the plaque off your teeth is to use the disclosing agents—tablets or liquids—now sold in all drugstores. The active ingredients are harmless dyes which stain plaque but not the clean surfaces of a tooth." 1975 Apr *Boys' Life* 53/2 "Plaque must be removed daily by conscientious use of your toothbrush, *dental floss*, and *disclosing wafers*—tablets whose harmless red vegetable dye makes plaque more visible." Additional references: 1972 Jan *Emory Mag* 6/3; Mar *Pop Sci* 83/1; 1974 Feb *Reader's Digest* 221/1

disclosure tablet *n* [*W3 disclosure*] Disclosing tablet (as in first quot sv DISCLOSING) 1972 Jan *Today's Health* 34/1 "One of the most outspoken leaders of the plaque control movement, Dr. Robert F. Barkley of McComb, Illinois, shuns the disclosure tablet." [Macomb?]

escalation index *n* 1974 June 1 *Between the Lines* (Newtown, Pa) 3/3 "What amounts to a cost-of-living clause may come to all of us. A debate is on in Administration circles about an 'escalation index' which would be attached to everything from wages, mortgages, income tax, interest rates, even for earnings by business firms. Dr. Milton Friedman, economist at the University of Chicago, discovered the system being used in Brazil where military dictators clamped it on to bring an 80 to 90 per cent annual inflation down to 18 per cent. (BTL, May 1)"

genesis bean; genesis rock; genesis stone *n* [*W3 genesis* "the origin or coming into being of anything"] Specimen of lunar or meteoritic material believed to retain characteristics of rock formed early in the development of the solar system 1972 Jan *McCall's* 74/2 "Among their finds: the white crystalline 'genesis rock' thought to be 4.15 billion years old." Jan 29 *Science News* 73/1 "They found a lunar object—a little green glass fragment dubbed 'Genesis bean'—that is similar in chemical composition to a class of meteorites called howardites." July *Reader's Digest* 129/1 (from *NY Times* 16 Apr) "As the melt cools, the various minerals crystallize—that is, become solid at different temperatures. The slag, which hardens first, is a white, aluminum, silicon-rich mix called anorthosite—the kind of rock found by astronaut David Scott which came to be dubbed Genesis rock." 1975 Jan *Sci Amer* 24/1 "Important clues to the origin of the solar system lie in 'genesis rocks.' These are rocks that have retained their character from nearly 4.6 billion years ago, when the planets were still accreting out of the cloud of dust and gas we call the solar nebula. Most meteorites are genesis rocks of a kind: their chemistry and mineralogy reveal that most of them were formed in environments characteristic of the early solar system. . . . [¶] Genesis rocks may exist on at least some of the asteroids, the huge swarm of small worlds in orbit at distances between 2.2 and 3.2 astronomical units from the sun." Ibid 32/3 "The astronauts who journeyed to the moon brought back very few genesis rocks. The moon was heavily cratered during the first half-billion years of its existence; most lunar rocks date from the end of that period." Jan 10 "CBS Late Movie: Stowaway to the Moon" WTOK-TV Ch 11 Meridian, Miss "What is a genesis stone?"

index *vt* [*BDNE* 1972; *World Book Dict* 1975 sense 4] Additional quots 1974 Apr 22 *Newsweek* 91/3 "[Milton] Friedman pointed out that Brazil has sharply lowered its rate of inflation in part by 'indexing' its economy. When the Brazilian consumer price index rises, not only does it increase wages but it also affects the amount Brazilians pay in taxes, interest rates and other items." May 25 *Bus Week* 148/2 "Both wages and old-age payments are now indexed in many European countries. . . . Enel, the Italian state electric company, is about to issue seven-year bonds with a variable interest rate and the principal indexed against inflation." Aug 15 *Forbes* 28/2 Quot sv NONINDEXED 1975 *World Book Yearbook* 590/3

index *n* 1971 Jan 23 *Sat Rev* 44/3 Quot sv INDEX BOND 1974 May 20 *Newsweek* 84/3 "'The only way to lessen inflation is by slowing the rate of monetary growth,' he [Milton Friedman] told *Newsweek's* Jeff B. Copeland. 'The key problem is how to do it without producing a recession. The index provides the means to slow down inflation without these effects. It eases the withdrawal pains and makes it a political possibility.'"

indexation *n* INDEXING 1974 May 25 *Bus Week* 147/1–2 "Basically, indexation simply means attaching escalator clauses based on some relevant yardstick of inflation to various long-term contracts. Wages and rents, for example, would be raised periodically to keep step with the cost of living. Interest payments on bonds and bank deposits would be adjusted upward or downward in line with the inflation rate . . . . And the tax system would be readjusted so that corporate and individual income gains that merely reflect inflation are not taxed away, resulting in a loss of real income." June 10 *USN&WR* 104/2 "Why not tie *everything* to the Consumer Price Index? . . . [¶] This is called 'indexation' (a clumsy word with a computer-like rasp to it) which would work this way: [¶] All wages would be linked directly to rises and falls in the cost of living. If inflation climbed 10 per cent, for example, so would everybody's pay. [¶] Interest rates, corporate bonds, mortgages and so on would be supplemented by a similar inflation adjustment. [¶] Business accounting practices—such as depreciation and the valuation of fixed assets like buildings and equipment—would be changed to reflect the impact of rising prices. [¶] Taxes would receive the same treatment." July *Fortune* 72/2 (editorial) "A sign that inflation has gone far past the threshold of pain is the increasing attention being paid to the notion of 'indexation'—wide application of price escalators to wage contracts, long-term bonds and loans, construction contracts, and much else." Ibid 94/1 "These obstacles to ending inflation can be substantially reduced through what has come to be called 'indexation'—the widespread use of price-escalator clauses in private and governmental contracts." July 5 *National Rev* 737/2 "'To be meaningful,' writes *The Economist*, 'indexation should cover all forms of earned, investment, and transfer income, contractual debts, and tax scales.'" July 8 *USN&WR* 45/1 "First of all, just what is 'indexation'? [¶] In the broadest sense, it means adjusting wages and salaries, the face value of life insurance and other assets, interest rates on loans, and even income taxes according to the trend of prices. Then the Government is supposed to do a better job of fighting inflation." 1975 Feb 2 *NY Times* (sect 4) 4/3 "Indexation is not a pretty word; but it is moving up fast in the vocabulary of international economics. . . . This is what indexing means: linking the prices charged for something, whether labor or oil, to the general rate of inflation." Additional references: 1974 June 15 *National Observer* 12/6 (letter); July *Fortune* 96/2

index bond *n* 1971 Jan 23 *Sat Rev* 44/3 "Perhaps we shall also come to experiment with index bonds, where the level of repayment is tied to the price level."

indexed *adj* 1974 Apr 7 *NY Times* F14/4 "Having learned that lesson, Brazil has now developed into what could be termed an 'indexed economy,' where practically every area of the economy has some sort of adjustment mechanism for inflation." Aug 25 *NY Times* F12/4 "Thus, it is feared that indexed incomes could generate a new round of cost increases."

indexing *n* Tying various money incomes to a cost-of-living index for the purpose of mitigating the costs of inflation on fixed money contracts, INDEXATION 1974 Albert Fishlow *Brookings Papers on Economic Activity* 1: 261–80 (cited 1974 Nov *Monthly Labor Rev* 57/1, 58/2 note; title of art) "Indexing Brazilian Style: Inflation Without Tears." Apr 7 *NY Times* F-14/3–8 (heading) "Indexing: An Inflation Lesson from Brazil." May 13 *Time* 110/2–3 "A band of conservative economists led by the provocative Milton Friedman of the University of Chicago are vigorously touting 'indexing,' a system that in theory preserves the buying power of money by tying all paper values to a price indicator. For example, if prices rise 7%, so does everything else: wages, prices specified in long-term business contracts, interest rates on bonds, savings and mortgages. Even taxes are included: a person whose salary rises 7% while prices are also going up 7% incurs no greater tax liability." May 20 *Newsweek* 84/1 "Many countries use indexing in a very limited way. But the country where the scheme has reached its most developed form is Brazil where 'monetary correction,' as the Brazilians call it, has helped to chop the staggering 92 per cent annual inflation rate of a decade ago to about 20 per cent today. Under the system, increases in the consumer price index automatically trigger a series of compensating adjustments in other areas of the economy: wages, taxes, interest rates and other items." July *Dun's* 11/1 "Economists seem to come up with one fad a year and 'indexing' is it for 1974. That is the notion that we can best face inflation by protecting everybody via an escalator clause. Indexing is neither a new idea (it was tried in Massachusetts in the eighteenth century) nor a good one." July *Reader's Digest* 52/1 "Faced with all these pressures, some economists contend that the best course is to accept inflation as permanent and make adjustments to anesthetize the pain. . . . [fn] One solution advocated by several prominent economists, and being tested in varying ways in Brazil, Canada and Europe, is 'indexing'—that is, raising or lowering incomes, taxes, savings or even debts in line with price trends. In theory, this arrangement would preserve real incomes and buying power." Aug 15 *Forbes* 28/1 Quot sv INDEXIZATION Aug 25 *NY Times* F12/8 "An ideal indexing system would be one that would adjust all incomes equally to relatively small price rises, so that when inflation quickens, adjustments would become more frequent." 1975 Feb 2 *NY Times* (sect 4) 4/3 Quot sv INDEXATION

indexization *n* INDEXING 1974 Aug 15 *Forbes* 26/3 "[David T] Kleinman is an advocate of indexization—that is, tying interest rates to inflation in such a way that lenders' capital is not eroded by rising price levels; the higher goes inflation, the higher go interest rates." Aug 15 *Forbes* 28/1 "Kleinman: I think there could be a very drastic depression, yes. Unless we move to a worldwide system of full monetary correction—indexization—and promptly resolve this recycling problem. What worries me is whether we can do it soon enough. You see, I think it is the artificial demand for credit—stimulated by cheap money—that's responsible for many of our problems. Indexing or monetary correction would eliminate that."

index-linking *n* INDEXING 1974 July 5 *National Rev* 738/1 "But there are, of course, examples of indexation accompanying accelerating, as well as decelerating, inflation. That simply shows 'that index-linking is no cure-all for inflation,' says *The Economist*." Aug *R Guide* 150/1 (subject heading; vol 74, no 11) "INDEX linking (economics)." 1975 [cf last quot sv INDEXATION] Feb 10 *R Guide* 156/2 (subject heading; vol 74, no 22) "INDEX linking (economics)."

monetary correction *n* INDEXING 1974 Jan 21 *Newsweek* 80/2–3 "After reducing inflation to about 30 per cent per year by 1967, it [Brazil] eased off. Simultaneously, however, it introduced purchasing-power escalator clauses into a wide range of contracts. The term used in Brazil is 'monetary correction.' If a Brazilian deposits money in a savings bank, the bank not only will pay him a stated interest rate, say 5 per cent, but also will periodically credit his account with a monetary correction equal to the rate of inflation over the period. Longer-term business loans, government securities, mortgages, and so on are handled the same way: the borrower pays the lender a stated rate plus a monetary correction." May 20 *Newsweek* 84/1 Quot sv INDEXING Aug 15 *Forbes* 28/1 Quot sv INDEXIZATION Nov *Monthly Labor Rev* 57/2 "Fishlow also states that Brazil's attempts at monetary correction by indexing prices and wages to measures of inflation were strictly limited during the first few years."

nonindexed *adj* 1974 Aug 15 *Forbes* 28/2 "If France decided to index its monetary sector, including the Eurodollar trading done out of Paris, there's no way for London to continue trading Eurodollar currencies in a nonindexed fashion."

partner dancing *n* TOUCH DANCING 1972 Oct *Harper's Bazaar* 72/2 "A big influence in this return to partner dancing has been all these shows coming back like *No, No, Nanette*, and, of course, all the movies on TV from the thirties and forties with all those really great stars."

string; The String; string bikini *n* 1974 June 14 "*W*" (Fairchild Pubs, NYC) 17 "The latest—The String—looks like a winner on the beaches of other countries too. [¶] It's the tiniest coverup. As a matter of fact, it makes the bikini look old-fashioned. Held by thin strings, it's just two tiny triangles—front and back—worn with a mini-bra." July 4 Roger Grimsby on "ABC News" "It all started here at Ipanema Beach—the string bikini. . . . The string is not yet found on the public beaches." Oct *Harper's Bazaar* 34/4 "However, do wear The String, at least, as swimming *au naturel* has not been approved legally everywhere." Nov *McCall's* 10/1 "Winter vacation time is coming and the string bikini is still with us—better, if not bigger, than ever. The string has come in for a lot of bad jokes but, actually, for a healthy, active woman, there's nothing immodest about it." 1975 June *Esquire* 152 (picture caption) "He likes her string bikini and shawl skirt by Gottex."

tot lot *n* Playground for small children, usu part of the facilities of an organized recreation program 1949 Nov 21 *Time* 24/1 "He had . . . roped off special streets for roller-skating and games, had set up 'tot-lots on unused property for the benefit of weary mothers." 1952 June *Amer City* 129/1 "Homeowners had to be assured that the new tot-lots and playgrounds and playfields would not become eyesores." 1953 Aug 4 *Lincoln* (Neb) *Journal* 1 (AP) "Attendance has dropped off sharply among the 8-year-olds at the Sharon Hill community YMCA's summer recreation club. [¶] Director Pete Ledonn found out why. Seems the kids objected to being put in an age-group called 'tots' and playing in an area called the 'Tot lot'." 1965 Feb *Recreation* 85/1 "The two fort-enclosed totlots include wigwam climbers and labyrinths . . . , cylinder-drum, candy mountains, sand areas, and other factors." Apr 1 *Friends Jour* 162/1 "The bang-bang fantasy is appropriate for four-year-olds on a tot lot, but it is inappropriate for men in their forties." 1966 Mar *Parks & Recreation* 295/2 (ad) "Now, you can make playgrounds, tot lots, tennis courts, and field event approaches *safe* . . . while holding resurfacing and maintenance costs to a minimum." 1973 Mar *Southern Living* 25 (ad) "Enjoy our scenic lake, putting greens, tennis courts, boutiques, tot-lots, and spray pools for the children." Apr *Intellectual Digest* 47/3 (subheading) "TOT LOTS NOT SO HOT."

touch dance *vi* [back-formation from *touch dancing*] 1972 Oct *Harper's Bazaar* 72/3 "Freddie doesn't touch dance at all."

touch dancing *n* Ballroom dancing, BODY-DANCING, CLOSE DANCING, PARTNER DANCING 1972 Oct *Harper's Bazaar* 72/1 "Dance experts agree that as the East goes, so goes the nation, and what you've heard by now is true—'touch,' 'partner,' 'ballroom' dancing is back." 1973 Sep 24 *Newsweek* 56/1 (ad) "And a few lessons are more important than ever now that real dancing is back, *touch* dancing—that exciting contact-to-music that brings out feelings no other kind of dancing ever did." Nov *Harper's Bazaar* 102/3 "That touch-dancing revival should get a big whirl from *The Waltz Emperor*—all about the Strauss family." 1974 Feb 9 *National Observer* 17/1 "To be sure, the ballroom-dance revival—that is, close or touch dancing as it is now called—has not yet reached epidemic proportions."

[Received August 1975]

AMONG THE NEW WORDS

I. WILLIS RUSSELL AND MARY GRAY PORTER
University of Alabama

UNTIL WE RECEIVED Peter Tamony's 1957 citation of *ball park*, we had assumed that the figurative use of the term was a development of the concrete sense '(satellite) capsule recovery area' as illustrated in the original entry (*American Speech* 44: 82–83). As this earlier quotation indicates, however, the semasiology is probably quite different, and we agree with Tamony's remark that "the 1957 example of usage of then Secretary of Defense Wilson and the persistence of usage (with variations) on the financial pages and in connection with money suggests that there may have been figurative usages of *ball park* prior to the 1960 Hawaii-area employment."

Thus, earlier citations might well show up, and we invite readers to be on the lookout for them and send us anything they find that throws light on the earlier history of *ball park* used figuratively.

Though *ball park, cliometrician, cliometrics,* and *mediagenic* are to be found in some dictionaries, we have set up full entries for them because we think the additional dated citations, especially those for *ball park*, will interest our readers. The 1976 edition of the *World Book Dictionary* (*WBD*) enters all four; *6,000 Words: A Supplement to Webster's Third New International Dictionary* (Springfield: G. & C. Merriam Co., 1976) enters *ball park* and *mediagenic*; *ball park* is also entered in the 1969 *Random House Dictionary* (*RHD*).

Acknowledgments: For citations, members of the American Dialect Society Committee on New Words: Dennis E. Baron (7), Joyce T. Fuller (1), Peter Tamony (18, including all the *ball park* quotations from 1957 to 1971); John Algeo (1), Walter S. Avis (2), Philip C. Kolin (1), Virginia McDavid (1), and Anne B. Russell (1). Dennis Baron and Peter Tamony contributed to the definitions of *ball park*.

ball park *n* 1: [*AS* 44: 82–83] Missile recovery area near Hawaii (additional quots) 1960 Aug 21 *San Francisco Examiner* sec I 10/3 (AP) "A C-119 . . . plucked the 19 foot long Discoverer XIV capsule from the air. . . . It came down some 200 miles from the center of its predicted impact area, but still within the designated 'ballpark' area 300 miles southsouthwest of Oahu, Hawaii." 1961 Sep 20 *San Francisco Examiner* 11/2 (UPI) "Surface ships in the Pacific 'ballpark' also were alerted to try to recover the capsule from the sea if the . . . cargo planes could not snare the parachuting capsule from the Discoverer." Oct 15 *San Francisco Chronicle* 17/6 (UP and AP) "Nine planes went out for the Discoverer, and seven of them flew into the 'ballpark,' the recovery area near Hawaii." 2: [*RHD* 1969; *WBD* 1976 sense 2] Figurative use; additional quots 1963 Nov 6 *San Francisco Call-Bulletin* 51/1 "Otherwise, they might find 'pockets of overbuilding in their own ball park.'" 1964 Feb 23 *This World* (*San Francisco Chronicle*) 24/3–5 (heading) "[Menotti's 'The Last] Savage' Looks Like a Hit in [Rudolph] Bing's Ballpark" 1965 Mar 28 *Book Week* (*San Francisco Examiner*) 6/2 "NAL guaranteed Whalen an advance of $100,000, which is not bad for a first book. 'The other bids were in the same ballpark,' Whalen said." 1971 Aug 10 *San Francisco Examiner* 18/2 "Perhaps your mother-in-law 'took over' because she is an R.N. and the hospital is her ballpark." 1975 July 9, mayor at the Mayors' Conference, Boston, Mass, over NBC-TV (in explanation of why the Conference should not criticize President Ford's defense budget) "We have no expertise; we should stay in our own ball park." —**hoot out of the ball park** [cf *laugh out of court*] 1962 June 19 *San Francisco Chronicle* 45/1–2 "Treasury Secretary Dillon was nearly hooted out of the ball park for suggesting that a stock that sells for 15 times its yearly earnings might be reasonably priced." —**in the ball park** [*WBD* 1976, *6000 Words* 1976 in etymology of *ball park* (*adj*)] Additional quots 1968 Oct 8 *San Francisco Examiner* 58/7–8 "However, the figures I have indicate this pay-out 'is in the ball park.'" 1969 Sep 8 *San Francisco Chronicle* 42/1 (editorial) "An executive amply qualified to speak, he has expressed doubt that his industry needs the SST. Increased operating costs, he said, are the big problem and 'They are just not in the ballpark for efficient and economic operation.'" 1971 Jan 29 *Life* 16/3–4 "An apartment in the ball park [by William Zinsser] . . . [My apartment didn't sell because it] wasn't in the ball park. . . . Would I lower the price? I did, and the ladies all said, 'Wonderful! Now at least it's in the ball park.' [¶] Though I am now in the ball park, nobody else is. . . . 'One of my clients wanted to make you an offer last week, but I told him not to bother. What he had in mind just wasn't in the ball park.' . . . In fact, I now realize that there's only one sentence I'm really waiting to hear: [¶] 'She doesn't like it, and he doesn't like it, and it's not right for them, and it isn't in the ball park, but frankly they're desperate and they don't want to look anymore.'" 1972 Apr 8 *Science News* 230/3 "For laser-induced fusion megajoule energies are necessary, and, says Alcock, 'Nobody's in that ball park.'" Dec *Esquire* 266/2 "One thing that didn't immediately connect was 'pain' that Schwarz [a psychic] saw behind Dr. Schram's eyes. 'I've never had any pain behind my eyes,' he says, 'but then I remembered that I had an operation on my eyes as a child so, again, he was in the ball park.'" 1974 Jan *Field & Stream* 16/2 "What the ultimate cost would run is known only to some celestial computer, but if you added another 110 percent or so you would probably be in the ballpark." 1975 Jan *Town & Country* 18/4 "As long as they continue to pay this rate, their yields will probably be in the same ball park as, and in some cases higher than, the yields on money-market funds." Mar 17 *NY Times* 31/4 "The consumer price index in December rose only 0.7 per cent; in January 0.6 per cent; and figures to be released later this week will be in that ball park." July 13 *Tuscaloosa News* B-1/1–2 "Webster has a pet theory about criticism. He is heavy on it with students, but in a light fashion. 'I'm a tough hombre,' he says, but in the next breath pampering. 'Feel okay? Maybe you came out a little too quick, huh? Atta girl, you're in the ball park." 1976 Jan 5 "Ironside" WSFA-TV Ch 12 Montgomery, Ala "Twenty milligrams of atropine sulfate . . . is that in the ballpark?" —**out of the ball park** 1967 Apr 23 *San Francisco Chronicle* 14/7–8 "The $35 fee is out of the ball park, from what I can determine." 1975 Aug 11 *Newsweek* 4/3 (letter) "In the second place, CIA deputy director Vernon Walters has confirmed publicly that the estimate given me was 'not out of the ball park.'" —**within the ball park** 1957 Aug 5 *San Francisco Examiner* sec II 15/2 (INS) "Wilson explained that 'I thought I would start with a figure that we could plus or minus a billion or so and be within the ball park.'" 1967 Dec 22 *San Francisco Examiner* 43/7–8 "There are various investment management approaches open to you. The one you used first is certainly 'within the ball park.'"

ball-park *adj* [*6000 Words* 1976] Within a reasonable or acceptable range; see also 1973 Aug 3 quot (William Safire) 1967 June 7 *Wall St Jour* 4 "'I gave them a guess of somewhere around $1.5 billion,' Mr. Roedel testified. 'I think they accepted it as a guess. I thought it was a ball-park figure.'" 1969 June 23 *San Francisco Examiner* 2/6 "A 'ballpark estimate' put the cost of such a plan at possibly $20 billion the first year, Fein said, but the actual price tag would ultimately depend on what kind of health care system the insurance would be expected to cover." 1970 Aug 28 *San Francisco Examiner* 16/1 (UPI) "'I think it's rather helpful,' said Howard W. Rathbun, president of the First National Bank of San Leandro. 'I don't think it's in the nature of coercion. It gives you kind of a ballpark estimate.'" 1972 Mar 25 *TV Guide* 12/2 "As a ball-park guess, I'd say at least 50 per cent of all court time is taken up by auto-accident cases.'" May 6 *New Yorker* 46/2 "Farthest from the center of action, but perhaps most important of all, around four million viewers in around two and a half million households—a ballpark figure based on Nielsen ratings, and most likely as accurate as police estimates of New Year's Eve crowds in Times Square—will later putatively enjoy themselves as well." 1973 June *Harper's Bazaar* 37/1 "Anything, anything but please don't eat it [egg], especially if you are male and in the general ball-park age range of 40." July *Woman's Day* 80/1 "Some ball-park figures on two-year leases: up to $250 monthly for a full-size luxury car, $80 to $90 for a compact." Aug *Progressive Farmer* 16/3 "However, sandy loam farms seldom sell, so it's hard to establish any kind of 'ball park' price on them." Aug 3 *NY Times Mag* 47/1–2 "*Ball-park figure:* In its meaning of 'rough estimate,' this comes from 'in the ball park,' a baseball reference reflecting a nostalgia for a once-national pastime now in decline. In the early sixties, this usage grew in government as the Air Force used 'ball park' to describe satellite recovery areas—delimited spaces like ball parks. A 'ball-park figure' is usually followed by a demand for 'the bottom line' or 'net net,' accounting terms." Nov 3 *Time* 50/1 "His uniform's cost? 'Two thousand,' said Elton. 'But that's just a ballpark figure.'" Nov *Woman's Day* 138/2 "You can get some ballpark estimates of repair prices from a repair guide published three times yearly." Nov 10 Tony Randall on "COS: Bill Cosby Special" ABC-TV "How much is this going to cost me? Just give me a ballpark figure."

beefalo *n* [*beef*+*buffalo*] 1974 Aug 17 *National Observer* 1/4 (picture caption) "Meet the beefalo, a mixture of beef cattle and buffalo. Its meat's leaner, cheaper, faster to cook than beef." Aug 21 *Sun-Times* (Chicago) 98 (picture caption) "A hybrid of beef animal and buffalo, the beefalo, breeders claim, produces meat that's leaner, tastier, and cheaper than beef." Sep 3 *Birmingham* (Ala.) *News* 12/1–2 "What do you get when you cross a beef cow with a buffalo? The answer, a beefalo." 1975 Apr 19 *Weekend Mag* (Montreal) 2/1 "The beefalo's eyes are probably the most visible buffalo feature—watchful and defiant and set so that the animal has wider vision—but the beefalo has inherited a whole bunch of unseen buffalo qualities and beefalo breeders say they're all the good ones, without the bad ones." May 31 *Sat Rev* 8/1 "Answering the call for a range-adapted animal, out of the West come the thundering hoofbeats of the *beefalo*, a massive, meaty cross between the legendary American bison and the modern beef cow." Oct 13 *Champaign-Urbana Courier* 5/6 (AP) "He said he is also interested in raising beefalo, a type of cattle resulting from a cross between domestic breeds and buffalo." Dec *Progressive Farmer* 22/1 "Beefalo is a name coined by D. C. Basolo of Burlingame, Calif., a meat broker who developed an interest in livestock genetics several years ago. In the early 1970's, he announced that he had found the secret to marrying the disease resistance, hardiness, and foraging ability of the buffalo with the meat characteristics and temperament of domestic cattle. The usual mix is three-eighths' buffalo, three-eighths' Charolais, and two-eighths' Hereford." 1976 Jan 6 *Globe and Mail* (Toronto) 9/3 "Len Lusk, a rancher near this Vancouver Island city, says he has the only beefalo ranch for sale in Canada."

cliometrician *n* [*WBD* 1976 without quots] 1974 May 6 *Newsweek* 77/1,3 "Robert William Fogel, who teaches economic history at the universities of Chicago and Rochester, and Stanley L. Engerman, his colleague at Rochester, are 'cliometricians.' The word, which hasn't yet made its way into standard dictionaries, denotes the wooing of Clio, the Greek muse of history, with advanced techniques of mathematical analysis, particularly the processing of huge quantities of previously intractable numerical data through computers." June 17 *Time* 98/1 "Together they are the leading edge of a new wing of historians known as cliometricians because their methods marry Clio, the muse of history, to the practice of quantifying the past with the help of computers." July 27 *National Observer* 15/1 (repr from *NY Rev of Books*) "The 'Cliometricians,' as they call themselves, have married the muse of history to the science of mathematics. These statistical historians are extremely sensitive and defensive about the union for they are aware that traditional devotees of Clio, most historians, regard the marriage as a *mesalliance*, a forced union of incompatibles." 1975 Apr 14 *NY Times* 28/4 "The heavy use of statistics and computerized historical research by cliometricians—historians who use such methods . . ." Aug 29 *Times Lit Supp* 971/1 "But cliometrics and cliometricians? These are

unfortunate coinages. It is as though astronomers, impressed by the power and versatility of their new instruments . . . should find astronomy and astronomers tame and out of date and decide to call their science uranometrics and themselves uranometricians. Professor [Robert] Fogel . . . is ill advised to allow his hard-won achievement to bear the taint of pretentiousness and Madison Avenue cleverness of the new title which he has bestowed upon it."

cliometrics *n* [*WBD* 1976] Additional quots 1974 June 9 *Atlanta Journal and Constitution* C-5 "Fogel and Engerman obtained their conclusions through the use of cliometrics, a sophisticated form of economic historical interpretation based on modern mathematical and statistical evidence. They scoured a large chunk of the rural South for 10 years in pursuit of census records, birth records, old plantation lists—anything which could shed light on how slaves lived and worked." June 17 *Time* 100/3 "Preliminarily, though, cliometrics seems to have scored heavily." 1975 Aug 29 *Times Lit Supp* 971/1 quot sv CLIOMETRICIAN

mediagenic *adj* [*WBD* 1976; *6000 Words* 1976] Additional quots 1971 Aug 23 *Newsweek* 15/2 "Tall, tanned and mediagenic as ever, Lindsay launched into an unrelenting critique of the Republican Party and the Nixon Administration, concluding with a promise 'to take an active part in 1972 to bring about new national leadership.'" 1973 June 18 *Newsweek* 19 (picture caption) "Haig (left) and Laird with the President [Nixon]: Mediagenic moments in the Rose Garden" 1974 June 17 *Newsweek* 42/1 "To the coldest eye, the trip is little more than an exercise in ceremony—and a brief, mediagenic escape from the Watergate scandals." Oct 7 *Newsweek* 63/3 "[Harold] Wilson . . . did not even try to match [Jeremy] Thorpe's mediagenic campaign style." 1975 Sep 8 *Newsweek* 21/2 "The new styles in politics reached into the Deep South last week as Mississippi held its Democratic primary runoff. The result was an up-to-the-minute slate: a woman for lieutenant governor, five blacks for the state legislature (where only one black sits at the moment) and, at the crest of the new wave, Cliff Finch, 48, a mediagenic 'workingman's candidate' for governor."

throw-weight *n* [*WBD* 1976] Additional quots 1972 July 10 *Time* 20/1 "There is no such thing as superiority,' says Adam Yarmolinsky, former Defense Department analyst. 'Throw weight, megatonnage, boosters, who cares? What is relevant is that both sides now have enough deliverable damage-inflicting capacity.'" 1974 July 8 *Newsweek* 24/2 "But along with MIRVing, the Kremlin will also have acquired a tremendous advantage in 'throw-weight' (the capacity to deliver heavier payloads and bigger clusters of MIRV's)."

veto-proof *adj* 1: Of legislation, so important that the President would not veto it, or supported by enough legislators to override a veto 1972 Sep 16 *National Observer* 2/5 "And the debt-limit extension, veto-proof because of its importance, could become a Christmas tree of Democratic proposals." 1974 Jan 25 *New Times* (NYC) 31/1 "He knew that to be a serious contender [for the Presidential nomination] he would need his name on a solid piece of legislation that was all his own, and it had to be veto-proof." 2: Able to override a veto, usu said of US Congress 1973 Sep 20 *San Francisco Examiner* 9/2 "The American Federation of Teachers, claiming 400,000 members, reacted to the vote by calling for the election of a 'veto-proof Congress . . . no longer intimidated by the big stick of a Nixon veto.'" 1974 Apr 11 *San Francisco Examiner* 2/1 (heading) "State labor looks to veto-proof Congress." June 17 *Newsweek* 13/3 "Mr. Nixon would be running the risk that his economic austerity program, added to the woes of Watergate, could so alienate voters that he could face a veto-proof Congress, two-thirds Democratic, after the turn of the year." Aug *Reader's Digest* 29/2 (editorial in *NY Daily News*) "A union-dominated, veto-proof Congress would block any budget-committee restrictions and open wide the gates to unlimited federal spending, further eroding public confidence in our political institutions." Oct *Reader's Digest* 98/1 "What do the leaders of organized labor want? The AFL-CIO puts it simply: a 'veto-proof Congress that could tell the President to jump in the lake.' Angered by Presidential vetoes that cut federal spending by $30.6 billion, labor demands a Congress that would override those vetoes and support its legislative agenda." Nov 3 *Washington Post* C-1/4 "The Democrats are asking the voters to elect a 'veto-proof' Congress, as if they really believe there is such a thing as a straight, unanimous, party-line vote on any major issue." 1975 Mar 30 *NY Times* sec 4 3/5 "Thus the House, where past farm bills often have bogged down, approved this year's version by a substantial, although not veto-proof, margin." June *NCEC* [National Committee for an Effective Congress, NYC] *Congressional Report* 2/1 "'What I see happening,' said Dick Conlon, director of the Democratic Study Group, 'is that reality has punctured the bloat of unreal expectations. There never was a veto-proof Congress. It was a phrase exploited by President Ford during the 1974 campaign to scare voters in the hope that the Republicans would not lose as many seats as they eventually did. The press picked up the phrase and popularized it.'"

[Received May 1976]

AMONG THE NEW WORDS

I. WILLIS RUSSELL AND MARY GRAY PORTER
University of Alabama

THE EXPLOSIVE INCREASE in the numbers of users of citizens band radio—in some months the number of license applications has approached half a million—has produced widespread interest in the many hundreds of CB slang terms. It sometimes seems as if each day brings another handbook for CB operators, each one with a glossary of CB slang; *The "Official" CB Slanguage Language Dictionary* by Lanie Dills has been on the *New York Times*'s list of paperback bestsellers; and newspapers, newsmagazines, and other periodicals consider the CB phenomenon newsworthy. The inclusion in this installment of a few CB slang terms—*bear, bear report, smokey, Smokey (the) Bear*, and *smokey report*—hardly constitutes a leap onto the citizens bandwagon; rather, it is a recognition that some CB slang has achieved a certain amount of currency outside the realm of CB radio.

In strong contrast to the exuberant growth of CB slang terms is the apparently short life of *action point*, which coincided with the life of the defunct World Football League.

Checkbook journalism appears to have been the model for *checkbook baseball*. We considered entering an adjective *checkbook* with the tentative definition 'involving the payment of unusually large sums of money in an attempt to reach a higher level of success, as evidenced, for example, by more wins for a team or higher ratings for a television program.' The fact that our files contain only one citation of *checkbook baseball*, however, suggests that such an entry is not yet warranted.

A *New Yorker* cartoon (25 August 1975, p. 26/2–3) depicts a practitioner of "preventive medicine," which seems to be *defensive medicine* carried to an extreme; the doctor tells his patient: "Nowadays, Mr. Lambert, we practice preventive medicine. In layman's terms, this means I don't do a damn thing until I talk to my lawyer."

Bleep and its variants carry into the electronic age the old tradition of disguising words considered vulgar or obscene. Like earlier devices—ciphers, asterisks, initials, blanks, and the words *blank* or *blankety-blank*—*bleep* and its kin may not be used solely to spare the reader's delicate sensibilities. As Carter Revard comments in "Deciphering *the* Four-letter Word in a Medieval Manuscript's Satire on Friars" (*Verbatim*, May 1977, p. 3/2): "The medieval scribe here was not really showing how shameful the words seemed to him but adding a little extra spice to the joke. . . . Instead of *obeying* a taboo . . . the scribe was *exploiting* it: this is a case of what Allen Walker Read (in *Language* vol. 40 no. 2, April–June 1964, pp. 162–66) has called 'a type of ostentatious taboo.' . . . We have lately enriched our vocabularies in this area, too, with the word *bleep* (*bleeping*), which has replaced earlier *blank, blankety-blank*, not to mention *s.o.b.* and the like."

Acknowledgments: For citations, two members of the American Dialect Society Committee on New Words, Dennis E. Baron (3, including the earliest for *checkbook journalism*) and Peter Tamony (5, including the earliest for *bananas* and *fruitcake* and note on *bleep* in combinations); and John Algeo (1). Thanks are also due Barbara Caughran and Evelyn McMillan for their proofreading of the typescript.

action point *n* In the World Football League, the point after touchdown, to be attempted by running or passing the football across the goal line 1974 Aug 3 *TV Guide* A62/1 "In less than 15 minutes, Weese passed for two TDs, ran for another and scampered across for an action point." Aug 13 *Tuscaloosa News* 10/4 "Chicago running back Mark Kellar continues to lead the league in scoring with nine touchdowns and one action point for 64 points." Dec 15 *Birmingham* (Ala) *News* C2/3 "The owners will be reflecting on a series of changes suggested by Bill Finneran, the New York systems analyst who invented the 'action point,' the required run or pass for the point-after-touchdown."

banana 1: *n* Crazy person, nut, zany or eccentric person 1976 Aug 8 *NY Times Book Rev* 8/3 "Part of that indefinable thing was a process appropriate to her own stage of life: putting down roots . . . in the very sort of . . . apartment that can save a stroller-pushing mother from turning into a banana." Oct 27 *Birmingham* (Ala) *Post-Herald* 1/2 "Mondale has called Bob [Dole] a bananna [*sic*]." 1977 June 18 "Alice" CBS-TV "If that banana doesn't stop screaming like that, she's gonna scare away all my customers." Aug 1 *New Yorker* 44/2 "To manage, you need the ability to hire and fire, to redeploy, to change responsibilities. And you don't have those things. . . . You could have the worst possible banana and still not be able to bring him up on charges." Aug 13 "Alice" CBS-TV "Will you leave me alone, banana."

2: *adj*, usu **bananas**, but attrib **banana** [*go bananas, BDNE* 1970; *bananas, adj, 6000 Words* 1976] Insane, crazy, nutty 1957 Mar 30 Al Capp "Li'l Abner" in *San Francisco News* 11/3 "They say you're bananas!!" 1966 Sep 2 Al Capp "Li'l Abner" in *San Francisco Examiner* 30/3–7 "I n-never knew goin' bananas was contagious!!" 1970 Sep 12 *TV Guide* 29 "The four of them drive the Redcoats bananas." 1973 "The Laughing Policeman" on "The ABC Sunday Night Movie" ABC-TV shown 30 Nov 1975 "He had a banana name, like . . . Rod-e-ney." Oct 1 *New Yorker* 48–50 "After fifty years of show-biz songs . . . and jokes . . . and sight gags . . . and street talk ('She's driving him bananas')—people are much more inclined to take it [the banana] with the utmost lack of seriousness." 1974 Aug *Fur-Fish-Game* 12/2 "The ten to fifteen pounders who live in the deep, dark waters of your home lake . . . are the ones I'm bananas about." 1977 Aug 13 "Alice" CBS-TV (repeat) "And get your banana self back to work." —**banana cake** *n* Eccentric person, nut, fruitcake 1975 July 24 "Barney Miller" ABC-TV "They've got some banana cake on top of a building with a pair of home-made wings." 1977 Mar 27 "Switch" CBS-TV "You didn't tell me she was a banana cake." —**bananafish**, in the phrase *go bananafish* [nonce variant of *go bananas*] 1972 Nov *Ms.* 77/2 "[The inner life] could keep a poet in solitary confinement in a Russian prison from going mad . . . , a soldier in Korea from being brainwashed, a scientist in a bathysphere from going bananafish." —**Bananasville** 1974 Erma Bombeck *I Lost Everything in the Post-Natal Depression* (Greenwich, Conn: Fawcett) 115 "At thirty-five most parents launch their first teen-ager. After that . . . it's Bananasville all the way." —**bananologist, bananology** *n* Nonce form 1974 Aug *Esquire* 55/1 (picture caption) "Anna Banana fancies herself a bananologist, one who practices the art of being bananas. Send her a dollar and she will happily issue you a master's in bananology." (see also WHAMFART-BANANAS)

barefoot doctor *n* [*World Book Dict* 1976] Earlier quots 1971 Nov *McCall's* 143/1 "The clinics are staffed for the most part by Barefoot Doctors. This is the name given to the thousands of young women and some young men whose job it is to watch over the health of peasant families throughout the rural areas of China. These people are trained in first aid, midwifery, and the treatment of simple diseases, and are able to perform minor surgery and any follow-up care necessary after a patient's illness or operation. They combine medical work with agricultural work, and during the winter go to hospitals for further training. [¶] One of the most important things the Barefoot Doctors do is to encourage family planning and the use of contraceptives. . . . [¶] Barefoot Doctors are trained in both traditional Chinese medicine and Western medicine." 1972 Feb 21 *USN&WR* 18/2 "She may also watch a 'barefoot doctor'—a medical worker with limited training who takes care of simple ailments." 1975 Mar 1 *Science News* 141/3 "The October 1974 issue of the *Chinese Medical Journal* reports that a million 'barefoot doctors'—that is, doctors' assistants—have been sent into China's rural areas." —**barefoot doctoring** *n* 1975 Mar 1 *Science News* 141/3 "The way Americans can really benefit from Chinese medicine . . . is by adopting some of their health care innovations—notably their 'barefoot doctoring.'"

bear (sometimes cap) *n* [prob shortened from SMOKEY (THE) BEAR] State trooper; any law enforcement officer (CB slang) 1975 May *Atlantic* 42/1 "There's a four-wheeler coming up fast behind me, might be a Bear wants to give us some green stamps." 1976 Jan 6 (and often) popular song "Convoy" WNPT, Tuscaloosa, Ala "They even had a bear in the air." June *CB Times* 28/3 (repr from *Heavy Duty Trucking Mag*) "Don't feed any of them cotton-pickin' bears there, guy." 1977 Feb 15 *Midnight* 17/3 (ad) "OUTWIT BEARS (RADAR TRAPS)" May *Reader's Digest* 129/2 "It was also a bit much when you kept referring to Moses the Lawgiver as the 'Sinai Bear.'" —**bear report** *n* Information broadcast by users of citizens band radios concerning the location of police officers 1975 Nov 16 *Parade* 27/4 "All those CB 'bear reports' were actually helping hold speeds down."

bleep *n* [imitative] 1: Toot, squeak, or other meaningless sound 1969 Sep *Electronics World* 38/1 "Groups record feedback and the bloops and bleeps of life outside the studio in the hope of finding the right sound that they can ride to a hit tune." 1971 July *Esquire* 97/1 "When I got there, the orchestra members were just arriving and starting to tune up, at first with solitary bleeps, then the whole hall buzzing and beginning to come alive with a weird but not unpleasant medley."

2: *Specif*, a: short high-pitched sound produced by various electronic devices [*W3* Addenda 1971] 1971 Feb 7 *Family Weekly* 8/1 "When the sound hits an object, it is bounced back to the lower cell which then translates it into a 'bleep' sound. Various objects have different-sounding bleeps."

b: Such a sound superimposed on the sound track of a televised program in order to eliminate certain words regarded as objectionable 1968 Apr 3 *Punch* 510/2 "Unfortunately the censor dictates that some offending words be erased, and they have been replaced by obvious bleeps." Apr 12 *Life* 18/3–4 "Courage at Last—or Just Bleeps? The Smothers Brothers Comedy Hour and Rowan and Martin's Laugh-In." 1970 Sep 12 *TV Guide* 15 "With the way movie morality has been going on the big screens, we can anticipate a busy year for the cutting-room experts in the video-projection rooms, with bleeps aplenty during the riper moments of dialogue." 1971 May 29 *TV Guide* 32/1 "[On a US television network, the BBC program *Till Death Do Us Part*] would wind up as a half hour of pantomime set to bleeps and station breaks."

bleep *vt* [*bleep, n*] Censor, used of broadcast and printed material [*6000 Words* 1976 enters *bleep vt* as a synonym of *blip vt* "to remove (recorded sound) from a videotape so that in the received television program there is an interruption in the sound"] 1970 Oct 24 *Sat Rev* 8/2 "Miss West . . . had just returned from a radio program in which she had had the disconcerting experience of being bleeped. . . . M. F. K. Fisher . . . had said something about there being 'sanctimonious bastards in the Quaker sect'—to which Miss West had replied, 'I may be sanctimonious, but I am not a bastard.' 'And do you know,' she told us, '*her* "bastard" wasn't bleeped—just mine.'" Winter *Northwestern Report* (Northwestern Univ) 47/2 "Rex Reed . . . commented uproariously on the filming of 'Myra Breckenridge' and . . . was bleeped into jumble several times." 1971 Feb 18 *Rolling Stone* 1/1 "Metromedia's stations all play bleeped or otherwise edited tapes of the song." 1974 May 20 *Newsweek* 25/2 "His first glimpse at the published version [of the transcripts of the White House tapes] shook his confidence, and he was not mollified when Mr. Nixon's lawyer, James St. Clair, told him that the White House had bleeped out an unflattering quote of John Ehrlichman's." 1975 Nov 8 *TV Guide* A6/1 (letter) "I bleep anything that I don't like by turning the set off." 1976 May *German Quarterly* 289 "In the back of Volume I [of the 1887 Weimar edition of Goethe's *Römische Elegien*] the editor, Gustav von Loeper, at last revealed that four more elegies were preserved in the same careful Roman script and on the same paper as the published twenty. He printed them there after the manner suggested by Schiller of bleeping certain passages."

bleep, bleep bleep, bleepers, bleeping, bleepity-bleep Substitutes for words regarded as vulgar, controversial, or otherwise censorable 1970 Oct 3 *TV Guide* 18/1 (cartoon caption) "A funny thing happened to me on the Moscow subway today. A man carrying a package came up to me and said, 'Comrade, can you BLEEP, BLEEP, BLEEP, BLEEP, to BLEEP, BLEEP, BLEEP, BLEEP, BLEEP, BLEEP for my wife?' 'No,' I said, 'you BLEEP, BLEEP, BLEEP, BLEEP, BLEEP, BLEEP, BLEEP, BLEEP, BLEEP and BLEEP, BLEEP, BLEEP, BLEEP, BLEEP go BLEEP, BLEEP.' Haw, haw, haw." Nov 14 *TV Guide* 19/1 "In *The Name of the Game* four of us were to crash a truck through a store window, crushing a customer to death.... But a bleeping censor ... walked in to tell us our little wreck was too horrible." 1971 Mar 6 *TV Guide* 35/2 "'*Bleep* with me and you're *bleeping* with dynamite,' roars [Broderick Crawford]." Mar 29 *National Observer* 14/3 "But I also know that in 8 or 10 years, nobody will give a bleep who Phil Esposito is." 1972 Apr 29 *TV Guide* 27/2 "But the critics still had it in for me. Because of my bleepity-bleep name. They wrote things like, 'A surprisingly good performance by Rock Hudson, of all people'... I still get some of that old bleep." June *True* 42/1 "Durocher soon showed he had lost none of his gift for casual obscenity and vituperative analysis. 'That *bleep*,' he said of one player, employing an Anglo-Saxonism that has long been his favorite noun, verb and adjective." 1973 Dec *Field & Stream* 12/2 "Run onto Yankee Point some dark night because you can't see that light and you won't think that old osprey is so bleep bleep beautiful." 1974 June 1 *TV Guide* 24/1 "'Good evening, ladies and *bleepers*—stop kicking my chair, Sonny!' 'Cut.' Now Freeman breaks himself up: 'Ladies and gentiles—ah, *bleep*... will you *please* get Sonny off the set, or tie him up?'" 1975 Sep 15 *Time* 7/1 (letter) "Imagine cutting the word virgin from the script of *M*A*S*H* because they are afraid some child is going to ask his parent what a virgin is.... Oh, and by the way, next Sunday's sermon concerns itself with Jesus and the BLEEP Mary." 1977 May *Verbatim* 3/2 Quot in prelim remarks —In combinations, esp as a substitute for *shit*. Peter Tamony has sent us the following comment: "I have a considerable number of examples of usage after 1965, including *bleep-out, bullbleep, chickenbleep, horsebleeped*." 1970 Mar 10 *Look* 58/1 "Anybody [on the team] who talked to a reporter could go on Durocher's bleep list." 1975 Jan *Field & Stream* 12/2 "You come skulking through the woods like a ruddy Indian as if you wanted to get shot, you... you bleephead, you." 1976 Jan 27 Milt Caniff "Steve Canyon" in *Champaign-Urbana Courier* 14 "Why grow old when you can charter Bughouse Beekman—who is scared bleepless!"

carpool *vi* [*W3, car pool, n*] Travel in a car pool 1973 June 25 *Newsweek* 60/3 "In announcing the proposals, acting EPA administrator Robert Fri said that they conceivably could result in... much greater use of car pooling and mass transportation just about everywhere." 1974 Jan 27 *NY Times Mag* 6/3 "The Government should encourage bundling as a nighttime fuel-saving equivalent to car pooling." July 13 *National Observer* 11/2 "We just car-pooled to Newport." 1977 Mar 8 *Family Circle* 78/3 (ad) "Car pool and combine trips." Mar 8 *Woman's Day* 18/2 (ad) "The U.S. Dept. of Transportation's Federal Highway Administration estimates a driver can save between $281 and $654 a year on a 20-mile daily round trip if he carpools." **—car-pool it** *vb ph* Travel in a car pool, POOL IT 1973 Dec *Ladies' Home Jour* 70/1 (ad) "Car pool it to the supermarket." Dec 10 *Newsweek* 117/3 "Drive in to any of several designated parking lots on your own wheels and then car-pool it to the slopes on somebody else's." 1974 May 27 *Newsweek* 92 (ad) "I began car pooling it to work in 1970." **—carpooler** *n* Member of a car pool 1972 July *Family Circle* 148/3 "I would even drive my daughter and assorted kiddies to nursery school imagining myself a part of a sweet sisterhood of car poolers." 1974 Feb 4 *Newsweek* 66/3 "Instead of paying a 50-cent daily toll, car poolers buy a $12-a-year ticket for an annual saving of about $100 in tolls." Oct *Woman's Day* 138/1 "If you fail to find potential car-poolers at work, check on whether your community has a car-pool program." 1976 June 10 "CBS Evening News" "... give carpoolers a break in California." (see also VAN POOL)

checkbook baseball *n* The practice of paying unusually large amounts of money for and to a few players on a baseball team in an effort to produce a winning or championship team 1977 Apr 23 *TV Guide* A59/1 "To weigh the effects of these developments on the national pastime, reporter Bill Moyers went to the Fort Lauderdale training camp of the team that many have singled out as the most flagrant practitioner of checkbook baseball—the New York Yankees."

checkbook journalism *n* 1: Payment of large sums of money to public figures for televised interviews 1975 Mar 25 *NY Times* 32/2 (editorial) "To avoid charges of 'checkbook journalism'—that is, buying and selling news to the highest bidder but otherwise remaining silent—CBS News maintained that the Haldeman interview was merely a 'memoir.'" Apr 14 *Newsweek* 96/3 "Last month television's ethics came under fire again, this time for the practice labeled checkbook journalism—the payment by broadcasters or publishers of large sums to public figures for exclusive interviews, such as the Haldeman appearance." Aug 25 *Time* 58/2–3 "The Frost–Nixon deal carries Watergate checkbook journalism to its greatest extreme to date.... Frost argues that since Nixon is out of office, the interviews are not news but a memoir and therefore immune to the checkbook charge." 1976 May 17 *Atlanta Constitution* A4/1 (editorial) "When the report, on CIA activities, appeared in full in New York's weekly newspaper, The Village Voice, charges of 'checkbook journalism' were raised again. Checkbook journalism is when a person who is part of a news story is paid to provide exclusive information." Oct 9 *TV Guide* 6/2 "CBS News president Richard Salant..., having paid a reported $50–150,000 for two interviews with former White House aide H. R. Haldeman, is no stranger to *old-style* checkbook journalism." 1977 May 9 *Time* 30/2 "CBS was shy of 'checkbook journalism' after having been widely criticized for buying an interview with Nixon's former chief of staff, Haldeman."
2: The practice of paying an anchorman a salary far above the usual ones in the hope of improving the local or network news program's ratings 1976 Oct 9 *TV Guide* 6/2 "Hunter and Pauley symbolize the *new* checkbook journalism: if you want a performer, *buy* him." Oct 16 *TV Guide* 43/1 "ABC's payment of a million dollars a year for five years to Barbara Walters, not so much for her journalistic excellence as for her star quality, is merely the most publicized example of this new 'checkbook journalism.'"

defensive medicine *n* Practices by physicians that serve more to protect the physician in case of a malpractice suit than to manage or treat the patient's ailment, such as the ordering of clinically unnecessary tests and X-rays 1973 May 26 *Science News* 339/1 "Claims have encouraged physicians to practice defensive medicine: to conduct extra tests that are not medically justified or not to conduct tests that might lead to a suit." 1974 Jan 27 *NY Times* 20/3 "Defensive medicine is the ordering by a physician of many extra, expensive X-rays and other laboratory tests that doctors generally consider unnecessary except for legal self-protection. The practice also includes the refusal to treat high-risk patients." July 20 *Science News* 38/2 "With PSRO decisions to back them, physicians should stop practicing defensive medicine—ordering unnecessary diagnostic tests—in order to ward off malpractice suits." 1975 Mar 31 *Barron's* 3/4 "HEW secretary Caspar Weinberger estimates that between $3 and $5 billion a year is being charged to the public in unnecessary defensive medicine practices." May 7 *Wall St Jour* 20/1 "But malpractice suits also have an indirect cost effect, since many doctors and hospitals now practice 'defensive medicine,' sometimes overtreating patients to avoid liabilities." 1976 Oct *Harper's* 7/1 (ad) "And there are indications [that malpractice premiums will] go even higher as doctors are forced to turn more and more to the practice of 'defensive' medicine. That is, taking X rays, ordering diagnostic tests, etc., etc., etc., when there may be little recognized medical need for them."

family hour, family time, family TV hour, family viewing (hour), family viewing time Two-hour period of prime television time during which programs may not be aired if they are unsuitable for children or if they might offend some viewers (Section 1, "Principles Governing Program Content," of the Television Code of the National Association of Broadcasters states: "Entertainment programming inappropriate for viewing by a general family audience should not be broadcast during the first hour of network entertainment programming in prime time and in the immediately preceding hour," quoted in *TV Guide*, 13 Sep 1975, p 10/1.) 1975 Sep 6 *TV Guide* A1/1 "April 8.... In the room, the 15 members of the Television Board of the National Association of Broadcasters voted 12–3 to insert a 'family viewing standards' regulation into the Code of the NAB. Thus the much publicized 'family hour' was born and the network censors rushed to sharpen their blue pencils, to excise 'gratuitous sex and violence' from early-evening programming." Ibid A5/1 "[Broadcasters] have created a 'family viewing time' that is controversial even before it has started. From 7 to 9 P.M. (ET) nothing may be shown that is not suitable for viewing by small children or anybody else who is easily offended. Now all they have to do is figure out what this means." Sep 13 *TV Guide* 9/1 "Effective this September, the TV stations that subscribe to the industry's Television Code have committed themselves to a principle known as family viewing time. This is an arrangement that sets up a two-hour family-viewing stretch every night of the week." Oct 13 *New Yorker* 142/3 "The networks have lately instituted a self-regulating policy of their own, called 'family viewing time,' which is supposed to keep programming from 7 to 9 P.M. fairly free of violence." Dec 7 *NY Times* Sec 2 D1/1 "The Family Viewing Hour... was designed to be 'a pause in the day's occupations' when the sex and mayhem that normally fills America's television screens is replaced by shows that, according to Tom Swafford, CBS's Vice-President of Program Practices, would embarrass neither parents nor children. The policy, which controls the nature of television programming between the hours of 7 and 9 P.M. (EST)... was put into effect by the networks on Sept. 8 and has been a source of conflict ever since." 1976 Jan 3 *TV Guide* A9/1 (letter) "Clearly, the family viewing concept, is, thus far, something that has not come across to the great mass of the American public in the way it was intended, and therefore, as I have believed from the outset, is doomed to failure." Apr *Psychology Today* 4/2 "All three networks, and notably CBS, have cut back violence on the new 'family hour,' that prime-time slot before nine p.m." June 12 *Sat Rev* 8/2 "The television networks and their tame Washington watchdogs have recently decided that the best way to curb the excess of violence and dunghill drama on TV is to create an antiseptic 'family viewing hour' in the early evening, effectively abandoning the rest of the prime-time schedule to rapes, murders, and other pathological entertainments." Aug 21 *TV Guide* 9/1 "Silverman realized that while violent action-adventure is *verboten* in family time, comic-book-style science fiction is something else." Sep 16 "Mary Hartman, Mary Hartman" WBRC-TV, Ch 6, Birmingham, Ala "Is this the family hour? 'Cause this is a lot of violence for the family hour." Oct 13 *Birmingham* (Ala) *News* 32/4 (heading) "'Baa Baa' too violent for family TV hours, CBS complaint says." Nov 7 *Birmingham* (Ala) *News* A33/1 (AP) "U.S. Dist. Judge Warren G. Ferguson of Los Angeles ruled Thursday that the Federal Communications Commission violated the First Amendment when it pressured networks to adopt the family time." **—post-family-hour** 1976 Dec 25 *TV Guide* A9/1 "The director reports they have deleted words like 'sanitary napkins' (although commercials for them are acceptable) and 'virgin' (although 'whore' can be used freely in other post-family-hour films)." (see also FVT, PTFP)

fruitcake *adj* [Wentworth & Flexner, *Dict of Am Slang, fruitcake, n* 1952] Crazy, nuts, BANANAS 1942 June 12 *San Francisco Examiner* 18/7

"If you had lost... I guess you would have gone fruitcake." 1976 Sep 17 Master of ceremonies on "Concentration" CBS-TV "The audience is going fruitcake, 'cause they know the answer."

fundraiser *n* [*World Book Dict* 1976 "a person who raises funds, especially for nonprofit organizations"] Party or other event held for the purpose of raising money for a cause, usu a political campaign or a charity 1972 Feb 21 *USN&WR* 44/1 (picture caption) "A Democratic fund-raiser; sale of tickets over $100 must be reported now." 1974 Feb 22 *New Times* (NYC) 16/1–2 "Some Republican members of the Judiciary Committee were not at all pleased when they found out Jenner... had sat on the dais at a Stevenson fund raiser." 1976 Feb 9 *Time* 14/1 "Not until December did he hold his first formal fund raiser, long after the other candidates had started collecting money." May 22 *TV Guide* A92/1 "The precision robbery of a charity fund-raiser ends in quite a surprise for the thieves, who learn that the stolen moneybags are filled with paper." Sep *Harper's Bazaar* 152 "I love to organize things, especially putting together a big-scale party—mostly as benefits or fund-raisers for the people and concerns we believe in." 1977 Jan 15 *TV Guide* 33/2 "' By moving the [Pro Bowl] game to locations never before exposed to it, we are hoping to draw better.' [¶] From Seattle, the permanently established floating fund-raiser will shift next to Tampa, where it also will be tied to the season-ticket sales of the home team."

FVT [family *viewing* time] FAMILY HOUR 1976 June 5 *TV Guide* 5/1 "It is possible for Family Viewing Time supporters to be encouraged by the 8-per-cent rise in awareness to [*sic*] FVT over *TV Guide*'s poll six months ago; but its detractors can point to the fact that 50 per cent of America's adults still don't even know that FVT exists, and only 11 per cent said FVT has had any effect on their viewing habits."

neural efficiency *n* The efficiency of the brain in processing information, as indicated by the speed with which it responds to flashes of light (Neural efficiency, tested with the neural efficiency analyzer, is believed by some to be a valid measure of intelligence, culture-free and unbiased by the subject's stress.) 1972 Feb *Pop Sci* 73/1 "The Neural Efficiency Analyzer computes the average time delay between the onset of the stimulus and each of two particular electrical responses of the brain. Readout—the neural efficiency 'score'—is the average time in milliseconds. Thus, the lower the number you score, the higher your neural efficiency." Ibid 73/3 "Now in production after a dozen years of research and development, the Neural Efficiency Analyzer is the invention of Dr. John Ertl, Director of the Center of Cybernetic Studies at the University of Ottawa." Winter *EDUCOM Bulletin* 21–22 "The machine, called a neural-efficiency analyzer, completes a test in less than three minutes. The machine has five basic parts: a helmet equipped with electrodes to pick up brain waves, a device to amplify the waves, an oscilloscope on which the waves can be monitored visually, a flashing light to stimulate the brain, and a computer to analyze the efficiency with which the brain processes the light flashes.... Ertl's invention reputedly yields a valid measure of native intelligence, whether the person being tested is illiterate, a newborn infant, or an established genius.... It has already discovered a number of very bright children who have been erroneously labeled dull or retarded on the basis of conventional IQ scores."

news hole *n* [cf *W3*, *hole*, *n* 2 b "an unfilled or blank area (as in a page or column printed or to be printed)"] Amount of space (in print journalism) or air time (in broadcast journalism) available for news stories 1973 Sep 17 *Newsweek* 76/3 "As a result, many smaller American newspapers—and some big ones, including The Wall Street Journal—were reducing their 'news holes,' restricting advertising and cutting back on the number of newsstand copies." 1974 May 27 *Newsweek* 87/1–2 "The problem [adequate coverage of other news when so much coverage is given Watergate] is most acute for TV, where the 'news hole' already is small.... Newspapers have much more room, and it is easier for them to expand the news hole." 1975 Feb 5 *NY Times* 14/2 "Another method of saving costs in the newsroom is to cut back on the 'news hole'—the amount of space devoted to news presentation—and many newspapers are doing that." 1976 Sep–Oct *Columbia Journ Rev* 30/2 "He contends that network news organizations no longer need the political conventions to prove their manhood.... 'The papers don't report all the dreck; when things are slow, they cut down the size of the news hole. Why shouldn't we do the same?'" Dec 25 *TV Guide* A5/2 "The men and women who fill the 'news hole' simply don't know anything about Japanese, Swedish (or anybody's) politics."

pool it *vb ph* Drive or ride in a car pool, CARPOOL (rr) 1974 Feb 4 *Newsweek* 66/1–2 (picture caption) "Pooling it to work at Ford: The 'in' method for saving gasoline." —**pooler** *n* CARPOOLER, member of a car pool 1973 Dec 31 *Newsweek* 7/2 "Computer printouts cross-match zip codes for three Boston insurance companies, while radio stations in Miami, Dallas, Lansing and Fort Worth, among other cities, have launched match-making services for potential poolers in their audiences." 1974 Feb 4 *Newsweek* 66/3 "[He] plunked down $700 two weeks ago for a full-page ad in a Chicago newspaper in an attempt to enlist potential poolers." —**poolmate** *n* Fellow member of a car pool 1974 Oct *Woman's Day* 4/2 "You may have to join the program of a nearby firm if you work for a small organization with no potential poolmates for you." —**pooling** 1976 Oct 16 *National Observer* 8/5 "The 3M company originated its plan in April 1973 with six vans; today it's a pooling leader with 79 vehicles in daily service."

PTFP [prime time family programming] FAMILY HOUR 1975 Sep 13 *TV Guide* 10/2 "We sense that a broadcaster consensus has already developed which considers extraneous violence, and explicit sexual subject matter as 'out of bounds' in PTFP. That is, Prime Time Family Programming—which is to lead into each evening's television fare."

smokey, smokey (the) bear (often cap *s* and *b*) *n* [from the similarity in the hats worn by many state troopers and that worn by Smokey Bear as pictured in advertising of the campaign for forest fire prevention] State trooper or other law enforcement officer, BEAR 1975 June 27 *New Times* (NYC) 42/2 "The van is trying to break 39 hours for the journey, and any interruption by the smokeys, the cops, would be excruciating." 1976 Apr

Progressive Farmer 119/1 "Their main purpose is to keep on the lookout for the highway patrol, lovingly called 'Smokey the Bear.'" May 10 *Time* 78/3 "Truck drivers installed the [CB] units to warn each other of lurking cops ('smokey bears') and radar cars ('Kojak with a Kodak')." Nov 7 *Birmingham* (Ala) *News* A15/1–2 "'Smokey' is truckers' jargon for a policeman." 1977 Aug *CB Bible* 8/2 "Oklahoma State Trooper Bob Carleton sat down and penned a pamphlet called 'CB's and Bear Facts,' designed to educate CBers as to what Smokey needs to know in an emergency." Aug 14 *Family Weekly* 14/3 "The truckers spoke in an elaborate code—highway patrolmen were 'Smokey the Bear' because of the wide-brimmed hats they wore." —**Smokey report** *n* CB radio reports on the location of police cars 1976 Feb 25 *Tuscaloosa News* 9/7 "Sure the constant Smokey reports get annoying." June *CB Times* 24/2 "Much criticism, in particular, has been focused on truckers' use of their two-ways to pass along 'Smokey reports'—the location of highway patrol vehicles."

van pool *n* [cf *W3*, car pool, *n*] 1974 Oct *Woman's Day* 138/2 "Van pools are working so well at Minnesota Mining and Manufacturing's huge complex just outside St. Paul that the company now has fifty-seven company-owned vans." 1976 Oct 16 *National Observer* 8/5 "The typical van pool works like this: An employer buys or leases a 12-passenger van and turns it over to a volunteer driver, who recruits a minimum of eight passengers. The company buys the gasoline and insurance and sets fares to cover the costs. The driver gets a free ride, personal use of the van in off hours at a low per-mile cost, and sometimes gets a percentage of the fares. Passengers get door-to-door transportation and freedom from commuting and parking." —**van pooling** *n* 1974 Oct *Woman's Day* 138/3 "Your own boss might be encouraged to try van-pooling if you tell him about governmental incentives offered." 1976 Oct 16 *National Observer* 8/4 "Van pooling is a new commuting style looking for a permanent place in transportation between private cars and mass-transit facilities." 1977 Mar 8 *Woman's Day* 21/1 (ad) "Vanpooling increased interest in carpooling too."

whamfartbananas *adj* [intens of BANANAS] 1977 Feb *Analog* 153/1 "I'm going whamfartbananas already. I'll be a basket case by the time I'm confirmed, you realize that?"

[Received August 1977]

AMONG THE NEW WORDS

I. WILLIS RUSSELL AND MARY GRAY PORTER

University of Alabama

THE APPEARANCE of *narrowcasting* 'cable television transmission' as an entry in the 1978 edition of the *World Book Dictionary* is interesting because the word has been around for a good many years, though not in this sense.

As will be seen from the quotations in our entry, the word in another sense appeared nearly 30 years ago in the 1949 *Britannica Book of the Year* article "Words and Meanings, New," but to our knowledge it never caught on, possibly because subscription radio and TV never caught on. Commenting on the word in the preliminary checklist for the *Britannica Book of the Year* article, which the American Dialect Society Committee on New Words then prepared, the late Atcheson L. Hench, a member of the Committee, wrote the chairman: "1932 I have an example of this word in a different meaning—the use of a beam of light to carry messages by voice. [¶] My point is that though your meaning is new, the word is not. [¶] Let me know if you want my quotation." Which, alas, the editor never did.

Underlying all the uses of *narrowcasting* in the second entry below is the idea of restriction of the audience, either to subscribers or to certain demographic groups. We hence list all citations in one chronological order.

Acknowledgments: Helen B. Lewis (1), Mamie Meredith (2), Michael Rainer (2), Anne B. Russell (1). Thanks are also due to Evelyn McMillan for help in the definition of -*gate*.

-**gate** *combining form* [*Watergate, World Book Dict* 1976] Scandal involving charges of corruption and usually of coverup (added to a noun that in some way suggests the particular scandal) —**Cartergate** 1978 Mar *Penthouse* 30/2 "I want to thank Craig S. Karpel for the immense amount of work he has put into his 'Cartergate' series." —**Cattlegate** 1976 Apr 11 *Tuscaloosa News* D14/7 (*Washington Post*) "[A Democrat in the Michigan legislature has said that state agencies have been slow to investigate the contamination of some cattle feed by PBB so as not to embarrass certain powers in the state Republican Party.] Farmers in Zuiderveen's Missaukee County have distributed bumper stickers that say, 'PBB: Cattlegate Bigger Than Watergate.'" —**Dallasgate** 1975 Oct 1 *Modern People* (Franklin Park, Ill) 1 (heading) "SHOCKING 'DALLASGATE' REVEALED" [concerning a JFK coverup] —**Hollywoodgate** 1978 Jan 23 *Newsweek* 55/3 "Rumors of a coverup spread, and journalists scurried to investigate what some were already calling Hollywoodgate." —**Koreagate** 1977 Jan 3 *Time* 84/1 "Actually, the Woodstein [Maxine Cheshire] of Koreagate is no stranger to Page One." Sep 20 *Star* 10/5-6 "Republicans call the scandal 'Koreagate' and plan to make it the chief issue in the 1978 congressional election." Nov 9 *Wall St Jour* 26/2 (editorial) "But it does occur to us that a society sated with Watergate, Koreagate, Bert Lance, the CIA and corporate layoffs might learn something from the program ['I, Claudius']." Dec 19 *Newsweek* 35/1 1978 Jan *Esquire* 40/3 Jan 12 "NBC News" "[Congress may be able to discipline some 20 senators] in connection with what may be called Koreagate." Feb 27 *Tuscaloosa News* 4/3-5 (cartoon) Mar 13 *Newsweek* 29/1 "[Tongsun] Park was seeing quite a lot of Leon Jaworski, special counsel for the House ethics committee's Koreagate probe. Jaworski dominated the early sessions in a hearing room of the Rayburn House Office Building, relentlessly trying to shake Park's assertion that he was working for himself—not for the Korean Government—when he gave hundreds of thousands of dollars to U.S. congressmen." —**Laborgate** 1974 Jan 5 *TV Guide* 10/1 "'Watergate' became an international symbol of corruption. (A French vintage scandal became 'Winegate'; crooked Southeast Asian unions produced a 'Laborgate.')" —**Lancegate** 1977 Oct 16 *NY Times Mag* (sec 6) 38/1 (Wm Safire) "Lancegate is no Watergate. The Nixon men had years to weave a tangled web of illegal eavesdropping and break-ins, and the Carter men had hardly a month to play what one may charitably call a downplaying of Bert Lance's problems" 1978 Jan *Esquire* 40/3 "And then there was Lancegate." —**Media-gate** 1978 May 2 *Atlanta Constitution* A-5/3 (Jesse Jackson) "You might say that when it comes to serving and recognizing blacks and other minorities, the press has its own coverup scandal—maybe we ought to call it Mediagate." —**Motorgate** 1976 Apr 3 (Cleveland) *Plain Dealer* A-12 "LOWELL, Mass. (AP)—A former auto service manager was sentenced to three to five years in prison yesterday in the first of a series of fraud cases resulting from the 'Motorgate' affair. [¶] Judge Henry Chmielinski called the case, which involves the submission of fradulent warranty claims to General Motors, 'a quagmire of corruption, a cesspool, a systematic, carefully organized case of wholesale corruption.'" —**Scrantongate** 1978 Feb 27 *Time* 20/3 "What is known is that *Post* Reporter Nancy Collins penetrated perhaps the most elaborate security precautions ever thrown around the birth of a book, and that her coup touched off a divisive row in the publishing community that some newsmen quickly dubbed 'Scrantongate.'" (H. R. Haldeman's *The Ends of Power* was bound at Scranton, Pennsylvania, where copies were apparently acquired by unauthorized persons.) —**Volgagate** 1973 Aug *National Lampoon* 27/2 "There have been persistent rumors in Russia of a vast scandal involving high-ranking members of the Communist bureaucracy in a serious conspiracy. Implicated in 'the Volgagate' are a group of liberal officers who were caught removing bugs from telephones, mixing actual letters and telegrams from Soviet citizens in with the usual phony ones, telling the truth to foreign newsmen, slipping real documents into fabricated official histories of the Khrushchev era, and trying to influence the outcome of normally rigged nominations to the Communist Party Presidium by surreptitiously introducing genuine ballots into the vote counts. Perhaps more seriously, all of them have refused to lie at their trials or participate in the traditional cover-up process." —**Winegate** 1973 Sep 10 *Newsweek* 66/2-3 "Last week the French wine industry was in ferment over the disclosure of a fraudulent scheme to peddle cheap wine as expensive Bordeaux.... 'You'll think it's exaggerating to say this, but the U.S. had Watergate and now we have our winegate,' a Bordeaux journalist told *Newsweek*'s Seth Goldschlager." Nov 20 *SR/World* 45/1 "At the very time Washington was going through its tortured inquiries, Bordeaux writhed in its great wine scandal. The cast included inspectors who didn't inspect, judges who didn't judge, officials who were more eager to camouflage the trickery than reveal it.... Inevitably, the brouhaha of Bordeaux became known as Wine-gate." Ibid 45/2 "Wine-gate has forced other feuds to the surface, notably the religious and social frictions between the *chartrons*, whose forebears were Protestant émigré traders, and the Roman Catholics, who are wine growers." 1974 Jan 5 *TV Guide* 10/1 Quot sv Labor-gate Nov 8 Garrick Utley NBC-TV "In France they call it the Winegate mentality." Nov 18 *Time* 45/1 1975 Feb *Harper's Bazaar* 71/1 "Although the recent Bordeaux 'Winegate' revelations have shaken everyone's faith, French wines marked VDQS or Appelation [*sic*] Controllée, Italian DOC wines and German Qualitätsweins still offer some reassurance." 1976 Helen MacInnes *Agent in Place* (Greenwich, Conn: Fawcett) 48 "'It's safer drinking bourbon than Bordeaux nowadays,' Brad suggested, and that launched Tony into a hilarious version of the 'Winegate' scandal in France."

narrowcast *vb* 1932 See preliminary remarks 1937 in 1938 *Am Sp* 13:160/1 "'Truly broadcasting is becoming less and less broadcast and more and more *narrowcast*,' commented a writer on the editorial page of the Lincoln (Nebraska) *Journal and Star* for August 25, 1937." 1948 Jan 31 *Sat Rev of Lit* 30/1 "Other broadcasters condemned it [subscription radio] as being 'narrowcasting' instead of 'broadcasting,' because the audience would be narrowed down to those who would pay a nickel a day for the service." Feb 2 *Time* 67/1 "Radiomen who like radio the way it is have an outraged squeal of their own ('Narrowcasting!') at the whole idea [of subscription radio]." 1949 *Brit Book of the Year* 773/1 "*narrowcasting, n* Term used by its opponents to describe subscription radio." 1970 July 18 *TV Guide* 20 "Don Durgin, NBC-TV president, lately has plumped for 'broadcasting rather than narrowcasting,' implying that too much prime-time programming has had older-age 'skew' and too little has appealed to *all* ages." 1972 May 27 *TV Guide* 12/1 "[Cable television's] chief advantage, he says, is its selectivity; candidates for lower-level offices need never again 'broadcast' their message prodigally to large masses of viewers who can't vote for them; instead, they'll 'narrowcast' it cheaply only to those who can." 1973 Mar 10 *TV Guide* 31/3-32/1 "Cable 10 [Vancouver, BC] might be compared—roughly—to a small U.S. public-television station.... But it's wired narrowcasting rather than broadcasting."

AMONG THE NEW WORDS

I. WILLIS RUSSELL AND MARY GRAY PORTER
University of Alabama

DECIMAL INCH seems to have been a word of the year 1963 that never caught on, judging by its absence from recent dictionaries and the paucity of citations in our files: only the ones given in our entry below.

On the other hand, *empty calorie*, though not yet entered in the dictionaries we have checked, still seems to be thriving in spite of the refusal of many nutritionists to use the term. As a former colleague in nutrition indignantly remarked back in the sixties when the term began to be used, a calorie is a calorie. Nevertheless, some writers continue to make a distinction between the calories in foods that supply other nutrients and the "empty" calories in foods that supply little more than calories.

Acknowledgments: Paul Alexander (2), R. F. Bauerle (2).

anti-gas guzzler 1977 Apr 25 "CBS News" "... the administration's anti-gas guzzler tax ..."

blocktime *n* 1972 June 19 *USN&WR* 102/3 "In this case, the mandatory hours—blocktime—run fom 8 to 11:40 a.m. and from 2 to 4 p.m." See also quots svv FLEXIBLE (WORK) TIME, etc and GLIDING SHIFT, etc

cafe coronary 1974 Dec 15 *Birmingham* (Ala) *News* D-26/3 (CS-T) "I've been very impressed with the fine publicity given to the 'Heimlich maneuver,' which can be lifesaving for someone who has 'cafe coronary' (food stuck in the throat)." 1978 Jan–Feb *Sat Eve Post* 87/1 "All too often, persons in restaurants are thought to have had a heart attack only to be found at autopsy with a large ball of steak wedged against the epiglottis. This mistaken diagnosis has become so common that the medical profession refers to these chokings as 'cafe coronaries.'"

CAT [BDNE 1970; WNCD8 1973; 6000 Words, WBD 1976] Earlier quots 1960 Apr 11 *Time* 63/2 "There appears an ominous possibility: that the aircraft was torn apart in mid-air by a phenomenon which airmen and meteorologists have taken to calling CAT—for 'clear air turbulence.' If the theory proves to be true, pilots will have to find ways to keep their ships out of CAT's claws." Oct 3 *Time* 54/1 "Clear air turbulence is exactly what it sounds like: an airplane speeding through a cloudless part of the sky can be ripped apart by an invisible tempest. CAT is most often met just above or just below the 30,000-35,000-ft. jet stream.... It has been agreed that CAT is caused by wind shear—the 'friction' between adjacent air masses moving at different speeds." 1965 *Brit Book of the Year* 869/1 "Words and Meanings, New"

cockapoo *n* [cocker spaniel + *-a-* + poodle] 1970 Nov 21 *TV Guide* 24/2 "[They share] a house with two female cockapoo dogs, an integrated mixture of cocker spaniel and poodle, respectively named Miss Carriage and Miss Cegenation." 1971 Oct *Atlantic* 84/1 "I have a cockapoo: it's a cross between a cocker and a poodle." 1975 Feb *Town & Country* 66/1 "Nor do we mean the 'newer breeds' that the purists dismiss as half-breeds (such as the Cockapoo, a Poodle/Cocker Spaniel combo)."

cockapopso *n* [cockapoo + Lhasa apso (with spelling change)] 1971 Dec 4 *TV Guide* 44/2 "Eve Arden has a cockapopso in addition to the Lhasa apso."

cowboy economics 1972 Adam Smith *Supermoney* (NY: Pop Libr) 249 "Thus, probably the corporation is not going to pay up unless the society compels it, induces, inveigles it or brings it about in some other way. The vision of good is simply too far removed from the vision of what has been perfectly good in the hundreds of years of cowboy economics."

cowboy economy 1972 Sep *Atlantic* 50/1 "To paraphrase University of Colorado economist Kenneth Boulding, man has lived through history in a 'cowboy economy' with 'illimitable plains' and 'reckless, exploitative, romantic, and violent behavior.' Consumption was 'linear'—that is, materials were extracted from supposedly infinite resources and waste was tossed into infinite dumps." (See SPACEMAN ECONOMY for continuation of this quot) 1976 Jan 12 *Harper's Weekly* 19/4-5 "The struggle is between those who would continue the growth-oriented sort of cowboy economy—man is the master of nature, the stock market, the last 150 years of this country—with the nuclear plants as the catalyst for the struggle with the group, probably influenced in some subtle way by Eastern religions, who are more into balance and harmony with nature, less dependence on technology, and certainly not the notion of compulsive growth which has been so critical to the nation's economic expansion."

decimal inch 1963 June 9 *NY Times* F-1/2 "Take a look at the decimal inch. It's an inch cut into 10 parts, and it represents an answer to backers of the metric system." 1964 *Brit Book of the Year* 868/1 "Words and Meanings, New"

empty calorie *usu pl* See *AS* 41: 138 Additional quots 1970 Aug 21 *Life* 47/1 "The meals above show another American diet problem: what we eat is chock full of things that have plenty of calories but little or no nutritional value. The carbonated and alcoholic beverages ... represent 'empty calories.'" 1971 Sep *Family Circle* 47/1 (ad) "If you like to nibble between meals, chances are you fill up on a lot of empty calories." Nov 1 *Moneysworth* 3/1 "The consumer advocate who rocked the country in July, 1970, with proof that most American dry breakfast cereals are devoid of nutrition and consist of 'empty calories,' reports that his revelations had an effect on the market for about three months." 1975 Jan 24 *Harper's Weekly* 2/3 "Recipe writers could do American readers a great favor by promoting the use of more fruit and fewer 'empty-calorie' sweets." 1977 Apr 9 *TV Guide* A5/1-2 "'Experts'... have complained that Americans are stuffing themselves with 'junk foods' and 'empty calories'—by which they mean such 'non-nutritious' fare as hot dogs, potato chips, white bread, dry cereals, cookies, candy, soda pop and other nationally popular snacks." Apr 15 *New Times* (NYC) 31/2 "In a country where... one-fifth of the public is dangerously overweight, most people need empty calories as much as Richard Nixon needs Carl Bernstein." —**empty-caloried** *adj* 1974 Feb *Family Circle* 20/1 "Chocolate... is also naturally bitter, so it requires huge amounts of empty-caloried sugar to sweeten it up."

energy guzzler *n* [prob after *gas guzzler*] 1977 Nov 15 *Family Circle* 115/2 "Use these methods to muzzle the energy guzzlers in your house and you'll begin to see really important savings in your gas and electric bills."

flexible (work) time; flex(i)time [*flextime*, 6000 Words 1976, World Book Dict 1978] 1972 June 19 *USN&WR* 100/1 "A novel plan that allows employes flexibility in choosing their own working hours is gaining favor abroad. . . . [¶] Flextime also is showing up in the U.S." 1973 Feb 4 *NY Times* F-1/2 "Flexible time, or flextime, allows an employe to choose—within guidelines—his own starting and finishing times." 1974 Feb *Nation's Cities* 42/2-3 "Relatively few American employers have heard of, much less tried, 'flextime,' but in Western Europe it has built a solid performance record in more than 5,000 firms and several governmental agencies since it was invented in 1967. [¶] Flextime permits employees some flexibility in setting their own work schedules. Workers have to be on the job certain core hours, but then have freedom—within certain limits—to decide when they want to start and when they want to finish, provided that they complete the required number of hours in that pay period." Spring *Occupational Outlook Quarterly* 6/3 "Another type of rearranged work schedule currently receiving much attention is the concept of 'flexi-time,' also called 'flexible work time' or 'gliding work hours.' This pattern, which usually retains a standard length workweek, generally requires workers to put in a certain number of hours each month. They may start work at any time within a certain band of hours in the morning, however, and quit any time during a similar afternoon time period. Timeclocks or other timekeeping devices usually keep track of the number of hours each employee works." Sep *Town & Country* 166/4 "Flextime applies mostly to employees at the paper-pushing level. Insurance and financial houses and government offices have had great success with flextime." 1975 Mar *Selected US Gov't Publications* 4/3 "*FLEXITIME.* A handbook for managers and employees who want to know more about developing a flexible work schedule. Produced by the U.S. Civil Service Commission, this handbook defines the 'Flexitime' program as a system which enables employees to determine their own hours of arrival and departure from the office." 1978 Mar 1 Madison *Wisconsin State Jour* sec 4, 1/1 "For Lois Rickens, flexitime means she can fix breakfast for her 11-year-old son and get him to school before she reports to work as a secretary for Control Data Corp. . . . [¶] For Control Data, the program of flexible work hours initiated in 1973 has meant happier and, presumably, more productive workers at virtually no cost."

gasahol, gasohol *n* 1973 Sep 9 *Family Weekly* inside front cover (Senator Roman L Hruska, replying to question "With gasoline supplies so tight, can't a substitute be found?") "Several years ago, the state of Nebraska experimented on something called 'gasohol.' It explored the utilization of alcohol distilled from grain and blended on a basis of ten percent alcohol to 90 percent gasoline. It was found that this mix can be successfully burned in any existing automobiles." 1974 Apr 27 *Business Week* 15/1 (letter) "Your item on 'gasahol' (Energy roundup, Mar. 16) reminds me of the Chemurgic Council organized by industry and government in the late 1930s to find industrial uses for the vast farm surpluses of that time. [¶] One result was the 90/10 blend of gasoline and denatured alcohol sold in the Midwest under the trade name Agrol." 1975 Jan 18 *Science News* 41/2 "To help meet the energy crisis, Nebraska is buying ethyl alcohol and other by-products of pulp mill waste liquor . . . to mix with gasoline for a fleet of state cars and trucks. They call the mixture, containing 10 percent ethanol, 'gasohol.'" 1976 July 14 Spokesman for Nebraska delegation, Democratic National Convention, CBS TV "Nebraska, whose efficient food producers are working to ease our energy shortage through the production of gasohol . . . casts its vote . . ." 1977 Dec 11 *Birmingham* (Ala) *News* A-12/1 (CDN) "The 'gasohol' that Robinson sold about two weeks ago was a mixture of 500 gallons of standard unleaded gasoline and 55 gallons of alochol [*sic*] made from corn stalks." 1978 June 1 *Wash Spectator and Between the Lines* (Public Concern Foundation, Inc) 4/2 "In Nebraska, a combination of gasoline and alcohol, called 'gasohol,' is being sold." Aug 13 *Birmingham* (Ala) *News* A-3/1 (AP) "Brazil's ultimate goal is to produce 'gasohol' not only from sugar cane but also from the common cassava plant and from the babacu palm which grows wild in the Amazon jungle." Sep 13 *Tuscaloosa News* 49/1 "Most cars run better on 'gasahol' than gasoline, especially older models."

gas guzzler *n* 1: Automobile that has a high rate of gasoline consumption per mile c1975 Anthony Sampson *The Seven Sisters* (NY: Bantam, 1976) 320 "The reign of Big Car seemed to have abruptly ended; in Detroit in the height of the crisis, there was a pervasive gloom about the prospects for the 'gas-guzzlers' on which the city's industry had so long depended." 1977 May 9 *Newsweek* 23/1-2 (cartoon caption; rpt from *New Yorker*) "[Car salesman to prospective buyer:] 'This may be your last chance to acquire a superpowered, oversize, hyperpolluting gas-guzzler. Don't blow it.'" June 16 AP Feature "Scope on Portland" Teleprompter Cable TV, Ch 7, Tuscaloosa, Ala "Keep those cars known as gas-guzzlers in the garage." Dec 8 *Birmingham* (Ala) *Post-Herald* 1/1 (AP) "Under the gas-guzzler agreement, the purchaser of a 1979-model car that gets between 14 and 15 miles per gallon would pay a tax of $200." 1978 Sep 25 *Newsweek* 74/2 "Under [EPA fuel-efficiency standards] each [automaker] must achieve a 'corporate average fuel economy' (CAFE) level of 19 miles per gallon in 1979 models—and 27.5 miles a gallon by 1985. To keep within the ceiling, a company must sell enough fuel-efficient compacts to offset sales of gas-guzzlers." 2: [Cf "*gas hog. Slang.* One using more than his share of rationed gasoline" in *Ten Eventful Years* (Chicago: Encyclopaedia Britannica, Inc, 1947) 4: 640/2] One who manufactures or drives such an automobile 1977 Sep 17 *TV Guide* 70/2 "The car was performing, and performing pretty well, on manure—or, more exactly, methane gas, which [he] extracts from manure. [He] told me he got his manure free from farmers and that barnyards were certain to outlast oil fields. [¶] It made me wonder who really was off the beam . . . he . . . or I, the gas-guzzler?" 1978 Apr 11 *Esquire* 100/2 "Like the guzzlers of the famous three-martini lunch, the gas guzzlers of Detroit have been put on warning: they can be fined for bad habits." See also ANTI-GAS GUZZLER, ENERGY GUZZLER, GUZZLER

gas-guzzling *adj* 1974 Jan 7 *Newsweek* 18/3 "Sales of gas-guzzling standard-size cars have plummeted in recent weeks, as conservation- and price-minded consumers rushed to buy the subcompact models." c1975 Anthony Sampson *The Seven Sisters* (NY: Bantam, 1976) 355 "For the substance that was burned up by gas-guzzling cars was also now the basis of petrochemicals, and fertilizers which could transform the agriculture of the poorer countries." 1977 May 2 *National Observer* 1/5 "PLEBISCITE BALLOT Do you approve President Carter's plan for a . . . Gas-Guzzling-Auto Tax?" June 24 radio newscast, WSGN, Birmingham, Ala "The Senate approved a watered-down version of President Carter's tax on gas-guzzling cars."

gliding shift; gliding work(ing) hours; gliding (working) time 1972 June 19 *USN&WR* 100/1 "The most-liberal and most-popular system—known as 'gliding working time'—allows employes to change working hours from day to day. [¶] Under this plan, workers must be on the job for certain fixed hours each day, five days a week. This is called 'blocktime,' often consisting of three hours in the morning and two in the afternoon." Ibid 102/1 "In 1970, Lufthansa German Airlines tried out the system in one of its offices. It then extended it to many other units and now is considering putting its technical workshops on a comparable program, with 'gliding shifts.'" Ibid 102/3 (continuation of quot SV BLOCKTIME) "'Gliding time' is from 6:30 a.m. to 8 and between 4 and 6 p.m." Ibid "Brown Boveri . . . has found that the 'psychological effect' of the change to flextime has been favorable. Most of its employes are on 'gliding working hours.'" 1973 Apr *Reader's Digest* 232/2-234/1 "Some firms . . . are adopting shorter work weeks or 'gliding time' (in which employes pick the eight hours each day they'd prefer to work)." 1974 Spring *Occupational Outlook Quarterly* 6/3 Quot SV FLEXIBLE (WORK) TIME, etc

guzzler *n* GAS GUZZLER 1975 Oct 6 *Newsweek* 74 (heading) "RATING THE '76 CARS: TURNING GUZZLERS INTO SIPPERS."

Heimlich hug /ˈhaɪmlɪk/ HEIMLICH MANEUVER 1978 Jan-Feb *Sat Eve Post* 87/2 "Many letters from rescuers describe the tremendous force with which the compacted food explodes from the mouth of the victim after the Heimlich 'hug.'"

Heimlich maneuver [*World Book Dict* 1977] Additional quots 1974 Dec 15 *Birmingham* (Ala) *News* D-26/3 Quot SV CAFE CORONARY 1975 Jan 31 *Harper's Weekly* 10/2 (quoted from *Parade,* 17 Nov 1974) "Ever hear of the 'Heimlich Maneuver'? . . . The maneuver consists of standing behind the choking victim, quickly clasping both arms around the victim's waist, one hand gripping the other wrist, and then pressing forcefully into the victim's diaphragm just below the ribs. This maneuver compresses the lung and expels the matter choking the victim." 1976 Jan *House & Garden* 16/3 "Here are the instructions for the Heimlich Maneuver, which has just been officially endorsed by the AMA as a lifesaving rescue device—but you should learn it through your Board of Health or First Aid Instruction Class and practice it only under approved medical supervision." Feb *Ladies' Home Jour* 40/2 "The surgeon describes his 'Heimlich Maneuver' in the *Journal of the American Medical Association:* 'Stand behind the victim and wrap your arms around his waist. Grasp your right fist with your left hand and place the thumb side of the fist against the victim's abdomen, just below the rib cage. Press your fist into the victim's abdomen with a *quick upward thrust.* Repeat several times, if necessary.'" Aug *Reader's Digest* 167/2 Aug *Southern Living* 25 (ad) See also quots SVV CAFE CORONARY, HUG OF LIFE

Heimlich sign Gesture made by grasping one's throat; recommended for use by food-choked victim who is conscious but unable to speak 1977 June 7 Public-service message by Dr Henry J Heimlich, WTCG-TV, Ch 17, Atlanta, Ga "Put your hand to your throat in the Heimlich sign that says 'I'm choking.'"

-hop See *AS* 47: 272-74; 48: 135-36 Additional illus **—bed-hop** 1975 Dec 21 Alistair Cooke on PBS ". . . in between the bed-hoppings . . ." 1978 June 5 *Time* 61/3 "Lesley Anne Down graduated to playing . . . a bed-hopping socialite in the film version of Harold Robbins' *The Betsy.*" **—city-hop** 1968 June 9 *NY Times* XX-15/6-8 (heading in ad) "City-Hopping Is The Thing That Makes Touring So Much Fun." 1972 Oct 6 *Life* 49/1 "Yet, up in his campaign plane, city-hopping across the country, the candidate himself is buoyant with optimism." **—foundation-hop** 1960 Vivienne Koch *Change of Love* 181 "There's a whole generation of writers who're nothing but foundation-hoppers. They've no sooner received one grant, than they're applying for the next." June 23 *Reporter* 17/1 "Professorial conversation abounds with references to promoters, operators, and foundation hoppers, and to academic boondoggling and projectitis." **—station-hop** 1961 Oct 8 *NY Times* XX-13/4 "Station hopping means riding slower trains, getting off at each interesting town along the way, spending two to three hours looking over each town and then continuing to the next spot by another passing local train."

hug of life HEIMLICH MANEUVER 1977 May 30 *Newsweek* 12/2 "Dr. Henry J. Heimlich . . . devised the technique. . . . Air pressure forces the obstruction from the windpipe like the cork from a champagne bottle. Endorsed by medical authorities and the American Red Cross, the 'hug of life' is now widely taught in schools, industry and the armed forces."

individual working time 1972 June 19 *USN&WR* 100/1-2 "The second plan in fairly common use is often termed 'individual working time.' Under this system, the employe each month may choose among several fixed working schedules for his plant or office."

personhood *n* [*BDNE* 1971; *World Book Dict* 1976] Earlier quots 1964 Aug 7 *Life* 40/4-71/1 "For, the more mature and emotionally secure a woman becomes, the less she turns to the looking glass to give her self-confidence and a sense of her own personhood and the more she looks into the eyes of the people she loves and who love her for the true reflection of her identity." 1967 Mar 3 *Time* 82/1 "Recalls the new religion editor: 'I found myself over my head with things like personhood, demythologizing, Bonhoeffer.'"

spaceman economy 1970 July *McCall's* 104 "One [program] would be aimed at stopping population growth, and the other at starting the transition from what economist Kenneth Boulding calls a 'cowboy economy' to a 'spaceman economy.'" July 27 *Sat Rev* 33 "This is clearly a call for what Kenneth Boulding has termed 'the space man economy'—a cyclical ecological system, without unlimited reservoirs of anything either for extraction or pollution. The call for a simpler space man economy has a special irony when it issues from commercial television, which is dedicated to education for 'the cowboy economy,' illimitable, reckless, exploitative, romantic, and violent, where consumption and production are regarded as good things in a context of infinite reservoirs from which material can be obtained and into which effluvia can be deposited." 1972 Sep *Atlantic* 50/1 "But we are shifting to a 'spaceman economy.' The earth is becoming finite, like a closed spaceship; consumption must become 'circular'—that is, to conserve what we have, resources must be continuously recycled through the system." 1974 Apr *Harper's* 48/1 "Institutionally, scarcity demands that we sooner or later achieve a full-fledged 'steady-state' or 'spaceman' economy. Thereafter, we shall have to live off the annual income the earth receives from the sun, and this means a forced end to our kind of abnormal affluence and an abrupt return to frugality."

AMONG THE NEW WORDS

I. WILLIS RUSSELL AND MARY GRAY PORTER
University of Alabama

Since the American support of Pakistan in the India-Pakistan conflict of 1971, *tilt* has appeared often, joining other words (for example, *slant, inclination, bias*) that denote both a deviation from the horizontal, the vertical, or the square and a deviation from strict neutrality. We think it likely that *tilt* is to be associated with the representation of Justice holding a balance, but this is not the only possible association. James J. Kilpatrick ("News Watch," *TV Guide,* 21 June 1975) seems to have in mind pinball machines that flash "TILT" when the player applies too much body English. He asks what the viewer will think when a newscaster reports on subjects about which he has editorialized, and answers, "I believe the viewer will think: *Tilt!*"

The *Wall Street Journal* (see quotation s.v. *wind shear*) is no doubt correct in attributing the recent prominence of the term *wind shear* in the press to crashes of airliners in which the phenomenon may have played a part. Almost all of our citations imply that even the largest aircraft are endangered by the powerful and violent forces present in wind shear. This usage appears to be both more restricted and less precise, or in any event less quantified, than the usage of meteorologists (see the bracketed quotations in the glossary). Apart from the cited definitions in technical dictionaries, all our quotations are in substantial agreement as to the meaning of *wind shear*, with one rather remarkable exception. Cleveland Amory, in the 4 October 1975 issue of *Saturday Review* (p. 8/3), quotes a well-known Midwestern newspaper: "Wind shear is the term used for two lawyers of air turbulence moving in opposite directions..." and wonders, "Does it take only *two* lawyers?"

Acknowledgments: For citations: John Algeo (1), Dennis E. Baron (1), Richard E. Ray (2). We are also grateful to M. W. Raven for her assistance in defining *wind shear*.

back burner Figurative use **1:** *n* [*Random House College Dict* 1975 *n* and *adj*; cf *OED back a* I. 2 "'Used to distinguish that one of two things (or sets of things) which lies behind the main or front one, and is more or less subsidiary to it'... 1535... back courte... 1592... a backe roome..."] Additional quots 1966 Feb 4 *Time* 39/1-2 "Still, the Negro, often economically and socially deprived at home, frequently finds the modern Army a haven... 'That uniform gives prestige and status to a guy who's been 100 years on the back burner,' says Jack Moskowitz, Deputy Assistant Secretary of Defense for civil rights and industrial relations." 1970 Oct 5 *USN&WR* 32/1 "Vietnam, as a rule, has been put on the 'back burner' as an issue, although most people would like to see that war ended one way or another." 1973 Dec 31 *Time* 46/1 "Yet the results of Mondrian's sojourn [in NYC] have to some extent been set on a back burner." 1974 July 1 *Time* 21/3 "It's on the back, back burner. Nobody here is working on it." Aug 24 *Time* 21/2 "Illinois Senator Charles Percy... said that his candidacy has been put 'on the back burner and maybe into the deep freeze.'" Sep 9 *Time* 14/3 "[He] called Ford's [amnesty] plan 'a very gutsy thing,' especially since [he] had assumed 'the issue was going to be on the back burner for a long time.'" 1975 Feb 16 Bill Munroe on "Meet the Press" NBC-TV "You're willing to put it on the back burner?" **2:** *adj* [*Dict of Amer Slang* Supp 1975; *RHCD* 1975] 1975 Nov 10 *Newsweek* 19/3 "Ford... and his people had taken a hands-off view of New York's problems from the first, and had in fact begun back-burner studies of the bankruptcy option as early as last July." See also **front burner**

Eurocommunism *n* [*World Book Dict* 1978] 1977 Apr 8 "Firing Line" PBS "I have written at length about this business of Eurocommunism." July 10 *NY Times Book Rev* 1/1-2 "Behind the temptation is the real target of the book, the phenomenon of 'Euro-Communism.' As is well known, the word stands for the well-publicized changes in doctrine and strategy recently announced by the principal Communist parties of Western Europe. They proclaim that they can now be trusted to behave as democratic parties ought to; they are pledged to respect the rules of the parliamentary game and constitutional guarantees of political freedom. They define themselves as national parties, independent of Moscow, and hence capable of preserving the integrity of their respective societies and, as the Italian C.P. has declared, participating in the system of European defense and economic cooperation." Aug 17 *The Bulletin* (Bonn) 123/2 Aug 22 *New Yorker* 23 (cartoon caption) Nov 16 *Wall St Jour* 1/3 "The controversial advocate of Eurocommunism crossed a picket line of striking university workers to make his appearance." 1978 Jan 30 *Newsweek* 50/2 "Eurocommunism has never been a totally cohesive political force, but the Communist parties of France, Italy and Spain do share some principles." Mar 25 *New Repub* 34/3 "The French electorate has just plain busted the hearts of all those journalists and intellectuals so eager to prove that a phenomenon they called Eurocommunism would turn out to be benign. Of course... Eurocommunism will still be the spoken dream of many who would not for a moment contemplate putting themselves under its rule. In western Europe... the only intrinsic and ultimate function of the Communist parties, their only genuine option, is to be ruthlessly extreme, on the Soviet model. The truth is that it has become their desire. This is why Laszek Kolakowski, the exiled Polish philosopher, says: 'Euro-communism is as possible as fried snowballs.'"

Eurocommunist **1:** *n* 1976 July 12 *Newsweek* 33/1-2 (picture caption) "Berlinguer (left) with Brezhnev: The 'Eurocommunists' went their separate way." 1978 Apr 23 *Birmingham News* A-4/1 "With great political acumen, he worked to give the Spanish Communist Party the image of a moderate, democratic movement that was determinedly independent of the Soviet Union. He had become a 'Eurocommunist.'" **2:** *adj* 1976 Oct *Harper's* 22/3 "To the foreign journalists who waited up with prepared copy about democracy in

peril or a Euro-Communist triumph, the results may have seemed anticlimactic." 1978 Mar 20 *New Times* (NYC) 16/2 "But, the students asked incredulously, what about the Committee to Save Italy (the pressure group Connally formed a few years ago to help keep a Eurocommunist government from coming to power there)." Apr 1 *New Repub* 38/1 "The danger of 'Eurocommunism' is... that the Eurocommunist movement will prevent the Socialist parties from ever gaining a majority... and in so doing destroy the legitimacy of the democracy in each country."

front burner Figurative use [perh by analogy with *back burner* (qv); *RHCD* 1975 *n* and *adj*] **1:** *n* 1976 Jan 18 *Tuscaloosa News* A-10/1 (AP) "'In dealing with the economy we're going to put jobs on the front burner,' the House Democratic chief said in an interview." **2:** *adj* 1975 Apr 10 John Chancellor over NBC "We don't have a lot of problems, what might be called front burner problems."

spacecraft earth 1971 Jan 9 *New Yorker* 67/1 "It may be that much of NASA's fascination with our planet—Spacecraft Earth, as ecology-minded space men call it—arises from the realization that the earth, with its closed ecological system, is far and away the biggest piece of space hardware of all."

spaceship earth *n* Earth viewed as a spaceship, as a body moving through space and carrying limited resources that must be conserved, esp through international cooperation [1972 Garrett Hardin *Exploring New Ethics for Survival: The Voyage of the Spaceship Beagle* (Baltimore: Penguin, 1973) 17 "Shortly before his death in 1965, Adlai Stevenson expressed the mood of the world-to-come with characteristic felicity: 'We travel together, passengers on a little spaceship, dependent on its vulnerable reserves of air and soil; all committed for our safety to its security and peace; preserved from annihilation only by the care, the work and, I will say, the love we give our fragile craft.'"] 1968 René Dubos *So Human an Animal* (NY: Scribner's) 264 "Even if we had enough learning and wisdom to achieve at any given time an harmonious state of ecological equilibrium between mankind and the other inhabitants and components of the spaceship Earth, it would be a dynamic equilibrium, which would be compatible with man's continuing development." June 2 *NY Times* E-10/2 (editorial) "This planet—which some call Spaceship Earth—also has limited resources, and as these approach exhaustion or are made unusable by pollution the margin of safety for all men declines." 1971 Sep 1 *Friends Jour* 424/2 "Another metaphor that we are having a considerable amount of trouble with is *spaceship earth*.... It is essentially a wrong metaphor.... This planet is not manmade.... If we treat it as if it were a spaceship that we built and control, we are going to have considerable difficulty in communication between Christian theology and modern science." 1972 John Maddox *The Doomsday Syndrome* (first McGraw-Hill paperback ed, NY: McGraw-Hill, 1973) 24-25 "The view from the moon has nevertheless made much more graphic the concept of the earth as a kind of spaceship, moving through a hostile vacuum with its rapidly growing burden of humanity and other forms of life.... Up to a point, the analogy of spaceship earth is helpful. Spaceships are indeed isolated and self-sufficient entities.... What will happen, this train of thought goes, if some essential material on spaceship earth should be exhausted?" 1975 May *Atlantic* 84/2-3 "[Buckminster Fuller] has given us the phrase 'spaceship Earth,' a hopeful phrase in his lexicon.... In his *operating manual for spaceship EARTH* he has reminded us that each of four billion inhabitants of the planet has for his potential use 200 billion tons of resources." 1976 Gerald Leinwand *The Future* (NY: Pocket Books) 50-51 "In its journey through the solar system those who are voyagers on 'spaceship earth' will have to content themselves with less, say the neo-Malthusians, because as the number of travelers grows, the resources available to them are consumed ever more rapidly and the earth's environment is polluted ever more poisonously." 1977 July *Harper's* 8/2 "... too poor to expect anything but a steerage passage on Spaceship Earth." Addit refs: 1968 Mar *McCall's* (rpt., 1976 Apr *McCall's* 70/3) 1970 July *Science Jour* 53/2 1971 July *Pop Sci* 106/2 Sep *Prevention* 83 1972 Caroline Bird *The Crowding Syndrome* (NY: David McKay) 268 1973 Aug 1-15 *Friends Jour* 388/1 1974 Ben Bova "The Role of Science Fiction" in *Science Fiction, Today and Tomorrow* ed Reginald Bretnor (Baltimore: Penguin, 1975) 4 Apr *Harper's* 50/1 1975 Feb *Reader's Digest* 76 June 29 *NY Times Book Rev* 2-3 (rev of R Buckminster Fuller *Synergetics* [NY: Macmillan]) 1976 Sep 13 *New Yorker* 98/3 Nov 22 *Green Bay* (Wisc) *Press-Gazette* A-9/5 (letter to Ann Landers) 1978 Feb *Esquire* 60/1-2 July 9 *Atlanta Journal and Constitution* C-12/1

tilt Figurative use **1:** *n* [cf *OED tilt sb²* II. 4 "'... inclination upward or downward.' [Implied in quots. 1562, 1658, 1706 in b.]" 1837] Tendency to favor one viewpoint or one side over another, bias (used esp of one who is or claims to be neutral) 1974 Dec 29 (NY) *Sunday News* 2/4 (UPI) "[Pres Ford] said his priorities now have a 'slight tilt' toward reversing the recession." 1975 Jan 11 *National Observer* 11/4 (heading) "FLORIDA TILT... Vacationers unexpectedly flood the state." June 10 *Wall St Jour* 20/3-5 (heading) "A Pro-Business Tilt in the Courts?" 1976 Mar 2 Barbara Walters on "Today" NBC-TV "... Massachusetts liberal tilt is obvious." Nov *Harper's* 29/1 "We hope you don't lift the embargo for at least another five years, by which time... Cuba's American orientation will have been eclipsed. The tilt will be more firmly toward us [the British] and the Japanese." **2:** *vi* 1972 Feb 19 *New Yorker* 91/1 "President Nixon... had made up his mind to support, or 'tilt toward,' the Pakistanis and castigate the Indians.... Still another element in the White House decision to tilt toward Pakistan undoubtedly concerned the Russians." 1974 Aug 5 *Time* 13/1 "But after reading the transcripts,' he said, '... I began tilting against the President, and my conviction grew steadily.'" 1976 Feb 29 Roberta Hornig on "Meet the Press" NBC-TV "How can you balance the two, or do you have to tilt?" Sep 18 *Sat Rev* 10/1 "When India went to war with Pakistan in 1971, Kissinger 'tilted' toward Yahya Khan." **3:** *vt* 1974 May 20 *Newsweek* 26/2 "The strain has been substantial, and Ford-watchers—Mr. Nixon among them—began wondering whether his ambivalence wasn't tilting him even farther from the boss." Nov 13 *Tuscaloosa News* 6/5 (Jack Anderson) "Ford's economic policies are tilted toward big business."

wind shear *n* [cf *OED shear sb²* II. 6; *W3 shear n* 5a: "a strain resulting from applied forces that cause or tend to cause contiguous parts of a body to slide relatively to each other in a direction parallel to their plane of contact... b: the stress giving rise to this strain..."] Weather phenomenon in which adjacent masses of the atmosphere move at different speeds or in different directions, exerting deforming and sometimes destructive forces at the boundary between the atmospheric currents [1959 *Dict of Guided Missiles and Space Flight* (Principles of Guided Missile Design, 5; Princeton: Van Nostrand) 679/2 "WIND SHEAR. The average wind gradient; the difference in wind velocity at two altitudes divided by the altitude increment. The units are ft per sec/ 1000 ft." 1974 *McGraw-Hill Dict of Scientific and Technical Terms* (NY: McGraw-Hill) 1615/1 "*wind shear* [meteorol] The local variation of the wind vector or any of its components in a given direction."] 1960 Oct 3 *Time* 54/1 (also cited *AS* 54: 38 sv *CAT*) "It has been agreed that CAT [clear air turbulence] is caused by wind shear—the 'friction' between adjacent air masses moving at different speeds." 1974 July 6 *Science News* 6/3 "Besides measuring mere winds in the atmosphere, the experiments aboard the rockets were planned to study wind shear (one layer of wind blowing past another) . . . and other features." 1975 May 10 *Science News* 305/1 "The [Great Red Spot on Jupiter] seems to show signs of a counterclockwise spiraling, while white cloud streams move from right to left on the south, forming triangular regions of wind shear at the Spot's 'ends.'" July 7 *Time* 9/3–10/1 "Wind shear carries a frightening connotation of lethal slicing forces, and with good reason. It is a highly unpredictable and violent weather phenomenon that results when opposing squall lines of high-velocity winds cross or collide. The result is a whirlwind, minitornado effect in which wildly thrashing air currents can throw even huge aircraft out of control when they are flying at relatively low landing speeds, generally around 180 knots. . . . [¶] 'We began defining wind shear and identifying it as hazardous only in the past decade,' explains Charles Miller, director of safety seminars for the Flight Safety Foundation. '. . . Only recently have we begun to appreciate the variations and magnitude of wind shear.' [¶] Although wind shear is invisible to the eye, the conditions that make it probable can be spotted by radar and detected by weather instruments." July 22 *Wall St Jour* 1/1 "The Eastern Airlines crash has brought into the open a subject previously the domain of pilots and meteorologists: the deadly phenomenon of low-level wind shear, or a rapid change in wind speed and direction close to the ground. The Air Lines Pilots Association says it has known for years that wind shear is a factor in many plane crashes, 'but nobody has been listening.'" July 31 *NY Times* 30/1 "The Air Lines Pilots Association today told a House subcommittee hearing on air safety that there was a 'major need' for installing wind-shear detectors in airliner cockpits to cut down on approach and landing accidents. [¶] Wind shear is a phenomenon in which adjacent air streams move in different directions and at varying velocities. Most experts believe wind shear figured significantly in the crash of an Eastern Airlines jet at Kennedy International Airport in New York on June 24."

AMONG THE NEW WORDS

I. WILLIS RUSSELL AND MARY GRAY PORTER
University of Alabama

IN THE PRELIMINARY REMARKS to the April 1948 installment of "Among the New Words" (*American Speech* 23: 147), the senior editor wrote:

> The war just completed gave us a number of terms for various types and shades of war: 'bacteriological warfare' (1937), 'total war' (1937), 'blitzkrieg' (1938), 'phoney war' (1939), 'psychological warfare' (1939), 'sitzkrieg' (1939), 'war of nerves' (1939), and 'shooting war' (1941) (see article 'Words and Meanings, New,' *Ten Eventful Years* [Encyclopaedia Brit., Inc., 1947] and *Am. Sp.* 18:65/2). A glance at the glossary below will reveal two new terms, 'cold war' and 'hot war.' Several of these are of especial interest. According to the dating, we have this progression: 'blitzkrieg,' 'phoney war' and 'sitzkrieg,' and finally 'shooting war.' Notice that the two middle terms imply the absence of the essential element in our concept of war; what that element is is made explicit in the last term, '*shooting* war.' A similar progression is seen in 'war,' 'cold war,' 'hot war.'

Since then, we have had the progression *skiing*, *water skiing*, *snow* (and *ice*) *skiing* (heard in conversation), and this installment of "Among the New Words" supplies another: *series*, *miniseries*, *maxiseries*.

Until he checked, the senior editor had assumed that some of the wartime terms, coined in a certain contemporary climate, would not have survived. Imagine his amazement to discover that all but *phoney war* are entered in either *Webster's Third* or *World Book Dictionary* (1976), the only dictionaries checked.

From the data in our files we can only conclude that there is some overlapping of meaning of *maxiseries*, *miniseries*, *multiseries*, and the phrase *limited series*. The last three terms clearly denote something different from an ordinary television series (whereas *maxiseries* may not). However, our evidence does not make clear how—or whether—they differ from one another. The first quotation under *miniseries* implies that *miniseries* and *multiseries* are synonymous. The limited series and the miniseries may be identical, or the miniseries may be one form of the limited series. Either interpretation seems plausible for the quotations from the *New York Times*, 12 December 1976, and the *Tuscaloosa News*, 12 September 1977. On the other hand, the *New Yorker* quotation seems to make a distinction between the miniseries and the limited series. Nowhere is the uncertainty surrounding the meaning and use of *miniseries* and *maxiseries* more evident than in reports about *Roots: The Next Generations*, the fourteen-hour sequel to the twelve-hour *Roots*. *Newsweek* (see quotation s.v. *maxiseries*) calls it a "maxiseries," but *TV Guide* (see quotation s.v. *miniseries*) refers to it as a "miniseries," an "epic miniseries," but miniseries nonetheless. Any reader with citations or expert knowledge that might shed light on these uncertainties is invited to comment.

In spite of the paucity and poverty of our evidence, we have set up entries for *short*, *steer*, and *upgrade* because they are germane to other entries in this installment. Although the shorting and upgrading mentioned in our single quotation (entered under *ping-pong*) are similar to the sharp, if not illegal, practices found in many kinds of merchandising, we think they are worth entering here because they are applied to abuses in the delivery of health care, not to the sale of more ordinary articles of commerce. In like manner, inclusion of *steer* seems justifiable since what it denotes here is sufficiently different from the act of the taxi driver who offers or is asked to steer his passenger to where the action is (an illegal gambling joint, for example, or a house of ill repute) or that of the tourist guide who receives a commission from a shopkeeper for steering his charges to a particular shop. The tourists may be deceived as to the quality of the goods, the passenger's destination may be disreputable, the steering itself may not be universally admired, but there is apparently no violation of the law. Until additional evidence is at hand, it is impossible to determine whether the "shorting," "steering," and "upgrading" of the quotation are the verbal nouns of transitive or intransitive verbs; we have, therefore, used the label "*vb*." Additional citations from our readers would be welcome for a supplement in a future issue.

Acknowledgments: The first two quotations in the *truth squad* entry were contributed by the late Mamie Meredith.

fraud squad *n* [*OEDS* sv *fraud* 1967, 1971] US illus 1977 Feb 26 *Nation* 242/2 "Within his department a four-year-old, twenty-nine-member 'fraud squad' audits and investigates Medicaid provider claims."

maxiseries *n* [*W3* Adden 1971 *maxi-*; *W3 series n* 1] Television series, esp as opposed to a MINISERIES 1976 Feb 7 *TV Guide* 32/1 "Later ['The Blue Knight'] came to TV as a miniseries with William Holden. And now it proceeds, with George Kennedy, as, presumably, a maxiseries." June 5 *TV Guide* 34/1 "If the maxiseries left something to be desired, there were new miniseries of high quality, such as *Rich Man, Poor Man* and *Family*." 1979 Feb 19 *Newsweek* 85/1 "While the seven-part maxiseries . . . seems unlikely to eclipse the impact of its ancestor, it is in many respects a superior achievement."

Medicaid mill *n* [*OEDS Medicaid* 1966 →; *World Book Dict* 1975 *Medicaid*; *W3 diploma mill* and *mill n* 6] Medical clinic in which individuals on Medicaid are often recommended for unnecessary services, sometimes administered below standard 1976 Feb 23 *Time* 37/1 "Working with investigators from Chicago's Better Government Association, a citizens' watchdog agency, the subcommittee last December set up a clinic near ghetto areas on the city's North Side. To all appearances, the operation was indistinguishable from other 'Medicaid mills' that have been hastily assembled to provide treatment for Chicago's poor and to collect payments from the federal and state governments." Apr 10 *TV Guide* A-96/1–2 "Following scenes of New York 'Medicaid mills,' (neighborhood centers that offer a range of medical services), one doctor discusses 'ping-ponging,' in which a 'mill' patient is shuttled among unneeded specialists or given unnecessary tests. Says one woman: 'I came in for a cold, and I came out with three or four prescriptions—and a prescription for glasses also.'" Sep 1 "CBS News" CBS-TV "There are . . . 350 Medicaid mills in New York." Sep 5 *NY Times* 1/1 "In an effort to check what it says are widespread abuses in Medicaid billings, the Federal Government has issued an order forbidding physicians as well as shared health facilities—commonly known as Medicaid mills—from selling their accounts receivable to collection agents." Sep 5 *NY Times*, sec 4, 1/2 "What they found was that the money was inadequately administered and thus proved a temptation to doctors to establish quasi-health clinics, known as 'Medicaid mills,' that dispensed services often substandard and unnecessary." Sep 6 *Newsweek* 18/1–2 "The Medicaid program, enacted by Congress in 1965 and jointly funded by the Federal, state, and local governments, helps to finance health services for the poor. But too often, committee investigators found, Medicaid money has become easy pickings for the unscrupulous. The staff report cites innumerable instances of phony bills for services that were unnecessary or never rendered. One investigator with perfect vision received three prescriptions for eyeglasses; another was X-rayed on a machine that had no film. 'Some people are ripping off vast amounts of money by setting up these Medicaid mills and running people through like cattle,' Moss told *Newsweek*'s Henry McGee last week."

mill patient *n* [Medicaid *mill* + *patient*] 1976 Apr 10 *TV Guide* A-96/1–2 Quot sv MEDICAID MILL

miniseries *n* [*OEDS mini-*; *W3 series n* 1] Television series of limited duration 1972 Oct 28 *TV Guide* 4/2 "And if a miniseries fails to earn healthy ratings, the network can replace only the parts viewers don't like—instead of scrapping an entire series." 1973 Jan 6 *TV Guide* 4/1 "Miniseries—a series of programs that would end after six, eight, 10 or whatever number the writers feel necessary either to tell one complete story or to turn out fresh, imaginative episodes of a series featuring the same characters in a new story each week. *The Forsyte Saga* took 26 episodes, *Elizabeth R* took six. . . . Many more miniseries are on the drawing boards." Apr 24 *World* 52/2 "The miniseries will be composed of four or more shows running in sequence, to be followed by another miniseries." June 2 *TV Guide* A-1/1 Dec *Esquire* 151/1 "*The Blue Knight* has been made into a four-hour TV 'mini-series,' with William Holden in the lead." 1976 Jan 18 *Tuscaloosa* (Ala) *News* C-10/6 "'Bluegrass Roots,' a new mini-series consisting of nine programs, will be presented by the Alabama Public Television Network illustrating the development of bluegrass music in America." Feb 9 *Time* 81/2 May 22 *TV Guide* 1 "*How the West Was Won*, a six-segment miniseries starring JAMES ARNESS, will be telecast on ABC next season." Dec 12 *NY Times* D-33/1 (heading) "Those Mini-Series Are Stretching A Point [¶] The concept of the limited series, long a staple abroad, is finally being explored seriously by the commercial networks." 1977 Sep 12 *Tuscaloosa News* 8/1 (AP) "The 12-hour miniseries . . . won Emmys for best limited series, directing and acting." 1979 Jan 21 *Family Weekly* 4/1 Feb 8 *TV Guide* A-93/1 Feb 26 *New Yorker* 26/1 "Robert A. Daly, of CBS, said that, although the pace was slower in the old days, before the success of the mini-series and the limited series, he thought that today we might be living in the golden age of television." Mar 3 *TV Guide* A-3/1 "In an expensive scheduling ploy, CBS and NBC threw high-powered specials and movies against ABC's telecast of *Roots: The Next Generations* and managed to blunt the ratings of the epic miniseries."

multiseries *n* One of several television series, with fewer segments than a regular series, that are scheduled to be televised in rotation in the same time slot; also such time-sharing shorter series collectively 1973 Jan 6 *TV Guide* 4/1 "Multiseries—several series running in the same time period. Examples would be *NBC Sunday Mystery Movie*, which alternates *McMillan and Wife, Columbo, McCloud* and *Hec Ramsey*; and ABC's *The Men*, which alternates *Assignment: Vienna, The Delphi Bureau* and *Jigsaw*. . . . [¶] The multiseries, the miniseries and the special all give the writers, directors and everyone else concerned more time to think and plan and, with luck, rehearse." Apr 24 *World* 52/2 "Other twelfth-floor vice-presidents use terms that are strictly part of the new Hollywood. They speak of 'the multiseries' and 'the miniseries' and the 'OTO.' The first stands for series such as 'Columbo,' 'McCloud,' etc., that share the same time spot and revolve every three or four weeks. Thus a series like 'Mannix' will have twenty-six new shows each year, while a multiseries like 'McMillan and Wife' will have only eight or nine new shows a year."

physical *adj* [*Webster's Sports Dict* 1976] Addit dated illus 1971 May 29 *TV Guide* 20/1 "I never fought or played stickball on the block. I wasn't a physical child and my father teased me about it." 1973 Jan 28 *Tuscaloosa News* B-2/4 (AP) "Phelps commented that 'UCLA is a very good, physical, aggressive team that plays well together.'" 1974 Mar 15 *Tuscaloosa News* 11/3 "It was a physical game, perhaps more physical than we had imagined and we did have some things happen that didn't help us much." Sep 29 *Birmingham* (Ala) *News* C-9/1 "'It was really a physical game,' . . . 'Vanderbilt is a lot better than last year and more physical.'" 1975 Jan 1 "NBC Sports: Orange Bowl" NBC-TV "Rutledge is the new quarterback, not as physical as Todd." Feb 13 "Archer" NBC-TV "I didn't like it, and if you don't want me to get physical, [you better shut up about it]." 1976 Jan 13 *Kansas City Star* 9/2 "Canadians often say that pro players cannot be developed in American colleges because of the restrictive rules on checking. . . . [¶] 'Any player with ability can come out of college and adjust to professional hockey. . . . There's plenty of physical hockey played in college.'" Jan 25 *Tuscaloosa News* B-2/5 "It was a very physical game and we got pretty roughed up."

ping-pong [cf *AS* 46: 296–97 *ping-pong vi* 1962, *vt* 1970; *World Book Dict* 1976] *Specif*, **1:** *vi* Refer a patient, esp one on Medicaid, to other doctors, particularly if such referral is not medically necessary 1976 Apr 10 *TV Guide* A-96/1–2 Quot sv MEDICAID MILL Sep 6 *Newsweek* 18/3 "Medicaid abuses, the investigators found, came in so many variations as to have a vocabulary of their own. Examples include 'Ping Ponging' (referring patients to other doctors within the clinic even when there is no medical need to do so), 'upgrading' (billing for additional services not provided), 'steering' (sending patients to a particular pharmacy, usually one affiliated with the mill) and 'shorting' (delivering fewer pills than prescribed)." **2:** *vt* 1976 Sep 5 *NY Times*, sec 4, 1/2 "The Senate investigators, all of whom had been pronounced in excellent health by Congressional doctors at the beginning of the inquiry, collected 'bushels full of prescriptions' (with directions where they were to be filled, which is illegal), were 'ping-ponged' to neurologists, gynecologists, internists, psychiatrists, podiatrists, dentists, ophthalmologists, pediatricians."

short *vb* [cf *W3 short vt* 2 "shortchange, cheat"; *OED short a* III "Not reaching to some standard. 15. Of things: . . . *Short measure, weight*: defective quantity by measure or weight; also, a measuring rod, vessel, etc., or a scale-weight, which defrauds the customer" 1789] *Specif*, dispense fewer pills than prescribed but charge the price of the prescribed quantity 1976 Sep 6 *Newsweek* 18/3 Quot sv PING-PONG

steer *vb* [cf *W3 vt* 1b "to entice (a prospective customer or victim) to an illicit or disreputable establishment"; *OED vt* 3d "Also, (*U.S. slang*) to manoeuvre or decoy (a person) to a place, or into doing something. . . . 1889 *Century Dict., Bunko-steerer*"] 1976 Sep 6 *Newsweek* 18/3 Quot sv PING-PONG

structural unemployment [1961 cited in *AS* 48: 142] Addit earlier illus 1932 Feb 20 *Sat Rev of Lit* 534/1–2 (Norman Angell, rev of Alvin Harvey Hansen, *Economic Stabilization in an Unbalanced World* [NY: Harcourt, Brace]) "Very well, says Professor Hansen in effect, suppose you *could* iron out the irregularities which cause these depressions and get rid largely of the unemployment due to the business cycle. What about the structural changes in the economic edifice—indispensable to progress—the new inventions, the change from coal to oil or water power, the tremendous improvement of machinery and technique? . . . [¶] Professor Hansen's point is that cyclical fluctuations have the effect of giving the whole economic structure a good shake up and keeping the system flexible and mobile. It means both transitory unemployment and new outlets constantly occurring to absorb it (and it might be added, create new transitory unemployment), but 'structural unemployment in a stabilized world will be a far more serious problem than it is in a world subject to cyclical fluctuations.'"

truth squad *n* 1952 Oct 10 *Daily Nebraskan* 2 "He has proved effective enough to cause the formation of a Republican 'Truth Squad,' . . . which has followed Mr. Truman along his whistle-stop route. The countermove is the GOP's rebuttal to the campaign aimed at cutting down Ike." Oct 20 *Newsweek* 29 "Treading on the President's heels, a Republican 'truth squad' kept busy answering the charges thrown at the GOP and Eisenhower. It followed the Truman campaign train and held press conferences at which such Republican senators as Homer Ferguson of Michigan, Bourke B. Hickenlooper of Iowa, and Francis Case of South Dakota rebutted Mr. Truman's statements." Oct 28 *Tuscaloosa News* 3/3 (UP) "The Republican 'truth squad' trailed President Truman to Minneapolis today after accusing him of getting election day mixed up with Hallowe'en." Nov 2 *NY Times* L-60/3 (UP) "A Republican 'Truth Squad' following President Truman said today he acted like 'a political cuckoo.'" Nov 3 *Tuscaloosa News* 12/5 (UP) "The Republican 'Truth Squad' after trailing President Truman across the country on his campaign trips, passed down its final verdict today that the President was 'guilty of over 100 lies, half-truths and distortions.'" 1976 Oct *Analog* 7/1–2 (editorial) "The leader of those critics, Lewontin, helped to organize an organization called the Sociobiology Study Group (SSG). Affiliated with Science for the People, the SSG has acted as a sort of 'truth squad' to point out what its members believe to be mistakes, oversimplifications, and errors of judgment in Wilson's work."

turf *n* **1:** [*World Book Dict* 1976 sense 4b] Addit dated illus 1962 Apr 28 *Sat Eve Post* 30/2 "Her [social worker's] turf: the lower Bronx." 1970 R Buckminster Fuller with Jerome Agel and Quentin Fiore, *I Seem To Be a Verb* (NY: Bantam) 161B "Before the invention and use of cables and the wireless, 99.9 per cent of humanity thought in terms of only their local turf." 1971 Jan *Amer Home* 14/1 (picture caption) "[She] is a stockbroker, and Wall Street is her turf, where the big city can be rough on a girl's complexion." Jan 10 *NY Times* XX-1/1 "I came to Beverly Hills . . . to see the stars' home turf (although today more stars probably live in Manhattan than in California)." Apr *House & Garden* 157/1 "TELEPHONE TURF Mr. Bell's tel has a special spot—a little fringed rug from Austria." July 5 *Newsweek* 55/1 "In Statehouses across the country, the reaction for years has been almost Pavlovian: governors and legislators alike salivated at the very thought of a huge industrial complex locating on their state's turf." **2:** Figurative use 1970 Oct 17 *Sat Rev* 67/3 "The lives of all our children and the very mindedness of society itself cannot be made whole as long as educators are obsessed by indecent needs to defend their own turfs, and academics regard those turfs as stinking kitchen middens." Nov 14 *Sat Rev* 28/2 (letter) "[The reviewer] seems to be jealously guarding a turf he feels is his own and resents anyone impinging on it." 1971 Mar 15 *Newsweek* 88/3 "Bernard (Bunny) Lasker, chairman of the New York Stock Exchange's Board of Governors, knew a threat when he saw it last week: Howard (The Horse) Samuels, president of New York's new Off-Track Betting Corporation, was trying to muscle in on his turf." June 14 *Newsweek* 76/3 "Today, to defend its campus turf, the AAUP is . . . reassessing its stand on unionization." Sep *Intellectual Digest* 19/1 (reprint from *Commonweal*) "Podhoretz is not at all loath to name one of the chief gangs with which he is contesting the intellectual turf." 1972 Feb 19 *New Yorker* 56/3 Sep 9 *Sat Rev* 82/2 "In November Lippincott will publish *Keep Off My Turf*, in which Mike Curtis, the Baltimore Colts' middle linebacker . . . ventures onto Jim Bouton's turf." 1973 Apr *Family Circle* 120/1 "Male occupations are a turf from which women are excluded." 1977 Jan 12 *Tuscaloosa News* 32/1–3 Feb 9 *Tuscaloosa News* 4/3–4 (David S Broder) "He concluded . . . that a vice president who sought responsibility for a specific area of government policy would confront . . . a brutal battle with the officials and bureaucrats of the department whose 'turf' he was invading." 1978 Mar *Academe* (AAUP) inside cover "It is also argued that [in] the bargaining process . . . administrators are transformed into resolute defenders of their (self-defined) 'turfs.'" Dec *Johns Hopkins Mag* 38/1 "Cone stayed on his home turf—science." 1979 Mar *Analog* 57/1 "It's a serious question that goes far beyond a fight over political turf. . . . [¶] The fight is between two approaches to science, two ideas of what it should be."

upgrade *vb* [cf *W3 vt* d "to substitute (a product of lower quality) for a product of higher quality in order to obtain a higher price"] Bill the agency administering Medicaid for more services than were provided Medicaid patients 1976 Sep 6 *Newsweek* 18/3 Quot sv PING-PONG

AMONG THE NEW WORDS

I. WILLIS RUSSELL AND MARY GRAY PORTER
University of Alabama

IN THE FALL 1978 number, we illustrated *-gate* as a combining form. Here we continue to present our material on what may be called "Watergate words." The material is of several kinds: dated citations for terms already entered in one or more dictionaries, fully attested terms not yet entered in any dictionary checked, and a number of terms which, to quote ourselves, "we believe will be of some interest to readers of this department because of their relationship, in one way or another, to more abundantly attested items" (*American Speech* 46: 291).

mini-Watergate *n* 1974 May 20 *Newsweek* 46/1 "For the first time since he was elected in 1955, Daley faces a Democratic primary challenge—and his 33-year-old rival . . . has a mini-Watergate to run against. Just four days before Daley fell ill . . . the mayor's city-council floor leader . . . was formally charged with twenty counts of mail fraud. That followed the indictment of . . . more than a dozen Daley ward bosses and functionaries on charges ranging from tax evasion to outright extortion." Sep 29 *Birmingham* (Ala) *News* A-24/2 "The Indianapolis Star has charged that they have uncovered a mini-Watergate—with widespread corruption in the criminal justice system—and that the officials in the system are using the grand jury and the courts to set a frame-up and discourage any more investigations." 1975 Aug *Esquire* 10/3 "In the movie, this [collapse of a studio set] becomes a grandiose disaster prefiguring the final Armageddon, and is followed by what Andrew Sarris has called a mini-Watergate: studio executives covering up a gross malpractice."

plumber *n* [*Dict of Amer Slang* 1975 supp; *World Book Dict* 1976 *n* 2] 1973 May 21 *Newsweek* 26/2 "It ended with the CIA supplying phony identification, disguises, spy equipment and other assistance to Hunt, G. Gordon Liddy and their undercover company—then part of the White House 'plumbers' team that was checking out security leaks." June 18 *Nation* 778/1 "The Watergate break-in was one of the direct results of Nixon's 'creation of a special investigative unit within the White House' which later came to be known as the 'plumbers.' Ehrlichman was in charge; Krogh, Young, Hunt and Liddy worked under him. Nixon continued: 'The unit operated under extremely tight security rules. Its existence and functions were known only to a very few persons at the White House. These included Messrs. Haldeman, Ehrlichman and Dean.' Nixon further explained that this small group in the White House was to stop security leaks and to investigate 'other sensitive security matters.' It should be noted that this group was authorized by Nixon to act independently of the FBI, the CIA and other federal intelligence agencies." Aug 20 *Time* 16/1–2 On the formation, composition, and activities of the "Special Investigations Unit, also known as the plumbers." Sep 26 "Watergate Hearings" NBC-TV testimony of E Howard Hunt that the term was put on a door to divert attention from the real nature of the operation 1974 Feb 18 *Time* 8/2 "Not long after President Nixon created his special investigations unit in June 1971 to plug 'leaks' of classified information, one of the group's members, in a wry acknowledgement of his assignment, tacked up a sign on his door: PLUMBER. Thus the appellation 'plumbers' came into being, and eventually such nefarious activities as tapping telephones, burglarizing offices and fabricating State Department cables came to be known as the work of the 'plumbers.'" Mar *Intellectual Digest* 63/3 (from Vincent Ostrom, *The Intellectual Crisis in Amer Public Administration,* rev ed, Univ of Ala Press, 1973-74) "Efforts to tighten the screws of administrative control will cause bureaucratic pipelines to leak like sieves. Plumbers will be needed." July 12 *New Times* (NYC) 29/1 "The unit was nicknamed the 'Plumbers' by [David] Young's grandmother, who asked, with pride, what Young's new important assignment was. Young told her he was to plug leaks. 'Oh, then you are a plumber,' she said, and the name stuck and was even hung on the door of Room 16 in the Executive Office Building ('This is where the Plumbers hang out')."

plumbing *n* [cf *W3* 2 b and *WBD76* sv *plumber n*] 1973 May 14 *Newsweek* 46/3 "Liddy and Hunt thought that they were attending to plumbing, and fixing leaks." Aug 27 *Time* 18/3 "Hunt still justifies his participation in Watergate and the plumbing activities on grounds of national security." —**plumbing crew** 1972 Sep 18 *Newsweek* 41/1 "In the fall of 1971, increasingly concerned about a rash of security leaks that began with the Pentagon Papers, Presidential assistant John D. Ehrlichman quietly tapped his able, aggressive deputy, Egil (Bud) Krogh, 31, to plug the leaks. Thus the White House 'plumbing' crew was born." —**plumbing union** 1973 June 17 *NY Times Mag* 6/3 "THEME: FAILURE OF ASSIGNED MISSION AND BLAME THEREFOR. [¶] MESSAGE: As is widely known among all agents of the K.G.B., F.B.I., White House plumbing union and American press, Comrade Petrosinov's supersecret, Eyes-Only-and-Burn-Bag, Ashes-to-Shredder Memorandum #05-90648-x8-ab-07 directed Special Negotiator Ulyanov to obtain U.S. agreement on three sights for Top Commissar Comrade Brezhnev to see during his U.S. visit."

post-Watergate *adj* [*post-* + *Watergate WBD75 n 1*] **1:** Existing or occurring after the Watergate revelations 1974 Sep 9 *Time* 14/3 "At the same time, the Government, which was guilty of widespread deception during the Viet Nam War, would foster much needed post-Watergate reconciliation by showing charity toward its dissenting young men." 1975 Feb 23 *NY Times Book Rev* 3/4 "This is, after all, in contrast with the confessions of incriminated insiders and the surmises of journalistic outsiders, the first real post-Watergate view of Nixon by someone who was both there and innocent." June *Harper's* 38/1 "The Cloak was designed for the man who has everything, including a bad case of post-Watergate paranoia, and who worries about being bugged all the time." Ibid 39/1 "He is not sanguine about the prospects for privacy in post-Watergate America." Sep 6 *Sat Rev* 44/1 "I confess to a certain queasiness before seeing *Three Days of the Condor,* the first 'big' post-Watergate film." Nov 1 *Sat Rev* 12/2 "The morality of the U.S. Congress in the post-Watergate era can best be summed up in the story of Mrs. Nelson Rockefeller's ashtrays." **2:** Characteristic of the mood or climate of American public life after the events of the Watergate scandal became known, typified by the public's decreased willingness to tolerate activities it regards as wrong, the anxiety of those in positions of power or prominence that their actions might be considered morally wrong, and a sincere desire for behavior that is morally right 1973 Dec 31 *Time* 17/2 "Beyond that are the kind of direct payoffs that Spiro Agnew thought had become offensive to ordinary citizens only in 'the new post-Watergate political morality.'" 1974 Jan 21 *New Yorker* 33 (cartoon caption) "[Corporation officer to board of directors:] 'Our recommendation, then, is that these plans be shelved till the post-Watergate morality blows over.'" 1975 Apr 4 *New Times* (NYC) 16/2 "Back in December, a highway patrolman stopped a car outside Santa Barbara, California, for going 61 in a 55 mph zone. The passenger in the chauffeur-driven vehicle turned out to be then-Governor Ronald Reagan, and no citation was given. After the story leaked out, an enraged San Diego Municipal Court Judge named Robert Cooney began refusing to fine anyone ticketed for speeding between 55 and 61 mph. The city attorney is taking the issue to Superior Court, but Cooney refuses to budge until the highway patrol offers an acceptable explanation for not citing Reagan's car. Post-Watergate politics prevail." July *Atlantic* 38/1 "John Connally, over a period of months before his indictment, had increasingly sounded troubled and disenchanted: public men were willy-nilly hounded, slandered, used for handy scapegoats in the post-Watergate morality (he said again and again) until the day might be fast approaching when good men would refuse to sacrifice themselves, their reputations, their families, their privacy." Aug 3 *Tuscaloosa News* D-2/3 "Happily, this time the approach is more cautious and sensible than that first great flight of post-Watergate Congressional morality, called the Federal Election Campaign Act of 1974." 1976 Feb 29 *NY Times Book Rev* 2/1 "He also seems unaware that he is writing for post-Watergate man, who is neither as gullible nor starry-eyed about the Great Game [espionage and counterintelligence activities] as Mr. Stevenson himself appears to be." Mar 22 *Time* 47/2 "Stirred by what he called 'post-Watergate pangs of conscience,' a knowledgeable source—possibly a member of the hospital staff—told New York *Times* Reporter M. A. Farber of his suspicions [in the mysterious death of at least 13 patients at a New Jersey hospital]." Sep 20 *Chron of Higher Educ* 3/4 "In the post-Watergate mood for more openness in government affairs, however, the [Academy of Sciences] now voluntarily makes available a good deal of information about its advisory bodies." Oct 16 *Sat Rev* 6/1 "[Andrew Young] possesses a rare set of assets that, in this time of post-Watergate disillusionment and Carter love politics, are uniquely suited to the national mood." Nov 15 Jack Anderson in *Crimson-White* (Univ of Ala) 5/3 "They are congressmen from the post-Watergate era and, hopefully, they may infect the House with the post-Watergate morality."

pre-Watergate *adj* 1973 Dec 24 *Newsweek* 21/3 "Now that the American public has become so much more familiar with courtroom parlance than we were in the innocent old Perry Mason, pre-Watergate days, the average mind can dream up authentic-sounding question-and-answer courtroom sequences without benefit of scriptwriter." 1975 Feb 23 *NY Times Book Rev* 2/4 "In Safire's pre-Watergate White House you will find an executive of scope and vision, supremely on top of his policies, from Cambodia to school busing." Apr 4 *New Times* (NYC) 16/3 "One of the pre-Watergate victims of Nixon politics is planning a comeback." 1976 Aug 8 *NY Times Book Rev* 8/3 "The unraveling of those questions, both emotional and ethical—particularly in the pre-Watergate climate—provides a case study of the American dream worth pondering." 1977 May *Reader's Digest* 169/2-170/1 (cond from *NY Times Mag* 14 Nov 1976) "These revelations of misdeeds, actual or possible, and their echoing traumas among the citizenry, are part of what is generally called 'the post-Watergate morality.' We have been living with that morality for many months now, and it seems to me there are two things to be said about it. First, it is far, far better than the pre-Watergate morality. Second, it may be too good for any of us to survive."

Spirit of Watergate 1973 May 21 *Newsweek* 4/3 (letter) "I never believed it was possible, but President Nixon has done what he promised the American people he would do if elected—he has brought us together. It took the Spirit of Watergate to do it." Sep 10 *Newsweek* 60/1-2 "Taiwan scored 57 runs in three [Little League World] Series games; their opponents made no runs and no hits—and their coaches responded with charges that the Chinese all-stars were above the league's 12-year age limit. Moments after pitcher Huang Ching-hui completed his team's no-hit streak, there was talk of a full-scale investigation of the players' birth records. Whether that comes about or not, the spirit of Watergate had clearly struck the Little League—revealing either rule-bending winners or, at the least, some of baseball's sorest losers."

Vatergatski *n* [pseudo-Russian] Watergate scandal 1973 Nov 12 *Time* 66/3 "Soviet newspapers, which had virtually ignored 'Vatergatski,' even began hinting to the Russian public that Nixon might not survive in office."

Waterbugger *n* [*Water*gate + *bugger* 'one who plants a concealed microphone,' perh influenced by *water bug,* an insect] 1973 May 17 Jack Anderson in *Tuscaloosa News* 4/5 "Not long after the Waterbuggers were arrested, our White House sources tipped us off that the plot had Haldeman's imprint all over it." May 21 *Newsweek* 18/1-2, 26/2, 28/2 May 28 *Newsweek* 26/2, 28/3, 31/1 June 14 Jack Anderson in *Tuscaloosa News* 4/2 "Our tax advisers say someone must pay taxes on the $460,000 at least that was paid to the Waterbuggers to buy their silence and to compensate their lawyers." July 2 *Newsweek* 14/2 "When the seven original Waterbuggers were indicted in September, Dean said, the President himself commended him on the 'good job' he had done." July 9 *Newsweek* 13/2 July 30 *Newsweek* 15/2-3, 20/3 1974 Sep 2 *Time* 46/1 "'The irony to me is that when we went to the Watergate and were called burglars, we didn't take anything,' said an indignant Barker after the robbery. 'As a matter of fact, we left something,' he added, referring presumably to the Waterbuggers' abandoned professional tools." Oct *Atlantic* 100/3 "Our final guest speaker in this section was Charles W. Bates, San Francisco bureau chief of the FBI. In introducing him I explained we were studying Waterbuggers and invited him to tell the students all about FBI surveillance of suspected subversives." —**Waterbuggery** *n* 1974 May *Atlantic* 96/1 "But then a dearth of issues is better than *counterproductive* issues, especially as long as the Republicans are suspect for Waterbuggery and malevolent incompetence." —**Waterbugging** *n* 1973 May 17 Jack Anderson in *Tuscaloosa News* 4/4 "Jeb Magruder has told prosecutors that ex-Attorney General John Mitchell opposed the Waterbugging, although he went along reluctantly in the end."

Waterbungler *n* One of the group that bungled the Watergate break-in 1973 Aug 6 *Newsweek* 25/2 "That Mr. Nixon would even think of clemency for the Waterbunglers is somewhat surprising—unless he already suspected that the burglary had been officially authorized."

Waterfallout; Watergate fallout *n* [*Watergate WBD75 n 1* + *fallout BDNE;* perh infl by *waterfall:* note punning use of "trickle" and "flood" in first quot] 1973 Sep 17 *Newsweek* 25/3 "WATERFALLOUT: Like the affair itself, the trade in Watergate trivia started as a trickle. But before long, quick-witted entrepreneurs across the country had turned out a flood of Watergate games, bumper stickers, posters, T shirts and even whisky labels." Sep 24 *Newsweek* 9/1 "Waterfallout included a neo-Chaucerian satiric poem (page 34), and Mr. Nixon elevated his profile (page 32)." 1974 Feb 11 *Newsweek* 24/1 "But in private, the party pros give a far different story, and in recent weeks more and more have been tormented by nightmares of Republican candidates drowning in a massive 'Waterfallout' at the polls this fall." July 27 *National Observer* 7/1 "That that record is being painstakingly reviewed this month on the fifth anniversary of Chappaquiddick says something about the Watergate fallout."

Watergaffe [*Water*gate + Fr *gaffe*] 1973 Dec 17 *Time* 49/1 "[One of *Le Canard*'s cartoonists had stumbled on an attempt to install bugging devices in the paper's new offices.] On the front page of its 'Watergaffe' issue, the editors jokingly boasted: 'Read *Le Canard Enchainé,* the most listened-to newspaper in France.'" See also WATERGOOF

Watergateana *n* [*Watergate* + *-ana W3 n pl suffix*] 1975 June *Esquire* 78/3 "'Frank is a wonderful guy, but he will probably self-destruct. . . . He did it with his law practice, he did it with the Peace Corps. . . .' Wouldn't it be wonderful if, now, he'd done it with Watergateana!" Sep *Esquire* 58/3

Watergateite *n* 1974 Oct 4 *New Times* (NYC) 27/3 "Then, when President Ford . . . attempted to recoup by floating a lead balloon saying all *forty-eight*(!) Watergateites were being considered for official mercy, the wailings and yowlings sounded like the Anvil Chorus getting its pitch from a buzz saw."

Watergateless *adj* 1974 May 27 *Newsweek* 87/2-3 (reprod of part of a page from *The Mercury,* Pottstown, Pa) "If you're interested, read about it, if not, toss this sheet away and you will have a 'Watergateless' newspaper."

Watergateman *n* 1973 Oct *Atlantic* 120/2 "A cynical soul can accept the duality of a man in need of a shield secluding himself with the co-producer of his foreign-policy extravaganzas—Henry Kissinger—on one flank, and the Watergatemen on the other."

Watergater *n* A participant in or one associated with the Watergate scandal 1973 July 9 *Newsweek* 29/3 "And that, dear children, is why 'Jonathan Livingston Seagull' wound up on the best-seller list, and the Watergaters are going to wind up in jail." 1974 Jan 5 *National Observer* 12/1 "Watergate has inspired a plethora of anti-Nixon [bumper] stickers . . . *See You Later, Watergater.*" Feb 7 *NY Rev of Books* 34/2 (letter) "Attorney Leonard Boudin has filed a suit against the government Watergaters on behalf of the Socialist Workers Party which has been continuously subjected to illegal government harassment and surveillance."

Watergatese *n* 1975 Oct 26 *NY Times Book Rev* 28/5 "Higgins criticizes such Watergatese as 'at that point in time.'"

Watergatish *adj* 1973 Fall *Bureaucrat* 267 "In such a case, it implies no disrespect for law and order to disagree with counsel and act even without his approval. Nor would such independence be Watergatish."

Watergatism *n* 1977 Oct *Analog* 152/1 "Senator Mike Pollock had arrived on the Hill five years earlier, the junior senator from California, one of the young Turks out to purge the government of Watergatism."

Watergative *adj* 1973 Nov *Harper's* 139/3 (Readers were asked to write a "poem parody, comic monologue, or new words to an old tune to immortalize this historic event" [Watergate].) "Listen my friends, and contemplate / The midnight raid on the Watergate. / . . . But the Presidency is inoperative / As long as the White House is Watergative."

Watergatology *n* 1973 Nov 5 *Newsweek* 62/2 (heading of a story about foreign reaction to "the spectacle of a U.S. President threatened by impeachment at home while he engaged the Soviet Union in a Mideast faceoff") "Watergatology."

Watergimmick *n* Novelty such as a sign or poster containing derogatory remarks on the Watergate affair 1973 June 25 *Newsweek* 21/1 (picture caption) "Watergimmicks: Signs, posters, towels."

Watergoof *n* 1975 May–June *Sat Eve Post* 113/1 "Aha, and in Paris, the S.D.E.C.E. [Service de la Documentation Extérieure et du Contre-espionage] was caught installing bugging devices in the offices of a leading humor magazine. The press dubbed this a 'Watergoof.'" See also WATERGAFFE

AMONG THE NEW WORDS

I. WILLIS RUSSELL AND MARY GRAY PORTER

University of Alabama

O NE OF THE WORDS in this installment, *lifeline*, has appeared in this department before, in *American Speech* 16 (1941): 308–9, where the then new sense of a vital supply route or line of communications is recorded. In spite of the great diversity of meaning, the original nautical term (*OED*, 1794→), the 1941 sense of *lifeline*, and our present entry all denote something that is essential to the preservation of life.

In addition to the two senses of *living museum* entered below, another is illustrated in *Webster's New Collegiate Dictionary* (8th edition, s.v. *living, adj* 2a): "the wilderness is a [living] museum . . . of natural history."

There seems to be no difference in meaning between *peak(-load) pricing* and *time-of-day pricing* (see the 1974 quotation under the first term). Presumably, the utility companies, on the basis of their experience with local patterns of consumption, specify certain hours of the day as the peak hours, unless their metering technology is sufficiently advanced to permit a more refined correlation between the time of consumption and the time of peak demand. Our citations, however, offer no justification for a distinction based on such metering methods.

Acknowledgment: Richard E. Ray for the 1978 *lifeline* citation.

hit lady *n* [cf *OEDS, hit man* 1970] Woman who commits murder for hire, HIT PERSON, HIT WOMAN 1976 *TV Season 74-75*, ed Nina David (Phoenix, Ariz: Oryx Press) 75/1 "*Hit Lady* Tuesday/Wednesday Movie of the Week ABC . . . Premiere date: 10/8/74." Oct 16 *TV Guide* A70/1 "'Hit Lady,' a 1974 TV-movie written by and starring Yvette Mimieux as an artist who works part-time as a syndicate assassin." 1978 Feb 10 "Wonder Woman" CBS TV Quot sv HIT PERSON

hit list *n* **1:** [*World Book Dictionary* 1979] List of targets for assassins 1976 Jan 5 *Time* 46/1 "One intelligence official, however, bitterly labeled *Counterspy's* roster of CIA agents as nothing more or less than 'a hit list.'" 1978 May 8 *Fortune* 117/2 "It is a fact of considerable symbolic importance that [he] is one of the very few corporate chief executives who carries a gun. . . . (He explains that his name has appeared on various 'hit lists.')" **2:** List of persons or programs against whom some concerted action is to be taken 1976 Jan 23 *New Times* (NYC) 30/1 "On a 'hit list' of 4,300 hoods Kennedy had designated for harassment and prosecution, Giancana, according to a former Kennedy aide, 'ranked number three on the list, maybe number two, with Hoffa, of course, claiming top spot.'" 1977 Apr 17 "Total News" WBRC-TV, Ch 6, Birmingham, Ala ". . . now that the Tennessee-Tombigbee waterway has been saved from President Carter's hit list . . ." 1979 Jan 11 Robert Pierpont CBS TV ". . . hit list of pork-barrel items that have to be eliminated." Jan 21

Tuscaloosa (Ala) *News* A–14/3 (AP) "The right-to-life forces already have announced a 'hit list' of senators who will be targeted for defeat in the 1980 elections." Apr 11 Jack Anderson in *Tuscaloosa News* 4/6 "As the pressure groups line up their sights for the 1980 elections, one prominent target is startled to find himself on one particular single-issue group's hit list. Sen. Frank Church, D-Idaho, has been marked for political extinction by the anti-abortionists despite his generally conservative stand."

hit man *n* [cf *OEDS, hit man* "a hired murderer" 1970; *Dict of Amer Slang* Supp 1975; *6000 Words;* for a similar change in meaning, cf *hatchet man (W3)*] 1974 July *Atlantic* 20/3 "Never review the work of an enemy. Unless you fancy yourself as a public assassin, a sort of licensed literary hit man, you will instinctively avoid this poisonous practice like the plague it is." Nov 9 *National Star* 48 (heading) "HOCKEY'S HIT MEN TRACK THE FLYERS." 1976 Mar *Reader's Digest* 34/1 "Every team employs swashbuckling 'hit men' and 'enforcers.' . . . The Philadelphia Flyers' Dave 'Hammer' Schultz is called a 'star'—and frequently credited with having made 'the big play of the game'—even though he rarely scores or blocks a puck. He excels at another job: ferocious attacks on opposing teams' stars." June 13 *NY Times Book Rev* 1/1, rev of Ring Lardner, Jr, *The Lardners: My Family Remembered* (NY: Harper & Row) "Curiously, the man whose very absence so impressed the killer sophisticates and one-line hit men of the Algonquin was a Midwestern sportswriter who wrote among other things funny items about his children for the papers, captions for a comic strip and the kind of dialect comedy some of them must have come to New York to get away from." 1977 Sep 30 *New Times* (NYC) 4/3 (letter) "The description of Roger Wood as my 'Australian hit-man' is typical. Roger is neither Australian nor a hit-man."

hit person *n* HIT LADY 1978 Feb 10 "Wonder Woman" CBS TV "[Man:] 'Violet used to be our number-one hit lady.' [Violet:] 'Hit person.'"

hit woman *n* HIT LADY 1977 Dec 10 *TV Guide* A7/1 "Of course he's got to be assassinated and an international hit woman is hired; she's a Bryn Mawr grad, a ruthless killer and a sexpot."

lifeline *n, usu attrib* [cf *OED, life sb* VI.17 "*Life-line,* a line or rope which is to be instrumental in saving life" 1794; *OEDS, life-line sb* 3 "The line of life . . . Also any essential supply route, a line of communication, etc." 1936] Minimum amount of electricity or other utilities needed in a home, the basis for a proposed rate structure under which the lowest rate would apply to the minimum and higher rates to higher amounts 1976 Mar 21 *Knoxville* (Tenn) *News-Sentinel* A-1/4-5 "Life-line rate, which would make the first few hundred kwhs used the least expensive—the reverse of what's now the case." Oct 30 *National Observer* 8/4 "In California the Legislature last year passed a law that said, 'Light and heat are basic human rights and must be made available to all the people at low cost for basic minimum quantities.' The statement reflected the 'lifeline' principle of utilities pricing: that certain quantities of gas, electricity, water, and telephone service are essential for survival and should be priced at levels that make them more widely affordable. Quantities exceeding the lifeline levels could be priced higher." Nov 8 *Newsweek* 69/3 "In Arkansas, seven cities have lifeline proposals on the ballot." Nov 13 *National Observer* 3/3 "Ohio voters turned down a state constitutional amendment establishing a 'lifeline' rate structure for natural gas and electricity users. Residential customers would have been charged a lower rate than now for the first 400 kilowatt hours of electricity or the first 3,000 cubic feet of gas. The rate would have climbed as consumption passed the minimum." 1977 Mar 15 *Washington Spectator and Between the Lines* (Washington Spectator, Inc) 2/1 "At the state level there is increasing agitation for 'lifeline' electricity rates which would fix the price of a minimum amount of electricity, shifting the burden forward onto the larger users." 1978 Jan 11 *Wall St Jour* 12/3 "The proposal will give the New Jersey Board of Public Utility Commissioners the power to set a 'lifeline increment' of natural gas and electricity, defined as a minimum amount of fuel and energy needed to live."

living *adj* Re-creating for study and observation the activities involved in the (usually everyday) life of the past —**living archeology** 1973 title cited in 1976 July *Archaeology* 177/2 "Errett Callahan, *Old Rag Report, a practical guide to living archeology* (Richmond, Virginia 1973)." 1976 July *Archaeology* 174/1 "The translation of data and artifacts into actual processes has been given a number of titles: action archaeology, living archaeology, imitative research, experimental research, replication research and so on. At the Colonial Pennsylvania Plantation the investigators are continually testing and refining their understanding of documents and artifacts by replicating colonial plantation life." Ibid 177/2 "It will be years before the Colonial Pennsylvania Plantation is running at a level that in any way approximates its historic prototypes, but the steps via living archaeology open new vistas for both observer and participant alike. This type of research, although still in its infancy, is adding new dimensions to historical and archaeological methodology. The possibilities of substantiating conjecture and establishing lifestyles by actual controlled experience are endless." —**living farm, living historical farm, living-history farm** 1973 Apr *Woman's Day* 122/3 "The Lincoln Boyhood Memorial, at Lincoln City, in southern Indiana, represents the most advanced living-history demonstration in the National Park System. The visitor can 'walk back into history' through the reconstructed farmstead of the Tom Lincoln family, bordered with a fairly large garden and growing orchard, then proceed to the ten-acre farm, where tobacco, cotton, flax and corn are raised. When members of the staff are not too busy, they allow visitors to walk behind the plow—this they like to call 'participatory history.' [¶] Living-history farms are in active operation, or under development, in every section." 1975 Aug *Progressive Farmer* 15/2 "The lead of two states, Iowa and Connecticut, can be followed and 'living farms' created. These living farms depict agriculture of long ago and are operated as nearly like the original as possible. Oxen pull the plow and tread the wheat. Housewives make candles and soap and perform other household chores just as did the housewives one and two centuries ago." Oct *Boys' Life* 63/2 "The Lincoln Boyhood Memorial Living Historical Farm is just one of the many 'living history' sites run by the U.S. National Park Service. The program includes farms, military parks, American Indian and colonial crafts, and outdoor life." —**living history 1:** [cf *W3 living adj* 4b "true to life or reality: vivid"] History made vivid by, for example, exhibits of documents or artifacts, reenactment of events, or demonstration of techniques and tools of the past [1972 June–July *Modern Maturity* 43/3 "History lives for many Americans when they thrill to the fife and drum corps at Minute Man National Historic Park in Concord, Mass."] 1975 June *Southern Living* 15/1 "We [women park rangers are] in uniform, learning the same things the men learn. Because when we go back to our national parks, we may have occasion to train men to fire muskets and cannons for the living history demonstrations." 1976 Mar 21 *Family Weekly* 9/1 "Philadelphia's major Bicentennial exhibit will be the Living History Center.... The main attraction here will be a 45-minute historical film charting events since the signing of the Declaration of Independence. It will use a projection technique which creates the illusion that the viewer is taking part in the film's activities." 1977 Dec 4 *Birmingham* (Ala) *News* A-27/1 "[He] says the park will be based on a 'living history' theme. No restorations are planned, only preservation of what remains of the ironworks, tramway and nailery." 1978 May *Southern Living* 16/3 "Travelers along the Natchez Trace Parkway in Mississippi have some special activities in store for them this summer. A living history at Mount Locust (milepost 15.5) began in March and will continue daily through October 28." 1979 Jan *Atlantic* 15/1 (ad) "Now, almost 40 years after the closing of the FTP, its voluminous files—production notebooks, newspaper clippings, poster art and set and costume designs—have at last been edited and reproduced in this stunningly illustrated history and scrapbook called FREE, ADULT, UNCENSORED: The Living History of the Federal Theatre Project." Apr 30 *New York Mag* A60/2 "Schedule a day at Stone Mountain Park ... Or drive to Plains for some living history." **2:** Re-creation, on a continuing or permanent basis, of the life of the past 1973 Apr *Woman's Day* 122/3 Quot sv LIVING FARM 1974 Aug *Southern Living* 41/3 "[She] lives her 18th-century life at the Gallegos House. A typical soldier's home, it is the only living history project on that long narrow street." 1975 Oct *Boys' Life* 63/2 Quot sv LIVING FARM 1977 Apr *Southern Living* 22/1-2 "Behind the spiked log walls at Pricketts Fort, the muted sounds of a cooper's tool rasping against wood mix with the shouted commands to a small militia. [¶] The rattle of a loom fits into the silent spots with an even tempo, and breaking the monotony of it all are the sharp barks of a dog playing with his young master. [¶] ... These activities make a living history and are the essential reason Pricketts Fort exists once again." Dec *Southern Living* 54/1 "In its living history program, Florewood has attempted to make the plantation come to life just as it was in 1850." —**living history park** 1977 Dec *Southern Living* 50/1 "The State of Mississippi's first living history park, Florewood River Plantation looks old, but it was practically born yesterday. The new $2.5 million project located near Greenwood, Mississippi, was built last year from the ground up to create a copy of a Mississippi cotton plantation of 1850." —**living museum 1:** Residence that houses a collection of objects such as might be found in a museum 1977 May *Ladies' Home Jour* 82/1-2 "His granddaughter would return to the Old World and become the Princess Grace married to Rainier III and help to rule a sovereign principality from a 200-room palace that is one of the most majestic living museums in all Europe." **2:** Building or other site where a bygone mode of living either is evoked by the reenactment of past events or the display of artifacts or is re-created by persons living at the site as people lived in the past 1975 Sep *Southern Living* 22/2 "[She] works in the Oldest Store Museum in St. Augustine, Florida. It's really a living museum of her own lifetime, with 100,000 items now on display, including ladies' high-topped shoes, front-laced corsets, automobile linen dusters, wicker perambulators, apple peelers, and old farm equipment." 1976 June *Woman's Day* 138/2 "[Another point of interest is] the Oconoluftee Village, an authentic living museum where old tribal ways and crafts are re-created and demonstrated." 1977 Nov 27 *Birmingham* (Ala) *News* D-18/3 "The beautiful old home in Demopolis, restored by the Marengo County Historical Society and operated as a living museum, has a special candle lit celebration each year called Christmas in the Canebrake." —**living ranch** Working ranch operated with the tools and methods of the past 1973 Apr *Woman's Day* 122/3 "This site at the base of the Vermillion Cliffs commemorates a frontier Mormon ranch—now a 'living ranch' with working cattle, even including spring roundup and branding. In the nineteenth-century ranch house, cooking, sewing, bread baking, quilting and carpet weaving are demonstrated."

peak(-load) pricing [*OEDS* 1933 *peak hour* (1903), *peak load* (1903)] Proposed rate structure under which the highest rates would be charged for electricity consumed at times of peak demand 1974 Nov *EDF Letter: A Report to Members of the Environmental Defense Fund* 2/1 "The major problem with current rates is that they disregard the *time* of consumption. Rates do not distinguish between consumption at periods of peak demand when power is expensive to produce and consumption off-peak. If a utility must serve an additional kilowatt hour on-peak, it makes no difference whether that kilowatt hour is demanded by a residential, commercial or industrial consumer, or how many hours that consumer usually uses per month. The critical factor remains the time of consumption. [¶] Time-of-day or peak-load pricing would charge each consumer the cost of serving the particular price he imposes on the system. A high price would be charged during peak hours, and a greatly reduced price would be charged off-peak. Time-of-day pricing offers consumers an option—the option of saving money by switching to an off-peak period. Many electricity uses could easily be shifted to a different time of day, and in view of the cost differential between on and off-peak, significant shifts are likely." 1975 *Environmental Defense Fund: A Report to Members 1974* 1/1 "In 1972 EDF intervened in a hearing before the Wisconsin Public Service Commission, arguing that a Wisconsin utility should adopt peak-load pricing. This system is designed to discourage the use of electricity at periods of peak demand by charging higher prices at such hours." Mar 25 *Wall St Jour* 15/3 "Mr. Zarb's announcement that his agency will intervene on behalf of a so-called peak-pricing arrangement puts the FEA on the side of consumer groups, which have long argued that utility regulators favor big business users." May *EDF Letter* 4/1 "On March 23 the California Public Utilities Commission (PUC) staff announced that the Pacific Gas and Electric Company (PG&E) has agreed to investigate implementation of peak-load pricing.... EDF advocated peak-load pricing in its testimony at PG&E hearings which began in March 1974.... Peak-load pricing would balance daily and seasonal use of electric power, reduce demand at peak periods, diminish the enormous environmental impact of peak-period power generation, and allow existing plants to be operated more efficiently." 1976 *Environmental Defense Fund: Annual Report for 1975*, np "Peak-load, or

time-of-day, pricing means that lower rates are charged during off-peak hours, as with telephone rates. This encourages consumers to reduce their use of electricity during peak hours, thus reducing the need to build more generating capacity."

time-of-day *adj* Of a proposed price structure for electricity: charging according to the time at which the electricity is used, with the highest rates set for electricity consumption at times of greatest demand 1975 Mar *EDF Letter: A Report to Members of the Environmental Defense Fund* 4/1 "In a final opinion issued January 23, the Commission requested further study and analysis of time-of-day pricing. EDF asserts that such pricing, which reflects a utility's higher production costs at periods of peak demand, would benefit the environment[,] the consumer, the utility investor and the utility itself. As demonstrated in France, the growth of demand for electricity on-peak can be reduced if consumers are given a price incentive to switch their electricity use to off-peak hours." June 29 *NY Times* F-1/2-3 "Mrs. Wells changed her housework habits because for part of the year it costs her more than six times as much to use electricity from 8 A.M. to 11 A.M. and 5 P.M. to 9 P.M. as it costs during the rest of the day. [¶] Mrs. Wells, one of 93,500 Vermont customers served by the Central Vermont Public Service Corporation, is one of the handful of residential electric customers in the United States whose electric bill is calculated on the basis of time-of-day rates." 1976 *Environmental Defense Fund: Annual Report for 1975* Quot sv PEAK(-LOAD) PRICING May 25 *Tuscaloosa News* 3/6 (AP) "A current TVA research study in Chattanooga is expected to provide information on special metering to determine what utility experts call 'time-of-day' pricing." Nov 8 *Newsweek* 69/1 "*Time of day pricing*. Instead of charging the same rate 24 hours a day, utilities would charge less for electricity consumed during off-peak hours, generally between 10 p.m. and 10 a.m." 1978 Jan 8 *Birmingham* (Ala) *News* G-6/4 "TVA and the Knoxville Utilities Board are preparing a time-of-day rate test which involves special metering and electricity pricing for 220 consumers in the Knoxville area. Purpose of the plan is to encourage consumers to postpone certain uses of electricity—such as washing clothes or baking—to hours when electric demand is not at peak levels. Charges for electricity in the test homes will be lower during these off-peak hours and higher during times of highest demand." Mar 21 *St Petersburg Times* B-2/5 "The company also got permission from the PSC to offer time-of-day pricing to 3,000 customers in Clearwater. The peak periods for those customers will be determined ahead of time by the company on the basis of its experience." Apr 24 *Family Circle* 22/3 "Under what they call 'time of day' pricing, utilities in about 22 states have begun charging increased rates during the peak daytime hours and lowered rates during off-peak hours (usually weekday nights). Already [some] heavily populated states ... offer special night rates for big manufacturing electricity users. Within five years many experts expect the new 'time of day' pricing system to be nationwide."

AMONG THE NEW WORDS

I. WILLIS RUSSELL AND MARY GRAY PORTER
University of Alabama

IN MARCH 1979, the senior editor received a query from Sol Steinmetz of Clarence L. Barnhart, Inc. Steinmetz had been examining our entry of *executive privilege* in *American Speech* 48 (1973): 254–55 and was unsure of the date of our first quotation (*Federal Bar Journal*), since. though it followed a 1954 quotation, that quotation was within square brackets.

A check revealed that the date of the *Federal Bar Journal* citation is indeed 1954, and a check of our typescript showed that the date 1954 had indeed preceded the title of the journal. An untidy manuscript at that point had presumably obscured the date, and its omission in proof had escaped both of us.

Since a correction clearly seemed in order, the senior editor decided to take a more careful look at the Conrad Philos article in the *Federal Bar Journal*. He first observed that the article was based on a talk the author had given the preceding July, which suggested the possibility of a 1953 date for the term. He then began checking cases cited by Philos and was rewarded by finding the 1951 quotation cited in the entry below.

As it turned out, finding this quotation was sheer luck. On the day the senior editor consulted the official version of the Supreme Court decision cited by Philos, the volume containing it was missing from the shelves of the Law Library. Thanks to a knowledgeable library attendant, the senior editor, himself unknowledgeable in legal bibliography, was guided to the Lawyer's Edition of the case, where the collocation *executive privilege*, with the definite article, appeared in Robert S. Erdahl's brief for the respondent. The senior editor's luck became apparent only after a subsequent examination of the official version of the case revealed that the arguments of the previous November were not included therein. The term *executive privilege* was not used in the decisions written by the Supreme Court.

The fact that *Touhy* v. *Ragen* had been argued before the Supreme Court in November 1950 suggested that the 1951 quotation had actually appeared in 1950. A chance encounter with a member of the Law School staff, with whom the matter was discussed, elicited the fact that the Supreme Court briefs are on microfiche. Voilà: four citations from the briefs for *Touhy* v. *Ragen,* with a reference to a British case containing the term *Crown privilege.* And the fact that the term is used, apparently independently, in the briefs for both the petitioner and the respondent suggests that it may not have been new in 1950.

In his March letter, Steinmetz had indicated that the Clarence L. Barnhart file contained a 1957 citation. The senior editor expressed interest in including it in the supplementary entry planned. In the meantime a second 1957 citation showed up in the Barnhart file from the same source, *The Wall Street Journal*, a week later. Significantly, this is the earliest date for the term in a nontechnical source, and in both quotations the term occurs without the definite article. Thanks are due Clarence Barnhart for letting us use these citations.

Finally, we have added a reference to the latest *Black's Law Dictionary*, which contains an entry of some 130 words for the term.

Acknowledgments for citations: Clarence L. Barnhart (6, including the 4 earliest for *court-ordered*), Edgar L. Frost (1), David Lowe (1), Richard E. Ray (3), and Eleanor Symons (1). Richard E. Ray supplied the definition of *down-size*. Thanks are due Timothy Hoff and John C. Payne for help on the entry *executive privilege*.

boat people   *n*   **1:** Yachtsmen, the yachting set   1972 July 14 *"W"* (Fairchild Pubs, NYC) 10/2–3 "The Boat People / When the big race from Newport is over, the parties in Bermuda go on . . . and on . . . and on. . . . After days of sailing or waiting, those BP (Boat People) show up looking natural and healthy."   **2:** People who live on junks, WATER PEOPLE   1979 Oct *Cuisine* 60/3 "Hire a boatman and row out to explore the life of the Tanka boat people. An estimated 50,000 gypsies have settled down to live on their junks, never moving, forever anchored in Aberdeen Harbor. They speak a dialect so strange it amounts to a different language from the universal Cantonese of Hong Kong. . . . Most of them live from hand to mouth, but there are always rumors of some great fortunes, some junks with paneled living rooms and beautiful, expensive furniture."   **3:** [*World Book Dict* 1979]   1978 Nov 27 *USN&WR* 29 "Usual havens such as Malaysia, Thailand and Indonesia are becoming more and more reluctant to grant the so-called boat people even temporary refuge."   Ibid 45/1–2 "The Vietnamese success story coincides with a move by the U.S. to admit additional 'boat people,' Indo-Chinese refugees who still are fleeing by the thousands in everything from rowboats to oceangoing freighters."   Dec 25 *Newsweek* 52/1–2 (picture caption) "Thousands of these 'boat people' ended up in crowded camps on the coast of Malaysia, but many more were turned away, and hundreds died of starvation or drowned when their overburdened craft capsized. . . . Eventually, some of the boat people were taken in by France and Canada, and the United States agreed to increase its quota of Vietnamese refugees by 40,000 early next year."

court-ordered   *adj*   [*court order*, W3 1961]   1957 Sep 23 *Time* 17/2 "Some court-ordered integration at the college level, none in elementary or secondary schools."   1958 Aug 8 *Wall St Jour* 16/2 "This would be advisable, he said, because of a bill now pending in the Senate that would exempt a court-ordered stock distribution from being treated as ordinary income."   1963 Feb 18 *Wall St Jour* 23/4 "Already, under court-ordered reapportionment, Birmingham's representation in the lower house of the Alabama legislature has been increased to 17 from seven, and Mobile's to 18 from 13."   1965 *Compton Yearbook* (events of 1964) 168/2 "Connecticut's November election for members of the General Assembly was canceled by a federal court after the Assembly in a special session had failed to meet a court-ordered September deadline for state legislative reapportionment."   1966 Jan 30 *Kansas City Star* D-6/1 "Legislators appear stunned by the imminence of court-ordered reapportionment."   1974 Nov *Ladies' Home Jour* 86/2 "Jennifer *was* given court-ordered custody of Billy eventually, but by that time her husband and child had been missing for six months—and her husband obviously was not personally served with a court order."   1975 July 21 *Time* 14/1 "Boston faces a $20 million departmental deficit, chiefly because of the cost of court-ordered school desegregation."   1976 Mar 1 *Time* 44/1 "The suit seeks a court-ordered ban on price fixing of boxes and any other products that the companies make."   Sep 1 *Ala School Jour* 1/1 "The lid bills, promoted by Wallace Administration floor leader Rep. Richard Manly of Demopolis and the Alabama Farm Bureau, would have placed a 20-per-cent increase on the amount of tax dollars a local government could have realized from the federal court-ordered reappraisal."   1977 Oct 28 *New Times* (NYC) 36/2 "The court-ordered election was held, and four of the seven 'expelled' members were elected to office."   1978 Mar 1 "Six O'Clock Report" WCFT-TV, Tuscaloosa, Ala ". . . changes which have been federally court-ordered."   1979 May *Reader's Digest* 147/1 "In April that year, as a result of a court-ordered FBI wiretap, he was indicted and arrested as part of an organized-crime bookmaking ring."

Crown privilege   See EXECUTIVE PRIVILEGE   1942 *Law Jour Reports* 3: 408 "'. . . the attention of the First Lord having been drawn to the nature and contents of the said documents the Treasury Solicitor has by his letter to the London agents of their solicitors dated August 13, 1940 . . . directed the defendant company not to produce the said documents and copies and to object to production thereof in these actions except under the order of this Honourable Court on the ground of Crown privilege.' [¶] The letter from the Treasury Solicitor therein referred to contained the following passage: 'The question of the production of the documents has been considered by Mr. Alexander, the First Lord of the Admiralty, and I am instructed to inform you that Crown privilege is claimed for all those in your list numbered 1–16 other than those numbered 4, 7 and 8, and with these three exceptions, the documents must accordingly not be produced. I assume that you will produce this letter to the plaintiffs' solicitors, and if necessary to the Master, and if it is not accepted as sufficient to found a claim for privilege, I will obtain an affidavit from Mr. Alexander making the claim formally'."   Ibid 416 "The withholding of documents, on the ground that their publication would be contrary to the public interest, is not properly to be regarded as a branch of the law of privilege connected with discovery. 'Crown privilege' is for this reason not a happy expression. Privilege, in relation to discovery, is for the protection of

the litigant and could be waived by him. But the rule that the interest of the State must not be put in jeopardy by producing documents which would injure it is a principle to be observed in administering justice, quite unconnected with the interests or claims of the particular parties in litigation, and indeed is a rule upon which the Judge should, if necessary, insist, even though no objection is taken at all."   1964 P G Osborne *A Concise Law Dict* 5th ed (London: Sweet & Maxwell) 98 "*Crown privilege*. The absolute right of the Crown to object to producing a document in court on the ground that it would be against the public interest to do so. Privilege is claimed by affidavit made by the Minister or the Permanent Secretary, stating that he has personally considered the documents in question. The court will not then look at those documents. See *Duncan* v. *Cammell Laird & Co.* [1942] A.C. 624; Crown Proceedings Act 1947, s. 28."

down-size   *vb*   [cf *down-grade*, *OEDS* 1930]   Reduce the length and weight (of a car)   1976 Sep 5 Leonard Woodcock on "Meet the Press" NBC-TV ". . . the down-sizing, as GM calls it. . . ."   Oct *Southern Living* 1/2 (ad) "Will 'downsized' cars have 'down-sized' prices?"   1977 May 29 Douglas A Fraser (UAW pres) on "Meet the Press" NBC-TV ". . . would be the down-sizing of cars. . . ."   1978 July 31 *Newsweek* 61/1 "The rush to down-size cars to meet tougher fuel-efficiency standards has only accelerated the trend."   May 8 *Fortune* 48/1 "While the new 'downsized' automobiles will require less flat-rolled steel, the growing truck and van market should absorb the loss."   Aug 30 *Pittsburgh Press* C-20/1 "Chrysler unveiled its smaller full-sized cars for the press today, and they're strikingly similar to the General Motors cars downsized in 1977. [¶] The Chrysler New Yorker, Chrysler Newport and Dodge St. Regis are roughly 700 pounds lighter and 5.5 inches shorter than their 1978 counterparts."   Sep 25 *Newsweek* 74/2 "Mighty General Motors, which started down-sizing its cars two years ahead of its rivals, has finished the job."   1979 Mar *Consumers' Research Mag* 13/2 "With auto makers down-sizing sedans and station wagons and with the addition of pollution control equipment which reduces engine power, large-trailer owners in increasing numbers are getting vans, suburbans, and pickups to replace tow vehicles formerly used."   Apr 2 *Forbes* 44/3   May 8 *Chr Sci Monitor* B-3/3 "As the industry moves onward in down-sizing, and car prices move ever upward, a question Detroit is asking is: Will motorists be willing to pay the price for small cars, or will they shun them, in turn slowing auto industry growth and eroding auto company profits?"   Aug 13 *Newsweek* 53/3

executive privilege   See preliminary remarks; see CROWN PRIVILEGE   1950 Supreme Court of the US, Oct Term 1950, No 83 US of Amer, ex rel, Roger Touhy, Petitioner, vs Joseph E Ragen . . . and George R McSwain, Respondents . . . Brief for Petitioner, p 8 (microfiche 340, US 462, Touhy v Ragen, US Sup Ct R & br, 1950, no 83, card 3) "This Court in *Marbury* v. *Madison*, 1 Cranch 137 (1803) . . . established the power in the Courts to enforce compliance with its processes as against a claim of Executive privilege."   Ibid Brief for the Respondent, pp 16–17 "That the executive privilege is constitutionally supported is evidenced, too, by the recognition accorded it by state legislatures and courts, as well as in the British law (see *Duncan* v. *Cammell, Laird & Co.* (1942) A.C. 624)."   Ibid Brief for the Respondent, p 32 "Nor can one ignore British judgments in the field of executive privilege."   Ibid Brief for the Respondent, p 44 (heading of part II) "THE COURT OF APPEALS CORRECTLY HELD THAT THE TRIAL COURT HAD IMPROPERLY REFUSED TO HONOR THE EXECUTIVE PRIVILEGE UNDER THE CIRCUMSTANCES OF THIS CASE."   1951 Supreme Court of the US 95, Lawyer's Ed 419/1–2 "Robert S. Erdahl . . . argued the cause, and with [others who are named] filed a brief for the respondent: . . . [¶] The Court of Appeals correctly held that the trial court had improperly refused to honor the executive privilege under the circumstances of this case."   [?1953] 1954 *Federal Bar Jour* 14: 113 (title of article by Conrad D Philos) "Executive Privilege and the Release of Military Records." (fn to title: "This article is based upon a talk which was delivered to the Institute of Military Law, Washington, D.C., in July 1953.")   1954 *Federal Bar Jour* 14: 117 "The Supreme Court, however, reversed the trial court, and held that the report could be withheld because it pertained to a 'military secret.' The Court also emphasized the fact that the cause of the accident could be determined without reference to the report. The *executive privilege* which protected the report was also recognized, but the case was not decided on that ground." [The case is *US* v *Reynolds*, in which the term *privilege* is used repeatedly but not *executive privilege*.]   1957 May 22 *Wall St Jour* 20/4 "Mr. Gray claimed the 'executive privilege' and refused to tell a Senate Antitrust subcommittee . . . precise details on the manner in which he informed four White House officials . . . of his April 10 decision before it was made public. . . . Under the 'executive privilege,' Administration officials claim the right to withhold from Congressional investigators details of conversations between top aides preliminary to official actions. . . . [¶] This claiming of Executive privilege, he asserted, was 'exactly the same situation in the Dixon-Yates controversy.'"   May 28 *Wall St Jour* 26/2 "Administration officials claim the right under 'executive privilege' to decline to tell Congressional investigators about executive department exchanges preliminary to official actions."   1979 *Black's Law Dict* 5th ed (St. Paul: West Pub Co) 511/2

fund-raiser   *n*   [cf *World Book Dict* 1976 *fund-raiser* "a person who raises funds, especially for nonprofit organizations"]   **1:** Event held to raise money, esp for a charitable or political organization   1974 Feb 22 *New Times* (NYC) 16/1–2 "Some Republican members of the Judiciary Committee were not at all pleased when they found out Jenner . . . had sat on the dais at a Stevenson fund raiser."   1975 Dec 12 *New Times* (NYC) 15/3 "He has been appearing regularly at Democratic forums and fund-raisers."   1976 Feb *Esquire* 46/2 "No one in his right mind would schedule a political fund-raiser in Westchester or Fairfield Counties on a Saturday night."   Nov 25 *New Times* (NYC) 47/1–2 "In Colorado, Senator Floyd Haskell refused a joint fund-raiser with Carter."   1978 June 19 *Fortune* 46/1 "It's true that all Presidents are occasionally required to lay it on thick for members of the party at fund-raisers."   Oct 1 *Family Weekly* 23/1–2 (heading) "HOW TO SUCCESSFULLY RAISE MONEY FOR CHARITY   Almost any event can be a good fund raiser if you know how to go about it."   1979 May 7 *New Yorker* 118/2 "Strauss will attend some fund-raisers in Washington next week. He attends about six to eight a week when fund-raisers are in season."   June *Sel US Govt Pubs* (Supt of Docs,

US GPO, Washington, DC) 13/1 "The next time your club or organization is planning a fund-raiser, family supper, or get-together, you should consider fish or seafood for the star attraction." Addit refs: 1977 July *McCall's* 24/2 1978 Dec *Junior League Rev* 17/2 1979 Aug 4 *TV Guide* A-16/1 Aug 7 *Woman's Day* 66/2 Aug 11 *TV Guide* 36/1 **2:** Product sold by members of an organization to raise money 1979 Jan 6 *TV Guide* A-75/2 (ad) "Can you imagine a more inspiring subject for any work of art . . . or a better fund-raiser for your group?"

micro *n* Microwave oven 1973 May *Weight Watchers* 19/1 "Sanyo's 'mini micro' (Model EM 8200) is a countertop oven priced pocketbook-wise at $249.95—an appliance of the future you can afford in the present." 1978 Dec *Good Housekeeping* 286/3 "Typical comments: . . . 'My micro is the easiest of all my appliances to clean, and I have many.'" 1979 Sep *Cuisine* 91/1 "Two more micro tips: to get more juice from a lemon or orange, microwave the fruit for 30 seconds before squeezing it. For after-dinner luxury, microwave brandy in snifters for 30 seconds; then flame it if you wish." Oct *Cuisine* 116/2 [Some recipes give, in addition to instructions for conventional cooking, the procedure to be followed when a microwave oven is used:] "MICRO DIRECTIONS."

microcook 1: *vt* 1976 Feb *Better Homes and Gardens* 85/1 "Using defrost cycle, micro-cook 7 to 8 minutes, turning package once." Ibid 85/3 "Instead of making a buttery roux or rich cream sauce for a vegetable or meat, micro-cook a sauce with broth, herbs, and a little cornstarch." 1979 Apr *Cuisine* 54/1 "For the rest, learn to use the technique of segmented cooking: partially microcooking one item while you prepare another, removing the first item from the oven while you cook a second dish, and then returning the first dish to the oven to complete its cooking." Apr 26 *Chicago Tribune* sec 1, 13/1 "Some special techniques are called for when you microcook muffins." **2:** *vi* 1976 May *Better Homes and Gardens* 72/4 "Meatballs micro-cook in a traditional Oriental sauce." 1977 Mar *Better Homes and Gardens* F-12/1 "Meats with bone micro-cook more evenly than rolled boneless cuts."

microwave *n* [*microwave oven, Random House College Dict* 1975; *6000 Words* and *World Book Dict* 1976] Microwave oven 1974 Aug 12 *New Yorker* 73/2 (ad) "Thermador takes you out of the kitchen and into any room you choose—indoors or out—with the new, quick-cooking portable microwave that goes wherever you want it." 1976 Apr *Bon Appétit* 29/2 "If you have a family that eats in relays, you'll find the microwave ideal for re-heating foods without the 'drying out' that can occur when the same food is warmed through in a conventional oven." 1977 May *Better Homes and Gardens* 233/1 "Most microwaves open from the right-hand side or from above." Nov *Amer Home* 61/2 Quot sv MICROWAVE (OVEN)-PROOF Nov *Southern Living* 186 (ad) "'A gimmick.' 'A gadget.' 'A toy in the kitchen.' You may still think of microwaves this way." 1978 July *Bon Appétit* 12/2 "If you're not content to use the microwave just to heat convenience foods but are anxious to use your oven to its greatest advantage, I think this dinner for two is one you might like to file away for your next uninterrupted evening together." Dec 4 *Newsweek* 33/1 (ad) "The first microwave to cook a complete meal all at once." 1979 Jan *Bon Appétit* 12/1 Quot sv MICROWAVE (OVEN)-PROOF Sep *Bon Appétit* 20/1 "Get your late summer barbecue off to a good start by precooking meats in the microwave, saving the coals for the final browning and crisping."

microwave *vb* Cook or heat in a microwave oven 1977 May *Amer Home* 66/2 "Microwave on defrost or low setting for 1 minute to loosen." 1978 June *Southern Living* 116 (ad) "The Microwave Cooking Center combines the speed and convenience of microwaving with the traditional benefits of conventional cooking." July *Bon Appétit* 12/2 "Mix the dessert right before dinner. Cover and refrigerate, then microwave just prior to serving." 1979 Apr *Cuisine* 54/1 "Foods that require longer cooking times and foods that adapt well to reheating . . . are microwaved early in the sequence." July *Book Digest* 121/1 (heading) "How to Microwave a Whole Chicken." July *Southern Living* 188/2 "Remember, the larger the quantity being microwaved, the more time it will take to heat." Sep *Cuisine* 91/1 Quot sv MICRO

microwave (oven)-proof *adj* Designed for or suitable for use in microwave cooking 1974 Dec *Family Circle* 27/4 (ad) "It's more than just oven-proof, it's microwave oven-proof." 1977 Nov *Amer Home* 61/2 "Place ribs on microwave rack in shallow glass or other microwave-proof baking dish." 1979 Jan *Bon Appétit* 12/1 "In general, glass, plastics, and paper products make the best cooking containers because, in each case, the microwave energy can penetrate the material to reach the food. Metal or metal-trimmed containers cannot be used because metal reflects the microwaves and prevents food from cooking. [¶] More important, metal will arc in the microwave. The electric current bouncing off the container onto the oven walls could damage the magnetron tube or set off sparks and start a fire. [¶] Most microwave products manufactured today are labeled 'microwave proof' or 'microwave safe.' Microwave-proof dishes can be used for cooking, while those marked microwave safe are only for reheating or warming."

microwave-safe *adj* Suitable for use as a container for foods to be heated in a microwave oven 1978 Dec *Good Housekeeping* 286/1 "Other often-used utensils were microwave-safe dinnerware, glass measuring cups, glass and plastic mixing bowls and paper products." 1979 Jan *Bon Appétit* 12/1 Quot sv MICROWAVE (OVEN)-PROOF July *Southern Living* 188/2 "Canned sauces must be poured into a microwave-safe dish for heating."

mini micro *n* Small microwave oven See first quot sv MICRO

mini-microwave oven *n* 1978 July *Bon Appétit* 24/1 "To the rescue comes a mini-microwave oven—just 13¼ inches high, 21⅞ inches wide and 14 inches deep."

water people *n* BOAT PEOPLE 2 1971 Feb *Reader's Digest* 128/2 "[Macao is] also a seaport whose 6800 'water people' live on creaking, salt-caked junks that venture daily into the water of China, trawling within range of the prowling Red gunboats."

AMONG THE NEW WORDS

I. WILLIS RUSSELL AND MARY GRAY PORTER
University of Alabama

TWO OF THE ENTRIES in this installment are related to old popular beliefs. The first, *China syndrome*, as is pointed out in the first 1979 citation (from the novelization of the movie), derives from the notion of many children that they will come out in China if they dig a hole straight down through the earth. The underlying belief of the sense of *creative* illustrated in the glossary, that imaginative or creative persons, poets especially, cannot be relied on for the truth, goes back at least to Aristotle, who cites a proverb to the effect that poets tell many lies (*Metaphysics* i.2.10).

Legionellosis (compare *salmonellosis* from *salmonella*) could not be coined until the bacillus (*Legionella*) that causes the disease was identified and named. Up to that time the illness was referred to in press reports by a variety of terms, among them "the baffling American Legion illness" (UPI dispatch in the *Birmingham* [Ala.] *Post-Herald*, 14 Aug. 1976, p. C–4/1) and "the American Legionnaires' Philadelphia fever" (*Time*, 16 Aug. 1976, p. 68/1), as well as the terms cited in the glossary. Officials of the American Legion asked reporters to use "Philadelphia Respiratory Disease" instead of "Legionnaire's Disease," a request that produced no better results than Jerry Rubin's request that the media stop identifying him as "a former Yippie leader" (*New Times*, 19 Aug. 1977, p. 68/2). Investigators have learned of other cases of the same illness, widely separated in time and space from the American Legion convention, but *Legionnaire's disease*, or one of its variants, seems to have caught on. It is certainly the name for which our files supply the most documentation.

Our entry for *Legionnaire's disease* is in some ways a departure from our usual practice. The 1978 edition of the *World Book Dictionary* enters *legionnaires'* or *legionnaire's disease*, and we have on other occasions offered citations that antedate dictionary entries. This is not our purpose here, however, for the earliest possible date would be in the first few days of August 1976, when health officials came to realize that an epidemic of some illness had broken out among the by then dispersed convention-goers. Rather, our aim has been to present quotations that illustrate the varied forms of the term in a very limited context, not in a more extensive context that would offer information of help in defining the term. Our citations vary in the use of the apostrophe and capitals. The most frequently occurring variant is *Legionnaire's disease* (11). The form next highest in frequency is *Legionnaires' disease* (8), followed by *legionnaire's disease* (4, plus one *legionaire's disease*); *Legionnaire's Disease, legionnaires disease,* and *Legionnaires Disease* (3 each); *Legionnaires disease* (2), and *legionnaires' disease* (1).

In spite of the ambiguity of certain citations in our files and perhaps also of some in the glossary, there seem to be enough unambiguous illustrations to justify setting up the two definitions of *profit center*.

Acknowledgments for citations: Walter S. Avis (1), Guy Bailey (5), Oliver Finley Graves (4), Anne B. Russell (1).

China syndrome Accident in which the failure of cooling systems causes the core of a nuclear reactor to overheat to the melting point of the fuel and the reactor vessel; meltdown 1970 June *Esquire* 76/4 "This 'fast-breeder reactor' required a large flow of coolant to keep control and prevent the 'China syndrome'—a constant worry to technicians, for once she starts melting, she'll melt her way all the way down to China." 1972 June *Reader's Digest* 98/1–2 "And here we come to the China Syndrome, the so-called 'maximum credible accident.' [¶] . . . with nothing to cool it, the uranium starts heating up at the amazing rate of about 40 degrees a second. In a matter of minutes . . . 200 tons of molten steel and uranium drip to the floor of the containment structure. [¶] So massive and hot is this molten glob that no existing structure can contain it. Thus it melts through the container floor and proceeds straight into the earth—hence, the China Syndrome." 1973 Sep *Pop Sci* 80/1 Dec 3 *New Yorker* 119/1 1975 Nov 23 *NY Times Book Rev* 53/2 1979 Burton Wohl *The China Syndrome* (NY: Bantam) 139–40 " 'What's a China Syndrome?' [¶] . . . 'If the core is exposed, for whatever reason, the fuel heats beyond core heat tolerance in a matter of minutes. Nothing can stop it. It melts then, right through the bottom of the core, the container, through the concrete basin and in fact, it melts right through the bottom of the plant. Remember your childhood myth? If you dig straight down and far enough, you'll get to China? Well, this is the same idea. Theoretically, that core could melt its way right through the center of the earth. But of course it couldn't actually, because sooner or later it would hit the water table. And when it did, the amount of steam generated by this incredible heat, would send a blast of vapor up through the rock and earth and into the atmosphere. Needless to say, that vapor would be intensely radioactive. . . . Possibly it might render an area the size of the state of Pennsylvania permanently uninhabitable. . . . And I'm not yet talking about the number of cancer cases that would be showing up later.' " Mar 19 *New Yorker* 23/1 Mar 30 *Washington Week in Review* PBS Apr 9 *Newsweek* 28/1 Apr 28 *TV Guide* 48/1 May 10 *Chr Sci Monitor* 13/1 May 22 *Esquire* 78/1–2 May 28 *USN&WR* 8/2 "The Silkwood wreck wound up as the basis for a scene in 'The China Syndrome,' an antinuclear movie released shortly before the March 28 Three Mile Island accident in Pennsylvania." Aug 4 *TV Guide* 6/2 Sep *Omni* 146/3 "It is chic to know the definition of China Syndrome, whereby reactor fuel melts into the ground toward China. But it is even more chic to know the precise antipodal point of the reactor. In the case of Three Mile Island, it was not China but Diamantina, a trench in the Indian Ocean." Oct 21 *Parade* 5/1

creative *adj* [Cf *OEDS* (1972) *creative a.* 1. b. "inventive . . . , imaginative"] Inventive or imaginative, especially for the purpose of conveying a false impression or perpetrating a fraud 1954 Feb 13 *Sat Rev* 18/2 "One of the community's most creative gossips begins to circulate the rumor that she is either a German spy or a saboteur." 1973 Jan *Esquire* 148/1 "It is part of American tax lore that nearly everybody who claims travel and entertainment expenses . . . resorts to at least some fiction. [¶] . . . and many of them perform this creative work the night before the audit." Nov *Harper's* 80/1 "The action [of secret intelligence agencies] . . . throughout the late Sixties . . . was bullish and 'creative' in the sense that stock-market promoters talk of 'creative accounting.'" 1974 Feb 10 *NY Times* F-1/3–4 "But there can be little doubt that the I.R.S. . . . will take strong measures against 'creative' tax devices and improper deduction—no matter what the inspiration." 1975 Leslie Charteris *Catch the Saint* (Roslyn, NY: Walter J Black for Detective Book Club, nd) 149 "You're very creative with numbers. For Carole's sake I wish you'd been a math professor instead of a crook." Sep 28 *NY Times Book Rev* 5/4 "May a lawyer give a client legal advice knowing that the client may use such advice in order to solve some legal problem by creative lying?" Nov 15 *Sat Rev* 10/1 "At 19 [he] was president of his own thriving electronic-equipment business, Creative Systems Enterprises. The 'creative' aspect of the business was that the equipment he sold belonged to the Pacific Bell Telephone Company." 1976 Feb 21 *Sat Rev* 17 (ad) June 6 *NY Times Book Rev* 34/4–5 [from the curriculum of the Famous Politician Writers School:] *"The Statesman's Memoirs 103.* Emphasis is placed on the importance of being boring as signification of statesmanly stature. To this end sessions will be devoted to such tried techniques as the Tangled Sentence, the Turgid Paragraph, . . . the Convenient Memory (Creative Amnesia) and so on." July 3 *Mary Tyler Moore Show* CBS TV "Don't think of it as lying—think of it as creative writing." 1977 Feb *Analog* 78/2 "Any [smuggled nuclear] fuel pellets they have on hand can easily be accounted for by creative paper work." Dec *Esquire* 106/1 "Once or twice his highly creative annual accounting was issued without benefit of an auditor's attestation." **—creative accountant** 1973 Aug 20 *New Yorker* 39/3 "Losses, then, of three hundred billion dollars in a year and a half, spread over more than thirty million investors—such were the bitter fruits . . . of the works of corporate fiction written by the 'creative' accountants, who found ways of justifying fanciful figures on their clients' earnings statements." **—creative accounting** 1973 Aug *Harper's* 72/2 "The extent to which Equity Funding's earnings before 1970 were the result of 'creative accounting' is still unclear." Aug 13 *New Yorker* 54/2 "The kind of figure-juggling that had come to be called 'creative accounting' continued to flourish, and accounting authorities continued to shrug." See also 1973 quot sv *creativity* Oct 15 *Newsweek* 114/3 Nov *Harper's* 80/1 Quot sv *creative*, above 1974 Mar *Harper's* 103/2 June 28 *New Times* (NYC) 15/1 1977 Kenneth S Most *Accounting Theory* (Columbus, Ohio: Grid Inc) 77–78 "Following the 1968 stock market crash the usual drive to blame the accountancy profession began. It was alleged that 'creative accounting' was responsible for fostering imaginary earnings growth. . . . [¶] The thrust of this criticism was that accountants had been 'managing' the income statement by selecting from different generally accepted accounting principles those methods which would result in the highest reported earnings per share. In a report to Congress on the Penn-Central bankruptcy, dated August 3, 1972, the SEC stated that: 'The whole pattern of income management which emerges here is made up of some practices which, standing alone, could perhaps be justified as supported by generally accepted accounting principles, and other practices which could be so supported with great difficulty, if at all. But certainly the aggregate of these practices produced highly misleading results.'" Dec 11 *Birmingham News* F-4/1–2 1978 Feb 13 *ABC News* ABC TV segment on "creative accounting" Feb 18 *New Republic* 5/2 "Creative accounting was employed to rescue the arms business from cuts that the new ceiling might otherwise have required." **—creative bookkeeping** 1978 Feb 26 *Birmingham News* D-6/5–6 "[They] are so mad they are talking of forming and controlling their own company to eliminate 'creative bookkeeping.' They say that movie companies now take the attitude, 'Oh, we owe you money. Swell, sue us.'" **—creativity** *n* 1970 Robert Townsend *Up the Organization* (Greenwich, Conn: Fawcett 1971) 98 "An early symptom of the mistress is a sudden surge of creativity in an executive's expense account." 1973 Aug 13 *New Yorker* 58/3 "Having predicted tripled earnings for a given year, he found himself forced to resort to creative accounting to make the prediction come true; then, having written artificially high earnings for that year, he was compelled by his game's inner dynamics to predict that those earnings would triple again in the following year—and then somehow goad his accountants to Parnassian heights of creativity to fulfill the new promise."

Legion disease LEGIONNAIRE'S DISEASE 1976 Aug 7 *NBC News* ". . . so-called Legion disease . . ." Aug 10 caption on ABC TV "The Legion Disease" Aug 16 *Time* 64/2 "Having heard that several Legionnaires had entered a Williamsport hospital with symptoms of something that soon came to be known as 'Legion Disease,' an official in the state's division of communicable diseases asked Hoak if he was aware of an unusual number of illnesses among his colleagues." Ibid 67/1 Sep 5 *NY Times* E-7/1–3 1978 Nov 12 *Tuscaloosa News* D-6/1–2 (heading) "Legion disease takes 2 forms."

Legionella pneumophila Name tentatively assigned to a previously unknown bacillus identified as the causative agent of Legionnaire's disease and a similar, but nonfatal, illness (Pontiac fever) 1979 June 17 *Birmingham News* A-34/1 (Knight News Service) "The germ that causes Legionnaires' disease has been given a new name. [¶] It's Legionella pneumophilia [*sic*]. The micro-organism is a bacillus, a form of bacterium. [¶] The name was proposed by Dr. Don J. Brenner, a bacteriology official at the Center for Disease Control in Atlanta, Ga." Oct *Sci Amer* 88/3–89/1 "The Legionnaires' disease agent turned out to have quite a few properties in common with other bacteria, but the overall pattern of its properties was quite different from that of any known species. [¶] Convincing evidence that the organism was a new species came when Donald J. Brenner, Arnold G. Steigerwalt and their CDC colleagues compared the genetic material of the Philadelphia bacterium with that of other bacteria by means of the elegant DNA-hybridization technique. . . . [¶] Attempts to hybridize single strands of DNA from the Legionnaires' disease bacterium with single strands from many other bacteria failed to identify any species that were related to the newly isolated organism. Although additional comparisons are still being made, the available evidence seems to justify the designation of the bacterium as a new genus and species. It has provisionally been named *Legionella pneumophila.*"

Legionellosis *n* [*Legionel*la pneumophila + *-osis*] 1979 Oct *Sci Amer* 89/2 "Legionellosis, as illness caused by *L. pneumophila* is now designated, has so far been seen in two basic forms: Legionnaires' disease and Pontiac fever."

Legion epidemic Outbreak of a mysterious and sometimes fatal respiratory disease among those who had attended the state convention of the American Legion in Philadelphia, 21–24 July 1976 1976 Sep 5 *NY Times* E-7/2 "The 'Legion epidemic' epitomizes some of the frustrations of modern medicine. With all that is apparently known of disease there is still not the slightest clue to its cause. It is not even known if the epidemic was an infectious disease, much less whether it was an infective virus, much less *which* virus."

Legion fever 1976 Oct 13 *Birmingham News* 44/1 (CS-T) "The mysterious 'Legion fever' that killed more than a score of Americans last summer 'is not the last outbreak we are going to encounter,' according to a prominent disease fighter." 1977 Dec 6 *National Enquirer* 37/3–4 (reprod of headline from Jan 10 *Daily News* [Chicago?], p C-2) "Link Legion Fever & New Germ."

Legionnaire; Legionnaires' LEGIONNAIRE'S DISEASE 1977 Oct 12 *Birmingham News* 1/6 (heading) "No Legionnaire cases in Nashville." Oct 23 *Florence* (Ala) *Times–Tri-Cities Daily* 9/1 (heading) "Legionnaires' In Arkansas."

Legionnaire disease 1976 Aug 9 *Knoxville News-Sentinel* 11/1 (heading) "'Legionnaire Disease' Death Toll Up to 27." 1977 Dec 6 *National Enquirer* 37/3–4 (reprod of headline from Nov 10 *Miami Herald*, p A-4) "Expert Fears Legionnaire Disease Could Cause 2,000 to 6,000 Deaths a Year."

Legionnaire's disease [*World Book Dict* 1978] 1976 Aug 5 (Kingston, Ont) *Whig Standard* 1/8 "the 'legionnaires disease' that has killed at least 22 persons." Aug 6 *Knoxville Journal* 3/2 "the so-called legionnaires disease." Aug 6 *Tuscaloosa News* 1/2 (AP) "the explosive outbreak of 'legionnaire's disease.'" Aug 7 *NBC Saturday News* Aug 8 *NBC News* Aug 9 *Knoxville News-Sentinel* 11/1 "the death toll from 'Legionnaire's disease.'" Aug 10 *Tuscaloosa News* 28/5 (AP) Aug 14 *Birmingham Post-Herald* A-2/2 (UPI) "the mysterious 'Legionnaires Disease.'" Aug 16 *Time* 66/1 "the rapid onset of the Legionnaires' disease." Aug 17 *Knoxville News-Sentinel* 10/6 Oct 12 *National Enquirer* 49/1 Nov 29 *Newsweek* 54/2 "the cause of the Legionnaires' disease." Ibid fn "the latest victim of Legionnaire's disease." 1977 Paul Dickson *The Future File* (NY: Avon 1979) 39 "the completely unanticipated and mysterious 'legionnaires' disease.'" Mar 19 *Sat Rev* 4/1 Aug 7 *Family Weekly* 13/2–4 (heading) "Tracking Down The Legionnaires' Disease." Aug 19 *New Times* (NYC) 68/2 "an official American Legion request that the media say Philadelphia Respiratory Disease instead of Legionnaire's Disease." Oct 2 (Memphis, Tenn) *Commercial Appeal* A-3/1 "the three diagnosed as having Legionnaires disease." Dec 6 *National Enquirer* 37/1 1978 Feb *Sci Amer* 80/3 May 31 *Today* NBC TV Oct 1 *Tuscaloosa News* D-4/5 (AP) 1979 June 17 *Birmingham News* A-34/1 (heading)

Legionnaire's fever 1976 Nov 29 *Newsweek* 54/2 "The specimen came from a victim of last summer's mysterious Legionnaire's fever."

Legionnaire's illness 1976 Sep 5 *Birmingham News* A-3/1–3 (heading) "Legionnaire's illness takes 29th victim?"

LOCA 1973 Feb *Intellectual Digest* 84/3 "The Intervenors charged that AEC estimates of core blockage in the event of a loss-of-coolant accident (LOCA, in the vernacular) were 'not technically supportable.' They argued that LOCAs in nuclear power plants would 'in all likelihood develop in uncontrollable ways and that there is at least a strong presumption that core meltdown and the release of unacceptable amounts of radioactivity to the environment will ensue.'" Sep *Pop Sci* 79/1 "The nightmare that everyone fears is a LOCA—'loss of coolant accident,' in which the reactor core suddenly loses its water and quickly becomes catastrophically overheated."

profit center *n* **1:** Organizational unit of a business enterprise for which data about expenses and revenue are gathered 1968 May–June *Harvard Business Rev* 80/1 "Almost all decentralized companies have some type of formal profit planning system. Theoretically, a profit budget system should assist top management in evaluating profit center managers." 1976 Sep 24 *Wall St Jour* 1/6 Dec *Financial Accounting Standards Board Statement No. 14,* "Financial Reporting for Segments of a Business Enterprise" paragraph 13 "Many enterprises presently accumulate information about revenue and profitability on a less-than-total-enterprise basis for internal planning and control purposes. Frequently, that type of information is maintained by profit centers for individual products and services or for groups of related products and services, particularly with respect to an enterprise's domestic operations. The term 'profit center' is used in this Statement to refer only to those components of an enterprise *that sell primarily to outside markets* and *for which information about revenue and profitability is accumulated.* An enterprise's existing profit centers—the smallest units of activity for which revenue and expense information is accumulated for internal planning and control purposes—represent a logical starting point for determining the enterprise's industry segments. If an enterprise's existing profit centers cross industry lines, it will be necessary to disaggregate its existing profit centers into smaller groups of related products and services (except as provided in paragraph 14). If an enterprise operates in more than one industry but does not presently accumulate any information on a less-than-total-enterprise basis (i.e., its only profit center is the enterprise as a whole), it shall disaggregate its operations along industry lines (except as provided in paragraph 14)." 1977 Dec *Fortune* 171/2 1978 Sep *Galileo* 24/1 1979 Apr 26 *Chicago Tribune* sec 4, 4/4 July–Aug *Columbia Jour Rev* 56/1.

2: Any highly profitable unit or activity of an enterprise; source of profit; moneymaker 1973 Aug 4 *TV Guide* 5/2 "Somewhat belatedly, they've discovered that the post-midnight hours seem to have potentialities never imagined before. They sniff a new 'profit center' here, and they are attempting to capitalize on it." 1977 Mar 5 *TV Guide* 38/2 "One of the networks' most important profit centers is Saturday morning." 1978 June 10 *TV Guide* 14/2 "Beginning as a penny-ante hobby for its parent, Time, Inc., in 1977 HBO suddenly turned into a profit center, controlling (with a subsidiary) about 80 per cent of a pay-cable industry worth $14.2 million in revenues monthly." Oct 20 *Wall St Jour* 23/3 "I wouldn't be surprised if the [*Kenyon Review*] turns out to be a profit center for the college in a few years." 1979 Apr 26 *Chicago Tribune* sec 4, 6/1 "Brunswick had been trying for some time to unload MacGregor, dissatisfied with it as a profit center." Oct 20 *TV Guide* 8/2 "With advertising, children's programming is profitable, and the center of those profits is Saturday morning. . . . [¶] . . . The pride of each network, though it is its afternoon dramatic series. '*Special Treat* is, quite honestly, not one of our profit centers,' says NBC's Dwyer."

AMONG THE NEW WORDS

I. WILLIS RUSSELL AND MARY GRAY PORTER
University of Alabama

READERS OF THIS DEPARTMENT are no doubt already aware of the publication of *The Second Barnhart Dictionary of New English* by Clarence L. Barnhart, Sol Steinmetz, and Robert K. Barnhart (Bronxville, N.Y.: Barnhart Books, 1980), cited in the glossary as *2BDNE*. Several of our entries are related to ones in this new dictionary of English neologisms.

The new Barnhart dictionary enters, for example, *back-to-basics* and derives it from the phrase *back to (the) basics*. We have set up an entry for the variant *back-to-the-basics*. The citations in our files show a preponderance of *back-to-basics*; however, both forms occur frequently, sometimes within a few lines of one another. Indeed, the back-to-(the)-basics concept is also known under a variety of other names, some of which are mentioned in the first quotation under the entry.

In 1975–76 the pet rock had a short-lived but commercially successful vogue, and accessories were added for the pampered pet rock: "pet rock food" (*New Times*, 23 Jan. 1976, p. 18/2), a "Pet Rock Obedience School Trainer" (T-shirt legend, noted 25 Aug. 1976, University of Alabama campus, Tuscaloosa), and for those called to that Great Gravel Pit in the Sky, a "pet rock cemetery" (*TV Guide*, 22 Mar. 1980, p. A-49/1). Diamonds were referred to as "pet rocks" ("*W*," Fairchild Publications, 26 Dec. 1975, p. 4: "pricey pet rocks"; advertisement in *Town & Country*, June 1976, p. 5: "the ultimate in pet rocks"; and *Green Bay Press-Gazette*, 21 Nov. 1976, p. A-5: PET ROCK. $2200."). *Newsweek* (6 Nov. 1976, p. 115/2), in what was surely an intentional pun, identified a party guest as "the Princess's pet rock singer." And for any good buddies who might consider the pet rock a silly investment, one company offered "Your Very Own Pet Transistor!" (*CB Radio/S9*, Mar. 1978, p. 63/2).

Although our earliest attestations of *RV* 'recreational vehicle' antedate the appearance of the abbreviation in dictionaries by only a few years, we have included our citations for the noun, as well as one each for *RV* as a verb and for *RV-cationer*. The phrase "for many years" in the first quotation and an account of the Eighth National Recreational Vehicle Exposition in *Outdoor Life* (Mar. 1971, p. 96) increase the probability that our earliest date for *RV* as an umbrella designation for trailers, campers, and motor homes—like the earliest date for any lexical item—is tentative and temporary.

back-to-the-basics **1:** *adj* [*2BDNE*, *back-to-basics*, *adj* (1975)] 1978 Feb-Mar *Today's Education* 34/1 "Proficiency in the basic skills, statewide assessment of minimal competency, tests of minimal competency, minimum achievement level testing, or testing of survival skills—no matter how it is described, this back-to-the-basics issue is attracting more and more legislative and public interest." Sep-Oct *Today's Education* 7/3 "Commenting on the test results, [he] points out that the back-to-the-basics movement and the cost of science labs and supplies have recently caused a decrease in emphasis on science." Ibid 18/3 (letter) "I feel that Fred Hechinger ('The Back-to-the-Basics Impact,' February-March) exaggerated the desires of the back-to-the-basics groups in order to ridicule them." **2:** *n* 1978 Mar 10 *Ala School Jour* 4/3 "Back-to-the-basics boosters had their knuckles rapped by sociologist Christopher Jencks in a recent Washington Post feature entitled 'The Wrong Answer for Schools: Back to the Basics.'" May-June *Humanist* 61/2 (AP) "Jackson's operation preaches a mixture of black pride, positive thinking, self-discipline, and educational 'back-to-the-basics.'" Nov-Dec *Today's Education* 35/1–2 "Back to the basics in reading instruction seems to imply a focus on single words and on linguistic units smaller than words. . . . [¶] As it concerns the content of reading, back to the basics can also mean exposure to approved 'classic' ideas and styles deemed to be essential to the educated person."

electronic-fuel-injected *adj* Equipped with an electronically controlled fuel injection system (see also FUEL-INJECTED) [1975 Apr 14 *New Yorker* 64/1 (ad) "A bigger engine . . . and a precise, computerized electronic fuel injection system that gives you both instant acceleration and great gas mileage." 1977 Aug *Fortune* 74/2 (ad) "The S-type is powered by the smooth, silent but amazingly powerful, electronically fuel-injected V-12." 1979 Mar *Consumers' Research Mag* 34–35 "The fuel injection system . . . is controlled by an electronic 'black box,' making it quite different from the CIS fuel injection system favored by several European makes."] 1975 May 26 *New Yorker* 61/1 (ad) "Cadillac's Electronic-Fuel-Injected, 5.7 Litre Engine is standard." 1976 Nov *Harper's* 8/2 (ad) "Seville is also a car of innovation—incorporating many of the latest American advancements. Such as its 5.7 Litre, Electronic-Fuel-Injected engine with an on-board analog computer." 1978 May *Atlantic* inside front cover (ad) "Only Seville offers both a 5.7 litre electronic-fuel-injected gasoline V8 or an available 5.7 litre fuel-injected diesel V8."

fuel-injected *adj* [*OEDS*, sv *fuel*, *sb* 3 b: *fuel injection* (1900); *fuel injector* (1914)] Of an engine, having the fuel supplied to the combustion chambers by a fuel injection system; of an automobile, powered by such an engine 1972 Feb *Esquire* 108/2 "The 183-cubic-inch engine is smaller than most found in U.S. economy cars, but it was a very potent Bosch fuel-injected engine and its 240 h.p. could pull the Gullwing to 160 m.p.h. with the right gearing." 1978 May *Psychology Today* 33 (ad) "TODAY A 2 YEAR OLD DATSUN 280-Z IS WORTH MORE THAN ITS ORIGINAL PRICE. IT'S A FUEL-INJECTED INVESTMENT." May *Atlantic* inside front cover (ad) "Impressive mileage is only the beginning when you select the 5.7 litre fuel-injected diesel V8." 1979 *The Tune-Up Book* (Shell Answer Book no 18, Shell Oil Co) [8]/2 "Fuel-injected engines are more sensitive to dirt than carbureted engines." Jan *Psychology Today* 60/2 (ad) "You might be as interested as the Swiss to know that you can't get a Renault with fuel injection. . . . But you can get a fuel-injected Rabbit." Nov 16 *Chr Sci Monitor* 19/3 "The [Volvo] 240 and 260 series, all fuel-injected, will be joined by a 250 sharing the 260's six-cylinder engine with the 240's body."

jiggle; jiggly *n* [*2BDNE*, *jiggly*, *jiggle*, *adj* (1978)] Sexually suggestive dress or behavior 1979 Sep 24 *People* 67/3 "Suddenly ABC's *Charlie's Angels* is threatening to junk the 'jiggle.' True, the series opened the season last week with bounteous Cheryl Ladd stuffed into a bikini." Nov 17 *TV Guide* 16/2 "And during what she refers to as 'the year of the jiggle,' when the networks were hurrying to modeling agencies to cast shows, she did receive offers from 'grade C and D *Charlie's Angels* ripoffs,' but she turned them all down." 1980 Jan 27 *Family Weekly* 18/1 "The monitors count up instances of profanity, scenes of 'suggested intercourse outside of marriage,' displays of what the trade calls 'jiggly,' and the like." Feb 16 *TV Guide* 13–14 "It [a no-cut contract for 'beat-up, 55-year-old Norman Fell'] constituted an astounding triumph for the uglies of the world—coming as it did from Silverman, the glamor-minded King of Jiggles on the female side." Mar *Good Housekeeping* 68/1 "Dainty footfalls rush to the rescue and, a few jiggles and giggles later, the door swings in." —**jiggle factor** 1979 Aug 11 *TV Guide* 35/2 "Meanwhile, the television critics are currently preoccupied with what they call 'the jiggle factor,' of which *Charlie's Angels* is considered the mother. But 'jiggle' has always been around." —**jiggle-o** *n* [play on *jiggle* and *gigolo*, perh also influenced by the brand name *Jell-O*] Quot under next subentry —**jiggly syndrome** 1979 Apr 30 *Time* 59/1 "In what Hollywood calls the 'jiggly' syndrome of successful TV series featuring winsome leading women, *Three's Company*'s Suzanne Somers has been one of the leading jiggle-os."

jiggle *vb* 1965 Jun 13 *NY Times* X-17/3 "An example of one who jiggles is the woman who wore high heels, blue jeans and a sequined halter to Monday's Giacometti opening." 1969 John Hallowell *The Truth Game* (NY: Simon & Schuster) 63 "Watching Kim [a man who has undergone sex-change surgery] jiggle her football frame and tell 'my very interesting story, darling' in stammering accented English, Dawn disengages herself from the stockbroker who wants to take her home." 1977 Robert Kimmel Smith *Sadie Shapiro in Miami* (NY: Fawcett Crest) 7 " 'The first time I saw Sadie I knew she was special,' Sam told me, 'because when she came jogging by, not one part of her was loose enough to jiggle.' " 1979 Burton Wohl *The China Syndrome* (NY: Bantam) 3–4 "And tell that belly dancer to keep it cool. . . . this is a *family* program. If she jiggles too much and pops out of that bikini top, we're in big trouble." Nov *Harper's* 8/3 (letter) "I . . . find that [public television] provides a thinking person's alternative to the mindless chase scenes and postpubescent jiggling of body parts that make up the bulk of network programming." Nov 3 *TV Guide* 33/2 "Silverman *loved* the idea of three jiggling detective-maidens."

meltdown *n* [*OEDS*, *meltdown*, *sb* a: 1937 (of ice cream), 1965 (of a reactor core)] Figurative sense 1979 May 13 "60 Minutes" CBS-TV "They're going to turn into the stretch, and they're going to have a real meltdown." 1980 Jan 14 *Newsweek* 37/3 "But his lead in a Des Moines Register state poll has dissipated from 49–26 last August to a 40–40 dead heat in December—the meltdown has reduced some of Kennedy's people to praying for a blizzard deep enough to snow in Carter's heavily rural and small-town constituency on caucus night—or for a farm-belt backlash against Carter's cutback on grain sales to the Soviets." Mar 28 Walter Cronkite CBS-TV "What happened was a meltdown of the optimism [? concerning nuclear power]." Apr 7 *Newsweek* 22/1 "What the returns revealed was not so much [Kennedy's] strength as Carter's deepening weakness—a showing that left his own people asking one another anxiously whether the meltdown of his Presidency has begun." May *Omni* 46/1 "This 'super bowl of tomfoolery' is calculated to give these brilliant students a chance to blow off pre-exam anxiety and to avert a cerebral meltdown." May 12 *Newsweek* 54/1 "Kennedy's slim chances rest on two assumptions: that Carter will come to be perceived as a sure loser . . . and that the Democratic Party will turn to Kennedy. . . . Kennedy's campaign handlers have devised a strategy to exploit such a Carter meltdown."

Miranda [*OEDS*, *Miranda* (1966), *Miranda warning* (1972); *2BDNE*, *Miranda*, *adj* (1967)] *n* Miranda warning 1977 Feb 13 *Tuscaloosa News* D-4/4 " 'I just read them (anyone taking the [polygraph] test) the Miranda (warning),' Fuller said." *vt* **1:** Read (a suspect) his rights as required by the US Supreme Court ruling in *Miranda vs Arizona* (1966) 1975 Nov 4 "Joe Forrester" NBC-TV " 'Be sure to give him his rights.'—I'll Miranda him all the way downtown.' " **2:** Bring into conformity with the requirements of the Miranda ruling 1979 Jan 12 *Birmingham Post-Herald* A-4/3–4 (letter) "The biggest problem with our legal system is lawyers and judges. . . . [¶] Years ago the police yelled that Miranda would ruin them. It has led to better policing, higher standards, and general improvement. [¶] I, for one, would like to see our legal system Miranda'd."

pet rock *n* **1:** Rock packaged with a "training manual" and sold as a novelty gift item [1958 Mar 8 *Sat Rev* 20/3 "When Ouida the novelist was an imaginative little girl named Louise Ramée in a tiny provincial town in England, she used sometimes in her walks to 'pick up a stone lying by the wayside, take it home, and make a sort of pet of it, saying it was lonely and uncared for.' This charming story, told by Ouida's first biographer, is related by her latest, Monica Stirling, in . . . 'The Fine and the Wicked,' which covers the years 1839 to 1908."] 1975 Dec 22 *Time* 4/1 (letter) "I can't understand why anyone would be willing to pay $4 for a pet rock, especially since it doesn't even come with a pedigree. [¶] I have a mongrel rock that may not have been purchased in a big fancy store like Bloomingdale's but does all the tricks mentioned in your article." 1976 Feb 6 *Wall St Jour* 6/2 (cartoon caption) "[Veterinarian on phone:] 'No, we don't board pet rocks.' " Feb 9 NBC News film clip on "Six O'Clock Report" WSFA-TV, Ch 12, Montgomery, Ala "It was the first pet rock show. . . . The Museum is not sure there will be a second annual pet rock show." Apr 17 *National Observer* 8/6 "If you are looking for companions for your pet rock, check out the U.S. Geological Survey leaflet, 'Collecting Rocks.' " 1977 Dec 11 *Tuscaloosa News* C-10/3 (*Washington Post*) "It was an idea conceived late at night in a Los Gatos, Calif., bar, and nine months later Gary Dahl's Pet Rock made him a near millionaire." 1979 Mar 13 *Woman's Day* 22/2 "When planted outdoors the tough young shoots will soon provide a scruffy-looking weedsward where one can romp and play with one's Pet Rock." **2:** Fad that brings considerable profit to its promoter 1976 Nov 6 *National Observer* 8/3 "Now novelty entrepreneurs, dreaming of a gimmick that could be this year's Pet Rock, are scrounging among the shreds of last year's money for this year's hot gift item." 1979 Apr 29 *NY Times Mag* 22/4 " 'In the beginning,' he says wistfully, 'I figured to make five, six million. I was going to quit Wall St. I really pictured this [Rent-A-Jogger service] like another Pet Rock, but it wasn't.' "

RV 1: *n* [*Random House Coll Dict* 1975; *6,000 Words* 1976; *2BDNE* (1976)] Earlier quots 1970 Sept *Pop Sci* 20/1 "California has led the way for many years not only in introducing the recreational vehicle, but in also providing many of its interesting innovations. And they seem to be in the vanguard of yet another new trend—the changeover of RV electrical systems to 12 volts, rather than 110." 1971 Mar *Outdoor Life* 100/2 "More and more RV's are being equipped with TV outlets and antenna domes on the roof." 1972 Mar-Apr *Consumers Digest* 4/1 "The key [to inexpensive family vacations] is the *Recreational Vehicle*, variously termed a '*Recvee*,' an '*R-Vee*' or simply (as it appears on the Illinois state license plates) as [*sic*] an '*RV*.' " **2:** *vi* Travel in a recreational vehicle 1978 Apr 16 *Family Weekly* 24/2 "Those statistics indicate that camping families either have more disposable income or that it costs them less to go RVing."

RV-cationer *n* [*RV* + *vacationer*] 1977 Apr 18 (rec'd) brochure, Harlingen (Tex) Area Chamber of Commerce unpag "TENS OF THOUSANDS OF RV-CATIONERS ENJOY HARLINGEN'S HOSPITALITY EACH YEAR."

AMONG THE NEW WORDS

I. WILLIS RUSSELL AND MARY GRAY PORTER
University of Alabama

With the assistance of Dennis E. Baron, *University of Illinois, Urbana*; Richard E. Ray, *Indiana University of Pennsylvania*; and Peter Tamony, *San Francisco*.

E VEN THOUGH *-gate* as a combining form has been entered in the *World Book Dictionary* since 1979, we have collected such a large number of examples over and above those already published in *American Speech* that we think one more go-round is justifiable. The short period during which *-gate* has established itself and *-gate* compounds have proliferated may, unhappily, have sociological implications.

A propos of *exit poll(ing)*, entered in the glossary below, Peter Tamony remarks that "in San Francisco, where the fire department had a demand at almost every election over the years, firemen took a *garbage poll* by gathering the crumpled sample ballots discarded all over town to get the trend, possibly for betting as well as for personal purposes."

Acknowledgments: This is the first installment of "Among the New Words" to be prepared by the ADS Committee on New Words according to the plan outlined in the *Newsletter of the American Dialect Society* (May 1981, p. 14). We hope to make this a permanent practice.

For citations: Walter S. Avis (4), Edgar L. Frost (1), Lena Frost (1), S. Paul Garner (3), Atcheson L. Hench (1), and Elizabeth P. McCurdy (1). Thanks are also due Mary M. Fish for help with the definitions of *bracket creep*, *demand-side*, and *supply-side*.

answer *vi, vt* [back formation from *unanswered*, *Sports Dict* 1976; cf *W3 adj* 3; cf *OED* sv *answer v* 25: 'to give back in kind' (1576); 26: *Obs* 'to return the hostile action of, . . . encounter' (ca 1400–1586)] Score after one's opponent has scored 1979 Mar 1 local sportscaster WCFT-TV, Ch 33, Tuscaloosa, Ala "Reggie King trying to answer [by making a basket after the opponents had scored one]." 1980 Oct-Nov *Modern Maturity* 34/2 "Baugh hit on a 55-yard touchdown strike. The Bears answered with a touchdown of their own." Oct 12 *Tuscaloosa News* A-2/3 "Alabama answered those points on its next possession with a 23-yard field goal."

anti-supply-sider *n* 1981 May 25 *Inquiry* 19/3 "The anti-supply-siders, both Democratic and Republican, are implicitly saying that inflation is caused by too much spending, private and public. . . . [¶] Anti-supply-siders sternly oppose tax cuts in an inflationary economy because they will encourage inflation, by increasing government deficits and private spending. For these critics of supply-side theory, government spending must be cut first, and at least proportionately to any tax cuts. In fact, they would prefer to cut spending and leave taxes alone until a balanced budget is achieved."

bracket creep *n* [Cf *OEDS* sv *bracket* 3c: *income bracket* F Scott Fitzgerald 1940. Cf *World Book Dict* (1975) sv *creeping adj: creeping inflation* in illus; 1951 cite of *creeping inflation* in ADS file] Movement of wage earners into higher income tax brackets as a result of wage increases intended to offset inflation 1980 May 16 *Chr Sci Monitor* 11/1 "[Milton Friedman] notes that Mr. Carter is able to claim a balanced budget involving modest spending cuts only by "leaning" on what will in fact be a $50 billion to $75 billion increase in taxes. These include new social security increases, the windfall-profits tax on oil companies, and the effect of inflation. [¶] The latter is 'bracket creep'—what happens when individuals, because of raises resulting from inflation, are pushed into higher tax brackets." Jul 14 *Newsweek* 57/2 "The particular tax bill put forth by Governor Reagan and the Republican congressmen . . . partially indexes the individual income-tax system for a short period of recent history—it merely removes part of the bracket creep." Jul 21 *Wall St Jour* sec 2 15/5 "A tax cut this year or next—$30 billion is often mentioned as a possible size—could ease the squeeze [on personal income]. However, analysts reckon that even $30 billion comes to less than tax payments will mount next year from 'bracket creep'— the tendency of inflation to push people into higher tax brackets." Aug 18 *Bus Wk* 130/1 (editorial) "*Business Week* opposed the original Kemp-Roth bill because there was no evidence that the tax cut would stimulate the economy enough to increase revenues as much as the cut reduced them. . . . Because the U.S. needs some tax relief to offset the impact of increases already legislated and the effect of bracket creep, which results when inflation pushes wage earners into higher tax brackets. Kemp-Roth II should be considered seriously—but only if it is accompanied by healthy cuts in spending." Aug 20 *Standard Fed Tax Reports: Taxes on Parade* 2 Sep 1 *Bus Wk* 86/1 (editorial) Oct 24 *Wall St Jour* sec 2 56/2 "Furthermore, Social Security taxes will go up in January, and 'bracket creep,' the inflation-caused pushing of people into higher tax brackets, is more substantial than five years ago." Dec 1 *Newsweek* 71/1

demand-side *adj* [perhaps inspired by SUPPLY-SIDE] Keynesian [1976 Donald W Moffat *Economics Dictionary* (NY: Elsevier) 76/2 sv *demand-pull inflation* "Also called *buyers' inflation*, it is an inflation in which the departure from stability originated on the demand side, with buyers demanding more of the nation's output at every level of prices."] 1980 Mar 5 *NY Times* D-2/1 "Demand-side economics (it was never called that until supply-side economics became a buzz word) is what used to be called 'the new economics' or 'Keynesian economics' in honor of John Maynard Keynes, whose 1936 work, 'The General Theory of Employment, Interest and Money,' was the bible of a great majority of the postwar generation of American and British economists. Mar 9 *NY Times* sec 3 1/5 "This [supply-side theory] is in contrast to the demand-side, or Keynesian, theory that to cure a lagging economy, one creates demand through government spending or tax cuts; and to cure inflation, one depresses demand by cutting spending or raising taxes." Mar 12 *NY Times* D-2/2 "There was a second major division that the conferees [of the American Assembly—business, labor, and government leaders] sought to resolve: those who believed that a cure for inflation during the next several years could be effected only by measures to curtail total demand versus those who favored 'supply-side' tax reductions and other incentives to spur work efforts, savings, investment and productivity. The issue wound up with a compromise between the demand-side and supply-side schools of thought. The conferees called for a 'balanced' economic program that would be 'as concerned about the supply side of the economy as about aggregate demand.' "   Mar 19 *Wall St Jour* 24/4 "The idea that a tax rate reduction might increase the revenue has been a standard proposition in economics for many years—possibly 40—but it has heretofore been derived from 'demand-side' or Keynesian reasoning."

exit poll(ing) *n* Poll of the preferences of voters taken as they leave the voting place   1980 Jul 5 *TV Guide* 29/2 "The latest fad in television political reporting is called the exit poll. It is a survey taken after voters have cast their ballots. This technique has been used extensively on primary nights this year. According to ABC's political director Hal Bruno, exit polling is extremely useful because it tells viewers *why* voters decided the way they did."   Sep 6 *TV Guide* 24/1 "The networks . . . are making increasing use of 'exit polls,' questionnaires filled in by voters just after they've cast their ballots. An advantage of exit polls is that they query actual—not 'potential' or 'likely'—voters."   Oct 25 *TV Guide* 6/2 "All three networks have been conducting nationwide polls right up to the last minute, and on Election Day all three will be conducting 'exit polls'—asking voters questions as they leave the polls in an attempt to reveal the subtleties of voter attitudes in this volatile election year. CBS started doing these exit polls in 1967; NBC in 1974; ABC just this year. The yield is so rich in sociological insights that they'll no doubt be a fixture in elections from now on."   Nov 6 *Atlanta Jour* B-1/1 "The emergence of exit polls, interviews with voters leaving polling places, began eight years ago, but in the last few years has been expanded into an obviously accurate predictor of results. . . . [¶] Despite NBC's claim that the proof was in the results, Mack Mattingly's victory over Sen. Herman Talmadge spoils the computer experts' pudding. . . . [¶] Either 'key precincts' were not located in Fulton, DeKalb and Cobb Counties, or there was no exit polling done in urban Georgia, where Mattingly was a smashing winner."   Nov 15 *TV Guide* A-3/2 "NBC also denied that it had based its projections on exit polling."

-gate [*World Book Dict* 1979, 1981 "scandal associated with _____, as in *Hollywoodgate, Lancegate*"; illus quot has *Koreagate*] See *AS* 53:215–17 (*-gate*); 54:285–98 (*Watergate* and derivs); 55:77–78 (David K Barnhart's note on *-gate* words); 56:151–52 Additional illustrations; see preliminary remarks —**Abdulgate** [*Abdul* Enterprises, Ltd, the fictitious Arab company of the Abscam operation]   1980 Feb 5 *Wall St Jour* 22/2 "It is almost as elementary a fact, though, that what Abdulgate is going to parade before the public over the next months is not going to be good for the institutions of government." —**aftergate** [*after* Water*gate*]   1975 Sep *Esquire* 99 (heading) "AFTERGATE Washington a year later—and let's face it, Nixon is missed." —**Billygate** [*Billy* Carter, brother of Pres Jimmy Carter]   1980 Jul 22 Sen Robert Dole on "ABC News" ABC TV " '. . . this Billy-gate or Billy-goat or whatever you call it."   Jul 25 "CBS News" CBS TV "Billygate was what Senator Robert Dole called it."   Jul 28 "Good Morning America" ABC TV " '. . . the deterioration of Carter's support because of Billy-goat or Billygate."   Aug 4 *Chr Sci Monitor* 1/4 (heading) " 'Billygate' inquiry will tread lightly till after convention."   Nov *Esquire* 129/1 "This was the instant exoneration of the President in the post-Billygate-press-conference analysis, the collective judgment that the President had put the issue behind him, thus causing the open-convention idea to die a sudden infant death and, in effect, deciding the convention a week before it convened.   —**coalgate**   1979 Nov 4 *Tuscaloosa News* D-3/5 (AP) "The coal industry case in Birmingham—it may all too easily be dubbed Alabama's Coalgate case—again focuses attention on the ethics dilemmas in the post-Watergate period."   —**diamondgate**   1979 Oct 22 *Maclean's* (Toronto) 32/2 "To some worried observers, what France's 'Diamondgate' served to reveal was not so much the Presidential taste in African souvenirs as his increasing predilection for a fettered press."   —**foodgate**   1979 Nov 12 *Maclean's* (Toronto) 44/1 "Khomeini received another reminder of the weakness of the flesh last week when the first major scandal since the revolution broke over the heads of three ministers. Known as 'Foodgate,' because it involves the purchase of imported foodstuffs, the scandal could threaten Commerce Minister Reza Sadr and Agriculture Minister Ali Mohammad Izadi as well as Health Minister Kazem Sami who coincidentally resigned his post on the grounds of 'lack of harmony' and 'factionalism' in the cabinet."   —**gategate** Quot *sv* GATENIK   —**Goldingate** Quot *sv* GATENIK   —**H₂Ogate** [H_2O the chemical formula for water]   1975 Feb 10 *Newsweek* 65/1 "Then [Gil Scott-Heron] spoke a scathing sequel to his 'H₂Ogate Blues'—'Pardon Our Analysis,' a poem about the 'Oatmeal Man's' pardoning of 'King Richard.' "   —**lettergate**   1979 Oct 22 *Maclean's* (Toronto) 25/3 "At week's end, creative writers Jack Kelly and Ron Greig had offered their resignations. But nobody else was willing to accept responsibility for Lettergate."   —**Libyagate**   1980 Jul 22 "ABC News" ABC TV [used during report on Billygate]   —**NASAgate**   1979 Sep-Oct *Galaxy* front cover "MOONWATCH—Is NASAGATE Covering Up Alien Landing On Our Moon?"   —**pajamagate**   1980 Jan 22 *Tuscaloosa News* 4/3–6 (Jack Anderson) "PAJAMAGATE? When Treasury Secretary William Miller learned from an aide—at 5 a.m. last Nov. 14—that the Iranian government was planning to withdraw its U.S. bank deposits, he immediately telephoned President Carter. [¶] NBC sketch artist Betty Wells of Baltimore drew a rumpled, pajama-clad Miller for the network news show. The secretary, in a thank-you note after receiving a copy of the sketch, couldn't resist a good-natured critique of the artist's work: [¶] 'Aside from the fact that the pajamas were the wrong pattern and that you had the subject on the wrong side of the bed and that it is my custom always to comb my hair before answering 5 a.m. phone calls (after all, you never know who may be calling), your sketch was completely accurate.' "   —**Panagate** [*Panama* Canal]   1977 Oct 15 *TV Guide* A-6/1 "Nor have the networks so far been willing to cover—much less themselves investigate—accusations from some conservatives that the treaty is at least partially motivated by the Administration's desire to bail out big New York banks. Supposedly, without the Canal—and Canal payments—Panama may default on roughly a billion dollars worth of loans held by big U.S. banks. Charges along these lines have been made by leading conservatives . . . but the bank aspect has not been covered by the networks. Rep. Floyd Spence has even gone so far as to talk of

'Panagate.' "   —**Pulitzergate**   1979 Mar-Apr *Columbia Jour Rev* 53/1 "[William Safire's] resultant *op-ed pillar* was the *sleeper* winner last year of a Pulitzer Prize for commentary in a *package deal* engineered by *opinion-makers* with *juice* inside the Pulitzer Advisory Committee. *Nobody drowned at Pulitzergate*, but it did not *play in Peoria.* The hitherto *silent majority* of Pulitzer jurors from the *boonies* angrily *blew the whistle* that their own *print picks* had been *deep-sixed* by the *inner circle* playing *hardball* in the *Big Apple.*"   —**Rashogate** [*Rasho*mon, title of Japanese film that depicted the same event from the viewpoint of several characters]   1978 Mar 4 *New Republic* 42/2 "*Movies*: 'Rashogate' (9 hrs., 45 min.)—37 people and things present 74 versions of the same event. Most unusual is the surrealistic testimony of the keyhole at DNC headquarters: the mixed feelings of personal violation, unwitting complicity, etc."   —**tailgate** [pun on *tailgate* and (Water)*gate*]   1978 Jun 30 Charles Osgood "CBS News" (A colonel in US Army Corps of Engineers had given orders to cover up the prominent *DATSUN* on the tailgates of government-owned pickup trucks.) "It's not Watergate, of course—it's more a tailgate."   —**Teapot Domegate**   1978 Jul 10 *Newsweek* 61 (ad) "Dan Rather would like to have been around during Teapot Domegate!"   —**troutgate**   1980 Sep 15 *Tuscaloosa News* 4/1 (editorial) "It was revealed last week, in what could become known as 'Troutgate,' that officials of the [National Fisheries] center near Leetown, W. Va., have taken to sneaking down to a stream on private property near the fishery where Carter likes to wet a line and stocking it with a few extra fish by cover of darkness on nights before the president shows up."   —**wienergate**   1978 Sep 20 *Wall Street Jour* 18/3 "The 32-year-old Redwood City biology teacher has ferreted out what he thinks may be the biggest scandal of the sports year: an unjustified nickel increase in the price of hot dogs and beer sold by vendors at Candlestick Park. He's calling it wienergate."

gatenik *n* Fancier of -*gate* words   1979 Apr 22 *NY Times Mag* 18/4 "The excessive use of this suffix is becoming a linguistic gategate. The only excuse for its perpetuation is in those instances where rhyme or punning gives special dispensation, as when the furor over New York City's Comptroller Harrison Goldin's dealings were dubbed 'Goldingate.' That bridged the gap for gateniks."

supply-side *adj* Pertaining to a view of economics advocating monetary restraint, reduction of the role of government in the economy, and a cut in the tax rate to stimulate investment and increase the production of goods and services   1979 Jul 9 *Barron's* 18/5–20/1 "In recent years, the CBO [Congressional Budget Office] began to find itself criticized because the models it relies upon—notably those of Data Resources Inc. and Wharton—tend to neglect the dynamic supply-side effects of cuts in the tax rate."   1980 Mar 5 *NY Times* D-2/2 "Although its champions present supply-side economics as a hot new idea, it is ancient. The Physiocrats, a group of early 18th-century French and Italian economic thinkers, put their stress on devising tax structures that would unfetter business enterprise and liberate labor to greater productive efforts. [¶] Later in the 18th century, supply-side economics was pushed to an extreme by Jean-Baptiste Say, whose main theorem was, 'Supply creates its own demand.' By this Say meant that a general glut in production or a depression was impossible because in producing goods employers had to pay out enough money for labor, materials, fuel, etc., to buy back those goods. The employers' profits would also be drawn into new spending for capital goods by the chance to earn interest or additional profits. Unfortunately, however, Say's beautiful theory was killed by the ugly fact of gluts and depressions."   Jun 2 *Newsweek* 65/2–3 "Supply-side economics is really a back-to-basics concept. 'We are re-establishing a number of classical economic ideas which also happen to coincide with educated common sense,' says Feldstein, 40, the high priest of supply stimulus. Unlike traditional Keynesians, who believe the government can effectively manage the economy by tinkering with demand, the younger economists hold the nineteenth-century view that if production is encouraged, less demand management will be required. Instead of dealing with inflation by slashing demand and causing higher unemployment, says economist Michael Evans, supply-siders argue that tax policies to raise production would eventually increase output and jobs—and that the cornucopia of efficiently manufactured goods would result in less pressure on prices. [¶] A major supply-side complaint against Keynesian policy is that it gives the government too large a role in the nation's economic life."   Oct 9 *Wall St Jour* 28/1 (editorial) "To grasp the difference [between the tax plans of Carter and Reagan], you have to start with an understanding of what has come to be called supply-side economics. As a catchword, this phrase has been abused by both its friends and enemies, but its fundamental proposition is clear enough historically and logically. The basic notion is that within a given monetary policy, presumably one anchored in a way to curb inflation, production and growth can be encouraged by increasing incentives for investment and work."   Oct 13 *Newsweek* 99/2–3 "Reagan's is basically a demand-pull tax cut, relying on consumer spending and saving to expand the economy. Carter's is more a supply-side cut, counting on tax incentives to encourage investment and expansion."   1981 Apr *Atlantic* 34/1 "Their major contention is that removing the burden of prohibitive taxation will unleash the creative energies of a competitive, return-motivated economy. People will work harder and more intelligently, invest more and better. The result will be an explosion in the supply of goods and services. The explosion will vanquish both inflation (money will have more goods to chase) and the initial government deficit (more activity will produce more tax revenue, even at lower rates). This is the meaning of supply-side economics."

supply-sider *n* Proponent of supply-side economics   1980 Feb 28 *Wall St Jour* 24/3 "Five years ago when Congressman Jack Kemp began talking about supply-side incentive economics, skeptics called him a snake-oil salesman. Reception to 'supply-siders' was still hostile a year later when they criticized the economic models being used by the congressional budget committees for assuming that higher government spending was better for the economy than lower tax rates."   Mar 5 *NY Times* D-2/3 "Modern supply-siders appear to be the descendants of Say. They appear to believe that if one provides the right incentives and stimulates supply enough, this will solve virtually all problems, including inflation."   Mar 9 *NY Times* sec 3 1/5 " 'Supply-siders' contend that the economy can be revived by such means as cutting business taxes, offering subsidies to investment and research, imposing regulatory reform and setting up a variety of measures to raise incentives and increase the productive efforts of business and workers." Jun 2 *Newsweek* 65/2–3 Quot sv SUPPLY-SIDE

AMONG THE NEW WORDS

I. WILLIS RUSSELL and MARY GRAY PORTER

The University of Alabama

With the assistance of Dennis E. Baron, *University of Illinois, Urbana;* Richard E. Ray, *Indiana University of Pennsylvania;* Peter Tamony, *San Francisco.*

asylee *n* [*asylum* + *refugee*] One who seeks political asylum in the United States but does not have official recognition as a refugee under the Refugee Act of 1980 1980 May 9 *Washington Week* PBS [Lee May referred to the Cuban asylees in Florida.] May 18 *Pittsburgh Press* B–1/4–5 "Here's a new word—'asylee.' That's how State Department is describing Cuban boat people fleeing here. Seems they can't be called 'refugees' under new Refugee Act of 1980 because that's a legal status. Thus, Cubans aren't officially 'refugees,' even though that's what everybody calls them, until government says they are. [¶] Meanwhile, they are 'asylees,' those in search of asylum."

blenderize *vt* [*blender* + *-ize*] Process in an electric blender 1974 Oct *Prevention* 81/2 "Use them [products of unsuccessful attempts to make yoghurt] as you would buttermilk—in baking or in blenderized drinks." 1980 Feb 10 *NY Times* D–43/2 "Each morning I blenderize the skins from one grapefruit, two oranges, two egg shells, banana skins and vegetable parings and add them to our compost pile."

discrimination in reverse [cf *reverse discrimination 2BDNE* 1971] See also RE-VERSED DISCRIMINATION, REVERSE DISCRIMINATORY 1965 June 29 *Tuscaloosa News* 2/6 "LeMaistre emphasized in his discussion with the businessmen that the law does not require companies and firms to 'discriminate in reverse.' This he explained as lowering company hiring standards simply as an attempt to put members of a minority group on the payroll. And he said firms were not to fire employes to hire members of some minority group. That he said would be discrimination in reverse."

gavel-to-gavel [cf *gavel, vt* 1926 in Mencken-McDavid-Maurer p. 237, note 5; cf *World Book Dict* 1981 sv *gavel, vt* esp quot "both sessions were gaveled into session ..."] **1:** *adj* [*World Book Dict* 1976] Earlier illustrations: See also quots sv PRE-GAVEL TO POST-GAVEL 1968 Aug 3 *TV Guide* 7/2 "CBS and NBC will square off this year for a classical gavel-to-gavel shoot-out ..." 1972 May *Harper's* 70/1 "In 1968, the network dropped the traditional 'gavel-to-gavel' coverage of the conventions ..." 1973 May 28 *Newsweek* 113/1 "In the first two days of hearings, each network offered gavel-to-gavel broadcasting, augmented by prime-time analysis of what it all meant." Oct 6 *National Observer* 3/5 "The Public Broadcasting Service (PBS) ... announced that it would continue to provide gavel-to-gavel replay of each day's session in evening prime time ..." 1974 Feb 23 *TV Guide* 8/1 "Some proponents of TV access are suggesting the best way around such fears might be to create a Congressional Broadcasting System (CBS!), possibly operated by the Library of Congress, which would man cameras and supply the media with gavel-to-gavel live or

taped pickups, the way the UN does."—**2:** *adv* 1972 July 8 *TV Guide* A–8 "NBC also covers gavel-to-gavel." 1976 Jan 31 *TV Guide* 5/2 "At both conventions, CBS and NBC will offer saturant coverage—gavel to gavel, and then some." July 8 network promo NBC TV "NBC will report it all, gavel to gavel." July 10 *TV Guide* A–12/2 "NBC also goes gavel-to-gavel, with David Brinkley and John Chancellor as anchormen." Aug 12 network promo NBC TV "NBC covered the Democratic convention gavel to gavel." 1980 July 12 *TV Guide* A–14/2 —**3:** *vi Nonce use* 1973 June 9 *New Yorker* 71 (cartoon caption) "Just drinks, buffet, and then, at eight o'clock, we'll gavel-to-gavel."

pre-gavel to post-gavel *adj* Beginning before the formal opening of a meeting and lasting until after the formal closing See also GAVEL-TO-GAVEL 1968 Aug 3 *TV Guide* 6/1 "This year, CBS and NBC will deliver their usual pre-gavel to post-gavel coverage for the expected four days of each conclave." 1972 July 8 *TV Guide* 10/1 "CBS and NBC, as usual, will offer pregavel to postgavel coverage at both conventions."

red sweat *n* Red-colored sweat on Eastern Airlines' flight attendants, caused by red ink on life jackets, but for a time believed to be a mysterious illness 1980 Mar 10 *Wall St Jour* 1/4 "The malady is also producing red spots on the skin of flight attendants' faces, chests, back and thighs. Mainly of pin-prick size, the tiny spots can last for hours." Mar 11 *NY Times* C–3/2–3 "The rash, which is generally described as consisting of small red dots that sometimes seem to ooze, occurs on the face as well as on other areas of the body. Some have called it 'red sweat.' ... 'Something involving cosmetic makeup' in combination with some other factor such as physical activity, or heat from an oven, seems to be a possibility, Dr. Millet said." Mar 21 *Wall St Jour* 13/2 "The mystery of the 'red sweat' that has been afflicting Eastern Airlines flight attendants has been solved. [¶] Eastern said red ink flaking off life vests used in safety demonstrations has been causing tiny red spots on the skin." Mar 24 *Newsweek* 64/3 "Dozens of the airline's flight attendants have recently experienced a bizarre symptom: tiny red spots on the skin that appear to ooze a crimson fluid. Eastern has called in medical detectives and aerospace specialists from Columbia and Duke universities, but so far, the sleuths have failed to track down the cause of the 'red sweat.' "

reindustrialization *n* [coined by Amitai Etzioni] Revitalization of the American economy through modernization of obsolescent and inefficient means of production in basic industries such as steel and transportation 1980 Aug 27 *Wall St Jour* sec 2, 17/4 "'Reindustrialization' is a word of some flaws. For one thing, it doesn't glide off the tongue. For another, it's nebulous. The goals behind it, depending on how they're defined, could take decades to accomplish." Ibid "Close your eyes and throw a dart at a map of the U.S.A., and it will land at a place where someone is holding a seminar on reindustrialization,' says Amitai Etzioni ... Prof. Etzioni ... is generally considered the originator of the buzzword." Sep 30 *Pittsburgh Post-Gazette* 6/2 "Even within business groups there is ambivalence. For example, a recent issue of *Financier* ... carried an editorial warning that reindustrialization could bring government 'co-option' of the private sector. But an article in the same issue called reindustrialization 'the only truly new idea on the horizon' ..." Oct 7 Amitai Etzioni in *Chr Sci Monitor* 23/2 "The need to shore up America's productive capacity is widely recognized these days. Some refer to it as revitalization; some as renewal; I coined the term reindustrialization. But whatever the name, the thesis is that economic problems run deeper than high inflation, unemployment, and interest rates; that after decades of public and private overconsumption and underinvestment the economic foundation—the infrastructure and the capital goods sector—has been neglected and needs the nation's attention and investment." Oct 14 *NY Times* A–19/4 "The city of Detroit has developed a plan to bulldoze several hundred houses and businesses in an old community in east Detroit in order to help provide General Motors with a 465–acre site for a $500 million Cadillac plant. It is part of the new process dubbed 'reindustrialization'—the rebuilding of our industrial plant, which has grown old and less-competitive than industries elsewhere in the industrialized world." 1981 Mar *Omni* 122/3 "If the reindustrialization of America is to be more than an empty slogan, Davidson believes, government and industry must form joint study groups to examine macro-engineering projects. One result might well be the establishment of a multibillion-dollar industry to develop supersonic ground transport." Mar 3 *Tuscaloosa News* 4/5 (Garry Wills) "Reindustrialization should be new modes of production and distribution, not the propping up of old ones."

reindustrialize *vi, vt* 1981 Jan 9 *Wall St Jour* 6/3 "[David Stockman] objected strongly to the idea of establishing a new Reconstruction Finance Corporation to involve the federal government in 'reindustrializing' the economy. The best way to reindustrialize, he argued, would be to reduce corporate tax rates, liberalize business-depreciation allowances, cut capital-gains taxes, reduce individual tax rates and bring the federal budget under control so as to reduce federal activity in private capital markets." Jan 11 *NY Times* sec 12, 66/1 "'Corporate spending for new, more efficient plant [sic] and equipment will undoubtably [sic] be less because of high interest rates and the shrinking bond market,' Richard Scott-Ram, vice president and economist at the Chemical Bank, said. 'This is not a welcome development, especially if you want to reindustrialize America.'"

reversed discrimination [sv *reverse discrimination 2 BDNE*1971] See also DISCRI-MINATION IN REVERSE 1974 June *WomenSports* 76/3 "USC football coach John McKay told the same seminar: 'We would have to eliminate men's athletics to comply with [Title IX], and we would have reversed discrimination.'"

reverse discriminatory *adj* 1979 Mar-Apr *Columbia Journ Rev* 25/2 "Calling for resistance to the lawsuit in a 1978 memo to A.P. personnel, Fuller stressed the need 'to preserve the high caliber of our news service by retaining the right to hire and promote the most qualified persons without regard to what could be irrelevant or reverse discriminatory factors.'"

rolling four-ten [*four ten*-hour workdays] Work pattern that alternately schedules two teams of workers for four ten-hour workdays followed by four days off. Each week, in an eight-week cycle, a crew begins its four workdays one day later than in the preceding week; hence *rolling.* 1979 Sep 20 *Indiana* (Pa.) *Evening Gazette* 2/5 "The 'rolling four-ten' concept, which means two crews alternate working four 10 hour days and then taking off four days, is an outgrowth of an imaginative and unprecedented partnership between labor and management." 1980 Mar 18 *Wall St Jour* 1/5 "About 1,500 building trades workers at a nuclear power plant near Baton Rouge, La., work four 10-hour days, then get off four days. Split into two teams, they earn overtime for the two extra hours daily and Sunday duty. This unusual 'rolling four-ten' schedule may lead to completion of the Gulf States Utilities plant a year sooner than expected."

warehouse (grocery) store, warehouse market, warehouse supermarket Large grocery store that lowers its operating costs and its prices by reducing or eliminating many of the services, products, or facilities available in traditional stores   1976 Sep 12 *Birmingham News* F–7/1 (CDN) "'Warehouse' supermarkets, which help consumers cut their grocery bills, are taking larger and larger bites of America's food dollar. [¶] Shopping in a budget supermarket feels a little like sneaking into your grocery's warehouse and writing your own prices. . . . [¶] Warehouse stores aim at cutting costs for the stores and passing along the savings to shoppers."   1979 Aug 26 *Pittsburgh Press* C–1/1 "In the wake of generic products and co-operative food plans, comes the warehouse grocery store. Its proponents call it a 'dramatic innovation' and say a customer can save 10 to 15 percent of his total grocery bill by shopping that way. [¶] The warehouse market has no overhead, no fancy equipment and hardly any advertising costs. [¶] Products are displayed in the crates in which they arrived at the store. Customers must bring their own bags and deal on a cash-and-carry basis."   Dec 3 *Wall St Jour* 26/4 "In a warehouse store, customers bag their own groceries and generally receive less service in an austere warehouse atmosphere."   1980 Aug 25 *Wall St Jour* sec 2, 17/3 "Some parts of the country have two kinds of supermarkets; the conventional ones and no-frills warehouse stores, which offer a more limited choice of goods at prices averaging 15% cheaper."

AMONG THE NEW WORDS

I. WILLIS RUSSELL AND MARY GRAY PORTER
The University of Alabama

With the assistance of Dennis E. Baron, *University of Illinois, Urbana-Champaign*; William W. Evans, *Louisiana State University*; Michael Montgomery, *University of South Carolina*; Thomas M. Paikeday, *New York Times Everyday Dictionary*; Richard E. Ray, *Indiana University of Pennsylvania*; and Catherine V. von Schon, *State University of New York, Stony Brook*

THE REPORTING OF THE COLLAPSE of two overhead, suspended walkways in the Hyatt Regency Hotel in Kansas City last summer, with considerable loss of life, brought forth several interesting variant terms for these structures. Two are deserving of comment. Senses *l f*, and especially *l g*, under the adjective *aerial* in *Webster's Third*, and sense *4* in the *World Book Dictionary*, were suggestive but only if one has a clear picture of the structure. We may thus be justified in listing *aerial walkway* along with the many dictionaries enter with *aerial* as the first member. With both of these dictionaries specifying narrowness as the characteristic of a *catwalk*—the hotel structures were certainly not narrow—it would be most surprising if the word in this sense ever catches on, but we include it because it was a variant.

A note on *skybridge* comes from an interesting paper read by Ellesa Clay High at the meeting of the South Atlantic Section of the American Dialect Society in Louisville, Kentucky, last fall, whose subtitle was "Place Names of the Red River Gorge." One of the place names in her paper was *Sky Bridge*. When we told her of our interest because of the use of the same term for a hotel structure, she agreed to write us what she knew about the place name. An excerpt from her letter follows:

Sky Bridge is one of the best known landmarks in the Red River Gorge, which is located in the Daniel Boone National Forest in eastern Kentucky. Approximately 75 feet long and 23 feet high, this arch may have been named for the way it juts against the skyline when viewed from certain vantage points on the banks of the Red River.

We are most grateful to Professor High for this material.

Although *The Second Barnhart Dictionary of New English* enters *platinum adj.* (1971) and cites a 1978 use of the phrase *go platinum*, it seems worthwhile to add a few citations from our files as examples of other phrases with *platinum*. The use of *platinum* in connection with record sales arose from the practice of presenting a platinum record to a performer whose album sells a million copies. In fact, the presentation record itself and not the sales it commemorates may be the sense of *platinum* in the December 20 quotation from the *Globe and Mail*.

aerial walkway   *n*   [cf *W3* sv *aerial* 1 f & 1 g; *World Bk Dict* sv *aerial* 4] Skybridge   1981 Jul 21 Memphis *Commercial Appeal* 9 "The death toll in the disastrous collapse of two aerial walkways at the Hyatt Regency Hotel was rolled back to 111 Monday by authorities who said two bodies had been counted twice at the city morgue."   Aug 3 *Newsweek* 26/1 "Outside the Hyatt Regency Hotel, where 111 people died in the collapse of two aerial walkways two weeks ago, 'No Trespassing' signs barred the curious and morbid."   Aug 18 *MacNeil-Lehrer Report* PBS "Two aerial walkways collapsed."

audit   *n*   [cf *W3* 1 b, *2BDNE* sv *energy audit*]   A survey of a building and its equipment to ascertain their condition and to recommend needs   1973 James H Filkins and Donald I Caruth *Lexicon of American Business Terms* (NY: Simon & Schuster) "Audit. . . . The systematic investigation of procedures and operations, or the appraisal thereof, for the purpose of determining conformity with prescribed criteria."   1976 Dec 5 *NY Times* 49/1 "Two previous audits by the Comptroller's Office . . . found the maximum-security hospital in the northeast Bronx 'unclean' and vermin-infested, lacking in effective patient care, seriously lax in record-keeping and financial accountability."   1978 Oct *Quad* (Univ of Ala) 8/2 "The decrease [in energy use] is handled by such practical-approach programs as . . . the study by graduate students on self-energy audits for small businesses."   1980 Aug 3 *Tuscaloosa News* A–2/1 "Personnel audits to determine the needs of various offices are being initiated."   1981 May *Better Homes and Gardens* 18/1 "Some utilities provide a home 'energy audit' for free; others charge a few dollars. It can be a valuable service, so call your utility company if they haven't informed you about how to get your audit."

audit   *vt*   [*2BDNE* energy audit 1977]   To make an energy audit of (a building)   1980 Apr 9 *Chr Sci Monitor* 3/1 " 'Honeywell,' he says, 'would audit a building, identify conservation possibilities, install the equipment, and monitor its operation.' "   1981 June 15 TVA official (heard orally) "We audited some 300,000 homes, suggesting insulation, etc."

catwalk   *n*   A skybridge   1981 July 19 Reporter on CBS-TV News

CFA   College Football Association   1981 Aug 17 *Tuscaloosa News* 11/5 (AP) "But the CFA can counter with another 'precedent.' "   Aug 22 *TV Guide* A-2/2 "The College Football Association (CFA), which includes . . . most of the top football powers, has reached an agreement with NBC that will give the network the right to televise the games of the 61 CFA members over a four-year period, 1982–85."   Sep 6 *Tuscaloosa News* B–7/5–8 (AP) "The NCAA has said CFA schools would be subject to probation for going with NBC."

creative finance, financing   *n*   Various tactics used to sell homes when interest rates are high, such as adjustable interest rates, assumption of existing low-interest mortgages, and barter or exchange   1981 Mar 23 *Barron's* 16/1 "These older loans, furthermore, aren't being paid off at the customary pace; home buyers, what few of them there are in these days of 15% interest rates, are indulging in 'creative financing'—assuming those venerable liens and tacking on second mortgages or working out wraparound financing deals with local lenders."   May 24 *Pittsburgh Press* B–8/4–6 "For existing houses, 'sellers are taking second mortgages and doing other creative financing,' Christian said."   May 28–Jun 3 *Baton Rouge Home Guide* 8/4–5 (heading) "Quail Hollow: Creative Design, Creative Finance"   Jul 6 *Barron's* 4/4 "What sets California apart, in addition to its sharply rising trend of deliquencies, is that California is the state that pioneered 'creative financing'."   Jul 20 *Newsweek* 58/1 "Many real-estate agents love seller financing (happily hyped as 'creative' financing) because it helps them put deals together at higher prices."

crowding out   *n*   Reducing the availability of credit to non-federal borrowers as a result of heavy borrowing by the US Treasury   [1952 Dec 1 *Birmingham News* 7/4 (AP) "A spokesman at the chief center of such inquiries—the Society of Genealogists—said the place sometimes is crowded out with American tourists searching through the files."]   1975 Apr 24 *Wall St. Jour* 14/4 "For this year's big national issue is 'crowding out,' a slogan for the question: Will the burgeoning demands of the federal government to finance a $60 billion to $100 billion deficit preempt private industry's credit needs in the capital market?"   1976 Donald W. Moffat *Economics Dict* (NY: Elsevier) 69/1 "CROWDING-OUT EFFECT. A MONETARIST view which holds that FISCAL POLICY loses some of its effect because, while government expenditures stimulate an economy, such expenditures must be financed and, at least in the long run, that financing reduces the ability of the private SECTOR to spend."   1981 Feb 23 *Barron's* 21/1 "The siren of inflation woos resources from productive use to 'riskless' government paper. In Israel, 'crowding out' is a melancholy reality."   Jul 27 *Newsweek* 60/3 "If the amount saved [by citizens after a tax cut] were less than that, the government would have to bid savings away from private borrowers. In the process it would raise interest rates, which would in turn reduce private investment. This 'crowding out' would make the deficit essentially neutral with respect to aggregate spending, but would be inflationary in the long run because it would reduce private output."   Aug 22 *Indiana* (Pa) *Evening Gazette* 14/1 " 'Crowding out' basically occurs when the Treasury borrows so much money from the public that there is not much left for corporations and, especially for municipalities to borrow."   Oct 19 *Wall St Jour*, sec 1, 1/5 " 'Crowding out' is a phrase that may have been overused in the past, but to the extent that the Treasury commandeers private resources, some private spending projects may get crowded out."

game-winner   *n*   [cf *2BDNE* sv *game-breaker*]   A hit in baseball or a kick in football which produces the run or puts the points on the scoreboard that win the game   1960 Nov 15 *Tuscaloosa News* 7/7 (AP) "The fullback who sets new national records every time he kicks a field goal kicked his fourth game-winner of the season despite severe pain from a hip injury suffered in the third quarter of the bruising Southeastern Conference clash."   1981 May 21 *Tuscaloosa News* 23/1 (AP) "His bat was hot again Wednesday night as he collected four hits, including the game-winner."   Oct 17 *Tuscaloosa News* 8/3 (AP) "He noted that two of his three home runs this season were game-winners."   Nov 15 *Tuscaloosa News* B–3/1 (AP) "It wasn't a game-winner, but Florida placekicker Brian Clark was still pleased with his record-breaking 55-yard field goal."

genetic engineer   *n*   [*BDNE* 1966]   Earlier quot 1954 Poul Anderson "The Big Rain" in *The Psychotechnic League* (NY: Pinnacle Books 1981) 218–19 (first pub in 1954 Oct *Astounding*) "Meanwhile giant pulverizers were reducing barren stone and sand to fine particles which would be mixed with fertilizers to yield soil; and the genetic engineers were evolving still other strains of life which could provide a balanced ecology; and the water units were under construction."

genetically engineered *adj* [cf *World Bk Dict* 1981, *6000 Words* sv *genetic engineering*] 1981 Jul 6 *Business Week* 39/3 "In late June, Genentech Inc. announced a new, genetically engineered vaccine against hoof-and-mouth disease." Jul 7 *Chr Sci Monitor* 3/3 "Making these or other agrichemicals from genetically engineered bacteria is no different from making other chemicals this way." Aug 28 *Wall St Jour*, sec 2, 38/2 "Genentech's Mr. Ross says, 'You can design the organism to do tricks for you. The better you tune up the bug, the less you have to tune up the fermentation process.' This fine tuning will also aim to prevent other problems, he adds. In fermenting genetically engineered microbes to produce methanol, for instance, 'you could cover England with bacteria,' Mr. Ross says. 'How the hell do you get rid of all the waste?' The solution would be to alter the genetic makeup of the bacteria to create more product and less waste." Sep 2 *Wall St Jour*, sec 2, 39/3 "The initial excitement [in genetic engineering] has centered on the possibilities for medicine in the use of genetically engineered bacteria to produce such substances as interferon and insulin, and for industry and agriculture in fermenting chemicals from corn and other plant life." Oct 9 *Wall St Jour*, sec 2, 29/4 "The Japanese are already world leaders in fermentation technology, the means by which most genetically engineered organisms will be mas produced."

mini-strike *n* A short-lived, usually localized labor strike 1975 Aug 8 "*W*" (Fairchild Pubs, NYC) 6/3 "The Italian couture collections, taking place amid mini-strikes and sweltering 90-plus-degree temperatures, were on the quiet side." 1979 Aug 21 *Wall St Jour* 3/4 "The United Auto Workers union said it may use a series of 'ministrikes' starting in the next two weeks as a prod against General Motors Corp. in an effort to obtain new local agreements on working conditions. [¶] Such work stoppages, amounting to one- or two-day strikes at selected GM plants, would occur before the UAW's national labor agreement with GM expires Sept. 14." Aug 22 *Pittsburgh Press* 7/4 "UAW Vice President Irving Bluestone, who pioneered the 'mini-strike' tactic in 1972, confirmed local strikes were being considered." Aug 22 *Wall St Jour* 2/3 "A union spokesman yesterday said the prospective ministrikes are related to disputes over local production standards." Aug 26 *Pittsburgh Press* E–3/2 "The United Auto Workers Union Thursday is expected to hit General Motors Corp. with mini-strikes in the morning."

negative amortization *n* The rise in the principal of a loan with a flexible interest rate, caused when the interest rises to the point that payments fail to cover the interest due 1981 Feb 24 *Wall St Jour*, sec 1, 10/2 "If the interest rate rose too fast, the payment wouldn't cover the full amount of the interest charges and the lender would recover the difference through 'negative amortization,' meaning increases in the unpaid balance of the loan." Apr 27 *Barron's* 25/1 "Another device boasts the elephantine name of negative amortization. While mortgage payments remain the same for a period of years, interest rates can rise and if they rise high enough, the principal will grow." Jun 29 *Barron's* 12/3 "Negative amortization means simply that the principal of the loan grows rather than declines. It can happen under an adjustable-rate mortgage if the loan contract allows the monthly payment level to remain flat over a period in which the interest payments are rising. If the rate increases wipe out the principal portion of the payment—which could easily occur in the early years of a loan—then the borrower's outstanding debt would increase." Aug 12 *MacNeil-Lehrer Report* PBS Sep *Amer Business* 32/2 "Each of these four plans allows what is called 'negative amortization.' This means that when interest rates rise but monthly payments are fixed, unpaid interest is added to what the home buyer owes. His unpaid balance temporarily grows."

out year, outyear *n* (usu pl exc attrib) [cf *OED* sv *out-* in comb B 12 . . . 'Out of or outside the thing named' 1885; *W3* sv *out adv* 8 a] The year(s) beyond the current budget year (US government) 1981 Apr 22 *Wall St Jour*, sec 1, 28/1 "But we see little need to alter out point of last Thursday, that the Republican Senator from New Mexico, in projecting out-year deficits substantially higher than those of the administration, stumbled into a trap laid by the Keynesians at the Congressional Budget Office." Jul 8 *MacNeil-Lehrer Report* PBS [Lehrer:] "What is an out year?" [Sen John Danforth, R-Mo:] " '83, '84." Sep 8 Pres Ronald Reagan *CBS News* "There would be more budget cuts in the out years beyond 1982." Sep 23 Roseburg, Ore *News-Review* 4/1 (editorial) "The [Reagon] administration is already putting its distinctive stamp on the language as it is sometimes incomprehensibly spoken in the highest official circles. [¶] As researched and defined recently in the Wall Street Journal . . . '[o]ut years' means long term." Oct 11 Pres Reagan CBS-TV ". . . 1983 and in the out year of 1984 . . ." Nov 17 *Birmingham Post-Herald* A–4/4 (Scripps-Howard News Service) "When Republican senators refused to vote for long–term revenue measures that indicated continuing deficits of $60 million a year, Stockman put an asterisk on the out-year budget designating how much future spending would have to be cut to meet goals." Nov 29 *NY Times Mag* 16/2–4 " 'I'm willing to consider revenue enhancement in outyears,' [Howard Baker] said. . . . 'Think "outyear," ' writes Senator Daniel P. Moynihan in his newsletter to 'Yorkers.' 'That is the term we use in the Senate Finance Committee for a tax provision that does not go into effect for one or two or three years after it is enacted.' [¶] 'Outyear'—one word as used by insiders, two words as misused by outsiders—is a contribution of the budget arts to the language arts. ' "Outyear" refers to future spending estimates,' explains Glen Goodnow of the Congressional Budget Office: 'The *current year* is fiscal '82; next January—1982—the President will present the *budget year* for fiscal '83; beyond that, fiscal '84, '85 and so on are the *outyears*.' " Dec *Atlantic* 39/2 "They're concerned about the out-year budget posture, not about the near-term economic situation."

platinum *n* [cf *2BDNE* sv *platinum adj* 1971] Sales of a million copies of a record album 1980 Mar 3 *Crimson-White* (Univ of Ala) 7/1 "Those albums are destined to go beyong [sic] gold, beyond platinum—in fact, there is no metalurgical [sic] way to qualify these awesome releases." Dec 20 Toronto *Globe & Mail* F–7 "It would have been very easy for Blondie to simply crank out 12 more versions of Call Me, taken the platinum and laughed all the way to the foreign exchange office." **—go double platinum** Sell two million copies 1977 Nov *Esquire* 8/1–2 "If the record hangs in there for a month, it may 'go platinum,' i.e., sell a million copies, or even 'double platinum.' " **—go**

platinum [cf *2BDNE* 1978 quot sv *platinum adj*] Thrive, prosper, do very well; sell in large numbers 1980 May *Life* 44 (ad) "Millions of young men and women are going to Dickies work clothes for the look of the Eighties. . . . [O]ur Dickies horseshoe is going platinum." Dec 22 Toronto *Globe & Mail* 17 "Jess's album has gone gold and his romance with Molly, his manager, has gone platinum." **—gone platinum** *adj* Designating an entertainer whose record album has sold a million copies 1980 Nov *In Cinema* 15/1 "Even for the gone platinum recording star, making a movie still represents the ultimate artistic validation." **—platinum-selling** *adj* 1980 Aug 29 Toronto *Globe & Mail* 14 "The very real inadequacies of this most popular, yet least commercial sounding of all platinum-selling groups, come bubbling to the fore." **—sell platinum** Sell a million copies 1980 Mar 31 *Crimson-White* (Univ of Ala) 4/3 (letter) "Their last four albums have sold platinum." **—triple platinum** Sales of three million copies 1979 Dec 27 *20/20* ABC-TV "It's headed for triple platinum, meaning three million sold." 1981 Nov 23 Toronto *Globe & Mail* 19 "The album has proved a significant and widespread hit, and Lodge is happy to rattle off such figures as 'two million in the U.S. alone, triple-platinum in Canada, platinum in Japan and Europe.' "

shootout *n* [cf *W3*, *2BDNE*] A hotly fought contest between evenly matched rivals (fig) 1968 Aug 3 *TV Guide* 7/2 "CBS and NBC will square off this year for a classical gavel-to-gavel shootout." 1979 Mar 1 *Tuscaloosa News* 19/5 "It was a shootout at Shea between a couple of the Bear's boys." Apr 23 Tom Brokaw on *Today* NBC-TV "There will be a real shootout [among the presidential candidates who are named]." 1981 Sep 7 *Tuscaloosa News* 13/1–4 (heading) "It was a wicked showdown, a lengthy tennis shootout." Dec 2 *Ellery Queen's Mystery Mag* 138 "And I suppose that during this Monopoly shootout, neither you nor Helmuth left the board for any reason?"

skybridge *n* An overhead suspended walkway across an enclosed court within a building such as a hotel 1981 Jul 20 NBC-TV News ". . . two skybridge walkways . . ." Jul 25 Memphis *Commercial Appeal* 5 "Two 45-ton skybridges crashed down into a crowded lobby July 17, killing 111 people and injuring at least 188 others." Jul 27 *Newsweek* 30/1–3 "The house was full—1,500 people, some on the dance floor, others clustered near the bar, still others watching from three 'sky bridges' overhead. . . . The majority of eyewitnesses had the impression that the top sky bridge went first, perhaps because of the strain caused by spectators swaying to the music." Aug 3 *Newsweek* 26/2 "The sole remaining 'sky bridge' had been dismantled."

skywalk *n* SKYBRIDGE 1981 Jul 21 Memphis *Commercial Appeal* 9 "The question of what caused the worst disaster in the city's history . . . was addressed briefly by the St. Louis subcontractor who designed the steel-and-concrete skywalk that collapsed onto revelers at a tea dance in the year-old hotel's lobby Friday night." Jul 22 *Tuscaloosa News* 9/3 "Two design changes and a missing washer combined to help cause the fatal collapse of two 'skywalks' at the Hyatt Regency Hotel, The Kansas City Times reported today." Aug 6 *Wall St Jour* 25/5 "The papers assigned 18 reporters to the story and hired engineers to analyze the design of the skywalks. The resulting articles told of design changes that apparently weakened the skywalks." Oct 1 Baton Rouge *State-Times* A–2/1 (AP) "It was from the restaurant the night of July 17 that diners watched in horror as two skywalks creaked, then dropped onto a crowded dance floor." Oct 2 Kittenning, Pa *Leader-Times* 2/3 "The 40-story Hyatt Regency Hotel, where the collapse of two lobby skywalks killed 113 people in July, filled only 100 rooms on its reopening night despite official reassurances of the hotel's safety."

skyway *n* [cf *World Bk Dict* 1981, sense 2] SKYBRIDGE 1981 Jul 19 David Garcia on ABC-TV News

AMONG THE NEW WORDS

I. WILLIS RUSSELL AND MARY GRAY PORTER

The University of Alabama

With the assistance of Dennis E. Baron, *University of Illinois, Urbana-Champaign*; William W. Evans, *Louisiana State University*; Michael Montgomery, *University of South Carolina*; Thomas M. Paikeday, *New York Times Everyday Dictionary*; Richard E. Ray, *Indiana University of Pennsylvania*; and Catherine V. von Schon, *State University of New York, Stony Brook*.

DURING THE TIME that Ronald Reagan has held public office, a number of terms derived from his name have been created. Whether they will become a part of the lexicon is, of course, impossible to predict, but the phenomenon itself seems to be of enough sociolinguistic interest for us to assemble in one place all the Reagan derivatives in our files. This we have done in this installment of "Among the New Words." Where there are enough citations to formulate a definition we have done so. For those terms lacking a sufficient number of citations, no definitions have been attempted. But we hope that readers who find defining quotations for any of these words—or, for that matter, quotations of any of the more fully documented terms that suggest modification or amplification of our definitions—will send them to us so that we may make the necessary modifications in our entries.

Acknowledgments for citations: David Frost (1), Marshall Winokur (1).

anti-Reagan, anti-Ronald Reagan *adj* 1971 Dec 20 *Newsweek* 28/2 "anti-Reagan feeling is gaining force in California . . ." 1978 Feb 26 *Birmingham News* F-3/3 "Which leaves the ultimate rationale of the anti-Reagan Republicans: Age." 1979 Nov 11 *Birmingham News* A-8/2 (AP) "Reagan analysts feel they can only benefit from having the anti-Reagan vote split among so many contenders—and this is one reason they have sat still so long." 1980 Sep 24 *Chr Sci Monitor* 22/1 "You don't have to be anti-Ronald Reagan to be concerned whether he has the intellectual depth to cope with the awesome decisionmaking of the presidency." Sep 23 *Chr Sci Monitor* 16/2 "Just as many of Palo Alto's likely Reagan votes are anti-Carter, so much of the Carter support here appears to be anti-Reagan." Oct 20 *Chron of Higher Educ* 4/1 "Anti-Reagan sentiment may motivate some students to go to the polls on election day, . . . but it has not inspired large numbers of students to hit the Presidential campaign trail."

Reaganaut *n* 1981 Aug 16 *NY Times Mag* 9/1 "When the Reaganauts recently needed votes in the Democratic-controlled House, this generation's conservative Democrats were not found wanting." Dec 9 CBS–TV News ". . . a dedicated Reaganaut."

Reaganesque *adj* [cf *BDNE* sv *-esque*] 1981 Nov 4 *Chr Sci Monitor* 17/3 (Rushworth M Kidder rev of Paul Tsongas *The Road from Here* [NY: Knopf]) "It's possibly a self-serving argument for a Democrat to make these days, as the political weather vane swings to the right in a Reaganesque wind." 1982 Jan 17 *Tuscaloosa News* A–17/3 (*LA Times*) "Norman J. Ornstein, an American Enterprise Institute specialist in congressional relations, sees more change ahead, in 'a Reaganesque direction.' "

Reaganism *n* The political, social, and economic ideas espoused by Ronald Reagan as Governor of California, candidate for the Presidency of the US, and President of the US 1971 May 29 *New Repub* 17/1 "*Reaganism in Connecticut* . . . [¶] Borrowing from an old Ronald Reagan script, Connecticut Governor Thomas Meskill has begun his first term by calling for tuition at the University of Connecticut, closing down the University's legal clinic, an end to most state-supported research and a 60 percent slash in antipoverty programs. On the other hand, he wants more money for drug enforcement, including more undercover agents, and tripled expenditures for industrial development. Connecticut faces an operating deficit similar to Rhode Island's and Pennsylvania's, both of which met their financial crises by passing an income tax. Not Governor Meskill, although salaries of high-paid executives in Fairfield and Hartford counties are an unworked goldmine. He wants a seven percent sales tax, extended to cover almost everything except groceries and shelter." 1973 Nov *Atlantic* 32/3 " 'California is behind most states in land conservation measures,' . . . 'Eight years of Reaganism have taken their toll.' " 1976 Jan 5 *Wall St Jour* 10/1 "Some months ago, with tongue in cheek, we coined the phrase: Reaganism is extremism in defense of Fordism. We could as easily have said that Fordism is pragmatism in pursuit of Reaganism, for either phrase suggests two men with common philosophies of government, but with differences in their approach for implementing same." 1981 Aug *Richmond Times-Dispatch* G–7/1 "Warnings to President Reagan by political aide Lyn Nofziger that AFL-CIO President Lane Kirkland intends to lead a labor-dominated Democratic Party to victory over Reaganism were given substance the past week in deteriorating relations between organized labor· and the White House."

Reaganite *n* Supporter of Ronald Reagan or his policies; a member of the Reagan staff or administration 1970 Oct 19 *National Observer* 11/2 " 'Mission impossible,' Reaganites scoff at Jess Unruh's guerrilla theater." 1973 May *Atlantic* 38/2 "We have also been called 'Nixonites' and 'Reaganites.' " 1976 Oct 9 *Birmingham News* 10/3 "[SC Gov James] Edwards, a Reaganite, calls the presidential race in South Carolina . . . a toss-up." 1977 Sep 4 *Parade* 16/1 "Ever since January, Dole has been crisscrossing the country, talking at party fund-raisers, conferring with such Reaganites as Lyn Nofziger, who heads Reagan's Citizens for the Republic, and John Sears, who managed the Reagan Presidential bid in 1976." 1980 May 12 *Newsweek* 25/1 "Ford almost certainly would not accept, but the Reaganites figure it can't hurt to let the former President know that he is first on their list [of possible vice-presidential candidates]." Sep 15 *Chr Sci Monitor* 10/3 "To some Reaganites, the challenger's troubles will start after next Sunday's Reagan-Anderson debate, which Carter has vowed to pass up." 1981 Jan 18 *Tuscaloosa News* A–13/5 (AP) "Sometimes they acted over the pained objections of Reaganites smoldering

with impatience to take the reins of power and suspicious about what the old crowd was up to." July 6 *Business Week* 113/2 "Unless the Reaganites can lift controls within 'a fairly short window,' the report says, Congress will be reluctant to tackle the politically sensitive task of accelerating the timetable, which now phases out [natural gas] controls by 1985." Sep 21 *Newsweek* 88/3 "But under the criteria the Reaganites are setting up, it is clear that the World Bank will be run more as a hard-nosed commercial establishment and less as a charitable agency." 1982 Jan 11 *Tuscaloosa News* 4/2–3 "It was hard to tell who was the champion Reaganite in Texas." —*attrib* 1980 Sep 8 *Newsweek* 78/ 2–3 "The pressure for conservative purity increased in Reagan's second term; his staff tried to fashion a legacy and to avoid the appointment of another Donald R. Wright, a supposedly Right-thinking state chief justice, who committed the Reaganite heresy of voting against the death penalty."

Reaganize *vt* **1:** To deal with in the manner of Ronald Reagan 1969 Mar 29 *New Repub* 7/2 "The Nixon Administration may think it's a good idea to Reaganize this issue . . . but they should understand that most university officials who have dealt successfully with students would prefer to be left alone." **2:** To bring under the influence of Ronald Reagan and his principles 1980 Jul 21 *Newsweek* 20 (heading) "A Reaganized GOP Sniffs Victory"

Reaganometrician *n* 1981 *Dupont Context* No. 2, 2 & 4 "Won't union leaders and workers wait for prices to come down before modifying demands for higher wages? [¶] No, argue Reaganometricians, people are rational. Just as investors in Wall Street discount the future, so will consumers on Main Street. When they spot a trend, when they know the President is purposeful in what he wants, they will act sensibly."

Reaganomic *adj* [prob from REAGANOMICS] 1981 Aug 6 *Crimson White* (Univ of Ala) 4/1 (editorial) "State governments have been waiting months to learn the impact of the Reaganomic budget cuts."

Reaganomics *n* [*Reagan* + *-omics*, AS 49: 252] Economic ideas of Pres Ronald Reagan; see quot from *Dupont Context* for a list of them 1981 Jan 30 *Chr Sci Monitor* 1/1–3 (heading) "Reaganomics: a chop, a freeze, then 'biggest-ever' budget cuts" Feb 16 *Newsweek* 70/2 "Given these dour possibilities, it is hardly surprising that the nation is rooting for Reaganomics to win." Mar 22 *Tuscaloosa News* A–14/3 "He was a builder and real estate man of great affluence. [¶] He said in principle he was for Reaganomics, particularly where it concerned the eliminating of federal government controls on business, and cracking down on environmentalists and welfare cheaters. [¶] Where he differed with Reagan, Stockman & Company was in their tax policies. [¶] 'But you will be getting a 10 percent cut like everybody else,' I told him. [¶] 'No, I won't,' he said. [¶] 'Why not?' [¶] 'Because I don't pay any taxes at all.' " *Dupont Context* No. 2, 2/1–2 "The Reagan program has a name: Reaganomics. It consists of 4 interrelated parts: federal tax reduction, federal spending restraint, reduced government intrusion in and regulation of business, and diminished use of the printing press—that is, the slower creation of money." Jun 22 *Media General Financial Weekly* 26/4 "The Reaganomics monetary policy appears to be committed to controlling the money supply despite the effects of high rates, and many are hopeful that this policy will curb inflation." Oct 4 *Manchester Guardian Weekly* 15/5 (*Wash Post*) "A review of the facts will show that, from the very beginning, respected Wall Street analysts . . . warned that the arithmetic of Reaganomics didn't add up, and no act of faith, for which the president had begged in his April 28 speech to Congress, could change the numbers. [¶] To me, the big mystery is not Wall Street's highly rational lack of confidence in Reagan, but why the Democrats continue to sidestep a golden opportunity to jump all over Reagan and Reaganomics." Oct 9 *Daily Reveille* (LSU, Baton Rouge) 1/1 "President Reagan's economic program is not a totally new approach. It is a 'putting together of a bunch of different ideas,' said David Johnson, professor of economics at the University, who added Reaganomics might be a fad which is not likely to stay as an economic philosophy." Nov 17 *Birmingham Post-Herald* A–4/3 "Now it turns out that those same doubts were being expressed more or less privately by one of the architects of Reaganomics even while he and the president were telling the nation that their plan was the greatest thing since sliced bread."

Reagan red *n* [Nancy *Reagan*, wife of Pres Ronald Reagan] 1981 Sep 15 *Chr Sci Monitor* B–3 & 5 "Aside from shots of Nancy Reagan's signature red, colors this year are muted, deep, often inky dark, with paisleys and plaids taking the tones of ancient madder silks and wools. [¶] . . . Color is also in vogue for black-tie evenings. A few of the options are a blazer in Reagan red for the dinner-party host, tartan trousers with a velvet jacket . . ., or a deep-toned plaid jacket with tuxedo trousers."

rehab *n* [*rehabilitation*; *2BDNE* 1963] (earlier quot) 1946 May 25 *Sat Eve Post* 59/2 "This low percentage of failures . . . is due to the thoroughness with which the 'rehab' candidates were screened before exchanging prison clothes for Army uniforms." —*attrib* [cf *2BDNE* rehab *n* 1963, *vt* 1978] 1980 May *Jour of Accountancy* 96/2 "The 'rehab' investment credit The Revenue Act of 1978 in sections 48(a)(1)(E) and 48(G) carved out certain exceptions where an investment credit may be taken for several types of commercial buildings, writes Philip W. Sandler in the *Tax Adviser* (February 1980). . . . [¶] In general, rehabilitation work done on factories, warehouses, etc., now qualifies as eligible investment credit property, writes the author."

zero-coupon *adj* Descriptive of a bond or other certificate of indebtedness that is offered at a discount, pays no annual interest, and is redeemed at face value upon maturity. The yield to the investor is the difference between the price at the time of purchase and the face value of the security. 1981 Jul 6 *Business Week* 83/1 "Pepsico Inc. has just raised $50 million with the first-ever deep-discount, zero-coupon Eurobond, with a yield to the investor of 13.67% over three years, which is 46 basis points below U. S. Treasury notes of a comparable maturity." Jul 21 *Wall St Jour* 45/3 "In the new issue market, Austria's export financing bank, Oesterreichische Kontroll-Bank, plans to offer $100 million of 'zero-coupon' notes. Underwriters tentatively priced the securities at 35.514 to yield 15⅜% to maturity in 1988." Aug 13 *Wall St Jour* 32/6 "The offering consisted of $65 million of deep-discount 12⅝% debentures, and $125 million of novel 'zero-coupon' notes, which don't pay any annual interest. [¶] The zero-coupon notes were priced at 25.653 to yield 17.75% to maturity in 1989, while the 12⅝% debentures were priced at 69.834 to yield 18.25% to maturity in 2003."

AMONG THE NEW WORDS

I. WILLIS RUSSELL AND MARY GRAY PORTER

The University of Alabama

With the assistance of William W. Evans, Michael Montgomery,
Richard E. Ray, and Peter Tamony

DAVID W. MAURER based his pioneering sociolinguistic studies of the argot of various subcultures on field work among users—they might be called native speakers—of the argot. One of these subcultures was that of the marijuana user, whose development and "relationship to the older subculture of hard drug users" he had commented upon in an article in the November 1946 *American Mercury.* In his preliminary note to the reprint of that article in his *Language of the Underworld* (Lexington: The University Press of Kentucky, 1981), from which the preceding quotation is drawn, he further remarks: "The subculture of the marijuana user has rapidly and widely diffused, taking the language as well as the drug to the heart of the dominant culture" (p. 156).

Our concern in this installment, which we offer as a tribute to David Maurer, is with the emergence into the language of the dominant culture of certain marijuana-related terms. In the hope of making some small contribution to the history of the appearance and diffusion of these terms in the mainstream culture, we have departed somewhat from our usual practice of entering in the glossary only words or meanings that are new, that is, not recorded in the general dictionaries. The glossary below includes both new terms and others that have found their way into nonspecialized dictionaries.

According to Maurer, the widespread smoking of marijuana in the United States is comparatively recent. The drug itself seems to have come in through New Orleans around 1910, and a marijuana "problem" became apparent in the middle 1930s (*Language of the Underworld*, p. 271). Maurer's dating is only apparently contradicted by the earliest quotations (1894) in *A Supplement to the Oxford English Dictionary.* The first appeared in the May 1894 issue of *Scribner's Magazine* and comes from an article by John G. Bourke entitled "The American Congo," which is essentially a travel article, whose nature may be seen in the following abbreviated quotation:

> There is an almost unvarying succession of the mesquite, or acacia, believed by the Mexicans to be especially subject to lightning-stroke; of the "nopal," or prickly pear . . .; of the melancholy "retama," . . .; of the "huisatchi," the "tasajillo," . . .; the awe-inspiring "coyotillo," of which such curious tales are on every lip . . .; the "toloachi," the "mariguan," and the "drago," the first two used by discarded women for the purpose of wreaking a terrible revenge upon recreant lovers, and the last one much employed by the "medicine-men" of the Indian tribes as a narcotic to induce prophetic dreaming [the list continues for another dozen lines].

Clearly this early occurrence of *mariguan* has no connection with Maurer's concern.

Maurer's statement of the date when marijuana smoking became a social issue receives some interesting corroboration from the *Reader's Guide to Periodical Literature.* A rather casual look at the volumes 1929 through the middle of 1981 shows that the term *marihuana* [*sic*] apparently does not occur until the 1935–37 volume, when it occurs as an entry head, indicating that it is already the "problem" that Maurer said it was. Under the heading are four articles from 1935 and 1936, three of them with the word *menace* in the title. In the 1937–39 volume, *marihuana* again gets a heading, with 16 articles, three of them on youth and the perils of the drug, five on the dangers of marijuana use.

Corroboration of another kind comes from a short piece in the "Miscellany" section of *American Speech* (Oct. 1940, pp. 336/2–337/1) by James A. Donovan, Jr. on the "Jargon of Marihuana Addicts." He notes that "Although the intoxicating powers of the hemp plant have been known for centuries, it is only within the past seven years that the use of it as a drug has become prevalent in the United States." After remarking that "A large and changeable jargon has grown up in connection with it"— Maurer has made the same observation somewhere—he lists some fifty terms.

A large number of terms and meanings related to the drug culture have found their way into the general dictionaries: the *Webster's Third Addenda Section* 1981, for example, contains a hundred-odd of them. For the glossary in this issue of "Among the New Words" we list a few, which though they lack the supportive number of citations to suggest permanence in the lexicon, illustrate the linguistic creativeness of marijuana users.

In the glossary Maurer's articles in *Language of the Underworld* are cited simply as "Maurer" followed by a page number; the date is that of the original publication. "Sabbag *Snowblind*" is Robert Sabbag's account of an American cocaine smuggler's activities, *Snowblind: A Brief Career in the Cocaine Trade* (New York: Avon, 1978; © 1976). The recent dictionary by Richard A. Spears, *Slang and Euphemism* (Middle Village, N.Y.: Jonathan David Publishers, 1981) we cite as "Spears."

Acknowledgment for citations: John Algeo (4).

Acapulco gold *n* [*2BDNE* 1969 (1967); Maurer 279/1 (1973); *Dict of Amer Slang* Sup 1975; *W3 Add* 1981; Spears] 1967 Jul 7 *Time* 21/2 "In the Hashbury, grass can be had for $10 to $15 a 'lid' (a one-ounce lot, capable of producing up to 40 joints); the finest variety is 'Acapulco Gold' from Mexico, undiluted and selling for $1 a joint ($5 for a matchboxful that can produce about ten joints."

Acapulco red *n* [Maurer 279/1 (1973)] 1971 Jan 10 *NY Times* NER-27/2 "Mr. Kessler noted, humorously, that the illegal drug traffic aped the conventions of business. 'Sometimes you listen to guys talking about Acapulco or Panama Red, about packaging and marketing techniques, of seasonal price fluctuations, and you have to laugh.' "

anti-marijuana *adj* 1970 Nov *Playboy* 66/2 "It is time that both the comedy and the tragedy of the U.S. anti-marijuana obsession be put in the dustbin of history alongside the Salem witch hangings and the laws against teaching evolution." 1971 Mar 7 *Parade* 18/2 "According to some experts on the medical, legal, and social aspects of drug use, our anti-marijuana laws are impracticable and unfair, and they may soon pass into disuse just as did the Volstead Act which prohibited the sale of liquor in this country." 1972 Summer *Fed Bar Jour* repr in 1973 Jan *Intellectual Digest* 52/3–54/1 "Scientific research has helped to illuminate the irrationalities of the first two antimarijuana propositions but not to expose the irrationalities of the third proposition: the belief that those who use marijuana are extreme dissidents and a very real threat to a stable social order." 1974 Apr *Atlantic* 88/1 "So it was that Liddy went to the Treasury Department, where he ramrodded Operation Intercept, the disastrous anti-marihuana blockade of the Mexican border, intended to bludgeon the Mexican government into stamping out production of the weed by fouling up tourist and itinerant-labor traffic at customs gates."

anti-pot *adj* [*pot* 'marijuana' *ShOED Add* 1974 "*slang*. *U.S.*)" 1951; *W3*] 1969 Dec 17 *Tuscaloosa News* 22/3 "The antipot adults are the same ones who can't get through the day or face the night without the most dangerous drug of all, alcohol." 1971 Mar 7 *Parade* 18/2 "John McCahey, deputy chief inspector of New York City's Narcotics Squad, admits that the anti-pot laws in effect are completely overshadowed by the problems of heroin peddling and addiction." 1981 Jan 11 *60 Minutes* CBS-TV "It's only with federal and state grants that counties can fund anti-pot programs." 1982 Mar 8 *Newsweek* 89/2 "Still, the report fails to support some of the more extreme views of the anti-pot forces. The committee found no convincing evidence that marijuana produces permanent damage to the central nervous system and brain. Nor is it addictive in the same manner as narcotics."

blonde from the coast See RUBIA DE LA COSTA 1976 Sabbag *Snowblind* 230 Quot sv RUBIA DE LA COSTA

bowl *n* Hookah, water pipe used by some marijuana smokers 1974 Sep 20 *New Times* (NYC) 38/3 " 'See that. I'll bet you don't know what that is, do you?' [¶] I look down at a very conventional hookah. [¶] 'No,' I say. [¶] 'Jeepers,' says Verdehan. 'That is a bowl . . . they call it a bowl. It's what they smoke marijuana out of.' "

dime bag *n* [Maurer 296/1 (1973); *Dict of Amer Slang* Sup 1975 svv *bag*, *dime bag*; *W3 Add* 1981 sv *dime n* b: "a packet containing 10 dollars worth of an illicit drug (as marijuana)"] 1970 Feb 20 *Life* 26/2 "Sometimes I'll buy two grams [of heroin] for $30 or $50, cut it, put it into eight or nine dime [$10] bags and sell it again." 1974 Feb *Harper's* 36/3 "Break that down to nickel and dime bags and you've got a town consuming smack at $6,000 to $10,000 a week. Let's say about $8,000 in heroin sold every week in nickel and dime bags. Some guys have been cutting it more than that."

domino theory *n* [Cf *SOED* sv *domino* 3.c, esp last quot; *World Book Dict* 1981 *domino theory* 2] See STEPPINGSTONE HYPOTHESIS 1975 Oct *Psychology Today* 41/ 2–3 "Eight out of 10 of them believe that drug use is immoral as well as illegal, and almost all believe that drugs are harmful and progressive toward danger of addiction—the domino theory of drugs."

Dread Weed, The [Cf Maurer 110/2 *weed* 'marijuana' (1938); Landy 1971] Marijuana 1972 Spring *Sat Eve Post* 61/2 "Zutty Singleton, a drummer born in Bunkie, Louisiana, in 1898, has never been on drugs or The Dread Weed."

Gainesville green [*Gainesville*, Fla; cf *SOED* sv *green* B. *sb* 7. f: "Marijuana of poor quality. *slang* (orig. *U.S.*)" 1957] 1976 Sabbag *Snowblind* 187 "Swan bought some coke, and Jimmy came across with some transplanted, homegrown, Gainesville Green from his tomato garden."

grass trap *n* [*grass* 'marijuana' *SOED* 1. e: "*slang* (orig. *U.S.*)" 1943; cf *speed trap W3*] A stretch of highway where the police stop long-haired or bearded drivers who may be transporting marijuana 1971 Feb 4 *Rolling Stone* 18/1 "Meanwhile the grass traps in downstate New Jersey are still in business, chiefly because business is good."

happy-time weed *n* [Cf DREAD WEED; *SOED* sv *happy* 5.e: " . . . *happy dust*, *cocaine* . . ." 1922] Marijuana 1971 Mar 22 *National Observer* 12/1 " . . . the principal reason for legalizing the happy-time weed is quite similar to the reason for repealing the prohibition against alcoholic beverages four decades ago. Both marijuana and alcohol seem to cause more trouble when they are illegal than when they are legal."

Hashbury, (The) [*Dict of Amer Slang* Sup 1975] 1967 Jul 7 *Time* 19/1 "Within The Hashbury circulate more than 25 undercover narcotics agents, who arrest an average of 20 hippies a week, usually for possession of marijuana." See also quot sv ACAPULCO GOLD 1979 Oct 22 *Ironside* (rerun) WBRC-TV, Ch 6, Birmingham, Ala "[She] lived in Hashbury for about a year."

hash pipe *n* [*SOED hash sb.*[3] 1959] 1970 Nov 12 *Crimson-White* (Univ of Ala) 12 (ad) "Newsom's Music Center has the best selection of posters, hash pipes, roach clips, sunglasses and incense in town."

head booth *n* [Cf *head shop BDNE* 1970: *W3 Add* 1981] A booth at an exhibition or fair where items of interest to drug users are shown 1971 Feb 4 *Rolling Stone* 18/4 "After an intensive investigation of all head booths, we found one new item: Snuff. Snuff is In. . . . Snuff is the new legal high."

Manhattan white *n* See NEW YORK WHITE 1981 Jul *Omni* 112/1 Quot sv SUBWAY SILVER

margie-wanna *n* Marijuana 1971 Mar *McCall's* 97/2 " 'Picked up two freaks loaded with margie-wanna,' one Task Force man will say, to open the ego contest."

marijuanaholic *n* [Cf *hashaholic* 1972 *2BDNE* sv *-aholic*] 1981 Dec *Reader's*

Digest 85/1 "In August 1981 Dr. Mark Gold completed a study of 100 teen-age and adult 'marijuanaholics'—chronic users of pot, who are psychologically, physiologically and socially disabled. Gold . . . is director of research at Fair Oaks Hospital in Summit, N.J., one of the few psychiatric hospitals in the country that specializes in treatment of the marijuanaholic."

Mexican *n* [Cf *Mexican red, Dict of Amer Slang* Sup 1975] Marijuana from Mexico; here, *specif* Michoacán 1976 Sabbag *Snowblind* 36 " 'When was the last time you smoked Mexican?' Swan asked."

Michoacan *n* Marijuana from the state of Michoacán, Mexico 1973 May *National Lampoon* 42/1 ". . . and just to show you how cool they are and everything they'll lay a nickel of Michoacan or a couple of tabs of sunshine on you so you'll know they're together . . ." 1976 Sabbag *Snowblind* 36 Quot sv PANAMA RED

New York City silver, New York white *n* In urban folklore, a variety of marijuana, of superb quality, that grows in the sewers of New York 1975 Nov *Psychology Today* 126/2 "A recent variation on the alligator story is the legendary 'New York white' strain of marijuana growing in the same prolific sewer system. The toilet was again the culprit, because heads flushed the incriminating weed down the drain as police rushed through the front door. The grass flourishes in the sewers, awaiting some harvester foolish enough to brave a horde of pale, drug-crazed reptiles." 1981 Oct *Omni* 12/2–3 (letter) "I must protest your assertion that the strain of marijuana known as New York City Silver is a rumor . . . [¶] Incidentally, one harvests the New York City Silver by prying open a manhole cover and dropping a bottle of cheap wine down the hole. The winos dive in after the wine, the alligators sate themselves on the winos, and you slip in and cop the pot."

nickel (bag) *n* [*Dict of Amer Slang* Sup 1975; *SOED* sv *nickel* 2 c 1967; *W3 Add* 1981; Spears] 1973 May *National Lampoon* 42/1 Quot sv MICHOACAN 1974 Feb *Harper's* 36/3 Quot sv DIME BAG 1977 Feb 24 *Crimson-White* (Univ of Ala) 4/3–6 (cartoon caption) [Shady-looking man to woman at coffee counter, where coffee is selling, "this week only!", for $6.25 a pound:] "Pssst! I got some nickel bags of some Grade-A Columbian [*sic*] ground brown!"

Panama (red) *n* [*W3 Add* 1981; Spears; cf *Dict of Amer Slang* Sup 1975 *Panamanian Red* = Mexican red] High-quality marijuana from Panama 1971 Jan 10 *NY Times* NER-27/2 Quot sv ACAPULCO RED 1976 Sabbag *Snowblind* 35 "Panama is getting very expensive." Sabbag *Snowblind* 36 " 'You went from Michocàn [*sic*] to Acapulco Gold and then to Panama Red.' [¶] 'That's right. Straight up the ladder.' "

pot bust *n* [*pot: ShOED "slang* (orig. *U.S.*)" 1951; Maurer 275 and 329/1: Mex Span *potación de guaya* 'drink of grief' or the telescoped form *potaguaya* as possible origin of Eng *pot*; *bust*: Maurer 237/1; *Dict of Amer Slang* Sup 1975] Arrest for the use, possession, or sale of marijuana 1970 Dec *Reader's Digest* 91/1 (from Sep 7 *Newsweek*) "There hasn't been a pot bust in Harvard dormitories for four years, even though estimates of undergraduate use range from 65 to 80 percent, and sharp-eyed passers-by can spot luxuriant plants growing inside some dorm windows."

pothead *n* [*BDNE* 1968; *W3 Add* 1971; *Dict of Amer Slang* Sup 1975; *World Book Dict* 1981; *BDNE* and *WBD* label the word *slang*] Marijuana user 1966 Jul 10 *NY Times Mag* 6/1 "Rumblings are audible which suggest that the arrest of Dr. Timothy Leary . . . on two separate occasions for violations of the Marijuana Tax Act of 1937 and the New York Narcotics Act (and his conviction . . . on the first of these) has provided the small but growing group of potheads, psychedelics and other mutants in this country with a leader who has the charisma, though not nearly the following, that the Rev. Dr. Martin Luther King Jr. has among Negroes."

pot hound *n* Dog trained to detect marijuana 1974 Nov *Reader's Digest* 173/1 "In fiscal 1973 alone, the U.S. Custom Service's formidable 'pot hounds' nosed out contraband narcotics worth $192.5 million on the street."

pot likker *n* Brewed marijuana 1967 Jul 7 *Time* 21/1–2 "Central to the drug scene is marijuana, the green-flowered cannabis herb that has been turning man on since time immemorial. . . . it is ubiquitous and easily grown, can be smoked in 'joints' (cigarettes), baked into cookies or brewed in tea ('pot likker')."

pot-phobe *n* One strongly opposed to the use of marijuana 1977 Apr 29 *New Times* (NYC) 18/2 "When in 1971 a group of British doctors said they had evidence that prolonged marijuana use shrinks brains, pot-phobes leaped at the findings as proof that dope dulls you upstairs."

pot plane *n* Airplane on which marijuana is smuggled into the country 1976 Mar 7 *Tuscaloosa News* E-12/4 (AP) "Roaring through tree tops at the end of a makeshift runway, the four-engine west Georgia pot plane which was landed on a perilous mountain airstrip last August has been flown out safely."

pot-prone *adj* Predisposed to the use of marijuana 1981 Dec *Reader's Digest* 82/2 "Marijuana use is now so endemic in every stratum of society that there is no longer such an identifiable entity as a pot-*prone* personality. Only one characteristic remains as a 'prone' factor: youth."

pot sniffer *n* See POT HOUND 1970 Nov 14 *Sat Rev* 59/3 (picture caption) "Pot sniffer—Customs now employs trained dogs to find hidden marijuana."

Pots' People Partier *n* Member of an *ad hoc* group of protesters at 1972 Democratic Convention 1972 Jul 11 *Greensboro* (NC) *Daily News* B-1/1 "The protestors are a rather disjointed lot. There are Zippies and Yippies and SDSers, and Viet vets, and poor folks and blacks, and the militant women and the militant gay, and the Peoples' [*sic*] Pot Partiers and the Pots' [*sic*] People Partiers, and the Jesus Freaks, and the Hare Krishna monks, and the Jews for Jesus, and the Buddhists for Mohammed, and God only knows what else."

pot-struck *adj* Under the influence of marijuana 1973 Jun *Esquire* 90/2 "His . . . shrewd analysis of what has happened to Marxism since it became the creed of neo-Slavophiles, resurrected Mandarins and pot-struck students . . . is masterly."

pot-vague *adj* Disoriented as a result of smoking marijuana 1970 Summer-Fall *Arts in Society* 164/1 "Sadly, some of our pot-vague and rock-happy young dissidents have been taken in by their patronizing elders and submissively misrationalize their freshness of artistic experience and their libertarian social motives by accepting the descriptions of themselves as mere symptoms of malaise."

primo, el-primo *adj* [Span] First-class, top-quality (esp of marijuana) 1979 Jan *Atlantic* 10/2 "Who's buying the primo stuff [marijuana]? None of my people can touch it—it goes for $120 to $200 an ounce, depending on the dealer." 1981 Dec 14 *Newsweek* 60/2 "He [an army captain in Vietnam] would still be standing there talking when the grunts had stampeded past him, racing toward oblivion, the juicers popping open cans of Carling Black Label, the smokers ripping up the barracks floorboards to get at their stashes of el-primo no seed, no stem marijuana laid in at $50 the 6-pound sandbag full."

rubia (de la costa) [Span 'blonde from the coast'] A rare strain of Colombian marijuana 1976 Sabbag *Snowblind* 230 ". . . he opened up a brick of the strangest-looking marijuana Swan had ever seen. It was white. . . . '*Rubia de la costa*, the blonde from the coast, the finest, complete dynamite 'up' grass in the world. . . .' [¶] While Swan explored the wonders of *rubia*, Black Dan gave him the rundown on the Mexican route."

Santa Marta gold *n* High-quality marijuana from Santa Marta, Colombia 1976 Sabbag *Snowblind* 93–94 "He gave Swan his first hit of Santa Marta Gold, and before long the two of them were old friends."

steppingstone hypothesis *n* Belief that marijuana use may or, in the view of some, must lead to heroin addiction 1977 Mar *Psychology Today* 8/1 (letter) "I'm not sure I can agree with Norman Zinberg that my study of initiation of drug use by heroin addicts 'shows—it does not simply indicate—that marijuana use does not lead to heroin use.' My study did, however, prove the falsity of the fallacy contained in those studies that seem[e]d to support the stepping-stone hypothesis. *Post hoc, ergo pro[p]ter hoc* is one of the classic logical fallacies but for some time it was elevated to the status of a research design in the field of marijuana research. [¶] What really 'shows' that marijuana is not a stepping-stone to heroin is how few marijuana smokers ever become heroin addicts." (See also DOMINO THEORY)

subway silver *n* See NEW YORK CITY SILVER 1981 Jul *Omni* 112/1 "There is a strain of albino marijuana growing in the New York City sewer system. The nutrient-rich sludge has germinated the seeds that were flushed down the toilet during drug raids, resulting in extremely powerful plants, known locally as Manhattan white or subway silver. It is hard to harvest, however, because it is guarded by all those alligators."

AMONG THE NEW WORDS

I. WILLIS RUSSELL AND MARY GRAY PORTER
The University of Alabama

CREATION SCIENCE and *scientific creationism* are interchangeable, to judge from the citations in our files. William W. Evans, a member of the Committee on New Words, commented, in reference to the quotation from *Civil Liberties* in the glossary s.v. *scientific creationism*: "But stylistic matters are sometimes involved."

Nouvelle cuisine, for which we supply some earlier dates, has given rise to an adjective *nouvelle* and a noun *nouvelle cuisinier*. Despite their French appearance, they seem to have originated in English, not in French. This is surely true of *nouvelle cuisinier*, two French words that several natives of France assure us no Frenchman would ever combine.

Acknowledgments for citations: to members of the Committee on New Words William W. Evans (4), Thomas M. Paikeday (1), and Richard E. Ray (5); our thanks also to Oliver Finley Graves (1), James B. McMillan (2), and Anne B. Russell (2). Two early quotations (for *call boy* and *parenting*) are from the files of the late Walter S. Avis and Mamie J. Meredith.

call boy *n* [by analogy with *call girl* (*Sup OED* sv *call n* 15) 1940] Male prostitute 1975 Nov 6 Toronto *Globe and Mail* 6/4 "I guess all the newspapers today refer quite casually to call girls; still I'm a bit jarred when the ones in New York refer to call boys." 1981 Nov 24 *NBC News* (segment on male prostitution in Washington, D.C.) Nov 26 *Tuscaloosa News* 9/5–6 (AP) "The report quoted the unidentified 'call boy' as saying, 'Information is being collected, being systematically collected, being systematically filtered to other places, not just the Soviets either.' " 1982 Jul 1 *CBS News* "They found the names of about 200 call boys."

cellular *adj* Using many low-powered transmitters, each forming a cell bounded by its transmitting range, within a large call area (thus making possible an increased number of simultaneous calls from mobile radio-telephones) 1981 Toronto *Globe and Mail* 6 "Satellites, earth stations, cellular radio, low-power TV, Telidon and two-way interactive cable systems will come increasingly under provincial and private jurisdiction." 1982 Jun 6 *Philadelphia Inquirer* D-1/3–4 "Cellular radio, a term likely to gain in recognition in coming years, will vastly expand the number of usable frequencies and thus permit hundreds of thousands of people to install phones in their cars." Jun 7 *Wall St Jour* Sec 2, 21/3 "Applicants are preparing to spend hundreds of millions of dollars to build the new systems, which will use so-called cellular transmission to greatly expand the volume of radiotelephone calls. Rather than relying on a single powerful transmitter to connect mobile-phone users with regular telephone lines, a cellular system employs low-power transmitters that each serve a small, limited area, or 'cell.' " Jun 28 *Barron's* 31/2 "What is cellular radio . . . ? Well, it's a way of carrying telephone messages, via a honeycomb-style system of low-power radio transmitters, which permits many more simultaneous calls than do conventional mobile phone systems." Jul 3 *Indiana* (Pa) *Gazette* 13/5 "Unlike the old mobile radio system where one big transmitter acts as a relay station in a metropolitan area, cellular radio uses several low-power transmitters. Each one will serve a small area or cell up to eight miles. As a vehicle drives from cell to cell, its call is automatically transferred without the usual delay and interference experienced with the prevailing mobile two-way radiotelephones." Jul 25 *Pittsburgh Press Family Mag* 3/2 "Cellular radio, long precluded by the scarcity of usable radio frequency channels, is now available because of advances in cellular technology, as well as decisions by the FCC to allocate more space on the radio spectrum to cellular services and to grant cellular franchises in 30 major metropolitan markets."

concrete, in *prep phr* Immovable, unalterable 1981 May 22 Richard A Gephardt (R-Mo) *McNeil-Lehrer Report* PBS-TV "He's not in concrete on that issue." June 1 *ABC-TV News* "[He] thought the President was locked in concrete." Jun 1 Thomas P O'Neill (D-Mass) as reported on *NBC-TV News* Sep 24 Pres Ronald Reagan on NBC-TV "Our feet were never embedded in concrete on this proposal." Sep 25 Haynes Johnson on *Washington Week* PBS-TV "[Pres Reagan] said his feet are not locked in concrete. . . . Are your feet locked in concrete on the defense budget?" 1982 May 6 *Tuscaloosa News* 4/5 (James J Kilpatrick) "But the structure of a tax reduction is not cast in concrete. As a tool for reducing the prospective deficits, the program of tax reduction can be adjusted." Aug 17 Prof emeritus of English, Univ of Ala "My memory is not set in concrete."

creation science *n* Belief that scientific evidence supports the biblical account, taken literally, of the creation of the universe (Adherents of this view adduce in its favor gaps in the fossil record and varying scientific theories regarding the mechanism of evolution and seek to have creation science taught as a scientific theory no less valid than the theory of evolution) (see also SCIENTIFIC CREATIONISM) 1981 Nov 23 Baton Rouge *State Times* B-5/6 "Louisiana's 'balanced treatment' law defines creation science as 'the scientific evidences for creation and inferences drawn from those scientific evidences.'" Dec 8 *Daily Reveille* (La State Univ) 16/2 "The ACLU's opening witnesses said the definition of creation-science in the Arkansas law is rooted in the language of Genesis." Dec 28 *State Times* A-13/1 "Overton is considering evidence and testimony introduced in the trial challenging Arkansas Act 590 of 1981 which requires the 'balanced' treatment of creation-science and evolution in the public schools." 1982 Jan 2 *Science News* 12/1 "What's ironic is that while its ultimate outcome will affect how science is taught in public schools throughout Arkansas—and presumably the nation—the question of whether 'creation science' truly constitutes science was not the legal issue." Feb *Civil Liberties* 1/1 quot sv SCIENTIFIC CREATIONISM May 16 *Tuscaloosa News* A-14/2 (from *LA Times*) "Indeed, the creationists are flooding state legislatures with bills and pressuring school boards to give 'creation science'—the assertion that the literal Bible account of origins is scientifically accurate—equal time with evolution in the nation's science classrooms." June 17 *Tuscaloosa News* 4 (letter) "The fact is that evolution cannot be experimentally tested and thus cannot ever be considered a true scientific theory: It does not meet the final criterion of the scientific method. Creation science also fails to meet this criterion—but this fact alone does not establish evolution as science." **—creation scientist** *n* 1982 Jan 2 *Science News* 13/1 "Noting a lack of 'transitional forms in the fossil record,' he claims that even 'Darwin had trouble with intermediates.' As a result, he says, 'I feel that if Darwin were alive today, he'd be a creation scientist."

endangered species *n* [*endangered* 'threatened with extinction' *BDNE* (1970); *World Book Dict* 1976; *W3* Add Sec 1981] Group of animate or inanimate objects that is threatened with extinction or destruction 1980 Spring–Summer *Ala Historical Qtrly* 102 "The buildings illustrated were selected on the basis of their presence on the endangered species list." [1981 Sep 11 *Tuscaloosa News* entertainment sec 3/1 "As reported by the AP, the composers spent most of their time complaining about how sterile the American environment is for their work, how endangered their species is because of National Endowment budget cuts."] 1981 Dec 8 *McNeil-Lehrer Report* PBS-TV (program on youth gangs) "The boys are our endangered species." 1982 Jan 11 *Newsweek* 72/1 "By now we've all been informed that public television is an endangered species. Drastic cutbacks in Congressional funding—along with competition from cable TV's new all-cultural channels—may eventually spell doom for the entire public-broadcasting system."

Jupiter effect *n* Meteorological and seismic disturbances that were predicted to occur in 1982 when all nine planets were located on the same side of the sun, according to John Gribbin and Stephen Plagemann, the authors of *The Jupiter Effect* (1974) 1974 Oct 7 *Time* 89/1 "In a new book, *The Jupiter Effect* . . . they prophesy that a major quake will devastate the Los Angeles area in 1982. . . . [¶] According to Gribbin . . . and Plagemann . . . the quake will strike in 1982 because the solar system's nine planets will be more or less aligned that year on one side of the sun, a configuration that occurs only once every 179 years. . . . [¶] As the planets line up, they say, the combined gravitational tug will raise large tides and cause great flare-ups on the sun, which will then be at the peak of its eleven-year sunspot cycle. The solar storms will spew out streams of charged particles more intense than usual, disrupting radio communications on earth, creating exceptionally bright northern (and southern) lights, and affecting global weather patterns. . . . Many quakes will occur in susceptible regions around the globe. . . ." 1975 Dec 13 *Science News* 377/2 "The 'Jupiter effect,' a theory of possible seismic activity on earth correlated with a 1982 alignment of planets in relation to the sun, has evoked little enthusiasm among geophysicists. . . . [¶] Sharp criticism has now come from astronomer Jean Meeus of the *Vereniging voor Sterrenkunde* in Belgium. . . . 'The "Jupiter effect," ' he says, 'does not exist.'" 1977 Mar *Smithsonian* 28/3 "With nuclear proponents adopting their environmental adversaries' tactic of crying catastrophe—however improbably—it is nice to know that one gloom-and-doom theory linking the tenets of astrology to those of science and predicting a terrible earthquake problem in 1982 seems to have been rendered inoperative, in the vernacular of bureaucracy. The theory was known as the Jupiter Effect; . . . it said that in 1982 several planets would all find themselves arranged in a straight line out from the sun, thus exciting an unusual gravitational force on our resident star."

loose cannon *n* Someone or something that has become uncontrollable 1981 Feb 6 *Washington Week in Review* PBS-TV "Is [he] a loose cannon?" 1982 May 6 *Tuscaloosa News* 4/5 (James J Kilpatrick) "These ruinous deficits are largely a product of the entitlement programs that have gone out of control. . . . Both Republicans and Democrats are responsible for these loose cannons." June 13 *Tuscaloosa News* A-26/6 (Jack Anderson) "The president's men realized that the Patman committee investigation was a loose cannon that might sink Nixon's re-election chances." May 28 Raleigh (NC) *News and Observer* A-5/1 (Jack W Germond and Jules Witcover) "After all, Young had been something of a loose cannon on the deck of the Carter administration as ambassador to the United Nations, a black who seemed quick to find racism all around him."

new cuisine *n* [tr of Fr phr NOUVELLE CUISINE (qv)] 1981 Oct *Gourmet* 135/1 "The dish [cold duck salad], or close variations thereof, is one of several instant clichés generated by the now-not-so-new new cuisine, though it's enjoyable nonetheless in its better manifestations."

nouvelle *adj* [Fr 'new', from Fr phr NOUVELLE CUISINE; *W3* Add Sec 1981] Prepared or served in the manner of the nouvelle cuisine 1977 May *Bon Appetit* 24/1 Quot sv NOUVELLE CUISINE 1981 Jan-Feb *Cuisine* 18/2 "But few of [the recipes] are for elaborate restaurant masterpieces buried under lavish decorations, nor are they the most ostentatiously *nouvelle* of the *nouvelle*." Apr *Food & Wine* 11/1 "The fact that the French boycotted the [Culinary Olympics] provoked much speculation. Was it, as some observers theorized, still 'sour grapes' after the disappointment of tying for third place with the U.S. at the '76 event? Or was a more likely explanation to be found in the philosophical rift between the traditionalist and the more progressive 'nouvelle' chefs of France?" May *Bon Appetit* 50/3 "Salads, side dishes and desserts were all created in keeping with the nouvelle theme of only the freshest and the best, usually in innovative combinations." Jul *Food & Wine* 40/3 "This seemed a polite stab at the cuisine in which scallops are combined with such things as gooseberries and pink peppercorns under the catchall label of *nouvelle*." Jul *Gourmet* 90/2 "Plates arrive from the kitchen under silver covers that are removed with a flourish to reveal distinctly *nouvelle* still-life-like [*sic*] arrangements on those handsome basket plates popularized by Michel Guérard."

nouvelle cuisine, (la) *n* [*W3* Add Sec 1981] (earlier quots) 1977 May *Bon Appetit* 24/1 "Theoretically, *la nouvelle cuisine*, or new French cooking, aims at producing clear, fresh flavors and light textures instead of self-defeating richness. . . . [¶] Where *la nouvelle cuisine* suggested a saner caloric intake, M. Guérard declared an all-out war on the calorie. Flour, butter and cream were cut back even below the nouvelle minimum. Steamed meats and poultry . . . vegetable purées . . . low-calorie sweeteners and non-fat dry milk came out of the closet." 1978 May 23 *Esquire* 68 (subheading) "La nouvelle cuisine may have started in the French provinces, but it has now taken Paris by storm." Ibid 69/3 "Gault and Millau claim to have invented in 1974 the now familiar term 'la nouvelle cuisine,' a cooking style that is 'light, imaginative, modern.'" Oct *Esquire* 32/1 "Of course, the body eventually adapts to even the most restricted diet (look today at the fast-food junkies, the bean-curd fiends, and the *nouvelle cuisine* enthusiasts)." **—nouvelle cuisiner** *n* [formed in English on the model of Fr *cuisinier*] Chef or restaurateur who specializes in the nouvelle cuisine 1981 Aug *Gourmet* 92/3 "Of these I'm particularly fond of an extraordinary mushroom '*gâteau*'—a sort of molded mousse (How these *nouvelle cuisiniers* play fast and loose with culinary terminology!) bound with cream and eggs and topped with poached beef marrow."

parenting *n* [2 *BDNE* 1974 (1963); *W3* Add Sec 1981; *World Book Dict* 1981] (earlier date) 1958 Feb 2 *NY Times Mag* 38/2 "And is the quantity of parenting necessarily more important than the quality?"

scientific creationism; science creationism *n* See CREATION SCIENCE 1981 Mar 30 *Birmingham* (Ala) *Post-Herald* A-7/3 "In case the lawmakers become jaded . . . they can take refuge in the quiet debate over scientific creationism. [¶] This pits a regiment of scientists who accept the Darwinian theory of evolution and a battalion of religious devotees espousing essentially that the world and universe were created, not evolved." Apr 4 *New Repub* 17/1 " 'Science creationism' consists almost exclusively of a multi-pronged attack on evolutionary biology and historical geology." (A cartoon on the same page depicts a monkey wearing a T-shirt with the legend: "SCIENTIFIC CREATIONISM.") Sep *Science Digest* 10/1 (letter) "I have recently read a number of books and pamphlets concerning 'scientific creationism.' My conclusion is that unless one wishes to redefine the word 'scientific,' it should not be used at all in the context of 'creationism.'" 1982 Jan *Harper's* 18/2 "For even as the polls, the media, and politicians respond to the popular nostalgia for a Norman Rockwell vision of Mom, Dad, Bud, and Sis enjoying a backyard barbecue, reality speaks of continuing chaos and disintegration, which classroom prayer, censored textbooks, or, eventually, the teaching of 'scientific creationism' can do little to reverse. Feb *Civil Liberties* 1/1 "U.S. District Judge William R. Overton ruled last month that Arkansas' scientific creationism statute was unconstitutional. 'Creation-science,' as anyone could see, was not science but religion, and had no place in a public school classroom." Mar 4 Baton Rouge *Enterprise* 8/3–4 "Public school teachers, as of yet, have no approved text from which to teach scientific creationism. . . . [¶] Religious leaders have lined up on both sides of the creation science issue. Some would like to see creationism given equal time with evolution in the classroom, but the Rev. James Stovall, executive director of the Louisiana Interchurch Conference, thinks that's a bad idea. . . . 'if scientific creationism is science, then there does not need to be a law to compel it's [*sic*] being taught in the classroom.'" Apr 1 *Daily Reveille* (La State Univ) 15/1–3 (AP) "A federal judge says he may dismiss the state suit seeking to require the teaching of creation science. . . . [State Senator Bill] Keith authored the 1981 law that says if public schools offer courses on the theory of evolution they also must teach courses in scientific creationism." **—scientific creationist** *n* 1981 Apr *Omni* 118/2 "An important symposium, for example, was held on evolution, which is currently under serious attack by so-called scientific creationists." 1982 May 16 *Tuscaloosa News* A-14/1 (*LA Times*) "Today evolutionists are fighting back, evolving a coordinated response to the so-called scientific creationists who believe that the world and the human race were suddenly created out of nothing by a divine intelligence."

subterranean economy; underground economic activity; underground economy *n* Segment of the economy in which transactions are based on cash or barter and are not reported to the Internal Revenue Service (such incomes may be derived from illicit activities, such as drugs, gambling, prostitution, but also from legal business activities).   1980 Jan-Feb *Economic Rev* (Fed Reserve Bank of Atlanta) 8/2 "It suggests increasing activity in the 'underground economy' (gambling, bartering, and other unreported income)."   May *Jour of Accountancy* 18/3 "A road map of the U.S. 'underground' economy—economic activity wholly or partially unreported to the Internal Revenue Service—is provided in a recent IRS study."   Ibid 20/2 "The U.S. is not alone in underground economic activity. In Europe, 'evading taxes is as ingrained' a custom 'as drinking wine with a meal,' according to an international business magazine."   Jul 22 *ABC News* "The subterranean economy is cash—out in the open but concealed from the Internal Revenue Service . . . two years ago when ABC first reported on the subterranean economy."   1981 Feb 9 *Barron's* 7/1 "The underground economy, as it was dubbed by Professor Peter M. Gutmann of Baruch College, City University of New York, first surfaced just a few years ago. Since then, estimates of its size, scope and rate of growth have been continuously revised upward."   1982 Jul 1 *Chr Sci Monitor* B-4/1 "Local custom means heavy traffic in illegal drugs and prostitution, an underground economy that is left alone as long as there is no trouble."

AMONG THE NEW WORDS

I. WILLIS RUSSELL AND MARY GRAY PORTER

The University of Alabama

With the assistance of William W. Evans, *Louisiana State University*; Michael Montgomery, *University of South Carolina*; and Richard E. Ray, *Indiana University of Pennsylvania*

A PROPOS OF OUR ENTRY *grief work*, mention may be made of Griefs Anonymous, "a group modeled on Alcoholics Anonymous to come to the assistance of people at the point of giving way to their grief" (*Newsweek* 11 Feb. 1952, p. 95).

Acknowledgments for citations: Jane Russell Johnson (2), James B. McMillan (3), and Mamie J. Meredith (1). Special thanks are due Ginny T. Raymond and Jennie S. Flowers for substantial contributions to the entry *grief work*. Mrs. Raymond supplied one citation and referred us to Mrs. Flowers, who researched the term and located six additional citations.

categorical *adj* [cf *W3 adj* 2, *World Book Dict* 1981 *adj* 1 b "explicit, direct"] Of a federal grant-in-aid designed for a specific project (cf *block grant* in *World Book Dict* 1981)   1973 Mar 1 Gov Calvin L Rampton on *Today* NBC-TV   1981 Aug 30 *Richmond Times-Dispatch* G-6/2 (David Broder) "No sooner had the president renewed his pledge to seek further shifts from narrow categorical programs to broad, flexible block grants than the attorney general's Task Force on Violent Crime came in with a recommendation for a new categorical aid program—this one for the construction of prisons."   1982 Aug 24 *Tuscaloosa News* 4/4 (James J Kilpatrick) "The Schmitt-Heckler bill proposes one more matching categorical grant program with all the trappings of guidelines, plans, applications, awards and reports that have become so familiar in recent years."

enterprise zone, (urban) *n* [cf *free enterprise*; also *enterprise capital* in *Ten Eventful Years* (Chicago: Ency Brit, Inc, 1947) 4: 630/2] Location, usually urban, with unemployment above the national average and concentrations of low and poverty-level incomes, and allowed to attract businesses by offering such incentives as lower payroll and capital gains taxes and favorable depreciation schedules   1981 Feb 11 *Chr Sci Monitor* 4/1 "Observers are beginning to worry that one of the apparently simple elements of the Reagan economic package—the plan for 'urban enterprise zones,' popularized by Mrs. Thatcher's Conservative Party in Britain—may be increasingly clouded by practical complexities. [¶] The zones, recently established in Belfast, Glasgow, Liverpool, and six other impoverished inner-city areas in Britain are designed as havens of entrepreneurial freedom. Businesses in them have something of a honeymoon from taxes and governmental regulation."   Aug 30 *Parade* 5/3 "Another of his ideas, for 'enterprise zones,' would make it cheaper for corporations to stay in decaying urban centers rather than flee to the suburbs

or the Sun Belt. The bill . . . would reduce payroll and capital gains taxes and depreciation schedules for businesses operating in areas of extreme unemployment."   Aug 31 Columbia (SC) *Record* D-9 (AP) "Pierce said cities would design projects under the 'enterprize zone program' using tax breaks, deregulation or other investment incentives such as job training."   1982 Jan *Atlantic* 14/2–3 "The GLC [Greater London Council] is also described as the strategic planning authority for the whole of London, but in the years since the council's birth, large-scale strategic planning has fallen out of fashion, though the central government has recently established an urban development corporation for London's blighted docklands and created an 'enterprize zone' with various fiscal and financial incentives for the regeneration of the inner city."   Feb 12 *Chr Sci Monitor* B-7/1 (ad) "ENTERPRISE ZONES: GREEN-LINING THE INNER CITIES by Stuart Butler [¶] Here is the first and only book available to fully explain what enterprise zones—just endorsed by the President—are all about. Stuart Butler first introduced the idea to the U.S., and is a leading authority on the subject."   Mar 10 *Wall St Jour* 1/5 "Over three years, tax breaks and regulatory exemptions to spur development and jobs would go to 75 urban and rural areas; the tax relief would top $10 million a year per zone. The White House improved passage chances by dropping a plan to waive minimum wages for teen-agers in enterprise zones. . . ."   Apr 5 *Newsweek* 28/3   May 19 *Chr Sci Monitor* 7/3–4   May 25 *Chr Sci Monitor* 5/3   Jun *Reader's Digest* 110–11   Aug 16 *Barron's* 1/2–3 "What has him [Arthur Laffer] teetering is a bunch of other dumb things in addition to the tax bill—monetary policy, retreat from free trade, failure to push enterprise zones."

gender gap *n* [*BDNE* sv *generation gap* 1970] Differences in the way men and women feel on an issue   1982 Sep 21 Bruce Morton CBS-TV "President Reagan has been suffering from what pollsters call a gender gap."   Oct 4 *Newsweek* 19/2 "The White House is opening the loophole to help close the 'gender gap'—data that show women are disproportionately dubious about administration policies."   Oct 18 *Chr Sci Monitor* 5/3–4 "Democratic National Chairman Charles Manett forecasts that the 'gender gap'—men's and women's differing voting patterns—will favor the Democrats more than ever in this year's elections. . . ."   Oct 20 *Birmingham* (Ala) *Post-Herald* A–7/1 "Wirthlin was among the first to note the significant gap between the way men and women feel about Reagan. . . . [¶] By now, the phrase 'gender gap' has become a part of the common vocabulary of this campaign. . . ."   1982 Nov 1 *Newsweek* 26/1–2 "Women in Politics: The Gender Gap [¶] . . . Increasingly they differ from men on the issues—and often at the expense of the GOP."

golden handcuff *n* [for GOLDEN see next entry; *World Book Dict* 1981 sv *handcuff* "2. *Figurative.* a restraint . . ."] Incentives or perquisites offered to key employees to keep them from taking a position with a different employer   1976 *Economics Dict* edited by Donald W Moffat (NY: Elsevier Scientific Pub Co) "Golden handcuffs: Benefits provided by employers in such a manner as to make it costly for employees to change jobs, thereby removing the competitive advantage an individual would otherwise have in selling his labor."   1981 Oct 4 *Pittsburgh Press* B-9/2 "Wood [Ernest O Wood, President, Pennsylvania Institute of CPAs] talks of the 'golden handcuff,' the 'golden handshake' and the 'golden parachute.' [¶] The handcuff symbolizes a corporation's grip on top performers it cannot afford to lose. The million dollar loan [at 2% interest] is an example."   1982 Feb 9 *Wall St Jour* (Sec 1) 16/3 "Getty Oil is trying to lock 'golden handcuffs' on explorationists by offering them four-year loans 'up front' equal to 80% of an employe's salary. Getty forgives 25% of the loan each year one stays with the company; after four years on the job, the loan is completely forgiven."   Aug 1 *Pittsburgh Press* B-6/2 "Even so, corporate loyalty remains an outmoded concept. . . . To reinforce the ties that bind, most corporations have been compelled to expand the concept of 'golden handcuffs'—perks that will keep valued employees locked in."

golden parachute *n* [*2BDNE* sv *golden handshake*: "*British.* 1. a large sum of money given as severance pay." 1963] Employment contract stipulating that in the event of a takeover by another company the employee, usually an important executive, may resign without loss of salary and various perquisites until his contract terminates   1981 Oct 4 *Pittsburgh Press* B-9/3 "Then there's the golden parachute. This refers to the protection top management may give itself when a corporate merger looms. What happened at Conoco is a good example. [¶] Last June when the Connecticut-based oil firm was being wooed by Mobil, DuPont and Seagram, the nine top Conoco officials struck a deal with their directors. Conoco Chairman Ralph E. Bailey was guaranteed his present annual pay of $637,716 for nearly eight years even if he lost his job. Eight other Conoco brass won similar agreements."   1982 May 3 *Wall St Jour* (sec 2) 33/6 "The payments [by Mohasco Corp] were part of a clause nine Mohasco officers signed last year that would allow them to leave the company with cash payments if an investor or other company gained 20% control of the carpet and furniture maker. Usually such 'golden parachutes' don't open until a third party gains actual control, or 51% of a company's stock."   Sep 1 Raleigh (NC) *News and Observer* B-8/3 (*NY Times* News Service) "Martin Marietta also disclosed that it had given so-called golden parachutes, or employment contracts, to 29 key executives Monday—five days after it received the takeover bid from Bendix. The terms, to be invoked if the company changed hands and the job status of the executives changed, provide that each may quit and still be paid his salary, other compensation, employee benefits and stock options until his employment contract ends."   Sep 27 Bill Moyer *CBS Evening News* CBS-TV   Oct 3 Raleigh (NC) *News and Observer* D-11/1 (*NY Times* News Service) "Because of the recent upsurge in hostile corporate takeover bids, 15 percent of the nation's largest companies have installed 'golden parachute' employment contracts for top management, according to a survey last week. . . . The long-term contracts provide for continued compensation in the event control of a company changes hands."

grief work *n* [*Sup OED* sv *grief therapy* 1963; *2BDNE* sv *grief therapy*] Steps necessary for a bereaved person to resolve his grief. (Quots supply details.)   [1917 Sigmund Freud "Mourning and Melancholia" *Collected papers* tr Joan Riviere (London: Hogarth Press & Inst of Psycho-Analysis 1950) 4: 169 "Just as the work of grief, by declaring the object to be dead and offering the ego the benefit of continuing to live, impels the ego to give up the object, so each single conflict of ambivalence, by disparaging the object, even as it were by slaying it, loosens the fixation of the libido to it."] 1944 Erich Lindemann "Symptomatology and Management of Acute Grief" *Amer Jour of Psychiatry* 101 (Sep) 143/1 "The duration of the grief reaction seems to depend upon the success with which a person does the *grief work*, namely, emancipation from the bondage of the deceased, readjustment to the environment in which the deceased is missing, and the formation of new relationships. One of the big obstacles to this work seems to be the fact that many patients try to avoid the intense distress connected with the grief experience and to avoid the expression of emotion necessary to it." 1970 Lydia Rapoport "Crisis Intervention as a Mode of Grief Treatment" in Robert W Roberts and Robert H Nee *Theories of Social Casework* (Chicago & London: Univ of Chicago Press) 282 "Lindemann notes that the duration of the grief reaction seems to be dependent on the success with which a person does his 'grief work.' " [1972] Colin Murray Parkes *Bereavement: Studies in Grief in Adult Life* (NY: International Universities Press, 1974 printing) 75 "The bereaved person continues to act, in many ways, as if the lost person were still recoverable and to worry about the loss by going over it in his mind. This activity has been termed 'grief work' by Freud (1917) and it can be assumed to have the same function as worry work in preparing the bereaved individual for a full acceptance of his loss." 1974 Ira O Glick and others *The First Years of Bereavement* (NY: John Wiley & Sons) 6–7 "By focusing his mind on the lost person and bringing to consciousness each relevant memory, the mourner gradually sets free the bound up energy. [¶] This process, which Freud called the 'work of mourning' (or 'grief work'), provides an explanation for the phenomenon we term 'obsessional review,' which is so prominent a feature of grief." 1975 Lois I Greenberg "Therapeutic grief work with children" *Social Casework* 56: 396/1–2 (heading) Otto S Margolis " in *Grief and the Meaning of the Funeral* edited by Otto S Margolis and others (NY: MSS Information Corp) 175 "The grief sufferer . . . should be encouraged to ventilate his feelings despite the pain that this causes. This is an essential part of grief work." 1982 Oct 8 Dr James Peterson *Over Easy* PBS "By grief work we mean grappling with our loss—work it through, don't deny it."

Ironman, Iron Man *n* **1:** Hawaii's very difficult and strenuous TRIATHLON 1979 May 14 *Sports Illus* 90/2 "The Iron Man contest was born when someone wondered what would happen if endurance tests in swimming, bicycling and running were piled on one another in a single event." 1982 Fall/Winter *International Male* 8.3: 36 "Perhaps the best known Triathlon is the Iron Man Triathlon in Hawaii which combines a 2.4 mile swim, a 112 mile bike ride and a 26.2 mile run." Sep 15 *Wall St Jour* 1/4 Quot sv TRIATHLON Oct 25 *Time* 75/1–2 Quot sv TRIATHLON (See TINMAN) **2: Iron Man, Iron Woman** Competitor who finishes the IRONMAN TRIATHLON 1979 May 14 *Sports Illus* 91/1 ". . . bearded Gordon Haller, a 28-year-old retired taxi driver, was delighted to read a short race report in a Honolulu newspaper. Better yet, friends started sending him mail addressed 'Iron Man.' " 1982 Fall/Winter *International Male* 8.3: 36 "We Iron Men and Women have conquered an event that surpasses what most of the rest of the world cannot accomplish in their wildest dreams."

measured *adj* Of a charge for telephone service based on the amount of actual use instead of, for example, a flat monthly rate 1978 Oct 22 *Tuscaloosa News* A-10/1–2 (AP) "The plan is called 'measured service' pricing and will, if shown to be feasible, allow telephoners to control the size of their bills by controlling the use of their phones. . . . [¶] 'Measured service' rates would be determined by the number of outgoing calls that are completed, the duration and distance of the calls and the time of day calls are made. . . ." 1979 Aug 12 *Family Weekly* 17/2 "Finally, if you are paying for flat-rate service but your conversations are always short, find out if your phone company offers 'measured rate' service. Charges are based on the length and frequency of calls." 1982 Jan *Bell Notes* (South Central Bell, Ala) "Basic measured service is priced below flat-rate service. The price includes a certain amount of calling each month. . . . Discounts are offered for evening, night or weekend calls."

recycle *vt* Reuse previously published material with little or no change 1982 May 4 *Tuscaloosa News* 5/2 (AP) "Editors of the more than 1,000 newspapers worldwide who buy her column and her estimated 70 million readers were not told she was recycling previously published letters, sometimes using only slight changes in wording and details like names and ages." May 5 *Tuscaloosa News* 6/1 (AP) "Messages of support flooded columnist Ann Landers' office and home Tuesday following an Associated Press report that found she recycled 15-year-old material in her column during the past 18 months. [¶] . . . Miss Landers said she had recycled 'very little' material. . . ." May 11 *Tuscaloosa News* 2/3–4 (AP) "Miss Landers acknowledged the recycled letters and promised to label reprinted portions of columns." May 17 *Newsweek* 107/2 "What provoked this outpouring of dismay was the news that star sob-sister Ann Landers (who is Abby's twin sister) had been caught recycling old letters in her syndicated advice column." Aug 9 *Tuscaloosa News* 4/3 "EDITOR'S NOTE: Art Buchwald is recycling some of his best columns whilst he and his family soak up the sun and enjoy the soft sea breeze of the Falkland Islands, otherwise known as 'Maggie's Vineyard.' "

smokestack *attrib* Manufacturing, in contrast to high-technology or service 1982 Oct 17 Alan Greenspan on *This Week with David Brinkley* ABC-TV "This is not a smokestack economy as it was 10 years ago." Oct 18 Participant on *McNeil-Lehrer Report* PBS "The United States is becoming less and less a smokestack society." Oct 18 *Chr Sci Monitor* 5/2 ". . . industry itself has changed from mass-production 'smokestack' factories to more technical and service jobs."

Tinman *n* TRIATHLON that is not as grueling as Hawaii's IRONMAN 1982 Sep 15 *Wall St Jour* 1/4 "Among veterans of the challenging Hawaii race, this sort of contest [a TRIATHLON consisting of a '1½ mile swim in Long Island's Noyac Bay, a 25-mile bike ride and a 20-mile run'] is known as a 'Tinman.' "

triathlete *n* [by analogy with *decathlete* (*Sup OED* 1968) and the earlier *pentathlete* (*OED* 1828)] Participant in a TRIATHLON 1982 Jun *Health* 46/1–3 (heading) "LYN BROOKS, TRIATHLETE" Fall/Winter *International Male* 8.3: 36 "It's estimated that perhaps 20,000 tri-athletes will participate in approximately 200 Triathlons of varying lengths this year." Sep 15 *Wall St Jour* 1/4 "More than 900 'triathletes,' about 10% of them women, have entered the next Ironman Oct. 9, including a large group of doctors, lawyers and business people." Oct 25 *Time* 75/3 "But living with a triathlete who may train 35 hours a week is not easy."

triathlon *n* [by analogy with *decathlon* (*Sup OED* 1912) and the earlier *pentathlon* (*OED pentathlum* 1706, *pentathlon* 1852)] Athletic event consisting, usually, of a swim, a bicycle ride, and a distance run, done without a break. (Quots supply specifics.) 1979 May 14 *Sports Illus* 90/1 "The athlete had been stung by a jellyfish and partially blinded by saltwater. . . . But still he kept on in this, the Hawaiian Iron Man Triathlon, an event that involved swimming 2.4 miles in perilously stormy seas, then bicycling 112 miles around the island of Oahu, followed by a 26.2 mile marathon run." 1981 Nov 6 *Daily Reveille* (La State Univ) 6/1 "The Office of Leisure Services is sponsoring a Tri-Athalon [*sic*], a combination of swimming, jogging and bicycling events. . . ." 1982 Jun 27 *Tuscaloosa News* B-1/1 "About five years ago, a group of runners were sitting in a bar in Hawaii satisfying their thirsts with hearty helpings of beer. [¶] As sometimes happens in such foamy situations, one of the runners started talking out of his mind. He wondered what would happen if an unusual triathlon, an offspring from the decathlon in the Olympic Games, was staged featuring three grueling events, a 2.4-mile ocean swim, a 112-mile bike ride and a 26.2-mile run. [¶] One drink led to another and the runners decided to propose such an undertaking to financial backers. Oh yeah, before they quit sipping, they decided the events should be held one after another without rest in between." Jul 19 *Tuscaloosa News* 12/1 "Ham not only survived the 440-yard swim, 25-mile bicycle race and 10-kilometer run, but also emerged as the winner of the first organized triathlon in the Tuscaloosa area." Fall/Winter *International Male* 8.3: 36 "In June 1982, nearly 800 men and women in top competitive condition plunged into the water at the start of the San Diego Triathlon. They swam 1.2 miles in 65 degree surf, then bicycled 21.7 miles over a hilly, twisting course and finally ran a 9 mile race to the finish line at Torrey Pines State Beach, San Diego, California. WHAT a Triathlon is is easier to report than WHY. A Triathlon is an uninterrupted event combining any three sports, usually swimming, cycling and running." Sep 15 *Wall St Jour* 1/4 "It is the triathlon, a contest that combines successive excesses of swimming, bicycling and running. To complete Hawaii's triathlon, appropriately named the Ironman, a competitor must swim 2.4 miles in the ocean, race the 112 miles around Oahu island on a bicycle, and then run a full 26.2-mile marathon." Oct 25 *Time* 75/1–2 "The [Hawaiian] Ironman is a kind of Super Bowl of the increasingly popular ultra-long-distance races called triathlons, contests consisting of three consecutive events. . . . The swim-bike-run events are the most popular, but the Tahoe Triathlon in April, for instance, featured cross-country skiing, biking and kayaking."

yellow rain *n* [from its color and because it is sprayed from aircraft and thus falls from the sky like rain] Mycotoxin allegedly supplied by the USSR to various governments in SE Asia and Afghanistan for use in chemical warfare 1981 Sep 21 *Wall St Jour* (Sec 1) 34/1 (editorial) "For some years there have been reports of some form of chemical warfare in Laos, Cambodia and Afghanistan. Refugees from these areas often referred to a 'yellow rain' sprayed from helicopters and airplanes that would cause a rapid and agonizing death from blistering, vomiting, violent convulsions and massive hemorrhaging." Nov 3 *Wall St Jour* (Sec 1) 34/1 (editorial) "The U.S. government has completed analysis of three more 'yellow rain' samples from Laos and Cambodia, showing the presence of mycotoxins of the trichot[h]ecene group, a deadly poison which can cause massive hemorrhaging, vomiting and blistering of the skin. Death, often with victims choking on their own blood, occurs within 45 minutes to an hour after exposure." Nov 17 *NY Times* A-30/2 (editorial) "The department [US Dept of State] has said yellow rain is so named because it patters on rooftops; yet it does not explain how particles large enough to patter are also small enough to breathe or to deliver a lethal dose to a clothed human." Nov 24 *NY Times* C-1/5 "The United States has been trying since 1976 to verify reports that chemical weapons, known popularly as 'the yellow rain,' are being used against remote villages in Laos, Cambodia and, more recently, Afghanistan." 1982 Feb 20 *Science News* 122/1 "Fred Celec, of the department's political-military affairs divisions, says that blood samples were drawn from nine individuals supposedly exposed to a 'yellow rain' gas attack in the fall of 1981. . . . Mirocha 'was able to tentatively identify' HT_2, a metabolite of the trichothecene mycotoxin T_2, in samples from only two of the alleged gas victims." 1982 Oct 7 *Chr Sci Monitor* 2/4 "Australian scientists are reported to have found no traces of the mycotoxin known as 'yellow rain'—nor of any other poison—on leaves and pebbles said to have been collected by anticommunist refugees in Laos."

AMONG THE NEW WORDS

I. WILLIS RUSSELL AND MARY GRAY PORTER
The University of Alabama

With the assistance of William W. Evans, *Louisiana State University;* Michael Montgomery, *University of South Carolina;* and Richard E. Ray, *Indiana University of Pennsylvania*

OUR ENTRY UNDER *card* in the glossary supplements the three examples given in *The Second Barnhart Dictionary of New English,* namely, "human rights card" (1978), "Chinese card" (1978), and "U.S. card" (1979). Not only are such *cards* metaphors for a variety of ploys in the game of power politics, but *the China card* has led one writer to a name for the game of US-USSR-Chinese political relations: *play Chinacard;* see the first citation under *card.* Card play appears to have inspired several writers to wordplay. *Newsweek*'s reference to Jimmy Carter's playing his *draft card* (see the 1981 July 6 citation in the glossary) is trumped by the *Columbia Journalism Review*'s heading for its story about Bob Hope's show from China: "The American card plays China" (Nov.-Dec. 1979, pp. 76–77).

Acknowledgments for citations: Dennis E. Baron (1), Lena Frost (3), Iredell Jenkins (1), Jane Russell Johnson (1), James B. McMillan (1), and Anne B. Russell (1).

birth *attrib* Blood, as opposed to adoptive 1975 May 11 *NY Times* 41/1 "between adopted persons and their 'birth parents,' a term he prefers to 'natural parents' because he feels the latter implies adopted parents are somehow less important." 1978 Nov 5 *Tuscaloosa News* C-12/1 (AP) "A group of women who as unwed mothers gave their children up for adoption believe they still have vital roles as their children's genetic parents. . . . [¶] The Connecticut United Birthparents, with 35 members, is interested in more than helping members overcome lingering emotional problems following the loss of their children." 1982 Nov 25 *MacNeil-Lehrer Report* (PBS) [used repeatedly in such collocations as "birth father," "birth mother," "birth parents" to describe the blood parents of an adopted child] Dec 22 *ABC-TV News* [reference to "birth mother" as opposed to the "adoptive mother"] 1983 Mar 7 *Chr Sci Monitor* 22/1–2 (letter) "I would like to point out that most adoptive parent organizations object to the term 'natural mother.' It implies that the adoptive mother is somehow unnatural. We prefer the terms birth mother and adoptive mother. [¶] Also in your editorial, you hinted at dangers that might exist by 'depriving' a child of his birth mother. Please allow me to point out that in adoption, an infant is usually relinquished by his birth parents for valid, unselfish, and loving reasons."

card *n* [*2BDNE* sv *card*[2] *n play the* (or *one's*)——*card* "to use a (particular) gambit or tactic so as to gain an advantage or attain a goal." 1973] Additional illus 1978 Aug 25 *Wall St Jour* 8/3 "Playing the China card (or playing Chinacard, for the sake of brevity) is an application of the balance of power, the venerable theory that assumes that relationships between states will always be fluid, with changes dictated by a shared interest in maintaining a power parity sufficient to prevent the eruption of overt conflict. . . . [¶] Inexperienced card players often imagine that only they are playing a strategic game. In fact, everyone plays Chinacard, but differently. The enduring Soviet interest is to prevent cooperation between the U.S. and China while attempting to encircle and contain China. The Soviets emphasize the common interest Washington and Moscow share against Peking. . . . [¶] Peking plays Chinacard by keeping both Moscow and Washington in high tension so that each will be willing to bid more for its cooperation." 1979 Feb 6 *Tuscaloosa News* 17/4–5 (AP) "The legislation introduced Monday would grant commercial credits to China and make changes in current restrictions on trade with the Soviet Union. 'To grant credits for the one and not the other would give credibility to the suspicion that the United States is playing a China card and with some risk of heightening anxieties of the Russians,' he said." May 6 Rep Toby Moffett on *Face the Nation* CBS-TV "[US negotiators are being outsmarted at the international oil bargaining table:] they don't play their Mexican card, they don't play their Canadian card. . . . " Jan 21 *Chr Sci Monitor* 23/2 "However, in talking to farmers and also to political leaders around the US, one becomes convinced that the American people are, as one Iowan puts it, 'ready for the President to play his Olympics-boycott card.' [¶] And now the President on 'Meet the Press' has apparently played this card—pushing for a boycott unless the Soviets pull out of Afghanistan by Feb. 15." 1981 Jul 6 *Newsweek* 64/3 "The case began in 1971 as a challenge by several men to the Vietnam-era draft. . . . After going unresolved for several years, the case was suspended in 1975, along with registration for the draft. It took on new meaning, however, after the Soviet invasion of Afghanistan, when Jimmy Carter decided to send the Russians a message by playing his draft card." 1982 Mar 31 *Wall St Jour* 22/2 (editorial) "But we are far from powerless, and it is a matter of fundamental national security that we not permit further Soviet intrusion into this hemisphere. The Soviets are dangerously mistaken if they think American public opinion will allow them to play a Cuba card, or even to bluff at it." Nov 3 *Chr Sci Monitor* 1/2 "Western newspapers have been full of speculation as to whether China was playing a 'Soviet card' against the United States, much as they speculated in an earlier period that Washington was playing a 'China card' against the Soviet Union." Nov 29 *Pittsburgh Press* B-2/1 "Whether or not it's now Russia's turn to play its 'China card' against the United States, there are definite signs of a thaw in relations between the Soviet Union and Communist China." Ibid B-2/2 "As for the Chinese, they seem to be showing their 'Russia card' in disapproval of the Reagan administration's failure to cut away from Taiwan far enough and fast enough and its caution in selling military equipment to mainland China."

dense pack 1: *n* Method of deploying ICBMs, specif the MX missile, in silos close to one another 1982 May 20 *Chr Sci Monitor* 1/1 "Of the various plans for housing this heavy intercontinental ballistic missile (ICBM), the front-runner now is 'dense pack.' The opposite of the hide-and-seek racetrack system spread over vast areas, this plan would crowd the missiles close together. [¶] With US missiles bunched together, the reasoning goes, incoming enemy missiles would have to be fired with extreme accuracy and precise timing in order to keep from blowing each other out of the sky—an effect strategic planners call 'fratricide.' " Ibid 6/3 "The dense pack plan may also include placing MX missiles in tunnels 2,000 feet underground. But this is thought to be technologically more difficult. Some form of ballistic missile defense also may be part of the dense-pack solution to housing the MX." Sep 15 Columbia (SC) *The State* A-9 (UPI) "The 'closely spaced basing' concept is known informally as 'dense pack.' It is estimated it will cost $23 billion to bury 100 MX missiles in superhardened capsules 1,000 to 2,000 feet from one another in an area of about 10 square miles. [¶] The Air Force theorizes that by crowding the missiles together and forcing the Soviets to home in on a small target, the first Soviet missile to explode would destroy other incoming missiles or deflect them from the site—creating what is called a fratricide factor." Nov 23 *Pittsburgh Post-Gazette* 3/1 "The close-spacing concept, which the Air Force calls 'dense pack,' represents a dramatic departure from past missile deployment plant, including the Carter administration's scheme for the MX." 1983 Apr 17 *Tuscaloosa News* A-16/3 (Art Buchwald) "[He] feels 'Dense Pack' basing is unfeasible and a waste of money." **2:** *vt* 1982 Nov 28 Sen Ernest Hollings on *This Week* ABC-TV "We can dense pack the Minuteman."

-flation *comb form* for *inflation* [See etymologies of *stagflation* in *BDNE, W3 Add Sec* 1981, *World Book Dict* 1981] **—adflation** *n* Increase in the cost of advertising space or time 1975 Feb 12 Radio commercial WALX-FM, Selma, Ala "Radio can help you fight adflation." 1976 Mar 22 *Time* 2nd of 4 unnumbered pages betw pp 18–19 "Radio, adflation fighter. Beat the rising cost of advertising. Use a lot more Radio." **—Euroflation** *n* Inflation in Europe 1979 Aug 27 *Newsweek* 41/2 (caption on chart showing rising prices of selected commodities and services in Britain, France, and Germany) "EURO FLATION" **—globflation** *n* [*glob*al in*flation* or *glob*al stag*flation*] Worldwide inflation 1979 Dec 5 *NY Times* D-2/3 "The chronic [balance-of-payments] deficits also undermine the value of the dollar, causing the oil exporters (who are paid in dollars) to raise their prices still higher, a new vicious cycle in global stagflation, or 'globflation.' " **—gradeflation** *n* [*grade inflation*] 1976 Jan 21 *Wall St Jour* 16/4 "But a much broader effort is called for if the evil of grade inflation, or 'gradeflation' as I prefer to call it, is to be brought under control." **—kidflation** *n* Inflation affecting children and businesses whose customers are principally children or young people 1981 Mar 2 *Wall St Jour* 1/6 "Many parents undoubtedly believe that the problem of 'kidflation' is child's play. . . . But many kids themselves feel quite harassed by increasing prices. So do manufacturers who vie for the estimated $45 billion that children aged six to 16 spend annually." Ibid 12/3–4 "The record and confection industries are among several that believe they have lost sales at the hands of 'kidflation.' When the recording industry, for example, fell into a slump in 1979, some industry officials said part of the reason was that the rising cost of albums was putting them beyond the financial reach of young people." 1982 Feb 28 *Greenville* (SC) *News and Greenville Piedmont* E-4 (heading) "Kidflation Today's children know something's up—prices" **—legis-flation** *n* 1982 Jun 10 *Ponca City* (Okla) *News* A-4/3 "Legis-flation: Cost of legislating in Oklahoma has more than doubled in seven years—from $5,017,982 in fiscal 1976 to an estimated $11,420,036 for the year just closing." **—medflation** *n* 1983 *PPG Products Mag* 91.1: 2/3 "About $220 of the sticker price of a new American-made automobile, for example, goes to pay the medical benefits for auto industry employees. Multiply this throughout industry and the effects of 'medflation' become readily apparent." **—musicflation** *n* 1982 Apr 18 Columbia (SC) *The State* F-4/1 (UPI) "When music becomes too expensive for people to enjoy, they buy fewer records and record companies make less money. When record companies make less money, they fire people and raise the price of records. [¶] So the price of records is going up and at least 80 people who were once employed by record companies have been laid off in the last two months. [¶] Enter Musicflation." **—oilflation** *n* Inflation caused by the high price of oil imports 1979 Dec 5 *NY Times* D-2/3 "Oilflation breeds huge trade and balance-of-payments deficits for this country. The resulting heavy outflow of dollars aggravates world inflation, including inflation in the oil-exporting countries." **—taxflation** *n* 1981 Jul 16 *Memphis Press-Scimitar* 7 "Armstrong said that when inflation hits the tax system—taxflation, he calls it—it penalizes the poor, wipes out periodic tax cuts passed by Congress, discourages savings and gives the government a 'windfall' of revenue. [¶] 'Indexation will stop taxflation dead in its tracks and it will keep the federal government from profiting from inflation,' he said." **—un-flation** (Trademark) Reduction in prices to counteract some effects of inflation 1978 Aug 16 *Tuscaloosa News* ad supp 1 "UN-FLATION® At Lowe's, the good old days are NOW! Because Un-flation Means Prices That Are As Low or Lower Than They Were Last Year, Or The Year Before!"

orphan drug *n* [Cf *SOED* sv *orphan* "*sb.* and *a.* 2 b. *slang.* A discontinued model of a motor vehicle . . . 1942 . . . B.2. *Path. orphan virus* 1954"; also *World Book Dict* 1981 sv *orphan n* 3 *Fig*] Drug that is not tested or manufactured because there are so few patients who might benefit from it 1982 Jun 3 Charleston (SC) *News & Courier* C-3/2–3 "A company spokesman says orphan drugs are given that name because, although there is a documented need for them for the treatment of a specific condition, the number of people afflicted is small, so the number of sales would not justify the cost of developing and marketing the drug from a business point of view. [¶] The result is that orphan drugs are usually not researched and marketed. [¶] Abbott laboratories has said it will sponsor hematin, an orphan drug for the treatment of hepatic porphyrias." Nov 29 *Today* NBC-TV "Orphan drugs are drugs known or thought to be useful in treating rare diseases [but that are not manufactured because pharmaceutical companies see no chance of making a profit on them]." 1983 Jan 4 Frank Reynolds on ABC-TV Jan 23 *Tuscaloosa News* A-20/2 (James Kilpatrick) "The much and justly maligned lame duck session of the 97th Congress did one good deed: it passed the Orphan Drug Act of 1982, and with the president's signature the measure is now law. The act offers hope to thousands of hopeless victims of rare diseases."

revenue enhancement *n* ; Euphemism for tax increase 1981 Oct 21 *NY Times* A-28/6 "The Reagan Administration's fiscal euphemist has been run to the ground. He is Lawrence A. Kudlow, who says he coined 'revenue enhancement,' the euphemism for tax increase used by the White House last month." Ibid D-2/3 "The recession is likely to swell the budget deficit for the fiscal year 1982 above the $43 billion the Administration was forecasting when it submitted its request to Congress for $13 billion in extra budget cuts and $3 billion in higher taxes, which it called 'revenue enhancement.' " Nov 8 *Pittsburgh Press* B-1/4–5 "Mrs. Rivlin may soon be back in trouble with Republicans because in public appearances she can't use Reagan administration's euphemism for tax increases, 'revenue enhancement,' without breaking up." Nov 12 *Pittsburgh Post-Gazette* 30/3 "The administration has asked for further budget cuts, but so far Congress hasn't appeared in any rush to approve them. And requests for small tax increases—called 'revenue enhancements' by Reagan officials—have been so ill-received that the administration has already said it won't press for them in the current fiscal year." Dec 20 *NY Times* E-16/1 "Ask for new taxes? Not me, says President Reagan; he has 'no plans for increasing taxes in any way.' And yet, it was quickly explained, his Administration is not above considering something called 'revenue enhancement.' ". 1982 Feb 24 *Pittsburgh Press* B-1/1 "And [Pres Reagan will] re-introduce $22 billion 'revenue enhancement' package, only this time compressed from three years to two to bring down fiscal 1983 deficit from $100 billion to $75 billion." 1983 Feb *Harper's* inside back cover (ad) "A tax increase in governmentese is 'revenue enhancement.' " Apr 20 *Tuscaloosa News* 1/5 " 'Revenue enhancement' or new taxes? [¶] It may boil down to a question of semantics, but whatever you call them, Gov. George C. Wallace, who prefers the former definition, proposed several new laws Tuesday night that could increase state revenues by as much as $82 million during the next two years." Apr 21 *Tuscaloosa News* 4/2 (editorial) "The need for the money is urgent but the proper amounts to alleviate true hardship cannot be raised with a euphemistic 'revenue enhancement' program."

revenue enhancer   *n*   Means of increasing the amount of monies available to a government   1983 Jan 22 Rep Jack Kemp on *Washington Week in Rev* PBS "[Taxes] are not revenue enhancers."

teleconferencing   *n*   [*2BDNE teleconference n* 1974]   1971 Fall *Educom* 8/2 "These [network applications] include teleconferencing, publishing, library services, and office paperwork filing and distribution." 1975 Sep *Change* 4 (heading) "On a foundation looking homeward, teleconferencing, the greening of Hanoi, a constitutional crisis at SUNY, the right to work." 1979 Jan 13 *Science News* 25/2 "Anik-B will continue such studies in areas including medical data exchange from remote regions, educational hookups, 'teleconferencing' and Eskimo broadcasting, as well as technical studies such as weather effects on high-frequency signal propagation." 1980 Jul 8 *Tuscaloosa News* 6/4–5 "At the different receiver sites, . . . telephones are equipped with speakers that broadcast the lecture and microphones participants can use to ask the lecturer questions. To cut down on the 'impersonality' of the set-up—one criticism of teleconferencing—visual aids such as slide shows are distributed in advance to receiving sites. [¶] . . . A major advantage of this type instruction, Balsamo emphasized, is that it eliminated the student's expenses for travel, lodging, food and gasoline. If teleconferencing is used for inservice training, there is a minimum loss of personnel work time, Balsamo added—about one hour a week." 1981 Jul 6 *Business Week* 54/2 (ad) "Our digital PBX (private branch exchange), one of the most advanced of its kind available, can help lower your phone costs with its computerized routing. It can handle both voice and data and has special features like wake-up calls for hotels and teleconferencing for offices." 1982 Sep 26 *Tuscaloosa News* A–27/1 "Teleconferencing refers to the University's joining a first-of-its-kind independent satellite network that can relay seminars from around the country to Alabama audiences, said Continuing Education Dean William Bryan." Dec 10 *Chr Sci Monitor* B-2/3 "Teleconferencing—the staging of business meetings over long distances via TV screens—will save time and cut millions of dollars in travel costs."

AMONG THE NEW WORDS

MARY GRAY PORTER AND I. WILLIS RUSSELL
The University of Alabama
With the assistance of William W. Evans, *Louisiana State University;*
Michael Montgomery, *University of South Carolina;*
and Richard E. Ray, *Indiana University of Pennsylvania*

IN OUR ENTRY for *cruise control*, we have used *Morrow* as a short-title citation for a fairly new compilation of recent additions to the lexicon: *The Morrow Book of New Words: 8500 Terms Not Yet in Standard Dictionaries* compiled and edited by N. H. and S. K. Mager (New York: Quill, 1982). Our definition of *cruise control* differs from that given in *Morrow*. The 1977 quotation clearly refers to a device that controls the car's speed, not to a signal that a certain speed has been exceeded. The experimental "smart cruise control" in the first 1979 quotation combines speed control with a proximity (not speed) warning. An earlier citation from the files of Mamie J. Meredith illustrates another, quite different use of the term: "Cruise control—that is, more efficient flying with the same equipment—has of itself almost doubled for each bomber the range provided in the original design" (August 27, 1948, General Motors program, Mutual Broadcasting System).

Our entry for the combining form *Euro-* offers additional illustrations of various senses that are already recorded. The definition of *Webster's Third New International Dictionary*, "European and," is seen in *Euro-Mediterranean*. Apart from some ambiguity in *Eurosteel, Eurosubsidy,* and *Eurotransplant*—does the *Euro-* of these words refer to the geographical entity or to the quasi-federation of the European Economic Community?—the terms listed in the glossary fit neatly into the three definitions for *Euro-* in *The Barnhart Dictionary of New English Since 1963*: (1) "of Europe, especially western Europe" *(Euromissile, Euro-nymphet, Euro strategic,* and *Euroterrorism);* (2) "of or relating to the European money market" *(Eurobanking, Eurodebt, Eurodeposit, Euro D-Mark, Eurofinancing, Euroloan, Euromark, Euromarket, Euronote, Euro[Swiss] franc,* and *Euroyen);* and (3) "of or relating to the European Economic Community or Common Market" *(Eurocompany, Eurounion,* and *Euroville).* The second *Euromissile* citation shows clearly that the word does not always refer to missiles of the western powers, especially of the United States; however, that does appear to be the predominant sense.

Guest worker, originally a translation of the German *Gastarbeiter,* was, like *Gastarbeiter,* restricted to workers from countries of southern Europe and the eastern Mediterranean who were employed in the countries of northern Europe, particularly in West Germany. The citations in the glossary illustrate the extension of the term to Mexican laborers in the United States. We have in our files no examples of the use of *Gastarbeiter* in this latter sense.

Acknowledgments for citations: Guy Bailey (2), James B. McMillan (1), Mamie J. Meredith (1), Michael Montgomery (1), and Marshall Winokur (1).

cruise control   *n*   [Cf *Morrow* 1982 *"cruise control* automobile device that provides warning when speed exceeds set levels."]   Device that maintains an automobile's cruising speed at the velocity set by the driver   1974 Jan 7 *New Yorker* 69/1 (ad) "Standard equipment includes electric windows, air conditioning, power-assisted steering and brakes, automatic transmission—even a cruise control." 1977 Sep *Gourmet* 17/2 (ad) *"Cruise Control with a memory*—It maintains any speed without your having to touch the gas pedal. Should you want to accelerate or slow down, simply touch a switch to return the car to your original speed." 1978 Nov 6 *Newsweek* 13 (ad) "CRUISE CONTROL WITH 5-SPEED STICK." 1979 Jan *Omni* 36/3–4 "One of the experimental cars, the Eagle II . . . features 'smart cruise control.' Using solid-state radar and a microcomputer, the cruise control system varies the car's speed to maintain a safe following distance behind any vehicles in front of it. It sounds a warning and automatically brakes to avoid crashes." Nov 4 Montgomery (Ala) *Advertiser—Ala Journal* B-9/1 (ad) "Half-day installations on Cruise Controls."

E-COM   /'i͵kɑm/   *Trademark* [Electronic Computer Originated Mail]   1981 Oct 11 *Atlanta Constitution—Journal* B-2 "E-COM, which stands for Electronic Computer Originated Mail, is really a half-stab at a complete electronic message delivery service. [¶] E-COM will not provide a point-to-point electronic message service. Instead, it will receive electronically generated messages of up to two pages, print them and deliver them through the regular postal delivery network. [¶] Companies using E-COM can either hook their computers to the post office system via phone lines, or deliver computer tapes directly to the post office for processing and printing." Dec 31 *Chattanooga* (Tenn) *Times* A-9/2 (AP) "The ECOM system would allow mass mailers to hook their computers up to new Postal Service computers in 25 cities around the country. The mailers' computers would transmit address lists and texts to the Postal Service computers. The actual letters would be printed, stuffed in envelopes and addressed in the post office before being delivered." 1982 Jan 4 *ABC-TV News* [screen legend:] "E-COM"; [reporter's pronunciation: /'i͵kɑm/] Mar 9 *Chr Sci Monitor* 23/4 "E-Com mailtapping legislation could include requiring coding of electronic correspondence or devices to detect tapping. . . . [¶] There is, however, an assumption in the E-COM service that privacy has a value and is to be protected. For instance, on arrival, an E-COM message is converted into hard copy, sealed, and delivered. But the message has been openly transmitted and made easy prey for interception by other computers and technological devices." 1983 May 30 *USN&WR* 13 (ad) "E-COM Service is a cooperative effort between private sector communication carriers and your Post Office. Here's how it works. Once your system is set up for E-COM Service, your computer operator simply prepares the message. It's then transmitted as data, by telephone or other communication carrier, to any one or more of 25 Serving Post Offices throughout the country."

Euro- *comb form* —**Eurobanking** *n* [Cf *2BDNE Eurobank n* 1966, *Eurobanker n* 1971] 1982 Aug *Atlantic* 13/1–2 "In Eurobanking, there is no deposit insurance. There are no rules, no regulators, no audits." Ibid 16/2–3 "It is past time for the world's central banks to offer the same liquidity guarantees to Eurobanking that they provide to their domestic banking systems. They should simultaneously impose similar rules and regulations." —**Eurocompany** 1971 Feb *Interplay* 31/1–2 "Now, at the start of 1971, enthusiasts for the European Economic Community, or Common Market, are suggesting . . . that the Common Market could by 1980 be seriously challenging the U.S. for the title of the undisputed world superpower. At that time, the expanded Community—possibly with as many as 15 or more members—could . . . have a kind [of] Community-wide Federal Reserve Board (with, of course, a common currency, or its equivalent, i.e. fixed parities), a vast number of giant Eurocompanies to challenge America's largest, and labor unions integrated right across national boundaries." Ibid 34 "However, there is now a growing realization that Eurocompanies as such must be facilitated if the Common Market is to have real meaning and if Europe is to produce powerful industrial complexes capable of withstanding American competition. . . . [¶] . . . The Eurocompany now on the Brussels drawingboard could be formed to merge two or more companies with head offices in different member-states; to form joint holding companies owned by corporations located in different states; to establish joint subsidiaries. . . . Officials in the EEC Secretariat in Brussels remain, as ever, optimistic that the Eurocompany will be a reality long before this decade is out. . . ." See also quot sv EUROUNION —**Eurodebt** *n* 1976 Jul 23 *Daily Beacon* (Univ of Tenn) 6/3 "The rub is that nobody knows how much Eurodebt is floating around the world." —**Eurodeposit** *n* 1974 Martin Mayer *The Bankers* (NY: Ballantine 1976) 229 "Our CD level was two thousand five hundred and ten (i.e., Morgan had $2.51 billion of CDs outstanding); Eurodeposits were forty-four negative (i.e. Morgan's European branches were taking $44 million out of the New York bank, not putting money into it). . . ." 1982 Aug *Atlantic* 13/1 "There is an additional $1 trillion of Eurodeposits that banks hold with one another. These are not counted, since they can be expanded without limit by a more magical sleight of hand. Suppose Chase Manhattan in London borrows a million dollars from Citicorp in London. Citicorp creates a million-dollar deposit for Chase and accepts a million-dollar IOU from Chase. Now suppose Chase offers to pay its obligation by creating a million-dollar deposit for Citicorp. The IOU is marked 'Paid' and returned to Chase, which opens the million-dollar checking account for Citicorp. Each bank has a new million-dollar liability, consisting of the other bank's deposit; and each bank has a new million-dollar asset, consisting of its own deposit at the other bank." —**Euro D-mark** *n* [Cf *Eurodollar BDNE* 1970, *6000 Words*] 1974 Martin Mayer *The Bankers* (NY: Ballantine 1976) 497 "Illustrating the range of options available to First National City on April 6, 1973, executive committee chairman Edward L. Palmer said, 'Euro D-marks are now available for six months on a one and a half percent basis. Domestic CDs are seven and a half percent. Are we willing to make a six-month bet that the D-mark won't be revalued more than three percent?' " —**Eurofinancing** *n* 1983 Jun 3 *International Herald Tribune* 12/1 (ad) "DGZ International S.A., the wholly-owned subsidiary, also contributed to the Bank's good results by strengthening its position in interbank money market activities and Eurofinancings." —**Euroflation** *n* See *AS* 58:361 —**Euroloan** *n* 1972 Apr 22 *New Yorker* 57/1 (ad) "We make loans to customers who've never had Euro-loans before. And we invent unusual forms for Euro-loans." —**Euromark** *n* [Cf *Eurodollar BDNE* 1970, EURO D-MARK, above] 1974 Martin Mayer *The Bankers* (NY: Ballantine 1976) 495 "As the dollar weakened, the Euromarket expanded into other currencies, and since the late 1960s, some of the loans that would once have been made in Eurodollars have been made instead in Euromarks, Euroyen, Eurosterling, and Euro(Swiss) francs. The nations that are the proprietors of these currencies did not like this at all . . . , but there is no way a government can control the trading or use of its currency outside its own borders." 1976 Jul 23 Nicholas Von Hoffman in *Daily Beacon* (Univ of Tenn) 6/3 "There are also units of bookkeeping currency called Euromarks . . . ; that is, obligations outside of West Germany . . . that can be cashed in back home in Bonn." —**Euromarket** *n* [Cf *Amer Heritage Dict* 1969 "The Common Market"] Market in Eurodollars or other Eurocurrency 1974 Mayer *The Bankers* (NY: Ballantine 1976) 489 "Nor can anybody criticize the Euromarkets for lending to operations in underdeveloped countries where the local financial markets could not conceivably raise the necessary funds. But there were also borrowers from cosmopolitan countries who were in the Euromarkets because they could no longer convince people to lend them money at home. . . ." 1982 *Morrow Book of New Words* 95/1 [See also first quot sv EUROMARK] —**Euromast** *n* Television tower in Rotterdam 1970 Oct 11 *NY Times Mag* 111/1 (ad) "From the canals of Amsterdam, to the palaces of The Hague to the Euromast of Rotterdam, there's probably more to see per square mile in Holland than in any other European country." —**Euro-Mediterranean** *adj* [*W3* EUR- or EURO- "European and"] 1980 Jan 11 *Chr Sci Monitor* 22/1 (letter) "The Renaissance of the 15th and 16th centuries may be seen in the broader context of world history as a Euro-Mediterranean 'florescence' without any inevitable consequences for Western influence in Africa or Asia." —**Euromissile** *n* Missile deployed in Europe 1980 Sep 17 *Chr Sci Monitor* 2/1 (heading) "US hopes to meet USSR on Euromissiles Oct. 15" 1983 Jun 13 *USN&WR* 27 "The President's performance at the Williamsburg summit convinced skeptics that Reagan is on track in his strategy to limit Euromissiles on both sides." Jul 4 *USN&WR* 26/2 "All of this, they say, contrasts with deepening Soviet economic problems, a continuing crisis over Poland, an interminable war in Afghanistan and the apparent failure of Moscow's drive to split the Atlantic Alliance over Euromissiles." —**Euronote** *n* Financial note sold in Europe but issued in non-European currency 1979 Aug 20 *Wall St Jour* 19/6 "The first Euronote to be denominated in Canadian dollars in three months was badly received. The $30 million (Canadian) five-year issue of Credit Foncier Franco-Canadien, a mortgage-finance company, was priced at par bearing 10.375% interest." —**Euro-nym-**

phet *n* [cf *W3 nymphet*] 1983 May 26 *Rolling Stone* 46/2–3 "Brooks, who's set this fall to film his own script, *Lost in America*, was seized with inspiration once the Euro-nymphet was out of earshot." —**Eurosteel** *n* European steel industry 1982 Jul 6 *Washington Times* A-7/1 "It found Eurosteel guilty as charged and recommended import penalties." —**Euro strategic** *adj* Of or dealing with European strategy 1982 Jan 15 *Chr Sci Monitor* B-6/2 (rev of Winston Churchill II *Defending the West* [Westport, Conn: Arlington House]) " 'The dawn of the eighties,' Mr. Churchill writes, 'ushered in an era in which every one of NATO's offsetting advantages in the field of nuclear weapons—at strategic, Euro strategic and battlefield level—has been lost.' " —**Eurosubsidy** *n* Government subsidy given to a European firm, esp one exporting its products to the US and underselling American manufacturers 1982 Jul 6 *Washington Times* A-7/1–2 "They also called Washington a Janus for two-facedly alleging Eurosubsidies while the U.S. itself was violating trade rules through DISCs. These allow U.S. firms tax deferrals through a $1.7 billion-a-year 'domestic international sale corporation' subsidy." —**Euro(Swiss) franc** *n* 1974 Mayer *The Bankers* 495 See quot sv EUROMARK —**Euroterrorism** *n* 1980 Jun 2 *Newsweek* 50/3 "In the past, Ponti and Gugliardo might have dodged the law simply by fleeing to another European country. But things are changing. To battle Euroterrorism, police all across Europe are sharing information and resources." —**Eurotransplant** *n* Computerized file of Europeans who need kidney transplants 1980 Sep *Reader's Digest* 60/1 "In May 1968, with a modest computer file of about 300 potential recipients, Dr. van Rood launched a system called Eurotransplant at the University of Leiden." —**Eurounion** *n* Labor union composed of workers in the countries of Europe, specif in the Common Market 1971 Feb *Interplay* 33–34 "And after Eurocompanies, Eurounions must be inevitable. A Europe of the Ten would have well over 30 million workers organized in trade unions, or considerably more than double the total membership of labor unions affiliated to the AFL-CIO. . . . [¶] The European labor unions . . . are, at least for the moment, themselves stopping short of actual mergers, but they accept that Eurocompanies will certainly dictate some parallel developments in the trade union movement." —**Euroville** *n* City in which the permanent headquarters of the European Economic Community were to be located 1958 Jan 20 *Newsweek* 30/1 "As for the 'Euroville' sweepstakes, it was still wide open—with Brussels on the inside track." —**Euroyen** *n* Japanese yen held by Europeans 1974 Mayer *The Bankers* 495 See quot sv EUROMARK

gridlock *n* *Fig* [Cf *Morrow* "a massive automobile traffic jam . . ."; *World Book Dict* 1983 "a complete stoppage of all vehicular traffic . . ."] Complete stoppage; failure to make any progress 1982 Dec 16 *MacNeil-Lehrer Report* PBS "The Senate has been described as being in a state of legislative gridlock." 1983 Apr *Atlantic* 102/2 "If U.S. management and labor could break this economic gridlock—if management had access to patient capital, labor had adequate retraining opportunities and sufficient job security, and both sides willingly restructured the organization of production—what would the resulting new American economy look like?" May 30 *Newsweek* 38/1 "It had taken 11 roll-call votes over nearly six hours after three weeks of legislative gridlock and an unusually fierce exchange of partisan rhetoric between Democratic leaders and Ronald Reagan." Jun 24 *MacNeil-Lehrer Report* PBS "and the gridlock that has taken place in our government."

guest worker *n* [Cf *guest worker* in *BDNE* 1970, *Morrow* 1982, and *World Book Dict* 1983] Mexican laborer legally in US 1981 May 23 *New Repub* 2/2 "The White House staff has subsequently explained that they are working on something like the old bracero, or guest worker, program. It was tried in 1941–64 with statutory authority granted in 1949. Braceros were restricted to areas certified by the secretary of labor as having a labor shortage. . . . [¶] Europe tried guest workers too, but Germany dropped the plan in 1973, France in 1974, and Switzerland and Holland have curtailed their programs." Jun 30 Report on ABC-TV News Jul 30 *Washington Week* PBS "[It] would allow 50,000 guest workers a year to enter the United States for a two-year period." 1982 Jan 25 *Chr Sci Monitor* 23/1 (editorial) "President Reagan's proposal for a pilot Mexican 'guestworker' program is an attempt to buy off domestic pressures for a large number of alien workers." Jan 26 *Chr Sci Monitor* 18/3 "The plan would tighten border control and provide emergency detention and deportation powers. At the same time, a two-year pilot program would allow 50,000 'guest workers' into the country each year. With this guest-worker system in place, employers caught knowingly hiring illegal aliens would face stiff fines."

leader board *n* **1:** *Golf* A board on which are listed the players with the best scores in a tournament 1981 Jun 20 Sportscaster ABC-TV "Still a very crowded leaderboard." 1982 Apr 11 *Tuscaloosa News* B-1 (picture legend) "Masters leaderboard" [followed by the names of the ten players with the lowest scores after three rounds in Masters tournament] Jun 21 *Tuscaloosa News* 11/7–8 (AP) "She said her father . . . wanted the victory as a Father's Day present. [¶] ' . . . I looked at the leader board and I didn't think I had much of a chance.' " Aug 21 Channel 13 News WVTM-TV, Ch 13, Birmingham, Ala "The leaderboard after 18 holes looks like this." 1983 Jul 12 *Tuscaloosa News* 15/1 "On the Professional Golf Association Tour, most folks keep their eyes on the leader board." Jul 17 *Tuscaloosa News* B-1/5 (*LA Times*) "Leader boards around the course dropped off the bottom names to report that England was leading New Zealand in its cricket test match in London." **2:** *Football* [trf meaning of sense 1] A listing of the teams with the best records 1982 Oct 23 Ara Parseghian on CBS-TV "Michigan [is] at the top of the leader board."

overnight letter *n* A letter which for a special fee is guaranteed to be delivered the next day 1981 Aug 13 Reported on ABC-TV News Sep 5 TV commercial on broadcast of Ala-LSU football game ABC-TV Oct 3 TV commercial CBS-TV "Introducing the Federal Express overnight letter." 1983 Mar 28 *Newsweek* 26 (ad) "It's the new Emery Urgent Letter. The overnight letter that lets you send up to twenty pages or four full ounces desk-to-desk across America for just eleven dollars."

steel-collar worker *n* [Cf *W3* svv *blue-collar, white-collar*] Robot 1981 Feb 11 *Chr Sci Monitor* 3/1 "With increasing frequency, union leaders see the ranks of blue-collar workers giving ground to 'steel-collar workers'—robots that can perform repetitive tasks tirelessly, quickly, and efficiently." 1982 Feb 16 *Wall*

St Jour 26/5 "If workers are retained as 'masters of robots,' they often take great pride in the 'steel-collar workers' now working for them." 1983 Apr 20 *Catalyst* 14/2 "The steel-collar worker is a reprogrammable automatic machine, sometimes called a robot."

AMONG THE NEW WORDS

MARY GRAY PORTER AND I. WILLIS RUSSELL

The University of Alabama

With the assistance of William W. Evans, *Louisiana State University;* Michael Montgomery, *University of South Carolina;* and Richard E. Ray, *Indiana University of Pennsylvania*

I N THIS INSTALLMENT we offer additional illustrations of words in *-gate,* a combining form entered in several dictionaries as well as in several earlier articles in *American Speech* (see the glossary). A third listing of *-gate* words here may seem a work of supererogation, but we believe that a record of these terms—however ephemeral most of them may be—is justifiable. Indeed, *Cartergate* is so ephemeral that it seems to have been coined, forgotten, and revived with a new meaning, all within a few years.

The *Barnhart Dictionary Companion* has dealt with *-speak* as a combining form "used to form nouns and meaning 'the typical language, jargon, or vocabulary of (something specified)'. *Informal.*" There, 1977 is given as the date of the earliest new formation with *-speak* abstracted from the *doublespeak* and *Newspeak* of George Orwell's 1949 novel *Nineteen Eighty-Four* (*BDC* 1.3 [1982]: 44/2–45/1). Entered in this and later issues (2.1 [1983]: 17/2; 2.2: 48/1–2) are *artspeak, discospeak, Olympspeak* (*Olympic +* *-speak*), *splitspeak* (1.3: 44/2–45/1); *nukespeak, Sportspeak, Valleyspeak, Videospeak, Warspeak* (2.1: 17/2); and *mellowspeak* (2.2: 48/1–2). Like the *BDC* entries, ours includes compounds with nouns (*computerspeak,* among others) and adjectives (*blandspeak,* for example) as the first element and blends with a first element that has been shortened (*medspeak*). In addition to these types, we have one compound with a personal name (*Haigspeak*), one with a two-word first element (*Valley Girlspeak*), and three derivatives (*anti-Nounspeak, Newspeakism,* and *out-Nounspeak*).

Acknowledgments for citations: the late Walter S. Avis (1), Edgar L. Frost (1), Lena Frost (1), Oliver Finley Graves (1), and Marshall Winokur (1).

anti-Nounspeak *adj* See NOUNSPEAK *sv* —SPEAK
—gate See 1978 ATNW *AS* 53:215–17, 1980 David K. Barnhart *AS* 55:77–78, 1981 *AS* [John Algeo and Charles Clay Doyle] 56:151–52 Additional illusts —**Altergate** [*alter vt* 'to change'] 1983 Jul 1 *Wash Wk in Rev* PBS ". . . Altergate, they call it." Aug 2 Jack Anderson in *Tuscaloosa News* 4/5–6 "But a few weeks ago, Reps. Judd Gregg, R-N.H., and John Hiler, R-Ind., were horrified to discover that some unflattering transcript changes had been made in their remarks at a hearing on environmental matters. . . . [¶] In their zeal to

pump 'Altergate' into a full-blown scandal that might embarrass the Democrats and share headlines with the purloined Jimmy Carter briefing book foofaraw, Gregg and Hiler charged that similar alterations had been made in the transcripts of still other hearings on the manipulation of the silver market in 1980." See also quot *sv* HEARINGSGATE —**Batgate** [baseball *bat*] 1983 Jul 31 Chicago *Sun-Times* 3 "*Batgate's* meaning[.] Everybody's talking about how American League President Lee MacPhail overruled his umpires and restored the home run George Brett lost for having too much pine tar on his bat."
—**Briefingate** [*briefing* cf Jul 18 *Newsweek* quot *sv* DEBATEGATE] 1983 Jul 6 William Safire in Montgomery (Ala) *Advertiser* A-4/3 "Briefingate—the penetration of the Carter campaign by the Reagan campaign, in order to give the Republican candidate an edge in 1980s televised debate—raises a legitimate issue of right and wrong." Jul 8 *Wall St Jour* 20/2 (editorial) "Commentary on the Briefingate scandal as it enters its third week has lacked its usual fervor, in no small part because Congress is not in session now." See also CARTERGATE DEBATEGATE —**Cartergate** [Jimmy *Carter*] See BRIEFINGATE DEBATE-GATE 1983 Jul 11 James Kilpatrick in *Tuscaloosa News* 4/1–2 "It seems to me absurd—on the basis of what we know now—to equate 'Cartergate' with 'Watergate.' " —**clamgate** 1983 Sep 22/23 *NBC News Overnight* "Stolen? Perhaps it's a clamgate, or only a chowder gap." —**debategate** [*debate* betw Pres Carter and Ronald Reagan during 1980 campaign] 1983 Jun 24 *NBC News Overnight* NBC-TV "Stolen briefing book? Debategate?" Jul 1 *Wall St Jour* 14/3 "And, lo and behold, it soon turned out that my colleague had exactly predicted the way in which the Debategate scandal would move on to Stage Four." Jul 3 *Sunday Oklahoman* A-18/6 "Is this going to become a shattering 'Debategate' in the Reagan administration or, as the president says, 'much ado about nothing'? . . . [¶] The story is that a briefing book and other documents, used to prepare Carter for his 1980 debate with Reagan came into the possession of Reagan's campaign organization. . . . [¶] First, the Reagan White House grossly mishandled the debate scandal—if you can call it that—when it was first divulged in a book by Laurence I. Barrett, of Time Magazine. [¶] He speculated, but had no proof, that the material was 'filched' by a Reagan 'mole' in the Carter White House. [¶] Instead of beating everyone to the punch with a complete and unassailable disclosure of everything that happened, top Reagan aides offered contradicting or incomplete stories, creating an appearance of that worst of all reactions—coverup—the Watergate crime that ruined Richard M. Nixon." Jul 18 *Newsweek* 14/2 "By last week the revelations that hundreds of documents from Jimmy Carter's White House—from a debate briefing book to sensitive National Security Council memos—had somehow been spirited to Reagan's 1980 campaign had tarnished the president's valued nice-guy reputation. . . . Amid what one aide called a 'feeding frenzy' in the media, the murky controversy dubbed 'Debategate' had the clear potential to damage Reagan's prospects for re-election in 1984." Jul 18 & 25 *New Repub* 10/1 "It seems virtually certain that a crime was committed when Carter campaign briefing documents were transferred to the Reagan campaign prior to the 1980 Presidential debate. What's not at all certain is whether the crime constitutes grand theft or petit larceny. Just how seriously 'Debategate' should be taken depends on answers not yet available." —**Floodgate** [Congressman Daniel *Flood* (Pa)] 1978 Mar 9 William Safire in *Crimson White* (Univ of Ala) 5/6 "[S]omeday . . . if President Carter can be shamed into appointing a special prosecutor to follow Koreagate and Floodgate where the Justice Department now fears to tread, the trail of rice may lead us to our takers." See also 1982 Tracey *AS* 57:263, 6 Mar 1978 quot in 1980 Barnhart *AS* 55:78. —**Hearingsgate** 1983 Jul 8 *Wall St Jour* 20/2 (editorial) "Republicans in the House were charging that Democratic committee staffers had altered the final text of a series of hearings on the EPA so as to make the Republicans look foolish, petulant and incompetent. 'Hearingsgate' is now before the House ethics committee." See also quot *sv* ALTERGATE —**Holly-woodgate** 1982 Aug 13 *Entertainment Tonight* ABC-TV "The David Begelman story—now termed Hollywoodgate—is far from over." Aug 22 *Entertainment Tonight* ABC-TV "The David Begelman story is being nicknamed Hollywoodgate." —**Lobogate** [*Lobos* nickname of Univ of N Mex athletic teams < Span *lobo* 'timber wolf'] 1983 Apr 3 *NY Times* "This is . . . the 17,121-seat arena that inspired one of college basketball's most notorious scandals, the arena where the coach who dealt in forged transcripts and phony credits, Norm Ellenberger, is still hailed by many Lobo rooters as a mod version of Albuquerque's original conqueror, the Spanish explorer Coronado. [¶] . . . And the scandal is still referred to here as Lobogate." —**lobster-gate** 1981 May 25 *Inquiry* 7/2 "When [he] was at the Massachusetts Port Authority he cultivated a taste for the high life that followed him to the governor's office, where it led to the now legendary 'lobstergate' scandal. After less than a year at the helm of the Bay State, [he] and his aides were accused of lunching regularly on the pricey crustaceans at taxpayer expense. The governor denied that he personally ate lobster at noontime, but his press office was forced to admit that lobster salad and lobster sandwiches had indeed become routine fare for [his] staff." —**mediagate** Sensational press treatment of a minor scandal; the minor scandal given such treatment in the media 1980 Aug 18 *Newsweek* 81/1 "The result is the unfolding tale of Billy Carter and his Libyan connection—an affair that many big-city dailies still call 'Billygate.' But thus far, at least, the story of First Brother Billy hardly seems to live up to that labeling—and many editors, reporters and journalism critics have begun wondering aloud whether the press has turned a minor-league scandal into a major-league miscalculation in judgment. 'This isn't Watergate,' fumes one angry editor. 'This is mediagate.' " —**Motorgate** 1975 Apr 24 *Wall St Jour* 1/6 (heading) "*Motorgate*/How a Floating Corpse Led to a Fraud Inquiry And Ousters by GM/Events Began Near Boston and Spread to Michigan; The Whys Are Uncertain/A Warranty Racket Alleged" 1978 Jul 13 *Wall St Jour* 28/3 "The former service manager of a Lowell, Mass., Chevrolet dealership was convicted here of the 1974 murder of a General Motors Corporation representative that triggered the tangled 'Motorgate' affair." —**Mounty-gate** [*W3 Mountie* or *Mounty* member of Royal Canadian Mounted Police] [1983 Aug *World Press Rev* 55/1 (from May 29 *Toronto Star*) "The Canadian Security Intelligence Service would be allowed to open mail, bug conversations, search homes, and scan tax files of subversion suspects—methods once used illegally by the Royal Canadian Mounted Police (RCMP).] 1981 Aug 25 *CBS-TV News* "In Canada they called it Mounty-

gate." **—Muldergate** [Cornelius P *Mulder* former South African cabinet member] 1979 Mar 25 Toronto *Sunday Star* A-17/1 "The information scandal—which has been dubbed 'Muldergate' after former minister Cornelius Mulder—began six months ago with a newspaper investigation into financial irregularities in Mulder's ministry." Mar 27 *Chr Sci Monitor* 3/1 "The turmoil has been caused by the so-called 'Muldergate scandal' in the government's Department of Information. Millions of dollars were spent on a variety of 'secret projects' that were supposed to improve the country's image abroad. [¶] Some of the money went on bribes. Much of it was misappropriated, and many millions were lost funding a daily newspaper . . . to give political support to the ruling National Party." 1981 Aug 23 *Manchester Guardian Weekly* 1/1 "No one outside South Africa's white laager expected a new dawn when the Muldergate saga finally engulfed Mr John Vorster and let Mr Botha sideslip into power." See also 2 Mar 1979 quot in 1980 Barnhart *AS* 55:78 **—Pornogate** [Cf *SOED porno- comb form* 1949, *porno adj* 1952, *n* 1958] 1981 Nov 18 *Birmingham News* A-9/1 (AP) "Nobody has called it Pornogate yet. But jokes about pornographic movies made in the Quebec National Assembly building are circulating furiously. [¶] Police say they are investigating whether erotic films were made with the television cameras and equipment normally used to broadcast sometimes hot debates in the provincial legislature." **—Rebelgate** [*Rebels* Univ of Miss nickname] 1983 Mar 22 *Daily Mississippian* (Univ of Miss student newspaper) 2/1 "In case you missed last Wednesday's report, a group led by the student body president-elect at Ole Miss invaded the campus newspaper and cut passages from an objectable [*sic*] story. . . . [¶] Rebelgate will lead to many other serious questions." **—Sewergate** Scandal concerning failure of EPA to act in cleaning up sites contaminated by hazardous wastes 1983 Feb 17 *Wash Wk in Rev* "Some of the critics are calling this sewergate." Feb 21 *Newsweek* 22/1–2 "But [the dismissal of Rita Lavelle from the EPA] quickly became a lightning rod for the nastiest controversy the Reagan administration has yet faced—complete with eerie overtones of Watergate, or 'Sewergate,' as one lawmaker dubbed it." Feb 28 *USN&WR* 26 "Tracking the EPA's 'Sewergate' " [Here follows a chronology of events in the controversy over the EPA Superfund from the Aug 1978 declaration of Love Canal as a disaster to Feb 17, 1983.] Mar 3 *Tuscaloosa News* 4/4–5 (letter) "President Reagan may be successful at heading off at the pass the scandal of 'Sewergate' as it is being called in Washington. Nevertheless he should be held personally responsible for the gutting of the EPA." Mar 28 *Time* 18/3 "Congressional committees continued to stumble over one another in their sometimes overzealous efforts to keep 'Sewergate' sizzling." See also 1978 quot in 1981 Barnhart *AS* 55:78, quot sv WASTE-WATERGATE **—Slaughtergate** Australian scandal involving the substitution of horse and kangaroo meat for beef in meat exported to US 1981 Oct 7 Columbia (SC) *State* A-2 (*Washington Post*) **—Stockmangate** [David *Stockman* director of Office of Management and Budget] 1981 Nov 12 Art Buchwald on *Today* NBC-TV "We've got ourselves a Stockmangate on our hands." **—Timbergate** 1982 Jan 10 *Tuscaloosa News* A-17/1 (*Washington Post*) "PEKING— Chinese headline writers might have named it 'Timbergate.' Greedy Communist officials in south China, taking everything from wristwatches to sexual favors, doled out tons of scarce lumber to wayward young women who then resold it on the black market for huge profits." **—Totegate** [*tote* shortened from *totalisator*] 1982 Feb 22 *New Yorker* 87/1 "Established in 1928 by an Act of Parliament, the Tote is a government-run concession, supervised by the Horse Race Totalisator Board. It has pari-mutuel windows at every major racecourse. . . . Like other government operations, the Tote has been mismanaged lately—plagued by creative accounting practices, which erupted in a 'Totegate' scandal." **—Walkergate** [Herschel *Walker* Univ of Ga football player] The events surrounding Walker's signing with a professional football team: rumors that he had signed, denials and investigations of the reports, and attempted coverup of the facts 1983 Feb 25 *Norman* (Okla) *Transcript* 10/1 (AP) "It takes only two words to capsule this week's football shenanigans which will hereafter be known as 'Walkergate.' One is a question: 'Why?' The other is an admonition: 'Shame.' " **—waste-watergate** [*W9NCD n waste water* 15c] 1983 Feb 18 *All Things Considered* NPR [Speaker believes EPA is attempting a coverup involving the Superfund for cleaning up hazardous wastes.] "We think it is waste-watergate." See also SEWERGATE

Newspeakism *n* [*Newspeak* 1949 (see preliminary remarks) + *-ism*] 1972 Oct *Atlantic* 34/3 "Apparently color—the color of blood—laced with fancyisms like 'historical perspective' and action words like 'convulsed' and 'wrenching' and Newspeakisms like 'confrontation' may be folded together into a reasonable facsimile of the New Journalism (*sic*)." Ibid 37/2 "On another front, such movements distort and corrupt further the language already savaged by the Establishment politicians when they conspire to eliminate the innocuous, and correct, locution, 'Everyone knows *he* has to decide for *himself*,' and to substitute the odious Newspeakism 'chairperson' for the sufficiently separate—and equal—'chairman' and 'chairwoman.' "

out-Nounspeak *vt* To surpass in the use of NOUNSPEAK See NOUNSPEAK sv —SPEAK *comb form* 1976 Oct 2 *Sat Rev* 52/2 "In a slick display of one-upmanship, he out-Nounspeaks Price. Admitting that 'U.S. Air Force aircraft fuel systems equipment mechanics course' is a fair specimen, he tells us that 'General Electric has issued an *earth resources technology satellite data collection platform field installation, operation and maintenance manual*, and the University of Michigan has produced a *shore erosion engineering demonstration project post-construction season progress interim report*.' "

—speak *comb form* [*Barnhart Dict Companion* 1.3:44–45; 2.1:17; 2.2:48] **—blandspeak** 1981 Feb *Foundation The Rev of Sci Fict* 61 "The book is written in the dead blandspeak that seems unique to science fiction experts, with a strictly functional use of the English language whose vocabulary is limited to a choice of the dullest and least evocative words, and the syntax is brain-crunching see what I mean?" **—businesspeak** 1983 Jim Fisk and Robert Barron *Buzzwords: The Official MBA Dictionary* (Wallaby Book; NY: Simon & Schuster) back cover "Talk your way to the top with this Berlitz course in businespeak." **—computerspeak** The jargon of computer users 1980 Sep *Omni* 102/1 "Broadcaster Edwin Newman charts the future of the English language, revealing how it will change in decades to come and explaining why Newspeak and Computerspeak may be the languages with which we communicate tomorrow." 1983 Fisk and Barron *Buzzwords: The Official MBA Dictionary* unpag sv *data* "*Data* Computerspeak for *information*. Properly pronounced the way Bostonians pronounce the word for a female child." **—Haigspeak** 1981 Jul *Harper's* 72/1 "Haigspeak is also a sign of civilization." 1982 Jul *Harper's* 64/3 "In both countries he was greatly ridiculed for his lapse into Haigspeak when he presented his credentials to the Queen." **—libspeak** [women's *lib*] 1974 Jun 1 *National Observer* 12/2 "Since gigging the girls about libspeak [Observations, April 13], I have been denounced as a chauvinist, a chauvinist pig, a chauvinist prig, a nonperson, a ratfink (a species I had supposed was extinct), and an enemy of the downtrodden." **—medspeak** 1983 Mar *Omni* 14/2 (letter) "I loved the article 'Medspeak,' by Mary Carpenter, in the September 1982 issue. Since I'm a registered nurse, I often have to interpret medspeak to my patients." **—Nounspeak** Style of writing or speech characterized by long strings of nouns used attributively 1976 Oct 2 *Sat Rev* 52/1 & 3 "I mention *Verbatim* because in the February, 1976, issue there was an article by Bruce D. Price, aptly called 'Noun Overuse Phenomenon Article.' Price discusses what both he and I consider to be one of the most distressing afflictions our language is suffering from these days. He calls it 'Nounspeak.' . . . [¶] . . . The body of anti-Nounspeak literature is growing. Jacques Barzun refers to the 'noun plague.' Nounspeak, nominalization, the noun plague—whatever you call it—is under attack." **—Safespeak** 1979 Sep 23 *NY Times Book Rev* 15/2 " 'Safespeak'—the consensus journalism wrought by market research—has absorbed the personal vision that once permeated the Chicago Tribune of Col. Robert McCormick and The Washington Herald of his cousin Eleanor 'Cissy' Patterson." **—Space-speak** 1982 Jan 30 *Chr Sci Monitor* 6/3 (heading) "Space-speak, Pentagon-style:" **—sportspeak** Language of sportswriters and announcers 1978 Dec 31 Harry Reasoner on *60 Minutes* CBS-TV "Sportspeak is not my mother tongue." **—Valley Girlspeak, Valspeak** [(San Fernando) *Valley Girl* title of recording by Frank Zappa; cf *Barnhart Dict Companion* 2.1 (1983):17 *Valleyspeak*] 1983 Jan 9 *Family Weekly* 5/1 "Like, you know, who can predict about, you know, language? I mean, like last year we got Valley Girlspeak." Apr 14 *Rolling Stone* 103/1 " 'The song ["Valley Girl"] hadn't even come out when I auditioned [for the part of Jennifer on *Square Pegs*],' she says. 'I was just trying to sound like the girls in my high school.' Tracy, as it happens, attended Westlake, a private girls school in L.A. Naturally, Westlake is chockfull of girls from the Valley. [¶] Jennifer DiNuccio is not, however, a Valspeak cliche." **—Whitespeak** 1983 Apr 18 *Newsweek* 100/1 "all the best people were themselves learning to speak a new racial argot at the same time: a kind of dissembling, hypocritical, ghastly Goody Two-shoes language of condescension, specially created by your tonier white people over the past couple of decades for discussions of—and with—blacks. I don't suppose for a moment that the feelings being disguised by the new Whitespeak are your violent, hater-type resentments. . . . They are more in the way of suspicions and ambivalences of which those who harbor them are vaguely ashamed."

AMONG THE NEW WORDS

MARY GRAY PORTER AND I. WILLIS RUSSELL

The University of Alabama

With the assistance of William W. Evans, *Louisiana State University*, Michael Montgomery, *University of South Carolina*, and Richard E. Ray, *Indiana University of Pennsylvania*

ERICH VON DÄNIKEN has authored a number of writings in which he puts forth the notion that beings from another world visited Earth untold ages ago. Man's myths and the artifacts of prehistoric civilizations he interprets as relics of our extraterrestrial visitors, the "ancient astronauts." "I am firmly convinced," he writes in his 1973 book *In Search of Ancient Gods*, "that 'gods' in mythology can only be a synonym for space traveller, for lack of a more accurate name for the flying phenomena" (translated by Michael Heron [New York: Bantam, 1975], p. 4).

A similar, but probably less seriously held, theory was popular among the Hungarian physicists in the Theoretical Division of Los Alamos. This Magyar-Martian theory claimed that the Martians left their planet several aeons ago and came to Earth, landing in Hungary, where they were forced to conceal their identity from the barbarians of Earth. On the whole, they were successful, but their partial failure provides "proof" of the theory. John McPhee summarizes the case thus: "the Martians had three characteristics too strong to hide: their wanderlust, which found its outlet in the Hungarian gypsy; their language (Hungarian is not related to any of the languages spoken in surrounding countries); and their unearthly intelligence. One had only to look around to see the evidence: Teller, Wigner, Szilard, von Neumann—Hungarians all" (*New Yorker*, 10 Dec. 1973, p. 52).

Space travellers of the present have made use of two new pieces of equipment, both denoted by the noun *backpack*. The first to be put into use was the pack that enabled the astronauts to walk on the moon. The second, also called *jet(-powered) backpack*, makes possible untethered movement and work outside a spacecraft.

The Cabbage Patch Kids must be acknowledged one of the toy industry's great successes. The demand was so great that Christmas shoppers turned violent when the dolls were not available in the stores—and rioted when they were available. Both the Hula Hoop fad of the Fifties and the Cabbage Patch Panic of 1983 have led at least one writer to take the toys as a synonym for *flash in the pan*. The question raised by Paul Duke in the last citation under *Cabbage Patch doll* is prefigured in an earlier evaluation of Ralph Nader's place in history: "But Ralph Nader has turned out not to be a hula hoop. He is in fact one of the most significant figures of this period" *(New York Times Book Review,* 19 Mar. 1972, p. 7/3).

Our entry under *-speak* supplements our earlier one in the Summer 1984 issue of *American Speech.* In our only citation for *Government-Speak,* the word is replaced in the body of the advertisement by *governmentese:* "A tax increase in governmentese is 'revenue enhancement.' There is no 'future' in this peculiar parlance. There are 'out years'" *(Harper's,* Feb. 1983, inside back cover). The ad writer also deplores the tendency of speakers of governmentese to use euphemisms excessively, a point illustrated in the citation for *recession-speak.*

Acknowledgment for citations: Edgar L. Frost (2).

ancient astronaut *n* [Cf *SOED* sv *ancient* 4b & c] Extraterrestrial traveller who, according to Erich von Däniken and others, visited Earth in prehistoric times and brought genetic, intellectual, and technological advances to the ancestors of modern man [1973 Dec *Esquire* 238/3 "Von Däniken declares that extraterrestrial beings visited us in prehistoric times. They tinkered (by interbreeding?) with the DNA of the hominids they found, to improve the intelligence of the species. Having created a rudimentary human civilization, they departed."] 1974 Dec 8 *NY Times Book Rev* 53/1 "In short, as well as achieving hardcover 'respectability,' the Bermuda Triangle phenomenon appears to be replacing flying saucers and ancient astronauts among sci-fi occult fans." 1978 Mar *Harper's* T29/2 (ad) "Have you ever seen an alleged landing field for ancient astronauts?" 1980 Oct *Omni* 158/2 "As further proof, Sitchin claims that the Sumerians considered Venus the eighth planet and Mars the sixth. The obvious conclusion, he says, is that the Sumerians were educated by ancient astronauts who landed on Earth approximately 450,000 years ago. Sitchin claims he found the phrase 'People of the Rocket Ships' in Sumerian writings. [¶] Astronomers and Sumerian scholars who have examined Sitchin's work doubt both his knowledge of astronomy and his grasp of Sumerian cuneiform." 1981 Jan *Omni* 14/1 (letter) "A society that gives open-armed acceptance to such notions as ancient astronauts, pyramid power, and astrology cannot be expected to scrutinize creationism with an informed or skeptical eye." 1982 Feb 1 *Analog* 146/1 (rev of *The Best Science Fiction of the Year #10* edited by Terry Carr) "Carr's picks include . . . MacIntyre's 'Martian Walkabout,' a predictable exercise in the 'ancient astronauts' subgenre." 1983 Feb *Omni* 130/1 "Such 'missing link' puzzles have prompted some outlandish speculations, ranging from Von Däniken's proposal that ancient astronauts arrived from the stars to breed man from ape, to astronomer Sir Fred Hoyle's Directed Panspermia theory that primitive life and even insects arrived from outer space along trails of cosmic dust."

backpack *n* [Cf *W3 backpack n* 2 "a piece of equipment (as a fire extinguisher) designed for operation while being carried on the back"; cf *SOED* sv: "Chiefly *U.S.* . . . A pack carried on the back; *spec.* one consisting of a folded parachute." (1946)] **1:** Portable life-support system for US astronauts outside their spacecraft 1969 Mar 9 *NY Times Mag* E-1/1 "Finally it also tested for the first time in space the life-supporting backpack that will enable astronauts to step onto the moon, severing the umbilical connection that, in the past, has kept them chained to their spacecraft. The umbilical provided oxygen, communcations and other links." **2:** Popular name of the jet-powered unit used by US astronauts to maneuver outside the Shuttle without a tether 1983 Dec 14 *Chr Sci Monitor* 8/1–2 (UPI) "The world's most expensive backpack, enabling spacewalking astronauts to venture away from their shuttle, is to be tested during the next shuttle mission. [¶] The manned maneuvering unit (MMU), which snaps onto the back of a spacesuit, will let astronauts do repair work in space, fetch ailing satellites, and even move large objects. The unit has two tanks containing pressurized nitrogen that feeds 24 small maneuvering jets. The 330-pound MMU, which is weightless in space, cost about $40 million to develop." 1984 Apr 5 *ABC News* "Then using one of the backpacks, Nelson will fly there." Apr 6 *CBS Evening News* "[He] will use a jet backpack to fly away from the shuttle." Apr 6 *Tuscaloosa News* 7/1 (AP) "The flight, in which astronaut George Nelson will use a jet-powered backpack to fly 200 feet from the ship and snare the satellite, began with a rumbling liftoff right on schedule."

be-Cabbaged *adj* [*be-* + CABBAGE PATCH KID™ + *-ed*] Having the Cabbage Patch Kid trademark or decorated with images of the Cabbage Patch Kids 1983 Dec 12 *Newsweek* 85/3 "There are new bits of finery in the Cabbage kingdom: lunch boxes, knee socks, sheets, tote bags, dinnerware, pajamas, children's cosmetics, jewelry, clocks, bikes—and licenses are growing fast. Coleco spokeswoman Kathleen McGowan has been dispatched to push the be-Cabbaged accessories as temporary substitutes for the genuine adorables."

Cabbage Kid *n* Another name for CABBAGE PATCH KID (qv) 1983 Dec 1 *Newsweek* 79/1 "On top of all their cuddly charms, the Cabbage Kids now have the lure of the unattainable." Ibid 81/3 "Coleco and its ad agency, Richard & Edwards, then assembled 'focus groups' throughout the nation last fall, charting the reactions of adults and children as they played with prototype Cabbage Kids."

Cabbage Patch *n* [CABBAGE PATCH KID™, DOLL, etc] Any item that sells spectacularly 1983 Dec 28 *Wall St Jour* 15/2 "The Muziks say that in only two months they have sold 75% of their initial factory run of 5,000 pairs. . . . [¶] 'It isn't a Cabbage Patch, but we're pleased,' Mrs. Muzik says, referring to this year's hottest selling item, the Cabbage Patch dolls."

Cabbage Patch doll *n* **1:** Another name for CABBAGE PATCH KID (qv) 1983 Dec 2 *McNeill-Lehrer News Hour* (PBS) "I didn't know a thing about Cabbage Patch dolls, but my son did." Dec 4 *Birmingham* (Ala) *News* D-10/1 (AP) "A mailman whose young daughter almost cried when she learned she wouldn't get a Cabbage Patch doll for Christmas took a whirlwind trip to London in search of the homely, chubby-cheeked plaything, and returned with five." Dec 12 *Newsweek* 79/1 "The problem, of course, is that if there were enough Cabbage Patch dolls for everyone who wanted one, there would be too many." **2:** Popular fad that passes quickly 1984 Apr 6 Paul Duke on *Wash Week in Rev* PBS "Is it possible that Gary Hart is a passing fancy, a kind of Cabbage Patch doll in American politics?"

Cabbage Patcher *n* [CABBAGE PATCH KID™ + *-er W3* 1c "native of : resident of : coming from"] Cabbage Patch Kid 1983 Dec 19 *Chr Sci Monitor* 27/1 "[She] kept her vigil because her two daughters, 18 and 15, want Cabbage Patchers for Christmas."

Cabbage Patch Kid *Trademark* [Cf 1983 Dec 12 *Newsweek* 80/3 "Although he is not adopted himself, he remembers being told as a child that babies are found in cabbage patches—a variation on the stork fairy tale—and he elaborated the same myth in the Cabbage Patch literature."] Soft-bodied doll sold with adoption papers (see quots for details) 1983 Nov 29 *Chr Sci Monitor* "The skirmish was over the Cabbage Patch Kids, the rage of the season's doll market." Dec 2 *Chr Sci Monitor* 31/3 "In a store in North Miami Beach, shoppers responding to an ad for the Cabbage Patch Kid doll turned into a mob when the stock ran out. . . . [¶] Two million Cabbage Patch Kid dolls will be sold by the end of the year, each with a given name, birth certificate, and adoption papers. [¶] There is something appealing, but a little sad, too, about this game of identity, as if the purchasers were Cabbage Patch Kids also, a bit lost and lonely at Christmas, looking for somebody to adopt them." Dec 12 *Newsweek* 78/1–2 "It was as if an army had been turned loose on the nation's shopping malls . . . searching for the legendary stockrooms said to be filled with thousands of the dough-faced, chinless, engagingly homely dolls that have become the Holy Grail of the 1983 Christmas shopping season: the Cabbage Patch Kids. . . . [¶] Without actually resembling any real baby that has ever walked the earth—for which the whole human race can be grateful—Cabbage Patch Kids caricature almost every characteristic of babyness: blunt, fat features; round cheeks; big eyes; short, pudgy little arms and legs."

CPK [CABBAGE PATCH KID] 1983 Nov 30 *Atlanta Jour* A-10/4 "Zayre is getting CPKs, but they won't be put out until all customers have gone on Saturday."

fast lane *n* [Cf *SOED* sv *fast a*: *"fast lane,* a traffic lane . . . intended for drivers who wish to overtake slower cars" (1966)] *Fig* The world of a certain segment of society, not unlike the jet set, sometimes characterized by the desire for immediate gratification, by excess, and by lack of restraint and commitment 1978 Apr 16 *Parade* 20/4 "Except for her, however, not a single person arrested fit the image usually associated with the superjet, 'fast-lane' set." 1980 Mar 19 *Crimson-White* (Univ of Ala) 8/5 "Jessica Lange is Angelique, the beautiful and inviting Death figure who hovers over Gideon's fast-lane living and personal excesses in sex, tobacco, and career." May 19 *Newsweek* 19/1 "'My life is not boring,' says Salk. 'It's like driving in the fast lane.'" 1981 Jul 18 *Channel 6 News* WBRC-TV, Ch 6, Birmingham, Ala "[He] is going to take you and I [*sic*] for one lap around this track and show us where the fast lane is." Oct 9 *Chr Sci Monitor* 14 (heading) "Cambodian united front talks in fast lane to nowhere" 1982 Jun 14 *Newsweek* 95/3 "Rogers neatly sketches life in Silicon Valley's fast lane, where venture capital reigns and everybody sips crisp California Chardonnay."

—speak [See 1984 ATNW *AS* 59:163-64 and references to *Barnhart Dict Companion* there.] Additional illustrations **—cablespeak** 1983 Jun 25 *TV Guide* A–4 (heading of letter about a requirement that cable-system operators reserve one channel for public-access TV) "CABLESPEAK" **—Government-Speak** *n* Jargon used by government officials, specifically those in the federal government 1983 Feb *Harper's* inside backcover (ad heading) "Government-Speak" **—machinespeak** *n* Computer language, esp low-level language 1983 Jul *Personal Computing* 131/3 "'I'm tired of hearing about the importance of "computer literacy,"' says one Commodore executive. 'Since the first high-level language, it's been obvious that computers can move toward English faster than people can can move toward machinespeak.'" **—Medspeak** *n* 1980 Nov *Esquire* 59/1 "During [1979] the *NEJM* published articles and letters on . . . the horrors of convoluted medical jargon ('How to Cure Medspeak')." **—recession-speak** *n* 1983 Jul *World Press Rev* 11/1 "Recession-speak is here, reports Jenny Tabakoff in the conservative *Sydney Morning Herald* [May 19]. When people are fired or laid off, their feelings are spared if they are described as 'disemployed,' 'dehired,' 'made redundant,' or 'surplus to requirements.'" **—sciencespeak** *n* Scientific sounding prose, esp in cosmetic advertising 1982 Apr *Science 82* 54/3 "Is all this sciencespeak just advertising gobbledygook, or is there something to it? A detailed review of the evidence for the claims yields two answers: yes and no." **—Valspeak** [Cf *BDC* 2.1: 24/2: "Valleyspeak, sometimes called *Valley talk,* the argot of the San Fernando Valley in Southern California, popular especially among teenagers. Informal (United States use.)."] 1983 Apr 4 *Today* NBC-TV "Valspeak. . . . Don't lose heart. Your Valgirl or dude can be cured." Aug *Creative Computing* 117/2–3 "'Cyberphobia' is a term of growing usage, import, and incidence. . . . The term is no passing bit of Valspeak or computer jargon. It describes a tangible and often socio-enconomically debilitating malady."

AMONG THE NEW WORDS

MARY GRAY PORTER AND I. WILLIS RUSSELL
The University of Alabama

With the assistance of William W. Evans, *Louisiana State University;*
Michael Montgomery, *University of South Carolina;*
and Richard E. Ray, *Indiana University of Pennsylvania*

WE HAVE IN OUR FILES twenty-six citations that contain the phrase *at* (or *on*) *the cutting edge* in the sense of 'at the limits of the known'. Our earliest example (1968) uses *at*, but *on* occurs more frequently (16 citations beginning in 1977).

Computer users describe their machines as *friendly* or *user-friendly* if a non-expert can easily learn to operate them. Very often complaints arise that the documentation—that is, the user's manual—is not *user-friendly*. The software may or may not be friendly; some buffs regard as *unfriendly* any software that compels them to read the instructions that come with it. Others consider clarity in the documentation the hallmark of *user-friendliness*. With one exception, the 1981 quotation about the user-friendly laser, all our citations for *friendly* and *user-friendly* refer to computer hardware or software.

There appears to be no general agreement on the origin of the *u* in *Yuppie*. The authors of *The Yuppie Handbook* tell us all about the Young Urban Professional; others take the *u* to stand for *Upwardly-mobile*. George Will (*Washington Post* 25 Mar. 1984, Sec. C, p. 7/1) deplores the appearance of the first of what he fears "will be a flood of books on Yuppies, young upwardly mobile professionals, a.k.a. Yaps (young aspiring professionals)." However, Will's evident lack of delight at the prospect of such a flood does not prevent him from expressing his admiration of Daniel Boorstin, whose writings cast light on "Yumpishness, as on almost everything else" (*Atlanta Journal and Constitution* 25 Mar. 1984, Sec. C, p. 3/2). An offshoot of *yuppie* can be seen in a photograph in *The Chronicle of Higher Education* (6 June 1984, p. 10): a 1984 graduate in his academic regalia is holding a sign "NUPPIE / non-working / urban-professional." Other spinoffs of *yuppie* have apparently been coined by Sherley Uhl, the politics editor of *The Pittsburgh Press*, who in a column of 1 April 1984—could the date be significant?—tells us of the "guppies (grown-up paupers) and serfs (suburban early-retired folks), who supposedly lean toward, if not on, Mr. Mondale."

Acknowledgment for citation: John Algeo.

build-down *n* Proposed reduction of nuclear weapons to be effected by eliminating more than one missile or warhead for each new one deployed 1983 May 6 Charles Corddry on *Wash Week in Rev* PBS "I think we can forget that buzzword freeze and get accustomed to a new one, build-down." May 11 *Chr Sci Monitor* 18/3–4 "One such 'build-down' suggestion, offered by Senate Armed Services Committee members William Cohen (R) of Maine and Sam Nunn (D) of Georgia, would require removing two old warheads from the strategic nuclear arsenal for every new one added. [¶] . . . Congress may require some form of a build-down as the price for deployment of any MX missiles, however." Jul 22 *Wall St Jour* 4/3 "In particular, the Georgia senator said he would like to see Mr. Reagan embrace some form of the 'build-down' proposal advocated by him, Rep. Gore and others." Sep 20 *MacNeil-Lehrer News Hour* PBS [Segment on Build-Down Resolution in the Senate] Oct 5 *Chr Sci Monitor* 1/2, 40/1 "The build-down concept would permit both superpowers to modernize their nuclear arsenals. But for every new warhead that is added, they would have to destroy a specific number of older warheads. . . . The new Reagan proposal calls for a guaranteed build-down of about 5 percent a year." Dec 16 *Chr Sci Monitor* 16/1 "Build-down is not effective in limiting the qualitative arms race. Its purpose is to cap the quantitative race, yet in so doing it channels competition into more dangerous areas such as superaccuracy and concealment." 1984 May *Games* 6/1 "[Peter] Thomas, professor of English at Lake Superior State College in Sault Ste. Marie, Michigan, . . . conducts an annual poll to see which words people would like to banish . . . [¶] After careful tabulation, the most offensive words of 1983 proved to be the over-used *high-tech* and *build-down*, the latter oxymoron referring to the reduction of nuclear arms." **—builddowning** 1983 Dec 9 *Chr Sci Monitor* 24/1 (letter heading) "Builddowning"

chiclet *adj* [from resemblance of keys to *Chiclets*, name of a brand of small rectangular pieces of candy-coated chewing gum] Of a computer keyboard, having keys that lack the full movement of a typewriter-style keyboard and are usually smaller and closer together than those on a typewriter [1983 Nov 14 *Newsweek* 81/1 "The keyboard may be the PCjr's weakest link: some users may not like its Chiclet-like keys."] 1983 Aug *Creative Computing* 50/1 "The Aquarius keyboard is a compromise between full-stroke and membrane—what we refer to as 'Chiclet' style. Unlike a flat membrane keyboard, each key on the Aquarius protrudes above the surface of the computer. To the delight of smaller children, and to the disappointment of touch typ[i]sts, the 49 light blue rubber keys are spaced rather close together." Dec *Science 83* 61 (spec ad sec) "A 'chiclet' keyboard has small keys that don't move quite as far as regular 'full' keyboards." Nov 2 *Today* NBC-TV "It's what we call in the industry a chiclet keyboard." 1984 Mar *Creative Computing* 81/3 "Critics say it is a cheap, 'Chiclet' keyboard, unworthy of a 'real' computer. . . . [¶] . . . this is no 'heads down, smoking fingers' professional data entry keyboard. . . . Neither is it like pressing a box of Chiclets into your lap. The keys move up and down; they click; you can feel them hit bottom." **—Chiclet Syndrome** 1983 Aug *Creative Computing* 17/1–2 "[F]or a further expose of the so-called 'Chiclet Syndrome,' see my review . . . in the December 1982 *Creative*."

consensus All-American *n* [Cf *World Bk Dict* 1983 sv consensus *n* sense 2; cf *SOED* sv consensus: "3. *attrib.* and *Comb.* 1966"] Football player chosen as a member of several All-American teams 1970 Dec *University Report* (Univ of Ala) 24/4–5 (picture caption) "Don McCauley—Consensus All-American" 1975 Sep 19 *Tuscaloosa News* 13/2 "Cunningham led the Tigers in receiving the last two seasons and last year became only the third consensus All-American in Clemson football history." Dec 22 Bud Wilkinson on ABC-TV " . . . a consensus All-American for two successive years." 1983 Nov 12 Keith Jackson on ABC-TV " . . . consensus All-American. . . . " Dec 11 *Tuscaloosa News* B-1/3 "Goode is leaving Alabama for his alma mater, Mississippi State, where he was a consensus All-American center-linebacker in 1960."

cutting edge 1: *n* Vanguard, frontier, forefront 1968 Mar *Alumni Review* (Univ of N Car, Chapel Hill) 9/1–2 " 'The Cutting Edge Symposia,' a one-semester project of the Danforth Associate Program, provides opportunities for UNC faculty members to discuss their own disciplines at their 'cutting edge'—where they're breaking new ground and how new developments are forcing re-evaluation of values, procedures, or the uses of knowledge." 1974 Jun 3 *USN&WR* 52/1 "At the cutting edge of these efforts ['aimed at understanding the global dynamics of weather'] is an array of weather satellites, observation platforms in space, that already have made possible quantum jumps in the accuracy of local forecasting." 1976 Sep 5 *Birmingham* (Ala) *News* E-2/1 "From my perspective, awash in a vast wave of albums, press releases and sales and play charts, it looks as if pop, and its cutting edge, rock, is in the doldrums." 1981 Dec 3 *NY Times* D-2/1 "To hear executives talk, the 'cutting edge' of technology in most industries must be very crowded. One reason so many companies can claim this position may be that their audiences are generally too polite to laugh. Another explanation could be that the executives doing the talking do not know any better." 1984 John Naisbitt *Megatrends* (NY: Warner Books) 246 "The megastates [California, Florida, Texas] share a number of interesting characteristics. All three are on the cutting edge of the whole immigration question, both legal and illegal; more than half of all Hispanic-Americans live in either Texas or California." — **2:** *adj* Advanced, innovative, pioneering, prominent 1978 Jul 12 *Meridian* (Miss) *Star* B-7/1 (UPI) " 'More than ever,' Mrs. Harris said, 'I am convinced the Action Grant program is a cutting edge example of President Carter's comprehensive national urban policy at work.' " 1981 Dec *Amer Business* 22/5 "These will be the cutting-edge issues of the '80s: Should government set targets, monitor and even participate in the capital formation process? How can government help restore the scientific and technological capability of industry? How can government monitor and assist in setting targets and rates of progress toward turning around productivity?" 1982 Nov 6 *Science News* 299/3 "With Japan embarking on such ambitious cutting-edge research as its fifth-generation computer project, Dertouzos warns that U.S. supremacy in semiconductors and computer science could be on the wane." 1984 Jan 12 *Chr Sci Monitor* 25/1 "For years no one had pretended that the English were particularly adept at marketing their potpourri of cutting-edge clothes." Feb *Harper's* 20/1–2 "The question of risk appears here also—with Thurow and others arguing that some large cutting-edge projects are too risky to be financed even by today's relatively healthy venture capital markets."

friendly *adj* USER-FRIENDLY 1982 Feb 22 *Newsweek* 53/1–2 "Part of the problem seems to be that software producers rarely test their materials with neophytes like me. . . . But there are programs, called 'friendly' in the industry, that offer heady relief." Jul-Aug *Science 82* 45/1 "To make the new electronics revolution more acceptable will require finding new ways of making technology useful to people who have no technical training. 'The challenge for the 1980s to the data processing industry,' says Lewis Branscomb, . . . 'is to bring computer capability—usefully and simply—to average citizens.' Partly because of the new memory devices, Branscomb says, 'we have a golden opportunity to create systems that are "friendly," that is, easy to use.' " 1983 Oct *PC Mag* 322/1 (ad) "Good personal software should be, as the computer people say, 'friendly.' Meaning that it helps you do what you want to do without getting in the way."

front edge *n* CUTTING EDGE 1984 Mar 6 *Chr Sci Monitor* 21/1 "On the campaign stump and behind the walls of academia, politicians and professors alike are arguing over the need for an 'industrial policy' that would aid not only 'smokestack' industries but also those on the front edge of technology, such as microelectronics and biotechnology."

-intensive *Comb form* [Cf *W9NCD* "*capital-intensive adj* (1959): having a high capital cost per unit of output; *esp*: requiring greater expenditure in the form of capital than of labor"] Requiring or containing a large quantity of that specified in the first part of the word **—calorie-intensive** 1980 Jun *Food & Wine* 60/1 "overly sweet, heavy, and calorie-intensive cocktails" **—disc-intensive** 1983 Nov *PC Mag* 346 (ad) "Disc intensive applications on the PC are accomplished at main frame speeds." **—earnings-intensive** 1972 Caroline Bird *The Crowding Syndrome* (NY: David McKay) 178 "[He] distinguished between 'time intensive' expenditures, which take a lot of time per dollar, such as reading a book, and 'earnings-intensive' commodities, which take a lot of dollars (presumably earned) per hour, such as night-clubbing." **—energy-intensive** 1971 Sep *Sci Amer* 139/3 "energy-intensive heavy industry" 1975 Dec 9 *Wall St Jour* 24/2 (editorial) "energy-intensive goods and services" 1976 Feb 9 *New Yorker* 54/2 "the power needed by a modern energy-intensive society" 1979 Dec 3 *Newsweek* 18/2–3 (letter) "our addiction to an extravagant, energy-intensive life-style" 1980 Aug *Omni* 6/2 "energy-intensive fertilizers." **—export-intensive** 1971 May 25 *The Bulletin* (Bonn: Press and Information Office of the Government of the Federal Republic of Germany) 130/2 "German industry traditionally has been 'export-intensive.' " **—fuel-intensive** 1982 Jan 25 *Chr Sci Monitor* 12/3 "[An airline is] fuel-intensive, labor-intensive, and capital-intensive" **—idea-intensive** 1981 Jan *Omni* 46/3 "tiny, idea-intensive, hardware-light creations" **—information-intensive** 1983 Nov 14 *Newsweek* 5th of 8 pages btw pp 56–57 (ad) "Add to this the high density of information-intensive companies in our region—plus a higher total annual income than any other part of the country—and you can see why the demand here for cellular mobile phone service is so large and so ready. [¶] Ameritech will continue to intensive region." —**instructor-intensive** 1984 Feb 14 *Chr Sci Monitor* 27/3 "Board sailing is instructor-intensive, and there should be no more than two pupils per teacher. A 1-to-1 ratio is even better." —**I/O-intensive** [*I/O* "input/output" (*6000 Words* and *World Bk Dict* 1976] 1980 Jun *Sci Amer* 140/2 (ad) "As a result, an HP 1000 L-series computer can perform I/O-intensive jobs that computers costing several times as much can't do." —**knowledge-intensive** 1974 May 20 *New Yorker* 111/1 "more knowledge-intensive, or highly technological, production, such as electronics, aviation products" 1980 Oct *Sci Amer* J28/2 (ad) "a more knowledge-intensive type structure of industries" 1982 Feb *Sci Amer* C3/3 (ad supp) "knowledge-intensive and technology-intensive industrial sectors" Aug 23 *Newsweek* 4/2 (letter) "a rapid structural change from old industry to knowledge-intensive industry" —**nontechnology-intensive** 1972 Feb 7 *USN&WR* 16/1 "those manufactured goods which are classed as 'nontechnology-intensive' " —**people-intensive** 1976 Feb 14 *Science News* 101/2 "The most promising methods [of agricultural pest control] will . . . need to be research- and people-intensive." —**personnel-intensive** 1975 Oct *Kulturbrief* (Bonn: Inter Nationes) 13/1 "a more personnel-intensive form of teaching" —**power-intensive** 1976 May 23 *Birmingham* (Ala) *News* B-1/5 "Power-intensive rather than labor-intensive, figures on employment [in primary production of aluminum] are harder to come by." —**R&D-intensive** [Cf *W9NCD R and D* (1966) <research *and development*] 1979 Jan 8 *Newsweek* 7/1 "the nation's trade surplus in R&D-intensive goods" —**research-intensive** 1976 Feb 14 *Science News* 101/2 Quot sv PEOPLE-INTENSIVE Mar-Apr *Columbia Journ Rev* 40/2 (ad) "[T]he pharmaceutical industry is the most research-intensive; it has the highest ratio of company-funded R&D to sales of any industry." —**skilled-labor intensive** 1980 Jan *Industrial and Labor Relations Rev* "Each of these industries [transportation, communication, and public utilities] tends to be highly concentrated (within an SMSA), publicly regulated, capital intensive, and skilled-labor intensive." —**steel intensive** 1980 Apr *Shelby Congressional Report to Alabama's Seventh Congressional District* 4/1 "steel intensive oil field equipment." —**technology-intensive** 1972 Feb 7 *USN&WR* 15/3 "As more countries compete in making shoes, clothing and other products that require less technology, he believes, the U.S. will become increasingly dependent on 'technology-intensive' items for export." 1977 Apr 15 *Wall St Jour* 25/1 "in certain capital and technology-intensive industries, such as petrochemical, steel, aluminum and telecommunications" —**time-intensive** 1972 Bird *The Crowding Syndrome* 178 Quot sv EARNINGS-INTENSIVE 1983 Apr *Harper's* 69/2 "What you save on raw furniture is often consumed in the finishing process—an activity I've always enjoyed but one that is discouragingly time-intensive." —**water-intensive** 1974 Apr *Harper's* 110/1 " . . . water intensive crops will suffer hugely and prices will rocket. Water intensive energy sources are: shale oil and Wyoming coal and nuclear power." 1977 Nov *Reader's Digest* 58/1 (cond from *NY Times Mag* 31 Jul) "water-intensive crops like alfalfa"

user-friendly *adj* Easy to operate, even for one without scientific or technical expertise; used chiefly, but not exclusively, of computer hardware and software [1966 Sep *Sci Amer* 181–82 "First, the languages by which men communicate with computers have evolved rapidly. Language forms have now begun to appear that are much more 'problem-oriented' or 'user-oriented' than the original languages; they are easy to learn because they resemble ordinary English and involve more or less conventional mathematical notation."] 1981 Sep 25 *Columbia* (SC) *Record* 7B (*NY Times*) "To deal with such concerns, leading laser manufacturers have concentrated on developing 'user friendly' systems that make it easier for the average worker to handle a laser. As a result, industry's 'comfort level' with lasers is rising steadily." 1983 Oct *Pop Computing* 11/3 (letter) "I have high praise for the Gemini but the supporting documentation is very technical and not user-friendly." 1984 Apr *Sci Amer* P4/2 (ad supp) "The standard QWERTY keyboard arrangement has been preserved in most word-processing equipment. Such a keyboard is considered 'user-friendly,' a term describing any computer operation that is performed with skills or knowledge learned in a non computer enviroment." July 23 *Fortune* 8/3–4 " 'Computer systems are generally very easy to penetrate,' says Geoffrey Goodfellow of SRI International, who himself has performed the feat. 'You've heard the phrase "user friendly"—some of them are downright "user affectionate." ' " —**user friendliness** *n* 1983 Jul *Personal Computing* 119/1 "There are some critics who feel that the currently available presentation-graphics systems still fall short when it comes to 'user friendliness.' John Durrett . . . believes that the software now on the market gives users the capability of making effective graphs, but not the knowledge of how to do so." Dec *Science 83* 64/1 (spec ad sec) "Evaluate the program for content, clarity, and what is known as 'user friendliness.' This means that you can use it with ease and that the documentation, if you should need to refer to it, is comprehensible. . . . It's worth noting that the term 'user friendly' is more and more beginning to mean that you can use the program with no documentation at all." 1984 Apr *Sci Amer* P4/3 (ad supp) "Xerox has developed a sophisticated 'electronic desktop' work station for professionals called the Xerox 8010 Star Information System, which combines computing, text editing, graphics creation and communications. Its 'user-friendliness' is suggested by the fact that a professional need use just the 'mouse' and four main function keys to store and retrieve information, print, send electronic mail, draw and even check spelling."

Yuppie *n* [*young urban* (or *upwardly mobile*) *professional* + *-ie*; perh also infl by *yippie*] 1984 Feb 18 *Pittsburgh Post-Gazette* 21/2 "Marissa Piesman and Marilee Hartley came up with the term in 'The Yuppie Handbook.' Before then, there wasn't a name for the Young Urban Professional—at least a name that stuck. [¶] A Yuppie, according to the authors, can be a person of either sex who lives in or near a major city, who claims to be between the ages of 25 and 45, and who 'lives on aspirations of glory, prestige, recognition, fame, social status, power, money or any and all combinations of the above.' " Mar 13 *CBS Morning News* "Advertising people call them yuppies—young, upwardly-mobile professionals. . . . Gary Hart devised a yuppie strategy." Mar 25 *NY Times* E-2/1 "This truly is the Year of the Yuppies, the educated, computer-literate, audiophile children of the baby boom." Jun 2 *All Things Considered* NPR " . . . in the young, upwardly mobile generation, the so-called yuppies."

AMONG THE NEW WORDS

MARY GRAY PORTER AND †I. WILLIS RUSSELL

The University of Alabama

With the assistance of William W. Evans, *Louisiana State University,* Michael Montgomery, *University of South Carolina,* and Richard E. Ray, *Indiana University of Pennsylvania*

SEVERAL OF OUR ENTRIES IN THIS installment are variants of or supplements to entries that have already appeared in compilations of new words.

The single citation for *altered-state* enumerates many kinds of persons who have entered into an altered state of consciousness. We have tentatively equated *alternate state of consciousness* with *altered* state of consciousness (*Second Barnhart Dictionary of New English*). Still another variation on the altered-state-of-consciousness theme is *state of altered consciousness*, for which we have only two citations.

The *Second Barnhart Dictionary of New English* defines *death squad* (citations from 1969) as "any of various unofficial vigilante groups in Latin America whose members murder petty criminals, suspected leftists, etc." The later examples quoted in the glossary extend the application of the term to other victims and to other regions of the world: Germany, Poland, the Philippines, and China, where the Peking authorities ordered the destruction of almost all dogs in the city, a task carried out, according to *Newsweek* (12 Dec. 1983, 60/2), by "doggie death squads." In other accounts there is the strong implication, if not a direct allegation, that government agencies or officials are involved in the killings.

Two senses—the name of the car model and 'flop'—can be read into the ad writer's use of *Edsel* in the *NY Times Book Review* (5 Jan. 1975, 5): "Henry Ford II, in 1957, unveiled the newest entry in automotive design. With vast hopes, large sums of money, technological know-how, and the first name of a family member, he had built an Edsel."

In its most common formulation the *Eleventh Commandment* enjoins Republicans not to bad-mouth other Republicans. Other imperatives, outside the political sphere, but also termed *the* (or *his own,* or *an*) *eleventh commandment,* are illustrated in the glossary; note particularly the two distinct *eleventh commandments* in the quotations from Andy Logan's article in the *New Yorker* for March 15, 1976.

Acknowledgments for citations: Joseph A. Fernandez (1), Edgar L. Frost (1), Joyce Mahan (1), James B. McMillan (3), Anne B. Russell (1).

altered-state [adj use of *altered state* of consciousness *2BDNE* (1972)] See also quot sv STATE OF ALTERED CONSCIOUSNESS 1982 Jan *Omni* 33/1 "Laboring in the altered-state vineyards at UCLA's Neuropsychiatric Institute, Siegel has mapped the visions of LSD users, returned war prisoners, isolation-chamber dreamers, UFO 'hostages,' children who have imaginary playmates, hypoglycemic hallucinators, tertiary syphilis sufferers, and NDE [near-death experience] survivors."

alternate state of consciousness *n* Altered state of consciousness 1982 Oct *Omni* 135/1–2 "Abnormalities in the limbic system around the amygdala can produce alternate states of consciousness. Patients with lesions in the area of the amygdala have feelings of *déjà vu* and *jamais vu,* when the unfamiliar seems familiar and the familiar, strange."

circuit breaker *n* [*Barnhart Dict Comp* 1: 3/2 (1979)] Earlier quots 1972 Dec 25 *USN&WR* 70–71 "[The Advisory Commission on Intergovernmental Relations] rejected these propositions of the staff—[¶] A federal grant of half a billion to 1.25 billion dollars a year to encourage the States to enact 'circuit-breaker' laws. Such statutes rebate some property taxes to low-income homeowners and renters, especially the elderly. . . . However, one Treasury official contended that a small federal grant for 'circuit breakers' to help the elderly still has Mr. Nixon's blessing." 1976 Apr 5 *Chr Sci Monitor* 23/3–4 "But he said economic troubles have dramatized the need for property-tax relief, making it necessary to 'totally reform the property tax system as we know it today.' His plan would include so-called 'circuit breaker' tax relief for those with low income and high property taxes." 1978 Sep-Oct *Today's Education* 47/1 "The potential of the property tax to irritate can be held within bounds by guarding against tax-burden overloads on low- and middle-income households, owners as well as renters. Measures already in use in about 30 states, known as circuit breakers, accomplish this: The state assumes part of the household's property tax (only for senior citizens in some states, for all ages in others) whenever the tax exceeds a specified percentage of income."

death squad *n* [*2BDNE* (1969)] Any group whose members murder the group's enemies or political opponents 1978 Jul 18 *Esquire* 47/1–2 "On April 7, 1977, Siegfried Buback, West Germany's federal Attorney General and the man in charge of the entire Baader-Meinhof prosecution, was murdered. While driving to work, two youths on a Suzuki motorcycle riddled Buback's Mercedes with machine-gun fire, killing Buback, his driver, and a bodyguard. The RAF [Rote Armee Fraktion] claimed responsibility for the murders the next day. Their open letter was signed 'Kommando Ulrike Meinhof.' . . . The members of this group were, on average, some six years younger than the original Baader-Meinhof members and came from even more affluent backgrounds. And despite their shrill political posturings, they were little more than a death squad with a distaste for the prosperous consumerism in what Gudrun Ensslin called 'the Raspberry Reich.' " 1980 Mar 10 *Newsweek* 46/3 "For five years, Al and Jeannie Mills had feared for their lives. Defectors from the People's Temple in 1975, they had become outspoken critics of the authoritarian Rev. Jim Jones. . . . [O]ne night last week, the couple was shot dead in their modest Berkeley, Calif., home. Their 16-year-old daughter, Daphene, was critically wounded and died two days later. [¶] . . . Former People's Temple attorney Charles Garry dismissed the idea of a 'hit list or death squad

[as] a figment of someone's imagination from the very beginning.'" 1983 Nov 21 *Newsweek* 64/1 "The killings were the latest in a right-wing campaign of slaughter that threatens to undo U.S. policy in El Salvador. American officials believe the murderers are former soldiers and moonlighting officers led by extremists in the officer corps. Since 1979 the death squads have killed thousands of people; after a two-year lull, they sprang back into action a few months ago, killing, kidnapping and threatening prominent moderates in an attempt to roll back land reform and thwart any government plans to negotiate with leftist guerrillas." 1984 Feb 24 *Chr Sci Monitor* 2/2 "A man claiming to belong to a Philippines military death squad filed an affidavit with Congress Wednesday attesting that he was asked by a top military official to assassinate political opposition leader Benigno Aquino." Nov 3 *CBS News* "The Solidarity priest . . . was allegedly killed by a security police death squad."

Edsel *n* [automobile manufactured by Ford Motor Co., named after *Edsel* Ford, son of Henry Ford] A product that does not correspond to the wishes or requirements of the time; a failure, frequently in spite of great effort on the part of the producer 1972 Oct 1 *Potomac* (*Washington Post*) 33/2 "One industry leader, Ratner, stayed with the [belted-back jacket] look, a move that prompted a commendation from a Sears spokesman, who said, 'You can't obsolete a style that fast. If the men's industry falls into that trap we'll have more and more Edsels on our hands. The belted-back jacket could be like the VW—a constant you can count on.'" 1977 Oct 23 *Birmingham News* A-32/1 (Knight News Service) "Indeed, one needn't stretch very far to call the Concorde a flying Edsel. The big mistake that the Ford Motor Co. made with the Edsel was to introduce a big car when Americans wanted small cars. At a time when airlines are interested primarily in fuel economy and low noise levels, the Concorde is the noisiest, thirstiest aircraft in the sky." 1979 *Galileo* #1 1–12 (Spec Double Issue) 6/3 "A pedal-powered vehicle could give the astronauts greater speed, more flexibility, and a lighter payload, all for a minimal output of human energy. But the bureaucrats of the space agency, sharing the average man's vision of the future, decided that exploration could best be achieved with an electric Edsel." 1980 Harry and Michael Medved *The Golden Turkey Awards: Nominees and Winners—The Worst Achievements in Hollywood History* (NY: G P Putnam's Sons) 157/2 "One of the few reviews received by *The Extraordinary Seaman* before it sank beneath the waves of well-deserved obscurity came from Kevin Thomas in the *Los Angeles Times*. 'There is absolutely not one honest-to-goodness laugh to be found in it,' he declares. '*The Extraordinary Seaman* is the most total fiasco since the Edsel.'" 1981 Sep 10 *CBS Morning News* "[The Concorde is] the Edsel of the jet age. It uses more fuel than conventional aircraft and, in addition, it carries far fewer seats." Dec 31 *CBS Evening News* "The Susan B. Anthony dollar is the Edsel of [US coinage]." 1984 Mar *Creative Computing* 246/2 "Since it will run MS-DOS, it is compatible with the IBM PC. Still, one can't help wondering if the Macintosh will turn out to be Apple's Edsel."

eleventh commandment *n* Any rule observed, or to be observed, as strictly as if it were an addition to the Ten Commandments of the Old Testament. Often humorous 1975 Nov 30 News announcer WBRC-TV, Ch 6, Birmingham, Ala "[Ronald Reagan] believes in the so-called eleventh commandment: Thou shalt not speak ill of other Republicans." 1976 Mar 15 *Time* 16/2 "A reporter asked Reagan if he were violating his promise to abide by the G.O.P.'s 'Eleventh Commandment'—thou shalt not smite thy fellow Republican." Mar 15 *New Yorker* 111–12 "[I]n August of 1974, after Gerald Ford designated Nelson Rockefeller as his choice for Vice-President, Mrs. Perry Duryea, in dramatic violation of the Eleventh Commandment according to Ronald Reagan—that a Republican should not speak ill of another Republican—announced in telegrams to Ford and legislative leaders that Rockefeller was not fit for the Vice-Presidency or any other office, because he was responsible for her husband's indictment, which she called 'tantamount to political assassination'." Ibid 114/3 "Even if the Moynihan candidacy comes to nothing, it will have a place in local political history as a case study of how to win political friends although one has repeatedly broken the Eleventh Commandment of New York politics: Do not offend the voters of an ethnic bloc big enough to get up a demonstration against you on the six-o'clock news." Mar 22 *Newsweek* 20/1–2 "As that single critical fact became evident, Reagan's war counselors nagged him to lay aside his Eleventh Commandment vows to be nice to the opposition and instead attack Ford head-on." May 29 *Sat Rev* 57/2 "Things began getting a bit nastier when Ronald Reagan came down Mount Sinai bearing a set of stone tablets with a new and improved eleventh commandment: 'No Republican shall speak ill of a fellow Republican.'" 1978 Aug 29 *Esquire* 33/3 "A confidant recalls that the Republicans' Eleventh Commandment ('Candidates shall not speak ill of one another') was inspired by Reagan's staff, after they realized their man was unlikely to attack his opponents." 1980 May *Book Digest* 127/1 (from John Fowles and Frank Horvat *The Tree* [Little, Brown & Co., 1979]) "It was almost as if he had let one of his cordons grow as it liked, a blasphemous breaking of his own eleventh commandment: Thou shalt prune all trees." 1982 Arthur Block *Murphy's Law Book ~~Four~~ Three: Wrong Reasons Why Things Go More* (LA: Price/Stern/Sloan) 25 "THE ELEVENTH COMMANDMENT: Thou shalt not commit-tee." 1984 Jun *Cuisine* 50/1 "I grew up believing in an Eleventh Commandment: 'Thou Shalt Always Eat a Good Breakfast.'" Jul-Aug *Summer Reading Issue* (Barnes & Noble catalog) 18/2 "Do English gentlemen have mistresses, or do they religiously observe the eleventh commandment: thou shalt not be found out?"

food stylist *n* One who prepares food to be photographed for advertisements, cook books, and the like 1977 May *Better Homes and Gardens* 2/2 (credit line under photo) "Food Stylist: Coena Coffee. Photograph: Maselli" 1983 Mar-Apr *Cook's Mag* 12/2 "Frequently these companies require Maggie's assistance for photography. She is a veteran food stylist, and never 'doctors' or otherwise tampers with the food." 1984 Feb *Cuisine* 10/2 "[She] combined a master's degree in nutrition with two years' experience as a free-lance food stylist and recipe developer before joining us three years ago." Sep *Bon Appetit* 83/1 "A food stylist's job is to design the presentation of food for magazine covers and feature articles, for advertisements or custom recipe cards."

mover and shaker *n* [Cf *W3 mover n* a (2) "one that incites or instigates to action or that promotes an action that has been begun"] Person of power and influence 1974 Apr 22 *Time* 61/2 "He had enormous influence among

the movers and shakers in Washington." 1975 Aug *Psychology Today* 46/3 "The corporate movers and shakers are dispersed throughout the 129 [Bohemian] Grove camps." 1979 Jan 14 *NY Times Book Rev* 36/2 "The public and the news media movers and shakers were ready for her revealing story." 1980 Aug 18 *Newsweek* 26/4 "Four years after the death of his legendary father, Illinois state Senator [Richard M] Daley has begun to emerge as a mover and shaker in his own right." 1984 Oct *Newsweek On Campus* 8/2 "Columbia [Business School], like its peers, is unashamedly trying to admit the movers and shakers of tomorrow." Oct 18 *Chr Sci Monitor* 36/3 "For an entire week, a veritable parade of Soviet movers-and-shakers faced questions from host Bryant Gumbel, who managed to glean a number of newsworthy snippets from them."

nuclear winter *n* The cooling of the earth that some scientists believe would result if the explosion of nuclear weapons injected vast quantities of dust and smoke into the atmosphere, thus preventing sunlight from reaching the surface of the earth 1983 Dec 14 *Chr Sci Monitor* 10/1 "A bold new theory states that with the explosion of even a fraction of the stored up arsenal of nuclear power presently on Earth, there will be a so-called 'nuclear winter,' caused by a devastating dust storm of soot and smoke, like that observed temporarily on Mars." 1984 Jan 6 *Chr Sci Monitor* 15/2 "The scientists contended that the ultimate danger of nuclear war is not the immediate concussion and blast of exploding missiles but the effect on the environment, the adjustment that makes life possible on Earth. When the missiles go off they may blow up soil and dust and smoke that create a cloud over the earth. Sun rays can't penetrate it. That drastically lowers temperature (30 or 40 degrees, maybe) and this creates a 'nuclear winter.'" Sep 11 *Birmingham Post-Herald* A-4/3 (Boston *Globe*) "But the bishops said abortion comes first because: 'While nuclear holocaust is a future possibility, the holocaust of abortion is a present reality.' Presumably they will allot nuclear war prime time during the nuclear winter."

oil patch *n* Oil region; the petroleum industry 1980 Mar 23 *Birmingham News* F-3/1 "Out in the Texas oil patch they tell the story of a young man, fresh from engineering school, who reported to one of the leases of a large oil company." 1982 May 21 *Chr Sci Monitor* 11/1–2 "Instead of being an aggressive explorer, Gulf is known in the oil patch for being cautious. It drills wells around already established basins, finding smaller amounts of oil or gas." 1983 Mar 5 *TV Guide* 52/2 "In Archer City, the local avant-garde—i.e., those whose fortunes have been freshened by the recent oil boom—regard the satellite dish as the most promising innovation. These dishes now bloom here and there throughout the oil patch like giant flowers."

outsource [Cf *Barnhart Dict Comp* 2:80/1–2 *out-sourcing n* (1982), esp 2nd citation headed "*Passing into verb.*"] *vt* To purchase (parts) from an outside supplier, either in the purchaser's own country or abroad [1974 Dec 9 *New Yorker* 132/2 "Management has less drastic alternatives to plant closings, of course, and these further weaken labor's bargaining power. Management can protect itself by arranging for what is called multiple worldwide sourcing—different plants in different countries producing the same component."] 1982 Feb 12 *CBS Morning News* " . . . that is likely to be outsourced." 1984 Sep 21 *Washington Week in Rev* PBS [Harry Ellis said in effect that companies had left themselves free to outsource spare parts and products from non-union shops.] Sep 24 *USA Today* B-2/2 "GM won more flexibility on work rules, job retraining and outside purchase of parts and supplies—but with a potential \$1 billion price tag. 'GM purchased a \$1 billion license to automate and outsource as it sees fit,' says MIT labor researcher Harley Shaiken." Sep 24 *Wall St Jour* 1/6 " 'In essence, GM has paid a billion for an unlimited license to automate and outsource,' says Harley Shaiken, an auto-industry automation expert at Massachusetts Institute of Technology."

state of altered consciousness *n* [Cf *2BDNE altered state of consciousness* (1972)] ALTERED STATE of consciousness 1972 Oct 14 *National Observer* 11/1 "The Washington Post for Oct. 1 carried an unusual article by Dr. Andrew Weil about what he views as the basic human need for occasional states of altered consciousness." 1981 Sep *Science Digest* 67/3 "Some experts theorize that the placebo response may be related to hypnosis, a state of altered consciousness in which people are more receptive to suggestion."

AMONG THE NEW WORDS

MARY GRAY PORTER AND †I. WILLIS RUSSELL
The University of Alabama

With the assistance of William W. Evans, *Louisiana State University,* Michael Montgomery, *University of South Carolina,* and Richard E. Ray, *Indiana University of Pennsylvania*

[I. Willis Russell died on February 12, 1985. His death brought to an end what was for me a delightful collaboration with one who was a gentle man, a considerate friend and mentor, and a meticulous editor and scholar. Citations from his files will continue to appear in "Among the New Words," but American lexicography has lost one of its great contributors. (M.G.P.)]

SEVERAL OF THE COMBINATIONS with *bio-* are formed with terms usually associated with inorganic, or at any rate with nonliving, matter: *biochip, biomining,* and *bio-reactor.* The last of these has had a varied career. According to the *Barnhart Dictionary Companion (BDC)* 2:2 (Summer 1983) 36/1, *bioreactor* means or has meant (1) a device for purifying polluted water (1972); (2) "large laboratory apparatus used to manufacture natural products such as food flavors and drugs" (1976, 1978); and (3) "a living organism which produces biologically useful materials or facilitates industrial processes" (1983). Our citation brings us back to the sense of a large vessel for the manufacture of products, but this time by the use of microorganisms and on an industrial scale.

Many of the *docu-* words cited in the glossary seem to imply that entertainment or other values outweigh historical accuracy. Whether this is true of *docuhistory* is not clear from the one citation. The reviewer notes that the work is composed of 1,677 documents and the editor's "voluminous" comments. Surely the combination of documents, however numerous, and editorial comment, however voluminous, cannot be "the new kind of historical production" to which the reviewer gives the name "docuhistory."

The cartoon by Whitney Darrow, Jr. depicting the "forever wild" Dunhams in their city clothes at a lakeside party demonstrates that the term is again in use, having attracted the attention of the *New Yorker* thirty-four years after our first citation.

We have no documented citation for what was, if memory serves, the earliest use of the term *squeaky-clean:* advertisements for a shampoo (Halo?) that promised "squeaky-clean" hair.

Acknowledgments for citations: Edgar L. Frost (2).

bio- *comb form* [W3 *bi-* or *bio- comb form* 2 "biology: biological"]—**bio business** *n* Development, manufacture, and distribution of advanced biological products 1980 May *Life* 57/1 "If all these maneuverings suggest high-powered industrial warfare rather than molecular biology, it is because gene splicing and the bio business in general are fast becoming the go-go darlings of Wall Street." —**biochip** *n* Proposed device composed of small proteins and capable of carrying out many of the electronic functions now performed by silicon chips 1983 Dec *Science 83* 87/1 "Forrest Carter of the Naval Research Laboratory recently organized an international workshop on molecular electronic devices, including conductors, insulators, switches, and memory devices—all no bigger than small proteins. The hope is that such devices could be assembled in incredibly tiny, cheap, self-replicating biochips, even complete organic computers, useful aids to health and intellectual capacity small enough to live inside the bloodstream or the brain." —**bioelement** *n* One of the lighter elements, esp those of which living matter is composed 1974 Nov *Analog* 98/2 "All elements are produced by the 'cooking' of hydrogen in the enormous fusion reactors we call the stars, and the physics of the fusion reactions is such that the formation of the lighter elements—the so-called bioelements—is vastly more probable than that of the heavier ones." —**biofuture** *n* Biological future; potential course of one's state of health 1982 Nov *Omni* 52/1–2 "In only the last decade some 80 diseases have been traced to predisposing genetic factors, and the hereditary components of dozens more disorders are being identified each year. These insights into our personal biofutures may range from knowledge of our likelihood of developing cancer to our vulnerability to pollutants and certain mental diseases." —**biomining** *n* Use of natural or genetically modified bacteria to extract metals from ores or pollutants from contaminated materials (See also BIOPRODUCTION and MICROBIAL MINING) 1984 Apr 24 *Chr Sci Monitor* 21/1 ". . . to use existing bacteria and genetically engineered organisms to help refine and recover metals such as gold, silver, copper, and uranium—and to help clean up industrial pollutants. [¶] Most of the research is experimental enough that metal-munching microbes won't be working alongside draglines for several years yet, if then. But, by one estimate, 'biomining' could be a $5 billion-a-year enterprise by the turn of the century." —**bioproduction** *n* Manufacture of industrial chemicals by the use of bacteria or similar organisms that have been developed specifically for the given task (See also BIOMINING and MICROBIAL MINING) 1981 Oct 28 *Chr Sci Monitor* 13/3 "Some other basic industrial chemicals, such as propylene oxide, widely used in the manufacture of plastics, also seem ripe for bioproduction. In fact, Cetus Corporation expects this to happen before 1990 and forecasts global sales worth $2 billion to $3 billion for biologically made propylene oxide. Beyond such basics, there are many end products which biotechnology can help manufacture. These will even include upgraded oil products such as lubricants made by biological processing of heavy oil and residuals. [¶] Developing the 'bugs' to do the job is only part of what will be needed." —**bio-reactor** *n* Tank for industrial-scale bioproduction 1984 Jun *Colorado Alumnus* Engineering supp 4/2 "Chemical engineers will play an important role designing the necessary equipment to facilitate large-scale production of chemicals and drugs. 'For example,' Davis added, 'we will need efficient bio-reactors, or tanks which hold the microorganisms, feedstocks and nutrients.'" —**biorobot** *n* Automated device designed to carry out certain laboratory procedures in molecular biology 1983 Dec *World Press Rev* 6 "A new Japanese 'bio-robot,' due to be introduced commercially next year, promises to revolutionize genetic engineering by automating cumbersome DNA analyses and manipulations."

docu- *comb form* [*docu*mentary] —**docu-autobio-musico-'Journey'** *n Nonce* [*docu*mentary-*autobio*graphical-*musico-* + "*Journey* through the Past" the title of the film] 1973 May 24 *Rolling Stone* 10 (heading) "Neil Young's First Film Shown: A docu-autobio-musico-'Journey'" —**docudramatize** *vt* [Cf *2BDNE docudrama n* 1976; *docudramatist n* 1977] Treat (a subject) in the style of a docudrama 1979 Jan 2 *Esquire* 72/2 (picture caption) "David Susskind wanted to docudramatize the Black Sox Scandal." —**docuhistory** *n* 1981 May 31 *Guardian* 18/1 (Lacey Baldwin Smith rev of *The Lisle Letters* edited by Muriel St. Clare Byrne [U of Chicago P]) "*The Lisle Letters* bear a deceptive title, for the 1,677 documents themselves compose only about one-half of the 4,000 pages and 2 million words; the remainder is Miss St. Clare Byrne's voluminous editorial comments. The combination is a new kind of historical production—docuhistory—in which the voice of the past speaks in concert with the imagination of the living, producing a duet between the living editor and the records of the dead." —**documusical** *n* 1974 Aug 3 *TV Guide* 36 "Johnny Cash, who used to have a segment about railroading on his weekly series, will do an hour-length ABC special, 'Ridin' the Rails,' Nov. 22. Producer Nick Webster calls it a 'documusical,' with songs and dramatic re-creations about America's railroads. Historic engines from the Baltimore and Ohio Railroad Museum will be used in sketches about the legend of John Henry, Casey Jones, a train robbery, and the completion of the first transcontinental railway at Promontory Point, Utah." —**docu-pulp** *n* [Cf *W3 pulp n* 5 b "tawdry or sensational writing"] 1983 Nov 19 *TV Guide* A-6/1 "How could a single creative team have generated this giddying patchwork of substance and fluff, serious history and mindless docu-pulp?" —**docu-re-creation** *n* See DOCU-REENACTMENT 1983 Jul 8 *Chr Sci Monitor* 10/3 "Narrated by Bill Kurtis, this 'docu-re-creation' was produced by Holly and Paul Fine, who received much attention when ABC News aired their 'The Saving of the President' last year. [¶] The line between news and entertainment is a thin one at best, often blurred by such news-magazine shows as '60 Minutes,' such 'reality' entertainment shows as 'Real People,' and innumerable entertainment 'docudramas' that tend to shade the truth in the name of dramatic license. Network news should not encourage any news form that, by its very nature, may confuse reality and the re-creation of reality in the minds of TV audiences." —**docu-reenactment** *n* Documentary film or program that uses little or no footage of the actual events it purportedly depicts but instead offers a re-creation 1983 Jul 15 *Chr Sci Monitor* 20/1 "That's the message one gets from an almost totally 'reenacted' documentary presented by ABC News's often innovative-or-bust 'Closeup' series. . . . [¶] Some basic matters are touched on too lightly in this docu-reenactment." —**docu-schlock** *n* [Cf *WNCD9 schlock adj* 1915; *BDNE schlock n* "something cheap or inferior; junk" 1967] 1983 Dec 14 *Chr Sci Monitor* 1/1 "TV executives call it 'reality programming,' like the news. But it isn't exactly news. Some call it 'infotainment,' meaning information that is entertaining. Others call it 'docu-schlock.' [¶] Whatever one calls it, shows like this have swept the airwaves. By now, the local channels nearly everywhere in the country carry at least one soft-feature, magazine-style TV show." —**docu-soap opera** *n* Docudrama in the manner of a soap opera 1979 May 17 *Chr Sci Monitor* 14/1 "'Blind Ambition' . . . is based on [John] Dean's book of the same name and 'Mo,' his wife's autobiography. Together, they constitute what is rapidly becoming a new television form: the docu-soap opera."

forever wild *adj* Legally protected against any form of commercial development; used esp of forest lands 1940 M L Fernald "The Problem of Conserving Rare Native Plants" *Annual Report of the Board of Regents of the Smithsonian Institution . . . 1939* (Washington: US GPO) 388 "When I first knew eastern Massachusetts, many public-spirited citizens gave freely to the State wild forest lands for State reservations which were to be kept forever wild." 1974 Jul 1 *New Yorker* 26 (cartoon caption) [Woman introducing cocktail party guests:] "The Dunhams have just been declared forever wild." 1975 Dec *Town & Country* 218/3 "A great deal of what one sees—some 9,425 square miles—has been designated 'forever wild' and makes up the largest state-owned park in the United States." 1980 Jan 28 *Sports Illus* 64/3, 77/2 "As a result of public protest against devastating logging practices in the 19th century, a unique clause in the state constitution decrees that this tract 'shall be forever kept as wild forest lands.' Except for maintenance of trails and campsites, no trees can be sold, removed or destroyed without constitutional amendment, and that would require passage by two successive legislatures and statewide approval by the voters. This protection has been in force since 1895, and in all that time no constitutional convention or session of the legislature has adopted any amendment to repeal the Forever Wild clause. . . . [¶] In this age of global pollution, a forever wild clause in a state constitution does not protect a region from contamination." —**forever wilder** *n* One who favors the preservation of forest lands in the wild state 1971 Nov 27 *New Yorker* 130/2 "These incursions . . . have caused a deep, bitter rift between commercial-minded people, who think that the Adirondack Forest Preserve is a waste of good land, and 'forever-wilders,' who think that the Preserve should be just that—an untouchable sanctuary, eternally free of the inroads of civilization."

microbial mining *n* Extraction of metals by microbes genetically engineered for such use (See also BIOMINING and BIOPRODUCTION) 1984 Apr 24 *Chr Sci Monitor* 21/2–3 "The allure of microbial mining lies largely in what it won't do. In theory, it will allow companies to extract metals without all the smoke-belching of smelters. It also is a less energy-intensive process. And it offers the potential of recouping riches from low-grade, uneconomic ores."

rockumentary *n* [*rock* (*BDNE* 1968) + *documentary* (*WNCD9 n* 1935)] Documentary movie, or one made in the style of a documentary, about rock music and musicians 1981 Dec 11 Columbia (SC) *The State* D-10 "*Beatlemania,* the former smash hit of Broadway, will appear at Carolina Coliseum next Thursday—a 'Rockumentary' that depicts in slides and music the turbulent '60s." 1983 Jan 7 *The State/Columbia Record* (SC) B-1 "The Beatles, 'The Compleat Beatles' (MGM UA): This two-hour, self-described 'rockumentary'—never shown on television or in theaters—is the first such. . . ." 1985 Jan 24 *Tusk* (entertainment supp to Univ of Ala student newspaper) 12/3 "*This is Spinal Tap*, the funniest movie of the year, took a rockumentary spoof look at Heavy Metal in particular and rock personalities in general." Mar 2 *TV Guide* A-6/2 "1984's *This Is Spinal Tap*, Rob Reiner's affectionate, sophisticated and very funny 'rockumentary' about a fictitious British heavy-metal group, is the ultimate sendup movie. Detailing, in documentary fashion, the disastrous American tour of the group that has, in 16 years, established itself as one of England's loudest bands, it's top satire and dandy entertainment."

squeaky-clean   *adj*   [Cf *W3 clean adj* 3 a & b]   Ethically or morally beyond reproach   [1972 Jun 23 *Tuscaloosa News* 9/1 (picture caption) "Starting with the important basic of squeaky-clean skin, she first applies a protective covering of moisturizer to keep the skin soft and fresh under make-up and to prepare the delicate tissues for the slap of the sun."]   1979 Mar 31 *Sat Rev* 44/1 "[Robin] Williams is supposed to be an innocent alien who lands in Boulder, Colorado, where he becomes the housemate of Mindy (played by Pam Dauber), a squeaky-clean schoolteacher."   1981 May 25 *Inquiry* 9/3 "As Billy Masiello noted about the squeaky-clean administration of Mike Dukakis, the incumbent beaten by King: 'The game . . . was over' when the Duke was elected."   1982 Feb 1 *Analog* 82/2 "He'd stay squeaky clean until then, even if the government couldn't."   1984 May 12 *TV Guide* 22/2 "Sexual consciousness goes only so far. Even when you have a squeaky-clean sex show."

sword and sorcery   *n*   Fantasy fiction, usu considered a sub-genre of science fiction, having as its dominant elements knightly quests, magic, and mythical creatures, and set in an era, past or future, that resembles the Middle Ages   1973 Aug *Vertex* 95/1 "If you're into hard science fiction, fantasy, sword and sorcery, 'new wave,' or any of the other sub-genres that make up the acronym SF, you may be interested in knowing that A Change of Hobbit is the place to go when you can't make it to . . . the only other places that boast SF specialty shops."   1981 [Feb *Foundation: The Rev of Sci Fict* 30–31 "SF writers try different dodges. One is to invent a social set-up something like the earlier ones in our own history. Hence the mock medievalism of some writers, including princesses and dragons."]   Mar *Science-Fiction Studies* 88 "[Ursula] Le Guin also polemicizes against sword and sorcery and the pretentiousness of the stolen myths found in so much SF; but she rarely cites particular examples."   Jul 13 *Newsweek* 81/2 "The Disney organization co-produced *Dragonslayer*, a dark slice of sword and sorcery that could have used some of Walt's old storytelling sense."   Nov *Science 81* 102/3 "United Artists' 3-D productions will include a science fiction film as well as a 'sword and sorcery fantasy.'"   —**swords and sorcery**   [var of SWORD AND SORCERY]   1984 Mar *Creative Computing* 153/3 "In some ways [*Enchanter*, a microcomputer adventure game] marks the return to the old Zorkish formulas of D&D (donuts and dragoons [*sic*]) style fantasy—sorcerers and warlocks, sweeping medieval stories of magical, untainted heroism and terrible, unthinkable evil. [¶] . . . *Enchanter* marks a welcome return to the swords and sorcery micro owners have come to know, love, and accept."

Tinseltown   *n*   [cf *W3 tinsel n* 3 "something superficially showy, attractive, or glamorous that actually has little real worth"]   Hollywood   1974 Sep 14 *TV Guide* 34/1 "You wrote me about checking maybe you could sign on with Les Brown if you decide to depart the Apple and come out here to Tinsel Town."   1976 May *Amer Home* 19/2–3 "Bring along the Kleenex to *Gable and Lombard* and watch James Brolin and Jill Clayburgh play pranks, dress up as glamour pusses and fall in love à la tinsel town."   1977 Dec 6 *National Enquirer* 12/4 "Legendary George Jessel, 79, May-Decembering with beautiful TinselTown psychic Tamara Rand—who is 28."   1980 Aug 16 *TV Guide* A-6/1 (letter) "As a pastor of a church, I'm not saying that we have all the answers, but at least we are not trying to make Jesus Christ out to be some tinseltown phantom who cannot be part of your life until you turn over all your finances to some fake 'high priest' of TV."   Nov *In Cinema* 6/1 "That's what [he] wants to say to virtually everyone he's come across in his varied Tinseltown career."   1981 Aug *Sat Rev* 57/1 (Henry Weil rev of Gary Carey *All the Stars in Heaven* [E P Dutton]) "This is as level-headed a tinsel-town bio as we're likely to see."

AMONG THE NEW WORDS

JOHN ALGEO   AND   MARY GRAY PORTER

University of Georgia and   *University of Alabama*
University College London

With the assistance of the British New Words Committee: Sylvia Chalker and Oonagh Sayce, and the additional assistance of Sidney Greenbaum, Robert Ilson, Thomas Lavelle, Tom McArthur, and René Quinault.

N EOLOGY IS NO RESPECTER of national boundaries.[1] New English words appear in any of the English-speaking countries of the world and make their way into the others, often so unobtrusively that it is difficult after the fact to tell where they originally came from. Moreover, what is a new word in one of the national varieties may be old hat in another. Thus the recent *Longman Guardian New Words* lists among its new words of 1986 *airbag, baglady, burrito,* and *credit union*—all words and things for some time familiar to Americans, however new they may be in Britain.

The words in this installment and in succeeding installments of this series are new British words in that they have been observed in British contexts but are not recorded in such dictionaries as the following:

> *Chambers 20th Century Dictionary.* New ed. Ed. E.M. Kirkpatrick. Edinburgh: Chambers, 1983.
> *Collins Dictionary of the English Language.* 2d ed. Ed. Patrick Hanks; Laurence Urdang, editorial director. London: Collins, 1986.
> *Longman Dictionary of the English Language.* London: Longman, 1984.
> *Longman Guardian New Words.* Ed. Simon Mort. London: Longman, 1986.
> *The Oxford Reference Dictionary.* Ed. Joyce M. Hawkins. Oxford: Clarendon, 1986.
> *Reader's Digest Great Illustrated Dictionary.* 2 vols. Ed. Robert Ilson. London: Reader's Digest, 1984, 1985.
> *A Supplement to the Oxford English Dictionary.* 4 vols. Ed. R.W. Burchfield. Oxford: Clarendon, 1972–86.

Some of the terms listed here are certainly not recent innovations in British English, and when long-standing use is suspected, it is noted in an entry. However, the working definition of *new word* for this column is a term or use not listed in the dictionaries mentioned above. If it has not been recorded, it is "new," whatever the facts of the matter may be.

Generally, slang terms have been avoided. However, the decision of what is to count as slang is itself often problematical. If a term occurs in an otherwise nonslang context or if it holds some promise of entering standard use, it may be included, despite an aura of slanginess. *A Dictionary of Slang and Unconventional English*, by Eric Partridge, 8th ed. by Paul Beale (London: Routledge, 1984) is cited as "Partridge" when it is relevant.

Some cautions about these entries are in order. It is possible that some of these words may already have been recorded in American dictionaries, although a number of them relate to specifically British phenomena and are therefore likely to be neologisms in any country. Also, there has been no opportunity to consult the various Merriam-Webster new words publications or *The Barnhart Dictionary Companion*, or other journals in which some of these forms may have been recorded. A number of the entries are for forms with sparse documentation; additional evidence is therefore needed for them.

As usual in this department, new uses of old words count as neologisms and are recorded. In the following glossary, definitions are given only when the illustrative citations are insufficiently self-defining.

airbridge   *n*   1986 Sep 10 *Times* 1/3 "The boy . . . scampered off and began to play with the controls of the airbridge, the movable walkway which is positioned by the aircraft door to allow passengers to disembark." (This use is distinct from the older meaning of the term as an air transportation link between two places.)

air motorway   *n*   1986 Sep 2 *Times* 7/7 "The key difference is that light aircraft are not allowed to fly in the 'air motorways' or controlled air space used by airliners in Britain, except under air traffic control."

alcohol arcade   *n*   1986 Oct 17 *Times* 13/1 "This was a fascinating glimpse into the brash new world of 'alcohol arcades,' where the under-age law seems to have suffered a de facto deregulation—where, indeed, 16-year-olds decline to enter certain pubs because these have been given over to 14-year-olds."

Alcometer   *n*   1986 Aug 27 *Times* 10/6 "But we are empowered to stop any motorist for routine reasons, . . . and we can then ask them to blow into the Alcometer if we think they might be over the limit." (The equivalent American term is *drunkometer*; the usual British term is *Breathalyzer*, a trademark, as the capital letter suggests this term may also be. Similar in form but distinct in sense is *alcoholometer* 'instrument for measuring the strength of alcohol in liquids'.)

all-ticket   *adj*   Accessible only by an admission ticket secured in advance   1986 Sep 22 *Times* 1/2 "The police chiefs believe that crowds can be better controlled if the games are not all-ticket because the ban meant frustrated fans caused trouble in town centres after being turned away from grounds."   Sep 30 *Guardian* 27/4 "Leaving an all-ticket discotheque at the hall attended mainly by black people, the victims were attacked." (A series of riots by out-of-town fans of visiting teams at soccer matches caused a concern for safety and crowd control that resulted in proposals to restrict attendance at matches; this term is probably connected with that reaction, although it is also used of entertainment events that are advance-ticket sale only because they are certain to be oversubscribed.)

Argy /arJi/ *n* Argentinian 1986 Aug 23 *Daily Mirror* 6/2 "British Actress Julie Christie has been signed to play the lead in an Argentinian film which has now been retitled Miss Mary. The original title gave both Julie and the Argies the heebie-jeebies. It was called Miss Maggie." Oct 12 *Sunday Times* 58/6 "Now there are two they make distinguished twins; clockwise and anti-clockwise chronicles of Thatcher's newly tumescent, patriotic, Argy-bashing Britain." (This term became common during the Falkland crisis of 1982 and is listed in Partridge. It follows a tradition of giving nursery-sounding and therefore dismissive nicknames to one's military foes. *Jerries* and *Japs* are older examples. A possible contributing etymon is the Briticism *argy-bargy* 'a wrangle, argument', which is semantically apposite.)

auto sales *n* Location for automatic vending machines (The term appears over machines selling candy and other products in the stations of the London Underground and has therefore probably existed for some years.)

bath sheet *n* Large bath towel (the usual term for oversized towels in department stores, for example John Lewis at Brent Cross Shopping Centre, but sometimes regarded as non-U)

bed show *n* 1986 Aug sign outside a London place of entertainment "Live Nude Bed Show"

Big Bang; Bang *n* **1:** Immediate consequences of the 1986 deregulation of the London Stock Exchange 1986 Oct 7 *Times* 37/1 "Technically Big Bang takes in two events. The abolition of fixed commissions charged by stockbrokers on transactions in equities and government securities (gilts), and the introduction of dual capacity, which will allow jobbers and brokers to do each other's jobs as well as to continue doing their own." (This nickname, which was much in the news in Britain in the fall of the year, is recorded in the *Longman Guardian New Words*, but is included here for the sake of the explanatory quotation and because of the related, but elsewhere unrecorded, terms BIG BANGER—the entry for which also includes a citation of the short form *Bang*—and LITTLE BANG. The term alludes to the *Big Bang* cosmological theory of the origin of the universe, itself a specialization of the general sense 'great explosion', perhaps with allusion to the explosion of atomic bombs.) **2:** Sudden forceful beginning 1987 Feb 9 "Day to Day" BBC1 "We proposed not to bring this [nonsmoking rule] in as a Big Bang approach." (The recent use of this more general sense, for which the *Collins* definition is cited here, is a topical allusion to sense 1.)

Big Banger *n* 1986 Oct 15 *Times* 14/1 "Michael Hawkes, chairman of Kleinwort Benson, is not your average Big Banger.... Apart from anything else, he knows that, in the short term at least, the Bang is bad news for profits."

black cab; black taxi *n* Licensed, metered taxicab, of a standard design and usually black (but sometimes blue or red) in color, available at taxi ranks or while cruising, distinguished from a minicab, which is an unmarked, usually nonmetered car of any of various designs and available chiefly by telephone 1986 Aug 27 *Times* 1/5 "The dead man, who was married with four children, drove a black cab in the nationalist Falls Road area of the city." Aug 28 *Hampstead Advertiser* 2/3 (listing under the heading "Helplines" with other services such as a Family Planning Clinic and a Gay Switchboard) "Black Taxis—01-455 9851" 1987 Feb 4 *London Evening Standard* 33/3 (letter) "I know for a fact that you will find a black cab in Hanover Square after 10 pm at night. In fact you will find many black cabs there and all the drivers will be sitting in the back of one of them, with the engine running, huddled round a cup of hot cocoa and having a chat and a game of cards. That is the mystery of the disappearing black cab." Feb 12 Morning News BBC1 "It is said that the black cabs [in Belfast]... also pay a levy to the Provos." Feb 12 *London Evening Standard* 39/1 (letter) "I often use minicabs and occasionally black taxis, and I don't tip."

black spot *n* Focus of deprivation or danger; a difficult place, event, or situation 1986 Aug 27 *Times* 22/2 "The real blackspot in Zimbabwean affairs derives from the difficulty of reaching a stable accommodation between the Africans who now rule the country, and specifically between the two main tribes, the Shona... and the Ndebele." Oct 30 *Times* 22 (picture caption) "The marchers have been collecting thousands of signatures for a petition urging help for unemployment black spots. It will be handed into the House of Commons next Wednesday." (A related, older sense of the term is 'a place on a roadway where accidents are frequent'. *Collins* records a generalization of that sense to "any dangerous or difficult place." But the term is also used in still broader senses without restriction to localities, as the first citation above shows.)

bluppy *n* 1986 Oct 12 *Sunday Times* 48/1 "Subsequently the categorisation was refined to include the guppy (gay urban professional) and the bluppy (black urban professional)." (part of the playful and ephemeral radiation from *yuppy*)

boil *n* **—on the boil** Under active consideration 1986 Sep 5 *Times* 21/8 (headline) "Vital Allied bid to buy Hiram still on the boil" (antonym: *on the back burner*)

Bombay mix *n* Cocktail food made of nuts and other crunchy ingredients flavored with Indian spices (identified by Robert Ilson during a party at the Survey of English Usage, University College London; also observed on a sign at Neal's Yard, a health-food store in London; one of a variety of such foods, for which numerous terms are used: *Caribbean mix, tropical mix,* and the American *gorp,* of uncertain origin but popularly etymologized as an acronym for "good old raisins and peanuts")

bonk *v* 1986 Oct 12 *Sunday Times* 48/7 "The important thing is that there is no one class represented here; it is a group of people, who share the same materialist ambitions, relaxing between getting, spending and bonking (yuppie for sex)." (perhaps a metaphorical extension of the informal sense 'hit resoundingly', terms for copulation often being based on expressions for 'strike')

boom *n* 1986 Aug 30 *Times* 1/4 "Then it smashed through two low-laying [*sic*] yellow and black booms which are used as out-going vehicles pass through the customs." (A variety of earlier recorded senses relate to ships and barriers on water; this use—one of a number of metaphorical extensions, another being the microphone boom—appears to refer to the arm of a land barrier.)

boot money *n* Money paid by a manufacturer to the members of a sport team, especially rugby, to use the company's product, specifically athletic shoes 1986 Sep 4 *Daily Telegraph* 12/4 (letter to editor) "But if, some years ago, Adidas were handing over enough 'boot money' to alert the Inland Revenue, who can doubt that increased sponsorship and other market forces have encouraged the spread and appreciation of such practices?... They must know about boot money, perks, expenses etc." Oct 17 *Times* 31/5 "If the game does take off, as the administrators hope—and television and sponsors' interest is threatening—it could get as mucky as rugby 'boot money.'"

breath pack *n* Implement for giving breath tests to persons suspected of being drunk drivers 1986 Aug 27 *Times* 10/5 "'I've not got a breath pack, can I borrow yours?' he said."

breath-test *vt* 1986 Aug 23 *Daily Mirror* 7/5 "Police breath-tested 300 anonymous volunteers in London in an experiment to show them the effects of drinking—and half of them failed."

brown *adj* Being of a racial category perceived as having a skin color between white and black, spec Asian, Indian 1986 Oct 19 *Sunday Times* 26/5–6 "'I just don't fit,' complains Corbett. 'I am not black (Afro-Caribbean); brown (Asian); White (UK); Irish or other.... So which box would I tick?'" (The use of *brown* for dark skin is well established; the *OED* defines the term "as a racial characteristic" and the *OEDS* as "mulatto." However, the sense 'Asian', apparently specifically 'Indian', is not recorded.)

brown off *vt* [backformation from the adj *browned-off*] Depress, sadden; annoy, irritate 1986 Oct 12 *Sunday Times* 52/1 "Shops shouldn't sell it. It's easy enough for someone to say, 'give it up'. It's all right at first, then it browns you off, makes you miserable." 1987 Feb 9 *London Evening Standard* 21/1 "Our experience of English beaches in the wet August of 1985 had so browned us off that I determined to head south for a real suntan." (Partridge attributes the verb to army use ca 1920.)

buttery *n* Small kitchen or coffee-making counter in the residence hall of an educational institution 1986 Oct 7 *Times* 14/5 "Butteries on landings are focal points for coffee-making and gossip, both favourite pastimes." (Several dictionaries define the term as a room in a college where food is stored and supplied or sold to students; this citation, however, referring to a place for coffee-making equipment in the dormitory of a public school, indicates a wider use of the term.)

cannibal *adj* [backformation from *cannibalize*] Produced by cannibalizing 1986 Aug 29 Newcastle *Evening Chronicle* 1/6 "One of the victims of the cannibal car scandal, Dawn Coultas,... is fighting for compensation after buying a Volvo that had been made from the halves of two wrecked cars.... The cars find their way on to the roads after being cut in half and then having parts that have been cannibalised from other wrecked cars welded on to them." (cf CAR CANNIBAL)

cap *vt* Put a limit on, restrict 1986 Oct 25 *Times* 35/1 "Members of the Association of British insurers (ABI), which includes virtually all the life companies, have decided to 'cap' the returns that can be used for illustrations of future benefits." (*Rate-capping* 'central government's placing a limit on the tax rate that local governments can levy' was much in the news in Britain in 1985–86. The resulting new sense of *cap* was recorded in *Collins* as "to impose an upper limit on the level of increase of (a tax, such as rates)"; however, as the citation above shows, the new sense is not limited to taxation.)

car cannibal *n* One who cannibalizes cars 1986 Aug 29 Newcastle *Evening Chronicle* 1/4 "Massive support came flooding into the offices of the Evening Chronicle today for our campaign to outlaw the North-East car cannibals." (cf CANNIBAL)

card-covered *adj* (Of a book) bound in stiff paper covers 1980 Stephen Skinner *Terrestrial Astrology* (London: Routledge) 161 "Nevertheless this text on geomancy was one of the few available this century, and has therefore been quite influential, appearing again by itself at a later date in a card-covered edition."

clapometer *n* Machine that registers the volume of an audience's response; applause meter 1986 Oct 12 *Times* 64/7 (summary of the TV version of Jeffrey Archer's *First among Equals*) "Fast-forwarding through the years, the fortunes of the famous four MPs rise and fall with clapometer rapidity."

clock *v* 1986 Oct 27 *Times* 3/5 "Used car buyers lose about £100 million a year as a result of 'clocking'—fraudulent reduction of the mileage recorded by the odometer—according to *Crime UK,* an economic, social and policy audit, published today." Idem "Mileage monitoring systems run by local authorities indicate that a fifth to a third of all used cars are clocked." (Partridge says in use since ca 1945)

close coupled *adj* (Of toilet fixtures) having the water tank joined in a single piece with the toilet bowl 1986 Aug 21 *Hampstead Advertiser* 11 (ad) "Large luxury close coupled w.c. with seat, panel extra" (a special application of the *OEDS* general sense 'coupled close together', attributed there specifically to electrical circuits)

cold-call *v* Attempt to sell a product, especially stock shares, over the telephone to an unprepared and unwilling potential customer 1986 Sep 13 *Times* 30 "Caution is the answer to the cold-caller [headline] /... but if you now get a call out of the blue from a smooth talker trying to sell you shares in companies you have never heard of, take care. At least one company based in Spain is cold-calling potential investors in the UK." Oct 13 *Times* 21/1 "Others, like the Bill's provisions relating to cold calling (the practice of seeking to enter into investment agreements following unsolicited calls), when read together with the SIB's [Securities and Investments Board's] proposals, are either unworkable or unacceptable." Oct 18 *Times* 4/2 "Almost any form of advertising or publicity except unsolicited telephone calls, known as 'cold calling' and knocking on doors will now be allowed." (*Collins* enters a noun *cold call* and a derivative noun *cold-calling*; but there is also a verb, as in the first citation above) **—cold-caller** See first citation above

collar bone *n* Thin strip of material used to stiffen a shirt collar, collar stay 1986 Sep 6 *Times* 1/7–8 (ad) "Sewn-in linings with removable collar bones... Seams are double stitched for strength and collars are fitted with removable bones." (*Bone,* as a term for whalebone and later other materials such as metal and plastic used to stiffen corsets, brassiers, and other garments, is of long standing. The combination *collar bone,* however, is not recorded, though it has doubtless existed for some time.)

comic *n* Tabloid newspaper (derogatory) 1986 Jul 23 *Atlanta Constitution*

A-11/1 "The British tabloids—the comics as they call them—spent the wedding week speculating madly about Sarah." (British use confirmed by personal query; so called because tabloids typically have comic strips, many photographs, large display type, and simple language on a low educational level)

compulsory-test vt Test compulsorily 1986 Sep 23 *Daily Mirror* 7/4 "The government is considering pleas that visitors from these countries should be compulsory tested."

computeracy n [*computer* + *literacy*] Knowledge about computers 1986 Aug 19 *Times* 21/4 "The answer is a definite yes, but first you must identify the various stages of computeracy so you can work out exactly how computerate you need to be for maximum career impact."

computerate adj [*computer* + *literate*] Knowledgeable about computers 1986 Tom McArthur *Worlds of Reference* (Cambridge UP) 5 "Finally, and quite soon at that, it is going to be hard for computerate generations to imagine a pre-electronic world." Aug 19 *Times* 21/4 "Is it then necessary to be 'computerate'? The answer is a definite yes." (See also the citation under COMPUTERACY.)

coolie n [perhaps a pun on *cool* in the jazz sense and *coolie* 'unskilled laborer'] Uncritical fan of popular music 1983 Kenneth Hudson *Language of the Teenage Revolution* (London: Macmillan) 50 "the people who buy such papers [as *Melody Maker*] regularly constitute a pop intelligentsia. Their part in the movement is to read and theorise about it and to listen to records in their own homes, leaving most of the up-front activity to the teenage coolies."

cost out vt Estimate or determine the cost of 1986 Sep 11 *Hampstead Advertiser* 12/3 "Last year I decided to cost out the gifts of the 12 Days of Christmas . . . and virtually all the winged variety of gifts could be furnished by London pet suppliers, from Colly Birds to Geese-a-laying." Sep 18 ibid 3/2 "Costing out the Heath [headline] / Running Hampstead Heath will put 1.6p on the rates." (The simplex *cost* is well established in this sense, but the combination *cost out* has not been recorded, although it has doubtless existed for some time. It is perhaps a blend of *cost* and *figure out, check out,* or the like.)

Little Bang n 1986 Oct 5 *Sunday Times Magazine* 43/1 "So in June 1984 that rule was scrapped, allowing brokers to incorporate themselves as limited companies; and even more important, letting outsiders, including banks, and even foreigners, buy their way in and start building up their infantry and their specialised assault units. At first they were limited to 29.9 per cent, but from March 1 this year [1986] ('Little Bang') that was raised to a full 100 per cent."

AMONG THE NEW WORDS

JOHN ALGEO

University of Georgia AND
University College London

With the assistance of the British New Words Committee:
Sylvia Chalker, Thomas Lavelle, Sarah Lawson, Tom McArthur,
René Quinault, and Oonagh Sayce, and the additional
assistance of Adele Algeo, Sidney Greenbaum, and Robert Ilson.

T HE MEMBERS OF THE BRITISH New Words Committee have been invaluable in contributing citations for neologisms and especially in answering questions about the currency of forms and in helping to explain what are great mysteries in their use to an outlander American. None of them, however, sees these installments in final form, and therefore they are not responsible for whatever errors remain. Whatever is right is due to their watchful eyes.

This installment of "Among the New Words" continues the reporting of new terms in British English begun in the last issue. Some of these terms are Briticisms, others are Common English and may be new in British but already recorded in American or new in both British and American English.

The question of what is a NEW word for our purposes is important. The last installment included *brown off* as a verb with the sense 'depress, sadden; annoy, irritate'. Allen Walker Read has kindly pointed out two earlier reports of the verb. H. L. Mencken wrote an article on "War Words in England," *American Speech* 19 (1944) 3–15, in which he quoted a letter of 30 August 1940 from Mrs. Jean Green in Hunsur, Mysore, India (n.16):

To brown off or to be browned off was first heard by me in Army circles at Aldershot in 1932, and when I came out to India later in the year it was also in use in Bangalore. Since then I have used it often, but gave it up a year or two ago, thinking it was overdone and dated. I am sure a great many other civilians have also been using it for a long time.

In addition, Lester V. Berrey in "English War Slang" (*Nation*, 9 Nov. 1940, 446–47) noted the following use:

To brown off (to be bored, fed up) is descriptive of the tedium endured during the protracted period of inactivity before the *Blitzkrieg* on England.

We are glad to add these citations to the evidence presented in the last installment. Although they report usage of fifty or more years ago, they

do not change the status of *brown off* as a NEW word for our purposes, because our criterion for newness is the nonappearance of a term in those current British dictionaries listed in the headnote to the last installment. A word may be—indeed, many of those we list certainly are—long established in the language but, for one reason or another, have not been recorded by lexicographers of the standard language. If we find evidence of their current use, we regard them as NEW words, whatever their actual age. Thus our definition of NEW is a purely stipulated and pragmatic one. Any other concept of NEW would be difficult to apply to our purpose, which is to note terms and senses not in current dictionaries.

We have a few general comments on the items in the following list.

Yuppy or *yuppie* is listed in some dictionaries and has already been documented in "Among the New Words" (*AS* 60 [1985]: 69) and in Fred R. Shapiro's article "Yuppies, Yumpies, Yaps, and Computer-Assisted Lexicology" (*AS* 61 [1986]: 139–46). The vogue for the term continues, illustrated here both in the entries for *appointments diary* and *Filofax* and by the radiation of the term into several others. *Bluppy* was cited in the last installment of "Among the New Words," and the entries below include *dumpy, guppy, sampy, yumpo, yuppiedom, yuppification, yuppify, yuppily,* and *yuppy-bashing.* *Longman Guardian New Words* lists in addition *droppies* [*di*sillusioned, *r*elatively *o*rdinary *p*rofessionals, *p*referring *i*ndependent *e*mployment *s*ituations], *guppie* [Green + *yuppie*], *huppie* [hippy + *yuppie*], and other radiations. Most of these terms are ephemera and, indeed, merely stunt words, but they are evidence of the sense of lexical play that pervades ordinary use of language and of the importance of *yuppy.*

Another term that has radiated vigorously is *golden handshake.* Its progeny are so numerous that it seems advisable to define *golden* as the key term and merely to illustrate its combinations.

The combining form *-bashing* in the sense 'malicious, unprovoked attack on' has been voguish on both sides of the Atlantic for some time. A long-established, bi-Atlantic form is *queer-bashing* 'beating up homosexuals' (also *fag-bashing,* at least in the US; cf. Bruce Rodgers, *The Queens' Vernacular: A Gay Lexicon* [San Francisco: Straight Arrow Books, 1972], s.v. *queer-bashing,* "[Brit teen sl] beating up homosexuals simply because they are homosexuals"). A recently newsworthy British form is *Paki-bashing* 'beating up Pakistanis'. The form is represented below by two entries: *yuppy-bashing* is a straightforward use of the form; *granny-bashing* has two senses, neither wholly predictable and the second a black-humorous but nonviolent use that may be school slang. Another such nonviolent use is *square-bashing* 'military drill'. In these nonviolent uses, the form applies to a dull and repetitive task.

The prolific combining form *Euro-* is represented by several new terms below. It is used so freely that it is entered independently in several dictionaries with the sense 'pertaining to (Western) Europe or the European Economic Community'; however, many of its combinations have senses that are not fully accounted for by their parts, so they must still be given separate treatment. Like any vogue form, this one has provoked a sense of ennui in some readers, as witnessed by the following letter to the editor of the *Daily Telegraph* (26 Mar. 1987): "SIR—Am I alone in feeling a pang of weary suspicion whenever I see anything proclaimed as being 'Euro', '2000' or, outside the context of aeroplane-engine description, 'Turbo'?"

Several terms in this installment are trade names: *Domestos, Filofax, Hush Puppy, Lilt,* and *Time Manager.* One does not expect to find such terms in a dictionary until they verge on generic use. Though some of these terms may be approaching that status, the reason for including them here is that they, or their uses, may be puzzling to an American observer of British English and they cannot be found in dictionaries.

appointments diary n Book with a day-by-day calendar in which appointments may be written; engagement book, date book, calendar 1987 Feb 22 *Sunday Telegraph* 21/6 "In the beginning there was the appointments diary. Then to contain the many and varied components of the work-hard-play-hard Yuppy lifestyle came the personal organiser—the Filofax." (This combination, a fuller specification of one sense of British *diary,* has doubtless been in use for some time, but has not been entered by lexicographers, who perhaps have regarded it as an analytical combination. Whereas American *diary* typically denotes a day-by-day record of past events, British *diary* also frequently refers to a day-by-day plan for future events.)

cash dispensing machine n See CASHPOINT sense 1 1986 Aug 19 (*Collins* and *Chambers* have *cash dispenser* in this sense.)

cashpoint n 1: Cash dispenser, automatic bank teller, often outside a bank, from which money can be withdrawn by inserting a card and keying in an identification number 1985 Nov Lloyds Bank leaflet "Lloyds Bank in the UK provides a straightforward way of saving at the full Deposit Account interest rate—with no-penalty instant cash withdrawals through Cashpoint. . . . No loss of interest on instant Cashpoint withdrawals. . . . Easy to control—you can check the balance in your Account at nearly 1,700 Cashpoint machines, including 170 LobbyService Cashpoints. [¶] Naturally your Deposit Account can be used without a Cashpoint card." 1986 Aug 19 *Times* 10/1 "Cashpoint flashpoint [headline] / Britain's 10,000 cash dispensing machines in banks could be shut down if a baronet succeeds in getting an injunction against the Queen's bankers Coutts and Co." Oct 12 *Sunday Times* 58/1 "its cashpoints feed out notes so new and clean they rasp the hand like fine sandpaper" (Each banking firm has a distinct name for its automatic cash dispensing system: Lloyds Bank, *Cashpoint,* perhaps the origin of the generic use in the last citations; Barclays Bank, *Express Till;* Midland Bank, *AutoBank;* National Westminster Bank, *Servicetill;* Royal Bank of Scotland, *Auto Teller.* In addition, *cashpoint* is also found in the US: *Cash Points* is a registered trade mark for the banking machines used by the Duke University Credit Union and doubltess by other credit unions around the US.) **2.** Cash register desk 1986 Sep sign at the checkout counter of a discount store, London "Cash Point" (This sense is recorded in *Chambers*; it is listed here because of its relationship to sense 1, it being unclear which has priority.)

Domestos *n* Trade name for a bleach or disinfectant used to clean toilets and sinks 1986 Aug 29 Newcastle *Evening Chronicle* 1/4 "A Tyneside shopkeeper had Domestos squirted into his face and was hit with a baseball bat when he was attacked by two masked and armed raiders."

dumpy *n* 1987 Mar 2 *London Evening Standard* 24/3 "First identified in America, Yuppy stands for Young Upwardly Mobile Professional. The Dumpy is a Downwardly, or Doubtfully, Mobile Professional (as an acronym this is, like Yuppy, something of a three-legged mule but it suits. And it is British). . . . Dumpies expect life to be a long trudge up the down escalator. One should strive but not to unseemly excess. Work is something one does between weekends." (stunt word)

Euro-banker *n* 1987 Mar 25 *London Evening Standard* 44/2 "Euro-bankers are agreed: there is still a great deal of mileage to be gained from the Euro-sterling convertible market, writes Joanna Hart."

Euro-bomb *n* 1986 Sep 23 *Guardian* 16/1 "'He said I believed in a Euro-bomb, and of course I don't,' Ashdown told me."

Euroconvertible *adj* 1986 Dec 10 *Times* 21/1 "He added that the Euroconvertible issue was the most cost effective way." 1987 Mar 25 *London Evening Standard* 44/2 "But the Euro-convertible market yields a very different story."

Eurodefence *n* 1987 Mar 22 *Sunday Times* 16/7 "Eurodefence shift. The EEC Commission's efforts to call a Euro-summit to discuss the zero-option missile deal seems unlikely to succeed."

Euro event *n* 1987 Mar *Camden Magazine* (London) 14/1 "As usual, among its 70 odd events, there are some real oddities—the fashionable French dance company Astrakhan, for example, whose new work *Waterproof* will be performed *in* the Swiss Cottage swimming pool on 2 and 3 of April. With music by cult Berlin group Einsturzende Neubaten, it will be a real Euro event."

Euro-summit *n* For citation see EURODEFENCE

Euro terrorist *n* 1987 Mar 24 *London Evening Standard* 7/2 "When the Euro terrorists announced two years ago that they had set up an international consortium to wage a 'Western European Revolutionary offensive' against the 'multi-national structure of NATO' old hands in the business of fighting terrorism tended to scoff."

Eurotunnel *n* 1986 Sep 23 *Guardian* 24/6 "The delayed £200 million issue of shares in Eurotunnel, the Anglo-French group chosen to build a Channel rail tunnel, is expected to start by the end of this week." Oct 28 *Times* 21/5 "Sir Nigel Broackes, chairman of Trafalgar House, is to join the board of Eurotunnel as a non-executive director if the Anglo-French consortium's £206 million international share placing is successfully completed by the deadline of 2 pm tomorrow." Dec 10 *Times* 20/1 "Officials of Eurotunnel, the Anglo-French consortium which is managing the plan for a 31-mile rail tunnel beneath the Channel, said yesterday that Morgan Grenfell, which has played a leading part in arranging finance for the tunnel so far, would stay with the group in a reduced role." (The name of the company formed to build a tunnel under the English Channel, connecting England and France, the term is also used for the tunnel itself, supplementing such earlier terms as *chunnel.*)

fast-forward *v* **1:** Move rapidly forward on a video-recorder tape 1987 Mar 12 *London Evening Standard* 21/1-2 "Time was when my greatest delight as a video-owner was to fast-forward through the commercials to watch the recorded programme without interruption. Nowadays I am hitting the fast-forward button through the programmes and stopping for the commercials." **2.** Move rapidly forward in time 1986 Oct 12 *Sunday Times* 64/7 (précis of the TV program based on Jeffrey Archer's *First among Equals*) "Fast-forwarding through the years, the fortunes of the famous four MPs rise and fall with clapometer rapidity." (from the fast-forward button on an audio or video player)

fattypuff *n* 1968 André Maurois *Fattypuffs and Thinifers* trans Norman Denny from *Patapoufs et Filifers* (Bodley Head) 1972 Anthony Price *Colonel Butler's Wolf* (London: Futura Book, Macdonald & Co, 1983), 92 "That's kind of you but golly—nothing to eat here. I'm much too much of a fattypuff to dare to eat stodge [heavy, starchy food] at lunch-time." 1984 Anthony Price *Sion Crossing* (London: Gollancz), 94–96 "'But I do have a rather miserable life. Always having to say "no" to steamed pudding seems to sharpen my tongue. So I'm not very popular with my subordinates.' He sighed. 'And they still call me "Fatso" behind my back.' 'But that's not fair!' Her eyes clouded. 'You're just . . . comfortably plump, Oliver.' She eyed him critically. 'Besides, you shouldn't take any notice of it. If you're not a *Filifer,* then so much the better for you—being a *Filifer* is no fun, anyway.' She smiled at him. 'If you're a *Patapouf*—then *be* a happy *Patapouf*—.' . . . Physically she was, of course, a perfect Thinifer—a sharp spaghetti-girl, of spires and minarets and flagpoles. But she lacked the Thinifer's intolerance. . . . It was after all a children's book, the story of the Great War between the Fat and the Thin, with its happy ending. . . . Latimer quailed for a moment. . . . He felt himself unquailing: as André Maurois had demonstrated, the Fattypuffs were easy to defeat, but utterly unconquerable."

fax *n pl* Facts 1987 Mar 6 *London Evening Standard* 25/1-2 "FOOD FAX" (heading to a list of restaurants with comments) Idem 27/4 "FILET 'O' FAX" (label on a McDonalds food container in a cartoon) Idem 43/5 "Fax of life" (heading to a letter to ed about FILOFAX) (spelling pun on *facts* echoing FILOFAX, ie "file of facts"; an early instance of the form is in *Ceefax,* ie "see facts," a BBC service broadcasting information such as stock market returns on a subscription channel)

Filofax *n* Trade name of a PERSONAL ORGANISER 1986 Oct 9 *Times* 16/6 "Diary entries. The Super-efficient person does not have a diary [appointment book] but a Filofax (if antiquarian by bent) or tiny computer (if modernistic)." 1987 Mar 5 *Midweek* 5/1–2 "Yuppie status symbols like Amstrads [a brand of personal computer] and Filofaxes are another case in point. People sneer at them because they are so *demode,* then go out and buy counterfeit products as soon as there's money in the bank. 'But mine's not a Filofax,' they argue, 'it's a Harper House Personal Planner. I'd hate to be one of the Filofax Brigade.'" Mar 6 *London Evening Standard* 22/5–6 "Within 10 years, say Wang, international business deals will be done from electronic briefcases containing portable telephones and the capacity to transmit images—the Filofax of the 90s and probably half as heavy." Idem 43/5 "My son is definitely a Yuppy but his idea of a Filofax is 'something my mother had when I was a little boy.' [¶] Come on, media! Filofaxes have been around for years. Where have you been?" See also citation under APPOINTMENTS DIARY

golden *adj* Pertaining to a large financial benefit given to an employee on association with or severance from a business in order to protect the interests of either the employee or the business; used in combination with a metaphorical noun **—golden goodbye** 1986 Oct 5 *Sunday Times Magazine* 43/1–2 "Those excluded from the bonanza, or dissatisfied with their share, promptly voted with their feet and sought greener pastures elsewhere. A whole new vocabulary of 'golden hellos', 'golden shackles' and 'golden goodbyes' had to be developed to describe the incentives devised to hold them, or to get them on the move." **—golden handcuff** 1986 Oct 9 *Times* 33/2 "The other problem is that they may be so locked into 'golden handcuffs'—cheap company loans or mortgages—that they hardly dare to move." (in *Longman Guardian New Words;* cf *AS* 58: 176–77) **—golden handshake** 1984 Kate Alexander *Paths of Peace* (NY: St Martin's) 217 "'No doubt something civilized could be arranged. You would be allowed to resign, there'd be a golden handshake for you.' 'And I'd be out of work—now, when the whole industry is in a state of flux!'" 1986 Aug 29 Newcastle *Evening Chronicle* 11/1 "Miss Monk wants the scheme . . . to direct its efforts to longer periods of retraining and see that there is more money available for training and less for 'golden handshakes.'" 1986 Oct 9 *Times* 33/1 "Further calculation may include the possibility of a takeover and the golden handshakes that usually result when the successful bidder brings on his own team." (widely recorded in dictionaries and doubtless the model on which the other expressions were formed) **—golden hello** 1986 Oct 18 *Times* 1/6 (reference to preparation for the Big Bang) "By the end of the rehearsal, firms will know whether the effort, the massive investment in equipment and the 'golden hello' transfer fees, sometimes running into seven figures, have given them a team ready for the real battle." 1987 Mar 2 *London Daily News* 3/1–3 "Town halls in London are offering cash bonuses—called 'golden hellos'—to attract more professional staff. . . . One of the pioneers of the municipal 'golden hellos'—a phrase first used in the US—is Hastings Council in East Sussex which recently advertised for a group accountant offering a £3,000 one-off payment." (in *Longman Guardian New Words*; cf *AS* 58: 176–77) **—golden parachute** 1986 Oct 9 *Times* 33/1 "In the United States one of the classic defences against takeovers is the 'golden parachute' whereby existing board memberes vote themselves huge severance terms. In Britain the scope for this is limited." (in *Longman Guardian New Words*; cf *AS* 58: 176–77) **—golden shackle** See GOLDEN GOODBYE **—golden welcoming shake** 1986 Oct 26 *Sunday Times* 48/7 "But for those who have received the notorious golden welcoming shakes, the pressure to perform will be enormous; and, save for the naturally ascetic, there can be a seductive pleasure." (reference to brokers paid large salaries to go to new firms in preparation for the Big Bang in the London stock market)

granny-bashing *n* **1:** Violent mistreatment of the elderly 1987 Mar 16 *London Evening Standard* 31/3 "Perhaps, given our unenviable record on child abuse and granny-bashing, with recent cases of pensioners murdered in their own homes, Spanish tourists might do well to boycott British holidays." **2:** Visiting old people as a form of community service to help them with shopping and odd jobs or merely to entertain them 1986 Oct 7 *Times* 14/5 "The Combined Cadet Force is no longer compulsory at most schools we visited. . . . Non-CCFers—and increasingly one and all—do afternoons of 'granny bashing', an apt description of school community welfare services."

guppy *n* **1:** 1986 Oct 12 *Sunday Times* 48/1 "Yuppie is the marketing acronym for young urban professional used in America to describe the getting and spending generation that emerged ambitious and unconfused in the late 1970s. Subsequently the categorisation was refined to include the guppy (gay urban professional) and the bluppy (black urban professional)." **2:** 1987 Mar 12 *London Evening Standard* 21/1 "Aimed smack dab at the people with the greatest spending power—the Guppies (Greedy Upwardly Mobile etc., etc.)—commercials are custom-built to impress and encourage their victims to wear the right clothes and listen to the right stereo in the right car they have bought from the right bank." (*Longman Guardian New Words* enters a different sense for *guppie* 'ecological-minded yuppie' [*Green* + *yuppie*]. In all senses it is a stunt word.)

hush puppy *n* 1986 Aug 21 *Hampstead Advertiser* 18/3 "The gentle sound of hush puppies being forced into open mouths as some of the more ironically minded of the audience decide that to chortle would upset the enjoyment of others—and then. Then it happened. The first full throated guffaw." (*Hush Puppy* is an Americanism known in Britain as the name of a brand of shoes. In this citation the term is used generically for feet or fashionable shoes, as part of a metaphor in which inappropriate laughter is stifled by putting one's foot into one's mouth. The choice of *hush puppies* is a covert judgment on the audience as either middle class, middle-aged, and tweedy, or as yuppy-like, according to various consultants. The original Southern American sense of the term as 'small cornmeal fritters', supposedly so called because thrown to dogs to keep them quiet, is unknown in Britain.)

Lilt *n* 1986 Oct 30 *Times* 18/3 "I declined a mug of vodka and Lilt." (trade name for a grapefruit and pineapple flavored carbonated beverage advertised as having "the totally tropical taste")

personal organiser *n* Notebook holding printed forms for organizing one's appointments, activities, and personal information 1987 Feb 22 *Sunday Telegraph* 21/6 "to contain the many and varied components of the work-hard-play-hard Yuppy lifestyle came the personal organiser—the Filofax. . . . that leather-bound status symbol got all your data into one place, combining such vital information as diary, address book, job checklists, personal accounts and the cat's blood group." Mar Kaleidoscope mail order catalog from Barclaycard 29 "Personal Organiser With 2-Year Diary / Executive-style leather organiser with personal goal and project pages, planners, schedules, notes, lists, address book, index and file tabs, plus 2-year diary, held in place by six ring binders. Inside back cover has credit card pocket, business card and season ticket slots. 7 1/2″ × 5 3/4″ × 1 1/2″. Two gilt corner protectors. Personalised with up to 3 initials."

personal planner *n* PERSONAL ORGANISER 1987 Mar 23 *London Evening Standard* 9/5 "Like punks, they are the victims of marketing tyrants who have now disappeared over the horizon. Now their Bible, Filofax, is going public, and the fad is fading. Soon not even the Grand Canyon will be deep enough to hold the discarded and absurd 'personal planners' no sensible person ever needed."

sampy *n* 1987 Mar 4 *London Evening Standard* 33/4 "Throughout this week, the four television channels are devoting considerable coverage to the subject of AIDS. In particular, attention is being focused upon a type of person fast becoming known to the rest of the population as a SAMPY: a sexually active, multiple partnered youth." (stunt term)

thinifer *n* See FATTYPUFF

Time Manager *n* Trademark 1987 Feb 22 *Sunday Telegraph* 21/6 "Enter phase three in the evolution of the life-file—the Time Manager. Even more bulky than the most compleat Yuppy's Filofax (this won't ruin the hang of your suit because you can't even get it into your pocket), the Time Manager's aim is to take all the information you need for your job and for life-outside-work, and get it organised so you actually achieve results."

yumpo *n* 1987 Feb 1 *Mail on Sunday* 21 (cartoon title) "The Yumpos (Youngish Upwardly-Mobile Property Owners) by Merrily Harpur" (stunt term)

yuppiedom *n* 1987 Mar 23 *London Evening Standard* 24/2 "Conspicuous drugs, conspicuous investment: in the North of the manor, around Tower Bridge especially, the tentacles of yuppiedom are snaking down from the City and Big Bang."

yuppification *n* 1987 Mar 5 *London Evening Standard* 8/4 "As for architectural gems, well, 'there's the outside toilets.' [¶] Colin is scathing about the yuppification of the East End." (reference to proposed "EastEnders" package tours in the wake of the popularity of the BBC TV soap opera of that name; a play on *yuppy* and *gentrification,* both much in the news at this time)

yuppify *v* 1987 Mar 19 *London Evening Standard* 39/3–4 "Marked door keys are good underworld currency, it seems. The police advise anyone who moves into converted or renovated property in newly yuppified areas to change their locks immediately."

yuppily *adv* 1987 Apr 3 *London Evening Standard* 23/1–2 "The Access city guides, an American series, are elegantly slim, well-groomed and Yuppily expensive at £10.95."

yuppy-bashing *n* 1987 Mar 20 *London Evening Standard* 19/4–5 "He makes no secret of the fact that he believes in the yuppy-bashing campaign, although he maintains he takes no part in violent acts."

NOTE

For support during the preparation of the material in this series of "Among the New Words," the editor is grateful to the John Simon Guggenheim Memorial Foundation and the Fulbright Commission.

AMONG THE NEW WORDS

JOHN ALGEO

University of Georgia AND
University College London

With the assistance of the British New Words Committee: Sylvia Chalker, Thomas Lavelle, Sarah Lawson, Tom McArthur, René Quinault, and Oonagh Sayce, and the additional assistance of Adele Algeo, Sidney Greenbaum, and Robert Ilson.

THIS INSTALLMENT CONTINUES THE LISTING of British new words from the last two issues.

audioconferencing *n* See TELECONFERENCING (*audio conference* as n in *Collins*)

backlighting *n* 1987 Feb 16 *Daily Telegraph* 11/2 "Since LCDs work by reflected light, you need a good source of illumination for the image to be clear. Further, many machines' displays can only be read over a very narrow angle. Both these limit the usefulness of laptops. Apart from generally improving the contrast on LCDs the latest solution is backlighting. As its name suggests, this simply uses an internal lighting source behind the screen." (As a general or photographer's term, the verb *backlight* 'illuminate from the rear' has been used for a generation; the specialized computer use of the verbal noun is recent.)

bhangra *n* A style of music combining traditional Indian modes and a disco beat 1987 June 3 morning news BBC1 "The leading bhangra bands can now attract huge audiences at musical venues."

care assistant *n* 1986 Sep 30 *Guardian* 2/6 "Care assistants and link workers with language skills should be employed to bring the Health Service closer to ethnic minority communities." 1987 Mar 11 *London Evening Standard* 13/1 "From behind the prison bars on Malaysia's Death Row, Gregory has struck up a remarkable friendship with 40-year-old care assistant Marnie Bennett and housewife Elizabeth McDonald." (probably a variant of *care attendant,* which *Collins* defines as a social welfare term for "a person who is paid to look after one or more severely handicapped people by visiting them frequently and staying when needed, but who does not live in")

code play *n* Play with a covert meaning 1987 Feb 20 *Daily Telegraph* 16/2-3 "Edward Albee has claimed that 'Who's Afraid of Virginia Woolf?' contains an attempt to examine American revolutionary principles, hence the names George and Martha, as in the first president and his wife. Others have suggested that it is a code play, in which all the characters are really male homosexuals." (This use of *code* is an extension from that in *code word* as a political term for slogans like *law and order* as a covert expression of racism. It suggests the development of a new sense for the attributive use of *code*: 'having a covert meaning'.)

dampish *adj* (Of Conservative politicians) inclined not to be firm in supporting right-wing Conservative policies 1986 Oct 26 *Sunday Times* 26/6 "Government ministers of a dampish persuasion are having nightmares about what might face them if Margaret Thatcher wins a third term in Downing Street. They fear they will encounter Thatcherism unrestrained by any attempt to balance the ticket with the sort of judicious mix of wet and dry to be found in her cabinet."(This joking nonce term reflects the established terms *wet* 'liberal in the Conservative Party' and *dry* 'hardcore Conservative'. Partridge gives *damp* 'soft-headed, stupid, foolish' in late 19c and early 20c and *wet* 'tearfully sentimental; in politics, unrealistic, visionary'; *Reader's Digest Great Illustrated* gives the sense 'feeble, faint-hearted,' perhaps from *wet behind the ears,* as well as the political sense of *wet.* Those general pejorative senses of *wet* are in the background of the current political use, but it derives from Margaret Thatcher's administration, as does *dry* as an obvious antonym also reflecting such general senses as 'without warmth or tenderness' and 'dull, wearisome'.)

department *n* Department store 1986 Oct 26 *Sunday Times* 9/4 "With 'only' 51 shopping days left to Christmas, a Santa Claus war is already breaking out in Britain's departments. (*Department store* is originally an Americanism, but this shortening seems to be a British innovation.)

designated Saturday *n* Saturday reserved for particular soccer matches 1986 Sep 19 *Times* 31/6 "Harlequins, for instance, see the logical consequence of the present competition as a fully-blown league with designated Saturdays and fixtures made by an outside agency."

doorstep *n* Sandwich made with thick slices of bread 1986 Aug, sign over sandwiches on a lunch counter at Woolworths in London "Doorsteps" (The term refers primarily to the thick slice of bread, in which use it is long established.)

DRAM *n* 1986 Oct 28 *Times* 27/5 "Analysts said that minimum prices for 256K DRAMs, or dynamic random access memory chips, which now range from about $4 to $8, were lowered to a range of between $2.50 and $4."

draw in *v* Stop a vehicle by the side of the road; pull over 1986 Oct 14 *Times* 31/1 "Stepping into the road, the policeman signalled the lorry driver to draw in." (Britons judge the term to be well established; possibly a blend of *draw up* and *pull in,* influenced by the sense used of trains, 'arrive at a platform'.)

drink driving *n* Driving a vehicle under the influence of alcohol; drunk driving 1986 Aug 20 *Daily Mirror* 7/3 "He booked her for drink driving—but magistrates cleared her yesterday because they weren't sure the mower was legally a road vehicle." Sep 22 *Times* 3/8 "Dennis Waterman, of the TV series, *Minder,* is to appear before Dorking magistrates in Surrey on November 20 accused of a drink-driving offence." (One consultant suggested a semantic distinction between *drink driving* as 'driving after having consumed an illegal quantity of alcohol, as measured by a breathalyzer' and *drunk driving* as 'driving in a noticeably drunken and dangerous way', the distinction being between a technological measurement and the observation of behavior. *Drink driving* is entered in the Australian *Macquarie Dictionary,* rev. ed. Arthur Delbridge [Dee Why, NSW: Macquarie Library, 1985].)

duck, break one's *v ph* Do a thing for the first time 1986 Aug 25 *Times* 11/1 (editorial) "Last week, a widowed lady 109 years old flew in an aeroplane for the first time. She had clearly decided that, having waited so long to break her duck, she ought to do it in style." (a generalization of the sense 'score one's first run in a game, especially cricket', with *duck* 'score of zero' from *duck's egg,* a metaphor for the shape of the numeral; an established expression for cricketers)

electronic meeting *n* Meeting of several persons by means of TELECONFERENCING 1986 Oct *Live-Net Newsletter* no 1 (Univ of London house organ) 3 ". . . the technical feasibility of electronic meetings does not guarantee that any of [the] possible benefits will become actual benefits."

excavationist *n* Archeological excavator 1986 Oct 28 *Times* 37/2 "This work, too is temporary and is usually carried out under pressure and against time, typifying the rather harsh conditions under which excavationists work." (The neologism serves to distinguish archeologists from construction workers and has the positive associations of *conservationist.*)

excursion class *n* Second class (on airplanes) (One of a number of euphemisms, such as *economy class* and *tourist class,* the latter favored by US airlines, the term echos such British expressions as *excursion fare/ticket* for off-hour travel at reduced rates.)

exhibition *attrib n* **1:** Model; serving as a typical or prime example of its type 1986 Aug 27 *Times* 16/3 "He said Wum was an exhibition village. 'The Government was rather proud of it and was inclined to show it off as an example of village life.' " **2:** Intended for demonstration or show rather than use 1987 Mar 6 *London Evening Standard* 46/2 "The process involved in erecting them [model houses], says John Attenborough of Wimpey's [house-building company,] is formidable. 'These are the real thing, fully habitable, not just exhibition models.' " (The reference in the second citation is to a house in a new development, which is exceptionally well built and furnished, serving as an advertisement of what the unbuilt houses are supposed to be. The implication of the citation, however, is that such houses are intended for demonstration rather than habitation, and so the use of the word *exhibition,* which was ameliorative, has become faintly pejorative.)

face square *n* Wash cloth 1986 Sep sign at John Lewis Department Store, Brent Cross Shopping Centre (synonym for *face cloth, face flannel*)

facility *n* Service, *spec* food service 1986 Aug 27 *Times* 3/5 "Although the full English breakfast is still largely available in most hotels which cater for businessmen, there appear to be surprisingly few London restaurants which offer the early morning facility." (The *OEDS* observes that the use of the term in the singular for "a specified amenity, service, etc." is originally US, but the use illustrated by this citation seems improbable in American. The term is currently voguish in English hotel and restaurant use, often with imprecise reference. One consultant observed that hotel rooms are sometimes offered "with facilities," which may represent either a bath and toilet or an electric kettle and packages of tea and instant coffee. Another consultant reported a sign from a pub, The East India Arms, on Fenchurch Street, reading "We have no facility for serving people in dirty clothing," in which the term is used as a bafflegab way of saying "We will not serve. . . .")

fanciable *adj* 1984 Sarah Caudwell *The Shortest Way to Hades* (New York: Penguin Books, 1986) 80 "Mind you, I don't say I mightn't have chatted her up a bit even if I hadn't had to—she was looking quite fanciable." (reported by one consultant to be well established colloquially; based on the British sense of the verb *fancy* 'be sexually attracted to', which is distinct from the common English sense 'want' as in "Do you fancy a game of squash?")

father (of a chapel) *n* Chairman of a printers' or journalists' local union 1986 Sep 10 *Times* 2/2 "Mr Clifford Longley, the father of *The Times* chapel of the National Union of Journalists, failed yesterday in his Court of Appeal attempt to prevent union disciplinary proceedings against him." Oct 20 *Times* 16/6 "The major problem—for managements and national union officials alike—was the Chapels (office branches); their power was absolute and their Fathers (chairmen) were baron-like." (*Reader's Digest Great Illustrated* has a combined sense "leader of a council, branch of a union, or similar organisation: *the city fathers, father of the chapel*"; whereas *city fathers* is a general and unspecific term typically used in the plural, *father of the chapel* refers to a specific office and therefore seems to merit separate treatment. Cf IMPERIAL FATHER.)

flag advertising *n* 1986 Oct 18 *Times* 4/2 "Solicitors will be able to put inserts in free newspapers and to join with other solicitors for 'flag' advertising under one logo or name." (perhaps a nautical allusion to ships sailing under the same flag, here a group of solicitors advertising under the same identification or heading)

flash *n* Piece of cloth sewn to a garment as an ornament, advertising, or identification 1986 Oct 16 *Midweek* published by *Ms London* 14/3 "I offer this information freely, of my own accord. I have not been paid a quarter of a million pounds fee, and I do not wear a Tesco's cat litter flash on my shorts." (extension of the British sense 'military shoulder patch')

footballing *adj* Resulting from or pertaining to football (ie, soccer) 1986 Aug 30 *Times* 8/1 "The latest tragic victim of a hitherto unknown footballing injury is Peter Whitehurst, who went down in agony when playing . . . in a pre-season friendly [a game not part of a competitive series] against Norwich City." Dec 10 *Times* 36/8 "Oxford, victors in the University rugby match at Twickenham yesterday, will today at Wembley seek their first footballing win over Cambridge for four years in the 103rd meeting between the clubs since the series began in 1874." (implied by *footballer* 'football player', as though from a verb; the *OED* verb *football* 'kick like a football, kick about with the feet' is not apposite)

fourth leader *n* Title of the third, and final, humorous editorial in the Saturday *Times* (eg) 1986 Sep 27 *Times* 9/1-3 (extension of the sense given by the *OEDS*: "from 1922 to 1966, the fourth leading article in *The Times*, usually of a light or humorous nature")

frame *n* Portable stand used by an incapacitated or handicapped person as an aid in walking; walker 1986 Oct 9 *Hampstead Advertiser* 23/3 "Now she has put away her dancing shoes for good . . . and she walks with a frame, but neighbours, friends and family all come to see her." (Two consultants report *walking frame* as a variant, and one *Zimmer*, a trademark according to the *Reader's Digest Great Illustrated.*)

gender struggle *n* Disagreement involving discrimination against a woman because of her sex 1986 Aug 27 *Times* 16/2 "A serious internal department matter which led to the suspension of Wendy Savage has been misrepresented as a gender struggle and a struggle between high technology and low technology, which is totally unrelated to this particular problem."

girly *adj* Pertaining to a group of women friends who meet frequently 1986 Oct 8 *Times* 15/1 "and on Sunday there was the usual girly lunch—just Annabel and Julia and all the regulars." (based on the noun *girl* 'woman of any age')

goulash communism *n* 1986 Oct 20 *Times* 21/2 (editorial) "Such relaxation can be welcomed on the commonsense grounds that it is better to be governed by a mild tyranny than by a cruel one. But the document both claims and exemplifies that 'goulash communism' has not succeeded in its principal aim of winning popular support for the satellite regimes [of Eastern Europe]." (established term, alluding to communism in Hungary; for the use of a food as a metonym for a country, compare *spaghetti western* 'cowboy film made in Italy')

hall *n* Place where sevices or commodities are sold; office, shop, department of a store—**booking hall** Office where reservations are made 1986 fall—**food hall** Grocery store or department 1986 "Classique Food Hall" (name of a grocery store on Baker Street) Aug 30 *Times* 8/4 "It was in the food hall [of Selfridges] that I caught sight of the pair again." Sep 17 *Times* 11/7 "For one thing, her presence in the competitor store was very unwelcome before contracts were signed, so for the past decade she has more or less confined her visits to the food halls." (This is a well-established use that is becoming even more common; several consultants cited the *food hall* at Harrods as a well-known example. Food halls are usually departments in a larger store, but the first citation shows the term used, doubtless for prestige sake, as part of the name of a shop.)

hazchem *n* Hazardous chemicals 1986 sign on the gate of the London School of Hygiene and Tropical Medicine "Warning Hazchem" (in common use on trucks and gates)

imperial father *n* 1986 Oct 20 *Times* 17/2 "The ballot form was set in metal but John Brown, Imperial Father of the composing room (head of all the Chapels combined) told the man putting the story into the page to stop work." (reportedly a title in the hierarchy of the National Graphical Association and the Society of Graphical and Allied Trades, NGA/SOGAT; cf FATHER (OF A CHAPEL)

infomercial *n* 1986 Oct 5 *Sunday Times* 47/2 "And the re-emergence of advertising magazines—now euphemistically known in the trade as 'infomercials'—are entirely acceptable to the Cable Authority." (Philip C. Kolin reported a similar US usage in *AS* 59 [1984]:379.)

instrument cowl *n* Frame and rim around the instrument panel of an automobile serving to protect it and shield it from external light 1986 Oct 30 *Times* 29/1 "Vehicle interiors are pretty well saturated with plastics, ranging from urethane foam with nylon upholstery for seating to instrument cowls, door handles, fascias, lock mechanisms and roof linings."

interior designed *pp* (Of a building's interior) with decorations and furnishings planned by an interior designer or decorator 1986 Oct 2 *Hampstead Advertiser* 40/2 (ad) "Style and luxury combine in this interior designed apartment in a prime residential location." Idem 40/6 (ad) "Tradition reigns with this majestic garden and ground floor family maisonette having been sympathetically modernised and lovingly interior designed." (*Interior design* and *interior designer* are listed as synonyms for *interior decoration* and *interior decorator* by several British dictionaries. The agent noun is doubtless the motive for the creation by backformation of the past participle from an underlying verb **to interior-design*.)

intervention *n* Comment or question following a speech 1986 Sep 5 *Times* 1/3 "But jobs provoked the most telling intervention when Mr. Laird, general secretary of the Amalgamated Engineering Union, warned Mr. Scargill and a future Labour government that they would fight any attempt to crush the industry." (common use at academic conferences, where contributions during the discussion period following a paper may be termed *interventions*; perhaps modeled on French use)

jam doughnut *n* Doughnut with a jam filling; jelly doughnut 1986 sign at the bakery counter of Waitrose Supermarket, Finchley Road (The usual variety of the food in England is a bun-shaped doughnut filled with jam or custard; hence the unmarked form *doughnut* refers to this, and the term *jam doughnut* seems mildly redundant. The torus-shaped doughnut, which is the norm in America, is also called a *dough ring* in England, according to one consultant. Definitions in British dictionaries typically try to cover both varieties and thus account for a nonexistent variety that is both filled and ring-shaped. Neither British nor American dictionaries define the full range of doughnut shapes, overlooking, for example, the twisted variety. The choice of the attributive *jam* in contrast to the American *jelly* is part of a general contrast: In American, typically *jelly* is made with fruit juice, whereas *jam* is made with the pulp of the fruit as well and is therefore thicker and less clear; in British, typically *jam* covers both those varieties, and *jelly* is a gelatin dessert, a jello.)

jet-lagged *adj* Affected or produced by jet lag 1978 Anthony Grey *The Chinese Assassin* (Pan Books, 1985) 13 " 'Forgive me, Moynahan, I'm jetlagged.' Scholefield switched on the light in the hall and closed the door quickly in the porter's leering face." Idem 55 "You'd know how self-sacrificial I'd been, coming back here last night and finding you in a jet-lagged coma." 1986 Sep 6 *Times* 16/5 "He said he was jet-lagged and tired, and there was much eye-rubbing and limb-stretching to emphasize the point." Oct 22 *Times* 21/2 "The scientists believe that the use of light therapy can help jet-lagged travellers adjust to new time zones." 1987 Mar 31 *Daily Telegraph* 14/6 "How did 'Mr Healey' and 'Mr Kinnock' actually know they were in the White House? After all, they must have been tired, flustered and jet-lagged." (an obvious form that has probably been in use for some time)

jitteringly *adv* 1986 Oct 30 *Times* 15/5 "At once a lament and a critique, these stories show the way SF is being rewired. Gibson, his finger jitteringly on the fast-forward button, shows the direction in which our literature might be headed." (probably a nonce form)

Kenya bean *n* A variety of thin string bean 1986 fall menu of Reform Club, London 1987 July advertising flier from Safeway grocery store, London "Information & Recipes for Kenya beans / A very young dwarf fine green bean which can be eaten raw or lightly cooked. . . . Fresh Kenya beans are a low fat, low energy (kilocalorie) vegetable rich in Vitamin C." (One consultant identifies this bean as an expensive import from Kenya and suggests *bobby bean*—another unrecorded term—as an analog.)

lagged *adj* Delayed 1986 Sep 12 *Guardian* 20/2 "Now, at last, it seems that the lagged effect of the oil shock earlier this year is taking hold, the economy is picking up and with it, demand for money." (This appears to be the past participle of the verb *lag*, but that verb is usually intransitive, so in this construction, the present participle *lagging* would be expected. The *OEDS* records a new transitive verb with the sense 'lag behind', but the past participle of that verb is not semantically appropriate in this citation: *effect* is the implied subject, not object of a verb *lag*. It appears that in this case, *lagged* is a derived adjective and not an inflected form of a verb.)

leaflet drop *n* Delivery of leaflets to the mail slot of houses 1986 Oct 27 *Times* 1/5 "Mr Newton indicated yesterday that senior ministers are pressing for a leaflet drop to every household rather than the television advertising campaign backed by most Aids specialists." (This use of *drop*, prominent during the educational campaign about the disease AIDS, may be an extension of the sense 'delivery of goods by parachute' recorded in the *Reader's Digest Great Illustrated* and a nominalization of the verbal senses 'send or post' and 'leave or deposit, especially at a specified place'. It is typical for mail, newspapers, advertising leaflets, etc to be "dropped" through a slot in or by the front door of English houses.)

leaving present *n* Present given to one who is leaving; goodby present 1986 Oct 9 *Marylebone Mercury* 1/7 "A Brazilian engineer was robbed of clothes and jewels worth £900 only four days before he returned home. His unpleasant leaving present happened when he left the window open in his room at the Stratford Court Hotel in Oxford Street." (Several consultants judge this to be a long-established use.)

legging suit *n* Knit pants and matching blouse 1986 Oct sign on a garment in a store window, London

link worker *n* Social worker who specializes in assisting disadvantaged foreigners having a poor command of English to cope with the complexities of British bureaucracy and customs 1986 Sep 30 *Guardian* 2/6 "Care assistants and link workers with language skills should be employed to bring the Health Service closer to ethnic minority communities."

lorry push *n* Stunt to raise money for charity by pushing a truck over a specified course 1986 Sep 12 *Daily Mirror* 3/1 "Jobless charity fund raisers have been warned they will lose their dole if they hold a six-week money-spinning event. Social Services say the group of 90 will not be paid because they won't be available for work during a lorry push from John O'Groats to Lands End." (One consultant observes that John O'Groats, in the extreme northeast of Scotland, and Land's End, in the extreme southwest of Cornwall, define the longest distance on mainland Britain and are therefore favorite termini for charity journeys, stunt trips by unusual modes of transportation, and bicycle tours, called *end to end* rides in cycling jargon.)

lurch *v* 1986 Oct 12 *Sunday Times* 48/7 "There is the Croydon Crusader for one. He comes with his shirt undone and possibly a gold chain round his neck. He will do a lot of sniffing and lurching (eyeing and chatting up women)." (Possibly a backformation from *lurcher* 'a crossbred hunting dog, especially one formerly used by poachers', as *Reader's Digest Great Illustrated* defines it, rather than a survival of the obsolete *lurch* 'lurk'. If so, the sense here is a metaphorical extension of 'hunt, poach', that is, 'attempt to attract, allure, seduce'.)

mailshot *n* Information campaign by mail, bulk mailing 1986 Aug 23 *Times* 23/1 "Some 4.2 million TSB customers were informed by a massive mailshot that they would be entitled to priority status in the sale of the bank on or about September 12." Oct 16 *Times* 1/3 "The mail shot, part of the publicity campaign by the Department of Health and Social Security, will offer explicit advice on safer sexual practices, warn against promiscuity and urge drug abusers not to share needles." (Several consultants say this has been around for several years and is increasing in its frequency of use.)

main *n* Main course 1986 Sep 12 *Guardian* 18/4 "Choice extends to three starters, mains and desserts."

masculist *n* 1986 Oct 17 *Times* 12/4 "There is a real danger that the profusion of the Hollywood brat stars will rouse a Masculist movement in protest at the concomitant exploitation of the young male as sex object." (*Chambers* has *masculinist* "an advocate of men's rights or privileges . . . coined on the analogy of *feminist*"; the form illustrated here is a closer formal analog.)

mega *adj* Big, important 1986 Aug 27 *Daily Mirror* 14/2 " 'Mandy is going to be really mega,' he says in his Americanised Scottish accent. Mega is Keith's favourite word." (*Mega-* as a combining form in several senses relating to 'large, long' has been voguish for some while and is entered in most dictionaries. An example of that established use is 1986 Aug 29 Newcastle *Evening Chronicle* 10/7 "It's a perfect mega-read for the beach, guaranteed to keep you happy for the whole fortnight." However, the main entry here shows the form in free word use and with an extended meaning.)

milk round [from a milkman's route] **1:** *n* Recruitment of college graduates by industry 1986 Sep 29 *Times* 23/3 "I have, of course, to consider my own suitability for a career in advertising; . . . but graduate entry into advertising is largely confined to the milk round which starts in December, so I have now to make the choice—teaching or advertising?" (*Collins* enters this sense as a modifier as in *milk-round recruitment*; Partridge dates the use since ca 1960 and defines it as a noun but exemplifies the term only in attributive use.) **2:** *v* with *up* (from *round up*) Recruit for employment in industry 1986 Oct 14 *Times* 28/1 "Young graduates, milk-rounded up by one of the major computer companies, are often led to believe that there is a job for life."

mimstud *n* 1986 Oct 19 *Sunday Times* 29/1 "Well, I've identified a new social group, too. They're the Mimstuds or middle-aged male stick-in-the muds. These little-known chaps wear the same old pinstripe suits they have worn for 30 years, drink the same old Wadworth 6X out of pint jugs in the same old pubs, believe there has been no worthwhile poetry since MacNeice and are said to be impossible to buy presents for." (stunt word)

narrow band *n* 1986 Oct 20 *Times* 27/1 "We have now entered into a world of 'narrow banded' exchange rates. Since early July, in the case of the yen and the Swiss franc and since early August, in the case of the mark, these major currencies have been held in a 'narrow band' of fluctuation with the dollar. . . . Meanwhile the effect of 'narrow banding' is to encourage foreigners to continue to expand their investments in the US, something that has the effect of keeping the dollar up—and keeping the trade deficit up." **—narrow banded** *adj* Citation above **—narrow banding** *n* Citation above and 1986 Oct 27 *Times* 21/3 "Contributing to this failure of the devaluation to work has been the co-operation of the New York Fed with the central banks of Japan, West Germany and Switzerland in 'narrow banding', the relationship between the dollar and their currencies. This has effectively frozen relative currency values at about their July-August levels."

netback pricing *n* 1986 Sep 22 *Times* 18/2 "The widespread use of netback pricing means the market has to rely on the Brent spot price to chart the movements of internationally traded crude. . . . Netback pricing means calculating the price of a cargo of crude oil with reference to the value of products made from it."

outhouse *vt* 1986 Sep 15 *Times* 13/4 (letter to ed) "Indeed the plans for a new library at St Pancras perpetuate the principle of fragmentation: the newspaper library will remain at Colindale, and large sections of printed material are to be outhoused in a separate depository in Islington."

over-jacket *n* 1986 Oct 17 *Times* 5/7 "Sussex police meanwhile laid on a massive force of 300 officers, many in luminous over-jackets, to stop every car on the road and ask the drivers if they had seen anything a week before." (The *OED* illustrates the term sv *over-* by an 1895 citation: "the elaborate over-jacket of the Louis XV period"; the use above is specifically to a vest-like garment worn to increase the wearer's visibility on a highway.)

page three **1:** *n* Third page of a tabloid newspaper, containing a large photograph of an unclothed young woman 1986 Sep 18 *Hampstead Advertiser* 4/3-4 "Page Three Girls—do they incite attacks on women, or are the topless tabloids just 'harmless fun'? . . . This is one of the women who breathes in and smiles for the bare-breasted photos which many consume as part of their British breakfast—a cup of tea, toast and Page Three." Sep 22 *Times* 12/6 "I'm not saying he's illiterate exactly, but he finds page 3 of the *Sun* very heavy going." **2:** *attrib* Appearing nude or seminude on the third page of a tabloid 1986 Aug 14 *Hampstead Advertiser* 6/3 "Page three girls seem to have come in for a lot more blame than they should deserve. . . . The fact is the girls who take their clothes off for the newspaper reading public do so not to degrade their so-called sisters, nor to incite men to rape them. They take their clothes off for the Nikon's lens purely and simply to make money." Sep 18 *Hampstead Advertiser* 4/4 "Pictured in The Sun almost continuously for two years she became a Page Three favourite and as a result can rarely walk out of her house without being hooted at." Oct 5 *Sunday Times Magazine* 58/1 "You often see Samantha Fox and Page Three girls wearing Jane's things when they're dressed up." **3:** *attrib* Beautiful, young, and like a pin-up girl 1985 Anthony Price *Here Be Monsters* (London: Grafton Books, 1986) 58 "And Del Andrew would always have told her the truth, the straight unvarnished truth: the bonus of Del's preference for pretty Page Three girls was that he treated Plain Janes (and even plainer Elizabeth) as *mates*, and not *playmates*, with no bourgeois sexual hang-ups."

playaholic *n* 1986 Oct 11 *Times* 39/6-8 (headline) "Davies the 'playaholic' falls foul of the invisible injury" (another of the numerous *-holic* terms radiating from *workaholic*)

teleconferencing *n* Meeting conducted by telephone 1986 Oct *Live-Net Newsletter* no 1 (Univ of London house organ) 3 "There has been a good deal of research and development on these matters. Most of it has been in the context of using teleconferencing for business meetings. . . . Research on teleconferencing so far has distinguished between 'audioconferencing' (in which more than two people are connected by telephone for an 'electronic meeting'); 'videoconferencing' (in which there are accompanying television pictures) and 'computer conferencing' (where written messages are typed in by participants and then stored and distributed to the others by means of a computer system)."

Note

For support during the preparation of the material in this series of "Among the New Words," the editor is grateful to the John Simon Guggenheim Memorial Foundation and the Fulbright Commission.

AMONG THE NEW WORDS

JOHN ALGEO

University of Georgia AND
University College London

With the assistance of the British New Words Committee:
Sylvia Chalker, Thomas Lavelle, Sarah Lawson,
Tom McArthur, René Quinault, and Oonagh Sayce,
and the additional assistance of Adele Algeo,
Ronald R. Butters, Sidney Greenbaum, and Robert Ilson

THIS FOURTH INSTALLMENT CONCLUDES the current series of British new words. The next installment of "Among the New Words" will return to our usual editorial practice of listing new words generally, with special attention to American sources.

The treatment of formatives like *-speak* and *-wise* is a problem. If the words produced by the formative are semantically transparent, so that their meaning can be predicted from those of the base of the word and the formative, the simplest lexicographical treatment is to enter the formative with a definition and a list of common, undefined formations containing it. The entries for *chestwise* and *socialwise* under *-wise* below are of that type. If, however, the words derived from the formative are semantically opaque, they must be defined independently. Of the latter type, *-speak* and its formations are examples. That formative is given an entry in several dictionaries (*OEDS*, *Reader's Digest Great Illustrated*, and *Collins Cobuild*) and illustrated by undefined formations. However, the meanings of words like *childspeak*, *Haigspeak*, and *Metspeak* (entered under *-speak* below) are not inferable from their parts. These words should be defined independently in a dictionary.

actorishness *n* 1987 Jun 8 *Daily Telegraph* 14/4 "In the final shot of this film, dancing in his own garden, with self-deflationary actorishness, defying sentimentality Olivier (and Patrick Garland) succeeded in bringing a lump to the throat."

fax *n pl* (additional citation for entry in *AS* Winter 1987) 1987 Jun 3 *Sun* 9/1 "Oddfax" (title of a cartoon featuring information such as "One of Queen Victoria's wedding presents was a 10 ft high wedge of cheese weighing half a ton")

hold-up *n* Hose with elasticized tops worn without garters or garter belt 1987 Jun 12 *London Evening Standard* 21/3 "However much hosiery manufacturers extol their virtue as the best things since Marilyn Monroe stood over the subway for boosting sales, hold-ups are still something of a conundrum to most women. [¶] The puzzle is: if hold-ups are going to stay up without wrinkling, then how can they without gripping you tightly and uncomfortably around the thigh? [¶] In a survey recently carried out by the trade newspaper, *Fashion Weekly*, nine separate brands of hold-ups were tested by women of varying heights, thigh sizes and life-styles." (One consultant reports as a synonym *stay-puts*.)

lustable *adj* 1987 Jun 8 *Daily Telegraph* 6/6 "Since Mr Archer became one of *Elle* magazine's 20 most lustable young men in Britain, more blondes press close to him with shy yearning smiles than can have touched Mr Nigel Lawson in a lifetime." (Several consultants cited *lust-afterable* or *lustable-after* as more expected forms.)

magicienne *n* 1986 Aug 21 *Hampstead Advertiser* 18/1 "Fay Presto is a talented, off beat magicienne. It was her show." (French loanword that goes against the vogue for sexually neutral vocabulary, cf PLOUGHPERSON's. The term is entered in the *OED* but labeled "Obs. rare" and has only one citation, from 1490; this is therefore certainly a new borrowing, part of the continuing French influence on British English.)

meach *v* 1986 Oct 19 *Sunday Times* 26/2 "A new verb has been coined by members of the cabinet: to meach. It's an acronym for 'makes extravagant additional commitments hourly.' You add 'er' for 'enrages Roy'." (stunt word that consultants explain as an allusion to Michael Meacher, left-wing Labour spokesman for Social Services, who tended to make commitments to increase benefits such as pensions and child support, and a reference to Roy Hattersley, right-wing Labour spokesman for the Exchequer, who would balance the budget)

noggie *n* 1986 Sept 30 *Guardian* 5/1 "Beside them lay Michael Frayn's mess bills . . . and the discharge papers of an unnostalgic 'noggie,' Mgr Bruce Kent." (perhaps 'draftee, conscript'; see next entry)

nogging *n* 1986 Sept 30 *Guardian* 5/1 "Mr John Biffen's army shorts, which would make a passable tent for a Conservative garden party, went on display yesterday at an exhibition about fizzers, skiving, and bull. Twelve years of 'nogging'—the call-up and National Service—are recalled at the Imperial War Museum in London with the help of Mr Biffen's bags."

nose *n* **—have a nose at** Poke one's nose into the business of; watch, observe, spy on TV play, fall 1986 "You're just upset because we didn't have a good nose at the new people."

off-the-ball *n* 1986 Sep 2 *Times* 1/3 "Mr Patrick Harrington, for the prosecution, told the court that Bishop had trapped Jarman on the ground in an off-the-ball incident and hit him with a single blow." (A consultant identifies this as a football, i.e. soccer, term, in full *off the ball foul*, that is, rough handling of one player by another while the referee's attention is on the ball. Fans and players understand such fouls to be vindictive, frequently revenge for some earlier encounter between the two players.)

paper curtain *n* 1986 Aug 21 *Guardian* 1/7 "The effect of this development is that journalists in South Africa can, for the first time since the declaration of the state of emergency on June 12, explain some of the cryptic references which have been appearing in overseas reports as to what has been happening behind the 'paper curtain' thrown up across the country by the emergency regulations." (An extension of *iron curtain* and *bamboo curtain*, with reference to blocking communication by censorship. The *OEDS* notes the existence of a variety of such terms sv *curtain*.)

pedestal booth *n* Public telephone on a post, partially enclosed in a transparent apwrap-around 1986 Aug 29 Newcastle *Evening Chronicle* 12/4–5 "They are to be replaced by the pedestal booth type which is the one used in areas of high vandalism."

perchery *n* 1986 Aug 28 *Hampstead Advertiser* 16/3 "There was a time when an egg was an egg. These days it can be . . . free range or perchery—the choice is bewildering." (A consultant observes that perchery or barn eggs are from hens kept 25 to a square meter of floor space in an indoor shed or barn; each bird must have at least 15 cm perching space. Battery hens are kept in stacked cages; free-range eggs are from hens that have all-day access to open air runs, one hen to every 10 square meters; semi-intensive eggs also come from hens with all-day access to open-air runs, but each hen has only 2.5 square meters.)

PET *n attrib* 1986 Oct 30 *Times* 31/1 "The UK, by contrast, saw the boom in the PET bottle for carbonated drinks, following its big success in the US. In just a few years the market for bottles made from PET, or polyethylene terephthalate to give it its correct designation, has grown to 700 million in the UK."

physia *n* Physiotherapist 1987 Jun 10 *London Evening Standard* 56/1-2 "Stefan had a groin injury that had been hanging around even after we had been to our normal physia and with a heavy programme looming we were getting worried. [¶] But just before the start of the French Open we were in the locker room at Roland Garros and the physia there mentioned he would not mind looking at Stefan's injury." (*OEDS, Chambers, Collins Cobuild* all enter *physio* in this sense with a final full-vowel pronunciation /o:/; this unrecorded spelling suggests a final schwa. Consultants were inclined to think this might be a misprint despite the double occurrence.)

pin **1:** *n* 1986 Sept 27 *Times* 9/5 (letter to ed) "What will happen to all the pins removed from the cheques attached to the TSB application forms?" **2:** *vt* 1986 fall sign in the office of London Electricity, Finchley Road "Avoid queuing / Customers not requiring a receipt should pin their cheque to the payment counterfoil and post here." (These senses of *pin* derive from the use of a straight pin to attach pieces of paper to each other. The contexts, however, imply nothing more than 'fastener' and 'fasten.')

plexipave *n* Kind of surface for a tennis court 1986 Oct 20 *Times* 38/5 "What was significant about yesterday's victory was that it came on plexipave, a hard court surface that particularly suits Lendl's game."

ploughperson's *n* Ploughman's lunch; cheese, bread and butter, pickles, and crudités 1986 Oct 13 *Times* 14/1 "Lunch sign outside the King's Head pub, Islington: 'Vegetables and Cheese Sauce, £2.00; Assorted Ploughperson's, £1.10'." (Several consultants remarked that it is what one would expect of Islington.)

porky pie *n* [rhyming slang] Lie 1986 Oct 11 *Times* 3/8 "In a statement the man allegedly said: 'I have been telling porky-pies.' He then admitted bursting into a house in Stockwell with two others and raping the girl, aged 24, a secretary, at knife point during rioting in September last year."

positively vet *v* Check a person's suitability for security clearance 1986 Oct 30 *Times* 5/2 "No one can be employed on work of this nature unless he or she has been positively vetted (PV). Though PV is a vital security safeguard, it has always been recognized that it cannot be regarded as a guarantee of trustworthiness." (Reference to young British service personnel assigned to duty on Cyprus. *Collins* enters *positive vetting* as 'security clearance,' and *vet* has the general British sense of 'examine, inspect, review, check.' One consultant suggests the motive behind the *positively* is to distinguish this term for choosing persons with unambiguously loyal sympathies from simple *vet* with a negative sense of 'exclude.')

punkette *n attrib* 1986 Aug 23 *Daily Mirror* 6/5 "Actress Tricia Ronane and pal Gabriella Palmano put on punkette style. Belts, buckles, straps."

pupil; pupil barrister *n* 1986 Oct 14 *Times* 2/4 (headline and article) "Ex-pupil sues chairman over child payment / Mr David Cocks, QC, acting chairman of the Criminal Bar Association, is being taken to court by his former pupil barrister over alleged arrears in maintenance payments for their child." (*Collins* and other recent dictionaries enter the related *pupillage* "period spent by a newly called barrister in the chambers of a member of the bar," a sense not in the *OED/S*. It is not clear whether the uses are new, or whether the *OED/S* thought them accounted for by the general senses of *pupil* and *pupillage*.)

PV **1:** *n* Positive vetting **2:** *part* Positively vetted (citation under POSITIVELY VET)

rah-rah accent *n* Upper-class speech, with associations of the hunting crowd 1983 Kenneth Hudson *Language of the Teenage Revolution* (London: Macmillan) 8 "Girls who arrive with a 'rah-rah' accent are teased into toning it down."

Roller *n* Rolls Royce automobile 1986 Aug 23 *Daily Mirror* 4/4 "It's the Roller that belonged to the King of Rock [Elvis Presley]." (Partridge enters as since ca 1950, an instance of the suffix found also in *rugger* 'rugby,' *champers* 'champagne,' and *fiver* 'five-pound note.')

salad sandwich *n* Sandwich made with salad ingredients: lettuce, tomato, cucumbers, onion, and "salad cream"—a thick mayonnaise dressing 1986 fall menu Woolworth, London (a frequent term)

sandwich junction *n* 1986 Oct 18 *Times* 20/4–6 (picture caption) "Bridge work: The sandwich junction linking the M25 and M1, showing, from the top, a slip road, a footbridge, the M1 flyover, a second slip road and the M25 itself." (Road intersections like the American cloverleaf are rare in Britain, where the normal intersection is on one plane with a traffic circle or roundabout connecting the roads.)

sanitary dressing *n* Sanitary napkin 1986 fall sign on disposal trash can in the women's toilet at the Barbican Centre, London "Ladies / This unit is for the hygienic disposal of sanitary dressings ONLY and will be serviced at regular intervals by SOUTHALLS personnel." (The usual British term is *sanitary towel*; other informal and in some cases vulgar terms reported by a consultant are *ST, pad, bunny, rag, mattress,* and *hammock plug*.)

self-standing *adj* Independent, self-contained, capable of being used alone 1987 John Sinclair *Collins Cobuild English Language Dictionary* (London: Collins) xvi "The main entries are self-standing and it is never necessary to consult the Extra Column for everyday purposes." (One consultant reports the term as used of furniture such as shelves and cupboards that do not require anchoring to a wall.)

send-in *n* 1987 Jun 7 *Sunday Telegraph* 19/1–2 "Connoisseurs squirm at the Royal Academy Summer Exhibition. . . . That . . . makes for horrendous problems in hanging the 1,320 works selected from a send-in of 13,570." (*Chambers* has a verb *send in* 'submit (an entry) for a competition.')

shadow *n attrib* **1:** Unreported, unrecorded 1986 Oct 17 *Times* 21/3–4 "But there is, says Mr Stephen Smith, senior research officer with the IFS [Institute for Fiscal Studies], a wider shadow economy, including do-it-yourself work, the work done by housewives and so on. This shadow economy does not involve normally taxable activities but it may mean that the size of the economy, as measured by the official statistics, is understated." (suggestive of *black economy,* based on *black market*) **2:** 1986 Oct 2 *Hampstead Advertiser* 1/1 "She stressed that the hospital would be fully functional under a 'shadow management' during an occupation. 'If there are patients in the wards, the nurses will look after them.' " (*OEDS* includes the sense "Designating organizations, structures, etc., built or instituted to substitute for or duplicate those existing in an emergency or to fulfil special needs, esp. before and during the war of 1939–45" with citations from 1936–46 and one from 1980 with ref to World War II. The second citation seems to be a similar sense in current use. A synonym for the phrase would be *skeleton staff*. Both senses echo the British use of *shadow* as in *shadow cabinet*.)

shriek alarm *n* 1986 Aug 25 *Times* 9/6 "We may buy 'shriek alarms' (Banham's sold out the other week) but we do not want pity or protection, beyond what a routinely decent society should give all citizens." (identified by one consultant as a compressed-air canister carried by women as a defense against mugging or rape)

skirting socket *n* 1986 Sep 27 *Times* 14/2 "Wall lights and skirting sockets are also available and can be wired into existing houses or at the building stage." (*Skirting [board]* is the American 'baseboard.' Consultants responded variously in identifying this term, locating the socket in, on, or just above the baseboard, and contrasting it with a *wall socket* located higher on the wall, or denying that such contrast exists. The diversity of response suggests that the term is technical jargon rather than common vocabulary.)

sky block *n* 1986 Aug 21 *Hampstead Advertiser* 3/2 "The lift dispute which stranded thousands of council sky-block tenants was settled last week." (A tall block of flats, apparently from *skyscraper* + *block*; a more familiar term is *tower block*.)

Sloaneish *adj* 1986 Oct 30 *Times* 13/1 "The Maclaren of Maclaren, Press Attaché to the British Embassy in Moscow, lives in a foreigners-only department [*sic*] block with a Sloaneish wife who has long abandoned her early inhibitions at knowing their bedroom to be the object of electronic eavesdropping." (The Sloane Ranger [from *Sloane Square*, a fashionable and affluent area of London, + *Lone Ranger*] is an upper-middle class young woman, characterized by dress, speech, and country connections. The spelling is typically British; cf *ageing*.)

sluppy *n* 1986 Oct 12 *Sunday Times* 48/6–7 "There were several false starts because yuppie groups do blend in with other classes. Jamie's Bar in Kensington, for example, seemed to offer a hybrid of the Sloane and the yuppie (presumably the Sluppy)."

smarm *adj* 1986 Aug 23 *Daily Mirror* 6/5 "DYNASTY'S Gordon Thompson and ex-Avengers girl Linda Thorson went to the same smarm school." (Cf *smarm* vb 'slick down (the hair) with oil or cream, ingratiate oneself'; n 'obsequiousness'; *smarmy* adj 'excessively ingratiating.' One consultant suggested a play on *charm school*.)

smuttery *n* 1986 Oct 16 *Times* 47/3 "More of a warning, really, than a recommendation: THE KENNY EVERETT VIDEO SHOW (BBC1, 8.30pm) is back for another series of 'smuttery' and 'naughty wobbling things of all denominations.' " (stunt word)

snap *n* 1986 Oct 23 *Times* 16/2 "At 7.31 on the night of Friday January 24 this year, the Press Association, Britain's national news agency, put out a 'snap' which said that the print unions at all four newspapers owned by News International had walked out." (One consultant identified this term as long in newsroom and news agency use in the sense 'news flash.')

snap tin *n* 1986 May 21 *Sun* 13 "OLD-STYLE 'snap tins' are being issued to miners at Denby Grange, West Yorks, to stop them throwing litter into the coal." (Cf *Street Talk: The Language of Coronation Street* [TV evening soap], London: Ward Lock, 1986: "**snap:** packed lunch, or other light meal, carried to work. Mining expression, but still commonly used in the Street." Partridge also enters *snap* as 'packed food' and adds "hence, *snap tin*, a container for a packed meal: railwaymen's: since ca. 1920." *The Sun* and *Coronation Street* agree that the term is associated with miners. Consultants were familiar with the use and observed that Stoke on Trent dialect calls the food *snappin'* and that Arthur Seaton, the protagonist of Alan Sillitoe's *Saturday Night, Sunday Morning*, carries his snap to the factory where he works as a machinist; the term is perhaps industrial working class rather than from a particular occupation.)

sniffer *n* Reporter 1986 Oct 19 *Sunday Times* 25/4 ". . . the Duke gathered a group of ocularly-suitable girls around him at a cultural performance in Kunming, demanded that the Fleet Street photographers record the event and barked to the sniffers (as Fleet Street reporters are known, from the rhyming slang 'sniffer and snorter') that 'I've got to do something right, haven't I?' " (a good example of rhyming slang since the clipped remainder of the rhyming phrase is semantically appropriate, suggesting the sniffing out of news and echoing *sniffer dog* 'police dog used to locate drugs or explosives by smell'; not in Franklyn's *Dictionary of Riming Slang*)

-speak *n formative* A style of language associated with a person or group, *pejorative* **—childspeak** Precocious or naively amusing language attributed to children in material intended for adults 1986 Oct 19 *Sunday Times* 49/7 "It is not a compilation of funny childspeak or cute little anecdotes aimed at amusing adults." **—Haigspeak** Language characterized by pompous obscurity resulting from redundancy, the semantically strained use of words, and verbosity, associated with Alexander Haig, Secretary of State during Ronald Reagan's first two years as president 1986 Sep 7 *Sunday Times* 13/8 "The answer was authentic Haigspeak: 'It's premature now for such posturing in a definitive way.' " (entered as an undefined example of the formative in *OEDS, Barnhart Dictionary Companion* 2:85, and *Cobuild*) **—Metspeak** Imprecise, verbose, bureaucratic language used to blunt the statement of unpleasant facts, associated with the London Metropolitan Police 1986 Oct 23 *Times* 13/1 "*The Queen's Peace* (BBC2) examined the police view of their role in a decade of anti-police riots. Riot situations, rather—riots plain and simple no longer occur in the linguistic GBH [grievous bodily harm—legal jargon] known as Metspeak. Straining in a flabby and otiose way to take the sting out of language, a respectful senior policeman informed his Commissioner (in advance of the anti-apartheid march to Clapham

Common), 'There could be a likelihood of possible disorder.' " (Consultants cite also *femspeak* and *streetspeak* 'rapping; trendy, up-to-the-moment jargon.')

splat gun *n* 1986 Oct 15 *Times* 16/1 "As well as helicopters, pyrotechnics and 'splat' guns (which cover victims in blood-coloured dye) the fee also includes a lunch of rabbit and chicken roasted in a hole in the ground, two nights in a hotel and champagne." (A consultant compares this with *splurge gun* from *Bugsy Malone*.)

sro *n* 1986 Oct 7 *Times* 37/2–3 "Alternatively, businesses can get their license by joining a self-regulating organization—sro. These mini-bodies will have their own rules for their own members—which must provide protection for investors, which is at least as good as that which the SIB [Securities and Investments Board] provides in its own rule book."

stay-put *n* HOLD-UP

stuffer *n* 1986 Oct 26 *Sunday Times* 3/2 "In the past six months customs investigators at Heathrow airport have discovered more than 100 Nigerians on flights from Lagos attempting to smuggle heroin packed inside contraceptive sheaths, which are swallowed or inserted in anal and vaginal passages. They are known to customs officers as 'stuffers and swallowers' and each can carry more than one lb of heroin in this way, worth about £50,000 at street value."

sug /sʌg/ *n* [acronym from *selling under guise*] Ostensible survey actually taken to discover the telephone number of a prospective buyer, esp for investment schemes 1986 Dec TV report on consumer fraud

swallower *n* STUFFER

taper relief *n* 1986 Sep 22 *Times* 32/2 "Reduced rates, known as taper relief, apply for gifts made between four and seven years before death."

three-hander *n* Play for three actors 1986 Sept 27 *Times* 10/8 "Jon Gaunt's ferociously dark three-hander, *Hooligans*, which follows after a short interval, also won a Fringe Award." (*Collins* enters *two-hander* 'play for two actors,' of which this is an extension.)

till point *n* Cash register desk 1986 sign at Covent Garden General Store, London (*Point* 'place, location' is popular in compounds in British English; cf *power point* 'wall socket.' *Till point* constellates with *cashpoint*, recorded in an earlier installment.)

top-up *n adjunct* 1986 Sep 8 *Times* 3/8 "The report says that the top-up mortgage is the cheapest way of raising cash for a new car or exotic holiday, and that it is the building societies which are unwittingly acting as middlemen. 'It is the easiest thing in the world to get say £10,000 through the top-up loophole,' Mr Bryan Hubbard, editor of the magazine, said. . . . 'Any street-wise borrower can claim a legitimate reason for the loan, and go out and buy a new Granada with tax relief,' he added. The Inland Revenue is aware of the problem, but said there was little that could be done [because] there was no policing of the top-up sector." (Consultants explain that a top-up mortgage involves further borrowing on an existing mortgage, properly for home improvements. Tax relief is given for mortgage interest payments on one's primary place of residence, not for other loans. So persons who have decreased their mortgages can take out a second loan to TOP UP the mortgage to the maximum of £30,000 allowed for tax relief. Such loan money is supposed to be used for house improvements, but it is often used for other purposes, such as automobile purchases. The term is a metaphor from topping up a drink, such as a glass of beer in a pub.)

tractor brush *n* Tractor with an attached brush for cleaning the ground 1986 Oct 18 *Times* 20/1 "Outside the site office, on the viaduct over the A1(M), Mr Tony Reegan, aged 30, a tractor brush driver, said he would be glad when it was all over."

traincard *n* Pass for use of the underground railway 1986 sign in the Finchley Road Station, London "7 Day Traincards can be renewed any time after mid-day on the day of expiry." (also *travelcard*)

TSO *n* [acronym for *trading standards officer*] 1986 Oct 14 *Times* 31/1 "Certain clues indicated that the vehicle might be grossly overloaded, so the TSO instructed the driver to report to a nearby weighbridge."

waxed *adj* Water-proofed 1986 Aug 30 *Times* 13 (ad) "Due to the success of our previous offers for waxed jackets we are again offering this new style waxed coat. It is made in the UK from 100% olive green waxed cotton and lined with a tartan lining." 1987 Jun 6 *Times* 9/6–8 (ad) "Due to the success of our previous offers for waxed garments we are now offering this new fashionable waxed kagoul. Designed to keep the weather out, protecting you from rain and harsh winds, and consequently ideal for both town and country."

wet-bag *n* Plastic- or rubber-lined container for toiletries, toilet kit; also called *sponge bag* or *wet pack* 1986 Sep 13 *Times* 8/7 "The toiletries and unguents are amazing: a sponge-bag is called a wet-bag."

whole-foodie *n* [from *wholefood* 'unprocessed or lightly processed health food'] 1986 Sep 24 *Times* 15/3 ". . . processed white bread, the very mention of which is usually enough to bring any modern self-respecting whole-foodie to boiling point."

wind-up *n* Practical joke, put-on, leg-pull 1986 Aug 23 *Daily Mirror* 5/3 "They didn't tell me it was a wind-up until they released me an hour later." (*Collins* has a verb *wind up* 'tease.')

winkie-wiggling *n* 1986 Oct 5 *Sunday Times* 47/7 "Spitting Image was back on Sunday on ITV with a winkie-wiggling contest. This involved close-ups of athletes' crotches and reflections like 'Marita Koch she may be, but she's not fooling anybody.' " (Partridge has *winkle* as children's or schoolboy's slang for 'penis' with a nursery variant *winkie*. Consultants maintain the contest in question is not a recognized sport in the UK, but think the reference is a WIND-UP [see above].)

winkle *v* Wriggle, force (one's way) 1986 Oct 19 *Sunday Times* 25/2 "By Thursday the whole tour had clearly managed to winkle its way right up Prince Philip's nose—leading to the celebrated backing escapade in Xian with the unfortunate Simon Kirby of Leamington Spa." (This use of the verb is a variant of the expression *get up one's nose* 'annoy severely, irritate' is apparently a generalization of *winkle (out)* 'extract, eject, force out'.)

-wise *adv formative* **1:** from nouns —**chestwise** 1986 Oct 12 *Sunday Times* 52/1 " 'I'm browned off,' Larry says, taking the tin out of his mouth. 'Chestwise I don't feel good.' " (ref to sniffing solvents) **2:** from adjectives —**socialwise** 1984 Sarah Caudwell *The Shortest Way to Hades* (New York: Penguin, 1986) 80 " 'Oh, like a shot—chuffed as chocolate about it. Grockle's breakfast parties are rather a big deal socialwise—I mean getting asked to them means you're part of a sort of intellectual élite.' " (Although other dictionaries do not

enter the second use of the formative, the *OED* has examples of adverbs in *-wise* formed on adjectives from *Beowulf's ealde wisan* to Kipling's 1903 "She . . . Treated them despiteful-wise.")

Worzel Gummidge *n* 1986 Oct 11 *Times* 17/1–2 (editorial) "It is not, as might be supposed, the fruits of some survey which has proved that the old-fashioned Worzel Gummidge scarecrow is in fact more successful at keeping birds away than any computerised system of bleeps and flashes; . . . True, the traditional Worzel Gummidge is a delightful figure, with his stick arms, battered hat, frayed waistcoat and straws in his hair, but he is surely sufficiently familiar, both from his many years of service in the fields and from his more recent television career." (From a scarecrow figure in a series of children's books by Barbara Euphan Todd, the first being *Worzel Gummidge; or, The Scarecrow of Scatterbrook* [1936], the stories were recently dramatized in a television series. One consultant observes that Michael Foot, Labour leader in the 1983 election, was often referred to as Worzel Gummidge, that is, wild looking with flying hair.)

yah-boo *adj* [*interj*, exclamation of scorn, derision, or contemptuous defiance] 1986 Oct 7 *Times* 16/1 "He assured me that he wants 'a lawyers' debate' led by Labour QCs John Smith and John Morris rather than a 'yah-boo affair between Neil and the Prime Minister,' and he believes Kinnock has no choice but to agree." (One consultant cited *yah-boo politics* as a familiar use.)

yarg *n* 1987 Jun 6 *Times* 3/4–7 "However the Horrells, tenants of a Duchy of Cornwall farm, have made a considerable commercial success of their own Cornish cheese, Yarg. . . . As for Yarg, in spite of its authentically rustic sounding name, the semi-hard, quick-ripening cheese distinctively wrapped in nettle-leaves is really a very recent introduction. [¶] The name is simply that of its inventor, a Mr Gray, spelt backwards."

NOTE

For support during the preparation of the material in this series of "Among the New Words," the editor is grateful to the John Simon Guggenheim Memorial Foundation and the Fulbright Commission.

AMONG THE NEW WORDS

JOHN ALGEO AND ADELE ALGEO
University of Georgia

With the assistance of William W. Evans, *Louisiana State University*; Raymond Gozzi, *University of Rhode Island*; Jonathan Lighter, *University of Tennessee*; Virginia G. McDavid, *Chicago State University*; James B. McMillan, *University of Alabama*; Louis Phillips, *School of Visual Arts*; and Mary Gray Porter, *University of Alabama*

THE YEAR 1987 WAS FULL OF CONTRASTS: presidential politics, Senate hearings, summitry, news control; New Agers converging harmonically; the stock market crash; and couch potatoes quietly cocooning. We prepared this installment of "Among the New Words" in the opening days of 1988, bringing together documentation for some of the voguish words of the past year. In the next installment we will continue the round-up.

Recently fashionable expressions sometimes have a long underground history. A case in point is *New Age*, popularized in 1987 by the Shirley MacLaine television program and the much publicized "Harmonic Convergence" weekend, and reminiscent of the 1960s *Age of Aquarius* (which sprouted from the musical *Hair* and enjoyed brief lexicographical existence as an entry in the Merriam *6,000 Words* and *The Barnhart Dictionary of New English since 1963*). Both expressions, however, are considerably older, going back at least to the turn of the century, when a millennialism natural to the end of a century was combined with unorthodox or avant-garde philosophy, politics, art, and what are today called "lifestyles," in a mix similar to that still associated with *New Age*. Something of its older uses are hinted at in the entry below, although an adequate history of the term remains to be written.

Acknowledgments for citations: Catherine Algeo, Thomas Algeo, Charles C. Doyle. For help with identifying early uses of *New Age*: Ted Davy.

action girl *n* 1987 Aug 15–16 *International Herald Tribune* 16 "Donna Rice, whose relationship with Gary Hart ended Hart's presidential campaign, was an 'action girl' who drifted from one party to another in search of rich or famous men, according to a profile in the latest edition of *Vanity Fair* magazine."

Black Monday *n* 1987 Oct 25 *Athens [Ga] Banner-Herald/Daily News* 1/5 "Wall Street, beginning on 'Black Monday', experienced its worst week of trading since the stock market crash of Oct. 28 and 29, 1929, which preceded the Great Depression of the 1930s." Nov 13 *Wall Street Journal* 17/4–6 (headline and article) "Black Monday Ends Bond Funds' Blues / . . . Before Oct. 19 became known as Black Monday, for instance, Strong Government Securities Fund held its entire portfolio in 90-day Treasury bills. In the week after that day's 22.6% stock market crash, its chairman, Dick Strong, went on a long-bond buying spree." Nov 20 *Time* 44/2 "Black Monday—Oct. 19—is already notorious as the darkest day in Wall Street history." Nov 22 Jack Anderson *Athens [Ga] Banner-Herald/Daily News* B-11/2 "With the usual 20-20 hindsight, many stock market experts have said that the 'meltdown' of Black Monday, Oct. 19, was not only inevitable but predictable. What the experts never seem to explain, though, is why they failed to predict the $500 billion drop in stock prices." Dec 7 *Time* 50/2 "Will the U.S. economy withstand the shock of the Black Monday stock-market crash, or will it slide into a prolonged recession?"

Bloody Monday (British) *n* BLACK MONDAY 1987 Nov 8 *Manchester Guardian Weekly* 3/3 "Investors such as Carl Icahn have already blamed the proposal for the severity of Bloody Monday's fall." Dec 20 *Manchester Guardian Weekly* 8/4 "Most retailer[s] are taking the sensible view that customers scared off expensive items by 'Bloody Monday' might be more willing to dip into their bank accounts in the hopes of grabbing a bargain."

boob tuber *n* [*boob tube* + *tuber* 'potato'] 1987 Oct 26 sv COUCH POTATO

bubble *n* 1987 Nov 17 *Wall Street Journal* 41/3 "Vernon L. Smith knows why the stock market crashed. He ought to. He's seen dozens of 'bubbles'—booms followed by sudden crashes—in the past three years. [¶] Almost every time, Mr. Smith says, the bubble occurred because inexperienced traders dominated the market. In fact, traders had to go through at least two booms and crashes before they collectively learned to avoid these bubbles." (ref to laboratory experiments in stock trading at Univ of Arizona)

channel *n* 1987 Nov 22 *Atlanta Journal/Constitution* J-10/2–3 "Doubleday/Dolphin, Crown/Harmony, E. P. Dutton, Alfred A. Knopf and others each have at least one New Age title on their fall list. Harper & Row has printed 40,000 copies of 'Channelling: The Intuitive Connection' by William A. Kautz; and Warner Books has issued 'State of Mind,' the autobiography of J. Z. Knight, the 'channel' for Ramtha."

channel *vt* 1987 Mar 18 *Today* NBC-TV "Now she channels spirits full-time. . . . I channel energy that I call . . . ." Dec 7 *Time* 66/1 "Not all the channeled voices are from outer space."

channeler *n* 1987 Aug *Ladies Home Journal* 48/3 " 'New Age has become a belief system,' says Alev [information officer of Cult Awareness Network]. 'Many followers are addicted to a hypnotic subculture.' Channelers such as Knight 'are often charismatic types who inspire absolute devotion and claim they are the sole source of revelations from God.' "

channeling *n* 1987 Aug *Ladies Home Journal* 48/3 "Made chic in large part because of Shirley MacLaine's best-seller and mini-series *Out on a Limb*, New Age blends Eastern and Western thought and encompasses self-help groups, healing crystals, reincarnation and channeling (communicating with spirits through a medium). [¶] CAN [Cult Awareness Network] says the New Age phenomenon, particularly channeling, shares characteristics with destructive cults." Nov 22 sv CHANNEL Dec 7 *Time* 66/1 "On the other hand, the extraterrestrials who turn up in the course of channeling—one of the most popular New Age sports—appear almost unfailingly wise and benevolent."

cocooning *n* 1987 Jun 15 *Newsweek* 46/1 "The Rustic Long Island cottage is her weekend retreat ('the cocooning trend') and it's smaller than her last place ('the downsizing trend')." Idem 47/3 "Similarly, Pillsbury has subscribed to her [Faith Popcorn's] notion that the 'cocooning' phenomenon will create new business opportunities in takeout foods. Says Pillsbury spokesman James R. Behnke: 'I *believe* in cocooning.' " Oct 26 John Schwartz *Newsweek* 73/1–2 "Professional trend watchers have coined a buzzword: 'cocooning.' . . . Some companies are trying to serve vidspuds at home. The Company Store, an upscale mail-order business, sells a sleeping-baglike item called the Couch Potato Down Comforter Featherbed. This is the ultimate cocooning aid: it *is* a cocoon." 1988 Jan 4 *Athens [Ga] Banner-Herald* 4/2–3 "Faith Popcorn (I did not make up that name) said that in her professional judgment everybody who was anybody would be staying home in 1988. Ensconced there, they will be found eating 'mom' food, putting on a few pounds, and in general doing the very latest thing trendwise: 'cocooning.' "

couch potato *n* 1982 Robert Armstrong and Jack Mingo *Dr. Spud's Etiquette for the Couch Potato* (pvtly pub). 1983 Jack Mingo and Robert Armstrong *The Official Couch Potato™ Handbook* (Santa Barbara: Capra Press) 63–67 "The Couch Potatoes, like almost everything good about Television, had their origins in sunny southern California. . . . Tom Iacino coined the term 'Couch Potato.' . . . Then, in 1979, the Couch Potatoes surfaced in Pasadena's famous Doo Dah Parade . . . . They dropped out the next year because motorized floats were outlawed, and no one wanted to pull the Ceremonial Couch." 1984 Mar 24 rev of *The Official Couch Potato Handbook* (Capra Press) *TV Guide* 34/1–2 "The Couch Potatoes were founded by Jack Mingo and illustrator Robert Armstrong as a loose association of Couch Rats and their like. Purporting to be a manual of style for those who repose, spud-like, in front of their sets all day, the 'Handbook' is filled with hints for the Truly Comatose." Sep/Oct *Ampersand* 14/2 "Couch potatoes rejoice. Thanks to Walter Annenberg, the man who brought America *TV Guide*, it may now be possible to partially work your way through many colleges and universities simply by turning on your television set." 1987 Jul 22 *Chicago Tribune* 1-15/1 "New York magazine is one of those publications that specialize in telling everyone what is fashionable. . . . [¶] So imagine my surprise when the magazine's latest issue reported in a cover story on night life that the latest trend in going out is, of all things, staying home. [¶] 'Couch Potatoes: The New Night Life,' says the cover, which features a contented couple of yuppies in spud suits, cuddling on their living room couch, eyes glued to their television. . . . [¶] It attributes the Couch Potato phenomenon to 'three increasingly important facts of baby boom life: marriage, children and home video (not necessarily in that order).' " Aug 4 *Athens [Ga] Banner-Herald* 7/4 "Dear Abby: My husband is a real couch potato. Now, don't get me wrong, I like TV as much as the next person, but here's my problem: He stays up until all hours watching old movies and reruns and then comes to bed late." Aug 4 *Atlanta Constitution* A-12/1 (headline) "Couch-potato teens found less fit but not fatter than other youths" Sep 2 *Atlanta Constitution* C-3/6 "Ms. Meredith noted the researchers chose athletic men, not passive 'couch potatoes' for study." Sep 3 *Atlanta Constitution* C-1/1 "If one must be more active than a couch potato on a holiday weekend, Callaway Gardens has just the ticket." Sep 8 *Star* 30/1 "Couch potatoes are sprouting up everywhere, say trend spotters across the U.S. What is a couch potato? According to *The Official Couch Potato Handbook*, by Jack Mingo (Last Gasp, $5.95), the answer can be found in your living room. It's that happy combination of your TV set, your couch—and you. While the rest of the world rushes madly about, endlessly pursuing excitement and the meaning of life, couch potatoes are at peace in front of their tubes, says Mingo." Sep 21 *Atlanta Constitution* C-6/6 "DEAR ABBY: 'Mrs. Couch Potato' complains because her husband stays up half the night watching reruns and old movies on TV—then he comes to bed at 2 or 3 a.m. wanting to be 'romantic.' " Oct 26 John Schwartz *Newsweek* 73/1–3 "Couch potatoes have long been with us, but they used to feel a little guilty about whiling away the midnight hours at home. Now they slouch on the couch with impunity and defiantly proclaim, 'Say it loud—I'm a spud and I'm PROUD.' . . . underground cartoonist Bob Armstrong . . . holds the federal trademark on the term 'Couch Potato' and has exacted licensing arrangements from manufacturers of a spud-ucopia of consumer goods while peddling his own line of T shirts, banners, buttons, hats and other potatophernalia. And he says he is gratified to see the increase in potato pride: 'No longer do you hear the terms "videot" or "boob tuber." ' " Nov 4 *Wall Street Journal* 39/3 "Sales this year should total about $1.25 billion, according to Paul Kagan Associates Inc., an entertainment media research firm in Carmel, Calif. And a recent forecast by the Roper Organization suggests that home-shoppers may be changing from 'couch potatoes' to busy consumers who are seeking greater control over their time. [¶] 'Home shopping is quick, clean (and) painless,' says the Roper study." Nov 20 *Atlanta Journal/Constitution* P-1/1 "The audience makes the theater a social event in an increasingly unsocial age. As VCRs help to create a vast national patch of couch potatoes, the theater performs a civic function. It lets us respond to responses other than our own." Nov 22 *Athens [Ga] Banner-Herald* 10/3 "Another charge is that having TV Twins encourages viewers to become couch potatoes. 'I don't recommend people watch more TV, but watch more quality TV or try to understand what they view,' Young said." Nov 23 *Wall Street Journal* 2-1/4 "Moreover, viewers may not take to interactive entertainment. Some critics say the format isn't suited for 'couch potatoes,' who want to sit back and be told a story."

couch potatoing *n* Lounging as a COUCH POTATO 1987 Dec 2 *Daily Beacon* (U of Tenn, Knoxville) 4/4 (heading) "Couch Potatoing"

couch rat *n* 1984 Mar 24 sv COUCH POTATO

couch tomato *n* 1983 Jack Mingo and Robert Armstrong *The Official Couch Potato™ Handbook* (Santa Barbara: Capra Press) 65 "The Couch Tomatoes were founded soon after as a women's fetch and adjust auxiliary. . . . Members were proud to be called Couch Potatoes or Couch Tomatoes, but to the rest of the world, they were bums."

Dr. Spin *n* SPIN DOCTOR 1988 Jan 2 *Atlanta Journal/Constitution* A-7/2 " 'Dr. Spin so far has got to be that group of people who are doing it for Bush,' Robert Squier, a Democratic political consultant, told a reporter. 'Because when he finished his first debate, and they convinced America—which means you guys—that not losing was winning, that's got to go into the "Spin Hall of Fame." ' "

finding *n* 1987 Aug 5 *Atlanta Constitution* A-15/4–5 "In the warped Poindexter thinking, the national security adviser has the authority to destroy secret presidential findings to avoid political embarrassment; he claims the power to seize the buck of accountability, keeping from his elected leader the secret of a venal diversion that would cause widespread revulsion." Aug 8 *Atlanta Journal/Constitution* A-14/3 " 'It's clear there will be no more oral findings, it's clear there will be no more retroactive findings.' [¶] A 'finding' is presidential authorization for covert actions, usually undertaken by the CIA."

free spinner *n* 1988 Jan 2 *Atlanta Journal/Constitution* A-1/4–5 "In political parlance, a free spinner is a consultant or academic who is untainted by association with a presidential campaign and, therefore, can be counted on to analyze political events with relative objectivity." (See SPIN.)

free spinning *n* 1988 Jan 2 *Atlanta Journal/Constitution* A-8/2 "To a certain extent, free spinning has become institutionalized in the 1988 campaign through television newsprograms and newsletters that rely heavily on such analysts to explain the presidential race."

front-running *n* 1987 Nov 6 *Atlanta Constitution* C-1/4 "An inability to sell shares as the market plunged may have wiped out profits or increased losses for investors. At the same time, a broker or firm that executed its own trades ahead of its customers' could have added to the downward pressure on prices while cutting its own losses. [¶] Attorneys and some brokerage officials said front-running may have taken place among individual brokers, but speculated the practice probably was not widespread." Idem C-8/1–2 "Complaints that some stockbrokers took better care of themselves than their customers when the market crashed last month are not surprising but are tough to prove, according to attorneys and brokerages. . . . [¶] David S. Ruder, chairman of the SEC, said in a television interview that 'there is some chance that in the confusion' institutional trades were made ahead of client trades on Black Monday. But he said no evidence of so-called 'front running' has surfaced yet to bear that out."

generational politician *n* 1987 Oct 9 sv GENERATIONAL POLITICS

generational politics *n* 1984 Jul 9 *Newsweek* 13/1 "By the 1970s and '80s Hart and Brown emerged as the two most successful practitioners of 'generational politics.' But neither was of the generation they were said to lead." 1987 Oct 9 *Atlanta Constitution* A-17/2 "As for the idea, rarely has there been one as empty as generational politics. At one level, it is an appeal based nakedly on age. It says: 'Elect me, I'm young.' But an aging population is not necessarily going to buy that. Some might even be offended by it. So generational politicians generally deny that what they offer is mere youth."

harmonic convergence *n* 1987 Aug 8 "Doonesbury" (comic strip) *Athens [Ga] Banner-Herald/Daily News* 8/5 "—She wants it to coincide with some big New Age event. I forget the name, something like 'moronic convergence' . . . —*Harmonic* convergence! —It's sort of a national Fruit Loops day. Lots of windchimes." Aug 13 *Athens Banner-Herald* 2/1 "Will a 'harmonic convergence' bathe the planet in good vibrations Sunday?" Aug 16 *Athens Banner-Herald/Daily News* 25/3 "National Forest rangers and others who keep order in the shadow of towering Mount Shasta girded Saturday for the two-day planetary purification that New Age exponents call 'harmonic convergence.' " Aug 17 *Atlanta Constitution* A-8/1 "Exemplifying the do-your-own-thing spirit of the 1960s, believers in 'harmonic convergence' greeted the dawn Sunday with Buddhist chants, pop music, their versions of Indian rituals and heartfelt hugs." Dec 7 *Time* 64/1 "Only on special occasions, like the highly publicized 'harmonic convergence' in August, do believers in I Ching or crystals gather together with believers in astral travel, shamans, Lemurians and tarot readers, for a communal chanting of om, the Hindu invocation that often precedes meditation. Led on by the urgings of José Argüelles, a Colorado art historian who claimed that ancient Mayan calendars foretold the end of the world unless the faithful gathered to provide harmony, some 20,000 New Agers assembled at 'sacred sites' from Central Park to Mount Shasta to—uh—provide harmony."

loop *n* **—in the loop** 1987 Aug 9 *Atlanta Journal/Constitution* C-2/3 "His [George Bush's] answer is that the failure to handle the matter in formal National Security Council meetings meant 'we were not in the loop. When you don't know something,' he told me, 'it's hard to react.' " **—out of the loop** 1983 Jun 25 *Atlanta Journal/Constitution* 23/1 "In the climactic scene of the movie 'WarGames,' a monster game-playing computer has taken control of the North American Defense Command and is moving the world relentlessly toward nuclear war. No one can stop it; in computer language, people are out of the 'loop,' or the decision-making process." 1987 Aug 17 "Shoe" comic strip *Atlanta Constitution* C-15 "[A:] How do those new circulation figures look, Chief? [B:] None of your business!! [C:] What was that all about? [A:] I think it was his way of telling me I'm out of the policy loop." Dec 19 *Atlanta Journal/Constitution* A-16/1 "Bush tries to portray himself as the indispensable right-hand man in his boss' successful enterprises, but, oddly enough, out of the loop in Reagan's most deplorable foreign policy debacle."

melt down *vi* 1987 Nov 16 *Wall Street Journal* 65/3 "Take the employees of Lowe's Cos., who hold 25% of the building-materials retailer in a couple of retirement-savings plans. The market value of their stock has melted down by 43%, to a post-crash $189 million from about $332 million earlier this year."

meltdown *n* **1:** Sudden catastrophic decline in financial value 1987 Oct 20 *USA Today* A-1 (headline and story) "Market 'Meltdown' . . . 'Whether today was a financial meltdown or not . . . I wouldn't want to be around for one worse than this,' said John Phelan, chairman of the New York Stock Exchange." (Jonathan Lighter notes that Phelan made this remark at a news conference broadcast live by Cable News Network the previous afternoon and that it was clear Phelan had been using the term for at least a few days before 19 Oct.) Oct 25 *Atlanta Journal/Constitution* A-10/2 "The plunge feeds on itself, as computers kick in to sell huge chunks of stock automatically. New York Stock Exchange chairman John J. Phelan Jr. calls the situation 'close to financial meltdown,' but President Reagan sees no reason for panic." Nov 8 *Manchester Guardian Weekly* 1/3 "And there is the ever present risk of a necessary fall in the value of the dollar turning into meltdown as happened on the share markets. It is not much help to say that the main industrialised nations willed this on themselves by abolishing exchange controls and freeing currency markets." Nov 20 morning news NBC-TV "The Wall Street Journal says that only the intervention of the Federal Reserve Board . . . saved the stock market from a total meltdown." Nov 22 sv BLACK MONDAY Dec 27 morning news CNN-TV "As troubles piled up after meltdown Monday, it [the stock market] went into collapse." **2:** Destruction from excessive use (hyperbole) Nov 2 *Athens [Ga] Banner-Herald* 4/1 "The telephone receiver may experience meltdown after being attached to the side of a teen-ager's head for 6 1/2 hours but her ear and her hearing will emerge unscathed." **3:** Critically dangerous state Nov 11 William Bennett (Secretary of Education) morning news CNN-TV "You've got close to educational meltdown here in Chicago." Nov 24 *Atlanta Constitution* A-10/1 (editorial) "In their desperation, the Cuban prisoners in these institutions have embarked on a tragic course. When the news broke Friday that the United States and Cuba had reached an agreement on deportation, they panicked. They have made an awful mistake, and they must be held accountable. [¶] At the same time, it is important to note that the Cuban inmates did not create this disaster alone. They had plenty of help from the U.S. Justice Department. From Day 1 of the Mariel boatlift in 1980, the feds have set the stage for this meltdown [the revolt of Cuban prisoners at the Federal detention center at Oakdale, Louisiana, and at the Atlanta Federal Penitentiary]." Dec 19 *Atlanta Journal/Constitution* A-17/4–5 "In the parkway meltdown, you may be sure—certainly DOT [Department of Transportation] and its attorneys were—that an intersection at Highland would have been legally fatal." (ref to legal battles over the construction of a road through a residential neighborhood)

New Age *n* esp *attrib* 1894–1938 *The New Age: A Democratic Review of Politics, Religion, and Literature* (a guild-socialist publication edited for a time after 1907 by A R Orage, a student of the Russian mystic George Gurdjieff) 1904– *New Age* (publication of Scottish Rite Freemasons) 1908–19 *Aquarian New Age: A Magazine of Aquarian Thought* (published in Boston and Los Angeles) 1944 Alice A Bailey *Discipleship in the New Age* (Lucis Pub Co, 3d ed 1948) 43 "What were the requirements for which we should look and what should be the technique to be applied in the New Age for the raising of the consciousness of men?" 1974– *New Age Journal* (publication devoted to "health, ecology, politics, spirituality, and lifestyles, with an emphasis on holism"; issue of Nov/Dec 1987, pp 52–53, has letters from readers defining the term) 1987 Aug *Ladies Home Journal* 48/3 "The middle-aged, especially middle-aged women, are primarily responsible for the popularity of the New Age movement—components of which, some say, represent a new kind of cult." Nov 22 *Atlanta Journal/Constitution* J-10/2 "Strange things are happening in the publishing business. Thanks to Shirley MacLaine—and probably the alignment of various planets, stars and asteroids—readers are coming out of the woodwork to clamor for 'New Age' books. [¶] For the unenlightened, New Age is a generic term for books in the spiritual, metaphysical, and holistic fields, including astrology, UFOs, and the occult." Dec Quality Paperback Bookclub ad leaflet "Books for the New Age" Dec 7 *Time* 62/3 "So here we are in the New Age, a combination of spirituality and superstition, fad and farce, about which the only thing certain is that it is not new. Nobody seems to know exactly where the term came from, but it has been around for several decades or more, and many elements of the New Age, like faith healing, fortune-telling and transmigration of souls, go back for centuries. . . . Bantam Books says its New Age titles have increased tenfold in the past decade. The number of New Age bookstores has doubled in the past five years, to about 2,500. New Age radio is spreading, with such stations as WBMW in Washington and KTWV-FM in Los Angeles offering dreamy light jazz that one listener described as 'like I tapped into a radio station on Mars.' The Grammys now include a special prize for New Age music (latest winner: Swiss Harpist Andreas Vollenweider)." Dec 29 *Atlanta Constitution* B-1/2–4/4 "In Los Angeles, an FM radio station nicknamed 'The Wave' offers its format of New Age music—soothing selections by artists such as pianist George Winston—with no disc jockeys. . . . New Age music—what some people call the beautiful music format for yuppies."

New Ager *n* 1987 Aug *Ladies Home Journal* 48/3 "Some New Agers, says Alev, are children of the sixties who still haven't found the answers they've been looking for. Others, adds Rubin, 'are now realizing that although they have become prosperous, material happiness is not enough.' " Dec 7 sv HARMONIC CONVERGENCE

Olliemania *n* 1987 Jul 19 *Chicago Tribune* 4-1/1 "Whatever happened to 'Olliemania'? [¶] . . . But by the week's end, Lt. Col. Oliver North who, it seemed, captivated the entire nation for nine days, was off the television screens and apparently out of mind." Sep 2 *Atlanta Constitution* C-1/2 "Keith Conquest doesn't need a public-opinion poll to know that Olliemania is fizzling. [¶] Conquest has a lot of evidence at his Fit-To-A-Tee Shirt store in a Washington shopping mall that support for charismatic Marine Lt. Col. Oliver L. North has waned: stacks of unsold T-shirts carrying the former presidential aide's picture." Sep 4 *Athens [Ga] Banner-Herald* 9/1 " 'Olliemania,' the national craze that followed the Marine lieutenant colonel's congressional testimony on his role in the Iran-Contra affair, has faded as fast as his image from the nation's TV screens."

paper trail *n* 1987 Nov 1 *Atlanta Journal/Constitution* A-3/2–4 "Unlike the defeated Bork, Ginsburg has left liberal sleuths a short paper trail. At 41, he has been a federal judge for the District of Columbia only a year, served a short time in the Justice Department and the Office of Management and Budget, and taught seven years at Harvard Law School. . . . [¶] The liberal groups, believing a paper trail can be found, say they have launched an exhaustive search of everything Ginsburg may have said or written." Nov 8 *Manchester Guardian Weekly* 19/2 (reprint from *Washington Post*) " 'What is most ominous about the nomination [of Douglas Ginsburg] at this stage is the suggestion that Ed Meese prevailed upon the President, with little consideration, to name an ideological clone of Judge Bork—a Judge Bork without a paper trail instead of a real conservative who would have broad support in the Senate,' Kennedy said." Nov 17 faculty member at department meeting, Univ of Georgia "A committee can make a strong recommendation or a weak recommendation, but we [the graduate faculty] should see the paper trail."

perestroika *n* 1987 Nov 5 *Atlanta Constitution* A-26/1 (editorial) "For all his talk of glasnost (openness) and perestroika (restructuring), the single solid proposal that Gorbachev made in the direction of democratization was to expand powers for local governments, presumably at Moscow's expense. But even this small gift was wrapped tightly in party ribbons." Nov 8 *Atlanta Journal/Constitution* A-1/1–2 "Shaking the Soviet people from their passivity and transforming the country into a modern, dynamic society is the main aim of perestroika, or restructuring—Gorbachev's program of social and economic reforms that he calls a 'revolution without shots.' [¶] As the Soviet Union marks the anniversary of the 1917 Bolshevik Revolution, it is clear that perestroika is entering a new, crucial phase that may determine the success or failure not only of the reform program, but also of Gorbachev." Nov 8 *Manchester Guardian Weekly* 1/2 "The resistance to Gorbachev's glasnost and perestroika is, by his own account, increasing, yet the effects of those reforms have still to be felt." Nov 13 *Atlanta Constitution* B-1/3 " 'In the Soviet Union, there is perestroika, so in the Hermitage, too, there must be perestroika,' said Vitaly Suslov, the museum's deputy director in charge of the renovation. [¶] In the age of perestroika, Soviet leader Mikhail Gorbachev's catchword for his plan to revitalize the Soviet economy, Suslov believes the Hermitage can finally rival the world's other great museums in services—as it does already with its staggering collection of art." Dec 7 *Time* 21/2 "In his new book, *Perestroika*, Gorbachev comes out as a Reagan booster." Dec 10 *Atlanta Constitution* A-12/4 " 'I have noticed that the skirts are shorter here than in Moscow,' Sergei Mikheyev observed Wednesday. 'I think that will cause some "perestroika" in the wardrobes of Soviet women.' " Dec 20 *Manchester Guardian Weekly* 10/5 "And his country is now heading into the hardest part of the perestroika, of the great economic dislocations, the price rises and the redundancies."

potato *n* COUCH POTATO 1987 Oct 26 John Schwartz *Newsweek* 73/1 "Madison Avenue has already picked up on the potato trend. . . . And the business world has heard the message; it has begun to pitch products directly to the potato market."

potatophernalia *n* 1987 Oct 26 sv COUCH POTATO

rolling vote *n* 1987 Oct 21 William Safire *Atlanta Constitution* A-11/1–2 "Putting pressure on a witness is a serious matter; if true, that might trouble some of the senators who were stampeded into a 'rolling vote' in the media on a matter better decided on the Senate floor. . . . [¶] But like many others on Capitol Hill, she [Linda Green, who warned a black professor of law not to testify for Bork] was caught up in the gotta-stop-Bork fever. Just as the ad people jumped in with lies, and senators stooped to the rolling vote, a staffer who taught law was swept over the ethical line."

self-spin *n* 1987 Dec 14 sv SPINNER

sofa spud *n* 1987 Dec 1 Ellen Goodman *Birmingham Post-Herald* A-5/1 "I am speaking of those maligned people known as couch potatoes. Or if you prefer, sofa spuds."

spin *n* Interpretation of an event for public presentation 1986 Oct 12 *This Week with David Brinkley* ABC-TV "So let's look at the most optimistic spin." 1987 Aug/Sep *Extra!* (newsletter of Fairness & Accuracy in Reporting) 1 (heading) "Media Put Reagan Spin on Arias Plan" Sep 15 *Atlanta Constitution* C-4/2 " 'We've always known if we weren't different, we wouldn't survive. So we try to anticipate the news, to look ahead. And we look for something with that USA Today spin,' Executive Editor Ron Martin said." Nov *Newsweek on Campus* 32/1 "Today's greeting-card poets don't necessarily spend their time writing tightly rhymed, flowery verse. Instead, many try to put an innovative spin on repetitive themes." Nov 7 *Atlanta Journal/Constitution* A-7/1–2 "In one oversight, staffers neglected to put the right spin on Carter's mention of his discussion with his daughter about nuclear warfare—what jokingly became known as 'Amy's nuclear nightmare.' " Dec 11 commentary on public radio "President Reagan attempted to put a positive spin on his report on the summit last night." Dec 18 *MacNeil/Lehrer NewsHour* ETV "For a final subject tonight we look at the editorial spin in Washington this week. . . . [picture of Reagan and Gorbachev labeled 'Summit Spin'] . . . Reporters frequently feel at the mercy of those they call the Sultans of Spin [press secretaries, etc]. . . . Is this a satisfactory way of informing the American public about something as important as the summit—leakage by spin?"

spin control *n* 1987 Nov 7 *Atlanta Journal/Constitution* A-7/1 "In political parlance, it is called 'spin control'—a campaign's attempt to influence reporters' interpretations of a news event. In the 1988 election, it is as critical as the candidate's performance, say some political operatives. In fact, 'it's too important,' said Newton Minow, a Chicago lawyer and national expert on presidential debates. 'Very often, before the public has had the chance to digest what they saw and heard, the spin control guys are out trying to affect that.' " 1988 Jan 2 *Atlanta Journal/Constitution* A-1/5–8/1 "The term [FREE SPINNER] was derived, apparently by Democratic media consultant and free spinner Robert Squier, from the phrase 'spin control,' which refers to the efforts of campaign officials to convince reporters of their candidate's genius and popularity."

spin doctor *n* 1986 Nov 19 Bernard Kalb lecture U of Tenn, Knoxville "The spin doctors came out after Reykjavik; the spin doctors came out after the 'Iranian connection.' " 1987 Dec 14 *Newsweek* 51/1 "To the average viewer [of the presidential candidates' debate], there were no big winners, no big losers and no dramatic turns in the bipartisan all-skate. This heightened the importance of the 'spin doctors,' whose subtle shadings are often invisible to the untrained eyes." 1988 Jan 2 *Atlanta Journal/Constitution* A-1/5–8/1 "Before the last television camera was flicked off at last week's Republican presidential debate, the 'spin doctors' were out in force. [¶] Candidates and their staffs swept through the press room at the George Brown Convention Center in Houston, hoping to attract reporters like honey does flies. Their goal: convincing journalists that their candidate had won the debate, or at least not lost it." (cf DR. SPIN)

Spin Hall of Fame *n* 1988 Jan 2 sv DR. SPIN

spinner *n* 1987 Dec 14 *Newsweek* 51/1 "When the debate was over, reporters crowded around spinners from the various camps; even the candidates engaged in protracted postdebate 'self-spin' on the Kennedy Center stage." 1988 Jan 2 *Atlanta Journal/Constitution* A-8/1 "The [free] spinners can be think-tank fellows, such as William Schneider and Norman Ornstein of the American Enterprise Institute or Stephen Hess of the Brookings Institution. They can be former campaign officials, such as Beckel and John Sears; pollsters, such as Peter Hart; political consultants, such as Squier and Eddie Mahe; or political scientists, such as Duke University's James David Barber."

spud *n* COUCH POTATO 1987 Oct 26 John Schwartz *Newsweek* 73/1 "Businesses are jumping to cash in on spud chic. Last week Coleco introduced a $35 couch-potato doll."

spud suit *n* 1987 Jul 22 sv COUCH POTATO

spud-ucopia *n* 1987 Oct 26 sv COUCH POTATO

spudismo *n* 1987 Oct 26 John Schwartz *Newsweek* 73/1–2 "The company had been preparing the item [a couch-potato doll] for 1988 but saw the advancing wave of *spudismo* and pushed up its schedule."

telespud *n* 1987 Nov *Newsweek on Campus* 14/1 "And we telespuds respond, gathering around the electronic hearth to watch everything from 'M*A*S*H' to 'Mr. Ed.' "

tuber *n* COUCH POTATO 1983 Jack Mingo and Robert Armstrong *The Official Couch Potato® Handbook* (Santa Barbara: Capra Press) 66 "The only outlet these Tubers had for their ideas at first was the Underground Comics."

ultraconsciousness *n* 1987 Oct 18 *Atlanta Journal/Constitution* H-1/5 " 'When I first got involved, there was a groundswell of interest in America in ultraconsciousness,' says Mark Thurston, who has spent the past 15 years as ARE's director of educational development."

up-day *n* 1987 Oct 25 *Atlanta Journal/Constitution* A-10/1 "Last week's Black Monday was followed by a record up-day, with the Dow soaring 102 points."

videot *n* 1987 Oct 26 sv COUCH POTATO

vidspud *n* COUCH POTATO 1987 Oct 26 sv COCOONING

wire around *vt* 1987 Aug 28 *Atlanta Constitution* A-1/1 "Clair George, the agency's deputy director for operations, said in testimony earlier this month before the committees investigating the Iran-contra affair that Casey had begun to 'wire around,' or circumvent, subordinates who weren't enthusiastic about the Iran deals."

AMONG THE NEW WORDS

JOHN ALGEO AND ADELE ALGEO

University of Georgia

With the assistance of George S. Cole, *Shippensburg University*; Lesa Dill, *Western Kentucky University*; William W. Evans, *Louisiana State University*; Raymond Gozzi, *University of Rhode Island*; William J. Kirwin, *Memorial University of Newfoundland*; Jonathan Lighter, *University of Tennessee*; Virginia G. McDavid, *Chicago State University*; James B. McMillan, *University of Alabama*; Patrick W. Merman, *School of Visual Arts*; Mary Gray Porter, *University of Alabama*; Sol Steinmetz, *Barnhart Books*; and Greg Williams

A CHARACTERISTIC FEATURE OF RECENT English is the shortening of a word to a part that is then used as a combining form for the original word, for example *parachute* to *para-* and *telephone* to *tele-*. As in those two examples, the shortened part is often identical in shape, though not in meaning, with a morphemic component of the original word. Another case in point is *eco-* from *ecology*. A large number of formations in *eco-* were recorded in an earlier installment of "Among the New Words" (*AS* 47 [1972], 268–71). In this issue we record a few more, together with some related words, *monkeywrench(ing)* and *social ecology*.

Electronic literally refers to electricity or electrons and by extension to computers or television. It freely forms combinations, however, whose meanings are by no means transparent. Consequently, dictionaries now enter the more frequent of the *electronic* combinations, such as *electronic banking*, *bulletin board*, *journalism*, and *mail*. In this installment we illustrate a few less frequent combinations. Of them, *electronic time bomb* is noteworthy as an earlier term for *computer virus*, which we will treat in a subsequent issue.

Voguish words tend to proliferate in form and meaning. An example, especially of proliferation of meaning, is *dumb down*, which seems originally to have been motion picture slang (see the citation from 1933 and that from 1928 for *dumb up*, both from the extensive collection of Jonathan Lighter). In the 1980s *dumb down* has been used mainly of simplifying the language and content of textbooks for less able students. Although that meaning is still prevalent, the citations below show various diversifications of it.

A complementary proliferating vogue term is *power*. It was noted by William Safire in "On Language," *New York Times Magazine* (13 July 1986, 6). Safire derived it from the baseball term *power hitter* and cited ten combinations with it. The entry below shows its continued and diversified use.

Another vogue is the "X-word" formula, in which "X" is any initial letter. A number of examples are cited here under *-word* and the related *-question* and *-people* spin-offs.

In contrast to terms like those of the "X-word" formula that spring up spontaneously in whole or part as jokes, other terms are deliberately and seriously invented to fill a hole in terminology. *Orature* is an example. It seems to have been invented several times independently.

Acknowledgments to others for citations: Catherine Algeo, Thomas Algeo, Walter S. Avis, Charles C. Doyle, I. Willis Russell; and for help in identifying and defining several of the ecological words: Frank Golley.

dumb down *vt* **1:** Revise so as to appeal to those of little education or intelligence 1933 Dec *Forum* 372 (H T Webster) "I can cheer, too, for the Hollywood gag men in conference on a comedy which has been revealed as too subtle when they determine they must dumb it down. That phrase saves time and wearying gestures." **a:** Write (a textbook) on a lower intellectual or educational level than that formerly expected of the group for whom it is intended 1984 Apr 11 *Athens [GA] Banner-Herald* 13/1 "Now, after a year of reports decrying the 'rising tide of mediocrity' in U.S. education, the secretary of education and other leaders say 'dumbed-down' children's textbooks are another piece in the puzzle in what went wrong in the American classroom.... William Honig, head of California's Department of Public Instruction and a vocal critic of 'dumbed-down texts,' said reading texts up to third grade level were effective in teaching basic skills. But from fourth grade on, he said, texts do a poor job of developing reading and thinking skills." 1985 Mar 12 *Knoxville Journal* 1 (headline) "Are we 'dumbing down' texts and minds?" 1987 Oct 22 *Atlanta Constitution* A-17/1 "They are generally blamed in education circles as having been a major force in dumbing-down textbooks nationwide. [¶] Because Texas made its textbook decisions statewide rather than district by district and because the Texas market was so large, textbook publishers tended to write and edit their texts to suit the Gablers." **b:** Reduce the requirements of (a job) for less-well educated workers 1988 Feb 21 *Harrisburg [PA] Sunday Patriot-News* F-4/3–4 (AP) "Although many employers realize they must bolster workers' skills to stay competitive, others are restructuring so employees often don't have to read, write or think—a change some educators call 'dumbing down.' ... 'There are jobs that will be dumbed down.' ... some companies opt for the dumbing-down approach simply because of the retraining costs." **2:** Teach (a student) with material intended for those at a lower grade-level 1983 Jul 3 *Atlanta Journal/Constitution* B-3/4 "In some schools, sixth-graders are taught with textbooks written for fourth-graders, a practice known in the trade as 'dumbing down.' Once out of school, former students, needing to break into a tough job market, are so used to being 'dumbed down' that they find reading this newspaper's job ads a difficult challenge." **3:** Cause (someone) to be or appear less intelligent 1985 quote under 1a 1988 Jan 13 *Washington Post* A-21/2–4 (William Raspberry) " 'Why do so many of the kids of the very poor seem dumber than the kids of the middle and upper income families?' he asks. 'Several things may be operating to "dumb them down." . . . In addition, some of those kids in poverty are in lead-laden environments where, after a few years, they are not just "dumbed down," they are brain-damaged as well.' "

dumb-down   *adj*   Reduced in requirements for basic skills of literacy and numeracy   1988 Feb 21 *Harrisburg [PA] Sunday Patriot-News* F-4/4   "Fast-food cashiering is a dumb-down job."   (perhaps a misspelling of *dumbed-down*)

dumb up   *vt*   DUMB DOWN   1928 Frank J Wilstach "Motion Picture Slang" scrapbook in NY Public Library np "Dumb it up! . . . Every thinker from Pythagoras to Nietzsche is rewritten in subway prose."

eco-anarchism   *n*   Anarchistic theory of ecology   1982 Murray Bookchin *The Ecology of Freedom* (Palo Alto, CA: Cheshire Books) 1–2 "For me, these changing emphases were not mere countercultural rhetoric; they marked a sweeping departure from my earlier commitment to socialist orthodoxies of all forms. I visualized instead a new form of libertarian social ecology—or what Victor Ferkiss, in discussing my social views, so appropriately called 'eco-anarchism.' "

ecocommunity   *n*   Human community living in balance with the environment   1982 Murray Bookchin *The Ecology of Freedom* Palo (Alto, CA: Cheshire Books) 46 "From this feeling of unity between the individual and the community emerges a feeling of unity between the community and its environment. Psychologically, people in organic communities must believe that they exercise a greater influence on natural forces than is actually afforded them by their relatively simple technology. Such a belief is fostered by group rituals and magical procedures. . . . The organic community is conceived to be part of the balance of nature—a forest community or a soil community—in short, a truly ecological community or *ecocommunity* peculiar to its ecosystem, with an active sense of participation in the overall environment and the cycles of nature."

ecodefender   *n*   One engaged in ECODEFENSE   1987 *Ecodefense: A Field Guide to Monkeywrenching,* ed Dave Foreman and Bill Haywood (Tucson, AZ: Ned Ludd) 15 "Ecodefenders pick their targets. Mindless, erratic vandalism is counterproductive."

ecodefense   *n*   Sabotage of companies and institutions exploiting or threatening the environment, ecotage (*AS* 47:270)   1987 *Ecodefense: A Field Guide to Monkeywrenching,* ed Dave Foreman and Bill Haywood (Tucson, AZ: Ned Ludd) title page

ecodisaster   *n*   Disappearance of many species in an environment   1978 Jan 24 *Atlanta Journal* C-2/4 "While he sympathized with the desire of the islands' residents for economic development, he said they are perhaps 'on the brink of ecodisaster.' [¶] Their coastal waters are 'ecologically rich and diverse,' he said, and the coral reef, marine lakes, mangrove swamps, sea grass beds and limestone island sustain thousands of species—82 of which are endangered, threatened or vulnerable."

ecofact   *n*   1984 "What Archaeologists Study" *World Book Science Annual* 371 "*Ecofacts* are natural objects found with artifacts or features. Ecofacts reveal how ancient people responded to their surroundings. Examples of ecofacts include seeds and animal bones."

ecomenu   *n*   Selection of simple, healthful foods that make minimal demands on the environment   1983 Apr 23 *Athens [GA] Daily News/Banner-Herald* 2/4 (UPI) "West Germany's environmentalist Greens Party said Friday they have no appetite for the frankfurters and sauerkraut usually served to the 498 members of Parliament who dine in the building's canteen. [¶] Instead, the party's 27 MPs who won seats in Parliament for the first time in March, have demanded an 'ecological menu' consisting of corn bread, corn rolls, Mueseli [*sic* for *muesli*] (a cereal favored by health food lovers), grain, potato and fresh vegetable dishes. . . . [¶] Greens representative Hannelore Saibold said fellow MPs should begin their switch in eating habits by doing without animal fats and eggs at least once a week for health reasons. [¶] Ms. Saibold said 'because of the indescribable hunger and thousands of deaths from starvation in many parts of the world,' the new ecomenu would 'symbolize new solidarity with people of the third world.' "

econote   *n*   Short article on ecology   1978 Jan *Audubon* 235/1 "Econotes" (title of a feature in the magazine)

ecoraider   *n*   ECODEFENDER   1982 Ann Ronald *The New West of Edward Abbey* (Albuquerque: U of New Mexico P) 183 "*The Monkey Wrench Gang* has more ambition than an ordinary propaganda novel of eco-raiders and environmental protest and speaks more profoundly than a vulgar little fairy tale." Ibid 190 "Some readers, however, may feel victimized by overkill on the part of both the ecoraiders and their creator."

electronic   *adj*   —**electronic battlefield**   1970 *Science News* 98:166 "Developed for the once-called 'McNamara Line' and now termed 'electronic battlefield,' the devices encompass many kinds of specially designed electronic and acoustical detectors for deployment in isolated regions [of Vietnam]."   —**electronic desk**   1987 fall *Plus: The College Guide to Consumer Electronics* 8/3–9/1 "The high-tech workstation of the future will start right under your nose—on your desk! The 'electronic desk' will combine the functions of a telephone, telephone dialer, calculator, typewriter, personal computer, appointments calendar, and address book."   (cf *Barnhart Dictionary Companion* 4 [1985]: 21, additional citation here)   —**electronic dialer**   1978 Jun 5 *New Yorker* 22/1 (ad) "You see, the Electronic Dialers are miniature computers that remember up to 16 phone numbers (any number you can dial direct) and then dial them for you. All at the touch of a button."   —**electronic evangelist**   1981 May *Harper's* 71/3 "Moral Majority, Inc., the political action program of the electronic evangelist Jerry Falwell, takes the position that by ignoring traditional moral and religious absolutes, Americans have dangerously restricted the system in which they live."   (cf Barbara Hunt Lazerson "Electronic Church Terms" *AS* 60 [1985]: 187–89, for this and similar terms)   —**electronic evangelistic peer**   Ibid 74/3 "The remnant utopianism we find in Dr. [Joyce] Brothers or Dr. [Billy] Graham, or in the Reverend [Jerry] Falwell and his numerous electronic evangelistic peers, either lacks theological sinew or has no sinew at all."   —**electronic kiosk**   1987 Aug 11 *International Herald Tribune* 16 "Two years ago, the department of telecommunications introduced a concept called the 'electronic kiosk' and invited newspapers and radio stations—which until then had seen videotex as a rival—to participate by providing information and other services."   —**electronic letter box**   Idem "Using Minitel, a subscriber can keep up with the news, . . . have a letter translated and keep up with friends around the country through an 'electronic letter box.' "   —**electronic press**   1977 Oct 8 *TV Guide* A-5/1 "Some years ago, the press—print and electronic—did its best to make itself and the public believe that the 'leftist bias' charges of the late '60s and early '70s were just a Nixonian fabrica

tion."   1979 May 19 *TV Guide* 10/2 "The problem is compounded by the division between the writing and the electronic press. The newspaper correspondents resent what they regard as the tendency of television to turn the [presidential press] conference into a 'show' that gets in the way of 'hard news.' "   —**electronic security arch**   1985 Jun 28 *[London] Times* 12/1 "Not so long ago, I am told, the boys in blue ushered into Parliament someone with 50 rounds of .22 ammunition in his pockets and not an alarm rang. My source—an amateur rifleman, not a terrorist—was taking the bullets to Bisley because they were defective and had dropped in to deliver a letter to an MP. It was only after he had passed through the electronic security arch that he realized what he had done. . . . the machine had been switched off because the area was being sprayed for deathwatch beetle and the spraying interfered with the mechanism."   —**electronic squealer**   1972 Jul 23 *Tuscaloosa [AL] News* A-3/1 (AP) "Each was required to present personal identification, submit hand luggage for search and undergo a body scanning by a metal-detecting device called an 'electronic squealer.' "   —**electronic time bomb**   1983 Oct 2 *Atlanta Journal/Constitution* A-6/2 "At the prestigious Massachusetts Institute of Technology, a punch line was surreptitiously programmed into the university's computer network. Without warning, when someone was working on a computer terminal, the screen would suddenly flash the word 'cookie.' If the person at the keyboard didn't respond rapidly by typing in a command of 'cookie,' the computer would start writing 'cookie' over and over on the screen until whatever was originally there was gobbled up. Then the computer would demand 'gimme cookie.' [¶] Questioned by Glickman, the head of computer security at Los Alamos National Laboratory, America's nuclear weapons test center, admitted that there's no sure way to know that a similar electronic 'time bomb' has not been secretly programmed into some computer at the center."   —**electronic vandalism**   1983 Sep 7 *International Herald Tribune* 1/2 "They say they're not malicious, but the victims lose all this computer time and they have some stranger roaming around in their system. I call it electronic vandalism."   —**electronic wallet**   1988 Jan 5 *PC Week* C-9/3 "Smart cards are being used by U.S. Marine recruits in place of money at Parris Island, S.C., in an application Mr. Dunham calls an 'electronic wallet.' "   —**electronic yoga**   1975 Dec 8 *Time* 58/1 "Glowingly described by fans as 'electronic yoga,' bio-feedback seemed to offer inner exploration without drugs, religion or psychotherapy."

monkey-wrench   *attrib*   [allusion to *The Monkey Wrench Gang* by Edward Abbey (Philadelphia: Lippincott, 1975), a novel about preservation of the environment by sabotaging exploiters and developers]   Pertaining to ECODEFENSE   1982 Ann Ronald *The New West of Edward Abbey* (Albuquerque: U of New Mexico P) 196 "To best the Team on a small scale and to thwart corporations on a large, Abbey delivers a monkey-wrench brand of justice, adjusting the gang's jaws whenever appropriate. No machine is too unimportant to leave incapacitated, no structure too gigantic to leave unscathed."

monkeywrencher   *n*   ECODEFENDER   1987 *Ecodefense: A Field Guide to Monkeywrenching,* ed Dave Foreman and Bill Haywood (Tucson, AZ: Ned Ludd) 15 "It is truly individual action. Because of this, communication among monkeywrenchers is difficult and dangerous."

monkeywrenching   *n*   ECODEFENSE   1987 *Ecodefense: A Field Guide to Monkeywrenching,* ed Dave Foreman and Bill Haywood (Tucson, AZ: Ned Ludd) 14 "Monkeywrenching is non-violent resistance to the destruction of natural diversity and wilderness. It is not directed toward harming human beings or other forms of life. It is aimed at inanimate machines and tools. Care is always taken to minimize any possible threat to other people (and to the monkeywrenchers themselves)."

orature   *n*   Oral literature   [1981] letter from Melbourne S Cummings, Assoc Dean, School of Communications, Howard U, Washington, DC, to Richard Allsopp, U of the West Indies, 16 Apr 1986 "At the First World Congress [on Communications and Development in Africa and the African Diaspora] the opening address was delivered by Micere Mugo, head of the Department of Literature at the University of Nairobi. She did not give us a copy of the paper that she presented in which she introduced the word 'orature'. That was in 1981, but she referred to an earlier time at which she either wrote or spoke about the term. She, too, spoke of the term as her own invention."   1983 Tom McArthur *Foundation Course for Language Teachers* (Cambridge UP) 41 "The early works of the Greeks, such as the Homeric epics, are generally described as part of their 'literature', but this is a term created after the event. Like the ancient Hindus, the Greeks had vast and complex oral heritages that might more accurately be called their 'orature', since the other term implies letters and literacy."   1986 Tom McArthur *Worlds of Reference* (Cambridge UP) 9 "What we may call the 'oratures' of pre-literate peoples belong also in World 3 [the interaction of material things and what has developed in our minds], but they are far less efficiently housed and safeguarded than the 'literatures' of literate societies."   Ibid 69–70 "Thus the Scholastics helped 'literature' to supersede 'orature'. Indeed, since the tenth century, the triumph of organized written-and-depicted material over the great oral heritages has been complete—so complete that some writers talk of 'oral literatures' to describe the earlier state, and I have been forced to invent 'orature' as a distinct term for that state."

-people   *Comb form*   (Cf -WORD)   —**S-people**   Socialists   1987/1988 Dec 26/Jan 2 *Nation* 790/2 "D.S.A. itself remained officially neutral in the campaign, not wanting to alienate its friends in labor and feminist circles who may not have been ready for a black presidential candidate. (Nobody on *The Times* ever called the S-people opportunists for *that* decision against Jackson.)"

power   *attrib*   Associated with, conducive to, or emblematic of power, esp political or economic; involving powerful people   1986 Nov 18 *PC Week* 141/4 "There is a perception that users who suffer from RAM-cram are power users who thrive on cramming their machines full of novel utilities in addition to their application software."   1987 conversation NYC book editor age ca 55 "I have a power breakfast in the morning, so I'll be unavailable most of this afternoon."   May 4 *New York* 45/2 "The Regency (540 Park Avenue, at 61st Street). Where the 'power breakfast' hype all began, this luxurious restaurant attracts a crowd that reads like an index to who's who in corporate America."   Oct 25 *Atlanta Journal/Constitution* J-3/4 "She can either send Elizabeth off with an American-Gothic couple who live in a *trailer park* (a cruel and unnecessary gag that grandstands to urban sensibilities). Or she can lug the kid along to power lunches."   Dec 3 Valerie Harper (TV actress) on *Larry King Live* CNN-TV "I wasn't there to hear my son's valedictorian address because I was at a power lunch [with network executives]."   Dec 9 *International Hour* CNN-TV "Mr. Gorbachev will be wearing a power suit to the summit meeting of superpowers." Dec 27 *Athens [GA] Daily News/Banner-Herald* B-8/2 "Some people play the frequent-flier bonus-mileage game the way others play the stock market, looking for every angle, even flying out of the way, to get some extra free miles later. For those 100,000-mile-a-year 'power fliers', there's—what else?—a new newsletter." Dec 27 *Atlanta Journal/ Constitution* G-1/1–2 "She noted that Gorbachev, in a dark blue suit and red power tie, was not intimidated by the dress at the formal dinner. 'To him, it wasn't the wrong kind of suit. None of the Soviets wore tuxedos.' " 1988 Jan 2 *Atlanta Journal/Constitution Weekend* mag 10/2 "Every morning, he [actor Michael Douglas] put on the Saville Row suit and the gold chain bracelet and the power suspenders and he slicked back his hair and he became Gordo [a character in the film *Wall Street*]." Jan 3 *Parade Magazine* 7/1 "Worst Fashion [of 1987] / The power necktie" Jan 4 *Athens [GA] Banner-Herald* 4/4 "It's bad enough admitting that you've quit running and taken up power-walking." Jan 28 *Wall Street Journal* 1/5 "Yellow ties are on their way out, says Field Brothers menswear stores, with pink and red the new 'power colors.' " Mar 15 *Los Angeles Times* V-1/2 "So as not to be brushed off during its power lunch, the leech anesthetizes as it bites—kind of like administering a shot of Novocain." Apr 2 *Atlanta Journal/Constitution* B-6 ("On the Fastrack" cartoon) "This is my first top-level Board meeting, Bob. What should I expect? / Well, you'll have to watch out for Ms. Trellis, of course. / She always plays power games." (drawing of couple going to a board meeting where they sit in chairs cut-down to floor level and look up at the executive at the table head) Apr 3 *Athens [GA] Daily News/Banner-Herald* D-7/1 "Connie Glaser, a communications specialist, helps private sector employers turn poor writing into power writing."

-question *comb form* (Cf -WORD) —**A-question** 1987 Jun 29 *Newsweek* 6/3 "As the nation's political-rumor mill rattled with talk of an impending GOP sex scandal, Vice President George Bush's eldest son and campaign adviser, George Jr., asked his father point-blank last week if he ever committed adultery . . . . Says George Jr., 'The answer to the Big A question is N.O.' "

social ecology *n* Study of ecological issues as the result of social and political factors 1982 Murray Bookchin *The Ecology of Freedom* (Palo Alto, CA: Cheshire Books) 1 "Owing to my early Marxian intellectual training, the article ["The Problems of Chemicals in Food" 1952] examined not merely environmental pollution but also its deep-seated social origins. Environmental issues had developed in my mind as social issues, and problems of natural ecology had become problems of 'social ecology'—an expression hardly in use at the time."

-word *comb form* Formative combined with the initial letter of a word under real or pretended taboo to make a jocular euphemism —**D-word** 1987 Dec 27 W Safire "On Language" *New York Times Magazine* 6/2 "Coinages [in connection with the Reagan-Gorbachev summit] were few; *the D word* was the chosen euphemism for unfashionable *détente*." —**F-word** 1987 Dec 7 *Time* 85/3 "After becoming the first man to utter the *f* word on British TV and 'devising' that quintessential artifact of the '60s sensibility, *Oh! Calcutta!*, [Kenneth] Tynan found a young woman whose masochistic fantasies matched his sadistic ones." —**H-word** 1988 Mar *Washington Monthly* 11/2–12/1 "The H word [subhead] . . . Fortunately, there is one word that can make a yuppie respect a public school teacher running against an attorney, one word that could have evened the playing field between my brother and The Opponent: Harvard. A Harvard-educated public school teacher is to so many people an oxymoron that it shatters their preconceptions." —**I-word** 1987 Nov 22 *Athens [GA] Daily News/Banner-Herald* 7/2 "Cohen, Rudman and other members of the Iran-Contra panels—including the most adamant of Reagan-bashers among the House Democrats—agreed on this central point. So did a range of political analysts and constitutional scholars interviewed last week, almost all of whom were sharply critical of the president's performance but nevertheless agreed that impeachment would not only have been unwarranted but also unwise. [¶] Probably the most compelling argument against the Democrats even uttering the 'I' word (it would be political masochism for a Republican to do so) is that they would have nothing to gain by it." —**L-word** 1988 Mar 15 *Birmingham [AL] Post-Herald* A-5/1 "Exit polling revealed that only 21 percent of the Southerners who voted for Mike Dukakis understood him to be a (shoo the children off to bed; I must use the L-word) liberal. —**N-word** Nigger 1988 Apr 19 *Red and Black* U of GA student newspaper 4/2 "There was a red BMW in front of me. A guy was standing up out of the sunroof of the moving car. [¶] On the sidewalk . . . was a black lady—probably in her 70s. . . . [¶] The guy, in the requisite Ray-Bans decided to gun her down with an arsenal of Arby's litter, while shouting the dreaded 'n' word. [¶] He actually hit the woman with garbage." —**O-word** 1988 Feb 20 CNN "What is the O-word? Olympics." —**P-word** Please 1988 Feb 14 reported by J B McMillan —**S-word** **1:** Socialism 1987 Dec 26 *Nation* 790/1 "Explicit in the article was the assumption that even the first initial of socialism is enough to sink a politician in that water [the mainstream]. 'The S word is definitely not something most politicians want to have anything to do with,' . . . [¶] Now, *The New York Times* is not normally in touch with leftists or the left (the S word is also enough to disqualify a source for its pages)." **2:** Sex 1988 Feb 14 reported by J B McMillan —**T-word** **1:** Taxes 1988 Mar 23 *Atlanta Constitution* A-10 (political cartoon of President Reagan talking to himself) "There's only one way to lower the deficit. We've got to raise ta . . / Oops . . . I almost said the 'T' word." **2:** Tornado 1988 Apr 6 Athens, GA, conversation about storm warning "You haven't heard the T-word, have you?" —**V-word** 1987 Oct 24 *Atlanta Journal/Constitution* B-1/1 "Sources tell me the usual solidarity of black leadership has been splintered in the cases of Eaves and Chuck Williams, the commissioner indicted along with him. Past local corruption cases didn't include the dread 'V-word'—as in videotape [of illegal actions]." —**W-word** Wimp 1988 Feb 14 Garrick Utley "Sunday Today" NBC-TV "I'm not going to mention the W-word."

AMONG THE NEW WORDS

JOHN ALGEO
AND
ADELE ALGEO
University of Georgia
Athens, Georgia

With the assistance of Robert K. Barnhart, *Barnhart Books*; George S. Cole, *Shippensburg University*; Lesa Dill, *Western Kentucky University*; William W. Evans, *Louisiana State University*; Raymond Gozzi, *University of Rhode Island*; William J. Kirwin, *Memorial University of Newfoundland*; Jonathan Lighter, *University of Tennessee*; Virginia G. McDavid, *Chicago State University*; James B. McMillan, *University of Alabama*; Patrick W. Merman; Louis Phillips, *School of Visual Arts*; Mary Gray Porter, *University of Alabama*; Sol Steinmetz, *Barnhart Books*; and Greg Williams

IN THE LATE SPRING OF 1988, the expression *kiss and tell* became prominent in news stories about books by former White House staff members and Reagan intimates. The expression is of long standing in English, though it is still recorded in few dictionaries. Lexicographers have apparently regarded the expression as an analytical verb phrase, despite its clearly idiomatic sense. The *OEDS* added it as a phrase to its entry for the verb *kiss*, defining it as "to recount one's sexual exploits," and illustrating it by quotations beginning with Congreve's 1695 *Love for Love*. The expression is older than that, however. It appears in Charles Cotton's 1675 *Burlesque upon Burlesque; or, The Scoffer Scoft* (66–67):

> *Juno.* But if (as now adayes thou know'st
> Men are too apt to make their boast)
> This *Rogue* so soon as he has done,
> As they all do, should straight-way run,
> And publish to the world, that he
> Has had his filthy will of me;
> Pray after such a fine Oration,
> Where then were *Juno*'s reputation?
> *Jup.* Should he do such a thing as that,
> I'de teach the *Rascal* how to prate,
> And if he needs must kiss, and tell,
> I'le kick him headlong into Hell.

Cotton's use of the expression suggests that it must have been proverbial already at the time he put it into Jupiter's mouth. It certainly was proverbial thereafter, being attested in Burton Stevenson's *Home Book of Proverbs, Maxims, and Familiar Phrases* (New York: Macmillan, 1948) and in F. P. Wilson's *Oxford Dictionary of English Proverbs*, 3d ed. (Oxford: Clarendon, 1970) with a number of quotations, including that from Cotton. B. J. Whiting's *Early American Proverbs and Proverbial Phrases* (Cambridge, MA: Belknap, 1977) cites an instance from an 1809 play by A. B. Lindsley, *Love and Friendship; or, Yankee Notions* (15), in which a black serving lad protests his honorable dealings:

> Me no de kiss and tell secret ob de fair sec.
> [I do not kiss and tell secrets of the fair sex.]

All of the early uses of the expression are in predicate function and have an explicitly sexual meaning. The currently voguish use, however, is attributive, refers to books, and has the more general sense 'revealing private or confidential matters that are embarrassing to the person written about'. That use has been around for several decades, the term being applied to books by associates of Presidents Johnson and Nixon before Reagan.

The recent vogue for the expression was occasioned by former Chief of Staff Donald Regan's publication of a book concerning his White House experience, in which he depicts Ronald Reagan as under the influence of his wife, who sought advice from an astrologer about the timing of presidential events. The President himself seems to have begun the vogue by using the expression in a television interview, although it is impossible to say who suggested it to him.

The term has spawned a number of imitations: *tattle-tale* as in "Nancy Reagan always seems to get a bum rap in the 'tattle-tale' book business" (Alan K. Simpson, Senator from Wyoming, *Atlanta Constitution* 19 May 1988, A-27/1) and *slap-and-yell* as in "Even two Reagan children, Patti and Michael, have written slap-and-yell books about the First Family" (*Time*, 23 May 1988, 14/1). They are doubtless nonce uses, but illustrate the current vigor of the source expression.

Acknowledgments to others for citations: Thomas Algeo, Walter S. Avis, Sheila Bailey, Charles Clay Doyle, Edgar L. Frost, and I. Willis Russell.

afterboomer *n* BABY BUSTER 1987 Nov 12 *Wall Street Journal* 41/1 "Running the gamut from teens to young adults, baby busters are an amorphous bunch who are harder to pigeonhole than the baby boomers. There isn't even total agreement on what to call them. While busters is most common, consultants also have coined such terms as 'afterboomers' and Flyers (Fun-loving youth en route to success)."

baby bust *n* Period of sharp decrease in the birthrate 1971 Sep 18 *National Observer* 8/4 "The 'baby boom' has turned into a 'baby bust,' and the U.S. population may stop growing before the end of the century." 1972 Mar 11 *Saturday Review* 40 "The grown-up babies of the post-World War II baby boom should be producing a baby boom of their own these days, but aren't. Instead, as front pages around the country have noted in recent months, the number of new babies actually has been decreasing, prompting talk of a 'baby bust.'" Apr 8 *Saturday Review* 16 "The Nazis encouraged a baby boom; Zero Population Growthers champion a baby bust." 1978 *Collier's Encyclopedia Yearbook* 453/1 "The aging of the U.S. population is partly a result of the 'baby bust' of the 1970's." Feb 8 *Toronto Globe and Mail* 11/1 "Postponement helped to contribute to the so-called baby bust—the dramatic drop in the United States birth rate in recent years." May 28 *Manchester Guardian Weekly* 1/4 "But the 'baby boom' in Japan ended in a 'baby bust' in the mid-1950's—some six years before a similar 'baby bust' in the United States and ten years before the birthrate dropped sharply in Germany." 1982 May 16 *Tuscaloosa [AL] News* 1/1 "The United States 'can't afford to waste or miseducate a single member' of the 'baby bust generation' if it is to survive and prosper during the economic revolution now occurring, former Vice President Walter Mondale told the University of Alabama graduating class Saturday." 1988 Winter *American Scholar* 64 "However, in contrast, from 1980 to 1986 the number of Americans aged fifteen to nineteen fell off by about 2.5 million, or 12 percent; these cohorts of the 'baby bust' are about to move into the labor market and, because of their smaller numbers, start a crunch on the funding of Social Security. With minor differences, this is also the situation in other industrial countries."

baby buster *n* One born during a BABY BUST, esp in the US 1965 to 1974 1987 Nov 12 *Wall Street Journal* 41/1 "Enough already about baby boomers. Marketers have analyzed them to death. Now get ready for the baby busters. They're the consumers born after the baby boom subsided—from about 1965 to 1974—and they're shaping up to be the next hot demographic group. [¶] 'They may be fewer in number than baby boomers, but young people today have lots of discretionary income,' says Barbara Fiegin, an executive vice president at Grey Advertising. . . . [¶] Running the gamut from teens to young adults, baby busters are an amorphous bunch who are harder to pigeonhole than the baby boomers."

bookend *vt* **1:** Enclose, bracket, precede and follow 1978 Dec 25 *Maclean's* 46/1 "At the centre of this 'hollywood novel' is 37-year-old Jill Peel, whose directorial career spans two films, which book-end her two 'love' stories." 1979 May 5 *Atlanta Journal/Constitution* T-58 "The hour-long show narrated by George Plimpton will be 'bookended' with a party at the publisher's Playboy Mansion West, with James Caan, Chevy Chase and Tony Curtis joining host Hefner." **2:** Close off, separate 1987 Sep 23 *Athens [GA] Banner-Herald* 4/4 "Only, Dantice had a story on her candidacy published first. O'Looney had none. A mistake on our part, I think. We should play tit-for-tat as much as possible: politicians and school partisans keep count. O'Looney didn't want to get 'bookended,' she said—that is, her story gets told weeks before the election while her opponent's story comes out within a week of the vote." **3:** End, conclude in a way appropriate to the beginning 1988 Jul 11 *Newsweek* 64/1 "[Architect Philip] Johnson has showcased this anything-goes style in a controversial new exhibition at the Museum of Modern Art in New York. It nicely bookends his long, trend-spotting career—in 1932 he was cocurator of the revolutionary 'International Style' exhibition at MOMA, which introduced stripped-down modern boxes to a wide public."

Britcom *n* [patterned on *sitcom*] British television comedy 1986 Mar 2 WGTV Atlanta/Athens (GA) fund-drive announcer "These British comedies—they call them Britcoms—they really do cost money." 1986 Jun *Fine Tuning* (Georgia Public TV program) 10 "*Solo* . . . Felicity Kendal . . . stars in this 13-part Britcom about a young woman making dramatic changes in her life." Ibid 11 "*Wodehouse Playhouse* . . . It's been several years since this popular Britcom played GPTV." 1987 Oct Ibid 20/2 "*Are You Being Served? / Premiere*. This 32-part Britcom, another GPTV exclusive, follows the rivalries at Grace Brothers department store, where Gentlemen's Ready To Wear battles Ladies' Separates and Underwear."

bunker atmosphere *n* Mood of last-ditch defensiveness in response to imminent loss of political power; cf BUNKER MENTALITY [1975 Oct 28 Mark Singer rev of G B Trudeau *Doonesbury Chronicles* in *Chronicle of Higher Education Rev* 11/3 "He has been able, for instance, to show the Nixon White House in its waning days as both a figurative *and* literal bunker, complete with a stone wall, armored tanks, machine-gun emplacements, and trigger-ready sentries."] 1974 Jan 21 *Newsweek* 3/1 "In the 'bunker atmosphere' at the Nixon White House, press secretary Ronald Ziegler has become a conspicuous insider. He is the last survivor of the original Nixon crowd—a young loyalist whose company seems to give comfort to a besieged President." 1975 Sep 15 *Time* 20/3 "Until late in the week, Abe Beame was struggling to prevent the loss of the power that he had exercised so inadequately during the months of mounting crisis. In the bunker atmosphere of city hall, one die-hard loyalist muttered that [NY governor Hugh] Carey and his aides were out to 'destroy' the mayor."

bunker mentality *n* Last-ditch defensive reaction, as to growing criticism or imminent loss of political power; cf BUNKER ATMOSPHERE 1981 Sep 14 *Time* 41 "'The reactionary regime has already receded into a bunker mentality,' Tehran-based Mousa Khiabani, chief of staff of anti-Khomeini guerrillas, told *Time* last week." 1986 Dec 22 *Newsweek* 7/3 "Amid signs of a bunker mentality in the White House, Attorney General Edwin Meese and Treasury Secretary James Baker are considering a set of 'new initiatives' to divert public attention from the Iran arms scandal."

buster *n* BABY BUSTER 1987 Nov 12 *Wall Street Journal* 41/1 "Busters also are characterized as driven people, preoccupied with success in school and in careers. 'They're definitely a materialistic group, but unlike yuppies, they're more into being entrepreneurs—starting their own health club or disco,' says Larry Graham, a marketing consultant who advises companies on the attitudes and spending habits of consumers 13-to-25 years old."

chat line *n* Computerized telephone service for engaging in conversation, often of a sexual or pornographic nature, with another subscriber to the service or with someone employed by the service for this purpose 1987 Oct 9 *Atlanta Constitution* C-4/4 "That may be what one messagerie had in mind when it called itself 'The Voice of the Paranoid.' But all the chat lines play the same theme. 'You're never alone on Minitel,' says one called Sophie, which shows a field of amorous bunnies in its advertisements."

double zero *attrib* ZERO-ZERO 1987 Sep 1 *Atlanta Constitution* A-17/2 "The United States and the Soviet Union are hurtling full-tilt toward the so-called 'double zero' option—the mutual removal of all theater-range nuclear missiles (between 300- and 3,000-mile ranges) in Europe."

flyer *n* 1987 Nov 12 sv AFTERBOOMER

gin up *vt* **1:** Create, produce 1970 Oct *Atlantic* 57/1 "Thus the White House goes to extra lengths to brief veterans' groups, who in turn gin up support for the President's war policy." 1987 Jun *Geology* 583 ". . . too many arguably parvenu scientists . . . offhandedly baptize a deep-sea topographic feature . . . that may have been known and well-explored—even if possibly unnamed—earlier, or even one bearing a long-established name in another language. They gin up a name, place it on an illustration, perhaps mention it in the text [of an article manuscript], get it by a harassed editor and into the technical literature, and consider that feature 'named' for posterity." **2:** Increase, encourage 1980 May 12 *New Yorker* 54 "We're still talking about doing things at the margins—cut taxes a little, gin up the economy a little." 1987 Oct 27 Edwin M Yoder *Atlanta Constitution* A-19/1 "In theory, the 'supply-side' tax cuts of 1981, adding substantially to the spendable income of upper-income taxpayers, were supposed to gin up the savings rate. That is what the supply-side apostles said. It didn't happen." (in *World Book Dictionary* 1980 and earlier with the 1970 quot, glossed 'stir up' and labeled "Dialect or Informal"; later uses show extended meanings and widened levels of use)

home-shopping *n* 1987 Nov 4 *Wall Street Journal* 39/3–5 (headline and article) "Home-Shopping Shakeout Forces Survivors to Find Fresh Approach / When cable-TV viewers sit down to watch home-shopping shows, the announcers periodically remind them that time is running out to buy a particular product. . . . [¶] The home-shopping business, which primarily sells goods and services at a discount to phone-in viewers of cable-TV, is still young. Although local shopping shows have been around for as long as a decade, most people date the industry's emergence to early 1985. That year, Clearwater, Fla.-based Home Shopping Network Inc. became the first broadcaster to go national." **—home-shopper** *n* Idem 39/3 "Sales this year should total about $1.25 billion, according to Paul Kagan Associates Inc., an entertainment media research firm in Carmel, Calif. And a recent forecast by the Roper Organization suggests that home-shoppers may be changing from 'couch potatoes' to busy consumers who are seeking greater control over their time. [¶] 'Home shopping is quick, clean (and) painless,' says the Roper study."

hub-and-spoke *attrib* 1984 Jul 2 *Newsweek* 60/2 "Control-tower tensions have grown worse with the airlines' new hub-and-spoke route systems, which make airport rush hours even more rushed. Carriers try to bring as many flights as possible into their hubs at the same time in the morning, then transfer the passengers to connecting flights; the process is reversed in the evening." 1987 *Americana Annual* 526 "Another post-deregulation trend that continued in 1986 was hub-and-spoke operations." Aug 13 *International Herald Tribune* 1 "Much of the difficulty travelers encounter arises from the airlines' use of the hub-and-spoke system of routing. In this system, carriers arrange their routes so that many flights converge at 'hub' airports. The idea is to maximize traffic. . . . But hub-and-spoke routes have proven prone to disruption. The hubs are often congested, and airports at the tips of the 'spokes' are short on backup equipment and repair capabilities." Nov 1 *New York Times Magazine* (Morton Hunt) 44 "Old air-travel joke: Whether you're going to heaven or hell, you have to change at Atlanta. [¶] That's because Atlanta's Hartsfield Airport is a major hub for both Delta and Eastern—a focal center in the 'hub-and-spoke' system that has dominated routing since deregulation."

kiss-and-tell *attrib* Revealing confidential or private matters known through personal intimacy 1970 Oct *Harper's* (Edwin M Yoder, Jr) 127/2 "It is kiss-and-tell time for Lyndon Johnson's White House inner circle. But those who relish bloody and Byzantine tales will be unsatisfied by this discreet chronicle of 'the transfer of power,' which covers LBJ's last months." 1974 Jul 19 *National Review* (Robert D Novak review of *An American Life: One Man's Road to Watergate* by Jeb Stuart Magruder) 824 "Magruder has always compensated for his shallowness and poor judgment by charm and an insouciant ruthlessness, and he now has used the kiss-and-tell method to ensure his financial security in the wake of personal disgrace." 1979 May 16 *Birmingham Post-Herald* (James P Herzog; Scripps-Howard) F-1/4 "She is out of prostitution, out of seven months of hiding that was inspired by her literary agent, and she is beginning a 10-day cross-country tour to promote her kiss-and-tell book called 'Defector's Mistress—The Judy Chavez Story.'" 1988 Apr 25 *Newsweek* 21/1 "It's as if the White House were infested with piranhas, all snapping furiously at the hands that once fed them. David Stockman's kiss-and-tell memoirs are history, and Michael Deaver's all-too-candid portrait of Ronald and Nancy Reagan was receding into memory last week." May 10 *Atlanta Constitution* A-9/3 "'The new book by Donald Regan,' [White House spokesman Marlin] Fitzwater said, 'is a kiss-and-tell story in the mold of all such books which seek to exploit the presidency or the first family for personal self-interest.'" May 12 *Atlanta Constitution* A-23/1 (William Safire) "President Reagan glowered and said he did not 'look kindly' on kiss-and-tell books, and struck his standard gallant pose as defender of his beleaguered bride." May 13 *Athens [GA] Banner-Herald* 4/1 (Carl Leubsdorf) "But the controversy over the recent 'kiss-and-tell' books by Mr. Regan and former spokesman Larry Speakes goes far beyond these and other titillating disclosures." May 13 *Atlanta Journal* A-19/1 (George Will) "Furthermore, authors of kiss-and-tell books are dishonorable. A necessary condition of government is a climate of candor in inner councils—strong convictions bravely expressed. Candor becomes rarer as government becomes an incubator for memoirists who attend meetings with book contracts in mind." May 15 *Atlanta Journal/Constitution* A-8/1–4 (Boston Globe service) "The 'kiss-and-tell' phenomenon is in full force. . . . [Donald] Regan's book is so hot a news topic that reporters are rounding up authors of other kiss-and-tell books to ask them what they think about it, and why they think such books are written, besides the presumed motivations of revenge, ego and greed. . . . [Larry] Speakes, in the midst of a major book-promotion tour, is being hounded by reporters seeking his insight on the kiss-and-tell trend. . . . 'I've been reading political memoirs since I was in high school nearly 40 years ago,' [Rolling Stone editor William] Greider said of the kiss-and-tell Reagan books. 'I don't think there's ever been an era that's produced anything like these. . . . These are totally different in tone and in their nastiness.'" Ibid sidebar "The Reagan kiss-and-tell library / 'Home Front,' a novel by daughter Patti Davis. Published March 1986. / 'The Triumph of Politics: Why the Reagan Revolution Failed,' by former budget director David Stockman. Published April 1986. / 'Man of the House,' by former Speaker of the House Tip O'Neill. Published September 1987. / 'Behind the Scenes,' by former White House aide Michael Deaver. Published January 1988. / 'On the Outside Looking In,' by adopted son Michael Reagan. Published March 1988. / 'Speaking Out,' by former press secretary Larry Speakes. Published May 1988. / 'For the Record: From Wall Street to Washington,' by former White House Chief of Staff Donald Regan. Published May 1988." May 22 *Atlanta Journal/Constitution* (Durward McAlister) C-2/2–3 "Is it possible that President Reagan exercises so little control that his underlings feel free to involve the United States in politically sensitive international adventures without consulting him? [¶] The answer, unfortunately, is yes. [¶] Forget the kiss-and-tell books; the evidence is as close at hand as this week's news." May 30 *Sports Illustrated* 83/1 "TV sports executives and announcers are a notoriously thin-skinned lot. It's no wonder, then, that the talk of the business right now is former ABC exec Jim Spences's kiss-and-tell memoir [*Up Close and Personal: The Inside Story of Network Television Sports*]. Donald Regan has nothing on Jim the Ripper." Jul 6 *Atlanta Constitution* ("Peanuts" cartoon) C-9 "[Lucy to Snoopy:] You know what you should write? You should write a 'kiss-and-tell book.'"

level playing field *n* Equal terms, par 1981 May 21 *Atlanta Constitution* (Gene Tharpe) A-5/3 "In 1980, Congress passed the Depository Institutions Deregulation and Monetary Control Act. The legislation provides for the lifting of government regulations over a period of years that will, in theory and somewhat in practice, put banks and S&Ls on an equal legal and business basis— a 'level playing field' is the description often used." 1987 *Americana Annual* 158 "Canadian unions lined up solidly against the government's free-trade initiative, not least because they feared that part of the 'level playing field' demanded by U.S. negotiators would be the antiunion environment that had already reduced U.S. unions to half the proportional strength of Canada's organized workers." Jun 15 *Newsweek* 53/2 "Even if the guests [on Ted Koppel's *Nightline*] are in a studio 50 feet away, they talk to him through the camera as if they were on the other side of the world. The physical arrangement provides a level playing field when other guests are somewhere else. It also puts them at a disadvantage; some guests find the earpiece—and the restricted visual contact with Koppel—uncomfortable." Oct 31 *Atlanta Journal/Constitution* A-24/3 "'I have come to realize that I am not on a level playing field with the rest of those people [institutional investers using computers],' he said. 'The market is a gopher hole—you poke money in, and you never get it back.'" 1988 Apr 1 economist interviewed on *Today Show* NBC-TV "We do need a trade bill to produce a level playing field between the United States and other countries." **—to level the playing field** To create equality 1987 Dec 21 *Athens [GA] Banner-Herald* 3/2 "'The current policy of allowing the states (and the District of Columbia) to design 51 different Medicaid programs, ranging from reasonably good to terrible, is unfair and must end,' the report said. [¶] It said an attempt to 'level the playing field' by having the federal government contribute a larger share of financing to poorer states has failed." (cf *even the playing field* sv WORD, *H-word* 1988 in the last installment of "Among the New Words")

messagerie *n* [Fr 'goods traffic, transport service'] CHAT LINE 1987 Feb 9 *Atlanta Constitution* (Richard Reeves) A-9/1 "Exchange lonely or not-so-lonely hearts messages via uncensored dating directories and 'messageries'—and, with luck, make a blind computer date for tonight along the Seine." Oct 9 *Atlanta Constitution* C-4/4–5 "But while the PTT likes to emphasize the Minitel's professional side, it is the soft-porn dialogue services that bring in the profit and the publicity. Depending on who is supplying the figures, these 'messageries' account for one-third to one-half of the Minitel hours. . . . The backlash began earlier this year, when mayors' offices around the country were bombarded by citizen complaints about the racy messagerie ads ('I'm Yours, Nothing but Yours, Call me Quickly,' was one poster showing a nude woman) that dominated street corner kiosks, subway stations, billboards and TV. . . . Messagerie advertising is now banned from TV, and most of the erotic posters are gone."

Minitel *n* [Fr fr *mini(stère)* 'ministry' + *tél(écommunication)* 'telecommunication'] **1:** French telecommunication system accessed by home computer terminals 1987 Aug 11 *International Herald Tribune* 16 "The poster is one of hundreds for privately operated message services on Minitel, the government-sponsored videotex system. [¶] Using Minitel, a subscriber can keep up with the news, seek an apartment, calculate taxes, consult a horoscope, settle bills, book an airline or train ticket, buy groceries and have them delivered, send a complaint to city hall, find a restaurant, get legal advice, look at what is playing at the movies, plan a trip, get a weather forecast, buy and sell shares, buy a used car or boat, get help with a child's homework, play chess, find a verse in the Bible, be told a joke, have a letter translated and keep up with friends around the country through an 'electronic letter box.'" **2:** A terminal in the French telecommunication system 1987 Feb 9 *Atlanta Constitution* (Richard Reeves) A-9/1 "The French government, determined to push the country into high-technology competitiveness, began offering Minitels free three years ago." Oct 9 *Atlanta Constitution* C-1/3–4 "Ms. Sagalyn, who has since moved to Paris, had discovered the Minitel, the home computer invented by the French government to coax its tradition-bound citizens into loving technology. . . . [¶] The Minitel terminal is given away free by the PTT, the French phone company. Everything is built in. There's no need to buy software or a modem, the extra piece of equipment that lets one computer communicate with another over phone lines. [¶] Dial a four-digit number, 3615, and press a button on the Minitel. A form appears on the screen. Type in a code name, and 4,500 services are available, from train reservations to information about the Communist Party." Dec 19 *Atlanta Journal/Constitution* C-1/2 "Today,

some 3.3 million French consumers use the Minitel—a 9-pound, lightweight computer terminal that plugs directly into a regular telephone outlet—to do much of their daily business." **—Minitelist** *n* A user of the Minitel system Idem C-1/4 "In the dark, in the office, at lunch and at midnight, the French are using the uncomplicated video terminals to talk to each other about lust, love and sometimes the cinema. . . . [¶] 'Looking for an intellectual,' one Minitelist typed after connecting to a dialogue service run by a former culture minister. In less than three minutes, 10 people who also were on the line sent anonymous responses."

near collision *n* 1987 Aug 22 *Atlanta Journal/Constitution* A-19/1 "Don't call them near-misses, these sticklers for terminological exactitude insist; the almost-accidents are complete misses, on the ancient theory that any miss is as good as a mile. Call them by their right name, as the Federal Aviation Administration does: 'near-collisions.' They demand that I, as a language maven, point out that a near-miss can only denote a girl entering puberty." Sep 5 *Atlanta Journal/Constitution* A-2/5 "In the wake of a near collision involving an off-course Delta Air Lines jet over the North Atlantic, the Federal Aviation Administration (FAA) is revamping its overseas navigational procedures, an agency spokesman in Washington said Friday. [¶] . . . The FAA action followed a report from the National Transportation Safety Board (NTSB) on Tuesday that said the Delta crew failed to verify the aircraft's position before coming within 30 feet of hitting a Continental Airlines jet in July." Dec 11 *Atlanta Constitution* A-1/1 "An error by an air traffic controller at Hartsfield International Airport's tower apparently caused a near-collision between two Delta Air Lines jets 15 miles west of the airport Tuesday night, government officials said Thursday." 1988 Apr 7 *Athens [Ga] Daily News* A-4 (James Kilpatrick) ". . . last year saw 1,063 near collisions in midair . . . ." May 15 *Atlanta Journal/Constitution* (Lewis Grizzard) B-1/1 "I don't want to know any more about how many midair near-collisions there are and about how we don't have enough air traffic controllers."

necklace *vt* 1987 *World Book Encyclopedia Year Book* 470 "The comrades executed many of those suspected collaborators, often by 'necklacing' them— setting fire to a gasoline filled automobile tire draped around the neck of the victim." Sep 29 *Athens [GA] Banner-Herald* 4/4 "Winnie Mandela has endorsed the use of 'necklacing' against her political opponents. This is when radical blacks place a tire laced with gasoline around the neck of a moderate black. The tire and victim are set ablaze. It is black South Africa's version of a lynching."

shopping network *n* System of advertising on cable television for products and services to be ordered by telephone 1987 Nov 28 *Athens [GA] Daily News/Banner Herald* 11/1 ("Shoe" cartoon, speaker sitting in front of a TV set) "That's weird. I've been sitting here all morning . . . / Watching this stupid shopping network. / And my feet are killing me."

shopping show *n* 1987 Nov 4 sv HOME-SHOPPING

AMONG THE NEW WORDS

JOHN ALGEO
AND
ADELE ALGEO
*University of Georgia
Athens, Georgia*

With the assistance of Robert K. Barnhart, *Barnhart Books*; George S. Cole, *Shippensburg University*; Lesa Dill, *Western Kentucky University*; William W. Evans, *Louisiana State University*; Raymond Gozzi, *University of Rhode Island*; William J. Kirwin, *Memorial University of Newfoundland*; Jonathan Lighter, *University of Tennessee*; Virginia G. McDavid, *Chicago State University*; James B. McMillan, *University of Alabama*; Patrick W. Merman, *Monroe, Michigan*; Louis Phillips, *School of Visual Arts*; Mary Gray Porter, *University of Alabama*; Sol Steinmetz, *Barnhart Books*; and Greg Williams, *University of Toronto*

IN ADDITION TO NEW TERMS FOR RELATIVELY new things or concerns (*caregiver* and *caregiving, emporiatrics, Hacky Sack*, and *jetway*) this installment includes stunt words like *buppie, dink(ie), dumpie, skippie, suppie, yappie, yuca*, and a number of other irradiations of *yuppie*. It also includes a number of old "new words"—terms that have been around for sometime but have not been recorded in dictionaries—such as *gomer, goofus*, and *tee ball*.

Most of the citations in the entry for *gomer* are from the extensive collections of Jonathan Lighter, who is writing a historical dictionary of slang. The unusually full entry for this term documents both its use and the attention that has been paid to it. It also shows how extensive is the evidence on which Lighter's dictionary will be based.

Other citations in this installment were supplied by Catherine M. Algeo, Thomas Algeo, Walter S. Avis, Shelia Bailey, Charles C. Doyle, and Claudia Kretzschmar. George E. Howard provided help with Hebrew.

animator *n* One who organizes or leads an activity, facilitator 1987 Jun 18 letter from M B L Nightingale, rep of British Council in Helsinki (answering a query about a brochure announcement of grants to "animators") "Thank you for your letter of 8 June 1987, enquiring about our use of the word 'animator'. . . . I think that our use in our brochure owes something to the French word 'animateur', that is someone who inspires or organises a function rather than actually does the lecturing or consultancy himself." Aug 11 *International Herald Tribune* 16 "Some [French Minitel] services hire 'animators' to handle several terminals at once and keep the conversation flowing." Nov

6 *Atlanta Constitution* C-4/4 "To satisfy their customers, most French messageries hire people they call animators. Their job is to send messages to the real customers calling the chat line, encouraging them to stay on the line. Sometimes the animators identify themselves. More often, they appear under a pseudonym just like the paying customers."

buppie *n* Black yuppie 1986 Aug 3 *Atlanta Journal/Constitution* G-1/1 "About 45 people . . . braved an afternoon downpour last week to attend a wine-tasting given . . . in honor of Fulton's top Buppie, [County Council Chairman] Michael Lomax." Aug 5 *Atlanta Constitution* A-14/4 "But Ponce [de Leon Avenue] fades fast before an onslaught of Yuppies and Buppies, many of them from the 'burbs." Nov 2 *Atlanta Journal/Constitution* G-1/1 "Although it's been bandied about town, you read it here first, folks. Atlanta's First Buppie will be bidding bye-bye to bachelorhood. [¶] It's true. Michael Lomax is getting married." 1987 Jul 29 *Atlanta Constitution* A-11/5 "Like affluent whites, many affluent blacks have drifted to the suburbs. According to Georgia Trend, in 1979, 'black families in Atlanta's central city earned less than half of what white families earned. But in the suburbs, black families earned two-thirds as much. The gap was narrowest for suburban black families where the wage earners were 25 to 34—the buppies.'"

caregiver *n* 1980 M Friel and C B Tehan in *Cancer Nursing* 3: 285 "Counteracting Burn-Out for the Hospice Caregiver." (article title) 1982 M Caroline Martin "Hospice Care Update" in *Sourcebook on Death and Dying* ed James A Fruehling (Chicago: Marquis) 209/2 "Still, there are hospice care elements such as bereavement and religious counseling, homemaker services, respite caregivers, shopping, transportation aides, and so forth, that are not reimbursable by the usual sources." Greg Owen and Robert Fulton "Hospice Care" in idem 218/2 "It is a philosophy; a philosophy that has the potential to change our view of what good health care is and to reorient our values such that the patient and his or her family, rather than a specific disease entity, become the focal point of the caregiver's attention." 1985 Jo Horne *Caregiving: Helping an Aging Loved One* (Washington, DC: AARP) 1 "For years caregivers—spouses, adult children, sons-in-law and daughters-in-law, sisters, brothers, friends—have taken on the job of caring for their aging relatives with little support and no compensation." 1987 Aug 14 *Atlanta Constitution* E-1/5 "The abject despair Frechette apparently felt before he killed his wife and then killed himself last month in Jonesboro can become the daily foe of an Alzheimer's 'caregiver,' the woman or man who tends to one of America's estimated 3 million victims of Alzheimer's disease, an irreversible deterioration of the brain that eventually leads to death." Aug-Sep *Modern Maturity* 30/1 "The question of who cares for Mom or Dad rarely comes down to who should, who can, or who wants to. It is almost always a female—a daughter or daughter-in-law, a sister, a niece. The word caregiver, as one expert put it, 'is a euphemism for unpaid female relative.'" Sep *AARP News Bulletin* 13/2 "Nevertheless, Engelter faulted employers for failing to meet one of the most critical needs of caregivers—job protection for those who must leave the work force temporarily."

caregiving *n* 1980 Hannelore Wass, et al, eds *Death Education: An Annotated Resource Guide* (Washington: Hemisphere) 290 "Caring and caregiving" (entry in index to audiovisual resources) 1985 Jo Horne *Caregiving: Helping an Aging Loved One* (Washington, DC: AARP) 6 "Caregiving is hard work, but it does not have to be unrewarding, sorrowful, or depressing. . . . In every caregiving situation there can be moments of incredible warmth and comfort and pleasure." 1987 Sep *AARP News Bulletin* 13/2 "To alleviate these pressures, some 100 companies during the last two years have launched initiatives—usually called 'elder care' programs—aimed at assisting employees with their caregiving needs." Idem "The Travelers Companies attracted 700 employees to its 'caregiving fair' and regularly draws 50 to 100 employees to seminars exploring the subject."

care recipient *n* 1985 Jo Horne *Caregiving: Helping an Aging Loved One* (Washington, DC: AARP) 32 "These are four brief descriptions of a care recipient and his or her incapacity."

dink; dinkie *n* 1987 Sep 13 sv SKIPPY Oct *Illustrated London News* 40/1 "Far from being envied by the fecund but impoverished, Dinkies (Double Income No Kids) are no longer fashionable but objects of sympathy." Nov 9 *Birmingham [AL] Post-Herald* A-5/3 "The yuppies and the dinks (double income, no kids) will become dumpies (downwardly mobile, middle-aged professionals), like the rest of us." Nov 17 *New York Times* 30 "'I read too much about "DINKS"—double-income no-kids couples,' she says, 'and successful bachelors who fear marriage, and once-gung-ho career women who have been won over to motherhood.'" 1988 Mar *Washington Monthly* 12/1 "Only one problem remained: in a ward populated by yuppies and DINKS (double income no kids), public school teachers are about as respected as a bear market."

dumpie *n* 1987 Nov 9 sv DINK

elder care *n* 1987 Sep sv CAREGIVING

emporiatrics *n* [Gk *emporos* 'traveler' + E *-iatrics* 'medical practice'] 1987 Sep 13 *Atlanta Journal/Constitution* F-2/1 "Emporiatrics, or travel medicine, is a relatively new specialization of medical practice which is growing due to the large number of people who travel for pleasure and business."

equitist *n* 1987 Jul 28 *Atlanta Constitution* A-10/3–4 (letter to ed) "Many of us who believe in equal rights and equal fairness under the law for all people, regardless of race, sex, nationality or religion, would feel more comfortable with a term that more fully encompasses the idea of equality. [¶] A better term is the word 'equitist,' a word that cannot now be found in dictionaries."

execu-crime *n* 1987 Aug 23 *Athens [GA] Banner-Herald/Daily News* B-4/1 "The amount of money lost to what Callahan labels 'execu-crime' isn't known because much of it goes unreported. But a congressional committee once pegged the cost of all forms of white-collar crime, from stock manipulation to antitrust violations at $44 billion annually."

footbag *n* 1982 sv HACKY SACK

gomer; goomer *n* [from or influenced by *Gomer* Pyle, a comic yokel character played by Jim Nabors on *The Andy Griffith Show*, CBS-TV, spring 1963 through summer 1964, and on *Gomer Pyle, USMC*, CBS-TV, fall 1964 through summer 1970. Everett Greenbaum, scriptwriter for the Griffith show, recalls naming the character after "Gomer Cool, a writer" (otherwise unidentified), quoted by Richard Kelly, *The Andy Griffith Show* (Winston-Salem, NC: John F Blair, 1981), 115. The variant *goomer* may be a blend with the vowel of *Goober*, Gomer's cousin and successor on *The Andy Griffith Show*. The acronymic etymology frequently asserted for the medical sense, 5 below, has not been substantiated and is therefore suspect, acronymic explanations being often ex post facto. Naaman's suggestion (sense 5, 1982 citation) that the term is from the Hebrew root GMR is morphologically possible but not semantically compelling, the senses of the Hebrew word being 'finishing, completing, deciding'. None of the other proposed sources is more convincing. The etymology is thus uncertain, but the name of the TV character is the most likely etymon. Proof of the term's use before 1963 would, however, require a different explanation.]

1: Military trainee, regarded as stupid and clumsy 1967 H Wentworth and S B Flexner *Dictionary of American Slang* suppl ed (NY: Crowell) "*Gomer gomar* n. A first-year or naive Air Force cadet. *Air Force use.*" 1980 Dan Cragg (S/MAJ, US Army, ret) "Lexicon Militaris" typescript 200 "*Gomer.* A trainee; any dull or stupid person."

2: Member of the US Marine Corps 1982 W T Tyler *Rogue's March* (NY: Harper & Row) 68 (ref to Colonel Selvey, defense attaché, from Tennessee) "She spent most of her idle hours drinking bourbon at the Marine house bar and knew their secret nicknames for the embassy staff as well as if she'd helped invent them. The door closed. 'Up yours too, Gomer Pyle.'" 1984 Lowell Ganz et al *Splash!* film "Up yours, Gomer—I'm waitin' for a fare."

3: A Communist Vietnamese soldier or airman (military slang, esp among combat aviators) 1978 Jul "Glossary of Common Viet Vet Terms" *National Lampoon* 67 "*goomers, V.C., Charlie, or bad guys* Our enemies." 1980 William C Anderson *BAT-21* (Englewood Cliffs, NJ: Prentice-Hall) 7 "If the Birddog pilot had homed in on his parachute beeper before he had clicked it off, chances are the gomers had too." Ibid 49 "Now he not only had a kid watching him, but also a dog that was going to start barking and bring every gomer in Vietnam." 1982 William Safire *What's the Good Word?* (NY: Times Books) 158–59 citing James M Pierce, Middletown, NY "I am currently a hospital administrator and have not (yet) heard 'gomer' used in the manner you described [as medical slang], but I did hear the term while serving in the air force in Southeast Asia in 1969. There the term 'gomer' meant a North Vietnamese or Vietcong soldier and supposedly was the acronym of 'guy on motorable enemy route [Ho Chi Minh Trail].' [¶] The term was used by forward air controllers and recce pilots, as in 'There are six gomers on route nine charlie at delta thirty-seven.' I also heard the term used by U.S. Army troops to refer to NVA or VC soldiers." 1984 Randy Cunningham (USN fighter ace) and Jeff Ethel *Fox Two* (Mesa, AZ: Champlin Fighter Museum) 3 "The Gomers, as someone had nicknamed the North Vietnamese early in the war, meant business." Ibid 78 "I turned to look the enemy pilot in the face—I could see the little Gomer inside [the cockpit] with his beady little Gomer eyes, Gomer hat, Gomer goggles and Gomer scarf." 1986 Stephen Coonts (former USN combat pilot) *Flight of the Intruder* (Annapolis, MD: Naval Institute Press) 24 "There's got to be some better targets in gomer country." 1987 Henry Zeybel (Lieut Col, USAF, ret) *Gunship: Spectre of Death* (NY: Pocket Books) 172 "Some non-Christian Gomers who couldn't speak English / Were shooting at us with a Communist gun."

4: A stupid person 1966 *The Beverley Hillbillies* CBS-TV "He sure is a funny-lookin' goomer." 1974 Dennis Ryan (Oshkosh, WI, U of TN grad student) "Who's that big goomer she's always with?" 1981 Don Ethan Miller *The Book of Jargon* (NY: Macmillan) 244 (list of tennis terms) "*goomer*: Also *gomer* (as in Pyle?), *goofer* and *goober*. A loser, not only in fact and habit, but also by preference or temperament. One who must value the thrill of agony, the victory of defeat."

5: A patient who is dirty, undesirable, senile, or unresponsive to treatment, esp a poor or homeless older man who frequently seeks emergency-room treatment for minor or imaginary complaints; an older patient requiring long-term care (hospital slang) 1972 July *National Lampoon* 76 "*Gomer.* A senile, messy, or highly unpleasant patient." 1973 Philip C Kolin "The Language of Nursing" *AS* 48: 209 "Those patients who require long-term care and who are usually sent to a nursing home are known to the RN as *gomers* (possibly derived from the dialectal *gomeral* 'simpleton')." 1978 Samuel Shem *The House of God* (NY: Dell, 1983) 38 "'Gomer is an acronym: Get Out of My Emergency Room—it's what you want to say when one's sent in from the nursing home at three A.M. . . . But gomers are not just dear old people,' said Fats. 'Gomers are human beings who have lost what goes into being human beings. They want to die, and we will not let them.'" Victoria George and Alan Dundes "The Gomer: A Figure of American Hospital Folk Speech" *Journal of American Folklore* 91: 570–73 "What precisely is a 'gomer'? He is typically an older man who is both dirty and debilitated. He has extremely poor personal hygiene and he is often a chronic alcoholic. A derelict or down-and-outer, the gomer is normally on welfare. . . . Because of the gomer's desire to stay in the hospital, he frequently pretends to be ill or he lacks interest in getting well on those occasions when he is really sick. . . . / Informants were unsure about the origin of the term 'gomer.' Some mentioned Gomer Pyle. . . . In the television series, Gomer Pyle was portrayed as a bumpkin and a loser (although sympathetically). The loser connotation would be akin to the gomer as he appears in hospital folklore. Other informants suggested a biblical source for the gomer (see Genesis 10:2–3; 1 Chronicles 1:5–6; Ezekiel 38:6; and Hosea 1:3), but this seems unlikely. . . . On the east coast of the United States, gomer is explained as an acronym for 'Get Out of My Emergency Room.' On the west coast, the interpretation more usually advanced is 'Grand Old Man of the Emergency Room.' There is agreement, however, that gomer always refers to a man. . . . [¶] It is difficult to determine just how long 'gomer' has been a part of American hospital folklore. One report took it back at least to 1964 when it was used by medical students at the University of Washington in / Seattle. Several informants thought they remembered its being used in the 1950's. Some doctors and nurses suggested 'gomer' might be of recent coinage because until the advent of Medicare and comparable state programs, a 'gomer' would not have been able to afford extensive and expensive medical treatment. . . . / Generally speaking, 'gomer' is a term used more by younger staff members." 1979 Frances J Storlie (RN, Tempe, AZ) "More on the Language of Nursing" *AS* 54: 37 "The patient will become a *gomer* 'unresponsive patient' within a short period of time." 1980 Nov 9 *New York Times Magazine* (William Safire) 16 "A *gomer* . . . is a patient . . . who is whining and otherwise undesirable. The term is said to be an acronym for 'Get Out of My Emergency Room,' but may originate in 'gomeral,' Scottish dialect for simpleton, influenced by the television hillbilly Gomer Pyle." 1982 William Safire *What's the Good Word?* (NY: Times Books) 156 quoting Adam Naaman, MD, Clifton Springs, NY "The noun 'gomer' comes from the Hebrew root G–M–R which means 'to finish.' 'Gomer' is the present tense of that verb, and a patient who is a gomer is not whining or otherwise undesirable. He is in the process of finishing his existence on the face of this earth. The term started in New York City, where many Jewish house staff officers sprinkled the medical language with words from Hebrew and Yiddish. Obviously WASP interns had to find other explanations for the term, and hence the acronym was invented for 'get out of my emergency room.'" Ibid 158 quoting Perry Chapman, Alexandria, VA "I would like to propose another explanation for the origin of the term 'gomer.'... When the doctor went on his daily [hospital] rounds, the patient whined, 'Can I go home today, Doc?' After a few days of this, the particularly persistent patient was perhaps referred to as the 'go-home-er.' Hence 'gomer.'" 1983 Stephen L Taller *Maledicta* 7: 38 "*gomer* a professional patient; a patient who regularly visits the emergency room for minor complaints. Acronym of '*g*et *o*utta *m*y *e*mergency *r*oom.'" David Paul Gordon (Institute of Human Learning, U of CA, Berkeley) *Language in Society* 12: 175 "Gomer: (1) Most commonly, an alcoholic or derelict with extremely poor personal hygiene and a record of multiple admissions to the hospital. Symptoms are predictable, and illness is often feigned. When sick, shows lack of interest in recovery; is often disoriented or hostile. (2) Less frequent, in intensive care units (I.C.U.), a person who is critically ill for an extended period of time and shows no sign of improvement." Jan 17 *Newsweek* 63/3 (on NBC-TV series *St Elsewhere*) "Doctors refer to chronically ill old folk as 'Gomers' (for 'Get out of my emergency room') and coolly prescribe 'DNR's' ('Do not resuscitate')." 1984 Jonathon Green *Newspeak* (London: Routledge & Kegan Paul) 108 "*GOMER* (medic/US) (acron) *g*et *o*ut of *m*y *e*mergency *r*oom: 1. a notation on the file of a patient (very often an elderly one) whose less than vital problems are withholding the possibility of real medical aid to someone near death. 2. patients, apparently too sick to stay at home but not so sick as to die, requiring long term care and keen to take every advantage of the hospital and its staff." 1985 Apr 13–14 *International Herald Tribune* 16/5 (quoting a senior medical student at George Washington U Medical Center) "You get angry at that stage when you hear patients called 'gomers' [an acronym for 'get out of my emergency room'], but when you're called at 3 A.M. and find a patient vomiting and incontinent and you're trying to put in an IV line and they're flailing around and as soon as you get the line in they'll knock it out and you start getting angry because you have nowhere else to put it." 1986 Robert L Chapman *New Dictionary of American Slang* (NY: Harper & Row) 172 "*gomer*... A patient needing extensive care, and usu sent to a nursing home [origin unknown; perhaps related to British *gomers* 'going-home clothes']." Ibid 175 "*gomer*... A hypochondriac [fr *get out of my emergency room*]." 1987 Alvin G Burstein, Prof of Psychology, U of TN, Knoxville, oral "I first encountered *goomer* about 1974 or '75 when I was at the University of Texas Health Services Center in San Antonio. It was interpreted as an acronym for 'get out of my emergency room.'... The gomer was typically a poor Mexican-American with a vague set of complaints, usually an older person. A gomer was essentially a patient that a doctor wouldn't want to touch." Oct 9 *Atlanta Constitution* C-4/1 "Even the hospital jargon underscored the lack of humanity. For example, Konner learned that hospital personnel describe children with third-degree burns as 'crispy critters.' 'Fly sign' referred to patients who lie with their mouths open, allowing flies to enter and leave. And 'gomer' was an acronym for 'get out of my emergency room,' describing any old, decrepit, hopeless patient whose care is guaranteed to be a thankless task." Nov *Discover* 30/1 "Hospitals have a reputation for... crude jargon: the difficult patients labeled gomers (Get Out of My Emergency Room), the doctors referred to as 007s (licensed to kill)."

gomere *n* Female GOMER 1978 Samuel Shem *The House of God* (NY: Dell, 1983) 38 "If I'm not mistaken, it's from one Ina Goober, whom I admitted six times last year. A gomer, or rather, the feminine, gomere." 1984 Jonathon Green *Newspeak* (London: Routledge & Kegan Paul) 108 "Female GOMERs are *GOMEREs*." (According to one physician, the pronunciation is /go'mɛr/.)

gomerette *n* Female GOMER 1978 Victoria George and Alan Dundes "The Gomer: A Figure of American Hospital Folk Speech" *Journal of American Folklore* 91: 571 "One informant claimed that the female version of a gomer was a 'gomerette.'"

gomeroid *adj* Resembling a GOMER, gomerlike (hospital slang, rare) 1982 William Safire *What's the Good Word?* (NY: Times Books) 152 "Patients have been known to turn 'gomeroid.'"

goofus *n* Stupid person 1987 Nov 10 *Atlanta Constitution* A-22/1 (editorial) "The United Nations has been righting some of its old wrongs. It has opened its World War II war crimes file, which should have been unsealed decades ago. The goofus who made a financial and political shambles of UNESCO—the United Nations' economic, social and cultural arm—has been replaced." (This pseudo-Latin form, noted in *AS* 49 [1974]: 204, is perhaps related to *goof* and *goof-up*. It has long-standing informal oral use in several related senses.)

Hacky Sack *n* 1982 John Cassidy *The Hacky-Sack Book: An Illustrated Guide to the New American Footbag Games* (Palo Alto, CA: Klutz Press) [8] "Hack Sack ® is a registered trademark of Wham-O Incorporated, San Gabriel, California." 1987 Oct 1 U of Georgia *Red and Black* 1/2–3 (picture caption) "Sherri DeProspero (left), Billy Lawless (right), both juniors, and Michelle Foster (center), a senior, spent the brisk fall afternoon playing Hacky-Sack in front of the main library. The game involves concentration in keeping the miniature leather beanbag in the air."

jet bridge *n* JETWAY 1987 Nov 23 conversation at Los Angeles airport "[passenger, checking in at a departure gate:] —What do you call that thing that we walk through to get from the gate to the airplane? [Delta Airline clerk:] —A jetway. —Is it called anything else? —Well, sometimes it's called a jet bridge, but usually a jetway." (The corresponding British term *airbridge* was reported in *AS* 62 [1987]: 243.)

jetway *n* Movable passageway connecting an airport boarding lounge with an aircraft 1986 Kathryn Lasky Knight *Trace Elements* (NY: Pocket Books) 238 "As the plane landed in Boston, Archie Baldwin just prayed to God that he would not cross paths with any of his extensive family.... [¶] He had just come out of the jetway into the gate area when a burly-looking fellow in his late forties approached." 1987 Aug 23 sv ROLLAWAY RAMP Nov 6 ABC-TV WLOS-13 news "The suspect apparently entered through the passenger jetway." (*Jetway* is listed by *RHD2* as a trademark.)

no-brainer *n* **1:** Decision easily made 1980 Dec 13 *TV Guide* (Edwin Kiester Jr) 43/2 "Sipping coffee afterward, she talked about the importance of the first, attention-getting item in a newscast. 'We talk all day long about what the lead should be. Sometimes the decision is a real no-brainer. If Iran releases the hostages we don't have to think twice about the lead.'" 1987 Sep 21 *Atlanta Constitution* A-14/2 "But when a major developer looks at the difference between the $400,000 a month a big tenant leasing 20,000 square feet of office space pays, versus the $1,500 a month a gay bar pays in rent, 'the business decision in that is what we call a no-brainer,' said the businessman, who did not want to be named." Dec 2 Haley Barbour *Today Show* NBC "It's almost a political no-brainer for Bush." **2:** Stupid or incoherent person 1987 Oct 25 *Atlanta Journal/Constitution* C-1/1 "Most [radio call-in] shows like Alan Colmes' screen their calls before allowing a caller to go on the air. [¶] But some months ago, Alan Colmes, for the heck of it, decided to stop doing that. If a no-brainer wants to talk on the radio—even if the message makes no sense whatsoever—he or she can do it." **3:** College course requiring little preparation or effort 1988 Jun 17 letter from George S Cole "On two occasions, last year, I overheard students referring to a certain course as being a 'no-brainer'."

ozone hole *n* 1987 Nov 9 *Atlanta Constitution* A-3/1–2 "Scientists studying the annual ozone 'hole' over Antarctica say they are increasingly concerned that the amount of the protective gas being destroyed is so great that the ozone balance of the planet may be affected.... [¶] Scientists who last month investigated the reappearance of the ozone hole say they were shocked at the size of the loss detected during the first few weeks of the Southern Hemisphere's spring." 1988 July 11 *Newsweek* 22/2–3 "Now there are signs that an ozone hole about the size of Greenland opens in the Arctic, too, and may drain ozone from the Northern Hemisphere." (cf *Barnhart Dictionary Companion* 5 [1986]: 25, later citations here)

patient zero *n* 1987 Randy Shilts *And the Band Played On: Politics, People, and the AIDS Epidemic* (NY: St Martin's) 147 "By the time Bill Darrow's research was done [in 1982], he had established sexual links between 40 patients in ten cities. At the center of the cluster diagram was Gaetan Dugas, marked on the chart as Patient Zero of the GRID epidemic." Oct 11 *Atlanta Journal/Constitution* A-1/1–11/1 (headline and article) "'Shoe-leather' work led to AIDS clue / Early cases traced to patient zero / His name, according to San Francisco Chronicle reporter Randy Shilts, the author of a new book on the AIDS epidemic, was Gaetan Dugas [an Air Canada flight attendant]. [¶] To frustrated public health authorities, struggling to understand the baffling new disease, he would soon be known as 'patient zero,' the man believed to have played a key role in the initial spread of the disease in America."

purpose-bred animal *n* [modeled on *purpose-built*] 1987 Sep 18 *Atlanta Constitution* A-25/2 "On the other hand, when animals bred specifically for research ('purpose-bred animals') are used, fewer animals are needed, and fewer animals suffer. Perhaps the slightly higher cost of purpose-bred animals will encourage careful treatment and efficient use of resources by researchers. Banning pound seizure will help put a stop to a lot of useless, redundant experiments that waste taxpayers' money."

rollaway ramp *n* Portable stairway on wheels for boarding an airplane and deplaning 1987 Aug 23 *Athens [GA] Banner-Herald/Daily News* B-9/2 "'At major airports,' she added, 'there are jetways. But if your route takes you to some smaller airport, you may find yourself being pushed onto the field and confronted with a rollaway ramp.'" (cf JET BRIDGE)

shoe-leather *attrib* Routinely investigative 1982 Nov 27 *Athens [GA] Banner-Herald/Daily News* 5/2 "The movie, which CBS will telecast Saturday, is a gem. Schillman is an old-fashioned shoe leather sleuth, and nobody does it better than Mitchum." 1987 Oct 11 *Atlanta Journal/Constitution* A-11/3 "The detective work that established the sexually transmitted nature of AIDS among homosexuals was 'pure shoe-leather epidemiology,' according to Dr. Donald Francis, a former director of laboratory research for the CDC, who is now an AIDS adviser for the state of California. [¶] Dr. Dritz made numerous trips to Atlanta, staying up late at night with CDC investigators at the Stafford Emory Inn across Clifton Road from the agency's headquarters to map out their investigation of the mysterious disease. [¶] They spent weeks drawing up the questions to ask—ranging from inquiries about pets and house plants to details of the infected person's sex acts and the names and addresses of their partners so they too could be interviewed. 'It was very exhausting work, but it was the only way we knew how to do it,' she said. 'It was our job.'" (cf PATIENT ZERO)

shrink-wrap; shrink-wrapped *adj* (Of computer software) wrapped in cellophane, the removal of which binds the purchaser to legal restrictions on the use of the software; hence, commercially available but with legally restricted use 1987 Dec 2 Tom West, Vice President of Data General, speaking to employees in Durham, NC "The things we like to buy are the dimestore [common, ordinary, generally available] shrink-wrap applications." Dec 8 *PCWeek: The National Newspaper of IBM Standard Microcomputing* 1/4 "PCWeek took a first look at the released, shrink-wrapped version of the IBM OS/2 Standard Edition 1.0 last week." (Many dictionaries enter the term as verb and noun in the general sense of wrapping and sealing products in plastic film or the film so used; the connotation of becoming legally liable to abide by conditions of use upon removal of the wrap appears to be a specialized sense in the computer industry.)

skippie *n* 1987 Sep 13 *Atlanta Journal/Constitution* G-12/3 "Upscale just put on sneakers. [¶] Look out, yuppies (young urban professionals). Step back, preppies, Dinks (double income, no kids) beware. Here come the skippies (school kids with income and purchasing power). [¶] The leading maker of school supplies [Mead Corporation] christened the group this summer to identify the market for its line of stylish and practical school products."

smokeless cigarette *n* 1987 Sep 28 *Atlanta Constitution* A-11/1 "The health community has been slogging through the trenches in the war against smoking,... and out comes RJR with a secret offensive weapon. It's the industry's Battle of the Bulge: the 'smokeless' cigarette. [¶] The product that they are developing is, they say, a cigarette that uses but does not burn tobacco. It's a cigarette that produces no ash and little sidestream smoke. In short, this product is supposedly 'safer,' although that word is never exhaled by a tobacco man. To say the word 'safer' would imply that regular cigarettes were unsafe. They call it, instead, 'the world's cleanest cigarette.' "

suppie *n* Southern yuppie 1987 Nov 22 review of *The Care and Feeding of Southern Men: A Survival Guide for the Unsuspecting Yankee* by Claudia Greco *Atlanta Journal/Constitution* J-11/3 "Ms. Greco's specimen lover is a nameless native of Richmond, Va., who is perfectly at home in his transplantation to New York and his Suppie wardrobe of Cardin shirts until certain atavistic urges come over him. When this happens, Ms. Greco learns all about Hound Dawgs, Footbawhl, Foah-by Foahs, and—her most outlandish spelling—'Fus' Famlya-vah-ginn-yuh.' "

tee ball, T-ball *n* A variety of baseball played by young children in which the ball is not pitched, but is hit from a stationary position atop a stake or tee 1966 Charles Nagel and Fredricka Moore *Skill Development through Games and Rhythmic Activities* (Palo Alto, CA: National Press) 265 "LONG BASE TEE BALL." (heading to rules of the game) 1976 Jun 22 Kingston (Ont) *Whig-Standard* 12/4 "Gone for the boys and girls playing in the league is the fear of facing a hard-throwing hurler. In T-Ball, the batter gets his or her swings at a stationary tee sitting on top of a rubber tee, about four-feet off the ground." Jun 27 *Tuscaloosa [AL] News* B-8/1 "The terminology sounds more like a [sic] exterminator's casebook, but is in reference to the four teams [Ants, Fleas, Skeeters, Ticks] in the YMCA tee-ball baseball league for ages six through eight." Ibid B-8/3–4 "In tee-ball competition, each team is permitted three outs, unless they score five runs, which immediately ends the inning. There is no pitcher since the ball is hit from a tee, which stands close to three feet in height." 1978 Glenn Kirchner *Physical Education for Elementary School Children* (Dubuque, IA: Wm C Brown) 345 "Tee Ball . . . This game is played in the same way as softball, with the following modification: [¶] 1. The batter is allowed one hit off the tee. [¶] 2. Since there is no pitcher, no one is permitted to steal a base." Aug 6 *Tuscaloosa [AL] News* B-7/1 (picture caption) "The Ants took the championship of the Northport T-Ball League this summer. Members of the seven-year-old team are. . . . " 1986 Monta Potter "Game Modifications for Youth Sport" in *Sport for Children and Youths* ed Maureen R Weiss and Daniel Gould (Champaign, IL: Human Kinetics) 206 "In addition, T-ball is enjoyed by the first and second grade children to ensure maximum batting success with this 'closed skill' version of the games of baseball and softball." 1988 Jun 3 *Athens [GA] Daily News* A-1/3 "The event was the annual meeting of parents and coaches for the start of the T-ball season. T-ball, a variant of baseball, is played by children ages 6 to 11."

yappie *n* 1986 Jun 18 *Toronto Globe and Mail* A-7/1 "Here [in Yellowknife, NWT] there are Yuppies with a penchant for building environmentally co-ordinated houses and going native in their dress. Call them Yappies—Young Arctic Professionals."

yuca *n* 1988 Jan 25 *Newsweek* 27/3–28/1 " . . . those born in Cuba but raised and educated in the United States . . . call themselves 'Yucas' (young, upwardly mobile Cuban-Americans), which is a bilingual pun on the Spanish word for a kind of cassava."

yup *n* Yuppie 1985 conversation attorney age 33 Knoxville, TN "She'll be there with all the other yups. . . . Greed is a hallmark of yup culture." 1987 Nov 6 *Atlanta Constitution* P-11/1 "Annie's now Ally, the favored daughter of a toy magnate and a powerful tycoon in her own right, with seemingly everything the Yup life has to offer—except true love."

yup *vi* Behave like a yuppie 1988 Jan 11 *Newsweek* 56/3 "It [Yuri Podnik's film *Is It Easy to Be Young?*] takes a close look at Soviet young people in Latvia—kids in the rock culture, Hare Krishnas, young professionals who would be Soviet Yuppies if the economy gave them some room to yup."

yuppieback *n* 1987 Aug 16 *Atlanta Journal/Constitution* J-11/1 "One of the major publishing phenomena of the 1980s is the rise of the 'quality' fiction paperback. After the success of Jay McInerney's 'Bright Lights, Big City,' which has sold more than 300,000 copies since 1984, younger authors have gladly bypassed traditional hard-cover publication in favor of slickly produced, aggressively marketed soft-cover series such as Bantam New Fiction and Vintage Contemporaries. Nicknamed 'yuppiebacks,' these paper editions are aimed at a young, upscale audience and are often written in the deadpan 'minimalist' style made popular by writers such as Raymond Carver and Ann Beattie."

yuppiecide *n* 1987 Dec 24 graffiti on wall of University Theatre, Toronto "Yuppiecide."

yuppie disease *n* 1987 Dec 30 *Atlanta Constitution* A-6/1 "Two independent researchers suggested Tuesday that rubella vaccines introduced in 1979 may have triggered an epidemic of Epstein-Barr syndrome, an exhausting illness that primarily strikes young adults. [¶] The syndrome, known as the 'yuppie disease,' causes chronic fatigue that has baffled doctors who are unable to explain why it has become so prevalent in recent years."

yuppieism *n* 1987 Dec 7 *Time* 72/1 "While some see in the New Agers' chants and nebulous slogans a revival of the shaggy '60s, others see the devotion of many New Agers to moneymaking as simply a new variant of yuppieism." (cf *Barnhart Dictionary Companion* 3 [1984]: 29, later citation here)

yuppism *n* 1987 Dec 19 *Nation* 757/1–2 " . . . the 'Yuppism' that has come to define our social competence: the inability to relate to others except as superiors, competitors or inferiors."

yup-scale *attrib* Upscale in a yuppie manner (nonce) 1987 Oct *Newsweek on Campus* 6/1 "Given today's Yup-scale yearnings, meanwhile, measuring up . . . means landing not merely a rewarding job, but a lucrative and prestigious one."

zero-zero *attrib* Pertaining to an arms-reduction proposal for each side to eliminate all weapons of a given type 1983 Feb 14 *New Yorker* 104/2 "When the Administration, after a big internal battle, settled on the 'zero-zero' approach to nuclear weapons in Europe—an approach opposed by then Secretary of State Alexander Haig—they leaked to friendly columnists the story of the struggle, with suggestions that Haig (of all people) was a bit soft. (Haig's view was that the zero-zero approach—asking the Soviet Union to dismantle all its intermediate-range missiles in exchange for an American pledge not to proceed with the deployment of intermediate-range missiles in Western Europe—would be difficult to move away from if, as he considered likely, it proved impossible to achieve, and this would cause more problems with our European allies.)" Ibid 105/1 "Even Paul Nitze, the United States negotiator

for the intermediate-range-nuclear-weapon talks, who, like Rostow, is an arms-control conservative, managed to run afoul of some Administration officials by exploring with his Soviet counterpart something other than the zero-zero option." Feb 28 *Atlanta Constitution* A-13/1 "At the American Legion, the headline was in the 'flexibility' he showed in being willing to listen to a serious counter to our zero-zero intermediate-range missile proposal, but the full text of the address—which Moscow's Americanologists read in detail—showed a cohesive world view far less accommodating." (See DOUBLE ZERO, "ATNW," *AS* 64 [1989]: 69.)

AMONG THE NEW WORDS

JOHN ALGEO   AND   ADELE ALGEO

University of Georgia   *Athens, Georgia*

With the assistance of Robert K. Barnhart, *Barnhart Books*; George S. Cole, *Shippensburg University*; Lesa Dill, *Western Kentucky University*; William W. Evans, *Louisiana State University*; Raymond Gozzi, *Bradley University*; William J. Kirwin, *Memorial University of Newfoundland*; Jonathan Lighter, *University of Tennessee*; Virginia G. McDavid, *Chicago State University*; James B. McMillan, *University of Alabama*; Patrick W. Merman, *Monroe, Michigan*; Michael Montgomery, *University of South Carolina*; Louis Phillips, *School of Visual Arts*; Mary Gray Porter, *University of Alabama*; Sol Steinmetz, *Barnhart Books*; and Greg Williams, *University of Toronto*

THE WORDS A PEOPLE USE MIRROR their interests and values. This installment of "Among the New Words" is in the nature of an "O tempora, o mores" look at late twentieth-century America. It includes some terms prominent during the presidential election of 1988 (*sound bite, photo op,* and their spin-offs), which characterized that election and foreshadow the probable future of American politics. When Ronald Reagan, the *Teflon-coated* president, has left office, the *Teflon* terms he inspired may retire with him, or they may acquire new vitality as a metaphor at once homely and technological.

As computers become more common and important parts of the lives of Americans, so do the problems associated with the machine. Those problems have been couched in an extended medical metaphor, from *virus* and *vaccine program* to *safe computer practice* (echoing a safe-sex response to the AIDS threat). The incredible marvels of computer technology, on the other hand, are expressed by the rollicking rime of *wait state*.

In recent years even the entertainment of Americans has assumed a serious mien. The citations for *dramedy,* however, document the rise and fall of a term. The earliest citation for the word in our files anticipates its recent popularity by almost a decade. Then, within a year's time, the term both rose to prominence and declined from favor, along with the television programs to which it was applied. That condensed life span is the lexical equivalent of a sound bite, or of the late Andy Warhol's fifteen minutes of celebrity for everyone.

Most of the terms in this installment do not appear in any of our dictionaries of record. A related form of one of them, *photo opportunity,* appears in *The Second Barnhart Dictionary of New English* with an earliest date of 1976, in the *World Book Dictionary* (1988 ed.), and in the *Random House Dictionary* (2nd ed. unabridged), where it is dated 1975–80. The shortening *photo op,* entered here, is more recent, but it has been very popular.

Teflon in the metaphorical sense is covered in *The Barnhart Dictionary Companion* 4: 113–14 with numerous citations from 1984–86. The term is given entry here to provide additional documentation, to show its continued use, and to record the origin proposed in the first citation, attributing the invention of the term to Representative Pat Schroeder of Colorado. It seems to have begun in the combination *Teflon-coated presidency,* from which it generalized.

The Barnhart Dictionary Companion (4: 152) has an entry for *virus* in the computer sense, with one illustrative citation and a query about the term's frequency. The entry in this installment answers the question about frequency: the term is now common. This entry also shows the variety of combinations into which the term has entered.

Acknowledgment to others for citations: Thomas Algeo, Charles Clay Doyle, and Betty Irwin.

bite *n* SOUND BITE 1988 Nov 21 *Newsweek* 137/1 "You're the one that was making the comparison, *Senator,*" Bentsen retorted. [¶] "Well, there's the bite," his debate coach, Michael Sheehan, said, watching in a room offstage. [ref to Lloyd Bentsen—Daniel Quayle vice-presidential debate]

dramedy, dramady *n* [*drama* + *comedy*] 1978 Oct 7 *TV Guide* 11 (ad) Richard Dreyfuss is MOSES WINE private investigator . . . *so go figure* the Big Fix /A Dramedy from Universal. 1987 Nov *Newsweek on Campus* 8/2 Tarses is among a handful of producers who've given TV a new, more serious sense of humor. This can be seen most strongly in a few influential shows that blend comedy and drama in varying proportions. The television industry has already coined a term for this kind of program, "dramedy." (It's a term that some, including Tarses, happen to hate.) Nov 9 *Time* 96/1 Sitcoms are trying to make you cry until you laugh this season. A new term has even been coined to describe the hybrid form: dramedies. Three new series—ABC's *Hooperman* and *The "Slap" Maxwell Story* and CBS's *Frank's Place*—are ostensibly comedies, but they go for few jokes and have no laughter on the sound track. Dec 16 *Miami Herald* E-3/3 The show [*Hill Street*] has a different feel. It's not really comedy. Some people call it 'dramedy.' Dec 28 *Wall Street Journal* 11/2 "Frank's Place" has been classified with a handful of other new series that exchange the flat, bright look of videotape and the stimulus of a laugh track for the rich depth of film and the challenge of combining comedy and drama in a genre dubbed "dramedy." 1988 Jan 25 *New York Times* 23/4 "I mean, how do you describe the funny and the serious elements?" [¶] He answered himself in mock serious critical tones: "It's a dramedy." Apr 6 *Atlanta Constitution* C-1/2 The movement away from laugh tracks has been noticeable this season on the so-called "dramadies"—part-comedy, part-drama shows, such as "The 'Slap' Maxwell Story" and "The Wonder Years," that rely more on rich characters and situations than one-liners. Jun 6 *Newsweek* 61/1–2 The "dramedy," that celebrated hybrid of drama and comedy, may expire before it has had a real chance to perform. When the networks finished announcing their fall schedules last week, gone were three of the four dramedies: ABC's "The Slap Maxwell Story," CBS's "Frank's Place" and NBC's "The Days and Nights of Molly Dodd." That leaves only ABC's "Hooperman" to represent a genre hailed by critics as the best thing to happen to TV since Howard Cosell retired his mouth. Dec 14 *Atlanta Journal/Constitution* D-4/1 And none dare call it [TV series *Annie McGuire*] "dramady," even though that's what it is. That term was applied to several new series last year that were part-comedy, part-drama. But most of them died, and now a TV executive would no more call a show a "dramady" than "a large vat of toxic waste."

photo op *n* 1988 Apr 2 *Nation* 451/2 If I had seen that tight little smile at a balloon bouncing a few weeks earlier, I would have figured that Dole was thinking, "When I find the scheduler who booked me in for this nonsense I'm going to cut him up in tiny pieces and feed him to the hogs at the next barnyard photo op." Oct 17 *Newsweek* 47/1 In private, senior Soviets at the conference talk confidently of 1989 as the year they will finally get a Gorbachev-Deng Xiaoping summit. This would be much more than the photo-op of the year; it would end 16 years of American advantage as the only member of the Washington-Moscow-Beijing triangle able to talk at the highest level to both of the other two. Nov 21 quot sv SOUND BITE Dec 2 *Athens [GA] Banner-Herald* 8/3–5 (cartoon) [Store manager to line of children waiting to see Santa Claus:] "Now remember, children. Santa and his elves are very very busy. So this is a photo op with a ten second sound bite for each of you." Dec 5 *Newsweek* 35/1 His sin: imposing nearly eight years of corrupt, abusive rule on his country. Last week former president Chun Doo Hwan, once the imperious, iron-fisted leader of South Korea, was in internal exile, a form of ritual humiliation. Or was it just a photo-op atonement? Cameras recorded Chun and his wife's teary departure from their suburban home; TV crews were tipped off to be on hand for their arrival at the remote monastery. By the weekend . . . the ex-strongman was expected to move into more comfortable lodgings on a nearby Army base.

photo opportunist *n* 1987 Oct 19 *Time* 77/1 Of course—because the joint is bound to be packed with publicists—photo opportunists and blaring lifestylists. The manufacture of quick and disposable illusions is an overwhelming reality in an era when the concept of image is replacing the value of reputation.

safe computer practice *n* [modeled on *safe sex*] 1988 Apr 19 *Atlanta Constitution* D-2/4–5 (heading and article) 'Safe computer practices' can stop spread of mindless viral vandalism . . . Just as single people of every persuasion are cautioned urgently about safe sexual practices, so are we in as monastic a pursuit as personal computering lectured about "safe computer practices"—much to the same end. May 3 (U of Georgia) *Red and Black* 4/4 (letter to ed) The only real prevention of infection is complete isolation and abstinence. Since this isn't practical to many computer users, "safe computer practices" should be used.

sound bite *n* 1987 Apr 13 *Newsweek* 25/3–26/1 Hart's refusal to reduce himself to a 30-second sound bite is an admirable—and difficult—stance in an age of media politics. Nov 16 *Time* 95/2 Many who watched the Bork hearings concluded that Kennedy and Utah's sycophantic Orrin Hatch vied in giving the worst performances. Yet Kennedy dominated the evening news coverage by crafting his wild charges into the little sound bites so dear to news producers. Idem They were earnest, perhaps a little verbose, sometimes eloquent, decidedly human, and a welcome change from the usual Washington sound-bite sophisticate. 1988 Jan 2 *Atlanta Journal/Constitution* A-8/2 "There are certain people—Squier, Sears, Schneider—who are instinctively quotable. They think in sound bites," said Republican media consultant Douglas Bailey, a co-founder of the Campaign Hotline. Jan 18 *Newsweek* 22/1–4 Some of these "sound-bites" sing; some sag. . . . The successful lines of the past—back to Abraham Lincoln's "A house divided against itself cannot stand" (a sound-bite that traveled by telegraph)—were not just catchy; they were also connected to the great themes and issues of the day. . . . It's still early, but this year's leader in the sound-bite sweepstakes is Gary Hart's antiestablishment slogan, "Let the people decide." Apr 24 *Atlanta Journal/Constitution* C-3/3 (George Will) Washington's attention span—longer than a television "sound bite," shorter than a senator's introduction at a Rotary luncheon—was momentarily filled by Larry Speakes' "Speaking Out," a book that is fresh evidence of the high ratio of dignitaries to dignity in public life today. May 18 *Atlanta Constitution* A-11/1 (Edwin M. Yoder) And if presidential elections turned on long, polite, rational debate rather than televised sound bites, it might sell. . . . Millions of voters, their minds uncontaminated by the slogans and subliminal messages of 30-second TV spots, would listen, march to the polls and reward the rational argument. Sep 25 *Athens [GA] Daily News/Banner-Herald* A-11/2 During the debate, the candidates want to accomplish at least two major goals—avoid major mistakes and provide some quotable comments, particularly those that can be used for a 15-second sound bite for television news shows. Sep 26 *Newsweek* 20/1 He has also taught Bush to use "sound bites"—telling quips and one-liners that are easily picked up by television news. Nov 14 *US News & World Report* 68/1–2 The collapse of political argument into sound bites looks like part of the same process [of moving away from logical exposition to fragmentary entertainment]. Nov 21 *Time* 144 You have just been massaged, pummeled—and maybe *had*—by some savvy movie publicists, the spin doctors of the entertainment industry. They operate in the slick new tradition of political handlers, whose job is to reduce a campaign to photo ops and sound bites, keep their candidates away from rancorous reporters and try, ever so discreetly, to manage the news. For a movie publicist, the methods and motives are the same; only the product is different. And by orchestrating the burgeoning infotainment press, a smart flack can detonate a bigger bang for the buck. Dec 2 quot sv PHOTO OP Dec 4 *Manchester Guardian Weekly* 30 (Waldemar Januszczak, rev of *America* by Jean Baudrillard) America, the book, is written in short, self-contained passages, pleasantly irreverent literary sound-bites.

Teflon; Teflon-coated; Teflon-skinned *attrib* Free of criticism for or unfavorable effects from one's own actions [1983 Aug 2] 1988 Apr 6 *Atlanta Constitution* C-4/5 Teflon's next frontier was the language. That breakthrough came the morning of Aug. 2, 1983, as Pat Schroeder was cooking eggs for the kids. Ms. Schroeder happens to be a Democratic congresswoman, and as she slid the eggs out of a frying pan, she reflected on the way political accountability, in her view, slid off President Reagan. [¶] "I said, 'He's just like this pan,' " she recalled last week. "Nothing sticks." [¶] Members of Congress may start the day's session with one-minute speeches, and this is how Rep. Schroeder started hers that day: "Mr. Speaker, after carefully watching Ronald Reagan, he is attempting a great breakthrough in political technology—he has been perfecting the Teflon-coated presidency." 1984 May 20 *Atlanta Journal/Constitution* J-6/2 (Andrew J Glass) Reagan is said to live a charmed political life as the proprietor of a Teflon-coated presidency in which nothing that goes wrong seems to stick to him. Jun 11 *Time* 13/2 (letter) By failing to mention Ronald Reagan's responsibility for the collapse of arms control, Hugh Sidey has convinced me that this is indeed a "Teflon President." Jun 25 *New Yorker* 91/1–2 Mondale says, "See, I think there's a perception that Reagan's flying high, with a Teflon coat around him, but the fact of it is that that campaign hasn't started yet." (Representative Patricia Schroeder, Democrat of Colorado, originated the phrase that Reagan's is a "Teflon-coated Presidency.") 1987 Jun 28 *Houston Chronicle* sec 3 4/1–4 (headline, subhead, and article) Teflon lawman / Head of South Houston police officers association weathers political storm to become chief / As head of South Houston's police officers association, Bill Butera was demoted, fired and labeled a coward, but none of the labels stuck and he now is chief of police. [¶] Led by the Teflon-skinned Butera, the association, along with an auxiliary mostly made up of feisty policemen's wives, played a major role in South Houston's high-stakes mayoral race in April. 1988 Jane Mayer and Doyle McManus *Landslide* (Boston: Houghton Mifflin) 12 But the public didn't seem to hold the president responsible [for loss of lives in the 1983 Beirut bombing], giving further currency to his reputation, in Colorado congresswoman Patricia Schroeder's phrase, as the Teflon president—nothing stuck to him. Mark Hartsgaard *On Bended Knee* (NY: Farrar Straus Giroux) 67 Presidential assistant Richard Darman told me that the so-called Teflon phenomenon—the fact that blame never seemed to stick to President Reagan, even after such disasters as the Beirut suicide bombing that claimed the lives of 241 marines—was directly related to journalists' tendency to emphasize personality over substance. (*Teflon* is a trademark.)

trapdoor *n* 1984 Feb 19 *Ventura County [CA] Star-Free Press* A-5 Here are some of the ways hackers pull off their computer capers: . . . [¶] TRAP DOOR—A code to get into the computer system devised by a programmer or designer that sidesteps the normal path and bypasses security safeguards. This is often used for an abuse of the system. 1988 Nov 5 *Atlanta Journal/Constitution* A-1/4 & A-9/1 The officials said users of the system could have closed the "trapdoor" in their systems that an unknown party used as an entry point. It is a program that lets the sender of information enter the receiver's computer and alter information. . . . [¶] "The intent of that trapdoor, if you will, is to help install it [the operating system] and take out any bugs," Dr. Cosgrove said.

"But then the system manager is expected to shut that [trapdoor] down." Nov 18 *Atlanta Constitution* B-1/2 'TRAPDOORS.' Unpublicized gaps that legitimate programmers sometimes leave in their programs. The idea is to give the inventor a pathway into the program when he wants to alter or improve his work. But intruders sometimes use trapdoors, too, as happened in the recent, well-publicized virus attack on a Department of Defense computer network, Arpanet.

vaccination program; vaccine program *n* 1988 Mar 27 *Philadelphia Inquirer* (Jim Detjen "Computers Falling Prey to Viruses") pn/a As more and more incidents of computer viruses have been reported, the demand for programs that protect computers has soared. At least 14 "vaccination" programs designed to protect computer disks from contamination are now available, said consultant [Harold] Highland. These programs check the computer program for viruses and prevent the bugs from destroying or altering data. Apr 19 *Atlanta Constitution* D-2/4–5 While vaccine programs are available now for all systems, Ms. Macon said "We urge our customers to use safe computing practices. Establish a routine of making frequent backups, keep your master disks write-protected and know the source of the software you are working with." Apr 28 (U of Georgia) *Red and Black* 1/2 "There are 'vaccine' programs for use against the viruses, but a different one must be developed for each virus due to their unique designs," he said.... [¶] "The only real way to prevent the viruses is to assure yourself that you have clean software," he said.

virus *n* —**computer virus** 1988 Jan 31 *New York Times* pn/a In the last nine months, computer viruses—which could subvert, alter or destroy the computer programs of banks, corporations, the military and the Government—have infected personal computer programs at several corporations and universities in the United States, as well as in Israel, West Germany, Switzerland, Britain and Italy. Feb 1 *Newsweek* 48/1 After several weeks experts found the culprit: a small, malicious program known as a computer "virus" had been injected into the system where it proceeded to destroy nearly 40 percent of the records. Mar 27 *Philadelphia Inquirer* pn/a A computer virus is a small, mischief-making program that is secretly inserted into a standard computer program or the computer's operating system. Since the virus copies itself, it has the ability to be spread from computer to computer by operators who unknowingly share contaminated software. Apr 2 *Atlanta Journal/Constitution* A-1/4 & A-13/1 So Sieczkowski, a computer engineering major, decided to investigate. He soon discovered that hundreds of computer disks had been contaminated with a computer "virus"—a small, mischief-making program that someone secretly had inserted onto the disks.... [¶] Computer viruses, depending on their instructions, can destroy data, display an unexpected message, make a disk unusable or wreak some other form of havoc. [¶] Like their biological namesake, they have the ability to replicate, spreading from computer to computer by attaching themselves to the operating systems of computers or other programs. Apr 19 *Atlanta Constitution* D-2/4 Basically, a computer virus is mindless vandalism. It is a program masquerading as something useful, but harboring a nasty little routine that attaches itself to your system file and will automatically leap to any other system file it comes across; thus they are easily spread by people who exchange disks or programs. Apr 28 (U of Georgia) *Red and Black* 1/1 Computer viruses—malicious subprograms designed to destroy or hinder normal computer operations—are affecting computers nationwide, but the University has been lucky to avoid the problem, a computer specialist said. —**electronic virus** 1988 Mar 20 *Athens [GA] Daily News/Banner-Herald* D-7/1–3 (headline and article) First electronic 'virus' strikes major U.S. software product / NEW YORK—For the first time in the United States, a software "virus," a type of computer program that can secretly spread from computer to computer and potentially destroy stored data, has infected a major commercial personal computer software product. —**silent virus** 1988 Nov 24 *Athens [GA] Daily News/Banner-Herald* D-11/2 "I fear viruses are evolving the next step up, to the silent virus that will find a way to escape detection, cause no trail to be left behind and cause random errors," said Dick tenEyck, telecommunications director for the Boston Computer Society, one of the largest associations of computer enthusiasts in the country. —**software virus** 1988 Mar 20 *Athens [GA] Daily News/Banner-Herald* D-7 Software viruses are so named because they parallel in the computer world the behavior of biological viruses. They are programs, or a set of instructions to the computer, that are deliberately planted on a floppy disk meant to be used with the computer or introduced when the computer is communicating over telephone lines or data networks with other computers. —**target virus** 1988 Nov 24 *Athens [GA] Daily News/Banner-Herald* D-11/2 Another virus tenEyck fears will be developed is a target virus. Such a destructive piece of code would attack programs from a specific manufacturer, such as Lotus Development Corp., or every data file created by that company's programs, such as 1–2–3. A target virus might also make its way into the portion of a computer's operating system that's permanently stored on a chip inside the computer, causing mammoth problems for buyers of particular computer brands, he said. —**virus attack** 1988 Nov 18 quot sv TRAPDOOR —**virus epidemic** 1988 May 3 (U of Georgia) *Red and Black* 4/3–4 (letter) This recent episode in the virus epidemic clearly discounts Everett's remarks. In fact, this particular strain of virus was designed to attach itself not to a legitimate application but to any system file it was exposed to, and could be contracted just as easily from bulletin board public domain software as from an illegally copied application. —**virus program** 1987 Dec 21 *Info World* 74/3 It was a classic virus program—a Christmas greeting that accessed the address files in the personal computers of each recipient then automatically launched more copies of the same greeting to every boss and customer on the list. 1988 Mar 20 *Athens [GA] Daily News/Banner-Herald* D-7/3 Canter said he discovered the virus program on March 2 when he turned his Macintosh on and the virus program, reading the computer's internal clock, was activated. He said the virus displayed its message and in his case was not harmless—it destroyed his computer's operating system file and work he was preparing. Apr 19 *Atlanta Constitution* D-2/4 Promulgating virus programs is "a criminal act," Ms. Macon said, and she promised that Apple will prosecute to the hilt, under federal and state computer-tampering laws, if it can find the author of this or any other virus.

wait state *n* 1988 May 1 *New York Times* F-8/1–3 A wait state is one indicator of the overall speed and performance of a computer system.... [¶] To match the C.P.U. [central processing unit] and the memory subsystem speeds, many computer makers insert a little extra bit of time—one cycle, or a wait state—into the C.P.U.'s performance. The length of the extra cycle is proportional to the performance of the processor. With a 16 MHz chip, one wait state equals 62.5 nanoseconds.... But those measly 62.5 nanoseconds are inserted into the process millions of times a second. A nanosecond here and a nanosecond there, and pretty soon you're talking real time. Oct 16 *Atlanta Journal/Constitution* E-8 (ad for Micro Center computer store) Now the 80386 power, advanced graphics and exclusive IBM MicroChannel Architecture of the Model 80 are available in a compact desktop configuration. The integrated, total-system design with no wait-states yields the expected IBM quality and reliability, as well as very fast processing.

zero wait state *n* 1988 May 1 *New York Times* F-8/1 & 5 We've been reading more and more lately about something called zero wait states, usually in the context of computer makers bragging about their machines being better than other computers.... [¶] If the cache memory is well engineered, that is, able to keep track of what areas are being used and how often, it will intercept almost all the calls to memory and eliminate the need for wait states. [¶] If the calls hit the cache 95 percent of the time, the performance is very close to zero wait state. It's not true zero wait state because 5 percent of the calls are misses instead of hits and are passed on to the slower memory. Oct 25 *Atlanta Journal/Constitution* D-2/1–2 That's a large hunk of change, but this is a large hunk of computer. It runs at 12 megahertz with zero wait states.... [¶] If you're interested, the difference between zero and one wait state is pretty significant in terms of speed. If you see a machine advertised at 12 megahertz clock speed with one wait state, this simply means that the computer's memory chips are fairly slow, on the order of 120 nanoseconds, and when the processor issues them an instruction, it must wait a click—a wait state—to allow them to recover before it issues the next instruction. A machine with zero wait state has something like 80-nanosecond chips, which can keep pace with the processor.

AMONG THE NEW WORDS

JOHN ALGEO   AND   ADELE ALGEO

University of Georgia   *Athens, Georgia*

With the assistance of the New Words Committee

THIS INSTALLMENT OF "AMONG THE NEW WORDS," like all others, is possible only because many persons look out for new words and send us citations of those words with their sources in the form of clippings or copies. The New Words Committee consists of those who help in that way, and membership is open to anyone who cares to contribute. Recently, the number of contributing committee members has increased gratifyingly. Indeed, the number has grown so much that it is no longer feasible to list contributors in every installment. Therefore, hereafter, in the last issue of each year we will give the names of persons who have served on the committee during that year. During the past year the following have been contributing members of the New Words Committee:

Catherine M. Algeo, *Amsterdam*
Thomas J. Algeo, *University of Michigan*
Robert K. Barnhart, *Barnhart Books*
Ronald R. Butters, *Duke University*
Sylvia Chalker, *London*
George S. Cole, *Shippensburg University*
Ludwig Deringer, *Katholische Universität Eichstätt*
Lesa Dill, *Western Kentucky University*
William W. Evans, *Louisiana State University*
Margery Fee, *Strathy Language Unit, Queen's University*
Raymond Gozzi, *Bradley University*
Betty J. Irwin, *University of Georgia*
William J. Kirwin, *Memorial University of Newfoundland*
Sarah Lawson, *London*
Jonathan Lighter, *University of Tennessee*
Virginia G. McDavid, *Chicago State University*
James B. McMillan, *University of Alabama*
Patrick W. Merman, *Monroe, Michigan*
Michael Montgomery, *University of South Carolina*
Thomas M. Paikeday, *Mississauga, Ontario*
Louis Phillips, *School of Visual Arts*
Mary Gray Porter, *University of Alabama*
Alan R. Slotkin, *Tennessee Technological University*
James C. Stalker, *Michigan State University*
Sol Steinmetz, *Barnhart Books*
John Tinkler, *University of Tennessee, Chattanooga*
Greg Williams, *University of Toronto*

In this installment we look at some words the New Words Committee members have sent us, clustering around a few themes. Science and its technological applications, as sources of new words, are as productive as the magic salt mill in the sea, which according to the Scandinavian myth is why the ocean tastes the way it does. The unwinding of the genetic code has made it possible to identify each person with practically perfect accuracy according to the unique structure of his or her DNA. In this installment we have a cluster of words relating to such *DNA* or *genetic fingerprinting*, a technique used forensically to identify murderers and rapists, either singly or in *pack rape*. Many rapists, however, turn out to be well-known to their victims, in the phenomenon of *acquaintance* or *date rape*.

Another application of science to help Big Brother keep us in order is the *eyealyzer*, which measures the alcohol we have consumed. To escape the penalties of an unfavorable measurement by that machine as well as the dangers resulting from over-indulgence, boozers are choosing *designated drivers*, especially at times traditional for imbibing, like New Year's Eve.

Those given to imbibing or otherwise taking steroids, a chemical enhancement for athletes, can fall prey to *steroid* or *roid rage* and may, together with those bored out of their skulls, find themselves confined with other *looney tunes* in a *rubber room*. Mechanical, rather than chemical, efforts to remold the human form nearer the heart's desire are *liposuction* and *lipofilling*.

The *notch* phenomenon began as a plea against assumed injustice but eventually came to be seen as a *low-rent* protest against *windfall* retirees. Such domestic fiscal complaints contrast oddly with the violent Near Eastern *intifada* uprisings. All these forms and some related ones are documented in this installment.

acquaintance rape *n* Forced sexual intercourse with a person known to the victim 1984 Apr 9 *Newsweek* 91/1 All these "nice" criminals add up to one grim statistic: according to law-enforcement officials and rape-treatment counselors, "acquaintance rape"—or "date rape," as it is popularly known—accounts for about 60 percent of all reported rapes. 1986 Jan 19 *Parade Mag* 16/2 In more than two-thirds of reported rapes, the rapist is someone the woman knows—a boyfriend, neighbor, family friend. And most women who survive a so-called 'acquaintance rape' report it neither to the police nor anyone else, since they consider it a very private, personal and embarrassing affair. 1988 Apr *Newsweek on Campus* 12/2 This phenomenon can take the form of gang rape or its first cousin, acquaintance or date rape. Jun 3 U of Georgia *Red and Black* 1/4 A campus minister has requested that the Georgia and Florida athletic boards change the location of the annual football game between the schools to make the atmosphere less conducive to acquaintance rape. 1989 Feb 2 U of Georgia *Red and Black* 1/1 The Georgia Center for Continuing Education will conduct a national video teleconference titled "A Seminar On Acquaintance/Date Rape" from 2 to 5 p.m. today. (cf DATE RAPE)
bonanza baby *n* WINDFALL BABY 1989 Apr 16 *Athens* [GA] *Daily News/Banner-Herald* D-7/3 That is why notch babies' checks look small compared with those of people born before them, who are sometimes known as "bonanza babies."
date rape *n* Sexual intercourse forced by a person with whom the victim has a social engagement 1983 May 18 U of Georgia *Red and Black* 1/1 But, according to some local rape counselors, "date rape" may be a hidden problem on campus that goes on with little notice but leaves frustrated, silent victims. 1988 Jun 3 U of Georgia *Red and Black* 1/4 "I don't want to give the impression that the situation is worse at the University, but one (date rape) is too many," he said. "If we can do anything to improve the environment, we should." Nov 20 *NY Times Mag* 28 I know a woman who got pregnant from a date rape, and another with a heart condition that could have killed her had she been forced to carry a child to term. 1989 Feb 2 *Athens Observer* 1/5–6 (headline and article) Date rape bill before assembly / A bill that would make it harder for information about a rape survivor's past or other personal information to be brought out in a trial may be up for a vote in the state House of Representatives next week. [¶] Prosecutors say the law would particularly help in "date rape" cases, where a woman is raped by someone she knows. (cf ACQUAINTANCE RAPE)
designated driver *n* Person selected to abstain from intoxicants at a party and to drive an automobile for other persons after the party [perh modeled on the baseball term *designated hitter*] 1988 Dec 30 *USA Today* D-2/4–5 (cartoon caption) "Here's to the life of the party, *the designated driver*." 1989 Jan 10 *USA Today* NBC Atlanta WXIA-11 (program segment on substance abuse) Is it your turn to be a designated driver?
DNA fingerprinting *n* Identification, especially for legal purposes, by analyzing the structure of the DNA in an individual's cells 1985 Dec 21–28 *Science News* 391/3 While DNA patterns have not yet condemned any criminals, forensic applications of molecular biology appear both imminent and powerful. "It is envisaged that DNA fingerprinting will revolutionize forensic biology particularly with regard to the identification of rape suspects," says geneticist Alec J. Jeffreys of the University of Leicester, U.K. 1987 May 30 *Science News* 344/1 Two papers appearing in the May 14 NATURE, however, show that "DNA fingerprinting"—an extraordinarily sensitive genetic technique developed for humans and used in forensic identification of individuals as well as paternity and maternity questions—can home in on genetic relations among wild sparrows as well as it does for humans. And other papers in press suggest that the technique applies to cats, dogs and mice as well. 1988 Feb 5 CBS *Evening News with Dan Rather* Officials are using DNA fingerprinting to positively identify suspects. Apr 24 *Atlanta Journal/Constitution* A-12/2 But at least 30 American police departments now are using "DNA fingerprinting" in active investigations. A Florida court recently convicted a rapist based on genetic evidence. Jun *Discover* 46/4–47/1 One afternoon in early August Berry [prosecutor of a rape case in Orlando, Florida] was visited by Jeffrey Ashton, another

attorney in his office, who told him of a TV news report he'd seen about a new technique called DNA fingerprinting. It had been used in a rape-murder case in Britain.... [¶] The DNA fingerprinting test used in Britain was developed by Alec Jeffreys, a geneticist at the University of Leicester. Jeffreys got the idea for the test while looking for genetic variations to serve as markers for inherited disease. It struck him that the techniques molecular biologists use to visualize variations in DNA could also be used to establish identity. 1989 Mar 17 *Wall Street Journal* B-1/1 Courtrooms are increasingly accepting "DNA fingerprinting." So far, courts in 24 states—in 79 cases—have permitted use of such evidence, usually by the prosecution, and the conviction rate in these cases is high.... [¶] DNA fingerprinting has been used in civil paternity cases even more frequently than in criminal investigations. (cf FINGERPRINTING, GENETIC FINGERPRINTING)
DNA print *n* GENETIC FINGERPRINT 1988 Jun *Discover* 48 (diagram caption) THE MAKING OF A DNA PRINT / Each person's DNA has individual patterns. Displayed as a "print," these patterns are a powerful forensic tool.
eyealyzer, eyelyzer *n* An instrument for detecting the amount of alcohol one has consumed by measuring alcohol in the vapors emitted from the eyes 1987 Dec *Discover* 14/1 Three years ago Giles started looking for alternatives to breath tests. First he tried to measure alcohol vapors leaving the palm of the hand, but he soon turned to the eye: its tear-covered surface provides an easy escape route for evaporating alcohol. [¶] Giles's device, called the eyelyzer, detects these vapors. 1988 Apr *Omni* 29/1–2 Giles has a possible solution. Working at the Addiction Research Foundation in Toronto, he has come up with a gadget he calls the Eyealyzer. Basically, it's a funnel that's placed over one of the subject's eyes for 15 seconds or so, during which time it gathers vapors emitted by the eye's lachrymal fluids. The vapors are then passed to a gas sensor that measures their alcohol content. So far Giles has tested the device on ten elderly alcoholic patients, checking the Eyealyzer measurements against results from both breathalyzers and blood tests. Not only is the Eyealyzer "quite sensitive," Giles reports, it is also "a little more accurate" than the standard balloon.
fingerprinting *n* DNA fingerprinting 1985 Nov 18 quot sv GENETIC FINGERPRINT 1987 May 30 *Science News* 344/1 In the fingerprinting technique, scientists essentially count the number of times a particular sequence of DNA base pairs (the chemical building blocks of the DNA molecule) repeats in sections of DNA.... And since parents pass down part of their variability patterns to their offspring, parentage can also be accurately determined.
genetic fingerprint *n* The distinctive structure of the DNA in an individual's cells, used as a means of identification 1985 Mar 8 Toronto *Globe and Mail* P-1 GENETIC FINGERPRINTS A BOON IN RAPE AND PATERNITY CASES / London —Scientists have discovered the genetic equivalent of the fingerprint, so that a single human cell could verify the attacker in a rape case, the father in a paternity suit and the identity of a body. Nov 18 Toronto *Globe and Mail* A-12 (dateline London) The key to the fingerprinting is then a "probe"—a piece of DNA (desoxyribonucleic acid, the building block of living matter) matching the core region of the selfish genes just like a key matches a lock. This probe then sticks to the DNA under test at just the places where the genes are placed. The positions of the probes on the DNA divide it into different lengths, and in the end it is not the variable regions themselves, but the spectrum of lengths into which the DNA is cut that finally makes up a person's "genetic fingerprint". 1989 Jan 24 London *Daily Telegraph* Reporting restrictions were lifted at the request of his solicitor, Mr Michael Lodge, who complained it had taken three months for police to arrest him after genetic fingerprint tests which he considered were evidence in only two of the eight offences. Jan 25 *San Francisco Chronicle* A-3/3 (headline and article) State OKs Use Of 'Genetic Fingerprints' / Palm Springs / State Attorney General John Van de Kamp yesterday approved the use of a genetic code technique that investigators may find more helpful than fingerprints in tracing crime suspects.
genetic fingerprinting *n* DNA fingerprinting 1985 Nov 18 Toronto *Globe and Mail* A-12 LONDON / A GENETIC technique called genetic fingerprinting has been used for the first time in an immigration case here, successfully proving that a boy was indeed the son of a British resident.... [¶] Moreover, the method would also work for the identification of criminals from the tiniest piece of skin or drop of blood left at the scene of a crime. Or from semen in case of rape. Not surprisingly, therefore, the British Home Office, which controls immigration into the United Kingdom, is also knocking at Dr. Jeffries' door, and apparently taking genetic fingerprinting very seriously. 1987 *McGraw-Hill Yearbook of Science and Technology* 153 Genetic fingerprinting enables virtually 100% discrimination between individuals from small samples of blood or semen. No two people have the same genetic fingerprint, unless they are identical twins. 1988 Apr 24 *Atlanta Journal/Constitution* A-12/2 "The most significant new technology we see today is the genetic 'fingerprinting,' " said Richard Frank, president of the American Academy of Forensic Sciences.... [¶] Since 1986, law enforcement officials have been learning to read the unique genetic identity stamped like a trademark in every human cell. Genetic tests may give police a virtually foolproof way to link a suspect to the blood, hair or body fluids at the scene of a crime. 1989 Mar 17 *Wall Street Journal* B-1/1 So-called DNA, or genetic, fingerprinting employs a complicated laboratory process to compare the genetic pattern in the blood sample of a suspect with that in blood, semen or other cellular material from the crime scene. Since every person except an identical twin has a unique genetic pattern, the process "gets a make" with absolute certainty.
intifada, intifadah *n* Palestinian uprising 1988 May 16 *Newsweek* 37/1 Yet signs of the uprising remain everywhere, in the shuttered shops of Arab centers like Nablus and Hebron, in the makeshift barriers that quarantine the refugee camps.... Still, with Israel squeezing the protesters and last week launching a pre-emptive strike against potential Palestine Liberation Organization staging areas in southern Lebanon, Israelis and Palestinians alike are starting to talk about a post-uprising environment, and about what this *intifada* meant. Jun *Atlantic* 24 The uprising, or what the Palestinians call the *intifada*, is emphatically not a revolt against the Israeli occupation alone. It is equally an internal revolution of children against fathers, women against husbands, poor against rich, refugees against the propertied classes. Jun 10 *Atlanta Constitution* A-23/1 (William Safire) The Israelis have finally figured out a way to contain the Palestinian intifada, or uprising, in the disputed territories.... [¶] But there

can be no denying the success of the new strategy of intifada (from the Arabic verb for "to shake loose") in the four-decade Arab war to destroy Israel. Dec 26 *Atlanta Journal/Constitution* A-19/4–5 (William Safire) The threat to Israelis from the Arab world is no chimera. Saudi Arabia proudly subsidizes the intifadah (uprising) violence. 1989 Jan 19 *Atlanta Journal/Constitution* A-9/3 State Department spokesman Charles E. Redman said the department had received a tape recording of comments Mr. Arafat made last week in which he said, "Whoever thinks of stopping the intifadah before it achieves its goals, I will give him 10 bullets in the chest." "Intifadah" is the Arabic word for the 13-month-long uprising by Palestinians against Israel's occupation of the West Bank and Gaza Strip.

lipofilling *n* Transfer of fat from one part of the body to another by suction and injection 1987 Sep 14 *Time* 70/2 An even newer trick, called lipofilling, makes use of the fat removed by liposuction to build up other areas, such as filling out cheeks on the face or redefining a jawline. 1988 *Colliers Encyclopedia Yearbook* 311/1 Liposuction, a procedure that vacuums fat from problem areas, surpassed breast augmentation as the most popular cosmetic procedure. And more people—mostly women—tried a new technique called lipofilling, which uses the fat removed by liposuction to build up other areas.

liposuction /ˈlaɪpoˌsəkšən/ **1:** *n* Removal of fat from the body by a process of suction 1987 Sep 14 *Time* 70/2 Tops on the list, for women, is suction lipectomy, an operation developed in France and introduced in the U.S. in 1982. Also called liposuction, it entails the insertion under the skin of a hollow, blunt-ended tube that is attached to a high-powered suction machine that vacuums out the fat. 1988 Aug 29 *New York Magazine* 44/2 . . . but there are strollers, too—chatting about divorce settlements, triglyceride terror, oat bran, IRAs, real estate in Aspen, liposuction . . . you know, life. 1989 Apr 11 *Atlanta Journal/Constitution* A-15/5 (Ellen Goodman) Liposuction, breast enhancement, face lifts are all best sellers. One doctor in San Francisco advertises his expertise, saying that he has made "dozens of TV appearances." **2:** *vb* To remove fat from the body by suction 1989 Jan 10 *Athens* [GA] *Banner-Herald* 9 (cartoon "Bloom County"; the penguin character is discussing what he would do differently from 1988) Actually, I wouldn't have my nose fat liposuctioned out, collapsing the superstructure into a "Q-tip"-like shape again.

looney tunes, loony tunes *adj* & *n* [from the Warner Bros animated cartoons] Illogical, erratic, absurd or crazy in behavior; a person or persons acting in such a manner 1985 Jul 6 *Saturday Night Live* NBC There was this looney tunes character. Jul 9 Toronto *Globe and Mail* (dateline Havana, Cuba) P-1 "And we are especially not going to tolerate these attacks from outlaw states run by the strangest collection of misfits, looney tunes and squalid criminals since the advent of (Nazi German dictator Adolf Hitler's) Third Reich," Mr. Reagan said. Jul 18 Toronto *Globe and Mail* P-7 Mr. Reagan specifically accused Libya, Iran, North Korea, Cuba and Nicaragua, describing their leaders, in a memorable phrase, as "the strangest collection of misfits, Looney Tunes and squalid criminals since the advent of the Third Reich." 1987 Dec 7 *Time* 66/2 As for channeling, "it's not a business; it's a labor of love." He adds a dark warning that others are less worthy. "There's some loony tunes out there," he says. 1988 Mar 24 *Atlanta Constitution* A-17/4 (Tom Teepen) The claim [by the Moral Majority that new civil-rights legislation will force churches to hire transvestite, homosexual, drug-addict AIDS victims as youth counselors] is Looney Tunes, of course, as attested to by support for the legislation from mainline Catholic, Baptist, Methodist, Episcopalian, Jewish, Presbyterian and Lutheran organizations. Oct 9 *Atlanta Journal/Constitution* M-10/3–4 [In Barry Goldwater's autobiography] Mr. Carter's United Nations Ambassador, Andrew Young, gets off no easier, and Mr. Goldwater characterizes Mr. Young and his aides as "looney tunes . . . leftovers from the hippie generation. . . . CIA agents called his staff the 'Manson family,' referring to the drug crazed California mass killers, because they believed their behavior at the U.N. was crazy."

low-rent *adj* Cheap, low on the socio-economic scale, crude, tasteless, tacky 1982 Mar 13 *Atlanta Journal/Constitution* B-2/5 Belushi was a low-rent junkie, if the word can be defined as one who uses the needle and syringe. 1987 Nov 9 "Dear Abby" *Athens* [GA] *Banner-Herald* 9/3 [At a small Virginia liberal arts college, the administration signaled the end of a party by removing the food and drink and blinking off and on the lights.] This, in my view, gave the guests the impression that they were simply "hired hands" being tolerated for two hours, not professionally respected colleagues. Is my perception inaccurate? Or was such behavior simply "low rent," as we used to say in the South? 1988 Mar *New York Monthly* 58 A few months before the shooting, the Italian publisher Longanesi brought out a low-rent docunovel titled *Sotto il vestito niente* (*Under Her Clothing, Nothing*), about sex, drugs, models, the Mafia and death in the Milanese fashion world. May 15 *Atlanta Journal/Constitution* J-10/2 (review of *All the Western Stars* by Philip Lee Williams) Jake has to tell the story because he's the one we can trust. He's a man who can use expressions such as "I be dog" or "deep-down sorry"; who can declare, "I don't care what anybody says, it's low-rent to allow chickens under your house." Dec 4 *New York Times Magazine* 84/3 Penn and Teller play "two low-rent types living off the land of show business," as Penn puts it. 1989 Jan 16 *Chicago Tribune* sec 5, 3/5 (headline to an article reviewing the book *Falling from Grace: The Experience of Downward Mobility in the American Middle Class* by Katherine S. Newman) Middle-class past, low-rent future Mar 17 *Atlanta Journal/Constitution* D-2/4 "Lower East Side Story" it's not. [¶] Rather, "Rooftops" is a low-rent drama with music about no-rent kids who make their homes (called "cribs") on the city's skyline.

notch *n* **1:** Reduction (in Social Security benefits for those born 1917–21) 1988 Jan 25 *New York Times* 22/3 (letter to ed) I am writing in response to "The Greed of Notch Babies" (editorial, Jan. 13), which does not explain fully the inequity of the notch in Social Security benefit levels for those born between 1917 and 1921. **2:** Period of five years (1917–21) spanning the birth dates of retirees who claim inequitable Social Security benefits 1988 Mar 30 *Atlanta Constitution* B-8/2–3 They are notch babies—people born in the "notch" between 1917 and 1921 who feel that in revamping the cost of living provisions of Social Security, the government cheated them out of 20 percent of the benefits they deserved. While officials contend they readjusted the payment schedule that short-changed those born between 1917 and 1921, the seniors say Congress' efforts have not corrected the five-year notch.

notch baby *n* One born during the NOTCH (sense 2) 1988 Sep 20 *Atlanta Constitution* A-10/5 (letter to ed) Let's be honest. The senior citizen "notch babies" are going to march because the government will not *give* them a fair share of Social Security money. [¶] . . . The "notch babies" do not show any concern for those born before 1917. 1989 Jan 25 *San Francisco Chronicle* C-3/1 This week Congress is holding more hearings on what to do about the so-called "notch babies"—people born from 1917 to 1921—who were part of the correction process adopted by Congress in 1977, and who for four years have been screaming because the [Social Security] benefits they got when they retired were lower than those for people born before 1917.

notchie *n* NOTCH BABY 1988 Mar 30 *Atlanta Constitution* B-8/2–3 The "notchies" claim they got an average of $660 less in 1987 than other Americans with identical work records.

notch year *n* Year within the NOTCH (sense 2) 1983 Nov 14 "Dear Abby" *Atlanta Constitution* B-2/1 It all started when I received a letter that read in part: "If you are drawing Social Security and were born in 1917, 1918, 1919, 1920 or 1921 (called 'the notch years') you are being unjustly penalized by receiving lower benefits than those born prior to and after the above-mentioned years." . . . I was incorrect in stating that those born in the notch years would receive lower benefits than those born after 1921. The fact is, everyone born after 1921 will be unjustly penalized by receiving lower benefits than those born before 1917.

pack rape *n* Forced sexual intercourse with several persons; gang rape (New Zealand use) 1988 Feb 27 *Auckland Sun* 1/1 Former Mongrel Mob secretary George Manfredos won an eight-year custody battle yesterday for his son Tony. . . . [¶] Mr Manfredos was a Mongrel Mob boss at the time of a brutal pack rape at a gang convention. He later fell out of favour with gang leaders.

reflag *vt* Register a foreign ship to permit it to fly the flag of the registering nation and thereby bring it under the diplomatic and military protection of that nation 1987 Jun 4 *Houston Chronicle* sec 1, 11/3 Nichols also expressed reservations about the Reagan administration's plans to put U.S. flags and captains on Kuwaiti oil tankers, bringing the ships under the protection of the United States against attacks from Iran. Iran and Iraq have been fighting a long, bloody war. Kuwait is a strong ally of Iraq, and the administration wants to "reflag" the Kuwaiti tankers to keep gulf oil flowing to the West. Jun 11 *Houston Chronicle* sec 1, 27 The Reagan administration's plan to temporarily "reflag" Kuwaiti vessels in order to extend a U.S. military presence in the Persian Gulf is not only highly dangerous, but also violates international law. [¶] The 1958 Geneva Convention on the High Seas requires that there be a "genuine link" between the flag state and vessel. There is no real link between the Kuwaiti vessels and the United States. Jun 29 *Newsweek* 25/1 Prodded by the Soviets' foray into a strategically vital region, the administration agreed to provide Navy escorts; it had already agreed in principle to reflag 11 Kuwaiti tankers as U.S. vessels. [¶] "Reflagging" means just that. Each ship will fly the U.S. flag, carry an American captain and bear an American name; the tanker Casbah, for example, will become the Ocean City. In theory, at least, reflagging the Kuwaiti tankers will force would-be attackers to think twice: opening fire on a U.S. vessel would be tantamount to an act of war against the United States, and Navy sources say the Iranian military has carefully avoided direct confrontation with the Great Satan. 1988 *World Book Yearbook* 408/1 As a result, in June, the United States agreed to *reflag* (reregister as American vessels) 11 Kuwaiti tankers and provide them with U.S. naval escorts through the gulf. **—reflagging** *part* 1987 Jun 4 *Houston Chronicle* sec 1, 11/3 Nichols, however, said the reflagging decision is bound to provoke an Iranian attack. [¶] "The Iranians would dearly love to twitch the nose of an American paper tiger and see what its reaction would be," he said. [¶] Nichols said he can find no precedent for the reflagging maneuver.

roid rage *n* Violent behavior resulting from the excessive use of anabolic steroids 1988 Sep 6 Columbia SC *State* B-1/3–4 "Roid rage"—the violent feelings experienced by athletes who take anabolic steroids—may be the newest affliction of sports medicine. Robert Voy, director of sports medicine and science of the U.S. Olympic Committee, said that if used in small amounts, the drugs may be innocuous. He said that many athletes take 10 to 15 times the therapeutic dose of the substances to build muscle, and that they can become violent. Oct 10 *Newsweek* 55/2 Even to the untrained eye, [Ben] Johnson [athlete who lost his gold medal for the Olympic 100-meter dash after testing positive for steroids] had many of the earmarks of a steroid user: extreme muscle definition, a remarkable improvement in performance over a short period of time, eyes yellowed by possible liver dysfunction. At times he also displayed what might be diagnosed as the fabled "roid rage." In Seoul, for instance, he once picked up a reporter and tossed him to one side without evident provocation.

rubber room *n* & *attrib* A room padded with foam rubber for violent, mentally deranged persons; a tedious, routine, pointless, or stressful job, especially in cramped, unpleasant working conditions 1976 Sep 6 *New Yorker* 39/1 (quoting an astronaut objecting to the routine imposed by Mission Control) . . . we have to work hard and do the best job we can, but, my gosh, you just couldn't do that stuff continuously. You'd be ready for the rubber room when they brought you back. 1988 May 13 *Atlanta Constitution* A-2/4–5 Without explanation, the railroad late last month stripped the clerks of all duties, reassigned them to overnight shifts and ordered them to sit for eight hours a night—sometimes in offices lacking telephones, paper and pencils—with permission to do nothing but read the company rule book. [¶] San Francisco-based Southern Pacific Transportation will not talk about the so-called "rubber room" assignments, insisting they are an issue for labor and management to discuss privately. . . . [¶] A handful of those rules are keys to understanding the rubber-room controversy—so-called, according to railroad watchers, not only because the no-work jobs create stress but because workers can be bounced from one office to another at the railroad's will. Oct 8 *San Francisco Chronicle* B-5/1–2 Before the agreement was reached, SP [Southern Pacific] had tried a markedly different tack. It placed union workers in so-called "rubber rooms" last May to persuade them to quit. [¶] The term "rubber room" was coined by the railroad unions, and applied to assignments in cramped, unpleasant quarters—comparable, the unions charged, to rubber-lined or padded rooms in mental hospitals.

steroid rage *n* ROID RAGE 1989 Jan 2 *Maclean's* 33/3 In both men and women, steroids can cause liver and kidney damage, increased cholesterol, acne, baldness, and dramatic mood swings and violent behavior known as "steroid rage."

windfall   *attrib*   Born between 1911 and 1916 and therefore entitled to higher Social Security benefits than those born later   **—windfall baby**   1989 Jan 25 *San Francisco Chronicle* C-3/4 Unhappily, this does not solve the problem of inequity between the windfall babies and the notch babies. . . . [¶] The fundamental flaw in all these bills is that they would perpetuate the original 1972 mistake—and overcompensate an even larger set of the elderly—and their inevitable phaseout would simply create new sets of notch babies to be dealt with down the line.   (cf BONANZA BABY)   **—windfall group**   Idem In fact, the notch babies, while receiving demonstrably lower benefits than the windfall group (those born from 1911 through 1916), continued to receive far higher benefits—as a share of their original income—than all other Social Security recipients, including those who retired before 1973–1974 and those who have retired since 1981—which is the peak year for benefits for those retiring at age 65.

AMONG THE NEW WORDS

JOHN ALGEO   AND   ADELE ALGEO
University of Georgia   *Athens, Georgia*

With the assistance of the New Words Committee

A NOTABLE DEVELOPMENT IN THE ENTERTAINMENT INDUSTRY has been an increase in violence, vulgarity, grotesquerie, and purported realism on television and radio shows, with a corresponding decrease in taste and manners. Because the new tendency echoes the style of tabloid magazines sold in supermarkets, it is sometimes called *supermarket TV* or *tabloid TV*. The violence has given rise to such terms as *confrontainment* and *crash* (*show, TV*); the vulgarity to *raunch* (*radio, TV*), *sleaze TV*, and *teleporn*; the presumed realism, offered by producers as defense of their product, to *nonfiction TV* and *reality* or *reality-based* (*show, TV*). The low level of taste in the programs of this form of broadcasting is reflected in the terms *junk TV show, trash TV*, and the related *trash-sport event*, as well as the highly productive *shock* (*artist, cabaret, jock, jocking, photojournalism, radio, TV, video*). *Me TV* emphasizes self-centeredness and lack of external standards.

Yesterday's fashions, like yesterday's tabloids, are fast forgotten. Clothing made of denim cloth—once typical of laborers—has long been fashionable wear, though unfashionable if it looks new. Consequently, various techniques to give new cloth an old appearance were developed, including the bleaching of the cloth in streaks. Jeans so treated have been called *stonewashed* (and a verb *to stonewash* is accordingly entered in the *Random House Dictionary*, 2nd Unabridged, although the word seems to be used chiefly in the participial form). For a brief period in late 1987 and early 1988 the alternative terms *acid* and *acid-wash* were used but seem to have faded, perhaps because their connotations were not what clothiers wanted. Bettersounding, but no more successful, are *frosted* and *iced jeans*.

Other fun, albeit less elegant, sartorial terms are *belt bag, fanny flask*, and *fanny pack*. For the last, a Norwegian equivalent, *rumptaske*, has also been reported.

Some years ago, *American Speech* documented the shift of the noun *fun* to adjectival use, first functionally and then formally (with *very fun* and *funner* eventually appearing). *Key* seems to be following a similar path, though more slowly. In the sense 'centrally important, fundamental', the word has been used attributively for some time and is now entered as an adjective in many dictionaries. The *OEDS* has a first citation of this use from 1913.

Throughout most of the twentieth century, however, the term was purely attributive in use: *key fact, key industry, key office, key position*, and the like. In such use it seems to be only an attributive noun. However, the last two citations of the *OEDS*, from 1970 and 1971, have the word in predicate use without a determiner: "two ideas were key" and "this is what's key"; such use clearly verges on the adjectival. We add other citations here to show that the adjectival use probably became widespread in the 1970s and is continuing. Full adjectival use would entail forms like *very key* and *keyer* or *keyest*. They will doubtless turn up.

The expression *postmodern* seems to have begun as an architectural term, though it has been extended to a variety of other fields, such as literary criticism; we hope to document some of those extensions in a subsequent installment of "Among the New Words." Meanwhile, however, this installment includes *deconstructivist architecture*, which may owe something to the lit-crit term *deconstruction*. If so, these terms demonstrate the circular flow of voguish words.

Otherwise, the entries in this installment range from the tragic (*atomic veteran*) to the trivial (*gack*) and embrace low finance (*bucket drive, chump change*), high technology (*copy code*), communication (*informate*), and the social order (*four-two-one syndrome*). They, like our language and our society, are a marvelous, motley bunch.

acid   *attrib n*   (Of clothing made from denim cloth) bleached, with light-colored streaks   **—acid jeans**   *n*   1987 Nov 20 *Wall Street Week* WGTV-8 Athens GA [Louis Rukeyser cited acid jeans as the top-selling item of clothing that Christmas season]   (cf FROSTED JEANS)   **—acid overalls**   *n*   1988 Jan sign in Melbourne, Australia, clothing-store window Westco Jeans/Acid Overalls/$45   **—acid-washed**   *attrib part ph*   1988 Jan 10 *New York Times Magazine* 14/2 [William Safire] *National Lampoon* magazine has issued a list of current euphemisms, including *the homeless* for those unfortunates the hard-hearted used to call *bums* or *derelicts*; *acid-washed* for what wearers of jeans used to call *faded*, and *private person* for the fellow who used to be a *grouchy recluse*.   **—acid-washing process**   *n*   1987 Dec 7 *Atlanta Constitution* C-2/1 In the first step of the acid-washing process, which refers to the pH balance of the wash bath rather than what the jeans are washed in, the inside-out jeans are given a regular washing.

atomic veteran; atomic vet   *n*   Veteran exposed to radiation from atomic weapons or testing   1983 May 15 *Atlanta Journal/Constitution* D-10/1–5 In 1979, the Kellys formed the National Association of Atomic Veterans, to lobby on behalf of an estimated 250,000 American servicemen who were exposed to radiation during the occupation of Hiroshima and Nagasaki and during the atmospheric tests conducted between 1946 and 1962. . . . / The Senate Veterans Committee has endorsed legislation that mandates a long-term epidemiological study of the atomic veterans in order to get better answers to some of the disturbing questions being raised. . . . it would provide atomic veterans a much better idea than they have now as to what price they and their children may have paid for their exposure.   1988 May 5 *Atlanta Constitution* A-24/1–2 (editorial) They are called "atomic veterans" because of their exposure to radiation during the 1945 occupation of Japan and the post-World War II tests of nuclear weapons. . . . [¶] The VA argues that the atomic veterans have not proved beyond a shadow of a doubt that their current health problems are directly related to their military service. Never mind that many atomic vets seem to suffer disproportionately from cancers and other illnesses for which a plausible, and most likely, explanation is the experience they all have in common: their exposure to radiation.   May 11 *Atlanta Constitution* B-1/2–4 The birth of the nuclear age began with a cataclysmic bang—but won't end with a whimper—for "atomic veteran" James C. Cox, an Atlanta native.   1989 Apr 17 *Atlanta Constitution* A-1/1 The case highlights the plight of almost 8,000 "atomic vets" who are trying to win compensation for health problems they say are related to atomic testing.

belt bag   *n*   FANNY PACK   1988 Dec 5 *Newsweek* 81/1 There's a new landmark on the urban waistland. Belt bags, those strange contraptions that used to be the sole province of rugged, outdoorsy types, are becoming increasingly popular with sidewalk hikers. Adweek magazine has named them one of the hottest products of 1988.

bucket drive   *vi*   Collect money for charity by public solicitation with bucket-like containers   1987 Apr 8 Ann Arbor *Michigan Daily* 4 [letter to ed] For the sake of tens of thousands of starving civilians in Lebanon, a number of Ann Arbor students, faculty, and residents will bucket drive today, Wednesday, April 8th, at five locations around Ann Arbor.

chump change   *n*   Small amount of money · 1987 Nov 14 *Atlanta Journal/Constitution* A-23/3 It's not the $350-a-month car allowance that makes the Fulton County Commission one of the most expensive in the state. It's not even the travel expenses, though the travel and miscellaneous expense money of Fulton's commissioners is not to be dismissed as chump change.   1988 May 9 *Time* 20/2 With the unemployment rate for black teenagers at 37%, little work is available to unskilled, poorly educated youths. The handful of jobs that are open—flipping burgers, packing groceries—pay only minimum wages or "chump change," in the street vernacular.   1989 Feb 26 *Washington Post Magazine* 14/1 " To ABC, however much money it [Ted Koppel's salary from *Nightline*] is, it's chump change," Kaplan says.

confrontainment   *n*   [*confront*ation + enter*tainment*]   TABLOID TV   1988 Nov 14 *Newsweek* 72/3 It [a brawl on TV in which the nose of the program host was broken] was a scene destined to live in TV-retrospective infamy, a testament both to Rivera's incendiary persona and the medium's most controversial programming ploy. Its designers call it "confrontainment." More objective observers have dubbed it "tabloid TV" or, when roused to the proper pitch of disgust, "trash TV."

copycode   *n*   A technique for preventing the copying of compact-disk recordings   1987 Oct 5 *Newsweek* 72/3 The industry is backing an antitaping technology called "Copycode," developed by CBS records. Under this system, CD's would be recorded with frequencies missing at fixed intervals. That absence could be picked up by microchips inserted into DAT machines. When those machines taped from CD's, the chip would register the drops in frequency and temporarily cause the machine to switch off, leaving gaps in the finished recording.   1988 Apr

8 *Athens* [GA] *Banner-Herald* 19/5 The "copycode" chip, developed by CBS and advocated by the record industry, was designed to prevent anyone from taping CDs onto blank digital audio tape. But the NBS [National Bureau of Standards] agreed with DAT proponents that the chip "degraded" the sound of the CD and "can be bypassed easily."

crash *attrib n* [pun on TRASH TV, with allusion to violent action] —**crash show** *n* 1989 Feb 22 *Detroit Free Press* B-1 [headline and article] CRASH TV / Will this new rash of shows smash ratings? / . . . "RollerGames" and two other shows being shopped by producers to America's television stations this winter are "crash TV.". . . [¶] "People are calling it the TV of the '90s," said Carol Healey, station manager at Philadelphia's WGBS-TV, which . . . will air a pilot of a second crash show, "Interceptor," in April. —**crash television; crash TV** *n* 1989 Jan 20 *Wall Street Journal* B-1/3–4 [headline and article] New Programming Recipe: Take Trash TV, Add Sports / First came trash television, the thriving genre of shows offering real-life sex and violence. Now comes the sequel, which the trade press has dubbed crash television. Jan 27 *Wall Street Journal* B-1/5 "Roller-games," a cross between roller derby and MTV, is being hailed as the favorite so far in a new genre called "crash TV" that's expected to appeal to action-minded young adults. Jan 29 quot SV REALITY SHOW

deconstructivist architecture *n* 1988 Jul 18 *U.S. News & World Report* 40/1 This time, it's an equally radical departure from the past that [Philip] Johnson is plugging: "Deconstructivist Architecture." Gleefully sabotaging traditional notions of stability and even gravity, deconstructivists are designing buildings that are—in the words of Mark Wigley, cocurator of the MOMA show, which opened last month—"dangerously deranged." These sleek, streamlined modernist buildings have been twisted and deformed: Walls slope, columns tilt, facades warp, ceilings gape. Right angles and symmetry give way to careening diagonals; buildings break through and distort one another. [¶] Although deconstructivism has its roots in abstract artistic and political theories—some of its architects even spent years refusing to design buildings that could be built—its ideas are starting to catch on.

fanny flask *n* 1988 Dec 5 *Newsweek* 81/1 [Christin] Ranger [marketing coordinator for Jan-Sport in Everett, WA] thinks the concept started with skiers' fanny flasks that evolved into belt packs for nonliquid essentials as the walking craze sent people into the streets. "The rest," she says, "is history."

fanny pack *n* Pouchlike container strapped around the waist 1971 May *Outdoor Life* 32/3 For the backpacker, there are many new or improved packs, pack-frames, and knapsacks, plus belt pockets, fanny packs, and duffelbags. 1988 Sep 4 *Columbia SC State* E-6/1 An adaption of the pouch that skiers wear to carry money, tissues, car keys, spare goggles and the like (and incidentally keep those form-fitting ski togs from bulging), they've become known as "fanny packs" by their users, because the slope set wears them at waist level, in back and above the hips. Non-skiers, however, are wearing them mostly in front. [¶] The little canvas or leather pouches are seen everywhere in New York and are beginning to dot the landscape elsewhere. Sep 25 *Atlanta Journal/Constitution* J-3/2 On New York's subways, the zippered waist pack is an everyday way for young people to safeguard wallets and other valuables. [¶] When these packs are advertised in catalogs for hikers or bikers, they are called "fanny packs" and are intended for wear in the back, but the subway riders turn them to the front so they are in a visible, clutchable position. Dec 5 *Newsweek* 81/1 Christin Ranger, marketing coordinator for Jan-Sport in Everett, Wash., says her company put out six versions this year (compared with only two last year), including larger fanny packs that hold lunches or tennis shoes and front-loaders with just enough room for a wallet.

four-two-one syndrome *n* Chinese family pattern of single children over three generations with its consequent social problems 1987 Dec 7 *Time* 38/2 Pampering is built into what is called the "four-two-one syndrome"—four grandparents and two parents, all doting on an only child. Many Chinese fear that when such children reach adulthood, they will be unwilling to care for aging parents and geriatric grandparents, forcing the elderly into the care of the state.

frosted jeans *n* ACID JEANS 1987 Dec 7 *Atlanta Constitution* C-1/2 Rachel Funk, 25, says she doesn't even like frosted jeans "because everyone's wearing them, and they're boring." 1988 Mar 20 *Atlanta Journal/Constitution* G-2/2 (picture caption) Fashion model Wanda Gayle Geddie wears a pullover with a graphic stripe pattern ($20) and frosted jeans ($32) from the Lane Bryant stores, in sizes 14 and up.

gack *n* 1988 Apr 15 *Atlanta Constitution* D-2/1 During the 60-second finale, it meant [contestants on the TV program *Double Dare*] running an oozy obstacle course that involved poking around inside a gigantic Swiss cheese, getting cranked through a giant wringer, wiggling down a huge, slimy model of an esophagus and sliding into a vat of pudding-like "gack," the program's own brand of sweet, gelatinous substance.

iced jeans *n* FROSTED JEANS 1987 Dec 7 *Atlanta Constitution* C-1/2 (subhead and article) 'Iced' jeans storm into fashion favor / . . . Now it's being pounded with chemically treated rocks—to satisfy the latest denim craze, frosted or iced (the name depends on the manufacturer) jeans.

informate *v* To share information and authority widely, especially in a business; to operate or communicate in a network pattern rather than hierarchically 1988 May 23 *Wall Street Journal* 17/4–5 [review of *In the Age of the Smart Machine: The Future of Work and Power* by Shoshana Zuboff] Ms. Zuboff argues that we should do away with conventional notions of the division of labor, whereby a firm is divided between operating personnel on the one hand, and the "guardians of all useful knowledge," such as staff specialists and middle management, on the other. Information flows would erode distinctions between those who act and those who think. Ms. Zuboff coins the word "informate" as a way of labeling the process of bringing the entire work force into the information stream, and thereby harnessing everybody's mind. Oct 17 *New York Times* 25 Now, workers are being given more powers—for example, the authority to deal with a problem involving one of the machines instead of turning to a superior, or to make production-line decisions. And they are being given more information about day-to-day operations so as to become more deeply involved in the factory's work. [¶] Manufacturing experts have coined a term for this new strategy: the "informated" factory.

junk TV show *n* TABLOID TV 1989 May 25 *Athens* [GA] *Banner-Herald* 4/3 [Mike Royko] The combination of items put the rumor [about Oprah Winfrey and her boyfriend] in full flight. And before long, it was passed along by various junk TV shows. [¶] I was ignorant of this because I seldom read dopey gossip columns and I don't watch those dippy celebrity TV shows.

key *pred adj* 1974 Edwin Newman *Strictly Speaking* (NY: Warner, 1975) 54–55 The arrival of spring was a key and/or major development in the calendar. In a recent period of three weeks the *Times* conferred keyness on a local news [*sic*]; labor and management negotiators (who were also top-level bargainers); Democrats in Congress; an election in West Germany; a cabinet post in Israel; the position of Herbert Kalmbach as a Watergate witness; a British insurance broker and parts of letters he was accused of forging; a piece of evidence in the Watergate affair, against which some witnesses were only potentially key; five initiatives that some Arizona citizens who had joined in a loose coalition wanted to put on the ballot in November; and a problem in the development of solar power. 1976 Paul E. Erdman *The Crash of '79* (NY: Pocket Books, 1977) 77 These men ran Switzerland's public affairs. They also fairly represented the diverse nature of the Swiss electorate: Gerber and Ulrich (the latter [Franz Ulrich, head of the Swiss espionage agency] not elected, but as key to the system as was the head of the CIA to the American power structure) were both German Swiss. . . . 1983 Mar 9 *Atlanta Constitution* A-15/3 [Arnold Rosenfeld] In the view of many in Israel who oppose total annexation of the West Bank, the issue is key, not only to an international settlement of the Palestinian issue, but to defining, or redefining, the nature of the Jewish state and the Zionist dream. 1985 Jan 9 Toronto *Globe and Mail* B-22 BNOC's prices are seen as key to prices charged by the Organization of Petroleum Exporting Countries. 1987 Nov 25 Daniel Patrick Moynihan, Senator from New York, *Letter to New York* 1 TWO PROPOSITIONS ARE KEY: *FIRST*, SOCIAL SECURITY IS FINE. IT IS NOT BROKE AND IT DOES NOT NEED FIXING. IT ASKS ONLY TO BE LEFT ALONE! 1988 Jun 26 *Atlanta Journal/Constitution* S-1/2 Sleep quality is just as key. Worry or anxiety can make it hard to drift off. Dec 3 *CNN Sports* Turner TV Network [LA Rams player interviewed] I know it's just a statistic, but it's key. Dec 9 NBC evening news (ad) It's key that I can prove that what we have to offer is best for them. 1989 May 7 *Atlanta Journal/Constitution* L-1/4 [headline] Rising Costs of Suits Makes Quality Key.

Me TV *n* TABLOID TV 1989 Jan 18–24 *Variety* 48/1–2 It's been called "Tabloid [*sic*] TV," "Trash TV," "Supermarket TV" and "Sleaze TV." [¶] Gerald Stone does not accept these easy labels. . . . [¶] Stone says "Me TV" is a more apt definition—"if there really needs to be one"—of the changing approach to news mags and talkshow formats. After 30 years of passively watching what others thought he should know, Stone asserts, this viewer has finally risen in protest "to impose the 'I' above the Eye."

nonfiction TV *n* REALITY TV 1989 Jan 15 *New York Times* sec 2, 37 Mr. Rivera, for instance, has defended not only his own show but others similar to it, saying, "These are all programs done outside the network news divisions. Nonfiction TV has become more diversified and more democratic. Overall, news programming is now more interesting, vital and less pretentious. An audience numbering in the tens of millions is not a lunatic fringe nor a gullible cult. It is America, and it is watching."

raunch *attrib n* —**raunch radio** *n* 1987 Dec 7 *Time* 61/2–3 In recent years the proliferation of "raunch radio" personalities like Howard Stern, the acid-tongued New York disk jockey, has raised a public outcry over broadcast vulgarity. Last April the FCC responded by altering its definition of what constitutes indecent programming. . . . The new ruling broadened the standard to include anything that depicts sexual or excretory activity in terms that are "patently offensive as measured by contemporary community standards for the broadcast medium." 1989 Jan 5 "USA Today" NBC Atlanta WXIA-11 Raunch radio is the product of the hands-off policy of the FCC [Federal Communications Commission] during the Reagan years. —**raunch television** *n* 1987 Dec 7 *Time* 61/3 Paul McGeady, general counsel for Morality in Media, complained that the decision will open the floodgates to post-midnight smut: "There's no reason that raunch radio-persons won't become raunch-television persons."

reality *attrib n* —**reality show** *n* 1989 Jan 29 Harrisburg PA *Sunday Patriot-News* A-11/1 Reality shows continued to be the order of the day. The only new genre seemed to be so-called "crash TV," prompted by the success of syndicated wrestling shows. —**reality television; reality TV** *n* 1988 Oct 17 *Newsweek* 87/1 Dubbed "Reality TV" by its advocates and "Tabloid TV" by its detractors, the genre aspires to reflect shards of viewers' own lives and encompasses everything from "thirtysomething" and "The Wonder Years" to Geraldo Rivera and Morton Downey Jr. 1989 Jan 27 *Wall Street Journal* B-1/4-5 For the same reason, viewers will see Paramount's "Tabloid," another entry in the hot genre of "reality television," even though some worry that there's a tabloid glut in the making. Apr 19 *Atlanta Constitution* B-1/4 When we *did* watch, it was a strange brew of talk shows that became shouting—and shoving—matches, something called "reality TV" (how's that for an oxymoron?), profanity and kinky sex. And occasionally, just to make sure we were paying attention, the clear, bright light of a "Murphy Brown" or "Lonesome Dove" reminded us that television could still be good, or even great, when it wanted to.

reality-based *adj* —**reality-based show** 1989 Jan 15 *New York Times* sec 2, 37 Although producers of some of the reality-based shows have made a habit of broadcasting the kinds of lurid stories that supermarket newspapers have long thrived on, others object to being placed in their class. "Don't call it tabloid TV," says Bob Young, one of the two producers of "Inside Edition." "Call it communication." Jan 29 Harrisburg PA *Sunday Patriot-News* A-11/1 "Group One Medical" was one of a wave of "reality-based" shows offered last year that did not make it through the season. May 15 *U.S. News & World Report* 14/3–16/1 So what happens when sex and violence scare away the sponsors? ABC wrestled with that question in a painful way last week. . . . Later it scuttled another crime program, "Scandals II," when ABC decided to rethink all of its reality-based shows, a k a "tabloid" or "trash TV," amid a wave of public threats to boycott advertisers. —**reality-based television** 1989 Jan 15 *New York Times* sec 2, 29/1–2 The half-dozen or so new shows and the old ones that remade themselves on a sex-and-mayhem model proved so successful that they have spawned a multibillion-dollar industry: reality-based television. . . . [¶] Whatever the particular shape, all are rooted, however loosely, in fact. Thus, the label "reality-based."

rumptaske *n* FANNY PACK 1988 Dec 5 *Newsweek* 81/1 Ben Pearson, camping buyer at L. L. Bean in Freeport, Maine, says Europeans love them (in Norway, the proper name is *rumptaske*).

shock *attrib n* —**shock artist** 1988 Nov 14 *Newsweek* 72 [headline and subhead] Trash TV / The industry's shock artists are all over the dial. They're lurid and they're loud and their credo is: anything goes as long as it gets an audience. —**shock-cabaret** 1988 Mar 4 Auckland *New Zealand Herald*, Entertainment sec,

3/2 There will be Chickens all over the stage at Ponsonby's Gluepot next Wednesday night when visiting Japanese shock-cabaret act *The Frank Chickens* will be sharing the bill with Auckland's own *Headless Chickens*.   —**shock jock** 1987 Jun 9 *Houston Chronicle* sec 4, 6/1 Recently, the FCC has been even stricter on what radio stations can broadcast, which is most evident in its reprimand of New York "shock jock" Howard Stern.   1989 Jan 5 "USA Today" NBC Atlanta WXIA-11 Morning shock jocks do attract attention, especially from young adults.   Mar 23 *Athens* [GA] *Banner-Herald* 2/4-5 San Jose, Calif. (AP) Critics of "shock jock" Perry Stone were pleased that KSJO-FM decided to fire the controversial disc jockey they had accused of using racial and sexist slurs in his popular morning talk show.   —**shock photojournalism** 1989 Jan 4 *Atlanta Constitution* A-14/3 [letter to ed] In a city where there is essentially one major newspaper there really is no need for "shock photojournalism" to attract attention and sell newspapers. The media should be responsible for reporting accurate, factual and sometimes educational news. The Dec. 23 front page of The Constitution, which had a large photo revealing the body of a passenger still strapped to the plane seat being lowered by a worker from a roof in Lockerbie, Scotland, is an example of poor taste and insensitivity rampant in the media coverage of recent tragic incidents.   —**shock radio** 1987 Jul 28 *Atlanta Constitution* A-10/5 [letter to ed] If WGST is convinced that "shock radio" is the way to boost its ratings, I'm sure it can find a "hired tongue" somewhere in this hemisphere who displays a modicum of class, a sufficiently broad vocabulary beyond the use and overuse of disgusting slang words and an ability to hear a caller out without screaming hysterical diatribes.   1988 *World Book Yearbook* 461/1 In the last two years, radio broadcasters in particular had come under increasing public pressure because some disk jockeys had gained popularity by use of "shock radio"—vulgar, often sexually oriented comments and stunts.   [¶] In April, the outcry against shock radio caused the FCC to warn broadcasters that it would begin imposing a broader definition of indecency.   May 18 *Wall Street Journal* 36/5 NBC's one-hour series include "Midnight Caller," about the host of a shock-radio talk show.   1989 Jan 5 "USA Today" NBC Atlanta WXIA-11 [New York shock jock Howard] Stern is known as the king of shock radio.   —**shock TV** 1988 Jul 11 *Newsweek* 62/2 It's been nearly a month since Morton Downey Jr.'s mouth went national, time enough to assess how the last word in Shock TV is playing. So far the returns have been fairly strong.   1989 Jan 16 *Newsweek* 65/4 In what may be the ultimate example of shock TV, Jim and Tammy Bakker came back to the airwaves last week and did not ask for money.   —**shock video** 1989 Jan 18–24 *Variety* 122/1 Trash tv, shock video, tabloid tv, exploitation tv—it has as many labels as there are television series. [¶] One thing is certain, however: It has become the hottest trend in tv programming, and viewers can't seem to get enough of it.

shock-jocking *gerund* 1988 May 21 *Nation* 698/3 [letter to ed] Yet radio has become so entrenched in shock-jocking and making money that our songs go to college radio or England for exposure.

sleaze television; sleaze TV *n* 1989 Feb 26 *Washington Post Magazine* 12 [subhead and headline] He's Koppel the Great, Emperor of 'Nightline,' Grand Inquisitor of the United States. But Sleaze TV is at the gates, and Uneasy Lies the Ted That Wears a Crown.   Ibid 17/1 Koppel's hand-wringing about sleaze television, meanwhile, might sound a trifle hollow considering how many times "Nightline" devoted itself to the gaudy travails of Jim and Tammy Bakker, the sex-scandaled televangelists.

stonewash *attrib v* [perh fr the participle *stonewashed* with final consonant-cluster simplification] 1988 Dec 10 *Athens* [GA] *Daily News/Banner-Herald* A-3 [Belk department store ad] . . . jeans . . . 100% cotton stonewash indigo denim in basic and fashion styles. (*RHD2* has *stonewash* vt "to wash (cloth) with pebbles or stones so as to give the appearance of wear" from which the attributive use is derived.)

supermarket TV *n* 1989 Jan 18–24 quot sv Me TV

tabloid (Of television) —**tabloid show** 1989 Jan 27 *Wall Street Journal* B-1/5 Another tabloid show, "Crimewatch Tonight," probably will make it because programmers think host Ike Pappas is credible, and this year's version is much slicker than last year's.   —**tabloid talk show** 1988 Oct 17 *Newsweek* 94/3 Add to all this the competition from syndicated "tabloid talk" shows, all-news and home video and you have the makings of a fatal erosion of the networks' franchise. Since 1980 the evening newscasts of ABC, CBS and NBC have lost almost a quarter of their combined audience.   —**tabloid television** 1988 May 18 *Wall Street Journal* 1/1 Tabloid television is luring an audience that is highly prized by advertisers: women, especially those between the ages of 18 and 49, who typically control a sizable portion of the family budget.   1989 Jan 10 *Athens* [GA] *Banner Herald* 8/6 This week also was the debut of "Inside Edition," the latest entry in the tabloid television roller derby. . . . [¶] While "Inside Edition" will follow NBC's "Nightly News" program, and while it may have the look and sound of a network news magazine, it isn't. [¶] A mix of investigative stories, celebrity interviews and other segments, "Inside Edition" . . .   Jan 15 *New York Times* sec 2, 29/2 But they make no bones about their intention to entertain first and inform second. Their forays into formerly taboo subjects, from neo-Nazism to violent sex, have earned them a variety of disparaging nicknames, including trash or tabloid television.   Jan 25 *Wall Street Journal* B-5/2 Michael Eisner, chairman and chief executive officer of Walt Disney Co., also complained about the lack of quality programs. And Mr. Eisner called tabloid television, the current hot trend featuring voyeuristic, explicit programming based on real life, "a fad that has to fade."   —**tabloid TV** 1988 Nov 14 quot sv CONFRONTAINMENT 1989 Jan 20 *Wall Street Journal* B-1/3 Trash television, also known as tabloid TV, has blossomed with the success of such programs as "A Current Affair" and "America's Most Wanted," and with the increasing luridness on the talk shows of hosts like Geraldo Rivera and Morton Downey Jr. Now some producers looking for the next hit genre, are adding sports to the mix.   Jan 27 *Wall Street Journal* B-1/5–6 Tabloid TV remains a hot topic and is a big draw at a panel discussion. . . . [¶] Asked to clap if they thought tabloid TV has gone too far, the audience applauds robustly.   Feb 26 *Washington Post Magazine* 17 Tabloid TV, right there in Koppel Kountry? "I don't put the Jim and Tammy show in that category," Koppel says huffily.   May 15 quot sv REALITY-BASED SHOW

teleporn *n* [*tele*vision + *porn*ography] 1988 Nov 14 *Newsweek* 73/1-2 The "Geraldo" show's studio brawl came barely a week after its host's NBC special on devil worship (bloodsoaked orgies, dismembered corpses, ritualistic child abuse) garnered such rhapsodic reviews as "an exercise in hysteria" (The Village Voice) and "dirty-minded teleporn" (The Washington Post).

trash-sport *attrib n* 1989 Jan 29 Harrisburg PA *Sunday Patriot-News* A-11/1 "American Gladiators" at least offered a peek at its stars, male and female athletes who will take on competitors in a series of "trash-sport" events.

trash television; trash TV *n* 1988 Nov 14 *Newsweek* 72 [headline and subhead] quot sv SHOCK ARTIST   Ibid 75/1 Quite obviously trash TV wouldn't be suddenly sweeping up those golden ratings if it wasn't fulfilling some deep human yearning, perhaps even a relatively fresh yearning. Some pop-culturists attribute the popularity of the genre to a spreading sense of powerlessness among TV's constituents.   Dec 14–20 *Variety* 39/1 [CBS News President Howard Stringer quoted] "Trash television is the dark at the end of the tunnel, and it is a journey to nowhere paid for with all our reputations. [¶] "I'm confident that trash tv will run its course."   1989 Apr 3 *Athens* [GA] *Banner-Herald* 10/5 Downey has written a letter to TV stations that carry his program, promising to restructure the program [The Morton Downey Jr. Show] that pioneered "trash TV."   May 15 quot sv REALITY-BASED SHOW

AMONG THE NEW WORDS

JOHN ALGEO   AND   ADELE ALGEO

University of Georgia   *Athens, Georgia*

With the assistance of the New Words Committee

Tʀᴜᴇ ᴛᴏ ɪᴛs ᴛʀᴀᴅɪᴛɪᴏɴ ᴏғ ʀᴇғʟᴇᴄᴛɪɴɢ ᴛʜᴇ spirit of the times, "Among the New Words" in this installment looks at violence, prejudice, fizzled technology, mendacious political rhetoric, international dickering, and drought. In future issues we hope to explore the happier side of neology.

Ballistic, its downtoned form *semiballistic*, and what appears to be its superlative, *nuclear*, are noteworthy for two reasons. First, as metaphorical transfers from armament to psychological states, they are chilling testimony of how we see the world around us as the mirror of our minds. Second, and less apocalyptically, they collocate frequently with *go* in an idiom that is already used in American English, as in *go bananas*, but that seems to be becoming more popular, especially in British use (as in *go missing* 'disappear').

Wilding, an innocuous-sounding word for a barbarous activity, is of uncertain origin. It is perhaps simply from the expression *running wild*, although it may suggest an acting out of the impulses symbolized by the monstrous-looking "Wild Things" of Maurice Sendak's children's book *Where the Wild Things Are*. The aim of wilding is a hunt for someone with whom to play *punch-out*. Gangs who engage in wilding are known as *wolf packs* (as in the April 29 citation), a term entered with an appropriate definition in *Webster's Third*, but ignored, in the relevant sense, by most dictionaries. The application of the simplex *wolf* to a member of such a pack is not recorded. The compound, in a less violent application, is also the source of a verb referring to the pack-like behavior of adolescents.

Technology does not always deliver the marvels it promises. *Cold fusion, tabletop fusion,* or *fusion in a jar,* so promising as a source of cheap, clean power, turned out to be a flash in the pan.

Globaloney was the invention of Clare Boothe Luce in 1943 and was first used to ridicule proposals for giving foreign aid from motives of humanitarianism or enlightened self-interest. Perhaps because the term has been used only sporadically and then as a political catchword of imprecise sense, it has not been entered in dictionaries. The term has staying power, however, since it will soon reach its golden anniversary and therefore merits notice.

The occasion for the revival of *globaloney* was the proposal of a *fifth basket* of negotiating topics between the US and Russia. The use of basket for a group of proposals in a negotiation, which originated in the 1970s, has been recorded in *The Second Barnhart Dictionary of New English* but is entered here for comparison. Another negotiating spin-off term is *third zero*, which echoes *zero-zero*.

The domestic political term *iron triangle* is notable for its semantic transmogrifications. About forty years ago, the form was used to denote a triangular-shaped area in North Korea used as a staging base by the Chinese Communist forces and threatened in 1951 by a drive of the UN forces; the northern point of the triangle was at Pyongyang, the southwestern at Chorwon, and the southeastern at Kumhwa. The term was too transient and too specific in application for dictionary entry, although our files contain a good many 1951 citations collected by I. Willis Russell and Mamie Meredith.

The term was reinvented, or perhaps revived, in the 1980s to denote an alliance of three groups that combine to ensure public funding for a shared interest: an agency of the executive branch of government, the corresponding Congressional committee, and the private industry manufacturing commodities bought by the government. Although the term is applicable to any such trio of reinforcing interests, military procurement is the most egregious example. This use, which may have deliberately echoed the older use from the Korean War, is a more contemporary version of the "military-industrial complex," warned against in Dwight Eisenhower's farewell address.

However, when Ronald Reagan ended his presidency and left the nation encumbered with a large debt to support the military-industrial complex, he redefined *iron triangle* to refer to Congress, the communication media, and "special interests" (a Reagan-years code word for those favoring domestic spending for education, health, and social welfare). If the earlier 1980s use of the term to denote the military-industrial complex was a borrowing from the Korean War use for a Chinese Communist military concentration, the semantic change involved an ironic identification of the American military-industrial complex with Chinese Communist militarism. Reagan's redefinition was another ironic reversal in applying the term to those who are natural budgetary opponents of the military-industrial iron triangle. The semantic history of *iron triangle* demonstrates that a struggle for mastery over words accompanies the struggle for power.

Personal economic issues are reflected in *glass ceiling*, *mommy track*, and its spin-off *daddy track*; psychological and less prejudicial ones in *thirtysomething* and *fortysomething*. The last are the spawn of the entertainment industry, which is also responsible for the nostalgic *Windy*. The final entries in this installment, *xeriscape* and *xeriscaping*, show that it is possible to make beauty out of deprivation and so end on a hopeful note.

Acknowledgments for citations: Catherine Algeo, Thomas Algeo, Sheila C. Bailey, George S. Cole, Ludwig Deringer, Betty Irwin, William J. Kirwin, Michael Montgomery, Virginia G. McDavid, Mary Gray Porter, †I. Willis Russell, James C. Stalker, Greg Williams.

ballistic *adj* [metaphor] Furious, raging, angry 1988 Oct 17 *Newsweek* 68/2 Was Lennon genuinely bisexual? Doubtful. [¶] **And so what if he was?** Exactly. It seems odd that Lennon's rigorously tolerant following has gone ballistic over claims that Lennon was doing stuff they don't think is wrong in the first place. Yoko Ono says that if he had really been caught in the act with Brian Epstein, Lennon himself would have been the first to tell the story. Nov 7 *NY Times* 17 (George Bush quoted) I get furious. I go ballistic. I really do and I bawl people out. Of course, everyone's running for cover. 1989 Feb 15 *International Herald Tribune* p n/a Administration sources said Mr. Mosbacher "went ballistic" during a meeting with the White House chief of staff, John H. Sununu, complaining that the White House personnel director, Chase Untermeyer, had set up an operation so slow and cumbersome that it would be weeks, if not months, before any key policymakers were in place at the Commerce Department. Apr 24 *Newsweek* 40/2 The unflattering dispatch produced a characteristic reaction from the former First Couple: Ronald Reagan was hurt, Nancy Reagan was ballistic. Apr 29 *Atlanta Journal/Constitution* A-23/4–5 Gwinnett, too, is showing some long-awaited glimmers of lucidity on the matter of mass transit. [¶] Now is not the time to go ballistic on them. . . . [¶] The suburbs are finally beginning to own up to their responsibilities in the metro community. This is no time to swing the city gates shut.

basket *n* [*BDNE2*] A group of negotiating proposals for consideration without linkage to other issues; the part of an agreement corresponding to a negotiating basket 1975 Aug 4 *Time* 17/1–2 The completed document [of the Helsinki declaration] has five parts: a preamble stating the conference's general goals (of "peace, security, justice and cooperation") and four major sections known for no discernible reason as "baskets." The area of greatest Soviet interest is Basket One, which covers the inviolability of frontiers, peaceful settlement of international disputes, nonintervention in internal affairs, the right of self-determination of peoples and other articles of cooperation and good faith. Basket Two, which was of particular interest to the East bloc and some smaller Western European nations, covers agreements regarding economic, scientific and environmental cooperation. [¶] Basket Three is the major area of Western concern. It deals with increased human contacts between East and West, includes the flow of information, the right of travel, improved working conditions for journalists and cooperation in matters of culture and education. The fourth basket—by far the weakest—involves follow-up arrangements. It merely provides that senior officials of the signature nations will meet in 1977 to see how the agreements are being observed. The charter is regarded as a single document rather than as four linked but separate agreements (which the Soviets wanted, presumably to be able to play down the importance of Basket Three). 1977 Aug 17 *Bulletin* (Bonn) 122/3 Neither have all the possibilities of "Basket 2" been exploited. The Soviet proposals for closer co-operation in environmental protection, traffic and energy could be considered. Nov *Atlantic* 6/3 It was the Swiss who hit upon the "basket" device for breaking procedural deadlocks during negotiations for the Helsinki agreements. They suggested that the various proposals should be divided into three groups, called "baskets." Thus, all ideas about principles of political cooperation, along with proposals for increasing military confidence, such as advance notification of army maneuvers, were placed in Basket One. Measures for improving economic cooperation were consigned to Basket Two. And finally, the controversial proposals involving cultural and humanitarian relations and agreement on principles of human rights were relegated to Basket Three. Over the next months, diplomats in Belgrade will be meeting first in plenary session and then in three separate commissions to look at how the agreements in each of these so-called "baskets" have been carried out. Idem While none of the Western or neutral delegations was proposing to suppress or ignore discussion of the humanitarian provisions signed at Helsinki—the so-called Basket Three agreements—they felt that the question had to be approached gingerly.

cold fusion; cold nuclear fusion *n* Nuclear fusion at ordinary temperature and without elaborate machinery 1989 Apr 11 *Athens [GA] Banner-Herald* 1/5 SALT LAKE CITY—If the modern fusion of major science and big business were a little different, Dallas would have been the scene Wednesday of an announcement to rock the research world—that the fearsome power in the core of the H-bomb and the sun might have been tamed and harnessed in a large economy-size test tube. [¶] Instead, the announcement was made in a news conference almost three weeks ago at the University of Utah. And Wednesday's visit to the Dallas meeting of the American Chemistry Society by Utah chemistry professor B. Stanley Pons will find his the largest scientific audience yet for "cold fusion." Apr 12 *Athens [GA] Daily News/Banner-Herald* C-6/1 ATLANTA—Georgia Tech researchers report attaining controlled, room-temperature nuclear fusion in their laboratory, apparently confirming a controversial report of "cold fusion" announced last month by chemists in Salt Lake City, Utah and Southampton, England. May 2 Harrisburg PA *Patriot-News* A-4 Tests fail to back cold-fusion claim / . . . The fusion-in-a-jar debate was ignited on March 23 when Dr. B. Stanley Pons of the University of Utah and Dr. Martin Fleischmann of the University of Southampton, England, announced that they had achieved "cold fusion" in an electrolytic cell. . . . [¶] The apparatus they used consisted of a glass cell filled with heavy water—water made using deuterium, a heavy form of hydrogen, instead of ordinary hydrogen—and two electrodes. Idem Nevertheless, [Dr. Steven E.] Jones [of Brigham Young University] said in a presentation prepared for the Baltimore meeting that his group "has accumulated considerable evidence for a new form of cold nuclear fusion which occurs when various hydrogen isotopes are loaded into various materials." Oct 15 *Atlanta Journal/Constitution* (comic strip "Shoe") Harley C. Scuggins from over in Bent Fence says he's achieved cold fusion energy on his bedside table.

daddy track *n* [modeled on MOMMY TRACK] Work arrangements that allow men time away from company business for parental responsibilities 1989 Apr 3 *Newsweek* 47/1 (headline and article) The Daddy Track / . . . So ends another day on the daddy track. It's about love, worrying, getting the kids dressed and making them put away the toys. It's closely related to the mommy track. Aug 13 *Ottawa Citizen* F-8/1–2 (headline and article) Following the Daddy Track / . . . The title of the talk is "The Fast Track and the Parent Track: You Can Have It All." And he [Douglas Hall, professor of organizational behavior at Boston U School of Management] means men, not women. Hall is talking about a new track—the "Daddy Track." . . . [¶] Even when men clearly are on the Daddy Track—without paying the price in salaries or promotions—most supervisors refuse to see it, although colleagues know immediately, Hall said.

fifth basket *n* 1989 May 5 *NY Times* 12/1 The fifth basket, cooperative efforts to deal with environmental problems, drugs, international terrorism and missile proliferation, will take its place alongside the four traditional areas on the Soviet-American agenda: arms control, human rights, bilateral relations and regional conflicts. [¶] In the transition period between President Bush's election and his assumption of office, Mr. Baker and two advisers . . . began tossing around the idea of adding this fifth basket to the agenda, to deal with issues that were clearly part of what the public perceived to be threats to its security but were not yet reflected in the fixed agenda of Soviet-American ministerial meetings. May 5 *Atlanta Journal/Constitution* A-20/3 Back in Washington, however, the arms controllers, Pentagon and State Department veterans of successive administrations, were quick to dub the fifth basket "global baloney." They say it only distracts the already overstretched policy-makers from the real issue at hand: reducing nuclear arms.

fortysomething *attrib* [modeled on THIRTYSOMETHING] Of persons in their forties 1989 Jul 5 *Wall Street Journal* A-9/1 Maybe they feared a fortysomething group couldn't possibly compete with memories of the days when, driven by Townshend's full-contact guitar attack, the band [The Who] set rock standards for power, volume, and demolition. Maybe they were fed up with all the "dinosaur" acts dominating this summer's concert calendar.

fusion in a jar; fusion in a bottle *n* COLD FUSION 1989 May 2 citation sv COLD FUSION May 14 Harrisburg PA *Patriot-News* G-20/3 To make a long story very short, Polaroid hasn't reversed the laws of physical science or created photography's version of fusion in a bottle. May 15 *US News & World Report* 13/1 "Mother Nature is tweaking us on the back of the head, reminding us to do the control experiments," said one chastened researcher in the great "fusion in a jar" chase that has seized the scientific world this spring. Physicists meeting in Baltimore last week wrote what was likely the final chapter on the story. Using words like "incompetence" and "delusion," the scientists said the results announced at a March 23 press conference by University of Utah chemist Stanley Pons were almost certainly the product of experimental errors. May 21 Harrisburg PA *Patriot-News* A-1/1–2 (headline and article) 'Mr. Wizard' lifts fog on fusion in a bottle / Who said the average basement scientist can't understand fusion in a jar? . . . [¶] "They've done it on the table-top—hopefully, theoretically—with a container with a couple of electrodes in it," said [Don] Herbert [1950s TV's "Mr. Wizard"]. "It's kind of like a mason jar."

glass ceiling *n* Unacknowledged prejudice based on race or sex that prevents corporate advancement in management 1988 Mar 27 Harrisburg PA *Sunday Patriot-News* G-12/1 But Bond, along with many of her counterparts, wonders just how long it will take for women to break what some refer to as the "glass ceiling," an invisible barrier that many women believe has kept them out of the executive hierarchy at the nation's biggest banks. Apr 17 *Atlanta Journal/Constitution* C-4/1 Few minority managers, meanwhile, have advanced in the line jobs—sales, finance and operations, for instance—that are the building blocks for careers in senior management, with many instead getting assignments in human resources, community relations and public affairs. [¶] To many women and minorities in business, the "glass ceilings" into which they are slamming provide clear evidence of nothing less than the abiding racism and sexism of the corporation.   1989 Jan 22 *Atlanta Journal/Constitution* E-6/3–4 (letter to ed) There are large inequalities between the opportunities available to women and men . . . with the easing of affirmative-action enforcement, a new phenomenon, the "glass ceiling," has widely appeared: Women are not being promoted because they are not guaranteed the right to compete equally at the workplace.   Jan 31 *Atlanta Journal/Constitution* A-11/1 Ronald H. Brown, the presumed winner of the chairmanship of the Democratic National Committee, faced a serious dilemma—the same one repeatedly encountered by black managers in corporate America: There is a "glass ceiling" blocking his climb up the ladder of success.   Apr 29 *Economist* 23/1 Mr Yuen [an engineer who learned he would not be promoted beyond section head in his firm], like many of his fellow Asians, had bumped his head on "the glass ceiling," the notion, conveniently subscribed to by the white majority, that Asian-American talents flower better in the back room, the laboratory or the class-room than in senior management.

globaloney *n* [blend of *global* + *baloney*] A foreign policy directed toward international welfare as distinct from narrowly national interests; any unrealistic foreign policy   1943 Oct 23 *Saturday Review of Literature* 10/1 (Stephen Naft) Was not this opinion frankly expressed after Pearl Harbor and after Mussolini's declaration of war against us by our reputedly most beautiful legislator in Washington, who is endowed with a "globaloney" knowledge of foreign affairs?   1944 *Britannica Book of the Year* 770 (Dwight L Bolinger "Words and Meanings, New") globaloney. Nonsense about matters affecting the world as a whole. (Global baloney. *Rep. Clare Luce*, Feb. 9, 1943.)   1946 *Saturday Review* 42/3 (Allen Walker Read " The Word Harvest of '45") An echo of Mrs. Luce's *globaloney* appears in the statement of a letter-writer in *Time*, August 27, that "the German woman sold the two G.I.'s a large slice of geobaloney."   1956 Dec 10 *Tuscaloosa [AL] News* 4/5 White House advisers are not unaware of the fact that a huge spending program will be viewed as Henry Wallace "Globaloney." They recall the derisive speech of Mrs. Clara [*sic*] Boothe Luce, in which she excoriated Roosevelt-Wallace-Truman foreign aid and coined the phrase "Globaloney." They also recall the derisive "milk for every Hottentot" criticism that was hurled at Wallace.   1978 William Safire *Safire's Political Dict* (NY: Random House) 41 Clare Boothe Luce, ridiculing Vice President Henry Wallace's foreign policy proposals in 1943 . . . used the [Alfred E.] Smith construction ["No matter how you slice it, it's still baloney"] with a new twist: "Much of what Mr. Wallace calls his global thinking is, no matter how you slice it, still Globaloney."   1989 May 5 *NY Times* 12/1 WASHINGTON, May 3—Its proponents call it the future. Its opponents call it global baloney, "globaloney" for short. [¶] Either way, what American and Soviet negotiators call "the fifth basket" of East-West issues is going to make its debut on the world stage when Secretary of State James A. Baker 3d and the Soviet Foreign Minister, Eduard A. Shevardnadze, meet in Moscow on Wednesday.

iron triangle *n* Threefold combination of governmental bodies and industries that influence federal appropriations to maintain funding for projects from which they benefit   1987 Mar 16 *Newsweek* 82/2 (George F Will) [Sen. Edward Kennedy] says the ability of the Senate to contribute is severely limited by the committee system constructed generations ago. It scatters jurisdictions. For example, on trade issues seven committees can shove their oars in. However, rationalization of the system would require dismantling some of the "iron triangles"—the linked committees that authorize programs, bureaucracies that administer them and client groups that benefit from them.   1988 Jan 25 *Newsweek* 47/2 Political scientists call it the "iron triangle"—a sturdy political alliance of Congress, industry and government agencies.   Dec 19 *Atlanta Journal/Constitution* A-13/1 (Lou Cannon) President Reagan gave a fire-and-brimstone valedictory last week, blaming Congress, the media and assorted special interests in "the Washington colony" for the fiscal mess he is leaving to the Bush administration. [¶] With geometrical sleight of hand, Mr. Reagan redefined the "iron triangle," a phrase that once described the interlocking network that enables federal programs to enjoy eternal life. . . . [¶] There is a leg missing from Mr. Reagan's version of the "iron triangle." He substitutes the media for the bureaucracy, absolving the executive branch from blame for a budget deficit that reflects both administration and congressional profligacy.   Dec 25 *Athens [GA] Daily News/Banner-Herald* D-3/2 (Patrick Buchanan, former White House director of communications) With a month yet before our 41st President takes his oath, Mr. Bush is already being boxed in by the "Iron Triangle" that sought his defeat. Congress, the media, the special interests—whom Ronald Reagan fingered as the inexorable engine of federal spending—is busy now canceling the mandate of '88. If Mr. Bush is not alert, the liberals he routed last fall will be setting his agenda by spring.   Dec 29 *NY Times* 18 (letter to ed from Myron Moskovit, professor of law at Golden Gate University) President Reagan complained in a speech to an enthusiastic audience of Administration officials that an "iron triangle" frustrated his supposed attempts to balance the budget (news story, Dec. 14). He defined this "iron triangle" as consisting of Congress, special interest groups and the news media—an interesting example of Orwellian newspeak. [¶] Hedrick Smith explains in his new book, "The Power Game: How Washington Works," that the iron triangle is a common Washington expression for an alliance that pushes sectarian interests over the general interest. It consists of (1) a particular agency in the executive department, (2) the Congressional committee that oversees it and (3) the industry it regulates. Mr. Reagan has omitted the agency (which works under his direction) from the triangle and replaced it with the news media!   1989 Jan 9–16 *Nation* 37/1 Ronald Reagan's favorite demons as he departs the White House are the news media, Congress and undefined special interests—what he loves to call "the Iron Triangle." He blames this mean combine for thwarting his efforts to balance the budget, blithely ignoring the fiscal predations of the real Iron Triangle: the Pentagon, military contractors and their staunch defenders on Capitol Hill.

mommy track *n* Work arrangements that permit flexible scheduling and fringe benefits for mothers, often perceived as blocking employment advancement   1989 Mar 13 *NY Times* 22/1–2 (headline and article) Why Not Many Mommy Tracks? / . . . He'll also quickly spot the second group—"willing to trade some career growth and compensation for freedom from the constant pressure to work long hours and weekends"—and put them on the mommy track. In other words,

ladies, take your choice. The big time belongs to the single, the childless, or the woman with a 24-hour nanny.   Mar 13 *Wall Street Journal* A-14/3-6 (headline) Mommy Track Is Good for Both Business and Families   Mar 17 *Atlanta Journal/Constitution* A-19/4 (Ellen Goodman) [In an article in *Harvard Business Review* in which she recommended two tracks for career women] Felice Schwartz—who has gotten something of a bad rap in this debate, she never once used the words "mommy track"—is an advocate for flexibility and all the goodies that come with it, from child care to respect.   Mar 24 *Atlanta Constitution* A-20/1–2 (headline and editorial) Trouble on the 'Mommy Track' / Alarmed by an explosion of interest in "mommy tracks," the heads of the nation's 40 largest women's organizations have joined forces to try to keep mommy-track thinking from being turned into mommy-track legislation. . . . [¶] But mommy-track solutions tend to become self-fulfilling prophecies, relegating mommies to subordinate roles, and women managers to childlessness. They discriminate against men as well as women, by attempting to define family issues, unfairly, as women's issues, and by denying some parents the job protections and child-care benefits intended for all.   Apr 3 *US News & World Report* 64/1 "Mommy Track" is one of those devastating journalistic catch phrases that come along now and then and overwhelm all rational discussion of some serious topic. . . . [¶] Just as the word *yuppie* has unmistakable overtones of callowness and mindless greed, *Mommy Track* smacks of derision toward child rearing and carries a heavy implication of a semipermanent caste system intended to hold women back. So any worthwhile plan that would allow workers to take time off or reduce their office duties to take care of children will be subject to recurrent spasms of Mommy Track bashing.   Apr 11 U of Georgia *Red and Black* 11/1 (comic strip "Bloom County") "... Please be assured ... we *value* your contribution to our little "Bloom County" family ... / ... but you'll understand that ... considering your new ... er ... condition ... / ... we'll have to lower your salary, position, hours ... and expectations." / ("The corporate 'mommy track'!") [pregnant moose being interviewed by The Big Cheese, with the moose's mental comment in parens]   Apr 15 *Economist* 30/3 And ambitious mothers are worried about taking time off to look after their children: a recent article in the *Harvard Business Review* infuriated feminists by suggesting that employers should put married women on a slow "mommy track" to reflect such absences.   May 23 *Wall Street Journal* A-1/5 THE "MOMMY TRACK" DEBATE boils as women ask: to track or not to track? [¶] A firestorm follows Felice Schwartz's proposal to separate women into "career primary" and "career and family oriented" tracks.   Jun 12 *Atlanta Journal/Constitution* B-7/2 (comic strip "On The Fastrack") [First frames of the comic strip show two businesswomen talking in an office; in the final frame the junior woman, trussed up and lying on a railroad track with a train coming—is thinking the comment in parens] "Wendy, you're being transferred." "But, Ms. Trellis! I just got back from maternity leave!" / "I know. Since you've had a baby, I'm transferring you from the 'career track' to the 'mommy track.'" / " The mommy track? What's that like?" / ("I should've guessed.") —**mom tracking**   1989 May 14 *Atlanta Journal/Constitution* M-2/5 So I have mixed emotions. If I had small children, I know subsidized child care would be a financial godsend. And I would appreciate "mom tracking" flex time to let me be with my children more. Yet it could be a dangerous way of labeling people. Much like: "I don't hire girls. They get pregnant."

nuclear *adj* [metaphor] BALLISTIC   1989 Jan 9 *Newsweek* (European edition) 40/1 Leahy [a practitioner of Cognitive Therapy] gave the couple "homework," asking them to prepare lists of what each wanted from the relationship. . . . "He also told us to meet once a week at a certain time to discuss things before they get out of proportion," says Mary. "Leahy's phrase with me was, 'Don't go nuclear. You can deal with things more rationally'."

punch-out *n* 1989 May 2 Harrisburg PA *Patriot-News* A-17/1 As a young New York City investment banker with a crushed skull lay struggling for life in Metropolitan Hospital last Sunday night, a group of Brooklyn youths went wilding. "We don't say no 'wilding,'" said the 16-year-old who told me about the Sunday night hunt. "We say we's goin' to play punch-out." [¶] The 16-year-old, who said he has never had a run-in with police, went on to describe punch-out: A group of teen-age boys decide who's going to throw the first punch, and the second; then they go on the prowl. Anyone who spots a likely target can start the chant, "Punch-out, punch-out," which cues the designated puncher to sock the stranger as hard as he can. If he knocks the victim down, he wins the round. "If the first guy don't punch him down, No. 2 tries. If that don't work, we all stomp him," the boy said.

semiballistic *adj* 1988 Dec 26 *Newsweek* 7/3 Bush at first "went semiballistic" over the leaks but ultimately cooled off and declined to confront the likely leakers.

tabletop fusion *n* COLD FUSION   1989 Apr 4 *Athens [GA] Banner-Herald* 10/1–2 Whether or not room-temperature fusion has been achieved by two Utah research teams should be verified within the next two weeks as dozens of laboratories race to duplicate the sensational results they claim, according to Joseph Lach, a Fermi National Laboratory physicist. [¶] At the same time, many scientists who originally greeted the initial reports with a great deal of skepticism are now beginning to believe that there may be something to tabletop fusion, he said.

third zero *n* [modeled on *zero-zero*, *AS* 64 (1989): 160] Complete elimination of nuclear missiles from Europe   1989 May 30 ABC morning news Atlanta WSB-TV/Channel 2 [George Bush at NATO news conference:] There will be no third zero.   1989 May 30 *Athens [GA] Banner-Herald* 1/3–4 Bush, in his remarks to reporters before leaving for a visit to the West German capital later today, ruled out elimination of the short-range nuclear missiles. " There will be no third zero," he said in a reference to arms control jargon for completely scrapping the missiles.

thirtysomething *n often attrib* or *adj* [title of a TV program] (Of) the thirties in age; (of) the generation of babyboomers, preoccupied with personal problems and approaching middle age; yuppie   1988 Dec 12 *Newsweek* 50/1 At the same time, the health-conscious "thirtysomething generation" has begun to shy away from fat-and-sodium laden fastfood fare.   Ibid 81/1 Thirtysomething (thur-tee-sum-thing) 1. *adj.* of or relating to an extended period of young-adult self-absorption, *viz.*: "Oh, shut up. Don't be so thirtysomething." 2. *n.* Emmy Award-winning drama returning for second season this week.   Dec 19 *Newsweek* 39/3 Professional trend-charter Faith Popcorn agrees that thirtysomething boomers are succumbing to cocooning instincts that are more easily satisfied outside of crowded cities.   1989 Jan 9 *US News & World Report* 41/1 These thirty-something Cuban Americans are bilingual, bicultural and, for the most part, economically secure. The majority wouldn't go back to Cuba if Fidel Castro and Communism disappeared overnight.   May 14 *Atlanta Journal/Constitution* L-1/4–5 (review of movie *High Hopes* by Eleanor Ringel) They are Cyril (Philip Davis) and Shirley

(Ruth Sheen)—working class, thirtysomething, unmarried and absolutely made for each other. Oct 8 *Atlanta Journal/Constitution* N-2/1–6 (headline and article) Fashion Mags: Something for Everyone but Thirtysomething Women / It's an awkward age, this thirtysomething. Too young for Lear's, too old for Seventeen. Too poor for Vogue and too far from Manhattan for Mirabella. Oct 8 *NY Times* 26/1 Flescher's "everybody" points a finger at Nissan and Toyota, which have recently gone mountain climbing with their Lexis and Infiniti nameplates, following the lead of Honda, which has done nicely with its thirty$omething Acura division. —**thirtysomethingish** 1989 Jul 17 *Newsweek* 6/2 Who are the thirty-somethingish hard chargers who are making it in the Bush administration?

wilding   *n*   1989 Apr 22 *NY Times* A-1 Chief of Detectives Robert Colangelo, who said the attacks appeared unrelated to money, race, drugs or alcohol, said that some of the 20 youths brought in for questioning had told investigators that the crime spree was the product of a pastime called "wilding." [¶] "It's not a term that we in the police had heard before," the chief said, noting that the police were unaware of any similar incidents in the park recently. "They just said, 'We were going "wilding."' In my mind at this point, it implies that they were going to go raise hell." Apr 23 Harrisburg PA *Patriot-News* A-3/2 Police said the teen-agers jumped the woman from the bushes and used a pipe and a rock to batter her unconscious during the attack, which was the final act of the gang's night of "wilding"—a street term for random pack violence. Apr 24 Harrisburg PA *Patriot-News* A-3/3 The attack on the woman came while the pack of youths was "wilding" in the park—their term for a rampage of random violence and thievery, police said. Apr 26 *NY Times* A-1 & A-15/1 On the streets of the neighborhood where the youths lived, there was little doubt that if those accused of the attack were indeed responsible they were typical teenagers who had been transformed into something else while wilding, a slang term that refers to the practice of marauding in bands to terrorize strangers and to swagger and bully. . . . [¶] Of "wilding," Troy said: "I ain't going to say it's fun. It's getting your anger out at somebody. It's like stealing fruit. It's not cause you are hungry." Apr 28 *Atlanta Journal/Constitution* A-6/2 The suspects are being held on charges of attempted murder, rape and assault and could face other charges. [¶] The woman [jogging in Central Park] apparently was one of several targets of the gang going "wilding" that night. [¶] The term was new to police, but not the activity: For years, loosely organized packs of marauding youths have roamed the streets and parks bullying, robbing and attacking victims at random. Apr 29 *Economist* 27/3 A new word, or at least new to the public, added to the alarm. Suspects described their activity—evenings spent mugging joggers and cyclists—as "wilding". Newspapers did their bit to fan the flames. The *NY Post* observed that calling the gang a "wolf pack" was libellous to wolves. May 1 *NY Times* 23 Wilding, they say, is not a thing of race. Anybody could be the victim—black, Hispanic, white, rich, poor. "It's animal, but it's beyond animal acts." Go out, do whatever you want, do it on impulse. If it means hurting someone, so be it. May 3 *Atlanta Journal/Constitution* E-4/1 But what hard evidence is there that television may have played a part in the teenage "wilding" that culminated in so brutal an attack? . . . [¶] Although studies are scarce on the connection between television watching and anything approaching the viciousness of the Central Park attack, Dr. Comstock holds that "a good primafacie case" can be made that action shows do stimulate aggression. May 8 *Maclean's* 54/1 But a nighttime incident last month, in which a gang of teenagers ambushed and then raped and beat a 28-year-old woman in Central Park, shocked many of the city's hardened citizens. . . . Police said that the youngsters, aged between 14 and 17, were part of a larger group of teenagers who were "wilding"—their slang for terrorizing and bullying—in the park. May 8 *Newsweek* 65/2 Originally, police say, about 35 youths, some as young as 13, had gone into the park "wilding"—a variety of bash-as-bash-can gang rampage that has disrupted some of the city's public places recently. . . . "They may have said, 'Let's go wilding,'" notes Franklin Zimring, director of the Earl Warren Legal Institute at the University of California, "but nobody said, 'Let's go raping'."

Windy   *n*   A fan of *Gone with the Wind* 1989 Aug 6 London *Sunday Telegraph Mag* 12/1 Mr Kaufman is one of 450 Gone With the Wind enthusiasts—let us call them Windies—whose replies to Dr [Helen] Taylor's questionnaire form the nucleus of her book [*Scarlett's Women: Gone with the Wind and Its Female Fans*], although, as he is one of only 40 men in the survey, his views do not carry their customary weight. Ibid 14/1 If Dr Taylor's studious research has emerged with any conclusion, it is that Gone With the Wind gives each individual Windy her own particular, personal experience; there are as many GWTWs as there are Windies.

wolf   *n*   [backformation from *wolf pack*, influenced by *wolf* 'rapacious person'] Member of a wolfpack, "a roving gang of roughneck teen-agers" (*W3*) 1989 May 1 *NY Times* 23 Did the young wolves attack her because she is white and they are black? Because she is rich and they are poor . . . [¶] Their discussion centers on why kids who committed a crime of such ferocity sang in their jail cell. . . . The Argus kids are convinced that even in jail the young wolves felt like celebrities. "They were hot news. Royalty. All the attention was focused on them."

wolf-pack   *vi*   [from the noun] 1989 Aug 12 Columbia SC *State* B-6/2 Other shopping centers are plagued by litter such as beer cans, paper and other trash left in the parking lots, where teenagers "wolf-pack," sit around on their cars and then leave.

xeriscape   *n*   [blend of *xeric* + land*scape*] Landscape with plants requiring little water 1987 Jul 17 *San Antonio Express-News* A-14 Statistics show that a large percentage of our water is used to maintain landscapes. In an attempt to conserve water in the landscape and to lower this high statistic, a new concept in landscaping has been developed. It is called xeriscape. Idem You are probably already familiar with many of these plants, and many of the plants that are considered "xeriscape plants" are plants that are native to Texas. [¶] You can see xeriscape plants in use and can obtain a list of these plants at the San Antonio Botanical Garden. 1989 May *News Edition, American Horticulturist* 1/1 "There's nothing new about Xeriscape concepts," says Donald Buma, executive director of Botanica, the Wichita Gardens, which will open its own Xeriscape garden this season. "It's really just a compilation of good horticultural practices." [¶] The movement was started by the Denver Water Department in 1981 in an effort to popularize the idea of landscaping to conserve water.

xeriscaping; xericscaping   *n*   [blend of *xeric* + land*scaping*] Landscaping with xeric plants 1987 Jul 17 *San Antonio Express-News* A-14 (heading and article) Xeriscaping an idea whose time has come / . . . Actually, the idea of xeriscaping has been around for quite a few years, but it is being practiced more and more each year. . . . [¶] One of the first major aspects of xeriscaping is the use of plants

that *at maturity* are relatively low water users. 1988 Sep 18 *Atlanta Journal/Constitution* P-1/2–4 (subhead and article) Now may be the time to apply the relatively new principle of xeriscaping: landscaping with drought-tolerant plants and a minimum of high-maintenance lawn areas. Both phrase and principle originated in the western United States, a region that has long had to cope with a limited water supply. . . . [¶] Regardless of whether your landscape is established or just getting started you can take a plan of action that will make it more water efficient. . . . [¶] This new concept in landscape design is called "xeriscaping," derived from the Greek "xeros" meaning dry, combined with landscaping. (The term was originally coined by a special task force of the Denver, Colorado Water Department, the Associated Landscape Contractors of Colorado and Colorado State University.) 1989 Apr 16 Harrisburg PA *Patriot-News* H-1/4 Welcome to xericscaping, a new style of gardening geared at coping with drought. May *News Edition, American Horticulturist* 1/1 In Denver, where Xeriscaping was conceived and named eight years ago, surveys show that 65 percent of the population has heard the word. But not everyone who has heard of Xeriscaping knows exactly what it means, let alone uses its principles. Formed from the Greek word for "dry," to many it still connotes landscapes dotted with cacti and swathed in white rock. In fact, Xeriscapes of cool-season turf, lush shrubs, and multi-hued perennials have reduced water use more than 60 percent.

AMONG THE NEW WORDS

JOHN ALGEO   AND   ADELE ALGEO

University of Georgia   *Athens, Georgia*

With the assistance of the New Words Committee

BUSINESS IS EXTRAORDINARILY RICH IN NEOLOGISMS, of which one in this installment, *cafeteria-style*, is an obvious metaphor. We hope to devote a future installment to other business terms. *Ahead of* and *behind the curve* are, for us, of obscure origin; the curve in question may be a business curve, although the curve of a surfer's wave seems apposite as well.

We dealt with terms for *caregiving* in a recent installment of "Among the New Words" (*AS* 64.2 [1989]). Here we have several more: *sandwich generation, daughter track,* and *granny track,* the last two modeled on *mommy track* (*AS* 65.2 [1990]).

Down and dirty, as we were told by Charles Hockett and Thomas Creswell, comes from poker. According to Thomas L. Clark's *Dictionary of Gambling & Gaming* (Cold Spring, NY: Lexik House, 1987), it is, "in seven-card stud, said of the last, or seventh, card dealt, which is face down." Hockett adds that when the earlier, face-up cards have the possibility of becoming a winning combination, the dealer uses this catchphrase to imply that the hidden card will spoil the prospect. The current voguish use of the term probably derives from the poker jargon, as extended by way of politics to general contexts. In the process of its extension, the term seems to have been contaminated semantically by expressions like *get down to the real nitty-gritty* and *dirty story.* As a result, its meaning has drifted in several directions so that in a given context the sense and associations of the term may not be clear.

Gazundering is a British neologism for the complement of a better established practice, *gazumping.* The latter involves a seller's frustrating a would-be property buyer by raising the price of the property between the initial agreement to sell and the closing of the contract. Gazumping was widespread when property values in England were high and rising. Its complement, gazundering, involves a prospective buyer's reducing the offer made for a property during the same interval and is feasible when housing prices are on the decline. Both forms of legal, but sharp, dealing are made possible by the glacial rate at which British solicitors do the legal work required for buying and selling property and by a refusal to streamline the procedures by which property exchanges hands, which seem to profit everyone except the buyers or sellers. The verb *gazump* is in the *OEDS* (1972) under the lemma *gazoomph* /gə'zumf/, with an earliest citation from 1928 referring to a swindle by dishonest auctioning. Its origin is uncertain, but has been attributed to Yiddish. The widespread current use, spelling, and presumably pronunciation /gəˈzəmp/ are illustrated by citations from 1971, but the term is not adequately defined in its current use, which was doubtless recent at the time the first *OEDS* volume was prepared. Other British dictionaries, such as *The Concise Oxford* (1982) and *Longman Dictionary of the English Language* (1984) give appropriate definitions. *Gazunder* looks like a blend of *gazump* (the last part of the word perhaps associated with *up*—by implication, an increase in price) and *under*—that is, a decrease in price.

Wedgy appears to be a term for a high-school prank carried into college use and thence spread to other contexts. Campbell Aycock tells us it was in high-school use in the 1970s. Frederic G. Cassidy reports a synonym *fishbite* (with various possible metaphorical interpretations), which we may hope to find in the second volume of the *DARE*. Connie Eble reports the synonyms *melvin* and *murphy*. *Dweeb* and *wussy* are other examples of adolescent slang percolating up to more general use.

Intifada and *perestroika* (with the stunt word *Pretoriastroika*) are instances of terms from international politics that were originally limited in geographical application but are broadening their reference and generalizing to wider use.

Needle stick sounds like medical jargon of older use, but the term has come into general use because of the spread of AIDS.

Wannabe is probably West Coast in origin; early citations connect it with the movies and surfing. Recent use is heavy in the rock music scene, but it is also a voguish term in many other contexts, as the entry below shows.

Acknowldgements for citations: Thomas Algeo, Lisa Buckley, Ronald R. Butters, Frederic G. Cassidy, Sylvia Chalker, George S. Cole, Lesa Dill, Charles C. Doyle, Connie Eble, Sidney Greenbaum, Charles Hockett, Betty Irwin, Michael Montgomery, Louis Phillips, Mary Gray Porter, Randy Roberts and the Tamony files at the University of Missouri, Anne Russell, Alan Slotkin, James Stalker, and Greg Williams.

cafeteria; cafeteria-style; cafeteria-type *n usu attrib* (Affording) choice from a list of options (as of fringe-benefit plans, contraceptives, etc) **1963** Feb 23 *San Francisco Examiner* 3/6 Addressing a Stanford Graduate School of Business seminar, Mason Haire of the U. C. Institute of Industrial Relations, said the idea for a "cafeteria-style" wage plan stemmed from a study of 2,000 unionized workers on the West Coast. [¶] This showed "wide variation" in the psychological value of pensions, hospital insurance and other fringe benefits to hourly paid workers. **1981** Oct 3 *Athens* [GA] *Daily News/Banner-Herald* 10/2 [Ellen Goodman] These packages, called "cafeteria plans," are only in operation in a dozen major corporations, but they are being considered by many others. [¶] Under a cafeteria plan, a worker can fill a tray of benefits to fit his or her own needs from a line of options, including everything from vacation time to legal insurance to dental care. A working parent with children, for example, might be able to pick child-care reimbursement rather than, say, vacation days, when the kids are small. **1982** Apr 29 Columbia SC *State* B -10/5 She [Dr. Elizabeth Connell, Emory University School of Medicine] does not recommend a single contraceptive method for all women. [¶] "You owe it to any woman," she says, "to go through the entire contraceptive cafeteria, as we call it, talking about benefits and risks." **1987** Nov 10 *Athens* [GA] *Banner-Herald* 8/1–2 A vote of the Clarke County Board of Education Thursday will determine whether school district employees will finally have a "cafeteria" type insurance plan. [¶] The issue, first raised eight months ago, may be resolved at Thursday's board meeting with members to vote on an agreement which gives employees the choice of signing up for a flexible fringe benefit program. The program would give workers several choices in the types of insurance coverages they would like to carry. **1988** Aug 1 *Newsweek* 39/3 In 1985 Steelcase became one of the few major U.S. companies to introduce a "cafeteria style" benefits plan. Workers are allotted "benefit dollars" and allowed to select from a menu of choices. There are eight medical plans, three dental options (including no coverage at all) and various forms of long- and short-term disability and life insurance. Employees who have money left over can put it in tax-free accounts to cover out-of-pocket health care or off-site day care. **1989** Oct 2 *Atlanta Journal/Constitution* C -1/2 Both applaud a new cafeteria-style fringe benefits program General Time installed recently to let employees shape their own benefit packages to meet their lifestyles. [¶] "I like having the flexibility to choose less in areas like health coverage and life insurance," said Ms. Pierce. "I like being able to buy more vacation time." Ibid C -1/5 Under this cafeteria-style plan, Ms. Pierce of General Time may conserve credits by choosing a modest medical insurance plan in order to buy extra vacation time. Nov memo to Tennessee Tech U personnel [heading] Schedule of cafeteria benefits information meetings Nov 6 *Atlanta Journal/Constitution* A-10/1 India was among the first to launch a government-sponsored family planning program. Since 1951, when the program was set up, the government has tried almost everything to check population growth, from cafeteria-type clinics distributing contraceptives to coercion during the 1975–77 state of emergency. Nov 23 *Atlanta Journal/Constitution* V-9/1 [comic strip "On The Fastrack"] "I've got a new system for giving out employee benefits, Bob. It's called a 'cafeteria plan'." / "From now on, workers can choose just a few benefits from a 'menu'. What do you think?" / "More gruel, Ma'am?"

curve *n* **—ahead of the curve** In the forefront, on the cutting edge, anticipating developments **1980** Dec 22 *New Yorker* 98/2 Bureaucrats and policy planners talk of "getting ahead of the curve." It is the current expression for anticipating the inevitable and making creative use of it—what used to be known as statesmanship. **1989** Jul 3 *Newsweek* 63/3 Perhaps Austin [Texas, which protects bats living under bridges] is just ahead of the curve, having already worked through its batophobia. Oct 3 *Atlanta Journal/Constitution* A-7/1 But there was one particular phone the little girl thought was the coolest phone in the whole store. It was black, with a rotary dial. A throwback, a relic, but no one had the heart to tell her. [¶] Or maybe she was ahead of the curve again. Idem The little girl wears funky hats and giant shirts and socks that look like bumblebees. . . . She's been known to reject thoroughly decent clothing suggestions from her mother with a simple, "That's not my style." [¶] The little girl is 8 years old. She loves to be ahead of her curve, though. Oct 6 *Atlanta Journal/Constitution* A-23/5 [Ellen Goodman] Whatever the motives, I have a sneaky feeling that Al [Neuharth] is onto something. We are talking trends. Call this new genre [an autobiography including chapters by two ex-wives and several children] a polygraphy or autobiography with detractors; the creator of USA Today is again ahead of the curve. Nov 11 *Athens* [GA] *Daily News/Banner-Herald* A-6/2–4 [comic strip "Doonesbury"] "Let's stop driving addicts underground and start helping them! Get out ahead of the curve, Bill! It's time to formulate policy for the *post*-prohibition era!" Dec 26 *Atlanta Journal/Constitution* F-3/1 The 1980s were the salad days for bizspeak, buzzwords and lousy metaphors. [¶] Business people tried to stay ahead of the curve by shooting from the lip with just the right jargon to show they were players, not bean counters. Dec 29 *Atlanta Journal/Constitution* A-11/2 [Ellen Goodman] Tongue-in-cheek, I wrote about Al Neuharth's autobusinessbiography as a new entry into the Eighties literature of egotism. [¶] It wasn't exactly a promo piece. But what do I find gracing the ads? One familiar half-sentence: " 'The creator of USA Today is again ahead of the curve.'—Ellen Goodman." **—behind the curve** Lagging behind current needs or trends **1989** Dec 14 Atlanta Ch 2 WSB-TV ABC *Good Morning America* [Sen Ted Kennedy] Once again, the politicians are behind the curve. The American people want. . . . **1990** Jan 14 CNN *Evans & Novak* [Robert Novak] I think the Republicans are behind the power curve on tax-cutting.

daughter track *n* [modeled on *mommy track*] Responsibility placed upon women to care for aging relatives; GRANNY TRACK **1990** Jan 8 *Atlanta Constitution* E-1/2–5 [headline and article] Life on the daughter track / . . . Sociologists have come up with a name for the way of life Martha shares with the daughters, daughters-in-law, granddaughters and nieces who care for America's elderly. [¶] The daughter track, they call it, an American cultural reality that insists women are responsible for caring for aging family members.

down and dirty *adj* Fiercely and unsportingly competitive, no holds barred, intensely applied; *also* crude, coarse, scandalous, or sexually suggestive **1988** Mar 27 *Atlanta Journal/Constitution* F-13/1 Into a crowded travel and food field that includes National Geographic, Travel & Leisure, Travel Today, Travel/Holiday and Gourmet comes Trips, a down-and-dirty—and likable—competitor that owes its birth to the marriage of yuppie consumers with safari shirts and pith helmets. Oct 2 *Atlanta Journal/Constitution* A-11/1–4 [headline and article] Race Is 'Down and Dirty' in 'Must-Win' Texas / "Texas elections are customarily down and dirty," said John C. White, a former Democratic national chairman who has run successfully for statewide office in the past. "You find out what a guy is really like when you push him right up to the wall." Oct 17 *NY Times* 23 [William Safire] Like George Bush in the campaign of 1970, he [Michael Dukakis] is unwilling to get down and dirty, and is also incapable of seizing the offensive by taking eloquent offense. Dec 5 *Newsweek* 4/2 Senate Democrats, still smarting from Bush's down-and-dirty tactics, plan to "turn [the hearings] into a seminar on the origins of the Willie Horton ad campaign," says one Democratic aide, and rough up Baker's "Mr. Clean" image. **1989** Jun 5 *Atlanta Constitution* E-2/3–6 [picture caption] Jonathan Keith, 19, has childhood memories of playing in this patch of woods near Market Square mall, now partly cleared for development. 'We really ought to get down and dirty with these developers who are disrespectful to the property,' he says. Jul 5 *Wall Street Journal* A-9/3 Daltrey's vocals [at The Who reunion] were down and dirty; Townshend slow-danced with his red Stratocaster. Aug 3 *Wall Street Journal* B-1/5 The initiative—which will take Gallo far from its early success in the '50s as maker of down-and-dirty wino potables such as Thunderbird—has gained new urgency at the behest of their three sons and a son-in-law, who run the company day to day, a Gallo spokesman says. Oct 9 *Atlanta Journal/Constitution* C-9/2–3 Some carriers, such as Continental and strike-plagued Eastern, and smaller lines like Southwest and Airwest airlines, continue to discount. But the big, better-heeled carriers believe they can fly above the fray—"the down and dirty discounting," in the words of one airline executive—by emphasizing quality. Oct 31 *Houston Chronicle* D-2/2 [Mike Royko, referring to Nancy Reagan's book *My Turn*] Enough of this elitist bickering. If you expect to capture our imagination, you had better get down and dirty. Dec 1 *Atlanta Journal/Constitution* D -4/6 This down-and-dirty tale [*Elvis* by Albert Goldman] became an instant collector's item three weeks after its publication—when Elvis Presley died. Dec 8 *Atlanta Journal/Constitution* D-3/3 [review of film *The War of the Roses*] Not that the fights don't get hair-raisingly down and dirty, but somehow smashed Staffordshire doesn't have the sting of crushed dreams (a la George and Martha in "Virginia Woolf"). Dec 11 U of Georgia *Columns* 3/3 After teaching for three years, "I realized I had to make a decision about getting down and dirty with my dissertation or remain employed as a TA the rest of my life," she says. **—downtown-and-dirty** **1990** Jan 7 *Atlanta Journal/Constitution* N-1/1 Tango (Mr. Stallone) is an Armani-suited do-gooder, a dandy with his stockbroker always on call. Cash (Mr. Russell) is a downtown-and-dirty kind of guy, a longhair with his barber always on hold. **—down if not dirty** **1990** Jan 15 *People* 82/2 [picture caption] Above, Donny and Marie [Osmond] were immaculate in 1977. At right, in concert recently, Donnie [*sic*] gets down, if not truly dirty.

dweeb *n* Unattractive, unsophisticated person; nerd, wimp (teenage slang) **1987** Sep *Newsweek On Campus* 18/3 Whatever the number of dweebs, they do not dominate the student body. Robert Vanderheide, a graduate student in Materials Science [at MIT], says: "Everybody knows at least one or two real nerds, but they're not all over the place." Dec 21 Steve Moore *Born in the Bleachers* (NY: Macmillan, 1989) 89 [caption to dated cartoon showing a tackily dressed, unshapely man] Total dweeb **1988** *Dream a Little Dream* [movie dialog] "Why is he being such a dweeb?" "I don't know, but he's my dweeb." **1989** Connie Eble *College Slang 101* (Georgetown CT: Spectacle Lane) 76 [heading and text] The Social Outcast / The Big L, Corndog, Donut Crew, Dork, Dweeb, Dweebie. Apr 7 *Atlanta Journal/Constitution* C-6/1 [comic strip "Kudzu"] [teenager:] "Do parakeets have souls?" [preacher:] "Good question, boy—I don't know." / [preacher's thought:] ("What a dweeb!") Apr 27 *Atlanta Journal/Constitution* B-5/1 Apr 28 U of Georgia *Red and Black* 7 May 7 *Philadelphia Inquirer* B-2/5 "*Aha!* It must have been cocaine," reasoned the dweebs from Tupelo who made their findings a national story. Jun *Smithsonian* 116/2 For another, etymological relics like "Cowabunga!" and "hodad" have been replaced [among surfers at Malibu] by essential phrases like "Awesome!" and "clueless dweeb" (i.e., nerd). Jun 1 *Wall Street Journal* B-1/1–2 They're certainly not to be confused with "dweebs," the newer moniker for what were once "nerds" or "geeks." Jun 8 *Atlanta Journal/Constitution* D-2/1 Although the '80s have brought us "dweeb," Dr. Chapman sees "geek" making a comeback among teenage name-callers. Sep 8 *Tuscaloosa* [AL] *News* A-7/5 ["Glossary" of teen talk] *Dweeb*—A person who is not cool. Example: "I just can't bring myself to go out with that dweeb." *Syn.* see dork, drip, goob. Nov 4 *Atlanta Journal/Constitution* C-12/1 [comic strip "Fox Trot"] "He's a drip! A dweeb! A loser! I can't believe you're sticking up for him!" Nov 6 *Atlanta Journal/Constitution* C-8/2 Nov 7 *Atlanta Journal/Constitution* D-7/2 Nov 20 *Newsweek* 54/3 A House Democratic aide reported being approached by "some dweeb" from the White House who suggested Bush would sign a congressional pay raise if the House would repackage capital gains in a must-pass bill. **—dweebish** *adj* **1987** Sep *Newsweek On Campus* 55/1 As the tape rolled for his audition to be a veejay on MTV, he smeared himself with shaving cream.... The audition ended abruptly as Seal shifted to the slow, dweebish whine favored by sitcom accountants: "I also have experience in cost estimation ... and project a-*nal*-ysis." **—protodweeb** *n* **1989** Sep 25 *Newsweek* 43/3 The three stars [of the TV show *Saturday Night Live* in 1984] formed an independent nucleus, and the memorable moments from that season were all theirs. Short brought the pointy-haired protodweeb Ed Grimley from Second City.

gazunder *vb* [*gazump* + *under*] (Of a potential property-buyer, usu of residential property) to frustrate a property-seller by lowering the amount of money offered between the agreement to buy and the closing of the contract, thus requiring the seller either to accept less than expected or to look for another buyer **1989** Jan 6 *Daily Telegraph* p n/a Media executive Matthew Lewin, 44, and his psychotherapist wife Vivienne have just been gazundered in Hampstead, one of London's most expensive areas, where a four-bedroom house can cost £400,000.... "We had a buying and selling deal set up during the property frenzy of August.... The hold-up was we hadn't yet found a place. Then we did and a day was nominated for the exchange. The day before it, our buyers pulled out." Jul 30 *Sunday Times* A-9/3 Ray Seaman thought he had struck lucky in a depressed housing market when a young couple offered the full asking price for his two-bedroomed flat in an old-fashioned 1930s block. [¶] Legal documents were drawn up and moving dates set, but on the eve of exchanging contracts his solicitor told him the terms had changed. [¶] Seaman, 27, had been "gazundered. " The buyers had cut their original offer of £73,000 by £3,000, and threatened to pull out if Seaman did not agree. **—gazunderer** *n* **1989** Jul 30 *Sunday Times* A-9/4 The gazunderer usually justifies his action as the result of last-minute "problems." ... The gazunderer is making a conscious decision to hold somebody to ransom. **—gazundering** *verbal n* **1989** Jan 6 *Daily Telegraph* p n/a The increasing pressure on sellers today, however, is brought about by ever-more ruthless tactics of the buyer. A new word has been coined for a common device to bring down the price of a house—gazundering. Here, the seller, often trapped by a vast bridging loan on a new property, is being undercut by the buyer, who legally can reduce his offer as often as he likes before the contract is signed. Jul 30 *Sunday Times* A-9/6–7 "Gazundering is symptomatic of the state of the market, but we abhor it completely," said Harvey Williams, national housing spokesman for the Royal Institution of Chartered Surveyors.... Estate agents and solicitors blame the long gap between accepting an offer and exchanging contracts, often three months or more, for the outbreak of gazundering. Ibid B-9/3 "Gazundering"—reneging on an agreed price—is on the march.

granny track *n* [modeled on *mommy track*] Responsibility to care for aging parents; DAUGHTER TRACK **1989** Aug 28–Sep 4 *US News & World Report* 92/1 Some 2 million Americans, mostly working women between the ages of 40 and 50, belong to the so-called sandwich generation, simultaneously caring for children and aging family members. Many quit or take less demanding jobs. "To keep workers off the granny track," notes Angela Heath of the American Association of Retired Persons, "more companies are helping with eldercare benefits."

intifada *n* [extended sense] Popular political uprising **1989** Mar 6 *Nation* 292/1 Ralph Nader and his public interest cadres have been fighting Congressional pay raises for years, without success, but this latest campaign caught on in ways the others had not.... [¶] Looking back, Nader says, the turning point came last December 16 ... when a listener called a radio talk show in Detroit to suggest a "tea bag party" to protest the pay raise. A populist nerve had been touched. Forty or more talk show hosts networked, Nader reports, and the *intifada* went national. Soon, hundreds of thousands of tea bags poured into Congressional offices. Apr 1 *Economist* 40/3 [headline and article] Intifada in the Balkans / VIOLENCE in Kosovo, another step towards the break-up of Yugoslavia: that is the price of the famous victory pulled off by Mr Slobodan Milosevic, Serbia's party leader, whom many Yugoslavs suspect of wanting to be another Tito.... [¶] Miners and other workers in Kosovo went on strike in February in protest against the proposed constitutional amendments [to return control of several autonomous provinces to the central parliament]. Dec 8 CBS evening news [journalist Bob Simon] Eastern Europe's intifada got results in two weeks.... The Palestinian intifada slogs on.

needle stick *n* usu *attrib* An injury from accidental stabbing by a hypodermic needle, particularly one contaminated by prior use on an AIDS-infected person **1987** Dec *Discover* 14/3 The first infected AIDS lab worker believes that safety procedures were generally followed and recalls no overt exposure to the virus, such as a needle stick or splash in the face, according to Emmett Barkley, head of the safety panel investigating the incident. **1988** Apr 22 *Atlanta Constitution* A-4/3 But because the source of infection among the 135 workers is unknown, the report raises the possibility that the number of AIDS cases resulting from job-related exposures could be higher than the dozen or so now believed to have occurred from needle stick injuries or other mishaps. Apr 26 CNN News 10 PM [reference to a policeman in San Francisco, said to be the first lawman to contract AIDS in the line of duty, having been stuck while searching a drug addict in the early 1980s] The needle-stick incident was not recorded at the time. **1989** Nov 9 Atlanta Ch 11 WXIA-TV [evening news] Health-care workers are still incurring needle-stick injury. Dec 11 *Atlanta Constitution* A-1/2 Dr. Melanie Thompson, president of the Atlanta AIDS Research Consortium, a group of doctors who treat AIDS patients, said a six-week preventive treatment with AZT is used by "physicians all over the city" for "significant needle-stick" injuries involving blood that is known to be contaminated.

perestroika *n* [extended sense] Radical change in economic policy **1989** Jan 14 *Economist* 39/1 Much has been made of the so-called "green *perestroika*" by which Colonel Moammar Qaddafi has tried to liberalise the Libyan economy. Private enterprise, which the colonel abolished a decade ago, has been temporarily rehabilitated. The old *souk* off Green Square, where the colonel once harangued his people with revolutionary gobbledygook from his "Green Book", reopened six months ago. Apr *Atlantic Monthly* 35 [George C. Lodge, heading and subhead] IT'S TIME FOR AN AMERICAN PERESTROIKA / While Japan plants its flag on the twenty-first century, an ideological fixation on the relations that should obtain between government and business prevents us from taking the steps necessary to ensure our future prosperity. May 13 *Economist* 46/1 India has begun to reexamine this carve-up. It is concluding that the economy would be better off if the state did a lot less and private business a lot more. [¶] Indian *perestroika* is at its most radical in the western state of Maharashtra, whose capital is Bombay. Maharashtra's sharp change of course was announced late last month.

Pretoriastroika *n* Restructuring of the political policies of the South African government **1989** Oct 8 *The Ottawa Citizen* A-8/1 [editorial] The ink is barely dry on President Frederik de Klerk's order not to break up lawful, peaceful protests in South Africa and there's already talk of "Pretoriastroika" and a "Pretoria spring."

sandwich generation *n* Person or persons with the responsibility of caring for both children and parents **1989** Apr 18 *USA Today* A-1 [heading and article] Hard times for 'sandwich generation' / "... But I am short-tempered, frazzled from all the responsibilities. I am the 'sandwich' generation, caught between kids and parents. I want to do the right thing." Apr 30 Harrisburg PA *Sunday Patriot-News* E-4/1–6 [headline and article] Politicians, employers must be aware of the growing 'sandwich generation' / ... This woman's profile is known by some sociologists as "the sandwich generation." ... [¶] She is sandwiched between raising children and caring for elderly parents. She must work to help support both. May 14 Harrisburg PA *Sunday Patriot-News* A-3/2–3 [headline and article] Millions of U.S. mothers face care-giver 'sandwich' / ... "Already," she said, "nearly two million women are part of the 'sandwich' generation, caring simultaneously for children and parents. Jul 24 *Wall Street Journal* A-1/5 "SANDWICH GENERATION": Over half of the 1.8 million women who are caring for children and parents at the same time are in the paid labor force, says the Older Women's League. But just 200 of six million employers offer elder-care aid. Aug 28–Sep 4 citation sv GRANNY TRACK Nov 19 *Gwinnett* [GA] *Daily* A-12 Tuck is part of the sandwich generation—a phenomenon sociologists say affects more women than men, since women are usually seen by society as the caregivers. [¶] Those in the sandwich generation are caught between their own children on the one hand and their aging parents on the other. As the elderly live longer, more and more adults are finding they raise their children just to turn around and play parent again—this time to their own mothers and fathers. **1990** Winter/Spring *Newsweek Special Issue* 63/2 'Sandwich generation': Grateful or not, many families will be hard pressed to support their elderly relations in the coming decades. Divorce, women working, parents having fewer children later in life and relocating to distant cities—these factors have all threatened the fabled "extended family" that took in aged relatives in decades past. The competing demands of work, children and aging parents on middle-aged working people have already popularized a new phrase—the "sandwich generation"—and many more families will feel squeezed as their elderly members retire.

ustabie *n* Has-been **1989** Jun 1 *Athens* [GA] *Banner-Herald* 8/3 [William Safire] "Ethics, shmethics," growls the Washington Establishment, an amalgam of office-holders, power brokers, wannabies, ustabies, thinktankers and a legion of world-weary thumbsuckers drawn up in vast, cumbrous array.

wannabe, wanna-be, wanna be, wannabee, wanna-bee, wannabie *n* also *attrib* One who imitates and identifies with another; one who aspires to hold a position or fill a role [**1971** May *Esquire* 123/1 Says Ray Mungo, founder of the Liberation News Service, "If you wanna be in the movie, you gotta have a costume."] **1981** Jul 6 *Newsweek* 82/2 The flood tide of surfers first started building in the early '60s. ... Before long the beaches were jammed with hordes of novices known as wannabees (as in, "I wanna be a surfer"). **1987** Oct *Illustrated London News* 21/2 Madonna's adoring fans, or Wannabees as they have come to be known because they "wannabee" like her, also vied for the prima donna's attention. Nov 1 *Atlanta Journal/Constitution* G-5/1 What bothers surfers is that only a quarter of that money is being spent on surfboards. The rest is spent by people surfers call "wanna bes." They don't surf but they want to, so they dress the part, as have non-participating fans of tennis and skiing. [¶] The clothes wanna bes wear are often only inspired by surf culture. **1989** Feb 3 *Atlanta Journal/Constitution* C-5/2 [review of the film *Sorceress*] Sometime in the 13th century, Etienne de Bourbon ..., a Dominican friar with high-born connections to the nobility, arrives in an isolated rural French village on a mission to seek out heresy. Told by the kindly local Cure ... that his people are "poor but pious," the friar begs to differ. "You must learn to look," he says with the self-righteous zeal of a witch-burner wanna-be. Mar 18 *Atlanta Journal/Constitution Weekend* mag 26/1 A then-unknown Peter O'Toole, eyes flashing bluer than any robin's egg, reinvents the fabled Oxfordshire cartographer and Bedouin wanna-be T.E. Lawrence as the most recklessly dashing, most irresistibly heroic, most punishingly beautiful legend in anyone's time. Mar 26 *Athens* [GA] *Daily News/Banner-Herald* D-3/3 This time the barbarians were Vandals, and they installed a Vandal emperor.... They were Roman wannabees, and let the bureaucracy and other vestiges of the Romans remain intact. Apr 6 *Atlanta Journal/Constitution* A-15/1 For drug traffickers, paramilitary extremists and Rambo wanna-bees, anti-personnel guns such as the Uzi, MAC-10 and MAC-11, TEC-9, AK-47 and AR-15 are becoming the new weapon of choice. Apr 10 *Newsweek* 68/3 He reports that he's figured out why Joan Rivers, Alan Thicke and all the other Carson wannabees never were. Jun 1 *Athens* [GA] *Banner-Herald* 8/3 citation sv USTABIE Jun 5 *US News & World Report* 42/1 A local clergyman has begun an antigang ministry to target would-be gang members, known as "wannabees." Jun 29 *Atlanta Journal/Constitution* A-15/1 None of this surprised me too much, to tell you the truth, because I've known about Elvis clones for years, and I once saw a whole crowd of Wannabes with about 15 Madonnas and nine Princes in it. Jul 12 *NY Times* C-15/3 [Caryn James] And like a sitcom with too much canned laughter, "When Harry Met Sally...," which opens today at the Beekman and other theaters, is a perfectly pleasant Woody Allen wannabe, full of canned romance. Jul 17 *Nation* 98/3 In *School Daze*, the entire film depends on the conflict between black people who are plainly, emphatically black and those who are wannabees—that is, who want to be white. Jul 24 *Wall Street Journal* A-12/6 His trading rules are few in number and simple: (1) Cut losses; (2) Ride winners; (3) Keep bets small; (4) Follow the rules without exception; (5) Know when to break the rules. After you understand those principles thoroughly, especially rules four and five, then all you wannabe super traders can just maybe begin to think about giving up your day jobs. Aug 7 *Newsweek* 56/2   Sep 18 *Newsweek* 74/3   Oct 1 *Atlanta Journal/Constitution* A-14/1–2 [headline to editorial concerning candidates for the governorship]   Let the Gubernatorial Wannabees Tell All   Oct 15 *Atlanta Journal/Constitution* A-2/1   Oct 26 *Athens* [GA] *Observer* B-3/3   These Dr. Joyce Brothers wannabes believe the costume you choose to wear for Halloween, Mardi Gras or whatever is psychologically revealing.   Oct 26 U of Georgia *Red and Black* 4/2   Oct 28 *Atlanta Journal/Constitution Weekend* mag 17/1   In the new film by Jonathan Kaplan ("The Accused"), Ms. Masterson plays unwed 17-year-old Lucy Moore—a blue-collar mom-to-be who captures the hearts and hopes of yupscale mom-and-pop-wannabes Linda and Michael Spector (Glenn Close and James Woods).   Oct 29 *Sunday Tennessean* G-1/2   As a result, most of the high court wanna-bes have been criss-crossing the state for months, shaking the hands of the politically connected Democrats whose votes they seek.   Nov *Ms* 47/2   When her [Glenn Close's] career was in start-up, directors felt comfortable casting her as what she calls "the earth mothers": . . . Teddy, the single working mother in *Jagged Edge*, who loved a Henry VIII wannabe.   Nov 24 *Atlanta Journal/Constitution* C-4/2   Dec 1 *Atlanta Journal/Constitution* D-4/2   Dec 13 *Atlanta Journal/Constitution* E-4/2–3   Dismissing her Christian wannabe daughter-in-law, Miss Daisy sniffs, "If I had a nose like that, I wouldn't go around saying 'Merry Christmas' to anyone."   **1990** Jan 11 Ibid A-22   Jan 15 *People* 74/1

wedgy, wedgie   *n*   Pulling of the cloth of one's underpants tightly between the buttocks, usu in the collocation *give someone a wedgy* (The pulling may be sudden or gradual, deliberate or accidental, malicious or playful; often done as a practical joke, the result is uncomfortable and undignified, but may also be painful if the testes are squeezed by the tightened cloth)   **1988** Dec 18 Washington DC WTTG-TV [Gary Shandling's Christmas program]   I think I've just given myself a wedgy.   **1989** Connie Eble *College Slang 101* (Georgetown CT: Spectacle Lane) 91   WEDGY Underwear pulled up tight from the back by someone else as a prank. "He gave me a *wedgy* so hard that the waistband ripped off my underwear."   Michael Moffatt *Coming of Age in New Jersey* (New Brunswick, NJ: Rutgers UP) 86   In vulgar male talk among the students of the 1980s, to "bust someone's balls" was usually metaphoric: to make verbal fun of them in an aggressive way.   The wedgie as an action collapsed the metaphor, making the phrase very literal indeed.   Sep 29 *USA Today* A-10/2–4   A group of protesters, including computer nerds, band members and thespians, broke security and demanded an end to abuse by The Popular Kids.   The Secret Service quickly pounced on the intruders, gave them all wedgies and released them on their own recognizance.   **—wedgie**   *vt*   To give (someone) a WEDGY   **1989** Michael Moffatt *Coming of Age in New Jersey* (New Brunswick, NJ: Rutgers UP) 86   Last year's juniors had wedgied last year's freshmen, and then each freshman victim had happily joined the patrol, its aficionados claimed.   **—wedgie attack**   *n*   Surprise infliction of a WEDGY as a practical joke   Idem   The correct manly response to a wedgie attack, according to its perpetrators, was to take it in good humor.   **—wedgiemaster**   *n*   One who organizes a WEDGIE PATROL   Ibid 87   Carrie really wanted to be friends with Tim, but she simply couldn't, she said, for in his heart all Tim really was was the "wedgiemaster."   **—wedgie patrol**   *n*   A group of college dormitory residents who make a WEDGY ATTACK as a form of hazing   Ibid 85   Something called the "wedgie patrol" was abroad in the late hours of the night on Hasbrouck Fourth, I was told.

wussy; wuss   *n*   [cf Robert L Chapman *New Dict of Am Slang* 1986]   Weak, ineffectual person; wimp   **1989** Nov 7 *Atlanta Journal/Constitution* D-2/1   And before you accuse me of being some kind of sherry-sipping, ascot-wearing, ballet-attending, "MacNeil/Lehrer News-Hour"-watching wussy, please note that I am a sports guy myself, having had a legendary athletic career consisting of nearly a third of the 1965 season on the track team at Pleasantville High School.   Nov 23–29 *Encore* 13/2–4 ["Life in Hell" by Matt Groening]   FORBIDDEN WORDS OF THE 1990s [list of vogue words] . . . WUSS   Nov 26 *Atlanta Journal/Constitution* G-7/1–5 [Tom Teepen]   The Battle of the El Salvador Sheraton revealed President George Bush at his wussy worst. . . . [¶] A wiser administration would have found out if the apparent attack was terrorism before calling it that. . . . Where Mr. Bush meant to look strong, he wound up looking silly.

AMONG THE NEW WORDS

JOHN ALGEO   AND   ADELE ALGEO

University of Georgia   *Athens, Georgia*

With the assistance of the New Words Committee

DURING 1989–1990, THE FOLLOWING PERSONS SERVED as members of the New Words Committee by sending citations for the files: Catherine M. Algeo, *Durham, NC;* Thomas J. Algeo, *Midland, TX;* Leonard R. N. Ashley, *Brooklyn College, CUNY;* Sheila Bailey, *University of Georgia;* Robert K. Barnhart, *Barnhart Books;* Dennis E. Baron, *University of Illinois;* Ronald R. Butters, *Duke University;* Frederic G. Cassidy, *University of Wisconsin,* emer.; Sylvia Chalker, *London;* George S. Cole, *Shippensburg University;* Betty Jean Craige, *University of Georgia;* Thomas J. Creswell, *Chicago State University,* emer.; Lesa Dill, *Western Kentucky University;* Charles Clay Doyle, *University of Georgia;* Connie C. Eble, *University of North Carolina, Chapel Hill;* Coburn Freer, *University of Georgia;* Allen Gardner, *University of Nevada, Reno;* Raymond Gozzi, Jr., *Bradley University;* Sidney Greenbaum, *University College, London;* Charles F. Hockett, *Cornell University,* emer.; Harry Homa, *Morris High School, Bronx, NY;* Betty J. Irwin, *University of Georgia;* Jennifer Jordan-Henley, *Middle Tennessee State University;* William J. Kirwin, *Memorial University of Newfoundland;* Enno Klammer, *Eastern Oregon State College;* William A. Kretzschmar, Jr., *University of Georgia;* Sarah Lawson, *London;* Robert H. Longshore, *University of Georgia,* emer.; Virginia G. McDavid, *Chicago State University,* emer.; James B. McMillan, *University of Alabama,* emer.; Patrick W. Merman, *Monroe, MI;* Michael B. Montgomery, *University of South Carolina;* Frank Nuessel, *University of Louisville;* Thomas M. Paikeday, *Mississauga, Ont.;* Louis Phillips, *School of Visual Arts, NYC;* Mary Grey Porter, *University of Alabama;* Linda L. Rapp, *University of Michigan, Dearborn;* Richard K. Redfern, *Bradenton, FL;* Randy Roberts, *University of Missouri, Columbia;* August Rubrecht, *University of Wisconsin, Eau Claire;* Anne Russell, *Tuscaloosa, AL;* Alan R. Slotkin, *Tennessee Technological University;* James C. Stalker, *Michigan State University;* Sol Steinmetz, *Random House;* John Tinkler, *University of Tennessee, Chattanooga;* Greg Williams, *University of Toronto;* Gordon R. Wood, *Southern Illinois University.*

The help provided by the persons listed above makes possible the preparation of the quarterly installments of "Among the New Words." Without the alertness of these helpers to the appearance of new words and the citations they send as documentation, we could not prepare the depart-

The automobile accessory variously called a *bra, car bra, nose bra, nose mask,* or *stealth auto* (or *car*) *bra* has been advertised as a protective device, presumably against bugs or scratches, and as a sporty decoration. In early 1990 it, or perhaps some new version of it, was declared to guard against radar detection. The adjective *stealth,* applied to it at that time, clearly echoes the *stealth bomber,* which was developed to elude radar. The earliest term in our files, *nose bra,* was abandoned perhaps because of its curiously mixed metaphor.

Toy boy and *boy toy* are semantically complex and intertwined, perhaps illustrating the fate of a borrowed word whose meaning is diversified because it is not clearly understood. *Toy boy* is a Briticism for a gigolo, a younger man kept by an older woman; it was introduced in American tabloids that imitate British publications and whose reporters are often expatriate Britishers. In a spirit of equal opportunity, the term was extended to homosexual liaisons. A variant, *boy toy,* was developed in American use (we have no British evidence for it). Our earliest citations for the variant reverse the roles as well as the words in the expression—that is, they use it for a young woman. Later it was used as a synonym for the British *toy boy* and then extended to denote any boyfriend, regardless of age. As a result of this semantic fluctuation, two of our citations for *boy toy* apply it to Madonna and Warren Beatty—one to her and the other to him.

Acknowledgments for citations in this issue: Thomas Algeo, Leonard R. N. Ashley, Ronald R. Butters, George S. Cole, Charles Clay Doyle, Betty Irwin, William J. Kirwin, Michael Montgomery, Mary Gray Porter, Linda L. Rapp, Anne Russell, and Alan Slotkin. In the spring issue of this year (65.1), the names of contributors of citations were omitted. They were Catherine M. Algeo, Thomas Algeo, George S. Cole, Raymond Gozzi, Jr., Betty Irwin, William J. Kirwin, James B. McMillan, Patrick Merman, Michael Montgomery, Thomas M. Paikeday, Sol Steinmetz, and Greg Williams.

boutique beer; boutique brew   *n*   MICROBREW   **1989** Nov 22 *Atlanta Journal/Constitution* D-4/5 [headline and article]   New Brews Seek Spot on the Shelf / Georgia boutique beer is here. . . . [¶] Like Anchor Steam (now a relative biggie), the boutique brews are closer in flavor to German domestic (not export) beers. They're generally darker, richer and more complex than generic Coors-Miller-Bud.

boy toy, boy-toy   *n*   **1:** A young woman as an object of sexual interest   **1989** Oct 30 *People* 75/1   An ambitious 20-year-old whose gold debut album, *Martika,* has spun off one No. 1 hit, "Toy Soldiers," and made her MTV's PG-rated Boy Toy of the month, Martika makes Madonna sound modest by comparison.   Dec 29 *USA Today* D-2/4-5 [picture caption]   PLAYBOY MEETS BOY TOY: Warren Beatty and Madonna have been out and about L.A., at trendy restaurants and nightclubs.   **2a:** TOY BOY 1   **1990** Feb 23 *Atlanta Journal/Constitution* D-7/2 [review of film *Men Don't Leave*] Meanwhile, the boys are making some peculiar new friends. Chris becomes the kept boy-toy of an eccentric older medical technician (Joan Cusack) who lives in the building. **b:** A man as an object of sexual interest Apr 2 *People* 75/1 As an unabashed Material Girl, she [Madonna] has earned $90 million in the past four years and has never wanted for available Boy Toys. . . . [¶] . . . "She's letting her aging Boy Toy [Warren Beatty] think he still has it," says one observer.

bra *n* NOSE MASK **1990** Feb 11 *Midland* [TX] *Reporter-Telegram* G-8 "The bra protects drivers from unfair readings that result in unjustified speeding tickets," he said. [¶] The bra, which starts at $299 depending on the auto make and model, is custom-made to fit most domestic and foreign cars.

brewpub, brew pub *n* A small brewery combined with a restaurant **1987** Feb 9 *Newsweek* 49/1 Since the nation's first brewpub, the Hopland Brewery, opened in Mendocino, Calif., in 1983, more than a dozen others have sprouted across the country. **1989** Jan 24 *USA Today* D-4/2 Maneo's Weeping Radish Brewery and Bavarian Restaurant, Milwaukee's Water Street Brewpub, and Berkeley's Triple Rock Brewing Co. serve up beer produced right on the premises. . . . [¶] It all began in 1982, when the Yakima Brewing Co. opened the USA's first brewpub in Yakima, Wash. . . . [¶] Today, about 35 brewpubs operate in California, Oregon and Washington. Feb 5 Columbia SC *State* G-5/1-5 [headline and article] Customers enjoy variety of beers offered by 'brewpubs' and 'microbreweries' / . . . The brothers restored Cleveland's first tavern last September and started brewing beer, part of a growing nationwide brewing trend as local brewers apply their craft in "brewpubs" and "microbreweries," offering a variety of beers to local clientele. **1990** Jan 11 Wheaton IL *Daily Herald* sec 6 p 7/1 "It's a shame, because the city [Philadelphia] has a real old tradition of breweries," said Jim Pericles, the beer brewer at the Samuel Adams, known as a brewpub because it doubles as a restaurant. Feb 22 *Wall Street Journal* B-1/4-5 Welcome to the brew pub, one of the hottest concepts in the restaurant industry. A combination of restaurants and microbreweries, brew pubs are capturing the fancy of folks looking to dine out and be diverted. . . . [¶] A longtime European tradition, brew pubs migrated to North America in 1984 after the U.S. and Canada changed federal regulations requiring that beer be kegged before it was sold—a way the government made sure it got its tax money. **—brewpublike** *adj* **1987** Feb 9 *Newsweek* 49/1 quot sv MICROBREWERY

car bra *n* NOSE MASK **1990** Feb 11 *Midland* [TX] *Reporter-Telegram* G-8 [picture caption] Denver inventor Kip Fuller holds a radar gun as he demonstrates his latest invention, a radar-deflecting car "bra", which deflects the radar used by police.

come out *v ph* (Of an athlete) to turn professional before eligibility to play on a college team is exhausted, esp at the end of the junior year **1990** Jan 13 NBC sports report of the Hula Bowl [Bobby Beathard] He's under a lot of pressure to come out. Jan 18 *Detroit Free Press* C-7 "Barry Sanders clearly opened the floodgates," said agent Richard Woods of Mobile, Ala. "He was a true junior, and they let him in. Now, players perceive that anyone can come out." . . . [¶] Cindrich said the only fear he has of loose draft rules is that self-serving agents will push juniors out of college before they are ready. [¶] "I'm afraid too many third parties will encourage kids to come out for reasons totally unrelated to the welfare of the player," he said. Apr 23 *Atlanta Journal/Constitution* F-1 / 2–8/1 While it has been theorized that many juniors were inspired by the success of running back Barry Sanders, who skipped his senior season at Oklahoma State and made All-Pro with Detroit, his agent, Atlanta's David Ware, doesn't agree. [¶] "I think most of them came out because, as the [NFL] commissioner [Paul Tagliabue] said on TV today, the wage scale is something they [the owners] want to do but they can't do it without an agreement with the union."

contract beer *n* A microbrew sold outside the area where it is made **1989** Nov 22 *Atlanta Journal/Constitution* D-4/5 Wild Boar Special Amber. This attractively packaged contract beer is made in Dubuque, Iowa, for the Georgia Brewing Co. It's somewhat darker than Helenboch, with more sweet bite and a bit of finish.

icehouse, ice house *n* [modeled on *greenhouse effect*] Cooling of the earth's surface and lower atmosphere, triggering an ice age **1987** Apr *Paleoceanography* 182/2 It has been previously argued that the change in planetary albedo due to the reflectivity of great expanses of polar ice could exert a large enough "force" on the climate of the Recent earth to drive it to a "runaway icehouse" state. Apr *Geological Society of America Bulletin* 482/2-3 Fischer attributed the Late Paleozoic lowstand to reduced plate activity expressed in continental thickening by the aggregation of the continents in Pangea, with an inferred decreased rate of volcanic activity and hence of atmospheric CO2 concentration, leading to a replacement of an Early Paleozoic greenhouse state by a Late Paleozoic icehouse state. **1988** Nov *JOI/USSAC Newsletter* (Washington DC: Joint Oceanographic Institutions Inc.) 5/2-3 . . . efforts should focus on three contrasting intervals—the Oligocene to late Miocene (the "ice house"), the middle Cretaceous (the "green house"), and the Paleocene to Eocene (the "doubt house").

inning *gerund* OUTING **1990** Apr 4 quot sv OUTING [After a station break, Sonya reported she had "been corrected to call it 'inning.'"]

lambada *n* An Afro-Brazilian dance involving close body contact, with positions and motions imitative of coitus **1989** Aug 21 *Time* 38/1 Spawned on the northeast coast of Brazil, the lambada has swept through France this summer. **1990** Jan 11 *Wall Street Journal* A-12/1 Born in the slums of Brazil in the 1920s, the lambada got its name from the Portuguese verb to whip or flog, referring to the smacking of thigh against thigh. Once banned as immoral in its home country, the dance achieved enormous popularity in Europe last summer with a heavily marketed single, "Lambada," by the French group Kaoma. Jan 29 *Newsweek* 60/3 . . . the lambada is cultural news so up to the minute that it hasn't even happened yet—not, anyway, at America's Dew Drop inns, wedding receptions and post-bar-mitzvah bashes. One reason real people aren't doing it may be that lambada . . . is so sensual that it was once banned in Brazil, . . . Borrowing from the tango and merengue, lambada is a fast-paced dance performed with the man's right leg placed between the thighs of his partner. Feb 23 *Atlanta Constitution* C-1/2 & C-4/3 As most media-aware Americans know, the lambada—a steamy, sexily undulating dance from Brazil—has already been declared the Next Big Thing. . . . [¶] Widely referred to as South America's "dirty dancing," the lambada was a smash throughout Europe last year, with the Kaoma single topping the charts in 15 countries. Mar 18 *Atlanta Journal/Constitution* G-1/1 [Lewis Grizzard] But now comes the lambada, a dance and movie of the same name. I began to notice television commercials for "Lambada"—the forbidden dance—a few weeks ago. [¶] Forget "Dirty Dancing." Do the lambada and somebody might think you're making love standing up. Mar 15 *Tuscaloosa* [AL] *News* 10/1 About the only thing hotter than lambada these days is the fever with which film-makers are trying to cash in on the bump-and-grind dance. . . . [¶] Born decades ago in Brazil's northern Bahia, lambada somewhat resembles other Latin dances, such as salsa. It is a close dance, with male and female partners entwined around each other, grinding their hips together.

lambaderia *n* A nightclub where the lambada is danced **1990** Jan 11 *Wall Street Journal* A-12/1 Aided by a steamy music video, the song (now incorporated in Kaoma's "World Beat" album along with tracks like "Lambareggae," "Lamba Caribe," "Dancando Lambada" and "Lambamor") topped the charts in 15 countries, and transformed Continental nightclubs into *lambaderias* overnight.

mallie *n* MALL RAT **1985** Aug 5 *International Herald Tribune* 12 [comic strip "Peanuts"; Charlie Brown:] Where are you girls going? / [Peppermint Patty:] Over to the shopping mall... / We're "mallies". We like to hang around with the other mallies. Aug 8 *International Herald Tribune* p n/a [comic strip "Peanuts"; Marcie:] Why are we standing by the telephone, sir? / [Peppermint Patty:] "Mallies" always hang around the pay telephones, Marcie. . . . / It makes us look like we've got something going. / [Marcie:] We could go into the book store. [Peppermint Patty:] Are you out of your mind?!

malling *n* **1:** (Esp of teenagers) congregating in a shopping mall for entertainment by meeting peers, eating, and window-shopping (cf MALLIE, MALL-JAM, and MALL RAT) **1989** Aug 12 Columbia SC *State* B-1/1-3 [headline and article] Bored, cruising and 'malling' / . . . Pick any night, and you'll find legions of teenagers cruising around or parking in mall parking lots, where they crank up their radios so loud that the rhythmic beat of bass guitars and drums makes the pavement pulsate. Or you may find them hanging out inside the malls, the "town squares" of suburbia. [¶] But this "malling" of Columbia also has caused a gigantic headache for law enforcement officials, mall managers, customers and store managers: some of the same teenagers who hang out are drinking, shoplifting, fighting, or just making a nuisance of themselves. **2:** [modeled on *greening (of America)*] Increase in the number of shopping malls (in a specified area) with loss of variety and quality in stores **1988** Jun 4 *Nation* 804/2-3 Indeed, that is pretty much how things stand now, and the anticipated malling of midtown into a sleaze-free *cordon sanitaire* can only accelerate the process. Dec 5 *US News & World Report* 53/1 The malling of America in recent years already has retailers scrambling for ways to distinguish themselves from an ever swelling pack. . . . As a result, most department stores end up trying to lure customers with low prices rather than top-of-the-line merchandise. **1989** Mar 25 *Atlanta Journal/Constitution* A-23/4 [Dick Williams] But as with Dante's, there are other Punch Line comedy clubs, other Fat Tuesdays, other Pilgreens' and another Barker's Hot Dogs. With the malling of America, there's almost another everything.

mall-jam *vi* To crowd together in a shopping area for social purposes **1989** Oct 1 *Atlanta Journal/Constitution* E-4/2 And though shopping centers are off the "in" list, some students like to mall-jam at Underground Atlanta, mostly to mingle and meet members of the opposite sex.

mall rat *n* One who frequents a shopping mall for social entertainment, a MALLIE **1988** May 13 *Wall Street Journal* R-7/1 [subhead and article] With time to kill and money to spend, teen-age 'mall rats' can't stay away / Outside . . . the nearby Catskills beckon . . . For the area's youthful "mall rats," however, the majestic vistas can't compete with the climate-controlled, neon-lit enticements inside.

microbrew *n* Beer produced by a MICROBREWERY **1987** Nov 9 *Time* 98/2-3 Microbrews accounted for only .03% of the 180 million bbl. of beer made in America last year, but sales are frothing. . . . Young though it is, the microbrew industry already has its rivalries. **1989** Nov 22 *Atlanta Journal/Constitution* D-4/5 Reassigned to California, I discovered Anchor Steam Beer, the microbrew that was to change the industry.

microbrewer *n* Brewer in a MICROBREWERY **1987** Nov 9 *Time* 98/1 And because of their limited distribution, microbrewers can turn out distinctive flavors.

microbrewery *n* A small brewery producing beer usually for local consumption **1987** Feb 9 *Newsweek* 49/1 Meantime the number of microbreweries, which sell their product both in bottles and at brewpublike taprooms, has grown from 40 in 1980 to 63 in 1985. Nov 9 *Time* 98/1 Enter the microbreweries—small local producers who generally turn out no more than 15,000 bbl. a year (in contrast to Anheuser-Busch's 72.3 million-bbl. ocean sold last year) and whose brews are primarily intended for regional consumption. **1989** Oct 13 *Atlanta Journal/Constitution* A-2/5 Atlanta native Dow Scoggins has gotten a taste of success as president of the new Helenboch brewery in Helen. The microbrewery's first offering, Helenbock [sic] Oktoberfest Beer, was awarded the prestigious ranking of 3.5 stars by World Beer Review magazine (four stars is tops). Nov 22 *Atlanta Journal/Constitution* D-4/5 Microbreweries—breweries producing less than 15,000 barrels annually—are where the market is growing. . . . [¶] Georgia now has a microbrewery—sort of. Friends Brewing Co. of Helen and Atlanta currently markets Helenboch Beer, an amber lager. **1990** Jan 11 Wheaton IL *Daily Herald* sec 6 p 7/3 By the end of 1988, there were 123 microbreweries in the United States, according to the directory, 71 of which were brewpubs. Nearly half of those microbreweries opened for business in 1988.

microbrewing *gerund* Producing beer in a MICROBREWERY **1987** Nov 9 *Time* 98/2-3 No one is more surprised than Fritz Maytag, scion of the washing-machine family, who in 1965 bought the Anchor Steam Beer Brewing Co. of San Francisco and went on to earn the title "the father of microbrewing."

nose bra *n* NOSE MASK **1984** Jun 24 *Athens* [GA] *Banner-Herald/Daily News* 19 [ad] WOLF / NOSE BRA / $49⁰⁰

nose mask *n* A cloth or plastic cover for the front end of a car, shielding the bumper and grill, with holes for the lights and front license plate, reputedly providing resistance to radar tracking **1989** spring brochure for Nissan Car Accessories 7/1 Nose Mask / Accentuate the sporty appearance of your 240SX while protecting your front end with a sleek, black vinyl nose mask. Custom designed for a smooth fit and allows your hood and headlights to be raised without removing the mask.

out *adv, adj* [clipped from *out of the closet*] Known and admittedly homosexual **1990** Apr 4 CNN *Sonya Live*—All people should be "out." But they shouldn't be forced out. . . .—I feel that the more people we have out, the less stigma there will be.

out *vt* To deliberately reveal the homosexuality of (especially a public person) **1990** Mar 30 CNN *Crossfire* Gerry Studds has become a very effective speaker for gay rights, even though he was in effect outed. **—outing** *gerund* **1990** Jan 29 *Time* 67/1-2 Gays have long gossiped about which public figures of past and present might be secret homosexuals. . . . This name dropping is defended as a way of giving the gay community role models and a sense of continuity. When the rumors involve living people, however, discussion about who is "in the closet" has generally been held to a discreet murmur—partly in deference to libel laws but mostly in defense of privacy. That consensus is fast breaking down with the spread of a phenomenon known as "outing," the intentional exposure of secret gays by other gays. [¶] . . . One outing victim had endorsed legislation allowing hospitals to test patients for AIDS without their consent. . . . [¶] While the idea of outing a fellow gay used to be considered repellent under any circumstances, the tactic has become increasingly acceptable to mainstream homosexual leaders. Mar 23 *Atlanta Journal/Constitution* C-4/1 And last week, New York's *OutWeek*, a gay-oriented weekly, followed with explicit details on the publishing tycoon's reported sex life. [¶] Mr. Forbes has become the latest target of "outing," a growing practice in which undeclared gay men, lesbians or bisexuals are involuntarily yanked from the sexual closet, typically by activists in the gay community. Mar 30 CNN *Crossfire* Welcome back. We're talking about "outing"—the practice in the gay community of forcing out closet homosexuals. Apr 4 CNN *Sonya Live* We're talking about "outing" or "inning," whatever you want to call it. It's about bringing gays out of the closet involuntarily. Apr 8 *Sunday Tennessean* G-3/1 [NY Times News Svc] A faction among American gay people has adopted a tactic that many find an alarming invasion of privacy: unmasking prominent people who homosexuals say are secretly gay. . . . [¶] Proponents of this tactic, known as outing—as in "out of the closet"—say homosexuals in positions of power have a responsibility to acknowledge proudly who they are . . . .

outage *n* Outing **1990** Apr 24 *Advocate* 37/1 Naming names—known as "outing" in *Time* magazine, called an "outage" by others, and termed "dragging people out of the closet" by an indignant columnist in the *New York Post*—is now all the rage in the gay press.

peace dividend *n* An anticipated saving in military spending due to improved relations with Russia **1989** Dec 20 L R N Ashley letter The relaxation of tension in the Cold War, with *glasnost* and All That, has led to the possibility that we can cut our military expenditures. This is being referred to as a *peace dividend*. Dec 25 *Newsweek* 49/1-2 All are good ideas that share one thing in common: they won't happen, because the whole idea of a colossal peace dividend is a fallacy. The $200 billion in cuts forecast by Secretary of Defense Dick Cheney last month are hardly cuts at all. They represent reductions from earlier plans that assumed growth in defense spending through 1994. . . . [¶] But the fact that the peace dividend is largely illusory is not likely to quell congressional debate on how to spend it. Dec 25 *Nation* 780/1 The $180 billion reduction in Cheney's proposed budgets will end up maintaining military spending at about the current level, though Pentagon spending will fall a little because of inflation. With these Potemkin Village cuts, President George Bush is right to note there will be no "peace dividend" from the thaw. **1990** Jan 11 *Midland* [TX] *Reporter-Telegram* A-6 [George Will] Jan 30 *Midland* [TX] *Reporter-Telegram* A-3/1 President Bush's first federal budget proposal, released Monday, was missing any "peace dividend" brought on by big cuts in defense spending. Feb 10 *Atlanta Journal/Constitution* A-22/3-5 [political cartoon showing eight empty boxes, each captioned sequentially:] Only the vaporous rustle of warm air . . . / . . . betrays the awesome stillness. / You can't hear it. / You can't see it. / You can't even feel it. / Infiniti? / Nope. / It's the Peace Dividend. Feb 11 *Atlanta Journal/Constitution* D-3/2 Since the military claims 24 cents out of every tax dollar, that typical family will pay $59.03 weekly to keep Uncle Sam in missiles, combat boots and the like. Now there's a "peace dividend" I can relate to. Feb 12 *Newsweek* 90/2 [George Will] The weakened Soviet threat makes Republicans willing, even eager, to have an across-the-board cut (half from defense) to meet Gramm-Rudman deficit reduction requirements. However, for tomorrow Gramm sees both promise and peril for both parties in the "peace dividend" from declining defense spending. Many Republicans say: Peace will be the only peace dividend; the defense budget will not rise but neither will it be a cornucopia of cuts. Feb 16 *Midland* [TX] *Reporter-Telegram* A-6/3-5 [political cartoon, showing Uncle Sam inquiring at the Capitol Hill Savings & Loan:] Pardon me, but isn't this where I pick up my "Peace Dividend"? Feb 19 *Midland* [TX] *Reporter-Telegram* A-6/6 [Jack Anderson] Feb 25 *Atlanta Journal/Constitution* F-5/4 [William F. Buckley] There are many hands out for whatever "peace dividend" we are scheduled to bask in, the most prehensile of them the savings and loan fiasco. Feb 26 *Midland* [TX] *Reporter-Telegram* A-5 [AP] Governors would like more federal money for education, health care, transportation and repairing bridges and roads. But most of the state officials say they'd just as soon see any "peace dividend" used to reduce the federal deficit. Mar 12 *Newsweek* 29/1 The superpowers should be able to take their fingers from the nuclear trigger and at the same time reap a peace dividend. Mar 19 *Newsweek* 18/3 The American soldier has historically drawn a bitter peace dividend. After World War I, when a Congress intoxicated by pacifism reduced the armed forces from 3 million to less than 300,000, the shrunken military nonetheless suffered short rations and squalid living conditions. Apr 15 *Atlanta Journal/Constitution* A-1/6 In hot pursuit of a so-called peace dividend amid lessened superpower tension, some lawmakers have urged cutbacks or even outright cancellation of high-cost weapons programs . . . .

signature beer *n* MICROBREW **1989** Nov 22 *Atlanta Journal/Constitution* D-4/5 Atlanta's Highland Brewing Co., an upscale pub-restaurant, contracted for production of several out-of-state signature beers and has since quit serving them. New Amsterdam, an outstanding New York microbrew, also foundered after initial raves.

slotting allowance *n* [Harold LeMay, Sid Lerner, and Marian Taylor *New New Words Dictionary* 1988] A charge made by a grocery store to a manufacturer for the use of shelf space to stock a product **1988** Dec 8 *Athens* [GA] *Daily News/Banner-Herald* C-3/1 Slotting allowances are the fees grocery companies charge for shelf space in their stores. Many small manufacturers question the legality and ethics of the fees, claiming they stifle new products, limit their ability to expand and cost consumers money. **1989** Oct 3 *NY Times* C-19/5 Many retailers now use a computerized system to determine the value of shelf space by the cubic inch. To increase that value, store owners are increasingly asking manufacturers for fees to stock a product, called "slotting allowances," which generally cost $4,000 a product for each store . . . . **1990** Jan 4 NBC *Today Show* People are

paying as much as $120,000 for these slotting allowances. . . . These highly confidential fees are called slotting allowances.

slotting fee *n* SLOTTING ALLOWANCE **1988** Dec 8 *Athens* [GA] *Daily News/Banner-Herald* C-3/1 "You just know that the big businesses aren't paying," she said. . . . "Can you see them telling Procter & Gamble that they won't stock Tide unless they pay a slotting fee?" **1990** Jan 4 NBC *Today Show* The merchant is trying to get as much as he can from slotting fees.

sound off *n* A competition of automobile stereo sound systems **1989** Jan 5 *Atlanta Constitution* E-1/4 The latest expression of automobile hip is a car stereo so big and so loud that it can blow out windshields and bulge car doors. The boom-boom-boom of a superstereo bass has become a common sound along popular cruising spots around the country, and hundreds of competitions called "sound-offs" have been held. Apr 1 *Asheville* [NC] *Citizen/Times* A-4/1 [editorial] **1990** Feb 8 *Athens* [GA] *Observer* A-1/1 & A-6/1 Brese indicated that most car owners who acquire these noise-makers are doing it for competitive reasons. "They're doing it strictly for the interest in Sound-Off competitions," he explained. [¶] At first these competitions were based purely on how much noise a system put out. But now the judging includes the installation, how the car looks, how clean the installation is and how pure the sound is. "Volume plays a very small role in it," said Brese. Apr 19 *Athens* [GA] *Observer* B-8/4 "Sound-off" competitions are growing rapidly in number nationwide, to the point that a sanctioning body, the International Auto Sound Challenge Association, was formed in 1987 to help regulate such events.

stealth auto bra; stealth car bra *n* NOSE MASK **1990** Feb 11 *Midland* [TX] *Reporter-Telegram* G-8 The inventor's [Kip Fuller's] latest innovation is known as a stealth car bra, so named because it resembles a brassiere strapped to the front of a vehicle. [¶] Made of radar-absorbing carbon fibers, the bra enables a car to fool police radar until it reaches close range, permitting drivers to spot the trap and slow down before their speed is clocked. Feb 23 *Atlanta Journal/Constitution* E-6/1-3 [headline] With stealth auto bra, speeding drivers can more easily give police radar the slip.

step dance *n* A synchronized, athletic African-American dance characteristic of black college fraternities and sororities **1989** Jul 10 *Wall Street Journal* A-1/4 [headline, subhead, and article] Steeped in Tradition 'Step Dance' Unites Blacks on Campus / Its Synchronized Movements Are a Fraternity Ritual And a Focus of Social Life / . . . It's also a dance tradition that, while long a mainstay of black collegiate life, has lately blossomed in popularity. A fraternity and sorority step-dance competition at the Philadelphia Civic Center Saturday drew an estimated 7,000 people, a record for the event. *Ibid* A-4/1 Erin Patton, strutting through his fraternity's signature step dance at a thunderous party in a Northwestern dorm, puts it more simply. "This is a way to express our identity," he says, a medallion in the shape of Africa bouncing against his chest.

step dancing *n* Performing a STEP DANCE **1989** Oct 2 *NY Times* A-9/5 [picture caption] Members of Alpha Phi Alpha [a black fraternity] practice step dancing at Morgan State University in Baltimore.

stepping *n* STEP DANCE; STEP DANCING **1989** Jul 10 *Wall Street Journal* A-1/4 It's mostly entertainment, but stepping is also a "touchstone" for black students, says Valerie Warnsby, an undergraduate at Drake University in Des Moines, Iowa, and a member of Delta Sigma Theta Sorority. "All day we're bombarded with stuff from white America. For us, it's an artistic expression of *our* history." *Ibid* A-4/1 Stepping draws from several music traditions—African drumming, minstrel shows, rap, church gospel—and has evolved into a uniquely American dance form. Its synchronized and syncopated moves date back to the 1940s, when lines of fraternity pledges marched in lockstep around campus in a rite of initiation. **1990** Apr 10 U of Ga *Red and Black* 2/4 [picture caption] Stepping: A member of the Kappa Alpha Psi [black fraternity] does one of his jumps for the show. **—stepping out** *gerund* **1989** Jul 10 *Wall Street Journal* A-1/4 Mr. Taylor quit a white fraternity [at Northwestern] in his freshman year to pledge Alpha Phi Alpha. He endured the ritual weeks of midnight practice sessions before "stepping out" as a pledge, and now views the synchronized group dance in more symbolic terms.

step show *n* A performance of STEP DANCE **1989** Oct 2 *NY Times* A-1 The groups [black fraternities and sororities] are also coming under greater scrutiny because of the crowds they attract to their precision dance routines, called step shows. **1990** Apr 10 U of Ga *Red and Black* 2/2 The step show was sponsored and performed by eight black Greek organizations.

tossing *n* OUTING **1990** Mar 23 *Atlanta Journal/Constitution* C-4/1 But outing, or "tossing" as it's also called, is not confined to dead folks incapable of having their privacy invaded or being libeled and retaliating with lawsuits. In the past two years, the hotly debated tactic has flourished, flinging more and more living celebrities out of their private sexual sanctums.

toy boy, toyboy *n* [John Ayto *Longman Register of New Words* 1985 "since the early 1980s"] **1:** A handsome young man, esp the lover of an older woman, supported by her; gigolo **1987** Feb 12 London *Hampstead Advertiser* 4/4 Matt Dillon, incidentally, has now been supplanted himself and I suppose his replacement at the moment is Tom Cruise, the fresh-faced toy boy of 'Top Gun'. Apr 17 London *Times* 11/5 The researcher who telephoned me [columnist Barbara Amiel] explained that they would like my comments on the phenomenon of "toy boys". The issue wasn't of much import to me, I said, and as far as I was concerned women were free to make fools of themselves over younger men, although I thought most such relationships were doomed and intrinsically unnatural. **1988** Oct 4 *Globe* [supermarket tabloid] 9/1 CHER is on the prowl for a new toy boy, say friends. [¶] The Oscar-winning actress has confided that she's grown tired of bagel-baker-turned-actor Rob Camilletti, 24, and needs a new beau in her life. . . . [¶] One pal says: "Cher likes to be around good-looking, younger guys." **2:** A young man supported by an older homosexual lover **1987** May 28 *London Evening Standard* 30/6 . . . an old-style Cockney gangster is locked in business rivalry with his former toyboy lover. **1990** Mar 27 *Globe* [supermarket tabloid] 3/1 Billionaire Malcolm Forbes was a homosexual who killed himself because he was dying of AIDS, his toyboy lover reveals.